The publisher and the University of California Press Foundation gratefully acknowledge the generous support of the Joan Palevsky Endowment Fund in Literature in Translation.

Valentinian Christianity

Valentinian Christianity

Texts and Translations

———

Geoffrey S. Smith

UNIVERSITY OF CALIFORNIA PRESS

University of California Press
Oakland, California

© 2020 by Geoffrey Smith

Library of Congress Cataloging-in-Publication Data

Names: Smith, Geoffrey S. (Geoffrey Stephen), 1983- translator, writer of
  introduction. | Container of (work): Valentinus, active 2nd century.
  Works. Selections.
Title: Valentinian Christianity : texts and translations / Geoffrey S. Smith.
Description: Oakland, California : University of California Press, [2019] |
  Includes bibliographical references and index. |
Identifiers: LCCN 2019016112 (print) | LCCN 2019019840 (ebook) |
  ISBN 9780520969803 (ebook) | ISBN 9780520297463 (cloth : alk. paper)
Subjects: LCSH: Valentinians—History—Sources. | Church history—
  Primitive and early church, ca. 30–600—Sources. | Gnostic literature.
Classification: LCC BT1475 (ebook) | LCC BT1475 .V35 2019 (print) |
  DDC 273/.1—dc23
LC record available at https://lccn.loc.gov/2019016112

Manufactured in the United States of America

26   25   24   23   22   21   20   19
10   9   8   7   6   5   4   3   2   1

Funding for this volume was made possible by a research sabbatical in the fall of 2017, generously granted by the University of Texas at Austin, and ongoing support from the Institute for the Study of Antiquity and Christian Origins.

For Marina

CONTENTS

Introduction

Valentinus and the Valentinian Tradition

To tell the story of the Valentinians is to embrace a series of enigmas. Second-century Christians accused Valentinus of heresy, but only decades earlier, he nearly became one of the most prominent leaders within the Roman church; the Valentinians were among the first Christians to write commentaries on the Bible, but they were also frequently accused of not taking the Scriptures seriously; and by the third century Valentinians were active throughout the Mediterranean world, from Gaul to Syria, and as far south as Egypt, yet by the end of the following century they would all but disappear from the historical record. But fortunately for us, they did not disappear without leaving a trace. Several texts written by Valentinus and his followers have survived. Some have been known since antiquity, but many more surfaced in 1945, when they were unearthed just outside of the Egyptian town of Nag Hammadi. This collection brings together for the first time all of the writings known to have been composed by the so-called Valentinians.

VALENTINUS

Little is known about Valentinus, the patriarch and namesake of the Valentinians. Around 135 C.E. Valentinus appears to have traveled from his homeland of Egypt,[1] where he may have received a formal Greek education in Alexandria, to Rome. Valentinus took his place alongside many other enterprising teachers, including Hermas, Marcion, and Justin, provincials who traveled to the empire's capital city to present their own understanding of the teachings of Jesus and carve out a niche

---

1. Epiph. *Pan.* 31.2.2–3.

1

within the ever-expanding network of semi-independent house churches.[2] Valentinus's writings survive only in excerpts embedded within the works of other authors. From these excerpts we learn that he offered instruction on a variety of topics, including cosmology,[3] anthropogony,[4] Christology,[5] and spiritual formation,[6] and that he found value in Jewish and Christian writings, as well as secular ones.[7] On account of his teaching and literary activity, Valentinus became well known in Rome and beyond. Tertullian reports that at one point Valentinus was considered for a prominent leadership position in Rome but failed to get the job because the other candidate was respected as a confessor, one who had remained faithful to Christ in a time of persecution.[8] Nothing certain is known about Valentinus after his departure from Rome, which may have occurred sometime in the 160s.[9] Epiphanius suggests that he continued teaching on the island of Cyprus, but many remain suspicious of this account.[10] The *Testimony of Truth* may refer to his death, but the passage in question is ambiguous.[11]

2. For a discussion of this model of Christianity in Rome, see Peter Lampe, *From Paul to Valentinus: Christians at Rome in the First Two Centuries* (Minneapolis: Fortress Press, 2003). See also Einar Thomassen, "Orthodoxy and Heresy in Second-Century Rome," *HTR* 97 (2004): 241–56.

3. Valentinus, frags. 5 and 8.

4. Valentinus, frag. 1.

5. Valentinus, frag. 3.

6. Valentinus, frag. 2.

7. Several allusions to the LXX and especially the New Testament appear in Valentinus's fragments. For an apparatus indicating some of these allusions, see Bentley Layton, *The Gnostic Scriptures: A New Translation with Annotations and Introduction* (Garden City, NY: Doubleday, 1995), 229–48. See frag. 6 for Valentinus's positive assessment of secular writings.

8. Tertullian, *Against the Valentinians* 4.1.

9. Irenaeus, *AH* 3.4.3; Tertullian, *Prescription* 30.2. On the basis of Irenaeus, *AH* 3.4.3, where Irenaeus claims that Valentinus "came to Rome in the time of Hyginus, flourished under Pius, and *remained* until Anicetus," some scholars maintain that Valentinus died in Rome. See Gerd Lüdemann, "Zur Geschichte des ältesten Christentums im Rom," *ZNW* 70 (1979): 91n12. For a critical response to this suggestion, see Einar Thomassen, *The Spiritual Seed: The Church of the "Valentinians"* (Leiden: Brill, 2008), 419n10.

10. Epiph. *Pan.* 31.7.1–2. For a critical assessment of the account, see Thomassen, *Spiritual Seed*, 419; and Christoph Markschies, *Valentinus Gnosticus? Untersuchungen zur valentinianischen Gnosis mit einem Kommentar zu den Fragmenten Valentins*, WUNT 65 (Tübingen: J. C. B. Mohr, 1992), 332n284.

11. Most editors reconstruct the text of 56.1–2 as ⲱⲕ ⲉ[ⲟ]ⲗ ⲡⲡⲱⲧ [ⲡ̄ⲟⲩⲁⲗ]ⲉⲛⲧⲓⲛⲟ ("He completed the course of Valentinus"). See Søren Giversen and B. Pearson, *Nag Hammadi Codices IX and X*, Nag Hammadi Studies 15 (Leiden: Brill, 1997); and Annie Mahé and Jean-Pierre Mahé, *Le témoignage véritable (NH IX, 3): Gnose et martyre*, BCNH: Textes 23 (Quebec City: Presses de l'Université Laval, 1996). Yet Uwe-Karsten Plisch, who follows the suggestion of H.–M. Schenke, offers an alternative reconstruction: ⲉ]ⲱⲕ ⲉ[ⲟ]ⲗ ⲡⲡⲱⲧ [ⲓ ⲟⲩⲁⲗ]ⲉⲛⲧⲓⲛⲟ ("after Valentinus completed the course"). See Uwe-Karsten Plisch, "Textverständnis und Übersetzung: Bemerkungen zur Gesamtübersetzung der Texte des Nag-Hammadi-Fundes durch den Berliner Arbeitskreis für Koptisch-Gnostische Schriften," *Hallesche Beiträge zur Orientwissenschaft* 26 (1998): 81–82. While many understand the phrase "complete the course" to refer to some sort of Valentinian curriculum, the expression appears as a

THE VALENTINIAN TRADITION

Even though nothing more is known about this early Christian teacher after his departure from Rome, his legacy becomes the subject of controversy throughout the next two centuries, with some, like Irenaeus and Epiphanius, bent on refuting Valentinian teaching and others, like Clement and Origen, making judicious use of it. Patristic authors single out several Christian teachers as Valentinian; most prominent among them are Ptolemy, Heracleon, and Theodotus. While scholars debate the extent to which later so-called Valentinians remained faithful to the teachings of Valentinus, most are confident that the Valentinians belonged to a distinct Christian group, distinguishable by their unique theology and rituals. The last credible evidence for the existence of Valentinian Christians appears in 388, when an anti-Semitic outburst in Callinicum, present-day Raqqa, led some Christians to set fire to a Jewish synagogue, a blaze that also destroyed an adjacent Valentinian church.[12]

If Valentinus's legacy was controversial to some, it was inspirational to others. From the second through the fourth century, Christians affiliated with the Valentinian movement composed numerous texts, many of which survive today, thanks in part to those who preserved their texts while writing against or about the Valentinians, and to the chance discovery of numerous papyrus codices of "heretical" early Christian writings near the Egyptian town of Nag Hammadi in 1945. Valentinian texts appear in codices I, II, XI, and XII. Codex I alone includes three Valentinian texts, the *Gospel of Truth*, the *Treatise on the Resurrection*, and the *Tripartite Tractate*, leading some of the first scholars to work on codex I to regard it as Valentinian and to assign the anonymous treatises therein to known Valentinians. The *Gospel of Truth* was thought to have been composed by Valentinus himself, and the *Tripartite Tractate* by Heracleon. Despite the fact that most scholars no longer regard all of the texts in codex I as Valentinian and have become more cautious about assigning these anonymous texts to known Valentinian teachers, the concentration of Valentinian texts in codex I remains intriguing. The discovery of the Nag Hammadi library in 1945 not only dramatically increased the number of known texts composed by Valentinians; it also provided access for the first time to Valentinian texts that survived independent of the patristic literary tradition.

Now that we have a wealth of texts written by Valentinians, we are confronted by a curious reality: though scholars often regard the Valentinians as a distinct Christian sect that thought of themselves as disciples of Valentinus, no surviving text composed by a so-called Valentinian actually uses the term Valentinian. This

---

euphemism for death earlier in the *Testimony of Truth* (34.10) and also in the Coptic translation of 2 Tim 4:7, where Pseudo-Paul predicts his imminent death. Both reconstructions are plausible, though I favor the latter on account of the literary parallels.

12. Ambrose, *Letter* 40.16.

designation appears only in the patristic sources—that is, in those writers who were largely interested in refuting the Valentinians. Even more striking is the fact that no text thought to have been composed by a Valentinian mentions Valentinus. In fact, in the Nag Hammadi texts, Valentinus's name appears only two times; he is twice named in a list of "heretics" in the *Testimony of Truth*.[13] Only one alleged Valentinian mentions Valentinus: Alexander, whose appeal to Valentinus and his writings is reported secondhand by an unsympathetic Tertullian. Yet given that little else is known about this Alexander, it is possible that Tertullian has dubbed him a Valentinian simply on the basis of his use of Valentinus's writings.[14] Justin himself admits that the Valentinians do not conceive of themselves as such when he openly states that his rivals "call themselves Christians," but "we call them after the name of the men from whom each doctrine and opinion had its origin."[15] Even Tertullian admits, "We call them Valentinians, though they seem not to be."[16] When Valentinians do refer to themselves, they call themselves "the spiritual seed" or simply "the church."

VALENTINIAN TEXTS

This collection includes only those texts written by Valentinus and the so-called Valentinians. I have chosen not to include the reports about the Valentinians for two reasons. First, including the numerous reports about the Valentinians would have made this volume impractically long; and second, many of the reports about the Valentinians are colored by bias to various degrees and are designed to cast the Valentinians in a negative light.

However, since no ancient authors identify themselves as Valentinian or follow-ers of Valentinus, we must determine how to identify texts composed by authors considered Valentinian—a process that admits that we have not completely bro-ken free of patristic influence. Texts are included in the present collection on the

---

13. *TestTruth* 55.1–59.9. The term *heretics* appears at 59.4.

14. Einar Thomassen is one of the few scholars who notes the dearth of references to Valentinus or the Valentinians in sources written by so-called Valentinians. Thomassen summarizes the evidence succinctly: "There is no doubt that [Valentinian] is a heresiological term. As far as we know, the 'Valen-tinians' never used that name for themselves." Yet Thomassen still believes that the Valentinians were a distinct sect, with their own theology and rituals. His argument is simply that they did not consider themselves Valentinians. Instead, Thomassen argues, Valentinians called themselves "Christians" and "identified themselves, in mythical terms, as 'the spiritual seed,' and in more religious-sociological language as an, or, rather, *the ekklesia*." Nevertheless, Thomassen asserts that "the movement must have possessed enough continuity, coherence, and specificity, and enough of a historical relation to Valentinus, to make it possible to identify various groups as 'Valentinian' over a span of at least 250 years." Thomassen, *Spiritual Seed*, 4–5.

15. Justin, *Dialogue* 35.

16. Tertullian, *Against the Valentinians* 4.

basis of one of two considerations: (1) a patristic author credibly identifies the text or author of the text as Valentinian; and (2) the theology, ritual practice, or technical terminology resembles to a high degree the theology, ritual practice, or technical terminology deemed Valentinian by patristic sources or found in texts deemed Valentinian by patristic sources.

Texts that ancient authors identify as Valentinian or attribute to known Valentinian teachers include the fragments of Valentinus, Heracleon's fragments, Ptolemy's *Letter to Flora,* the anonymous *Commentary on the Prologue of John,* the Anonymous *Letter,* the *Excerpts of Theodotus,* the anonymous *Commentary on Valentinus's "Summer Harvest,"* and perhaps the *Gospel of Truth.* That the *Gospel of Truth* belongs to this category is less certain (see the introduction to the *Gospel of Truth).* Nevertheless, on the basis of its theology and hermeneutical mode, and the striking similarities between its language and that of the *Tripartite Tractate,* a text whose Valentinian characteristics are not in doubt, we can with confidence include the *Gospel of Truth* within the Valentinian corpus, even if it may not be identical with the text mentioned by Irenaeus.

The rest of the texts in this collection are included on the basis of their striking affinities to the texts identified as Valentinian by ancient sources.[17] When attempting to isolate meaningful ritual, theological, and terminological similarities between texts known to be Valentinian and those suspected to be, I find it helpful to draw upon Ludwig Wittgenstein's notion of "family resemblance." Wittgenstein illustrates this concept by way of an appeal to gaming:

> Consider for example the proceedings that we call "games." I mean board-games, card-games, ball-games, Olympic games, and so on. What is common to them all?— Don't say: "There must be something common, or they would not be called 'games'"— but look and see whether there is anything common to all.—For if you look at them you will not see something that is common to all, but similarities, relationships, and a whole series of them at that. To repeat: don't think, but look!—Look for example at board-games, with their multifarious relationships. Now pass to card-games; here you find many correspondences with the first group, but many common features drop out, and others appear. When we pass next to ball-games, much that is common is retained, but much is lost.—Are they all "amusing"? Compare chess with noughts

17. For the most detailed discussion of which texts are Valentinian, see Einar Thomassen, "Notes pour la délimitation d'un corpus valentinien à Nag Hammadi," in *Les textes de Nag Hammadi et le problème de leur classification: Actes du colloque tenu à Quebec du 15 au 19 septembre 1993,* ed. L. Painchaud and A. Pasquier, BCNH: Études 3 (Quebec City: Presses de l'Université Laval, 1995), 243–59. I agree largely with his assessments, though I am not convinced that some of the texts he considers Valentinian in fact are. As a result, my collection is slightly smaller. See also Thomassen's revised assessment of the First Apocalypse of James in "The Valentinian Materials in *James* (NHC V,3 and CT,2)," in *Beyond the Gnostic Gospels: Studies Building on the Work of Elaine Pagels,* ed. Eduard Iricinschi et al., STAC 82 (Tübingen: Mohr Siebeck, 2013), 79–90.

and crosses. Or is there always winning and losing, or competition between players? Think of patience. In ball games there is winning and losing; but when a child throws his ball at the wall and catches it again, this feature has disappeared. Look at the parts played by skill and luck; and at the difference between skill in chess and skill in tennis. Think now of games like ring-a-ring-a-roses; here is the element of amusement, but how many other characteristic features have disappeared! And we can go through the many, many other groups of games in the same way; can see how similarities crop up and disappear. And the result of this examination is: we see a complicated network of similarities overlapping and crisscrossing: sometimes overall similarities, sometimes similarities of detail.[18]

When considering what we mean by "games," Wittgenstein urges us to look not for "something that is common to all" games, but for "similarities" and "relationships" among them. These relationships he characterizes as "multifarious," and "correspondences" from one kind of game to another continue, while others drop out as new features replace them. Games, then, can be conceived of as a range of related activities with a constellation of features in common, with several features shared by a few, and occasional features unique to some.

Conceptualizing the relationships among Valentinian texts in terms of family resemblance rather than "something that is common to all" provides us with a fitting corrective to the way that Valentinian texts are often conceptualized and grouped together. Already by the late second century C.E., Irenaeus sought to summarize what he considered to be the core of Valentinian theology, which he refers to metaphorically as "their fruit-bearing."[19] In *Against the Heresies* 1.1–8, Irenaeus offers a summary of the Valentinian Wisdom myth—that is, a story about a heavenly being named Wisdom who makes a mistake that leads to the rupture of the divine realm and, eventually, to the creation of an inferior creator who, in turn, creates the material world. In the modern era, it was François Sagnard who, in his 1947 study of the Valentinians, termed Irenaeus, *AH* 1.1–8 the *grande notice* and asserted that the Wisdom myth lies at the heart of Valentinianism.[20] In his words, the *grande notice* "remains the principal source (*la source capitale*) among the writings of the Valentinian gnosis and helps to give a coherent and characteristic overall impression (*ensemble*), out of which only some secondary features still remain obscure."[21] Sagnard made his claim two years after the discovery of the Nag Hammadi library, though at the time no editions or transcriptions of the newly discovered texts were available to scholars. Despite the availability of the new writings

18. Ludwig Wittgenstein, *Philosophical Investigations*, trans. G. E. M. Anscombe (Oxford: Basil Blackwell, 1986), I 66.

19. Irenaeus, *AH* 1.4.4.

20. François Sagnard, *La gnose valentinienne et le témoignage de saint Irénée*, Études de philosophie médiévale 36 (Paris: J. Vrin, 1947).

21. Sagnard, *La gnose valentinienne*, 567 (trans. mine).

from the Nag Hammadi discovery, the pride of place Sagnard assigned to the so-called *grande notice* remains; many scholars continue to view the Wisdom myth as Irenaeus recounts it as a foundational myth shared by all Valentinians, or in Wittgenstein's words, as "something common to all."

Yet rather than approach the writings of the Valentinians with assumptions about their mythology and theology, this collection seeks to encourage readers to encounter Valentinian writings on their own terms. In some texts, such as the *Tripartite Tractate* and the *Excerpts of Theodotus,* knowledge of something like the Wisdom myth as Irenaeus recounts it is certain. However, in others, such as the *Gospel of Truth,* where wisdom is not a lesser god who introduces deficiency in the divine realm of fullness, but an impersonal cognitive faculty of the Father, knowledge of the Wisdom myth is less likely. What binds this collection of writings together, therefore, is not adherence to a common myth, but a family resemblance.

I have divided the texts in this collection into three groups: Greek texts quoted by patristic authors, Coptic texts from Nag Hammadi, and a lone Valentinian inscription in Greek. I offer new transcriptions of texts of the Nag Hammadi writings, the Excerpts of Theodotus, and the Flavia Sophe inscription. I rely on scholarly editions for texts with more complicated textual histories. In general, my editorial method is conservative; I have avoided speculative reconstructions in fragmentary texts such as the *Valentinian Exposition,* and I refrain from emendations wherever possible. Additionally, I have attempted to make the Greek and Coptic texts as accessible as possible so that students too may benefit from this collection. Therefore, I have not included a comprehensive apparatus but offer only occasional notes on difficult constructions. I have also departed from the convention in Nag Hammadi studies to include paratextual marks added to the text by scribes, the functions of which are still little understood, and have instead punctuated the Coptic text in line with the custom of editors of Greek texts (comma and period indicate English comma and full stop, middot indicates English colon or semicolon, and semicolon indicates English question mark). Finally, I have chosen not to include *nomina sacra,* abbreviations of sacred names common in Christian manuscripts, preferring to report the full noun instead. Additional sigla used in the Greek and Coptic texts generally follow the conventions found in the Coptic Gnostic Library, which I reproduce here, with slight modification, for the convenience of the reader.

.   A dot placed under a letter in the transcription indicates that the letter is visually uncertain, even though the content may make the reading certain. A dot on the line outside of brackets in the transcription indicates an uncertain letter from which some vestiges of ink remain.

[ ]   Square brackets in the transcription indicate a lacuna in the MS where writing most probably at one time existed. When the text cannot be reconstructed, but the number of missing letters can be reasonably estimated, that number is

indicated by a corresponding number of dots or a numerical estimation; where the number of missing letters cannot be reasonably estimated, the space between the brackets is filled with three dashes. In the translation the square brackets are used only around words that have been substantially restored. Dots within brackets used in the translation do not indicate the number of missing letters, only that some text is missing.

⟦ ⟧   Double square brackets indicate letters canceled by the scribe.

{ }   Braces indicate letters unnecessarily added by the scribe.

` ´   High strokes indicate that the letter so designated was secondarily written above the line by the scribe.

< >   Pointed brackets in the transcription indicate an editorial correction of a scribal omission. In the translation, they indicate words that have been editorially emended.

( )   Parentheses in the translation indicate material supplied by the translator for the sake of clarity.

Greek Texts

I. FRAGMENTS OF VALENTINUS

Valentinus was an influential Christian teacher during his own lifetime. Tertullian reports that Valentinus was the runner-up for a prominent ecclesiastical position in Rome.[1] Yet Valentinus's sphere of influence was not limited to Rome. Within years of his death, his influence had spread to Gaul, Egypt, and perhaps even Syria.

His prolific writings contributed to his early and widespread influence. The author of the *Testimony of Truth* claims that Valentinus "has spoken [many words, and he has] written many [books]."[2] The surviving fragments of Valentinus suggest that his writings spanned several genres, including psalms,[3] homilies,[4] and letters.[5] Pseudo-Tertullian reports that Valentinus even composed a "gospel," which many scholars have speculated may be the *Gospel of Truth* from Nag Hammadi, an identification that remains tantalizing, if improbable.

Perhaps Valentinus's best-known work was his psalm book, which is surprisingly well attested by ancient authors, considering the fact that only one short "psalm" from the collection survives today (see "Summer Harvest"). Tertullian reports that a certain Alexander found support for his Christological views in the "psalms of Valentinus," which Alexander regards confidently "as the production of

---

1. Tertullian, *Against the Valentinians* 4.1.
2. *Testimony of Truth* 56.
3. Fragment 8.
4. Fragments 4 and 6.
5. Fragment 3.

[a] respectable author";[6] Origen, likewise, refers to the "psalms of Valentinus"; at the end of the Muratorian fragment, a book of psalms is mentioned, perhaps in association with Valentinus; and Hippolytus characterizes Valentinus's "Summer Harvest" as a psalm. That Valentinus's psalms were known in North Africa and Egypt in the late second century, perhaps in Rome in the third century, and wherever the Muratorian fragment was composed in the fourth century illustrates the broad geographical distribution and longevity of Valentinus's psalm book.

Unfortunately, only a few fragments of Valentinus's writings survive. They have come to us not as scraps of papyrus, but as quotations embedded within the writings of other early Christians. The seven fragments in this collection hail from Clement and Hippolytus. An additional fragment survives in Photius, but since Photius does not provide a direct quotation of Valentinus, I have chosen not to include it in this collection. Similarly, I have not included a passage from Hippolytus, *Refutation of All Heresies* 6.42.2, known as fragment 7, since it does not preserve a direct quotation from Valentinus. Together these fragments give the impression that Valentinus was a well-read and creative teacher who found inspiration for his theology in the Scriptures.

The Greek text below is based on E. Heitsch, *Die griechischen Dichterfragmente der römischen Kaiserzeit,* 2nd ed., vol. 1 (Göttingen: Vandenhoeck & Ruprecht, 1963).

6. Tertullian, *On the Flesh of Christ* 17.

Fragment 1 (Clement of Alexandria, Strom. 2.36.2–4)

2 καὶ ὡσπερεὶ φόβος ἐπ᾽ ἐκείνου τοῦ πλάσματος ὑπῆρξε τοῖς ἀγγέλοις, ὅτε μείζονα ἐφθέγξατο τῆς πλάσεως διὰ τὸν ἀοράτως ἐν αὐτῷ σπέρμα δεδωκότα τῆς ἄνωθεν οὐσίας καὶ παρρησιαζόμενον· 3 οὕτω καὶ ἐν ταῖς γενεαῖς τῶν κοσμικῶν ἀνθρώπων φόβοι τὰ ἔργα τῶν ἀνθρώπων τοῖς ποιοῦσιν ἐγένετο, οἷον ἀνδριάντες καὶ εἰκόνες καὶ πάνθ᾽ ἃ χεῖρες ἀνύουσιν εἰς ὄνομα θεοῦ· 4 εἰς γὰρ ὄνομα Ἀνθρώπου πλασθεὶς Ἀδὰμ φόβον παρέσχεν προόντος Ἀνθρώπου, ὡς δὴ αὐτοῦ ἐν αὐτῷ καθεστῶτος, καὶ κατεπλάγησαν καὶ ταχὺ τὸ ἔργον ἠφάνισαν.

Fragment 2 (Clement of Alexandria, Strom. 2.114.3–6)

3 εἷς δέ ἐστιν ἀγαθός, οὗ παρρησία ἡ διὰ τοῦ υἱοῦ φανέρωσις, καὶ δι᾽ αὐτοῦ μόνου δύναιτο ἂν ἡ καρδία καθαρὰ γενέσθαι, παντὸς πονηροῦ πνεύματος ἐξωθουμένου τῆς καρδίας. 4 πολλὰ γὰρ ἐνοικοῦντα αὐτῇ πνεύματα οὐκ ἐᾷ καθαρεύειν, ἕκαστον δὲ αὐτῶν τὰ ἴδια ἐκτελεῖ ἔργα πολλαχῶς ἐνυβριζόντων ἐπιθυμίαις οὐ προσηκούσαις. 5 καί μοι δοκεῖ ὅμοιόν τι πάσχειν τῷ πανδοχείῳ ἡ καρδία· καὶ γὰρ ἐκεῖνο κατατιτρᾶταί τε καὶ ὀρύττεται καὶ πολλάκις κόπρου πίμπλαται ἀνθρώπων ἀσελγῶς ἐμμενόντων καὶ μηδεμίαν πρόνοιαν ποιουμένων τοῦ χωρίου, καθάπερ ἀλλοτρίου καθεστῶτος. 6 τὸν τρόπον τοῦτον καὶ ἡ καρδία, μέχρι μὴ προνοίας τυγχάνει, ἀκάθαρτος, πολλῶν οὖσα δαιμόνων οἰκητήριον· ἐπειδὰν δὲ ἐπισκέψηται αὐτὴν ὁ μόνος ἀγαθὸς πατήρ, ἡγίασται καὶ φωτὶ διαλάμπει. καὶ οὕτω μακαρίζεται ὁ ἔχων τὴν τοιαύτην καρδίαν, ὅτι ὄψεται τὸν θεόν.

Fragment 3 (Clement of Alexandria, Strom. 3.59.3)

πάντα ὑπομείνας ἐγκρατὴς ἦν. θεότητα Ἰησοῦς εἰργάζετο· ἤσθιεν καὶ ἔπινεν ἰδίως οὐκ ἀποδιδοὺς τὰ βρώματα. τοσαύτη ἦν αὐτῷ ἐγκρατείας δύναμις, ὥστε καὶ μὴ φθαρῆναι τὴν τροφὴν ἐν αὐτῷ, ἐπεὶ τὸ φθείρεσθαι αὐτὸς οὐκ εἶχεν.

Fragment 4 (Clement of Alexandria, Strom. 4.89.2–3)

2 ἀπ᾽ ἀρχῆς ἀθάνατοί ἐστε καὶ τέκνα ζωῆς ἐστε αἰωνίας καὶ τὸν θάνατον ἠθέλετε μερίσασθαι εἰς ἑαυτούς, ἵνα δαπανήσητε αὐτὸν καὶ ἀναλώσητε, καὶ ἀποθάνῃ ὁ θάνατος ἐν ὑμῖν καὶ δι᾽ ὑμῶν. 3 ὅταν γὰρ τὸν μὲν κόσμον λύητε, ὑμεῖς δὲ μὴ καταλύησθε· κυριεύετε τῆς κτίσεως καὶ τῆς φθορᾶς ἁπάσης.

Fragment 5 (Clement of Alexandria, Strom. 4.89.6–90.1)

89.6 ὁπόσον ἐλάττων ἡ εἰκὼν τοῦ ζῶντος προσώπου, τοσοῦτον ἥσσων ὁ κόσμος τοῦ ζῶντος αἰῶνος. 90.1 τίς οὖν αἰτία τῆς εἰκόνος; μεγαλωσύνη τοῦ προσώπου παρεσχημένου τῷ ζωγράφῳ τὸν τύπον, ἵνα τιμηθῇ δι᾽ ὀνόματος αὐτοῦ· οὐ γὰρ αὐθεντικῶς εὑρέθη μορφή, ἀλλὰ τὸ ὄνομα ἐπλήρωσεν τὸ ὑστερῆσαν ἐν πλάσει. συνεργεῖ δὲ καὶ τὸ τοῦ θεοῦ ἀόρατον εἰς πίστιν τοῦ πεπλασμένου.

Fragment 1 (Clement of Alexandria, Strom. 2.36.2–4)

2 And fear, so to speak, fell over the angels in the presence of the molded form when he spoke things greater than his molding (should have allowed), on account of the one who invisibly placed a seed of superior substance within him and who spoke with boldness. 3 Thus also among the races of earthly people the works of people become frightening to those who made them, such as statues and images and all things crafted by human hands in the name of a god. 4 For as one molded in the name of a human, Adam brought about fear of the preexistent human, since that very one stood within him, and they were terrified and immediately hid their work.

Fragment 2 (Clement of Alexandria, Strom. 2.114.3–6)

3 "There is one who is good," whose bold speech is the manifestation through the Son, and through whom alone is a heart able to become pure, after every evil spirit is driven out of the heart. 4 For the many spirits inhabiting the heart do not allow it to be pure. Instead, each of them accomplishes its own works, in many ways inflicting it with inappropriate desires. 5 And it seems to me that the heart suffers something like what occurs in a motel. For it is trashed and dug up and frequently filled with the feces of wanton visitors showing little regard for the place, since they live elsewhere. 6 It is the same way with the heart, until it is shown care, it is impure, inhabited by many demons. But when the only good one, the Father, oversees it, he makes it holy and illuminates it. And in this way one who has such a heart is blessed, since that person will see God.

Fragment 3 (Clement of Alexandria, Strom. 3.59.3)

He had self-control, enduring all things. Jesus performed divinity: he ate and drank in his own way without defecating. Such was the power of self-control in him that the nourishment in him did not become waste, since he did not possess corruption.

Fragment 4 (Clement of Alexandria, Strom. 4.89.2–3)

2 From the beginning you are immortal, and you are children of eternal life. You wanted to divide death within you, so that you might consume and destroy it, and so that death might die in you and through you. 3 For when you destroy the world, you yourselves are not destroyed; you rule over creation and all corruption.

Fragment 5 (Clement of Alexandria, Strom. 4.89.6–90.1)

89.6 As much as the image of a living face is inferior (to a living face), the world is inferior to the living eternity. 90.1 What then is the cause (of the power) of the image? The greatness of the face provides the painter with a figure, so that the images might be honored by his name. For the form was not intended to be perfectly accurate, but the name filled what was lacking in the molded form. The invisibility of God cooperates with what has been molded for (the sake of) fidelity.

Fragment 6 (Clement of Alexandria, Strom. 6.52.4)

πολλὰ τῶν γεγραμμένων ἐν ταῖς δημοσίαις βίβλοις εὑρίσκεται γεγραμμένα ἐν τῇ ἐκκλησίᾳ τοῦ θεοῦ· τὰ γὰρ κοινὰ ταῦτα ἔστι τὰ ἀπὸ καρδίας ῥήματα, νόμος ὁ γραπτὸς ἐν καρδίᾳ· οὗτός ἐστιν ὁ λαὸς ὁ τοῦ ἠγαπημένου, ὁ φιλούμενος καὶ φιλῶν αὐτόν.

Fragment 8 (Hippolytus, Ref. 6.37.7)

θέρος
πάντα κρεμάμενα πνεύματι βλέπω,
πάντα δ' ὀχούμενα πνεύματι νοῶ·
σάρκα μὲν ἐκ ψυχῆς κρεμαμένην,
ψυχὴν δὲ ἀέρος ἐξεχομένην,
ἀέρα δὲ ἐξ αἴθρης κρεμάμενον,
ἐκ δὲ βυθοῦ καρποὺς φερομένους,
ἐκ μήτρας δὲ βρέφος φερόμενον.

Fragment 6 (Clement of Alexandria, Strom. 6.52.4)

Much of what is written in the public books is found in the writings of God's church. For the things in common are the words from the heart, the law that is written in the heart. These are the people of the beloved, who are beloved and love him.

Fragment 8 (Hippolytus, Ref. 6.37.7)

Summer Harvest
I see in spirit that all are hung,
I know in spirit that all are borne.
Flesh hanging from soul,
Soul clinging to air,
Air hanging from upper atmosphere,
Crops rushing forth from the deep,
A babe rushing forth from the womb.

II. PTOLEMY'S *LETTER TO FLORA*

Multiple sources confirm that Ptolemy was a prominent and early student of Valentinus, active in the second century C.E.; however, little is known about his life. Yet a letter he wrote does survive. Embedded within Epiphanius's *Panarion* is a lengthy letter written by Ptolemy to a woman named Flora. In this letter, Ptolemy offers his views on what was a fundamental question for early Christians: what is the status of the law of Moses now that Jesus has fulfilled God's plan of salvation? He opens the letter by carving out a middle position between two extremes. On the one hand are those who assert that God the Father ordained the entire law. On the other hand are those who claim that the entire law is the work of the devil. Ptolemy situates his own view between these two. He posits the existence of three heavenly beings, the Perfect God, the just god, and the devil, and argues that the law is not the product of a single author, but of three: the just god, Moses, and the elders. Further, he argues that the portion of the law revealed by the just god itself divides into three parts: the pure but imperfect part, the part interwoven with injustice, and the symbolic part. When the Savior comes and announces the truth of the Perfect God, Ptolemy claims that the imperfect part becomes fulfilled, the unjust part becomes abolished, and the symbolic part takes on a spiritual meaning.

Ptolemy does not discuss first principles, the aspect of his theology he is best known for among the heresiologists, but he does end his *Letter to Flora* with a promise of future teaching "once you have been deemed worthy of the apostolic tradition," an advanced lesson that would cover the "origin and generation" of the cosmic beings and substances.

The Greek text below is based on K. Holl, *Epiphanius, Ancoratus und Panarion,* vols. 1–3, GCS 25, 31, 37 (Leipzig: Hinrichs, 1915, 1922, 1933).

3.1 Τὸν διὰ Μωσέως τεθέντα νόμον, ἀδελφή μου καλὴ Φλώρα, ὅτι μὴ πολλοὶ προκατελάβοντο, μήτε τὸν θέμενον αὐτὸν ἐγνωκότες μήτε τὰς προστάξεις αὐτοῦ ἀκριβῶς, ἡγοῦμαι καὶ σοὶ εὐσύνοπτον ἔσεσθαι μαθούσης τὰς διαφωνούσας γνώμας περὶ αὐτοῦ.

3.2 Οἱ μὲν γὰρ ὑπὸ τοῦ θεοῦ καὶ πατρὸς νενομοθετῆσθαι τοῦτον λέγουσιν, ἕτεροι δὲ τούτοις τὴν ἐναντίαν ὁδὸν τραπέντες ὑπὸ τοῦ ἀντικειμένου φθοροποιοῦ διαβόλου τεθεῖσθαι τοῦτον ἰσχυρίζονται, ὡς καὶ τὴν τοῦ κόσμου προσάπτουσιν αὐτῷ δημιουργίαν, πατέρα καὶ ποιητὴν τοῦτον λέγοντες εἶναι τοῦδε τοῦ παντός.

3.3 <Πάντως δὲ> διέπταισαν οὗτοι, διᾴδοντες ἀλλήλοις καὶ ἑκάτεροι αὐτῶν διαμαρτόντες παρὰ σφίσιν αὐτοῖς τῆς τοῦ προκειμένου ἀληθείας.

3.4 Οὔτε γὰρ ὑπὸ τοῦ τελείου θεοῦ καὶ πατρὸς φαίνεται τοῦτον τεθεῖσθαι, ἑπόμενος γάρ ἐστιν, ἀτελῆ τε ὄντα καὶ τοῦ ὑφ᾽ ἑτέρου πληρωθῆναι ἐνδεῆ, ἔχοντά τε προστάξεις ἀνοικείας τῇ τοῦ τοιούτου θεοῦ φύσει τε καὶ γνώμῃ.

3.5 Οὔτ᾽ αὖ πάλιν τῇ τοῦ ἀντικειμένου ἀδικίᾳ νόμον προσάπτειν <τὸ> ἀδικεῖν ἀναιροῦντα. τῶν τε ἑξῆς ἐστι μὴ συνορώντων τὰ ὑπὸ τοῦ σωτῆρος εἰρημένα· «οἰκία γὰρ ἢ πόλις μερισθεῖσα ἐφ᾽ ἑαυτὴν ὅτι μὴ δύναται στῆναι» ὁ σωτὴρ ἡμῶν ἀπεφήνατο.

3.6 Ἔτι τε τὴν τοῦ κόσμου δημιουργίαν ἰδίαν λέγει εἶναι «τά τε πάντα δι᾽ αὐτοῦ γεγονέναι καὶ χωρὶς αὐτοῦ γεγονέναι οὐδὲν» ὁ ἀπόστολος. προαποστερήσας τὴν τῶν ψευδηγορούντων ἀνυπόστατον σοφίαν, καὶ οὐ φθοροποιοῦ θεοῦ, ἀλλὰ δικαίου καὶ μισοπονήρου. ἀπρονοήτων δέ ἐστιν ἀνθρώπων, τῆς προνοίας τοῦ δημιουργοῦ μὴ αἰτίαν λαμβανομένων καὶ μὴ μόνον τὸ τῆς ψυχῆς ὄμμα, ἀλλὰ καὶ τὸ τοῦ σώματος πεπηρωμένων.

3.7 Οὗτοι μὲν οὖν ὡς διημαρτήκασιν τῆς ἀληθείας δῆλόν σοί ἐστιν ἐκ τῶν εἰρημένων· πεπόνθασι δὲ τοῦτο ἰδίως ἑκάτεροι αὐτῶν, οἱ μὲν διὰ τὸ ἀγνοεῖν τὸν τῆς δικαιοσύνης θεόν, οἱ δὲ διὰ τὸ ἀγνοεῖν τὸν τῶν ὅλων πατέρα, ὃν μόνος ἐλθὼν ὁ μόνος εἰδὼς ἐφανέρωσε.

3.8 Περιλείπεται δὲ ἡμῖν ἀξιωθεῖσί γε τῆς ἀμφοτέρων τούτων <γνώσεως> ἐκφῆναί σοι καὶ ἀκριβῶσαι αὐτόν τε τὸν νόμον, ποταπός τις εἴη, καὶ τὸν ὑφ᾽ οὗ τέθειται, τὸν νομοθέτην, ῥηθησομένων ἡμῖν τὰς ἀποδείξεις ἐκ τῶν τοῦ σωτῆρος ἡμῶν λόγων παριστῶντες, δι᾽ ὧν μόνον ἔστιν ἀπταίστως ἐπὶ τὴν κατάληψιν τῶν ὄντων ὁδηγεῖσθαι.

3.1 As for the law that has been established through Moses, my noble sister Flora, not many have grasped it, having no accurate knowledge of him who established it or of its ordinances; I believe that it will be easily grasped by you once you have learned the different opinions about it.

3.2 For some say that it was ordained by God and Father, but others, turning toward the opposite path, maintain confidently that it was established by the opposite, the destructive devil, just as they also credit him with the creation of the world, claiming that he is the father and maker of this entirety.

3.3 <But> they are <utterly> mistaken, refuting one another, and each of them failing utterly to find the truth of the subject.

3.4 For it is apparent that the law was not established by the Perfect God and Father, for it is derivative, being imperfect and in need of fulfillment by another, since it includes ordinances foreign to the nature and opinion of such a God.

3.5 Nor can one attribute the law to the unjust of the opposite one, since it abolishes what is unjust. It is fitting of those who do not understand the things said by the Savior: "For a house or city divided against itself is not able to stand," our Savior proclaimed.

3.6 Still the apostle says that the creation of the world is his own, "All things came to be through him, and apart from him nothing came to be," preemptively taking away the foundationless wisdom of the false accusers, and (demonstrating that creation comes) not from a god that causes destruction, but from (a God who is) just and who despises evil. But (this idea) comes from ignorant people, those who do not grasp the providence of the creator and have blinded not only the eye of the soul, but also that of the body.

3.7 It is clear to you from what has been said that these people miss the truth entirely; each of them has suffered this, the first group because they are ignorant of the God of justice, and the second group because they are ignorant of the Father of the entirety, who was revealed by the one who came alone and alone knew him.

3.8 But it remains for those of us who have been made worthy of the <knowledge> of both of these to reveal to you and to make clear the law itself, of what sort it is, and the lawgiver by whom it was established, presenting proofs of what we say from the words of our Savior, through which alone it is possible to grasp the things that exist without error.

4.1 Πρῶτον οὖν μαθητέον ὅτι ὁ σύμπας ἐκεῖνος νόμος ὁ ἐμπεριεχόμενος τῇ Μωσέως πεντατεύχῳ οὐ πρὸς ἑνός τινος νενομοθέτηται, λέγω δὴ οὐχ ὑπὸ μόνου θεοῦ, ἀλλ' εἰσί τινες αὐτοῦ προστάξεις καὶ ὑπ' ἀνθρώπων τεθεῖσαι. Καὶ τριχῇ τοῦτον διαιρεῖσθαι οἱ τοῦ σωτῆρος λόγοι διδάσκουσιν ἡμᾶς.

4.2 Εἴς τε γὰρ αὐτὸν τὸν θεὸν καὶ τὴν τούτου νομοθεσίαν διαιρεῖται, <διαιρεῖται> δὲ καὶ εἰς τὸν Μωσέα, οὐ καθὰ αὐτὸς δι' αὐτοῦ νομοθετεῖ ὁ θεός, ἀλλὰ καθὰ ἀπὸ τῆς ἰδίας ἐννοίας ὁρμώμενος καὶ ὁ Μωσῆς ἐνομοθέτησέν τινα, καὶ εἰς τοὺς πρεσβυτέρους τοῦ λαοῦ διαιρεῖται, καὶ πρῶτον εὑρίσκονται ἐντολάς τινας ἐνθέντες ἰδίας.

4.3 Πῶς οὖν τοῦτο οὕτως ἔχον ἐκ τῶν τοῦ σωτῆρος δείκνυται λόγων, μάθοις δ' ἂν ἤδη.

4.4 Διαλεγόμενός που ὁ σωτὴρ πρὸς τοὺς περὶ τοῦ ἀποστασίου συζητοῦντας αὐτῷ, ὃ δὴ ἀποστάσιον ἐξεῖναι νενομοθέτητο, ἔφη αὐτοῖς ὅτι «Μωσῆς πρὸς τὴν σκληροκαρδίαν ὑμῶν ἐπέτρεψεν τὸ ἀπολύειν τὴν γυναῖκα αὐτοῦ. Ἀπ' ἀρχῆς γὰρ οὐ γέγονεν οὕτως. Θεὸς γάρ,» φησί, «συνέζευξε ταύτην τὴν συζυγίαν, καὶ ὁ συνέζευξεν ὁ κύριος, ἄνθρωπος,» ἔφη, «μὴ χωριζέτω.»

4.5 Ἐνταῦθα ἕτερον μὲν τοῦ θεοῦ δείκνυσι νόμον, τὸν κωλύοντα χωρίζεσθαι γυναῖκα ἀπὸ ἀνδρὸς αὐτῆς, ἕτερον δὲ τὸν τοῦ Μωσέως, τὸν διὰ τὴν σκληροκαρδίαν ἐπιτρέποντα χωρίζεσθαι τοῦτο τὸ ζεῦγος.

4.6 Καὶ δὴ κατὰ τοῦτο ἐναντία τῷ θεῷ νομοθετεῖ ὁ Μωσῆς· ἐναντίον γάρ ἐστι τῷ μὴ διαζευγνύναι. Ἐὰν μέντοι καὶ τὴν τοῦ Μωσέως γνώμην, καθ' ἣν τοῦτο ἐνομοθέτησεν, ἐξετάσωμεν, εὑρεθήσεται τοῦτο οὐ κατὰ προαίρεσιν ποιήσας τὴν ἑαυτοῦ, ἀλλὰ κατὰ ἀνάγκην διὰ τὴν τῶν νενομοθετημένων ἀσθένειαν.

4.7 Ἐπεὶ γὰρ τὴν τοῦ θεοῦ γνώμην φυλάττειν οὐκ ἠδύναντο οὗτοι, ἐν τῷ μὴ ἐξεῖναι αὐτοῖς ἐκβάλλειν τὰς γυναῖκας αὐτῶν, αἷς τινες αὐτῶν ἀηδῶς συνῴκουν, καὶ ἐκινδύνευον ἐκ τούτου ἐκτρέπεσθαι πλέον εἰς ἀδικίαν καὶ ἐκ ταύτης εἰς ἀπώλειαν,

4.8 τὸ ἀηδὲς τοῦτο βουλόμενος ἐκκόψαι αὐτῶν ὁ Μωσῆς, δι' οὗ καὶ ἀπόλλεσθαι ἐκινδύνευον, δεύτερόν τινα. ὡς κατὰ περίστασιν ἧττον κακὸν ἀντὶ μείζονος ἀντικαταλλασσόμενος, τὸν τοῦ ἀποστασίου νόμον ἀφ' ἑαυτοῦ ἐνομοθέτησεν αὐτοῖς,

4.9 ἵνα, ἐὰν ἐκεῖνον μὴ δύνωνται φυλάσσειν, κἂν τοῦτόν γε φυλάξωσιν καὶ μὴ εἰς ἀδικίας καὶ κακίας ἐκτραπῶσι, δι' ὧν ἀπώλεια αὐτοῖς ἔμελλε τελειοτάτη ἐπακολουθήσειν.

4.1 First, then, one must learn that the whole law encompassed within the Pentateuch of Moses has not been furnished by one being, I mean, not by one God alone, but some commandments are from him, and some were given by men. The words of the Savior teach us about this threefold division.

4.2 For it is allocated to God himself and his ordinances, but <it is allocated> also to Moses, not meaning that God legislates through him, but that Moses legislated some things that arose from his own thoughts, and (another) is allocated to the elders of the people, and at the beginning they devised some commandments of their own.

4.3 How, then, this occurred in this way is demonstrated by the words of the Savior, you will learn now.

4.4 When conversing with those who argue with him about divorce, which has been legislated to be allowed, the Savior said, "Moses permitted a man to divorce his wife on account of your hard-heartedness. For from the beginning it was not this way. For God," he says, "joined this marriage, and what the Lord has joined," he said, "let no one separate."

4.5 Here he demonstrates that there is a law of God, which prevents a wife from divorcing her husband, and another law, of Moses, which permits the breaking of this union on account of hard-heartedness.

4.6 And according to this, Moses legislates contrary to God; for not joining is contrary (to joining). If, however, we consider the opinion of Moses, according to which he legislated, it will be discovered that he did not give his own law willingly, but out of necessity on account of the weakness of those furnished with the laws.

4.7 For since they were not able to preserve God's opinion, in which it is not possible for them to reject their wives, with whom some of them lived unhappily, and because of this they ran the risk of turning to more unrighteousness and because of this to destruction,

4.8 Moses wanted to eradicate for them this unhappiness, on account of which they ran the risk of being destroyed. Thus, given the circumstances, exchanging a lesser evil for a greater one, he established for them a law of divorce from himself,

4.9 so that, if they were not able to observe the first, they might observe this one and not turn to unrighteousness and wickedness, through which total destruction is destined to follow for them.

4.10 Αὕτη μὲν ἡ τούτου γνώμη, καθ' ἣν ἀντινομοθετῶν εὑρίσκεται τῷ θεῷ. πλὴν ὅτι γε Μωσέως αὐτοῦ δείκνυται ἐνταῦθα ἕτερος ὢν παρὰ τὸν τοῦ θεοῦ νόμον, ἀναμφισβήτητόν ἐστι, κἂν δι' ἑνὸς τὰ νῦν ὦμεν δεδειχότες.

4.11 Ὅτι δὲ καὶ τῶν πρεσβυτέρων εἰσίν τινες συμπεπλεγμέναι παραδόσεις ἐν τῷ νόμῳ, δηλοῖ καὶ τοῦτο ὁ σωτήρ. «Ὁ γὰρ θεός» φησίν «εἶπεν· τίμα τὸν πατέρα σου καὶ τὴν μητέρα σου, ἵνα εὖ σοι γένηται·

4.12 «Ὑμεῖς δέ,» φησίν, «εἰρήκατε,» τοῖς πρεσβυτέροις λέγων· «δῶρον τῷ θεῷ ὃ ἐὰν ὠφεληθῇς ἐξ ἐμοῦ, καὶ ἠκυρώσατε τὸν νόμον τοῦ θεοῦ διὰ τὴν παράδοσιν ὑμῶν τῶν πρεσβυτέρων.»

4.13 Τοῦτο δὲ Ἡσαΐας ἐξεφώνησεν εἰπών· «ὁ λαὸς οὗτος τοῖς χείλεσί με τιμᾷ, ἡ δὲ καρδία αὐτῶν πόρρω ἀπέχει ἀπ' ἐμοῦ, μάτην δὲ σέβονταί με, διδάσκοντες διδασκαλίας ἐντάλματα ἀνθρώπων.»

4.14 Σαφῶς οὖν ἐκ τούτων εἰς τρία διαιρούμενος ὁ σύμπας ἐκεῖνος δείκνυται νόμος· Μωυσέως τε γὰρ αὐτοῦ καὶ τῶν πρεσβυτέρων καὶ αὐτοῦ τοῦ θεοῦ εὕρομεν νομοθεσίαν ἐν αὐτῷ. Αὕτη μὲν οὖν ἡ διαίρεσις τοῦ σύμπαντος ἐκείνου νόμου ὧδε ἡμῖν διαιρεθεῖσα τὸ ἐν αὐτῷ ἀληθὲς ἀναπέφαγκεν.

5.1. Πάλιν δὲ δὴ τὸ ἓν μέρος, ὁ αὐτοῦ τοῦ θεοῦ νόμος, διαιρεῖται εἰς τρία τινά· εἴς τε τὴν καθαρὰν νομοθεσίαν τὴν ἀσύμπλοκον τῷ κακῷ, ὃς καὶ κυρίως νόμος λέγεται, ὃν οὐκ ἦλθε καταλῦσαι ὁ σωτὴρ ἀλλὰ πληρῶσαι, οὐ γὰρ ἦν ἀλλότριος αὐτοῦ ὃν ἐπλήρωσεν, οὐ γὰρ εἶχεν τὸ τέλειον· καὶ εἰς τὸν συμπεπλεγμένον τῷ χείρονι καὶ τῇ ἀδικίᾳ, ὃν ἀνεῖλεν ὁ σωτὴρ ἀνοίκειον ὄντα τῇ ἑαυτοῦ φύσει.

5.2 Διαιρεῖται δὲ καὶ εἰς τὸ τυπικὸν καὶ συμβολικὸν τὸ κατ' εἰκόνα τῶν πνευματικῶν καὶ διαφερόντων νομοθετηθέν, ὃ μετέθηκεν ὁ σωτὴρ ἀπὸ αἰσθητοῦ καὶ φαινομένου ἐπὶ τὸ πνευ-ματικὸν καὶ ἀόρατον.

5.3 Καὶ ἔστι μὲν ὁ τοῦ θεοῦ νόμος, ὁ καθαρὸς καὶ ἀσύμπλοκος τῷ χείρονι, αὐτὴ ἡ δεκάλογος, οἱ δέκα λόγοι ἐκεῖνοι οἱ ἐν ταῖς δυσὶ πλαξὶ δεδιχασμένοι, εἴς τε ἀπαγόρευσιν τῶν ἀφεκτέων καὶ εἰς πρόσταξιν τῶν ποιητέων. οἳ καίπερ καθαρὰν ἔχοντες τὴν νομοθεσίαν, μὴ ἔχοντες δὲ τὸ τέλειον, ἐδέοντο τῆς παρὰ τοῦ σωτῆρος πληρώσεως.

5.4 Ὁ δέ ἐστιν συμπεπλεγμένος τῇ ἀδικίᾳ, οὗτος ὁ κατὰ τὴν ἄμυναν καὶ ἀνταπόδοσιν τῶν προαδικησάντων κείμενος, ὀφθαλμὸν ἀντὶ ὀφθαλμοῦ καὶ ὀδόντα ἀντὶ ὀδόντος ἐκκόπτεσθαι κελεύων καὶ φόνον ἀντὶ φόνου ἀμύνασθαι. οὐδὲν γὰρ ἧττον καὶ ὁ δεύτερος ἀδικῶν ἀδικεῖ, τῇ τάξει μόνον διαλλάσσων, τὸ αὐτὸ ἐργαζόμενος ἔργον.

4.10 This was his reason for devising laws contrary to God. Therefore, that the law of Moses is different from the law of God is beyond dispute here, even if we have demonstrated this from one (passage).

4.11 That there are some traditions of the elders embedded in the law the Savior also makes clear. "For God," he says, "said, 'Honor your father and your mother so that it may be well with you.'"

4.12 "But you," he says when speaking to the elders, "have deemed as a gift to God what you have received from me, and you have nullified the law of God through the tradition of your elders."

4.13 This Isaiah also uttered, saying, "This people honors me with their lips, but their heart is far from me; in vain they honor me, teaching teachings that are the commandments of humans."

4.14 Therefore, clearly it is shown from these things that the whole law is divided into three; for we find within it the legislation of Moses himself and of the elders, and of God himself. This division of the entire law, then, as divided by us, has revealed what is true in it.

5.1 Moreover, this part, the law of God himself, is divided into three parts: the pure legislation that is not mixed with evil, which also is properly called law, which the Savior did not come to destroy but fulfill, for what he fulfilled was not foreign to him, for it did not have perfection; and the legislation mixed with inferiority and injustice, which the Savior abrogated, because it was dissimilar to his own nature.

5.2 And it is divided into legislation that is typological and symbolic, which is an image of the spiritual and differentiated, which the Savior transformed from the perceptible and phenomenal to the spiritual and invisible.

5.3 The law of God, pure and not mixed with what is inferior, is the Decalogue, those ten teachings engraved upon two tablets, that prohibit the abstention from things and commanding things to be done. These include pure legislation, though the legislation is not perfect, and they are in need of fulfillment by the Savior.

5.4 There is also the law mixed with injustice, one established for retaliation and repayment of prior injustices, an eye to be cut out for an eye and a tooth for a tooth, and a murder to be repaid with a murder. For the second unjust one is no less unjust, changing in order alone while doing the same thing.

5.5 Τοῦτο δὲ τὸ πρόσταγμα δίκαιον μὲν ἄλλως καὶ ἦν καὶ ἔστι, διὰ τὴν ἀσθένειαν τῶν νομοθετηθέντων ἐν παρεκβάσει τοῦ καθαροῦ νόμου τεθέν. ἀνοίκειον δὲ τῇ τοῦ πατρὸς τῶν ὅλων φύσει τε καὶ ἀγαθότητι.

5.6 Ἴσως δὲ τοῦτο κατάλληλον, ἐπάναγκες δὲ μᾶλλον· ὁ γὰρ καὶ τὸν ἕνα φόνον οὐ βουλόμενος ἔσεσθαι ἐν τῷ λέγειν «οὐ φονεύσεις,» προστάξας τὸν φονέα ἀντιφονεύεσθαι, δεύτερον νόμον νομοθετῶν καὶ δυσὶ φόνοις βραβεύων, ὁ τὸν ἕνα ἀπαγορεύσας, ἔλαθεν ἑαυτὸν ὑπ᾽ ἀνάγκης κλαπείς.

5.7 Διὸ δὴ ὁ ἀπ᾽ ἐκείνου παραγενόμενος υἱός, τοῦτο τὸ μέρος τοῦ νόμου ἀνήρηκεν, ὁμολογήσας καὶ αὐτὸ εἶναι τοῦ θεοῦ. ἔν τε τοῖς ἄλλοις καταρυθμεῖται τῇ παλαιᾷ αἱρέσει καὶ ἐν οἷς ἔφη· «ὁ θεὸς εἶπεν· ὁ κακολογῶν πατέρα ἢ μητέρα θανάτῳ τελευτάτω.»

5.8 Τὸ δέ ἐστι μέρος αὐτοῦ τυπικόν, τὸ κατ᾽ εἰκόνα τῶν πνευματικῶν καὶ διαφερόντων κείμενον, τὰ ἐν προσφοραῖς λέγω καὶ περιτομῇ καὶ σαββάτῳ καὶ νηστείᾳ καὶ πάσχα καὶ ἀζύμοις καὶ τοῖς τοιούτοις νομοθετηθέντα.

5.9 Πάντα γὰρ ταῦτα, εἰκόνες καὶ σύμβολα ὄντα, τῆς ἀληθείας φανερωθείσης μετετέθη. κατὰ μὲν τὸ φαινόμενον καὶ <τὸ> σωματικῶς ἐκτελεῖσθαι ἀνηρέθη, κατὰ δὲ τὸ πνευματικὸν ἀνελήφθη, τῶν μὲν ὀνομάτων τῶν αὐτῶν μενόντων, ἐνηλλαγμένων δὲ τῶν πραγμάτων.

5.10 Καὶ γὰρ προσφορὰς προσφέρειν προσέταξεν ἡμῖν ὁ σωτήρ, ἀλλὰ οὐχὶ τὰς δι᾽ ἀλόγων ζῴων ἢ τούτων τῶν θυμιαμάτων, ἀλλὰ διὰ πνευματικῶν αἴνων καὶ δοξῶν καὶ εὐχαριστίας καὶ διὰ τῆς εἰς τοὺς πλησίον κοινωνίας καὶ εὐποιίας.

5.11 Καὶ περιτομὴν περιτετμῆσθαι ἡμᾶς βούλεται, ἀλλ᾽ οὐχὶ τῆς ἀκροβυστίας τῆς σωματικῆς, ἀλλὰ καρδίας τῆς πνευματικῆς.

5.12 Καὶ τὸ σάββατον φυλάσσειν, ἀργεῖν γὰρ θέλει ἡμᾶς ἀπὸ τῶν ἔργων τῶν πονηρῶν.

5.13 Καὶ νηστεύειν δέ, ἀλλὰ οὐχὶ τὴν σωματικὴν βούλεται νηστείαν ἡμᾶς νηστεύειν, ἀλλὰ τὴν πνευματικήν, ἐν ᾗ ἐστιν ἀποχὴ πάντων τῶν φαύλων. Φυλάσσεται μέντοι γε καὶ παρὰ τοῖς ἡμετέροις ἡ κατὰ τὸ φαινόμενον νηστεία, ἐπεὶ καὶ ψυχῇ τι συμβάλλεσθαι δύναται αὕτη μετὰ λόγου γινομένη, ὁπότε μήτε διὰ τὴν πρός τινας μίμησιν γίνεται μήτε διὰ τὸ ἔθος μήτε διὰ τὴν ἡμέραν, ὡς ὡρισμένης <εἰς> τοῦτο ἡμέρας.

5.5 To be sure, this commandment was and still is just, on account of the weakness of those who received the legislation, put in place so that they would not deviate from the pure law. But it is foreign to the nature and goodness of the Father of the whole.

5.6 Likewise this is appropriate, and even necessary. For the one who does not want there to be a murder when saying, "You shall not murder," while commanding that a murder be responded to by another murder, has legislated a second law commanding two murders, although he had forbidden murder setting in motion himself as one being tricked by necessity.

5.7 Therefore, when his Son arrived, he abrogated this part of the law, even though he confessed that it came from God. He recounts this (part of the law as it was) in the old sect, both in other passages and in those in which he said, "God said, 'The one who slanders father or mother will die.'"

5.8 And there is the typological part, established in the image of the spiritual and differentiated elements; I am speaking about legislation concerning offerings and circumcision and the Sabbath and fasting and Passover and unleavened bread and other topics.

5.9 For all of these things being images and symbols, when the truth appeared, they were transformed. With respect to their phenomenal and corporeal (meanings) they were annulled as accomplished, but with respect to their spiritual (meaning) they were restored, the names remaining the same, but the meanings changed.

5.10 For the Savior enjoined us to make offerings, but not of irrational animals or incense of this sort, but of spiritual praise and glory and thanksgiving and of fellowship and benefaction with those near us.

5.11 And he wanted us to be circumcised, but not with reference to our bodily foreskin, but our spiritual heart.

5.12 And to keep the Sabbath, for he wants to be at rest when it comes to wicked deeds.

5.13 And to fast, but he does not want us to fast bodily, but spiritually, in which there is distance from all things trivial. To be sure, literal fasting is also practiced among us, since it is capable of building up the soul when done within reason, when it comes not from the imitation of others or from habit or on a particular day, as a day set apart <for> this.

5.14 Ἅμα δὲ καὶ εἰς ἀνάμνησιν τῆς ἀληθινῆς νηστείας, ἵνα οἱ μηδέπω ἐκείνην δυνάμενοι νηστεύειν ἀπὸ τῆς κατὰ τὸ φαινόμενον νηστείας ἔχωσιν τὴν ἀνάμνησιν αὐτῆς.

5.15 Καὶ τὸ πάσχα δὲ ὁμοίως καὶ τὰ ἄζυμα, ὅτι εἰκόνες ἦσαν, δηλοῖ καὶ Παῦλος ὁ ἀπόστολος «τὸ δὲ πάσχα ἡμῶν,» λέγων «ἐτύθη Χριστός,» καὶ «ἵνα ἦτε,» φησίν, «ἄζυμοι, μὴ μετέχοντες ζύμης»—ζύμην δὲ νῦν τὴν κακίαν λέγει—«ἀλλ᾽ ἦτε νέον φύραμα.»

6.1 Οὕτως γ᾽ οὖν καὶ αὐτὸς ὁ τοῦ θεοῦ εἶναι νόμος ὁμολογούμενος εἰς τρία διαιρεῖται, εἴς τε τὸ πληρούμενον ἀπὸ τοῦ σωτῆρος, τὸ γὰρ «οὐ φονεύσεις, οὐ μοιχεύσεις, οὐκ ἐπιορκήσεις» ἐν τῷ μηδ᾽ ὀργισθῆναι μηδὲ ἐπιθυμῆσαι μηδὲ ὀμόσαι περιείληπται.

6.2 Διαιρεῖται δὲ καὶ εἰς τὸ ἀναιρούμενον τελείως. Τὸ γὰρ «ὀφθαλμὸν ἀντὶ ὀφθαλμοῦ καὶ ὀδόντα ἀντὶ ὀδόντος» συμπεπλεγμένον τῇ ἀδικίᾳ καὶ αὐτὸ ἔργον τῆς ἀδικίας ἔχον, ἀνηρέθη ὑπὸ τοῦ σωτῆρος διὰ τῶν ἐναντίων.

6.3 Τὰ δὲ ἐναντία ἀλλήλων ἐστὶν ἀναιρετικά· «ἐγὼ γὰρ λέγω ὑμῖν μὴ ἀντιστῆναι ὅλως τῷ πονηρῷ, ἀλλὰ ἐάν τίς σε ῥαπίσῃ, στρέψον αὐτῷ καὶ τὴν ἄλλην σιαγόνα.»

6.4 Διαιρεῖται δὲ καὶ εἰς τὸ μετατεθὲν καὶ ἐναλλαγὲν ἀπὸ τοῦ σωματικοῦ ἐπὶ τὸ πνευματικόν, τὸ συμβολικὸν τοῦτο <τὸ> κατ᾽ εἰκόνα τῶν διαφερόντων νενομοθετημένον.

6.5 Αἱ γὰρ εἰκόνες καὶ τὰ σύμβολα παραστατικὰ ὄντα ἑτέρων πραγμάτων καλῶς ἐγίνοντο μέχρι μὴ παρῆν ἡ ἀλήθεια· παρούσης δὲ τῆς ἀληθείας τὰ τῆς ἀληθείας δεῖ ποιεῖν, οὐ τὰ τῆς εἰκόνος.

6.6 Ταῦτα δὲ καὶ οἱ μαθηταὶ αὐτοῦ καὶ ὁ ἀπόστολος Παῦλος ἔδειξε, τὸ μὲν τῶν εἰκόνων, ὡς ἤδη εἴπομεν, διὰ τοῦ πάσχα δι᾽ ἡμᾶς καὶ τῶν ἀζύμων δείξας, τὸ δὲ τοῦ συμπεπλεγμένου νόμου τῇ ἀδικίᾳ, εἰπὼν «τὸν νόμον τῶν ἐντολῶν ἐν δόγμασιν κατηργῆσθαι,» τὸ δὲ τοῦ ἀσυμπλόκου τῷ χείρονι, «ὁ μὲν νόμος,» εἰπών, «ἅγιος, καὶ ἡ ἐντολὴ ἁγία καὶ δικαία καὶ ἀγαθή.»

7.1 Ὡς μὲν οὖν συντόμως ἔστιν εἰπεῖν, αὐτάρκως οἶμαί σοι δεδεῖχθαι καὶ τὴν ἐξ ἀνθρώπων παρεισδύσασαν νομοθεσίαν καὶ αὐτὸν τὸν τοῦ θεοῦ νόμον τριχῇ διαιρούμενον.

7.2 Περιλείπεται δὲ εἰπεῖν ἡμῖν τίς ποτέ ἐστιν οὗτος ὁ θεὸς ὁ τὸν νόμον θέμενος. Ἀλλὰ καὶ τοῦτο ἡγοῦμαί σοι δεδεῖχθαι ἐπὶ τῶν προειρημένων, εἰ ἐπιμελῶς ἀκήκοας.

5.14 But at the same time it is a reminder of the true fast, so that those not as yet able to fast truly might have a reminder of it from the literal fasting.

5.15 In a similar way, Paul the apostle makes clear that the Passover and the unleavened bread were images when he says "Our Passover, Christ, has been sacrificed," and "so that you might be," he says, "unleavened bread, not sharing in leaven"—but by leaven he means evil—"but you might be a new dough."

6.1 Thus the law of God itself is agreed upon as being divided into three parts, into the part fulfilled by the Savior, for the (commandments) "You shall not murder, you shall not commit adultery, you shall not make false oaths" are covered by the prohibition of anger and desire and swearing.

6.2 It is also divided into a part abrogated entirely, for "An eye for an eye and a tooth for a tooth," mixed with injustice and having the same work of injustice, was destroyed by the Savior through the opposite.

6.3 Things opposite to each other are mutually destructive: "for I say to you, do not oppose the wicked man, but if anyone hits you, turn the other cheek to him."

6.4 And it is divided into the part transformed and changed from the bodily to the spiritual, the symbolic which is the image of the surpassing things.

6.5 For the images and the symbols standing in for other things were good before the truth had come; but now that the truth has arrived it is necessary to do things of the truth, not things of the image.

6.6 These things his disciples and the apostle Paul demonstrated, that of the images, as we have already mentioned, through the Passover for us and the unleavened bread; for the law mixed with injustice, when he says, "The law of the commandments in dogmas was annulled"; and for the law not mixed with anything deficient, when he says, "The law is holy, and the commandment is holy and just and good."

7.1 As one speaking concisely, I think I have demonstrated clearly to you the legislation added by humans and the threefold division of the law of God itself.

7.2 Now it remains for us to say who this God is who established the law. But I think that this also has been demonstrated to you in what has been said, if you have listened carefully.

7.3 Εἰ γὰρ μήτε ὑπ᾽ αὐτοῦ τοῦ τελείου θεοῦ τέθειται οὗτος, ὡς ἐδιδάξαμεν, μήτε μὴν ὑπὸ τοῦ διαβόλου, ὃ μηδὲ θεμιτόν ἐστιν εἰπεῖν, ἕτερός τίς ἐστι παρὰ τούτους οὗτος ὁ θέμενος τὸν νόμον.

7.4 Οὗτος δὲ δημιουργὸς καὶ ποιητὴς τοῦδε τοῦ παντός ἐστιν κόσμου καὶ τῶν ἐν αὐτῷ, ἕτερος ὢν παρὰ τὰς τούτων οὐσίας μέσος τούτων καθεστὼς, ἐνδίκως καὶ τὸ «τῆς μεσότητος» ὄνομα ἀποφέροιτο ἄν.

7.5 Καὶ εἰ ὁ τέλειος θεὸς ἀγαθός ἐστιν κατὰ τὴν ἑαυτοῦ φύσιν, ὥσπερ καὶ ἔστιν, ἕνα γὰρ μόνον εἶναι ἀγαθὸν θεόν, τὸν ἑαυτοῦ πατέρα ὁ σωτὴρ ἡμῶν ἀπεφήνατο, ὃν αὐτὸς ἐφανέρωσεν, ἔστιν δὲ καὶ ὁ τῆς τοῦ ἀντικειμένου φύσεως κακός τε καὶ πονηρὸς ἐν ἀδικίᾳ χαρακτηριαζόμενος, τούτων δὲ οὖν μέσος καθεστὼς καὶ μήτε ἀγαθὸς ὢν μήτε μὴν κακὸς μήτε ἄδικος, ἰδίως γε λεχθείη ἂν δίκαιος, τῆς κατ᾽ αὐτὸν δικαιοσύνης ὢν βραβευτής.

7.6 Καὶ ἔσται μὲν καταδεέστερος τοῦ τελείου θεοῦ καὶ τῆς ἐκείνου δικαιοσύνης ἐλάττων οὗτος ὁ θεός, ἅτε δὴ καὶ γεννητὸς ὢν καὶ οὐκ ἀγέννητος, εἷς γάρ ἐστιν ἀγέννητος ὁ πατήρ, ἐξ οὗ τὰ πάντα, ἰδίως τῶν πάντων ἠρτημένων ἀπ᾽ αὐτοῦ. μείζων δὲ καὶ κυριώτερος τοῦ ἀντικειμένου γενήσεται καὶ ἑτέρας οὐσίας τε καὶ φύσεως πεφυκὼς παρὰ τὴν ἑκατέρων τούτων οὐσίαν.

7.7 Τοῦ μὲν γὰρ ἀντικειμένου ἐστὶν ἡ οὐσία φθορά τε καὶ σκότος, ὑλικὸς γὰρ οὗτος καὶ πολυσχιδής, τοῦ δὲ πατρὸς τῶν ὅλων τοῦ ἀγεννήτου ἡ οὐσία ἐστὶν ἀφθαρσία τε καὶ φῶς αὐτοόν, ἁπλοῦν τε καὶ μονοειδές. ἡ δὲ τούτου οὐσία διττὴν μέν τινα δύναμιν προήγαγεν, αὐτὸς δὲ τοῦ κρείττονός ἐστιν εἰκών.

7.8 Μηδέ σε τὰ νῦν τοῦτο θορυβείτω θέλουσαν μαθεῖν πῶς ἀπὸ μιᾶς ἀρχῆς τῶν ὅλων <ἁπλῆς> οὔσης τε καὶ ὁμολογουμένης ἡμῖν καὶ πεπιστευμένης, τῆς ἀγεννήτου καὶ ἀφθάρτου καὶ ἀγαθῆς, συνέστησαν καὶ αὗται αἱ φύσεις, ἥ τε τῆς φθορᾶς καὶ <ἡ> τῆς μεσότητος, ἀνομοούσιοι αὗται καθεστῶσαι, τοῦ ἀγαθοῦ φύσιν ἔχοντος τὰ ὅμοια ἑαυτῷ καὶ ὁμοούσια γεννᾶν τε καὶ προφέρειν.

7.9 Μαθήσῃ γάρ, θεοῦ διδόντος, ἑξῆς καὶ τὴν τούτων ἀρχήν τε καὶ γέννησιν, ἀξιουμένη τῆς ἀποστολικῆς παραδόσεως, ἣν ἐκ διαδοχῆς καὶ ἡμεῖς παρειλήφαμεν, μετὰ καὶ τοῦ κανονίσαι πάντας τοὺς λόγους τῇ τοῦ σωτῆρος ἡμῶν διδασκαλίᾳ.

7.10 Ταῦτά σοι, ὦ ἀδελφή μου Φλώρα, δι᾽ ὀλίγων εἰρημένα οὐκ ἠτόνησα· καὶ τὸ τῆς συντομίας προέγραψα ἅμα τε τὸ προκείμενον ἀποχρώντως ἐξέφηνα, ἃ καὶ εἰς τὰ ἑξῆς τὰ μέγιστά σοι συμβαλεῖται, ἐάν γε ὡς καλὴ γῆ καὶ ἀγαθὴ γονίμων σπερμάτων τυχοῦσα τὸν δι᾽ αὐτῶν καρπὸν ἀναδείξῃς.

7.3 For if this law was not established by the Perfect God himself, as we have taught, or by the devil, a notion that is not permitted by God to speak, the one who established the law is someone other than these two.

7.4 Thus he is the creator and maker of the whole universe and everything within it, and since he is different than these two in essence, occupying a place between them, he ought fittingly also to be called "the intermediate."

7.5 And if the Perfect God is good according to his nature, as indeed he is, for our Savior professed that there is only one good God, his Father, whom he made known, and if the one with the opposite nature is evil and wicked and characteristically unjust, then the one between these two is not good, evil, or unjust, but might uniquely be called just, since he administers the justice that is his.

7.6 This god will be inferior to the Perfect God and lesser than his righteousness, inasmuch as he is begotten and not unbegotten, for there is one unbegotten Father, from whom come all things, because all things depend upon him in kind. Yet he is also greater and more powerful than the adversary, and he has another essence and nature in addition to the essences of the other two.

7.7 For the essence of the adversary is destruction and darkness, for he is material and divided, but the essence of the unbegotten Father of the whole is incorruption and autonomous light, unified and simple. The essence of the unbegotten Father brought forward a twofold power, and the Savior is an image of the greater one.

7.8 But at this time do not be troubled by your desire to learn how from one origin of the whole, being <simple>, and confessed and believed by us, unbegotten and incorruptible and good, these three natures of destruction and the intermediate were contrived, having been established as dissimilar, yet the good has a nature to put forth things that are like itself and of the same substance.

7.9 For God willing, you shall later learn about their origin and generation, once you have been deemed worthy of the apostolic tradition, which we also have received by succession, and we too are able to guarantee the authority of all our words by the teaching of our Savior.

7.10 By offering you these brief teachings, my sister Flora, I have not become fatigued; and I have at once written about this matter concisely, and I have disclosed a sufficient amount, which also in the future will contribute to you greatly, if, like beautiful and good soil receiving fertile seeds, you bring forth their fruit.

III. FRAGMENTS OF HERACLEON

Little is known about Heracleon other than that he was a student of Valentinus. What we know about his teachings comes from fragments of his writings preserved by church fathers. Heracleon's commentary on John survives only in brief excerpts quoted by Origen in his own commentary on John. Clement of Alexandria preserves two additional fragments, one on Matthew (frag. 49) and another on Luke (frag. 50), but I have included only the latter, since the former is not a direct quotation of Heracleon. Heracleon is considered to have been one of the first Christians to compose commentaries on New Testament writings. Though his commentary on John does not survive in its entirety, from the excerpts we gather that he interpreted the Gospel of John allegorically, with mundane details of the biblical narrative signaling deeper spiritual realities. For example, in fragment 27, Heracleon understands the words "They departed from the city" to signify "the overthrow of their prior worldly way of being."

Heracleon's precise dates are not known, but he likely composed these commentaries sometime during the last quarter of the second century C.E. Given that his writings survive only in Clement and Origen, his teachings may have been particularly influential among educated Christians in Egypt.

The Greek text is based on C. Blanc, *Origène: Commentaire sur saint Jean,* 5 vols., SC 120, 157, 222, 290, 385 (Paris: Éditions du Cerf, 1966, 1970, 1975, 1982, 1992); and L. Früchtel, O. Stählin, and U. Treu, *Clemens Alexandrinus,* 4th ed., vol. 2, GCS 52.15 (Berlin: Akademie, 1985).

Fragment 1 (Jn 1:3)

«Πάντα δι' αὐτοῦ ἐγένετο»
οὐ τὸν αἰῶνα ἢ τὰ ἐν τῷ αἰῶνι γεγονέναι διὰ τοῦ λόγου.

Ὅτι οὐχ ὡς ὑπ' ἄλλου ἐνεργοῦντος αὐτὸς ἐποίει ὁ λόγος, ἀλλ' αὐτοῦ ἐνεργοῦντος ἕτερος ἐποίει.

«Καὶ χωρὶς αὐτοῦ ἐγένετο οὐδὲ ἕν»
τῶν ἐν τῷ κόσμῳ καὶ τῇ κτίσει

Fragment 2 (Jn 1:4)

«Ὃ γέγονεν ἐν αὐτῷ ζωὴ ἦν»
εἰς τοὺς ἀνθρώπους τοὺς πνευματικούς.

Αὐτὸς γὰρ τὴν πρώτην μόρφωσιν τὴν κατὰ τὴν γένεσιν αὐτοῖς παρέσχε, τὰ ὑπ' ἄλλου σπαρέντα εἰς μορφὴν καὶ εἰς φωτισμὸν καὶ περιγραφὴν ἰδίαν ἀγαγὼν καὶ ἀναδείξας.

Fragment 3 (Jn 1:18)

«Οὐδεὶς τὸν θεὸν ἑώρακεν πώποτε»
εἰρῆσθαι οὐκ ἀπὸ τοῦ βαπτιστοῦ ἀλλ' ἀπὸ τοῦ μαθητοῦ.

Fragment 4 (Jn 1:21)

ὡς ἄρα Ἰωάννης ὡμολόγησεν μὴ εἶναι ὁ Χριστός, ἀλλὰ μηδὲ προφήτης μηδὲ Ἠλίας.

Fragment 5 (Jn 1:23)

Ὁ λόγος μὲν ὁ σωτήρ ἐστιν, φωνὴ δὲ ἡ ἐν τῇ ἐρήμῳ ἡ διὰ Ἰωάννου διανοουμένη, ἦχος δὲ πᾶσα προφητικὴ τάξις.

Fragment 6 (Jn 1:25)

περὶ τοῦ ὀφείλεσθαι τὸ βαπτίζειν Χριστῷ καὶ Ἠλίᾳ καὶ παντὶ προφήτῃ, οἷς μόνοις ὀφείλεται τὸ βαπτίζειν

Fragment 7 (Jn 1:26)

οὐ πρὸς ὃ ἐκεῖνοι ἐπηρώτων, ἀλλ' ὃ αὐτὸς ἐβούλετο

Fragment 8 (Jn 1:26)

«Μέσος ὑμῶν στήκει» ἀντὶ τοῦ «Ἤδη πάρεστιν καὶ ἔστιν ἐν τῷ κόσμῳ καὶ ἐν ἀνθρώποις, καὶ ἐμφανής ἐστιν ἤδη πᾶσιν ὑμῖν.»

Fragment 1 (Jn 1:3)

"All things came about through him"
    The eternity and the things in the eternity did not come about through the Word.

    Because it was not the Word who made all things as under some other agent, but the Word himself was the agent, and another did the making.

"And apart from him nothing came to be"
    ("Nothing") in the world or in creation

Fragment 2 (Jn 1:4)

"What came to be in him was life"
    ("In him" means) to those people who are spiritual.

    The Word supplied them with their first form when they were born by drawing out and revealing the things that had been sown by another into a form and a light and into its own sketch.

Fragment 3 (Jn 1:18)

"No one has seen God at any time"
    (This was) spoken not by the Baptizer, but by the disciple.

Fragment 4 (Jn 1:21)

As indeed John admitted that he was not the Christ, nor a prophet nor Elijah.

Fragment 5 (Jn 1:23)

The Word is the Savior, and the voice that was in the wilderness that was meant by John, but the sound is the entire prophetic order.

Fragment 6 (Jn 1:25)

(The question implies that) to baptize belongs to the Christ and Elijah and every prophet, by whom alone baptism ought to be done.

Fragment 7 (Jn 1:26)

(John's answers refer) not to what (the Pharisees) asked, but to what he desired.

Fragment 8 (Jn 1:26)

"He stands among you" is the same as "Already he is here, and he is in the world and among humanity, and he is already visible to you all."

Fragment 9 (Jn 1:28)

Ταῦτα ἐν Βηθανίᾳ ἐγένετο.

Fragment 10 (Jn 1:29)

«Ἀμνὸς τοῦ θεοῦ» ὡς προφήτης φησὶν ὁ Ἰωάννης, τὸ δὲ «Ὁ αἴρων τὴν ἁμαρτίαν τοῦ κόσμου» ὡς περισσότερον προφήτου.

Fragment 11 (Jn 2:12)

«Μετὰ τοῦτο κατέβη εἰς Καφαρναοὺμ αὐτὸς»

τὴν Καφαρναοὺμ σημαίνειν ταῦτα τὰ ἔσχατα τοῦ κόσμου, ταῦτα τὰ ὑλικὰ εἰς ἃ κατῆλθεν· καὶ διὰ τὸ ἀνοίκειον εἶναι τὸν τόπον οὐδὲ πεποιηκώς τι λέγεται ἐν αὐτῇ ἢ λελαληκώς.

Fragment 12 (Jn 2:13)

Αὕτη... ἡ μεγάλη ἑορτή· τοῦ γὰρ πάθους τοῦ σωτῆρος τύπος ἦν, ὅτε οὐ μόνον ἀνηρεῖτο τὸ πρόβατον, ἀλλὰ καὶ ἀνάπαυσιν παρεῖχεν ἐσθιόμενον, καὶ θυόμενον τὸ πάθος τοῦ σωτῆρος τὸ ἐν κόσμῳ ἐσήμαινεν, ἐσθιόμενον δὲ τὴν ἀνάπαυσιν τὴν ἐν γάμῳ.

Fragment 13 (Jn 2:13–16)

Οὐ γὰρ ἐκ δέρματος ... νεκροῦ ἐποίησεν αὐτό, ἵνα τὴν ἐκκλησίαν κατασκευάσῃ οὐκέτι λῃστῶν καὶ ἐμπόρων σπήλαιον, ἀλλὰ οἶκον τοῦ πατρὸς αὐτοῦ.

Fragment 15 (Jn 2:19)

«Ἐν τρίτῃ»
ἐν τρισὶν

τὴν πνευματικὴν ἡμέραν

Fragment 16 (Jn 2:20)

τὸν Σαλομῶντα, τεσσεράκοντα καὶ ἓξ ἔτεσιν κατεσκευακέναι τὸν ναὸν, εἰκόνα τυγχάνοντα τοῦ σωτῆρος

ὃ τετρὰς ἐστίν ... ἡ ἀπρόσπλοκος, εἰς τὸ ἐμφύσημα καὶ τὸ ἐν τῷ ἐμφυσήματι σπέρμα.

Fragment 17 (Jn 4:12–15)

ἄτονον καὶ πρόσκαιρον καὶ ἐπιλείπουσαν ἐκείνην γεγονέναι τὴν ζωὴν καὶ τὴν κατ᾽ αὐτὴν δόξαν· κοσμικὴ γάρ ... ἦν·

Ὃ δὲ δίδωσιν ὕδωρ ὁ σωτήρ ... εἶναι ἐκ τοῦ πνεύματος καὶ τῆς δυνάμεως αὐτοῦ.

«Οὐ μὴ διψήσῃ δὲ εἰς τὸν αἰῶνα»

Fragment 9 (Jn 1:28)

These things occurred in Bethany.

Fragment 10 (Jn 1:29)

"Lamb of God" John says as a prophet, but "Who takes away the sin of the world," as more than a prophet.

Fragment 11 (Jn 2:12)

"After this he went down into Capernaum."

> Capernaum indicates the things at the extreme edge of the world, these material things into which he went down. And because the place is uninhabitable, he is not said to have done or said anything in it.

Fragment 12 (Jn 2:13)

This . . . is the great feast; for it was a type of the suffering of the Savior, when not only was the sheep snatched up, but eating it brought rest, and killing indicates the suffering of the Savior in the world, but eating indicates the rest that occurs in marriage.

Fragment 13 (Jn 2:13–16)

For not out of dead leather did he make it, so that he might build the church up no longer as a den of thieves and vagrants, but as the house of his father.

Fragment 15 (Jn 2:19)

"On the third (day)"
in three days

(The third day is) the spiritual day.

Fragment 16 (Jn 2:20)

Solomon, being forty-six when building the temple, is an image of the Savior.

(Forty) is the tetrad, that which is unmixed, for the inspiration and seed that is in the inspiration.

Fragment 17 (Jn 4:12–15)

Weak and fleeting and lacking was the life and the glory corresponding to it, for it was of this world.

But the water that the Savior gives is from his Spirit and power.

"But he shall not thirst forever"

αἰώνιος γὰρ ἡ ζωὴ αὐτοῦ καὶ μηδέποτε φθειρομένη, ὡς καὶ ἡ πρώτη ἡ ἐκ τοῦ φρέατος, ἀλλὰ μένουσα· ἀναφαίρετος γὰρ ἡ χάρις καὶ ἡ δωρεὰ τοῦ σωτῆρος ἡμῶν, καὶ μὴ ἀναλισκομένη μηδὲ φθειρομένη ἐν τῷ μετέχοντι αὐτῆς.

Φθειρομένην δὲ τὴν πρώτην διδοὺς εἶναι ζωήν

«Ἀλλομένου»

τοὺς μεταλαμβάνοντας τοῦ ἄνωθεν ἐπιχορηγουμένου πλουσίως καὶ αὐτοὺς ἐκβλύσαι εἰς τὴν ἑτέρων αἰώνιον ζωὴν τὰ ἐπικεχορηγημένα αὐτοῖς.

ὡσὰν ἐνδειξαμένην τὴν ἀδιάκριτον καὶ κατάλληλον τῇ φύσει ἑαυτῆς πίστιν, μὴ διακριθεῖσαν ἐφ᾽ οἷς ἔλεγεν αὐτῇ

«Δός μοι τοῦτο τὸ ὕδωρ»

ὡς ἄρα βραχέα διανυχθεῖσα ὑπὸ τοῦ λόγου ἐμίσησεν λοιπὸν καὶ τὸν τόπον ἐκείνου τοῦ λεγομένου ζῶντος ὕδατος.

«Δός μοι τοῦτο τὸ ὕδωρ, ἵνα μὴ διψῶ μηδὲ διέρχωμαι ἐνθάδε ἀντλεῖν»

Ταῦτα λέγει ἡ γυνὴ ἐμφαίνουσα τὸ ἐπίμοχθον καὶ δυσπόριστον καὶ ἄτροφον ἐκείνου τοῦ ὕδατος.

Fragment 18 (Jn 4:16–18)

«Λέγει αὐτῇ»

δῆλον ὅτι τοιοῦτό τι λέγων, «εἰ θέλεις λαβεῖν τοῦτο τὸ ὕδωρ, ὕπαγε φώνησον τὸν ἄνδρα σου»·

οὐ γὰρ περὶ ἀνδρός . . . κοσμικοῦ ἔλεγεν αὐτῇ, ἵνα καλέσῃ, ἐπείπερ οὐκ ἠγνόει ὅτι οὐκ εἶχεν νόμιμον ἄνδρα.

αὐτῇ τὸν σωτῆρα εἰρηκέναι· «Φώνησόν σου τὸν ἄνδρα καὶ ἐλθὲ ἐνθάδε,» δηλοῦντα τὸν ἀπὸ τοῦ πληρώματος σύζυγον·

Ἀλλ᾽ ἐπεί . . . κατὰ τὸ νοούμενον ἠγνόει τὸν ἴδιον ἄνδρα, κατὰ δὲ τὸ ἁπλοῦν ᾐσχύνετο εἰπεῖν ὅτι μοιχόν, οὐχὶ δὲ ἄνδρα εἶχεν, πῶς οὐχὶ μάτην ἔσται προστάσσων ὁ λέγων· «Ὕπαγε, φώνησον τὸν ἄνδρα σου, καὶ ἐλθὲ ἐνθάδε»;

«Ἀληθὲς εἴρηκας ὅτι ἄνδρα οὐκ ἔχεις»
ἐπεὶ ἐν τῷ κόσμῳ οὐκ εἶχεν ἄνδρα ἡ Σαμαρεῖτις· ἦν γὰρ αὐτῆς ὁ ἀνὴρ ἐν τῷ αἰῶνι.

For his life is eternal and never is destroyed, as also (is the case with) the first (life) from the well, rather it endures. For not to be taken away is the grace and the gift of our Savior, and it cannot be stolen or destroyed when one participates in it.

But the first life given is destroyed.

"Leaping"

(Leaping refers to) those who have a part in what is richly provided for them from above, and they allow the things provided to them to leap out for the eternal life of others.

(Regarding the Samaritan woman,) she exhibited an impartial faith proper to her own nature, showing no hesitation about the things he said to her.

"Give me this water"

As when she had been pricked a bit by the word, she then despised even the place of that so-called living water.

"Give me this water, so that I may not thirst nor come here to draw water"

The woman says these things indicating that the water is laborious, hard to come by, and lacking in nutrition.

Fragment 18 (Jn 4:16–18)

"He says to her"

It is clear that this is what he is saying: "If you want to receive this water, go call your husband."

For he did not speak to her about a worldly husband whom she might summon, since he would not have been unaware that she did not have a husband according to the law.

The Savior said to her: "Call your husband and come here," indicating her companion from the fullness.

But since she did not know about her own husband from an intellectual perspective, but from a straightforward perspective she felt ashamed to say that she had an adulterer, not a husband, how will the one who says, "Go, call your husband and come here" not give a meaningless command?

"Truly you say that you don't have a husband"

(This was said) because the Samaritan did not have a husband in the world, since her husband was in the eternity.

«Πέντε ἄνδρας ἔσχες·»

«Ἓξ ἄνδρας ἔσχες.»

Διὰ τῶν ἓξ ἀνδρῶν, ἧ συνεπέπλεκτο καὶ ἐπλησίαζεν παρὰ λόγον πορνεύουσα καὶ ἐνυβριζομένη καὶ ἀθετουμένη καὶ ἐγκαταλειπομένη ὑπ᾽ αὐτῶν.

Fragment 19 (Jn 4:19)

«Εὐσχημόνως ὡμολογηκέναι τὴν Σαμαρεῖτιν τὰ ὑπ᾽ αὐτοῦ πρὸς αὐτὴν εἰρημένα·»

προφήτου γὰρ μόνου . . . ἐστὶν εἰδέναι τὰ πάντα·

ὡς πρεπόντως τῆ αὐτῆς φύσει ποιήσασαν τὴν Σαμαρεῖτιν, καὶ μήτε ψευσαμένην μήτε ἄντικρυς ὁμολογήσασαν τὴν ἑαυτῆς ἀσχημοσύνην· πεπεισμένην . . . αὐτὴν ὅτι προφήτης εἴη, ἐρωτᾶν αὐτὸν ἅμα τὴν αἰτίαν ἐμφαίνουσαν δι᾽ ἣν ἐξεπόρνευσεν, ἅτε δι᾽ ἄγνοιαν θεοῦ καὶ τῆς κατὰ τὸν θεὸν λατρείας ἀμελήσασαν καὶ πάντων τῶν κατὰ τὸν βίον αὐτῇ ἀναγκαίων. καὶ ἄλλως <ταπεινὴν> ἐν τῷ βίῳ τυγχάνουσαν, οὐ γὰρ ἄν . . . αὐτὴ ἤρχετο ἐπὶ τὸ φρέαρ ἔξω τῆς πόλεως τυγχάνον.

Ὅτι βουλομένη μαθεῖν πῶς καὶ τίνι εὐαρεστήσασα καὶ θεῷ προσκυνήσασα ἀπαλλαγείη τοῦ πορνεύειν λέγει τὸ «Οἱ πατέρες ἡμῶν ἐν τῷ ὄρει τούτῳ προσεκύνησαν» καὶ τὸ ἑξῆς.

Fragment 20 (Jn 4:21)

Ἐπὶ μὲν τῶν προτέρων μὴ εἰρῆσθαι αὐτῇ· «Πίστευέ μοι, γύναι,» νῦν δὲ τοῦτο αὐτῇ προστετάχθαι,

ὅρος μὲν τὸν διάβολον λέγεσθαι ἢ τὸν κόσμον αὐτοῦ, ἐπείπερ μέρος ἐν ὁ διάβολος ὅλης τῆς ὕλης . . . ἦν. ὁ δὲ κόσμος τὸ σύμπαν τῆς κακίας ὅρος, ἔρημον οἰκητήριον θηρίων, ᾧ προσεκύνουν πάντες οἱ πρὸ νόμου καὶ οἱ ἐθνικοί· Ἱεροσόλυμα δὲ τὴν κτίσιν ἢ τὸν κτίστην, ᾧ προσεκύνουν οἱ Ἰουδαῖοι.

Δευτέρως ὅρος μὲν . . . εἶναι τὴν κτίσιν ἢ ἐθνικοὶ προσεκύνουν· Ἱεροσόλυμα δὲ τὸν κτίστην <ᾧ> οἱ Ἰουδαῖοι ἐλάτρευον.

Ὑμεῖς οὖν . . . οὔτε τῇ κτίσει οὔτε τῷ δημιουργῷ προσκυνήσετε, ἀλλὰ τῷ πατρὶ τῆς ἀληθείας, καὶ συμπαραλαμβάνει γε . . . αὐτὴν ὡς ἤδη πιστὴν καὶ συναριθμουμένην τοῖς κατὰ ἀλήθειαν προσκυνηταῖς.

Fragment 21 (Jn 4:22)

«Ὑμεῖς»

ἀντὶ τοῦ «Οἱ Ἰουδαῖοι <καὶ οἱ> ἐθνικοὶ» διηγήσατο

"You have had five husbands"

"You have had six husbands." (*Variant reading in Heracleon's text*)

Through the six husbands, with whom she united and whom she associated with without good reason, fornicating and being disparaged and rejected and abandoned by them.

Fragment 19 (Jn 4:19)

"The Samaritan responded fittingly to the things said to her by him."

For it is a prophet alone who knows all things.

(The Samaritan is to be praised) since the Samaritan acted in keeping with her own nature, and neither concealing nor disclosing her own lack of decorum. Having been persuaded that he was a prophet, she asked him, at once disclosing the cause through which she had committed sin, as if out of ignorance of God and neglectful of the service of God and of all things necessary for her concerning life. And moreover she occupied a <low position> in life, for, if not, she would not have come to a well outside of the city.

Since she wants to learn how, by being pleasing to anyone and giving worship to God, she might be set free from sin, she says "Our fathers worshipped upon this mountain," and so forth.

Fragment 20 (Jn 4:21)

In what was said earlier, it was not said to her: "Believe me, woman," but now this is commanded to her,

The mountain indicates the devil or his world, since the devil . . . was one part of all matter. But the world is the whole mountain of wickedness, a desert inhabited by beasts, which all those before the law and the gentiles were worshipping. But Jerusalem is the creation of the creator, which the Jews were worshipping.

The second mountain . . . is the creation that gentiles were worshipping. But Jerusalem is the creation <where> the Jews were serving.

You, then, . . . shall not worship the creation or the creator, but the Father of truth, and he included . . . her because (she is) already faithful and counted among those who worship according to truth.

Fragment 21 (Jn 4:22)

"You"

It means the same as "the Jews <and the> gentiles."

μὴ δεῖν καθ᾽ Ἕλληνας προσκυνεῖν, τὰ τῆς ὕλης πράγματα ἀποδεχομένους καὶ λατρεύοντας ξύλοις καὶ λίθοις, μήτε κατὰ Ἰουδαίους σέβειν τὸ θεῖον, ἐπείπερ καὶ αὐτοὶ μόνοι οἰόμενοι ἐπίστασθαι θεὸν ἀγνοοῦσιν αὐτόν, λατρεύοντες ἀγγέλοις καὶ μηνὶ καὶ σελήνῃ.

Fragment 22 (Jn 4:22–23)

Τὸ «Ἡμεῖς προσκυνοῦμεν» . . . εἶναι ὁ ἐν αἰῶνι καὶ οἱ σὺν αὐτῷ ἐλθόντες· οὗτοι γάρ . . . ᾔδεσαν τίνι προσκυνοῦσιν κατὰ ἀλήθειαν προσκυνοῦντες. Ἀλλὰ καὶ τὸ «Ὅτι ἡ σωτηρία ἐκ τῶν Ἰουδαίων ἐστὶν» ἐπεὶ ἐν τῇ Ἰουδαίᾳ . . . ἐγενήθη, ἀλλ᾽ οὐκ ἐν αὐτοῖς, οὐ γὰρ εἰς πάντας αὐτοὺς εὐδόκησεν, καὶ ὅτι ἐξ ἐκείνου τοῦ ἔθνους ἐξῆλθεν ἡ σωτηρία καὶ ὁ λόγος εἰς τὴν οἰκουμένην. Κατὰ δὲ τὸ νοούμενον ἐκ τῶν Ἰουδαίων τὴν σωτηρίαν . . . γεγονέναι, ἐπείπερ εἰκόνες οὗτοι τῶν ἐν τῷ πληρώματι αὐτῷ εἶναι νομίζονται.

«Ἐν πνεύματι καὶ ἀληθείᾳ προσκυνεῖσθαι τὸν θεὸν»

οἱ πρότεροι προσκυνηταὶ ἐν σαρκὶ καὶ πλάνῃ προσεκύνουν τῷ μὴ πατρί. ὥστε . . . πεπλανῆσθαι πάντας τοὺς προσκεκυνηκότας τῷ δημιουργῷ. . . . ἐλάτρευον τῇ κτίσει, καὶ οὐ τῷ κατ᾽ ἀλήθειαν κτίστῃ, ὅς ἐστιν Χριστός, εἴ γε «Πάντα δι᾽ αὐτοῦ ἐγένετο, καὶ χωρὶς αὐτοῦ ἐγένετο οὐδέν.»

Fragment 23 (Jn 4:23)

Ἀπολωλέναι . . . ἐν τῇ βαθείᾳ ὕλῃ τῆς πλάνης τὸ οἰκεῖον τῷ πατρί, ὅπερ ζητεῖται, ἵνα ὁ πατὴρ ὑπὸ τῶν οἰκείων προσκυνῆται.

Fragment 24 (Jn 4:24)

«Πνεῦμα ὁ θεός»

ἄχραντος γὰρ καὶ καθαρὰ καὶ ἀόρατος ἡ θεία φύσις αὐτοῦ.

«Τοὺς προσκυνοῦντας ἐν πνεύματι καὶ ἀληθείᾳ δεῖ προσκυνεῖν»

ἀξίως τοῦ προσκυνουμένου πνευματικῶς, οὐ σαρκικῶς· καὶ γὰρ αὐτοὶ τῆς αὐτῆς φύσεως ὄντες τῷ πατρὶ πνεῦμά εἰσιν, οἵτινες κατὰ ἀλήθειαν καὶ οὐ κατὰ πλάνην προσκυνοῦσιν, καθὰ καὶ ὁ ἀπόστολος διδάσκει λέγων λογικὴν λατρείαν τὴν τοιαύτην θεοσέβειαν.

Fragment 25 (Jn 4:25)

Προσεδέχετο ἡ ἐκκλησία τὸν Χριστὸν καὶ ἐπέπειστο περὶ αὐτοῦ, ὅτι τὰ πάντα μόνος ἐκεῖνος ἐπίσταται.

Fragment 26 (Jn 4:26–27)

«Ἐγώ εἰμι, ὁ λαλῶν σοι»

It is not fitting to worship as the gentiles do, since they approve of material things and honor wood and stone, nor is it fitting to honor God as the Jews do, since, although they think they alone know God, they too are ignorant of him, serving angels and the month and the moon.

Fragment 22 (Jn 4:22–23)

The words "We worship" mean the one in the eternity and those coming with him. For these had known the one they worship, since they worship in truth. But also the words "Because salvation is from the Jews" (were said) because he was born in Judea, but not among them, for he was not pleased with all of them, and because salvation and the word spread from that nation to the world. But on an intellectual level salvation has come about from the Jews, since they are thought to be images of those in the fullness.

"God is worshipped in spirit and truth"

Those who worshipped earlier, gave worship in flesh and error not to the Father. Therefore, all who have worshipped the creator are in error. They served the created thing and not the creator in truth, who is Christ, since indeed "All things came about through him, and apart from him nothing came to be."

Fragment 23 (Jn 4:23)

In the deep material of error . . . has been lost what belongs to the Father, which is being sought after, so that the Father might be worshipped by his own.

Fragment 24 (Jn 4:24)

"God is spirit"

For his divine nature is undefiled and pure and invisible.

"It is necessary for those who worship to worship in spirit and truth"

(These words are) worthy of the one who worships spiritually, not fleshly. For those having the same nature with the Father are also spirit; they worship in spirit and not in error, just as the apostle also teaches, saying that such piety is rational service.

Fragment 25 (Jn 4:25)

The church received Christ and was persuaded about him, that only he knows all things.

Fragment 26 (Jn 4:26–27)

"I am he, the one speaking to you"

ἐπεὶ ἐπέπειστο ἡ Σαμαρεῖτις περὶ τοῦ Χριστοῦ ὡς ἄρα ἐλθὼν πάντα ἀπαγγελεῖ αὐτῇ, φησί «Γίνωσκε ὅτι ἐκεῖνος, ὃν προσδοκᾷς, ἐγώ εἰμι, ὁ λαλῶν σοι.» Καὶ ὅτε ὡμολόγησεν ἑαυτὸν τὸν προσδοκώμενον ἐληλυθέναι, «ἦλθον . . . οἱ μαθηταὶ πρὸς αὐτόν,» δι' οὓς ἐληλύθει εἰς τὴν Σαμάρειαν.

Fragment 27 (Jn 4:28–30)

Τὴν ὑδρίαν τὴν δεκτικὴν ζωῆς . . . εἶναι διάθεσιν καὶ ἔννοιαν τῆς δυνάμεως τῆς παρὰ τοῦ σωτῆρος. ἥντινα καταλιποῦσα . . . παρ' αὐτῷ, τουτέστιν ἔχουσα παρὰ τῷ σωτῆρι τὸ τοιοῦτο σκεῦος, ἐν ᾧ ἐληλύθει λαβεῖν τὸ ζῶν ὕδωρ. ὑπέστρεψεν εἰς τὸν κόσμον εὐαγγελιζομένη τῇ κλήσει τὴν Χριστοῦ παρουσίαν· διὰ γὰρ τοῦ πνεύματος καὶ ὑπὸ τοῦ πνεύματος προσάγεται ἡ ψυχὴ τῷ σωτῆρι.

«Ἐξῆλθον δὲ ἐκ τῆς πόλεως»

τοῦ ἐκ τῆς προτέρας αὐτῶν ἀναστροφῆς οὔσης κοσμικῆς· καὶ ἤρχοντο διὰ τῆς πίστεως . . . πρὸς τὸν σωτῆρα.

Fragment 28 (Jn 4:31)

Ἐβούλοντο κοινωνεῖν αὐτῷ ἐξ ὧν ἀγοράσαντες ἀπὸ τῆς Σαμαρείας κεκομίκεισαν.

Fragment 30 (Jn 4:33)

Σαρκικῶς . . . ταῦτα λέγεσθαι . . . ὑπὸ τῶν μαθητῶν, ὡς ἔτι ταπεινότερον διανοουμένων καὶ τὴν Σαμαρεῖτιν μιμουμένων λέγουσαν· «Οὔτε ἄντλημα ἔχεις, καὶ τὸ φρέαρ ἐστὶν βαθύ.»

Fragment 31 (Jn 4:34)

Διὰ τοῦ «Ἐμὸν βρῶμά ἐστιν ἵνα ποιήσω τὸ θέλημα τοῦ πέμψαντός μέ» . . . διηγεῖσθαι τὸν σωτῆρα τοῖς μαθηταῖς, ὅτι τοῦτο ἦν ὃ συνεζήτει μετὰ τῆς γυναικός, βρῶμα ἴδιον λέγων τὸ θέλημα τοῦ πατρός· τοῦτο γὰρ αὐτοῦ τροφὴ καὶ ἀνάπαυσις καὶ δύναμις ἦν. Θέλημα δὲ πατρὸς ἔλεγεν εἶναι τὸ γνῶναι ἀνθρώπους τὸν πατέρα καὶ σωθῆναι, ὅπερ ἦν ἔργον τοῦ σωτῆρος τοῦ ἕνεκα τούτου ἀπεσταλμένου εἰς Σαμάρειαν, τουτέστιν εἰς τὸν κόσμον.

Fragment 32 (Jn 4:35)

Τὸν τῶν γεννημάτων λέγει θερισμόν, ὡς τούτου μὲν ἔτι διωρίαν ἔχοντος τετράμηνον, τοῦ δὲ θερισμοῦ, οὗ αὐτὸς ἔλεγεν, ἤδη ἐνεστῶτος. . . . Ἤδη ἀκμαῖοι καὶ ἕτοιμοί εἰσιν πρὸς θερισμὸν καὶ ἐπιτήδειοι πρὸς τὸ συναχθῆναι εἰς ἀποθήκην, τοῦτ' ἔστιν διὰ πίστεως εἰς ἀνάπαυσιν, ὅσαι γε ἕτοιμοι· οὐ γὰρ πᾶσαι· αἱ μὲν γὰρ ἤδη ἕτοιμοι ἦσαν . . . αἱ δὲ ἔμελλον, αἱ δὲ μέλλουσιν, αἱ δὲ ἐπισπείρονται ἤδη.

(It is) because the Samaritan had been persuaded that Christ would proclaim all things to her when he came that he says, "Know that this one, who speaks to you, I am he, the one speaking to you." And when he confirmed that he, the one who was expected, had come, "the disciples came to him," on behalf of whom he had gone to the Samaritan.

Fragment 27 (Jn 4:28–30)

The water container is the disposition capable of receiving life and thought of the power from the Savior. She left it . . . with him, that is, she had this sort of vessel with the Savior, in which she had proceeded to receive the living water. She returned to the world proclaiming the coming of Christ to the calling. For through the spirit and by the spirit the soul is led to the Savior.

"They departed from the city"

> The overthrow of their prior worldly way of being. And they came through faith to the Savior.

Fragment 28 (Jn 4:31)

They wanted to share with him some of the goods that had been purchased from the Samaritans.

Fragment 30 (Jn 4:33)

In a fleshly way . . . these things were said . . . by the disciples, since they were thinking lower and they imitated the Samaritan when she said, "You have nothing to draw with, and the well is deep."

Fragment 31 (Jn 4:34)

With the words "My food is that I should do the will of the one who sent me" . . . the Savior explains to the disciples that this was what he was talking about with the woman when he said that his own food is the will of the Father. For this was his nourishment and rest and power. But the will of the Father is that humanity knows the Father and is saved, which was the work for which the Savior was sent into Samaria, that is, into the world.

Fragment 32 (Jn 4:35)

He speaks about the reaping of crops, since this had an interval of four months, but the reaping about which he spoke was already at hand. . . . They are already mature and ready for reaping and able to be brought together in a storehouse, that is, into rest through faith, indeed, as many as are mature, for not all are. For some were already mature . . . but others were about to be, and others will be, and others are still being sown.

Fragment 33 (Jn 4:35)

Τῷ κατὰ τὸ «Ὁ θερισμὸς πολύς, οἱ δὲ ἐργάται ὀλίγοι» σημαινομένῳ ὁμοίως ταῦτα εἴρηται, τῷ ἑτοίμους πρὸς θερισμὸν καὶ ἐπιτηδείους πρὸς τὸ ἤδη συναχθῆναι εἰς τὴν ἀποθήκην διὰ τῆς πίστεως εἰς ἀνάπαυσιν εἶναι, καὶ ἐπιτηδείους πρὸς σωτηρίαν καὶ παραδοχὴν τοῦ λόγου·

Fragment 34 (Jn 4:36)

τὸ «Ὁ θερίζων μισθὸν λαμβάνει» εἰρῆσθαι . . . ἐπεὶ θεριστὴν ἑαυτὸν λέγει . . . ὁ σωτήρ. Καὶ τὸν μισθὸν τοῦ κυρίου ἡμῶν . . . εἶναι τὴν τῶν θεριζομένων σωτηρίαν καὶ ἀποκατάστασιν τῷ ἀναπαύεσθαι αὐτὸν ἐπ᾽ αὐτοῖς. Τὸ δὲ «Καὶ συνάγει καρπὸν εἰς ζωὴν αἰώνιόν» . . . εἰρῆσθαι, ἢ ὅτι τὸ συναγόμενον καρπὸς ζωῆς αἰωνίου ἐστίν, ἢ καὶ αὐτὸ ζωὴ αἰώνιος.

Fragment 35 (4:36–37)

«Ἵνα ὁ σπείρων ὁμοῦ χαίρῃ καὶ ὁ θερίζων»

χαίρει μὲν γάρ . . . ὁ σπείρων ὅτι σπείρει, καὶ ὅτι ἤδη τινὰ τῶν σπερμάτων αὐτοῦ συνάγεται ἐλπίδα ἔχων τὴν αὐτὴν καὶ περὶ τῶν λοιπῶν· ὁ δὲ θερίζων ὁμοίως ὅτι καὶ θερίζει. ἀλλ᾽ ὁ μὲν πρῶτος ἤρξατο σπείρων· ὁ δεύτερος θερίζων. Οὐ γὰρ ἐν τῷ αὐτῷ ἐδύναντο ἀμφότεροι ἄρξασθαι· ἔδει γὰρ πρῶτον σπαρῆναι, εἶθ᾽ ὕστερον θερισθῆναι. Παυσαμένου μέντοι γε τοῦ σπείροντος σπείρειν, ἔτι θεριεῖ ὁ θερίζων· ἐπὶ μέντοι τοῦ παρόντος ἀμφότεροι τὸ ἴδιον ἔργον ἐνεργοῦντες ὁμοῦ χαίρουσιν κοινὴν χαρὰν τὴν τῶν σπερμάτων τελειότητα ἡγούμενοι.

«Ἐν τούτῳ ἐστὶν ὁ λόγος ἀληθινὸς ὅτι ἄλλος ἐστὶν ὁ σπείρων καὶ ἄλλος ὁ θερίζων»

ὁ μὲν γὰρ ὑπὲρ τὸν τόπον υἱὸς ἀνθρώπου σπείρει· ὁ δὲ σωτήρ, ὢν καὶ αὐτὸς υἱὸς ἀνθρώπου, θερίζει καὶ θεριστὰς πέμπει τοὺς διὰ τῶν μαθητῶν νοουμένους ἀγγέλους, ἕκαστον ἐπὶ τὴν ἑαυτοῦ ψυχήν.

Fragment 36 (Jn 4:38)

οὐ δι᾽ αὐτῶν οὐδὲ ἀπ᾽ αὐτῶν ἐσπάρη ταῦτα τὰ σπέρματα . . ., οἱ δὲ κεκοπιακότες εἰσὶν οἱ τῆς οἰκονομίας ἄγγελοι, δι᾽ ὧν ὡς μεσιτῶν ἐσπάρη καὶ ἀνετράφη.

«Ὑμεῖς εἰς τὸν κόπον αὐτῶν εἰσεληλύθατε»

οὐ γὰρ ὁ αὐτὸς κόπος σπειρόντων καὶ θεριζόντων· οἱ μὲν γὰρ ἐν κρύει καὶ ὕδατι καὶ κόπῳ τὴν γῆν σκάπτοντες σπείρουσιν, καὶ δι᾽ ὅλου χειμῶνος τημελοῦσιν σκάλλοντες καὶ τὰς ὕλας ἐκλέγοντες· οἱ δὲ εἰς ἕτοιμον καρπὸν εἰσελθόντες θέρους εὐφραινόμενοι θερίζουσιν.

Fragment 33 (Jn 4:35)

With the same meaning as "The reaping is great, but the workers are few" were these things said, (referring) to those ripe for the reaping and ready now to be brought together in the storehouse through faith, to be in rest, and are suitable for salvation and the acceptance of the Word.

Fragment 34 (Jn 4:36)

The words "The one who reaps receives a reward" were said because the Savior calls himself a reaper. And the reward of our Lord is the salvation and restoration of those who are reaped by his resting upon them. But the words "And he gathers fruit for eternal life" are made either because what is gathered is the fruit of eternal life, or (because) even it itself is eternal life.

Fragment 35 (4:36–37)

"So that the one who sows and the one who reaps might rejoice together"

For the one who sows rejoices because he sows, and because some of his seeds have already been gathered, he has the same hope also concerning the rest. But the one who reaps similarly rejoices because he also reaps. But the one who sows began first; the one who reaps, second. For both were not able to start at the same time. For it was necessary to sow first, then to reap later. However, after the one who sows stopped sowing, the reaper will still reap. Yet at present, both rejoice together doing their respective work, because they deem the fruition of the seeds a shared joy.

"In this is the saying true, that it is one who sows and another who reaps"

For the Son of Man above the place sows, but the Savior, being also himself a Son of Man, reaps and sends the angels, being conceptualized as the disciples, as reapers, each for his own soul.

Fragment 36 (Jn 4:38)

Not through them or by them were these seeds sown, but those who have toiled are the angels of the assembly, through whom, as intermediaries, they were sown and brought up.

"You have entered into their labor"

For sowing and reaping are not the same labor, for those who sow do so in the frost and water and with fatigue when digging the earth, and through the whole winter they care for it by digging and weeding. But the others during summer happen upon fruit, and in good spirits they reap.

Fragment 37 (Jn 4:39)

«Ἐκ τῆς πόλεως»

ἀντὶ τοῦ «ἐκ τοῦ κόσμου»

«Διὰ τὸν λόγον τῆς γυναικός»

τουτέστιν διὰ τῆς πνευματικῆς ἐκκλησίας·

καὶ ἐπισημαίνεταί γε τὸ «Πολλοί» ὡς πολλῶν ὄντων ψυχικῶν· τὴν δὲ μίαν ... τὴν ἄφθαρτον τῆς ἐκλογῆς φύσιν καὶ μονοειδῆ καὶ ἑνικήν.

Fragment 38 (Jn 4:40)

«παρ᾽ αὐτοῖς» ἔμεινεν καὶ οὐκ «ἐν αὐτοῖς,» καὶ δύο ἡμέρας, ἤτοι τὸν ἐνεστῶτα αἰῶνα καὶ τὸν μέλλοντα τὸν ἐν γάμῳ, ἢ τὸν πρὸ τοῦ πάθους αὐτοῦ χρόνον καὶ τὸν μετὰ τὸ πάθος, ὃν παρ᾽ αὐτοῖς ποιήσας πολλῷ πλείονας διὰ τοῦ ἰδίου λόγου ἐπιστρέψας εἰς πίστιν, ἐχωρίσθη ἀπ᾽ αὐτῶν.

Fragment 39 (Jn 4:42)

«Οὐκέτι διὰ τὴν σὴν λαλιὰν πιστεύομέν»

λείπειν τὸ «μόνην.»

«Αὐτοὶ γὰρ ἀκηκόαμεν, καὶ οἴδαμεν ὅτι οὗτός ἐστιν ὁ σωτὴρ τοῦ κόσμου»

οἱ γὰρ ἄνθρωποι τὸ μὲν πρῶτον ὑπὸ ἀνθρώπων ὁδηγούμενοι πιστεύουσιν τῷ σωτῆρι, ἐπὰν δὲ ἐντύχωσιν τοῖς λόγοις αὐτοῦ, οὗτοι οὐκέτι διὰ μόνην ἀνθρωπίνην μαρτυρίαν, ἀλλὰ δι᾽ αὐτὴν τὴν ἀλήθειαν πιστεύουσιν.

Fragment 40 (Jn 4:46–53)

βασιλικὸν ... τὸν δημιουργόν, ἐπεὶ καὶ αὐτὸς ἐβασίλευεν τῶν ὑπ᾽ αὐτόν· διὰ δὲ τὸ μικρὰν αὐτοῦ καὶ πρόσκαιρον εἶναι τὴν βασιλείαν ... βασιλικὸς ὠνομάσθη, οἱονεὶ μικρός τις βασιλεὺς ὑπὸ καθολικοῦ βασιλέως τεταγμένος ἐπὶ μικρᾶς βασιλείας· τὸν δὲ ἐν Καφαρναοὺμ υἱὸν αὐτοῦ ... τὸν ἐν τῷ ὑποβεβηκότι μέρει τῆς μεσότητος τῷ πρὸς θάλασσαν, τουτέστιν τῷ συνημμένῳ τῇ ὕλῃ. ὁ ἴδιος αὐτοῦ ἄνθρωπος ἀσθενῶν, τουτέστιν οὐ κατὰ φύσιν ἔχων, ἐν ἀγνοίᾳ καὶ ἁμαρτήμασιν ἦν.

«Ἐκ τῆς Ἰουδαίας εἰς τὴν Γαλιλαίαν»

ἀντὶ τοῦ «ἐκ τῆς ἄνωθεν Ἰουδαίας»

«Ἤμελλεν ἀποθνήσκειν»

ἀνατρέπεσθαι τὰ δόγματα τῶν ὑποτιθεμένων ἀθάνατον εἶναι τὴν ψυχὴν

αὐτὴν ... εἶναι τὸ ἐνδυόμενον ἀφθαρσίαν φθαρτὸν καὶ ἀθανασίαν θνητόν, ὅταν «καταποθῇ ὁ θάνατος αὐτῆς εἰς νῖκος.»

Fragment 37 (Jn 4:39)

"Out of the city"

(Means) the same as "out of the world."

"On account of the word of the woman"

That is, through the spiritual church.

And "many" indicates that there are many soulish people. But the one woman is the uncorrupted nature of the elect, both uniform and singular.

Fragment 38 (Jn 4:40)

"With them" he remained and not "in them," and two days (means) either the present age and the coming age that is in marriage, or the time prior to his passion and after his passion, which he passed with them and turned many more through his own word to faith, (before) being separated from them.

Fragment 39 (Jn 4:42)

"We no longer believe because of your saying"

"Only" is lacking.

"For we ourselves have heard, and we know that this is the Savior of the world"

For humans believe in the Savior first by being guided by humans, but when they encounter his words, no longer do they believe solely on account of human witness, but on account of the truth itself.

Fragment 40 (Jn 4:46–53)

The official . . . is the creator, since he also reigned over those beneath him. But because his kingdom is small and temporary, he was deemed an official, as though he was some parochial king placed over a small kingdom by the worldwide king. But his son in Capernaum . . . is in the bottom part of the middle (region), which is by the sea, that is, what has been joined together with matter. His own man was weak, that is, not being according to nature, and he was in ignorance and sins.

"From Judea into the Galilee"

Means the same as "from the Judea above"

"He was about to die"

The teachings of those who consider the soul to be immortal are overthrown.

(The soul) is corruption cloaked in incorruption and mortality in immortality, when "its death is consumed in victory."

τὸ «Ἐὰν μὴ σημεῖα καὶ τέρατα ἴδητε, οὐ μὴ πιστεύσητε» λέγεσθαί ...
οἰκείως πρὸς τὸ τοιοῦτον πρόσωπον δι᾽ ἔργων φύσιν ἔχον καὶ δι᾽ αἰσθήσεως
πείθεσθαι καὶ οὐχὶ λόγῳ πιστεύειν.

Τὸ δὲ «Κατάβηθι πρὶν ἀποθανεῖν τὸ παιδίον μου» διὰ τὸ τέλος εἶναι τοῦ
νόμου τὸν θάνατον ... ἀναιροῦντος διὰ τῶν ἁμαρτιῶν· πρὶν τελέως οὖν ...
θανατωθῆναι κατὰ τὰς ἁμαρτίας δεῖται ὁ πατὴρ τοῦ μόνουσωτῆρος, ἵνα
βοηθήσῃ τῷ υἱῷ, τουτέστιν τῇ τοιᾷδε φύσει.

τὸ «Ὁ υἱός σου ζῇ» κατὰ ἀτυφίαν εἰρῆσθαι τῷ σωτῆρι ... ἐπεὶ οὐκ εἶπεν·
«ζήτω,» οὐδὲ ἐνέφηνεν αὐτὸς παρεσχῆσθαι τὴν ζωήν. Λέγει δὲ ὅτι καταβὰς
πρὸς τὸν κάμνοντα καὶ ἰασάμενος αὐτὸν τῆς νόσου, τουτέστιν τῶν
ἁμαρτιῶν, καὶ διὰ τῆς ἀφέσεως ζωοποιήσας εἶπεν· «Ὁ υἱός σου ζῇ.»

τὸ «Ἐπίστευσεν» ὁ ἄνθρωπος, ὅτι εὔπιστος καὶ ὁ δημιουργός ἐστιν, ὅτι
δύναται ὁ σωτὴρ καὶ μὴ παρὼν θεραπεύειν.

Δούλους δὲ τοῦ βασιλικοῦ ... τοὺς ἀγγέλους τοῦ δημιουργοῦ, ἀπαγγέλλοντας
ἐν τῷ «Ὁ παῖς σου ζῇ,» ὅτι οἰκείως καὶ κατὰ τρόπον ἔχει, πράσσων μηκέτι
τὰ ἀνοίκεια· καὶ διὰ τοῦτο ... ἀπαγγέλλειν τῷ βασιλικῷ τοὺς δούλους τὰ
περὶ τῆς τοῦ υἱοῦ σωτηρίας, ἐπεὶ καὶ πρώτους ... βλέπειν τὰς πράξεις τῶν
ἐν τῷ κόσμῳ ἀνθρώπων τοὺς ἀγγέλους, εἰ ἐρρωμένως καὶ εἰλικρινῶς
πολιτεύοιντο ἀπὸ τῆς τοῦ σωτῆρος ἐπιδημίας.

διὰ τῆς ὥρας χαρακτηρίζεται ἡ φύσις τοῦ ἰαθέντος.

«Ἐπίστευσεν αὐτὸς καὶ ἡ οἰκία αὐτοῦ ὅλη»

ἐπὶ τῆς ἀγγελικῆς εἰρῆσθαι τάξεως καὶ ἀνθρώπων τῶν οἰκειοτέρων αὐτῷ.

Ζητεῖσθαι δέ ... περί τινων ἀγγέλων εἰ σωθήσονται, τῶν κατελθόντων ἐπὶ τὰς
τῶν ἀνθρώπων θυγατέρας. Καὶ τῶν ἀνθρώπων δὲ τοῦ δημιουργοῦ τὴν
ἀπώλειαν δηλοῦσθαι ... ἐν τῷ· «Οἱ υἱοὶ τῆς βασιλείας ἐξελεύσονται εἰς τὸ
σκότος τὸ ἐξώτερον.»

«Υἱοὺς ἐγέννησα καὶ ὕψωσα, αὐτοὶ δὲ μὲ ἠθέτησαν»

οὕστινας υἱοὺς ἀλλοτρίους, καὶ σπέρμα πονηρὸν καὶ ἄνομον ... καὶ ἀμπελῶνα
ἀκάνθας ποιήσαντα.

The words "unless you see the signs and wonders, you will not believe" are said fittingly to such a person who has a nature through works and who is persuaded through perception and does not believe the word.

The words "come down before my child dies" are made because death is the end of the law that destroys by means of sins. Therefore, before (the son) is ultimately put to death because of sins, the Father is in need of the only Savior so that he might help the son, that is, this sort of nature.

The words "your son lives" are said by the Savior without arrogance, since he did not say, "Let him live," nor did he disclose that it was he who poured life into him. Rather he says that after going down to the ill child and curing him of his ailment, that is, of his sins, and through forgiveness having made him alive, he said, "Your son lives."

That the man "believed" (means) that even the creator believes that the Savior can heal even when not present.

The servants of the official are the angels of the creator, those who announce in the words "Your child lives," that he lives properly and in the right manner, no longer preoccupied with unfitting matters. And because of this the servants announce the news about the salvation of the son to the official, since the angels are first to see the actions of humans in the world, whether they are conducting themselves influentially and purely since the arrival of the Savior.

The nature of the one who has been healed is characterized in the course of the hour.

"He believed along with his entire house"

(This) refers to the angelic and human order, those more like him.

To be questioned is whether certain angels, those who went down to the daughters of humans, will be saved. And the destruction of the humans of the creator is made clear in the words "The children of the kingdom will depart into outer darkness."

"Children I have begotten and exalted, but they have rejected me"

Such are foreign children, an evil and lawless seed, and a vineyard that yields thorns.

Fragment 41 (Jn 8:21)

«Ὅπου ἐγὼ ὑπάγω ὑμεῖς οὐ δύνασθε ἐλθεῖν»

πῶς ἐν ἀγνοίᾳ καὶ ἀπιστίᾳ καὶ ἁμαρτήμασιν ὄντες ἐν ἀφθαρσίᾳ δύνανται γενέσθαι;

Fragment 42 (Jn 8:22)

«Μήτι ἀποκτενεῖ ἑαυτόν;»

πονηρῶς διαλογιζόμενοι οἱ Ἰουδαῖοι ταῦτα ἔλεγον καὶ μείζονας ἑαυτοὺς ἀποφαινόμενοι τοῦ σωτῆρος καὶ ὑπολαμβάνοντες ὅτι αὐτοὶ μὲν ἀπελεύσονται πρὸς τὸν θεὸν εἰς ἀνάπαυσιν αἰώνιον, ὁ δὲ σωτὴρ εἰς φθορὰν καὶ εἰς θάνατον ἑαυτὸν διαχειρισάμενος, ὅπου ἑαυτοὺς οὐκ ἐλογίζοντο ἀπελθεῖν. ᾤοντο λέγειν τὸν σωτῆρα οἱ Ἰουδαῖοι ὅτι ἐγὼ ἐμαυτὸν διαχειρισάμενος εἰς φθορὰν μέλλω πορεύεσθαι, ὅπου ὑμεῖς οὐ δύνασθε ἐλθεῖν.

Fragment 43 (Jn 8:37)

«Ὅτι ὁ λόγος ὁ ἐμὸς οὐ χωρεῖ ἐν ὑμῖν»

οὐ χωρεῖ ὅτι ἀνεπιτήδειοι ἤτοι κατ᾽ οὐσίαν ἢ κατὰ γνώμην

Fragment 44 (8:43–44a)

αἰτίαν ἀποδίδοσθαι τοῦ μὴ δύνασθαι αὐτοὺς ἀκούειν τὸν Ἰησοῦ λόγον μηδὲ γινώσκειν αὐτοῦ τὴν λαλιὰν ἐν τῷ «Ὑμεῖς ἐκ τοῦ πατρὸς τοῦ διαβόλου ἐστέ.» Αὐταῖς γοῦν λέξεσίν φησι· «Διατί δὲ οὐ δύνασθε ἀκούειν τὸν λόγον τὸν ἐμόν, ἢ ὅτι ὑμεῖς ἐκ τοῦ πατρὸς τοῦ διαβόλου ἐστέ;» ἀντὶ τοῦ «ἐκ τῆς οὐσίας τοῦ διαβόλου,» φανερῶν αὐτοῖς λοιπὸν τὴν φύσιν αὐτῶν, καὶ προελέγξας αὐτοὺς ὅτι οὔτε τοῦ Ἀβραάμ εἰσιν τέκνα—οὐ γὰρ ἂν ἐμίσουν αὐτόν—οὔτε τοῦ θεοῦ, διὸ οὐκ ἠγάπων αὐτόν.

Fragment 45 (Jn 8:44a)

πρὸς οὓς ὁ λόγος ἐκ τῆς οὐσίας τοῦ διαβόλου ἦσαν·

Fragment 46 (Jn 8:44a)

«Ἐκ τοῦ πατρὸς τοῦ διαβόλου»
ἀντὶ τοῦ ἐκ τῆς οὐσίας τοῦ πατρός.

«Τὰς ἐπιθυμίας τοῦ πατρὸς ὑμῶν θέλετε ποιεῖν»
τὸν διάβολον μὴ ἔχειν θέλημα ἀλλ᾽ ἐπιθυμίας

ταῦτα εἴρηται οὐ πρὸς τοὺς φύσει τοῦ διαβόλου υἱούς, τοὺς χοϊκούς, ἀλλὰ πρὸς τοὺς ψυχικούς, θέσει υἱοὺς διαβόλου γινομένους. ἀφ᾽ ὧν τῇ φύσει δύνανταί τινες καὶ θέσει υἱοὶ θεοῦ χρηματίσαι.

Fragment 41 (Jn 8:21)

"Where I am going, you are not able to come"

How are they able to come to be in incorruption while they are in ignorance and unbelief and sin?

Fragment 42 (Jn 8:22)

"Will he kill himself?"

The Jews said these things because they contemplated wickedly and presented themselves as greater than the Savior, and they assumed that they would depart to God into eternal rest, but the Savior, slaying himself into destruction and death, where they thought they would not return. The Jews supposed that the Savior said, "I am about to get rid of myself by going into destruction, where you are not able to come."

Fragment 43 (Jn 8:37)

"Because my word has no place in you"

It has no place because they are unfit either according to substance or according to their outlook.

Fragment 44 (8:43–44a)

The reason given as to why they were not able to hear the word of Jesus or know what he said is found in the words "You are from your father, the devil." He said these words: "Why are you not able to hear my word, is it because you are from your father, the devil?" (These words) mean "of the essence of the devil," making clear to them their nature, after telling them that they are not children of Abraham—for they would not have despised him—nor of God, since they do not love him.

Fragment 45 (Jn 8:44a)

(Those) to whom the Word (came) were of the essence of the devil.

Fragment 46 (Jn 8:44a)

"From your father, the devil"
(These words) mean of the substance of the father.

"You desire to do the desires of your father"
The devil does not have a will, only desires.

These things were said not to those who by nature are children of the devil, the earthly, but to the soulish ones, who have become children of the devil by adoption. Some from this nature are able to be called children of God by adoption.

παρὰ τὸ ἠγαπηκέναι τὰς ἐπιθυμίας τοῦ διαβόλου καὶ ποιεῖν τέκνα οὗτοι τοῦ διαβόλου γίνονται, οὐ φύσει τοιοῦτοι ὄντες.

τριχῶς δεῖ ἀκούειν τῆς κατὰ τέκνα ὀνομασίας, πρῶτον φύσει, δεύτερον γνώμῃ, τρίτον ἀξίᾳ· καὶ φύσει μέν ... ἐστὶν τὸ γεννηθὲν ὑπό τινος γεννητοῦ, ὃ καὶ κυρίως τέκνον καλεῖται· γνώμῃ δέ, ὅτε τὸ θέλημά τις ποιῶν τινος διὰ τὴν ἑαυτοῦ γνώμην τέκνον ἐκείνου οὗ ποιεῖ τὸ θέλημα καλεῖται· ἀξίᾳ δέ, καθ' ὃ λέγονταί τινες γεέννης τέκνα καὶ σκότους καὶ ἀνομίας, καὶ ὄφεων καὶ ἐχιδνῶν γεννήματα. Οὐ ἀρ γεννᾷ ... ταῦτά τινα τῇ ἑαυτῶν φύσει· φθοροποιὰ ἀρ καὶ ἀναλίσκοντα τοὺς ἐμβληθέντας εἰς αὐτά· ἀλλ' ἐπεὶ ἔπραξαν τὰ ἐκείνων ἔργαν τέκνα αὐτῶν εἴρηται ... τέκνα τοῦ διαβόλου νῦν λέγει τούτους, οὐχ ὅτι γεννᾷ τινας ὁ διάβολος, ἀλλ' ἄότι τὰ ἔργα τοῦ διαβόλου ποιοῦντες ὡμοιώθησαν αὐτῷ.

Fragment 47 (Jn 8:44b)

Οὐ γὰρ ἐκ τῆς ἀληθείας ἡ φύσις ἐστὶν αὐτοῦ, ἀλλ' ἐκ τοῦ ἐναντίου τῇ ἀληθείᾳ, ἐκ πλάνης καὶ ἀγνοίας. Διό ... οὔτε στῆναι ἐν ἀληθείᾳ οὔτε σχεῖν ἐν αὐτῷ ἀλήθειαν δύναται, ἐκ τῆς αὐτοῦ φύσεως ἴδιον ἔχων τὸ ψεῦδος, φυσικῶς μὴ δυνάμενός ποτε ἀλήθειαν εἰπεῖν. ... οὐ μόνος αὐτὸς ψεύστης ἐστίν, ἀλλὰ καὶ ὁ πατὴρ αὐτοῦ. ἰδίως «πατὴρ αὐτοῦ» ἐκλαμβάνων τὴν φύσιν αὐτοῦ, ἐπείπερ ἐκ πλάνης καὶ ψεύσματος συνέστη.

Fragment 48 (Jn 8:50)

τὸ «Ἔστιν ὁ ζητῶν καὶ κρίνων» οὐκ ἀναφέρει ἐπὶ τὸν πατέρα· ὁ ζητῶν καὶ κρίνων ἐστὶν ὁ ἐκδικῶν με, ὁ ὑπηρέτης ὁ εἰς τοῦτο τεταγμένος, ὁ μὴ εἰκῇ τὴν μάχαιραν φορῶν, ὁ ἔκδικος τοῦ βασιλέως· Μωσῆς δέ ἐστιν οὗτος, καθ' ἃ προείρηκεν αὐτοῖς λέγων· «Εἰς ὃν ὑμεῖς ἠλπίσατε». ὁ κρίνων καὶ κολάζων ἐστὶν Μωσῆς, τουτέστιν αὐτὸς ὁ νομοθέτης. πῶς οὖν οὐ λέγει τὴν κρίσιν πᾶσαν παραδεδόσθαι αὐτῷ; καλῶς λέγει· ὁ γὰρ κριτὴς ὡς ὑπηρέτης τὸ θέλημα τούτου ποιῶν κρίνει, ὥσπερ καὶ ἐπὶ τῶν ἀνθρώπων φαίνεται γινόμενον.

Fragment 50 (Lk 12:8)

ὁμολογίαν εἶναι τὴν μὲν ἐν πίστει καὶ πολιτείᾳ, τὴν δὲ ἐν φωνῇ. ἡ μὲν οὖν ἐν φωνῇ ὁμολογία καὶ ἐπὶ τῶν ἐξουσιῶν γίνεται, ἣν μόνην, φησίν, ὁμολογίαν ἡγοῦνται εἶναι οἱ πολλοὶ οὐχ ὑγιῶς, δύνανται δὲ ταύτην τὴν ὁμολογίαν καὶ οἱ ὑποκριταὶ ὁμολογεῖν. ἀλλ' οὐδ' εὑρεθήσεται οὗτος ὁ λόγος καθολικῶς εἰρημένος· οὐ γὰρ πάντες οἱ σωζόμενοι ὡμολόγησαν τὴν διὰ τῆς φωνῆς ὁμολογίαν καὶ ἐξῆλθον, ἐξ ὧν Ματθαῖος, Φίλιππος, Θωμᾶς, Λευὶς καὶ ἄλλοι πολλοί. καὶ ἔστιν ἡ διὰ τῆς φωνῆς ὁμολογία οὐ καθολική, ἀλλὰ μερική. καθολικὴ δὲ ἦν νῦν λέγει, ἡ ἐν ἔργοις καὶ πράξεσι καταλλήλοις τῆς εἰς αὐτὸν πίστεως. ἕπεται δὲ ταύτῃ τῇ ὁμολογίᾳ καὶ ἡ μερικὴ ἡ ἐπὶ τῶν ἐξουσιῶν, ἐὰν δέῃ καὶ ὁ λόγος αἱρῇ. ὁμολογήσει γὰρ οὗτος καὶ τῇ φωνῇ, ὀρθῶς

Since they have loved the desires of the devil, they are able to be made into children of the devil, although they were not such by nature.

It is necessary to understand the term "children" in three ways: first by nature, second by outlook, third by worth. By "nature" means one begotten by someone begotten, which is properly called "child." By "outlook" is when one doing the will of another through his own outlook is called a child of the one whose will he does. But "by worth" is when some are called children of Gehenna and darkness and lawlessness, and the products of snakes and vipers. For these do not beget anything by their own nature; for they cause destruction and kill what is thrown to them. But since they enacted their works, they are called their children. He calls them now children of the devil not because the devil begets any of them, but because when they do the deeds of the devil they came to resemble him.

Fragment 47 (Jn 8:44b)

For his nature is not of the truth, but of the opposite of the truth, of error and ignorance. Therefore, he is not able to stand in truth or bear truth within himself, since from his nature he has a lie as his own, and naturally he is not ever able to speak truth. Not only is he himself a liar, but he is also its father. "His father" indicates his nature, since it derives from error and a lie.

Fragment 48 (Jn 8:50)

The words "There is one who seeks, and he judges" do not refer to the Father. The one who seeks and judges is the one who vindicates me, the service person summoned for this, the one who does not bear the sword without a plan, the one who vindicates the king. This is Moses, according to what he said to them earlier, saying, "in whom you have hoped." The one who judges and chastises is Moses, that is, the lawgiver himself. How then does he not say that all judgment has been given over to him? Correctly he speaks, for the judge judges as a servant when he does the will of this one, as it appears to come to be among humans.

Fragment 50 (Lk 12:8)

Confession is made in faith and conduct on the one hand, and by voice on the other. The confession in voice occurs before the authorities, which many incorrectly consider to be the only confession, for even the hypocrites are able to make this confession. But it will not be found that this word was said universally. For not all those who are saved confessed through the voice, among whom are Matthew, Philip, Thomas, Levi, and many more. The confession through the voice is not universal, but partial. But universal is the confession in works and deeds, which corresponds to faith in him. But the

προομολογήσας πρότερον τῇ διαθέσει. καὶ καλῶς ἐπὶ μὲν τῶν ὁμολογούντων «ἐν ἐμοὶ» εἶπεν ἐπὶ δὲ τῶν ἀρνουμένων τὸ «ἐμὲ» προσέθηκεν. οὗτοι γάρ, κἂν τῇ φωνῇ ὁμολογήσωσιν αὐτόν, ἀρνοῦνται αὐτόν, τῇ πράξει μὴ ὁμολογοῦντες. μόνοι δ᾽ ἐν αὐτῷ ὁμολογοῦσιν οἱ ἐν τῇ κατ᾽ αὐτὸν πολιτείᾳ καὶ πράξει βιοῦντες, ἐν οἷς καὶ αὐτὸς ὁμολογεῖ ἐνειλημμένος αὐτοὺς καὶ ἐχόμενος ὑπὸ τούτων. διόπερ «ἀρνήσασθαι αὐτὸν οὐδέποτε δύνανται.» ἀρνοῦνται δὲ αὐτὸν οἱ μὴ ὄντες ἐν αὐτῷ. οὐ γὰρ εἶπεν «ὃς ἀρνήσηται ἐν ἐμοί,» ἀλλ᾽ «ἐμέ»· οὐδεὶς γάρ ποτε ὢν ἐν αὐτῷ ἀρνεῖται αὐτόν. τὸ δὲ «ἔμπροσθεν τῶν ἀνθρώπων,» καὶ τῶν σῳζομένων καὶ τῶν ἐθνικῶν δὲ ὁμοίως παρ᾽ οἷς μὲν καὶ τῇ πολιτείᾳ, παρ᾽ οἷς δὲ καὶ τῇ φωνῇ. διόπερ ἀρνήσασθαι αὐτὸν οὐδέποτε δύνανται· ἀρνοῦνται δὲ αὐτὸν οἱ μὴ ὄντες ἐν αὐτῷ.

partial one before the authorities comes after this confession, if it should be necessary and the word should convict. For this person will confess with the voice, who has previously confessed correctly in disposition. And rightly about those who confess he said, "In me." But for those who deny he added, "Me." For even if they confess him with their voice, they deny him, since they do not confess in deed. But only those who live in conduct and deed in relation to him confess in him, among them he also confesses, since he has embraced them and is held by them. For this reason they are not ever able to deny him. Rather those who are not in him deny him. For he did not say, "Whoever denies in me," but "Me," for no one who was ever in him will deny him. And "before people" (the confession is made as it is), also before those who are saved and the gentiles, before those who are saved also by conduct, but before the gentiles by voice. For this reason they are never able to deny him. But those not in him are the ones who deny him.

IV. EXCERPTS OF THEODOTUS

In his *Excerpts of Theodotus* Clement of Alexandria records a series of extracts from a variety of Valentinian sources. Despite the title of the work, not all of the extracts come from Theodotus, a Valentinian teacher who is known only from Clement's extracts. He is named only five times in the entire text. In other instances Clement may be citing Theodotus, but he does not do so by name. Another challenge the text poses to interpreters is that unlike the *Gospel of Philip,* which, if it is a collection of extracts, does not seem to include additions by the person responsible for compiling the extracts, Clement has added his own comments to many of the extracts, and his additions are not always easily distinguishable from the texts he excerpts from his Valentinian sources.

While questions remain about the precise nature of the sources Clement uses, scholars often divide the *Excerpts* into four groups: (A) 1–28, (B) 29–43:1, (C) 43.2–65, and (D) 66–86. Group C has affinities with Irenaeus, *AH* 1.4.5–7.1 and may draw upon the source used by Irenaeus.

The *Excerpts* survive in two late manuscripts, one directly copied from the other. The earliest of the two is *Laur.* V 3, which dates to the eleventh century C.E. Clement likely produced the collection, however, in the latter part of the second century C.E. The following Greek text comes from my own transcription of *Laur.* V 3, in consultation with Sagnard's edition.

ΕΚ ΤΩΝ ΘΕΟΔΟΤΟΥ ΚΑΙ ΤΗΣ ΑΝΑΤΟΛΙΚΗΣ ΚΑΛΟΥΜΕΝΗΣ
ΔΙΔΑΣΚΑΛΙΑΣ ΚΑΤΑ ΤΟΥΣ ΟΥΑΛΕΝΤΙΝΟΥ ΧΡΟΝΟΥΣ ΕΠΙΤΟΜΑΙ

1 «Πάτερ,» φησί, «παρατίθεμαί σοι εἰς χεῖρας τὸ Πνεῦμά μου.» Ὅ προέβαλε, φησί,
σαρκίον τῷ Λόγῳ ἡ Σοφία, τὸ πνευματικὸν σπέρμα, τοῦτο στολισάμενος κατῆλθεν
ὁ Σωτήρ.

Ὅθεν ἐν τῷ πάθει τὴν Σοφίαν παρατίθεται τῷ Πατρί, ἵνα αὐτὴν ἀπολάβῃ παρὰ
τοῦ Πατρός, καὶ μὴ κατασχεθῇ ἐνταῦθα ὑπὸ τῶν στερίσκειν δυναμένων.

Οὕτως πᾶν πνευματικὸν σπέρμα, τοὺς ἐκλεκτούς, διὰ τῆς προειρημένης φωνῆς
παρατίθεται.

Τὸ ἐκλεκτὸν σπέρμα φαμὲν καὶ «σπινθῆρα» ζωοποιούμενον ὑπὸ τοῦ Λόγου καὶ
«κόρην ὀφθαλμοῦ» καὶ «κόκκον σινάπεως» καὶ «ζύμην» τὰ δόξαντα καταδιῃρῆσθαι
γένη ἑνοποιοῦσα<ν> εἰς πίστιν.

2 Οἱ δ' ἀπὸ Οὐαλεντίνου, πλασθέντος φασὶ τοῦ ψυχικοῦ σώματος, τῇ ἐκλεκτῇ ψυχῇ
οὔσῃ ἐν ὕπνῳ ἐντεθῆναι ὑπὸ τοῦ Λόγου σπέρμα ἀρρενικόν, ὅπερ ἐστὶν ἀπόρροια
τοῦ ἀγγελικοῦ, ἵνα μὴ ὑστέρημα ᾖ. Καὶ τοῦτο ἐζύμωσεν, τὰ δόξαντα καταδιῃρῆσθαι
ἑνοποιοῦν, τὴν ψυχὴν καὶ τὴν σάρκα, ἃ καὶ ἐν μερισμῷ ὑπὸ τῆς Σοφίας προηνέχθη.
Ὕπνος δὲ ἦν Ἀδὰμ ἡ λήθη τῆς ψυχῆς, ἣν συνεῖχε μὴ διαλυθῆναι <τὸ σπέρμα> [7] τὸ
πνευματικόν, ὅπερ ἐνέθηκεν τῇ ψυχῇ ὁ Σωτήρ. Τὸ σπέρμα ἀπόρροια ἦν τοῦ ἄρρενος
καὶ ἀγγελικοῦ. Διὰ τοῦτο λέγει ὁ Σωτήρ· «Σώζου σὺ καὶ ἡ ψυχή σου.»

3 Ἐλθὼν οὖν ὁ Σωτὴρ τὴν ψυχὴν ἐξύπνισεν, ἐξῆψεν δὲ τὸν σπινθῆρα. δύναμις γὰρ οἱ
λόγοι τοῦ Κυρίου. Διὰ τοῦτο εἴρηκεν· «Λαμψάτω τὸ φῶς ὑμῶν ἔμπροσθεν τῶν
ἀνθρώπων.» Καὶ μετὰ τὴν ἀνάστασιν, ἐμφυσῶν τὸ Πνεῦμα τοῖς Ἀποστόλοις, τὸν μὲν
χοῦν καθάπερ τέφραν ἀπεφύσα καὶ ἐχώριζεν, ἐξῆπτε δὲ τὸν σπινθῆρα καὶ ἐζωοποίει.

4 Ὁ Κύριος, διὰ πολλὴν ταπεινοφροσύνην, οὐχ ὡς ἄγγελος ὤφθη, ἀλλ' ὡς
ἄνθρωπος. Καὶ ὅτε ἐν δόξῃ ὤφθη τοῖς Ἀποστόλοις ἐπὶ τοῦ Ὄρους, οὐ δι' ἑαυτὸν
ἐποίησεν δεικνὺς ἑαυτόν, ἀλλὰ διὰ τὴν Ἐκκλησίαν, ἥτις ἐστὶ «τὸ γένος τὸ
ἐκλεκτόν,» ἵνα μάθῃ τὴν προκοπὴν αὐτοῦ μετὰ τὴν `ἐκ´ τῆς σαρκὸς ἔξοδον.

Αὐτὸς γὰρ καὶ ἄνω Φῶς ἦν, καὶ ἐστι τὸ «ἐπιφανὲν ἐν σαρκὶ» καὶ τὸ ἐνταῦθα ὀφθὲν
οὐχ ὕστερον τοῦ ἄνω· οὐδὲ διεκέκοπτο, ἢ ἄνωθεν μετέστη δεῦρο, τόπον ἐκ τόπου
ἀμεῖβον, ὡς τὸν μὲν ἐπιλαβεῖν, τὸν δὲ ἀπολιπεῖν. ἀλλ' ἦν τὸ πάντη Ὄν, καὶ παρὰ
τῷ Πατρὶ κἀνταῦθα, δύναμις γὰρ ἦν τοῦ Πατρός.

7. MS reads ὥς.

Excerpts of Theodotus and the So-Called Eastern School at the Time
of Valentinus

1 "Father," he says, "I commit into your hands my Spirit." Wisdom, he says, set
forth the flesh for the Word, the spiritual seed; dressed with flesh, the Savior
descended.

For this reason, at the passion he commits Wisdom to the Father, so that he might
receive her from the Father, and not be restrained down here by those who are able
to deprive him.

Thus he commits the entire spiritual seed, the elect, by the aforementioned utterance.

We agree that the elect seed is both a "spark" made alive by the Word and a "pupil
of the eye" and a "mustard seed" and "leaven" that joins in faith the genuses that
seem to be divided.

2 But the followers of Valentinus say that when the psychic body was molded a
male seed was implanted by the Word into the elect soul while it was asleep, wherefore it is an emission of the angelic, so that there might be no lack. And this (seed)
leavened, unifying things appearing to have been divided, the soul and flesh,
which had been brought forth separately by Wisdom. Adam's sleep was the forgetfulness of the soul, which maintained (it) lest the spiritual <seed> be dissolved,
which the Savior placed within the soul. The seed was an emission of the male and
angelic. For this reason the Savior says, "Be saved, you and your soul."

3 Therefore, when he arrived, the Savior awakened the soul and kindled the spark. For
the words of the Lord are power. For this reason he said, "Let your light shine before
people." And following the resurrection, when he breathed the Spirit upon the Apostles, dust like ashes he blew off and scattered, but he kindled and enlivened the spark.

4 The Lord, on account of his great humility, did not appear as an angel, but as a
human. And when in glory he appeared to the Apostles on the mountain, he did
not reveal himself (this way) for his own sake, but for the sake of the church, which
is "the chosen race," so that it might understand his progress after his departure
from the flesh.

For he was light also while above, and "that which appeared in the flesh" and
appeared here is not later than what is above; nor was it interrupted, as if it
descended here from above, changing from place to place, as gain in one place, and
loss in the other. But he was the one present in all, and he is with the Father while
here, for he was the power of the Father.

Ἄλλως τε ἐχρῆν κἀκεῖνον πληρωθῆναι τὸν λόγον τοῦ Σωτῆρος ὃν εἶπεν· «Εἰσί τινες τῶν ὧδε ἑστηκότων, οἳ οὐ μὴ γεύσονται θανάτου, ἕως ἂν ἴδωσι τὸν Υἱὸν τοῦ Ἀνθρώπου ἐν δόξῃ.» Εἶδον οὖν καὶ ἐκοιμήθησαν ὅ τε Πέτρος καὶ Ἰάκωβος καὶ Ἰωάννης.

5 Πῶς οὖν τὴν μὲν ὄψιν τὴν φωτεινὴν ἰδόντες οὐκ ἐξεπλάγησαν, τὴν δὲ φωνὴν ἀκούσαντες ἔπεσον ἐπὶ γῆν; Ὅτι ὦτα τυγχάνει ἀπιστότερα ὀφθαλμῶν, καὶ ἡ παρὰ δόξαν φωνὴ μᾶλλον ἐκπλήσσει.

Ὁ δὲ Ἰωάννης ὁ βαπτιστὴς τῆς φωνῆς ἀκούσας οὐκ ἐφοβήθη, ὡς ἂν ἐν πνεύματι ἀκούσας, συνήθει τῆς τοιαύτης φωνῆς. καθὸ δὲ ἄνθρωπός τίς ἐστι μόνον ἀκούσας κατεπλάγη. Διὸ καὶ λέγει αὐτοῖς ὁ Σωτήρ· «Μηδενὶ εἴπητε ὃ <ἑ>ἴδετε.»

Καίτοι οὐδὲ σαρκικοῖς ὀφθαλμοῖς τὸ φῶς ἑωράκεισαν (οὐδὲν γὰρ συγγενὲς καὶ οἰκεῖον ἐκείνῳ τῷ φωτὶ καὶ τῇδε τῇ σαρκί), ἀλλ᾽ ὡς ἡ δύναμις καὶ ἡ βούλησις τοῦ Σωτῆρος ἐνεδυνάμωσεν τὴν σάρκα εἰς τὸ θεάσασθαι. ἄλλως τε καὶ ὃ ἡ ψυχὴ εἶδεν μετέδωκεν κοινωνούσῃ τῇ σαρκὶ <διὰ τὸ> συμπεπλέχθαι αὐτῇ.

Τὸ δὲ «μηδενὶ εἴπητε», ἵνα μὴ ὅ ἐστιν ὁ Κύριος νοήσαντες, ἀπόσχωνται <τοῦ>[8] ἐπιβάλλειν τῷ Κυρίῳ τὰς χεῖρας, καὶ ἀτελὴς ἡ οἰκονομία γένηται, καὶ ὁ θάνατος ἀπόσχηται τοῦ Κυρίου, ὡς μάτην πειράζων ἐπὶ ἀνηνύτῳ.

Καὶ ἔτι ἡ μὲν ἐν τῷ Ὄρει φωνὴ τοῖς ἤδη συνιεῖσιν ἐκλεκτοῖς ἐγένετο, διὸ καὶ ἐθαύμασαν μαρτυρουμένου τοῦ πιστευομένου. Ἡ δὲ ἐπὶ τῷ Ποταμῷ τοῖς μέλλουσι πιστεύειν. διὸ καὶ ἠμελήθη ἡ φωνὴ αὐτοῖς, προκατεχομένοις ἐπὶ τῇ τῶν νομοδιδασκάλων ἀγωγῇ.

6 Τὸ «Ἐν Ἀρχῇ ἦν ὁ Λόγος καὶ ὁ Λόγος ἦν πρὸς τὸν Θεὸν καὶ Θεὸς ἦν ὁ Λόγος» οἱ ἀπὸ Οὐαλεντίνου οὕτως ἐκδέχονται· [9]

«Ἀρχὴν» μὲν γὰρ «τὸν Μονογενῆ» λέγουσιν, ὃν καὶ Θεὸν προ<σ>αγορεύεσθαι, ὡς καὶ ἐν τοῖς ἑξῆς ἄντικρυς Θεὸν αὐτὸν δηλοῖ λέγων· «Ὁ Μονογενὴς Θεός, ὁ ὢν εἰς τὸν κόλπον τοῦ Πατρός, ἐκεῖνος ἐξηγήσατο.»

Τὸν δὲ Λόγον τὸν «ἐν τῇ Ἀρχῇ» τοῦτον τὸν, ἐν τῷ Μονογενεῖ ἐν τῷ Νῷ καὶ τῇ Ἀληθείᾳ μηνύει τὸν Χριστόν, τὸν Λόγον καὶ τὴν Ζωήν. ὅθεν εἰκότως καὶ αὐτὸν Θεὸν λέγει, τὸν ἐν τῷ Θεῷ τῷ Νῷ ὄντα.

---

8. MS reads τοῖς.
9. ἐκδέχονται: read as ἐνδέχονται by Sagnard in both L and P.

Besides, it was necessary that the word spoken by the Savior be fulfilled: "There are some among those standing here who will not taste death until they see the Son of Man in glory." Then Peter and James and John saw and fell asleep.

5 How then were they not terrified upon seeing the luminous vision, but fell upon the ground when hearing the voice? Because the ears are more suspicions than the eyes, and the unexpected voice is more shocking.

But John the Baptist was not afraid upon hearing the voice, as if he had heard in spirit, (which is) accustomed to such a voice. But it is just as any person would be terrified when he simply hears. Therefore, the Savior said to them, "Tell no one what you saw."

And yet they had not seen the light with fleshly eyes (for there is not a kinship and affiliation between that light and this flesh), but as the power and will of the Savior endowed the flesh with the ability to see. Additionally, what the soul saw it shared with the accompanying flesh <because> it was intertwined with it.

And "Tell no one" (was said), lest once they know what the Lord is, they might avoid laying hands upon the Lord, and the arrangement might become imperfect, and death might avoid the Lord, as something making an attempt in vain toward the impossible.

And yet the voice on the mountain came to the elect who already perceived, wherefore they also marveled when what they believed was testified about. But the (voice) in the river was for those who were to believe. Wherefore the voice was ignored by them, since they were bound by the training of the teachers of the law.

6 The (verse) "In the beginning was the Word and the Word was with God and the Word was God" the Valentinians receive in this way:

"Beginning" they call the "Only Begotten," whom God is also addressed as, as also in what immediately follows it is clear that he is God, saying, "The Only-Begotten God, who is in the bosom of the Father, he has explained him."

The Word, the one "in the beginning," this one in the Only-Begotten, in the Mind and the Truth indicates the Christ, the Word and the Life. Wherefore he fittingly calls him God, the one who is in God and in the Mind.

«Ὃ γέγονεν ἐν αὐτῷ,» τῷ Λόγῳ, «Ζωὴ ἦν,» ἡ σύζυγος. διὸ καί φησιν ὁ Κύριος· «Ἐγώ εἰμι ἡ Ζωή.»

7 Ἄγνωστος οὖν ὁ Πατὴρ ὤν, ἠθέλησεν γνωσθῆναιτοῖς Αἰῶσι, καὶ διὰ τῆς Ἐνθυμήσεως τῆς ἑαυτοῦ, ὡς ἂν ἑαυτὸν ἐγνωκώς, Πνεῦμα γνώσεως οὔσης ἐν γνώσει, προέβαλε τὸν Μονογενῆ. Γέγονεν οὖν καὶ ὁ ἀπὸ γνώσεως, τουτέστι τῆς πατρικῆς Ἐνθυμήσεως, προελθὼν Γνῶσις, τουτέστιν ὁ Υἱός, ὅτι «δι' Υἱοῦ ὁ Πατὴρ ἐγνώσθη.»

Τὸ δὲ τῆς ἀγάπης Πνεῦμα κέκραται τῷ τῆς γνώσεως, ὡς Πατὴρ Υἱῷ καὶ Ἐνθύμησις Ἀληθείᾳ, ἀπ' Ἀληθείας προελθὸν ὡς ἀπὸ Ἐνθυμήσεως ἡ γνῶσις.

Καὶ ὁ μὲν μείνας «Μονογενὴς Υἱὸς εἰς τὸν κόλπον τοῦ Πατρός,» τὴν Ἐνθύμησιν διὰ τῆς γνώσεως ἐξηγεῖται τοῖς Αἰῶσιν, ὡς ἂν καὶ ὑπὸ τοῦ κόλπου αὐτοῦ προβληθείς. ὁ δὲ ἐνταῦθα ὀφθεὶς οὐκέτι «Μονογενής,» ἀλλ' «ὡς Μονογενὴς» πρὸς τοῦ Ἀποστόλου προσαγορεύεται, «δόξαν ὡς Μονογενοῦς,» ὅτι εἷς καὶ ὁ αὐτὸς ὤν, ἐν μὲν τῇ κτίσει Πρωτότοκός» ἐστιν Ἰησοῦς, ἐν δὲ Πληρώματι «Μονογενής.» Ὁ δὲ αὐτός ἐστι, τοιοῦτος ὢν ἑκάστῳ τόπῳ οἷος κεχωρῆσθαι δύναται.

Καὶ οὐδέποτε τοῦ μείναντος ὁ καταβὰς μερίζεται. Φησὶ γὰρ ὁ Ἀπόστολος· «Ὁ γὰρ ἀναβὰς αὐτός ἐστι καὶ ὁ καταβάς.»

Εἰκόνα δὲ τοῦ Μονογενοῦς τὸν Δημιουργὸν λέγουσιν. Διὸ καὶ <τ>αῦτα[10] τῆς εἰκόνος τὰ ἔργα. Ὅθεν καὶ ὁ Κύριος, εἰκόνα τῆς πνευματικῆς ἀναστάσεως ποιήσας τοὺς νεκροὺς οὓς ἤγειρεν, οὐκ ἀφθάρτους τὴν σάρκα, ἀλλ' ὡς αὖθις ἀποθανουμένους ἤγειρεν.

8 Ἡμεῖς δὲ τὸν ἐν ταὐτότητι Λόγον Θεὸν ἐν Θεῷ φαμεν, ὃς καὶ «εἰς τὸν κόλπον τοῦ Πατρὸς» εἶναι λέγεται, ἀδιάστατος, ἀμέριστος, εἷς Θεός.

ὁ Σωτὴρ καὶ {Ἡσαΐας· «καὶ ἀνταποδώσω τὰ ἔργα αὐτῶν εἰς τὸν κόλπον αὐτῶν,» εἰς τὴν ἔννοιαν αὐτῶν, τὴν ἐν τῇ ψυχῇ, ἀφ' ἧς πρώτης ἐνεργεῖται}[11] «Πρωτότοκος πάσης κτίσεως.»

---

10. <τ>αῦτα: Sagnard suggests λυτὰ.
11. This phrase is a possible marginal note.

"That which came about in him," in the Word, "was Life," the Companion. Therefore, the Lord also says. "I am the life."

7 Therefore, the Father, who was unknown, wanted to be known to the eternities,
and through his own consideration, as if he had come to know himself—a spirit of
knowledge being within knowledge—he emanated the Only-Begotten. He too who
came to be from knowledge, that is from the Father's consideration, went forth as
knowledge, that is, the Son, because "through the Son the Father was known."

But the Spirit of love has been mixed with that of knowledge, as the Father with the
Son and the Consideration with Truth, having come from Truth as knowledge
from Consideration.

And the one who remained "Only-Begotten Son in the bosom of the Father"
explains Consideration to the eternities through knowledge, as if he also had been
emanated from his bosom. But the one who appeared here is no longer called
by the Apostle "Only-Begotten," but "as Only-Begotten," "glory as of an Only-
Begotten," because since he is one and the same, Jesus is the "Firstborn" in creation, but "Only-Begotten" in fullness. But he is the same, since he is such as can be
discerned in each place.

The one who descended is also never divided from the one who remained. For the
Apostle says, "For the one who ascended is also the one who descended."

They call the Creator an image of the Only-Begotten. Therefore, even these things
are the works of the image. And, therefore, the Lord, after he made the dead whom
he raised an image of the spiritual resurrection, raised them not with incorruptible
flesh, but as if to die again.

8 But we say that the identical Word is God in God, who is also said to be "in the
bosom of the Father," unceasing, undivided, one God.

"All things came about by him," according to the activity affiliated with the identical Word, (all things) spiritual and intellectual and aesthetic. "This one explained
the bosom of the Father," the Savior and Firstborn of all creation.[12]

---

12. Isaiah: "And I will repay their works into their bosom," into their thought, which is in the soul,
from which it is initially activated.

Ὁ δὲ ἐν ταὐτότητι Μονογενής, οὗ κατὰ δύναμιν ἀδιάστατον ὁ Σωτὴρ ἐνεργεῖ, οὗτός ἐστι «τὸ Φῶς» τῆς Ἐκκλησίας, τῆς πρότερον ἐν σκότῳ καὶ ἐν ἀγνοίᾳ οὔσης.

«Καὶ ἡ σκοτία αὐτὸν οὐ κατέλαβεν.» οἱ ἀποστατήσαντες καὶ οἱ λοιποὶ τῶν ἀνθρώπων οὐκ ἔγνωσαν αὐτόν, καὶ ὁ θάνατος οὐ κατέσχεν αὐτόν.

9 Ἡ πίστις οὐ μία, ἀλλὰ διάφορος. Ὁ γοῦν Σωτήρ φησι· «Γενηθήτω σοῦ κατὰ τὴν πίστιν.» Ὅθεν εἴρηται τοὺς μὲν τῆς κλήσεως ἀνθρώπους κατὰ τὴν παρουσίαν τοῦ Ἀντιχρίστου πλανηθήσεσθαι· ἀδύνατον δὲ τοὺς ἐκλεκτούς· διό φησι· «Καὶ εἰ δυνατόν, τοὺς ἐκλεκτούς μου.»

Πάλιν ὅταν λέγῃ· «Ἐξέλθετε ἐκ τοῦ οἴκου τοῦ Πατρός μου,» τοῖς κλητοῖς λέγει. Πάλιν τῷ ἐξ ἀποδημίας ἐλθόντι καὶ κατεδηδοκότι τὰ ὑπάρχοντα, ᾧ τὸν σιτευτὸν ἔθυσεν μόσχον, τὴν κλῆσιν λέγει· καὶ ὅπου ὁ βασιλεὺς εἰς τὸ δεῖπνον τοῦ γάμου τοὺς ἐν ταῖς ὁδοῖς κέκληκεν.

Πάντες μὲν οὖν κέκληνται ἐπ᾽ ἴσης, «βρέχει γὰρ ἐπὶ δικαίους καὶ ἀδίκους, καὶ τὸν ἥλιον ἐπιλάμπει πᾶσιν»· ἐκλέγονται δὲ οἱ μᾶλλον πιστεύσαντες, πρὸς οὓς λέγει· «Τὸν Πατέρα μου οὐδεὶς ἑώρακεν εἰ μὴ ὁ Υἱός,» καὶ «Ὑμεῖς ἐστε τὸ φῶς τοῦ κόσμου,» καὶ «Πάτερ ἅγιε, ἁγίασον αὐτοὺς ἐν τῷ ὀνόματί σου.»

10 Ἀλλ᾽ οὐδὲ τὰ πνευματικὰ καὶ νοερά, οὐδὲ οἱ Ἀρχάγγελοι <καὶ> οἱ Πρωτόκτιστοι, οὐδὲ μὴν οὐδ᾽ αὐτὸς ἄμορφος καὶ ἀνείδεος καὶ ἀσχημάτιστος καὶ ἀσώματός ἐστιν, ἀλλὰ καὶ μορφὴν ἔχει ἰδίαν καὶ σῶμα ἀνάλογον τῆς ὑπεροχῆς τῶν πνευματικῶν ἁπάντων, ὡς δὲ καὶ οἱ Πρωτόκτιστοι ἀνάλογον τῆς ὑπεροχῆς τῶν ὑπ᾽ αὐτοὺ<ς> οὐσιῶν.

Ὅλως γὰρ τὸ γενητὸν οὐκ ἀνούσιον μέν, οὐχ ὅμοιον δὲ μορφὴν καὶ σῶμα ἔχουσι τοῖς ἐν τῷδε τῷ κόσμῳ σώμασιν. Ἄρρενά τε γὰρ καὶ θήλεα τὰ ἐνταῦθα καὶ διάφορα πρὸς αὐτά, ἐκεῖ δὲ ὁ μὲν Μονογενὴς καὶ ἰδίως νοερός ἰδέᾳ ἰδίᾳ καὶ οὐσίᾳ ἰδίᾳ κεχρημένος ἄκρως εἰλικρινεῖ καὶ ἡγεμονικωτάτῃ, καὶ προσεχῶς τῆς τοῦ Πατρὸς ἀπολαύων δυνάμεως. οἱ δὲ Πρωτόκτιστοι, εἰ καὶ ἀριθμῷ διάφοροι καὶ ὁ καθ᾽ ἕκαστον περιώρισται καὶ περιγέγραπται, ἀλλ᾽ ἡ ὁμοιότης τῶν πραγμάτων ἑνότητα καὶ ἰσότητα καὶ ὁμοιότητα ἐνδείκνυται.

Οὐ γὰρ τῷδε μὲν πλέον, τῷδε δὲ ἧττον παρέσχηται τῶν Ἑπτά· οὐδ᾽ ὑπολείπεται τις αὐτοῖς προκοπή, ἐξ ἀρχῆς ἀπειληφότων τὸ τέλειον, ἅμα τῇ πρώτῃ γενέσει παρὰ τοῦ Θεοῦ διὰ τοῦ Υἱοῦ.

Καὶ ὃ μὲν «Φῶς ἀπρόσιτον» εἴρηται, ὡς Μονογενής» καὶ «Πρωτότοκος,» «ἃ ὀφθαλμὸς οὐκ εἶδε καὶ οὖς οὐκ ἤκουσεν οὐδὲ ἐπὶ καρδίαν ἀνθρώπου ἀνέβη,» οὐδὲ ἔσται τις τοιοῦτος οὔτε τῶν Πρωτοκτίστων οὔτε ἀνθρώπων.

But the identical Only-Begotten, according to whose unceasing power the Savior acts, is "the Light" of the church, which was formerly in darkness and ignorance.

"And the darkness could not overtake him." The apostates and the rest of humanity had not known him, and death did not bind him.

9 The faith is not single, but differing. Indeed then the Savior says, "May it be according to your faith." Wherefore it is said that those of the calling will stray at the arrival of the Antichrist; but (this would be) impossible for the elect. Therefore, he says, "And if possible, my elect."

Again when he says,"Get out of my Father's house," he is speaking to the calling. Again he mentions the call in (the story about) the one who returned from a trip and consumed his goods, on behalf of whom he slaughtered the fattened calf; and where the king summoned those on the roads to the wedding feast.

Therefore all have been called equally, "For he rains upon righteous and unrighteous, and the sun he shines upon all"; but elect are those who believe exceedingly, to whom he says, "No one has seen my Father except the Son," and "You are the light of the world," and "Holy Father, sanctify them in your name."

10 But neither the spiritual nor the intellectual things, nor the archangels <and> those created first, nor even he is shapeless and formless and figureless and incorporeal, but he also has his own shape and body proportionate to his superiority over all spiritual things, just as also those created first (have their own shape and body) proportionate to their superiority over the beings beneath them.

For in general what has come to be is not without substance, but unlike the bodies in this world, they have form and body. For male and female here differ from each other, but there the Only-Begotten and uniquely intellectual one has been furnished with his own form and substance that is utterly pure and sovereign, and he has the immediate benefit of the Father's power. The ones created first, even if in number they are distinct and each is bounded and delineated, in any case the likeness of their deeds demonstrates their unity, equality, and likeness.

For no superiority nor inferiority was given among the seven; no progress remains for them, since from the beginning they have received perfection, at the same time as the first creation from God through the Son.

And he is said to be "light unapproachable," as "Only-Begotten" and "Firstborn," "what no eye has seen and no ear has heard, nor has it entered into a person's heart," and such a person dwells not among those first created nor among humanity.

οἳ δὲ «διὰ παντὸς τὸ πρόσωπον τοῦ Πατρὸς βλέπουσιν·» πρόσωπον δὲ Πατρὸς ὁ Υἱός, δι᾽ οὗ γνωρίζεται ὁ Πατήρ. Τὸ τοίνυν ὁρῶν καὶ ὁρώμενον ἀσχημάτιστον εἶναι οὐ δύναται οὐδὲ ἀσώματον. ὁρῶσι δὲ ὀφθαλμῷ οὐκ αἰσθητῷ, ἀλλ᾽ οἵῳ παρέσχεν ὁ Πατήρ νοερῷ.

11 Ὅταν οὖν εἴπῃ ὁ Κύριος· «Μὴ καταφρονήσητε ἑνὸς τῶν μικρῶν τούτων. ἀμὴν λέγω ὑμῖν· τούτων οἱ ἄγγελοι τὸ πρόσωπον τοῦ Πατρὸς διὰ παντὸς βλέπουσιν,» οἷον τὸ προκέντημα, <τ>οἷοι ἔσονται οἱ ἐκλεκτοί, τὴν τελείαν ἀπολαβόντες προκοπήν. «Μακάριοι δὲ οἱ καθαροὶ τῇ καρδίᾳ, ὅτι αὐτοὶ τὸν Θεὸν ὄψονται.»

Πρόσωπον δὲ τοῦ ἀσχηματίστου πῶς ἂν εἴη; Σώματα γοῦν ἐπουράνια εὔμορφα καὶ νοερὰ οἶδεν ὁ Ἀπόστολος. πῶς δ᾽ ἂν καὶ ὀνόματα διάφορα αὐτῶν ἐλέγετο, εἰ μὴ σχήμασιν ἦν περιγεγραμμένα, μορφῇ καὶ σώματι; «Ἄλλη δόξα ἐπουρανίων, ἄλλη ἐπιγείων, ἄλλη ἀγγέλων, ἄλλη ἀρχαγγέλων.»

Ὡς πρὸς τὴν σύγκρισιν τῶν τῇδε σωμάτων, οἷον ἄστρων, ἀσώματα καὶ ἀνείδεα, ὡς πρὸς τὴν σύγκρισιν τοῦ Υἱοῦ σώματα μεμετρημένα καὶ αἰσθητά, οὕτως καὶ ὁ Υἱὸς πρὸς τὸν Πατέρα παραβαλλόμενος.

Καὶ δύναμιν μὲν ἰδίαν ἔχει ἕκαστον τῶν πνευματικῶν καὶ ἰδίαν οἰκονομίαν, καθὸ δὲ ὁμοῦ τε ἐγένοντο καὶ τὸ ἐντελὲς ἀπειλήφασιν οἱ πρωτόκτιστοι, κοινὴν τὴν λειτουργίαν καὶ ἀμέριστον.

12 Οἱ πρωτόκτιστοι οὖν τόν τε Υἱὸν ὁρῶσι καὶ ἑαυτοὺς καὶ τὰ ὑποβεβηκότα, ὥσπερ καὶ οἱ Ἀρχάγγελοι τοὺς πρωτοκτίστους. Ὁ δὲ Υἱὸς ἀρχὴ τῆς πατρικῆς ὑπάρχει θέας, πρόσωπον τοῦ Πατρὸς λεγόμενος.

Καὶ οἱ μὲν Ἄγγελοι, νοερὸν πῦρ καὶ πνεύματα νοερά, τὴν οὐσίαν ἀποκεκαθαρμένοι. φῶς δὲ νοερὸν ἡ μεγίστη προκοπὴ ἀπὸ τοῦ νοεροῦ πυρός, ἀποκεκαθαρμένου τέλεον, «εἰς ἃ ἐπιθυμοῦσιν ἄγγελοι παρακύψαι,» ὁ Πέτρος φησίν·

ὁ δὲ Υἱὸς ἔτι τούτου καθαρώτερος· «ἀπρόσιτον φῶς» καὶ «δύναμις θεοῦ» καὶ κατὰ τὸν Ἀπόστολον, «τιμίῳ καὶ ἀμώμῳ καὶ ἀσπίλῳ αἵματι ἐλυτρώθημεν.» Οὗ «τὰ μὲν ἱμάτια ὡς φῶς ἔλαμψεν, τὸ πρόσωπον δὲ ὡς ὁ ἥλιος,» ᾧ μηδὲ ἀντωπῆσαι ἔστι ῥᾳδίως.

13 Οὗτός ἐστιν «Ἄρτος» ἐπουράνιος καὶ πνευματικὴ Τροφὴ ζωῆς παρεκτικὴ κατὰ τὴν βρῶσιν καὶ γνῶσιν, «τὸ Φῶς τῶν ἀνθρώπων,» τῆς Ἐκκλησίας δηλονότι.

Rather they "always behold the face of the Father"; the face of the Father is the Son, through whom the Father is made known. Therefore that which sees and is seen is not able to be without form or body. But they see not with a sense-preceiving eye, but with a mental eye of the sort the Father supplied.

11 Therefore when the Lord said, "Do not despise one of these little ones. Truly I say to you, their angels always behold the face of the Father," as is the template, so will the elect be, once they receive the perfect progress. "But blessed are the pure in heart, for they will see God."

But how could there be a face of the formless one? Indeed the Apostle knows bodies that are heavenly, beautiful, and noetic. But how could different names be given to them, unless they were defined by shapes, form, and body? "(There is) a glory of heavens, a glory of earth, a glory of angels, and a glory of archangels."

Just as when compared to bodies here, such as stars, they are without body and form, (and) as when compared to the Son, they are measurable and perceivable bodies, so too is the Son when compared to the Father.

And each of the spiritual beings has its own power and its own administration, just as those created first came to be together and received completion, a shared and undivided ministry.

12 Therefore, those created first behold the Son and themselves and the subordinate things, just as also the archangels behold those first begotten. But the Son is the beginning of the fatherly vision, which is called the face of the Father.

And the angels, (being) noetic fire and noetic spirits, have been made pure in their nature. But the greatest progress from the noetic fire, having been made pure completely, is noetic fire "into which the angels desire to look," Peter says.

But the Son is still purer than this; "inaccessible light" and "power of God" and according to the Apostle, "by costly and blameless and spotless blood we were redeemed." Whose "garments illuminate like light, and face as the sun," which is not easy to gaze into.

13 He is heavenly "bread" and spiritual nourishment producing life concerning bread and knowledge, "the light of humanity," namely, of the church.

Οἱ μὲν οὖν «τὸν οὐράνιον ἄρτον φαγόντες ἀπέθανον,» ὁ δὲ «τὸν ἀληθινὸν Ἄρτον» τοῦ Πνεύματος ἐσθίων οὐ τεθνήξεται.

Ὁ «ζῶν Ἄρτος» ὁ «ὑπὸ τοῦ Πατρὸς δοθεὶς» ὁ Υἱός ἐστι τοῖς ἐσθίειν βουλομένοις.

«Ὁ δὲ ἄρτος ὃν ἐγὼ δώσω,» φησίν, «ἡ σάρξ μού ἐστιν,» ἤτοι ᾧ τρέφεται ἡ σάρξ διὰ τῆς Εὐχαριστίας, <ἤ> ὅπερ καὶ μᾶλλον, ἡ σάρξ τὸ σῶμα αὐτοῦ ἐστιν, «ὅπερ ἐστὶν ἡ Ἐκκλησία,» «ἄρτος οὐράνιος,» συναγωγὴ εὐλογημένη.

τάχα δὲ ὡς ἐκ τῆς αὐτῆς οὐσίας <καὶ> τῶν ἐκλεκτῶν κατὰ τὸ ὑποκείμενον γενομένων, καὶ ὡς τοῦ αὐτοῦ τέλους τευξομένων.

14 Τὰ δαιμόνια «ἀσώματα» εἴρηται, οὐχ ὡς σῶμα μὴ ἔχοντα, ἔχει γὰρ καὶ σχῆμα· διὸ καὶ συναίσθησιν κολάσεως ἔχει, ἀλλ᾿ ὡς πρὸς σύγκρισιν τῶν σῳζομένων σωμάτων πνευματικῶν σκιὰ ὄντα ἀσώματα εἴρηται.

Καὶ οἱ Ἄγγελοι σώματά εἰσιν· ὁρῶνται γοῦν. Ἀλλὰ καὶ ἡ ψυχὴ σῶμα. Ὁ γοῦν Ἀπόστολος· «Σπείρεται μὲν γὰρ σῶμα ψυχικόν, ἐγείρεται δὲ σῶμα πνευματικόν.»

Πῶς δὲ καὶ αἱ κολαζόμεναι ψυχαὶ συναισθάνονται μὴ σώματα οὖσαι; «Φοβήθητε,» γοῦν λέγει, «τὸν μετὰ θάνατον δυνάμενον καὶ ψυχὴν καὶ σῶμα εἰς γέενναν βαλεῖν·»

τὸ γὰρ φαινόμενον οὐ πυρὶ καθαίρεται, ἀλλ᾿ εἰς γῆν ἀναλύεται. Ἄντικρυς δὲ ἀπὸ τοῦ Λαζάρου καὶ τοῦ πλουσίου διὰ τῶν σωματικῶν μελῶν σῶμα εἶναι δείκνυται ἡ ψυχή.

15 «Ὡς δὲ ἐφορέσαμεν τὴν εἰκόνα τοῦ χοϊκοῦ, φορέσωμεν καὶ τὴν εἰκόνα τοῦ ἐπουρανίου,» τοῦ πνευματικοῦ, κατὰ προκοπὴν τελειούμενοι· πλὴν πάλιν «εἰκόνα» λέγει, ὡς εἶναι σώματα πνευματικά.

Καὶ πάλιν· «Ἄρτι βλέπομεν δι᾿ ἐσόπτρου ἐν αἰνίγματι, τότε δὲ πρόσωπον πρὸς πρόσωπον.» Αὐτίκα γὰρ ἀρχόμεθα γινώσκειν. Οὗ δὲ «πρόσωπον» <καὶ> ἰδέα καὶ σχῆμα καὶ σῶμα. Σχῆμα μὲν οὖν σχήματι θεωρεῖται, καὶ πρόσωπον προσώπῳ, καὶ ἐπιγινώσκεται τὰ γνωρίσματα τοῖς σχήμασι καὶ ταῖς οὐσίαις.

16 Καὶ ἡ περιστερὰ δὲ σῶμα ὤφθη—ἣν οἱ μὲν τὸ ἅγιον Πνεῦμά φασιν, οἱ δὲ ἀπὸ Βασιλείδου τὸν διάκονον, οἱ δὲ ἀπὸ Οὐαλεντίνου τὸ Πνεῦμα τῆς Ἐνθυμήσεως τοῦ Πατρός—<τὸ> τὴν κατέλευσιν πεποιημένον ἐπὶ τὴν τοῦ Λόγου σάρκα.

17 Ἔστιν Ἰησοῦς καὶ ἡ Ἐκκλησία καὶ ἡ Σοφία δι᾿ ὅλων κρᾶσις τῶν σωμάτων δυνατή, κατὰ τοὺς Οὐαλεντινιανούς.

Therefore "those eating the heavenly bread died," but the one who eats "the true bread" of the Spirit will not die.

The Son is the "living bread" that "was given by the Father" to those wanting to eat.

"But the bread that I will give," he says, "is my flesh," truly to the one whose flesh is nourished by the Eucharist, <or> even better, the flesh is his body, "which is the church," "heavenly bread," a blessed gathering.

Perhaps just as the elect come from the same substance according to their placement, so too they will arrive at the same destination.

14 The demons are called "incorporeal," not because they do not have bodies, for even they have a shape; therefore they also can feel pain, but because when compared to spiritual bodies which are saved they are shadows, they are said to be incorporeal.

The angels are also bodies; at least they are visible. Yet even the soul is a body. The Apostle (says), "For it is sown a soul body, but raised a spiritual body."

How can souls that are punished feel (it) unless they are bodies? "Be fearful," he certainly says, "of the one who, after death, is able to cast soul and body into Gehenna."

For what is visible is not purified by fire, but into dust it is dissolved. But from (the story) of Lazarus and the rich man, the soul is clearly shown to be a body by means of its bodily limbs.

15 "As we have born the earthly image, we will also bear the heavenly image," of the spiritual, as we are perfected in accordance with our progress. Again he says "image," meaning spiritual bodies.

And again: "Now we see in a mirror dimly, but then face-to-face." For at once we begin to know. There is not "face" <and> form and shape and body. Shape is observed by shape, and face by face, and recognizable things are recognized by shapes and substances.

16 The dove appeared also as a body—the dove that some call the Holy Spirit, but the followers of Basilides call the minister, and the followers of Valentinus call the Spirit of the Father's thought—when descending upon the Word's flesh.

17 Jesus and the church and wisdom are a complete and powerful mixture of bodies, according to the Valentinians.

Ἡ γοῦν ἀνθρωπίνη μίξις ἡ κατὰ γάμον ἐκ δυεῖν μεμιγμένων σπερμάτων ἑνὸς γένεσιν παιδίου ἀποτελεῖ, καὶ τὸ σῶμα εἰς γῆν ἀναλυθὲν κέκραται τῇ γῇ καὶ τὸ ὕδωρ τῷ οἴνῳ. τὰ δὲ κρείττω καὶ διαφορώτερα σώματα ῥᾳδίαν ἴσχει τὴν κρᾶσιν· πνεῦμα γοῦν πνεύματι μίγνυται.

Ἐμοὶ δὲ δοκεῖ κατὰ παράθεσιν τοῦτο γενέσθαι, ἀλλ᾽ οὐ κατὰ κρᾶσιν. Μή τι οὖν ἡ θεία δύναμις διήκουσα τὴν ψυχὴν ἁγιάζει αὐτὴν κατὰ τὴν τελευταίαν προκοπήν; «Ὁ γὰρ Θεὸς πνεῦμα· ὅπου θέλει πνεῖ.»

ἡ γὰρ δύναμις οὐ κατ᾽ οὐσίαν διήκει, ἀλλὰ κατὰ δύναμιν καὶ ἰσχύν· παράκειται δὲ τὸ πνεῦμα τῷ πνεύματι, ὡς τὸ πνεῦμα τῇ ψυχῇ.

18 Ὁ Σωτὴρ ὤφθη κατιὼν τοῖς Ἀγγέλοις. Διὸ καὶ «εὐηγγελίσαντο» αὐτόν. Ἀλλὰ καὶ τῷ Ἀβραὰμ καὶ τοῖς λοιποῖς δικαίοις, τοῖς ἐν τῇ ἀναπαύσει οὖσιν ἐν τοῖς δεξιοῖς, ὤφθη. «Ἠγαλλιάσατο» γάρ, φησίν, «ἵνα ἴδῃ τὴν ἡμέραν τὴν ἐμήν,» τὴν ἐν σαρκὶ παρουσίαν.

Ὅθεν, ἀναστὰς ὁ Κύριος εὐηγγελίσατο τοὺς Δικαίους τοὺς ἐν τῇ ἀναπαύσει, καὶ μετέστησεν αὐτοὺς καὶ μετέθηκεν, καὶ πάντες «ἐν τῇ σκιᾷ αὐτοῦ ζήσονται.» Σκιὰ γὰρ τῆς δόξης τοῦ Σωτῆρος τῆς παρὰ τῷ Πατρὶ ἡ παρουσία ἡ ἐνταῦθα, φωτὸς δὲ σκιὰ οὐ σκότος, ἀλλὰ φωτισμός ἐστιν.

19 «Καὶ ὁ Λόγος σὰρξ ἐγένετο,» οὐ κατὰ τὴν παρουσίαν μόνον ἄνθρωπος γενόμενος, ἀλλὰ καὶ «ἐν ἀρχῇ.» ὁ ἐν ταυτότητι Λόγος, κατὰ «περιγραφὴν» καὶ οὐ κατ᾽ οὐσίαν γενόμενος ὁ Υἱός.

Καὶ πάλιν «σὰρξ ἐγένετο» διὰ προφητῶν ἐνεργήσας. Τέκνον δὲ τοῦ ἐν ταυτότητι Λόγου ὁ Σωτὴρ εἴρηται. Διὰ τοῦτο «ἐν Ἀρχῇ ἦν ὁ Λόγος, καὶ ὁ Λόγος ἦν πρὸς τὸν Θεόν· ὃ γέγονεν ἐν αὐτῷ, Ζωή ἐστιν.» Ζωὴ δὲ ὁ Κύριος.

Καὶ ὁ Παῦλος· «Ἔνδυσαι τὸν καινὸν Ἄνθρωπον τὸν κατὰ Θεὸν κτισθέντα,» οἷον εἰς αὐτὸν πίστευσον τὸν ὑπὸ τοῦ Θεοῦ «κατὰ Θεόν,» τὸν ἐν Θεῷ Λόγον, «κτισθέντα.» Δύναται δὲ τὸ «κατὰ Θεὸν κτισθέντα» τὸ εἰς ὃ μέλλει τέλος προκοπῆς φθάνειν ὁ ἄνθρωπος μηνύειν, ἐπ᾽ ἴσης τῷ «ἀπεβάλετο εἰς ὃ ἐκτίσθη<ς> τέλος.»

Καὶ ἔτι σαφέστερον καὶ διαρρήδην ἐν ἄλλοις λέγει· «Ὅς ἐστιν εἰκὼν τοῦ Θεοῦ τοῦ ἀοράτου.» Εἶτα ἐπιφέρει· «Πρωτότοκος πάσης κτίσεως.» «Ἀοράτου» μὲν γὰρ «Θεοῦ εἰκόνα» τὸν Λόγον <λέγει> τοῦ Λόγου τοῦ ἐν ταυτότητι «Πρωτότοκον δὲ πάσης κτίσεως.» Γεννηθεὶς ἀπαθῶς, κτίστης καὶ γενεσιάρχης τῆς ὅλης ἐγένετο κτίσεώς τε καὶ οὐσίας, «ἐν αὐτῷ» γὰρ ὁ Πατὴρ τὰ πάντα ἐποίησεν.

Indeed the human mixing in marriage from two mingled seeds produces the birth of one child, and the body when dissolved into the earth mixes with the earth and water mixes with wine. And the better and more distinguished bodies are capable of mixing easily; wind mixes with wind.

Yet to me it seems like this occurs by juxtaposition not mixture. Therefore doesn't the divine power pervading the soul make it holy in the final stage of progress? "For God is Spirit; he inspires where he desires."

For the power does not pervade according to substance, but power and might; and spirit accompanies spirit, as spirit accompanies soul.

18 The Savior was seen by the angels as he descended. Therefore they proclaimed him. But he was also seen by Abraham and the rest of the righteous ones, those who are in the (place of) rest among those on the right. For "He rejoiced," he says, "to see my day," the return in flesh.

Wherefore the risen Lord proclaimed good news to the righteous ones in the (place of) rest, and he changed and transposed them, and they all "will live in his shadow." For the return to this place is a shadow of the Savior's glory, which is with the Father, but a shadow of light is not darkness but illumination.

19 "And the Word became flesh," becoming human not only at his arrival, but also "in the beginning." The identical Word became the Son by limitation and not by essence.

And again "he became flesh" when working though the prophets. The Savior is called a child of the identical Word. Therefore "in the beginning was the Word, and the Word was with God; that which came about in him is life." Life is the Lord.

And Paul: "Put on the new human created according to God," as though (he said,) "Believe in him who was 'created' by God 'according to God,' the Word in God." "Created according to God" can refer to the end of progress to which the person hastens, as in the (expression) "He cast off the end for which he was created."

And in other (passages) he speaks even more openly and distinctly: "Who is an image of the invisible God." Then he adds, "Firstborn of all creation." For <he calls> the Word of the identical Word "an image of the invisible God" and "First-born of all creation." Since he was begotten without passion, he became founder and creator of all creation and substance, for "by him" the Father made all things.

Ὅθεν καὶ «μορφὴν δούλου λαβ<ε>ῖν» εἴρηται, οὐ μόνον τὴν σάρκα κατὰ τὴν παρουσίαν, ἀλλὰ καὶ τὴν οὐσίαν ἐκ τοῦ ὑποκειμένου· δούλη δὲ ἡ οὐσία, ὡς ἂν παθητὴ καὶ ὑποκειμένη τῇ δραστηρίῳ καὶ κυριωτάτῃ αἰτίᾳ.

20 Τὸ γὰρ «πρὸ ἑωσφόρου ἐγέννησά σε» οὕτως ἐξακούομεν, ἐπὶ τοῦ πρωτοκτίστου Θεοῦ Λόγου, καὶ «πρὸ ἡλίου» καὶ σελήνης καὶ πρὸ πάσης κτίσεως «τὸ Ὄνομά σου.»

21 Τὸ «κατ᾽ εἰκόνα Θεοῦ ἐποίησεν αὐτούς, ἄρσεν καὶ θῆλυ ἐποίησεν αὐτούς.» τὴν προβολὴν τὴν ἀρίστην φασὶν οἱ Οὐαλεντινιανοὶ[13] τῆς Σοφίας λέγεσθαι, ἀφ᾽ ἧς τὰ μὲν ἀρρενικὰ ἡ ἐκλογή, τὰ δὲ θηλυκὰ ἡ κλῆσις. Καὶ τὰ μὲν ἀρρενικὰ ἀγγελικὰ καλοῦσι, τὰ θηλυκὰ δὲ ἑαυτούς, τὸ διαφέρον πνεῦμα.

Οὕτως καὶ ἐπὶ τοῦ Ἀδάμ, τὸ μὲν ἀρρενικὸν ἔμεινεν αὐτῷ, πᾶν δὲ τὸ θηλυκὸν σπέρμα ἀρά<μενον> ἀπ᾽ αὐτοῦ Εὔα γέγονεν, ἀφ᾽ ἧς αἱ θήλειαι, ὡς ἀπ᾽ ἐκείνου οἱ ἄρρενες.

Τὰ οὖν ἀρρενικὰ μετὰ τοῦ Λόγου συνεστάλη, τὰ θηλυκὰ δὲ ἀπανδρωθέντα ἑνοῦται τοῖς Ἀγγέλοις καὶ εἰς Πλήρωμα χωρεῖ. Διὰ τοῦτο ἡ γυνὴ εἰς ἄνδρα μετατίθεσθαι λέγεται, καὶ ἡ ἐνταῦθα Ἐκκλησία εἰς Ἀγγέλους.

22 Καὶ ὅταν εἴπῃ ὁ Ἀπόστολος, «Ἐπεὶ τί ποιήσουσιν, οἱ βαπτιζόμενοι ὑπὲρ τῶν νεκρῶν;» ὑπὲρ ἡμῶν γάρ, φησίν, οἱ Ἄγγελοι ἐβαπτίσαντο, ὧν ἐσμεν μέρη.

Νεκροὶ δὲ ἡμεῖς οἱ νεκρωθέντες τῇ συστάσει ταύτῃ, ζῶντες δὲ καὶ ἄρρενες οἱ μὴ μεταλαβόντες τῆς συστάσεως ταύτης.

«Εἰ νεκροὶ οὐκ ἐγείρονται, τί καὶ βαπτιζόμεθα;» Ἐγειρόμεθα οὖν ἡμεῖς ἰσάγγελοι τοῖς ἄρρεσιν ἀποκατασταθέντες, τοῖς μέλεσι τὰ μέλη, εἰς ἕνωσιν.

«Οἱ βαπτιζόμενοι» δέ, φασίν, «ὑπὲρ ἡμῶν τῶν νεκρῶν,» οἱ Ἄγγελοί εἰσιν οἱ ὑπὲρ ἡμῶν βαπτιζόμενοι, ἵνα ἔχοντες καὶ ἡμεῖς τὸ Ὄνομα μὴ ἐπισχεθῶμεν κωλυθέντες εἰς τὸ Πλήρωμα παρελθεῖν τῷ Ὅρῳ καὶ τῷ Σταυρῷ.

Διὸ καὶ ἐν τῇ χειροθεσίᾳ λέγουσιν ἐπὶ τέλους, «εἰς λύτρωσιν ἀγγελικήν,» τουτέστιν ἣν καὶ Ἄγγελοι ἔχουσιν, ἵν᾽ ᾖ βεβαπτισμένος ὁ τὴν λύτρωσιν κομισάμενος τῷ αὐτοῦ Ὀνόματι ᾧ καὶ ὁ Ἄγγελος αὐτοῦ προβεβάπτισται.

---

13. Οὐαλεντινιανοὶ: MSS read οἱ Οὐαλεντινιανοῦ.

For this reason it is also said "he received a form of a servant," (referring) not only to his flesh at coming, but also to his underlying substance. Substance is a slave, since it suffers and is subordinate to the efficacious and decisive cause.

20 For "I begot you before the morning star" we understand in this way, with reference to the first-created Word of God, and "before the sun is your name" and moon also before all creation.

21 "He created them according to the image of God, male and female he created them." The Valentinians say that spoken about (in this verse) is the first emanation of Wisdom, the males from the emanation are the election, but the females are the calling. And they call the males angelic, and the females themselves, the superior spirit.

Thus also, with the (example) of Adam, the male remained in him, but all of the female seed, having been removed from him, became Eve, from whom (come) the females, as from him (come) the males.

Therefore, the males are gathered together with the Word, but the females, when they become male, are joined to the angels and advance into the fullness. Therefore, the woman is said to be transformed into a man and the church here (is said to be transformed) into angels.

22 And when the Apostle said, "Otherwise what will they do, those baptized on behalf of the dead?" For on our behalf, he says, the angels, of whom we are parts, were baptized.

But we are dead who are made dead by this structure, but males are alive who did not take part in this structure.

"If the dead are not raised, why are we baptized?" Therefore we are raised equal to angels, having been returned to the males in oneness, the members with the members.

"Those baptized on our behalf, the dead," they say, are the angels who are baptized on our behalf, so that when we also have the name, we might not be restrained, prevented by the limit and the cross from entering into the fullness.

Wherefore when laying on hands they say at the end, "For the angelic redemption," that is, what the angels have, so that the one receiving the redemption might be baptized in his name, in which his angels had also been baptized.

Ἐβαπτίσαντο δὲ ἐν ἀρχῇ οἱ Ἄγγελοι, ἐν λυτρώσει τοῦ Ὀνόματος τοῦ ἐπὶ τὸν Ἰησοῦν ἐν τῇ περιστερᾷ κατελθόντος καὶ λυτρωσαμένου αὐτόν.

Ἐδέησεν δὲ λυτρώσεως καὶ τῷ Ἰησοῦ, ἵνα μὴ κατασχεθῇ τῇ Ἐννοίᾳ ᾗ ἐνετέθη τοῦ ὑστερήματος, προ᾽σ᾽ερχόμενος διὰ τῆς Σοφίας, ὥς φησιν ὁ Θεόδοτος.

23 Τὸν Παράκλητον οἱ ἀπὸ Οὐαλεντίνου τὸν Ἰησοῦν λέγουσιν, ὅτι πλήρης τῶν Αἰώνων ἐλήλυθεν, ὡς ἀπὸ τοῦ Ὅλου προελθών.

Χριστὸς γάρ, καταλείψας τὴν προβαλοῦσαν αὐτὸν Σοφίαν, εἰσελθὼν εἰς τὸ Πλήρωμα, ὑπὲρ τῆς ἔξω καταλειφθείσης Σοφίας ᾐτήσατο τὴν βοήθειαν. καὶ ἐξ εὐδοκίας τῶν Αἰώνων Ἰησοῦς προβάλλεται Παράκλητος τῷ παρελθόντι Αἰῶνι. Ἐν τύπῳ δὲ Παρακλήτου ὁ Παῦλος ἀναστάσεως Ἀπόστολος[14] γέγονεν.

Αὐτίκα μετὰ τὸ πάθος τοῦ Κυρίου καὶ αὐτὸς ἀπεστάλη κηρύσσειν. Διὸ καὶ καθ᾽ ἕ<κά>τερον ἐκήρυξε τὸν Σωτῆρα· γενητὸν καὶ παθητὸν διὰ τοὺς ἀριστ<ερ>ούς, ὅτι τοῦτον γνῶναι δυνηθέντες, κατὰ τὸν τόπον τοῦτον δεδίασιν, καὶ κατὰ τὸ πνευματικὸν ἐξ ἁγίου Πνεύματος καὶ Παρθένου, ὡς οἱ δεξιοὶ Ἄγγελοι γινώσκουσιν.

Ἰδίως γὰρ ἕκαστος γνωρίζει τὸν Κύριον καὶ οὐχ ὁμοίως πάντες. «Τὸ πρόσωπον τοῦ Πατρὸς ὁρῶσιν οἱ Ἄγγελοι τούτων τῶν μικρῶν,» τῶν ἐκλεκτῶν, τῶν ἐσομένων ἐν τῇ αὐτῇ κληρονομίᾳ καὶ τελειότητι.

Τάχα δὲ τὸ πρόσωπον ἔστι μὲν καὶ ὁ Υἱός, ἔστι δὲ καὶ ὅσον καταληπτὸν τοῦ Πατρὸς δι᾽ Υἱοῦ δεδιδαγμένοι θεωροῦσι. τὸ δὲ λοιπὸν ἄγνωστόν ἐστι τοῦ Πατρός.

24 Λέγουσιν οἱ Οὐαλεντινιανοὶ ὅτι ὃ κατὰ εἷς τῶν προφητῶν ἔσχεν Πνεῦμα ἐξαίρετον εἰς διακονίαν, τοῦτο ἐπὶ πάντας τοὺς τῆς Ἐκκλησίας ἐξεχύθη. διὸ καὶ τὰ σημεῖα τοῦ Πνεύματος, ἰάσεις καὶ προφητεῖαι, διὰ τῆς Ἐκκλησίας ἐπιτελοῦνται.

Ἀγνοοῦσι δὲ ὅτι ὁ Παράκλητος, <ὁ> προσεχῶς ἐνεργῶν νῦν τῇ Ἐκκλησίᾳ, τῆς αὐτῆς[15] οὐσίας ἐστὶ καὶ δυνάμεως τῷ προσεχῶς ἐνεργήσαντι κατὰ τὴν παλαιὰν διαθήκην.

25 Τὸν ἄγγελον ὡρίσαντο οἱ ἀπὸ Οὐαλεντίνου λόγον ἀπαγγελίαν ἔχοντα τοῦ Ὄντος. Λέγουσι δὲ καὶ τοὺς Αἰῶνας ὁμωνύμως τῷ λόγῳ λόγους.

14. Ἀπόστολος: MSS read Ἀποστολή.
15. αὐτῆς: MSS read αὐτοῦ.

The angels were baptized in the beginning, in the redemption of the name that descended upon Jesus in the dove and redeemed him.

Redemption was necessary even for Jesus, so that he might not be detained by the mind of the deficiency in which he was placed while approaching through Wisdom, as Theodotus says.

23 The followers of Valentinus call Jesus the helper, because he has come filled with the eternities, since he comes forth from the whole.

For Christ, leaving behind the one who brought him forth, Wisdom, and entering into the fullness, requested help for Wisdom, who was left outside. And Jesus was brought forth by the goodwill of the eternities as a helper for the eternity that had transgressed. In the type of the helper, Paul became the Apostle of the resurrection.

Right after the passion of the Lord he too was sent off to preach. Therefore, he preached the Savior according to <both> (understandings): created and subject to suffering for those on the <left>, because since they are able to know him, they fear him in this place, and spiritual from the Holy Spirit and virgin, as the angels on the right know (him).

For each one knows the Lord in his own (way) and not all in the same (way). "The angels of the little ones behold the face of the Father," that is, of the elect, those who will be in the same inheritance and perfection.

But perhaps the face is also the Son, and the extent of the graspability of the Father as those who have been taught by the Son perceive. But the rest of the Father is unknown.

24 The Valentinians say that the Spirit that each of the prophets had chosen for service was poured forth upon all those of the church. Therefore, the signs of the Spirit, healings and prophecies, are also made perfect through the church.

But they do not know that the helper, <who> now works directly through the church, is of the <same> substance and power as the one who worked directly throughout the Old Testament.

25 The followers of Valentinus defined the angel as a Word having a message from the One Who Is. And they also call the eternities "words," using the same word.

Οἱ Ἀπόστολοι, φησί, μετετέθησαν τοῖς δεκαδύο ζῳδίοις, ὡς γὰρ ὑπ' ἐκείνων ἡ γένεσις διοικεῖται, οὕτως ὑπὸ τῶν Ἀποστόλων ἡ ἀναγέννησις <ἐφ>ορᾶται.

26 Τὸ ὁρατὸν τοῦ Ἰησοῦ ἡ Σοφία καὶ ἡ Ἐκκλησία ἦν τῶν σπερμάτων τῶν διαφερόντων, ἣν ἐστολίσατο διὰ τοῦ σαρκίου, ὥς φησιν ὁ Θεόδοτος. τὸ δὲ ἀόρατον <τὸ> Ὄνομα, ὅπερ ἐστὶν ὁ Υἱὸς ὁ Μονογενής.

Ὅθεν ὅταν εἴπῃ, «Ἐγώ εἰμι ἡ θύρα,» τοῦτο λέγει ὅτι μέχρι τοῦ Ὅρου οὗ εἰμι ἐγὼ ἐλεύσεσθε, οἱ τοῦ διαφέροντος σπέρματος.

Ὅταν δὲ καὶ αὐτὸς εἰσέρχηται, καὶ τὸ σπέρμα συνεισέρχεται αὐτῷ εἰς τὸ Πλήρωμα, διὰ τῆς θύρας συναχθὲν καὶ εἰσαχθέν.

27 Ὁ ἱερεὺς εἰσιὼν ἐντὸς τοῦ καταπετάσματος τοῦ δευτέρου, τό τε πέταλον ἀπετίθει παρὰ τῷ θυσιαστηρίῳ τοῦ θυμιάματος. αὐτὸς δὲ ἐν σιγῇ, τὸ ἐν τῇ καρδίᾳ ἐγκεχαραγμένον Ὄνομα ἔχων, εἰσήει, δεικνὺς τὴν ἀπόθεσιν <τοῦ σώματος> τοῦ καθάπερ πετάλου χρυσοῦ καθαροῦ γενομένου καὶ κούφου διὰ τὴν κάθαρσιν τοῦ ὥσπερ σώματος τῆς ψυχῆς ἀπόθεσιν, ἐν ᾧ ἐγκεχάρακτο τὸ γάνωμα τῆς θεοσεβείας δι' οὗ ταῖς Ἀρχαῖς καὶ ταῖς Ἐξουσίαις ἐγινώσκετο τὸ Ὄνομα περικείμενος.

Ἀποτίθεται δὲ τοῦτο τὸ σῶμα, τὸ πέταλον τὸ ἀβαρὲς γενόμενον, «ἐντὸς τοῦ καταπετάσματος τοῦ δευτέρου,» ἐν τῷ νοητῷ κόσμῳ, ὅ ἐστι δεύτερον ὁλοσχερὲς καταπέτασμα τοῦ παντός, «παρὰ τὸ θυσιαστήριον τοῦ θυμιάματος,» παρὰ τοὺς λειτουργοὺς τῶν ἀναφερομένων εὐχῶν Ἀγγέλους.

Γυμνὴ δὲ ἡ ψυχὴ ἐν δυνάμει τοῦ συνειδότος, οἷον σῶμα τῆς δυνάμεως γενομένη, μεταβαίνει εἰς τὰ πνευματικά, λογικὴ τῷ ὄντι καὶ ἀρχιερατικὴ γενομένη, ὡς ἂν ἐμψυχουμένη ὡς εἰπεῖν ὑπὸ τοῦ Λόγου προσεχῶς ἤδη, καθάπερ οἱ Ἀρχάγγελοι τῶν Ἀγγέλων ἀρχιερεῖς γενόμενοι, καὶ τούτων πάλιν οἱ Πρωτόκτιστοι.

Ποῦ δὲ ἔτι γραφῆς καὶ μαθήσεως κατόρθωμα τῇ ψυχῇ ἐκείνῃ τῇ καθαρᾷ γενομένῃ, ὅπου καὶ ἀξιοῦται «πρόσωπον πρὸς πρόσωπον» Θεὸν ὁρᾶν;

Τὴν γοῦν ἀγγελικὴν διδασκαλίαν ὑπερβᾶσα καὶ τὸ Ὄνομα τὸ διδασκόμενον ἐγγράφως, ἐπὶ τὴν γνῶσιν καὶ κατάληψιν τῶν πραγμάτων ἔρχεται, οὐκέτι νύμφη, ἀλλ' ἤδη Λόγος γενόμενος, καὶ παρὰ τῷ νυμφίῳ καταλύων μετὰ τῶν Πρωτοκλήτων καὶ Πρωτοκτίστων, φίλων μὲν δι' ἀγάπην, υἱῶν δὲ διὰ τὴν διδασκαλίαν καὶ ὑπακοήν, ἀδελφῶν δὲ διὰ τὸ τῆς γενέσεως κοινόν.

The Apostles, he says, were translated into the twelve signs of the zodiac, for as birth is managed by them, so too is rebirth <overseen> by the Apostles.

26 The visible part of Jesus was Wisdom and the church of the superior seeds, which he put on through the flesh, as Theodotus says. But the invisible part is <the> name, which is the Only-Begotten Son.

For which reason when he says, "I am the door," he is saying that as those of the superior seed, you shall come up to the boundary where I am.

And when he enters, the seed accompanies him into the fullness, gathered together and brought forward through the door.

27 When entering into the second veil, the priest set aside the plate at the incense altar. He entered in silence, having the name engraved upon his heart, displaying the putting aside <of the body,> which has become pure like the golden plate and bright through the purification (and) which is like a setting aside of a body of the soul, from which the brightness of the piety was engraved through which he, having been enveloped in the name, was known by the principalities and the powers.

He sets aside this body, the plate that had become weightless, "within the second veil," in the noetic world, which is the second complete veil of the entirety, "at the incense altar," with the angels who perform the prayers offered up.

The soul, stripped by the power of the one who knows, such that it becomes a body of power, changes into spiritual things, becoming in essence rational and high priestly, so as to be ensouled, so to speak, directly by the Word, just as the archangels become the high priests of the angels, and the firstborn in turn become the high priests of the archangels.

But where is the correct (teaching) of scripture and doctrine for that soul that has come to be pure, and where is it permitted to see God "face-to-face"?

Therefore, after going beyond the angelic teaching and the name that is taught in Scripture, it comes to the knowledge and apprehension of the facts, no longer a bride, but now a Word, and takes up residence with the bridegroom along with those first-called and firstborn, friends by love, children by teaching and obedience, and siblings by common origin.

Ὥστε τὸ μὲν τῆς οἰκονομίας ἦν τὸ πέταλον περικεῖσθαι καὶ μανθάνειν εἰς γνῶσιν, τὸ δὲ δυνάμεως τὸ θεοφόρον γίνεσθαι τὸν ἄνθρωπον, προσεχῶς ἐνεργούμενον ὑπὸ τοῦ Κυρίου καὶ καθάπερ σῶμα αὐτοῦ γινόμενον.

28 Τό· «Θεὸς ἀποδιδοὺς ἐπὶ τρίτην καὶ τετάρτην γενεὰν τοῖς ἀπειθοῦσι,» φασὶν οἱ ἀπὸ Βασιλείδου κατὰ τὰς ἐνσωματώσεις. Οἱ δὲ ἀπὸ Οὐαλεντίνου τοὺς τρεῖς τόπους δηλοῦσθαι τοὺς ἀριστερούς, τετάρτην δὲ γενεὰν τὰ σπέρματα αὐτῶν· «Ἔλεον δὲ ποιῶν εἰς χιλιάδας,» ἐπὶ τὰ δεξιά.

29 Ἡ Σιγή, φασί, Μήτηρ οὖσα πάντων τῶν προβληθέντων ὑπὸ τοῦ Βάθους, ὃ μὲν οὐκ ἔσχεν εἰπεῖν, περὶ τοῦ Ἀρρήτου σεσίγηκεν, ὃ δὲ κατέλαβεν, τοῦτο ἀκατάληπτον προσηγόρευσεν.

30 Εἶτα, ἐκλαθόμενοι τῆς δόξης τοῦ Θεοῦ, παθεῖν αὐτὸν λέγουσιν ἀθέως. Ὁ γὰρ συνεπάθησεν ὁ Πατήρ, «στερεὸς ὢν τῇ φύσει», φησὶν ὁ Θεόδοτος, «καὶ ἀνένδοτος», ἐνδόσιμον ἑαυτὸν παρασχών, ἵνα ἡ Σιγὴ τοῦτο καταλάβῃ, πάθος ἐστίν.

ἡ γὰρ συμπάθεια, πάθος τινὸς διὰ πάθος ἑτέρου. Ναὶ μήν καὶ τοῦ πάθους γενομένου, τὸ Ὅλον συνεπάθησεν καὶ αὐτό, εἰς διόρθωσιν τοῦ παθόντος.

31 Ἀλλὰ καὶ εἰ ὁ κατελθὼν εὐδοκία τοῦ Ὅλου ἦν, «ἐν αὐτῷ γὰρ πᾶν τὸ Πλήρωμα ἦν σωματικῶς», ἔπαθεν δὲ οὗτος, δῆλον ὅτι καὶ τὰ ἐν αὐτῷ σπέρματα συνέπαθεν, δι᾽ ὧν τὸ Ὅλον καὶ τὸ Πᾶν εὑρίσκεται πάσχον.

Ἀλλὰ καὶ διὰ τῆς τοῦ δωδεκάτου Αἰῶνος πείσεως τὰ Ὅλα «παιδευθέντα,» ὥς φασι, συνεπάθησεν.

Τότε γὰρ ἐπέγνωσαν ὅτι <ὅ> εἰσιν, «χάριτι τοῦ Πατρός εἰσιν,» Ὄνομα ἀνωνόμαστον, Μορφὴ καὶ Γνῶσις. Ὁ δὲ βουληθεὶς Αἰὼν τὸ ὑπὲρ τὴν Γνῶσιν λαβεῖν ἐν ἀγνωσίᾳ καὶ ἀμορφίᾳ ἐγένετο.

Ὅθεν καὶ κένωμα Γνώσεως εἰργάσατο, ὅπερ ἐστὶ σκιὰ τοῦ Ὀνόματος, ὅπερ ἐστὶν Υἱός, Μορφὴ τῶν Αἰώνων. Οὕτως τὸ κατὰ μέρος ὄνομα τῶν Αἰώνων ἀμελεῖ ἐστι τοῦ Ὀνόματος.

32 Ἐν Πληρώματι οὖν, ἑνότητος οὔσης, ἕκαστος τῶν Αἰώνων ἴδιον ἔχει πλήρωμα, τὴν συζυγίαν. Ὅσα οὖν ἐκ συζυγίας, φασί, προέρχεται, πληρώματά ἐστιν· ὅσα δὲ ἀπὸ ἑνός, εἰκόνες.

And so it was in the divine plan to wear the plate and to advance toward knowledge, but it was (the goal) of power that humanity should become the bearer of God, energized directly by the Lord and becoming, in a sense, his body.

28 Regarding "God rendering to the disobedient to the third and fourth generation," the followers of Basilides (understand it as a reference) to reincarnations. But the followers of Valentinus (maintain) that the three places indicate those on the left, while the fourth generation is their seed; "having mercy upon thousands" (refers) to those on the right.

29 Silence, they say, being the mother of all who were put forth by Depth, about which she had nothing to say, remained silent about the Ineffable one, but what she received, she termed incomprehensible.

30 Next forgetting God's glory, they irreverently say that he suffered. For the Father shared in suffering, "although stubborn and unyielding by nature," says Theodotus, by presenting himself as yielding, in order that Silence might comprehend this, it is suffering.

For sympathy is the suffering of one on account of the suffering of another. And indeed during the passion, the whole suffered the same (suffering) for the healing of the one who suffered.

31 But if the one who came down was the goodwill of the whole, "for in him was the entire bodily fullness," and he suffered, it is clear that the seed in him also suffered, (and that) through them the whole and the entirety are found suffering.

Additionally though the suffering of the twelfth eternity the whole "was instructed," as they say, sharing in passion.

For then they knew that "they are" what they are "by the grace of the Father," a name without a name, form and knowledge. But the eternity that wanted to grasp what is beyond knowledge came to be in ignorance and formlessness.

For which reason it worked at a void of knowledge that is a shadow of the name, which is the Son, form of the eternities. Thus the partial name of the eternities is doubtless from the name.

32 Therefore, although there is unity in the fullness, each of the eternities has its own fullness, the syzygy. Therefore, whatever comes from a syzygy, they say, are fullnesses; but whatever come from one are images.

Ὅθεν ὁ Θεόδοτος τὸν Χριστὸν, ἐξ ἐννοίας προελθόντα τῆς Σοφίας, εἰκόνα τοῦ Πληρώματος ἐκάλεσεν.

Οὗτος δέ, καταλείψας τὴν Μητέρα, ἀνελθὼν εἰς τὸ Πλήρωμα, ἐκράθη ὥσπερ τοῖς Ὅλοις, οὕτω δὲ καὶ τῷ Παρακλήτῳ.

33 Υἱόθετος μέντοι γέγονεν ὁ Χριστός, ὡς πρὸς τὰ πληρώματα «Ἐκλεκτὸς» γενόμενος καὶ «Πρωτότοκος» τῶν ἐνθάδε πραγμάτων.

Ἔστιν οὖν ὁ λόγος οὗτος παράκουσμα τοῦ ἡμετέρου, ἐκ τοῦ ὑποκειμένου «Πρωτότοκον» λέγοντος τὸν Σωτῆρα, καὶ ἔστιν ὡσπερεὶ Ῥίζα καὶ «Κεφαλὴ» ἡμῶν, ἡ δὲ Ἐκκλησία καρποὶ αὐτοῦ.

Χριστοῦ, φασί, τὸ ἀνοίκειον φυγόντος <καὶ> συσταλέντος εἰς τὸ Πλήρωμα, ἐκ τῆς μητρῴας γεννομένου ἐννοίας, ἡ Μήτηρ αὖθις τὸν τῆς οἰκονομίας προηγάγετο Ἄρχοντα εἰς τύπον τοῦ φυγόντος αὐτήν, κατ᾽ ἐπιπόθησιν αὐτοῦ, κρείττονος ὑπάρχοντος, ὃς ἦν τύπος τοῦ Πατρὸς τῶν ὅλων.

Διὸ καὶ ἥττων γίνεται, ὡς ἂν ἐκ πάθους τῆς ἐπιθυμίας συνεστώς[[α]]. {Ἐμυσάχθη} μέντοι ἐνιδοῦσα τὴν «ἀποτομίαν» αὐτοῦ, ὥς φασιν αὐτοί.

34 Ἀλλὰ καὶ <αἱ> εὐώνυμοι δυνάμεις, πρῶται προβληθεῖσαι τῶν δεξιῶν ὑπ᾽ αὐτῆς, ὑπὸ τῆς τοῦ Φωτὸς παρουσίας οὐ μορφοῦνται, κατελείφθησαν δὲ αἱ ἀριστεραὶ ὑπὸ τοῦ Τόπου μορφωθῆναι.

Τῆς Μητρὸς οὖν μετὰ τοῦ Υἱοῦ καὶ τῶν σπερμάτων εἰσελθούσης εἰς τὸ Πλήρωμα, τότε ὁ Τόπος τὴν ἐξουσίαν τῆς Μητρὸς καὶ τὴν τάξιν ἀπολήψεται ἣν νῦν ἔχει ἡ Μήτηρ.

35 Ὁ Ἰησοῦς, «τὸ Φῶς» ἡμῶν, ὡς λέγει ὁ Ἀπόστολος, «ἑαυτὸν κενώσας,» τουτέστιν, ἐκτὸς τοῦ Ὅρου γενόμενος, κατὰ Θεόδοτον, ἐπεὶ «Ἄγγελος» ἦν τοῦ Πληρώματος, τοὺς Ἀγγέλους τοῦ διαφέροντος σπέρματος συνεξήγαγεν ἑαυτῷ.

Καὶ αὐτὸς μὲν τὴν λύτρωσιν, ὡς ἀπὸ Πληρώματος προελθών, εἶχεν. τοὺς δὲ Ἀγγέλους εἰς διόρθωσιν τοῦ σπέρματος ἤγαγεν.

Ὡς γὰρ ὑπὲρ μέρους δέονται καὶ παρακαλοῦσι, καὶ δι᾽ ἡμᾶς κατεχόμενοι, σπεύδοντες εἰσελθεῖν, ἄφεσιν ἡμῖν αἰτοῦνται ἵνα συνεισέλθωμεν αὐτοῖς·

Therefore, Theodotus called the Christ, who came forth from the thought of Wisdom, an image of the fullness.

But he left behind the mother, (and) when ascending into the fullness, he was mixed as if with the whole, and in this way also with the helper.

33 To be sure, Christ became adopted as a son because he became "elect" among the fullnesses and "Firstborn" of the things here.

This teaching is a misunderstanding of ours, which maintains that the Savior is the "Firstborn" of what has been established, and he is just as our root and "head," and the church is its fruits.

Christ, they say, upon fleeing that which was foreign <and> being drawn up into the fullness, after he had been begotten by the thought of the mother, the mother in turn brought forth the ruler of the organization as a type of the one that had fled from her, according to a desire for him, since he was greater, (since) he was a type of the Father of the whole.

Therefore, he became less, as if produced by the passion of desire. To be sure, "she was disgusted" when observing his "brutality," as they say.

34 But also <the> powers on the left, first to be put forth by her from those on the right, not formed by the arrival of the light, but those on the left remained behind to be formed by the place.

Therefore, after mother with the Son and the seeds entered into the fullness, then the place will receive the power of the mother and the order that the mother now has.

35 Jesus, our "light," as the Apostle says, "emptied himself," that is, going beyond the limit, according to Theodotus, since he was an "angel" of the fullness, he led out the angels of the superior seed with him.

And he had the redemption since he had gone forth from the fullness. But he led the angels into the rectifying of the seed.

For as they are bound and they entreat for the sake of parts, and for our benefit they are restrained, zealous to enter, they request exemption for us so that we might enter with them.

σχεδὸν γὰρ ἡμῶν χρείαν ἔχοντες ἵνα εἰσέλθωσιν, ἐπεὶ ἄνευ ἡμῶν οὐκ ἐπιτρέπεται αὐτοῖς—διὰ τοῦτο γὰρ οὐδὲ ἡ Μήτηρ συνελήλυθεν ἄνευ ἡμῶν, φασίν—εἰκότως ὑπὲρ ἡμῶν δέονται.

36 Ἐν ἑνότητι μέντοι γε προεβλήθησαν οἱ Ἄγγελοι ἡμῶν, φασίν, εἷς ὄντες, ὡς ἀπὸ ἑνὸς προελθόντες.

Ἐπεὶ δὲ ἡμεῖς ἦμεν οἱ μεμερισμένοι, διὰ τοῦτο ἐβαπτίσατο ὁ Ἰησοῦς τὸ ἀμέριστον μερισθῆναι, μέχρις ἡμᾶς ἑνώσῃ αὐτοῖς εἰς τὸ Πλήρωμα, ἵνα ἡμεῖς, οἱ πολλοί, ἓν γενόμενοι, {οἱ} πάντες τῷ ἑνὶ τῷ δι᾽ ἡμᾶς μερισθέντι ἀνακραθῶμεν.

37 Οἱ ἀπὸ Ἀδὰμ ἐξελθόντες, οἱ μὲν Δίκαιοι, διὰ τῶν ἐκτισμένων τὴν ὁδὸν ποιούμενοι, παρὰ τῷ Τόπῳ κατείχοντο, κατὰ τοὺς Οὐαλεντινιανούς. οἱ δὲ ἕτεροι, ἐν τῷ τοῦ σκότου ἐκτισμένῳ ἐν τοῖς ἀριστεροῖς, ἔχοντες συναίσθησιν τοῦ πυρός.

38 «Ποταμὸς ἐκπορεύεται πυρὸς ὑποκάτω τοῦ θρόνου» τοῦ Τόπου, καὶ ῥεῖ εἰς τὸ κενὸν τοῦ ἐκτισμένου, ὅ ἐστιν ἡ Γέεννα, ἀπὸ κτίσεως τοῦ πυρὸς ῥέοντος μὴ πληρουμένη. Καὶ αὐτὸς δὲ ὁ Τόπος πύρινός ἐστι.

Διὰ τοῦτο, φησί, καταπέτασμα ἔχει ἵνα μὴ ἐκ τῆς προσόψεως ἀναλωθῇ τὰ πνεύματα. Μόνος δὲ ὁ Ἀρχάγγελος εἰσέρχεται πρὸς αὐτόν, οὗ κατ᾽ εἰκόνα καὶ ὁ ἀρχιερεὺς ἅπαξ τοῦ ἐνιαυτοῦ εἰς τὰ ἅγια τῶν ἁγίων εἰσῄει.

Ἔνθεν καὶ ὁ Ἰησοῦς παρακληθεὶς συνεκαθέσθη τῷ Τόπῳ, ἵνα μένῃ τὰ πνεύματα καὶ μὴ προαναστῇ αὐτοῦ, καὶ ἵνα τὸν Τόπον ἡμερώσῃ καὶ τῷ σπέρματι δίοδον εἰς Πλήρωμα παράσχῃ.

39 Ἡ Μήτηρ, προβαλοῦσα τὸν Χριστὸν ὁλόκληρον καὶ ὑπ᾽ αὐτοῦ καταλειφθεῖσα, τοῦ λοιποῦ οὐκέτι οὐδὲν προέβαλεν ὁλόκληρον, ἀλλὰ τὰ δυνατὰ παρ᾽ αὐτῇ κατέσχεν, ὥστε καὶ τοῦ Τόπου καὶ τῶν κλητῶν[16] τὰ ἀγγελικὰ αὐτὴ προβαλοῦσα παρ᾽ αὐτῇ κατέχει, τῶν ἐκλεκτῶν τῶν ἀγγελικῶν ὑπὸ τοῦ Ἄρρενος ἔτι πρότερον προβεβλημένων.

40 Τὰ μὲν γὰρ δεξιὰ πρὸ τῆς τοῦ Φωτὸς αἰτήσεως προηνέχθη ὑπὸ τῆς Μητρός, τὰ δὲ σπέρματα τῆς Ἐκκλησίας μετὰ τὴν τοῦ Φωτὸς αἴτησιν, ὅτε ὑπὸ τοῦ Ἄρρενος τὰ ἀγγελικὰ τῶν σπερμάτων προεβάλετο.

41 Τὰ διαφέροντα σπέρματά, φησι, μήτε ὡς πάθη, ὧν λυομένων συνελύθη ἂν καὶ τὰ σπέρματα, μήτε ὡς κτίσιν προεληλυθέναι,

---

16. MS reads ρ.

For perhaps because they need us in order to enter, since without us it is not permitted for them—therefore, the mother has not entered with them without us, they say—fittingly they are fettered for our sake.

36 Indeed our angels were put forth in unity, they say, being one, since they came forth from one.

Since we were separated, Jesus was baptized to divide the undivided, until he might unite us with them in the fullness, so that we, the many, having become one, might all be joined in the one who was divided on our account.

37 Those who came from Adam, the righteous, making their way through the created things, were restrained at the place, according to the Valentinians. But the others (were restrained) at the place created for darkness among those on the left, sensing the fire.

38 "A river of fire flows from under the throne" of the place, and runs into the void of creation, which is Gehenna; though the fire flows from creation it is never filled. And the place itself is fiery.

Therefore, he says, it has a veil so that the spiritual things might not be destroyed by the sight (of it). But the archangel alone enters into it, as a representation of this also the high priest once a year enters into the holy of holies.

From there Jesus was called and sat down with the place so that the spirituals might not remain and rise before him, and so that he might overcome the place and permit the seed to pass into the fullness.

39 The mother, having brought forth Christ complete and having been left behind by him, henceforth no longer brought forth anything complete, but she kept with her the things possible, so that even of the place and allotment then having produced the angelic things, she keeps them with her, for the angelic elect had been put forth earlier by the male.

40 For those on the right were brought forth by the mother before the demand for the light, but the seeds of the church after the demand of the light, when the angelic things of the seeds had been put forth by the male.

41 The superior seeds, he says, came forth neither as passions, the seeds of which would have been destroyed when they were destroyed, nor as a creation,

ἀλλ' ὡς τέκνα, ἀπαρτιζομένης γὰρ τῆς κτίσεως, συναπηρτίσθη ἂν καὶ τὰ σπέρματα.

Διὸ καὶ τὴν οἰκειότητα ἔχει πρὸς τὸ Φῶς, ὃ πρῶτον προήγαγεν, τουτέστι τὸν Ἰησοῦν, ὁ αἰτησάμενος τοὺς Αἰῶνας Χριστός, ἐν ᾧ συνδιυλίσθη κατὰ δύναμιν καὶ τὰ σπέρματα συνελθόντα αὐτῷ εἰς τὸ Πλήρωμα. Διότι πρὸ καταβολῆς κόσμου εἰκότως λέγεται ἡ Ἐκκλησία ἐκλελέχθαι, ἐν ἀρχῇ τοίνυν συνελογίσθημεν, φασί, καὶ ἐφανερώθημεν.

Διὰ τοῦτο ὁ Σωτὴρ λέγει, «Λαμψάτω τὸ Φῶς ὑμῶν,» μηνύων περὶ τοῦ Φωτὸς τοῦ φανέντος καὶ μορφώσαντος, περὶ οὗ ὁ Ἀπόστολος λέγει, «Ὃ φωτίζει πάντα Ἄνθρωπον ἐρχόμενον εἰς τὸν κόσμον,» τὸν τοῦ διαφόρου σπέρματος.

Ὅτε γὰρ «ἐφωτίσθη» ὁ Ἄνθρωπος, τότε «εἰς τὸν κόσμον ἦλθεν,» τουτέστιν ἑαυτὸν ἐκόσμησεν, χωρίσας αὐτοῦ τὰ ἐπισκοτοῦντα καὶ συναναμεμιγμένα αὐτῷ πάθη. Καὶ τὸν Ἀδὰμ ὁ Δημιουργὸς ἐννοίᾳ προσχών, ἐπὶ τέλει τῆς δημιουργίας αὐτὸν προήγαγεν.

42 Ὁ Σταυρὸς τοῦ ἐν Πληρώματι Ὅρου σημεῖόν ἐστιν, χωρίζει γὰρ τοὺς ἀπίστους τῶν πιστῶν ὡς ἐκεῖνος τὸν κόσμον τοῦ Πληρώματος.

Διὸ καὶ τὰ σπέρματα ὁ Ἰησοῦς, διὰ τοῦ σημείου, ἐπὶ τῶν ὤμων βαστάσας, εἰσάγει εἰς τὸ Πλήρωμα. Ὦμοι γὰρ τοῦ σπέρματος ὁ Ἰησοῦς λέγεται· Κεφαλὴ δὲ ὁ Χριστός.

Ὅθεν εἴρηται, «Ὃς οὐκ αἴρει τὸν Σταυρὸν αὐτοῦ καὶ ἀκολουθεῖ μοι, οὐκ ἔστι μου ἀδελφός.» Ἦρεν οὖν τὸ σῶμα τοῦ Ἰησοῦ, ὅπερ ὁμοούσιον ἦν τῇ Ἐκκλησίᾳ.

43 Λέγουσιν οὖν ὅτι αἱ δεξιαὶ ᾔδεσαν τοῦ Ἰησοῦ καὶ τοῦ Χριστοῦ τὰ ὀνόματα καὶ πρὸ τῆς παρουσίας, ἀλλὰ τὸ σημεῖον οὐκ ᾔδεσαν τὴν δύναμιν.

Καὶ δόντος πᾶσαν τὴν ἐξουσίαν τοῦ πνεύματος, συναινέσαντος δὲ καὶ τοῦ Πληρώματος, ἐκπέμπεται «ὁ τῆς βουλῆς Ἄγγελος.» Καὶ γίνεται Κεφαλὴ τῶν ὅλων μετὰ τὸν Πατέρα.

«Πάντα γὰρ ἐν αὐτῷ ἐκτίσθη τὰ ὁρατὰ καὶ τὰ ἀόρατα, Θρόνοι, Κυριότητες, Βασιλεῖαι,» Θεότητες, Λειτουργίαι.

«Διὸ καὶ ὁ Θεὸς αὐτὸν ὑπερύψωσεν καὶ ἔδωκεν αὐτῷ Ὄνομα τὸ ὑπὲρ πᾶν ὄνομα, ἵνα πᾶν γόνυ κάμψῃ καὶ πᾶσα γλῶσσα ἐξομολογήσηται ὅτι Κύριος τῆς δόξης Ἰησοῦς Χριστὸς» Σωτήρ. «ἀναβὰς αὐτὸς καὶ καταβάς.»

«τὸ δὲ ἀνέβη τί ἐστιν, εἰ μὴ ὅτι καὶ κατέβη; Ὁ καταβὰς αὐτός ἐστιν εἰς τὰ κατώτατα τῆς γῆς καὶ ἀναβὰς ὑπεράνω τῶν οὐρανῶν.»

but as children, since when creation was completed, the seeds would have been included. Therefore, it also has a connection to the light, which was put forth first, which is Jesus, the Christ who adjures the eternities, by whom also the seeds were strained as much as possible while going with him into the fullness. Since the church is fittingly said to have been chosen before the foundation of the world, they say we were counted and revealed in the beginning.

For this reason the Savior says, "Let your light shine," with reference to the light that appeared and gave form, concerning which the Apostle says, "Which illuminates every person coming into the world," (meaning) the superior seed.

For when the human "was enlightened," then "into the world he came," that is, he adorned himself, separating the passions that were casting a shadow over him and mixing with him. And the Creator, who earlier had held Adam in thought, put him forth when he had finished creating.

42 The cross is a sign of the boundary in the fullness, for it divides the unfaithful from the faithful as it divides the world from the fullness.

Therefore, Jesus, by the sign, having carried the seeds upon his shoulders, leads them into the fullness. For Jesus is called the shoulders of the seed; but Christ is the head.

Wherefore it is said, "The one who does not take up his cross and follow me, is not my brother." Therefore, he took the body of Jesus, which was of one substance with the church.

43 They say that those on the right knew the names of Jesus and Christ even prior to the coming, but they did not know the sign, the power.

And after the Spirit has given all power, and the fullness assents, "the Angel of the counsel" is sent forth. And he becomes the head of the whole after the Father.

"For all things were created by him, things visible and invisible, thrones, dominions, kingdoms," deities, ministries.

"Therefore, God exalted him and gave him a name above every name, so that every knee should bow and every tongue should confess that Jesus Christ, Savior, is the Lord of Glory." "The one who ascended also descended."

"What does the ascent suggest, if not that he also descended? He is the one who descended into the lowest parts of the earth and ascended above the heavens."

44 Ἰδοῦσα δὲ αὐτὸν ἡ Σοφία ὅμοιον τῷ καταλιπόντι αὐτὴν Φωτί ἐγνώρισεν, καὶ προσέδραμεν καὶ ἠγαλλιάσατο καὶ προσεκύνησεν. τοὺς δὲ ἄρρενας Ἀγγέλους τοὺς σὺν αὐτῷ ἐκπεμφθέντας θεασαμένη, κατῃδέσθη καὶ κάλυμμα ἐπέθετο.

Διὰ τούτου τοῦ μυστηρίου ὁ Παῦλος κελεύει τὰς γυναῖκας «φορεῖν ἐξουσίαν ἐπὶ τῆς κεφαλῆς διὰ τοὺς Ἀγγέλους.»

45 Εὐθὺς οὖν ὁ Σωτὴρ ἐπιφέρει αὐτῇ μόρφωσιν τὴν κατὰ γνῶσιν καὶ ἴασιν τῶν παθῶν, δείξας ἀπὸ Πατρὸς ἀγεννήτου τὰ ἐν Πληρώματι καὶ τὰ μέχρι αὐτῆς.

Ἀποστήσας δὲ τὰ πάθη τῆς πεπονθυίας, αὐτὴν μὲν ἀπαθῆ κατεσκεύασεν, τὰ πάθη δὲ διακρίνας ἐφύλαξεν. καὶ οὐχ ὥσπερ <τὰ> τῆς ἔνδον διεφορήθη, ἀλλ᾿ εἰς οὐσίαν ἤγαγεν αὐτά τε καὶ <τὰ> τῆς δευτέρας διαθέσεως.

Οὕτως διὰ τῆς τοῦ Σωτῆρος ἐπιφανείας, ἡ Σοφία γίνεται, καὶ τὰ ἔξω κτίζεται, «Πάντα γὰρ δι᾿ αὐτοῦ γέγονεν, καὶ χωρὶς αὐτοῦ γέγονεν οὐδέν.»

46 Πρῶτον οὖν ἐξ ἀσωμάτου πάθους καὶ συμβεβηκότος εἰς ἀσώματον ἔτι τὴν ὕλην αὐτὰ μετήντλησεν καὶ μετέβαλεν, εἶθ᾿ οὕτως εἰς συγκρίματα καὶ σώματα. ἀθρόως γὰρ οὐσίαν ποιῆσαι τὰ πάθη οὐκ ἐνῆν.

καὶ τοῖς σώμασι κατὰ φύσιν ἐπιτηδειότητα ἐνεποίησεν.

47 Πρῶτος μὲν οὖν Δημιουργὸς ὁ Σωτὴρ γίνεται καθολικός. «ἡ δὲ Σοφία, » δευτέρα, «οἰκοδομεῖ οἶκον ἑαυτῇ καὶ ὑπήρεισεν στύλους ἑπτά.»

Καὶ πρῶτον πάντων προβάλλεται εἰκόνα τοῦ Πατρὸς Θεόν, δι᾿ οὗ ἐποίησεν «τὸν οὐρανὸν καὶ τὴν γῆν,» τουτέστι «τὰ οὐράνια καὶ τὰ ἐπίγεια,» τὰ δεξιὰ καὶ τὰ ἀριστερά.

Οὗτος ὡς εἰκὼν πατρὸς πατὴρ γίνεται, καὶ προβάλλει πρῶτον τὸν ψυχικὸν Χριστόν Υἱοῦ εἰκόνα, ἔπειτα τοὺς Ἀρχαγγέλους Αἰώνων εἰκόνας, εἶτα Ἀγγέλους <Ἀρχ>αγγέλων, ἐκ τῆς ψυχικῆς καὶ φωτεινῆς οὐσίας ἥν φησιν ὁ προφητικὸς λόγος· «Καὶ Πνεῦμα Θεοῦ ἐπεφέρετο ἐπάνω τῶν ὑδάτων,» κατὰ τὴν συμπλοκὴν τῶν δύο οὐσιῶν τῶν αὐτῷ πεποιημένων, τὸ εἰλικρινὲς «ἐπιφέρεσθαι» εἰπών, τὸ δὲ ἐμβριθὲς καὶ ὑλικὸν ὑποφέρεσθαι, τὸ θολερὸν καὶ παχυμερές.

44 Seeing him, Wisdom discovered that she was similar to the light that had abandoned her, and she ran to (him) and rejoiced and worshipped. But when she beheld
the male angels who were sent out with him, she stood in awe and put on a veil.

On account of this mystery, Paul urges the women "to wear power upon their
heads on account of the angels."

45 Immediately, then, the Savior placed upon her a form in accordance with
knowledge and healing from the passions, demonstrating from the unbegotten
Father the (contents) of the fullness and the (emanations) down to her.

After removing the passions of the one who had suffered, he rendered her without
passion, and once he separated the passions, he kept them. And they were not differentiated as from <those> within, but he brought into being them and <the>
orders of the second (level).

Thus through the manifestation of the Savior, Wisdom came into being, and the
things outside were created, "For all things came to be through him, and apart
from him nothing came to be."

46 First then from incorporeal passions and chance he drew these things and
changed them into something incorporeal yet still material, then in the same way
into compounds and bodies. For it was not possible to change the passions directly
into substance.

And he endowed the bodies with things suitable according to their nature.

47 The Savior became the first universal creator. "But Wisdom," second, "built a
home for herself and she erected seven columns."

And first of all she put forward a god as an image of the Father, and through him
she made "the heaven and the earth," that is, "the heavenly things and the terrestrial things," the things on the right and the things on the left.

This, as an image of the Father, came to be a father, and put forward the soulish
Christ as an image of the Son, the archangels as images of the eternities, then
angels of <archangels>, from the soulish and luminous substance about which the
prophetic word speaks "And the Spirit of God was born upon the waters," concerning the combination of the two substances that had been made for him, the pure
substance is said to be "born upon," but the heavy and material substance, the
thick and rough substance, is born under.

Ἀσώματον δὲ καὶ ταύτην ἐν ἀρχῇ αἰνίσσεται τὸ φάσκειν «ἀόρατον»· οὔτε γὰρ ἀνθρώπῳ τῷ μηδέπω ὄντι ἀόρατος ἦν, οὔτε τῷ Θεῷ· ἐδημιούργει γάρ. ἀλλὰ τὸ ἄμορφον καὶ ἀνείδεον καὶ ἀσχημάτιστον αὐτῆς ὧδέ πως ἐξεφώνησεν.

48 Διακρίνας δὲ ὁ Δημιουργὸς τὰ καθαρὰ ἀπὸ τοῦ ἐμβριθοῦς, ὡς ἂν ἐνιδὼν τὴν ἑκατέρου φύσιν, φῶς ἐποίησεν, τουτέστιν ἐφανέρωσεν καὶ εἰς φῶς καὶ ἰδέαν προσήγαγεν, ἐπεὶ τό γε ἡλιακὸν καὶ οὐράνιον φῶς πολλῷ ὕστερον ἐργάζεται.

Καὶ ποιεῖ τῶν ὑλικῶν τὸ μὲν ἐκ τῆς λύπης, οὐσιωδῶς κτίζων «Πνευματικὰ τῆς πονηρίας, πρὸς ἃ ἡ πάλη ἡμῖν,» διὸ καὶ λέγει ὁ Ἀπόστολος· «Καὶ μὴ λυπεῖτε τὸ Πνεῦμα τὸ ἅγιον τοῦ Θεοῦ, ἐν ᾧ ἐσφραγίσθητε.»

τὸ δὲ ἐκ τοῦ φόβου, τὰ θηρία, τὸ δὲ ἐκ τῆς <ἐκ>πλήξεως καὶ ἀπορίας, τὰ στοιχεῖα τοῦ κόσμου.

Ἐν δὲ τοῖς τρισὶ στοιχείοις τὸ πῦρ ἐναιωρεῖται καὶ ἐνέσπαρται καὶ ἐμφωλεύει καὶ ὑπὸ τούτων ἐξάπτεται καὶ τούτοις ἐπαποθνήσκει, μὴ ἔχον τύπον ἀποτακτὸν ἑαυτοῦ ὡς καὶ τὰ ἄλλα στοιχεῖα ἐξ ὧν τὰ συγκρίματα δημιουργεῖται.

49 Ἐπεὶ δὲ οὐκ ἐγίνωσκεν τὴν δι᾽ αὐτοῦ ἐνεργοῦσαν, οἰόμενος ἰδίᾳ δυνάμει δημιουργεῖν, φίλεργος ὢν φύσει, διὰ τοῦτο εἶπεν ὁ Ἀπόστολος· «Ὑπετάγη τῇ ματαιότητι τοῦ κόσμου, οὐχ ἑκών, ἀλλὰ διὰ τὸν ὑποτάξαντα, ἐπ᾽ ἐλπίδι ὅτι καὶ αὐτὸς ἐλευθερωθήσεται,» ὅταν συλλεγῇ τὰ σπέρματα τοῦ Θεοῦ.

Τεκμήριον δὲ μάλιστα τοῦ ἀκουσίου τὸ «εὐλογεῖν τὸ σάββατον» καὶ τὴν ἀπὸ τῶν πόνων ἀνάπαυσιν ὑπερασπάζεσθαι.

50 «Λαβὼν χοῦν ἀπὸ τῆς γῆς»—οὐ τῆς ξηρᾶς, ἀλλὰ τῆς πολυμεροῦς καὶ ποικίλης ὕλης μέρος—ψυχὴν γεώδη καὶ ὑλικὴν ἐτεκτήνατο ἄλογον καὶ τῆς τῶν θηρίων ὁμοούσιον· οὗτος «κατ᾽ εἰκόνα» ἄνθρωπος.

Ὁ δὲ «καθ᾽ ὁμοίωσιν,» τὴν αὐτοῦ τοῦ Δημιουργοῦ, ἐκεῖνός ἐστιν ὃν εἰς τοῦτον «ἐνεφύσησέν» τε καὶ ἐνέσπειρεν, ὁμοούσιόν τι αὐτῷ δι᾽ Ἀγγέλων ἐνθείς.

Καθὸ μὲν ἀόρατός ἐστι καὶ ἀσώματος, τὴν οὐσίαν αὐτοῦ «πνοὴν ζωῆς» προσεῖπεν, μορφωθὲν δὲ «ψυχὴ ζῶσα» ἐγένετο, ὅπερ εἶναι, καὶ αὐτὸς ἐν ταῖς προφητικαῖς γραφαῖς ὁμολογεῖ.

But it is also intimated that this was incorporeal in the beginning, the calling (of it) "invisible." But it was never invisible to anyone living, nor to God; for he created (it). But he has in some way proclaimed the formlessness and shapelessness and figurelessness of it.

48 After the Creator divided the pure things from the coarse ones, since he knew the nature of each, he made light, that is, he revealed and brought it out to light and form, since he made the solar and heavenly light much later.

And of the material things he made one out of grief, giving substance to the "spiritual things of wickedness, against which is our struggle, and, therefore, the Apostle says, "And do not grieve the Holy Spirit of God, by which you were sealed."

And (he made another) out of fear, the wild beasts, and another from <terror> and confusion, the elements of the world.

In the three elements fire is suspended and sown and loiters and is inflamed by them and dies with them, since it has no particular type of its own like the other elements from which the compounds are created.

49 Since he did not know the one that worked through him, believing that he created by his own power, since he was not hardworking by nature, for this reason the Apostle said, "He was subject to the purposelessness of the world, not wittingly, but on account of the one who subjected it, with the hope that it will be freed," when the seeds of God are gathered.

A particular indication of his unwillingness is his "blessing the Sabbath" and embrace of the respite from work.

50 "Taking dust from the earth"—not from the land, but from the diverse and multicolored part of matter—he made an earthly and material soul, irrational and of the same substance as that of the animals. This is human "according to the image."

But the (human) "according to the likeness" of the Creator himself, this one is the one into whom he "breathed" and implanted when he placed (within him) by angels something with the same substance as himself.

Insofar as he is invisible and incorporeal, he called his substance "breath of life," but what was given form became "a living soul," and he proclaims that it is this way in the prophetic writings.

51 Ἄνθρωπος γοῦν ἐστιν ἐν ἀνθρώπῳ, ψυχικὸς ἐν χοϊκῷ, οὐ μέρει μέρος, ἀλλὰ ὅλῳ ὅλος συνὼν ἀρρήτῳ δυνάμει Θεοῦ. Ὅθεν ἐν τῷ Παραδείσῳ, τῷ τετάρτῳ οὐρανῷ, δημιουργεῖται.

Ἐκεῖ γὰρ χοϊκὴ σὰρξ οὐκ ἀναβαίνει, ἀλλ᾽ ἦν τῇ ψυχῇ <τῇ> θείᾳ οἷον σὰρξ ἡ ὑλική. Ταῦτα σημαίνει· «Τοῦτο νῦν ὀστοῦν ἐκ τῶν ὀστῶν μου,»—τὴν θείαν ψυχὴν αἰνίσσεται τὴν ἐγκεκρυμμένην τῇ σαρκὶ καὶ στερεὰν καὶ δυσπαθῆ καὶ δυνατωτέραν—«καὶ σὰρξ ἐκ τῆς σαρκός μου,»—τὴν ὑλικὴν ψυχὴν σῶμα οὖσαν τῆς θείας ψυχῆς.

Περὶ τούτων τῶν δυεῖν καὶ ὁ Σωτὴρ λέγει «φοβεῖσθαι δεῖν τὸν δυνάμενον ταύτην τὴν ψυχὴν καὶ τοῦτο τὸ σῶμα» τὸ ψυχικὸν «ἐν γεέννῃ ἀπολέσαι.»

52 Τοῦτο τὸ σαρκίον «ἀντίδικον» ὁ Σωτὴρ εἶπεν καὶ ὁ Παῦλος «νόμον ἀντιστρατευόμενον τῷ νόμῳ τοῦ νοός μου,» καὶ «δῆσαι» παραινεῖ καὶ «ἁρπάσαι ὡς ἰσχυροῦ τὰ σκεύη» τοῦ ἀντιπολεμοῦντος τῇ οὐρανίῳ ψυχῇ, ὁ Σωτήρ. καὶ «ἀπηλλάχθαι αὐτοῦ» παραινεῖ «κατὰ τὴν ὁδόν, μὴ τῇ φυλακῇ περιπέσωμεν καὶ τῇ κολάσει.»

ὁμοίως δὲ καὶ «εὐνοεῖν» αὐτῷ, μὴ τρέφοντας καὶ ῥωννύντας τῇ τῶν ἁμαρτημάτων ἐξουσίᾳ, ἀλλ᾽ ἐντεῦθεν νεκροῦντας ἤδη καὶ ἐξίτηλον ἀποφαίνοντας ἀποχῇ τῆς πονηρίας, ἵνα ἐν τῇ διαλύσει ταύτῃ διαφορηθὲν καὶ διαπνεῦσαν λάθῃ, ἀλλὰ μὴ καθ᾽ αὐτό τινος ὑποστάσεως λαβόμενον, τὴν ἰσχὺν ἔχῃ παράμονον ἐν τῇ διὰ πυρὸς διεξόδῳ.

53 Τοῦτο «ζιζάνιον» ὀνομάζεται συμφυὲς τῇ ψυχῇ, τῷ χρηστῷ σπέρματι· τοῦτο καὶ «σπέρμα τοῦ Διαβόλου,» ὡς ὁμοούσιον ἐκείνῳ, καὶ «ὄφις» καὶ «διαπτερνιστὴς» καὶ «λῃστὴς» ἐπιτιθέμενος κεφαλῇ βασιλέως.

Ἔσχεν δὲ ὁ Ἀδὰμ ἀδήλως αὐτῷ ὑπὸ τῆς Σοφίας ἐνσπαρὲν τὸ σπέρμα τὸ πνευματικὸν εἰς τὴν ψυχήν, «διαταγείς,» φησί, «δι᾽ Ἀγγέλων, ἐν χειρὶ Μεσίτου. ὁ δὲ μεσίτης ἑνὸς οὐκ ἔστιν, ὁ δὲ Θεὸς εἷς ἐστιν.»

«Δι᾽ Ἀγγέλων» οὖν τῶν ἀρρένων τὰ σπέρματα ὑπηρετεῖται, τὰ εἰς γένεσιν προβληθέντα ὑπὸ τῆς Σοφίας, καθὸ ἐγχωρεῖ γίνεσθαι.

Ἅτε γὰρ Δημιουργός, ἀδήλως κινούμενος ὑπὸ τῆς Σοφίας, οἴεται αὐτοκίνητος εἶναι, ὁμοίως καὶ οἱ ἄνθρωποι.

Πρῶτον οὖν σπέρμα πνευματικὸν τὸ ἐν τῷ Ἀδὰμ προέβαλεν ἡ Σοφία, ἵνα ᾖ «τὸ ὀστοῦν,» ἡ λογικὴ καὶ οὐρανία ψυχή, μὴ κενή, ἀλλὰ μυελοῦ γέμουσα πνευματικοῦ.

51 Therefore man is in man, soulish in earthly, not part to part, but joined whole to whole by God's ineffable power. Therefore in paradise, in the fourth heaven, he was created.

For there earthly flesh does not ascend, but it was to the divine soul as material flesh. These things are indicated by "Now this is bone of my bones"—he hints at the divine soul which is concealed within the flesh and (is) firm and invulnerable and very powerful—"and flesh of my flesh"—the material soul which is a body of the divine soul.

Concerning these two the Savior also says, "To be feared is what can destroy this soul and this body," the soulish one, "in Gehenna."

52 This body the Savior called "an adversary" and Paul said "a law at war with the law of my mind," and the Savior urges us "to bind" and "plunder its belongings as those of a strong man" who is at war against the heavenly soul. And he also urges us "to be reconciled with him on the road, lest we fall into prison and chastisement."

And likewise "to be kind" to it, not nourishing and strengthening it with the power of sin, but here and now putting it to death and denouncing it as obsolete in our abstinence from evil, so that in its destruction it might be separated and blown away in secret, but not receiving any existence of its own, (thus) having power of its own in its journey though the fire.

53 This is termed "a tare" which unites with the soul, the good seed; this is also "a seed of the devil," since it shares a substance with him, and "a snake" and "a heel biter" and "a thief" who attacks the head of a king.

But unknown to him, Adam had the spiritual seed sown into his soul by Wisdom, "ordained," he says, "through angels by the hand of a mediator. The mediator is not of one, but God is one."

Therefore, the seeds put forth into becoming are ministered to to the extent that they are able to come to be "through" male "angels."

For just as the Creator, being moved by Wisdom unwittingly, thinks that he is self-moved, so also do humans.

Therefore, Wisdom first put forward a spiritual seed which was in Adam, so that it might be "the bone," the rational and heavenly soul which is not empty, but filled with spiritual marrow.

54 Ἀπὸ δὲ τοῦ Ἀδὰμ τρεῖς φύσεις γεννῶνται· πρώτη μὲν ἡ ἄλογος, ἧς ἦν Κάιν· δευτέρα δὲ ἡ λογικὴ καὶ ἡ δικαία, ἧς ἦν Ἄβελ· τρίτη δὲ ἡ πνευματική, ἧς ἦν Σήθ.

Καὶ ὁ μὲν χοϊκός ἐστι «κατ᾽ εἰκόνα,» ὁ δὲ ψυχικὸς «καθ᾽ ὁμοίωσιν» Θεοῦ· ὁ δὲ πνευματικὸς κατ᾽ ἰδίαν. ἐφ᾽ οἷς τρισίν, ἄνευ τῶν ἄλλων παίδων τοῦ Ἀδάμ, εἴρηται· «Αὕτη ἡ βίβλος γενέσεως ἀνθρώπων.»

Ὅτι δὲ πνευματικὸς ὁ Σήθ, οὔτε ποιμαίνει, οὔτε γεωργεῖ, ἀλλὰ παῖδα καρποφορεῖ, ὡς τὰ πνευματικά. Καὶ τοῦτον, ὃς «ἤλπισεν ἐπικαλεῖσθαι τὸ Ὄνομα Κυρίου,» «ἄνω» βλέποντα, οὗ «τὸ πολίτευμα ἐν οὐρανῷ,» τοῦτον ὁ κόσμος οὐ χωρεῖ.

55 Τοῖς τρισὶν ἀσωμάτοις ἐπὶ τοῦ Ἀδὰμ τέταρτον ἐπενδύεται ὁ χοϊκός[17] τοὺς «δερματίνους χιτῶνας.»

Οὔτ᾽ οὖν ἀπὸ τοῦ Πνεύματος, οὔτ᾽ οὖν ἀπὸ τοῦ ἐμφυσήματος, σπείρει ὁ Ἀδάμ, θεῖα γὰρ ἄμφω, καὶ δι᾽ αὐτοῦ μέν, οὐχ ὑπ᾽ αὐτοῦ δέ, προβάλλεται ἄμφω.

Τὸ δὲ ὑλικὸν αὐτοῦ ἐνεργὸν εἰς σπέρμα καὶ γένεσιν, ὡς ἂν τῷ σπέρματι συγκεκραμένον, καὶ ταύτης ἐν ζωῇ τῆς ἁρμονίας ἀποστῆναι μὴ δυνάμενον.[18]

56 Κατὰ τοῦτο, πατὴρ ἡμῶν ὁ Ἀδάμ, «ὁ πρῶτος ἄνθρωπος ἐκ γῆς χοϊκός.»

Εἰ δὲ καὶ ἐκ ψυχικοῦ ἔσπειρεν καὶ ἐκ πνευματικοῦ, καθάπερ ἐξ ὑλικοῦ, πάντες ἂν ἴσοι καὶ δίκαιοι ἐγεγόνεισαν, καὶ ἐν πᾶσιν ἂν ἡ διδαχὴ ἦν. Διὰ τοῦτο πολλοὶ μὲν οἱ ὑλικοί, οὐ πολλοὶ δὲ οἱ ψυχικοί, σπάνιοι δὲ οἱ πνευματικοί.

Τὸ μὲν οὖν πνευματικὸν φύσει σῳζόμενον· τὸ δὲ ψυχικόν, αὐτεξούσιον ὄν, ἐπιτηδειότητα ἔχει πρός τε πίστιν καὶ ἀφθαρσίαν, καὶ πρὸς ἀπιστίαν καὶ φθοράν, κατὰ τὴν οἰκείαν αἵρεσιν. τὸ δὲ ὑλικὸν φύσει ἀπόλλυται.

Ὅταν οὖν τὰ ψυχικὰ «ἐγκεντρισθῇ τῇ καλλιελαίῳ» εἰς πίστιν καὶ ἀφθαρσίαν, καὶ μετάσχῃ «τῆς πιότητος τῆς ἐλαίας,» καὶ ὅταν «εἰσέλθῃ τὰ ἔθνη,» τότε «οὕτω πᾶς Ἰσραήλ.»

Ἰσραὴλ δὲ ἀλληγορεῖται ὁ πνευματικός, ὁ ὀψόμενος τὸν Θεόν, ὁ τοῦ πιστοῦ Ἀβραὰμ υἱὸς γνήσιος ὁ «ἐκ τῆς ἐλευθέρας,» οὐχ ὁ «κατὰ σάρκα,» ὁ ἐκ τῆς δούλης τῆς Αἰγυπτίας.

17. MS reads τὸν χοϊκόν.
18. δυνάμενον: MSS read δυνάμενος.

54 From Adam three natures were produced: the first was irrational, which was Cain's (nature); the second was rational and just, which was Abel's (nature); and the third was spiritual, which was Seth's (nature).

And what is earthly is "according to the image," what is physical "according to the likeness" of God, and the spiritual according to one's own. With reference to these three, without the other children of Adam, it has been said, "This is the book of the generation of people."

Because Seth is spiritual, he does not shepherd nor does he plow, but he bears a child, as (do) spiritual things. And this one, who "hoped to call upon the name of the Lord," looking "upward," whose "citizenship is in heaven," this one the world does not contain.

55 On the three incorporeal (layers) upon Adam, a fourth, the earthly, is draped as the "garments of skin."

Therefore, neither from the Spirit nor from what was breathed into him does Adam sow, for both are divine and both are put forth through him, not by him.

But his material (nature) works toward seed and generation, as if mixed with seed, and (it is) not able to be away from the same harmony in life.

56 For this reason, our father Adam is "the first earthly human of the earth."

But if he had sown also from soulish and from spiritual as well as from material, all would have become equal and righteous, and the teaching would have been in all. On account of this, many are material, but not many are soulish, and few are spiritual.

The spiritual is saved by nature, but the soulish, which has free will, has a propensity for both faith and incorruption, and for lack of faith and corruption according to its own choice. But the material by nature is destroyed.

Therefore when the soulish "are grafted onto the olive tree" into faith and incorruption, and participate in "the girth of the olive tree," and when "the gentiles should enter in," then "thus all Israel . . ."

But Israel is interpreted allegorically, the spiritual one who will see God, the lawful son of faithful Abraham, who is "from the free woman," not the one "according to the flesh," the one from the Egyptian slave.

57 Γίνεται οὖν, ἐκ τῶν γενῶν τῶν τριῶν, τοῦ μὲν μόρφωσις τοῦ πνευματικοῦ, τοῦ δὲ μετάθεσις τοῦ ψυχικοῦ ἐκ δουλείας εἰς ἐλευθερίαν.

58 Μετὰ τὴν τοῦ θανάτου τοίνυν βασιλείαν, μεγάλην μὲν καὶ εὐπρόσωπον τὴν ἐπαγγελίαν πεποιημένην, οὐδὲν δὲ ἧττον διακονίαν θανάτου γεγενημένην, πάσης ἀπειπούσης Ἀρχῆς καὶ Θεότητος, ὁ μέγας Ἀγωνιστής, Ἰησοῦς Χριστός, ἐν ἑαυτῷ δυνάμει τὴν Ἐκκλησίαν ἀναλαβών, τὸ ἐκλεκτὸν καὶ τὸ κλητόν, τὸ μὲν παρὰ τῆς τεκούσης τὸ πνευματικόν, τὸ δὲ ἐκ τῆς οἰκονομίας τὸ ψυχικόν. ἀνέσωσεν καὶ ἀνήνεγκεν ἅπερ ἀνέλαβεν, καὶ δι᾽ αὐτῶν καὶ τὰ τούτοις ὁμοούσια·

«Εἰ γὰρ ἡ ἀπαρχὴ ἁγία, καὶ τὸ φύραμα· εἰ ἡ ῥίζα ἁγία, καὶ οἱ κλάδοι.»

59 Σπέρμα μὲν οὖν πρῶτον παρὰ τῆς τεκούσης ἐνεδύσατο, οὐ χωρηθείς, ἀλλὰ χωρήσας αὐτὸ δυνάμει, ὃ κατὰ μικρὸν μορφοῦται διὰ γνώσεως.

Κατὰ δὲ τὸν Τόπον γενόμενος, εὗρεν Ἰησοῦν Χριστὸν ἐνδύσασθαι τὸν προκεκηρυγμένον, ὃν κατήγγελλον οἱ Προφῆται καὶ ὁ Νόμος, ὄντα εἰκόνα τοῦ Σωτῆρος.

Ἀλλὰ καὶ οὗτος ὁ ψυχικὸς Χριστός, ὃν ἐνεδύσατο, ἀόρατος ἦν. ἔδει δὲ τὸν εἰς κόσμον ἀφικνούμενον, ἐφ᾽ ᾧτε ὀφθῆναι, κρατηθῆναι, πολιτεύσασθαι, καὶ αἰσθητοῦ σώματος ἀνέχεσθαι.

Σῶμα τοίνυν αὐτῷ ὑφαίν<ετ>αι τῆς ἐκ τῆς ἀφανοῦς ψυχικῆς οὐσίας, δυνάμει δὲ θείας ἐγκατασκευῆς[19] εἰς αἰσθητὸν κόσμον ἀφιγμένον.

60 Τὸ οὖν· «Πνεῦμα ἅγιον ἐπὶ σέ,» τὴν τοῦ σώματος τοῦ Κυρίου <γένεσιν> λέγει, «Δύναμις δὲ ὑψίστου ἐπισκιάσει σοι,» τὴν μόρφωσιν δηλοῖ τοῦ Θεοῦ, ἣν ἐνετύπωσεν τὸ σῶμα ἐν τῇ Παρθένῳ.

61 Ὅτι μὲν οὖν αὐτὸς ἕτερος ἦν ὧν[20] ἀνείληφεν δῆλον ἐξ ὧν ὁμολογεῖ· «Ἐγὼ ἡ Ζωή,» «ἐγὼ ἡ Ἀλήθεια,» «ἐγὼ καὶ ὁ Πατὴρ ἕν ἐσμεν.»

Τὸ δὲ πνευματικὸν ὃ ἀνείληφεν, καὶ τὸ ψυχικόν, οὕτως ἐμφαίνει· «Τὸ δὲ παιδίον ηὔξανεν καὶ προέκοπτεν σφόδρα.» Σοφίας μὲν γὰρ τὸ πνευματικὸν δεῖξαι, μεγέθους δὲ τὸ ψυχικόν.

---

19. ἐγκατασκευῆς: MSS read ἐκ κατασκευῆς.
20. ὧν: ὧι L ᾧ P.

57 Therefore, from three races, the formation of the spiritual comes to be on the one hand, but on the other the transposition of the psychic from slavery to freedom comes to be.

58 After the kingdom of death, which had made the great and equitable promise, but had just as well become a ministry of death, after every ruler and divinity had refused, the Great Competitor, Jesus Christ, took for himself by power the church, the elect and the called, the spiritual one from the mother and the soulish from the arrangement. He rescued and carried up what he had received, and through them things similar to them.

"For if the firstfruits are holy, so too is the dough; if the root is holy, so too are the branches."

59 A seed from the mother he put on first, not being removed, but holding it with power, it is formed gradually through knowledge.

Upon arriving in the place, he found Jesus Christ, whom it was prophesied he would put on, whom the prophets and law proclaimed, being an image of the Savior.

But even this soulish Christ, whom he put on, was invisible. It was necessary when coming into the world to be seen here, to be supported, to be a citizen, and to bear up an aesthetic body.

Therefore a body <was woven> for him from the substance from the invisible soulish (element), (a body) that arrived in the perceptible world with power from divine constitution.

60 Therefore, "Holy Spirit upon you" refers to the <creation> of the body of the Lord, "and power of the Most High shall overshadow you" makes apparent the fashioning of God, which the body imprinted in the Virgin.

61 That he was something other than what he took upon himself is clear from what he proclaims: "I am the life," "I am the truth," "I and the Father are one."

But the spiritual (nature) that he received and the soulish he discloses in this way: "The child grew and progressed exceedingly." For the spiritual (nature) ought to exhibit wisdom, but the soulish ought to exhibit size.

Διὰ δὲ τῶν ἐκρυέντων ἐκ τῆς πλευρᾶς ἐδήλου ταῖς ἐκρύσεσι²¹ τῶν παθῶν ἀπὸ τῶν ἐμπαθῶν, ἀπαθεῖς γενομένας τὰς οὐσίας σεσῶσθαι.

Καὶ ὅταν λέγῃ «Δεῖ τὸν Υἱὸν τοῦ Ἀνθρώπου ἀποδοκιμασθῆναι, ὑβρισθῆναι, σταυρωθῆναι,» ὡς περὶ ἄλλου φαίνεται λέγων, δηλονότι τοῦ ἐμπαθοῦς.

Καί· «Προάξω ὑμᾶς,» λέγει, «τῇ τρίτῃ τῶν ἡμερῶν εἰς τὴν Γαλιλαίαν.» αὐτὸς γὰρ προάγει πάντα· καὶ τὴν ἀφανῶς σῳζομένην ψυχὴν ἀναστήσειν ᾐνίσσετο, καὶ ἀποκαταστήσειν οὗ νῦν προάγει.

Ἀπέθανεν δὲ ἀποστάντος τοῦ καταβάντος ἐπ᾽ αὐτῷ ἐπὶ τῷ Ἰορδάνῃ Πνεύματος, οὐκ ἰδίᾳ γενομένου, ἀλλὰ συσταλέντος, ἵνα καὶ ἐνεργήσῃ ὁ θάνατος, ἐπεὶ πῶς, τῆς Ζωῆς παρούσης ἐν αὐτῷ, ἀπέθανεν τὸ σῶμα; οὕτω γὰρ ἂν καὶ αὐτοῦ τοῦ Σωτῆρος ὁ θάνατος ἐκράτησεν ἄν, ὅπερ ἄτοπον. Δόλῳ δὲ ὁ θάνατος κατεστρατηγήθη·

ἀποθανόντος γὰρ τοῦ σώματος καὶ κρατήσαντος αὐτὸ{ν} τοῦ θανάτου, ἀναστείλας τὴν ἐπελθοῦσαν ἀκτῖνα τῆς δυνάμεως, ὁ Σωτὴρ ἀπώλεσε μὲν τὸν θάνατον, τὸ δὲ θνητὸν σῶμα, ἀποβαλὼν πάθη, ἀνέστησεν.

Τὰ ψυχικὰ μὲν οὖν οὕτως ἀνίσταται καὶ ἀνασῴζεται, πιστεύσαντα δὲ τὰ πνευματικὰ ὑπὲρ ἐκεῖνα σῴζεται, «ἐνδύματα γάμων» τὰς ψυχὰς λαβόντα.

62 Κάθηται μὲν οὖν ὁ ψυχικὸς Χριστὸς ἐν δεξιᾷ τοῦ Δημιουργοῦ, καθὸ καὶ ὁ Δαβὶδ λέγει· «Κάθου ἐκ δεξιῶν μου,» καὶ τὰ ἑξῆς.

Κάθηται δὲ μέχρι συντελείας, «ἵνα ἴδωσιν εἰς ὃν ἐξεκέντησαν.» Ἐξεκέντησαν δὲ τὸ φαινόμενον, ὃ ἦν σὰρξ τοῦ ψυχικοῦ. «Ὀστοῦν γὰρ αὐτοῦ οὐ συντριβήσεται,» φησί, καθάπερ ἐπὶ τοῦ Ἀδὰμ τὴν ψυχὴν ὀστοῦν ἠλληγόρησεν ἡ προφητεία.

Αὕτη γὰρ ἡ ψυχὴ τοῦ Χριστοῦ, πάσχοντος τοῦ σώματος, ἑαυτὴν «εἰς τὰς χεῖρας τοῦ Πατρὸς παρακατέθετο.» τὸ δ᾽ ἐν τῷ ὀστέῳ πνευματικὸν οὐκέτι παρακατατίθεται, ἀλλ᾽ αὐτὸς σῴζει.

63 Ἡ μὲν οὖν τῶν πνευματικῶν ἀνάπαυσις ἐν κυριακῇ, ἐν Ὀγδοάδι, ἣ Κυριακὴ ὀνομάζεται, παρὰ τῇ Μητρί, ἐχόντων τὰς ψυχάς, τὰ ἐνδύματα, ἄχρι συντελείας. αἱ δὲ ἄλλαι πισταὶ ψυχαί, παρὰ τῷ Δημιουργῷ, περὶ δὲ τὴν συντέλειαν, ἀναχωροῦσι καὶ αὗται εἰς Ὀγδόαδα.

21. ταῖς ἐκρύσεσι: MSS read τὰς ἐκρύσεις.

Through the effluences that flowed from his side he demonstrates that the flow of the passions from the things with passion saves the substances that have become passionless.

And when he says, "It is necessary that the Son of Man be rejected, insulted, crucified," he appears to be speaking about someone else, that is, about the one with passion.

And "I will go before you," he says, "on the third day into Galilee." For he goes before all, and intimated that he will raise up the soul that is invisible as saved and restore (it to the place) toward which he now goes.

He died upon the departure of the Spirit that came down upon him in the Jordan, not by becoming its own thing, but by being drawn in so that death might also act, since how, with life present within him, did the body die? For in this way death would have ruled over the Savior himself, which is incorrect. But death was outmaneuvered by cunning.

For after the body died and death prevailed upon it, the Savior sent up the beam of power that had come upon and destroyed death and raised up the mortal body that had cast off passion.

Thus the soulish elements are raised up and saved, but the believing spiritual elements are saved above these, receiving their souls as "wedding garments."

62 The soulish Christ is seated at the right hand of the Creator, as David says, "Sit at my right hand," etc.

He sits until the consummation, "so that they might see the one they pierced." But they pierced the appearance, which was the flesh of the soulish one. "For his bone will not be broken," it says, just as in the case of Adam the prophecy employs bone as an allegory for the soul.

For the very soul of Christ, while the body suffered, "deposited" itself "into the Father's hands." But the spiritual nature in the bone is no longer deposited, but he retains it.

63 The resting of the spirituals on the Lord's Day, in the Ogdoad, which is termed the Lord's Day, is with the mother, wearing their souls, the garments, until the culmination. But the other faithful souls are with the Creator, but at the culmination they also go up into the Ogdoad.

Εἶτα, τὸ δεῖπνον τῶν γάμων κοινὸν πάντων τῶν σωζομένων, ἄχρις ἂν ἀπισωθῇ πάντα καὶ ἄλλη`λα´ γνωρίσῃ.

64 Τὸ δὲ ἐντεῦθεν, ἀποθέμενα τὰ πνευματικὰ τὰς ψυχάς, ἅμα τῇ Μητρὶ κομιζομένη τὸν Νυμφίον, κομιζόμενα καὶ αὐτὰ τοὺς νυμφίους, τοὺς Ἀγγέλους ἑαυτῶν, εἰς τὸν Νυμφῶνα ἐντὸς τοῦ Ὅρου εἰσίασι, καὶ πρὸς τὴν τοῦ Πατρὸς ὄψιν ἔρχονται, Αἰῶνες νοεροὶ γενόμενα, εἰς τοὺς νοεροὺς καὶ αἰωνίους γάμους τῆς συζυγίας.

65 Ὁ δὲ τοῦ δείπνου μὲν «ἀρχιτρίκλινος,» τῶν γάμων δὲ παράνυμφος «τοῦ Νυμφίου δὲ Φίλος, ἑστὼς ἔμπροσθεν τοῦ νυμφῶνος, ἀκούων τῆς φωνῆς τοῦ Νυμφίου, χαρᾷ χαίρει.»

Τοῦτο αὐτοῦ «τὸ Πλήρωμα τῆς χαρᾶς» καὶ τῆς ἀναπαύσεως.

66 Ὁ Σωτὴρ τοὺς Ἀποστόλους ἐδίδασκεν, τὰ μὲν πρῶτα τυπικῶς καὶ μυστικῶς, τὰ δὲ ὕστερα παραβολικῶς καὶ ἠνιγμένως, τὰ δὲ τρίτα σαφῶς καὶ γυμνῶς κατὰ μόνας.

67 «Ὅτε ἦμεν ἐν τῇ σαρκί,» φησὶν ὁ Ἀπόστολος, ὥσπερ ἔξω τοῦ σώματος ἤδη λαλῶν. Σάρκα οὖν λέγειν αὐτόν φησιν ἐκείνην τὴν ἀσθένειαν, τὴν ἀπὸ τῆς ἄνω Γυναικὸς προβολήν.

Καὶ ὅταν ὁ Σωτὴρ πρὸς Σαλώμην λέγῃ «μέχρι τότε εἶναι θάνατον ἄχρις ἂν αἱ γυναῖκες τίκτωσιν,» οὐ τὴν γένεσιν κακίζων ἔλεγεν ἀναγκαίαν οὖσαν διὰ τὴν σωτηρίαν τῶν πιστευόντων.

Δεῖ γὰρ εἶναι τὴν γένεσιν ταύτην ἄχρις ἂν τὸ σπέρμα προσενεχθῇ τὸ προλελογισμένον·

ἀλλὰ περὶ τῆς ἄνω Θηλείας αἰνίττεται, ἧς τὰ πάθη κτίσις γέγονεν, τῆς καὶ τὰς ἀμόρφους οὐσίας προβαλ<λ>ούσης. δι᾽ ἣν καὶ ὁ Κύριος κατῆλθεν, ἀπὸ μὲν τοῦ πάθους ἡμᾶς ἀποσπάσων, ἑαυτῷ δὲ εἰσποιησόμενος.

68 Ἄχρι μὲν γὰρ ἦμεν τῆς Θηλείας μόνης τέκνα, ὡς ἂν αἰσχρᾶς συζυγίας, ἀτελῆ καὶ νήπια καὶ ἄφρονα καὶ ἀσθενῆ καὶ ἄμορφα, οἷον ἐκτρώματα προ<σ>ενεχθέντα, τῆς Γυναικὸς ἦμεν τέκνα. ὑπὸ δὲ τοῦ Σωτῆρος μορφωθέντες,[22] Ἀνδρὸς καὶ Νυμφῶνος γεγόναμεν τέκνα.

69 Ἡ Εἱμαρμένη ἐστὶ σύνοδος πολλῶν καὶ ἐναντίων δυνάμεων. αὗται δέ εἰσιν ἀόρατοι καὶ ἀφανεῖς, ἐπιτροπεύουσαι τὴν τῶν ἄστρων φορὰν καὶ δι᾽ ἐκείνων πολιτευόμεναι.

---

22. μορφωθέντες: MSS read μορφωθέντας.

Then the marriage feast shared by all who are saved, until all are made equal and know each other.

64 Thereupon the spiritual elements that have laid aside their souls, together with the mother who escorts the groom, also escort the grooms, their angels, enter into the bridal chamber within the boundary, and come to the vision of the Father, becoming intellectual eternities, in the intellectual and eternal marriages of the syzygy.

65 The "master" of the banquet, the best man of the marriage "and friend of the groom who stands before the bridal chamber, hearing the voice of the groom, rejoices."

This is his "fullness of joy" and rest.

66 The Savior initially instructed the Apostles figuratively and mystically, but later in parables and riddles, and finally plainly and openly when alone.

67 "When we were in the flesh," the Apostle says, as though he is already speaking outside of the body. Then he says that by flesh he means that weakness that was an emanation of the woman above.

And when the Savior says to Salome, "Death exists as long as women give birth," he is not offering a reproach of birth because it is necessary for the salvation of those who believe.

For it is necessary that this birth exist until the previously considered seed be brought forth.

But he is hinting at the woman above whose passions became creation because she put forward those amorphic beings. On her account the Lord came down pulling us out of passion and adopting us for himself.

68 For while we were children of the female alone, as if from a shameful union, incomplete and infants and mindless and weak and formless, brought forth like miscarriages, we were children of the woman. But having been formed by the Savior, we have become children of man and bridal chamber.

69 Fate is a gathering of many contrary powers. They are invisible and not seen, managing the circuit of the stars and governing through them.

Καθὸ γὰρ ἕκαστον αὐτῶν ἔφθακεν, τῇ τοῦ κόσμου κινήσει συναναφερόμενον, τῶν κατ᾽ αὐτὴν τὴν ῥοπὴν γεννωμένων εἴληχεν τὴν ἐπικράτειαν, ὡς αὐτοῦ τέκνων.

70 Διὰ τῶν ἀπλανῶν τοίνυν καὶ πλανωμένων ἄστρων, αἱ ἐπὶ τούτων ἀόρατοι δυνάμεις ἐποχούμεναι, ταμιεύουσι τὰς γενέσεις καὶ ἐπισκοποῦσι·

τὰ δὲ ἄστρα αὐτὰ μὲν οὐδὲν ποιεῖ, δείκνυσι δὲ τὴν ἐνέργειαν τῶν κυρίων δυνάμεων, ὥσπερ καὶ ἡ τῶν ὀρνίθων πτῆσις σημαίνει τι, οὐχὶ ποιεῖ.

71 Τὰ τοίνυν δεκαδύο ζῴδια καὶ οἱ ταῦτα ἐπιόντες ἑπτὰ ἀστέρες, τοτὲ μὲν συνοδεύοντες, τοτὲ δὲ ὑπαπαντῶντες, ἀνατέλλοντες, οὗτοι, πρὸς τῶν δυνάμεων κινούμενοι, κίνησιν τῆς οὐσίας δηλοῦσιν εἰς γένεσιν τῶν ζῴων καὶ τὴν τῶν περιστάσεων τροπήν.

Διάφοροι δ᾽ εἰσὶν καὶ οἱ ἀστέρες καὶ αἱ δυνάμεις, ἀγαθοποιοὶ κακοποιοί, δεξιοὶ ἀριστεροί, ὧν κοινὸν τὸ τικτόμενον· ἕκαστον δὲ αὐτῶν γίνεται κατὰ καιρὸν τὸν ἴδιον, τοῦ δυναστεύοντος τὰ κατὰ φύσιν ἀποτελοῦντος, τὸ μὲν ἐν ἀρχῇ, τὸ δὲ ἐπὶ τέλει.

72 Ἀπὸ ταύτης τῆς στάσεως καὶ μάχης τῶν δυνάμεων ὁ Κύριος ἡμᾶς ῥύεται, καὶ παρέχει τὴν εἰρήνην ἀπὸ τῆς τῶν δυνάμεων καὶ τῆς τῶν Ἀγγέλων παρατάξεως, ἢν οἳ μὲν ὑπὲρ ἡμῶν, οἳ δὲ καθ᾽ ἡμῶν παρατάσσονται.

Οἳ μὲν γὰρ στρατιώταις ἐοίκασι, συμμαχοῦντες ἡμῖν, ὡς ἂν ὑπηρέται Θεοῦ, οἳ δὲ λησταῖς· ὁ γὰρ Πονηρὸς οὐ παρὰ Βασιλέως ἐζώσατο λαβὼν τὴν μάχαιραν, ἑαυτῷ δὲ ἐξ ἀπονοίας ἁρπάσας.

73 Διὰ δὴ τοὺς ἀντικειμένους οἵ, διὰ τοῦ σώματος καὶ τῶν ἐκτός, ἐπιβατεύουσι τῆς ψυχῆς καὶ ἐνεχυράζουσιν εἰς δουλείαν. οἱ δεξιοὶ οὔκ εἰσιν ἱκανοὶ παρακολουθοῦντες σῴζειν καὶ φυλάσσειν ἡμᾶς.

Οὐ γὰρ εἰσι τέλεον προνοητικοί, ὥσπερ ὁ ἀγαθὸς Ποιμήν, ἀλλὰ μισθωτῷ παραπλήσιος ἕκαστος, τὸν λύκον ὁρῶντι προσιόντα καὶ φεύγοντι καὶ οὐ προθύμῳ τὴν ψυχὴν ὑπὲρ τῶν ἰδίων προβάτων ἐπιδιδόναι.

Προσέτι δὲ καὶ ὁ ἄνθρωπος, ὑπὲρ οὗ ἡ μάχη, ἀσθενὲς ὂν ζῷον, εὐεπίφορόν ἐστι πρὸς τὸ χεῖρον καὶ τοῖς μισοῦσι συλλαμβανόμενον· ὅθεν καὶ πλείω τὰ κακὰ ὑπάρχει αὐτῷ.

For just as each of them came, having been carried around by the motion of the world, it obtained dominion over those born at that moment, as though they were its children.

70 Therefore, through the fixed and wandering stars, the invisible powers transcend them, they oversee and manage births.

But the stars accomplish nothing themselves, but exhibit the activity of the ruling powers, just as the flight of birds signals something but accomplishes nothing.

71 The twelve signs of the zodiac and the seven stars moving around them, at times with them, and at times against them when rising up, these, when moved by the powers, exhibit the motion of substance toward the generation of animals and the changing of affairs.

But the stars and the powers are different, good and bad, right and left, and what is brought forth shares (in both natures). Each of them comes to be at its own time, the powerful accomplishing according to its nature, in part at the beginning, and in part at the end.

72 From this state of affairs and contest of the powers the Lord rescues us, and he provides peace from the squabbles of powers and angels, in which some are assembled for us but others against us.

For some are like soldiers who fight for us as God's staff officers, but others are like pirates. For the wicked one armed himself, not taking up a sword on behalf of the king, but by treacherously plundering for himself.

73 So on account of the opponents who, through the body and things outside, usurp the soul and pledge it to slavery. Those on the right are not qualified when following to save and protect us.

For providences are not perfect like the Good Shepherd, but each resembles a hired servant who sees the wolf nearby and flees and is not willing to give up his soul on behalf of his own sheep.

And, besides, the man, over whom is the battle, since he is a weak animal, is inclined to what is inferior and imprisoned by those who hate him. Whence also he takes on even greater evil.

74 Διὰ τοῦτο ὁ Κύριος κατῆλθεν εἰρήνην ποιήσων, τοῖς ἀπ᾽ οὐρανοῦ τοῖς ἀπὸ γῆς ὥς φησιν ὁ Ἀπόστολος·

«Εἰρήνη ἐπὶ τῆς γῆς καὶ δόξα ἐν ὑψίστοις.» Διὰ τοῦτο ἀνέτειλεν ξένος ἀστὴρ καὶ καινός, καταλύων τὴν παλαιὰν ἀστροθεσίαν, καινῷ φωτί, οὐ κοσμικῷ, λαμπόμενος, ὁ καινὰς ὁδοὺς καὶ σωτηρίους τρεπόμενος, αὐτὸς ὁ Κύριος, ἀνθρώπων Ὁδηγός, ὁ κατελθὼν εἰς γῆν ἵνα μεταθῇ τοὺς εἰς τὸν Χριστὸν πιστεύσαντας ἀπὸ τῆς Εἱμαρμένης εἰς τὴν ἐκείνου Πρόνοιαν.

75 Ὅτι δέ ἐστι, φασίν, Εἱμαρμένη τοῖς ἄλλοις, τὰ ἀποτελέσματα προλεγόμενα δείκνυσιν, ἐναργὴς δὲ ἀπόδειξις καὶ ἡ τῶν μαθημάτων θεωρία.

Αὐτίκα οἱ Μάγοι οὐ μόνον «εἶδον τὸν ἀστέρα» τοῦ Κυρίου, ἀλλὰ καὶ τὸ ἀληθὲς ἔγνωσαν ὅτι «Βασιλεὺς ἐτέχθη,» καὶ ὧν Βασιλεύς, ὅτι θεοσεβῶν. Τότε Ἰουδαῖοι μόνοι διαβόητοι ἦσαν ἐπὶ θεοσεβείᾳ.

Διὰ τοῦτο γὰρ καὶ ὁ Σωτήρ, πρὸς θεοσεβεῖς κατιών, ἐπὶ τούτους ἦλθεν πρώτους τοὺς τότε ἐπὶ θεοσεβείᾳ δόξαν ἀποφερομένους.

76 Ὡς οὖν ἡ γέννησις τοῦ Σωτῆρος γενέσεως ἡμᾶς καὶ Εἱμαρμένης ἐξέβαλεν, οὕτως καὶ τὸ βάπτισμα αὐτοῦ πυρὸς ἡμᾶς ἐξείλετο, καὶ τὸ πάθος πάθους, ἵνα κατὰ πάντα ἀκολουθήσωμεν αὐτῷ.

Ὁ γὰρ εἰς Θεὸν βαπτισθεὶς εἰς Θεὸν ἐχώρησεν καὶ εἴληφεν «ἐξουσίαν ἐπάνω σκορπίων καὶ ὄφεων περιπατεῖν,» τῶν Δυνάμεων τῶν πονηρῶν.

Καὶ τοῖς Ἀποστόλοις ἐντέλλεται· «Περιιόντες, κηρύσσετε, καὶ τοὺς πιστεύοντας βαπτίζετε εἰς Ὄνομα Πατρὸς καὶ Υἱοῦ καὶ ἁγίου Πνεύματος,»

εἰς οὓς ἀναγεννώμεθα, τῶν λοιπῶν Δυνάμεων ἁπασῶν ὑπεράνω γινόμενοι.

77 Ταύτῃ θάνατος καὶ τέλος λέγεται τοῦ παλαιοῦ βίου τὸ βάπτισμα, ἀποτασσομένων ἡμῶν ταῖς πονηραῖς Ἀρχαῖς, ζωὴ δὲ κατὰ Χριστόν, ἧς μόνος αὐτὸς κυριεύει.

Ἡ δύναμις δὲ τῆς μεταβολῆς τοῦ βαπτισθέντος οὐ περὶ τὸ σῶμα, ὁ αὐτὸς γὰρ ἀναβαίνει, ἀλλὰ περὶ ψυχήν.

Αὐτίκα δοῦλος Θεοῦ ἅμα τῷ ἀνελθεῖν τοῦ βαπτίσματος καὶ πρὸς τῶν ἀκαθάρτων λέγεται Πνευμάτων, καὶ εἰς ὃν πρὸ ὀλίγου ἐνήργουν, τοῦτον ἤδη «φρίσσουσιν.»

78 Μέχρι τοῦ βαπτίσματος οὖν ἡ Εἱμαρμένη, φασίν, ἀληθής· μετὰ δὲ τοῦτο οὐκέτι ἀληθεύουσιν οἱ ἀστρολόγοι.

74 On account of this the Lord came down bringing peace for those from heaven, those from the earth, as the Apostle says,

"Peace on earth and glory in the heights." On account of this a strange and new star rose up, bringing to an end the old arrangement of planets, illuminating with a new light that is not of this world, revolving around a new path of salvation, the Lord himself, humanity's guide, who descended to earth so that he might move those who believed in Christ from fate to providence.

75 They say that the events foretold demonstrate that fate exists for the others, and that the contemplation of the sciences is visible proof.

For example, the Magi not only "beheld the star" of the Lord, but they also perceived the truth that "a king was born," and whose king (he was), namely, of the pious ones. In that time the Jews alone were famous for piety.

For this reason the Savior, when descending to the pious ones, went first to those who at that time had gained glory in reference to piety.

76 As, then, the birth of the Savior freed us from becoming and from fate, so too his baptism removed us from fire, and his passion rescued us from passions, so that we might follow him in all things.

For the one baptized into God went forward into God and received "power to walk upon scorpions and snakes," the wicked powers.

And he commands the Apostles, "As you go about, preach, and baptize the faithful in the name of the Father and Son and Holy Spirit,"

in whom we are reborn, becoming higher than all the remaining powers.

77 In this sense, baptism is called death and an end to the old life, once we get rid of the wicked rulers, but it is also life according to Christ, of which he is the only Lord.

But the power of the transformation of the one baptized is not concerning the body, for the one who comes up, but concerning the soul.

As soon as he comes up from baptism he is called a servant of God even by the unclean spirits, and now "they tremble" at the one upon whom they recently acted.

78 Then until baptism, they say, fate is real, but after it the astrologers are no longer correct.

Ἔστιν δὲ οὐ τὸ λουτρὸν μόνον τὸ ἐλευθεροῦν, ἀλλὰ καὶ ἡ γνῶσις τίνες ἦμεν, τί γεγόναμεν, ποῦ ἦμεν, ποῦ ἐνεβλήθημεν, ποῦ σπεύδομεν, πόθεν λυτρούμεθα, τί γέννησις, τί ἀναγέννησις.

79 Ἕως οὖν ἀμόρφωτον, φασίν, ἔτι τὸ σπέρμα, Θηλείας ἐστὶ τέκνον· μορφωθὲν δὲ μετετέθη εἰς ἄνδρα καὶ υἱὸς Νυμφίου γίνεται· οὐκέτι ἀσθενὴς καὶ τοῖς κοσμικοῖς ὑποκείμενος ὁρατοῖς τε καὶ ἀοράτοις, ἀλλ᾽ ἀνδρωθεὶς ἄρρην γίνεται καρπός.

80 Ὃν γεννᾷ ἡ Μήτηρ εἰς θάνατον ἄγεται καὶ εἰς κόσμον· ὃν δὲ ἀναγεννᾷ Χριστὸς εἰς ζωὴν μετατίθεται, εἰς Ὀγδόαδα.

Καὶ ἀποθνήσκουσιν μὲν τῷ κόσμῳ, ζῶσι δὲ τῷ Θεῷ, ἵνα θάνατος θανάτῳ λυθῇ, ἀναστάσει δὲ ἡ φθορά.

Διὰ γὰρ Πατρὸς καὶ Υἱοῦ καὶ ἁγίου Πνεύματος σφραγισθεὶς ἀνεπίληπτός ἐστι πάσῃ τῇ ἄλλῃ δυνάμει, καὶ διὰ τριῶν Ὀνομάτων πάσης τῆς ἐν φθορᾷ τριάδος ἀπηλλάγη. «φορέσας τὴν εἰκόνα τοῦ χοϊκοῦ, τότε φορεῖ τὴν εἰκόνα τοῦ ἐπουρανίου.»

81 Τοῦ πυρὸς τὸ μὲν σωματικὸν σωμάτων ἅπτεται πάντων, τὸ δὲ καθαρὸν καὶ ἀσώματον ἀσωμάτων φασὶν ἅπτεσθαι, οἷον Δαιμόνων, Ἀγγέλων τῆς πονηρίας, αὐτοῦ τοῦ Διαβόλου. Οὕτως ἐστὶ τὸ ἐπουράνιον πῦρ δισσὸν τὴν φύσιν, τὸ μὲν νοητόν, τὸ δὲ αἰσθητόν.

Καὶ τὸ βάπτισμα οὖν διπλοῦν ἀναλόγως· τὸ μὲν αἰσθητὸν δι᾽ ὕδατος, τοῦ αἰσθητοῦ πυρὸς σβεστήριον· τὸ δὲ νοητὸν διὰ Πνεύματος, τοῦ νοητοῦ πυρὸς ἀλεξητήριον.

Καὶ τὸ σωματικὸν πνεῦμα τοῦ αἰσθητοῦ πυρὸς τροφὴ καὶ ὑπέκκαυμα γίνεται, ὀλίγον ὄν. πλεῖον δὲ γενόμενον σβεστήριον πέφυκεν. Τὸ δὲ ἄνωθεν δοθὲν ἡμῖν Πνεῦμα, ἀσώματον ὄν, οὐ στοιχείων μόνων, ἀλλὰ καὶ Δυνάμεων κρατεῖ καὶ Ἀρχῶν πονηρῶν.

82 Καὶ ὁ ἄρτος καὶ τὸ ἔλαιον ἁγιάζεται τῇ δυνάμει τοῦ Ὀνόματος· οὐ τὰ αὐτὰ ὄντα κατὰ τὸ φαινόμενον οἷα ἐλήφθη, ἀλλὰ δυνάμει εἰς δύναμιν πνευματικὴν μεταβέβληται.

Οὕτως καὶ τὸ ὕδωρ, καὶ τὸ ἐξορκιζόμενον καὶ τὸ βάπτισμα γινόμενον, οὐ μόνον χωρ<ίζ>ει τὸ χεῖρον, ἀλλὰ καὶ ἁγιασμὸν προσλαμβάνει.

But it is not only washing that sets one free, but also the knowledge of who we were, what we have become, where we were, where we were placed, where we are going, from what we are ransomed, what birth is, what rebirth is.

79 While the seed remains unformed, they say, it is a child of the female. But when it was formed, it was changed into a male, and it becomes a child of the groom. No longer is it weak and subject to the cosmic elements, both visible and invisible, but once it is made masculine, it becomes male fruit.

80 The one whom the mother births is led into death and into the world. But the one whom Christ rebirths is transposed into life in the Ogdoad.

And they die in the world, but live in God, so that death might be destroyed by death, and destruction by resurrection.

For the one sealed by the Father and Son and Holy Spirit is not open to attack by every other power, and by three names has been delivered from the entire triad of destruction. "When bearing on the image of the earthly, it bears the image of the heavenly."

81 The corporeal element of fire is in contact with all corporeal things, and the pure and incorporeal element is in contact with all immaterial things, like demons, angels of wickedness, and the devil himself. This heavenly fire is double in nature, in part intellectual, and in part sensible.

Then, baptism is analogously also double, the sensible part through water, which puts out the sensible fire, but the intellectual part through Spirit, a defense against the intellectual fire.

And the corporeal Spirit becomes nourishment and fuel for the sensible fire when it is small. But when it grows larger it has become an extinguisher. But the Spirit given to us from on high, since it is incorporeal, reigns not only over the elements, but over the powers and wicked rulers.

82 And the bread and the oil are made holy by the power of the name; they are not the same as they seemed to be when they were received, but they have been transformed into spiritual power by power.

Thus also the water, becoming both the exorcism and the baptism, not only <distinguishes> what is inferior, but also provides holiness.

83 Ἐπὶ τὸ βάπτισμα χαίροντας ἔρχεσθαι προσῆκεν, ἀλλ᾽ ἐπεὶ πολλάκις συγκαταβαίνει τισὶ καὶ ἀκάθαρτα πνεύματα, παρακολουθοῦντα καὶ τυχόντα μετὰ τοῦ ἀνθρώπου τῆς σφραγῖδος, ἀνίατα τοῦ λοιποῦ γίνεται, τῇ χαρᾷ συμπλέκεται φόβος, ἵνα τις μόνος καθαρὸς αὐτὸς κατέλθῃ.

84 Διὰ τοῦτο νηστεῖαι, δεήσεις, εὐχαί, <θέσεις> χειρῶν, γονυκλισίαι, ὅτι ψυχὴ «ἐκ κόσμου» καὶ «ἐκ στόματος λεόντων» ἀνασῴζεται· διὸ καὶ πειρασμοὶ εὐθέως ἀγανακτούντων τῶν ἀφ᾽ ὧν ἀφῃρέθη, κἄν τις φέρῃ προειδώς, τά γε ἔξω σαλεύουσιν.

85 Αὐτίκα ὁ Κύριος μετὰ τὸ βάπτισμα σαλεύεται, εἰς ἡμέτερον τύπον, καὶ γίνεται πρῶτον «μετὰ θηρίων» ἐν τῇ ἐρήμῳ. εἶτα κρατήσας τούτων καὶ τοῦ Ἄρχοντος αὐτῶν, ὡς ἂν ἤδη βασιλεὺς ἀληθής, «ὑπ᾽ Ἀγγέλων ἤδη διακονεῖται.»

Ὁ γὰρ Ἀγγέλων ἐν σαρκὶ κρατήσας εὐλόγως ὑπ᾽ Ἀγγέλων ἤδη δουλεύεται.

Δεῖ οὖν ὡπλίσθαι τοῖς κυριακοῖς ὅπλοις, ἔχοντας τὸ σῶμα καὶ τὴν ψυχὴν ἄτρωτον, «ὅπλοις σβέσαι τὰ βέλη τοῦ Διαβόλου δυναμένοις,» ὥς φησιν ὁ Ἀπόστολος.

86 Ἐπὶ τοῦ προ<σ>κομισθέντος νομίσματος ὁ Κύριος εἶπεν οὐ· «Τίνος τὸ κτῆμα;» ἀλλά· «Τίνος ἡ εἰκὼν καὶ ἡ ἐπιγραφή; Καίσαρος»· ἵνα οὗ ἐστιν, ἐκείνῳ δοθῇ.

Οὕτως καὶ ὁ πιστός· ἐπιγραφὴν μὲν ἔχει διὰ Χριστοῦ τὸ Ὄνομα τοῦ Θεοῦ, τὸ δὲ Πνεῦμα ὡς εἰκόνα. Καὶ τὰ ἄλογα ζῷα διὰ σφραγῖδος δείκνυσι τίνος ἐστὶν ἕκαστον, καὶ ἐκ τῆς σφραγῖδος ἐκδικεῖται. Οὕτως καὶ ἡ ψυχὴ ἡ πιστή, τὸ τῆς ἀληθείας λαβοῦσα σφράγισμα, «τὰ στίγματα τοῦ Χριστοῦ» περιφέρει.

Οὗτοί εἰσιν «τὰ παιδία τὰ ἤδη ἐν τῇ κοίτῃ συναναπαυόμενα» καὶ «αἱ Παρθένοι αἱ φρόνιμοι,» αἷς αἱ λοιπαὶ αἱ μέλλουσαι οὐ συνεισῆλθον εἰς τὰ «ἡτοιμασμένα ἀγαθά,» «εἰς ἃ ἐπιθυμοῦσιν Ἄγγελοι παρακύψαι.»

83 It is befitting to go to baptism joyfully, but since frequently descending with some are unclean spirits, following and receiving the seal with the person, they become incurable in the future, (and) fear is intertwined with joy, so that only the one who is pure may descend.

84 For this reason, fast, petition, pray, <raise up> hands, kneel, because a soul is saved "from the world" and "from the mouth of lions." Therefore, there are immediate trials for those who are vexed about the things from which they have been separated, and even if someone should endure with foreknowledge, the outer person is shaken.

85 For example, the Lord after baptism was shaken, as a type for us, and he was initially "with the beasts" in the desert. Then when he gained authority over them and their ruler, as if already a true king, "he was already ministered to by angels."

For the one who had ruled over angels in the flesh is appropriately served already by angels.

It is necessary, therefore, that we put on the Lord's armor, keeping the body and soul protected, "armor able to extinguish the arrows of the devil," as the Apostle says.

86 In the (story of the) coin brought to him, the Lord did not say, "Whose possession (is this)?" but "Whose image and inscription? Caesar's," so that it might be given to the one whose it is.

Thus also the faithful; he has the name of God through Christ as an inscription, but the Spirit as an image. And irrational animals demonstrate by a seal to whom each belongs, and they are claimed by the seal. Thus also the faithful soul, having received a seal of truth, bears "the marks of Christ."

These are "the children who already are resting together in the bed" and "the wise virgins," with whom the others who are late did not enter into the "prepared goods," "upon which the angels want to look."

V. ANONYMOUS *COMMENTARY ON THE PROLOGUE OF JOHN*

Irenaeus quotes this brief commentary on John's prologue in *Against the Heresies* 1.8.5. The commentary is followed by the words "And Ptolemy indeed (teaches) in this way" (*Et Ptolemaeus quidem ita.*). However, there are two uncertainties about this attribution. First, the sentence does not appear in the surviving Greek, only in the Latin translation, which leaves open the possibility that Irenaeus did not write the sentence. Second, the sentence comes at the end of Irenaeus's presentation of Valentinian theology, specifically the theology of Ptolemy's followers, or as Irenaeus says in his preface: "I refer particularly to the disciples of Ptolemy, whose school may be described as a bud from that of Valentinus."[23] Thus the attribution to Ptolemy may refer back to all of the material in *AH* 1.1–8, and not narrowly to the prologue commentary. If this is the case, Irenaeus does not mean by the expression "And Ptolemy indeed (teaches) in this way" that Ptolemy composed all of this material, but rather that it represents Ptolemy's brand of Valentinian theology. I am more persuaded by the latter interpretation of the sentence and thus include the prologue commentary as an anonymous Valentinian text.

What is clear about the Valentinian commentary, however, is its exegetical mode. The author understands the prologue as John's disclosure of the first ogdoad, or set of eight eternities that populate the highest tier of the divine realm of fullness. The author of the commentary discovers the names of the first eight eternities in the nouns that John uses in the prologue, resulting in an ogdoad comprised of Father, Grace, Only-Begotten, Truth, Word, Life, Man, and Church. From these, presumably, the commentator believes the rest of the heavenly eternities receive their beginning. While we cannot be sure who composed this prologue commentary, it is worth noting that Ptolemy was reputed to have been the first Valentinian to posit the existence of "eternities regarded as animate beings having their existence apart from God."[24] Thus we should not be surprised that the anonymous commentary is the work of either Ptolemy or someone influenced by him.

The Greek text is based on W. W. Harvey, *Sancti Irenaei episcopi Lugdunensis libri quinque adversus haereses,* vol. 1 (Cambridge: Cambridge University Press, 1857). In the Greek and English I have formatted the text to correspond to the three voices in the text: that of Irenaeus, the commentator, and the New Testament. Unindented passages belong to Irenaeus, those with a single indent belong to the commentator, and those indented twice are quotations from the Gospel of John.

---

23. Irenaeus, *AH* praef.2.
24. Tertullian, *Against the Valentinians* 4.

Ἔτι τε Ἰωάννην, τὸν μαθητὴν τοῦ Κυρίου, διδάσκουσι τὴν πρώτην ὀγδοάδα μεμηνυκέναι, αὐταῖς λέξεσι λέγοντες οὕτως·

Ἰωάννης, ὁ μαθητὴς τοῦ Κυρίου, βουλόμενος εἰπεῖν τὴν τῶν ὅλων γένεσιν, καθ᾿ ἣν τὰ πάντα προέβαλεν ὁ Πατὴρ, «ἀρχήν» τινα ὑποτίθεται, τὸ πρῶτον γεννηθὲν ὑπὸ τοῦ Θεοῦ, ὃν δὴ καὶ Υἱὸν, Μονογενῆ, καὶ Θεὸν κέκληκεν, ἐν ᾧ τὰ πάντα ὁ Πατὴρ προέβαλε σπερματικῶς. Ὑπὸ δὲ τούτου, φησὶ, τὸν Λόγον προβεβλῆσθαι, καὶ ἐν αὐτῷ τὴν ὅλην τῶν Αἰώνων οὐσίαν, ἣν αὐτὸς ὕστερον ἐμόρφωσεν ὁ Λόγος. Ἐπεὶ οὖν περὶ πρώτης γενέσεως λέγει, καλῶς ἀπὸ τῆς ἀρχῆς, τουτέστι τοῦ Θεοῦ καὶ τοῦ Λόγου, τὴν διδασκαλίαν ποιεῖται. λέγει δὲ οὕτως·

«Ἐν ἀρχῇ ἦν ὁ Λόγος, καὶ ὁ Λόγος ἦν πρὸς τὸν Θεὸν, καὶ Θεὸς ἦν ὁ Λόγος· οὗτος ἦν ἐν ἀρχῇ πρὸς τὸν Θεόν.»

Πρότερον διαστείλας τὰ τρία, Θεὸν, καὶ Ἀρχὴν, καὶ Λόγον, πάλιν αὐτὰ ἑνοῖ, ἵνα καὶ τὴν προβολὴν ἑκατέρων αὐτῶν δείξῃ, τοῦ τε Υἱοῦ καὶ τοῦ Λόγου, καὶ τὴν πρὸς ἀλλήλους ἅμα καὶ τὴν πρὸς τὸν Πατέρα ἕνωσιν. Ἐν γὰρ τῷ Πατρὶ, καὶ ἐκ τοῦ Πατρὸς ἡ ἀρχὴ, καὶ ἐκ τῆς ἀρχῆς ὁ Λόγος. Καλῶς οὖν εἶπεν· «Ἐν ἀρχῇ ἦν ὁ Λόγος,» ἦν γὰρ ἐν τῷ Υἱῷ· «καὶ ὁ Λόγος ἦν πρὸς τὸν Θεὸν,» καὶ γὰρ ἡ ἀρχή· «καὶ Θεὸς ἦν ὁ Λόγος,» ἀκολούθως, τὸ γὰρ ἐκ Θεοῦ γεννηθὲν Θεός ἐστιν· «οὗτος ἦν ἐν ἀρχῇ πρὸς τὸν Θεόν,» ἔδειξε τὴν τῆς προβολῆς τάξιν.

«πάντα δι᾿ αὐτοῦ ἐγένετο, καὶ χωρὶς αὐτοῦ ἐγένετο οὐδ᾿ ἕν.»

πᾶσι γὰρ τοῖς μετ᾿ αὐτὸν Αἰῶσι μορφῆς καὶ γενέσεως αἴτιος ὁ Λόγος ἐγένετο. Ἀλλὰ

«ὃ γέγονεν ἐν αὐτῷ,» φησὶ, «ζωή ἐστιν.»

ἐνθάδε καὶ συζυγίαν ἐμήνυσε· Τὰ μὲν γὰρ ὅλα, ἔφη, δι᾿ αὐτοῦ γεγενῆσθαι, τὴν δὲ ζωὴν ἐν αὐτῷ. Αὕτη οὖν ἡ ἐν αὐτῷ γενομένη οἰκειοτέρα ἐστὶν ἐν αὐτῷ τῶν δι᾿ αὐτοῦ γενομένων. σύνεστι γὰρ αὐτῷ, καὶ δι᾿ αὐτοῦ καρποφορεῖ. ἐπειδὴ γὰρ ἐπιφέρει,

«καὶ ἡ ζωὴ ἦν τὸ φῶς τῶν ἀνθρώπων,»

Ἄνθρωπον εἰπὼν ἄρτι, καὶ τὴν Ἐκκλησίαν ὁμωνύμως τῷ Ἀνθρώπῳ ἐμήνυσεν, ὅπως διὰ τοῦ ἑνὸς ὀνόματος δηλώσῃ τὴν τῆς συζυγίας κοινωνίαν. Ἐκ γὰρ τοῦ Λόγου καὶ τῆς Ζωῆς Ἄνθρωπος γίνεται καὶ Ἐκκλησία. Φῶς δὲ εἶπε τῶν ἀνθρώπων τὴν Ζωὴν, διὰ τὸ πεφωτίσθαι αὐτοὺς ὑπ᾿ αὐτῆς, ὃ δή ἐστι μεμορφῶσθαι καὶ πεφανερῶσθαι. Τοῦτο δὲ καὶ ὁ Παῦλος λέγει· «Πᾶν γὰρ τὸ φανερούμενον φῶς

Still they teach that John, the disciple of the Lord, discloses the first ogdoad, when they speak with these words in this way:

John, the disciple of the Lord, wanting to speak about the origin of the whole, in relation to which the Father emanated all things, sets forth a certain "beginning," that which was first begotten by God, whom indeed he has called also Son, Only-Begotten, and God, in whom the Father emanated all things seminally. By this one, he says, the Word was emanated, and in him was the whole of the eternities, which the Word himself later shaped. Since, then, he speaks about the first origin, rightly from the beginning, that is to say, from God and the Word, he composes the teaching. He speaks in this way:

"In the beginning was the Word, and the Word was with God, and the Word was God; this one was in the beginning with God."

After first differentiating the three, God, Beginning, and Word, again (he makes) them into one so that in fact he might make known the emanation of each of them, of the Son and of the Word, and at the same time he might unite the one with one another and with the Father. For in the Father and from the Father is the beginning, and from the beginning is the Word. Rightly, then, he said, "In the beginning was the Word," since he was in the Son; "and the Word was with God," for indeed (he is) the beginning; "and the Word was God," consequently, since that which is generated from God is God; (and when he said,) "This one was in the beginning with God," he made known the order of the emanation.

"All things came about through him, and apart from him not one thing came about."

For the Word was a cause of form and origin to all the eternities that came about after him. But

"That which came about in him," he says, "is life."

Here in fact he disclosed a union. For on the one hand the whole, he was saying, has come about through him, but life (has come about) in him. This, therefore, that comes about in him is more properly in him than are the things that come about through him. For it is with him, and through him it bears fruit. For when he adds,

"And life was the light of man,"

having just now said Man, he discloses also Church synonymously with Man, thus through the name of one he might indicate the fellowship of the union. For from Word and Life come Man and Church. But Light he called the Life of Man, because they have been enlightened by her, that is, shaped and made manifest. This is what Paul also says: "For life is that which

ἐστιν. » Ἐπεὶ τοίνυν ἐφανέρωσε καὶ ἐγέννησε τόν τε Ἄνθρωπον καὶ τὴν Ἐκκλησίαν ἡ Ζωή, φῶς εἰρῆσθαι αὐτῶν. Σαφῶς οὖν δεδήλωκεν ὁ Ἰωάννης διὰ τῶν λόγων τούτων, τά τε ἄλλα, καὶ τὴν τετράδα τὴν δευτέραν, Λόγον καὶ Ζωήν, Ἄνθρωπον καὶ Ἐκκλησίαν. Ἀλλὰ μὴν καὶ τὴν πρώτην ἐμήνυσε τετράδα. διηγούμενος γὰρ περὶ τοῦ Σωτῆρος καὶ λέγων πάντα τὰ ἐκτὸς τοῦ πληρώματος δι᾽ αὐτοῦ μεμορφῶσθαι, καρπὸν εἶναί φησιν αὐτὸν παντὸς τοῦ πληρώματος.

« φῶς, » εἴρηκεν αὐτὸν, « τὸ ἐν τῇ σκοτίᾳ φαινόμενον, καὶ μὴ καταληφθὲν ὑπ᾽ αὐτῆς. »

ἐπειδὴ πάντα τὰ γενόμενα ἐκ τοῦ πάθους ἁρμόσας ἠγνοήθη ὑπ᾽ αὐτῆς. Καὶ υἱὸν δὲ, καὶ ἀλήθειαν, καὶ ζωὴν λέγει αὐτὸν καὶ

« λόγον σάρκα γενόμενον· οὗ τὴν δόξαν ἐθεασάμεθά, » φησι, « καὶ ἦν ἡ δόξα αὐτοῦ οἵα ἦν ἡ τοῦ μονογενοῦς, ἡ ὑπὸ τοῦ πατρὸς δοθεῖσα αὐτῷ, πλήρης χάριτος καὶ ἀληθείας. »

Λέγει δὲ οὕτως· « Καὶ ὁ λόγος σὰρξ ἐγένετο, καὶ ἐσκήνωσεν ἐν ἡμῖν, καὶ ἐθεασάμεθα τὴν δόξαν αὐτοῦ, δόξαν ὡς μονογενοῦς παρὰ Πατρὸς, πλήρης χάριτος καὶ ἀληθείας. »

Ἀκριβῶς οὖν καὶ τὴν πρώτην ἐμήνυσε τετράδα, Πατέρα εἰπών, καὶ Χάριν, καὶ τὸν Μονογενῆ, καὶ Ἀλήθειαν. Οὕτως ὁ Ἰωάννης περὶ τῆς πρώτης καὶ μητρὸς τῶν ὅλων Αἰώνων ὀγδοάδος εἴρηκε. Πατέρα γὰρ εἴρηκε, καὶ Χάριν, καὶ Μονογενῆ, καὶ Ἀλήθειαν, καὶ Λόγον, καὶ Ζωήν, καὶ Ἄνθρωπον, καὶ Ἐκκλησίαν.

manifested everything." Since, therefore, Light manifested and begat Man and Church, she is called their Light. Clearly, therefore, has John disclosed through these words both other things and the second tetrad, Word and Life, Man and Church. But indeed further the first tetrad he disclosed. For while discoursing about the Savior and saying that all things that are outside of the fullness have been shaped by Him, he says that He is the fruit of the entire fullness. For indeed,

> "Light," he terms Him, "is that which shines in the darkness, and it (light) was not comprehended by it (darkness)."

Since he fits together all things that come about from passion, he was not recognized by it. He also calls him Son, Truth, Life, and

> "Word become flesh. Whose glory we beheld," he says, "and his glory was like that of the Only-Begotten, the (glory) given to him by the Father, full of grace and truth."

But (John) speaks in this way: "And the Word became flesh, and dwelt among us, and we beheld His glory, the glory as of the Only-Begotten of the Father, full of grace and truth."

> Clearly, then, does he disclose the first tetrad when he speaks about the Father, Grace, Only-Begotten, and Truth. In this way John speaks about the first ogdoad and the mother of the whole of the eternities. For he names Father, Grace, Only-Begotten, Truth, Word, Life, Man, and Church.

VI. ANONYMOUS *LETTER*

In his treatise against heretics, the *Panarion*, Epiphanius quotes from a work written by an unnamed Valentinian. He claims to provide the text "word for word" from "their book." The work opens like a letter, using the traditional epistolary expression "Greetings!" However, the *Letter* also takes on a metaphysical character; the author purports to be the product of a certain "Indestructible mind" who writes to "those indestructible among the prudent, soulish, fleshly, and cosmic." The *Letter* focuses on the names of the heavenly eternities and the processes by which they populated the heavens, which the author describes as "mysteries unnameable and unspeakable and supercelestial." The date of composition of the *Letter* and the identity of its author remain unknown, but the *Letter* may hail from the late second or early third century C.E. Greek text is adapted from K. Holl, *Epiphanius, Ancoratus und Panarion*. Vols. 1–3. GCS 25, 31, 37. Leipzig: Hinrichs, 1915, 1922, 1933.

5:1 Παρὰ φρονίμοις, παρὰ δὲ ψυχικοῖς, παρὰ δὲ σαρκικοῖς, παρὰ δὲ κοσμικοῖς, παρὰ δὲ τῷ Μεγέθει νοῦς ἀκατάργητος τοῖς ἀκαταργήτοις χαίρειν.

5:2 Ἀνονομάστων ἐγὼ καὶ ἀρρήτων καὶ ὑπερουρανίων μνείαν ποιοῦμαι μυστηρίων πρὸς ὑμᾶς, οὔτε ἀρχαῖς οὔτε ἐξουσίαις οὔτε ὑποταγαῖς οὔτε πάσῃ συγχύσει περινοηθῆναι δυναμένων, μόνῃ δὲ τῇ τοῦ Ἀτρέπτου Ἐννοίᾳ πεφανερωμένων.

5:3 ὅτε γὰρ <ἐπ'> ἀρχῆς ὁ Αὐτοπάτωρ αὐτὸς ἐν ἑαυτῷ περιεῖχε τὰ πάντα, ὄντα ἐν ἑαυτῷ ἐν ἀγνωσίᾳ,—ὃν καλοῦσί τινες Αἰῶνα ἀγήρατον, ἀεὶ νεάζοντα, ἀρρενόθηλυν, ὃς πάντοτε περιέχει τὰ πάντα καὶ οὐκ ἐνπεριέχεται,—

5:4 τότε ἡ ἐν αὐτῷ Ἔννοια ἠθέλησεν ἐκείνη, ἥν τινες Ἔννοιαν ἔφασαν, ἕτεροι Χάριν οἰκείως, διὰ τὸ ἐπικεχορηγηκέναι αὐτὴν θησαυρίσματα τοῦ Μεγέθους τοῖς ἐκ τοῦ Μεγέθους. οἱ δὲ ἀληθεύσαντες Σιγὴν προσηγόρευσαν, ὅτι δι' ἐνθυμήσεως χωρὶς λόγου τὰ ἄπαντα τὸ Μέγεθος ἐτελείωσεν—

5:5 ὡς οὖν προεῖπον, ἡ ἄφθαρτος <Ἔννοια>, αἰώνια βουληθεῖσα δεσμὰ ῥῆξαι, ἐθήλυνε τὸ Μέγεθος ἐπ' ὀρέξει ἀναπαύσεως αὐτοῦ. καὶ αὕτη αὐτῷ μιγεῖσα ἀνέδειξε τὸν Πατέρα τῆς ἀληθείας, ὃν οἰκείως οἱ τέλειοι Ἄνθρωπον ὠνόμασαν, ὅτι ἦν ἀντίτυπος τοῦ προόντος Ἀγεννήτου.

5:6 μετὰ τοῦτο δὲ ἡ Σιγή, φυσικὴν ἑνότητα Φωτὸς προενεγκαμένη σὺν τῷ Ἀνθρώπῳ,—ἦν δὲ αὐτῶν ἡ συνέλευσις τὸ θέλειν—ἀναδείκνυσι τὴν Ἀλήθειαν. Ἀλήθεια δὲ ὑπὸ τῶν τελείων οἰκείως ὠνομάσθη, ὅτι ἀληθῶς ὁμοία ἦν τῇ ἑαυτῆς μητρὶ Σιγῇ—τῆς Σιγῆς τοῦτο βουληθείσης, ἀπομερισμὸν φώτων τοῦ τε ἄρρενος καὶ τῆς θηλείας ἴσον εἶναι, ὅπως δι' ἑαυτῶν καὶ ἡ ἐν αὐτοῖς φανερωθῇ τοῖς ἐξ αὐτῶν [ἐν αὐτῷ] εἰς αἰσθητικὰ φῶτα μερισθεῖσι.

5:7 μετὰ τοῦτο ἡ Ἀλήθεια, μητρικὴν προενεγκαμένη προυνικίαν, ἐθήλυνε τὸν Πατέρα ἑαυτῆς εἰς ἑαυτήν. καὶ συνῆεσαν ἑαυτοῖς ἀφθάρτῳ μίξει καὶ ἀγηράτῳ συγκράσει, καὶ ἀναδεικνύ<ου>σι τετράδα πνευματικὴν ἀρρενόθηλυν, ἀντίτυπον τῆς προούσης τετράδος, ἥτις ἦν Βυθός, Σιγή, Πατήρ, Ἀλήθεια. αὕτη δὲ ἡ ἐκ τοῦ Πατρὸς καὶ τῆς Ἀληθείας τετράς· Ἄνθρωπος, Ἐκκλησία, Λόγος, Ζωή.

5:8 τότε τοῦ πάντα περιέχοντος Βυθοῦ θελήματι, ὁ Ἄνθρωπος καὶ ἡ Ἐκκλησία, πατρικῶν μνησθέντες λόγων, συνῆεσαν ἑαυτοῖς καὶ ἀναδεικνύουσι δωδεκάδα προυνίκων ἀρρενοθηλύν<των>. οἱ οὖν ἄρρενές εἰσι Παράκλητος, Πατρικός, Μητρικός, Ἀείνους, Θελητός—ὅ ἐστι, Φῶς—Ἐκκλησιαστικός. αἱ δὲ θήλειαι· Πίστις, Ἐλπίς, Ἀγάπη, Σύνεσις, Μακαρία, Σοφία.

5:1 Indestructible mind to those indestructible among the prudent, soulish, fleshly, and cosmic in the presence of the Great One. Greetings!

5:2 I mention to you mysteries unnameable and unspeakable and supercelestial, not able to be comprehended by authorities or powers or subordinates or any combination, but having been manifest only to the Thought of the Unchangeable One.

5:3 When, <from> the beginning, the Self-Progenitor himself surrounded all things within himself, while they were within him in ignorance—he whom some call Ageless Eternity, Ever-Young, Male-Female, who surrounds all things and is not surrounded—

5:4 then the Thought within him willed her, whom some have called Thought, (but) others properly (call her) Grace, since she has supplied treasures of the Great One for those from the Great One. But those who have spoken the truth call (her) Silence, because the Great One has perfected all things by conception without speech.

5:5 As I said before, the incorruptible Thought, desiring to shatter eternal shackles, softened the Great One with a longing for his rest. And after uniting with him, she brought forth the Father of Truth, whom the Perfect have appropriately named Man, because he was the copy of the previous Unbegotten One.

5:6 After this Silence, after bringing forth a natural union of Light with Man—but their union was what was willed—brings forth Truth. She was fittingly named Truth by the Perfect, because she was truly like her own mother Silence—this being the desire of Silence, that the allocation of the lights of male and female be equal, so that through themselves that which is among them might be made manifest to those separated from them as perceptible lights.

5:7 After this Truth, having displayed a sexual desire like her mother's, softened her own Father to her. And they came together in immortal intercourse and ageless mixing, and they brought forth a male and female spiritual tetrad, a copy of the prior tetrad, which was Depth, Silence, Father, and Truth. But this is the tetrad from Father and Truth: Man, Church, Word, and Life.

5:8 Then by the will of the all-surrounding Depth, Man and Church, recalling the words of their father, came together and brought forth a duodecad of male and females (filled with) sexual desire. The males are Helper, Paternal, Maternal, Eternal Mind, Willed—that is, Light—and Ecclesiasticus. And the females: Faith, Hope, Love, Understanding, Blessed One, and Wisdom.

5:9 μετέπειτα δὲ Λόγος καὶ Ζωή, καὶ αὐτοὶ τὸ τῆς ἑνώσεως μεταπλάσαντες δώρημα, ἑαυτοῖς ἐκοινώνησαν—ἦν δὲ ἡ κοινωνία αὐτῶν τὸ θέλημα—καὶ συνελθόντες ἀνεδείξαντο δεκάδα προυνίκων καὶ αὐτῶν ἀρρενοθηλύντων. οἱ μὲν ἄρρενές εἰσι Βύθιος, Ἀγήρατος, Αὐτοφυὴς, Μονογενὴς, Ἀκίνητος. οὗτοι τὴν προσωνυμίαν <εἰς> τὴν δόξαν τοῦ Πάντα Περιέχοντος <περι>εποιήσαντο. αἱ δὲ θήλειαι· Μῖξις, Ἕνωσις, Σύγκρασις, Ἑνότης, Ἡδονή. καὶ αὗται τὴν προσωνυμίαν εἰς δόξαν τῆς Σιγῆς περιεποιήσαντο.

6:1 Τετελειωμένης οὖν τῆς κατὰ Πατέρα Ἀληθείας τριακάδος, ἣν οἱ ἐπίγειοι μὴ ἐπιστάμενοι ἀριθμοῦσι καὶ ὁπόταν ἔλθωσιν ἐπ᾽ αὐτήν, μηκέτι ἀριθμὸν εὑρίσκοντες, ἀνακυκλοῦσι πάλιν ἀριθμοῦντες αὐτήν—ἔστι δὲ Βυθὸς, Σιγὴ, Πατὴρ, Ἀλήθεια, Ἄνθρωπος, Ἐκκλησία, Λόγος, Ζωὴ, Παράκλητος, Πατρικὸς, Μητρικὸς, Ἀείνους, Θελητὸς, Ἐκκλησιαστικὸς, Πίστις, Ἐλπὶς, Ἀγάπη, Σύνεσις, Μακαρία, Σοφία, Βύθιος, Ἀγήρατος, Αὐτοφυὴς, Μονογενὴς, Ἀκίνητος, Μῖξις, Ἕνωσις, Σύγκρασις, Ἑνότης, Ἡδονή—

6:2 τότε ὁ τὰ πάντα περιέχων συνέσει τῇ ἀνυπερβλήτῳ, δογματίσας τε κληθῆναι ἑτέραν Ὀγδοάδα ἀντὶ τῆς προούσης αὐθεντικῆς Ὀγδοάδος, ἥτις ἐν τῷ ἀριθμῷ τῆς Τριακάδος μείνῃ—οὐ γὰρ ἦν Μεγέθους φρόνημα εἰς ἀριθμὸν πίπτειν—ἀντέστησεν ἀντὶ τῶν ἀρρένων τοὺς ἄρρενας Μόνον, Τρίτον, Πέμπτον, Ἕβδομον, καὶ τὰς θηλείας Δυάδα, Τετράδα, Ἑξάδα, Ὀγδοάδα.

6:3 αὕτη οὖν ἡ Ὀγδοάς, ἡ ἀντικληθεῖσα ἀντὶ τῆς προούσης Ὀγδοάδος—Βυθοῦ, Πατρὸς, Ἀνθρώπου, Λόγου καὶ Σιγῆς, Ἀληθείας, Ἐκκλησίας, Ζωῆς—ἡνώθη τοῖς φωσὶ καὶ ἐγένετο Τριακὰς ἀπηρτισμένη.

6:4 καὶ <ἦν> ἡ προοῦσα Ὀγδοὰς ἀναπαυομένη. ὁ δὲ Βυθὸς ἐξῆλθεν Μεγέθους στηρίγματι ἐνωθῆναι τῇ Τριακάδι· συνήει γὰρ τῇ Ἀληθείᾳ, καὶ ὁ Πατὴρ τῆς Ἀληθείας συνήρχετο τῇ Ἐκκλησίᾳ, καὶ ὁ Μητρικὸς εἶχε τὴν Ζωὴν καὶ ὁ Παράκλητος τὴν Ἑνάδα καὶ ἡ Ἑνὰς ἡνοῦτο τῷ Πατρὶ τῆς Ἀληθείας καὶ ὁ Πατὴρ τῆς Ἀληθείας ἦν μετὰ τῆς Σιγῆς. ὁ Λόγος δὲ ὁ πνευματικὸς ἐκοινώνει πνευματικῇ μίξει καὶ ἀφθάρτῳ συγκράσει, ποιοῦντος τὸ τέλος τοῦ Αὐτοπάτορος ἀδιχοτόμητον τὴν ἑαυτοῦ ἀνάπαυσιν.

6:5 ἡ οὖν Τριακὰς ἀπαρτίσασα βύθια μυστήρια τελειώσασα γάμον ἐν ἀφθάρτοις, ἀνέδειξε φῶτα ἄφθαρτα. ἅτινα μεσότητος ὠνομάσθησαν τέκνα καὶ ἀχαρακτήριστα ἦσαν—τοῦ νοϊκοῦ μὴ παρακειμένου—ἐκτὸς φρονήσεως ἀναπαυόμενα χωρὶς Ἐννοίας. περὶ γὰρ οὗ τις πράσσει, ἐὰν μὴ νοῇ καθολικῶς, οὐ πράσσει.

6:6 τότε γενομένων τῶν φώτων, ὧν τὴν πολυπληθίαν πρὸς ἀριθμὸν ἐξειπεῖν οὐκ ἀναγκαῖον, περινοεῖν δέ—ἕκαστον γὰρ τὸ ἴδιον ὄνομα κεκλήρωται δι᾽ ἐπίγνωσιν ἀρρήτων μυστηρίων.

5:9 Then Word and Life, after they changed the gift of union, had intercourse with each other—but their intercourse was what was willed—and by coming together they brought forth a decad of (beings filled with) sexual desire, themselves also male and female. The males are Deep, Ageless, Self-Grown, Only-Begotten, and Immovable. These received (their) names to the glory of the All-Surrounding. And the females: Mixing, Union, Intercourse, Unity, and Pleasure, and they received (their) names to the glory of Silence.

6:1 Having completed the triacad from the Father of Truth, which the terrestrial ones count without understanding and whenever they return to (the matter) and double back to count it again, still not finding the total—but it is Depth, Silence, Father, Truth, Man, Church, Word, Life, Helper, Paternal, Maternal, Eternal Mind, Willed, Ecclesiasticus, Faith, Hope, Love, Understanding, Blessed One, Wisdom, Deep, Ageless, Self-Grown, Only-Begotten, Immovable, Mixing, Union, Intercourse, Unity, and Pleasure—

6:2 Then the one who surrounds all things with unsurpassable understanding, declaring that another Ogdoad be summoned forth corresponding to the prior principal Ogdoad, which would remain in the sum of the Triacad—for it was not the purpose of the Great One to be counted—raised up in the place of the males Alone, Third, Fifth, and Seventh, and the females Dyad, Tetrad, Hexad, and Ogdoad.

6:3 This Ogdoad, summoned forth corresponding to the prior Ogdoad—Depth, Father, Man, and Word and Silence, Truth, Church, and Life—was joined with the lights and became a complete Triacad.

6:4 And the prior Ogdoad was at rest. But Depth went out with the support of the Great One to be united with the Triacad. For he joined with Truth, and the Father of Truth came together with Church, and Maternal had Life, and Helper had Henad, and Henad was united with the Father of Truth, and the Father of Truth was with Silence. But the spiritual Word joined by spiritual intercourse and immortal mixing, once the Self-Progenitor at last procured his undivided rest.

6:5 Then the Triacad, after completing deep mysteries and perfecting marriage among immortals, brought forth immortal lights. These were named the children of the middle, and they were indistinguishable—since (their) intellectual (faculty) was not present—resting senseless without Thought. For one who studies (this), unless he understands completely, does not study (this).

6:6 Then, following the creation of the lights, whose large number we do not need to tally, but consider carefully—for each has been called by its own name thanks to the knowledge of ineffable mysteries.

6:7 ἡ οὖν Σιγή, βουληθεῖσα εἰς ἐκλογὴν γνώσεως ἅπαντα σῶσαι, συνῆγε τῇ δευτέρᾳ ἀντιτεθείσῃ Ὀγδοάδι ἀφθάρτῳ μίξει νοϊκῇ δὲ βουλήσει. ἦν δὲ αὐτῆς ἡ νοϊκὴ βούλησις Πνεῦμα τὸ Ἅγιον, τὸ ἐν μέσῳ τῶν ἁγίων ἐκκλησιῶν. τοῦτο οὖν εἰς τὴν δευτέραν Ὀγδοάδα πέμψασα ἔπεισε καὶ αὐτὴν ἑνωθῆναι αὐτῇ.

6:8 γάμος οὖν ἐτελειοῦτο ἐν τοῖς τῆς Ὀγδοάδος μέρεσιν, ἑνουμένου τοῦ Ἁγίου Πνεύματος τῷ Μόνῳ καὶ τῆς Δυάδος τῷ Τρίτῳ καὶ τοῦ Τρίτου τῇ Ἑξάδι καὶ τῆς Ὀγδοάδος τῷ Ἑβδόμῳ καὶ τοῦ Ἑβδόμου τῇ Δυάδι καὶ τῆς Ἑξάδος τῷ Πέμπτῳ.

6:9 ὅλη δὲ ἡ Ὀγδοὰς συνῆλθε μετὰ ἡδονῆς ἀγηράτου καὶ ἀφθάρτου μίξεως—οὐ γὰρ ἦν χωρισμὸς ἀλλήλων, ἦν δὲ σύγκρασις μεθ᾽ ἡδονῆς ἀμώμου—καὶ ἀνέδειξε πεντάδα προυνίκων ἀθηλύντων. ὧν τὰ ὀνόματά ἐστι ταῦτα· Καρπιστὴς, Ὁροθέτης, Χαριστήριος, Ἄφετος, Μεταγωγεύς. οὗτοι τῆς Μεσότητος ὠνομάσθησαν υἱοί.

6:10 βούλομαι δὲ ὑμᾶς γινώσκειν· Ἀμψίου, Αὐραὰν, Βουκοῦα, Θαρδουοῦ, Οὐβουκοῦα, Θαρδεδδεῖν, Μερεξὰ, Ἀτὰρ, Βαρβὰ, Οὐδουὰκ, Ἐστὴν, Οὐανανὶν, Λαμερτάρδε, Ἄθαμες, Σουμὶν, Ἀλλωρὰ, Κουβιαθὰ, Δαναδαρία, Δαμμὼ, Ὠρὴν, Λαναφὲκ, Οὐδινφὲκ, Ἐμφιβοχὲ, Βάρρα, Ἀσσίου, Ἀχὲ, Βελὶμ, Δεξαριχὲ, Μασεμών.

6:7 Now Silence, wanting to save all things for the election of knowledge, united by immortal intercourse and intellectual will with the second, contrasting Ogdoad. Now her intellectual will is the Holy Spirit, which dwells in the midst of the holy church. By sending this one (Holy Spirit), then, to the second Ogdoad, she persuaded it too to become one with her.

6:8 Marriage, then, was perfected by the members of the Ogdoad, Holy Spirit united to Sole, Dyad with Third, Third with Hexad, Ogdoad with Hebdomad, Hebdomad with Dyad, and Hexad with Fifth.

6:9 Now the entire Ogdoad joined together with ageless pleasure and immortal intercourse—for there was no separation from each other, but (their) commixture was with blameless pleasure—and brought forth a Pentad of femaleless sexual desire. Their names are these: Emancipator, Terminator, Thanksgiving, Free Ranging, and Leader. These were named the sons of the Middle.

6:10 I want you to know: Ampsiou, Auraan, Boukoua, Thardouou, Ouboukoua, Thardeddein, Merexa, Atar, Barba, Oudouak, Esten, Ouananin, Lamertarde, Athames, Soumin, Allora, Koubiatha, Danadaria, Dammo, Oren, Lanaphek, Oudinphek, Emphiboche, Barra, Assiou, Ache, Belim, Dexiarche, and Masemon.

VII. ANONYMOUS *COMMENTARY ON VALENTINUS'S "SUMMER HARVEST"*

Immediately following his quotation of Valentinus's hymn "Summer Harvest," Hippolytus reproduces an interpretation of the hymn that begins with the words "Thus with these words he means . . . " While there is some debate concerning the source of this commentary—Is it a Valentinian interpretation of the hymn or Hippolytus's own understanding of what Valentinus meant?—I find it likely that Hippolytus here quotes an allegorical interpretation of the hymn by a follower of Valentinus. Hippolytus introduces "Summer Harvest" as a "psalm," which means that it likely hails from Valentinus's famous psalm book. We know from Tertullian of a certain Alexander who appealed to Valentinus's psalm book when debating Christology. Thus it is likely that the psalm book was, for some, an important Christian work worthy of careful interpretation. Greek text adapted from Miroslav Marcovitch, *Hippolytus: Refutatio Omnium Haeresium* (Berlin: De Gruyter, 1986).

οὕτως ταῦτα νοῶν· σάρξ ἐστιν ἡ ὕλη ... ἥτις κρέμαται ἐκ τῆς ψυχῆς, τοῦ δημιουργοῦ. ψυχὴ δὲ ἔρος ἐξέχεται, τουτέστιν ὁ δημιουργὸς τοῦ Πνεύματος ἔξω πληρώματος. ἠρ δὲ αἴθρης ἐξέχεται, τουτέστιν ἡ ἔξω Σοφία τοῦ ἐντὸς Ὅρου καὶ παντὸς πληρώματος. ἐκ δὲ βυθοῦ καρποὶ φέρονται, ἡ ἐκ τοῦ Πατρὸς πᾶσα προβολὴ τῶν αἰώνων γενομένη.

Thus with these words he means: flesh is matter . . . which hangs on soul, from the creator. Soul clings to air, that is, the creator clings to Spirit, which is outside the fullness. Air clings to ether, that is, the external Wisdom clings to the internal boundary and complete fullness. From depth fruit is born, the Father's complete emanation of the eternities comes to be.

Coptic Texts

VIII. *GOSPEL OF TRUTH*

The *Gospel of Truth* is the modern title given to the untitled third text in Nag Hammadi codex I. Fragments of another version of the writing survive in Nag Hammadi codex XII. The version in codex I is translated into a subdialect of Lycopolitan, whereas the version in codex XII is Sahidic. Though the version in codex XII is fragmentary, it is clear that the two versions differ in length and content. The version in codex XII is more concise and appears to have undergone a redaction in response to theological debates that took place in the fourth century. Given the secondary nature of the version in codex XII, I have included only the version from codex I.

Since the beginning and end do not survive in the version from codex XII, it is unclear whether that version of the *Gospel of Truth* was given a title in the codex in antiquity. Modern editors have assigned the text the title *Gospel of Truth* on the basis of the text's opening line: "The gospel of truth is a joy." While some ancient books received titles on the basis of their incipits, others did not, and it is unclear whether the so-called *Gospel of Truth* would have been known as such in antiquity.

It has become customary to attribute the *Gospel of Truth* to Valentinus. This attribution depends in part upon an uncritical conflation of two ancient reports. Irenaeus claims that the Valentinians had among them a *Gospel of Truth* (*evangelium veritatis*), and Pseudo-Tertullian claims that Valentinus composed a "Gospel of his own" (*Evangelium . . . suum*).[1] When conflated, these references give the

---

1. Ps.-Tertullian, *AH* 4.6.

impression that Valentinus is reported to have composed a *Gospel of Truth*. To be sure, the *Gospel of Truth* mentioned by Irenaeus may be the same *Gospel* known to Pseudo-Tertullian, but such an association requires speculation beyond the available evidence. Unfortunately, Irenaeus says little else about the Valentinian *Gospel of Truth* other than "it was written not long ago" (*non olim conscriptum est*) and that it "accords in no way with the gospels of the apostles" (*in nihilo conveniens apostolorum evangeliis*), hardly enough to establish a secure link with the *Gospel of Truth* from Nag Hammadi. Nevertheless, on the basis of its theology, hermeneutical mode, and striking similarities with the language of the *Tripartite Tractate,* a text whose Valentinian characteristics are not in doubt, we can with confidence include the *Gospel of Truth* within the Valentinian corpus, even if it may not be identical with the text mentioned by Irenaeus.

In a strict sense, the Nag Hammadi *Gospel of Truth* is not a gospel, but a homily on the gospel, as the author understands it. The text opens with a cosmic myth of Error that sets the stage for the coming of the Savior, who will bring humanity back to the Father. Finding the Entirety adrift and searching in vain for the Father, Error creates a molded form and traps the Entirety within it. In this way, Error partitions the Entirety off from the Father and ensures that it will live in ignorance and darkness. Salvation arrives when the Savior comes into the world to put an end to the reign of Error. He brings knowledge and light, and teaches humanity, the embodiment of the Totality, about its true origins in the Father. The *Gospel of Truth* is laced with biblical allusions. Jacqueline Williams has identified approximately sixty "probably" or "possible" biblical allusions in the text, with references to Genesis, Matthew, John, Romans, 1 and 2 Corinthians, Ephesians, Philippians, Colossians, 2 Timothy, Hebrews, 1 John, and Revelation.[2] If much about the author of the *Gospel of Truth* remains in doubt, his intimate familiarity with Scripture, particularly the New Testament, is certain.

2. Jacqueline A. Williams, *Biblical Interpretation in the Gnostic "Gospel of Truth" from Nag Hammadi* (Atlanta: Scholars Press, 1988), 179–83.

[16.31] ΠΕΥΑΓΓΕΛΙΟΝ Ν̅ΤΜΗΕ ΟΥΤΕΛΗΛ ΠΕ [32] Ν̅ΝΕΕΙ Ν̅ΤΑ2ΧΙ ΠΙ2ΜΑΤ ΑΒΑΛ 2ΪΤΟΟΤϤ̅ [33] Μ̅ΠΙΩΤ Ν̅ΤΕ ΤΜΗΕ ΑΤΡΟΥCΟΥΩΝϤ̅ [34] 2Ν̅ ΤΘΑΜ Μ̅ΠΙϢΕΧΕ Ν̅ΤΑ2Ϊ ΕΒΑΛ 2Ν̅ [35] ΠΙΠΛΗΡΩΜΑ, ΠΕΕΙ ΕΤ2Ν̅ ΠΙΜΕΕΥΕ [36] ΟΥΑ2Α ΠΙΝΟΥC Ν̅ΤΕ ΠΙΩΤ, ΕΤΕ [37] ΠΕΕΙ ΠΕ ΕΤΟΥϢΕΧΕ ΑΡΑϤ ΧΕ [38] ΠCΩΤΗΡ, ΕΠΡΕΝ Μ̅ΦΩΒ ΕΤϤ̅ΝΑ- [39] ΕΕΙϤ, ΠΕ ΑΠCΩΤΕ Ν̅ΝΕΕΙ Ν̅ΤΑ2Ρ̅ [17.1] ΑΤCΟΥΩΝ ΠΙΩΤ. ΕΠΙΡΕΝ ΔΕ [Μ]- [2] ΠΕΥΑΓΓΕΛΙΟΝ ΠΕ ΠΟΥΩΝ2 Α- [3] ΒΑΛ Ν̅ΤΕ †2ΕΛΠΙC, ΕΠΘΙΝΕ ΠΕ [4] Ν̅ΝΕΕΙ ΕΤΚΩΤΕ Ν̅CΩϤ.

ΕΠΙΔΗ [5] ΠΤΗΡϤ̅ ΑΥΚΑΤΟΥ Ν̅CΑ ΠΕΝΤΑΥ- [6] ΕΙ ΑΒΑΛ Ν̅2ΗΤϤ̅—ΑΥΩ ΝΕΡΕΠΤΗ- [7] ΡϤ̅ 2Ϊ CΑΝ2ΟΥΝ Μ̅ΜΑϤ, ΠΙΑΤϢΑ- [8] Π̅Ϥ̅ Ν̅ΑΤΜΕΕΥΕ ΑΡΑϤ, ΠΕΕΙ [9] ΕΤCΑΤΠ̅ ΑΜΕ2 ΝΙΜ—ΕΤΜ̅Ν̅Τ- [10] ΑΤC{Ν̅}ΟΥΩΝ ΠΙΩΤ ΑCΡ̅ ΟΥΝΟΥϢϤ̅ [11] ΜΝ̅ ΟΥ2Ρ̅ΤΕ. ΠΙΝΟΥϢϤ̅ ΔΕ ΑϤ- [12] ΩΡΧ̅ Μ̅ΠΡΗΤΕ Ν̅ΟΥ2ΛΑCΤΝ̅ [13] ΚΑΑCΕ ΧΕ ΝΕϢΛΑΥΕ ΝΕϤ [14] ΑΒΑΛ. ΕΤΒΕ ΠΕΕΙ ΑCΘΜΘΑΜ [15] Ν̅ΘΙ ΤΠΛΑΝΗ. ΑCΡ̅ 2ΩΒ ΑΤ2ΥΛΗ [16] Ν̅ΤΕC 2Ν̅Ν ΟΥΠΕΤϢΟΥΕΙΤ [17] ΕΜΠΕCCΟΥΩΝ Ν̅†ΤΜ̅Ν̅Τ- [18] ΜΗΕ. ΑCϢΩΠΕ 2ΝΝ ΟΥΠΛΑCΜΑ, [19] ΕCCΑΒΤΕ 2Ν̅ ΤΘΑΜ 2Ν̅ ΟΥΜ̅Ν̅Τ- [20] CΑΕΙΕ Ν̅ΤΧΒΒΙΩ Ν̅†ΤΜ̅Ν̅Τ- [21] ΜΗΕ.

ΠΕΕΙ ΘΕ ΝΕΥΘΒΒΙΟ ΝΕϤ [22] ΕΝ ΠΕ, ΠΙΑΤϢΑΠϤ̅ ΝΑΤΜΕΥΕ [23] ΑΡΑϤ, ΝΕΟΥΛΑΥΕ ΓΑΡ ΠΕ [24] ΠΙΝΟΥ- ϢΠ̅, ΜΝ̅ †ΒϢΕ ΜΝ̅ ΠΙΠΛΑCΜΑ [25] Ν̅ΤΕ ΠΘΑΛ. ΕΤΜ̅Ν̅ΤΜΗΕ ΕΤ- [26] CΜΑΝΤ̅ ΟΥΑΤϢΒ<Τ>C̅ ΤΕ ΟΥΑΤ- [27] ϢΤΑΡΤΡ̅ ΤΕ ΟΥΑΤ<Τ>CΑΕΙΑC ΤΕ. [28] ΕΤΒΕ ΠΕΕΙ ΚΑΤΑΦΡΟΝΙ Ν̅†- [29] ΠΛΑΝΗ.

ΤΕΕΙ ΤΕ ΘΕ Μ̅Ν̅ΤΕC [30] ΝΟΥΝΕ Μ̅ΜΕΥ. ΑCϢΩΠΕ 2Ν̅ [31] ΟΥ2ΛΑCΤΝ̅ ΕΠΙΩΤ, ΕCϢΟΟΠ [32] ΕCCΑΒΤΕ Ν̅2ΕΝΕΡΓΟΝ ΜΝ̅ 2Ν̅- [33] ΒϢΕ ΜΝ̅ 2Ν̅2Ρ̅ΤΕ ϢΙΝΑ ΧΕ [34] ΑΒΑΛ 2Ν̅ ΝΕΕΙ Ν̅CCΩΚ Ν̅ΝΑ- [35] ΤΜΗΤΕ Ν̅CΡ̅ ΑΙΧΜΑΛΩΤΙΖΕ Μ̅- [36] ΜΑΥ.

†ΒϢΕ Ν̅ΤΕ †ΠΛΑΝΗ ΝΕC- [37] ΟΥΑΝ2 ΑΒΑΛ ΕΝ. CΟΕΙ Ν̅ΝΟΥ- [18.1] [. . . .] ΕΝ 2ΑΤΜ̅ ΠΙΩΤ. †ΒϢΕ Ν- [2] ΤΑCϢΩΠΕ ΕΝ 2ΑΤΜ̅ ΠΙΩΤ, ΕΙϢ- [3] ΠΕ Ν̅ΤΑCϢΩΠΕ ΘΕ ΕΤΒΗΗΤϤ̅. [4] ΠΕΤϢΩΠΕ Ν̅ΤΑϤ Ν̅2ΗΤϤ̅ ΠΕ ΠΙCΑΥ- [5] ΝΕ, ΠΕΕΙ Ν̅ΤΑϤΟΥΩΝ2 ΑΒΑΛ ϢΙ- [6] ΝΑ Ν̅CΒΩΛ ΑΒΑΛ Ν̅ΘΙ †ΒϢΕ [7] ΑΥΩ ΠΙΩΤ Ν̅CΕΟΥΩΝϤ̅, ΕΠΙΔΗ [8] Ν̅ΤΑCϢΩΠΕ Ν̅ΘΙ †ΒϢΕ ΧΕ ΝΕϤ- [9] CΑΥΝΕ Μ̅ΠΙΩΤ ΕΝ, ΤΟΤΕ ΕΥϢΑΝ- [10] CΟΥΩΝ ΠΙΩΤ CΝΑϢΩΠΕ ΕΝ ΧΙ- [11] Ν̅{ΧΙ} ΠΙΝΕΥ Ν̅ΘΙ †ΒϢΕ.

ΠΕΕΙ <ΠΕ> ΠΕΥ- [12] ΑΓΓΕΛΙΟΝ Μ̅ΠΕΤΟΥΚΩΤΕ Ν̅- [13] CΩϤ, Ν̅ΤΑϤΟΥΑΝ2Ϥ̅ Ν̅ΝΕΤ- [14] ΧΗΚ ΑΒΑΛ 2ΙΤΝ̅ ΝΙΜ̅Ν̅ΤϢΑΝ2ΤΗϤ̅ [15] Ν̅ΤΕ ΠΙΩΤ, ΠΙΜΥCΤΗΡΙΟΝ ΕΘΗΠ, [16] ΙΗCΟΥC ΠΕΧΡΙCΤΟC, ΠΕΕΙ ΑΒΑΛ 2ΙΤΟΟΤϤ̅ [17] ΑϤΡ̅ ΟΥΑΕΙΝ ΑΝΕΤ2Μ̅ ΠΚΕΚΕΙ [18] ΑΒΑΛ 2ΙΤΟΟΤC̅ Ν̅†ΒϢΕ. ΑϤΡ̅ ΟΥΑ- [19] ΕΙΝ ΑΡΑΥ ΑϤ† Ν̅ΟΥΜΑΕΙΤ. ΠΙ- [20] ΜΑΕΙΤ Ν̅ΔΕ ΠΕ †Μ̅Ν̅ΤΜΗΕ ΕΝ- [21] ΤΑϤΤΑΜΑΥ ΑΡΑC.

ΕΤΒΕ ΠΕΕΙ [22] ΑCΒΩΛΚ̅ ΑΡΑϤ Ν̅ΘΙ †ΠΛΑΝΗ. ΑC- [23] ΠΩΤ Ν̅CΩϤ ΑC2Ρ̅Ϣ Ν̅2ΗΤϤ̅. [24] ΑCΟΥΩCϤ̅. ΑΥΑϤΤϤ̅ ΑΥϢΕ. ΑϤ- [25] ϢΩΠΕ Ν̅ΝΟΥΤΑ2 Μ̅ΠΙCΑΥΝΕ Ν̅- [26] ΤΕ ΠΙΩΤ. Ν̅ΤΑϤΤΕΚΟ

16.36 ΟΥΑ2Α: variation of ΑΥΩ. 18.11 ΠΕΕΙ <ΠΕ>: see similar emendation at 34.35.

[16.31] The good news of truth is a joy [32] for those who have received grace from [33] the Father of the truth to know him by [34] the power of the Word who has come forth from [35] the fullness, this one who is in the thought [36] and mind of the Father, [37] the one called [38] Savior, since it is the name of the task that he will [39] accomplish, salvation for those who have become [17.1] ignorant of the Father. The name [of] [2] the gospel is the appearance [3] of hope, discovery [4] for those who search for him.

When [5] the Entirety sought after the one [6] from whom they had come—in fact, the Entirety was [7] inside of him, the [8] incomprehensible, unknowable one [9] who is greater than every thought—[10] ignorance of the Father gave rise to frenzy [11] and fear. Frenzy [12] thickened like a mist [13] such that no one was able to see. [14] On account of this Error [15] became powerful. She worked on her matter [16] vainly, [17] since she did not know the [18] truth. She brought about a modeled form, [19] preparing in power and [20] beauty a surrogate for the [21] truth.

Yet this was not a humiliation for him, [22] the incomprehensible, unknowable one, [23] since they are nothing, the frenzy [24] and the forgetfulness and the creation [25] of deception. But the truth that is established is unchanging, [26] undisturbable, and incapable of being made more beautiful. [27] For this reason ignore [29] Error.

Thus she has no [30] root. She became [31] a mist in relation to the Father, existing [32] to prepare works and [33] forgetfulnesses and fears so that [34] by means of these things she might lure those in [35] the middle and imprison [36] them.

The forgetfulness of Error was [37] not apparent. It is not a [18.1] [. . .] from the Father. The forgetfulness [2] did not come about by the hand of the Father, [3] although it did indeed come about because of Him. [4] That which came about in him is knowledge, [5] which appeared so [6] that forgetfulness might disappear [7] and the Father might be known, since [8] forgetfulness came about because [9] the Father was not known, then when [10] the Father is known forgetfulness [11] will cease to exist from then on.

This <is> the [12] good news of the one who is sought [13] after, who revealed himself to the [14] perfect through the mercies [15] of the Father, the hidden mystery, [16] Jesus the Christ, through whom [17] he (the Father) enlightened those in darkness [18] through forgetfulness. He enlightened [19] them and gave (them) a path. The [20] path is the truth [21] that he explained to them.

For this reason [22] Error was angry with him. She [23] persecuted and tormented him. [24] She was brought to naught. He was nailed to a tree. He [25] became the fruit of the

ϭⲉ ⲉⲛ ϫⲉ ²⁷ ⲁϩⲟⲩⲁⲙϥ̄, ⲛⲉⲛⲧⲁϩⲟⲩⲁⲙϥ ⲇⲉ ²⁸ ⲁϥϯ ⲛⲉⲩ ⲁⲧⲣⲟⲩϣⲱⲡⲉ ⲁⲩⲣⲉ- ²⁹ ϣⲉ
ⲛϩⲣⲏⲓ̈ ⲛϩⲛ̄ ⲡⲓϭⲓⲛⲉ. ⲛ̄ⲧⲁϥ ⲛ̄- ³⁰ ϫⲉ ⲛⲉⲉⲓ ⲛ̄ⲧⲁϥϭ̄ⲛⲧⲟⲩ ⲛ̄ϩⲏⲧϥ̄, ³¹ ⲁⲩⲱ ⲛ̄ⲧⲁϥ ⲁⲩϭⲛⲧϥ̄
ⲛ̄ϩⲏⲧⲟⲩ.

ⲡⲓ- ³² ⲁⲧϣⲁⲡϥ̄, ⲛ̄ⲁⲧⲙⲉⲉⲩⲉ ⲁⲣⲁϥ, ⲡⲓ- ³³ ⲱⲧ ⲡⲉⲉⲓ ⲉⲧϫⲏⲕ, ⲡⲉⲉⲓ ⲛ̄ⲧⲁϩ- ³⁴ ⲧⲉⲛⲟ ⲙ̄ⲡⲧⲏⲣϥ̄,
ⲉⲣⲉⲡⲧⲏⲣϥ̄ ⲛ̄- ³⁵ ϩⲏⲧϥ̄, ⲁⲩⲱ ⲡⲧⲏⲣϥ̄ ⲉϥϣⲁⲁⲧ ⲙ̄ⲙⲁϥ. ³⁶ ⲉⲁϥⲁⲙⲁϩⲧⲉ ⲙ̄ⲡⲓϫⲱⲕ ⲛ̄ⲧⲉⲩ ³⁷
ⲛ̄ϩⲏⲧϥ̄, ⲡⲉⲉⲓ ⲉⲧⲉⲙ̄ⲡⲉϥⲧⲉⲉⲓϥ ³⁸ ⲙ̄ⲡⲧⲏⲣϥ̄, ⲛⲉϥⲣ̄ ⲫⲑⲟⲛⲓ ⲉⲛ ⲛ̄ϭⲓ ³⁹ ⲡⲓⲱⲧ. ⲉⲩ ϭⲉ ⲙ̄ⲫⲑⲟⲛⲟⲥ
ⲡⲉⲧⲟⲩ- ⁴⁰ ⲧⲁϥ ⲙⲛ̄ ⲛⲉϥⲙⲉⲗⲟⲥ; ⲉⲛⲉⲑⲉ ¹⁹·¹ ⲛ̄ⲅⲁⲣ ⲛ̄ⲧⲁⲡⲓⲁⲓⲱⲛ ϫ[ⲓ ⲡϫⲱⲕ] ² ⲛ̄ⲧⲉⲩ,
ⲛⲉⲩⲛⲁϣ ⲉⲓ ⲉⲡⲓ [...] ³ ⲡⲓⲱⲧ ⲡⲉ. ⲉϥⲁⲙⲁϩⲧⲉ ⲙ̄ⲡ[ⲓ]- ⁴ ϫⲱⲕ ⲛ̄ⲧⲉⲩ ⲛ̄ϩⲣⲏⲓ ⲛ̄ϩⲏⲧϥ̄, ⲉ[ϥ]- ⁵ ϯ
ⲙ̄ⲙⲁϥ ⲛⲉⲩ ⲛ̄ⲟⲩⲥⲧⲟ ϣⲁⲣⲁϥ ⁶ ⲙⲛ̄ ⲟⲩⲥⲁⲩⲛⲉ ⲟⲩⲉⲉⲓ ϩⲛ̄ ⲟⲩ- ⁷ ϫⲱⲕ. ⲛ̄ⲧⲁϥ ⲡⲉ ⲛ̄ⲧⲁϥⲧⲥⲉⲛⲟ
⁸ ⲙ̄ⲡⲧⲏⲣϥ̄. ⲁⲩⲱ ⲡⲧⲏⲣϥ̄ ⲉϥⲛ̄ϩⲏ- ⁹ ⲧϥ̄, ⲁⲩⲱ ⲛⲉⲣⲉⲡⲧⲏⲣϥ̄ ϣⲁⲁⲧ ¹⁰ ⲙ̄ⲙⲁϥ ⲡⲉ.

ⲙ̄ⲡⲣⲏⲧⲉ ⲁⲃⲁⲗ ϩⲓ̈- ¹¹ ⲧⲟⲟⲧϥ̄ ⲛⲟⲩⲉⲉⲓ ⲉⲩⲛ̄ϩⲁⲉⲓⲛⲉ ¹² ⲉⲩⲟⲉⲓ ⲛ̄ⲁⲧⲥⲁⲩⲛⲉ ⲁⲣⲁϥ, ϣⲁϥ- ¹³
ⲟⲩⲱϣⲉ ⲁⲧⲣⲟⲩⲥⲟⲩⲱⲛϥ̄ ⲁⲩⲱ ¹⁴ ⲁⲧⲣⲟⲩⲙ̄ⲣ̄ⲣⲓⲧϥ̄, ⲙ̄ⲡⲣⲏⲧⲉ—ⲉⲩ ¹⁵ ⲅⲁⲣ ⲡⲉⲛⲉⲣⲉⲡⲧⲏⲣϥ̄
ϣⲁⲁⲧ ⲙ̄- ¹⁶ ⲙⲁϥ ⲉⲓⲙⲏⲧⲓ ⲁⲡⲓⲥⲁⲩⲛⲉ ⲁ- ¹⁷ ⲡⲓⲱⲧ—ⲁϥϣⲱⲡⲉ ⲛ̄ⲭⲁⲩⲙⲁⲓ̈ⲧ, ¹⁸ ⲉϥⲥⲟⲣⲁϩⲧ̄
ⲁⲩⲱ ⲉϥⲥⲣⲁϥⲧ̄. ⲙ̄ⲙⲁ ¹⁹ ⲛ̄ϫⲓ ⲥⲃⲱ ⲁϥⲓ ⲁⲧⲙⲏⲧⲉ ⲁϥϫⲉ ²⁰ ⲡⲓϣⲉϫⲉ ⲉϥⲟⲉⲓ ⲛ̄ⲟⲩⲥⲁϩ. ²¹ ⲁⲩⲉⲓ
ϣⲁⲣⲁⲉⲓ ⲛ̄ϭⲓ ⲛ̄ⲥⲟⲫⲟⲥ ²² ⲛ̄ϩⲣⲏⲓ̈ ϩⲙ̄ ⲡⲟⲩϩⲏⲧ ⲟⲩⲁⲉⲉ- ²³ ⲧⲟⲩ ⲉⲩⲡⲓⲣⲁⲍⲉ ⲙ̄ⲙⲁϥ. ⲛ̄ⲧⲁϥ ²⁴ ⲇⲉ
ⲛⲉϥϫⲡⲓⲟ ⲙ̄ⲙⲁⲩ ϫⲉ ⲛⲉ- ²⁵ ϩⲛ̄ⲡⲉⲧϣⲟⲩⲉⲓⲧ ⲛⲉ. ⲁⲩⲙⲉⲥ- ²⁶ ⲧⲁϥ ϫⲉ ⲛⲉϩⲛ̄ⲣⲙ̄ⲛ̄ϩⲏⲧ ⲉⲛ ²⁷ ⲛⲉ
ⲙⲁⲙⲛⲉ.

ⲙⲛ̄ⲛⲥⲁ ⲛⲉⲉⲓ ⲧⲏ- ²⁸ ⲣⲟⲩ ⲁⲩⲉⲓ ϣⲁⲣⲁⲓ̈ ⲛ̄ϭⲓ ⲛ̄ⲕⲉⲕⲟⲩⲓ̈ ²⁹ ϣⲏⲙ, ⲛⲉⲉⲓ ⲉⲧⲉ ⲡⲱⲟⲩ
ⲡⲉ ³⁰ ⲡⲥⲁⲩⲛⲉ ⲙ̄ⲡⲓⲱⲧ. ⲉⲁⲩⲧⲱⲕ ³¹ ⲛⲉⲁⲩϫⲓ ⲥⲃⲱ ⲁⲛⲓⲙⲟⲩⲛⲧ̄ ³² ⲛ̄ϩⲟ ⲛ̄ⲧⲉ ⲡⲓⲱⲧ. ⲁⲩⲥⲁⲩⲛⲉ,
³³ ⲁⲩⲥⲟⲩⲱⲛⲟⲩ. ⲁⲩϫⲓ ⲉⲁⲩ, ⲁⲩϯ ³⁴ ⲉⲁⲩ. ⲁϥⲟⲩⲱⲛϩ̄ ⲁⲃⲁⲗ ϩⲙ̄ ⲡⲟⲩ- ³⁵ ϩⲏⲧ ⲛ̄ϭⲓ ⲡⲓϫⲱⲱⲙⲉ
ⲉⲧⲁⲛϩ̄ ³⁶ ⲛ̄ⲧⲉ ⲛⲉⲧⲁⲛϩ̄, ⲡⲉⲉⲓ ⲉⲧⲥⲏϩ ϩⲣⲏ- ³⁷ ⲉⲓ ϩⲙ̄ ⲡⲓⲙⲉⲉⲩⲉ ⲟⲩⲁϩⲙ̄ ⲡⲓ- ³⁸ ⲛⲟⲩⲥ ²⁰·¹ [ⲛ̄ⲧⲉ
ⲡ]ⲓⲱⲧ, ⲁⲩⲱ ϫⲓⲛ ϩⲁⲑⲏ ⲛ̄ⲧⲕⲁ- ² [ⲧⲁ]ⲃⲟⲗⲏ ⲙ̄ⲡⲧⲏⲣϥ̄ ⲉϥⲛ̄ϩⲣⲏⲓ̈ ϩⲛ̄ ³ ⲛⲓⲁⲧⲧⲉϩⲁⲩ ⲛ̄ⲧⲟⲟⲧϥ̄,
ⲡⲉⲉⲓ ⁴ ⲉⲧⲉ ⲙⲛ̄ ϭⲁⲙ ⲛ̄ⲗⲁⲩⲉ ⲁϥⲓⲧϥ̄ ⲉⲡⲓ- ⁵ ⲇⲏ ⲉⲥⲕⲏ ⲙ̄ⲡⲉⲧⲛⲁϥⲓⲧϥ̄ ⲛ̄ⲥⲉϩⲗ̄- ⁶ ϩⲱⲗϥ̄.
ⲉⲙⲡⲉⲗⲁⲩⲉ ϣⲟⲩⲁⲛϩ̄ ⁷ ⲁⲃⲁⲗ ϩⲛ̄ ⲛⲉⲉⲓ ⲛ̄ⲧⲁⲩⲛ̄ϩⲟⲩⲧⲟⲩ ⁸ ⲁⲡⲟⲩϫⲉⲉⲓ ⲉⲛⲉⲙ̄ⲡⲉϥⲉⲓ ⲉ- ⁹ ⲧⲙⲏⲧⲉ
ⲛ̄ϭⲓ ⲡ`ⲓ´ϫⲱⲱⲙⲉ ⲉⲧⲙ̄ⲙⲉⲩ. ¹⁰ ⲉⲧⲃⲉ ⲡⲉⲉⲓ ⲡⲓϣⲁⲛϩⲏⲧ ⲡⲓⲡⲓⲥⲧⲟⲥ, ¹¹ ⲓⲏⲥⲟⲩⲥ, ⲁϥϣⲁⲣ`ϣ´ϩⲏⲧ
ⲉϥϣⲱⲡ ⲛ̄ⲛⲓϩⲓⲥⲉ ¹² ϩⲁⲛⲧⲉϥϭⲓ ⲙ̄ⲡⲓϫⲱⲱⲙⲉ ⲉⲧⲙ̄- ¹³ ⲙⲉⲩ, ⲉⲡⲓⲇⲏ ϥⲥⲁⲩⲛⲉ ϫⲉ ⲡⲓⲙⲟⲩ ¹⁴
ⲛ̄ⲧⲟⲟⲧϥ̄ ⲟⲩⲱⲛϩ̄ ⲛ̄ϩⲁϩ ⲡⲉ.

ⲙ̄- ¹⁵ ⲡⲣⲏⲧⲉ ⲛ̄ⲛⲟⲩⲇⲓⲁⲑⲏⲕⲉ ⲉⲙⲡⲁ- ¹⁶ ⲧⲟⲩⲏⲛ ⲁⲣⲁⲥ, ⲉⲥϩⲏⲡ ⲛ̄ϭⲓ ϯⲟⲩⲥⲓⲁ ¹⁷
ⲙ̄ⲡⲛⲉⲡ ⲙ̄ⲡⲛⲉⲓ ⲉⲛⲧⲁϩⲙⲟⲩ, ¹⁸ ⲙ̄ⲡⲣⲏⲧⲉ ⲇⲉ ⲙ̄ⲡⲧⲏⲣϥ̄, ⲉⲧⲉ ¹⁹ ⲛⲉϥⲥⲏⲡ ⲉⲣⲉⲡⲓⲱⲧ

18.27 ⲁϩⲟⲩⲁⲙϥ̄: read ⲁϩⲟⲩⲟⲩⲁⲙϥ̄.
18.40 ⲉⲛⲉⲑⲉ: variation of ⲉⲛⲉ?
19.21 ϣⲁⲣⲁⲉⲓ: read ϣⲁⲣⲁⲉϥ?
19.28 ϣⲁⲣⲁⲓ̈: read ϣⲁⲣⲁϥ?
20.1–2 ⲕⲁ[ⲧⲁ]ⲃⲟⲗⲏ ⲙ̄: reported as ⲕⲁ[ⲧⲁ]ⲃⲟⲗ<ⲏ> {ϩ}ⲙ̄ by Attridge, but the reading in the earliest
image is clear.

knowledge of [26] the Father. But it (the fruit) did not corrupt because [27] it was eaten. Rather to those who had eaten it, [28] it gave them cause to rejoice [29] in the discovery. He [30] discovered them in himself, [31] and him they discovered in themselves.

As for the [32] incomprehensible, unknowable one, the [33] Father, the perfect one, the one who [34] created the Entirety, within him is [35] the Entirety, yet the Entirety needs him. [36] Although he held their perfection [37] within himself, which he had not given [38] to the totality, the Father was not jealous. [39] For what jealousy (could there be) [40] between himself and his members? For if [19.1] the eternity had [received] [2] their [perfection], they would have been able to come to the [. . .] [3] the Father. He held [4] their perfection within himself, [5] giving it to them as a return to him [6] and a knowledge unified [7] perfectly. He is the one who created [8] the Entirety. Although the Entirety was within [9] him, the Entirety needed [10] him.

Just as [11] (it is with) a person of whom [12] some are ignorant, he [13] wants them to know and [14] love him, so too—[15]for what did the Entirety lack [16] except knowledge of [17] the Father—he became an instructor, [18] gentle and persevering. In the midst of places [19] of learning he appeared and spoke [20] the word, since he was a teacher. [21] Those wise [22] in their own hearts came to me [23] to test him. But he [24] chastised them, since they were [25] vacuous. They hated [26] him, since they were not actually [27] wise.

After all these things [28] the little children came to me, [29] those to whom [30] the knowledge of the Father belongs. Being strengthened, [31] they learned about the countenances [32] of the Father. They came to know, [33] they were known. They received glory, they [34] gave glory. Manifest in their [35] heart was the living book [36] of the living, the one written [37] in the thought and [38] mind [20.1] [of the] Father, which prior to the [2] foundation of the Entirety was within [3] his incomprehensibility, this one [4] that no one took, since [5] it remains for the one who will take it [6] to be killed. No one would have been able to become manifest [7] from among those who had believed [8] in salvation unless [9] that book came to the middle. [10] On account of this the merciful one, the faithful one, [11] Jesus, was patient and took on sufferings [12] until he took that book, [13] since he knows that his death [14] is life for many.

[15] Just as (it is with) a will not yet [16] opened, the property [17] of the deceased master of the house is hidden, [18] so too (it is for) the Entirety, which [19] was hidden while

19.22 "to me": "to him"?
19.28 "to me": "to him"?

ⲘⲠⲦⲎⲢϤ ⲟ ²⁰ ⲚⲀϨⲞⲢⲀⲦⲞⲤ, ⲈⲞⲨⲈⲈⲒ ⲀⲂⲀⲖ Ⲛ̄- ²¹ ϨⲚⲦϤ̄ ⲠⲈ, ⲠⲈⲈⲒ ⲈⲦⲈϢⲀⲢⲈⲘⲀ- ²² ⲈⲒⲦ ⲚⲒⲘ ⲈⲒ
ⲀⲂⲀⲖ ϨⲒ̈ⲦⲞⲞⲦϤ̄. Ⲉ- ²³ ⲦⲂⲈ ⲠⲈⲈⲒ ⲀϤⲞⲨⲀⲚϨ̄ ⲀⲂⲀⲖ Ⲛ̄ϬⲒ ²⁴ ⲒⲎⲤⲞⲨⲤ. ⲀϤϬⲀⲖⲈϤ Ⲙ̄ⲠⲒⲬⲰⲘⲈ Ⲉ- ²⁵
ⲦⲘ̄ⲘⲈⲨ. ⲀⲨⲀϤⲦϤ̄ ⲀⲨϢⲈ· ⲀϤ- ²⁶ ⲦⲰϬⲈ Ⲙ̄ⲠⲆⲒⲀⲦⲀⲄⲘⲀ ⲀⲂⲀⲖ Ⲛ̄- ²⁷ ⲦⲈ ⲠⲒⲰⲦ ϨⲒ̈ ⲠⲈⲤⲦⲀⲨⲢⲒ̈Ⲥ.
ⲰⲘⲚ̄ ²⁸ ϮⲚⲀϬ Ⲛ̄ⲤⲂⲰ Ⲛ̄ⲦⲈⲈⲒϬⲀⲦ. ⲈϤⲤⲰⲔ ²⁹ Ⲙ̄ⲘⲀϤ ⲀⲠⲒⲦⲚ̄ ⲀⲠⲘⲞⲨ ⲈⲢⲈⲠⲰⲚϨ̄ ³⁰ Ⲛ̄ⲀⲚⲎϨⲈ
ⲦⲞ ϨⲒ̈ⲰⲞϤ. ⲈⲀϤⲂⲰϢ ³¹ Ⲙ̄ⲘⲀϤ Ⲛ̄ⲚⲒⲠⲖϬⲈ ⲈⲦⲦⲈⲔⲀⲒ̈Ⲧ ³² ⲀϤϮ ϨⲒ̈ⲰⲰϤ Ⲛ̄ⲦⲘⲚ̄ⲦⲀⲦⲦⲈⲔⲞ, ³³
ⲠⲈⲈⲒ ⲈⲦⲈ ⲘⲚ̄ ϢϬⲀⲘ Ⲛ̄ⲖⲀⲨⲈ ³⁴ Ⲁϣ ϤⲒⲦϤ̄ Ⲛ̄ⲦⲞⲞⲦϤ̄. ⲈⲀϤϢⲈ ⲀϨⲞⲨⲚ ³⁵ ⲀⲚⲒⲘⲀⲈⲒⲦ ⲈⲦϢⲞⲨⲈⲒⲦ
Ⲛ̄ⲦⲈ ³⁶ ⲚⲒϨⲢ̄ⲦⲈ, ⲀϤⲤⲒⲚⲈ ⲀⲂⲀⲖ ϨⲒ̈ⲦⲞⲞⲦⲞⲨ ³⁷ Ⲛ̄ⲚⲈⲈⲒ ⲈⲦⲂⲚϢ ⲀⲂⲀⲖ Ⲛ̄ⲦⲞⲞⲦⲤ̄ ³⁸ Ⲛ̄ⲦⲂⲰϢⲈ, ⲈϤⲞⲈⲒ
Ⲛ̄ⲚⲞⲨⲤⲀⲨⲚⲈ ³⁹ ⲘⲚ̄ ⲞⲨϬⲰⲔ, ⲈϤϢⲰ Ⲛ̄ⲚⲈⲦⲚ̄ϨⲎⲦ. ²¹·¹ [.] [.]Ⲧ Ⲛ̄ⲦⲀⲢ[. .] [. . .] ² ⲦⲤⲈⲂⲞ
Ⲛ̄ⲚⲈⲈⲒ ⲈⲦⲀⲬⲒ ⲤⲂ[Ⲱ].

³ ⲚⲈⲦⲚⲀⲬⲒ ⲤⲂⲰ ⲆⲈ [Ⲛ]Ⲉ ⲚⲈ- ⁴ ⲦⲀⲚϨ̄ ⲈⲦⲤϨϨ̄ ⲀⲠⲒⲬⲰⲰⲘⲈ ⁵ Ⲛ̄ⲦⲈ ⲚⲈⲦⲀⲚϨ̄. ⲈⲨⲬⲒ ⲤⲂⲰ Ⲁ- ⁶
ⲢⲀⲨ ⲞⲨⲀⲈⲈⲦⲞⲨ, ⲈⲨⲬⲒ Ⲙ̄ⲘⲀⲨ ⁷ Ⲛ̄ⲦⲞⲞⲦϤ̄ Ⲙ̄ⲠⲒⲰⲦ, ⲈⲨⲤⲦⲞ Ⲙ̄ⲘⲀⲨ ⁸ ⲀⲢⲀϤ Ⲛ̄ⲔⲈⲤⲀⲠ. ⲈⲠⲒⲆⲎ
ⲈⲢⲈⲠ- ⁹ ⲬⲰⲔ Ⲛ̄ⲦⲈ ⲠⲦⲎⲢϤ̄ ϨⲘ̄ ⲠⲒⲰⲦ ¹⁰ ⲀⲚⲀⲄⲔⲎ ⲀⲦⲢⲈⲠⲦⲎⲢϤ̄ ϢⲈ Ⲁ- ¹¹ ϨⲢⲎⲒ̈ ϢⲀⲢⲀϤ. ⲦⲞⲦⲈ
ⲈⲢⲈⲠⲞⲨ- ¹² ⲈⲈⲒ ⲤⲀⲨⲚⲈ, ϢⲀϤⲬⲒ Ⲛ̄ⲚⲈⲦⲈ ¹³ ⲚⲞⲨϤ ⲚⲈ, ⲀⲨⲰ ϢⲀϤⲤⲰⲔ Ⲙ̄- ¹⁴ ⲘⲀⲨ ϢⲀⲢⲀϤ.
ⲠⲈⲦⲞⲈⲒ ⲄⲀⲢ Ⲛ̄- ¹⁵ ⲀⲦⲤⲀⲨⲚⲈ ϤϢⲀⲀⲦ, ⲀⲨⲰ ⲞⲨ- ¹⁶ ⲚⲀϬ ⲠⲈ ⲈⲦϤϢⲀⲀⲦ Ⲙ̄ⲘⲀϤ, ⲈⲠⲒ- ¹⁷ ⲆⲎ
ⲈϤϢⲀⲀⲦ Ⲙ̄ⲠⲈⲦⲚⲀ- ¹⁸ ⲬⲀⲔϤ̄. ⲈⲠⲒⲆⲎ ⲈⲢⲈⲠⲬⲰⲔ Ⲛ̄ⲦⲈ ¹⁹ ⲠⲦⲎⲢϤ̄ ϢⲞⲞⲠ ϨⲘ̄ ⲠⲒⲰⲦ, ⲀⲚⲀⲄ- ²⁰
ⲔⲎ Ⲛ̄ⲆⲈ ⲀⲦⲢⲈⲠⲦⲎⲢϤ̄ ϢⲈ ²¹ ⲀϨⲢⲎⲒ̈ ϢⲀⲢⲀϤ Ⲛ̄ⲦⲈⲠⲞⲨⲈⲈⲒ ⲠⲞⲨ- ²² ⲈⲈⲒ {ⲠⲞⲨⲈⲈⲒ} ⲬⲒ ⲚⲚⲈⲦⲈ
ⲚⲞⲨϤ ²³ ⲚⲈ. Ⲛ̄ⲦⲀϤⲢ̄ ϢⲢ̄Ⲡ Ⲛ̄ⲤⲀϨⲞⲨ, ⲈⲀϤ- ²⁴ ⲤⲂⲦⲰⲦⲞⲨ ⲀⲦⲈⲈⲒ Ⲛ̄ⲚⲈⲈⲒ Ⲛ̄- ²⁵ ⲦⲀϨⲒ̈ ⲀⲂⲀⲖ
Ⲛ̄ϨⲎⲦϤ̄.

ⲚⲈⲈⲒ Ⲛ̄- ²⁶ ⲦⲀϤⲢ̄ ϢⲀⲢⲠ Ⲛ̄ⲤⲀⲨⲚⲈ Ⲙ̄ⲠⲞⲨ- ²⁷ ⲢⲈⲚ ⲀⲐⲀⲚ ⲀⲨⲘⲞⲨⲦⲈ ⲀⲢⲀⲨ, ²⁸ ϨⲰⲤ ⲞⲨⲈⲈⲒ
ⲈϤⲤⲀⲨⲚⲈ Ⲛ̄ⲦⲀϤ ²⁹ ⲠⲈ Ⲛ̄ⲦⲀϤⲦⲈⲨⲞ Ⲙ̄ⲠⲈϤⲢⲈⲚ Ⲛ̄- ³⁰ ϬⲒ ⲠⲒⲰⲦ. ⲠⲈⲦⲈⲘ̄ⲠⲞⲨⲬⲞⲨ ⲄⲀⲢ Ⲙ̄- ³¹
ⲠⲈϤⲢⲈⲚ ϤⲞⲈⲒ Ⲛ̄ⲀⲦⲤⲀⲨⲚⲈ. ³² Ⲙ̄ⲘⲀⲚ ⲈϢ Ⲛ̄ⲢⲎⲦⲈ ⲈⲢⲈⲞⲨ- ³³ ⲈⲈⲒ ⲚⲀⲤⲰⲦⲘ̄ ⲈⲘⲠⲞⲨϢⲰ Ⲙ̄- ³⁴
ⲠⲈϤⲢⲈⲚ; ⲠⲈⲦⲞⲈⲒ ⲄⲀⲢ Ⲛ̄ⲀⲦ- ³⁵ ⲤⲀⲨⲚⲈ ϢⲀ ⲦϨⲀⲎ ⲞⲨⲠⲖⲀⲤⲘⲀ ³⁶ ⲠⲈ Ⲛ̄ⲦⲈ ⲦⲂϢⲈ, ⲀⲨⲰ ϤⲚⲀ- ³⁷
ⲂⲰⲖ ⲀⲂⲀⲖ Ⲛ̄Ⲙ̄ⲘⲈⲤ. ⲈⲒϢⲠⲈ Ⲙ̄- ³⁸ ⲘⲀ`Ⲛ´ ⲚⲒⲤϢⲰ ⲀϨⲢⲀⲨ ⲘⲚ̄ⲦⲈⲨ Ⲙ̄- ²²·¹ [Ⲙ]Ⲉ[Ⲩ] Ⲛ̄ⲚⲞⲨⲢⲈⲚ
Ⲙ̄ⲘⲚ̄ⲦⲈⲨ ² Ⲙ̄ⲘⲈⲨ Ⲛ̄ⲦⲤⲘⲎ; ϨⲰⲤⲦⲈ ⲞⲨ- ³ ⲈⲈⲒ ⲈϤϢⲀⲤⲀⲨⲚⲈ, ⲞⲨⲀⲂⲀⲖ ⲠⲈ ⁴ ϨⲘ̄ ⲠⲤⲀⲚϨⲢⲈ.
ⲈⲨϢⲀⲘⲞⲨⲦⲈ Ⲁ- ⁵ ⲢⲀϤ, ϢⲀϤⲤⲰⲦⲘ̄, ϢⲀϤⲢ̄ ⲞⲨⲰ, ⁶ ⲀⲨⲰ ϢⲀϤⲚⲀϨϬϤ̄ ⲀⲠⲈⲦⲘⲞⲨⲦⲈ ⁷ ⲀⲢⲀϤ
Ⲛ̄ϤϢⲈ ⲀϨⲢⲎⲒ̈ ϢⲀⲢⲀϤ. ⲀⲨⲰ ⁸ ϢⲀϤⲘ̄ⲘⲈ ⲬⲈ ⲈⲨⲘⲞⲨⲦⲈ ⲀⲢⲀϤ Ⲛ̄- ⁹ ⲈϢ Ⲛ̄ⲢⲎⲦⲈ. ⲈϤⲤⲀⲨⲚⲈ,
ϢⲀϤⲈⲒⲢⲈ ¹⁰ Ⲙ̄ⲠⲞⲨⲰϢ`Ⲉ´ Ⲙ̄ⲠⲈⲚⲦⲀϨⲘⲞⲨⲦⲈ ¹¹ ⲀⲢⲀϤ, ϢⲀϤⲞⲨⲰϢⲈ ⲀⲢ̄ ⲈⲚⲈϤ, ϢⲀϤ- ¹² ⲬⲒ
Ⲙ̄ⲦⲀⲚ. ϢⲀⲢⲈⲠⲢⲈⲚ Ⲙ̄ⲠⲞⲨⲈⲈⲒ ¹³ ϢⲰⲠⲈ ⲚⲈϤ. ⲠⲈⲦⲚⲀⲤⲀⲨⲚⲈ Ⲙ̄- ¹⁴ ⲠⲒⲢⲎⲦⲈ ϢⲀϤⲘ̄ⲘⲈ
ⲬⲈ Ⲛ̄ⲦⲀϤ Ⲛ̄- ¹⁵ ⲦⲞⲚ ⲀⲨⲰ ⲬⲈ ⲈϤⲚ̄ⲚⲀ ⲀⲦⲞⲚ. ¹⁶ ϢⲀϤⲘ̄ⲘⲈ Ⲙ̄ⲠⲢⲎⲦⲈ Ⲛ̄ⲞⲨⲈⲈⲒ ¹⁷ ⲈⲀϤϨⲈ,
ⲀϤⲚⲀϨϬϤ̄ ⲀⲂⲀⲖ ϨⲘ̄ ¹⁸ ⲠⲈϤϨⲈ, ⲈⲀϤⲚⲀϨϬϤ̄ ⲀⲢⲀϤ ⲞⲨ- ¹⁹ ⲀⲈⲈⲦϤ̄, ⲀϤⲦⲈϨⲞ Ⲛ̄ⲚⲈⲦⲈ ⲚⲞⲨϤ ²⁰
ⲀⲢⲈⲦⲞⲨ ⲚⲈ.

ⲀϤⲤⲦⲞ Ⲛ̄ϨⲢⲀϨ ²¹ ⲀⲂⲀⲖ ϨⲚ̄ ⲦⲈⲠⲖⲀⲚⲎ. ⲀϤⲤⲰⲔ ²² ϨⲒ̈ⲐⲎ Ⲙ̄ⲘⲀⲨ ϢⲀ ⲚⲒⲘⲀⲈⲒⲦ ²³ Ⲛ̄ⲦⲞⲞⲦⲞⲨ,
Ⲛ̄ⲦⲀⲨⲔⲒⲘ ⲀⲂⲀⲖ Ⲛ̄- ²⁴ ϨⲎⲦⲞⲨ, ⲈⲚⲦⲀⲨⲬⲒ Ⲛ̄ⲦⲈⲠⲖⲀⲚⲎ ²⁵ ⲈⲦⲂⲈ ⲠⲒⲂⲀⲐⲞⲤ, Ⲙ̄ⲠⲈⲦ{Ⲁ}ⲔⲦⲀ- ²⁶ ⲈⲒⲦ
ⲀⲘⲀⲈⲒⲦ ⲚⲒⲘ, ⲈⲘⲚ̄ ⲠⲈ- ²⁷ ⲦⲔⲦⲀⲈⲒⲦ ⲀⲢⲀϤ. ⲚⲈⲨⲚⲀϬ Ⲙ̄- ²⁸ ⲘⲀⲈⲒϨⲈ ⲦⲈ ⲬⲈ ⲚⲈⲨϨⲚ̄ ⲠⲒⲰⲦ, ²⁹

the Father of the Entirety was [20] invisible, being something [21] from him, he from whom [22] every space comes forth. [23] For this reason Jesus appeared. [24] He clothed himself with that book. [25] He was nailed to a tree; [26] he published the decree [27] of the Father upon the cross. O [28] such great teaching! He draws [29] himself down to death though eternal life [30] clothes him. After stripping [31] himself of perishable rags [32] he clothed himself with incorruption, [33] which no one [34] can take from him. Having entered [35] the empty spaces of [36] fears, he passed through [37] those stripped naked by [38] forgetfulness, being knowledge [39] and perfection, proclaiming the things of the heart. [21.1] . . . after . . . [2] teach those who will receive teaching.

[3] But those who will receive teaching [are] [4] the living who are inscribed in the book [5] of the living. They receive teaching about [6] themselves alone, receiving it [7] from the Father, turning themselves [8] to him again. Since the [9] perfection of the Entirety is in the Father [10] it is necessary for the Entirety to [11] go up to him. Then if one [12] has knowledge, he receives those [13] who belong to him, and he draws [14] them to himself. For the one who is [15] ignorant is lacking, and [16] what he lacks is great, since [17] he lacks that which will [18] perfect him. Since the perfection of [19] the Entirety exists in the Father, [20] it is necessary for the Entirety to go up [21] to him and for each [22] one to receive what belongs to him. [23] He preregistered them, having [24] prepared them to give to those who [25] had come forth from him.

Those [26] whose name he knew [27] first, at the end were called, [28] so that one who comes to know is [29] the one whose name the Father [30] has proclaimed. For the one whose name [31] has not been uttered is ignorant. [32] Truly how will one [33] hear if his name has not [34] been called? For the one who is [35] ignorant to the end is a modeled form [36] of forgetfulness, and he will [37] be destroyed with it. For if not, [38] (how is it that) these despised ones have [22.1] no name and no [2] call? Thus [3] if one knows, he is [4] from above. If he is called, [5] he hears, he answers, [6] and he turns to the one who calls [7] him and goes to him. [8] He knows the manner in which he [9] is called. Coming to know, he does [10] the will of the one who called [11] him, he desires to be pleasing to him, he [12] receives rest. The name of each [13] comes to him. The one who will know in [14] this way knows whence he comes [15] and where he is going. [16] He knows as one [17] who, after becoming intoxicated, has turned away from [18] his intoxication, returning to himself, [19] has made upright the things that [20] belong to him.

He has turned many [21] from Error. He has gone [22] before them to their spaces, [23] from which they had departed, [24] because they received Error [25] on account of the depth, that which surrounds [26] all spaces, while there is none that [27] surrounds it. It was a great [28] marvel that they were in the Father, [29]

ⲉⲩⲥⲁⲩⲛⲉ ⲙ̄ⲙⲁϥ ⲉⲛ, ⲁⲩⲱ ⲛⲉⲩ- ³⁰ ⳓⲙⳓⲁⲙ ⲛ̄ⳓⲓ ⲁⲃⲁⲗ ⲟⲩⲁⲉⲉⲧⲟⲩ ³¹ ⲡⲉ, ⲉⲡⲓⲇⲏ ⲛⲉⲩϣ̄ ⳓⲙⳓⲁⲙ ⲉⲛ ⲁϣ- ³² ⲱⲡ ⲁⲣⲁⲩ ⲁⲩⲱ ⲁⲥⲁⲩⲛⲉ ⲙ̄ⲡⲉ- ³³ ⲧⲛⲉⲩⲛ̄ϩⲏⲧϥ̄. ⲉⲛⲉⲑⲉ ⲅⲁⲣ ⲉ- ³⁴ ⲛⲉⲙ̄ⲡⲉϥⲓ ⲁⲃⲁⲗ ⲛ̄ϩⲏⲧϥ̄ ⲛ̄ⳓⲓ ³⁵ ⲡⲉϥⲟⲩⲱϣⲉ—ⲁϥⲟⲩⲁⲛϩ̄ϥ ⲅⲁⲣ ³⁶ ⲁⲃⲁⲗ ⲁⲩⲥⲁⲩⲛⲉ ⲉⲩⲧⲏⲧ ⲛ̄ⲙ̄- ³⁷ ⲙⲉⲥ ⲧⲏⲣⲟⲩ ⲛ̄ⳓⲓ ⲛⲓⲧⲛ̄ ⲛ̄ⲧⲟⲟⲧⲥ̄, ³⁸ ⲉⲧⲉ ⲡⲉⲉⲓ ⲡⲉ ⲡⲓⲥⲁⲩⲛⲉ ⲛ̄ⲧⲉ ³⁹ ⲡⲓⲭⲱⲱⲙⲉ ⲉⲧⲁⲛϩ̄ ⲉⲛⲧⲁϥ- ⁴⁰ ⲟⲩⲁⲛϩ̄ϥ ⲛ̄ⲛⲓ- ²³·¹ ⲁⲓⲱⲛ ⲁⲧⲑⲁⲛ ⲛ̄ⲛⲓⳓϩⲉⲉⲓ ⲛⲧⲟ]- ² ⲟⲧϥ̄, ⲉϥⲟⲩⲁⲛϩ̄ ⲁⲃⲁⲗ ⲉⲓϣⲉ]- ³ ϫⲉ ⲉϩ̄ⲛ̄ⲧⲟⲡⲟⲥ ⲉⲛ ⲛⲉ ⲛ̄ⲧⲉ ⁴ ϩ̄ⲛ̄ⲥⲙⲏ ⲟⲩⲇⲉ ϩ̄ⲛ̄ⲥϩⲉⲉⲓ ⲉⲛ ⁵ ⲛⲉ ⲉⲩϣⲁⲁⲧ ⲛ̄ⲛⲟⲩϩⲣⲁⲩ ⁶ ϣⲓⲛⲁ ⲛ̄ⲧⲉⲟⲩⲉⲉⲓ ⲁϣⲟⲩ ⲛ̄ϥ- ⁷ ⲙⲉⲩⲉ ⲁⲩⲡⲉⲧϣⲟⲩⲉⲓⲧ. ⁸ ⲁⲗⲗⲁ ϩ̄ⲛ̄ⲥϩⲉⲉⲓ ⲛⲉ ⲛ̄ⲧⲉ ϯ- ⁹ ⲙⲛ̄ⲧⲙⲏⲉ ⲛ̄ⲧⲁⲩ ⲉⲩϣⲉϫⲉ ¹⁰ ⲉⲩⲥⲁⲩⲛⲉ ⲙ̄ⲙⲁⲩ ⲟⲩⲁⲉⲉⲧⲟⲩ. ¹¹ ⲉⲟⲩⲙⲉ<ⲉⲩⲉ> ⲉϥϫⲏⲕ ⲡⲉ ⲡⲥϩⲉⲉⲓ ¹² ⲡⲥϩⲉⲉⲓ ⲙ̄ⲡⲣⲏⲧⲉ ⲛ̄ⲛⲟⲩϫⲱ- ¹³ ⲱⲙⲉ ⲉϥϫⲏⲕ ⲁⲃⲁⲗ, ⲉϩ̄ⲛ̄ⲥϩⲉ- ¹⁴ ⲉⲓ ⲛⲉ ⲁⲩⲥⲁϩⲟⲩ ⲁⲃⲁⲗ ϩⲓⲧⲟⲟⲧⲥ ¹⁵ ⲛ̄ϯⲙⲛ̄ⲧⲟⲩⲉⲉⲓ. ⲉⲁϩⲣⲁⲡⲱⲧ ¹⁶ ⲥⲁϩⲟⲩ <ⲛ̄>ⲛⲓⲁⲓⲱⲛ ϣⲓⲛⲁ ⲁⲃⲁⲗ ¹⁷ ϩⲓⲧⲟⲟⲧⲟⲩ ⲛ̄ⲛⲓⲥϩⲉⲉⲓ ⲛ̄ⲧⲟⲟⲩ ¹⁸ ⲉⲁⲥⲟⲩⲱⲛ ⲡⲓⲱⲧ.

ⲉϯⲥⲟⲫⲓⲁ ¹⁹ ⲛ̄ⲧⲟⲟⲧϥ̄ ⲉⲥⲣ̄ ⲙⲉⲗⲉⲧⲁ ⲙ̄- ²⁰ ⲡⲓϣⲉϫⲉ·
ⲉⲣⲉϯⲥⲃⲱ ⲛ̄ⲧⲟⲟⲧϥ̄ ²¹ ⲉⲥϣⲉϫⲉ ⲙ̄ⲙⲁϥ.
ⲡⲓⲥⲁⲩⲛⲉ ⲛ̄- ²² ⲧⲟⲟⲧϥ̄ ⲁϥⲟⲩⲁⲛϩ̄ ⲁⲃⲁⲗ.
²³ ⲡⲓⲁⲥⲟ ⲛ̄ⲧⲟⲟⲧϥ̄ ⲉϥⲟⲉⲓ ⲛ̄- ²⁴ ⲛⲟⲩⲕⲗⲁⲙ ⲁϫⲱϥ·
ⲉⲣⲉⲡⲓ- ²⁵ ⲣⲉϣⲉ ⲛ̄ⲧⲟⲟⲧϥ̄ ⲉϥⲧⲏⲧ ²⁶ ⲛⲙ̄ⲙⲉϥ.
ⲡⲓⲉⲁⲩ ⲛ̄ⲧⲟⲟⲧϥ̄ ²⁷ ⲁϥϫⲓⲥⲉ ⲙ̄ⲙⲁϥ.
ⲡⲓⲥⲙⲁⲧ ²⁸ ⲛⲧⲟⲟⲧϥ̄ ⲁϥⲟⲩⲁⲛϩ̄ϥ ⲁ- ²⁹ ⲃⲁⲗ.
ⲡⲓⲙ̄ⲧⲁⲛ ⲛ̄ⲧⲟⲟⲧϥ̄ ⲁϥ- ³⁰ ϣⲁⲡϥ̄ ⲁⲣⲁϥ.
ϯⲁⲅⲁⲡⲏ ⲛ̄ⲧⲟ- ³¹ ⲟⲧϥ̄ ⲁⲥⲣ̄ ⲟⲩⲥⲱⲙⲁ ϩⲓⲱⲱϥ.
ⲡⲓ- ³² ⲛⲁϩⲧⲉ ⲛ̄ⲧⲟⲟⲧϥ̄ ⲁϥⲁⲙⲁϩⲧⲉ ³³ ⲙ̄ⲙⲁϥ.

ⲡⲓⲣⲏⲧⲉ ⲉⲣⲉⲡⲓϣⲉ- ³⁴ ϫⲉ ⲛ̄ⲧⲉ ⲡⲓⲱⲧ ⲉϥⲙⲁⲁϩⲉ ³⁵ ⲁⲃⲁⲗ ϩⲛ̄ ⲡⲧⲏⲣϥ̄ ⲉⲡⲟⲩⲧⲁϩ ²⁴·¹ [ⲛ̄ⲧⲉ] ⲡⲓϩⲏⲧ ⲛ̄ⲧⲟⲟⲧϥ̄ ⲡⲉ ⲁⲩⲱ ² ⲟⲩⲙⲟⲩⲛⲅ̄ ⲛ̄ϩⲟ ⲛ̄ⲧⲉ ⲡⲉϥⲟⲩ- ³ ⲱϣⲉ. ⲉϥϥⲓ ⲛ̄ⲧ`ⲁϥ´ ϩⲁ ⲡⲧⲏⲣϥ̄, ⲉϥ- ⁴ ⲥⲱⲧⲡ̄ ⲙ̄ⲙⲁⲩ, ⲁⲩⲱ ⲁⲛ ⲉϥϫⲓ ⲙ̄- ⁵ ⲡⲙⲟⲩⲛⲅ̄ ⲛ̄ϩⲟ ⲛ̄ⲧⲉ ⲡⲧⲏⲣϥ̄, ⁶ ⲉϥⲥⲱⲧϥ̄ ⲙ̄ⲙⲁⲩ, ⁷ ⲉϥ`ⲥ´ⲧⲟ ⲙ̄ⲙⲁⲩ ⁷ ⲁϩⲟⲩⲛ ⲁⲡⲓⲱⲧ, ⲁϩⲟⲩⲛ ⲁϯⲙⲉⲉⲩ ⁸ ⲓⲏⲥⲟⲩⲥ ⲛ̄ⲧⲉ ϯⲙⲛ̄ⲧ<ⲁⲧ>ⲁⲣⲏⲝ̄ⲥ̄ ⲛ̄ⲧⲉ ⁹ ⲡⲓϩⲗⲁⳓ.

ⲉϥⳓⲱⲗⲡ̄ ⲙ̄ⲡⲉϥⲧⲁⲡ ¹⁰ ⲁⲃⲁⲗ ⲛ̄ⳓⲓ ⲡⲓⲱⲧ—ⲡⲉϥⲧⲁⲡ ⲇⲉ ¹¹ ⲡⲉ ⲡⲓⲡⲛⲉⲩⲙⲁ ⲉⲧⲟⲩⲁⲁⲃ—ⲉϥⲟⲩ- ¹² ⲱⲛϩ̄ ⲁⲃⲁⲗ ⲙ̄ⲡⲓⲡⲉⲑⲏⲡ ⲛ̄ⲧⲟ- ¹³ ⲟⲧϥ̄. ⲡⲓⲡⲉⲑⲏⲡ ⲛ̄ⲧⲟⲟⲧϥ̄ ⲡⲉ ¹⁴ ⲡⲉϥϣⲏⲣⲉ ϣⲓⲛⲁ ϫⲉ ⲁⲃⲁⲗ ¹⁵ ϩⲛ̄ ⲛⲓⲙⲉϩⲧ ⲛ̄ⲧⲟⲟⲧϥ̄ ⲙ̄ⲡⲓⲱⲧ ¹⁶ ⲛ̄ⲥⲉⲥⲟⲩⲱⲛϥ̄ ⲛ̄ⲥⲉⲗⲟ ⲉⲩϩⲁ- ¹⁷ ⲥⲓ ⲛ̄ⳓⲓ ⲛⲓⲁⲓⲱⲛ ⲉⲩϣⲓⲛⲉ ⲛ̄ⲥⲁ ¹⁸ ⲡⲓⲱⲧ ⲉⲩⲙⲁⲧⲛ̄ ⲙ̄ⲙⲁⲩ ⲙ̄- ¹⁹ ⲙⲁⲩ ⲛ̄ϩⲣⲏⲓ ⲛ̄ϩⲏⲧϥ̄ ⲉⲩⲥⲁⲩ- ²⁰

22.36–37 ⲛⲙ̄ⲙⲉⲥ . . . ⲛ̄ⲧⲟⲟⲧⲥ̄: read ⲛⲙ̄ⲙⲉϥ . . . ⲛ̄ⲧⲟⲟⲧϥ̄ (referring to ⲥⲁⲩⲛⲉ; as Grobel notes, the gender here is possibly confused on account of the feminine Greek noun γνῶσις, which ⲥⲁⲩⲛⲉ presumably translates).

23.22 ⲁϥⲟⲩⲁⲛϩ̄: possibly ⲁϥⲟⲩⲁⲛϩ̄<ϥ>.

not knowing him, and that they were [30] able to come forth alone, [31] since they were not able to [32] comprehend themselves or to know the [33] one in whom they were. For if [34] his will had not come forth from him [35]—for he revealed it [36] in a knowledge with which [37] all its emanations agree, [38] namely, the knowledge of [39] the living book that he [40] revealed to the [23.1] eternities at the end as his letters, [2] revealing that [3] they are not in places of [4] voices nor in letters [5] lacking sound [6] so that one might read them and [7] think about something deficient. [8] Rather, they are letters of [9] truth that only those [10] who know them speak. [11] Each letter is a complete <thought> [12] as though a complete book, [13] since they are letters [14] written by the [15] unity. The Father has [16] written them <for> the eternities so that [17] by means of his letters [18] they might know the Father.

His wisdom [19] meditates on [20] the word;
his teaching [21] proclaims it.
His knowledge [22] has been made manifest.
[23] His restraint is [24] a crown upon it;
[25] his joy mingles [26] with it.
His glory [27] has exalted it.
His image [28] has revealed it. [29]
His rest has [30] received it into himself.
His love [31] made a body upon it.
[32] His trustworthiness has prevailed upon [33] it.

In this manner the word [34] of the Father proceeds [35] into the Entirety as the fruit [24.1] [of] his heart and [2] countenance of his will. [3] It bears the totality, [4] choosing them, and receives [5] the countenance of the Entirety, [6] purifying them, bringing them [7] into the Father, into the Mother, [8] Jesus of the bound<less> [9] sweetness.

The Father reveals [10] his bosom—his bosom [11] is the Holy Spirit—by manifesting [12] his hidden aspect. [13] His hidden aspect is [14] his son so that from [15] the Father's compassion [16] the eternities might know him [17] and cease toiling in search of [18] the Father by resting themselves [19] in him, since they know [20] that

22.31–32 "to comprehend themselves": this verb is difficult to translate, but appears to have a late meaning of χωρεῖν (spiritual capacity to know).

22.33–34 "For if his will had not come forth from him": the second half of this sentence may have been lost in transmission.

23.21–22 "His knowledge has been made manifest": or "His knowledge has revealed <it>."

23.23 "His restraint": or "His value."

24.2 "countenance": literally, "form of face."

24.10–11 "his bosom is the Holy Spirit": This sentence may be a later, Trinitarian gloss.

ⲛⲉ ϫⲉ ⲡⲉⲉⲓ ⲡⲉ ⲡⲓⲙⲧⲁⲛ. ⲉⲁϥ-²¹ ⲙⲟⲩϩ ⲙⲡⲓⲱⲧⲁ, ⲁϥⲃⲱⲗ ⲁⲃⲁⲗ ²² ⲙ̄ⲡⲓⲥⲭⲏⲙⲁ—ⲡⲓⲥⲭⲏⲙⲁ
ⲛ̄ⲧⲟⲟ-²³ ⲧϥ̄ ⲡⲉ ⲡⲕⲟⲥⲙⲟⲥ ⲡⲉⲉⲓ ⲉⲛ-²⁴ ⲧⲁϥϣ̄ⲙ̄ϣⲉ ⲛ̄ϩⲏⲧϥ̄. ²⁵ ⲡⲙⲁ ⲅⲁⲣ ⲉⲧⲉ ⲟⲩⲛ̄ ⲕⲱϩ
ⲙ̄ⲙⲉⲩ ²⁶ ϩⲓ̈ⲧ ⲧⲱⲛ ⲟⲩϣⲧⲁ ⲡⲉ. ⲡⲙⲁ ²⁷ ⲇⲉ ⲉⲧⲉ ϯⲙ̄ⲛ̄ⲧⲟⲩⲉⲉⲓ ⲟⲩ-²⁸ ϫⲱⲕ ⲡⲉ ⲉⲡⲓⲇⲏ
ⲛ̄ⲧⲁϥϣⲱⲡⲉ ²⁹ ⲛ̄ϭⲓ ⲡⲓϣⲧⲁ ϫⲉ ⲛⲉⲩⲥⲁⲩⲛⲉ ³⁰ ⲉⲛ ⲙ̄ⲡⲓⲱⲧ ⲡⲉ. ⲧⲟⲧⲉ ⲉⲩϣⲁⲛ-³¹ ⲥⲟⲩⲱⲛ
ⲡⲓⲱⲧ, ϥⲛⲁϣⲱⲡⲉ ⲉⲛ ³² ϫⲓⲛ ⲡⲓⲛⲉⲩ ⲛ̄ϭⲓ ⲡⲓϣⲧⲁ. ⲙ̄ⲡⲣⲏⲧⲉ ³³ ⲁⲃⲁⲗ ϩⲓ̈ⲧⲟⲟⲧⲥ̄ ⲛ̄ⲧⲙⲛ̄ⲧⲁⲧⲥⲁⲩ-
³⁴ ⲛⲉ ⲛ̄ⲧⲉ ⲟⲩⲉⲉⲓ, ⲧⲟⲧⲉ ⲉϥϣⲁ-³⁵ ⲥⲁⲩⲛⲉ, ϣⲁⲥⲃⲱⲗ ⲁⲃⲁⲗ ϩⲓⲧⲟⲟ-³⁶ ⲧⲥ̄ ⲛ̄ϭⲓ ⲧⲙⲛ̄ⲧⲁⲧⲥⲁⲩⲛⲉ
ⲛ̄ⲧⲟ-³⁷ ⲟⲧϥ̄, ⲙ̄ⲡⲣⲏⲧⲉ ⲙ̄ⲡⲕⲉⲕⲉⲓ ⲉϣⲁϥ-³⁸ ⲃⲱⲗ ⲁⲃⲁⲗ ⲉϥϣⲁⲛⲟⲩⲱⲛϩ̄ ²⁵·¹ ⲛ̄ϭⲓ ⲡⲟⲩⲁⲉⲓⲛ,
ⲙ̄ⲡⲓⲣⲏⲧⲉ ⲁⲛ ² ⲡⲓϣⲧⲁ ϣⲁϥⲃⲱⲗ ⲁⲃⲁⲗ ϩⲣⲏ[ⲓ̈] ³ ϩⲛ̄ ⲡⲓϫⲱⲕ. ⲉϥⲟⲩⲁⲛϩ̄ ϭⲉ ⲉⲛ ⁴ ϫⲓⲛ ⲡⲓⲛⲉⲩ
ⲛ̄ϭⲓ ⲡⲓⲥⲭⲏⲙⲁ, ⲁⲗ-⁵ ⲗⲁ ⲉϥⲛⲁⲃⲱⲗ ⲁⲃⲁⲗ ⲛ̄ϩⲣⲏⲓ ⁶ ϩⲛ̄ ⲡⲧⲱⲧ ⲛ̄ⲧⲉ ϯⲙ̄ⲛ̄ⲧⲟⲩ-⁷ ⲉⲉⲓ. ϯⲛⲟⲩ
ⲅⲁⲣ ⲛⲟⲩϩⲃⲏⲩⲉ ⁸ ⲥⲉⲕⲏ ⲛⲉⲩ ⲉⲩϣⲏϣ ϩⲛ̄ ⲡⲟⲩⲁ-⁹ ⲉⲓϣ ⲉⲣⲉϯⲙⲛ̄ⲧⲟⲩⲉⲉⲓ ⲛⲁϫⲱⲕ ¹⁰
ⲙ̄ⲙⲁⲉⲓⲧ ⲁⲃⲁⲗ. ⲛ̄ϩⲣⲏⲓ ϩⲛ̄ ϯ-¹¹ ⲙⲛ̄ⲧⲟⲩⲉⲉⲓ ⲉⲣⲉⲡⲟⲩⲉⲉⲓ ⲡⲟⲩ-¹² ⲉⲉⲓ ⲛⲁϫⲓ ⲙ̄ⲙⲁϥ· ⲛ̄ϩⲣⲏⲓ ϩⲛ̄ ¹³
ⲟⲩⲥⲁⲩⲛⲉ ⲉϥⲛⲁⲥⲱⲧϥ̄ ⲙ̄ⲙⲁϥ ¹⁴ ⲁⲃⲁⲗ ϩⲛ̄ⲛ ⲟⲩⲧⲟ ⲛ̄ⲣⲏⲧⲉ ⲁϩⲟⲩⲛ ¹⁵ ⲁⲩⲙⲛ̄ⲧⲟⲩⲉⲉⲓ, ⲉϥⲟⲩⲱⲙ
¹⁶ ⲛ̄ϩⲩⲗⲏ ⲛ̄ϩⲣⲏⲓ̈ ⲛ̄ϩⲏⲧϥ̄ ⲙ̄-¹⁷ ⲡⲣⲏⲧⲉ ⲛ̄ⲛⲟⲩⲥⲉⲧⲉ ⲁⲩⲱ ⲡⲕⲉ-¹⁸ ⲕⲉⲓ ϩⲛ̄ ⲟⲩⲁⲉⲓⲛ, ⲡⲙⲟⲩ ϩⲛ̄
ⲟⲩ-¹⁹ ⲱⲛϩ̄.

ⲉⲓϣⲡⲉ ⲁⲛⲉⲉⲓ ϭⲉ ϣⲱⲡⲉ ²⁰ ⲙ̄ⲡⲟⲩⲉⲉⲓ ⲡⲟⲩⲉⲉⲓ ⲙ̄ⲙⲁⲛ, ²¹ ⲟⲩⲛ ⲡⲉⲧⲉϣϣⲉ ⲁⲣⲁⲛ ϭⲉ ²²
ⲛ̄ⲧⲛ̄ⲙⲉⲩⲉ ⲁⲡⲧⲏⲣϥ̄ ϣⲓⲛⲁ ²³ ⲉⲣⲉⲡⲓⲏⲉⲓ ⲛⲁϣⲱⲡⲉ ⲉϥⲟⲩⲁ-²⁴ ⲁϥ ⲁⲩⲱ ⲉϥⲥⲟⲣⲁϩⲧ̄ ⲁ†ⲙⲛ̄ⲧ-²⁵
ⲟⲩⲉⲉⲓ. ⲙ̄ⲡⲣⲏⲧⲉ ⲛ̄ϩⲁⲉⲓⲛⲉ ²⁶ ⲉⲁⲩⲡⲱⲛⲉ ⲁⲃⲁⲗ ϩⲛ̄ ϩⲛⲙⲁ ²⁷ ⲉⲩⲛ̄ⲧⲉⲩ ⲙ̄ⲙⲉⲩ ⲛ̄ϩⲉⲛ-²⁸ ⲥⲕⲉⲩⲟⲥ
ⲛ̄ϩⲣⲏⲓ ϩⲛ̄ ϩⲛ̄-²⁹ ⲧⲟⲡⲟⲥ ⲉⲛⲁⲛⲟⲩⲟⲩ ⲉⲛ. ³⁰ ⲛⲉϣⲁⲩⲟⲩⲁϭⲡⲟⲩ ⲁⲩⲱ ⲙⲁϥ-³¹ † ⲁⲥⲓ ⲛ̄ϭⲓ ⲡⲛⲉⲡ
ⲙ̄ⲡⲏⲉⲓ ⲁⲗ-³² ⲗⲁ ϣⲁⲥⲣⲉϣⲉ ϫⲉ ⲛ̄ϩⲣⲏⲓ̈ ⲅⲁⲣ ³³ ϩⲛ̄ ⲡⲙⲁ ⲛ̄ⲛⲓⲥⲕⲉⲩⲟⲥ ⲉ-³⁴ ⲑⲁⲩ ⲛⲉⲧⲙⲏϩ
ⲛⲉⲧⲉϣⲁⲩ-³⁵ ϫⲁⲕⲟⲩ ⲁⲃⲁⲗ. ϫⲉ ⲧⲉⲉⲓ ⲧⲉ ³⁶ ⲧⲉⲕⲣⲓⲥⲓⲥ ⲛ̄ⲧⲁϩⲉⲓ ⲁⲃⲁⲗ ²⁶·¹ ⲙ̄ⲡⲥⲁ ⲛⲧⲡⲉ· ⲉⲁⲥⲧ
ϩⲉⲡ ⲁⲟⲩ-² ⲁⲛ ⲛⲓⲙ. ⲉⲩⲥⲛϭⲉ ⲧⲉ ⲉⲥϣⲁⲗⲙ̄, ³ ⲙ̄ϥⲟ ⲥⲛⲉⲩ, ⲉⲥϣⲱⲧ ⲛ̄-⁴ ⲥⲁ ⲡⲓⲥⲁ ⲙⲛ̄ ⲡⲉⲉⲓ.
ⲉⲁϥⲓ ⲁⲧⲙⲏ-⁵ ⲧⲉ ⲛ̄ϭⲓ ⲡⲓϣⲉϫⲉ, ⲉⲧⲛ̄ϩⲣⲏⲓ ⁶ ϩⲛ̄ ⲡⲣⲏⲧ ⲛ̄ⲛⲉⲧϣⲉϫⲉ ⲙ̄ⲙⲁϥ ⁷—ⲟⲩⲣⲁⲩ
ⲟⲩⲁⲉⲉⲧϥ̄ ⲉⲛ ⲡⲉ, ⲁⲗ-⁸ ⲗⲁ ⲁϥⲣ̄ ⲟⲩⲥⲱⲙⲁ—ⲟⲩⲛⲁϭ ⲛ̄-⁹ ϣⲧⲁⲣⲧⲣ̄ ⲁϥϣⲱⲡⲉ ⲛ̄ϩⲣⲏⲓ ϩⲛ̄ ¹⁰
ⲛ̄ⲥⲕⲉⲩⲟⲥ ϫⲉ ϩⲁⲉⲓⲛⲉ ⲁϩⲟⲩ-¹¹ ϣⲟⲩⲱⲟⲩ ϩⲛⲕⲁⲩⲉ ⲁϩⲟⲩⲙⲁ-¹² ϩⲟⲩ ϫⲉⲥ ϩⲛ̄ⲕⲁⲩⲉ ⲁϩⲟⲩⲥ̄ⲛⲏ-
¹³ ⲧⲟⲩ ϩⲛ̄ⲕⲁⲩⲉ ⲁϩⲟⲩⲡⲁⲛⲟⲩ, ¹⁴ ϩⲁⲉⲓⲛⲉ ⲁϩⲟⲩⲧⲟⲩⲃⲁⲩ ϩⲛ̄ⲕⲉ-¹⁵ ⲕⲁⲩⲉ ⲁϩⲟⲩⲡⲱϣⲉ. ⲙⲁⲉⲓⲧ
¹⁶ ⲛⲓⲙ ⲁⲩⲕⲓⲙ, ⲁⲩⲱ ⲁⲩϣⲧⲁⲣⲧⲣ̄ ¹⁷ ϫⲉ ⲙⲛ̄ⲧⲟⲩ ⲥⲙ̄ⲛⲉ ⲙ̄ⲙⲉⲩ ¹⁸ ⲟⲩⲧⲉ ⲙ̄ⲛ̄ⲧⲉⲩ ⲥⲧⲁⲥⲓⲥ. ⲉⲥⲉⲗⲁ-
¹⁹ ⲗⲧ ⲛ̄ϭⲓ ϯⲡⲗⲁⲛⲏ ⲉⲛⲥ̄ⲙⲉ ²⁰ ⲉⲛ ϫⲉ ⲉⲩ ⲡⲉ ⲉⲧⲥ̄ⲛⲁⲉⲉⲓϥ. ⲉ[ⲥ]-²¹ ⲙⲁⲕϩ̄ ⲛ̄ϩⲏⲧ ⲉⲥⲛⲉϣⲡⲉ
ⲉⲥ-²² ⲱⲥϥ̄ ⲙ̄ⲙⲁⲥ ⲁⲃⲁⲗ ϫⲉ ⲥⲙ̄ⲙⲉ ²³ ⲉⲛ ⲁⲗⲁⲩⲉ. ⲉⲡⲓⲇⲏ ⲁϥϩⲱⲛ ²⁴ ⲁⲣⲁⲥ ⲛ̄ϭⲓ ⲡⲓⲥⲁⲩⲛⲉ—
ⲉⲧⲉ ⲡⲉⲉⲓ ²⁵ ⲡⲉ ⲡⲓⲧⲉⲕⲟ ⲛ̄ⲧⲉⲥ ⲙⲛ̄ ⲛⲉⲥϯ ²⁶ ⲧⲏⲣⲟⲩ—ϯⲡⲗⲁⲛⲏ ⲥϣⲟⲩⲉⲓⲧ ⲉ-²⁷ ⲙⲛ̄ ⲗⲁⲩⲉ
ⲛ̄ϩⲏⲧⲥ̄.

ⲁⲥⲉⲓ̈ ⲁⲧⲙⲏ-²⁸ ⲧⲉ ⲛ̄ϭⲓ ϯⲙⲛ̄ⲧⲙⲏⲛⲉ, ⲁϩⲟⲩ-²⁹ ⲥⲟⲩⲱⲛⲥ̄ ⲛ̄ϭⲓ ⲛⲓϯ ⲧⲏⲣⲟⲩ ⲛ̄ⲧⲉⲥ ³⁰ ⲁⲩⲣ̄
ⲁⲥⲡⲁⲍⲉ ⲙ̄ⲡⲓⲱⲧ ϩⲛ̄ ⲟⲩⲙⲛ̄-³¹ ⲉ ⲙⲛ̄ ⲟⲩϭⲁⲙ ⲉⲥϫⲏⲕ ⲁⲃⲁⲗ ⲉⲥ-³² ⲧⲱⲧ ⲙ̄ⲙⲁⲩ ⲙⲛ̄ ⲡⲓⲱⲧ. ϫⲉ
ⲟⲩ-³³ ⲁⲛ ⲅⲁⲣ ⲛⲓⲙ ⲉⲧⲙⲁⲓ̈ⲉ ⲛ̄ϯⲙⲛ̄ⲧ-³⁴ ⲙⲏⲛⲉ—ϫⲉ ϯⲙⲛ̄ⲧⲙⲏⲛⲉ ⲡⲉ ⲣⲱϥ ³⁵ ⲙ̄ⲡⲓⲱⲧ· ⲡⲓⲗⲉⲥ
ⲛ̄ⲧⲟⲟⲧϥ̄ ⲡⲉ ⲡⲓ-³⁶ ⲡⲛⲉⲩⲙⲁ ⲉⲧⲟⲩⲁⲁⲃ—ⲡⲉⲧⲧⲱϭⲉ ⲙ̄-²⁷·¹ ⲙⲁϥ ⲁϯⲙⲛ̄ⲧⲙⲏⲛ[ⲉ] ⲉϥⲧⲱϭⲉ ²

25.32 ϣⲁⲥⲣⲉϣⲉ: read ϣⲁϥⲣⲉϣⲉ?
26.12 ϫⲉⲥ: read ϫⲉ ⲉⲓⲥ (Till).
26.22 ⲱⲥϥ̄: read ⲱϩⲥ.

this one is the rest. After he had [21] filled the deficiency, he destroyed [22] the sem-blance—the semblance is [23] the world in which [24] he served. [25] For the place where there is envy [26] and quarreling is deficient. But [27] the place where there is unity [28] is perfect, since the deficiency [29] came about because the [30] Father was not known. Therefore, when [31] the Father comes to be known, the deficiency will cease to exist [32] from that time on. Just as (it is with) [33] a person's ignorance, [34] when he comes to know, [35] his ignorance [36] vanishes by itself, [37] just as when darkness [38] vanishes once light appears, [25.1] so also [2] deficiency vanishes [3] in perfection. Therefore, the sem-blance is not manifest [4] from that time on, rather [5] it will vanish [6] in mingling with unity. [7] Now their works [8] lie scattered; in time [9] the unity will perfect [10] the spaces. Within [11] unity each [12] one will receive himself; within [13] knowledge he will purify himself [14] from a multitude of likenesses into [15] a unity by consuming [16] matter within him [17] like a fire, and darkness [18] by light, death by [19] life.

If then these things have come about [20] for each one of us, [21] then it is fitting for us [22] to be mindful of the Entirety so that [23] this house will be holy [24] and tranquil in the unity. [25] Just as (it is with) some [26] who leave from places [27] having vessels [28] that in places [29] are not great. [30] They would break them, and [31] the master of the house does not suffer loss. Instead [32] <he> rejoices because [33] in place of the bad vessels [34] there are full ones that are [35] perfect. This is the [36] judgment that has come from [26.1] above; it has passed judgment on [2] everyone. It is a sword wielded, [3] double-edged, cutting with [4] both sides. After the Word had come to the middle, [5] the one within [6] the heart of those who utter it [7]—it is not merely a sound, but [8] it became a body—a great [9] disturbance occurred among [10] the vessels because some were [11] empty and others were full, [12] since some had been stocked [13] and others had been poured out, [14] some had been sealed and others [15] had been cracked open. All [16] spaces were jolted, and they became disturbed, [17] since they did not have steadfastness [18] nor did they have stability. [19] Error grew anxious, since she did not know [20] what she would do. She was [21] suffering, in mourning, [22] tearing herself down because she did not know [23] anything. When [24] knowledge—which is the [25] undoing of her and all her emanations [26]—approached her, Error became empty [27] having nothing within.

Truth came to the middle, [28] and all its emanations [29] knew it. [30] They welcomed the Father of truth [31] with a perfect power that joins [32] them with the Father. [33] For, concerning everyone who loves truth [34]—truth is the mouth of [35] the Father; his tongue is the [36] Holy Spirit—the one joined [27.1] to the truth is joined [2] to the Father's

24.18 "resting themselves": or "resting there."

ⲙ̄ⲙⲁϥ ⲁⲣⲱϥ ⲙ̄ⲡⲓⲱⲧ ⲁⲃⲁⲗ ³ ϩⲙ̄ ⲡⲓⲗⲉⲥ ⲛ̄ⲧⲟⲟⲧϥ̄, ⲉϥⲁ- ⁴ ϫⲓ ⲙ̄ⲡⲓⲡⲛⲉⲩⲙⲁ ⲉⲧⲟⲩⲁⲁⲃ, ⁵ ⲉⲡⲉⲉⲓ ⲡⲉ ⲡⲟⲩⲱⲛϩ̄ ⲁⲃⲁⲗ ⲙ̄ⲡⲓ- ⁶ ⲱⲧ ⲁⲩⲱ ⲡϭⲱⲗⲡ̄ ⲁⲃⲁⲗ ⲛ̄ⲧⲉϥ ⁷ ϣⲁ ⲛⲉϥⲁⲓⲱⲛ.

ⲁϥⲟⲩⲱⲛϩ̄ ⲁⲃⲁⲗ ⁸ ⲙ̄ⲡⲓⲡⲉⲑⲏⲡ ⲛ̄ⲧⲟⲟⲧϥ̄· ⲁϥⲃⲁⲗϥ̄ ⁹ ⲁⲃⲁⲗ. ⲛⲓⲙ ⲅⲁⲣ ⲡⲉⲧϣⲱⲡⲉ ⲓ- ¹⁰ ⲙⲏⲧⲓ ⲁⲡⲓⲱⲧ ⲟⲩⲁⲉⲉⲧϥ̄; ⲙⲁ- ¹¹ ⲉⲓⲧ ⲛⲓⲙ ϩⲛ̄ϯ ⲛ̄ⲧⲉϥ ⲛⲉ ⲛ̄ⲧⲁⲩ- ¹² ⲥⲟⲩⲱⲛϥ̄ ϫⲉ ⲛ̄ⲧⲁⲩⲉⲓ ⲁⲃⲁⲗ ¹³ ⲛ̄ϩⲏⲧϥ̄ ⲙ̄ⲡⲣⲏⲧⲉ ⲛ̄ϩⲛ̄ϣⲏ- ¹⁴ ⲣⲉ ⲉⲩϩⲛ̄ ⲟⲩⲣⲱⲙⲉ ⲉϥ- ¹⁵ ϫⲏⲕ ⲁⲃⲁⲗ. ⲛⲉⲩⲥⲁⲩⲛⲉ ⲙ̄- ¹⁶ ⲙⲁϥ ⲡⲉ ϫⲉ ⲛⲉⲙ̄ⲡⲁⲧⲟⲩ- ¹⁷ ϫⲓ ⲙⲟⲣⲫⲏ, ⲟⲩⲧⲉ ⲙ̄ⲡⲁ- ¹⁸ ⲧⲟⲩϫⲓ ⲣⲉⲛ, ⲉⲧⲁϥⲙⲓⲥⲉ ¹⁹ ⲙ̄ⲡⲟⲩⲉ̈ⲓ ⲡⲟⲩⲉⲉⲓ ²⁰ ⲛ̄ϭⲓ ⲡⲓⲱⲧ. ⲧⲟⲧⲉ ⲉⲩϣⲁⲛϫⲓ ⲫⲟⲣⲙⲏ ²¹ ⲙ̄ⲡⲓⲥⲁⲩⲛⲉ ⲛⲧⲟⲟⲧϥ̄, ²² ⲉ̄ⲙ̄ⲙⲁⲛ ⲉⲩⲛ̄ϩⲏⲧϥ̄, ⲥⲉ- ²³ ⲥⲁⲩⲛⲉ ⲙ̄ⲙⲁϥ ⲉⲛ. ⲡⲓⲱⲧ ⲛ̄- ²⁴ ⲧⲁϥ ϥϫⲏⲕ ⲁⲃⲁⲗ, ⲉϥⲥⲁ- ²⁵ ⲛⲉ ⲁⲙⲁⲉⲓⲧ ⲛⲓⲙ ⲉⲧⲛ̄ϩⲏⲧϥ̄. ²⁶ ⲉϣⲱⲡⲉ ⲉϥϣⲁⲛⲟⲩⲱϣⲉ, ²⁷ ⲡⲉⲧϥ̄ⲟⲩ`ⲁ´ϣϥ̄ ϥⲟⲩⲱⲛϩ̄ ⲙ̄ⲙⲁϥ, ²⁸ ⲉϥϯ ⲙⲟⲣⲫⲏ ⲛⲉϥ ⲁⲩⲱ ⲉϥϯ ²⁹ ⲣⲉⲛ ⲛⲉϥ. ⲁⲩⲱ {ⲁⲩⲱ} ϣⲁϥϯ ⲣⲉⲛ ³⁰ ⲛⲉϥ ⲁⲩⲱ ⲉϥⲧⲣⲟ ⲙ̄ⲙⲁϥ ³¹ ⲁⲧⲣⲟⲩϣⲱⲡⲉ, ⲛ̄ⲛⲉⲉⲓ ⲉⲧⲉⲙ̄- ³² ⲡⲁⲧⲟⲩϣⲱⲡⲉ, ⲥⲉⲟⲉⲓ ⲛ̄ⲁⲧ- ³³ ⲥⲁⲩⲛⲉ ⲙ̄ⲡⲉⲛⲧⲁϩⲧⲥⲉⲛⲁⲩ.

³⁴ ⲛⲉⲉⲓϫⲟⲩ ϭⲉ ⲙ̄ⲙⲁⲥ ⲉⲛ ϫⲉ ³⁵ ϩⲛ̄ⲗⲁⲩⲉ ⲛⲉ ⲛⲉⲉⲓ ⲉⲧⲉⲙ̄ⲡⲁ- ³⁶ ⲧⲟⲩϣⲱⲡⲉ. ⲁⲗⲗⲁ ⲥⲉϣⲟⲟⲡ ²⁸·¹ ϩⲙ̄ ⲡⲉⲧⲛⲁⲟⲩⲱϣⲉ ² ⲁⲧⲣⲟⲩϣⲱⲡⲉ ⲉϥϣⲁⲛ- ³ ⲟⲩⲱϣⲉ, ⲙ̄ⲡⲣⲏⲧⲉ ⁴ ⲙ̄ⲡⲕⲁⲓⲣⲟⲥ ⲉⲧⲛ̄ⲛⲏⲩ. ϩⲛⲉⲉⲩ ⁵ ⲛⲓⲙ ⲉⲙⲡⲁⲧⲟⲩⲱⲛ ⲁⲃⲁⲗ ⁶ ϥⲥⲁⲩⲛⲉ ⲛ̄ⲧⲁϥ ⲙ̄ⲡⲉⲧⲛ̄ⲁ- ⁷ ⲛ̄ⲧϥ̄ ⲁⲃⲁⲗ. ⲡⲕⲁⲣⲡⲟⲥ ⲛ̄ⲧⲁϥ ⁸ ⲉⲧⲉⲙ̄ⲡⲁⲧϥ̄ⲟⲩⲱⲛ ⲁⲃⲁⲗ ⁹ ϥⲥⲁⲩⲛⲉ ⲛ̄ⲗⲁⲩⲉ ⲉⲛ, ⲟⲩⲇⲉ ¹⁰ ϥ̄ⲣ̄ ⲗⲁⲩⲉ ⲛ̄ϩⲱⲃ ⲉⲛ. ⲁⲛ ⲡⲓ- ¹¹ ⲣⲏⲧⲉ ⲙⲁⲉⲓⲧ ⲛⲓⲙ ⲉⲧϣⲟⲟⲡ ¹² ϩⲱⲱϥ ϩⲛ̄ ⲡⲓⲱⲧ ϩⲛⲁⲃⲁⲗ ¹³ ϩⲛ̄ ⲡⲉⲧϣⲟⲟⲡ ⲛⲉ, ⲡⲉⲛ- ¹⁴ ⲧⲁϥⲧⲉϩⲁϥ ⲛ̄ⲧⲁϥ ⲁ- ¹⁵ ⲣⲉⲧϥ̄ ⲁⲃⲁⲗ ϩⲛ̄ ⲡⲉⲧϣⲟⲟⲡ ¹⁶ ⲉⲛ. ϫⲉ ⲡⲉⲧⲉⲙ̄ⲛ̄ⲧⲉϥ ⲛⲟⲩ- ¹⁷ ⲛⲉ ⲙ̄ⲙⲉⲩ ⲙⲛ̄ⲧⲉϥ ⲟⲩ- ¹⁸ ⟦ⲁ..⟧ⲧⲁϩ ⲙ̄ⲙⲉⲩ ⲁⲛ, ⲁⲗ- ¹⁹ ⲗⲁ ⲉϥⲙⲉⲩⲉ ⲛⲉϥ ²⁰ ϫⲉ « ⲁϩⲓ̈ϣⲱⲡⲉ » ⲉⲓⲧⲉ ⲁⲛ ²¹ ϥⲛⲁⲃⲱⲗ ⲁⲃⲁⲗ ϩⲓ̈ⲧⲟⲟⲧϥ̄. ²² ⲉⲧⲃⲉ ⲡⲉⲉⲓ ⲡⲉⲧⲉⲛⲉϥϣⲟ- ²³ ⲟⲡ ⲡⲧⲏⲣϥ̄ ⲉⲛ ⲉϥⲛⲁ- ²⁴ ϣⲱⲡⲉ ⲉⲛ ⲁⲛ. ⲉⲩ ϭⲉ ⲡⲉⲧ`ⲁ´ϥ- ²⁵ ⲟⲩⲁϣϥ̄ ⲁⲧⲣⲉϥⲙⲉⲩⲉ ⲁⲣⲁϥ; ²⁶ ϫⲉ « ⲁⲉⲓϣⲱⲡⲉ ⲙ̄ⲡⲣⲏⲧⲉ ⲛ̄ⲛⲓ- ²⁷ ϩⲁⲉⲓⲃⲉ ⲙⲛ̄ ⲛⲓⲫⲁⲛⲧⲁⲥⲓⲁ ²⁸ ⲛ̄ⲧⲟⲩϣⲏ ». ⲡ̄ϭⲓⲛ̄ⲧⲣⲉϥⲣ̄ ²⁹ ⲟⲩⲁⲉⲓⲛ ⲛ̄ϭⲓ ⲡⲟⲩⲁⲉⲓⲛ ⲉⲑ̄ⲣ̄ⲧⲉ ³⁰ ⲉⲛⲧⲁϥϫⲓⲧⲥ ⲛ̄ϭⲓ ⲡⲉⲉⲓ ⲉⲧⲙ̄- ³¹ ⲙⲉⲩ, ⲉϥϣⲁϥⲙ̄ⲙⲉ ϫⲉ ⲟⲩⲗⲁⲩ- ³² ⲉ ⲡⲉ.

ⲡⲣⲏⲧⲉ ⲛⲉⲩⲟⲉⲓ ⲛ̄ⲁⲧ- ³³ ⲥⲁⲩⲛⲉ ⲁⲡⲓⲱⲧ, ⲉⲛⲧⲁϥ ⲡⲉ ²⁹·¹ ⲉⲛⲉⲩⲛⲉⲩ ⲁⲣⲁϥ ⲉⲛ. ⲉⲡⲓⲇⲏ ⲛⲉ- ² ϥⲟⲉⲓ ⲛ̄ⲟⲩϩⲣ̄ⲧⲉ ⲙⲛ̄ ⲟⲩϣⲧⲣ̄- ³ ⲧⲣ̄ ⲙⲛ̄ ⲟⲩⲙⲛ̄ⲧⲁⲧⲧⲱⲕ ⲁⲣⲉⲧⲥ̄ ⁴ ⲙⲛ̄ ⲟⲩⲙⲛ̄ⲧϩⲏⲧ ⲥⲛⲉⲩ ⲙⲛ̄ ⲟⲩ- ⁵ ⲡⲱϣⲉ, ⲛⲉⲩⲛ̄ ϩⲁϩ ⲙ̄ⲙⲛ̄ⲧⲁ- ⁶ ⲡⲟⲗⲁ ⲉⲩⲣ̄ ϩⲱϥ ⲁⲃⲁⲗ ϩⲓⲧⲟ- ⁷ ⲟⲧϥ̄ ⲛ̄ⲛⲉⲉⲓ, ⲟⲩⲁϩⲛ̄ <ϩⲛ̄>ⲙⲛ̄<ⲧ>ⲁⲧ- ⁸ ⲥⲃⲱ ⲉⲩϣⲟⲩⲉⲓⲧ ⲙ̄ⲡⲣⲏⲧⲉ ⁹ ⲉϣⲁⲣⲟⲩⲥⲙ̄ⲛ̄ⲧⲟⲩ ⲁⲡⲛ̄ⲕⲁⲧ- ¹⁰ ⲕⲉ, ⲛ̄ⲥⲉⲥⲓⲛⲉ ⲙ̄ⲙⲁⲩ ϩⲛ̄ ⲛ̄ⲣⲉ- ¹¹ ⲥⲟⲩⲉ ⲉⲩϣ̄ⲧⲣ̄ⲧⲁⲣⲧ. ⲏ ⲟⲩⲙⲁ ¹² ⲡⲉⲧⲟⲩⲡⲱⲧ ⲁⲣⲁϥ, ⲏ ⲉⲩⲟ ⲛ̄- ¹³ ⲁⲧⲛⲁⲙⲧⲉ ⲉⲩⲉⲓ ⲉⲁⲩⲡⲱⲧ ¹⁴ ⲛ̄ⲥⲁ ϩⲛ̄ϩⲁⲉⲓⲛⲉ, ⲏ ⲉⲩϩⲛ̄ ϩⲛ̄- ¹⁵ ⲙⲛ̄ⲧⲧⲁⲉⲓⲥϣⲉ, ⲏ ⲉⲩϣⲟⲡ ¹⁶ {ϩ}ⲛ̄ϩⲛ̄ⲥⲱϣⲉ ⲛ̄ⲧⲉⲩ, ⲏ ⲉⲁⲩϩⲁ- ¹⁷ ⲉⲓⲉ ⲁⲃⲁⲗ ϩⲛ̄ ϩⲛ̄ⲙⲁ ⲉⲩϫⲁⲥⲓ, ¹⁸ ⲏ ⲉⲩⲥⲱⲕ ⲁϩⲣⲏⲓ̈ ⲁⲃⲁⲗ ¹⁹ ϩⲓⲧⲟⲟⲧϥ̄ ⲙ̄ⲡⲁⲏⲣ ⲉⲙⲛ̄ ⲧⲛ̄ϩ ⲣⲱ ⲙ̄ⲙⲁⲩ. ²⁰ ϩⲛ̄ⲥⲁⲡ ⲁⲛ ⲉⲓϣϫⲉ ϩⲁⲉⲓⲛⲉ ²¹ ⲛⲉⲧϩⲁⲗϩⲗ̄ ⲙ̄ⲙⲁⲩ ⲉⲙⲛ̄ ⲡⲉⲧ- ²² ⲡⲱⲧ ⲣⲱ ⲛ̄ⲥⲱⲟⲩ, ⲏ ⲛ̄ⲧⲁⲩ ⲉⲩ- ²³ ⲙⲟⲩⲟⲩⲧ ⲛ̄ⲛⲉⲧϩⲓ̈ⲧⲟⲩϣⲟⲩ ²⁴ ϫⲉ ⲁⲩϫⲱϩⲙ̄ ⲁⲃⲁⲗ ϩⲓⲧⲟⲟ- ²⁵ ⲧϥ̄ ⲙ̄ⲡⲥⲛⲁϥ ⲛ̄ⲛⲉⲉⲓ. ϣⲁ ²⁶ ⲡⲥⲁⲡ ⲉⲧⲉϣⲁⲩⲛⲉϩⲥⲉ ⲛ̄ϭⲓ ²⁷ ⲛⲉⲉⲓ· ⲉⲧⲉϣⲁⲩϣⲉ

27.9–10 ⲡⲉⲧϣⲱⲡⲉ ⲓⲙⲏⲧⲓ: can also be understood as ⲡⲉⲧϣⲱⲡ ⲉⲓⲙⲏⲧⲓ.

27.11 ϯ: Grobel and others understand this to be a variant form of ϯⲏ.

29.6 ϩⲱϥ: read ϩⲱⲃ.

mouth [3] by his tongue, [4] having received the Holy Spirit, [5] since this is the appearance of the Father [6] and his revelation [7] to his eternities.

He revealed [8] his hidden aspect; he explained it. [9] For who exists except [10] the Father alone? [11] All spaces are his gifts. They [12] knew that they had come from [13] within him like children [14] who are within an adult man. [15] They knew [16] that they had not yet [17] received form, nor had [18] they received names, each one of which [19] the Father births. [20] When they receive form [21] from his knowledge, [22] while indeed they are within him, they [23] do not know him. His Father [24] is perfect, knowing [25] all the spaces within him. [26] If he wills, [27] the one he wills he reveals, [28] giving form to him and naming [29] him. He names [30] him and makes him [31] so that those come to be who, [32] before they come into existence, are [33] ignorant of the one who formed them.

[34] I have not said, therefore, that [35] those who have not yet come into being are nothing. [36] Rather, they exist [28.1] in the one who shall will [2] that they come into being when he [3] wills, like [4] the time that is coming. [5] Before everything comes into being, [6] he knows what he will [7] make. (But) his fruit [8] that has not yet come into being [9] does not know anything, nor [10] does it do anything. Moreover, [11] every space that also exists within [12] the Father is from [13] the one that exists, the one [14] who established it [15] out of that which does not exist. [16] The one who does not have a root [17] also has [18] no fruit, but [19] although he thinks about himself [20] "I have come to be," [21] he will be destroyed by his own means. [22] For this reason, the one who did not exist [23] at all will [24] not come to be. What, then, is it that he [25] desired to lead him to believe about himself? [26] That "I have come to be like the [27] shadows and phantasms [28] of the night." When the light shines [29] on the fear [30] that that person has endured, [31] he knows that it is [32] nothing.

Thus they were [33] ignorant of the Father, because he is the one whom [29.1] they did not see. Since [2] it was fear and disturbance [3] and insecurity [4] and double-mindedness and [5] dissension, there were many illusions [6] at work by means of [7] these, and (there were) many vain [8] falsehoods as though [9] they were deep in sleep, [10] finding themselves in a nightmare. [11] Either (there is) a place [12] to which they are hastening, or [13] powerless they arrive after having chased [14] after others, or they are [15] fighting, or they are [16] being fought, or they have fallen [17] from high places, [18] or they glide up into [19] the air without even having wings. [20] Occasionally, moreover, (it seems as) if some [21] kill them even though there is no one [22] even chasing them, or they are the ones [23] killing those beside them [24] because they have been defiled by [25] their blood. [26] Once those who [27]

27.4 "having received": or "whenever he receives."
27.9 "For who exists": or "For who contains."
27.11 "gifts": or "emanations."
27.14 "adult man": or "perfect man."

ϩⲛ̄ ⲛⲉⲉⲓ [28] ⲧⲏⲣⲟⲩ, ⲙⲁⲩⲛⲉⲩ ⲁⲗⲁⲩⲉ [29] ⲛ̄ϭⲓ ⲛⲉⲉⲓ ⲉⲧⲉ ⲛⲉⲟⲩⲛ ϩⲣⲏⲓ̈ [30] ϩⲛ̄ ⲛⲉⲉⲓ ⲧⲏⲣⲟⲩ
ⲛ̄ϣⲧⲁⲣⲧⲣ̄ [31] ⲁⲃⲁⲗ, ϫⲉ ⲛⲉϩⲛ̄ⲗⲁⲩⲉ ⲛⲉ [32] ⲛⲉⲉⲓ. ⲙ̄ⲡⲓⲣⲏⲧⲉ ⲡⲣⲏⲧⲉ ⲡⲉ [33] ⲡⲉⲉⲓ ⲛ̄ⲛⲉⲛⲧⲁⲩⲛⲟⲩϫⲉ
[34] ⲛ̄ⲧⲙⲛ̄ⲧⲁⲧⲥⲁⲩⲛⲉ ⲁⲃⲁⲗ [35] ⲙ̄ⲙⲁⲩ ⲙ̄ⲡⲣⲏⲧⲉ ⲙ̄ⲡⲛ̄ⲕⲁ- [36] ⲧⲕⲉ, ⲉⲙⲁⲅⲁⲡϥ̄ ϫⲉ ⲟⲩⲗⲁⲩⲉ [37] ⲡⲉ,
ⲟⲩⲇⲉ ⲙⲁⲩⲱⲡ ⲛ̄ⲛⲉϥ- [30.1] ⲕⲉϩⲃⲏⲩⲉ ϫⲉ ϩⲛ̄ϩⲃⲏⲩⲉ ⲉⲩ- [2] ⲥⲙ̄ⲙⲁⲛⲧ̄ ⲛⲉ. ⲁⲗⲗⲁ ϣⲁⲟⲩ- [3] ⲕⲁⲁⲩ
ⲛ̄ⲥⲱⲟⲩ ⲙ̄ⲡⲣⲏⲧⲉ ⲛ̄- [4] ⲟⲩⲣⲉⲥⲟⲩⲉ ϩⲛ̄ ⲧⲟⲩϣⲏ. ⲡⲓⲥⲁⲩ- [5] ⲛⲉ ⲛ̄ⲧⲉ ⲡⲓⲱⲧ ⲛ̄ⲥⲉϣⲓⲧϥ̄ ⲉ- [6]
ⲡⲟⲩⲁⲉⲓⲛ ⲡⲉ. ⲡⲣⲏⲧⲉ ⲡⲉ ⲡⲉⲉⲓ [7] ⲛ̄ⲧⲁϥⲉⲉⲓϥ, ⲉϥⲛ̄ⲕⲁⲧⲕⲉ ⲛ̄- [8] ϭⲓ ⲡⲟⲩⲉⲓ ⲡⲟⲩⲉⲉⲓ ⲙ̄ⲡⲥⲁⲡ [9]
ⲉⲛⲉϥϭⲟⲉⲓ ⲛ̄ⲁⲧⲥⲁⲩⲛⲉ. [10] ⲟⲩⲁϩⲁ ⲡⲣⲏⲧⲉ ⲡⲉ ⲡⲉⲉⲓ ⲛ̄- [11] ⲧⲣⲉϥⲥⲁⲧⲛⲉ ⲕⲁⲧⲁ ⲑⲉ ⲛ̄- [12] ⲧⲁϥⲛⲉϩⲥⲉ,
ⲁⲩⲱ ⲟⲩⲡⲉⲧⲛⲁ- [13] ⲛⲟⲩϥ ⲙ̄ⲡⲣⲱⲙⲉ ⲉⲧⲁⲥⲧⲁϥ [14] ⲛ̄ϥ̄ⲛⲉϩⲥⲉ, ⲟⲩⲁϩⲛ̄ ⲟⲩⲙⲁⲕⲁ- [15] ⲣⲓⲟⲥ ⲡⲉ
ⲡⲉⲉⲓ ⲛ̄ⲧⲁϥⲟⲩⲏⲛ [16] ⲁⲛⲃⲉⲗ ⲛ̄ⲛⲓⲃⲗ̄ⲉⲉⲩ.

ⲟⲩⲁϩ [17] ⲁϥⲡⲱⲧ ⲛⲥⲱϥ ⲛ̄ϭⲓ ⲡⲓⲡⲛⲉⲩⲙⲁ [18] ⲉⲧⲏⲥ ⲁⲃⲁⲗ ϩⲛ̄ ⲡⲧⲣⲉϥ- [19] ⲧⲟⲩⲛⲁⲥϥ̄. ⲉⲁϥϯ
ⲧⲟⲟⲧϥ̄ [20] ⲙ̄ⲡⲉⲧϣⲏϣ ⲁϩⲣⲏⲓ̈ ϩⲓ ⲡⲉ- [21] ⲥⲛⲧ ⲁϥⲧⲣⲉϥⲧⲱⲕ ⲁⲣⲉⲧϥ̄ [22] ⲁϫⲛ̄ ⲛⲉϥⲟⲩⲉⲣⲓⲧⲉ ϫⲉ
ⲛⲉ- [23] ⲙ̄ⲡⲁⲧϥ̄ⲧⲱⲟⲩⲛ. ⲇⲉ ⲡⲉ ⲡⲓⲥⲁⲩ- [24] ⲛⲉ ⲛ̄ⲧⲙ̄ ⲡⲓⲱⲧ ⲟⲩⲁϩⲁ ⲡⲟⲩ- [25] ⲱⲛϩ̄ ⲁⲃⲁⲗ
ⲙ̄ⲡⲉϥϣⲏⲣⲉ ⲁϥ- [26] ϯ ⲛⲉⲩ ⲣⲓⲧⲉ ⲁⲙⲙⲉ. ⲛ̄- [27] ⲧⲁⲣⲟⲩⲛⲉⲩ ⲅⲁⲣ ⲁⲣⲁϥ ⲁⲩⲱ ⲁⲩ- [28] ⲥⲱⲧⲙ̄
ⲁⲣⲁϥ, ⲁϥϯ ⲛⲉⲩ ⲁⲧⲣⲟⲩ- [29] ϫⲓ ϯⲡⲉ ⲁⲃⲁⲗ ⲙ̄ⲙⲁϥ, ⲟⲩⲁϩⲛ̄ [30] ⲁⲧⲟⲩϣⲁⲗⲙⲉϥ, ⲟⲩⲁϩⲛ̄ⲛ
ⲧⲟⲩⲉⲙⲁϩⲧⲉ ⲁϫⲛ̄ ⲡϣⲣⲙⲛ̄- [31] ⲣⲓⲧ.

ⲉⲁϥⲟⲩⲱⲛϩ̄ ⲁⲃⲁⲗ [32] ⲉϥⲧⲁⲙⲟ ⲙ̄ⲙⲁⲩ ⲁⲡⲓⲱⲧ, ⲡⲓ- [33] ⲁⲧϣⲁⲡϥ̄. ⲉⲁϥⲛⲓϥⲉ ⲛ̄ϩⲏⲧⲟⲩ [34] ⲙ̄ⲡⲉⲧϩⲛ̄
ⲡⲓⲙⲉⲉⲩⲉ, ⲉϥⲉⲓ- [35] ⲣⲉ ⲙ̄ⲡⲉϥⲟⲩⲱϣⲉ, ⲉⲁⲩϫⲓ ⲙ̄- [36] ⲡⲟⲩⲁⲉⲓⲛ ⲛ̄ϭⲓ ϩⲁϩ. ⲁⲩⲕⲁⲧⲟⲩ [31.1] ⲁⲣⲁϥ.
ϫⲉ ⲛⲉⲩϭⲉⲓ ⲛ̄ϣⲙ̄ⲙⲟ ⲡⲉ ⲁⲩⲱ ⲛⲉⲩⲛⲉⲩ ⲁⲡⲉϥⲉⲓⲛⲉ ⲉⲛ [3] ⲡⲉ, ⲁⲩⲱ ⲛⲉⲙ̄ⲡⲟⲩⲥⲟⲩⲱ- [4] ⲛϥ̄ ⲛ̄ϭⲓ
ⲑⲩⲗⲏ. ϫⲉ ⲛ̄ⲧⲁϥⲉⲓ ⲁ- [5] ⲃⲁⲗ ϩⲓⲧⲟⲟⲧⲥ̄ ⲛ̄ⲟⲩⲥⲁⲣⲝ ⲛ̄- [6] ⲥⲙⲁⲧ, ⲉⲙⲡⲉⲗⲁⲩⲉ ϩⲱⲥ ⲛ̄ⲧϭⲛ- [7]
ⲙⲁⲁⲣⲉ ⲛ̄ⲧⲟⲟⲧϥ̄ ϫⲉ ϯⲙⲛ̄ⲧ- [8] ⲁⲧⲧⲉⲕⲟ <ⲟⲩ>ⲙⲛ̄ⲧⲁⲧⲉⲙⲁϩⲧⲉ [9] ⲙ̄ⲙⲁⲥ ⲧⲉ. ⲉϥϣⲉϫⲉ ⲁⲛ [10]
ϩⲛ̄ ϩⲃⲃⲣⲉ ϫⲓⲛ ⲉϥϣⲉϫⲉ ⲁ- [11] ⲡⲉⲧϩⲛ̄ ⲫⲏⲧ ⲙ̄ⲡⲓⲱⲧ, ⲉⲁϥ- [12] ⲉⲓⲛⲉ ⲁⲃⲁⲗ ⲙ̄ⲡϣⲉϫⲉ ⲛⲁⲧ- [13]
ϣⲧⲁ.

ⲉⲁϥϣⲉϫⲉ ⲁⲃⲁⲗ ϩⲛ̄ [14] ⲣⲁϥ ⲛ̄ϭⲓ ⲡⲟⲩⲁⲉⲓⲛ, [15] ⲟⲩⲁϩⲛ̄ ϯⲥⲙⲏ ⲛ̄ⲧⲟⲟⲧϥ̄ [16] ⲛ̄ⲧⲁⲥⲙⲓⲥⲉ ⲙ̄ⲡⲓⲱⲛϩ̄,
ⲁϥ- [17] ϯ ⲛⲉⲩ ⲙⲉⲩⲉ ϩⲓ ⲙⲛ̄ⲧⲣⲙ̄ⲛ̄ϩⲏⲧ [18] ϩⲓ ⲛⲁϩ ϩⲓ ⲟⲩⲭⲉⲉⲓⲇⲉ ϩⲓ ⲡⲓⲡⲛⲉⲩⲙⲁ ⲛ̄- [19] ϭⲁⲙ ⲁⲃⲁⲗ
ϩⲛ̄ ϯⲙⲛ̄<ⲁⲧ>ⲁⲣⲏϫⲥ̄ ⲛ̄- [20] ⲧⲉ ⲡⲓⲱⲧ ⲟⲩⲁϩⲛ̄ ϯⲙⲛ̄ⲧϩⲗⲁϭ. [21] ⲉⲁⲩⲧⲣⲟⲩⲱϫⲛ̄
ⲛ̄ϭⲓ ⲛⲓⲕⲟⲗⲁⲥⲓⲥ [22] ⲙⲛ̄ ⲛⲓⲙⲁⲥⲧⲓⲅⲝ—ϫⲉ ⲛ̄ⲧⲁⲩ ⲡⲉⲧⲉ- [23] ⲛⲉⲩⲥⲁⲣⲙ̄ ⲛ̄ϩⲣⲉϥ ⲛ̄ⲛⲓϩⲁⲉⲓⲛⲉ [24]
ⲛ̄ⲧⲁⲩⲣ ϩⲁⲉ ⲙ̄ⲡⲓⲛⲁϩ ⲛ̄ϩⲣⲏⲓ ϩⲛ̄ [25] ϯⲡⲗⲁⲛⲏ ⲟⲩⲁϩⲛ̄ ϩⲛ̄ⲥⲛⲉϩ—[26] ⲁⲩⲱ ⲙⲛ̄ ⲟⲩϭⲁⲙ ⲁϥⲃⲁⲗⲟⲩ
ⲁ- [27] ⲃⲁⲗ, ⲁⲩⲱ ⲁϥϫⲡⲁⲩ ϩⲛ̄ ⲡⲥⲁⲩⲛⲉ [28] ⲡⲉ. ⲁϥϣⲱⲡⲉ ⲉϥⲟⲉⲓ ⲛ̄ⲟⲩ- [29] ⲙⲁⲉⲓⲧ ⲛ̄ⲛⲉⲉⲓ
ⲉⲛⲉⲩⲥⲁⲣⲙ̄ [30] ⲁⲩⲱ ⲟⲩⲥⲁⲩⲛⲉ ⲛ̄ⲛⲉⲉⲓ ⲉⲧⲟⲓ̈ [31] ⲛ̄ⲁⲧⲥⲁⲩⲛⲉ, ⲟⲩϭⲓⲛⲉ ⲛ̄ⲛⲉⲉⲓ ⲉ- [32] ⲛⲉⲩϣⲓⲛⲉ
ⲟⲩⲁϩⲛ̄ ⲟⲩⲧⲁϫⲣⲟ [33] ⲛ̄ⲛⲉⲉⲓ ⲉⲧⲉⲛⲉⲩⲛⲁⲉⲓⲛ ⲁⲣⲁⲩ, [34] ⲟⲩⲙⲛ̄ⲧⲁⲧϫⲱϩⲙ̄ ⲛ̄ⲛⲉⲉⲓ ⲉⲧⲉ- [35]
ⲛⲉⲩϫⲁϩⲙ̄.

ⲉⲛⲧⲁϥ ⲡⲉ ⲡϣⲱⲥ [36] ⲉⲛⲧⲁϩⲕⲱⲉ ⲛ̄ⲥⲱϥ ⲙ̄ⲡⲓⲡⲥⲧⲉ- [32.1] ϯⲥ ⲛ̄ⲉⲥⲁⲩ ⲉⲧⲉⲙ̄ⲡⲟⲩⲥⲱⲣⲙ̄. [2] ⲁϥⲉⲓ
ⲁϥϣⲓⲛⲉ ⲛ̄ⲥⲁ ⲡⲉⲉⲓ ⲛ̄ⲧⲁϥ- [3] ⲥⲱⲣⲙ̄. ⲁϥⲣⲉϣⲉ ⲛ̄ⲧⲁⲣⲉϥ- [4] ϭⲓⲛⲉ ⲙ̄ⲙⲁϥ ϫⲉ ⲡⲓⲡⲥⲧⲉⲩⲉⲓⲥ [5]
ⲟⲩⲱⲡ ⲡⲉ ⲉϥϩⲛ̄ ⲧϭⲓϫ ⲛ̄ϭⲃⲟⲩⲣ [6] ⲉⲥⲉⲙⲁϩⲧⲉ ⲙ̄ⲙⲁϥ. ⲡⲥⲁⲡ [7] ⲛ̄ⲧⲁϥ ⲉⲧⲟⲩⲛⲁϭⲓⲛⲉ ⲙ̄ⲡⲟⲩ- [8]

30.11 ⲥⲁⲧⲛⲉ: read ⲥⲁⲩⲛⲉ.

31.23 ⲥⲁⲣⲙ̄: variant of ⲥⲱⲣⲙ̄.

endure [28] all these things awaken, they do not see anything, [29] those who experienced [30] all these disturbances, [31] because these things are nothing. [32] This is the way [33] of those who have cast out [34] ignorance from [35] them like sleep, [36] since they do not consider it to be anything, [37] nor do they consider its [30.1] other works as [2] established works. Rather they [3] leave them behind like [4] a dream in the night. The knowledge [5] of the Father they crave [6] as though it is the light. This is the way [7] each one has acted, [8] as one sleeping when [9] he was ignorant. [10] And this is the way [11] he has come to know, as though [12] he has awakened, and good [13] it is for the man who will return [14] and awaken, and blessed [15] is the one who has opened [16] the eyes of the blind.

And [17] the Spirit [18] who hastened from [19] rousing him pursued him. Having extended his hand [20] to the one lying on the [21] ground, he helped him [22] to his feet, since [23] he was not yet standing. The knowledge [24] of the Father and the revelation [25] of his son he [26] gave them a way to know. [27] For once they saw and [28] heard him, he made it possible for them to [29] taste him, [30] to smell him, and to grasp the beloved [31] son.

When he had appeared [32] he informed them about the Father, the [33] incomprehensible one. Having breathed into them [34] that which is within the thought, doing [35] his will, many received [36] the light. They turned [31.1] to him. Because they were strangers, [2] and they had not seen his image, [3] the material ones had not known [4] him. He came [5] by means of a fleshly [6] form, and nothing hindered [7] his journey because incorruption [8] is indomitable. [9] Moreover, he speaks [10] new things, since he speaks about [11] what is in the heart of the Father, who has [12] brought forth the immaculate [13] word.

When light had spoken through [14] his mouth, [15] along with his voice [16] that generated life, he [17] gave them thought and understanding [18] and mercy and salvation and the spirit of [19] power from the limitlessness and sweetness of [20] the Father. [21] Having brought chastisements [22] and lashings to an end—because they were [23] leading away from his face [24] in error and in fetters some [25] who needed mercy—[26] with might he destroyed them, [27] and he convicted them with knowledge. [28] He became a [29] path for those who had gone astray [30] and knowledge for those who are [31] ignorant, discovery for those who [32] were seeking and strength [33] for those who were trembling, [34] purification for those who were [35] defiled.

He is the shepherd [36] who left behind the ninety-nine [32.1] sheep that had not strayed. [2] He went and sought after the one that [3] had strayed. He rejoiced when he [4] found it because ninety-nine [5] is the number in the left hand [6] since it holds it. When [7] the one is found, [8]

30.23 "not yet standing": or "not yet risen."
31.8 "indomitable": or "incomprehensible."

ⲉⲉⲓ, ϣⲁⲣⲉⲡⲱⲡ ⲧⲏⲣϥ̄ ⟦ⲁⲧⲟⲩ⟧ ⁹ ⲡⲱϣⲛⲉ ⲁⲧⲟⲩⲛⲉⲙ. ⲡⲓⲣⲏⲧⲉ ¹⁰ ⲡⲉⲧϣⲁⲁⲧ ⲙ̄ⲡⲟⲩⲉⲉⲓ—
ⲉⲧⲉ ¹¹ ⲧⲉⲉⲓ ⲧⲉ ⲧⲟⲩⲛⲉⲙ ⲧⲏⲣⲥ̄—ⲉⲧⲉ- ¹² ϣⲁⲥⲥⲱⲕ ⲙ̄ⲡⲉⲛⲧⲁϩⲣ̄ ϣⲧⲁ ⲛ̄ⲥ- ¹³ ϫⲓ ⲙ̄ⲙⲁϥ ⲁⲃⲁⲗ
ϩⲓⲧⲟⲟⲧⲥ̄ ⲛ̄ⲧ̄- ¹⁴ ⲧⲁⲉⲓⲉ ⲛ̄ⲅⲃⲟⲩⲣ ⲛ̄ϥⲡⲱⲛⲉ ⲛ̄ⲧⲟⲩ- ¹⁵ ⲛⲉⲙ, ⲁⲩⲱ ⲡⲓⲣⲏⲧⲉ ⲛ̄ⲧⲉⲡⲱⲡ ¹⁶ ⲣ̄ ϣⲉ.
ⲡⲓⲙⲁⲉⲓⲛⲉ ⲙ̄ⲡⲉⲧⲛ̄ ¹⁷ ⲡⲟⲩϩⲣⲁⲩ. ⲡⲉ ⲡⲓⲱⲧ ⲡⲉ ⲡⲉⲉⲓ. ¹⁸ ⲕⲁⲛ ϩⲛ̄ ⲧⲁⲃⲁⲧⲧⲟⲛ ⲉⲡⲉⲥⲁⲩ ¹⁹
ⲛ̄ⲧⲁϥϭⲓⲛⲧϥ̄ ⲉⲁϥϩⲁⲉⲓⲉ ⲁⲡⲓ- ²⁰ ϩⲓⲉⲓⲧ ⲁϥⲣ̄ ϩⲱⲃ ⲁⲣⲁϥ. ⲁϥⲧⲛ̄ϩⲟ ²¹ ⲙ̄ⲡⲉⲥⲁⲩ ⲉⲁϥⲛ̄ⲧϥ̄ ⲁϩⲣⲏⲓ̈
²² ϩⲛ̄ ⲡⲓϩⲓⲉⲓⲧ ϫⲉⲕⲁⲥⲉ ⲉⲣⲉⲧⲁ- ²³ ⲙ̄ⲙⲉ ⲛ̄ϩⲏⲧ ³⁸—ⲛ̄ⲧⲱⲧⲛ̄ ⲛⲉ ⲛⲓϣⲏⲣⲉ ⲛ̄ⲧⲉ ⲡⲙ̄ⲙⲉ ³⁹
ⲛ̄ϩⲏⲧ—²³ cont'd. ϫⲉ ⲉⲩ ⲡⲉ ⲡⲥⲁⲃ- ²⁴ ⲃⲁⲧⲟⲛ, ⲡⲉⲉⲓ ⲉⲧⲉⲙⲉϣϣⲉ ⲛ̄- ²⁵ ⲧⲉⲡⲟⲩϫⲉⲉⲓ ⲟⲩⲱⲥϥ̄
ⲛ̄ϩⲏⲧϥ̄, ²⁶ ϫⲉⲕⲁⲥⲉ ⲉⲣⲉⲧⲛ̄ϣⲉϫⲉ ⲁⲃⲁⲗ ²⁷ ϩⲛ̄ ⲡⲓϩⲱⲟⲩ ⲉⲧⲛ̄ϩⲣⲏⲉⲓ, ⲡⲉⲉⲓ ²⁸ ⲉⲧⲉ ⲙⲛ̄ⲧⲉϥ
ⲟⲩϣⲏ ⲙ̄ⲙⲉⲩ, ²⁹ ⲟⲩⲁϩⲛ̄ ⲁⲃⲁⲗ ϩⲙ̄ ⲡⲟⲩⲁⲉⲓⲛ ³⁰ ⲉⲧⲉⲙⲁϥϩⲱⲧⲡ̄ ϫⲉ ϥϫⲏⲕ ⲁⲃⲁⲗ.

³¹ ϣⲉϫⲉ ϭⲉ ⲁⲃⲁⲗ ϩⲙ̄ ⲫⲏⲧ ϫⲉ ³² ⲛ̄ⲧⲱⲧⲛ̄ⲛⲉ ⲡⲉ ⲡⲓϩⲱⲟⲩ ⲉⲧϫⲏⲕ ³³ ⲁⲃⲁⲗ ⲁⲩⲱ ⲉϥⲟⲩⲏϩ ϩⲛ̄
ⲧⲏⲛⲉ ³⁴ ⲛ̄ϭⲓ ⲡⲟⲩⲁⲉⲓⲛ ⲉⲧⲉⲙⲁϥϫⲱⲭⲛ̄. ³⁵ ϣⲉϫⲉ ⲁⲧⲙⲏⲉ ⲙⲛ̄ ⲛⲉⲉⲓ ⲉⲧϣⲓ- ³⁶ ⲛⲉ ⲛ̄ⲥⲱⲥ ⲁⲩⲱ
ⲡⲥⲁⲩⲛⲉ ⲛ̄ⲛⲉⲉⲓ ³⁷ ⲛ̄ⲧⲁⲩⲣ̄ ⲛⲁⲃⲓ ⲛ̄ϩⲣⲏⲉⲓ ϩⲛ̄ ⲧⲟⲩⲡⲗⲁⲛ`ⲏ´. ³³·¹ ⲧⲁϩⲣⲟ ⲛ̄ⲧⲟⲩⲣⲓⲧⲉ ⲛ̄ⲛⲉⲉⲓ ⲛ̄- ²
ⲧⲁϩⲥⲗⲁⲧⲉ, ⲟⲩⲁϩⲁ ⲥⲱⲧ ⲛ̄ⲛⲉ- ³ ⲧⲛ̄ϭⲓϫ ⲁⲛⲉⲉⲓ ⲉⲧϣⲱⲛⲉ. ⲥⲁⲛϣ̄ ⁴ ⲛ̄ⲛⲉⲉⲓ ⲉⲧϩⲕⲉⲉⲓⲧ, ⲁⲩⲱ
ⲛⲉⲧϩⲁ- ⁵ ⲥⲓ ⲛ̄ⲧⲉⲧⲛ̄ⲧ ⲙ̄ⲧⲁⲛ ⲛ̄ⲛⲉⲩ, ⲛ̄ⲧⲉ- ⁶ ⲧⲛ̄ⲧⲟⲩⲛⲉⲥ ⲛⲉⲉⲓ ⲉⲧⲟⲩⲱϣⲉ ⲁ- ⁷ ⲧⲱⲟⲛ,
ⲛ̄ⲧⲉⲧⲛ̄ⲛⲉϩⲥⲉ ⲛ̄ⲛⲉⲧⲛ̄- ⁸ ⲕⲁⲧⲕⲉ. ⲛ̄ⲧⲱⲧⲛ̄ ⲛ̄ⲅⲁⲣ ⲧⲉ ⲧⲙⲛ̄ⲧ- ⁹ ⲣⲙ̄ⲛϩⲏⲧ ⲉⲧⲧⲁⲕⲙ̄. ⲉϣⲱⲡⲉ
ⲉⲣⲉ- ¹⁰ ϣⲁⲛⲡⲧⲱⲕ ⲣ̄ ϯϩⲉ, ϣⲁϥⲧⲱⲕ ¹¹ ⲛ̄ϩⲟⲩⲟ. ϫⲓ ϩⲣⲏⲧⲛ̄ ⲁⲣⲱⲧⲛ̄ ⲙ̄ⲙⲓⲛ ¹² {ⲙⲓⲛ} ⲙ̄ⲙⲱⲧⲛ̄.
ⲙ̄ⲡⲣ̄ϫⲓ ϩⲣⲏⲧⲛ̄ ⲁϩⲛ̄- ¹³ ⲕⲁⲩⲉ ⲉⲧⲉ ⲛⲉⲉⲓ ⲛⲉ ⲛ̄ⲧⲁⲧⲉⲧⲛ̄- ¹⁴ ⲛⲁϫⲟⲩ ⲁⲃⲁⲗ ⲙ̄ⲙⲱⲧⲛ̄. ⲛⲉⲛⲧⲁⲧⲉ-
¹⁵ ⲧⲛ̄ⲕⲁⲃⲁⲗ ⲙ̄ⲙⲁⲩ ⲙ̄ⲡⲣⲥⲱⲧⲉ ¹⁶ ⲁⲣⲁⲩ `ⲁ´ⲟⲩⲁⲙⲟⲩ. ⲙ̄ⲡⲣⲣ̄ ϫⲁⲗⲉⲥ. ¹⁷ ⲙ̄ⲡⲣⲣ̄ ϥⲛⲧ, ϫⲉ
ⲁⲧⲉⲧⲛ̄ⲟⲩⲱ ¹⁸ ⲉⲣⲉⲧⲛ̄ⲛⲟⲩϩⲉ ⲙ̄ⲙⲁϥ ⲁⲃⲁⲗ. ¹⁹ ⲙ̄ⲡⲣϣⲱⲡⲉ ⲉⲣⲉⲧⲛ̄ⲛⲟⲉⲓ ⲛ̄ⲧⲟ- ²⁰ ⲡⲟⲥ
ⲙ̄ⲡⲇⲓⲁⲃⲟⲗⲟⲥ, ϫⲉ ⲁⲧⲉ- ²¹ ⲧⲛ̄ⲟⲩⲱ ⲉⲣⲉⲧⲛ̄ⲟⲩⲱⲥϥ̄ ⲙ̄ⲙⲁϥ. ²² ⲙ̄ⲡⲣⲧⲁϩⲣⲟ ⲛ̄ⲛⲉⲧⲛ̄ϫⲣⲟⲡ, ⲛⲉ-
²³ ⲉⲓ ⲉⲧϩⲁⲉⲓϩ, ϩⲱⲥ ⲟⲩⲥⲟϩⲉ ⲡⲉ. ²⁴ ⲟⲩⲗⲁⲩⲉ ⲅⲁⲣ ⲡⲉ ⲡⲓⲁⲧϩⲉⲡ ⲁϫⲓ- ²⁵ ⲧϥ̄ ⲛ̄ϭⲁⲛⲥ̄ ⲛ̄ϩⲟⲩⲟ
ⲁⲡⲓϩⲉⲡ. ²⁶ ϫⲉ ⲛ̄ⲧⲁϥ ⲅⲁⲣ ⲡⲉⲧⲙ̄ⲙⲉⲩ ²⁷ ϭⲓⲣⲉ ⲛ̄ⲛⲉϥϩⲃⲏⲩⲉ ϩⲱⲥ ⲟⲩ- ²⁸ ⲁⲧϩⲉⲡ ⲡⲉ ⲡⲉⲉⲓ ⲛ̄ⲧⲁϥ,
ϩⲱⲥ ²⁹ ⲟⲩⲇⲓⲕⲁⲓⲟⲥ ⲡⲉ ϭⲓⲣⲉ ⲛ̄ⲛⲉϥ- ³⁰ ϩⲃⲏⲩⲉ ϩⲛ̄ ϩⲛ̄ⲕⲉⲕⲁⲩⲉ. ⲉⲓⲣⲉ ³¹ ϭⲉ ⲛ̄ⲧⲱⲧⲛ̄ ⲙ̄ⲡⲟⲩⲱϣ
ⲙ̄ⲡⲓⲱⲧ, ³² ϫⲉ ⲛ̄ⲧⲱⲧⲛ̄ ϩⲛ̄ⲁⲃⲁⲗ ⲙ̄ⲙⲁϥ.

³³ ϫⲉ ⲡⲓⲱⲧ ⲅⲁⲣ ϥϩⲁⲗϭ, ⲁⲩⲱ ϩⲛ̄ ³⁴ ⲡⲓⲟⲩⲱϣⲉ ⲛ̄ⲧⲟⲟⲧϥ̄ ⲟⲩⲡⲉⲧⲛⲁ- ³⁵ ⲛⲟⲩϥ. ⲛⲉⲁϥϫⲓ
ⲥⲁⲩⲛⲉ ⲁⲛⲉⲧⲉ ³⁶ ⲛⲟⲩⲧⲛ̄ ⲛⲉ ⲛ̄ⲧⲉⲧⲛ̄ⲙ̄ⲧⲁⲛ ⲙ̄- ³⁷ ⲙⲱⲧⲛ̄ ⲁⲭⲱⲟⲩ. ⲁⲃⲁⲗ ⲅⲁⲣ ϩⲛ̄ ⲛⲓ- ³⁸
ⲟⲩⲧⲱⲱϩ ϣⲁⲩϫⲓ ⲥⲁⲩⲛⲉ ⲁⲛⲉ- ³⁹ ⲧⲉ ⲛⲟⲩⲧⲛ̄ ⲛⲉ, ϫⲉ ⲛ̄ϣⲏⲣⲉ ⲙ̄ⲡⲓⲱ`ⲧ´ ³⁴·¹ ⲛ̄ⲧⲁⲩ ⲛⲉ
ⲡⲉϥⲥⲧⲁⲉⲓ, ϫⲉ ϩⲛ̄ⲁ- ² ⲃⲁⲗ ⲛⲉ ϩⲛ̄ ⲧⲭⲁⲣⲓⲥ ⲛ̄ⲧⲉ ⲡⲉϥ- ³ ϩⲟ. ⲉⲧⲃⲉ ⲡⲉⲉⲓ ⲡⲓⲱⲧ ⲙⲁⲉⲓ ⁴
ⲙ̄ⲡⲉϥⲥⲧⲁⲉⲓ, ⲁⲩⲱ ϥⲟⲩⲱⲛϩ ⲙ̄ⲙⲁϥ ⁵ ⲁⲃⲁⲗ ϩⲙ̄ ⲙⲁ ⲛⲓⲙ, ⲁⲩⲱ ⲉϥϣⲁⲧⲱϩ ⁶ ⲙⲛ̄
ϯϩⲩⲗⲏ ϣⲁϥ ⲙ̄ⲡⲉϥⲥⲧⲁⲉⲓ ⁷ ⲁⲡⲟⲩⲁⲉⲓⲛ, ⲁⲩⲱ ϩⲛ̄ ⲡⲉϥⲥϭⲣⲁϩⲧ̄ ⁸ ϣⲁϥⲧⲣⲉϥⲣ̄ ⲥⲁ
ⲧⲡⲉ ⲛ̄ⲥⲙⲁⲧ ⲛⲓⲙ, ⁹ ⲛ̄ϩⲣⲁⲩ ⲛⲓⲙ. ⲙ̄ⲙⲉϣϫⲉ ⲅⲁⲣ ⲉⲛ ⲛⲉⲧ- ¹⁰ ϣⲱⲗⲙ̄ ⲁⲡⲥⲧⲁⲉⲓ, ⲁⲗⲗⲁ
ⲡⲥⲧⲁⲉⲓ ¹¹ ⲡⲉⲡⲛⲉⲩⲙⲁ ⲡⲉⲧⲉ ⲟⲩⲛⲧⲉϥ ⲙ̄ⲙⲉⲩ ⲛ̄- ¹² ⲡⲱⲗⲙ̄ ⲁⲩⲱ ϣⲁϥⲥⲱⲕ ⲙ̄ⲙⲁϥ ¹³

32.23 A symbol in the margin indicates that lines 38–39 are to be inserted here.

the entire number [9] moves over to the right (hand). Just as [10] the one lacking the one—that [11] is the entire right (hand)—[12] draws the one that is deficient and [13] receives it through the [14] left part, and it moves over to the right (part), [15] so too the number [16] becomes one hundred. It is the sign of the one who is in [17] their voice. This is the Father. [18] Even on the Sabbath, the sheep [19] he found that had fallen into the [20] pit he worked to find. He revitalized [21] the sheep when he brought it up [22] from the pit so that you might [23] know within—[38] you who are children of internal knowledge [39]—[23 contd.] what the Sabbath is, [24] the (day) upon which it is inappropriate for [25] Salvation to be idle, [26] so that we might speak from [27] the day above, which [28] does not have night, [29] and from the light [30] that does not set because it is perfect.

[31] Therefore, say from the heart that [32] you are the perfect day [33] and among you [34] dwells the light that does not dim. [35] Speak about the truth with those who seek [36] after it and (about) the knowledge of those [37] who have sinned in their error. [33.1] Make firm the foot of those [2] who have stumbled, and extend [3] your hands to those who are sick. Feed [4] those who are hungry, and to those who are tired [5] give rest, and [6] lift up those who desire to [7] rise, and wake up those who are [8] asleep. For you are the understanding [9] that is attracted. When [10] strength works in this way, it becomes even [11] stronger. Worry about yourselves [12] alone. Do not worry about [13] others whom you have [14] cast out from among you. The things [15] you have vomited do not return [16] to and eat. Do not be moths. [17] Do not be worms, because already [18] you are shaking it off. [19] Do not become a (dwelling) place [20] for the devil, because [21] already you have neutralized him. [22] Do not establish (those who are) your obstacles, those [23] who stumble, as though (you were their) support. [24] For the unrighteous one is someone to [25] harm rather than the righteous one. [26] For the former [27] does his deeds as one [28] unrighteous, [29] (but the latter) as one righteous does his [30] deeds among others. Then as for you, do [31] the will of the Father, [32] because you are from him.

[33] For the Father is sweet, and in [34] his will is something good. [35] He had received knowledge of the things [36] that are yours, and you have rested [37] yourselves in them. For by the [38] fruits knowledge is received about the things [39] that are yours, because the children of the Father [34.1] are his aroma, because [2] they are from the grace of his [3] countenance. For this reason the Father loves [4] his aroma, and he manifests it [5] everywhere, and when it mixes [6] with matter he gives his aroma [7] to the light, and in his rest [8] he makes it surpass every form, [9] every sound. For the ears do not [10] smell the aroma, but [11] the spirit is that which has [12] the (sense of) smell, and it draws it [13]

33.9 "that is attracted": or "that attracts."
33.13 "others whom": or "other things that."
33.36 "and you have rested": possibly "so that you can rest."
34.7 "rest": or "silence."

ⲛⲉϥ ϣⲁⲣⲁϥ, ⲁⲩⲱ ⲛϥϣⲱⲙⲥ̅ ⲁϩⲣⲏⲓ̈ [14] ϩⲛ̅ ⲡⲥⲧⲁⲉⲓ ⲙ̅ⲡⲓⲱⲧ, ⲛ̅ⲧϥⲙⲁ- [15] ⲛⲉϥ ⳪ⲉ, ⲛϥⳲⲓⲧϥ̅ ⲁϩⲣⲏⲓ̈ ⲁⲡⲙⲁ [16] ⲛ̅ⲧⲁϥⲉⲓ ⲁⲃⲁⲗ ⲙ̅ⲙⲉⲩ, ⲁⲃⲁⲗ [17] ϩⲙ̅ ⲡⲓⲥⲧⲁⲉⲓ ⲛ̅ϣⲁⲣⲡ̅ ⲉⲧⲁ- [18] ⲣⲁϥ. ⲟⲩⲉⲉⲓ ϩⲛⲛ ⲟⲩⲡⲗⲁⲥⲙⲁ [19] ⲙ̅ⲯⲩⲭⲓⲕⲟⲛ ⲡⲉ, ⲉϥⲟⲉⲓ [20] ⲙ̅ⲡⲣⲏⲧⲉ ⲛ̅ⲟⲩⲙⲁⲩ ⲉϥⲁⲣⲁϥ [21] ⲉⲛⲧⲁϩⲱⲧⲉ, ⲉϥϩⲛ̅ ⲟⲩⲕⲁϩ ⲉϥ- [22] ⲧⲏⲕ ⲉⲛ, ⲉⲧⲉϣⲁⲣⲟⲩⲙⲉⲩⲉ [23] ⲁⲣⲁϥ ⲛ̅ϭⲓ ⲛⲉⲧⲛⲉⲩ ⲁⲣⲁϥ ϫⲉ ⲟⲩ- [24] ⲕⲁϩ ⲡⲉ. ⲙⲛ̅ⲛⲥⲱⲥ ⲉϣⲁϥⲃⲱⲗ [25] ⲛ̅ⲕⲉⲥⲁⲡ, ⲉⲣⲉϣⲁⲛⲟⲩⲛⲓϥⲉ [26] ⲥⲁⲕϥ̅, ϣⲁϥϩⲙⲁⲙ. ⲛⲓⲥⲧⲁⲉⲓ [27] ϭⲉ ⲉⲧⲁⲣϥ̅ ϩⲛⲁⲃⲁⲗ ϩⲛ̅ ⲡⲓⲡⲱϣⲉ [28] ⲛⲉ. ⲉⲧⲃⲉ ⲡⲉⲉⲓ ⲁϥⲓ ⲛ̅ϭⲓ ⲡⲛⲁ[ϩ]- [29] ⲧⲉ ⲁϥⲃⲱⲗ ⲙ̅ⲡⲓⲡⲱϣⲉ ⲁⲃⲁⲗ, [30] ⲁⲩⲱ ⲁϥⲉⲓⲛⲉ ⲙ̅ⲡⲓⲡⲗⲏⲣⲱⲙⲁ [31] ⲉⲧϩⲏⲙ ⲛ̅ⲧⲉ ⲧ̅ⲁⲅⲁⲡⲏ ϫⲉⲕⲁⲥⲉ [32] ⲡⲁⲣⲁϣ ⲛⲉϥⲥⲱⲧⲉ ⲁϣⲱⲡⲉ [33] ⲁⲗⲗⲁ ⲧ̅ⲙⲛ̅ⲧⲟⲩⲉⲉⲓ ⲧⲉ ⲛ̅ⲧⲉ [34] ⲡⲓⲙⲉⲉⲩⲉ ⲉⲧϫⲏⲕ ⲁⲃⲁⲗ.

ⲡⲉ- [35] ⲉⲓ <ⲡⲉ> ⲡⲗⲟⲅⲟⲥ ⲙ̅ⲡⲓϣⲙⲛⲟⲩϥⲉ ⲛ̅- [36] ⲧϭⲓⲛⲉ ⲛ̅ⲧⲉ ⲡⲓⲡⲗⲏⲣⲱⲙⲁ ⲛ̅ⲛⲉ- [37] ⲉⲓ ⲉⲧⲥⲁⲙⲧ ⲁⲃⲁⲗ ϩⲁϫⲱϥ [35.1] ⲙ̅ⲡⲓⲟⲩⲭⲉⲉⲓ ⲧⲉ{ⲉⲓ} ⲉⲧⲛⲛⲏⲩ [2] ⲁⲃⲁⲗ ⲙ̅ⲡⲥⲁ ⲛϩⲣⲉ. ⲉⲥⲥⲁⲙⲧ [3] ⲛ̅ϭⲓ ⲧⲟⲩϩⲉⲗⲡⲓⲥ ⲉⲧⲟⲩⲥⲁⲙⲧ [4] ⲁⲃⲁⲗ ϩⲛⲧⲥ̅—ⲉⲧⲉ ⲡⲉⲩⲉⲓⲛⲉ [5] ⲡⲉ ⲡⲟⲩⲁⲉⲓⲛ ⲉⲧⲉ ⲙⲛ̅ ϩⲁⲉⲓⲃⲉⲥ [6] ⲛ̅ϩⲏⲧϥ̅—ⲉⲓϫⲉ ⲙ̅ⲡⲥⲁⲡ ⲉ- [7] ⲧⲏⲙⲉⲩ ϣⲁϥⲙⲁⲁϩⲉ ⲁⲉⲓ ⲛ̅ϭⲓ [8] ⲡⲓⲡⲗⲏⲣⲱⲙⲁ. ⲉⲛⲧⲁϥϣⲱⲡⲉ [9] ⲉⲛ ⲛ̅ϭⲓ ⲡⲓϣⲧⲁ ⲛ̅ⲧϩⲩⲗⲏ ⲁⲃⲁⲗ ϩⲓⲧⲟ- [10] ⲟⲧⲥ̅ ⲛ̅ⲧ̅ⲙⲛ̅ⲧⲁⲧⲁⲣⲏϫⲥ̅ ⲛ̅ⲧⲉ [11] ⲡⲓⲱⲧ ⲉⲧⲛ̅ⲛⲏⲩ ⲁⲧⲛ̅ <ⲡ>ⲟⲩⲁⲉⲓϣ ⲙ̅- [12] ⲡⲓϣⲧⲁ, ⲕⲁⲓⲧⲟⲓⲅⲉ ⲙ̅ⲡⲉⲗⲁⲩⲉ [13] ϭⲙϭⲁⲙ ⲛ̅ϫⲟⲟⲥ ϫⲉ ϥⲛⲁⲉⲓ ⲙ̅ⲡ- [14] ⲣⲏⲧⲉ ⲛ̅ϭⲓ ⲡⲓⲁⲧⲧⲉⲕⲟ. ⲁⲗⲗⲁ ⲁϥⲁ- [15] ϣⲉ{ⲉ}ⲉⲓ ⲛ̅ϭⲓ ⲡⲓⲃⲁⲑⲟⲥ ⲛ̅ⲧⲉ ⲡⲓ- [16] ⲱⲧ[[ϩⲁ`ϩ´ⲧⲛϥ ⲉⲛ]], ⲁⲩⲱ ⲛⲉϥϣⲟⲟⲡ [17] ϩⲁϩⲧⲛϥ ⲉⲛ ⲛ̅ϭⲓ ⲡⲓⲙⲉⲩⲉ ⲛ̅ⲧⲉ [18] ⲧ̅ⲡⲗⲁⲛⲏ. ⲟⲩϩⲱϥ ⲛ̅ⲥⲉϩ ⲡⲉ, [19] ⲟⲩϩⲱϥ ⲉϥⲙⲁⲧⲛ̅ ⲛ̅ⲥⲉϩⲱϥ [20] ⲁⲣⲉⲧϥ̅ ⲡⲉ ϩⲛ̅ ⲡⲓϭⲓⲛⲉ ⲙ̅ⲡⲉⲉⲓ [21] ⲛ̅ⲧⲁϩⲓ ϣⲁ ⲡⲉⲉⲓ ⲉⲧⲉϥⲛⲁⲧⲁ- [22] ⲥⲧⲟ ⲙ̅ⲙⲁϥ. ⲡⲓⲧⲁⲥⲧⲟ ⲅⲁⲣ ⲥⲉ- [23] ⲙⲟⲩⲧⲉ ⲁⲣⲁϥ ϫⲉ ⲙⲉⲧⲁⲛⲟⲓⲁ.

[24] ⲉⲧⲃⲉ ⲡⲉⲉⲓ ⲁⲧ̅ⲙⲛ̅ⲧⲁⲧⲧⲉⲕⲟ [25] ⲛⲓϥⲉ ⲁⲃⲁⲗ, ⲁⲥⲟⲩⲁϩⲥ̅ ⲛ̅ⲥⲁ ⲡⲉⲛ- [26] ⲧⲁϥⲣ̅ ⲛⲁⲃⲓ ϫⲉⲕⲁⲥⲉ ⲉϥⲉⲙ̅- [27] ⲧⲁⲛ ⲙ̅ⲙⲁϥ. ⲡⲕⲱ ⲅⲁⲣ ⲁⲃⲁⲗ ⲡⲉ [28] ⲡⲁϣⲱϫⲡ ⲁⲡⲟⲩⲁⲉⲓⲛ ϩⲛ̅ ⲡⲓϣⲧⲁ, [29] ⲡⲓϣⲉϫⲉ ⲛ̅ⲧⲉ ⲡⲓⲡⲗⲏⲣⲱⲙⲁ. [30] ⲡⲥⲁⲉⲓⲛ ⲅⲁⲣ ϣⲁϥⲡⲱⲧ ⲁⲡⲙⲁ ⲉ- [31] ⲧⲉ ⲟⲩⲛ̅ ϣⲱⲛⲉ ⲛ̅ϩⲏⲧϥ̅ ϫⲉ ⲡⲓⲟⲩ- [32] ⲱϣⲉ ⲛ̅ⲧⲁϥ ⲡⲉ ⲉⲧϣⲟⲟⲡ [33] ⲛ̅ϩⲏⲧϥ̅. ⲡⲉⲧⲣ̅ ϣⲧⲁ ϭⲉ ⲙⲁϥϩⲁ- [34] ⲡϥ̅ ϫⲉ ⲟⲩⲛ̅ⲧⲉϥ ⲙ̅ⲙⲉⲩ ⲙ̅ⲡⲉ- [35] ⲧ̅ϥϣⲁⲁⲧ ⲙ̅ⲙⲁⲩ. ⲡⲓⲣⲏⲧⲉ ⲡⲓⲡⲗⲏ- [36] ⲣⲱⲙⲁ ⲉⲧⲉ ⲛϥ̅ⲣ̅ ϣⲧⲁ ⲉⲛ, ⲡⲱⲧⲁ [37] ⲛ̅ⲧⲁϥ ϥⲙⲟⲩϩ ⲙ̅ⲙⲁϥ ⲡⲉⲛⲧⲁϥ- [36.1] ⲧⲉⲉⲓϥ ⲁⲃⲁⲗ ϩⲓⲧⲟⲟⲧϥ̅ ⲁⲙⲁϩ [2] ⲡⲉⲧϥ̅ϣⲁⲁⲧ ⲙ̅ⲙⲁϥ ϫⲉⲕⲁⲥⲉ [3] ϭⲉ ⲡⲓϩⲙⲁⲧ ⲉϥⲁϫⲓⲧϥ̅. ϫ<ⲉ> ⲙ̅ⲡⲥⲁⲡ [4] ⲉⲧⲉⲛⲉϥϣⲁⲁⲧ, ⲛⲉⲙⲛⲧⲉϥ ⲙ̅- [5] ⲙⲉⲩ ⲙ̅ⲡⲉϩⲙⲁⲧ. ⲉⲧⲃⲉ ⲡⲉⲉⲓ [6] ⲛⲉⲩⲧⲥⲃ̅ⲕⲟ ⲡⲉ ⲉⲧϣⲟⲟⲡ ϩⲛ̅ [7] ⲡⲙⲁ ⲉⲧⲉⲣⲉⲡⲉϩⲙⲁⲧ ⲙ̅ⲙⲉⲩ [8] ⲉⲛ. ⲡⲥⲁⲡ ⲉⲛⲧⲁⲩϫⲓ ⲙ̅ⲡⲉⲉⲓ ⲉ- [9] ⲧⲥⲁⲃⲕ̅ ⲡⲉⲧϥ̅ϣⲁⲁⲧ ⲙ̅ⲙⲁϥ ⲁϥ- [10] ⲟⲩⲁⲛϩϥ̅, ⲉϥⲟⲉⲓ [11] ⲛ̅ⲛⲟⲩⲡⲗⲏⲣⲱⲙⲁ, ⲉⲧⲉ ⲡⲉⲉⲓ ⲡⲉ ⲡϭⲓⲛⲉ ⲙ̅ⲡⲟⲩⲁⲉⲓⲛ [12] ⲛ̅ⲧⲙⲏⲉ, ⲉⲛⲧⲁϣⲁⲉⲓⲉ ⲁⲣⲁϥ ϫⲉ [13] ⲟⲩⲁⲧϣ̅ⲃ̅ⲧϥ̅ ⲡⲉ.

ⲉⲧⲃⲉ ⲡⲉⲉⲓ {ⲙ̅}- [14] ⲡⲭⲣⲓⲥⲧⲟⲥ ⲁⲩϣⲉϫⲉ ⲁⲣⲁϥ ϩⲛ̅ ⲧⲟⲩ- [15] ⲙⲏⲧⲉ, ϣⲓⲛⲉ ⲛ̅ⲥⲉϫⲓ ⲛ̅ⲛⲟⲩⲥⲧⲟ [16] ⲛ̅ϭⲓ ⲛⲉⲉⲓ ⲛ̅ⲧⲁϩϣⲧⲁⲣⲧ̅ⲣ̅, ⲛ̅ϥⲧⲁϩ- [17] ⲥⲟⲩ ⲙ̅ⲡⲓⲧⲱϩⲥ̅—ⲡⲓⲧⲱϩⲥ̅ ⲡⲉ [18] ⲡⲛⲁⲉ ⲙ̅ⲡⲓⲱⲧ ⲉⲧⲉϥⲛⲁⲛⲁⲉ [19] ⲛⲉⲩ. ⲛⲉⲛⲧⲁϥⲧⲁϩⲥⲟⲩ ⲇⲉ [20] ⲛⲉ ⲛⲉⲉⲓ ⲛ̅ⲧⲁϩϫⲱⲕ ⲁⲃⲁⲗ. [21] ⲛ̅ⲥⲕⲉⲩⲟⲥ ⲅⲁⲣ ⲉⲧⲙⲏϩ ⲛⲉⲧⲉ- [22] ϣⲁⲟⲩⲧⲁϩⲥⲟⲩ. ⲡⲥⲁⲡ ⲇⲉ· ⲉⲧⲉ [23] ⲡⲧⲱϩⲥ̅ ⲛ̅ⲟⲩⲉⲉⲓ ⲛⲁⲃⲱⲗ ⲁ- [24]

35.9 ϣⲧϣ̅: read ϣⲧⲁ.
35.35 ⲙ̅ⲙⲁⲩ: read ⲙ̅ⲙⲁϥ.

to itself, and it sinks down [14] into the aroma of the Father, and he [15] then harbors it, and he takes it down to the place [16] that it came from, within [17] the first aroma that grows cold. [18] It is something in a soulish [19] form, existing [20] like cold water [21] that has been flowing, which is upon soil that is [22] not firm, (and) of which those who see it think that [23] it is soil. [24] Later it dissolves [25] again. When a breath [26] draws it, it becomes hot. The cold aromas, [27] then, are from the division. [28] For this reason <faith> came [29] and destroyed the division, [30] and it brought the warm fullness [31] of love so that [32] the cold would not return, [33] but that there might be the unity of [34] the perfect thought.

This [35] <is> the word of the good news of [36] the discovery of the fullness for [37] those who wait for [35.1] the salvation that is coming [2] from above. [3] Their hope, which they await, waits [4]—those whose image [5] is the light that has no shadow [6] in it—because at that time [7] the fullness is about to come. [8] The <deficiency> of matter did not [9] come about by means of [10] the limitlessness of [11] the Father, who comes at <the> time of the deficiency, [12] although no one [13] was able to say that the undefiled one would come [14] in this way. But [15] the depth of the Father multiplied, [16] and the mind of [17] Error was not existing with him. [18] It is a thing that falls, [19] a thing that is easy to set [20] upright in the discovery of the one [21] who has come to the one he will [22] bring back. For the bringing back is [23] called the repentance.

[24] For this reason undefilement [25] breathed forth, it set out after the one [26] who had sinned so that it might give [27] him rest. For forgiveness is [28] the remainder for the light in the deficiency, [29] the word of the fullness. [30] For the physician goes to the place [31] where there is sickness because [32] it is his desire that dwells [33] in him. The one who is deficient, then, does not conceal it [34] because he has what [35] he (another?) lacks. Just as the fullness, [36] which is not deficient, [37] fills his deficiency, <the fullness> that he [36.1] gave from himself to fill [2] that which he lacks so that [3] he then might receive grace. For at the time [4] he was deficient, he did not have [5] grace. For this reason [6] there was a diminishing that existed in [7] the place where there was no grace. [8] Once that which was diminished was received, [9] what he lacked he [10] revealed, since it was their fullnesses, [11] which is the discovery of the light [12] of truth, which shined upon him because [13] he is immutable.

For this reason [14] Christ was spoken about in their [15] midst, so that those who are disturbed might receive a bringing back, [16] and he might anoint [17] them with ointment—the ointment is [18] the mercy of the father who will have mercy [19] upon them. But those whom he anointed [20] are those who were perfected. [21] For full vessels are

35.11 "who comes at <the> time of": also possible though less likely "who comes to give time for."
35.26–27 "it might give him rest": or "he might rest."

ⲃⲁⲗ ϣⲁϥϣⲟⲩⲟ, ⲟⲩⲉ⳿ⲏ ⲧⲗⲁ- ²⁵ ⲉⲓϭⲉ ⲁⲧⲣⲉϥⳅ̄ ϣⲧⲁ ⲡⲉ ⲡ⳿ϩⲱⲃ ²⁶ ⲉⲧⲉ {ⲙ̄}ⲡⲉϥⲧⲱϩⲥ̄·
ⲛⲁⲃⲱⲕ ²⁷ ⲛ̄ⲧⲟⲟⲧϥ̄. ⲡⲥⲁⲡ ⲅⲁⲣ ⲉⲧⲙ̄ⲙⲉⲩ ²⁸ ϣⲁⲣⲉⲟⲩⲛⲓϭⲉ ⲥⲁⲕϥ̄, ⲟⲩⲉⲉⲓ ²⁹ ϩⲛ̄ ⲧϭⲁⲙ
ⲙ̄ⲡⲉⲧⲛⲙ̄ⲙⲉϥ. ⲁⲗ- ³⁰ ⲗⲁ ϩⲁⲧⲛ̄ ⲡⲉⲉⲓ ⲛ̄ⲧⲁϥ ⲉⲧⲉ ⲟⲩⲁⲧ- ³¹ ϣⲧⲁ ⲡⲉ ⲙⲁⲩⲛⲁϩ ⲧⲃ̄ⲃⲉ ⲛ̄ⲗⲁⲁⲩ ³²
ϩⲁϩⲧⲏϥ, ⲟⲩⲇⲉ ⲙⲁⲩϣⲟⲩⲉ ⲗⲁⲩⲉ, ³³ ⲁⲗⲗⲁ ⲡⲉⲧϥ̄ϣⲁⲁⲧ ⲙ̄ⲙⲁϥ ϣⲁϥ- ³⁴ ⲙⲁϩϥ̄ ⲁⲛ ⲙ̄ⲙⲁϥ
ⲛ̄ϭⲓ ⲡⲓⲱⲧ ⲉϥ- ³⁵ ϫⲏⲕ ⲁⲃⲁⲗ. ⲟⲩⲁⲅⲁⲑⲟⲥ ⲡⲉ· ϥⲥⲁⲩ- ³⁶ ⲛⲉ ⲛ̄ⲛⲓⲭⲟ ⲛ̄ⲧⲟⲟⲧϥ̄ ϫⲉ ⲛ̄ⲧⲁϥ ⲡⲉ ³⁷
ⲛ̄ⲧⲁϥϫⲟ ⲙ̄ⲙⲁⲩ ϩⲛ̄ ⲡⲓⲡⲁⲣⲁⲇⲓⲥ- ³⁸ ⲥⲟⲥ ⲛ̄ⲧⲟⲟⲧϥ̄. ⲡⲉ⳿ϥ⳿ⲡⲁⲣⲁⲇⲓⲥⲥⲟⲥ ⲇⲉ ³⁹ ⲡⲉ ⲡⲉϥⲙⲁ
ⲛ̄ⲙ̄ⲧⲁⲛ.

ⲡⲉⲉⲓ ³⁷·¹ ⲡⲉ ⲡⲓϫⲱⲕ ⲁⲃⲁⲗ ϩⲛ̄ ⲡⲓⲙⲉⲩⲉ ² ⲛ̄ⲧⲉ ⲡⲓⲱⲧ, ⲟⲩⲉϩⲛ̄ ⲛⲉⲉⲓ ⲛⲉ ³ ⲛ̄ϣⲉϫⲉ ⲛ̄ⲧⲉ
ⲡⲉϥⲙⲁⲕⲙⲉⲕ. ⁴ ⲡⲟⲩⲉⲓ ⲡⲟⲩⲉⲉⲓ ⲛ̄ⲧⲉ ⲛⲉϥϣⲉ- ⁵ ϫⲉ ⲡⲉ ⲡϩⲱⲃ ⲛ̄ⲧⲉ ⲡⲉϥⲟⲩⲟ- ⁶ ϣⲉ ⲟⲩⲉⲉⲓ
ϩⲙ̄ ⲡⲟⲩⲱⲛϩ̄ ⲁⲃⲁⲗ ⁷ ⲛ̄ⲧⲉ ⲡⲉϥϣⲉϫⲉ. ϫⲓⲛ ⲉⲩⲟ ⲛ̄ⲃⲁ- ⁸ ⲑⲟⲥ ⲛⲧⲉ ⲡⲉϥⲙⲉⲩⲉ, ⲡⲗⲟⲅⲟⲥ
ⲛ̄- ⁹ ⲧⲁϩⲣ̄ ϣⲁⲣⲡ̄ ⲛ̄ⲉⲓ ⲁⲃⲁⲗ ⲁϥⲟⲩⲱⲛϩ̄ ¹⁰ ⲙ̄ⲙⲁⲩ ⲁⲃⲁⲗ ⲟⲩⲁϩⲛ̄ ⲟⲩⲛⲟⲩⲥ ⲉϥ- ¹¹ ϣⲉϫⲉ,
ⲡⲗⲟⲅⲟⲥ ⲟⲩⲉⲉⲓ ϩⲛ̄ⲛ ⲟⲩ- ¹² ⲭⲁⲣⲓⲥ ⲉⲥⲕⲁⲣⲁⲉⲓⲧ· ⲁⲩⲙⲟⲩⲧⲉ· ¹³ ⲁⲣⲁϥ ϫⲉ ⲡⲓⲙⲉⲉⲩⲉ ⲉⲡⲓⲇⲏ ⲛⲉⲩ-
¹⁴ ϣⲟⲟⲡ ⲛ̄ϩⲏⲧϥ̄ ⲉⲙⲡⲟⲩⲱⲛϩ ¹⁵ ⲁⲃⲁⲗ. ⲁⲥϣⲱⲡⲉ ϭⲉ ⲁⲧⲣⲉϥ- ¹⁶ ⲣ̄ ϣⲁⲣⲡ̄ ⲛ̄ⲉⲓ ⲁⲃⲁⲗ ⲙ̄ⲡ- ¹⁷
ⲥⲁⲡ ⲛⲧⲁϥⲣ̄ ϩⲛⲉϥ ⲛ̄ϭⲓ ⲡⲟⲩ- ¹⁸ ϣⲉ ⲙ̄ⲡⲉⲛⲧⲁϩⲟⲩⲱϣⲉ. ¹⁹ ⲡⲟⲩⲱϣⲉ ⲇⲉ ⲡⲉⲧⲉ ⲡⲓⲱⲧ
ⲙⲁ- ²⁰ ⲧⲛ̄ ⲙ̄ⲙⲁϥ ⲛ̄ϩⲏⲧϥ̄ ⲟⲩⲁϩⲛ̄ ²¹ ⲡⲉⲧⲣ̄ ⲉⲛⲉϥ. ⲙⲁⲣⲉⲗⲁⲩⲉ ϣⲱ- ²² ⲡⲉ ⲁϫⲛ̄ⲧϥ̄, ⲟⲩⲇⲉ
ⲙⲁⲣⲉⲗⲁⲩ- ²³ ⲉ ϣⲱⲡⲉ ⲁϫⲛ̄ ⲡⲟⲩⲱϣⲉ ⲛ̄ⲧⲉ ²⁴ ⲡⲓⲱⲧ. ⲁⲗⲗⲁ ⲟⲩⲁⲧⲧⲉϩⲉⲣⲉⲧϥ̄ ²⁵ ⲡⲉ
ⲡⲉϥⲟⲩⲱϣⲉ ⲡⲉϥⲓ̈ϫⲛⲟⲥ ²⁶ ⲡⲉ ⲡⲟⲩⲱϣⲉ, ⲁⲩⲱ ⲙⲛ̄ ⲗⲁⲩⲉ ²⁷ ⲛⲁⲙⲙⲉ ⲁⲣⲁϥ ⲟⲩⲧⲉ ⲛϥ̄ϣⲟⲟⲡ
²⁸ ⲉⲛ ⲁⲧⲣⲟⲩⲧ̄ ϩⲧⲏⲩ ⲁⲣⲁϥ ϣⲓⲛⲁ ²⁹ ⲛ̄ⲥⲉⲉⲙⲁϩⲧⲉ ⲙ̄ⲙⲁϥ. ⲁⲗⲗⲁ ³⁰ ⲡⲥⲁⲡ ⲉⲧⲉϥⲟⲩⲱϣⲉ
ⲡⲉⲧϥ̄ⲟⲩ- ³¹ ⲁϣϥ̄ ⲡⲉⲉⲓ ⲡⲉ—ⲕⲁⲛ ⲉϣⲱⲡⲉ ³² ⲉⲡⲛⲉⲩ ⲁⲃⲁⲗ ⲉⲛϥ̄ⲣ̄ ⲉⲛⲉⲩ ⲉⲛ ³³ ϩⲛ̄ ⲗⲁⲩⲉ
ⲛ̄ⲛⲁϩⲣⲛ̄ ⲡⲛⲟⲩⲧⲉ—ⲡⲟⲩ- ³⁴ ϣⲉ ⲡⲓⲱⲧ. ϥⲥⲁⲩⲛⲉ ⲅⲁⲣ ⲛ̄ⲧⲟⲩ- ³⁵ ϩⲟⲩⲉⲓⲧⲉ ⲧⲏⲣⲟⲩ ⲙⲛ̄
ⲧⲟⲩϩⲁⲏ. ³⁶ ϩⲛ̄ ⲧⲟⲩϩⲁⲏ ⲅⲁⲣ ϥⲛⲁϣⲛ̄ⲧⲟⲩ ³⁷ ⲁϩⲣⲉⲩ. ⲧϩⲁⲏ ⲇⲉ ⲡⲉ ⲡϫⲓ ⲥⲁⲩⲛⲉ ³⁸ ⲁⲡⲉⲉⲓ
ⲉⲑⲏⲡ. ⲡⲉⲉⲓ ⲇⲉ ⲡⲉ ⲡⲓⲱⲧ, ³⁸·¹ ⲡⲉⲉⲓ ⲛ̄ⲧⲁⲧⲉⲣⲟⲩⲉⲓⲧⲉ ⲉⲓ ⲁ- ² ⲃⲁⲗ ⲙ̄ⲙⲁϥ, ⲡⲉⲉⲓ ⲉⲧⲟⲩⲛⲁⲥⲱ- ³
ⲧⲉ ⲁⲣⲁϥ ⲧⲏⲣⲟⲩ ⲛ̄ϭⲓ ⲛⲉ{ⲉⲓ} ⲛ̄ⲧⲁϩ- ⁴ ⲉⲓ ⲁⲃⲁⲗ ⲙ̄ⲙⲁϥ. ⲁⲩⲟⲩⲱⲛϩ̄ ⁵ ⲇⲉ ⲁⲃⲁⲗ ⲁⲩⲉⲁⲩ ⲙⲛ̄
ⲟⲩ- ⁶ ⲧⲉⲗⲏⲗ ⲛ̄ⲧⲉ ⲡⲉϥⲣⲉⲛ.

ⲡⲣⲉⲛ ⁷ ⲇⲉ ⲙ̄ⲡⲓⲱⲧ ⲡⲉ ⲡϣⲏⲣⲉ. ⲛ̄ⲧⲁϥ ⲛ̄- ⁸ ϣⲁⲣⲡ̄ ⲡⲉⲛⲧⲁϥϯ ⲣⲉⲛ ⲁⲡⲉⲛ- ⁹ ⲧⲁϩⲉⲓ ⲁⲃⲁⲗ
ⲙ̄ⲙⲁϥ ⲉⲛⲧⲁϥ ⲣⲱ ¹⁰ ⲡⲉ, ⲁⲩⲱ ⲁϥⲙⲉⲥⲧϥ̄ ⲛ̄ⲛⲟⲩϣⲏ- ¹¹ ⲣⲉ. ⲁϥϯ ⲡⲉϥⲣⲉⲛ ⲁⲣⲁϥ ⲉⲧⲉ ⲛⲉ- ¹²
ⲟⲩⲛ̄ⲧⲉϥϥ. ⲛ̄ⲧⲁϥ ⲡⲉ ⲉⲧⲉ ⲟⲩⲛ̄- ¹³ ⲧⲉϥ ⲛ̄ⲕⲉⲉⲓ ⲛⲓⲙ ⲉⲩϣⲟⲟⲡ ϩⲁϩ- ¹⁴ ⲧⲏϥ. {ⲛ̄ϭⲓ} ⲡⲓⲱⲧ
ⲟⲩⲛ̄ⲧⲉϥ ⲙ̄ⲡⲣⲉⲛ· ¹⁵ ⲟⲩⲛ̄ⲧⲉϥ ⲙ̄ⲡϣⲏⲣⲉ. ⲟⲩⲛ̄ ϭⲁⲙ ¹⁶ ⲛ̄ⲥⲉⲛⲉⲩ ⲁⲣⲁϥ. ⲡⲣⲉⲛ ⲇⲉ ⲛ̄- ¹⁷ ⲧⲁϥ
ⲟⲩⲁⲧⲛⲉⲩ ⲁⲣⲁϥ ⲡⲉ ϫⲉ ¹⁸ ⲛ̄ⲧⲁϥ ⲟⲩⲁⲉⲉⲧϥ̄ ⲡⲉ ⲡⲙⲩ- ¹⁹ ⲥⲧⲏⲣⲓⲟⲛ ⲙ̄ⲡⲁⲧⲛⲉⲩ ⲁⲣⲁϥ ²⁰
ⲉⲧⲛ̄ⲛⲏⲩ ⲁϩⲛ̄ⲙⲉϣϫⲉ ⲉⲩⲙⲏϩ ²¹ ⲙ̄ⲙⲁϥ ⲧⲏⲣⲟⲩ ⲛ̄ⲧⲟⲟⲧϥ̄. ⲕⲁⲓ ⲅⲁⲣ ²² ⲡⲓⲱⲧ ⲥⲉϫⲟⲩ ⲙ̄ⲡⲉϥⲣⲉⲛ
²³ ⲉⲛ. ϥⲟⲩⲁⲛϩ̄ ⲇⲉ ⲁⲃⲁⲗ ϩⲛ̄ ⲟⲩ- ²⁴ ϣⲏⲣⲉ.

ⲡⲓⲣⲏⲧⲉ ϭⲉ ⲟⲩⲛⲁϭ ⲡⲉ ⲡⲣⲉⲛ. ²⁵ ⲛⲓⲙ ϭⲉ ⲡⲉⲧⲁϣ ⲧⲉⲩⲉ ⲣⲉⲛ ⲛⲉϥ, ²⁶ ⲡⲓⲛⲁϭ ⲛ̄ⲣⲉⲛ, ⲛ̄ⲥⲁⲃⲏⲗ
ⲁⲣⲁϥ ²⁷ ⲟⲩⲁⲉⲉⲧϥ̄, ⲡⲉⲉⲓ ⲉⲧⲉ ⲡⲱϥ ⲡⲉ ²⁸ ⲡⲣⲉⲛ ⲟⲩⲁϩⲛ̄ ⲛ̄ϣⲏⲣⲉ ⲙ̄ⲡⲣⲉⲛ, ²⁹ ⲛⲉⲉⲓ ⲉⲧⲉⲛⲉϥⲙⲁⲧⲛ̄
ⲙ̄ⲙⲁϥ ³⁰ ⲛ̄ϩⲏⲧⲟⲩ ⲛ̄ϭⲓ ⲡⲣⲉⲛ ⲙ̄ⲡⲓⲱⲧ, ³¹ ⲡⲁⲗⲓⲛ ⲛⲉⲩⲙⲁⲧⲛ̄ ⲙ̄ⲙⲁⲩ ϩⲱⲟⲩ ³² ϩⲙ̄ ⲡⲉϥⲣⲉⲛ;

37.5 ϩⲱϥ: read ϩⲱⲃ.

37.25 ⲓ̈ϫⲛⲟⲥ: read ⲓ̈ⲭⲛⲟⲥ.

38.2–3 ⲥⲱⲧⲉ: variant of ⲥⲱⲧ.

those [22] that are anointed/sealed. But once [23] the ointment of one dissolves [24] it becomes empty, and the cause [25] for it becoming deficient is the thing [26] through which its ointment will [27] go. For at that time [28] a breath draws it, one [29] in the power of what is with it. But [30] from him who is not deficient [31] no seal is removed, [32] nor is anything emptied out, [33] but what he lacks the perfect Father [34] fills again. [35] He is good; he knows [36] his sowings, that it is he [37] who has sown them in his paradise. [38] But his paradise [39] is his place of rest.

This [37.1] is the perfection in the thought [2] of the Father, and these are [3] the words of his contemplation. [4] Each of his words [5] is a matter of his unified will [6] in the revelation [7] of his word. When they were in the depth [8] of his thought, the word [9] that was first to come forth revealed [10] them along with a mind that [11] speaks, the unified word in silent grace. [12] He was called [13] thought, since they were [14] in it when they had not yet been revealed. [15] It happened then that he was [16] first to come forth [17] when the will [18] of the one who had willed willed it. [19] Now it is the will that the Father rests [20] himself in and [21] is pleased with. Nothing comes [22] about apart from him, nor does anything [23] come about apart from the will of [24] the Father; rather, his will [25] is inscrutable. His footprint [26] is the will, and no one [27] will know it nor will anyone [28] be mindful of it in order to [29] grasp him. Rather, [30] when he wills what he wills [31] is this—even if [32] the vision is not pleasing to them [33] in some (way) before God—[34] desiring the Father. For he knows the [35] beginning of all of them and their end. [36] For in the end he will ask them [37] to their face. The end is the reception of knowledge [38] about that which is hidden. This is the Father, [38.1] the one from whom the beginning came, [2] the one to whom all who have [3] come from him will return. [4] They have been manifest [5] for the glory and [6] joy of his name.

The name [7] of the Father is the Son. He first [8] gave a name to the one who [9] had come forth from him, since he was the same, [10] and he gave birth to him as a child. [11] He give to him a name [12] that was his. It is he who has [13] all that exists around [14] him. The Father has the name; [15] he has the Son. It is possible [16] for him to be seen. But his name [17] is invisible because [18] it alone is the mystery [19] of the invisible one [20] which comes to the ears that are entirely [21] filled with it by him. For indeed [22] as for the Father, his name is not spoken. [23] Rather it is manifest through a [24] Son.

In this way, then, the name is great. [25] Who, then, will be able to produce a name for him, [26] the great name, except him [27] alone, this one to whom the name belongs [28] and the children of the name, [29] these among whom the name of the Father [30] rests itself, [31]

37.7 "they were in the depth": or "they were depths."

επιΔΗ ογατϣωπε [33] πε πιωτ, Ντας ογαεετς πεν- [34] τασμιсε Μμας νες Νογρεν,
[35] ϩαθΗ εμπατεςτсενο Ννаι- [36] ωΝ, ϣινα Νςϣωπε αχΝ τογα- [37] πε Νϭι πρεν
Μπιωτ εςοεї [38] Νχαειс, ετε πεει πε πρεν [39.1] μαμΗε, εταρχ ϩΜ πες- [2] ογαϩ саϩνε
ϩΝ τϭαΜ ετχΗκ [3] αβαλ. χε πιρεν ογαβαλ εν [4] πε ϩΝ ϩΝλεζιс, ογαϩΝ ϩΝ- [5]
ΜΝτταειρεν πε πεςρεν, [6] αλλα ογατνεγ αρας πε. [7] ας† ρεν αρας ογαεετς, [8]
εςνεγ αρας ογαεετς, εν- [9] τας ογαεετς πετε ογ- [10] Ν ϭαΜ Ν† ρεν αρας. [11] χε
πετενςϣοοπ [12] εν ΜΝτς ρεν Μμεγ. [13] εγνа† εγ γαρ Νρεν αρας [14] πεει ετε Νςϣοοπ
εν· [15] πεει Ντας ετϣοοπ ςϣο- [16] οπ ΜΝ πεςκερεν, αγω [17] ςсαγνε Μμας ογαεετς,
[18] αγω ατρες† ρεν αρας ογ- [19] αεετς. πιωτ πε· πϣΗρε [20] πε πεςρεν. Ντас- [21]
ϩαπς ϭε εν ϩΝ πιϩως· [22] αλλα νεςϣοοπ. [23] πϣΗρε νεςς ρεν ογαε- [24] ετς. πρεν ϭε
πα πιω`τ´ [25] πε, Νθε ετε πρεν Μ- [26] πιωτ πε πϣΗρε. πιμεϩτ [27] επει εςνаϭΝ ρεν
τον Ν- [28] саβΗλ απιωτ;

αλλα παν- [29] τωс ςναχοос Νϭι ογεει [30] ϩαϩτΝ πεςϣβΗρ, χε « νιΜ πε [31] ετνа† ρεν
απεει ετενες [32] ϣρπ Νϣοοπ ϩαθΗ μμας, [33] ϩωс ϭε πρεν εϣαρογχιτς [40.1] εν Νϭι
Μμιсε Ντοοτς Ν- [2] νεει Νταϩμεстογ; » ϣαρπ [3] ϭε ογπετεϣϣε αραν πε [4] аρ νοει
Μπιϩωβ, χε ογεγ [5] πε πρεν; χε Ντас πε πρεν [6] μαμΗε. Ντас εν ϭε πε [7] πρεν αβαλ
Μπιωτ, χε Ν- [8] τας πε πετϣοοπ Νχαειс [9] Νρεν. Ντασχι ϭε Μπρεν [10] εν απογϣεπ
ΜπρΗτε [11] Νϩνκαγε, κατα πεсмат [12] Μπογεει πογεει ετογ- [13] Να{с} τενας Νϩητς.
πεει [14] Δε πε πχαειс Νρεν. Νκε- [15] λαγε εν πε Νταστεεις [16] арас. αλλα ογατ† ρεν
[17] арас πε, ογαττεογας νε, [18] ϣα πсαπ Ντας Νταπεει [19] ετχΗκ `αβαλ´ ϣεχε αρας
ογ- [20] αεετς, αγω Ντας πετε [21] ογΝ ϭαΜ Μμας αχογ [22] Μπεςρεν αγω ανεγ [23]
арас.

Νταρε⟦[сс]⟧ϣωκ ϭε [24] εςνϩΗτς χε πεςρεν ετ- [25] ογαϣς πεςϣΗρε πε, αγω [26]
ας† Μπρεν αρας Νϭι πεει [27] Νταϩϊ αβαλ ϩΝ πιβαθος, ασϣε- [28] χε ανεςπεθΗπ,
εςсαγνε [29] χε πιωτ ογαττεϩαγ πε. [30] ετβε πεει ρω ασΝ πεει α- [31] βαλ, χεκαсε
εςαϣεχε [32] ϩα πτοπος αγω πεςμα [33] ΝΜταν Νταςι αβαλ Ν- [34] ϩΗτς. [41.1] αγω νς†
εαγ ΜπιπλΗρωμα, [2] †μΝτναϭ Ντε πεςρεν, αγω [3] πιϩλаϭ Ντε πιωτ. πογεει πογ- [4]
εει πμα Ντασει αβαλ Νϩητς [5] ςναϣεχε ϩαρας, αγω ϩΝ †τа- [6] ειε Ντασχι
Μπεςτεϩο αρε- [7] τς Ντοοτς ςναπωτ ατстο [8] αρετς Νκεсαπ αγω ασι αβαλ [9] ϩΜ `
π`μα´ ετΜμεγ—πμα Ντασ- [10] ϩε αρετς Νϩητς—εςχι †πε α- [11] βαλ ϩΜ πμα
ετΜμεγ αγω [12] εςχι сανϣ, εςχι αειεγ. αγω [13] πεςμα ΝΜταν Μμιν Μμας [14] πε
πεςπλΗρωμα.

νι†Η ϭε [15] τΗρογ ΝτΝ πιωτ ϩΝπιπλΗ- [16] ρωμα νε, αγωϩΝ νες†Η [17] τΗρογ, τογνογνε
πε ϩΝ [18] πενταςτρογρωτ αβαλ Ν- [19] ϩητς τΗρογ. ας† νεγ Ν- [20] νογτωϣ. сεογανϩ
ϭε α- [21] βαλ Νϭι πογεει πογεει [22] χεκαсε αβαλ ϩΝ πογμε- [23] εγε Μμιν Μμαγ

39.21 ϩϣς: read ϩωβ.
40.17 νε: read πε.

(who) moreover rest themselves [32] in his name? Since the Father is ungenerated, [33] he alone is the one [34] who bears himself to himself as a name, [35] before he had created the eternities, [36] so that the name of the Father might exist over [37] their head as [38] a crown, which is the name [39.1] truly, which is firm in his [2] command in the perfect power. [3] The name is not [4] from words, nor (is his name) from [5] speech; [6] instead it is invisible. [7] He gave a name to him alone, [8] since he alone saw him, he [9] who alone had [10] the power to give a name to him. [11] The one who does not exist [12] does not have a name. [13] For what name could be given to [14] the one who does not exist? [15] The one who exists exists also [16] with his name, and [17] he knows it only, and [18] (knows how) to give it to him [19] alone. He is the Father; the Son [20] is his name. He, [21] therefore, did not hide in it a thing; [22] instead it existed. [23] The Son alone gave a name. [24] The name, therefore, belongs to the Father, [25] just as the name of [26] the Father is the Son. Where would compassion [27] find a name [28] except from the Father?

But doubtless [29] one will say [30] to his neighbor, "Who is it [31] that will give a name to the one [32] who existed before himself, [33] as if children do not receive [40.1] a name from [2] those who give birth to them?" First, [3] therefore, it is fitting for us [4] to consider this matter: what [5] is the name? It is the name [6] truly. It, therefore, is not [7] the name from the Father, because it [8] is the one that is the proper [9] name. Therefore, he did not receive the name [10] as a loan as [11] others (do), in accordance with the manner [12] in which each one [13] will be made. But this [14] is the proper name. There is [15] no other who gave it [16] to him. Rather, he is unnameable, [17] he <is> indescribable, [18] until the time in which he who [19] is perfect spoke about him alone, [20] and he is the one who [21] has the power in him to say [22] his name and to see [23] him.

Therefore, when he was content [24] that his name that [25] is willed is his Son, and [26] the one who had come forth from the depth [27] gave this name to him, he spoke [28] about his hidden things, knowing [29] that the Father is without evil. [30] For this very reason, he brought this one forth, [31] in order to speak [32] about the place and his place [33] of rest from which he had [34] come. [41.1] And he gave glory to the fullness, [2] the greatness of his name, and [3] the sweetness of the Father. About [4] the place from which each one came [5] he will speak, and to the place [6] where he received his establishment [7] he will hasten to return again [8] and take from [9] that place—the place where [10] he stood—tasting [11] from that place and [12] receiving nourishment, experiencing growth. And [13] his own place of rest [14] is his fullness.

Therefore, [15] all emanations from the Father are fullnesses, [16] and as for all his emanations, [17] their root is within [18] the one who caused them all to grow up [19] within himself. He gave them [20] their destinies. Therefore, [21] each one was manifest so that [22] through

40.23 "him": or "it" (referring to "the name").
41.23 < . . . >: a verb has likely been accidentally omitted here, resulting in a sentence fragment.

< . . . >. ⲡⲙⲁ ²⁴ ⲅⲁⲣ ⲉⲧⲟⲩⲭⲁⲩ ⲙ̄ⲡⲟⲩⲙⲉⲉⲩⲉ ²⁵ ϣⲁⲣⲁϥ, ⲡⲙⲁ ⲉⲧⲙ̄ⲙⲉⲩ, ²⁶ ⲧⲟⲩⲛⲟⲩⲛⲉ,
ⲧⲉⲧϥⲓ ⲙ̄ⲙⲁⲩ ²⁷ ⲁⲧⲡⲉ ⲍⲛ ⲛⲓϫⲓⲥⲉ ⲧⲏⲣⲟⲩ ²⁸ ϣⲁ ⲡⲓⲱⲧ. ⲟⲩⲛ̄ⲧⲉⲩ ⲛ̄ⲧⲉϥ- ²⁹ ⲁⲡⲉ ⲉⲥⲟⲉⲓ
ⲛ̄ⲙ̄ⲧⲁⲛ ⲛⲉⲩ, ³⁰ ⲁⲩⲱ ⲥⲉⲉⲙⲁⲍⲧⲉ ⲛⲙ̄ⲙⲉⲩ ³¹ ⲁⲍⲟⲩⲛ, ⲉⲩⲍⲏⲛ ⲁⲍⲟⲩⲛ ³² ⲁⲣⲁϥ, ⲍⲱⲥ
ⲁⲧⲣⲟⲩϫⲟⲟⲥ ϫⲉ, ³³ « ⲁⲩϫⲓ ⲁⲃⲁⲗ ⲍ̄ⲛ ⲡⲉϥⲍⲟ ³⁴ ⲁⲃⲁⲗ ⲍⲓ̈ⲧⲟⲟⲧϥ ⲛ̄ⲛⲓⲁⲥⲡⲁⲥ- ³⁵ ⲙⲟⲥ ».
ⲥⲉⲟⲩⲁⲛⲍ ⲇⲉ ⲉⲛ ⁴²·¹ ⲁⲃⲁⲗ ⲛ̄ϭⲓ ⲛⲉⲉⲓ ⲙ̄ⲡⲓⲣⲏⲧⲉ ² ϫⲉ ⲙⲡⲟⲩⲣ̄ ⲧⲡⲉ ⲙ̄ⲙⲓⲛ ⲙ̄ⲙⲁⲩ, ³ ⲟⲩⲧⲉ
ⲙ̄ⲡⲟⲩϣⲱⲱⲧ ⲙ̄ⲡⲉⲩ ⁴ ⲙ̄ⲡⲓⲱⲧ, ⲟⲩⲧⲉ ⲛ̄ⲥⲉⲙⲉⲩⲉ ⲁⲣⲁϥ ⁵ ⲉⲛ ⲍⲱⲥ ϣⲏⲙ, ⲟⲩⲧⲉ ϫⲉ ϥⲥⲁϣⲓ,
⁶ ⲟⲩⲧⲉ ϫⲉ ⲟⲩⲃⲁⲗⲕϥ̄ ⲡⲉ. ⲁⲗⲗⲁ ⲟⲩ- ⁷ ⲁⲧⲡⲉⲑⲁⲩ ⲡⲉ, ⲟⲩⲁⲧⲱⲧⲁⲣⲧⲣ̄ ⲡⲉ, ⁸ ⲟⲩⲍⲗⲁϭ ⲡⲉ,
ⲉϥⲥⲁⲩⲛⲉ ⲁⲙⲁ- ⁹ ⲉⲓⲧ ⲛⲓⲙ ⲉⲙⲡⲁⲧⲟⲩϣⲱⲡⲉ, ⲁⲩⲱ ¹⁰ ⲛⲉϥⲣ̄ ⲭⲣⲓⲁ ⲉⲛ ⲁⲧⲣⲟⲩⲧⲥⲉⲃⲉ ⲉⲓ- ¹¹ ⲉⲧϥ̄
ⲁⲃⲁⲗ.

ⲡⲉⲉⲓ ⲡⲉ ⲡⲣⲏⲧⲉ ⲛ̄- ¹² ⲛⲉⲧⲉⲟⲩⲛ̄ⲧⲉⲩ ⲙ̄ⲙⲉⲩ ¹³ ⲁⲃⲁⲗ ⲍ̄ⲛ ⲡⲥⲁ ⲍⲣⲉ ⲛ̄ⲧⲟⲟⲧⲥ̄ ⲛ̄ⲧ̄- ¹⁴ ⲙⲛ̄ⲧⲛⲁϭ
ⲛⲁⲧⲱϫⲓⲧⲥ̄, ⲉⲟⲩⲥⲁ- ¹⁵ ⲙⲧ̄ ⲛ̄ⲥⲁ ⲡⲓⲟⲩⲉⲓ ⲟⲩⲁⲉⲉⲧϥ̄ ¹⁶ ⲁⲩⲱ ⲡⲉⲧϫⲏⲕ ⲁⲃⲁⲗ, ⲡⲉⲧⲟⲉⲓ ⲙ̄- ¹⁷ ⲙⲉⲩ
ⲛⲉⲩ. ⲁⲩⲱ ⲙⲁⲩϣⲉ ⲁⲍⲣⲏ- ¹⁸ ⲉⲓ ⲁⲉⲙⲛ̄ⲧⲉ, ⲟⲩⲧⲉ ⲙⲛ̄ⲧⲉⲩ ¹⁹ ⲫⲑⲟⲛⲟⲥ ⲙ̄ⲙⲉⲩ, ⲟⲩⲧⲉ ²⁰ ⲁϣⲉⲣⲁⲙ
ⲟⲩⲧⲉ ⲙⲛ̄ ⲙⲟⲩ ⲛ̄- ²¹ ⲍⲣⲏⲓ̈ ⲛ̄ⲍⲏⲧⲟⲩ. ⲁⲗⲗⲁ ⲉⲩⲙⲁ- ²² ⲧⲛ̄ ⲙ̄ⲙⲁⲩ ⲍ̄ⲛ ⲡⲉⲧⲙⲁⲧⲛ̄ ²³ ⲙ̄ⲙⲁϥ,
ⲉⲩⲣⲁⲥⲓ ⲉⲛ, ⲟⲩⲧⲉ ²⁴ ⲉⲩϭⲗ̄ⲙ̄ⲗⲁⲙⲛ̄ⲧ ⲉⲛ ⲙ̄ⲡⲕⲱ- ²⁵ ⲧⲉ ⲙ̄ⲧⲙⲏⲉ. ⲁⲗⲗⲁ ⲛ̄ⲧⲁⲩ ²⁶ ⲣⲱ ⲡⲉ ⲧⲙⲏⲉ,
ⲁⲩⲱ ⲉϥϣⲟ- ²⁷ ⲟⲡ ⲛ̄ⲍⲏⲧⲟⲩ ⲛ̄ϭⲓ ⲡⲓⲱⲧ, ⲁⲩⲱ ⲛ̄- ²⁸ ⲧⲁⲩ ⲉⲩⲍ̄ⲛ ⲡⲓⲱⲧ ⲉⲩϫⲏⲕ ⲁ- ²⁹ ⲃⲁⲗ ⲉⲩⲟⲉⲓ
ⲛ̄ⲁⲧⲡⲱϣⲉ ⲍ̄ⲛ ³⁰ ⲡⲓⲁⲅⲁⲑⲟⲥ ⲛⲁⲙⲏⲉ, ⲉⲩϯ ³¹ ϣⲧⲁ ⲗⲁⲩⲉ ⲉⲛ ⲍ̄ⲛ ⲗⲁⲩⲉ, ⲁⲗⲗⲁ ³² ⲉⲩϯ ⲙ̄ⲧⲁⲛ,
ⲉⲩⲗⲏⲕ ⲍ̄ⲛ ⲡⲉ- ³³ ⲡⲛⲉⲩⲙⲁ. ⲁⲩⲱ ⲉⲩⲛⲁⲥⲱⲧⲙ̄ ⲁⲧⲉⲩ- ³⁴ ⲛⲟⲩⲛⲉ ⲉⲩⲛⲁⲥⲣϥⲉ ⲁⲣⲁⲩ ³⁵ ⲛⲉⲉⲓ
ⲉⲧϥⲛⲁϭⲛ̄ ⲧⲉϥⲛⲟⲩⲛⲉ ³⁶ ⲛ̄ⲍⲏⲧⲟⲩ, ⲛ̄ϥⲧⲙⲣ̄ ⲡⲁⲥⲓ ⲛ̄ⲧⲉϥ- ³⁷ ⲯⲩⲭⲏ. ⲡⲉⲉⲓ ⲡⲉ ⲡⲧⲟⲡⲟⲥ ⲛ̄ⲛⲓ- ³⁸
ⲙⲁⲕⲁⲣⲓⲟⲥ· ⲡⲉⲉⲓ ⲡⲉ ⲡⲟⲩⲧⲟ- ³⁹ ⲡⲟⲥ.

ⲡⲕⲉϣⲱϫⲡ̄ ϭⲉ ⲙⲁⲣⲟⲩ- ⁴⁰ ⲙ̄ⲙⲉ ⲍ̄ⲛ ⲛⲟⲩⲧⲟⲡⲟⲥ ϫⲉ ⲟⲩ- ⁴¹ ⲡⲉⲧⲉϣϣⲉ ⲁⲣⲁⲉⲓ ⲉⲛ ⲡⲉ, ⁴³·¹
ⲉⲁⲥⲓϣⲱⲡⲉ ⲍ̄ⲙ ⲡⲙⲁ ⲛ̄ⲙ̄ⲧⲁⲛ, ² ⲁϣⲉϫⲉ ⲁⲕⲉⲍⲱⲃ. ⲁⲗⲗⲁ ⲛ̄ⲧⲁϥ ³ ⲡⲉⲧⲛⲁϣⲱⲡⲉ ⲛ̄ⲍⲏⲧϥ̄,
ⲁⲩⲱ ⲁ- ⁴ ⲥ̄ⲣϥⲉ ⲛ̄ⲛⲉⲩ ⲛⲓⲙ ⲁⲡⲓⲱⲧ ⲛ̄ⲧⲉ ⁵ ⲡⲧⲏⲣϥ̄ ⲟⲩⲱϣ̄ⲛ ⲛⲓⲥⲛⲏⲩ ⲛⲁ- ⁶ ⲙⲏⲉ, ⲛⲉⲉⲓ
ⲉⲣⲉϯⲁⲅⲁⲡⲏ ⲙ̄- ⁷ ⲡⲓⲱⲧ ϣⲟⲩⲟ ⲁϫⲱⲟⲩ ⲁⲩⲱ ⲙⲛ̄ ⁸ ϣⲧⲁ ⲛ̄ⲧⲉϥ ϣⲟⲟⲡ ⲍ̄ⲛ ⲧⲟⲩⲙⲏⲧⲉ. ⁹ ⲛⲉⲉⲓ
ⲛ̄ⲧⲁⲩ ⲉⲧⲟⲩⲱ[[ⲍ]]ⲛ[[ⲙ]]ⲍ̄ ¹⁰ ⲙⲁⲙⲏⲉ[[ⲓ]], ⲉⲩϣⲟⲟⲡ ⲍ̄ⲙ ⲡⲓⲱⲛⲍ ¹¹ ⲛⲁⲙⲏⲉ ⲁⲩⲱ ⲛ̄ⲛⲁⲛⲏⲍⲉ,
ⲁⲩⲱ ¹² ⲉⲩϣⲉϫⲉ ⲁⲡⲟⲩⲁⲉⲓⲛ ⲉⲧ- ¹³ ϫⲏⲕ ⲁⲃⲁⲗ ⲁⲩⲱ ⲉⲧⲙⲏⲍ ⲍ̄ⲛ ¹⁴ ⲡⲓⲥⲡⲉⲣⲙⲁ ⲛ̄ⲧⲉ ⲡⲓⲱⲧ
ⲁⲩⲱ ¹⁵ ⲉⲧⲍ̄ⲛ ⲡⲉϥⲍⲏⲧ ⲁⲩⲱ ⲍ̄ⲛ ⲡⲓⲡ- ¹⁶ ⲗⲏⲣⲱⲙⲁ. ⲉⲩⲧⲉⲗⲏⲗ ⲛ̄ⲍⲏⲧϥ̄ ¹⁷ ⲛ̄ϭⲓ ⲡⲉϥⲡⲛⲉⲩⲙⲁ,
ⲁⲩⲱ ⲉϥϯ ⲉⲁⲩ ¹⁸ ⲙ̄ⲡⲉⲧⲉⲛⲉϥϣⲟⲟⲡ ⲛ̄ⲍⲏⲧϥ̄ ¹⁹ ϫⲉ ⲛⲁⲛⲟⲩϥ. ⲁⲩⲱ ⲥⲉⲭⲏⲕ ²⁰ ⲁⲃⲁⲗ ⲛ̄ϭⲓ
ⲛⲉϥϣⲏⲣⲉ ⲁⲩⲱ ²¹ ⲥⲉⲙ̄ⲡϣⲁ ⲙ̄ⲡⲉϥⲣⲉⲛ, ϫⲉ ²² ⲛ̄ⲧⲁϥ ⲅⲁⲣ ⲡⲓⲱⲧ ⲍ̄ⲛ ⲍ̄ϣⲏ- ²³ ⲣⲉ ⲛ̄ⲧⲉⲉⲓⲙⲓⲛⲉ
ⲛⲉⲧϥⲟⲩⲁ- ²⁴ ϣⲟⲩ.

their ²³ own thought < . . . >. For the place ²⁴ where they send their thought, ²⁵ that place, ²⁶ their root, <is> that which lifts them ²⁷ up in all the heights ²⁸ to the Father. They have his ²⁹ head, since it is rest for them, ³⁰ and they are supported, ³¹ drawing near ³² to him, as it is said, ³³ "They partake of his face ³⁴ through kisses." ³⁵ But they are not manifest ^{42.1} in this way ² because they themselves were not elevated, ³ (and yet) they did not lack the glory ⁴ of the Father, nor did they consider him ⁵ to be small, ⁶ or embittered, or angry. Rather, ⁷ he is without evil, he is undisturbable, ⁸ he is sweet, knowing all spaces ⁹ before they have come about, and ¹⁰ he did not need to be ¹¹ taught.

This is the way of ¹² those who have ¹³ (a thing) from above by the limitless ¹⁴ greatness, those awaiting ¹⁵ the one alone ¹⁶ and the perfect one, the one who is ¹⁷ there for them. And they do not go down ¹⁸ to Hades, nor do they have ¹⁹ jealousy nor ²⁰ deep sighing nor death ²¹ within them. But resting ²² themselves in the one who rests, ²³ they are not troubled, nor ²⁴ are they entangled in the fence ²⁵ around the truth. But they are themselves ²⁶ the truth, and the Father dwells ²⁷ within them, and ²⁸ they are in the Father since they are perfect, ²⁹ undivided in ³⁰ the one who is truly good, ³¹ not deficient in anything, but ³² at rest, refreshed in the ³³ Spirit. And they will listen to their ³⁴ root, since they will be occupied ³⁵ with these things in which he will find his root, ³⁶ and he will not suffer the loss of his ³⁷ soul. This is the place of the ³⁸ blessings; this is their ³⁹ place.

As for the rest, then, let them ⁴⁰ know in their places that ⁴¹ it is not fitting for me, ^{43.1} since I have arrived at the place of rest, ² to say anything. But it is ³ that in which I have come to be, and ⁴ (it is fitting) to be concerned at all times with the Father of ⁵ the Entirety and those who are truly brothers, ⁶ those upon whom the love of ⁷ the Father pours and in whose midst no ⁸ deficiency of him exists. ⁹ Those are the ones who are manifest ¹⁰ truly, dwelling in life ¹¹ truly and eternally, and ¹² speaking the light that is ¹³ perfect and filled with ¹⁴ the seed of the Father and ¹⁵ that is in his heart and in the ¹⁶ fullness. His spirit rejoices within him, ¹⁷ and it glorifies ¹⁸ the one within which it dwelled ¹⁹ because he is good. And his children ²⁰ are perfect, and ²¹ they are worthy of his name, for ²² he is the Father, (and) children ²³ of this sort are those whom he ²⁴ desires.

42.17 "there": or "thought."

IX. *TREATISE ON THE RESURRECTION*

The *Treatise on the Resurrection*, also called the *Epistle to Rheginos*, is the title of the fourth text in Nag Hammadi codex I. The text purports to be a letter written to an otherwise unknown Christian named Rheginos, who may have asked the author for special teaching regarding the nature of the Savior's resurrection. Of particular interest is the nature of the Savior's resurrected self, possibly occasioned by confusion over Paul's teaching in 1 Corinthians 15. Unfortunately, the author's own understanding of the reality of the fleshly resurrection remains elusive on account of an elliptical question that can be taken plainly or rhetorically: "Why will you not receive flesh when you ascend into the eternity?" Whatever the author's own view, the *Treatise on the Resurrection* contributes to our knowledge of the kinds of debates that occupied early Christians concerning the nature of the self after death. The *Treatise on the Resurrection* was likely composed in the late second century C.E. in Greek.

43.25 ΟΥΝ ϨⲀⲈΙⲚⲈ, ΠⲀϢⲎⲢⲈ ⲢⲎ- 26 ⲄΙⲚΟⲤ, ⲈⲨϢϢⲈ ⲀⲤⲂⲰ ⲀϨⲀϨ. 27 ΟΥⲚⲦⲈⲨ ⲘⲘⲈⲨ ⲘⲠΙⲤⲔΟⲠΟⲤ
28 ⲈⲨⲈⲘⲀⲢⲦⲈ ⲚϨⲚϨⲎⲦⲎⲘⲀ 29 ⲈⲨϢⲀⲀⲦ ⲘⲠⲈⲨⲂⲰⲖ. ⲀⲨⲰ 30 ⲈⲨϢⲀⲚⲘⲈⲈⲦⲈ ⲀⲚⲈⲈΙ, ϢⲀⲨ- 31
ⲘⲈⲨⲈ ⲀϨⲚⲘⲚⲦⲚⲀϬ ⲚϨⲢⲎ- 32 Ï ⲚϨⲎⲦΟⲨ. ⲚⲦⲘⲈⲨⲈ ⲚⲆⲈ ⲈⲚ 33 ϪⲈ ⲀⲨⲀϨⲈ ⲀⲢⲈⲦΟⲨ ⲘⲪΟⲨⲚ
Ⲙ- 34 ⲠⲖΟⲄΟⲤ ⲚⲦⲘⲎⲈ ⲈⲨϢΙⲚⲈ 35 ⲚϨΟⲨΟ ⲀⲠⲈⲨⲘⲦⲀⲚ, ⲠⲈⲈΙ 36 ⲚⲦⲀϨⲚϪΙⲦϤ ϨΙⲦⲘ ⲠⲚⲤⲰ- 37
ⲦⲎⲢ, ⲠⲚϪⲀⲈΙⲤ ⲠⲈⲬⲢⲎⲤⲦΟⲤ. 44.1 ⲚⲦⲀϨⲚϪΙⲦϤ ⲚⲦⲀⲢⲈⲚⲤΟⲨ- 2 ⲰⲚ ⲦⲘⲎⲈ ⲀⲨⲰ ⲀⲚⲘⲦⲀⲚ 3
ⲘⲘⲀⲚ ⲀϨⲢⲎΪ ⲀϪⲰⲤ. ⲀⲖⲖⲀ 4 ⲈⲠⲈΙⲆⲎ ⲈⲔϢΙⲚⲈ ⲘⲘⲀⲚ 5 ⲀⲠⲈⲦⲈϢϢⲈ ϨⲚ ΟΥϨⲖⲀϬ 6 ⲈⲦⲂⲈ
ⲦⲀⲚⲀⲤⲦⲀⲤΙⲤ, ⲦⲤϨⲈ- 7 ⲈΙ ⲚⲈⲔ ϪⲈ ΟΥⲀⲚⲀⲄⲔⲀΙΟⲚ 8 ⲦⲈ. ⲀⲨⲰ ΟΥⲚ ϨⲀϨ ⲘⲘⲈⲚ Ο- 9 ⲈΙ
ⲚⲀⲠΙⲤⲦΟⲤ ⲀⲢⲀⲤ, ϨⲚⲔΟⲨ- 10 ⲈΙ ⲚⲆⲈ ⲚⲈⲦϬΙⲚⲈ ⲘⲘⲀⲤ 11 ⲈⲦⲂⲈ ⲠⲈⲈΙ ⲘⲀⲢⲈⲠⲖΟⲄΟⲤ 12 ϢⲰⲠⲈ
ⲚⲈⲚ ⲈⲦⲂⲎⲦⲤ.

Ⲛ- 13 ⲦⲀϨⲀⲠϪⲀⲈΙⲤ Ⲣ ⲬⲢⲰ ⲚⲈϢ 14 ⲚϨⲈ ⲚⲚϨⲂⲎⲨⲈ ⲈⲨϢΟ- 15 ΟⲠ ϨⲚ ⲤⲀⲢⲜ ⲀⲨⲰ ⲚⲦⲀ- 16
ⲢⲈϤΟⲨⲀⲚϨϤ ⲀⲂⲀⲖ ⲈⲨϢⲎ- 17 ⲢⲈ ⲚⲚΟⲨⲦⲈ ⲠⲈ; ⲀϤϨⲘⲀϨⲈ 18 ϨⲚ ⲠΙⲦΟⲠΟⲤ ⲠⲈⲈΙ ⲈⲦⲔϨ- 19
ⲘⲀⲤⲦ ⲚϨⲎⲦϤ, ⲈϤϢⲈϪⲈ 20 ⲀⲠⲚΟⲘΟⲤ ⲚⲦϤⲨⲤΙⲤ—ⲈⲈΙϪΟⲨ 21 ⲚⲆⲈ ⲘⲘⲀϤ ϪⲈ «ⲠⲘΟⲨ».
ⲠϢⲎ- 22 ⲢⲈ ⲚⲆⲈ ⲘⲠⲚΟⲨⲦⲈ, ⲢⲎⲄΙⲚⲈ, 23 ⲚⲈⲨϢⲎⲢⲈ ⲚⲢⲰⲘⲈ ⲠⲈ. ⲀⲨ- 24 Ⲱ ⲚⲈϤⲈⲘⲀⲢⲦⲈ ⲀⲢⲀⲨ
ⲘⲠⲈ- 25 ⲤⲚⲈⲨ, ⲈⲨⲚⲦⲈϤ ⲘⲘⲈⲨ ⲚⲦ- 26 ⲘⲚⲦⲢⲰⲘⲈ ⲘⲚ ⲦⲘⲚⲦⲚΟⲨ- 27 ⲦⲈ ϪⲈⲔⲀⲤⲈ ⲈϤⲚⲀⲬⲢΟ
ⲘⲘⲈⲚ 28 ⲀⲠⲘΟⲨ ⲀⲂⲀⲖ ϨΙⲦⲘ ⲠⲦⲢϤ- 29 ϢⲰⲠⲈ ⲚϢⲎⲢⲈ ⲚⲚΟⲨⲦⲈ, 30 ϨΙⲦΟΟⲦϤ ⲆⲈ ⲘⲠϢⲎⲢⲈ
Ⲙ- 31 ⲠⲢⲰⲘⲈ ⲈⲢⲈⲦⲀⲠΟⲔⲀⲦⲀⲤⲦⲀ- 32 ⲤΙⲤ ⲚⲀϢⲰⲠⲈ ⲀϨΟⲨⲚ ⲀⲠ- 33 ⲠⲖⲎⲢⲰⲘⲀ, ⲈⲠⲈΙⲆⲎ
ⲚϢⲀ- 34 ⲢⲠ ⲈϤϢΟΟⲠ ⲀⲂⲀⲖ ϨⲘ ⲠⲤⲀ Ⲛ- 35 ⲦⲠⲈ ⲚⲤⲠⲈⲢⲘⲀ ⲚⲦⲘⲎⲈ ⲈⲘ- 36 ⲠⲀⲦⲈⲦⲤⲨⲤⲦⲀⲤΙⲤ
ϢⲰⲠⲈ. 37 ϨⲚ ⲦⲈⲈΙ ⲀϨⲚⲘⲚⲦϪⲀⲈΙⲤ ⲘⲚ 38 ϨⲚⲘⲚⲦⲚΟⲨⲦⲈ ϢⲰⲠⲈ ⲈⲚⲀ- 39 ϢⲰⲨ.

ⲦⲤⲀⲨⲚⲈ ϪⲈ ⲈⲈΙⲦⲈⲨΟ 45.1 ⲘⲠⲂⲰⲖ ϨⲚ ϨⲚϨⲂⲎⲨⲈ Ⲛ- 2 ⲆⲨⲤⲔΟⲖΟⲚ, ⲀⲖⲖⲀ ⲘⲚ ⲖⲀⲨⲈ Ⲛ- 3
ⲆⲨⲤⲔΟⲖΟⲚ ϢΟΟⲠ ϨⲘ ⲠⲖΟ- 4 ⲄΟⲤ ⲚⲦⲘⲎⲈ. ⲀⲖⲖⲀ ⲈⲠⲈΙⲆⲎ Ⲉ- 5 ⲦⲢⲈ ⲠⲂⲰⲖ ⲚⲦⲀϤⲈΙ ⲀⲂⲀⲖ
Ⲁ- 6 ⲦⲘⲎⲦⲈ ⲀⲦⲘⲔⲈ ⲖⲀⲨⲈ ⲈϤϬⲎⲠ, 7 ⲀⲖⲖⲀ ⲀⲦⲢⲈϤΟⲨⲰⲚϨ ⲀⲂⲀⲖ 8 ⲘⲠⲦⲎⲢϤ ϨⲀⲠⲖⲰⲤ ⲈⲦⲂⲈ
Ⲡ- 9 ϢⲰⲠⲈ, ⲠⲂⲰⲖ ⲀⲂⲀⲖ ⲘⲘⲈⲚ 10 ⲘⲠⲠⲈⲐⲀⲨ ⲠΟⲨⲰⲚϨ ⲆⲈ Ⲁ- 11 ⲂⲀⲖ ⲘⲠⲈⲦⲤⲀⲦⲠ. ⲦⲈⲈΙ ⲦⲈ
12 ⲦⲠⲢΟⲂΟⲖⲎ ⲚⲦⲘⲎⲈ ⲘⲚ ⲠⲈ- 13 ⲠⲚⲈⲨⲘⲀ, ⲦⲈⲬⲀⲢΙⲤ ⲦⲀ ⲦⲘⲎ- 14 Ⲉ ⲦⲈ.

ⲠⲤⲰⲦⲎⲢ ⲀϤϢⲰⲘⲔ Ⲙ- 15 ⲠⲘΟⲨ—ⲚⲔⲎⲠ ⲈⲚ ⲀⲢ ⲀⲦⲤⲀⲨⲚⲈ—16 ⲀϤⲔⲰ ⲚⲄⲀⲢ ⲀϨⲢⲎΪ ⲘⲠⲔΟ-
17 ⲤⲘΟⲤ ⲈϢⲀϤⲦⲈⲔΟ. ⲀϤϢϤⲦ[ϥ] 18 ⲀϨΟⲨⲚ ⲀⲨⲀΙⲰⲚ ⲚⲀⲦⲦⲈⲔΟ, 19 ⲀⲨⲰ ⲀϤⲦΟⲨⲚⲀⲤϤ ⲈⲀϤϢⲰ-
20 ⲘⲚⲔ ⲘⲠⲈⲦΟⲨⲀⲚϨ ⲀⲂⲀⲖ 21 ⲀⲂⲀⲖ ϨΙⲦΟΟⲦϤ ⲘⲠⲀⲦⲚⲈⲨ 22 ⲀⲢⲀϤ. ⲀⲨⲰ ⲀϤϮ ⲚⲈⲚ Ⲛ- 23
ⲦⲈϨΙⲎ ⲚⲦⲚⲘⲚⲦⲀⲦⲘΟⲨ. ⲦΟ- 24 ⲦⲈ ϬⲈ ⲚⲐⲈ ⲚⲦⲀϨⲀⲠⲀⲠΟⲤⲦΟ- 25 ⲖΟⲤ ϪΟΟϤ ϪⲈ, «ⲀⲚϢⲠ
ϨΙⲤⲈ 26 ⲚⲘⲘⲈϤ, ⲀⲨⲰ ⲀⲚⲦⲰⲰⲚ 27 ⲚⲘⲘⲈϤ, ⲀⲨⲰ ⲀⲚⲂⲰⲔ ⲀⲦⲠⲈ 28 ⲚⲘⲘⲈϤ». ⲈΙϢⲠⲈ ⲦⲚϢΟ-
29 ΟⲠ ⲚⲆⲈ ⲈⲚΟⲨⲀⲚϨ ⲀⲂⲀⲖ ϨⲘ 30 ⲠΙⲔΟⲤⲘΟⲤ ⲈⲚⲢ ⲪΟⲢⲈΙ Ⲙ- 31 ⲘⲀϤ, ⲈⲚϢΟΟⲠ ⲚⲀⲔⲦΙⲚ 32
ⲘⲠⲈⲦⲘⲘⲈⲨ, ⲀⲨⲰ ⲈⲨⲈ- 33 ⲘⲀϨⲦⲈ ⲘⲘⲀⲚ ⲀⲂⲀⲖ ϨΙⲦΟ- 34 ΟⲦϤ ϢⲀ ⲠⲚϨⲢⲰⲦⲠ, ⲈⲦⲈ ⲠⲈ- 35 ⲈΙ
ⲠⲈ ⲠⲈⲚⲘΟⲨ ϨⲘ ⲠⲈⲈΙⲂΙ- 36 ΟⲤ. ⲈⲨⲤⲰⲔ ⲘⲘⲀⲚ ⲀⲦⲠⲈ Ⲁ- 37 ⲂⲀⲖ ϨΙⲦΟΟⲦϤ ⲚⲐⲈ ⲚⲚΙⲀⲔⲦΙⲚ 38
ϨΙⲦⲘ ⲠⲢⲎ, ⲈⲚⲤⲈⲈⲘⲀϨⲦⲈ Ⲙ- 39 ⲘⲀⲚ ⲈⲚ ϨΙⲦⲚ ⲖⲀⲨⲈ. ⲦⲈⲈΙ ⲦⲈ 40 ⲦⲀⲚⲀⲤⲦⲀⲤΙⲤ ⲚⲠⲚⲈⲨⲘⲀ- 46.1
ⲦΙⲔⲎ ⲈⲤⲰⲘⲚⲔ ⲚⲦⲮⲨⲬΙⲔⲎ 2 ϨΟⲘΟΙⲰⲤ ⲘⲚ ⲦⲔⲈⲤⲀⲢⲔΙⲔⲎ.

44.13 Ⲣ ⲬⲢⲰ: following Schenke, I understand this verb to be χρᾶν, "to impart an oracle."
44.17 ⲀϤϨⲘⲀϨⲈ: Following Barns, I suspect that metathesis has occurred between ϥ and Ϩ and that
the MS should read ⲀϤϩⲙⲁϩⲉ, "he walked."
45.4–5 ⲈⲦⲢⲈ: read ⲈⲦⲂⲈ (following Polotsky).

43.25 There are some, my son Rheginos, 26 who desire to learn many things. 27 They have this objective 28 when captivated by questions 29 lacking answers. 30 If they are successful in these things, they often 31 think highly of 32 themselves. But I do not think 33 that they have stood within the word 34 of truth, since they seek 35 instead their own rest, which 36 we have received from our 37 Savior, our Lord Christ. 44.1 We received it once we came to know 2 the truth and rested 3 ourselves upon it. But 4 since you ask us 5 earnestly about what is fitting (to believe) 6 concerning the resurrection, I write 7 to you that it is necessary. 8 Indeed many 9 lack faith in it, but a few 10 find it. 11 For this reason let 12 us explore the topic.

13 How did the Lord proclaim 14 things while 15 in the flesh and after 16 he revealed himself as Son 17 of God? He walked about 18 in this place where you 19 reside, speaking 20 about the law of nature—but I 21 call it "death." Moreover, the Son 22 of God, Rheginos, 23 was Son of Man. 24 He possessed them 25 both, having 26 humanity and divinity 27 so that he might conquer 28 death by 29 being Son of God, 30 and by being the Son of 31 Man the restoration 32 might occur into the 33 realm of fullness, since initially 34 he was from above 35 as a seed of truth before 36 his ordering had come to be. 37 Within this (ordering) rulers and 38 divinities came into existence 39 in abundance.

I know that I am offering 45.1 the answer in terms 2 that are perplexing, but there is nothing 3 perplexing about the Word 4 of truth. But since 5 on account of the answer he (the Word) came into 6 the middle so that nothing else would remain hidden, 7 but he would reveal plainly 8 everything about 9 existence, both the destruction 10 of evil and the revelation 11 of the elect. This is 12 the emanation of truth and 13 spirit; grace belongs to 14 truth.

The Savior swallowed 15 death—you are not thought to be ignorant (about this)—16 for he set aside the world, 17 since it is perishing. He transformed [himself] 18 into an imperishable eternity, 19 and he raised himself up after swallowing 20 the visible 21 through the invisible. 22 He gave us 23 the path of our immortality. Then, 24 therefore, as the apostle 25 said, "We suffered 26 with him, and we rose 27 with him, and we went to heaven 28 with him." If we 29 appear in 30 this world bearing 31 him, we are the rays 32 of that one, and we 33 are grasped by 34 him until our setting, 35 that is, our death in this 36 life. We are drawn to heaven 37 by him like rays 38 by the sun, and 39 we are not detained by anything. This is 40 the spiritual resurrection 46.1 that swallows the soulish 2 just like the fleshly.

43.37 "our Lord Christ": hereafter alternatively "our Lord, the Excellent One."

44.11–12 "For this reason let us explore the topic": literally, "For this reason let the teaching come about to us on account of it (i.e., the resurrection)."

44.19–20 "speaking about the law of nature": or "speaking *against* the law of nature."

³ ειϣπε ογν ογεει ν̄Δε εμϥ- ⁴ πιστεγε εν, μ̄ν̄τεϥ μ̄μεγ μ̄- ⁵ π̄ρ πειθε. πτοπος γαρ ν̄τπι- ⁶ стιс πε παϣηρε αγω πα π̄ρ ⁷ πειθε εν πε. πετμααγτ να- ⁸ τωων. αγω ογν πετρ̄ πιστεγ- ⁹ ε ϩν̄ ν̄φιλοσοφος ετν̄νιμα· ¹⁰ αλλα ϥ̄νατωων. αγω πφιλο- ¹¹ софос ετν̄νιμα, μ̄πωρ ατρεϥ- ¹² πιστεγε ογρεϥκτο μ̄μαϥ ογ- ¹³ [α]εετϥ—αγω ετβε τν̄πιстιс. ¹⁴ [α]ϩν̄соγν̄ πϣηρε ν̄γαρ μ̄- ¹⁵ πρωμε, αγω αϩν̄πιστεγε ¹⁶ Χε αϥτωογν αβαλ ϩν̄ νετ- ¹⁷ μαογτ. αγω πεει πετν̄χογ ¹⁸ μ̄μαϥ Χε· «αϥϣωπε ν̄βωλ ¹⁹ αβαλ μ̄πμογ ϩως ογναϭ ²⁰ πε `π´ετογρ̄ πιστεγε αραϥ». ϩν̄- ²¹ ναΤ νε νετρ̄ πιστεγε.

ν̄ϥνα- ²² τεκο εν ν̄ϭι πμεγε ν̄νε- ²³ τογαχ. ν̄ϥνατεκο εν ν̄ϭι ²⁴ πνογс ν̄νεταϩсογωνϥ. ²⁵ ετβε πεει τν̄сατπ αϩογν ²⁶ απογχεει μ̄ν πсωτε ε- ²⁷ αϩογταϣν̄ Χιν ν̄ϣαρπ̄ ²⁸ ατρ̄ν̄τμ̄ϩαειε ϩν̄ τμ̄ν̄τ- ²⁹ αθητ ν̄νετοει ν̄ατсαγνε, ³⁰ αλλα εναει αϩογν ατμ̄ν̄τ- ³¹ ρ̄μ̄<ν>ϩητ ν̄νεταϩсογων τ- ³² μηε. τμηε ϭε ετογραεις α- ³³ ραс μ̄ν ϣϭαμ ν̄κλαс α- ³⁴ βαλ, ογτε νεсϣωπε. ογ- ³⁵ Χωρε πε <π>сγстημα μ̄π- ³⁶ πληρωμα. ογκογει πε πεν- ³⁷ ταϩβωλ αβαλ, αϥϣωπε ³⁸ μ̄κοςμος. πτηρϥ ν̄Δε πε ³⁹ πετογεμαϩτε μ̄μαϥ ατρεϥ- ⁴⁷·¹ ϣωπε, νεϥϣοοπ πε. ϩως- ² τε μ̄πωρ αρ̄ Διстαζε ετβε ³ τανастаςιс, παϣηρε ρηγινε. ⁴ ειϣπε νεκϣοοπ ν̄γαρ εν ⁵ ϩν̄ сαρ̄ζ, ακΧι сαρ̄ζ ν̄ταρεκ- ⁶ ει αϩογν απικοсμος. ετβε ⁷ εγ ν̄κναΧι εν ⁸ ν̄τсαρ̄ζ εκϣαν- ⁸ βωκ αϩρηι αϩογν απαιων; ⁹ πετсατπ̄ ατсαρ̄ζ πετϣο- ¹⁰ οπ νες ναιτιος μ̄πωνϩ. ¹¹ πετϣωπε ετβητκ̄ μη μ̄- ¹² πωκ εν πε; πετε πωκ πε ¹³ μη ν̄ϥϣοοπ εν ν̄μμεκ; ¹⁴ αλλα εκν̄νιμα εγ πε ετκ- ¹⁵ ϣαατ μ̄μαϥ; πεει πε ν̄τα- ¹⁶ κ̄ρ̄ спογΔαζε αсβο αραϥ.

¹⁷ πΧοριον μ̄πсωμα ετε πε- ¹⁸ ει πε τμ̄ν̄τϩλλο, αγω κ- ¹⁹ ϣοοπ ν̄τεκο. ογν̄τεκ μ̄- ²⁰ μεγ ν̄ταπογсια νογϩηγ. ²¹ ν̄κναϯ ν̄γαρ εν μ̄πετ- ²² сατπ εκϣανβωκ. πεθαγ ²³ ογν̄τεϥ μ̄μεγ μ̄πϭωχ̄β, ²⁴ αλλα ογν̄ ϩματ αραϥ.

μ̄ν λα- ²⁵ αγε ϭε сωτ μ̄μαν αβαλ ²⁶ ν̄νιμα, αλλα πτηρϥ, ετε α- ²⁷ ναν πε, τν̄ογαχ. αϩν̄Χι ²⁸ μ̄πογχεει Χινρ αρηχϥ ²⁹ ϩα θαη. μαρν̄μεγε ν̄ϯϩε- ³⁰ ες. μαρν̄Χι ν̄ϯϩεες.

46.3 εμϥ̄: read ενϥ. ¦ 10 αλλα . . . αγω: read αγω . . . αλλα (following Barns).
46.21 ναΤ: read ναϭ (following Barns).
46.39 ατρεϥ: transcribed as μ̄πεϥ by Peel, but the reading is clear in the earliest photo.
47.28 Χινρ αρηχϥ: read Χινν αρηχϥ.
47.29 ϩα: read ϣα (following Till).
47.30 ϯϩεες: previous scholars have read this word as ϩεεс, and explained it as either ϩε ("way") plus εс (the AF form of the adjective "old") (so Schenke), or as a variant of the noun ϩε (so Till, Layton, Peel).

[3] Yet if then someone does not [4] believe, he does not have [5] the persuasion. For it is the realm of faith, [6] my son, and it is not that belonging to the (realm of) [7] persuasion. The dead will [8] rise. There is one who believes [9] among the philosophers of this world; [10] he will rise. But as for the philosopher [11] of this world, let him not be made [12] to believe that he alone [13] returns himself—indeed (we return) on account of our faith. [14] For we have known the Son of [15] Man, and we have believed [16] that he rose from among the [17] dead. This is the one about whom we say, [18] "He became death's destruction, [19] as he is great, [20] the one in whom they believe." [21] Great are those who believe.

[22] The thought of those [23] who are saved will not be destroyed. [24] The mind of those who have known him will not be destroyed. [25] On account of this we are chosen [26] for salvation and redemption, [27] since we are destined from the beginning [28] not to fall into the [29] senselessness of those who are ignorant, [30] but we will enter into the [31] wisdom of those who have known the [32] truth. Indeed as for the truth that is guarded, [33] it is not possible to abandon it, [34] nor ought it be (abandoned). [35] Strong is <the> ordering of the [36] fullness. Small is that which [37] became separated; it produced [38] (the) world. But the entirety is [39] what is detained in order for it (the world) [47.1] to come into being; it existed. Therefore, [2] do not be in doubt concerning [3] the resurrection, my son Rheginos. [4] For when you did not exist [5] in the flesh, you received flesh once you [6] entered into this world. Why [7] will you not receive flesh when you [8] ascend into the eternity? [9] That which is better than the flesh is that which is [10] for it a cause of life. [11] Isn't it true that what came about on your account [12] belongs to you? Does not that which is yours [13] exist with you? [14] But while you are in this world what do you [15] lack? This is what [16] you have hoped to learn.

[17] The afterbirth of the body is [18] old age, and you [19] are in defilement. You have [20] absence as a benefit. [21] For you will not surrender what is [22] better when you leave. That which is evil [23] has inferiority, [24] but there is grace for it.

There is nothing, [25] therefore, that redeems us from [26] this world, but as for the entirety, which [27] we are, we are saved. We have received [28] salvation from one end [29] to the other. Let us think in this way. [30] Let us learn in this way.

46.34 "nor ought it be (abandoned)": alternatively "nor has it been (abandoned)."

ⲁⲗⲗⲁ ³¹ ⲟⲩⲛ̄ ϩⲁⲉⲓⲛⲉ ⲟⲩⲱϣⲉ ⲁⲙ- ³² ⲙⲉ, ⲛ̄ⲁϩⲣⲉ ⲡϣⲓⲛⲉ ⲉⲧⲃⲉ ³³ ⲛⲉⲧⲟⲩϣⲓⲛⲉ ⲉⲧⲃⲏⲧⲟⲩ, ⲉⲓϣ- ³⁴ ⲡⲉ ⲡⲉⲧⲟⲩⲁϫ, ⲉϥϣⲁⲛⲕⲱ- ³⁵ ⲉ ⲛ̄ⲥⲱϥ ⲙ̄ⲡⲉϥⲥⲱⲙⲁ, `ⲉ´ϥⲛⲁ- ³⁶ ⲟⲩϫⲉⲉⲓ ⲛ̄ⲧⲟⲩⲛⲟⲩ. ⲙ̄ⲡⲣ̄ⲧⲣⲉ- ³⁷ ⲗⲁⲩⲉ ⲣ̄ ⲇⲓⲥⲧⲁⲍⲉ ⲉⲧⲃⲉ ⲡⲉⲉⲓ. ³⁸ ⲛ̄ⲛⲉⲥ ⲛ̄ϩⲉ ϭⲉ ⲛ̄ⲙⲉⲗⲟⲥ ⲉⲧⲟⲩ- ³⁹ ⲁⲁⲛ̄ϩ ⲁⲃⲁⲗ ⲉⲧⲙⲁⲟⲩⲧ ⲛ̄ⲥⲉ- ⁴⁸·¹ ⲛⲁⲟⲩϫⲉⲉⲓ ⲉⲛ, ϫⲉ ⲛ̄ⲙⲉⲗ[ⲟ]ⲥ ⲉ- ² ⲧⲁⲁⲛ̄ϩ ⲉⲧϣⲟⲟⲡ ⲛ̄ϩⲣⲏⲓ̈ ⲛ̄- ³ ϩⲏⲧⲟⲩ ⲛⲉⲩⲛⲁⲧⲱⲟⲩⲛ ⲡⲉ;

ⲉⲩ ⁴ ϭⲉ ⲧⲉ ⲧⲁⲛⲁⲥⲧⲁⲥⲓⲥ; ⲡϭⲱⲗⲡ̄ ⁵ ⲁⲃⲁⲗ ⲡⲉ ⲛ̄ⲟⲩⲁⲉⲓϣ ⲛⲓⲙ ⲛ̄- ⁶ ⲛⲉⲧⲁϩⲧⲱⲟⲩⲛ. ⲉⲓϣⲡⲉ ⲁⲕⲣ̄ ⁷ ⲡⲙⲉⲩⲉ ⲛ̄ⲅⲁⲣ ⲉⲕϭⲱϣ ϩⲙ̄ ⲡⲉⲩ- ⁸ ⲁⲅⲅⲉⲗⲓⲟⲛ ϫⲉ ⲁϩⲏⲗⲉⲓⲁⲥ ⲟⲩ- ⁹ ⲱⲛ̄ϩ ⲁⲃⲁⲗ ⲁⲩⲱ ⲙⲱⲩⲥⲛ̄ⲥ ¹⁰ ⲛⲙ̄ⲙⲉϥ, ⲙ̄ⲡⲱⲣ ⲁⲙⲉⲩⲉ ⲁⲧⲁ- ¹¹ ⲛⲁⲥⲧⲁⲥⲓⲥ ϫⲉ ⲟⲩϥⲁⲛⲧⲁⲥⲓⲁ ¹² ⲧⲉ. ⲟⲩϥⲁⲛⲧⲁⲥⲓⲁ ⲉⲛ ⲧⲉ, ⲁⲗⲗⲁ ¹³ [ⲟ]ⲩⲙⲏⲉ ⲧⲉ ⲛ̄ϩⲟⲩⲟ ⲛ̄ⲇⲉ ⲟⲩ- ¹⁴ ⲡⲉⲧⲉⲥϣⲉ ⲡⲉ ⲁϫⲟⲟⲥ ϫⲉ ⲟⲩ- ¹⁵ ϥⲁⲛⲧⲁⲥⲓⲁ ⲡⲉ ⲡⲕⲟⲥⲙⲟⲥ ¹⁶ ⲛ̄ϩⲟⲩⲟ ⲁⲧⲁⲛⲁⲥⲧⲁⲥⲓⲥ, ⲧⲉⲉⲓ ¹⁷ ⲉⲛⲧⲁⲥϣⲱⲡⲉ ⲁⲃⲁⲗ ϩⲓⲧⲟ- ¹⁸ ⲟⲧϥ̄ ⲙ̄ⲡⲉⲛϫⲁⲉⲓⲥ, ⲡⲥⲱ- ¹⁹ ⲧⲏⲣ, ⲓⲏⲥⲟⲩⲥ ⲡⲉⲭⲣⲏⲥⲧⲟⲥ.

ⲉⲧ- ²⁰ ⲃⲉ ⲉⲩ ⲛ̄ⲇⲉ ⲉⲉⲓⲧⲁⲙⲟ ⲙ̄- ²¹ ⲙⲁⲕ ⲛ̄ⲧⲉⲩⲛⲟⲩ; ⲛⲉⲧⲁ- ²² ⲁⲛ̄ϩ ⲥⲉⲛⲁⲙⲟⲩ. ⲡⲱⲥ ²³ ⲉⲩⲁⲛ̄ϩ ϩⲛ̄ ⲟⲩϥⲁⲛⲧⲁ- ²⁴ ⲥⲓⲁ; ⲛ̄ⲣⲙ̄ⲙⲁⲉⲓ ⲁⲩⲣ̄ ϩⲏ- ²⁵ ⲕⲉ, ⲁⲩⲱ ⲛ̄ⲛⲣⲁⲉⲓ ⲁⲩⲱ̄ⲣ̄- ²⁶ ϣⲱⲣⲟⲩ. ⲡⲧⲏⲣϥ̄ ϣⲁⲣⲉ- ²⁷ ϣ̄ⲃⲉⲓⲉ. ⲟⲩϥⲁⲛⲧⲁⲥⲓⲁ ²⁸ ⲡⲉ ⲡⲕⲟⲥⲙⲟⲥ—ϫⲉⲕⲁⲥⲉ ²⁹ ϭⲉ ⲛⲓⲣ̄ ⲕⲁⲧⲁⲗⲁⲗⲉⲓ ⲥⲁ ⲛ- ³⁰ ϩⲃⲏⲩⲉ ⲁⲡⲉϩⲟⲩⲟ.

ⲁⲗⲗⲁ ³¹ ⲧⲁⲛⲁⲥⲧⲁⲥⲓⲥ ⲙⲛ̄ⲧⲉⲥ ⲙ̄ⲙⲉⲩ ³² ⲙ̄ⲡⲓⲥⲙⲁⲧ ⲛ̄ⲧⲙⲓⲛⲉ, ϫⲉ ³³ ⲧⲙⲏⲉ ⲧⲉ {ⲡⲉ} ⲡⲉⲧⲁϩⲉ ⲁⲣⲉⲧϥ̄. ³⁴ ⲁⲩⲱ ⲡⲟⲩⲱⲛ̄ϩ ⲁⲃⲁⲗ ⲙ̄ⲡⲉ- ³⁵ ⲧϣⲟⲟⲡ ⲡⲉ, ⲁⲩⲱ ⲡⲁϣⲃⲉⲓ- ³⁶ ⲉ ⲡⲉ ⲛ̄ⲛϩⲃⲏⲩⲉ ⲁⲩⲱ ⲟⲩ- ³⁷ ⲙⲉⲧⲁⲃⲟⲗⲏ ⲁϩⲟⲩⲛ ⲁⲩⲙⲛ̄ⲧ- ³⁸ ⲃⲣ̄ⲣⲉ. ⲧⲙⲛ̄ⲧⲁⲧⲧⲉⲕⲟ ⲛ̄ⲅⲁⲣ ⁴⁹·¹ [ⲥϩⲉϯ] [[ⲁϩⲣⲏⲓ]] ⲁⲡⲓⲧⲛ̄ ⲁⲭⲙ̄ ² ⲡⲧⲉⲕⲟ, ⲁⲩⲱ ⲡⲟⲩⲁⲉⲓⲛ ϥϩⲉ- ³ ϯ ⲁⲡⲓⲧⲛ̄ ⲁⲭⲙ̄ ⲡⲕⲉⲕⲉⲓ, ⲉϥ- ⁴ ⲱⲙⲛ̄ⲕ ⲙ̄ⲙⲁϥ. ⲁⲩⲱ ⲡⲡⲗⲏ- ⁵ ⲣⲱⲙⲁ ϥ̄ϫⲱⲕ ⲁⲃⲁⲗ ⲙ̄ⲡⲉϣ- ⁶ ⲧⲁ. ⲛⲉⲉⲓ ⲛⲉ ⲛ̄ⲥⲩⲙⲃⲟⲗⲟⲛ ⲙⲛ̄ ⁷ ⲛ̄ⲧⲁⲛⲧⲛ̄ ⲛ̄ⲧⲁⲛⲁⲥⲧⲁⲥⲓⲥ. ⁸ ⲛ̄ⲧⲁϥ ⲡⲉ ⲉⲧⲧⲁⲙⲓⲟ ⲙ̄ⲡⲉ- ⁹ ⲧⲛⲁⲛⲟⲩϥ.

ϩⲱⲥⲧⲉ ⲙ̄ⲡⲱⲣ ⲁ- ¹⁰ ⲣ̄ ⲛⲟⲉⲓ ⲙⲉⲣⲓⲕⲱⲥ, ⲱ ⲣⲏⲅⲓ- ¹¹ ⲛⲉ, ⲟⲩⲧⲉ ⲙ̄ⲡⲣ̄ⲣ ⲡⲟⲗⲓⲧⲉⲩⲉ- ¹² ⲥⲑⲁⲓ ⲕⲁⲧⲁ ⲧⲉⲉⲓⲥⲁⲣⲝ ⲉⲧⲃⲉ ¹³ ⲧⲙⲛ̄ⲧⲟⲩⲉⲉⲓ, ⲁⲗⲗⲁ ⲁⲙⲟⲩ ⲁ- ¹⁴ ⲃⲁⲗ ϩⲛ̄ ⲛ̄ⲙⲉⲣⲓⲥⲙⲟⲥ ⲙⲛ̄ ⲛ̄- ¹⁵ ⲙ̄ⲣⲣⲉ ⲁⲩⲱ ⲏⲇⲏ ⲟⲩⲛ̄ⲧⲉⲕ ⲙ̄- ¹⁶ ⲙⲉⲩ ⲛ̄ⲧⲁⲛⲁⲥⲧⲁⲥⲓⲥ. ⲉⲓϣ- ¹⁷ ⲡⲉ ⲡⲉⲧⲛⲁⲙⲟⲩ ⲛ̄ⲅⲁⲣ ϥ̄ⲥⲁⲩ- ¹⁸ ⲛⲉ ⲁⲣⲁϥ ⲟⲩⲁⲉⲉⲧϥ̄ ϫⲉ ⲉϥ- ¹⁹ ⲛⲁⲙⲟⲩ—ⲕⲁⲛ ⲉϥϣⲁⲛⲣ̄ ϩⲁϩ ²⁰ ⲛ̄ⲣⲁⲙⲡⲉ ϩⲙ̄ ⲡⲉⲉⲓⲃⲓⲟⲥ, ⲥⲉ- ²¹ ⲉⲓⲛⲉ ⲙ̄ⲙⲁϥ ⲁϩⲟⲩⲛ ⲁⲡⲉⲉⲓ—²² ⲉⲧⲃⲉ ⲉⲩ ⲛ̄ⲧⲁⲕ ⲛ̄ⲕⲛⲉⲩ ⲁⲣⲁⲕ ²³ ⲉⲛ ⲟⲩⲁⲉⲉⲧⲕ̄ ⲉⲁⲕⲧⲱⲟⲩⲛ ⲁⲩ- ²⁴ ⲱ <ⲉ>ⲥⲉⲉⲓⲛⲉ ⲙ̄ⲙⲁⲕ ⲁϩⲟⲩⲛ ⲁⲡⲉ- ²⁵ ⲉⲓ; ⲉⲓϣⲡⲉ ⲟⲩⲛ̄ⲧⲉⲕ ⲙ̄ⲙⲉⲩ ⲙ̄- ²⁶ ⲡⲧⲱⲟⲩⲛ ⲁⲗⲗⲁ ⲕϭⲉⲉⲧ· ϩⲱⲥ ²⁷ ⲉⲕⲛⲁⲙⲟⲩ, ⲕⲁⲓⲧⲟⲓⲅⲉ ⲡⲏ ϥ̄ⲥⲁⲩ- ²⁸ ⲛⲉ ϫⲉ ⲁϥⲙⲟⲩ, ⲉⲧⲃⲉ ⲉⲩ ϭⲉ ²⁹ ϯⲕⲱ ⲁⲃⲁⲗ ⲛ̄ⲥⲁ ⲧⲉⲕⲙⲛ̄ⲧ- ³⁰ ⲁⲧⲣ̄ ⲅⲩⲙⲛⲁⲍⲉ; ϣϣⲉ ⲁⲡⲟⲩ- ³¹ ⲉⲉⲓ ⲡⲟⲩⲉⲉⲓ ⲁⲧⲣⲉϥⲣ̄ ⲁⲥⲕⲉⲓ ³² ⲛ̄ⲟⲩⲁⲡⲥ̄ ⲛ̄ϩⲉⲉⲥ, ⲁⲩⲱ ⲛ̄ⲥⲉ- ³³ ⲃⲁⲗϥ̄ ⲁⲃⲁⲗ ⲙ̄ⲡⲓⲥⲧⲟⲓⲭⲉⲓⲟⲛ ³⁴ ϫⲉⲕⲁⲥⲉ ⲛ̄ϥⲣ̄ ⲡⲗⲁⲛⲁ, ⲁⲗⲗⲁ ⲉϥ- ³⁵ ⲛⲁϫⲓ ⲙ̄ⲙⲁϥ ⲟⲩⲁⲉⲉⲧϥ̄ ⲛ̄ⲕⲉ- ³⁶ ⲥⲁⲡ ⲡⲉⲉⲓ ⲉⲧϣⲣ̄ⲡ̄ ⲛ̄ϣⲟ- ³⁷ ⲟⲡ.

47.38 ⲛ̄ⲛⲉⲥ ⲛ̄ϩⲉ: read ⲛ̄ⲛⲉϣ ⲛ̄ϩⲉ (following Barns).

48.25 ⲛ̄ⲛⲣⲁⲉⲓ: read ⲛ̄ⲣ̄ⲣⲁⲉⲓ. | 26 ϣⲁⲣⲉⲃ: read ϣⲁⲣⲉϥ. 49.1 ⲁⲭⲙ̄: read ⲁⲭⲙ̄. 49.24 <ⲉ>ⲥⲉⲉⲓⲛⲉ: I accept Peel's emendation.

Yet [31] there are some (who) desire to understand, [32] in the search for [33] the things they investigate, whether [34] the one who is saved, when he leaves [35] behind his body, will he [36] be saved immediately. Let [37] no one be in doubt about this. [38] How then will the visible parts [39] that are dead [48.1] not be saved, since the living parts [2] that exist within [3] them will rise?

What [4] then is the resurrection? [5] It is the revelation on every occasion of [6] those who have risen. For if you [7] remember reading in the Gospel [8] that Elijah appeared [9] along with Moses, [10] do not consider the resurrection [11] to be an illusion. [12] It is not an allusion; [13] it is true. It is more [14] suitable to say that [15] the world is an allusion [16] rather than the resurrection, which [17] has come about through [18] our Lord, the Savior, [19] Jesus Christ.

[20] What am I telling [21] you now? Those alive [22] will die. How [23] do they live in an illusion? [24] The rich have become poor, [25] and the kings have been dethroned. [26] Everything is [27] transformed. The world [28] is an illusion—lest, [29] indeed, I pontificate about [30] matters too much.

But [31] the resurrection does not have [32] this kind of nature, because [33] truth is that which is established. [34] It is the revelation [35] of what is, and it is the transformation [36] of things and a [37] migration to something [38] new. For incorruption [49.1] [pours] down upon [2] corruption, and light pours [3] down upon darkness, [4] swallowing it. The fullness [5] fills the deficiency. [6] These are the symbols and [7] images of the resurrection. [8] It is He (Christ) who makes the [9] good.

Therefore, do not [10] know in part, O Rheginos, [11] nor live [12] as a citizen according to this flesh on account of [13] unity, but flee [14] from the divisions and the [15] chains and already you have [16] the resurrection. For if [17] the one who will die knows [18] about himself that he [19] will die—if he has many [20] years in this life, he is [21] brought this—[22] why not see yourself [23] as risen and [24] brought to this? [25] If you have [26] the resurrection but remain as though [27] you will die, and yet that one knows [28] that he has died, why then [29] do I overlook your [30] lack of training? It is fitting for each [31] one to train [32] in numerous ways, and [33] he will be released from this element [34] so that he might not commit error, but he [35] himself will receive again [36] that which existed first. [37]

ⲛⲉⲉⲓ ⲛ̄ⲧⲁϩⲓϫⲓⲧⲟⲩ ⲁⲃⲁⲗ ³⁸ ϩⲛ̄ ⲧⲙⲛ̄ⲧⲁⲧⲣ̄ ⲫⲑⲟⲛⲉⲓ ⲙ̄ⲡⲁ- ^{50.1} ϫⲁⲉⲓⲥ, ⲓⲏⲥⲟⲩⲥ ⲡⲉⲭⲣⲏⲥⲧ̣[ⲟⲥ.
ⲁⲓⲧ]ⲥ̣ⲉ- ² ⲃⲁⲕ ⲁⲣⲁⲩ ⲙⲛ̄ ⲛⲉⲕⲥⲛ[ⲏⲩ], ⲛⲁϣⲏ- ³ ⲣⲉ, ⲉⲙⲡⲓⲕⲉ ⲗⲁⲩⲉ ⲛ̄ⲥⲱⲉⲓ ϩⲛ̄ ⁴ ⲛⲉⲧⲉⲥϣⲉ
ⲁⲡⲧⲁϫⲣⲉ ⲧⲏⲩⲧⲛ̄. ⁵ ⲉⲓϣⲡⲉ ⲟⲩⲛ ⲟⲩⲉⲉⲓ ⲛ̄ⲇⲉ ⲥⲛϩ ⁶ ⲉϥϣⲏⲕ ϩⲛ̄ ⲧⲁⲡⲁⲅⲅⲉⲗⲓⲁ ⲙ̄- ⁷ ⲡⲗⲟⲅⲟⲥ,
ϯⲛⲁⲃⲁⲗⲁϥ̄ ⲁⲣⲱⲧⲛ̄ ⲉ- ⁸ ⲣⲉⲧⲛ̄ϣⲓⲛⲉ. ϯⲛⲟⲩ ⲛ̄ⲇⲉ, ⲙ̄- ⁹ ⲡⲣ̄ⲡⲣ̄ ⲫⲑⲟⲛⲉⲓ ⲁⲗⲁⲩⲉ ⲉⲧⲏⲡ ⲁ- ¹⁰ ⲣⲁⲕ
ⲉⲩⲛ̄ ϭⲁⲙ ⲙ̄ⲙⲁϥ ⲛ̄ⲣ̄ ⲱ- ¹¹ ⲫⲉⲗⲉⲓ.

ⲟⲩⲛ ϩⲁϩ ϭⲱϣⲧ̄ ⲁϩⲟⲩⲛ ¹² ⲁⲡⲉⲉⲓ ⲡⲉⲉⲓ ⲛ̄ⲧⲁⲉⲓⲥϩⲉⲉⲓ ⲙ̄- ¹³ ⲙⲁϥ ⲛⲉⲕ. ⲛⲉⲉⲓ ϯⲧⲁⲙⲟ ⲙ̄ⲙⲁⲩ· ¹⁴
ⲁϯⲣⲏⲛⲏ ⲛ̄ϩⲏⲧⲟⲩ ⲙⲛ̄ ⲧⲉⲭⲁⲣⲓⲥ. ¹⁵ ϯϣⲓⲛⲉ ⲁⲣⲁⲕ ⲙⲛ̄ ⲛⲉⲧⲙⲁⲉⲓⲉ ¹⁶ ⲙ̄ⲙⲱⲧⲛ̄ ⲉⲩⲟⲉⲓ ⲙ̄ⲙⲁⲉⲓⲥⲁⲛ.

¹⁷ ⲡⲗⲟⲅⲟⲥ ⲉⲧⲃⲉ ⲧⲁ- ¹⁸ ⲛⲁⲥⲧⲁⲥⲓⲥ

These things I have received [38] freely from my [50.1] Lord, Jesus Christ. [I have] taught [2] you and your brothers, my [3] children, about them, and I have overlooked none of [4] the things suitable for strengthening you. [5] But if there is one thing written [6] that remains opaque in my exposition of [7] the word, I will interpret it for you [8] if you ask. But now, [9] do not envy anyone who numbers among [10] you if he is able to assist. [11]

Many are examining [12] what I have written [13] to you. I say to these, [14] Peace (be) among them and grace. [15] I greet you and those who love [16] you in brotherly love.

[17] The Treatise on the [18] Resurrection

X. TRIPARTITE TRACTATE

The *Tripartite Tractate* is the fifth text in Nag Hammadi codex I. Since no title appears in the manuscript, the *Tripartite Tractate* has received its editorial title on the basis of its division into three parts by scribal decoration. Spanning eighty-seven manuscript pages, the *Tripartite Tractate* offers a comprehensive account of salvation history, beginning with the ineffable God and the population of the heavenly realm of fullness with eternities, and culminating in humanity's final return to the Father. While the anonymous *Tripartite Tractate* was once thought to be the work of Heracleon, scholars now reject this attribution on the basis of theological differences between the work and Heracleon's surviving writings.

Part 1 of the *Tripartite Tractate* describes the Father largely by way of negative theology, before turning to the emanation of two additional beings, Son and Church. Next comes a detailed discussion of the introduction of deficiency into the divine realm. Whereas other Valentinian texts attribute the introduction of deficiency to Wisdom, the *Tripartite Tractate* places the Word at the center of this drama. Part 2, the shortest of the three sections, describes the creation of the first human being, who is a dual creation. The lower creator god supplies his material and soulish parts, whereas his spiritual element comes from the heavenly Word. Adam's three substances give rise to the creation of three classes of humanity. The final part focuses on the salvation of the three classes of humanity. Each class responds to the advent of the Savior differently. The material ones reject him completely; the spiritual ones rush to him; and the soulish ones hesitate before embracing him. The text then concludes with a discussion of the final return to the Father, which culminates in a hymn to the Savior.

While the precise date of the *Tripartite Tractate*'s composition remains uncertain, affinities with Origen's *First Principles* may suggest a date of composition sometime in the middle of the third century C.E. The original language of composition was Greek.

⁵¹·¹ ϫⲉ ⲡ[ⲉ]ⲧⲁⲛⲛⲁϣ ϫⲟⲟϥ ϩⲁ ⲛⲉⲧϫⲁ- ² ⲥⲓ, ⲡⲉⲧⲉϣϣⲉ ⲡⲉ ⲛ̄ⲧⲛ̄ⲣ ϣⲁ- ³ ⲣⲡ̄ ⲙ̄ⲡⲓⲱⲧ,
ⲉⲧⲉ ⲧⲛⲟⲩⲛⲉ ⲛ̄ⲇⲉ ⁴ ⲡⲉ ⲙ̄ⲡⲧⲏⲣϥ̄, ⲡⲉⲉⲓ ⲛ̄ⲧⲁⲛϫⲓ ⁵ ⲛ̄ⲧⲟⲟⲧϥ̄ ⲛ̄ⲛⲟⲩϩⲙⲁⲧ ⲁⲧⲣⲛ̄- ⁶ ϣⲉϫⲉ
ⲁⲣⲁϥ.

ϫⲉ ⲛⲉϥϣⲟⲟⲡ ⁷ ⲉⲙⲡⲁⲧⲉⲗⲁⲩⲉ ϣⲱⲡⲉ ⲥⲁⲃⲁⲗ ⁸ ⲁⲣⲁϥ ⲟⲩⲁⲉⲉⲧϥ̄. ⲡⲓⲱⲧ ⲟⲩⲉⲉⲓ ⲛ̄- ⁹ ⲟⲩⲱⲧ
ⲡⲉ, ⲉϥⲟ ⲙ̄ⲡⲣⲏⲧⲉ ⲛ̄ⲛⲟⲩ- ¹⁰ ⲏⲡⲉ, ϫⲉ ⲡϣⲁⲣⲡ̄ ⲡⲉ ⲁⲩⲱ ⲡⲉⲧⲉ ¹¹ ⲛ̄ⲧⲁϥ ⲟⲩⲁⲉⲉⲧϥ̄ ⲡⲉ. ⲉϥⲟ̄
ⲙ̄ⲡⲣⲏ- ¹² ⲧⲉ ⲛ̄ⲟⲩⲉⲉⲓ ⲟⲩⲁⲉⲉⲧϥ̄ ⲉⲛ, ⲏ̄ ¹³ ⲙ̄ⲙⲁⲛ ⲛ̄ⲉϣ ⲛ̄ϩⲉ ⲟⲩⲓ̈ⲱⲧ ⲡⲉ; ¹⁴ ⲉⲓⲱⲧ ⲅⲁⲣ ⲛⲓⲙ ⲟⲩⲛ
ⲟⲩⲣⲉⲛ ⲥⲱⲕ ¹⁵ ⲛ̄ⲥⲱϥ, ϫⲉ « ϣⲏⲣⲉ. » ⲁⲗⲗⲁ ⲡⲟⲩⲉ ⲛ̄- ¹⁶ ⲟⲩⲱⲧ, ⲉⲧⲉ ⲛⲧⲁϥ ⲟⲩⲁⲉⲉⲧϥ̄ ⲡⲉ ¹⁷
ⲡⲓⲱⲧ, ⲉϥⲟ ⲙ̄ⲡⲣⲏⲧⲉ ⲛ̄ⲛⲟⲩⲛⲟⲩ- ¹⁸ ⲛⲉ ⲙⲛ̄ⲛ ⲟⲩϣⲏⲛ ⲙⲛ̄ ϩⲉⲛⲕⲗⲁ- ¹⁹ ⲇⲟⲥ ⲙⲛ̄ ϩⲉⲛⲟⲩⲧⲁϩ.
ⲉⲩϫⲟⲩ ⲙ̄- ²⁰ ⲙⲁⲥ ⲁⲣⲁϥ ϫⲉ ⲟⲩϫⲁⲉⲓⲥ ⲛ̄- ²¹ ⲓ̈ⲱⲧ ⲡⲉ ⲉⲩⲟⲩⲁⲧ<ⲧ>ⲣⲉⲗⲁⲩⲉ ²² ⲣ̄ ⲙⲓⲛⲉ ⲙ̄ⲙⲁϥ
ⲡⲉ ⲛⲙ̄ⲙⲉϥ ²³ ⲡⲉ ⲁⲩⲱ ⲟⲩⲁⲧⲡⲁⲛⲉϥ. ⲉⲧⲃⲉ ²⁴ ⲡⲉⲉⲓ ϫⲉ ⲟⲩϫ[[ⲡ]]ⲁⲉⲓⲥ ⲛ̄ⲟⲩⲱⲧ ²⁵ ⲡⲉ ⲁⲩⲱ
ⲟⲩⲛⲟⲩⲧⲉ ⲡⲉ ϫⲉ ⲙⲛ̄ ²⁶ ⲗⲁⲩⲉ ⲟ̄ ⲛ̄ⲛⲟⲩⲧⲉ ⲛⲉϥ, ⲁⲩⲱ ⲙⲛ̄ ²⁷ ⲗⲁⲩⲉ ⲉϥⲟ ⲛ̄ⲓⲱⲧ ⲛ̄ⲛⲉϥ. ⲟⲩ- ²⁸
ⲁⲧϫⲡⲁϥ ⲅⲁⲣ ⲡⲉ ⲟⲩⲇⲉ ⲛ̄ⲕⲉ- ²⁹ ⲟⲩⲉⲉⲓ ⲉⲛ ⲡⲉ ⲛ̄ⲧⲁϩϫⲡⲁϥ, ⲁⲩⲱ ³⁰ ⲛ̄ⲕⲉⲟⲩⲉⲉⲓ ⲉⲛ ⲡⲉ
ⲛ̄ⲧⲁϩⲧⲥⲉⲛⲁϥ. ³¹ ⲡⲉⲧⲉ ⲡⲓⲱⲧ ⲅⲁⲣ ⲛ̄ⲟⲩⲉⲉⲓ ⲡⲉ ³² ⲏ̄ ⲡϥ̄ⲣⲱⲙⲉϥⲧⲥⲉⲛⲟ, ⲟⲩⲛ̄- ³³ ⲧⲉϥ ⲓ̈ⲱⲧ
ϩⲱⲟϥ ⲁⲛ ⲁⲩⲱ ⲡⲉⲛ- ³⁴ ⲧⲁϩⲧⲥⲉⲛⲁϥ. ⲟⲩⲛ̄ 6ⲁⲙ ⲙⲉⲛ ³⁵ ⲛ̄ⲧϥ̄ϣⲱⲡⲉ ⲛ̄ⲓⲱⲧ ⲁⲩⲱ ⲣⲱⲙⲉ- ³⁶
ϥⲧⲥⲉⲛⲟ ⲙ̄ⲡⲉⲛⲧⲁϩϣⲱⲡⲉ ⲁ- ³⁷ ⲃⲁⲗ ⲙ̄ⲙⲁϥ ⲁⲩⲱ ⲡⲉⲛⲧⲁϩⲧⲥⲉ- ³⁸ ⲛⲁϥ. ⲟⲩⲉⲓⲱⲧ ⲛ̄ⲅⲁⲣ ⲉⲛ
ⲡⲉ ³⁹ ϩⲛ̄ⲛ ⲟⲩⲙⲛ̄ⲧϫⲁⲉⲓⲥ ⲡⲉ ⲁⲩⲱ ⲟⲩ- ⁴⁰ ⲛⲟⲩⲧⲉ ⲁⲃⲁⲗ ϫⲉ ⲟⲩⲛ̄ⲧⲉϥ <ⲙ̄>- ⁵²·¹ ⲙⲉⲩ
ⲙ̄ⲡⲉⲛⲧⲁϩϫⲡ[ⲁϥ] ⲁⲩⲱ ⲡ[ⲉ]- ² ⲧⲁϩⲧⲥⲉⲛⲁϥ. ϩⲛ̄ ⲟⲩⲙⲛ̄[ⲧϫ]ⲁⲉⲓⲥ 6ⲉ ³ ⲡⲓⲱⲧ ⲟⲩⲁⲉⲉⲧϥ̄ ⲁⲩⲱ
ⲡⲛⲟⲩⲧⲉ ⁴ {ⲙ̄}ⲡⲉⲧⲉⲙ̄ⲡⲉⲗⲁⲩⲉ ϫⲡⲁϥ. <ⲛⲓ>ⲡⲧⲏ- ⁵ ⲣϥ̄, ⲉⲛⲧⲁϥ ⲉⲧⲁϩϫⲡⲁⲟⲩ ⲉⲁϥ- ⁶
ⲧⲥⲉⲛⲁⲟⲩ. ⲟⲩⲁⲧⲧⲁⲣⲭⲏ ⲡⲉ· ⁷ ⲟⲩⲁⲧϩⲁⲏ ⲡⲉ.

ϫⲉ ⲟⲩ ⲙⲟⲛⲟⲛ ⲟⲩ- ⁸ ⲁⲧϩⲁⲏ ⲡⲉ, ⲉⲧⲃⲉ ⲡⲉⲉⲓ ⲟⲩⲁⲧⲙⲟⲩ ⁹ ⲡⲉ ⲁⲃⲁⲗ ϫⲉ ⲟⲩⲁⲧϫⲡⲁϥ ⲡⲉ. ¹⁰
ⲁⲗⲗⲁ ⲟⲩⲁⲧⲣⲓⲕⲉ ⲁⲛ ⲡⲉ ⲙ̄ⲡⲉ- ¹¹ ⲧϥ̄ϣⲟⲟⲡ ⲙ̄ⲙⲁϥ ⲁⲛⲏϩⲉ ⲧⲙⲉⲧ ¹² ⲁⲩⲱ ⲡⲉⲧⲉ ⲛ̄ⲧⲁϥ ⲡⲉ ⲁⲩⲱ
ⲡⲉⲧϥ̄- ¹³ ⲥⲙⲁⲛⲧ ⲙ̄ⲙⲁϥ ⲡⲉ ⲁⲩⲱ ⲡⲉⲧϥ̄- ¹⁴ ⲟⲉⲓ ⲛ̄ⲛⲟ6 ⲙ̄ⲙⲁϥ ⲡⲉ. ⲟⲩⲇⲉ ⲛ̄- ¹⁵ ⲧⲁϥ ϥⲛⲁϥⲓⲧϥ̄
ⲉⲛ ⲙ̄ⲡⲉⲧϥ̄ⲟ- ¹⁶ ⲉⲓ ⲙ̄ⲙⲁϥ, ⲟⲩⲇⲉ ⲙⲛ̄ ⲕⲉⲟⲩⲉ- ¹⁷ ⲉⲓ ⲛⲁϫⲓⲧϥ̄ ⲛ̄6ⲟⲛⲥ̄ ⲁⲧⲣⲉ<ϥ>ϫⲡⲉ ¹⁸ ⲟⲩϩⲁⲛ
ⲉⲙⲡⲉϥⲣ̄ ϩⲉⲛⲉϥ ¹⁹ ⲁⲣⲁⲥ ⲛ̄ⲛⲟⲩⲁⲉⲓϣ. ⲉⲣⲉⲁϫⲓ ²⁰ ⲉⲛ ⲙ̄ⲡⲉϥⲣ̄ ϩⲏⲧⲥ̄ ⲛ̄ϣⲱⲡⲉ. ²¹ ⲧⲉⲉⲓ ⲧⲉ ⲑⲉ
ⲉ{ⲛ}ⲧⲉ<ⲛ>ϥϣⲃⲃⲓⲁⲓ̈ⲧ ²² ⲛ̄ⲧⲁϥ ⲉⲛ, ⲟⲩⲇⲉ ⲙⲛ̄ ⲕⲉⲟⲩⲉ- ²³ ⲉⲓ ⲛⲁϣ ϥⲓⲧϥ̄ ⲁⲃⲁⲗ ⲙ̄ⲡⲉⲧϥ̄- ²⁴
ϣⲟⲟⲡ ⲙ̄ⲙⲁϥ ⲁⲩⲱ ⲡⲉⲧⲉ ⲛ̄- ²⁵ ⲧⲁϥ ⲡⲉ ⲁⲩⲱ ⲡⲉⲧϥ̄ⲟⲉⲓ ⲙ̄ⲙⲁϥ ²⁶ ⲡⲉ ⲙⲛ ⲧⲉϥⲙⲛ̄ⲧⲛⲟ6, ⲁⲧⲙ̄-
²⁷ ⲧⲣⲟⲩϣ ⲃⲓⲧϥ̄ ⲟⲩⲇⲉ ⲙⲛ̄ 6ⲁⲙ ²⁸ ⲁⲧⲣⲉⲕⲉⲟⲩⲉⲉⲓ ϣⲱⲧϥ̄ ⲁⲕⲉ- ²⁹ ⲣⲏⲧⲉ ⲏ ⲁ6ⲁϫϥ̄ ⲏ ⲁϣⲱⲧϥ̄
³⁰ ⲏ ⲁⲧⲥ̄ⲃⲕⲁϥ ⲉⲡⲓⲇⲏ ⲧⲉⲉⲓ ⲧⲉ ³¹ ϩⲛ̄ ⲟⲩⲙⲛ̄ⲧϫⲁⲉⲓⲥ ⲙ̄ⲙⲏⲉ, ⲉ- ³² ⲧⲉ ⲡⲓⲁⲧϣⲱⲧϥ̄ ⲡⲉ,
ⲛ̄ⲁⲧⲡⲁⲛⲉϥ, ³³ ⲉⲡⲓⲁⲧⲡⲱⲛⲉ ⲧⲱⲉⲓⲉ ϩⲉⲉⲓⲱϥ.

³⁴ ϫⲉ ⲡⲉⲉⲓ ⲟⲩⲁⲉⲉⲧϥ̄ ⲉⲛ ⲡⲉⲧⲟⲩ- ³⁵ ⲙⲟⲩⲧⲉ ⲁⲣⲁϥ ⲙ̄ⲙⲁϥ ϫⲉ ³⁶ « ⲟⲩⲁⲧⲁⲣⲭⲏ ⲡⲉ » ϫⲉ
« ⲟⲩⲁⲧϩⲁⲏ ³⁷ ⲡⲉ ⲁⲃⲁⲗ » ϫⲉ ⲟⲩⲁⲧϫⲡⲁϥ ³⁸ ⲡⲉ ⲁⲩⲱ ⲟⲩⲁⲧⲙⲟⲩ ⲡⲉ, ⲁⲗ- ³⁹ ⲗⲁ ⲕⲁⲧⲁ ⲡⲣⲏⲧⲉ
ⲉⲧⲉⲙⲛ̄- ⁴⁰ ⲧⲉϥ ⲁⲣⲭⲏ ⲙ̄ⲙⲉⲩ ⲁⲩⲱ ⲙⲛ̄- ⁴¹ ⲧⲉϥ ϩⲁⲏ ⲁⲛ ⲙ̄ⲡⲣⲏⲧⲉ ⲉⲧⲉϣⲟ- ⁴² ⲟⲡ ⲙ̄ⲙⲁϥ,
ⲟⲩⲁⲧϣⲁⲃⲉϥ ⲡⲉ ⁵³·¹ ϩⲛ̄ [ⲧ]ⲉϥ[ⲙ̄]ⲛⲧⲛⲟ6, ⲟⲩⲁⲧⲛ̄ ⲣⲉⲧϥ̄ ² ⲡⲉ ϩ[ⲛ̄] ⲧⲉϥⲥⲟⲫⲓⲁ, ⲟⲩⲁⲧⲉⲙⲁϩ- ³
ⲧⲉ ⲙ̄ⲙⲁϥ ⲡⲉ ϩⲛ̄ ⲧⲉϥϫⲟⲩ- ⁴ ⲥⲓⲁ, ⲟⲩⲁⲧϩⲉⲧϩⲱⲧ<ϥ̄> ⲡⲉ ϩⲛ̄ ⲧⲉϥ- ⁵ ⲙⲛ̄ⲧϩⲗ6ⲉ

ϫⲉ ϩⲛ̄ ⲟⲩⲙⲛ̄ⲧϫⲁⲓⲥ ⁶ ⲛ̄ⲧⲁϥ ⲟⲩⲁⲉⲉⲧϥ̄—ⲡⲓⲁⲅⲁⲑⲟⲥ, ⁷ ⲡⲓⲁⲧϫⲡⲁϥ ⲛ̄ⲓⲱⲧ, ⲁⲩⲱ ⲡⲓⲁⲧ- ⁸
ϣⲧⲁ ⲉⲧϫⲏⲕ—ⲡⲉⲉⲓ ⲡⲉ ⲡⲉⲧⲙⲏϩ ⁹ {ⲡⲉⲧⲙⲏϩ} ⲁⲃⲁⲗ ⲛ̄ϫⲡⲟ ⲛⲓⲙ ⲛ̄- ¹⁰ ⲧⲉϥ, ⲙⲛ̄ ⲁⲣⲉⲧⲏ ⲛⲓⲙ,

⁵¹·¹ As for what we will be able to say about the things that are exalted, ² what is fitting is for us to begin with ³ the Father, who is the root of the ⁴ entirety, this one ⁵ from whom we have received grace ⁶ to speak about him.

He existed ⁷ before anything except ⁸ he alone came to be. The Father is ⁹ a single one, existing like a number, ¹⁰ since he is the first and the one ¹¹ who is himself alone. He exists not like ¹² a single one, or ¹³ truly how is he a father? ¹⁴ Because (in the case of) every father there is a name that ¹⁵ follows, "son." But the single ¹⁶ one, who alone is ¹⁷ the Father, exists like a root ¹⁸ and a tree and branches ¹⁹ and fruit. It is said ²⁰ about him that he is a proper ²¹ Father, since he is inimitable ²² and immutable. Because of ²⁴ this he is properly alone ²⁵ and a god because no ²⁶ one is god to him, and no ²⁷ one is a father of him. For he is unbegotten, ²⁸ and there is no other ²⁹ who has begotten him, and ³⁰ there is no other who created him. ³¹ For the one who is the father of someone ³² or his creator, ³³ he also has a father and ³⁴ a creator. It is indeed possible ³⁵ for him to become a father and a ³⁶ creator of the one who came to be ³⁷ from him and the one whom he created. ³⁸ For he is not a father ³⁹ in the proper sense nor a ⁴⁰ god, since he has ⁵²·¹ one who has begotten [him and one] ² who created him. Then only a proper ³ father and god ⁴ is the one whom no one has begotten. As for <the> entireties, ⁵ he is the one who has begotten them and ⁶ created them. He is without beginning; ⁷ he is without end.

Not only is he ⁸ without an end, for this reason he is immortal ⁹ because he is unbegotten. ¹⁰ But he is unwavering in that which ¹¹ he dwells eternally, ¹² and in that which he is, and in that ¹³ by which he is established, and in that by which he ¹⁴ is great. ¹⁵ He will not take himself from that which he is, ¹⁶ nor will any other ¹⁷ compel him with violence to make him produce ¹⁸ an end that he has never desired. ¹⁹ He has not received ²⁰ his making of the limit of existence. ²¹ Thus he is unchanged, ²² and others ²³ will not be able to take him from his ²⁴ existence or that which ²⁵ he is or that which is his being ²⁶ and his might, so that he cannot ²⁷ be taken nor is it possible ²⁸ for anyone to change him into another ²⁹ thing, or to lessen him, or change him, ³⁰ or reduce him, since this is ³¹ properly true, which ³² is the unchangeable one, immutable one, ³³ with immutability clothing him.

³⁴ This one is not only ³⁵ called ³⁶ "without a beginning" and "without ³⁷ end" because he is unbegotten ³⁸ and immortal, but ³⁹ in the way that he does not have ⁴⁰ a beginning nor ⁴¹ an end as he ⁴² is, he is unsurpassable ⁵³·¹ in his greatness, inscrutable ² in his wisdom, ungraspable ³ in his power, ⁴ unexaminable in his ⁵ sweetness.

Properly ⁶ he alone—the good one, ⁷ the unbegotten Father, and the complete ⁸ perfect one—is filled ⁹ with all his children, ¹⁰ and with every virtue, and ¹¹ with

ⲁⲩⲱ ⲙ̅- ¹¹ ⲡⲉⲧⲣ̅ ϣⲉⲩ ⲛⲓⲙ. ⲁⲩⲱ ⲟⲩⲛⲧⲉϥ ¹² ϩⲟⲩⲟ, ⲉⲧⲉ ⲧⲁⲉⲓ ⲧⲉ ϯⲙⲛ̅ⲧⲁⲧ- ¹³ ⲃⲟⲟⲛⲉ,
ϫⲉⲕⲁⲥⲉ ⲉⲩⲛⲁϭⲛ̅ⲧⲥ̅ ¹⁴ ⲉⲩⲛ̅ⲧⲉϥ ⲉⲡⲉⲧⲉⲩⲛ̅ⲧⲉϥ ⲧⲏ- ¹⁵ ⲣϥ̅, ⲉϥϯ ⲙ̅ⲙⲁϥ ⲉⲩⲙⲁϣⲱ ϫⲁⲃ- ¹⁶ ⲉϥ
ⲁⲩⲱ ⲉϥϩⲁⲥⲉ ⲉⲛ ⲁⲃⲁⲗ ¹⁷ ϩⲛ̅ ⲡⲉⲧϥ̅ϯ ⲙ̅ⲙⲟϥ, ⲉϥⲟ ⲛ̅ⲣⲙ̅- ¹⁸ ⲙⲁⲟ ϩⲛ̅ ⲛⲉⲧϥ̅ϯ ⲙ̅ⲙⲟⲟⲩ, ¹⁹ ⲁⲩⲱ
ⲉϥⲙⲁⲧⲛ̅ ⲙ̅ⲙⲁϥ ⲁⲃⲁⲗ ²⁰ ϩⲛ̅ ⲛⲉⲧϥ̅ⲣ̅ ϩⲙⲟⲧ ⲙ̅ⲙⲁⲩ.

²¹ ϫⲉ ⲡⲉⲉⲓ ϭⲉ ⲛ̅ⲧⲉⲉⲓϩⲉ ⲁⲩⲱ ⲡⲓ- ²² ⲥⲙⲁⲧ ⲁⲩⲱ ⲡⲓⲛⲁϭ ⲛ̅ϯⲁⲉⲓⲏ ²³ ϫⲉ ⲙⲛ̅ ⲕⲉⲟⲩⲉⲉⲓ
ϣⲟⲟⲡ ⲛⲙ̅- ²⁴ ⲙⲉϥ ϫⲓⲛ ⲛ̅ϣⲁⲣⲡ̅, ⲏ ⲟⲩⲧⲟⲡⲟⲥ ²⁵ ⲉϥϣⲟⲟⲡ ⲛ̅ϩⲏⲧϥ̅ ⲏ ⲁϥⲉⲓ ⲁⲃⲁⲗ ²⁶
ⲙ̅ⲙⲁϥ ⲏ ⲉϥⲛⲁⲛⲁϩⲟⲩϥ ⲉϩⲟⲩⲛ ²⁷ ⲁⲣⲁϥ. ⲏ ⲟⲩⲥⲙⲁⲧ ⲛⲁⲣⲭⲁⲓⲟⲛ ²⁸ ⲉϥⲣ̅ ⲭⲣⲁⲥⲑⲁⲓ ϩⲛ̅ⲛ
ⲟⲩⲧⲁⲛⲧⲛ̅ ²⁹ ⲉϥⲣ̅ ϩⲱⲃ. ⲏ ⲟⲩⲙ̅ⲕⲁϩ ⲉϥϣⲟⲟⲡ ³⁰ ⲛⲉϥ ⲉϥⲟⲩⲏϩ ⲛ̅ⲥⲱϥ ⲙ̅ⲡⲉⲧϥ̅ⲉⲓ- ³¹ ⲣⲉ
ⲙ̅ⲙⲁϥ. ⲏ ⲟⲩϩⲩⲗⲏ ⲉⲥⲕⲏ ³² ⲛⲉϥ ⲁϩⲣⲏⲓ̈ ⲉⲥⲧⲥⲉⲛⲟ ⲁⲃⲁⲗ ⲛ̅- ³³ ϩⲏⲧⲥ̅ ⲛ̅ⲛⲉⲧϥ̅ⲧⲥⲉⲛⲟ ⲙ̅ⲙⲁϥ. ³⁴
ⲏ̅ ⲟⲩⲥⲓⲁ ⲉⲥⲙ̅ⲡⲉϥϩⲟⲩⲛ ⲁⲃⲁⲗ ³⁵ ⲙ̅ⲙⲁⲥ ⲉϥϫⲡⲟ ⲛ̅ⲛⲉⲧϥ̅ϫⲡⲟ ⲙ̅- ³⁶ ⲙⲁⲩ. ⲏ ⲕⲉϣⲃⲏⲣ ⲛ̅ⲙⲙⲉϥ
ⲣ̅ ϩⲱⲃ ³⁷ ⲉϥⲣ̅ ϩⲱⲃ ⲛ̅ⲙⲙⲉϥ ⲁⲛⲉⲧⲣ̅ ϩⲱⲃ ³⁸ ⲁⲣⲁⲩ. ⲁⲧⲣⲉϥϫⲟⲟⲥ ⲛ̅ⲧⲉⲉⲓϩⲉ ³⁹ ⲟⲩⲙⲛ̅ⲧⲁⲧⲥⲃⲱ
ⲧⲉ, ⲁⲗⲗⲁ ϩⲱⲥ ⁴⁰ ⲁⲅⲁⲑⲟⲥ, ⲛ̅ⲛⲁⲧⲱⲧⲁ, ⲉϥϫⲏⲕ, ⁵⁴·¹ ⲉϥⲙⲏϩ ⲉⲛⲧⲁϥ ⲡⲉ ⲡ[ⲧ]ⲏⲣϥ̅ ⲙ̅- ² ⲙⲓⲛ
ⲙ̅ⲙⲁϥ

ϫⲉ ⲙⲛ̅ ⲟⲩⲁⲛ ⲙ̅ⲙⲁⲩ ³ ⲛ̅ⲧⲉ ⲛⲓⲣⲉⲛ ⲉⲧⲟⲩⲣ̅ ⲛⲟⲉⲓ ⲙ̅ⲙⲁⲩ ⁴ ⲏ ⲛⲉⲧⲟⲩϫⲟⲩ ⲙ̅ⲙⲁⲩ ⲏ ⲛⲉⲧⲟⲩⲛⲉⲩ
⁵ ⲁⲣⲁⲩ ⲏ ⲛⲉⲧⲟⲩⲁⲙⲁϩⲧⲉ ⲙ̅ⲙⲁⲩ, ⁶ ⲙⲛ̅ ⲟⲩⲁⲛ ⲙ̅ⲙⲁⲩ ⲧⲟⲉⲓⲉ ⲁⲣⲁϥ, ⁷ ⲕⲁⲛ ⲉⲩⲡⲣⲉⲓϣⲟⲩ
ⲙ̅ⲡϣⲁ ⲉⲅⲟⲩⲁ- ⁸ ⲉⲓⲉⲓ ⲉⲩⲧⲁⲉⲓⲁⲉⲓⲧ. ⲁⲗⲗⲁ ⲛⲉ- ⁹ ⲉⲓ ⲙⲉⲛ ⲟⲩⲛ ϭⲟⲙ ⲛ̅ϫⲟⲟⲩ ⲁⲩⲉⲁϥ ¹⁰ ⲛⲉϥ
ⲙⲛ̅ ⲟⲩⲧⲁⲉⲓⲟ ⲕⲁⲧⲁ ⲧϭⲁⲙ ¹¹ ⲙ̅ⲡⲟⲩⲉⲉⲓ ⲡⲟⲩⲉⲉⲓ ⲛ̅ⲛⲉⲧϯ ⲉⲁⲩ ¹² ⲛⲉϥ. ⲛ̅ⲧⲁϥ ⲛ̅ⲇⲉ, ⲛ̅ⲑⲉ
ⲉⲧϥ̅ϣⲟ- ¹³ ⲟⲡ ⲙ̅ⲙⲁⲥ ⲁⲩⲱ ⲛ̅ⲑⲉ ⲉⲧϥ̅ⲟ- ¹⁴ ⲉⲓ ⲙ̅ⲙⲁⲥ ⲁⲩⲱ ⲡⲥⲙⲁⲧ ⲉⲧϥ̅ ⲙ̅- ¹⁵ ⲙⲁϥ, ⲙⲛ̅ ϭⲁⲙ
ⲁⲧⲣⲉⲛⲟⲩϭ ⲣ̅ ⲛⲟⲓ̈ ¹⁶ ⲙ̅ⲙⲁϥ, ⲟⲩⲇⲉ ⲙⲛ̅ ϣⲉϫⲉ ¹⁷ ⲛⲁϣ ⲟⲩⲁϩⲙⲉϥ, ⲟⲩⲇⲉ ⲙⲛ̅ ⲃⲉⲗ ¹⁸ ⲛⲁϣ ⲛⲉⲩ
ⲁⲣⲁϥ, ⲟⲩⲇⲉ ⲙⲛ̅ ⲥⲱⲙⲁ ¹⁹ ⲛⲁϣ ⲁⲙⲁϩⲧⲉ ⲙ̅ⲙⲁϥ ⲉⲧⲃⲉ ϯ- ²⁰ ⲙⲛ̅ⲧⲛⲟϭ ⲛ̅ⲧⲉϥ ⲛ̅ⲛⲁⲧⲛ̅ ⲣⲉⲧⲥ̅
²¹ ⲁⲩⲱ ⲡⲓⲃⲁⲑⲟⲥ ⲛ̅ⲧⲉϥ ⲛ̅ⲁⲧⲧⲉϩⲁϥ ²² ⲁⲩⲱ ⲡⲓϫⲓⲥⲉ ⲛ̅ⲧⲉϥ ⲛ̅ⲁⲧ`ϣ´ⲓⲧϥ̅ ²³ ⲁⲩⲱ ⲡⲓⲟⲩⲱϣⲉ
ⲛ̅ⲧⲉϥ ⲛ̅ⲁⲧϣⲁ- ²⁴ ⲡϥ̅. ⲧⲉⲉⲓ ⲧⲉ ⲧⲫⲩⲥⲓⲥ ⲙ̅ⲡⲓⲁⲧ- ²⁵ ϫⲡⲁϥ, ⲉⲛⲉϩⲓⲟⲩⲉ ⲉⲛ ⲛ̅ⲧⲟⲟⲧⲥ̅ ²⁶ ϩⲛ̅
ⲕⲉⲟⲩⲉⲉⲓ, ⲟⲩⲇⲉ ⲛ̅ⲥⲁϩⲧⲣⲉ ²⁷ ⲉⲛ ⲙ̅ⲡⲓⲣⲏⲧⲉ ⲛ̅ⲇⲉ ⲡⲉⲧⲧⲛϣ. ²⁸ ⲁⲗⲗⲁ ⲡⲓⲧⲉϩⲟ ⲁⲣⲉⲧϥ̅
ⲟⲩⲛ̅ⲧⲉ<ϥ> ²⁹ ⲙⲙⲉⲩ, ⲉⲙⲛ̅ⲧⲉϥ ⲙ̅ⲙⲉⲩ ⲛ̅ⲛⲟⲩ- ³⁰ ϩⲟ ⲟⲩⲇⲉ ⲟⲩⲥⲭⲏⲙⲁ, ⲛⲉⲉⲓ ⲉⲧⲉ- ³¹
ϣⲁⲣⲟⲩⲙⲉⲉⲩⲉ ⲁⲣⲁⲩ ϩⲛ̅ⲛ ⲟⲩ- ³² ⲉⲥⲑⲏⲥⲓⲥ, ⲉⲁⲃⲁⲗ ⲙ̅ⲙⲁϥ ⲡⲉ « ⲡⲁⲧ- ³³ ⲧⲉϩⲁϥ » ⲁⲛ.
ⲉϣϫⲉ ⲟⲩⲁⲧⲧⲉϩⲁϥ ³⁴ ⲡⲉ, ϩⲓ̈ⲉ ⲡϩⲱϥ ⲟⲩⲏϩ ⲛ̅ⲥⲱϥ ϫⲉ ⲟⲩ- ³⁵ ⲁⲧⲥⲟⲩⲱⲛϥ̅ ⲡⲉ, ϫⲉ
ⲡⲓⲁⲧⲣ̅ ⲛⲟⲉⲓ ³⁶ ⲙ̅ⲙⲁϥ ϩⲛ̅ ⲙⲉⲩⲉ ⲛⲓⲙ, ⲛ̅ⲛⲁⲧ- ³⁷ ⲛⲉⲩ ⲁⲣⲁϥ ϩⲛ̅ ϩⲱⲃ ⲛⲓⲙ, ⲛ̅ⲛⲁⲧ- ³⁸ ϣⲉϫⲉ
ⲁⲣⲁϥ ϩⲛ̅ ϣⲉϫⲉ ⲛⲓⲙ, ⲛ̅- ³⁹ ⲛⲁⲧϫⲱϩ ⲁⲣⲁϥ ϩⲛ̅ ⲧϭⲓϫ ⲛⲓⲙ. ⲛ̅- ⁴⁰ ⲧⲁϥ ⲟⲩⲁⲉⲉⲧϥ̅ ⲙ̅ⲙⲓⲛ ⲙ̅ⲙⲁϥ
⁴¹ ⲡⲉⲧⲥⲁⲩⲛⲉ ⲙ̅ⲙⲁϥ ⲛ̅ⲑⲉ ⲉⲧϥ̅- ⁵⁵·¹ ϣⲟⲟⲡ ⲙ̅ⲙⲁⲥ ⲙⲛ̅ ⲡⲉϥⲥⲙⲁⲧ ² ⲙⲛ̅ ⲧⲉϥⲙⲛ̅ⲧⲛⲟϭ
ⲙⲛ̅ ⲧⲉϥϩⲁⲓ̈- ³ ⲏ, ⲁⲩⲱ ⲉⲩⲛ ϭⲟⲙ ⲙ̅ⲙⲟϥ ⲛ̅ⲣ̅ ⲛⲟ- ⁴ ⲉⲓ ⲙ̅ⲙⲁϥ, ⲁⲛⲉⲩ ⲁⲣⲉⲩ, ⲁϫⲉ ⲣⲉⲛ ⁵
ⲁⲣⲁϥ, ⲁⲉⲙⲁϩⲧⲉ ⲙ̅ⲙⲁϥ, ⲉⲛⲧⲁϥ ⁶ ⲡⲉⲧⲟ ⲛ̅ⲛⲟⲩⲥ ⲛⲉϥ ⲟⲩⲁⲉⲉⲧϥ̅, ⲉϥⲟ ⁷ ⲛ̅ⲃⲉⲗ ⲛ̅ⲛⲉϥ
ⲟⲩⲁⲉⲉⲧϥ̅, ⲉϥⲟ ⲛ̅- ⁸ ⲣⲱϥ ⲛ̅ⲛⲉϥ ⲟⲩⲁⲉⲉⲧϥ̅, ⲉϥⲟ ⲙ̅ⲫⲟⲣ- ⁹ ⲙⲏ ⲛⲉϥ ⲟⲩⲁⲉⲉⲧϥ̅, ⲁⲩⲱ ⲡⲉⲧϥ̅- ¹⁰
ⲣ̅ ⲛⲟⲓ̈ ⲙⲙⲁϥ, ⲉⲧ[ϥⲛ]ⲉⲩ ⲁⲣⲁⲩ, ¹¹ ⲉⲧϥ̅ϣⲉϫⲉ ⲙ̅ⲙⲁϥ, ⲉⲧϥ̅ⲁⲙⲁϩ- ¹² ⲧⲉ ⲙⲙⲁϥ ⲙ̅ⲙⲓⲛ ⲙ̅ⲙⲟϥ,
ⲛ̅- ¹³ ϭⲓ ⲡⲓⲁⲧⲣ̅ ⲛⲟⲉⲓ ⲙⲙⲁϥ, ⲛ̅ⲁⲧϣⲉ- ¹⁴ ϫⲉ ⲁⲣⲁϥ, ⲛ̅ⲁⲧϣⲁⲡϥ̅, ⲛ̅ⲁⲧⲡⲁⲛϥ̅, ¹⁵ ⲉⲩⲧⲣⲟⲫⲏ

53.32 ⲉⲥⲧⲥⲉⲛⲟ: read ⲉϥⲧⲥⲉⲛⲟ.
54.26 ⲛ̅ⲥⲁϩⲧⲣⲉ: read ⲛ̅ⲥϩⲁⲧⲣⲉ.
54.34 ⲡⲓϩⲱϥ: read ⲡⲓϩⲱⲃ.
55.4 ⲁⲣⲉⲩ: read ⲁⲣⲁϥ.

every valued thing. And he has [12] more, namely, the lack of [13] evil, so that it might be discovered [14] that he has the one who has everything, [15] because he gives it unreachable being, [16] and he is not bothered [17] by that which he gives, since he is rich [18] in the things he gives, [19] and he rests himself [20] in the gifts he gives.

[21] This one, then, is of such a sort and [22] image and great size [23] that no one dwells with [24] him from the beginning, nor is there a place [25] within which he dwells or from which he has come [26] or for which he will separate [27] himself. Nor is there an ancient form [28] that he consults as a model [29] while he works. Nor is there for him any difficulty [30] that follows him in what he makes. [31] Nor for him is there any matter that exists [32] with which <he> creates [33] the things he creates. [34] Nor is there a substance within him from [35] which he begets the things he begets. [36] Nor is there any coworker [37] working with him on the things on which he is working. [38] To speak in this way [39] is ignorant, but (one should speak of him) as [40] good, without fault, perfect, [54.1] and complete, since he is [2] himself the entirety.

None [3] of the names that are thought, [4] nor those said, nor those seen, [5] nor those grasped, [6] not one of these are fitting to him, [7] even though they are radiantly glorious, increasing, [8] and honored. Rather, [9] it is possible to speak these (names) for his glory [10] and honor in accordance with the potential [11] of each one of those that glorify [12] him. But as for him, in his [13] existence, being, [14] and form, [15] it is not possible for mind to contemplate [16] him, nor will any voice [17] be able to articulate him, nor will any eye [18] be able to see him, nor will any body [19] be able to grasp him on account of [20] his inscrutable greatness [21] and his incomprehensible depth [22] and his immeasurable height [23] and his illimitable will. [24] This is the nature of the unbegotten [25] one, not coming into contact [26] with another thing, nor is he paired (with anything) [27] like something limited. [28] Instead he has this stature, [29] not having a [30] face or a form, those things that [31] are understood by means of [32] sense perception, (the stature) from which also arises (the name) [33] "the incomprehensible." If he is incomprehensible, [34] then it follows that [35] he is unknowable, that he is the one who is inconceivable [36] by every thought, invisible [37] to any thing, unutterable [38] by every word, [39] untouchable by any hand. He [40] alone is [41] the one who knows himself in the way he [55.1] is and his form [2] and his greatness and his immensity, [3] and because it is possible for him to conceive of [4] himself, to see himself, [5] to name himself, and to grasp himself, he [6] is the one who is his own mind, he is [7] his own eye, he is [8] his own mouth, he is [9] his own form, and the one who [10] is what he thinks, what he sees, [11] what he says, what he [12] himself grasps, [13] namely, the one who is incomprehensible, unutterable, [14] incom-

ⲡⲉ, ⲉⲩⲟⲩⲛⲁϥ ⲡⲉ, [16] ⲟⲩⲁⲗⲏⲑⲓⲁ ⲡⲉ, ⲟⲩⲣⲉϣⲉ ⲡⲉ, ⲟⲩ- [17] ⲙ̄ⲧⲁⲛ ⲡⲉ, ⲡⲉⲧϥ̄ⲣⲛⲟⲉⲓ ⲙ̄ⲙⲁϥ, [18] ⲡⲉⲧϥ̄ⲛⲉⲩ ⲁⲣⲁϥ, ⲡⲉⲧϥ̄ϣⲉϫⲉ [19] ⲁⲣⲁϥ, ⲡⲉⲧⲉⲩⲛ̄ⲧⲉϥ ⲙ̄ⲙⲉⲩ [20] ⲙⲙⲉⲉⲩⲉ. ϥⲛⲉⲣⲥⲉ ⲁⲉⲣⲏⲓ̈ [21] ⲛ̄ⲥⲟⲫⲓⲁ ⲛⲓⲙ, ⲁⲩⲱ ϥⲛ̄- [22] ⲧⲡⲉ ⲛ̄ⲛⲟⲩⲥ ⲛⲓⲙ, ⲁⲩⲱ ϥⲛ̄- [23] ⲧⲡⲉ ⲛ̄ⲉⲁⲩ ⲛⲓⲙ, ⲁⲩⲱ ϥⲛ̄- [24] ⲧⲡⲉ ⲛ̄ⲥⲁⲉⲓⲉ ⲛⲓⲙ ⲁⲩⲱ ⲙⲛ̄ⲧ- [25] ⲉⲗϭⲉ ⲛⲓⲙ ⲁⲩⲱ ⲙⲛ̄ⲧⲛⲁϭ ⲛⲓⲙ [26] ⲁⲩⲱ ⲃⲁⲑⲟⲥ ⲛⲓⲙ ⲁⲩⲱ ϫⲓⲥⲉ [27] ⲛⲓⲙ.

ϫⲉ ⲡⲁⲉⲓ ϭⲉ, ⲉⲧⲉ ⲟⲩⲁⲧ- [28] ⲥⲟⲩⲱⲛϥ̄ ⲡⲉ ⲛ̄ϩⲣⲏⲓ̈ ϩⲛ̄ ⲧⲉϥⲫⲩ- [29] ⲥⲓⲥ, ⲉⲧⲁⲣⲉⲛⲓⲙ̄ⲛ̄ⲧⲛⲟϭ ⲉⲛ̄ⲧⲁⲓ̈- [30] ⲣ̄ ϣⲣⲡ̄ ϫⲟⲟⲩ ⲧⲏⲣⲟⲩ ⲉⲣⲟϥ, ⲉϣ- [31] ϫⲉ ϥⲟⲩⲱϣⲉ ⲁϯ ⲙ̄ⲡⲥⲁⲩⲛⲉ ⲁ- [32] ⲧⲣⲟⲩⲥⲟⲩⲱⲛϥ̄ ⲁⲃⲟⲗ ⲙ̄ⲡⲣⲟⲩⲟ [33] ⲛ̄ⲧⲉϥⲙ̄ⲛ̄ⲧϩⲗϭⲉ, ⲟⲩϣⲓⲕⲁⲛⲟⲥ ⲡⲉ. [34] ⲟⲩⲛ̄ⲧⲉϥ ⲙ̄ⲙⲉⲩ ⲛ̄ⲧⲉϥϭⲁⲙ, ⲉ- [35] ⲧⲉ ⲡⲉϥⲟⲩⲱϣⲉ ⲡⲉ. ⲧⲉⲛⲟⲩ ⲇⲉ [36] ⲉϥⲁⲙⲁϩⲧⲉ ⲙ̄ⲙⲓⲛ ⲙⲙⲟϥ ϩⲛ̄ [37] ⲟⲩⲙⲛ̄ⲧⲕⲁⲣⲱⲥ, ⲉⲧⲉ ⲛ̄ⲧⲁϥ [38] ⲡⲉ ⲡⲛⲟϭ, ⲉϥϣⲟⲟⲡ ⲛ̄ⲗⲁⲉⲓϭⲉ [39] ⲛ̄`ⲡ´ϫⲡⲟ ⲛ̄ⲧⲉ ⲛⲓⲡⲧⲏⲣϥ̄ ⲉⲡⲟⲩ- [40] ϣⲱⲡⲉ ϣⲁ ⲁⲛⲏϩⲉ.

[56.1] ϫⲉ ⲛ̄ⲧⲁϥ ⲙ̄ⲙⲓⲛ ⲙⲙⲟϥ ϩⲛ̄ [2] ⲟⲩⲙⲛ̄ⲧⲭⲁⲉⲓⲥ ⲉϥϫⲡⲟ ⲙ̄- [3] ⲙⲁϥ ⲛ̄ⲁⲧϣⲉϫⲉ ⲙ̄ⲙⲁϥ ⲉⲩ- [4] ⲟⲩϫⲡⲟϥ ⲙ̄ⲙⲓⲛ ⲙ̄ⲙⲟϥ ⲟⲩⲁⲉ- [5] ⲉⲧϥ̄ <ⲡⲉ>, ⲉϥⲣ̄ ⲛⲟⲓ̈ ⲙ̄ⲙⲁϥ, ⲁⲩⲱ ⲉϥ- [6] ⲥⲁⲩⲛⲉ ⲙ̄ⲙⲁϥ ⲛ̄ⲑⲉ ⲉⲧϥ̄ϣⲟ- [7] ⲟⲡ ⲙ̄ⲙⲁⲥ. ⲡⲉⲧⲙ̄ⲡϣⲁ ⲛ̄- [8] ⲧⲉϥⲑⲁⲩⲙⲁ ⲙⲛ̄ ⲡⲉⲁⲩ ⲙⲛ̄ ⲡⲁ- [9] ⲥⲱ ⲙⲛ̄ ⲡⲧⲁⲉⲓⲟ ⲉϥⲉⲓⲛⲉ ⲙ̄- [10] ⲙⲁϥ ⲁⲃ[ⲁ]ⲗ ⲉⲧⲃⲉ ϯⲙⲛ̄ⲧⲁⲧ- [11] ⲁⲣⲏϫⲥ̄ ⲛ̄ⲧⲉϥⲙⲛ̄ⲧⲛⲟϭ ⲁⲩⲱ ϯ- [12] ⲙⲛ̄ⲧⲁⲧϩⲉⲧϩⲱⲧϥ̄ ⲛ̄ⲧⲉ ⲧⲉϥ- [13] ⲥⲟⲫⲓⲁ ⲙⲛ̄ ϯⲙⲛ̄ⲧⲁⲧϣⲓⲧϥ̄ [14] ⲛ̄ⲧⲉ ⲧⲉϥⲉϫⲟⲩⲥⲓⲁ ⲙⲛ̄ ϯ- [15] ⲙⲛ̄ⲧϩⲗϭⲉ ⲛ̄ⲧⲉϥ ⲛ̄ⲁⲧⲧⲁⲡⲥ. [16] ⲡⲉⲉⲓ ⲡⲉ ⲉⲧⲕⲱ ⲙ̄ⲙⲟϥ ⲉϩⲣⲏⲓ̈ [17] ⲛ̄ⲧⲉⲉⲓϩⲉ, ⲛ̄ϫⲡⲟ ⲉⲩⲛ̄ⲧⲉϥ [18] ⲙ̄ⲙⲉⲩ ⲛ̄ⲛⲉⲁⲩ ϩⲓ̈ ⲧⲁⲉⲓⲟ ⲛ̄- [19] ⲙⲁⲉⲓⲉ ⲛ̄ⲛⲁⲅⲁⲡⲏ, ⲉⲧⲉ ⲛ̄- [20] ⲧⲁϥ ⲡⲉⲧϯ ⲉⲁⲩ ⲛⲉϥ ⲙ̄- [21] ⲙⲓⲛ ⲙ̄ⲙⲟϥ, ⲉⲧⲣ̄ ⲙⲁⲉⲓⲉ ⲉ<ⲧ>- [22] ⲧⲁⲉⲓⲟ, ⲉⲧⲣ̄ ⲁⲅⲁⲡⲏ ⲁⲛ, [23] ⲡⲁⲉⲓ ⲉⲧⲉ ⲟⲩⲛ̄ⲧⲉϥ ⲙ̄ⲙⲉⲩ [24] ⲛ̄ⲛⲟⲩϣⲏⲣⲉ ⲉϥⲕⲁⲁⲧ ⲛ̄- [25] ⲧⲟⲟⲧϥ̄, ⲉϥⲕⲁⲣⲁⲓ̈ⲧ ⲁⲣⲁϥ, ⲉⲧⲉ [26] ⲡⲉⲉⲓ ⲡⲉ ⲡⲓⲁⲧϣⲉϫⲉ ⲙ̄ⲙⲁϥ [27] ϩⲛ̄ ⲡⲓⲁⲧϣⲉϫⲉ ⲙ̄ⲙⲁϥ, ⲡⲓⲁⲧ- [28] ⲛⲉⲩ ⲁⲣⲁϥ, ⲡⲓⲁⲧⲁⲙⲁϩⲧⲉ ⲙ̄- [29] ⲙⲁϥ, ⲡⲓⲁⲧⲣ̄ ⲛⲟⲉⲓ ⲙ̄ⲙⲁϥ ϩⲛ̄ [30] ⲡⲓⲁⲧⲣ̄ ⲛⲟⲓ̈ ⲙ̄ⲙⲁϥ. ⲧⲉⲉⲓ ⲧⲉ ⲑⲉ [31] ⲉⲧϥ̄ϣⲟⲟⲡ ⲙ̄ⲙⲁϥ ⲁⲛⲏϩⲉ ⲧⲙⲉⲧ. [32] ⲡⲓⲱⲧ, ⲛ̄ⲑⲉ ⲉⲛⲧⲁⲛϣⲣⲡ̄ ⲛ̄ϫⲟⲟⲥ, [33] ϩⲛ̄ⲛ ⲟⲩⲙⲛ̄ⲧⲁⲧϫⲡⲁⲥ ⲡⲉⲧϥ̄- [34] ⲥⲁⲩⲛⲉ ⲙ̄ⲙⲁϥ ⲙ̄ⲙⲁϥ ⲙ̄ⲙⲓⲛ [35] ⲙ̄ⲙⲁϥ, ⲉⲧⲁϥϫⲡⲟ ⲙ̄ⲙⲁϥ ⲉϥ- [36] ϣⲟⲟⲡ ⲉⲩⲛ̄ⲧⲉϥ ⲙ̄ⲙⲉⲩ ⲛ̄ⲛⲟⲩ- [37] ⲙⲉⲉⲩⲉ, ⲉⲧⲉ ⲡⲉⲉⲓⲙⲉⲩⲉ ⲛ̄- [38] ⲧⲉϥ ⲡⲉ, ⲉⲧⲉ ⲧⲉⲉⲓ ⲧⲉ ϯⲁⲓⲥ- [57.1] ⲑⲏⲥⲓⲥ ⲛ̄ⲧⲉϥ ⲉⲧ.[.].̣.̣.ⲡ [2] ⲛ̄ⲧⲉ ⲡⲓϩⲁⲉ ⲣⲉⲧϥ̄ ⲛ̄ⲧⲉϥ ⲡⲉ [3] ϣⲁ ⲁⲛⲏϩⲉ. ⲉⲧⲉ ⲡⲉⲉⲓ ⲡⲉ [4] ϩⲛ̄ ⲟⲩⲙⲛ̄ⲧⲭⲁⲉⲓⲥ ⲛ̄ⲇⲉ <ϯ>- [5] ⲙⲛ̄ⲧⲕⲁⲣⲱⲥ ⲁⲩⲱ ϯⲥⲟⲫⲓⲁ [6] ⲙⲛ̄ ϯⲭⲁⲣⲓⲥ, ⲉⲩϣⲁⲙⲟⲩⲧ[ⲉ] [7] ⲁⲣⲁⲥ ⲟⲛ ϩⲛ̄ ⲟⲩⲙⲛ̄ⲧⲭⲟⲉⲓⲥ ⲙ̄- [8] ⲡⲓⲣⲏⲧⲉ.

ϫⲉ ⲡⲓⲣⲏⲧ[ⲉ] ⲉⲧⲉⲣⲉ[ⲡⲓ]- [9] ⲱⲧ ϣⲟⲟⲡ ϩⲛ̄ⲛ ⲟ[ⲩ]ⲙⲛ̄ⲧⲭⲟ[ⲉⲓⲥ], [10] ⲡⲉⲉⲓ ⲉⲧⲉ ⲙⲛ̄ ⲕ[ⲉⲟⲩⲉⲓ [11] ϣⲟⲟⲡ] ϩⲁ ⲧⲉϥⲉϩⲏ ⲁⲩ[ⲱ ⲡⲉⲉⲓ ⲉⲧⲉ] [12] ⲙⲛ̄ ⲕⲉⲁⲧϫⲡⲟϥ ⲛⲥ̣[ⲱϥ ⲧⲉⲉⲓ] [13] ⲧⲉ ⲑⲉ ϩⲱⲱϥ ⲁⲛ [14] ⲙ̄[ⲡϣⲏⲣⲉ ⲉϥ]- [14] ϣⲟⲟⲡ ϩⲛ̄ⲛ ⲟⲩⲙ̣[ⲛ̄ⲧ]ⲭ̣ⲁ̣- [15] ⲉⲓⲥ, ⲡⲉⲉⲓ ⲉⲧⲉ ⲙⲛ̄ ϭⲉ ϩⲁ ⲧⲉϥ- [16] ⲉϩⲏ ⲁⲩⲱ ⲙⲛ̄ ϭⲉ ⲙⲛ̄ⲛⲥⲱϥ [17] ⲛ̄ϣⲏⲣⲉ ϣⲟⲟⲡ {ϩⲁ ⲧⲉϥⲉϩⲏ}. [18] ⲉⲧⲃⲉ ⲡⲉⲉⲓ ⲟⲩϣⲣⲡ̄ ⲙ̄ⲙⲓⲥⲉ ⲡⲉ [19] ⲁⲩⲱ ⲟⲩϣⲏⲣⲉ ⲛⲟⲩⲱⲧ ⲡⲉ, [20] « ⲡϣⲣⲡ̄ ⲙ̄ⲙⲓⲥⲉ » ⲙⲉⲛ ϫⲉ' ⲙⲛ̄ ⲗⲁⲩⲉ [21] ϣⲟⲟⲡ ϩⲁ ⲧⲉϥⲉϩⲏ « ⲡϣⲏⲣⲉ ⲛ̄- [22] ⲟⲩⲱⲧ » ⲛⲇⲉ ϫⲉ ⲙⲛ̄ ⲗⲁⲩⲉ ⲙⲛ̄- [23] ⲛ̄ⲥⲱϥ. ⲁⲩⲱ ⲟⲩⲛ̄ⲧⲉϥ ⲙ̄- [24] ⲙⲉⲩ ⲙ̄ⲡⲓⲕⲁⲣⲡⲟⲥ ⲛ̄ⲧⲉϥ, ⲡⲉ- [25] ⲉⲓ ⲉⲧⲉⲙⲁⲩⲥⲟⲩⲱⲛϥ̄ ⲉⲧⲃⲉ [26] ⲡϩⲟⲩⲟ ⲛ̄ⲧⲉϥⲙⲛ̄ⲧⲛⲟϭ. [27] ⲁⲩⲱ ⲛⲉϥⲟⲩⲱϣⲉ ⲁⲧⲣⲟⲩⲥⲟⲩⲱⲛϥ̄ ⲡⲉ [28] ⲉⲧⲃⲉ ⲧⲙⲛ̄ⲧⲣⲙ̄ⲙⲁⲟ ⲛ̄ⲧⲉϥ- [29] ⲙⲛ̄ⲧϩⲗϭⲉ.

57.2 ⲡⲓϩⲁⲉ: read ⲡⲓϩⲁⲉ.

prehensible, unchangeable, [15] while being vigorous, joyful, [16] sincere, glad, [17] restful, what he knows, [18] what he sees, what he says, [19] what he has [20] as thought. He surpasses [21] all wisdom, and he [22] transcends all intellect, and he [23] transcends all glory, and he [24] transcends all beauty and all sweetness [25] and all greatness [26] and all depth and [27] all superiority.

If then this one, who [28] is unknowable in his nature, [29] to whom will be all the lofty things that I [30] already mentioned, if [31] he desires out of the excess of his sweetness to give knowledge [32] so that he might be known, [33] he is capable (of so doing). [34] He has his power, [35] which is his will. But now [36] he restrains himself in [37] silence, he who [38] is great, being the cause [39] of the birthing the totalities into their [40] eternal existence.

[56.1] He alone [2] properly begets himself [3] as unutterable, since [4] he alone is self-begotten, [5] since he conceives of himself, and since he [6] knows himself for what he [7] is. What is worthy of [8] his admiration and glory and forbearance [9] and honor he makes [10] on account of the limitlessness [11] of his greatness and the [12] unexaminability of his [13] wisdom and the immeasurability [14] of his power and [15] his untasteable sweetness. [16] This is the one who puts forth himself [17] in this way, as a generation that has [18] glory and an honor [19] wonderful and lovely, [20] he being the one who glorifies [21] himself, who marvels, <who> [22] honors, who also loves, [23] the one who has [24] a son who exists by [25] his hand, who is silent about him, [26] this is the one who is the unutterable one [27] in the unutterable one, the invisible [28] one, the ungraspable [29] one, the inconceivable one in [30] the inconceivable one. Thus [31] he dwells in him eternally. [32] The Father, just as we have said before, [33] in an unbegotten manner is the one [34] in whom he knows himself, [35] who begot him [36] when he had a [37] thought, which is the thought [38] of him, that is, the [57.1] sense perception of he who [. . .] [2] of his stature [3] forever. But that is [4] properly <the> [5] silence and wisdom [6] and grace, when it is termed [7] properly in [8] this way.

Just as [the] Father [9] exists [properly,] [10] this one whom no [other] [11] preexists and [this one apart from whom] [12] there is no other unbegotten one, [13] so too also [the son] [14] properly exists, [15] this one whom no other preexists [16] and after whom no other [17] son exists. [18] Because of this he is a firstborn, [19] and he is an only son, [20] "firstborn" because no one [21] preexists him and "only son" [22] because there is no one [23] after him. He also has [24] his fruit, which [25] cannot be known on account of [26] the abundance of its greatness. Yet [27] he wanted it to be known [28] on account of the richness of his [29] sweetness.

55.37 "silence": or "sleepiness."

ⲁⲩⲱ ⲧϭⲁⲙ ⲛ̄ⲁⲧⲧⲟⲩ- ³⁰ ϩⲁⲙⲙⲉⲥ ⲁϥⲟⲩⲁⲛϩ̄ⲥ̄ ⲁⲃⲁⲗ, ⲁⲩⲱ ³¹ ⲡϩⲟⲩⲟ ⲉⲧⲛⲁϣⲱϥ <ⲛ̄>ⲧⲉ ⲧⲉϥⲙⲛ̄ⲧ- ³² ⲁⲫⲑⲟⲛⲟⲥ ⲁϥⲙⲁϫⲧⲥ̄ ⲛ̄ⲙⲙⲉϥ.

³³ ϫⲉ ⲟⲩ ⲙⲟⲛⲟⲛ ⲡϣⲏⲣⲉ ϣⲟⲟⲡ ³⁴ ϫⲓⲛ ⲛ̄ϣⲟⲣⲡ̄, ⲁⲗⲗⲁ ⲧⲕⲉⲉⲕⲕⲗⲏⲥⲓⲁ ³⁵ ϩⲱⲱⲥ ⲁⲛ ⲥϣⲟⲟⲡ ϫⲓⲛ ⲛ̄ϣⲁⲣⲡ̄. ³⁶ ⲡⲉⲧⲙⲉⲉⲩⲉ ϭⲉ ⲛⲉϥ ϫⲉ `ⲡ´ⲧⲣⲟⲩϭⲛ ³⁷ ⲡϣⲏⲣⲉ ⲉϥⲟ ⲛ̄ϣⲏⲣ ⲛ̄ⲟⲩⲱⲧ ³⁸ ⲉϥϯ ⲁϩⲟⲩⲛ ⲛ̄ⲛⲁϩⲣⲛ̄ ⲡϣⲉϫⲉ, ³⁹ ⲉⲧⲃⲉ ⲡⲙⲩⲥⲧⲏⲣⲓⲟⲛ ⲛ̄ⲇⲉ ⲙ̄ⲡϩⲱϫ, ⁴⁰ ⲙ̄ⲡⲓⲣⲏⲧⲉ ⲉⲛ ⲡⲉ. ⲙ̄ⲡⲓⲣⲏⲧⲉ ⲅⲁⲣ ⁵⁸·¹ ⲙ̄ⲡⲓⲱⲧ ⲉⲧⲉ ⲟⲩⲉⲉⲓ ⲛ̄- ² ⲟⲩⲱⲧ ⲡⲉ ⲁⲩⲱ ⲁϥⲟⲩⲁⲛϩ̄ϥ ³ ⲁⲃⲁⲗ ⲉϥⲟⲉⲓ ⲛ̄ⲓⲱⲧ ⲛ̄ⲛⲉϥ ⁴ ⲟⲩⲁⲉⲉⲧϥ̄, ⲧⲉⲉⲓ ⲧⲉ ⲑⲉ ϩⲱ- ⁵ ⲱϥ ⲁⲛ ⲙ̄ⲡϣⲏⲣⲉ ⲁⲩϭⲓⲛⲉ ⲙ̄- ⁶ ⲙⲁϥ ⲉϥⲟ ⲛ̄ⲥⲁⲛ ⲛⲉϥ ⲙ̄ⲙⲓⲛ ⁷ ⲙ̄ⲙⲟϥ, ϩⲛ̄ ⲟⲩⲙⲛ̄ⲧⲁⲧϫⲡⲁⲥ ⁸ ⲙⲛ̄ ⲟⲩ[ⲙⲛ]ⲧⲁⲧⲁⲣⲭⲏ. ⲛ̄ⲧⲁϥ ⲛ̄- ⁹ ⲇⲉ [ⲉ]ϥⲣ̄ [ⲙⲁ] ϩⲉⲓⲉ ⲙ̄ⲙⲁϥ ⲙ̄ⲙⲓⲛ ¹⁰ ⲙ̄ⲙⲟϥ ⲙⲛ ⲡⲉ]ⲓⲱⲧ, ⲁⲩⲱ ⲉϥϯ ⲉ- ¹¹ [ⲁⲩ ⲛⲉϥ] ⲁⲩⲱ ⲉϥⲧⲁⲓⲟ ⲉϥⲣ̄ ¹² [ⲁⲅⲁⲡⲏ]. ⲁⲩⲱ ⲛ̄ⲧⲁϥ ϩⲱⲱϥ ¹³ ⲁ[ⲛ ⲡ]ⲉⲧϥ̄ⲣ̄ ⲛⲟⲉⲓ {ⲙⲙⲓⲛ} ¹⁴ ⲙ̄ⲙⲟϥ ⲛ̄ϣⲏⲣⲉ ⲕⲁⲧⲁ ⲛⲓⲇⲓ- ¹⁵ ⲁⲑⲉⲥⲓⲥ ϫⲉ· ϩⲛ̄ « ⲟⲩⲙⲛ̄ⲧⲁⲧ- ¹⁶ {ⲁⲧ}ⲁⲣⲭⲏ » ⲙⲛ̄ « ⲟⲩⲙⲛ̄ⲧ<ⲁⲧ>ϩⲁⲛ. » ⲉ- ¹⁷ ⲡϩⲱϫ ϣⲟⲟⲡ ⲙ̄ⲡⲓⲣⲏⲧⲉ ⲉⲩ- ¹⁸ ⲡⲉⲧⲥⲙⲁⲛⲧ̄ ⲡⲉ. ⲉϩⲉⲛ- ¹⁹ ⲁⲧⲁⲡⲟⲩ ⲛⲉ ⲉϩⲉⲛⲁⲧⲁ- ²⁰ ⲣⲏⲭⲟⲩ ⲛⲉ, ϩⲛⲁⲧⲡⲁⲣⲭⲟⲩ ²¹ ⲁⲃⲁⲗ ⲛⲉ ⲛⲉϥϫⲡⲟ. ⲛⲉⲉⲓ ⲉⲧ- ²² ϣⲟⲟⲡ ⲛ̄ⲧⲁⲩϣⲱⲡⲉ ⲁⲃⲁⲗ ²³ ⲙ̄ⲙⲁϥ, ⲡϣⲏⲣⲉ, ⲙⲛ̄ ⲡⲓⲱⲧ ²⁴ ⲙ̄ⲡⲓⲣⲏⲧⲉ ⲛ̄ϩⲛⲏⲡⲓ ⲉⲧⲃⲉ ⲡϩⲟⲩⲟ ²⁵ ⲛ̄ϩⲉⲛϩⲟⲉⲓⲛⲉ ⲉⲩϯ ⲡⲓ ⲉⲣⲛ̄ ²⁶ ⲛⲉⲩⲉⲣⲏⲩ ϩⲛ̄ⲛ ⲟⲩⲙⲉⲉⲩⲉ ²⁷ ⲉⲛⲁⲛⲟⲩϥ ⲛ̄ⲁⲧⲥⲓ, ⲉⲩⲟⲩⲉⲓⲉ ²⁸ ⲛ̄ⲟⲩⲱⲧ ⲧⲉ ϯⲡⲓ ⲉϥϣⲟⲟⲡ ⲛ̄ϩⲣⲏⲓ ²⁹ ϩⲛ̄ ϩⲁϩ <ⲙ̄>ⲡⲉⲓⲉⲓ. ⲉⲧⲉ ⲧⲉⲉⲓ ⲧⲉ ϯ- ³⁰ ⲉⲕⲕⲗⲏⲥⲓⲁ ⲛ̄ϩⲁϩ ⲛ̄ⲣⲱⲙⲉ, ⲧⲉⲧ- ³¹ ϣⲟⲟⲡ ϩⲁ ⲑⲏ ⲛ̄ⲛⲁⲓⲱⲛ, ⲧⲉⲉⲓ ³² ⲉⲧⲟⲩⲙⲟⲩⲧⲉ ⲁⲣⲁⲥ ϩⲛ̄ ⲟⲩⲙⲛ̄ⲧ- ³³ ϫⲁⲉⲓⲥ ϫⲉ· « ⲛⲓⲁⲓⲱⲛ ⲛ̄ⲧⲉ ⲛⲓⲁⲓⲱⲛ. » ³⁴ ⲉⲧⲉ ⲧⲁⲉⲓ ⲧⲉ ⲧⲫⲩⲥⲓⲥ ⲛ̄ⲧⲉ ⲛⲓ- ³⁵ ⲡⲛⲉⲩⲙⲁ ⲉⲧⲟⲩⲁⲁⲃ ⲛ̄ⲁⲧⲧⲉⲕⲟ, ⲧⲉ- ³⁶ ⲉⲓ ⲉⲧⲉⲣⲉⲡϣⲏⲣⲉ ⲙⲁⲧⲛ̄ ⲙ̄ⲙⲁϥ ³⁷ ⲁϫⲱⲥ, ϩⲱⲥ ⲧⲉϥⲟⲩⲥⲓⲁ ⲧⲉ ⲛ̄ⲑⲉ ³⁸ ⲙ̄ⲡⲓⲱⲧ, ⲉⲧⲉϥⲙⲁⲧⲛ̄ ⲙ̄ⲙⲁϥ ⁵⁹·¹ ⲁϫⲛ̄ ⲡϣⲏⲣⲉ.

ϫ[ⲉ . . . .] ² ϯⲉⲕⲕⲗⲏⲥⲓⲁ ⲥϣ[ⲟ]ⲟⲡ [ⲛ]ϩⲣⲏⲓ ϩⲛ ⲛⲓ- ³ ⲇⲓⲁⲑⲉⲥⲓⲥ ⲙⲛ̄ ⲛⲓⲁⲣⲉⲧⲏ ⲛⲉⲉⲓ ⁴ ⲉⲧⲉ ⲡⲓⲱⲧ ⲙⲛ̄ ⲡϣⲏⲣⲉ ϣⲟⲟⲡ ⁵ ⲛ̄ϩⲏⲧⲟⲩ, ⲛ̄ⲑⲉ ⲛ̄ⲧⲁⲓϫⲟⲟⲥ ϫⲓⲛ ⁶ ϣⲁⲣⲡ. ⲉⲧⲃⲉ ⲡⲉⲉⲓ ⲥⲕⲛ ⲙ̄ⲙⲉⲩ] ⁷ ⲛ̄ⲛⲓϫⲡⲟ ⲛ̄ⲛⲁⲓⲱⲛ ⲛ̄ⲛⲁⲧⲁ[ⲡⲟ]ⲩ. ⁸ ⲁⲩⲱ ϩⲛ̄ⲛ ⲟⲩⲙⲛ̄ⲧ[ⲁ]ⲧⲁⲡⲥ̄ ⲛ̄[ⲧⲁⲩ] ⁹ ϩⲱⲟⲩ ⲥⲉϫⲡⲟ ϩⲛ ⲛ̄[ⲓ]ⲁⲣⲉⲧⲏ [ⲙⲛ] ¹⁰ ⲛⲓⲇⲓⲁⲑⲉⲥⲓⲥ ⲉ[ⲧⲥϣⲟⲟⲡ] ϩⲣ[ⲏⲓ] ¹¹ ⲛ̄ϩⲏⲧⲟⲩ. ⲛⲉⲉ[ⲓ ⲅⲁⲣ ⲛⲉ ⲡⲉⲥⲡⲟ]- ¹² ⲗⲓⲧⲉⲩⲙⲁ ⲡⲉⲧ[ⲟⲩⲉⲓⲣⲉ ⲙⲙⲁϥ] ¹³ ϣⲁ ⲛⲟⲩⲉⲣⲏⲩ ⲁⲩ[ⲱ ⲛⲉⲉⲓ] ¹⁴ ⲉⲛⲧⲁⲩⲉⲓ ⲉⲃⲟⲗ ⲙ̄[ⲁⲩ ⲁ]ⲛ ¹⁵ ϣⲁ ⲡϣⲏⲣⲉ, ⲡⲉⲉⲓ ⲉⲧⲟⲩϣⲟⲟⲡ ¹⁶ ⲛ̄ⲉⲁⲩ ⲉⲧⲃⲏⲧϥ̄. ⲉⲧⲃⲉ ⲡⲉⲉⲓ ¹⁷ ⲙⲛ̄ ϭⲟⲙ ⲁⲧⲣⲉⲛⲟⲩⲥ ⲣ̄ ⲛⲟⲉⲓ ⲙ̄- ¹⁸ ⲙⲁϥ—ⲛⲉⲡϫⲱⲕ ⲁⲃⲁⲗ ⲙ̄ⲡⲙⲁ ¹⁹ ⲉⲧⲙ̄ⲙⲉⲩ ⲡⲉ—ⲟⲩⲇⲉ ⲛⲉϣϣⲉ- ²⁰ ϫⲉ ϫⲟⲟⲩ, ϩⲛⲁⲧϣⲉϫⲉ `ⲅⲁⲣ´ ⲁⲣⲁⲩ ⲛⲉ ²¹ ⲁⲩⲱ ϩⲛⲛⲁⲧϯ ⲣⲉⲛ ⲁⲣⲁⲩ ⲛⲉ ϩⲛ̄- ²² ⲁⲧⲣ̄ ⲛⲟⲓ̈ ⲙ̄ⲙⲁⲩ ⲛⲉ. ⲛ̄ⲧⲁⲩ ⲛ̄ⲇⲉ ²³ ⲟⲩⲁⲉⲉⲧⲟⲩ ⲛⲉⲧⲉ ⲟⲩⲛ̄ ϭⲁⲙ ⲙ̄- ²⁴ ⲙⲁⲩ ⲛ̄ϫⲓ ⲣⲉⲛ ⲁⲣⲁⲟⲩ ⲁⲣ̄ ⲛⲟⲉⲓ ²⁵ ⲙ̄ⲙⲁⲩ, ⲛ̄ⲥⲉⲭⲁⲉⲓⲧ ⲅⲁⲣ ⲉⲛ ²⁶ ⲛ̄ⲛⲓⲙⲁ.

ϫⲉ ⲛⲁ ⲡⲙⲁ ⲉ- ²⁷ ⲧⲙ̄ⲙⲉⲩ ϩⲛ̄ⲛⲁⲧϫⲟⲟⲩⲉ ⲛⲉ, ²⁸ ϩⲛⲁⲧⲁⲡⲟⲩ ⲛⲉ ϩⲁⲧⲛ̄ ²⁹ ϯⲥⲩⲥⲧⲁⲥⲓⲥ, ⲉⲧⲉ ⲧⲉⲉⲓ ⲧⲉ ³⁰ ϫⲉ ⲁⲩⲱ ⲡⲓⲣⲏⲧⲉ ⲡⲉ ⲁⲩⲱ ⲧⲉⲉⲓ- ³¹ ϭⲁⲧ ⲡⲉ, ⲡⲓⲣⲉϣⲉ ⲡⲉ, ⲡⲓⲁⲗⲏⲗ ³² ⲡⲉ ⲛ̄ⲧⲉ ⲡⲓⲁⲧϫⲡⲁϥ, ⲛ̄ⲛⲁⲧ- ³³ ϫⲓ ⲣⲉⲛ ⲁⲣⲁϥ, ⲛ̄ⲛⲁⲧϯ ⲣⲉⲛ ⲁⲣⲁϥ, ³⁴ ⲛ̄ⲛⲁⲧⲣ̄ ⲛⲟⲉⲓ ⲙ̄ⲙⲁϥ, ⲛ̄ⲁⲧⲛⲉⲩ ³⁵

57.39 ⲙ̄ⲡϩⲱϥ: read ⲙ̄ⲡϩⲱⲃ.
58.17 ⲡϩⲱϥ: read ⲡϩⲱⲃ.
58.28 ⲉϥϣⲟⲟⲡ: read ⲉⲥϣⲟⲟⲡ.
59.35 ⲁⲣⲁⲩ: read ⲁⲣⲁϥ.

And the unexplainable power [30] he revealed, and [31] he mixed with it the great abundance of his [32] generosity.

[33] Not only does the son exist [34] from the beginning, the church [35] also exists from the beginning. [36] (In response to) the one who thinks that the discovery that [37] the son was an only son [38] contradicts the statement (regarding the church), [39] because of the mystery of the matter [40] it is not so. For just as [58.1] the Father is a unitary [2] one and revealed himself [3] as the Father for him [4] alone, so too [5] the Son was discovered [6] to be a brother to himself alone, [7] by being unbegotten [8] and without a beginning. He [9] marvels at himself [10] [and the] Father, and he gives [11] him [glory] and honor and [12] [love.] He too, [13] moreover, is the one whom he contemplates [14] as Son in accordance with the [15] dispositions: "without beginning" [16] and "without end." [17] This matter thus [18] is established. Since [19] they are innumerable and illimitable, [20] his children are indivisible. [21] These that [22] exist have come about [23] from him, the Son, and the Father, [24] like kisses because of the abundance [25] of some who give kisses to [26] each other with a thought [27] good and insatiable, since [28] the kiss is singular despite existing in [29] many kisses. This is the [30] church of many people, which [31] preexists the eternities, this [32] which is called [33] properly "the eternities of the eternities." [34] This is the nature of the [35] incorruptible holy spirits, this [36] upon which the Son rests, [37] since his substance is like [38] the Father, who rests himself [59.1] upon the Son.

[. . .] [2] The church exists in the [3] dispositions and abilities [4] in which the Father and Son dwell, [5] as I have said from the [6] beginning. For this reason it lies there among [7] the births of innumerable eternities. [8] And innumerably [they] [9] too beget by the properties [and] [10] dispositions [that exist] [11] among them. [For] these [are its] charter [12] that [they make] [13] with one another and [those] [14] who have come forth from [them] [15] to the Son, the one on account of whose glory they dwell. [16] For this reason [17] it is not possible for mind to contemplate [18] him—He was the perfection of that place[19]—nor was it possible for words [20] to express them, since they are ineffable [21] and unnameable and [22] inconceivable. But they [23] alone are able to take names [24] for themselves and to conceive of [25] themselves, since they have not taken root [26] in these places.

Those of that place [27] are ineffable, [28] they are innumerable within [29] the system, which is [30] both the manner and the [31] form, it is the joy, it is the delight [32] of the unbegotten, [33] nameless, unnameable, [34] inconceivable, invisible, [35] ungraspable

ⲁⲣⲁⲩ, ⲛ̄ⲛⲁⲧⲁⲙⲁⲣⲧⲉ ⲙ̄ⲙⲁϥ ³⁶ ⲡⲉ. ⲡⲓⲡⲗⲏⲣⲱⲙⲁ ⲡⲉ ⲛ̄ⲧⲉ ϯⲙⲛ̄ⲧ- ³⁷ ϯⲉⲓⲱⲧ ϩⲱⲥⲇⲉ
ⲛ̄ⲧⲉⲡⲉϥϩⲟⲩⲟ ³⁸ ϣⲱⲡⲉ ⲛ̄ⲛⲟⲩϭⲛ̄ϫⲡⲟ ⁶⁰·¹ [.] [.]ⲛ̄[. .] [.]ⲧⲁⲥ ⲛ̄ⲛⲁⲓⲱⲛ.

ϫⲉ ² ⲛⲁϥϣⲟⲟⲡ ⲁⲛⲓϩⲉ ⲧⲙⲉⲧ ϩⲛ̄ ³ ⲡⲙⲉⲉⲩⲟⲩⲉ, ϫⲉ ⲡⲓⲱⲧ ⲉϥⲟ ⁴ ⲙ̄ⲡⲣⲏⲧⲉ ⲛ̄ⲛⲟⲩⲙⲉⲉⲩⲉ ⁵
ⲛⲉⲩ ⲙⲛ̄ <ⲟⲩ>ⲧⲟⲡⲟⲥ. ⲉⲁⲩⲧⲉϩⲟ ⲇⲉ ⁶ [ⲛ]ϭⲓ ⲛϫⲡⲟⲟⲩⲉ, ⲁϥⲟⲩⲱϣϣⲉ ⁷ ⲛⲭⲓ ⲡⲉⲧⲉⲩⲛ
ϭⲟⲙ ⲙ̄ⲙⲁϥ ⲁ- ⁸ [ⲡ]ⲧⲏⲣϥ̄ [ⲁⲉ]ⲙⲁⲣⲧⲉ ⲁⲉⲓⲛⲉ ⁹ [ⲁ]ⲃⲁ[ⲗ] ⲙ̄[ⲡⲉⲧ]ⲁϥϣⲱⲱⲧ ϩⲛ̄ ⲡ- ¹⁰ [. . .
ⲁϥⲉⲓⲛ]ⲉ ⲁⲃⲁⲗ ⲛ̄ⲛⲉⲧ—¹¹ [. . . . .ϩ]ⲏⲧϥ̄. ⲁⲗⲗⲁ ⲉϥϣⲟ- ¹² [ⲟⲡ ⲛⲑⲉ] ⲉⲧϥ̄ϣⲟⲟⲡ ⲙ̄ⲙⲁⲥ, ¹³
[ⲉϥϣⲟⲟ]ⲡ ⲛ̄ⲛⲟⲩⲡⲏⲅⲛ, ⲉⲙⲁⲥ- ¹⁴ ϭⲱϫⲃ̄ <ⲛ̄>ϩⲏⲧϥ̄ ⲙ̄ⲡⲙⲁⲟⲩ ⲉⲧⲣ̄- ¹⁵ ϩⲟⲩⲉ ϩⲉⲧⲉ ⲁⲃⲁⲗ
ⲙ̄ⲙⲁⲥ. ¹⁶ ϣⲁ ⲡⲛⲉⲩ ⲙⲉⲛ ⲉⲧⲟⲩϣⲟⲟⲡ ¹⁷ ϩⲙ̄ ⲡⲙⲉⲩⲉ ⲙ̄ⲡⲓⲱⲧ, ⲉⲧⲉ ⲡⲁ- ¹⁸ ⲉⲓ ⲡⲉ, ⲉⲩϣⲟⲟⲡ ϩⲛ̄
ⲡⲃⲁⲑⲟⲥ ¹⁹ ⲉⲧϩⲏⲡ, ⲛⲉⲩⲥⲁⲩⲛⲉ ⲙⲉⲛ ⲙ̄- ²⁰ ⲙⲁⲩ ⲛ̄ⲭⲓ ⲡⲃⲁⲑⲟⲥ, ⲛ̄ⲧⲁⲩ ⲛ̄ⲇⲉ ²¹ ⲙⲛ̄ ϭⲁⲙ
ⲙ̄ⲙⲁⲩ ⲛ̄ⲥⲟⲩⲱⲛ ²² ⲡⲃⲁⲑⲟⲥ ⲉⲧⲉⲛⲉⲩϣⲟ- ²³ ⲟⲡ ⲛ̄ϩⲏⲧϥ̄, ⲟⲩⲇⲉ ⲙⲛ̄ ²⁴ ϭⲟⲙ ⲙ̄ⲙⲁⲩ
ⲁⲧⲟⲩⲥⲟⲩⲱⲛⲟⲩ ²⁵ ⲙ̄ⲙⲓⲛ ⲙ̄ⲙⲟⲟⲩ, ⲟⲩⲇⲉ ²⁶ ⲁⲧⲟⲩⲥⲟⲩⲱⲛ ϭⲉ. ⲉⲧⲉ ²⁷ ⲡⲉⲉⲓ ⲡⲉ ⲛⲉⲩϣⲟⲟⲡ
ⲙⲉⲛ ²⁸ ⲙⲛ̄ ⲡⲓⲱⲧ· ⲛⲉⲩϣⲟⲟⲡ ²⁹ ⲛ̄ⲧⲁⲩ ⲛⲉⲩ ⲉⲛ ⲡⲉ. ⲁⲗⲗⲁ ³⁰ ⲙⲟⲛⲟⲛ ⲛⲉⲩⲛ̄ⲧⲉⲩ ⲙ̄ⲙⲉⲩ ³¹
ⲙ̄ⲡⲧⲣⲟⲩϣⲱⲡⲉ ⲙ̄ⲡⲣⲏⲧⲉ ³² ⲛ̄ⲛⲟⲩⲥⲡⲉⲣⲙⲁ, ⲁⲧⲟⲩϭⲛ̄ⲧⲥ̄ ³³ ⲉⲩϣⲟⲟⲡ ⲙ̄ⲡⲣⲏⲧⲉ ⲛ̄ⲛⲟⲩ- ³⁴
ⲃⲉⲕⲉ. ⲛ̄ⲑⲉ ⲙ̄ⲡⲗⲟⲅⲟⲥ ⲙⲉⲛ ³⁵ ⲁϥϫⲡⲁⲟⲩ. ⲁϥⲕⲏ ⲁϩⲣⲏⲓ ϩⲛ̄ ⲟⲩ- ³⁶ ⲙⲛ̄ⲧⲥⲡⲉⲣⲙⲁ. ⲉⲙⲡⲁⲧⲟⲩ- ³⁷
ϣⲱⲡⲉ ⲇⲉ ⲛ̄ϭⲓ ⲛⲉⲉⲓ ⲉⲧϥⲛⲁ- ³⁸ ϫⲡⲟⲟⲩ ⁶¹·¹ ⲁⲃⲁⲗ ⲙ̄[ⲡ]ⲗⲁⲉⲓ. [. .] ⲡⲉⲛⲧⲁϥⲣ̄ ² ϣⲁⲣⲡ ⲙ̄ⲙⲉⲩ[ⲉ]
ⲁⲣⲁⲟⲩ, ⲡⲓⲱⲧ ³—ⲟⲩ ⲙⲟⲛⲟⲛ ⲁⲧⲟⲩϣⲱⲡⲉ ⲛⲉϥ, ⁴ ⲁⲗⲗⲁ ⲁⲧⲟⲩϣⲱⲡⲉ ⲛⲉⲩ ϩⲱⲟⲩ ⁵
ⲁⲛ, ⲁⲧⲟⲩϣⲱⲡⲉ ϭⲉ ϩⲙ̄ ⲡⲉϥ]- ⁶ ⲙⲉⲩⲉ ϩⲱⲥ ⲟⲩⲥⲓⲁ ⲙ̄ⲙⲉⲩ[ⲉ,] ⁷ ⲁⲧⲟⲩϣⲱⲡⲉ ⲇⲉ
ⲛⲉⲩ ϩⲱⲟⲩ—ⲁ[ϥ]- ⁸ ⲥⲓⲧⲉ ⲛ̄ⲛⲟⲩⲙⲉⲉⲩ[ⲉ] ϩⲱ[ⲥ] ⲟⲩⲥⲡⲉ[ⲣ]- ⁹ ⲙⲁ ⲡⲉ ⲛ̄ⲙⲛ̄ⲧⲥⲡ[ⲉⲣⲙⲁ.]
ⲁⲧ[ⲣⲟⲩ]- ¹⁰ ⲣ̄ ⲛⲟⲉⲓ ⲙ̄ⲙⲉⲛ ϫⲉ ⲟ[ⲩ ⲡⲉⲧ]ϣ[ⲟ]- ¹¹ ⲟⲡ ⲛⲉⲩ ⲁϥⲣ̄ ϩⲙⲁⲧ [ⲁϯ ⲛ̄ϯϣⲁ]- ¹² ⲣ̄ⲡ̄
ⲙ̄ⲫⲟⲣⲙⲏ. ⲁⲧⲟⲩⲙ̄[ⲙⲉ ⲇⲉ ϫⲉ] ¹³ ⲛⲓⲙ ⲡⲉ ⲡⲓⲱⲧ ⲉⲧϣⲟⲟ[ⲡ ⲛⲉⲩ,] ¹⁴ ⲡⲣⲉⲛ ⲙⲉⲛ ⲙ̄ⲡⲓⲱⲧ
ⲁϥⲧⲉⲉⲓϥ ¹⁵ ⲛⲉⲩ ϩⲁⲧⲛ̄ ⲟⲩⲥⲙⲏ ⲉⲥϯ ϩⲣⲁⲟⲩ ¹⁶ ⲛⲉⲩ ϫⲉ ⲡⲉⲧϣⲟⲟⲡ ϥϣⲟⲟⲡ ⲁⲃⲁⲗ ¹⁷ ϩⲙ̄ ⲡⲣⲉⲛ
ⲉⲧⲙ̄ⲙⲉⲩ, ⲡⲉⲧⲉⲩⲛ̄- ¹⁸ ⲧⲉⲩ<ϥ̄> ⲙ̄ⲡⲧⲣⲟⲩϣⲱⲡⲉ, ϫⲉ ⲡϫⲓⲥⲉ ¹⁹ ⲇⲉ ϩⲙ̄ ⲡⲣⲉⲛ, ⲉⲛⲧⲁϥⲁⲃⲉϣ
²⁰ ⲁⲣⲁⲟⲩ.

ⲉϥϣⲟⲟⲡ ⲇⲉ ⲙ̄ⲡⲉⲥ- ²¹ ⲙⲁⲧ ⲛ̄ⲛⲟⲩⲃⲉⲕⲉ, ⲉⲩⲛⲧⲉϥ ⲙ̄- ²² ⲙⲉⲩ ⲙ̄ⲡⲉϥⲣⲱϣⲉ ⲛ̄ϭⲓ ⲡⲗⲓⲗⲟⲩ ²³
ⲉⲙⲡⲁⲧ`ϥ´ⲛⲉⲩ ⲇⲉ ⲁⲛⲏϩⲉ ⲁⲡⲉⲛ- ²⁴ ⲧⲁϩⲥⲓⲧⲉ ⲙ̄ⲙⲟϥ. ⲉ[ⲧ]ⲃⲉ ⲡⲉⲉⲓ ⲛⲉⲩ- ²⁵ ⲛ̄ⲧⲉⲩ ⲙ̄ⲡⲓϩⲱⲃ
ⲟⲩⲁⲉⲉⲧϥ̄ ²⁶ ⲁⲧⲟⲩϣⲓⲛⲉ ⲛ̄ⲥⲱϥ, ⲉⲩⲣ̄ ⲛⲟⲓ ⲙⲉⲛ ²⁷ ϫⲉ ϥϣⲟⲟⲡ, ⲉⲩⲟⲩⲱϣⲉ ⲇⲉ ⲁϭⲛ̄ⲧϥ̄ ²⁸
ϫⲉ ⲱ ⲡⲉⲧϣⲟⲟⲡ. ⲁⲗⲗⲁ ⲉⲡⲓⲇⲏ ⲟⲩ- ²⁹ ⲁⲅⲁⲑⲟⲥ ⲡⲉ ⲡⲓⲱⲧ ⲉϥϫⲏⲕ, ⲛ̄- ³⁰ ⲑⲉ ⲉⲧⲉⲙ̄ⲡⲉϥⲥⲱⲧⲙ̄
³¹ ⲁⲣⲁⲟⲩ ϣⲁⲃⲟⲗ ⲁⲧⲟⲩϣⲱⲡⲉ ³² ϩⲛ̄ ⲡⲉϥⲙⲉⲩⲉ, ⲁⲗⲗⲁ ⲁϥϯ ⲛⲉⲩ ³³ ⲁⲧⲟⲩϣⲱⲡⲉ ϩⲱⲟⲩ,
ⲧⲉⲉⲓ ⲧⲉ ⲑⲉ ³⁴ ⲁⲛ ⲉⲧϥ̄ⲛⲁⲣ̄ ϩⲙⲁⲧ ⲙ̄ⲙⲁϥ ³⁵ ⲛⲉⲩ ⲁⲧⲟⲩⲙ̄ⲙⲉ ϫⲉ ⲉⲩ ⲡⲉⲧϣⲟ- ³⁶ ⲟⲡ, ⲉⲧⲉ
ⲡⲁⲉⲓ, ⲡⲉⲧⲥⲁⲩⲛⲉ ⲙ̄ⲙⲁϥ ³⁷ ⲁⲛⲏϩⲉ ⲧⲙⲉⲧ ⲙ̄ⲙⲓⲛ ⲙ̄ⲙⲟϥ. ⁶²·¹ [. . . . .] . [.] . [.] . ² ⲙⲟⲣⲫⲏ
ⲛ̄[ⲥⲁⲩ]ⲛⲉ ϫⲉ ⲟⲩ ⲡⲉⲧϣ[ⲟ]- ³ ⲟⲡ ⲛ̄ⲑⲉ ⲉⲧⲟⲩϫⲡⲟ ⲙ̄ⲙⲁⲩ ⲙ̄ⲡⲓ- ⁴ ⲙⲁ. ⲉϥϣⲁⲙⲉⲥⲧⲟⲩ,
ⲉϥϣⲟⲟⲡ ϩⲙ̄ ⁵ ⲡⲟⲩⲟⲉⲓⲛ ⲉⲛⲉⲩ ⲁⲛⲉⲛⲧⲁϩϫⲡⲟⲟⲩ.

⁶ [ϫ]ⲉ ⲡⲧⲏⲣϥ̄ ⲁⲡⲓⲱⲧ ⲉⲓⲛⲉ ⲙ̄ⲙⲁⲩ ⁷ [ⲁ]ⲃⲁⲗ, ⲙ̄ⲡⲣⲏⲧⲉ ⲛ̄ⲛⲟⲩⲗⲓⲗⲟⲩ ϣⲏⲙ, ⁸ ⲙ̄ⲡⲣⲏⲧⲉ
ⲛ̄ⲛⲟⲩⲧⲗ̄ⲧⲗⲉ ⲛ̄ⲧⲉ ⲟⲩ- ⁹ ϩⲁⲗⲙⲉ, ⲙ̄ⲡⲣⲏⲧⲉ ⲛⲛⲟⲩⲕⲟⲩⲡⲣ ¹⁰ ⲛ̄ⲧⲉ ⲟ[ⲩϩⲉⲗⲁ]ⲗⲉ, ⲙ̄ⲡⲣⲏⲧⲉ ⲛ̄ⲛⲟⲩ-

---

59.37 ϩⲱⲥⲇⲉ: read ϩⲱⲥⲧⲉ.
60.7 ⲛ̄ⲭⲓ: read ⲛ̄ϭⲓ.
60.20 ⲛ̄ⲭⲓ: read ⲛ̄ϭⲓ.
61.28 ⲱ: read ⲉⲩ.

one. [36] He is the fullness of the [37] fatherly so that his [38] abundance is a begetting [60.1] [. . .] of the eternities.

[2] They existed eternally [3] in thought, since the Father was [4] like a thought [5] and <a> place to them. After the begettings had been established, [6] the one who is able to prevail over [7] [the] entirety desired [8] to bring [9] forth [what] was lacking in the [10] [. . . He brought] forth those who [11] [. . . in] him. But he is [12] [the way] he is, [13] [he is] a spring, which is not [14] lessened by the water that [15] flows abundantly from it. [16] When they were [17] in the thought of the Father, that [18] is, while they were in the hidden depth, [19] the depth knew them, [20] but it was [21] not possible for them to know [22] the depth in which they dwelled, [23] nor was it [24] possible for them to know [25] themselves, nor [26] for them to know anything (else). That [27] is, they were [28] with the Father; they did not exist [29] for themselves. Instead, [30] they only had [31] being like [32] a seed, so that it is discovered that [33] they existed like a [34] fetus. Like the word [35] he begot them. He was established [36] spermatically. [37] But those whom he would [38] beget had not yet come to be [61.1] from him. [. . .] The one who [2] first thought about them, the Father [3]—not only so that they come to be for him, [4] but so that they come to be for themselves [5] as well, that they, therefore, come to be in [his] [6] thought as a thought substance, [7] and that they might come to be for themselves too—[8] sowed thought like a [spermatic] [9] seed. So that [they might] [10] know [what exists] [11] for them, he graciously [gave the] first [12] form. [But] so that they might [understand] [13] who the Father who exists [for them] is, [14] he gave the name of the Father [15] to them by means of a voice telling [16] them that what exists exists [17] in that name, which they have [18] from their coming into being, because their exaltation, [19] which has been forgotten [20] by them, is in the name.

The child, while in the [21] form of a fetus, has [22] enough for itself [23] when it has not yet seen the one who [24] sowed it. For this reason they had [25] the singular task of [26] searching after him by recognizing [27] that he exists, desiring to discover [28] what exists. But since [29] the perfect Father is good, [30] just as he did not ever hear [31] them so that they would exist [32] in his thought, but he granted [33] that they also might exist, so too [34] will he give [35] them grace to know what exists, [36] that is, the one who knows himself [37] eternally. [62.1] [. . .] [2] form to [know] what exists [3] just as they are begotten in this [4] place. When they are born, they are in [5] the light with the result that they see those who have begotten them.

[6] The Father brought forth the entirety, [7] like little children, [8] like the dripping of a [9] fountain, like a bud [10] from a [vine,] like a [11] [flower,] like a <plant> of [12] [. . .] need-

[11] [ⳅⲣ]ⲉ[ⲣⲉ, ⲙⲡⲣ]ⲏⲧⲉ ⲛ̄ⲛⲟⲩⲧⲱⲕⲥ̄ ⲙ̄- [12] [. . . . .]ⲱⲡ ⲉⲩⲣ̄ ⲭⲣⲓⲁ ⲛ̄ⲛⲟⲩϫⲓ ⲥⲁ- [13] [ⲛⲉⳍ] ⲙⲛ̄
ⲟⲩⲡⲁⲩⲣⲉ ⲙⲛ̄ ⲟⲩⲙⲛ̄ⲧ- [14] ⲁ̣[ⲧⳃ]ⲧⲁ. ⲁⳅⲉⲙⲁⳍⲧⲉ ⲙ̄ⲙⲟⲥ [15] ⲁⳍⲟⲩⲁⲉⲓⳃ. ⲡⲉⲧⲉⲁⳅⲙⲉⲩⲉ [16] ⲁⲣⲁⲥ
ϫⲛ ⲛ̄ⳃⲁⲣⲡ̄ ⲛ̄ⲧⲁⳅ ⲙ̄ⲙⲉⲛ [17] ⲟⲩⲛ̄ⲧⲉⳅⲥ̄ ⲙⲙⲉⲩ ϫⲛ ⲛ̄ⳃⲁⲣⲡ̄. [18] ⲁⳅⲛⲉⲩ ⲁⲣⲁⲥ, ⲁⳅⳍⲱⲧⲡ̄ ⲇⲉ
ⲙ̄ⲙⲟⲥ [19] ⲁⲛⲁⲉⲓ ⲉⲛⲧⲁⲣ̄ ⳃⲟⲣⲡ̄ ⲛ̄ⲉⲓ ⲁⲃⲁⲗ [20] ⲙ̄ⲙⲁⳅ. ⳍⲛ̄ⲛ ⲟⲩⲫⲑⲟⲛⲟⲥ ⲉⲛ, ⲁⲗ- [21] ⲗⲁ ϫⲉⲕⲁⲥⲉ
ⲛ̄ⲥⲉⲧⲙ̄ϫⲓ ϫⲛ̄ [22] ⲛ̄ⳃⲁⲣⲡ̄ ⲛ̄ⲧⲟⲩⲙⲛ̄ⲧⲁⲧⲱⲧⲁ <ⲛ̄>ϫⲓ ⲙ̄- [23] ⲁⲓⲱⲛ ⲛ̄ⲥⲉⲧⲙ̄ϥⲓⲧⲟⲩ ⲁⳍⲣⲏ̈
ⲁⲡⲓ- [24] ⲉⲁⲩ, ⳃⲁ ⲡⲓⲱⲧ, ⲛ̄ⲥⲉⲙⲉⲩⲉ ⲛⲉⲩ [25] ⲟⲩⲁⲉⲉⲧⲟⲩ ϫⲉ ⲁⲃⲁⲗ ⲙ̄ⲙⲟⲟⲩ [26] ⲟⲩⲛ̄ⲧⲉⲩ ⲙ̄ⲡⲁⲉⲓ
ⲙ̄ⲙⲉⲩ. {ⲁ} ⲁⲗⲗⲁ [27] ⲙ̄ⲡⲣⲏⲧⲉ ⲛ̄ⲇⲉ ⲉⲛⲧⲁⳅⲣ̄ ⳍⲛⲉⳅ [28] ⲁϯ ⲛⲉⲩ ⲁⲧⲣⲟⲩⳃⲱⲡⲉ, ⲡⲉⲉⲓ [29] ⲡⲉ
ⲡⲣⲏⲧⲉ ⲁⲛ, ⲁⲧⲣⲟⲩⳃⲱⲡⲉ ⲛⲁⲧ- [30] ⳃⲧⲁ, ⲛ̄ⲧⲁⲣⲉⳅⲣ̄ ⳍⲛⲉⳅ, ⲁⳅϯ ⲛⲉⲩ [31] ⲙ̄ⲡⲓⲙⲉⲉⲩⲉ ⲉⲧϫⲏⲕ
ⲁⲃⲁⲗ ⲛ̄- [32] ⲧⲉ ϯⲙⲛ̄ⲧⲡⲉⲧⲣ̄ ⲡⲉⲧⲛⲁⲛⲟⲩⳅ [33] ⲁⲣⲁⲩⲟⲩ.

ϫⲉ ⲡⲁⲉⲓ ϭⲉ ⲉⲛⲧⲁⳅϫⲁⲉⲓ- [34] ⲁⳅ ⲛ̄ⲛⲟⲩⲁⲉⲓⲛⲉ ⲁⲛⲉⲛⲧⲁⲩⲉⲓ ⲉ- [35] ⲃⲟⲗ ⲙ̄ⲙⲟⳅ ⲙ̄ⲙⲓⲛ ⲙ̄ⲙⲟⳅ,
ⲡⲉ- [36] ⲧⲟⲩⲙⲟⲩⲧⲉ ⲁⲣⲁⲩ ⲙ̄ⲙⲟⳅ, ⲛ̄- [37] ⲧⲁⳅ ⲡⲉ ⲡⳃⲏⲣⲉ, ⲉⲧⲙⲏⳍ, ⲉⲧϫⲏⲕ, [38] ⲛ̄ⲛⲁⲧⲱⲧⲁ.
ⲁⳅⲛ̄ⲧⳅ ⲁⲃⲁⲗ ⲉⳅ- [39] ⲧⲏⲧ ⲙⲉⲛ ⲙⲛ̄ ⲡⲉⲛⲧⲁⲉⲓ ⲁⲃⲁⲗ [63.1] [ⲙ]ⲙⲁ̣ⳅ ⲉ̣[. .]ⳃ[. . . . .] [2] ⲉⳅⲣ̄
ⳃⲃ[ⲏ]ⲣ̣ ⲛ̣ϫ̣ⲓ̣ [. . . .]ⲙ̣ [. .] [3] ⲡⲧⲏⲣⳅ̄ ⲕⲁⲧⲁ [. .] [.] [.] ⲉⲣⲉⲡⲟⲩⲉ[ⲓ] [4] ⲡⲟⲩⲉⲓ ⲛⲁⳃⲁ[ⲡⳅ] ⲁⲣⲁⳅ
ⲙ̄ⲙⲁⳅ, [5] ⲉⲧⳅⲙⲛ̄ⲧⲛⲁϭ ⲉⲛ ⲧⲉ ⲧⲉⲉⲓ [6] ⲉⲙⲡⲁⲧⲁⲩⳃⲁⲡⳅ ⲙ̄ⲙⲟⳅ. ⲁⲗⲗ[ⲁ] [7] ⳅⳃⲟⲟⲡ ⲛ̄ⲧⲁⳅ
ⲛ̄ⲧⲁⲉⲓⲉ ⲉⲧⲉ[ⳅ]- [8] ⳃⲟⲟⲡ ⲙ̄ⲙⲁⳅ. ⲙ̄ⲡⳅⲣⲏⲧⲉ ⲙⲛ̄ [ⲡⲉ]- [9] ⳅⲥⲙⲁⲧ ⲙⲛ̄ ⲧⲉⳅⲙⲛ̄ⲧⲛⲟϭ [10] ⲉⲩⲛ̄
ϭⲁⲙ ⲙ̄ⲙⲁⳅ [ⲁⲧ]ⲣⲟⲩⲛⲉⲩ [ⲁ]- [11] ⲣⲁⳅ ⲛ̄ⲥⲉϫⲟⲟⲥ ⲁ[ⲡ]ⲉⲧ[ⲟ]ⲩⲥⲁ̣[ⲩⲛⲉ] [12] ⲙ̄ⲙⲁⳅ, ⲛ̄ⲧⲉⳅ ⲉⲩⲣ̄
ⲫⲟⲣ̣ⲓ̣ [ⲙ]- [13] ⲙⲁⳅ ⲉⳅⲣ̄ ⲫⲟⲣⲓ ⲙ̄ⲙⲁⳅ, [ⲁⲩⲱ] [14] ⲟⲩⲛ̄ ϭⲟⲙ ⲙ̄ⲙⲁⳅ ⲛ̄ⲧⲉⳍ̣[ⲁⳅ. ⳅ]- [15] ⳃⲟⲟⲡ ⲛ̄ⲧⲁⳅ
ⲛ̄ⲑⲉ ⲉⲧⳅⳃ̣[ⲟ]ⲟⲡ [16] ⲙ̄ⲙⲁⲥ ⲛ̄ⲇⲉ· ⲡⲓⲁⲧⳃ ⲉⲣ ⲙⲓⲛⲉ [17] ⲙ̄ⲙⲁⳅ. ϫⲉⲕⲁⲥⲉ ⲉⳅⲛⲁϫⲓ [18] ⲉⲁⲩ ⲁⲃⲁⲗ
ⳍⲛ̄ ⲡⲟⲩⲉⲓ ⲡⲟⲩⲉⲓ, [19] <ⲁ>ⳅⲟⲩⲁⲛⳍ̄ϥ ⲉⲃⲟⲗ ⲙ̄ⲙⲓⲛ ⲙ̄ⲙⲟⳅ [20] ⲛ̄ϭⲓ ⲡⲓⲱⲧ ⲁⲩⲱ ⳍⲛ̄ ⲧⲉⳅⲙⲛ̄ⲧⲁⲧ-
[21] ⳃⲉϫⲉ ⲁⲣⲁⳅ, ⲉⳅⳍⲏⲡ ⲛ̄ⲁⲧⲛⲉⲩ [22] ⲁⲣⲁⳅ, ⲉⲩⲣ̄ ⲑⲁⲩⲙⲁ ⲙ̄ⲙⲁⳅ [23] ⳍⲛ̄ⲛ ⲟⲩⲛⲟⲩⳍ. ⲉⲧⲃⲉ ⲡⲉⲉⲓ
ⲧⲙⲛ̄ⲧ- [24] ⲛⲁϭ ⲙ̄ⲡⲉⳅϫⲓⲥⲉ ⳍⲙ̄ ⲡⲧⲣⲟⲩ- [25] ⳃⲉϫⲉ ⲁⲣⲁⳅ ⲛ̄ⲥⲉⲛⲉⲩ ⲁⲣⲁⳅ. [26] ⳅⳃⲱⲡⲉ ⲉⳅⲟⲩⲁⲛ̄ⳍ̄
ⲁⲃⲁⲗ [27] ⲉⲩⲛⲁⳍⲱⲥ ⲁⲣⲁⳅ ⲉⲧⲃⲉ ⲡⳍⲟⲩⲟ [28] ⲛ̄ⲧⲉⳅⲙⲛ̄ⲧⳍⲗ̄ϭⲉ ⳍⲛ̄ ϯⲭⲁⲣⲓⲥ [29] ⲛ̄ⲇⲉ
< . . . > ⲁⲩⲱ ⲙ̄ⲡⲣⲏⲧⲉ {ⲁⲩⲱ ⲙ̄- [30] ⲡⲣⲏⲧⲉ} ⲛ̄ⲛⲓⲙⲛ̄ⲧⲣ̄ⲙ̄ⲙⲁ- [31] ⲉⲓⳍⲉ ⲛ̄ⲧⲉ ⲛⲓⲙⲛ̄ⲧⲕⲁⲣⲱⲥ
[32] ⳍⲛ̄ⲙⲓⲥⲉ{ⲥⲉ} ⲛⲉ ⳃⲁ ⲉⲛⲏⳍⲉ [33] ⲛ̄ⲧⲁⲩ ⲛ̄ⲇⲉ ⳍⲛ̄ϫⲡⲟ ⲛⲛⲟⲩⳅ ⲛⲉ, [34] ⲧⲉⲉⲓ ⲧⲉ ⲑⲉ ⳍⲱⳅ
ⲁⲛ ⲛ̄ⲛⲓⲇⲓⲁ- [35] ⲑⲉⲥⲓⲥ ⲛ̄ⲧⲉ ⲡⲗⲟⲅⲟⲥ ⳍⲛ̄ⲡⲣⲟⲃⲟ- [36] ⲗⲏ ⲛⲉ ⲙ̄ⲡⲛⲉⲩⲙⲁⲧⲓⲕⲏ. ⲛ̄ⲧⲁⲩ ϭⲉ
ⲙ̄- [37] ⲡⲉⳅⲛⲉⲩ, ⳍⲱⲥ ⲉⲛⲁⲩⲗⲟⲅⲟⲥ ⲡⲉ, [64.1] [ⳍⲉ]ⲛⲥ̣[ⲡⲉⲣⲙⲁ] ⲛⲉ ⲁⲩⲱ ⳍⲉⲛ- [2] ⲙⲉⲩⲉ ⲛ̄[ⲧⲉ ⲛ]
ⲉⳅⲙⲓⲥⲉ ⲛⲉ, [3] ⲁⲩⲱ ⳍⲉⲛⲛⲟⲩⲛⲉ ⲉⲩⲁⲛ̄ⳍ̄ [4] ⲁⲛⲏⳍⲉ ⲧⲙⲉⲧ, ⲉⲩⲟⲩⲁⲛ̄ⳍ̄ ϫⲉ [5] ⳍⲉⲛϫⲡⲟ ⲛⲉ ⲛ̄ⲧⲁⲉⲓ
ⲁⲃⲁⲗ ⲙ̄- [6] ⲙⲁⲩ, ⳍⲛ̄ⲛⲟⲩⳅ ⲛⲉ ⲁⲩⲱ ⳍⲛ̄- [7] ⲡⲛⲉⲩⲙⲁⲧⲓⲕⲟⲛ ⲛⲉ ⲛ̄ϫⲡⲟ ⲉⳍⲟⲩⲛ ⲉⲩ- [8] ⲉⲁⲩ
ⲙ̄[ⲡ]ⲓⲱⲧ.

ϫⲉ ⲙⲛ̄ ⲭⲣⲓⲁ [9] ⲛ̄ⲥⲙⲏ ⳍ[ⲓ ⲡ]ⲛⲉⲩⲙⲁ, ⲛ̄ⲛⲟⲩⲥ ⲁⲩⲱ ⲛ̄- [10] ⲗⲟⲅ[ⲟ]ⲥ̣, [ϫⲉ] ⲟⲩⲇⲉ ⲙⲛ̄ ⲭⲣⲉⲓⲁ-
ⲛⲣ̄ [11] [ⳍⲱ]ⲃ [ⲁ]ⳍⲟⲩ[ⲛ] ⲁⲡⲉⲧⲟⲩⲣ̄ ⳍⲛⲉⲩ ⲛ̄- [12] [ⲉⳅϥ], ⲁⲗⲗⲁ ⳍⲙ̄ ⲡⲥⲙⲁⲧ ⲉⲧⲉ- [13] [ⲛⲉⳅ]ⳃⲟⲟⲡ
ⲙ̄ⲙⲁⳅ, ⲧⲉⲉⲓ ⲧⲉ ⲑⲉ [14] [ⲛ̄ⲛⲉ]ⲧⲁⳍⲉⲓ ⲁⲃⲁⲗ ⲙ̄ⲙⲁⳅ, ⲉⲩ- [15] ϫⲡⲟ ⲙ̄ⲡⲉⲧⲟⲩⲁⳃⳅ ⲧⲏⲣⳅ̄.
ⲁⲩⲱ [16] ⲡⲉⲧⲟⲩⲣ̄ ⲛⲟⲉⲓ ⲙ̄ⲙⲁⳅ, ⲙⲛ̄ ⲡⲉ- [17] ⲧⲟⲩϫⲟⲩ ⲙ̄ⲙⲁⳅ, ⲙⲛ̄ ⲡⲉⲧⲟⲩ- [18] ⲕⲓⲙ ⲁⲣⲁⲩ ⲉⳍⲟⲩⲛ
ⲉⲣⲟⳅ, ⲙⲛ̄ [19] ⲡⲉⲧⲟⲩⲕⲁⲁⲧ ⲁⳍⲣⲏ̈ ⲙ̄ⲙⲁⳅ, ⲁⲩⲱ [20] ⲡⲉⲧⲟⲩⳍⲱⲥ ⲙ̄ⲙⲟⳅ ⲉⲩϯ ⲉⲟ- [21]

62.11 ⲧⲱⲕⲥ̄: ⲧⲱϭⲉ (Kasser)?
62.18 ⳍⲱⲧⲡ̄: read ⲱⲧⲡ̄?
62.22 <ⲛ̄>ϫⲓ: read <ⲛ̄>ϭⲓ.
63.7–8 ⲛⲧⲁⲉⲓⲉ . . . ⲙ̄ⲙⲁⳅ: read ⲛⲧⲟⲉ . . . ⲙ̄ⲙⲁⲥ.
63.10 ⲙ̄ⲙⲁⳅ: read ⲙ̄ⲙⲁⲩ
63.16 ⲛ̄ⲇⲉ: possibly read ϫⲉ.

ing to receive [13] [nourishment] and growth and [14] faultlessness. He retained it [15] for a while. The one who had known [16] it from the very beginning [17] had it from the beginning. [18] He saw it, but he <shut> it <off> [19] from those who first came from [20] him. (He did this) not in jealousy, but [21] so that the eternities might not receive their faultlessness from [22] the beginning [23] and might not elevate themselves to the glory, [24] to the Father, and might think [25] that from themselves alone [26] they have this. [27] But just as he was pleased to give them [28] being, so [29] too, so that they might become faultless, [30] when he willed, he gave them [31] the perfect thought of [32] beneficence [33] toward them.

It is this one, then, whom he shown forth [34] as a light for those who had come [35] from himself, the [36] one from whom they receive a name, [37] he is the son who is full, perfect, [38] and faultless. He brought him forth [39] intertwined with what had come forth from [63.1] him [. . .] [2] joining in receiving [. . .] [3] the entirety according to [. . .] each [4] one will take [him] for himself, [5] yet this was not his greatness [6] before they had received it from him. But [7] he is <as> he [8] is. In his manner and [9] his form and his might [10] it is possible for <them> to see [11] him and to speak about what they know of [12] him, because they wear [13] him while he wears them, [and] [14] it is possible for them to reach him. [He] [15] is as he is: [16] incomparable. [17] So that he might receive [18] glory from each one, [19] the Father <has revealed> himself [20] and in his ineffability, [21] hidden and invisible, [22] while they marvel at him [23] intellectually. For this reason the greatness [24] of his exaltation (resides) in their [25] speaking about and seeing him. [26] He becomes manifest [27] so that they might hymn him on account of the greatness [28] of his sweetness in the grace [29] of < . . . > And just as [30] the marvels [31] of the silences [32] are eternal generations [33] and cognitive offspring, [34] so too are the dispositions [35] of the word spiritual emanations. [36] The two, [37] therefore, since they belong to a word, [64.1] are [seeds] and [2] thoughts [of] his children, [3] and roots that live eternally, [4] revealing [5] that they are children who have come forth from [6] themselves, since they are minds and [7] spiritual children within the [8] glory of [the] Father.

There is no need for [9] voice and spirit, mind and [10] word, [because] neither is there a need to [11] [work] at what they are pleased [12] [to do,] but the form by which [13] [he was] existing, so are [14] those who have come forth from him, [15] begetting all that they desire. And [16] the one they contemplate, and the [17] one they speak about, and the one toward whom [18] they move, and [19] the one in whom they reside, and [20] the one they hymn

ΟΥ M̄ΜΟϤ, ΟΥN̄ΤΕϤ M̄ΜΕΥ ²² N̄ϢΗΡΕ. ΤΕΕΙ ΓΑΡ ΤΕ ΤΟΥϬΟΜ ²³ N̄ΡΩΜΕϤϪΠΟ, N̄ΘΕ ϨΩΩϤ
ΑΝ ²⁴ N̄ΝΕΕΙ ΕΝΤΑϤΕΙ ΕΒΟΛ M̄ΜΟΟΥ, ²⁵ ΚΑΤΑ ΤΟΥΜN̄Τ̄ϯ ΤΟΟΤϤ̄ MN̄ ΝΕΥ- ²⁶ ΕΡΗΥ, ΕΥϯ
N̄ΤΟΟΤϤ̄ N̄ΝΕΥ- ²⁷ ΕΡΗΥ M̄ΠΣΜΑΤ ΝΝΙΑΤϪΠΟΟΥ.

²⁸ ϪΕ ΠΙΩΤ ΜΕΝ, ΚΑΤΑ ΠΕΤϤ̄- ²⁹ ϪΑΣΙ M̄ΜΑϤ ΑΝΙΠΤΗΡϤ, ΕϤΟ N̄- ³⁰ ΑΤΣΟΥΩΝϤ̄ ΑΥΩ
N̄ΑΤϢΑΠϤ̄, ³¹ ΕΥN̄ΤΕϤ M̄ΜΕΥ N̄ϯΜN̄ΤΝΟϬ ³² M̄ΠΙΡΗΤΕ MN̄ ϯΑΕΙΗ N̄ΘΕ, ³³ ΕΝΕΝΤΑϤΟΥΑΝϨϤ̄
ΑΒΑΛ N̄ΣΕ- ³⁴ ϨΗΤϤ̄ ϨN̄ ΟΥϢΩΩΤ ΑΒΑΛ Α- ³⁵ ΝΕΤϪΑΣΙ ΤΗΡΟΥ N̄ΤΕ ΝΙΑΩΝ ³⁶ ΕΝΤΑϤΕΙ
ΑΒΑΛ M̄ΜΑϤ, ΝΕΥ- ³⁷ ΝΑΤΕΚΟ ΠΕ. ΕΤΒΕ ΠΑΕΙ ΠΕϤ- ³⁸ ϪΙΝ MN̄ ΤΕϤΜN̄ΤΑΤϨΙΣΕ ΑϤΑ- ³⁹
ΜΑϨΤΕ M̄ΜΟΣ ϨΡΗΪ ϨN̄ ΠΕΤϤ̄- ⁶⁵·¹ ϢΟΟΠ{Ϥ̄} M̄ΜΑϤ. [N̄ΤΑϤ ϤϢΟΟΠ N̄]- ² ΑΤϢΕϪΕ ΑΡΑϤ
[ΑΥΩ N̄]N̄ΑΤϪΕ ΡΕ[N̄] ³ ΑΡΑϤ, ΑΥΩ ΕϤ[Ϫ]ΑΣΙ ΑΝΟΥϬ ΝΙΜ ⁴ ΑΥΩ ΑϢΕϪΕ ΝΙΜ. ΠΑΕΙ ΔΕ
ΑϤΣΑ[Υ]- ⁵ ΤN̄ M̄ΜΑϤ ΑΒΑΛ M̄ΜΙΝ M̄Μ[ΟϤ,] ⁶ ΑΥΩ ΠΕΝΤΑϤΠΑΡΕϢϤ̄ ΑΒ[ΑΛ] ⁷ ΠΕΕΙ
ΠΕN̄ΤΑϨϯ N̄ΝΟΥΤΑϪΡΟ Μ[N̄] ⁸ ΟΥΤΟΠΟΣ MN̄ ΟΥΜΑ N̄ϢΩΠΕ N̄- ⁹ ΠΙΤΗΡϤ̄, ΕΟΥΡΕΝ N̄ΤΕϤ
ΠΕ « ΠΕϨ[Ι] ¹⁰ ΕΤΕ ΑΒΑΛ ϨΪΤΟΟΤϤ̄, » ΕϤϢΟΟΠ ¹¹ N̄ΙΩΤ M̄ΠΤΗΡϤ̄, ΑΒΑΛ N̄ΤΕϤΜ̣[N̄Τ]- ¹²
ϢΟΠ ϨΪΣΕ ΑΡΑΥ <N̄>ΕΤϢΟΟΠ, ΕΑϤ- ¹³ ΣΕΤϤ̄ ΑϨΡΗΪ ΑΠΟΥΜΕΥΕ ΑΤΡ[ΟΥ]- ¹⁴ ϢΙΝΕ N̄ΣΩϤ.
ΠϨΟΥΟ N̄ΤΕ Τ.[. . . .] ¹⁵ ΑΒΑΛ ϨΜ ΠΤΡΟΥϨ ΝΟΕΙ ϪΕ ϤϢΟ- ¹⁶ [ΟΠ Α]ΥΩ N̄ΣΕϢΙΝΕ ϪΕ ΕΥ
ΠΕ[[N̄]]- ¹⁷ [ΤΕ]ΝΕϤϢΟΟΠ. ΠΕΕΙ ΔΕ ΑΥΤΕ- ¹⁸ [ΕΙ]Ϥ ΝΕΥ ΕΥΑΠΟΛΑΥΣΙΣ MN̄ ¹⁹ ΟΥΣΑΝΕϢ MN̄
ΑΛΗΛ MN̄ ΟΥϨΟΥΟ ²⁰ N̄ΤΕ ϯΜN̄Τ̄Ρ ΟΥΟΕΙΝ, ΕΤΕ ϯ- ²¹ ΤΜN̄ΤϢΒΗΡ ϢΟΠ ϨΪΣΕ N̄ΤΕϤ ΤΕ,
²² ΠΙΣΑΥΝΕ N̄ΤΕϤ, ΑΥΩ ΠΙΜΟΥϨϬ ²³ N̄ΤΕϤ ϢΑΡΑϤ, ΕΤΕ ΠΑΕΙ ΠΕ, ²⁴ ΕΤΟΥΜΟΥΤΕ ΑΡΑϤ
ΑΥΩ N̄ΤΑϤ ²⁵ ΠΕ ΠϢΗΡΕ, ΕΝΤΑϤ ΠΕ ΝΙΠΤΗΡϤ̄, ²⁶ {Ϫ} ΑΥΩ ΠΕΝΤΑϤΣΟΥΩΝϤ̄ ϪΕ ΝΙΜ ²⁷
ΠΕ ΑΥΩ ΕϤΤΕΕ[Ι]Ε ϨΪΩΩϤ. ²⁸ ΠΑΕΙ ΠΕ ΕΤΟΥΜΟΥΤΕ ΑΡΑϤ M̄- ²⁹ ΜΑϤ ϪΕ « ϢΗΡΕ, » ΑΥΩ
ΕΤΟΥϨ ΝΟΪ ³⁰ M̄ΜΑϤ ϪΕ ϤϢΟΟΠ ΑΥΩ ΝΕΥϢΙ- ³¹ ΝΕ N̄ΣΩϤ ΠΕ. ΠΕΕΙ ΠΕ ΠΕΤϢΟΟΠ ³²
N̄ΕΙΩΤ ΑΥΩ ΠΕΤΟΥΝΑϢ ϢΕϪΕ ³³ ΑΡΑϤ ΕΝ ΑΥΩ ΠΕΤΟΥϨ ΝΟΕΙ M̄- ³⁴ ΜΑϤ ΕΝ ΠΕΕΙ ΠΕ ΕΤΡ̄
ϢΡΠ N̄ϢΑ- ³⁵ ΠΕ.

ϪΕ MN̄ ϬΟΜ N̄ΛΑΥΕ ΑΡ̄ ΝΟΪ ³⁶ M̄ΜΑϤ Η ΑΜΕΥΕ ΑΡΑϤ. Η ΕΥΝΑϢ ³⁷ ϨΩΝ ΕϨΟΥΝ ΑΜΕϤ, ΟΥΒΕ
ΠΕΤϪΑΣΙ, ³⁸ ΟΥΒΕ ΠΑϢΡΠ N̄ϢΩΠΕ ϨN̄ ΟΥΜN̄Τ- ³⁹ ϪΑΕΙΣ; ΑΛΛΑ ΡΕΝ ΝΙΜ ΕΥΡ̄ ΝΟΕΙ M̄- ⁴⁰ ΜΑϤ
⁶⁶·¹ Η ΕΥ{Ρ̄ ΝΟΕ[Ι] M̄ΜΑϤ Η ΕΥ}ϪΟΥ ² M̄ΜΑϤ ϨΑΡΟϤ ΕϨΕΙΝΕ M̄ΜΑΥ ³ ΑΒΑΛ ΑΥΕΑΥ, N̄ΝΟΥϪΝΟΣ
⁴ N̄ΤΕϤ, ΚΑΤΑ ΤϬΟΜ M̄ΠΟΥΕΕΙ ⁵ [ΠΟ]ΥΕΕΙ N̄ΝΕΤϯ ΕΑΥ ΝΕϤ. ΠΕΝ- ⁶ [Τ]ΑϨϢΑΕΙ ε´ ϬΕ ΑΒΑΛ
M̄ΜΑϤ ΕϤΣΑΥ- ⁷ [Τ]N̄ M̄ΜΑϤ ΑΒΑΛ ΑΥϬΝϪΠΟ MN̄- ⁸ Ν ΟΥΣΑΥΝΕ N̄ΤΕ ΝΙΠΤΗΡϤ̄, N̄ΤΑϤ ⁹ [. .]
. Ε ΝΙΡΕΝ ΤΗΡΟΥ ϨN̄ ΟΥΜN̄Τ- ¹⁰ ΑΤϪΕ ϬΑΛ, ΑΥΩ ΝΤΑϤ ΠΕ ΠϢΑ- ¹¹ Ρ̄Π ΟΥΑΕΕΤϤ̄ ϨN̄
ΟΥΜN̄ΤϪΑΪΣ, ¹² [Π]ΡΩΜΕ N̄ΤΕ ΠΙΩΤ, ΕΤΕ ΠΑΕΙ ΠΕ, ΕϤ- ¹³ [ϪΩ] M̄ΜΟϤ

ΤΜΟΡΦΗ N̄ΤΕ ΠΙΑΤΜΟΡ- ¹⁴ ΦΗ,
ΠΣΩΜΑ N̄ΤΕ ΠΙΑΤΣΩΜΑ,
ΠϨΟ Μ- ¹⁵ ΠΙΑΤΝΕΥ ΑΡΑϤ,
ΠΛΟΓΟΣ M̄[ΠΙΑΤΟΥ]- ¹⁶ ΑϨΜΕϤ,
ΠΝΟΥΣ M̄ΠΙΑΤΡ̄ N̄[ΟΕΙ M̄]- ¹⁷ ΜΑϤ,
ΤΠΗΓΗ ΕΝΤΑ<Ϩ>ϨΕΤΕ ΑΒΑΛ [M̄]- ¹⁸ ΜΑϤ,
ΤΝΟΥΝΕ N̄ΤΕ ΝΕΤϪΑΕΙΤ,
¹⁹ ΠΝΟΥΤΕ ΔΕ N̄ΝΕΤΚΗ ΑϨΡΗΪ,
ΠΟΥΟΪΝ ²⁰ N̄ΝΕΤ`Ϥ Ρ̄ ΟΥΟΕ<ΙΝ> ΑΡΑΥ,

while glorifying [21] him, he has [22] children. For this is their [23] reproductive power, like [24] those from whom they have come forth, [25] according to their mutual giving, [26] since they give to one another [27] the form of the unbegotten ones.

[28] The Father, in accordance with his [29] superiority to the entireties, since he is [30] unknown and incomprehensible, [31] has such greatness [32] and weightiness that [33] had he revealed himself suddenly [34] and immediately to [35] all those exalted among the eternities [36] who had come forth from him, they [37] would have died. For this reason his [38] power and his indefatigability he [39] held back within that in which he [65.1] is. [He is] [2] ineffable and unnameable, [3] and he is exalted over every mind [4] and every word. This one, however, extended [5] himself, [6] and it was that which he stretched out [7] that gave a firmness and [8] a location and a dwelling place to [9] the entirety, one of his names being "the one [10] through whom," because he is [11] Father of the entirety, from his [12] laboring for those who exist, having [13] sown into their mind (the desire to) [14] seek him. The abundance of the [. . .] [15] from their knowing that he [16] exists and their asking about [17] what existed. But this one was given [18] to them for enjoyment and [19] nourishment and delight and abundance [20] of illumination, which [21] is his co-laboring, [22] his knowledge, and his mixing [23] with them, that is, [24] the one called and who [25] is the son, since he is the entireties, [26] and the one whom they have known who [27] he is and that it is he who clothes. [28] This one who is called [29] "Son," and about whom it is known [30] that he exists and that they sought. [31] This is the one who exists [32] as Father and the one about whom they will not be able to speak [33] and the one about whom they do not know. [34] This is the one who first came to [35] be.

It is not possible for anyone to know [36] him or to think about him. Or is it possible [37] to go there, toward the exalted one, [38] toward the first being properly (speaking)? [39] All names conceived of [40] or spoken about [66.1] him are brought [3] in honor, as his footprint, [4] in accordance with the power of each [5] one of those who honor him. [6] Then the one who arose from him when he stretched [7] himself out for begetting [8] and knowledge of the entireties, he [9] [. . .] all the names truthfully, [10] and he is [11] properly the only first one, [12] [the] man of the Father, that is, the one I [13] [call]

the form of the formless, [14]
the body of the bodiless,
the face of [15] the invisible,
the word of [the] [16] ineffable,
the mind of the inconceivable, [17]
the fountain that flowed from [18] him,
the root of those who are planted,
[19] and the god of those who are,
the light [20] of those whom he enlightens,

ⲡⲟⲩⲱϣⲉ ⲛ̄ⲛⲉⲛ- ²¹ ⲧⲁϥⲟⲩⲁϣⲟⲩ,
ⲧⲡⲣⲟⲛⲟⲓⲁ ⲛ̄ⲛⲉⲧϥ̄- ²² ⲣ̄ ⲡⲣⲟⲛⲟⲓⲁ ⲙ̄ⲙⲁⲩ,
ⲧⲙⲛ̄ⲧⲣⲙ̄ⲛ̄ϩⲏⲧ ²³ ⲛ̄ⲛⲉⲛⲧⲁϥⲉⲉⲩ ⲛ̄ⲣⲙ̄ⲛ̄ϩⲏⲧ,
ⲧϭⲟⲙ ²⁴ ⲛ̄ⲛⲉⲧϥ̄ϯ ϭⲟⲙ ⲛ̄ⲛⲉⲩ,
ⲡⲥⲱⲟⲩϩ ⲁ- ²⁵ ϩⲟⲩⲛ ⲛⲉⲧϥ̄ⲥⲁϩⲟⲩ ⲁⲣⲁⲩ,
ⲡϭⲱⲗⲡ̄ ²⁶ ⲁⲃⲁⲗ ⲛ̄ⲛⲉⲧⲟⲩϣⲓⲛⲉ ⲛ̄ⲥⲱⲟⲩ,
ⲡⲃⲉⲗ ²⁷ ⲛ̄ⲛⲉⲧⲛⲉⲩ ⲁⲃⲁⲗ,
ⲡⲛⲉⲩⲙⲁ ⲛ̄ⲛⲉⲧⲛⲓ- ²⁸ ϥⲉ,
ⲡⲱⲛϩ̄ ⲛ̄ⲛⲉⲧⲁⲛϩ̄,
ⲧⲙⲛ̄ⲧⲟⲩⲉⲓ ²⁹ ⲛ̄ⲟⲩⲱⲧ ⲛⲛⲉⲧⲙⲁϫϭ ⲛⲛⲓⲡⲧⲏⲣϥ.

³⁰ ⲛ̄ⲧⲁⲩ ⲧⲏⲣⲟⲩ ⲉⲩϣⲟⲟⲡ ϩⲙ̄ ⲡⲟⲩⲉⲉⲓ ³¹ ⲛ̄ⲟⲩⲱⲧ, ⲉϥⲧⲟⲉⲓ ϩⲓ̈ⲱⲱϥ ⲧⲏⲣϥ̄ ⲙ̄- ³² ⲙⲓⲛ ⲙ̄ⲙⲟϥ, ⲁⲩⲱ ⲛ̄ϩⲣⲏⲓ̈ ϩⲙ̄ ⲡⲓⲣⲉ<ⲛ> ⲛ̄- ³³ ⲟⲩⲱⲧ ⲛ̄ⲧⲉϥ ⲥⲉⲙⲟⲩⲧⲉ ⲁⲣⲁϥ ⲙ̄- ³⁴ ⲙⲁϥ ⲉⲛ ⲁⲛⲏϩⲉ ⲧⲙⲉⲧ. ⲁⲩⲱ ⲕⲁ- ³⁵ ⲧⲁ ⲡⲓⲣⲏⲧⲉ ⲛ̄ⲟⲩⲱⲧ, ⲛ̄ⲧⲁⲩ ⲁⲩⲥⲁϣ ³⁶ ⲡⲟⲩⲉⲉⲓ ⲛ̄ⲟⲩⲱⲧ ⲛⲉ ⲁⲩⲱ ⲛⲓⲡⲧⲏⲣϥ̄ ³⁷ ⲛⲉ. ⲟⲩⲇⲉ ⲛ̄ϥⲡⲛϣ ⲉⲛ ⲛ̄ⲥⲱⲙⲁ- ³⁸ ⲧⲓⲕⲟⲥ, ⲟⲩⲇⲉ ϥⲡⲁⲣⲭ ⲉⲛ ⲁⲛⲓⲣⲉⲛ ³⁹ ⲉⲛⲧⲁϥϣⲟⲟⲡ ⲙ̄ⲙⲁⲩ, ⲟⲩⲉⲧ ⁴⁰ ⲡⲉⲉⲓ ⲙⲉⲛ ⲙ̄ⲡⲓⲣⲏⲧⲉ ⲟⲩⲱⲧ ⁶⁷·¹ ⲡⲉⲉⲓ ⲛ̄ⲇⲉ ⲙ̄ⲡ̣[ⲓⲕⲉⲣⲏⲧⲉ. ⲟⲩⲇⲉ] ² ⲁⲛ ⲙⲁϥϣⲓⲃⲉ ϩⲛ̄ [. . .] ϣ, ⲟⲩⲇ̣[ⲉ] ³ ⲙⲁϥⲡⲱⲱⲛⲉ ⲁ[ⲛⲓⲣ]ⲉ̣ⲛ ⲉⲛⲧⲁϥ[ⲣ ⲛ]- ⁴ ⲟⲉⲓ ⲙ̄ⲙⲁⲩ, ϥⲣ ⲡⲉⲉⲓ ⲧⲉⲛⲟⲩ ϥⲣ ⁵ ⲡⲉⲉⲓ ⲁⲕⲉⲣⲏⲧⲉ, ⲉⲟⲩⲱⲧ ⲡⲁⲉⲓ ⲧⲉ̣- ⁶ ⲛⲟⲩ ⲁⲩⲱ ⲟⲩⲱⲧ ⲡⲁⲉⲓ ⲁⲕⲉϩⲁ[ⲧⲉ.] ⁷ ⲁⲗⲗⲁ ⲛ̄ⲧⲁϥ ⲧⲏⲣϥ̄ ⲡⲉ ϣⲁⲃⲟⲗ. [ϥⲟ]- ⁸ ⲉⲓ ⲙ̄ⲡⲟⲩⲉⲉⲓ ⲡⲟⲩⲉⲉⲓ ⲛ̄ⲛⲓⲡⲧⲏⲣϥ̄ ⁹ ⲁⲛⲏϩⲉ ⲧⲙⲉⲧ ϩⲓ̈ ⲟⲩⲥ[ⲁ]ⲡ. ϥⲟⲉⲓ ⲛ- ¹⁰ ⲛⲉⲧⲉ ⲛ̄ⲧⲁⲩ ⲧⲏⲣⲟⲩ ⲛⲉ. ⲛ̄ⲧⲁϥⲙ ¹¹ ⲡⲓⲱⲧ ⲛ̄ⲛⲓⲡⲧⲏⲣϥ̄. ⲛ̄ⲧⲁϥ ⲁⲛ ⲛⲉ ⲛⲓ- ¹² ⲡⲧⲏⲣϥ̄ ϫⲉ ⲛ̄ⲧⲁϥ ⲡⲉⲧⲟⲉⲓ <ⲛ̄>ⲥⲁⲩⲛⲉ ¹³ ⲛⲉϥ ⲙ̄ⲙⲓⲛ ⲙ̄ⲙⲁϥ ⲁⲩⲱ ⲉϥⲟⲉⲓ [ⲛ]- ¹⁴ ⲧⲟⲩⲉⲓⲉ ⲧⲟⲩⲉⲓⲉ ⲛ̄ⲛⲓⲁⲣⲉⲧⲏ. ⲟⲩ[ⲛ]- ¹⁵ ⲧⲉϥ ⲙⲉⲛ ⲛ̄ⲛⲓϭⲟⲙ ⲁⲩⲱ <ⲉϥⲟ>ⲉⲓ ⲛ̄ⲃⲉⲗ ¹⁶ ⲙ̄ⲡⲉⲧϥⲥⲁⲩⲛⲉ ⲙ̄ⲙⲁϥ ⲧⲏⲣϥ̄, ¹⁷ ⲉϥⲛⲉⲩ ⲁⲣⲁϥ ⲙ̄ⲙⲁϥ ⲙ̄ⲙⲓⲛ ⲙ̄ⲙⲁϥ ¹⁸ [ⲧ]ⲏⲣϥ̄, ⲉⲩⲛ̄ⲧⲉϥ ⲙ̄ⲙⲉⲩ ⲛ̄ⲛⲟⲩ- ¹⁹ ϣⲏⲣⲉ ⲁⲩⲱ ⲙ̄ⲙⲟⲣⲫⲏ. ⲉⲧⲃⲉ ⲡⲉ- ²⁰ ⲉⲓ ϩⲉⲛⲁⲧⲁⲡⲟⲩ ⲛⲉ ⲛⲉϥϭⲟⲙ ²¹ ⲙⲛ̄ ⲛⲉϥⲁⲣⲉⲧⲏ ⲁⲩⲱ ϩⲛ̄ⲁⲧⲥⲱ- ²² ⲧⲙ̄ ⲁⲣⲁⲟⲩ ⲛⲉ, ⲉⲧⲃⲉ ⲡⲓϫⲡⲟ ⲉⲧϥ̄- ²³ ϫⲡⲟ ⲙ̄ⲙⲁⲩ <ⲙ̄ⲙⲁϥ>. ϩⲛ̄ⲁⲧⲁⲡⲟⲩ ⲛⲉ ²⁴ ⲁⲩⲱ ϩⲛ̄ⲁⲧⲡⲁⲣⲭⲟⲩ ⲁⲃⲁⲗ ⲛⲉ {ⲛⲉ} ²⁵ ⲛⲓϫⲡⲟ ⲛ̄ⲧⲉ ⲛⲉϥⲗⲟⲅⲟⲥ ⲁⲩⲱ ⲛⲓ- ²⁶ ϩⲱⲛ ⲛ̄ⲧⲉϥ ⲁⲩⲱ ⲛⲓⲡⲧⲏⲣϥ̄ ⲛ̄ⲧⲉϥ. ²⁷ ϥⲥⲁⲩⲛⲉ ⲙ̄ⲙⲁⲩ ⲉⲧⲉ ⲛ̄ⲧⲁϥ ⲡⲉ ⲙ̄- ²⁸ ⲙⲓⲛ ⲙ̄ⲙⲁϥ, ⲉϥϣⲟⲟⲡ ⲛ̄ϩⲣⲏⲓ̈ ⲛ̄ϩⲛ̄ ²⁹ ⲡⲓⲣⲉⲛ ⲛ̄ⲟⲩⲱⲧ ⲉⲛⲧⲁⲩ ⲧⲏⲣⲟⲩ ³⁰ ⲉⲩϣⲟⲟⲡ ⲛ̄ϩⲏⲧϥ̄ ⲉⲩϣⲉϫⲉ. ⲁⲩⲱ ³¹ ⲉϥⲓⲛⲉ ⲁⲃⲁⲗ ϫⲉⲕⲁⲥ ϩⲛ̄ ⲟⲩⲙⲛ̄ⲧ- ³² ⲟⲩⲉⲓ ⲛ̄ⲟⲩⲱⲧ ⲉⲩϭⲁⲛⲧϭ̄ ⲉⲩ- ³³ ϣⲟⲟⲡ ⲕⲁⲧⲁ ⲧⲟⲩⲉⲓⲉ ⲧⲟⲩⲉⲓⲉ ⲛ̄ⲁⲣⲉ- ³⁴ ⲧⲏ. ⲁⲩⲱ ⲡⲁϣⲉⲉⲓⲇⲉ ³⁵ ⲁⲛ ⲙ̄ⲡⲉϥⲟⲩ- ³⁵ ⲁⲛϩ̄ϥ ⲁⲃⲁⲗ ⲛ̄ⲛⲓⲡⲧⲏⲣϥ̄ ϩⲓ̈ ⲟⲩⲥⲁⲡ, ³⁶ ⲁⲩⲱ ⲡⲓϣⲱϣ ⲛ̄ⲧⲉϥ ⲙ̄ⲡⲉϥⲟⲩⲁⲛϩ̄ϥ ³⁷ ⲁⲛⲉⲛⲧⲁϥⲉⲓ ⲁⲃⲁⲗ ⲙ̄ⲙⲁϥ.

ϫⲉ ⲛⲉ- ³⁸ ⲧⲁ<ϩ>ⲉⲓ ϭⲉ ⲁⲃⲁⲗ ⲙ̄ⲙⲁϥ ⲧⲏⲣⲟⲩ, ⲛ̄ⲧⲉ ³⁹ ⲛⲉⲉⲓ ⲛⲉ ⲛⲓⲁⲓⲱⲛ ⲛ̄ⲧⲉ ⲛⲓⲁⲓⲱⲛ, ⁶⁸·¹ [ⲉ] ϩⲛ̄ⲡⲣⲟ[ⲃⲟⲗ]ⲏ ⲛⲉ ⲛ̄ϫⲡⲟ ⲛⲉ ⲛ̄- ² ⲧⲉⲩⲫⲩⲥⲓⲥ ⲛ̄ⲣⲱⲙⲉϥϫⲡⲟ, ³ ⲛ̄ⲧⲁⲩ ϩⲱⲟⲩ ϩⲣⲏⲓ̈ ϩⲛ̄ ⲧⲟⲩⲫⲩⲥⲓⲥ ⁴ ⲛ̄ⲣⲱⲙⲉ ⲉϥϫⲡⲟ ⲁⲩ<ϯ> ⲉⲁⲩ ⲙ̄- ⁵ ⲡⲓⲱⲧ, ⲛ̄ⲑⲉ ⲉⲛⲧⲁϥϣⲱⲡⲉ ⁶ ⲛ̄ⲗⲁⲉⲓϭⲉ ⲛⲉⲩ ⲛ̄ⲧⲉ ⲡⲟⲩⲧⲉ- ⁷ ϩⲟ ⲁⲣⲉⲧϥ̄. ⲉⲧⲉ ⲡⲉⲉⲓ ⲡⲉ ⲛ̄- ⁸ ⲧⲁⲛⲣ̄ ϣⲣ̄ⲡ ⲛ̄ϫⲟⲟⲥ, ϫⲉ ϥⲉⲓⲣⲉ ⁹ ⲛ̄ⲛⲁⲓⲱⲛ ⲛ̄ϩⲉⲛⲛⲟⲩⲛⲉ ⲁⲩⲱ ϩⲛ̄- ¹⁰ ϩⲁⲗⲙⲏ ⲁⲩⲱ ϩⲛ̄ⲉⲓⲁⲧⲉ, ϫⲉ ⲡⲉⲉⲓ ¹¹ ⲉⲧⲟⲩϯ ⲉⲁⲩ ⲛⲉϥ.

66.35 ⲁⲩⲥⲁϣ: ϩⲛ̄ⲛ ⲟⲩϣⲱϣ?
67.38 ⲛ̄ⲧⲉ: read ⲉⲧⲉ.
68.2 ⲧⲉⲩⲫⲩⲥⲓⲥ: read ⲧⲉϥⲫⲩⲥⲓⲥ.

the love of those [21] whom he loved,
the providence of those [22] about whom he cares,
the wisdom [23] of those whom he made wise,
the power [24] of those to whom he gives power,
the gathering [25] of those whom he gathers to him,
the revelation [26] of the things sought after,
the eye [27] of those who see,
the breath of those who [28] breathe,
the life of those who live,
the unity [29] of those who blend with the eternities.

[30] They all exist in the singular [31] one, since he clothes himself entirely, [32] and by his singular [33] name he is [34] never called. And in [35] this unique way, they are at once [36] the singular one and the entireties. [37] He is not divided bodily, [38] nor is he divided into the names [39] that he has (been given), (lest he be) one [40] thing in one way but another [67.1] thing in [another way. Neither] [2] does he change in [. . .] nor [3] does he change [the] names that he [conceives,] [4] (lest he be this now and [5] that later, being a certain one now [6] and another one later. [7] Instead he is entirely himself forever. [He] [8] is each one of the entireties [9] eternally and at once. He is [10] what they all are. He brought [11] the Father to the eternities. He is the [12] entireties because he is the one who is knowledge [13] of himself, and he is each [14] one of the virtues. He has [15] the powers and <he is> beyond [16] all that he knows, [17] yet he sees himself in him-self [18] entirely, having a [19] Son and form. For this reason [20] his powers [21] and virtues are innumerable and inaudible, [22] because of the begetting <by which> he [23] begets them. Innumerable [24] and indivisible are [25] the begettings of his words and his [26] eternities and his entireties. [27] He knows them, which he [28] himself is, since they dwell in [29] the solitary name, and all [30] dwell in it while speaking. And [31] he brings (them) forth so that in solitary [32] unity it might be discovered that they [33] exist in accordance with the virtue of each one. [34] And he did not [35] reveal the multitude of entireties at once, [36] nor did he reveal his equality [37] to those who had come forth from him.

[38] Then all those that had come forth from him, [39] these <who> are the eternities of the eternities, [68.1] [being] emanations and children of [2] <his> reproductive nature, [3] they too in their reproductive nature [4] have <given> honor to [5] the Father, since he had brought about [6] a cause for them for their [7] establishment. This is [8] what we said earlier, that he made [9] the eternities as roots and [10] springs and fathers, and that he is

ⲁⲩⲭⲡⲟ ⲭⲉ ¹² ⲟⲩⲛ̅ⲧⲉϥ ⲙ̅ⲙⲉⲩ ⲛ̅ⲛⲟⲩⲉⲡⲓⲥⲧⲏ- ¹³ ⲙⲏ ⲙⲛ̅ ⲟⲩⲙ̅ⲛ̅ⲧⲣⲙ̅ⲛ̅ϩⲏⲧ, ⲁⲩⲱ ¹⁴ ⲁⲩⲙ̅ⲙⲉ ⲭⲉ
{ⲁⲩⲙ̅ⲙⲉ ⲭⲉ} ⲛ̅- ¹⁵ ⲧⲁⲩⲉⲓ ⲁⲃⲁⲗ ϩⲛ̅ ϯⲉⲡⲓⲥⲧⲏⲙⲏ ¹⁶ ⲙⲛ̅ ϯⲙⲛ̅ⲧⲣⲙ̅ⲛ̅ϩⲏⲧ ⲛ̅ⲇⲉ ⲛⲓ[ⲡⲧⲏ]- ¹⁷
ⲣϥ̅. ⲛⲉⲩⲛⲁⲉⲓⲛⲉ ⲁⲃⲁⲗ ⲛ̅ⲛⲟⲩ- ¹⁸ ⲉⲁⲩ ⲉϥⲧⲛ̅ⲧⲁⲛⲧ̅—« ⲡⲓⲱⲧ ⲡⲉ ⲡⲉ- ¹⁹ ⲉⲓ ⲉⲧⲉ ⲛ̅ⲧⲁϥ ⲡⲉ
ⲛⲓⲡⲧⲏⲣϥ̅ »—²⁰ ⲉⲛⲉⲑⲉ ⲛ̅ⲧⲁⲩϥⲓⲧⲟⲩ ⲁϩⲣⲏⲓ̈ ⲁϯ ²¹ ⲉⲁⲩ ⲕⲁⲧⲁ ⲧⲟⲩⲉⲓⲉ ⲧⲟⲩⲉⲓⲉ ⲛ̅- ²² ⲛⲉⲱⲛ.
ⲉⲧⲃⲉ ⲡⲉⲉⲓ ⲛ̅ϩⲣⲏⲓ̈ ϩⲛ̅ ⲡⲓ- ²³ ϩⲱⲥ ⲁϩⲟⲩⲛ ⲁϯ ⲉⲁⲩ ⲁⲩⲱ ²⁴ ϩⲣⲏⲓ̈ ϩⲛ̅ ϯϭⲟⲙ ⲛ̅ⲧⲉ ϯⲙⲛ̅ⲧⲟⲩⲉⲓ- ²⁵
{ⲉⲓ} ⲛ̅ⲟⲩⲱⲧ ⲙ̅ⲡⲉⲧⲁⲩⲉⲓ ⲁⲃⲁⲗ ²⁶ ⲙ̅ⲙⲁϥ, ⲁⲩⲥⲱⲕ ⲁϩⲟⲩⲛ ⲁⲩⲙⲟⲩⲭϭ ²⁷ ⲙ̅ⲛ̅ⲛ ⲟⲩⲧⲱⲧ
ⲙⲛ̅ ⲟⲩⲙⲛ̅ⲧⲟⲩ- ²⁸ ⲉⲉⲓ ⲛⲟⲩⲱⲧ ϣⲁ ⲛⲟⲩⲉⲣⲏⲩ. ²⁹ ⲁⲩⲉⲓⲣⲉ ⲛ̅ⲛⲟⲩⲉⲁⲩ ⲉϥⲙ̅ⲡϣⲁ ⲙ̅- ³⁰ ⲡⲓⲱⲧ
ⲁⲃⲁⲗ ϩⲙ̅ ⲡⲓⲡⲗⲏⲣⲱⲙⲁ ³¹ ⲛ̅ⲧⲉ ϯⲥⲁⲟⲩϩⲥ̅, ⲉϥⲟⲉⲓ ⲛ̅ⲟⲩ- ³² ⲉⲓⲛⲉ ⲛ̅ⲟⲩⲱⲧ ⲉϩⲁϩ ⲡⲉ, ⲁⲃⲁⲗ ³³
ⲭⲉ ⲛ̅ⲧⲁⲩⲛⲧϥ̅ ⲁⲃⲁⲗ ⲁⲩⲉⲁⲩ ³⁴ ⲙ̅ⲡⲟⲩⲉⲉⲓ ⲛ̅ⲟⲩⲱⲧ ⲁⲩⲱ ⲁⲃⲁⲗ ³⁵ ⲭⲉ ⲁⲩⲉⲓ ⲁⲃⲁⲗ ϣⲁ ⲡⲉⲉⲓ
ⲉⲧⲉ ⲛ̅- ³⁶ ⲧⲁϥ ⲡⲉ ⲛⲓⲡⲧⲏⲣϥ̅. ⲛⲉ ⲡⲁⲉⲓ ϭⲉ ⁶⁹·¹ ⲛⲉⲩⲧⲁⲉⲓⲟ ⲡⲉ ⲙ̅ⲛ̅[. . .] ⲡⲉⲁⲩ[. .] ² ⲡⲁⲉⲓ
ⲉⲛⲧⲁϩⲉⲓ[ⲉ ⲁⲃ]ⲁⲗ ⲛ̅ⲛⲓⲡ̅ⲧ̅[ⲏ]- ³ ⲣϥ̅, ⲉⲟⲩⲁⲡⲁⲣⲭⲏ ⲛ̅ⲛⲓⲁⲧⲙⲟⲩ ⲡⲉ[ ] ⁴ ⲁⲩⲱ ⲟⲩϣⲁ ⲉⲛⲏϩⲉ
ⲡⲉ ⲁⲃⲁⲗ ⲭⲉ, ⲉ- ⁵ ⲁϥⲉⲓ ⲁⲃⲁⲗ ϩⲛ̅ ⲛⲓⲁⲓⲱⲛ ⲉⲧⲁⲛϩ̅, ⲉ[ϥ]- ⁶ ϩⲏⲕ ⲁⲃⲁⲗ ⲉϥⲙⲏϩ ⲉⲧⲃⲉ
ⲡⲉⲧⲭ̅[ⲏⲕ] ⁷ ⲉⲧⲙⲏϩ, ⲁϥⲕⲁⲟⲩ ⲉϩⲣⲏⲓ̈ ⲉⲩⲙⲏϩ ⁸ ⲉⲩⲭⲏⲕ ⲛⲉⲉⲓ ⲉⲛⲧⲁϩϯ ⲉⲁⲩ ϩⲛ̅- ⁹ ⲛ ⲟⲩⲭⲱⲕ
ⲁⲃⲁⲗ ⲁⲃⲁⲗ ϩⲛ̅ ϯⲕⲟ[ⲓ]- ¹⁰ ⲛⲱⲛⲓⲁ. ⲙ̅ⲡⲣⲏⲧⲉ ⲅⲁⲣ ⲙ̅ⲡⲓⲱⲧ ⲛ̅- ¹¹ [ⲁ]ⲧⲱⲧⲁ, ⲉⲩϯ ⲉⲁⲩ ⲛⲉϥ
ϣⲁⲣⲉϥ- ¹² ⟦ⲧ̅ⲥ̅ⲧ̅⟧ⲥⲱ`ⲧ´ⲙ̅ ⲡⲉⲁⲩ ⲁⲛ ⲉⲧϯ ⲉⲁⲩ ⲛⲉ[ϥ, ¹³ ⲁ]ⲟⲩⲁⲛϩⲟⲩ ⲁⲃⲁⲗ ⲙ̅ⲡⲉⲉⲓ ⲉⲧⲉ ⲛ̅- ¹⁴
[ⲧ]ⲁϥ ⲡⲉ.

ⲭⲉ ⲧⲗⲁⲉⲓϭⲉ ⲙ̅ⲡⲓⲙⲁϩ ¹⁵ ⲉⲁⲩ ⲥⲛⲉⲩ ⲉⲛⲧⲁⲥϣⲱⲡⲉ ¹⁶ [ⲛ]ⲉⲩ {ⲟⲩ} ⲡⲉⲧⲉ ⲡⲁⲉⲓ ⲉⲛⲧⲁⲩⲧⲥⲧⲁϥ
¹⁷ [ⲁ]ⲭⲱⲟⲩ ⲁⲃⲁⲗ ϩⲙ̅ ⲡⲓⲱⲧ ⲉⲁⲩⲙ̅ⲙⲉ ¹⁸ [ⲁ]ⲧⲭⲁⲣⲓⲥ ⲧⲁⲉⲓ ⲉⲛⲧ[ⲁ]ⲩϯ ⲕⲁⲣⲡⲟⲥ ¹⁹ ⲙ̅ⲙⲁⲥ
ⲁⲃⲁⲗ ϩⲙ̅ ⲡⲓⲱⲧ ϣⲁ ⲛⲟⲩⲉ- ²⁰ ⲣⲏⲩ ⲭⲉⲕⲁⲥⲉ, ⲙ̅ⲡⲣⲏⲧⲉ ⲉⲛⲧⲁⲩ- ²¹ ⲉⲓⲛⲉ ⲁⲃⲁⲗ <ⲙ̅ⲙⲁⲩ> ϩⲛ̅ⲛ
ⲟⲩⲉⲁⲩ ⲙ̅ⲡⲓⲱⲧ, ²² ⲡⲉⲉⲓ ⲡⲉ ⲡⲣⲏⲧⲉ ⲁⲛ, ⲁⲡⲧⲣⲟⲩⲱⲛϩ̅ ²³ ⲁⲃⲁⲗ ⲉⲩⲭⲏⲕ, ⲁⲩⲱⲛϩ̅ ⲁⲃⲁⲗ ⲉⲩ- ²⁴
ⲉⲓⲣⲉ ϩⲛ̅ ϯⲙⲛ̅<ⲧ>ϯ ⲉⲁⲩ.

ⲭⲉ ⲛⲉϩⲉⲛ- ²⁵ ⲉⲓⲁⲧⲉ ⲙ̅ⲡⲓⲙⲁϩ ϣⲁⲙⲧ ⲛ̅ⲉⲁⲩ <ⲛⲉ> ²⁶ ⲕⲁⲧⲁ ⲧⲙⲛ̅ⲧⲁⲩⲧⲉϩⲟⲩⲥⲓⲟⲥ ⲙⲛ̅ ²⁷ ⲧϭⲟⲙ
ⲉⲛⲧⲁⲩⲭⲡⲁⲥ ⲛ̅ⲙⲙⲉⲟⲩ, ²⁸ ⲉⲡⲟⲩⲉⲉⲓ ⲡⲟⲩⲉⲉⲓ ⲙ̅ⲙⲁⲩ ⲉⲛⲥⲉ- ²⁹ ϣⲟⲟⲡ ⲉⲛ ⲙ̅ⲙⲁϥ ⲁϯ ⲉⲁⲩ ϩⲛ̅
ⲟⲩ- ³⁰ ⲙⲛ̅ⲧⲟⲩⲉⲓ ⲛ̅ⲟⲩⲱⲧ ⲙ̅ⲡⲉⲧϥ̅ⲟⲩ- ³¹ ⲁϣϥ̅.

ⲭⲉ ⲡⲓϣⲁⲣⲡ̅ ϭⲉ ⲙⲛ̅ ⲡⲓⲙⲁϩ ³² ⲥⲛⲉⲩ ⲛⲉ, ⲁⲩⲱ ⲡⲓⲣⲏⲧⲏ ⲥⲉⲭⲏⲕ ⲙ̅ⲡ- ³³ ⲥⲛⲉⲩ ⲁⲩⲱ ⲥⲉⲙⲏϩ ⲭⲉ
ϩⲛ̅ⲟⲩⲱⲛϩ̅ ³⁴ ⲁⲃⲁⲗ ⲛⲉ ⲛ̅ⲧⲟⲟⲧϥ̅ ⲙ̅ⲡⲓⲱⲧ ⲉⲧⲭⲏⲕ ³⁵ ⲁⲃⲁⲗ ⲉⲧⲙⲏϩ, ⲙⲛ̅ ⲛⲉⲛⲧⲁϩⲉⲓ ⲁⲃⲁⲗ, ³⁶
ⲉⲧⲭⲏⲕ ⲁⲃⲁⲗ ϩⲙ̅ ⲡⲧⲣⲟⲩϯ ⲉⲁⲩ ⲙ̅- ³⁷ ⲡⲉⲧⲭⲏⲕ. ⲡⲓⲕⲁⲣⲡⲟⲥ ⲇⲉ ⲛ̅ⲧⲁϥ ⲙ̅- ³⁸ ⲡⲙⲁϩ ϣⲁⲙⲛ̅ⲧ
ϩⲛ̅ⲛⲉⲁⲩ ⲛⲉ ⲛ̅ⲧⲉ ³⁹ ⲡⲟⲩⲱϣⲉ ⲙ̅ⲡⲟⲩⲉ ⲡⲟⲩⲉ ⲛ̅ⲛⲁⲓⲱⲛ ⁴⁰ ⲁⲩⲱ ⲧⲟⲩⲉⲓⲉ ⲧⲟⲩⲉⲓⲉ ⲛ̅ⲛⲁⲣⲉⲧⲏ.
⁴¹—ⲟⲩⲛ̅ⲧⲉ ⲡⲓⲱⲧ ⲙⲉⲛ ϭⲟⲙ.—ϥϣⲟⲟⲡ ⁷⁰·¹ [ϩ]ⲛ̅ ⲟⲩ[ⲡⲗⲏⲣ]ⲱⲙⲁ, ⲉϥⲭⲏⲕ ² ⲁⲃⲁⲗ ⲙ̅[ⲡⲙⲉ]
ⲅⲉ ⲉⲧⲉ ⲁⲃⲟⲗ ³ ϩⲛ̅ⲛ ⲟⲩⲧⲱⲧ, ϩⲱⲥ ⲉⲁⲃⲟⲗ ⁴ ϩⲛ̅ⲛ ⲟⲩⲕⲁⲧⲁ `ⲡ´ⲟⲩⲉⲓ ⲡⲟⲩⲉⲉⲓ ⁵ ⲛ̅ⲛⲁⲓⲱⲛ ⲡⲉ.
ⲡⲉⲧϥ̅ⲟⲩⲁϣϥ̅ ⁶ [ⲁ]ⲩⲱ ⲡⲉⲧⲉⲟⲩⲛ ϭⲁⲙ ⲙ̅<ⲙ>ⲁϥ ⲁⲣⲁϥ ⁷ ⲉϥϯ ⲉⲁⲩ ⲙ̅ⲙⲁϥ ⲙ̅ⲡⲓⲱⲧ.

68.16 ⲛ̅ⲇⲉ: read ⲛ̅ϭⲓ.

69.12 ⟦ⲧ̅ⲥ̅ⲧ̅⟧ⲥⲱ`ⲧ´ⲙ̅ ⲡⲉⲁⲩ: The scribe may have corrected ⲧⲥⲧⲱ (ⲧⲥⲧⲟ?) ⲙ̅ⲡⲉⲁⲩ to ⲥⲱⲧⲙ̅ ⲡⲉⲁⲩ.

the one whom [11] they glorify. They have begotten, since [12] he has knowledge [13] and wisdom, and [14] the entireties knew that [15] they had come forth from knowledge [16] and wisdom. [17] They would have brought forth an [18] ostensible honor—"the Father is the one who is the entireties"—[20] if (the eternities) had risen to give [21] honor according to each one of [22] (themselves). For this reason in the [23] song of glorification and [24] in the power of the unity [25] from whom they had come forth, [26] they were drawn into a mixing [27] and a mingling and a unity [28] with each other. [29] They brought glory worthy of [30] the Father from the fullness [31] of the gathering, which is a [32] single image even though it is many, because [33] it was brought forth as a glory [34] for the single one and [35] because they came forth toward the one who [36] himself is the entireties. This (glory), then, [69.1] was an honor for the [. . .] [2] this one who brought forth the entireties, [3] since it is a firstfruit of those who are immortal [4] and eternal because, since [5] it came forth from the living eternities, being [6] perfect and complete on account of the [perfect] one [7] who is complete, it established as complete [8] and perfect those who had given glory [9] perfectly from the fellowship. [10] For, as with the faultless Father, [11] when he is glorified he [12] hears also the glory that glorifies [him, [13] so that] they are revealed as that which [14] he is.

The cause of the [15] second honor that came about [16] for them is that which had been returned [17] to them by the Father once they had known [18] the grace by which they bore fruit [19] with one another [20] from the Father so that, just as they [21] <were> brought forth in glory of the Father, [22] so too, to appear [23] perfect, they appeared [24] giving glory.

They [25] <were> fathers of the third glory [26] in accordance with the free choice and [27] power that was produced with them, [28] since each one of them [29] does not exist by himself to give glory in a [30] unified manner to him whom he [31] loves.

Therefore, they are the first and [32] second, and in this way both are perfect [33] and complete because they are manifestations [34] of the Father who is perfect [35] and complete, as well as of those who had come forth, [36] who are perfect in their giving of glory to [37] the perfect one. Now the fruit of [38] the third are honors of [39] the will of each one of the eternities [40] and each one of the qualities. [41]—The Father has Power.—It (the fruit) exists [70.1] fully, perfect [2] in [the thought] that is from [3] agreement, since it is from [4] the unanimity [5] of the eternities. That which he loves [6] and over which he has power [7] gives glory to him, the Father.

⁸ ϫⲉ ⲉⲧⲃⲉ ⲡⲉⲉⲓ ϩⲉⲛⲛⲟⲩⲥ ⲛⲉ ⲛ̄- ⁹ ⲇⲉ ϩⲉⲛⲛⲟⲩⲥ, ⲉⲩϭⲁⲛⲧⲥ̄ ⲉϩⲛ̄- ¹⁰ ⲗⲟⲅⲟⲥ ⲛⲉ ⲛ̄ⲧⲉ ϩⲛ̄ⲗⲟⲅⲟⲥ, ⲉϩⲛ̄- ¹¹ ⲡⲣⲉⲥⲃⲩⲧⲉⲣⲟⲥ ⲛⲉ ⲛ̄ⲧⲉ ϩⲉⲛⲡⲣⲉ- ¹² ⲥⲃⲩⲧⲉⲣ[ⲟ]ⲥ, ⲉϩⲛ̄ⲃⲁⲑⲙⲟⲥ ⲛⲉ ¹³ [ⲛ̄]ⲇⲉ ϩⲛ̄ⲃⲁⲑⲙⲟⲥ ⲛⲉ, ⲉⲩϫⲁ[ⲥⲉ] ¹⁴ ⲁⲛⲟⲩⲉⲣⲏⲩ. ⲡⲟⲩⲉⲉⲓ ⲡⲟⲩⲉ̄- ¹⁵ ⲉⲓ ⲛ̄ⲛⲉⲧϯ ⲉⲁⲩ ⲉⲩⲛ̄ⲧⲉϥ ⲙ̄- ¹⁶ ⲙⲉⲩ ⲙ̄ⲡⲉϥⲧⲟⲡⲟⲥ ⲙⲛ̄ ⲡⲉ[ϥ]- ¹⁷ ϫⲓⲥⲉ ⲙⲛ̄ ⲧⲉϥⲙⲟⲛⲏ ⲙⲛ̄ ⲧⲉϥ- ¹⁸ ⲁⲛⲁⲡⲁⲩⲥⲓⲥ, ⲉⲧⲉ ⲡⲉⲁⲩ ⲡⲉ ¹⁹ ⲉⲧϥⲉⲓⲛⲉ ⲙ̄ⲙⲁϥ ⲁⲃⲁⲗ.

ϫⲉ ²⁰ ⲛⲉⲧϯ ⲉⲁⲩ ⲙ̄ⲡⲓⲱⲧ ⲧⲏⲣⲟⲩ ⲟⲩ- ²¹ ⲛ̄ⲧⲉⲩ ⲙ̄ⲙⲉⲩ ⲙ̄ⲡⲟⲩϫⲡⲟ ²² ⲁⲛⲏϩⲉ ⲧ[ⲙ]ⲉⲧ,— ⲥⲉϫⲡⲟ ⲕⲁⲧⲁ ²³ ϯϭⲛ̄ϯ ⲧⲟⲟⲧⲟⲩ ⲛ̄ⲛⲟⲩⲉⲣⲏⲩ—²⁴ ⲉϩⲛ̄ⲁⲧⲁⲣⲏϫⲛⲟⲩ ⲛⲉ ⲁⲩⲱ ϩⲛ̄- ²⁵ ⲁⲧϣⲓⲧⲟⲩ ⲛⲉ ⲛⲓⲡⲣⲟⲃⲟⲗⲏ ⲉⲙⲛ̄ ⲗⲁ- ²⁶ ⲁⲩⲉ ⲙ̄ⲫⲑⲟⲛⲟⲥ ϣⲟⲟⲡ ⲁⲃⲁⲗ ²⁷ ⲙ̄ⲡⲉⲓⲱⲧ ϣⲁ ⲛⲉⲧ<ⲁ>ϩⲉⲓ ⲉⲃⲟⲗ ²⁸ ⲙ̄ⲙⲁϥ ⲁⲧⲣⲟⲩϫⲡⲟ ⲙ̄ⲡⲉϥ- ²⁹ ϩⲓ̈ⲥⲟⲛ ⲙⲛ̄ ⲡⲉϥⲉⲓⲛⲉ, ⲉⲛⲧⲁϥ ⲡⲉⲧ- ³⁰ ϣⲟⲟⲡ ϩⲣⲏ̈ ϩⲛ̄ ⲛⲓⲡⲧⲏⲣϥ̄, ⲉϥϫⲡⲟ ³¹ ⲉϥⲟⲩⲱⲛϩ̄ ⲙ̄ⲙⲁϥ ⲁⲃⲁⲗ. ⲁⲩⲱ ⲡⲉ- ³² ⲧϥ̄ⲟⲩⲁϣϥ̄ <ϥ>ⲉⲓⲣⲉ ⲙ̄ⲙⲟϥ ⲛ̄ⲉⲓⲱⲧ, ³³ ⲛⲉⲉⲓ ⲉⲧⲉ ⲛ̄ⲧⲁϥ ⲡⲉ ⲡⲟⲩⲉⲓⲱⲧ, ³⁴ ⲁⲩⲱ ⲛ̄ⲛⲟⲩⲧⲉ, ⲛⲁⲉⲓ ⲉⲧⲉ ⲛ̄ⲧⲁϥ ³⁵ ⲡⲉ ⲡⲟⲩⲛⲟⲩⲧⲉ, ⲉϥⲉⲓⲣⲉ ⲙ̄ⲙⲁⲩ ³⁶ ⲛ̄ⲛⲓⲡⲧⲏⲣϥ̄, ⲛⲉⲉⲓ ⲉⲧⲉ ⲛ̄ⲧⲁϥ ⲡⲉ ³⁷ ⲡ<ⲟⲩ>ⲧⲏⲣϥ̄. ⲉⲛⲓⲣⲉⲛ ⲧⲏⲣⲟⲩ ⲉⲧⲛⲁ- ⁷¹·¹ ⲛⲟⲩ ⲕⲁⲁⲧ ⲙ̄ⲡⲙⲁ ⲉⲧⲙ̄- ² ⲙⲉⲩ ϩⲛ̄ ⲟⲩⲙⲛ̄ⲧϫⲁⲉⲓⲥ, ³ [ⲛ]ⲉⲉⲓ ⲛ̄ⲧⲁⲩⲣ̄ ⲕⲟⲓⲛⲱⲛⲓ ⲁⲣⲁⲟⲩ ⁴ ⲛ̄ϭⲓ ⲛⲓⲁⲅⲅⲉⲗⲟⲥ, ⲉⲛⲧⲁϣⲱⲡⲉ ϩⲛ̄ ⁵ ⲡⲕⲟⲥⲙⲟⲥ ⲙⲛ̄ ⲛⲁⲣⲭⲱⲛ, ⲉⲙⲛ̄ⲧ- [ⲉⲩ] ⁶ ⲙ̄ⲙⲉⲩ ⲛ̄ⲧⲟⲩⲙⲛ̄ⲧⲣ̄ ⲙⲓⲛⲉ ⲙ̄ⲙ[ⲁⲩ] ⁷ ⲙⲛ̄ ⲛⲓⲁⲛⲏϩⲉ.

ϫⲉ ⲧⲥⲩⲥⲧⲁⲥ[ⲓⲥ] ⁸ ϩⲉ ⲧⲏⲣⲥ̄ ⲛ̄ⲛⲓⲁⲓⲱⲛ ⲟⲩⲛⲧⲉⲥ ⲙ̄ⲙ[ⲉⲩ] ⁹ ⲛ̄ⲛⲟⲩⲙⲁⲉⲓⲉ ⲙⲛ̄ ⲟⲩϭⲛ̄ϣⲓⲛⲉ ¹⁰ ⲛ̄ⲥⲉ ⲡⲓϭⲓⲛⲉ ⲉⲧϫⲏⲕ ⲁⲃⲁⲗ ⲧⲏⲣ[ϥ] ¹¹ ⲙ̄ⲡⲓⲱⲧ, ⲁⲩⲱ ⲡⲉⲉⲓ ⲡⲉ ⲡⲟⲩⲧⲱⲧ ¹² ⲛⲁⲧϭⲣⲁⲡ. ⲉϥⲟⲩⲱⲛϩ̄ ⲙ̄ⲙⲁϥ ⲁ- ¹³ [ⲃ]ⲁⲗ ⲙ̄ⲙⲓⲛ ⲙ̄ⲙⲁϥ ⲛ̄ϭⲓ ⲡⲓⲱⲧ ⲁⲛ[ⲏ]- ¹⁴ ϩⲉ ⲧⲙⲉⲧ, ⲙ̄ⲡⲉϥⲟⲩⲁϣϥ̄ ⲁⲧⲣⲟ[ⲩ]- ¹⁵ ⲥⲟⲩⲱⲛϥ̄, ⲉϥϯ ⲙ̄ⲙⲟϥ ⲁⲧⲣⲟⲩⲣ̄ ¹⁶ ⲛⲟⲉⲓ ⲙ̄ⲙⲁϥ ⲁϣⲓⲛⲉ ⲛ̄ⲥⲱϥ, ⲉϥⲣⲁ- ¹⁷ [ⲉⲓ]ⲥ ⲁⲣⲁϥ ⲙ̄ⲡⲉⲧϥ̄ ϣⲣⲡ̄ ⲛ̄ϣⲟⲟⲡ ⲙ̄- ¹⁸ [ⲙ]ⲁϥ ⲛⲁⲧϣⲓⲛⲉ ⲛ̄ⲥⲱϥ.

ϫⲉ ⲛ̄ⲧⲁϥ ¹⁹ [ⲡ]ⲱⲧ ⲡⲉⲧⲁϩⲧϯ ⲛ̄ⲛⲁ{ⲁ}ⲫⲟⲣⲙⲏ ²⁰ [ⲛⲛ]ⲟⲩⲛⲉ ⲛ̄ⲛⲓⲁⲓⲱⲛ, ⲉϩⲛ̄ⲧⲟⲡⲟⲥ ⲛⲉ ²¹ ⲙ̄ⲡⲓⲙⲁⲓⲧ[[ⲛ̄]] ⲉⲧⲙⲁⲧⲛ̄ ϣⲁⲣⲁϥ ²² ⲙ̄ⲡⲣⲏⲧⲉ ϣⲁ ⲟⲩⲁⲛⲥⲏⲃ ⲙ̄ⲡⲟ- ²³ [ⲗ]ⲓⲧⲓⲁ, ⲉⲁϥⲡⲱⲣϣ̄ ⲛ̄[ⲉⲩ] ⲛ̄ⲟⲩⲛⲁ- ²⁴ [ϩ]ⲧⲉ ⲙ̄ⲛ̄ ⲟⲩⲥⲁⲡⲥⲡ̄[ⲥ] ⲁⲡⲉⲧⲉ- ²⁵ [ⲛ]ⲥⲉϭⲁϣⲧ̄ ⲁⲣⲁϥ ⲉⲛ, ⲁⲩⲱ ⲟⲩϩⲉⲗ- ²⁶ [ⲡ]ⲓⲥ ⲉⲥϫⲟⲟⲣ ⲁⲡⲉⲧⲉⲛ̄ⲥⲉⲣ ⲛⲟ- ²⁷ [ⲉ]ⲓ ⲙ̄ⲙⲁϥ ⲉⲛ, ⲁⲩⲱ ⲟⲩⲁⲅⲁⲡⲏ ²⁸ [ⲉ]ⲥϫⲡⲟ ⲉⲥϭⲁϣⲧ̄ ⲁϩⲟⲩⲛ ⲁⲡⲉⲧⲥ̄- ²⁹ [ⲛ]ⲉⲩ ⲁⲣⲁϥ ⲉⲛ, ⲁⲩⲱ ⲟⲩⲙⲛ̄ⲧⲣⲙ̄ⲛ̄- ³⁰ [ϩⲏ]ⲧ ⲉⲥϣⲏⲡ ⲛ̄ⲧⲉ ⲡⲓⲛⲟⲩⲥ ϣⲁ ⲁⲛⲏ- ³¹ [ϩⲉ,] ⲁⲩⲱ ⲟⲩⲙⲁⲕⲁⲣⲓⲥⲙⲟⲥ ³² [ⲉ]ⲧⲉ ⲡⲉⲉⲓ ⲡⲉ ϯⲙⲛ̄ⲧⲣⲙ̄ⲙⲁⲟ ⲙⲛ̄ ³³ ϯ<ⲙⲛ̄ⲧ>ⲣⲙ̄ϩⲉ, ⲁⲩⲱ ⲟⲩⲥⲟⲫⲓⲁ ⲛ̄ⲇⲉ ⲡⲉ- ³⁴ ⲧⲟⲩⲱϣ ⲙ̄ⲡⲉⲁⲩ ⲙ̄ⲡⲓⲱⲧ ⲁ- ³⁵ ⲡⲟⲩⲙⲉⲉⲩⲉ.

ϫⲉ ⲡⲓⲱⲧ ⲙⲉⲛ ³⁶ ⲡⲁⲉⲓ ⲉⲧⲭⲁⲥⲓ ⲉⲩⲥⲟⲟⲩⲛ ⲙ̄ⲙⲟϥ ⁷²·¹ ⲙ̄ⲡⲉϥⲟ[ⲩ]ⲱϣⲉ ⲉⲧⲉ ⲡⲉⲉⲓ [ⲡⲉ] ² ⲡⲓⲡⲛⲉⲩⲙⲁ ⲉⲧⲛⲓϥⲉ ϩⲛ̄ ⲛⲓⲡⲧⲏⲣⲥ̄ ³ ⲁⲩⲱ ⲉϥϯ ⲛⲉⲩ ⲛ̄ⲛⲟⲩⲙⲉ- ⁴ ⲉⲩⲉ ⲁⲧⲣⲟⲩϣⲓⲛⲉ ⲛ̄ⲥⲁ ⲡⲓⲁⲧ- ⁵ [ⲥ]ⲟⲩⲱⲛϥ̄, ⲛ̄ⲑⲉ ⲉϣⲁⲣⲟⲩⲥⲱⲕ ⁶ [ⲛ̄]ⲟⲩⲉⲉⲓ ⲁⲃⲁⲗ ϩⲓⲧⲛ̄ⲛ ⲟⲩⲥϯ ⁷ ⲛⲟⲩϥⲉ ⲁⲧⲣⲉϥϣⲓⲛⲉ ⲛ̄ⲥⲁ ⲡϩⲱ[ⲃ] ⁸ ⲉⲧⲉⲣⲉⲡⲓⲥϯ ⲛⲟⲩϥⲉ ϣⲟⲟⲡ ⲉⲧⲃ[ⲏ]- ⁹ ⲏⲧϥ̄, ⲉⲡⲓⲇⲏ ⲡⲓⲥϯ ⲛⲟⲩϥⲉ ⲛ̄- ¹⁰ ⲧⲉ ⲡⲓⲱⲧ ϥⲣ̄

70.8–9 ⲛ̄ⲇⲉ: read ⲛ̄ⲧⲉ.
70.13 [ⲛ̄]ⲇⲉ: read ⲛ̄ⲧⲉ.
70.24 ⲁⲧⲁⲣⲏϫⲛⲟⲩ: read ⲁⲧⲁⲣⲏϫⲟⲩ.
71.33 ⲛ̄ⲇⲉ: read ⲛ̄ⲧⲉ.
71.35 ⲡⲟⲩⲙⲉⲉⲩⲉ: read ⲡⲉϥⲙⲉⲉⲩⲉ.
72.10 ⲟⲩϩⲟ: read ϩⲟⲩⲟ.

[8] For this reason they are minds of [9] minds, which are found to be [10] words of words, [11] elders of [12] elders, ranks [13] of ranks, which are elevated [14] over one another. Each one [15] of those who give glory has [16] his place and [his] [17] rank and his station and his [18] rest, which is the glory [19] that he brings forth.

[20] Those who glorify the Father all [21] have their begetting [22] eternally—they beget [23] by giving of themselves to each other—[24] since they are limitless and [25] immeasurable emanations (and) since no [26] jealousy exists between [27] the Father and those who <have> come forth [28] from him regarding their begetting of his [29] equal or his likeness, since he is the one who [30] exists in the entireties, begetting [31] and manifesting himself. And [32] whomever he wills, <he> makes into a father, [33] over whom he is Father, [34] and gods, over whom he [35] is God, and he makes them [36] entireties, over whom he is [37] the Entirety. All great names [71.1] reside there [2] properly, [3] those with whom angels commune, [4] who have come to be in [5] the world along with the rulers, though they do not have [6] any resemblance [7] to the eternal ones.

Therefore, the entire system [8] of the eternities has [9] a love and a seeking [10] after the perfect and complete discovery [11] of the Father, and this is their [12] unhindered agreement. While the Father manifests [13] himself eternally, [14] he did not want them [15] to know him, since he makes it possible for him to be [16] conceived of as one sought after, [17] while reserving for [18] himself his primordial and unsearchable being.

He, [19] [the] Father, the one who gave the root origins [20] to the eternities, since they are places [21] on the path that leads toward him [22] just as toward a school of conduct, [23] he extended to [them] faith in [24] and petition to the one [25] they did not see, and a [26] strong hope in the one who is not known, [27] and a bountiful love [28] that looks toward the one whom it does not [29] see, and a longed-for understanding [30] of the mind eternal, [31] and a blessing, [32] that is, riches and [33] freedom, and a wisdom of the one [34] who desires the glory of the Father in [35] <his> thought.

The Father, [36] who is exalted, is known [72.1] by his will, that [is,] (through) [2] the spirit that breathes into the entireties [3] and giving them a mind [4] for seeking after the [5] unknowable one, just as one is drawn [6] in by a (pleasing) aroma [7] to seek after the thing [8] from which the aroma comes, [9] since the aroma of [10] the Father

ⲟⲩⳉⲟ ⲁⲛⲉⲉⲓ ⲛ̅ⲁ̣[ⲧ]- [11] ⲙ̅ⲡⳉⲁ. ⲧⲙ̅ⲛ̅ⲧⳉⲗ̅ϭⲉ ⲅⲁⲣ ⲛ̅ⲧⲉ[ϥ] [12] ⲥⲕⲱ ⲁⳉⲣⲏⲓ̈ ⲛ̅ⲛⲓⲁⲓⲱⲛ ⳉⲛ̅ⲛ ⲟⲩ- [13] ⳉⲏⲇⲟⲛⲏ ⲛ̅ⲁⲧⳉⲉϫⲉ ⲁⲣⲁⲥ, [14] ⲁⲩⲱ ⲥϯ ⲛⲉⲩ ⲛⲛⲟⲩⲙⲉⲉⲩⲉ ⲁ- [15] ⲧⲣⲟⲩⲙⲟⲩⳉ ⲙⲛ ⲡⲉⲉⲓ ⲉⲧⲟ̣[ⲩ]- [16] ⲱϣⲉ ⲁⲧⲣⲟⲩⲥⲟⲩⲱⲛϥ̅ ⲕⲁ̣[ⲧⲁ] [17] ⲟⲩⲙ̅ⲛ̅ⲧⲟⲩⲉⲉⲓ, ⲛ̅ⲥⲉϯ ⲧ̣[ⲟⲟ]- [18] ⲧϥ̅ ⲛ̅ⲛⲉⲩⲉⲣⲉⲩ ⲙ̅ⲡ̅ⲛⲉⲩⲙⲁ ⲉ[ⲧ]- [19] ⲥⲁⲧⲉ ⲛ̅ⳉⲏⲧⲟⲩ. ⲉⲩⲕⲁⲁⲧ ⲛ̅- [20] ⳉⲣⲏⲓ̈ ⳉⲛⲛ ⲟⲩⲛⲁϭ ⲛ̅ⳉⲣⲏϣⲉ ⲉⲛ[ⲁ]- [21] ϣⲱⲥ, ⲉⲩⲣ̅ ⲃ̅ⲣ̅ⲣⲉ ⳉⲛ̅ⲛ ⲟⲩⲙ̅ⲛ̅ⲧⲁⲧ- [22] ϫⲟⲟ[ⲥ], ⲉⲙⲛ̅ⲧⲉⲩ ⲙ̅ⲙⲉⲩ ⲙ̅- [23] ⲡⲧⲣⲟⲩⲛⲁⲩⳉⲟⲩ ⲁⲃⲁⲗ ⲙ̅ⲡ[ⲉ]- [24] ⲧⲁⲩⲕⲁⲁⲩ ⲙ̅ⲙⲁϥ ⳉⲛ̅ⲛ ⲟⲩⲙ̅[ⲛⲧ]- [25] ⲁⲧⲣ̅ ⲛⲟⲉⲓ ⲁⲃⲁⲗ, ϫⲉ ⲥⲉⲛⲁϣⲁ[ϫⲉ] [26] ⲉⲛ, ⲉⲩⲕⲁⲣⲁⲉⲓⲧ ⲁⲡⲉⲁⲩ ⲙ̅[ⲡⲓ]- [27] ⲱⲧ, ⲁⲡⲉⲧⲉⲩⲛ̅ ϭⲟⲙ ⲙ̅ⲙⲁ[ϥ] [28] ⲁϫⲟⲟⲥ, ⲛ̅ⲥⲉϫⲓ ⲙⲟⲣⲫⲏ [ⲙ]- [29] ⲙⲟϥ. ⲁϥⲟⲩⲱⲛⳉ̅ ⲁⲃⲁⲗ ⲙ̅ⲙ̣[ⲁϥ, ⲉ]- [30] ⲙⲛ̅ ϭⲟⲙ ⲛ̅ⲗⲉ ⲁϫⲟⲟϥ. ⲟ̣[ⲩ]ⲛ̅- [31] ⲧⲉⲩ<ϥ> ⲙ̅ⲙⲉⲩ ⲉϥⳉⲏⲡ ⳉⲣⲏ[ⲓ ⳉ]ⲛ̅- [32] ⲛ ⲟⲩⲙⲉⲉⲩⲉ ⳉⲱⲥ ⲉ<ⳉⲉⲛ>ⲁⲃⲁⲗ ⲙ̅- [33] ⲡⲉⲉⲓ [ⲛⲉ]. ⲥⲉⲕⲁⲣⲁⲉⲓⲧ ⲙⲉⲛ ⲁⲡⲱⲧ [34] ⲙ̅ⲡⲣⲏⲧⲉ ⲉⲧϥ̅ϣⲟⲟⲡ ⲙ̅ⲙⲁϥ [35] ⳉⲙ̅ ⲡⲉϥⲥⲙⲁⲧ ⲙⲛ̅ ⲧⲉϥⲙⲓⲛⲉ [36] ⲙⲛ̅ ⲧⲉϥⲙ̅ⲛ̅ⲧⲛⲟϭ. [73.1] ⲉⲁⲩⲣ̅ ⲙ̅ⲡϣⲁ ⲇⲉ ⲛ̅ϫⲓ ⲛⲓⲁⲓⲱⲛ ⲛ̅ⲥⲟⲩ- [2] ⲱⲛ ⲡⲉⲉⲓ ⲁⲃⲁⲗ ⳉⲓⲧⲟⲟⲧϥ̅ ⲙ̅ⲡⲡ̅ⲛⲉⲩⲙⲁ [3] ϫⲉ ⲟⲩⲁⲧϫⲉ ⲣⲉⲛ ⲁⲣⲁϥ ⲡⲉ ⲁⲩⲱ [4] ⲟⲩⲁⲧⲧⲉⳉⲁϥ ⲡⲉ. ⲁⲃⲁⲗ ⳉⲓⲧⲛ̅ ⲡⲓ- [5] ⲡⲛⲉⲩⲙⲁ ⲛ̅ⲧⲉϥ, ⲉⲧⲉ ⲡⲉⲉⲓ ⲡⲉ ⲡⲓⲓ̈ⲭⲛⲟⲥ [6] ⲛ̅ⲧⲉ ⲡⲓϭⲛ̅ϣⲓⲛⲉ ⲛⲥⲱϥ, ⲉϥϯ ⲙ̅ⲙⲁϥ [7] ⲛⲉⲩ ⲁⲧⲣⲟⲩⲣ̅ ⲛⲟⲉⲓ ⲙ̅ⲙⲁϥ ⲛ̅ⲥⲉ- [8] ϣⲉϫⲉ ⲁⲣⲁϥ.

ϫⲉ ⲡⲟⲩⲉⲉⲓ ⲡⲟⲩⲉⲉⲓ ⲛ̅- [9] ⲧⲉ ⲛⲓⲁⲓⲱⲛ ⲟⲩⲣⲉⲛ ⲡⲉ, <ⲉⲧⲉ ⲧⲉⲉⲓ> ⲧⲉ ⲧⲟⲩⲉⲓⲉ ⲧⲟⲩ- [10] ⲉⲓⲉ ⲛ̅ⲛⲉϥⲁⲣⲉⲧⲏ ⲙⲛ̅ ⲛⲓϭⲟⲙ ⲛ̅ⲧⲉ [11] ⲡⲓⲱⲧ, ⲉϥϣⲟⲟⲡ ⳉⲛ̅ ⳉⲁⳉ ⲛ̅ⲣⲉⲛ ⳉⲛ̅ [12] ⲟⲩⲙⲟⲩⳉ ⲙⲛ̅ ⲟⲩϯⲙⲉⲧⲉ ⲙⲛ̅ ⲛⲟⲩ- [13] ⲉⲣⲏⲩ. ⲟⲩⲛ̅ ϭⲁⲙ ⲁⲧⲣⲟⲩϫⲟⲟϥ ⲉⲧⲃⲉ [14] ⲧⲙ̅ⲛ̅ⲧⲣⲙ̅ⲙⲁⲟ ⲙ̅ⲡⲗⲟⲅⲟⲥ, ⲛ̅ⲑⲉ ⲙ̅ⲡⲓ- [15] ⲱⲧ ⲉⲟⲩⲣⲉⲛ ⲛ̅ⲟⲩⲱⲧ ⲡⲉ̣ ⲁⲃⲁⲗ ϫⲉ [16] ⲟⲩⲉⲉⲓ ⲛ̅ⲟⲩⲱⲧ ⲡⲉ, ⲟⲩⲁⲧⲁⲡϥ̅ ⲛ̅- [17] ⲇⲉ ⲡⲉ ⳉⲛ̅ ⲛⲉϥⲁⲣⲉⲧⲏ ⲡⲉ ⲙⲛ̅ ⲛⲓ- [18] [ⲣ]ⲉⲛ.

ϫⲉ ⲧⲡⲣⲟⲃⲟⲗⲏ ϭⲉ ⲛ̅ⲧⲉ [19] [ⲛ]ⲓⲡⲧⲏⲣϥ̅, ⲉⲧϣⲟⲟⲡ ⲁⲃⲁⲗ ⳉⲛ̅ ⲡⲉⲧ- [20] [ϣ]ⲟⲟⲡ, ⲉⲣⲉⲛⲧⲁⲥϣⲱⲡⲉ ⲉⲛ ⲕⲁ- [21] [ⲧ]ⲁ̣ ⲟⲩϣⲱⲱⲧ ⲁⲃⲁⲗ ⲛⲛⲟⲩⲉⲣⲏⲩ, [22] [ⳉ]ⲱⲥ ⲉ<ⲩ>ⲛⲟⲩⳉⲉ ⲁⲃⲁⲗ ⲙ̅ⲡⲉⲧⲭⲡⲟ [23] ⲙ̅ⲙⲁⲩⲟ ⲡⲉ. ⲁⲗⲗⲁ ⲉϥⲟ ⲙ̅ⲡⲥⲙⲁⲧ [24] ⲛ̅ⲛⲟⲩⲡⲱⲣϣ̅ ⲁⲃⲁⲗ ⲛ̅ϭⲓ ⲡⲟⲩϫⲡⲟ, [25] ⲉϥⲡⲱⲣϣ̅ ⲙ̅ⲙⲁϥ ⲁⲃⲁⲗ ⲛ̅ϭⲓ [26] [ⲡ]ⲓⲱⲧ ⲁⲛⲉⲧϥ̅ⲟⲩⲁϣⲟⲩ ϫⲉⲕⲁⲥⲉ [27] [ⲛ]ⲉⲛⲧⲁⳉⲉⲓ ⲁⲃⲁⲗ ⲙ̅ⲙⲟϥ ⲉⲩⲛⲁ- [28] ϣⲱⲡⲉ ⲛ̅ⲧⲁϥ ⲁⲛ ⲡⲉ.

ϫⲉ ⲡⲓⲣⲏⲧⲉ [29] ⲙ̅ⲡⲓⲁⲓⲱⲛ ⲧⲉⲛⲟⲩ ⲉⲟⲩⲉⲉⲓ [30] ⲡⲉ ⲛ̅ⲟⲩⲱⲧ ⲉϥⲡⲏϣ ⳉⲛ̅ ⲟⲩⳉⲟ- [31] ⲉⲓϣ, ⲁⲩⲱ {ⳉⳉ} ⲉⲛⲟⲩⲁⲉⲓϣ ⲡⲏϣ ⲁⳉⲉⲛ- [32] ⲣⲁⲙⲡⲉ, ⲉⲛⲣⲁⲙⲡⲉ ⲡⲏϣ ⲁⳉⲛ̅- [33] ⲥⲛⲟⲩ, ⲛ̅ⲥⲛⲟⲩ ⲇⲉ ⲁⳉⲉⲛⲉⲃⲉⲧⲉ, ⲛⲉ- [34] ⲃⲉⲧⲉ ⲇⲉ ⲁⳉⲉⲛⳉⲟⲟⲩ, ⲛ̅ⳉⲟⲟⲩ [35] ⲁⳉⲉⲛⲟⲩⲛⲁⲩⲉ, ⲁⲩⲱ ⲛⲟⲩⲛⲁⲩⲉ [36] ⲁⳉⲛ̅ⲥⲟⲩⲥⲟⲩ, ⲡⲉⲉⲓ ⲡⲉ ⲡⲣⲏⲧⲉ [74.1] ⳉⲱⲱϥ ⲁⲛ ⲙ̅ⲡⲓⲁⲓⲱⲛ ⲛ̅ⲧⲉ [2] ⲧⲙⲏⲉ, ⲉⲟⲩⲉⲉⲓ ⲡⲉ ⲛ̅ⲟⲩⲱⲧ [3] ⲉⲛⲁϣⲱϥ, ⲉϥϫⲓ ⲉⲁⲩ ⳉⲛ̅ ⲛ̅ϣⲏⲙ [4] ⲙⲛ̅ ⳉⲛ̅ ⲛⲟϭ ⲛ̅ⲣⲉⲛ ⲕⲁⲧⲁ ⲡⲉ<ⲧⲉ> ⲟⲩ- [5] ⲛ̅ ϭⲁⲙ ⲙ̅ⲙⲁϥ ⲁϣⲁⲡϥ̅—ⲕⲁⲧⲁ <ⲧⲁ>ⲛ̅- [6] ⲧⲛ̅ ⲇⲉ ⲁⲛ—ⲙ̅ⲡⲣⲏⲧⲉ ⲛ̅ⲛⲟⲩⳉⲁⲗ- [7] ⲙⲛ ⲉⲥϣⲟⲟⲡ ⲙ̅ⲡⲉⲧⲥ̅ϣⲟⲟⲡ [8] ⲙ̅ⲙⲁϥ, ⲉⲥⳉⲉⲧϯ ⲁⳉⲛ̅ⲛⲓⲣϣⲟⲩ [9] ⲙⲛ̅ ⳉⲛ̅ⲗⲓⲙⲛⲏ ⲙⲛ̅ ⳉⲛ̅ⲉⲓⲟⲟⲣ [10] ⲙⲛ̅ ⳉⲉⲛⲃⲁⲉⲓⲉ, ⲙ̅ⲡⲣⲏⲧⲉ ⲛⲟⲩ- [11] ⲛⲟⲩⲛⲉ ⲉⲥⲡⲁⲣϣ̅ ⲁⲃⲁⲗ ⳉⲁ ⳉⲛ̅- [12] ϣⲏⲛ ⲁⲩⲱ ⳉⲛ̅ⲕⲗⲁⲇⲟⲥ ⲙⲛ̅ [13] ⲛⲉϥⲕⲁⲣⲡⲟⲥ, ⲙ̅ⲡⲣⲏⲧⲉ ⲛ̅ⲟⲩ- [14] ⲥⲱⲙⲁ ⲛ̅ⲣⲱⲙⲉ, ⲉϥⲡⲏϣ ⳉⲛ̅ [15] ⲟⲩⲙ̅ⲛ̅ⲧⲁⲧⲡⲱϣⲉ ⲁⳉⲛ̅ⲙⲉⲗⲟⲥ [16] ⲛ̅ⲧⲉ ⳉⲛ̅ⲙⲉⲗⲟⲥ, ⳉⲛ̅ⲙⲉⲗⲟⲥ ⲛ̅ϣⲁ- [17] ⲣⲡ̅ ⲙⲛ̅ ⳉⲛ̅ ⳉⲁⳉⲟⲩ, ⲁⳉⲛ̅ⲛⲁϭ ⳉ[ⲓ] [18] ϣⲏⲙ.

72.30 ⲛ̅ⲗⲉ: read ⲇⲉ.

73.1 ⲛ̅ϫⲓ: read ⲛ̅ϭⲓ.

74.10 ⲃⲁⲉⲓⲉ: probably from ϥⲟ.

surpasses those less [11] worthy. For [his] sweetness [12] leaves the eternities in [13] indescribable pleasure, [14] and it gives them a mind for [15] mixing with the one who [16] wants them to know him in accordance [17] with a unified way, and they assist one another through [18] the spirit that [19] is sown among them. Though they lie [20] under a heavy weight, [21] they are made new indescribably, [22] since they do not have (the ability) [23] to be separated from what [24] they are placed under [25] incomprehensibly, because they will not [speak,] [26] since they remain silent about the glory of the [27] Father, about the one who is able [28] to speak, and they receive form [29] from him. He revealed [himself,] [30] but it is not possible to speak about him. [31] They have <him> hidden in [32] a thought, since <they are> from [33] him. They remain silent about [34] the way the Father is [35] in his form and his nature [36] and his greatness. [73.1] But the eternities have become worthy of [2] knowing through his spirit [3] that he is unnameable and [4] incomprehensible. Through [5] his spirit, that is, the footprint [6] of the search for him, he gives [7] them (the ability) to conceive of him and [8] speak about him.

Each one of [9] the eternities is a name, <that is,> each [10] of the Father's virtues and his abilities, [11] since he exists in many names, [12] mixed and agreeing with each other. [13] It is possible for him to be spoken about because [14] of the richness of language, just as the [15] Father is a single name because [16] he is singular, yet he is innumerable [17] in his virtues and [18] names.

The emanation of [19] [the] entireties, which exist from the one who [20] exists, did not come to be according to [21] a separation from each other, [22] as if cast from the one who begets [23] them. Instead their begetting is a form [24] of extension, [25] since the Father extends himself [26] to those he loves so that [27] those who have come from him might [28] also come to be in him.

Just as [29] the current eternity, though [30] it is singular, is divided by time, [31] and time is divided into [32] years, and years are divided into [33] seasons, and seasons into months, [34] and months into days, and days [35] into hours, and hours [36] into seconds, so [74.1] too the eternity of [2] truth, since it is singular [3] and manifold, receives honor in small [4] and great names in accordance with the ability [5] of each to grasp it, analogously, [6] like a spring [7] which is what it is, [8] but flows into rivers [9] and lakes and streams [10] and canals, (or) like a [11] root spreading out under [12] trees and branches and [13] its fruit, (or) like a [14] human body, which is divided [15] indivisibly into members [16] of members, first members [17] and last, large [and] [18] small.

ϫⲉ ⲛⲓⲁⲓⲱⲛ ⲇⲉ ⲁⲩⲛ̄ⲧ[ⲟⲩ] ¹⁹ ⲁⲃⲁⲗ ⲕⲁⲧⲁ ⲡⲓⲙⲁϩ ϣⲁⲙⲛ̄ⲧ ⲛ̄- ²⁰ ⲕⲁⲣⲡⲟⲥ ⲁⲃⲁⲗ ϩⲓ̈ⲧⲛ̄
ⲧⲙⲛ̄ⲧ[ⲁⲩ]- ²¹ ⲧⲉϫⲟⲩⲥⲓⲟⲥ ⲛ̄ⲧⲉ ⲡⲟⲩⲱϣⲉ ²² ⲁⲩⲱ ⲁⲃⲁⲗ ϩⲓ̈ⲧⲛ̄ ϯⲥⲟⲫⲓⲁ ⲉⲛ- ²³ ⲧⲁϥⲣ ϩⲙⲁⲧ
ⲙ̄ⲙⲁⲥ ⲛⲉⲩ ⲁⲡⲟⲩⲙⲉⲩⲉ. ²⁴ ⲛ̄ⲥⲉⲟⲩⲱϣⲉ ⲉⲛ ⲁϯ ⲉⲁⲩ ⲙ[ⲛ̄] ²⁵ ⲡⲉⲉⲓ ⲉⲧⲉ ⲁⲃⲁⲗ ϩⲛ̄ ⲟⲩⲧⲱⲧ ⲡⲉ,
[ⲉ]- ²⁶ ⲁⲩⲛ̄ⲧϥ̄ ⲁⲃⲁⲗ ⲁϩⲛ̄ⲗⲟⲅⲟⲥ ⲛⲉ[ⲁⲩ] ²⁷ ⲙ̄ⲡⲟⲩⲉⲉⲓ ⲡⲟⲩⲉⲉⲓ ⲛ̄ⲧⲉ ⲛⲓⲡⲗ[ⲏ]- ²⁸ ⲣⲱⲙⲁ. ⲟⲩⲇⲉ
ⲁⲛ ⲛ̄ⲥⲉⲟⲩⲱϣⲉ ²⁹ ⲉⲛ ⲁϯ ⲉⲁⲩ ⲙⲛ̄ ⲡⲧⲏⲣϥ̄. ⲟⲩⲇⲉ ⲁⲛ ³⁰ ⲛ̄ⲥⲉⲟⲩⲱϣⲉ ⲉⲛ ⲙⲛ̄ ⲕⲉⲟⲩⲉⲉⲓ ³¹ ⲉⲁϥⲣ̄
ϣⲁⲣⲡ ⲁⲡⲥⲁ ⲛϩⲣⲉ ⲙ̄- ³² ⲡⲃⲁⲑⲟⲥ ⲙ̄ⲡⲉⲧⲙ̄ⲙⲉⲩ ⲏ ⲡϥ̄- ³³ ⲧⲟⲡⲟⲥ, ⲉⲓⲙⲏⲧⲓ ⲛ̄ⲧⲟϥ ⲡⲉⲧⲕⲏ ³⁴
ⲉϩⲣⲏⲓ̈ ϩⲙ̄ ⲡⲣⲉⲛ ⲉⲧϫⲁⲥⲓ ⲁⲩⲱ ³⁵ ϩⲛ̄ ⲡⲧⲟⲡⲟⲥ ⲉⲧϫⲁⲥⲓ, ⲉⲓ ⲙⲏ ϥϫⲓ ³⁶ ⲛ̄ⲧⲟⲟⲧϥ̄ ⲙ̄ⲡⲉⲧⲁϩⲟⲩⲱϣⲉ,
⁷⁵·¹ ⲉϥϫⲓⲧϥ̄ ⲛⲉϥ ⲁϩⲣⲏⲓ̈ ⲁⲡⲉⲧⲛ̄ⲧⲡⲉ ² ⲙ̄ⲙⲁϥ, ⲁⲩⲱ <ⲛ̄>ϥϫⲡⲁϥ, ⲙ̄ⲡⲣⲏⲧⲉ ³ [ⲛ̄]ϫⲟⲟⲥ ϫⲉ,
ⲙ̄ⲙⲓⲛ ⲙ̄ⲙⲟϥ ⲁⲩⲱ ⁴ ⲁⲃⲁⲗ ϩⲓ̈ⲧⲛ̄ ⲡⲉⲧⲙ̄ⲙⲉⲩ ϥϫⲡⲁϥ ⁵ ⲙⲛ̄ ⲡⲉⲧⲉ ⲛ̄ⲧⲁϥ ⲡⲉ, ϥ{.}ⲣ ⲃⲣ̄ⲣⲉ ⲙ̄- ⁶
ⲙⲓⲛ ⲙ̄ⲙⲟϥ ⲙⲛ̄ ⲡⲉⲧⲁϩⲓ̈ ⲁϫⲱϥ ⁷ ⲁⲃⲁⲗ ϩⲓ̈ⲧⲛ̄ ⲡⲉϥⲥⲁⲛ, ϥⲛⲉⲩ ⲁⲣⲁϥ ⁸ ⲛ̄ϥⲥⲁⲡⲥⲡ̄ⲥ ⲙ̄ⲙⲁϥ
ⲁⲡⲓϩⲱⲃ, ϫⲉ ⁹ ⲡⲉⲧⲁϩⲟⲩⲱϣⲉ ⲁϣⲉ ⲁϩⲣⲏⲓ̈ ⲁϫⲱϥ.

¹⁰ ⲁⲧⲥϣⲱⲡⲉ ϭⲉ ⲙ̄ⲡⲓⲣⲏⲧⲉ ⲙⲁϥϫⲉ ¹¹ ⲗⲁⲩⲉ ⲛⲉϥ ⲁⲡⲁⲉⲓ ⲛ̄ϭⲓ ⲡⲉⲛⲧⲁϩ- ¹² ⲟⲩⲱϣⲉ
ⲁϯ ⲉⲁⲩ, ⲥⲁⲃⲗ̄ⲗⲉϥ ⲟⲩ- ¹³ ⲁⲉⲉⲧϥ̄ ϫⲉ ⲟⲩⲛ ⲟⲩϩⲟⲣⲟⲥ ¹⁴ ⲛ̄ϣⲉϫⲉ ⲉϥⲕⲏ ϩⲙ̄ ⲡⲗⲏⲣⲟⲩⲙⲁ,
ⲁⲧ- ¹⁵ [ⲣ]ⲟⲩⲕⲁⲣⲱⲟⲩ ⲙⲉⲛ ⲁⲧⲙⲛ̄ⲧⲁⲧⲉ- ¹⁶ ϩⲁⲥ ⲙ̄ⲡⲓⲱⲧ, ⲁⲧⲟⲩϣⲉϫⲉ ⲇⲉ ⲁⲡⲉ- ¹⁷ ⲧ[ⲟ]
ⲩⲱϣⲉ ⲁⲧⲉⲣⲁϥ. ⲁⲥⲉⲓ ⲁϩⲣⲏⲓ̈ ⲁ- ¹⁸ [ϫ]ⲛ̄ ⲟⲩⲉⲉⲓ ⲛ̄ⲛⲁⲓⲱⲛ ⲁⲧⲣⲉϥϫⲓ ⲧⲟ- ¹⁹ [ⲟ]ⲧϥ̄ ⲁⲧⲉϩⲟ
ⲛ̄ϯⲙⲛ̄ⲧⲁⲧⲣ ⲛⲟⲓ̈ ⲙ̄- ²⁰ ⲙⲁⲥ ϥⲧ ⲉⲁⲩ ⲛⲉⲥ ⲙⲛ̄ ϯⲙⲛ̄ⲧⲁⲧ- ²¹ [ϣ]ⲉϫⲉ ⲁⲣⲁⲥ ⲛ̄ⲧⲉ ⲡⲓⲱⲧ ⲛ̄ϩⲟⲩⲟ.
²² [ⲉ]ⲩⲗⲟⲅⲟⲥ ⲛ̄ⲧⲉ ϯⲙⲛ̄ⲧⲟⲩⲉⲉⲓⲉ ⲡⲉ ²³ [ⲟ]ⲩⲉⲉⲓ ⲡⲉ, ⲉⲛⲟⲩⲁⲃⲁⲗ ⲉⲛ ⲡⲉ ϩⲛ̄ ²⁴ ⲡⲧⲱⲧ ⲛ̄ⲇⲉ
ⲛⲓⲡⲧⲏⲣϥ̄ ⲡⲉ, ⲟⲩⲇⲉ ²⁵ ⲁⲃⲁⲗ ⲉⲛ ϩⲛ̄ ⲡⲉⲛⲧⲁϥⲛ̄ⲧⲟⲩ ⲁⲃⲁⲗ, ²⁶ ϫⲉ ⲡⲉⲧⲁϩⲛ̄ ⲡⲧⲏⲣϥ̄ ⲁⲃⲁⲗ
ⲡⲓⲱⲧ.

²⁷ ϫⲉ ⲡⲓⲁⲓⲱⲛ ⲛⲉⲩⲟⲩⲁⲃⲁⲗ ⲡⲉ ϩⲛ̄ ⲛⲉⲉⲓ ²⁸ ⲉⲧⲉⲁⲩϯ ⲛⲉⲩ ⲛ̄ⲧⲥⲟⲫⲓⲁ, ⲉⲧϥ̄ⲣ ²⁹ ϣⲣ̄ⲡ ⲛ̄ϣⲟⲟⲡ
ⲡⲟⲩⲉⲉⲓ ⲡⲟⲩⲉⲉⲓ ³⁰ ⲙ̄ⲡⲉϥⲙⲉⲩⲉ. ⲙ̄ⲡⲉⲧϥ̄ⲟⲩⲁϣϥ̄ ³¹ ⲉⲩⲉ{ⲟⲩ}ⲛⲧⲟⲩ ⲁⲃⲁⲗ. ⲉⲧⲃⲉ ⲡⲉⲉⲓ ³² ⲁϥϫⲓ
ⲛ̄ⲛⲟⲩⲫⲩⲥⲓⲥ ⲛ̄ⲥⲟⲫⲓⲁ ³³ ⲁⲧⲣⲉϥϣⲁⲧϥ̄ ⲛ̄ⲥⲁ ⲡⲥⲙⲓⲛⲉ ³⁴ ⲉⲧⲏⲡ, ϩⲱⲥ ⲉⲩⲕⲁⲣⲡⲟⲥ ⲛ̄ⲥⲟ- ³⁵
ⲫⲓⲁ ⲡⲉ, ϫⲉ ⲡⲓⲟⲩⲱϣⲉ ⲛ̄ⲛⲁⲩⲧⲉ{ⲩ}- ³⁶ ϫⲟⲩⲥⲓⲟⲥ ⲉⲧⲁⲩϫⲡⲁ{ⲩ}ϥ ⲙⲛ̄ ³⁷ ⲛⲓⲡⲧⲏⲣϥ̄
ⲛⲉϥϣⲟⲟⲡ ⲛ̄ⲛⲟⲩⲗⲁⲓ̈ϭⲉ ³⁸ ⲛ̄ⲡⲓⲟⲩⲉⲉⲓ, ⲡⲓⲣⲏⲧⲉ ⲁⲧⲣⲉϥⲣ̄ ⁷⁶·¹ ⲡⲉⲧⲁϥⲟⲩⲁϣϥ̄ ⲉⲙⲛ̄ ⲗⲁⲩⲉ ² ⲣ̄
ⲕⲁⲧⲉⲭⲉ ⲙ̄ⲙⲁϥ.

ϫⲉ ⲧⲡⲣⲟ- ³ ⲁⲓⲣⲉⲥⲓⲥ ϭⲉ ⲙ̄ⲡⲗⲟⲅⲟⲥ ⲉⲧⲉ ⲡⲉ- ⁴ ⲉⲓ ⲡⲉ ⲛⲉⲟⲩⲡⲉⲧⲛⲁⲛⲟⲩϥ ⲡⲉ. ⁵ ⲉⲁϥϯ
ⲙ̄ⲡⲉϥⲟⲩⲁⲉⲓ, ⲁϥϯ ⲉ- ⁶ ⲁⲩ ⲙ̄ⲡⲓⲱⲧ, ⲕⲁⲛ ⲁⲩⲟⲩⲱϣ ⁷ ⲉⲧⲟⲟⲧϥ̄ ⲁⲩϩⲱⲃ ⲉⲛⲉⲉⲩ ⲁⲧϭⲟⲙ, ⁸
ⲉⲁϥⲟⲩⲱϣⲉ ⲁⲉⲓⲛⲉ ⲛ̄ⲟⲩⲉⲉⲓ ⁹ ⲁⲃⲁⲗ ⲉϥϫⲏⲕ ⲁⲃⲁⲗ ϩⲛ̄ ⲟⲩ- ¹⁰ ⲧⲱⲧ ⲡⲉⲉⲓ ⲉⲧⲉⲛⲉϥϣⲟⲟⲡ
ⲙ̄- ¹¹ ⲙⲁϥ ⲉⲛ ⲁⲩⲱ ⲉⲙⲛ̄ⲧⲉϥ ⲙ̄ⲡⲟ[ⲩ]- ¹² ⲁϩ ⲥⲁϩⲛⲉ ⲙ̄ⲙⲉⲩ ⲁⲣⲁϥ.

75.1 ⲉϥϫⲓⲧϥ̄: read ⲛϥ̄ϫⲓⲧϥ̄. ⲉ{ϥ}ϫⲓⲧϥ̄ also possible.
75.5 ϥ{.}ⲣ̄: read ⲛϥ̄ⲣ.
75.7 ϥⲛⲉⲩ: read ⲛϥ̄ⲛⲉⲩ.

The eternities brought [themselves] [19] forth in accordance with the third [20] fruit by the free [21] choice of the will [22] and by the wisdom [23] that he gifted them for their thought. [24] They did not want to give glory [with] [25] that which comes from agreement, [though] [26] it came from words of [glory] [27] of each one of the [28] fullnesses. Nor did they want [29] to give glory with the entirety. Nor, moreover, [30] did they want (to give glory) with any other [31] who was initially above [32] the depth of that one or his [33] location, except for the one who exists [34] in the name that is exalted and [35] in the place that is exalted, (and) only if he receives [36] from the one who willed, [75.1] and receives him to himself from the one above [2] him, and begets him himself, so [3] to speak, and [4] through that one begets himself [5] and what he is, and renews [6] himself and the one who came upon him [7] from his brother, and sees him [8] and petitions him concerning the matter, namely, [9] the one who desired to ascend to him.

[10] Therefore, in order that it might come to be in this way, the one who wanted to give glory does not say [11] anything to him about this, [12] except only [13] that there is a limit [14] to speech established in the fullness, so that [15] they are silent about the incomprehensibility [16] of the Father, but they speak about the one [17] who wants to know him. It occurred [18] to one of the eternities that he should attempt to [19] reach the incomprehensibility and give glory [20] to it and even more to the ineffability [21] of the Father. [22] Since he is a Word from the unity, [23] he is one, but he is not from the [24] agreement of the entireties, nor [25] (is he) from the one who brought them forth, [26] namely, the one who brought forth the totality, the Father.

[27] This eternity was among those [28] who were given wisdom, so that he might [29] dwell first in the thought of each one. [30] By what he wills [31] they will be brought forth. For this reason [32] he received a wise nature [33] in order to inquire into the hidden order, [34] since he is a wise fruit, [35] because the free will [36] that was begotten with [37] the entireties existed as a cause [38] for this one, the way to lead him to do [76.1] what he desired without anyone [2] restraining him.

The inclination [3] of the Word, that [4] is, was good. [5] Once he had advanced, he gave glory [6] to the Father, even if it brought about [7] something impossible, [8] since he had wanted to bring forth one [9] who is perfect from an [10] agreement that did not exist [11] and without having the [12] order (to do so).

ϫⲉ ¹³ ⲡⲓⲁⲓⲱⲛ ⲛⲉ ⲟⲩϩⲁⲉ ⲡⲉ ⲉⲁϥⲛ- ¹⁴ ⲧⲟⲩ ⲁⲃⲁⲗ ⲕⲁⲧⲁ ⲟⲩϯ ⲧⲟⲟⲧϥ ¹⁵ ⲛ̄ⲛⲉⲩⲉⲣⲏⲩ, ⲁⲩⲱ
ⲟⲩϣⲏⲙ ¹⁶ ⲡⲉ ϩⲛ̄ ⲧⲉϥⲁⲉⲓⲏ. ⲁⲩⲱ ϩⲁⲑⲏ ⲙ̄- ¹⁷ ⲡⲁⲧϥϫⲡⲉ ϭⲉⲗⲁⲅⲉ ⲁⲩⲉⲁⲩ ⲙ- ¹⁸ ⲡⲟⲩⲱϣⲉ ϩⲛ̄
ⲡⲧⲱⲧ ⲇⲉ ⲛ̄ⲛⲓⲡ[ⲧⲏ]- ¹⁹ ⲣϥ, ⲁϥⲉⲓⲣⲉ ϩⲛ̄ ⲟⲩⲙⲛ̄ⲧⲛⲟϭ ²⁰ ⲙ̄ⲙⲉⲉⲩⲉ ⲁⲃⲁⲗ ϩⲛ̄ ⲟⲩⲁⲅⲁⲡⲏ ²¹ ⲉⲥⲣ̄
ϩⲟⲩⲟ, ⲁϥϯ ⲡⲉϥⲟⲩⲁⲉⲓ[ⲉ] ²² ⲁⲡⲉⲉⲓ ⲉⲧⲕⲁⲁⲧ ⲁϩⲣⲏⲓ ⲙ̄ⲡⲕϣ- ²³ ⲧⲉ ⲙ̄ⲡⲓⲉⲁⲩ ⲉⲧϫⲏⲕ, ϫⲉ ⲁ- ²⁴
ϫⲛ̄ ⲡⲟⲩⲱϣⲉ ⲉⲛ ⲛ̄ⲧⲉ ⲡⲓⲱⲧ ²⁵ ⲡⲉⲧⲁⲩϫⲡⲟ ⲙ̄ⲡⲓⲗⲟⲅⲟⲥ, ⲉⲧⲉ ⲡⲉ- ²⁶ ⲉⲓ ⲡⲉ, ⲟⲩⲇⲉ ⲁⲛ ⲁϫⲛ̄ⲧϥ
ⲉϥ- ²⁷ ⲛⲁϯ ⲡⲉϥⲟⲩⲁⲉⲓⲉ. ⲁⲗⲗⲁ ⲛ̄- ²⁸ ⲧⲁϥ ⲡⲓⲱⲧ ⲛⲉⲁϥⲛ̄ⲧϥ ⲁⲃⲁⲗ ⲁ- ²⁹ ⲛⲉⲉⲓ ⲉⲧϥⲥⲁⲩⲛⲉ ϫⲉ
ⲡⲉⲧⲉϣ- ³⁰ ϣⲉ ⲡⲉ ⲁⲧⲣⲟⲩϣⲱⲡⲉ.

ϫⲉ ⲡⲓⲱⲧ ϭⲉ ³¹ ⲁⲩⲱ ⲛⲓⲡⲧⲏⲣϥ̄ ⲁⲩⲥⲁⲕⲟⲩ ⲛⲉⲩ ⲥⲁ- ³² ⲃⲟⲗ ⲙ̄ⲙⲟϥ, ⲁⲧⲣⲉϥϣⲱⲡⲉ ³³
ⲉϥⲧⲁϫⲣⲁⲉⲓⲧ ⲛ̄ϫⲉ {ⲁ}ⲡϩⲟⲣⲟⲥ ³⁴ ⲉⲛⲧⲁ<ϩ>ⲁⲡⲓⲱⲧ ⲧⲁϣϥ̄,—ϫⲉ ⲟⲩⲁ- ³⁵ ⲃⲁⲗ ⲉⲛ ⲡⲉ
ⲛ̄ⲧⲉⲣⲱ ⲛ̄ⲧⲙⲛ̄ⲧⲁⲧ- ³⁶ ⲧⲉϩⲁⲥ, ⲁⲗⲗⲁ ϩⲙ̄ ⲡⲟⲩⲱϣⲉ ⁷⁷·¹ ⲙ̄ⲡⲓⲱⲧ—ⲁⲩⲱ ϫⲉⲕⲁⲥⲉ ⲁⲛ ⲉⲩⲛⲁ- ²
ϣⲱⲡⲉ ⲛ̄ϭⲓ ⲛⲓϩⲃⲏⲩⲉ ⲉⲛⲧⲁⲩϣⲱ- ³ ⲡⲉ ⲁⲩⲟⲓⲕⲟⲛⲟⲙⲓⲁ ⲉⲥⲛⲁϣⲱⲡⲉ. ⁴ ⲉϣⲁⲥϣⲉ ⲉ<ⲛ>
ⲛⲁⲥⲛⲁϣⲱⲡⲉ ⲉⲛ ⲡⲉ ⁵ [ϩ]ⲙ̄ ⲡⲟⲩⲱⲛϩ̄ ⲁⲃⲁⲗ ⲙ̄ⲡⲗⲏⲣⲱⲙⲁ. ⁶ [ⲁ]ⲃⲁⲗ ϭⲉ ⲙ̄ⲡⲁⲉⲓ ⲙⲁⲥϣⲉ ⲁⲣ̄
ⲕⲁ- ⁷ [ⲧ]ⲏⲅⲟⲣⲓ ⲙ̄ⲡⲕⲓⲙ ⲉⲧⲉ ⲡⲗⲟⲅⲟⲥ ⲡⲉ, ⁸ [ⲁ]ⲗⲗⲁ ⲡⲉⲧⲉϣϣⲉ ⲡⲉ ⲁⲧⲣⲛ̄ϣⲉϫⲉ ⲁ- ⁹ [ⲡ]ⲕⲓⲙ
ⲛ̄ⲧⲉ ⲡⲗⲟⲅⲟⲥ ϫⲉ ⲟⲩⲗⲁⲉⲓϭⲉ ⲡⲉ ¹⁰ [ⲛ]ⲟⲩⲟⲓⲕⲟⲛⲟⲙⲓⲁ ⲉⲥⲧⲛ̄ϣ ⲁⲧⲣⲉⲥ- ¹¹ ϣⲱⲡⲉ.

ϫⲉ ⲡⲗⲟⲅⲟⲥ ⲙⲉⲛ ⲁϥϫⲡⲁϥ ¹² ⲙ̄ⲙⲓⲛ ⲙ̄ⲙⲁϥ, ⲉϥϫⲏⲕ ⲛ̄ⲟⲩⲉⲉⲓ ⲛ̄- ¹³ [ⲟ]ⲩⲱⲧ, ⲁⲩⲉⲁⲩ ⲙ̄ⲡⲓⲱⲧ,
ⲡⲉⲛⲧⲁϥ- ¹⁴ [ⲟⲩ]ⲁϣϥ̄, ⲁⲩⲱ ⲉϥϭⲱⲕ ⲉⲧⲏϥ ⲙ̄ⲙⲟϥ, ¹⁵ ⲛⲉⲉⲓ ⲇⲉ ⲛ̄ⲧⲁϥⲟⲩⲱϣⲉ ⲁϫⲓⲧⲟⲩ ¹⁶ ϩⲛ̄
ⲟⲩⲧⲉϩⲟ ⲁϥϫⲡⲁⲩ ϩⲛ̄ ϩⲉⲛϩⲁⲓⲃⲉⲥ ¹⁷ ⲙ̄[ⲛ̄] ϩⲉⲛⲉⲓⲇⲱⲗⲟⲛ ⲙⲛ̄ ϩⲛ̄ⲧⲁⲛⲧⲛ̄. ¹⁸ ϫⲉ ⲙ̄ⲡⲉϥϭⲓ ⲃⲓ ϩⲁ
ⲡⲉⲛϭⲱϣⲧ ⲙ̄- ¹⁹ [ⲡ]ⲟⲩⲁⲉⲓⲛ, ⲁⲗⲗⲁ ⲁϥϭⲱϣⲧ ⲁ- ²⁰ [ⲡ]ⲃⲁⲑⲟⲥ ⲁϥⲣ̄ ϩⲏⲧ ⲥⲛⲉⲩ. ⲁⲃⲁⲗ ⲙ̄- ²¹
[ⲡ]ⲉⲉⲓ ⲟⲩⲡⲱϣⲉ ⲡⲉ—ⲛ̄ⲧⲁϥⲛ̄ⲕⲁϩ ⲙ̄- ²² [ⲡϣ]ⲁ—ⲙ̄ⲛ̄ ⲟⲩⲣⲓⲕⲉ ⲁⲃⲁⲗ ϩⲛ̄ ⲧⲙⲛ̄ⲧ- ²³ ϩⲏⲧ
ⲥⲛⲉⲩ ⲙⲛ̄ ⲡⲱϣⲉ, ⲟⲩⲃϣⲉ ²⁴ ⲙⲛ̄ ⲟⲩⲙⲛ̄ⲧⲁⲥⲁⲩⲛⲉ ⲛ̄ⲧⲉϥ ⲁⲩⲱ ²⁵ <ⲙ̄ⲡ>ⲉⲧϣⲟⲟⲡ.

ϫⲉ ⲡϥϭⲓⲛϥⲓⲧϥ ⲁϩⲣⲏⲓ ⲙⲛ̄ ²⁶ ⲡⲉϥϭⲛ̄ϭⲱϣⲧ ⲁⲃⲁⲗ ⲁ[ⲧ]ⲉϩⲟ ⲙ̄- ²⁷ ⲡⲓⲁⲧⲧⲉϩⲁϥ ⲁϥⲧⲱⲕ
ⲁⲣⲉⲧϥ ⲛⲉϥ ²⁸ ⲛⲉϥϣⲟⲟⲡ ⲛ̄ϩⲏⲧϥ. ⲛ̄ϣⲱⲛⲉ ⲛ̄ⲇⲉ ²⁹ ⲉⲛⲧⲁⲩⲟⲩⲁϩⲟⲩ ⲛ̄ⲥⲱϥ ⲉϩⲟⲩⲛ ³⁰
ⲛ̄ⲧⲁⲣⲉϥϣⲱⲡⲉ ⲛ̄ⲥⲁ ⲛⲃⲁⲗ ⲙ̄- ³¹ ⲙⲁϥ ⲟⲩⲁⲉⲉⲧϥ, ⲉⲁⲩϣⲱⲡⲉ ⲁ- ³² ⲃⲁⲗ ϩⲛ̄ ϯⲙⲛ̄ⲧϩⲏⲧ ⲥⲛⲉⲩ
ϫⲉ ⲡⲓ- ³³ ⲧⲣⲙ̄ⲧⲉϥϩⲟ ⲙ̄ⲡⲓϩⲟⲩⲧⲟϭⲧϥ ⲛ̄- ³⁴ ⲛⲉⲁⲩ ⲛ̄ⲧⲉ ⲡⲓⲱⲧ, ⲡⲉⲧⲉ ⲡϫⲓⲥⲉ ³⁵ ⲛ̄ⲧⲉϥ
ⲛ̄ⲛⲁⲧⲁⲣⲏϫϥ. ⲡⲉⲉⲓ ⲛ̄ⲇⲉ ³⁶ ⲉⲙⲡϥ̄ⲧⲉϩⲁϥ ϫⲉ ⲙ̄ⲡϥ̄ϣⲁⲡϥ.

³⁷ ϫⲉ ⲡⲉⲧⲉⲁϥⲛ̄ⲧϥ ϭⲉ ⲁⲃⲁⲗ ⲙ̄ⲙⲓⲛ ⁷⁸·¹ ⲙ̄ⲙⲟϥ ⲛ̄ⲛⲟⲩⲁⲓⲱⲛ ⲙ̄ⲙⲛ̄ⲧⲟⲩ- ² ⲉ ⲛ̄ⲟⲩⲱⲧ ⲁϥⲡⲱⲧ
ⲁϩⲣⲏⲓ ⲁⲡⲉ- ³ ⲧⲉ ⲡⲱϣ ⲡⲉ, ⲁⲩⲱ ⲁⲡⲓⲥⲩⲛⲅⲉⲛⲏⲥ ⁴ ⲛ̄ⲧⲉϥ ⲙ̄ⲡⲗⲏⲣⲟⲩⲙⲁ ⲁⲩⲕⲱ ⁵ ⲙ̄ⲡⲉⲧⲁϩϣⲱⲡⲉ
ϩⲙ̄ ⲡϣⲧⲁ ⲙ̄[ⲛ̄] ⁶ ⲛⲉⲛⲧⲁⲩⲉⲓ ⲁⲃⲁⲗ ⲙ̄ⲙⲁϥ [ϩⲛ̄]- ⁷ ⲛ ⲟⲩⲫⲁⲛⲧⲁⲥⲓⲁ, ϩⲱⲥ ⲉⲛⲛⲟ[ⲩϥ] ⁸
ⲉⲛ ⲛⲉ.

76.13–14 ⲉⲁϥⲛ̄ⲧⲟⲩ: read ⲉⲁⲩⲛ̄ⲧϥ.
76.33 ⲛ̄ϫⲉ: read ⲛ̄ϭⲓ.
77.4 ⲉϣⲁⲥϣⲉ ⲉ<ⲛ>: also possible ⲉϣⲁⲥϣⲉ{ⲉ}.
77.18 ⲃⲓ: read ϥⲓ.
77.21 ⲛ̄ⲧⲁϥⲛ̄ⲕⲁϩ: read ⲛ̄ⲧⲁϥⲙ̄ⲕⲁϩ.
77.32–33 ⲡⲓⲧⲣⲙ̄ⲧⲉϥϩⲟ ⲙ̄ⲡⲓϩⲟⲩⲧⲟϭⲧϥ: possibly ⲡⲓⲙ̄ⲧⲣⲉϥⲧⲉϩⲟ ⲙ̄ⲡⲓϩⲟⲩ ⲧⲟⲟⲧϥ.

[13] This eternity was last to have <been> brought [14] forth by cooperation, [15] and he is small [16] in size. And before [17] he begot anything else for the glory of [18] the will and with the agreement of the eternities, [19] he acted thoughtfully [20] from an abundance of love, [21] and he advanced [22] toward that which surrounds [23] the perfect glory, because [24] the Word was not made apart from the will of the Father, [25] that is, [26] not apart from it [27] will he advance. But [28] he, the Father, brought him forth for [29] those about whom he knows that it is fitting [30] that they would come to be.

Then the Father [31] and the entireties withdrew [32] from him, so that [33] the boundary [34] that the Father had supplied might be established—since [35] it is not from comprehending the incomprehensibility, [36] but from the will [77.1] of the Father—and, moreover, (they withdrew) so that the things that [2] had come about might [3] become an arrangement that will come to be. [4] If it (the arrangement) were not to come (to be), it would not come into being [5] by the appearance of the fullness. [6] Therefore, it is not fitting to [7] denounce the movement that is the Word, [8] but it is fitting for us to say about [9] [the] movement of the Word that it is a cause for [10] an order that is destined to [11] come to be.

The Word himself produced it, [12] being perfect and unified, [13] for the glory of the Father, the one whom he [14] desired, and (he produced it) being content with it, [15] but those he desired to grasp [16] firmly he begot in shadows [17] and phantoms and likenesses. [18] For he was not able to bear the sight of [19] [the] light, but he gazed into [20] [the] depth and doubted. From [21] this came a division—he was greatly [22] distressed—and a turning away on account of [23] doubt and division, forgetting [24] and ignorance of himself and [25] <of what> is.

His self-exaltation and [26] his expectation of comprehending [27] the incomprehensible one became resolute in him [28] and was within him. But the ailments [29] followed him [30] once he went beyond [31] himself, having come [32] to be in doubt on account of [33] his inability to accomplish the grasping of [34] the glories of the Father, the one whose exaltation [35] is among limitless things. This one [36] did not grasp him because he did not receive him.

[37] The one that he himself brought forth [78.1] as a unified eternity [2] went up to the [3] one who is his, and the one like [4] him in the fullness abandoned [5] the one who had come to be from the deficiency along with [6] those who merely appeared to have come from him, [7] since they are not [8] his.

ϫⲉ ⲛ̄ⲧⲁⲣⲉϥⲛ̄ⲧϥ̄ ⲁⲃⲁⲗ ⁹ ⲙ̄ⲙⲁϥ ⲛ̄ϫⲉ ⲡⲉⲧⲁϩⲛ̄ⲧϥ̄ ⲁⲃⲁⲗ [ⲙ]- ¹⁰ ⲙⲓⲛ ⲙ̄ⲙⲟϥ ⲉϥϫⲏⲕ, ⲛ̄ϩⲟⲩⲟ ¹¹ ⲁϥⲣ̄ ϭⲱⲃ ⲙ̄ⲡⲥⲙⲁⲧ ⲛ̄ⲛⲟⲩⲫⲩⲥⲓⲥ ¹² ⲛ̄ⲥϩⲓ̈ⲙⲉ ⲉⲁⲥⲣ̄ ϫⲁⲉⲓⲉ ⲛ̄ⲧⲉⲥⲙ̄[ⲛⲧ]- ¹³ ϩⲁⲩⲟⲩⲧ.

ϫⲉ ⲁⲃⲁⲗ ⲙⲉⲛ ⲙ̄ⲡⲉ[ⲉⲓ] ¹⁴ ⲉⲧⲁϩϣⲧⲁ ⲙ̄ⲙⲓⲛ ⲙ̄ⲙⲁϥ ⲛ̄[ⲉⲩ]- ¹⁵ ϣⲟⲟⲡ ⲙⲉⲛ ⲛ̄<ϭⲓ> ⲛⲉⲧⲁϩϣⲱ[ⲡⲉ] ⲁ- ¹⁶ ⲃⲁⲗ ϩⲙ̄ ⲡⲉϥⲙⲉⲟⲩⲉ ⲙⲛ̄ ⲡ[ⲉϥ]- ¹⁷ ϫⲓⲥⲉ ⲛ̄ϩⲏⲧ. ⲁⲃⲁⲗ ⲛ̄ⲇⲉ ϩⲙ̄ ¹⁸ ⲡⲉⲧϫⲏⲕ ⲛ̄ⲧⲉϥ ⲁϥⲕⲁⲁϥ ⲁϥϫ[ⲓⲧϥ] ¹⁹ ⲁϩⲣⲏⲓ̈ ⲁⲛⲉⲧⲉ ⲛⲟⲩϥ ⲛⲉ. ⲛⲉϥ[ϣⲟ]- ²⁰ ⲟⲡ ⲙ̄ⲡⲗⲏⲣⲱⲙⲁ ⲉϥϣⲟⲟⲡ ⲙ̄[ⲉⲛ] ²¹ ⲛ̄ⲛⲟⲩⲣ̄ ⲡⲙⲉⲩⲉ ⲛⲉϥ ϫⲉ ⲉϥ[ⲛⲁ]- ²² ⲛⲟⲩϩⲙⲉ ⲁⲃⲁⲗ ϩⲛ̄ ⲡⲉϥϫⲁϭⲓϩ[ⲏ]ⲧ.

²³ ϫⲉ ⲡⲉⲛⲧⲁϩⲣⲱⲧ ⲁⲡϫⲓⲥⲉ ⲙⲛ̄ ²⁴ ⲡⲉⲛⲧⲁϩⲥⲁⲕϥ̄ ⲛⲉϥ ⲙ̄ⲡⲟⲩϣⲱ- ²⁵ ⲡⲉ ⲉⲩⲟⲩⲁⲥϥ̄. ⲁⲗⲗⲁ ⲉⲩⲉⲓⲛⲉ ²⁶ ⲁⲃⲁⲗ [ⲛ]ⲛⲟⲩⲕⲁⲣⲡⲟⲥ ϩⲛ̄ ⲡⲗⲏⲣⲱ- ²⁷ ⲙⲁ, ⲁⲩϣⲁⲣϣ̄ⲣ̄ ⲛ̄ⲛⲉⲉⲓ ⲛ̄ⲧⲁϩ- ²⁸ ϣⲱⲡⲉ ϩⲛ̄ ⲡϣⲧⲁ.

ϫⲉ ⲛⲉⲛⲧⲁ[ⲩ]- ²⁹ ϣⲱⲡⲉ ⲁⲃⲁⲗ ϩⲛ̄ ⲡⲓⲙⲉⲉⲩⲉ ⲙ̄- ³⁰ ⲙⲛ̄ϫⲁⲥⲓϩⲏⲧ ⲉⲩⲣ̄ ⲙⲓⲛⲉ ⲙ̄- ³¹ ⲙⲁⲩ ⲙⲉⲛ ⲙⲛ̄ ⲛⲓⲡⲗⲏⲣⲱⲙⲁ, ⲛⲁⲓ̈ ³² ⲉⲧⲉ ϩⲛ̄ⲧⲁⲛⲧⲛ̄ ⲛⲉ ⲛ̄ⲧⲉⲩ ⲛⲉ ³³ ϩⲉⲛⲉⲓⲇⲱⲗⲟⲛ `ⲛⲉ´ ⲙⲛ̄ ϩⲛ̄ϩⲁⲉⲓⲃⲉⲥ ³⁴ ⲙⲛ̄ ϩⲛ̄ⲫⲁⲛⲧⲁⲥⲓⲁ, ⲉⲩⲟ ⲛ̄ϫⲁⲉⲓⲉ ³⁵ ⲙ̄ⲡⲗⲟⲅⲟⲥ ⲙⲛ̄ ⲡⲟⲩⲟⲉⲓⲛ, ⲛⲉⲉⲓ ⲉ- ³⁶ ⲧⲉ ⲛⲁ ⲡⲓⲙⲉⲉⲩⲉ ⲉⲧϣⲟⲩⲉⲓⲧ, ⲉϩⲛ̄- ³⁷ ϫⲡⲟ ⲛⲗⲁⲩⲉ ⲉⲛ ⲛⲉ. ⲉⲧⲃⲉ ⲡⲉⲉⲓ ⲁⲛ ⁷⁹·¹ ⲁⲣⲉⲧⲟⲩϩⲣⲁⲛ ⲛⲁϣⲱⲡⲉ ⲛ̄ⲑⲉ ² ⲛ̄ⲧⲟⲩⲁⲣⲭⲏ· ⲁⲃⲁⲗ ϩⲛ̄ ⲡⲉⲧⲉⲛⲉϥ- ³ [ϣ]ⲟⲟⲡ ⲉⲛ ⲁⲧⲣⲟⲩⲧⲥⲧⲁ ⲁⲛ ⲁⲡⲉ- ⁴ [ⲧ]ⲛ̄ⲛⲁϣⲱⲡⲉ ⲉⲛ. ⲛ̄ⲧⲁⲩ ⲛ̄ⲇⲉ ⲕⲁⲧⲁ- ⁵ [ⲣⲁ]ⲩ ⲟⲩⲁⲉⲉⲧⲟⲩ ⲉⲧϣⲟⲟⲡ ⲙ̄ⲙⲁⲩ ⁶ [ⲉⲩ]ⲟⲉⲓ ⲛⲁϭ ⲉⲩⲟⲉⲓ ⲛ̄ⲣⲙⲛ̄ϭⲁⲙ ⁷ [ⲉⲩⲧⲁⲉ]ⲓⲁⲉⲓⲧ ⲛ̄ⲇⲉ ⲛ̄ϩⲟⲩⲟ ⲁⲛⲓⲣⲉⲛ ⁸ [ⲉⲧⲧⲟ]ⲉⲓ ⲁⲣⲁⲩ, ⲛⲉⲉⲓ ⲉⲧⲉ ϩⲛ̄ϩⲁⲓ̈ⲃⲉⲥ ⁹ [ⲛ̄ⲧⲉⲩ] ⲛⲉ, ⲉⲩⲧⲥⲁⲉⲓⲁⲉⲓⲧ ϩⲛⲛ ⲟⲩⲧⲁⲛ- ¹⁰ [ⲧⲛ. ⲫⲟ] ⲅⲁⲣ ⲙ̄ⲡⲓⲇⲱⲗⲟⲛ ϣⲁϥϫⲓ ⲥⲁⲉⲓ- ¹¹ [ⲉ ⲛ̄]ⲧⲟⲟⲧϥ̄ ⲙ̄ⲡⲉⲉⲓ ⲉⲧⲉ ⲟⲩ<ⲉⲓ>ⲇⲱⲗⲟⲛ ¹² [ⲛ̄]ⲧⲉϥ ⲡⲉ.

ϫⲉ ⲛⲉⲩⲙⲉⲉⲩⲉ ⲁⲣⲁⲟⲩ ¹³ [ⲙ]ⲙⲓⲛ ⲙ̄ⲙⲁⲩ ϫⲉ ϩⲛ̄ϣⲱⲡⲉ ⲟⲩⲁ- ¹⁴ [ⲉ]ⲉⲧⲟⲩ ⲛⲉ ⲁⲩⲱ ϩⲛⲛⲁⲧⲁⲣⲭⲏ ⲛⲉ, ¹⁵ [ϩ]ⲱⲥ ⲉⲛⲥⲉⲛⲉⲩ ⲁϭⲉⲗⲁⲩⲉ ⲉⲛ ⲉϥ- ¹⁶ [ϣ]ⲟⲟⲡ ϩⲁ ⲧⲟⲩⲉϩⲛ. ⲉⲧⲃⲉ ⲡⲉⲉⲓ ⲛⲉⲩ- ¹⁷ [ⲱ]ⲛϩ ⲁⲃⲁⲗ ϩⲛ̄ ⲧⲙⲛ̄ⲧⲁⲧⲣ̄ ⲡⲓⲑⲉ ¹⁸ [ⲙ]ⲛ̄ ⲛⲓⲙⲛ̄ⲧⲁⲡⲟⲥⲧⲁⲧⲏⲥ, ⲉⲙⲡⲟⲩ- ¹⁹ [ⲑⲃ]ⲃⲓⲁⲩ ⲙ̄ⲡⲉⲛⲧⲁⲩϣⲱⲡⲉ ⲉⲧⲃⲏⲛ- ²⁰ [ⲧϥ]

ϫⲉ ⲛⲉⲩⲟⲩⲱϣⲉ ⲁⲟⲩⲉϩ ⲥⲁ- ²¹ [ϩⲛ]ⲉ ⲛⲛⲉⲩⲉⲣⲏⲩ, ⲉⲩϭⲣⲱ ⲁⲣⲁⲟⲩ ²² [ϩⲛ̄] ⲧⲟⲩⲙⲛ̄ⲧⲙⲁⲉⲓⲉⲁⲟⲩ ⲉⲧϣⲟⲩ- ²³ ⲉ[ⲓ]ⲧ, ⲉⲡⲉⲁⲩ ⲉⲧⲉⲩⲛ̄ⲧⲉⲩϥ ⲉⲩⲛ̄- ²⁴ ⲧⲉϥ ⲙ̄ⲙⲉⲩ ⲛ̄ⲛⲟⲩⲗⲁⲉⲓⲥⲉ ²⁵ [ⲛ̄ⲧ]ⲉ ⲧⲥⲩⲥⲧⲁⲥⲓⲥ ⲉⲧⲛⲁϣⲱⲡⲉ.

²⁶ [ϫ]ⲉ ϩⲛⲧⲁⲛⲧⲛ̄ ⲛⲉ ϭⲉ ⲛ̄ⲧⲉ ⲛⲉⲧϫⲁ- ²⁷ [ⲥ]ⲓ. ⲁ<ⲩ>ϥⲓⲧⲟⲩ ⲁϩⲣⲏⲓ̈ ⲁⲩⲙⲛ̄ⲧⲙⲁⲓ̈- ²⁸ ⲟⲩⲉϩ ⲥⲁϩⲛⲉ ⲙ̄ⲡⲟⲩⲉ ⲡⲟⲩⲉ ⲙ̄- ²⁹ ⲙⲁⲩ, ⲕⲁⲧⲁ ⲡⲁⲉⲓⲟⲩ ⲙ̄ⲡⲣⲉⲛ ³⁰ ⲉⲧϥϣⲟⲟⲡ ⲛ̄ϩⲁⲉⲓⲃⲉⲥ ⲛⲉϥ, ⲉϥⲣ̄ ³¹ ⲫⲁⲛⲧⲁⲥⲉ ⲁⲧⲣⲉϥϣⲱⲡⲉ ⲉϥⲁ- ³² ⲉⲓ ⲁⲛⲉϥⲉⲣⲏⲩ.

ϫⲉ ⲡⲙⲉⲉⲩⲉ ϭⲉ ⲛ̄ⲛⲓ- ³³ ⲕⲉⲕⲟⲟⲩⲉ ⲙⲡⲉϥϣⲱⲡⲉ ⲉϥⲟⲩⲁ- ³⁴ ⲥϥ̄, ⲁⲗⲗⲁ ⲕⲁⲧⲁ ⲡⲧⲁⲛⲧⲛ̄ <ⲛⲛ>ⲉⲧⲟⲩ- ³⁵ ϣⲟⲟⲡ ⲛⲉⲩ ⲛ̄ϩⲁⲉⲓⲃⲉⲥ, ⲡⲉⲧⲁⲩ{ⲁ}- ³⁶ ⲙⲉⲩⲉ ⲁⲣⲁϥ ⲧⲏⲣϥ̄ ⲟⲩⲛ̄ⲧⲉⲩϥ ⲙ̄ⲙⲉⲩ ³⁷ ⲛ̄ϣⲏⲣⲉ ⁸⁰·¹ ⲛⲁⲩⲱ. ⲛ̄ⲧⲁⲩ ⲛⲉⲧⲁⲩⲙⲉⲩⲉ ⲁ- ² ⲣⲁⲩ ⲙ̄ⲙⲁⲩ, ⲛⲉⲟⲩⲛ̄ⲧⲉⲩⲥⲟⲩ ³ ⲙ̄ⲙⲉⲩ

78.9 ⲛ̄ϫⲉ: read ⲛ̄ϭⲓ.
80.1 ⲁⲩⲱ: read ⲉⲩⲱ.

After the one who brought himself [9] forth perfect had brought [10] him forth, [11] he became quite weak like a female form of nature [12] that has deserted its masculine [13] (partner).

From what [14] was itself deficient [15] came the things that came to be [16] from his thought and [his] [17] arrogance. But from [18] what is perfect in him he left it and [brought himself] [19] up to those who are his. He was dwelling [20] in the fullness as [21] a memorial for him so that he [might] [22] be saved from his arrogance.

[23] The one who went up and [24] the one who drew him to himself were not [25] barren. Rather, by bringing [26] forth fruit in the fullness, [27] they agitated those who [28] were in the deficiency.

The things that had [29] come forth from the [30] arrogant thought resemble [31] the full-nesses, [32] which are their likenesses, [33] images, shadows, [34] and phantasms, devoid [35] of reason and light, these [36] that belong to the vain thought, since they are [37] not born of anything. For this reason, [79.1] their end will be like [2] their beginning: from what did [3] not exist (they must) [4] return again to what will not be. But it is they [5] by themselves who are [6] greater, more powerful, [7] and more honored than the names [8] [that are given] to them, those that are [their] shadows, [9] since they are beautiful in reflection. [10] For [the face] in the image receives [11] its beauty from that which [12] is its image.

They thought about [13] themselves that they are beings that exist alone [14] and with-out beginning, [15] since they do not see anything else [16] existing prior to them. For this reason they were [17] [living] in disobedience [18] [and] rebelliousness, having not [19] humbled themselves to the one on account of [20] [whom] they had come to be.

They wanted to command [21] each other, lording themselves over each other [22] [in] their vain self-importance, [23] while the glory that they have [24] contains a cause [25] [of] the system that will come into being.

[26] They are likenesses of the things that are exalted. [27] They were brought to a love [28] of power in each one of them, [29] in accordance with the greatness of the name [30] of which (each) is a shadow, [31] imagining that (each) is greater [32] than his peers.

The thought of these [33] others was not barren, [34] but just as <those> [35] of which they are shadows, everything they thought [36] about they have as [37] potential offspring. [80.1] Those about whom they thought, [2] they had as [3] children. Thus [4] it happened

ⲛ̄ϫⲡⲟ. ⲁⲃⲁⲗ ⲙ̄ⲡⲉ[ⲉⲓ] ⁴ ⲁⲥϣⲱⲡⲉ ⲁⲧⲣⲉϩⲁϩ ⲉⲓ ⲁⲃⲁⲗ ⲙ̄- ⁵ ⲙⲁⲩ ⲛ̄ϫⲡⲟ, ⲉϩⲛ̄ⲣⲉϥⲙ̄ⲗⲁ[ϩ] ⁶ ⲛⲉ
ⲉϩⲛ̄ⲣⲉϥⲙⲓϣⲉ ⲛⲉ ⲉϩⲛ̄- ⁷ ⲣⲉϥϯ ϣ̄ⲧⲁⲣⲧ̄ⲣ ⲛⲉ ⲉϩⲛ̄ⲁⲡⲟⲥⲧⲁ- ⁸ ⲧⲏⲥ ⲛⲉ. ϩ̄ⲛⲁⲧ̄ⲣ ⲡⲓⲑⲉ ⲛⲉ ⲉϩⲛ̄- ⁹
ⲙⲁⲉⲓⲟⲩⲉϩ ⲥⲁϩⲛⲉ ⲛⲉ. ⲁⲩ[ⲱ ⲛ]- ¹⁰ ⲕⲉϩⲁⲉⲓⲛⲉ ⲧⲏⲣⲟⲩ ⲙ̄ⲡⲓⲣⲏ[ⲧⲉ ⲁ]- ¹¹ ⲃⲁⲗ ϩ̄ⲛ ⲛⲉⲉⲓ.

ϫⲉ ⲡⲗⲟⲅⲟⲥ ϭⲉ ⲁ[ϥ]- ¹² ϣⲱⲡⲉ ⲛ̄ⲗⲁⲉⲓϭⲉ ⲛ̄ⲛⲉⲉⲓ ⲛ̄[ⲧⲁⲩ]- ¹³ ϣⲱⲡⲉ. ⲁϥⲟⲩⲱϩ ⲁⲧⲟⲟⲧϥ
ⲛ̄[ϩⲟⲩⲟ] ¹⁴ ⲛ̄ϩⲟⲩⲟ ⲁⲣ̄ ⲁⲡⲟⲣⲓⲥ, ⲁϥⲉⲓⲱⲣⲙ. ¹⁵ ⲁⲛⲧⲓ ⲟⲩϫⲱⲕ ⲁϥⲛⲉⲩ ⲁⲩⲱⲧ[ⲁ]· ¹⁶ ⲁⲛⲧⲓ
ⲟⲩⲙⲟⲩϫϭ ⲁϥⲛⲉⲩ ⲁ[ⲩⲡ]- ¹⁷ ϣⲱϣⲉ· ⲁⲛⲧⲓ ⲟⲩⲥⲙⲓⲛⲉ ⲁϥ[ⲛⲉⲩ] ¹⁸ ⲁϩⲛ̄ϣ̄ⲧⲟⲣⲧ̄ⲣ· ⲁⲛⲧⲓ
ϩⲉⲛⲏ[ⲧⲁⲛ] ¹⁹ ⲁϩⲛ̄ⲧⲁⲣⲁⲭⲏ. ⲟⲩⲇⲉ ⲁⲛ ⲙⲛ̄ [ϭⲁⲙ] ²⁰ ⲙ̄ⲙⲁϥ ⲁⲗⲁϭⲉ ⲁⲧⲣⲟⲩⲙ̄ⲣ[ⲣⲉ ϣ]- ²¹
ⲧⲁⲣⲧ̄ⲣ, ⲟⲩⲇⲉ ⲙⲛ̄ ϭⲁⲙ ⲙ̄ⲙ̣[ⲁϥ] ²² ⲁⲧⲉⲕⲁⲥ. ⲛⲉⲁϥⲣ̄ ⲁⲧϭⲁⲙ ⲧ̣[ⲏⲣϥ] ²³ ⲛ̄ⲧⲁⲣⲉⲡ̄ϥⲧⲏⲣϥ̄
ⲁⲩⲱ ⲡⲩ̄ϫ̣[ⲓ]ⲥ̣[ⲉ] ²⁴ ⲕⲁⲁϥ ⲛ̄ⲥⲱϥ.

ϫⲉ ⲛⲉⲧⲁϩϣ̄ϣ̣ⲡ̣[ⲉ] ²⁵ ϭⲉ {ⲡⲉ} ⲉ̣ⲙⲡⲟⲩⲥⲟⲩⲱⲛⲟⲩ ⲙ̣ⲙ̣[ⲓⲛ] ²⁶ ⲙ̄ⲙⲟⲟⲩ ⲁⲩⲱ ⲙ̄ⲡⲟⲩⲥⲟⲩⲱ[ⲛ]
²⁷ ⲙ̄ⲡⲗⲏⲣⲱⲙⲁ ⲉⲛⲧⲁⲣⲉⲓ ⲁⲃⲁ[ⲗ] ²⁸ ⲙ̣ⲙⲁⲩ, ⲁⲩⲱ ⲙ̄ⲡⲟⲩⲥⲟⲩⲱⲛ ²⁹ ⲡⲉⲛⲧⲁϣⲱⲡⲉ ⲛ̄ⲗⲁⲉⲓϭⲉ
ⲙ̄- ³⁰ ⲡⲧⲣⲟⲩϣⲱⲡⲉ.

ϫⲉ ⲡⲗⲟⲅⲟⲥ ³¹ ϭⲉ, ⲉϥϣⲟⲟⲡ ϩⲣⲏ̣ⲓ̈ ϩ̄ⲛ ⲛⲓⲧⲱϣⲉ ³² ⲙ̄ⲡⲓⲣⲏⲧⲉ ⲛⲛⲁⲧⲥⲙⲓⲛⲉ, ⲙ̄- ³³ ⲡⲉϥⲟⲩⲱϩ
ⲁⲧⲟⲟⲧϥ̄ ⲁⲉⲓⲛⲉ ⲁ- ³⁴ ⲃⲁⲗ ⲙ̄ⲡⲓⲣⲏⲧⲉ ⲛ̄ϩⲉⲛⲡⲣⲟⲃⲟ- ³⁵ ⲗⲏⲟⲩ, ⲛⲉⲧϣⲟⲟⲡ ϩ̄ⲛ ⲡⲗⲏⲣⲟⲩ- ³⁶ ⲙⲁ,
ⲛⲉⲁⲩ ⲉⲛⲧⲁϩϣⲱⲡⲉ ⲁⲩⲟⲩⲉⲁⲩ ³⁷ ⲙ̄ⲡⲓⲱⲧ. ⲁⲗⲗⲁ ⲉⲣⲉⲁϥⲉⲓⲛⲉ ⁸¹·¹ [ⲁ]ⲃ̣ⲟⲗ <ⲛ>ϩ̄ⲛ̣{ϩⲓ}
ⲙ̄ⲛ̄ⲧϭⲱⲃ ⲉⲩⲥⲁⲃⲕ̄, ⲉⲩ- ² [ⲥⲁ]ϣ̣ⲧ̄ ⲛ̄ⲧⲟⲟⲧϥ̄ ⲛ̄ⲛⲓϣⲱⲛⲉ ⲛⲉⲉⲓ ³ [ⲛⲧ]ⲁ̣ϥⲥⲁϣ̄ⲧ̄ ⲛ̄ⲧⲟⲟⲧⲟⲩ
ϩⲱⲱϥ ⲁⲛ. ⁴ [ⲡⲧ]ⲁ̣ⲛⲧⲛ̄ ⲛ̄ϯⲇⲓⲁⲑⲉⲥⲓⲥ ⲡⲉ ⲉⲧⲁϩ- ⁵ ⲣ̄ ⲟⲩⲉⲓ ⲛ̄ⲟⲩⲱⲧ ⲡⲉⲉⲓ ⲉⲧⲁϩ- ⁶ ϣⲱⲡⲉ
ⲛ̄ⲗⲁⲉⲓϭⲉ ⲛ̄ⲛⲉϩⲃⲏⲩⲉ ⁷ ⲉⲧⲉⲛ̄ⲥⲉϣⲟⲟⲡ ⲛ̄ϣⲁⲣⲡ̄ ⲉⲛ ⲙ̄ⲙⲓⲛ ⁸ ⲙ̄ⲙⲟⲟⲩ.

ϫⲉ ϣⲁ ⲡⲉⲉⲓ ⲡⲉⲧⲁϩⲉⲓⲛⲉ ⁹ ⲁⲃⲁⲗ ⲛ̄ⲛⲉⲉⲓ ⲙ̄ⲡⲓⲣⲏⲧⲉ ⲉⲧⲁϩⲣ̄ ¹⁰ ϩⲣⲱϩ ⲉⲡϣ̄ⲧⲁ, ϣⲁ ⲡⲓⲛⲉⲩ
ⲉⲧⲁϥ- ¹¹ ⲧⲁϩⲟ ⲛ̄ⲛⲉⲉⲓ ⲉⲛⲧⲁⲩϣⲱⲡⲉ ⲉⲧ- ¹² ⲃⲏⲧϥ̄ ⲕⲁⲧⲁ ⲗⲟⲅⲟⲥ ⲉⲛ—ⲉⲧⲉ ⲡⲓⲧⲁ- ¹³ ϫⲟ
ⲡⲉ ⲉⲧⲁϩϣⲱⲡⲉ ⲛ̄ⲛⲟⲩⲕⲣⲓⲥⲓⲥ—¹⁴ ⲉϥϯ ⲟⲩⲃⲛⲟⲩ ⲁⲩⲧⲉⲕⲟ ¹⁵ [ⲉ]ⲧⲉ ⲛⲉⲉⲓ ⲛⲉ ⲛ̄ⲧⲁϩ
ⲟⲩⲃⲉ ⲧⲕⲣⲓⲥⲓⲥ ¹⁶ [ⲉ]ⲥⲟⲩⲏϩ ⲛ̄ⲥⲱⲟⲩ ⲛ̄ϭⲓ ⲧⲃⲁⲗⲕⲉ, ⲉⲟⲩ- ¹⁷ [ⲣ]ⲉ̣[ϥ]ϣⲱⲡ{ⲉ} ⲇⲉ ⲁⲩⲱ
ⲟⲩⲣⲉϥⲥⲱ- ¹⁸ [ⲧⲉ] ⲧⲉ ⲛ̄ⲧⲟⲩⲅⲛⲱⲙⲏ ⲙⲛ̄ ⲧⲟⲩ- ¹⁹ [ⲙ]ⲛ̄ⲧⲁⲡⲟⲥⲧⲁⲧⲏⲥ, ⲉⲁⲃⲁⲗ ⲙ̄ⲙⲁⲥ ²⁰
[ⲡⲉ] ⲡⲓⲛⲟⲩⲟⲩϩ ⲁϩⲟⲩⲛ ⲡⲉⲧⲉϣⲁ- ²¹ [ⲙ]ⲟⲩⲧⲉ ⲁⲣⲁϥ ⲁⲛ ϫⲉ « ⲙⲉⲧⲁⲛⲟⲓ- ²² [ⲁ. »] ⲁ̣ϥ
ⲡⲱⲱⲛⲉ ⲉϩⲟⲩⲛ ⲛ̄ϭⲓ ⲡⲗⲟⲅⲟⲥ ²³ ⲁ̣[ⲕⲉ]ⲅⲛⲱⲙⲏ ⲁⲩⲱ ⲕⲉⲙⲉⲉⲩⲉ. ²⁴ ⲉⲁ̣[ϥ]ⲛⲁⲟⲩϩϥ̄ ⲁⲃⲁⲗ
ⲛ̄ⲛⲉⲑⲁⲩ, ²⁵ ⲁϥⲛⲁⲟⲩϩϥ̄ ⲉϩⲟⲩⲛ ⲉⲛⲉⲧⲛⲁⲛⲟⲩ- ²⁶ ⲟⲩ. ⲡⲛⲟⲩϩ ⲉϩⲟⲩⲛ ⲁϥⲟⲩⲁϩϥ̄ ⲛ̄- ²⁷ ⲥⲱϥ
ⲛ̄ϭⲓ ⲡⲓⲙⲉⲩⲉ ⲛ̄ⲧⲉ ⲛⲉⲧϣⲟⲟⲡ ²⁸ ⲙⲛ̄ ⲡⲓⲥⲁⲡⲥ̄ ϩⲁ ⲡⲣⲁ ⲙ̄ⲡⲣⲉϥⲛⲁⲟⲩϩϥ̄ ²⁹ ⲁⲣⲁϥ ⲙ̄ⲙⲓⲛ ⲙ̄ⲙⲁϥ
ⲙ̄ⲡⲉⲧⲛⲁⲛⲟⲩϥ.

³⁰ ϫⲉ ⲛⲧⲁϥ ⲛ̄ϣⲁⲣⲡ̄ ⲡⲉⲧϩⲛ̄ ⲡⲗⲏⲣⲟⲩ- ³¹ ⲙⲁ ⲡⲉⲧⲁⲣⲧⲱⲃϩ ⲙ̄ⲙⲁϥ ⲁⲩⲱ ⲉϥ- ³² ⲣ̄ ⲡⲙⲉⲉⲩⲉ.
ⲉⲓⲇⲁ ⲛⲉϥⲥⲛⲏⲩ ³³ ⲕⲁⲧⲁ ⲟⲩⲉⲓ ⲟⲩⲉⲓ ⲁⲩⲱ ⲥⲉⲡ ⲧⲏⲣϥ̄ ³⁴ ⲙⲛ̄ ⲛⲉϥⲉⲣⲏⲩ. ⲉⲓⲧⲁ ⲛ̄ⲧⲁⲩ ⲧⲏⲣⲟⲩ.
³⁵ ϩⲁⲑⲏ ⲇⲉ ⲛ̄ⲛⲉⲉⲓ ⲧⲏⲣⲟⲩ ⲡⲱⲧ. ⁸²·¹ ⲛⲉⲣⲉⲡⲓⲥⲁⲡⲥ̄ ϭⲉ ⲛ̄ⲧⲉ ⲡⲓⲡⲱⲧ [ⲡⲉ] ² ⲛⲉⲟⲩⲃⲟⲏⲑⲓⲁ ⲡⲉ
ⲁⲧⲣⲉⲩ- ³ ⲧⲥⲁϥ ⲉϩⲟⲩⲛ ⲙ̄ⲙⲓⲛ ⲙ̄ⲙ̣[ⲁϥ] ⁴ ⲁⲩⲱ ⲡⲧⲏⲣϥ̄, ϫⲉ ʼⲛⲉʼ ⲟⲩⲗⲁⲉⲓϭⲉ ⁵ ⲛⲉϥ ⲡⲉ

that many children came forth ⁵ from them, being fighters, ⁶ attackers, ⁷ disturbers, and rebels. ⁸ They are disobeyers and ⁹ lovers of power. All [the] ¹⁰ others of this sort are ¹¹ from these.

The Word ¹² was a cause for those [who] ¹³ came to be. He continued still more ¹⁴ to be perplexed, and he was astonished. ¹⁵ Instead of perfection, he saw deficiency; ¹⁶ instead of unity, he saw division; ¹⁷ instead of order, he [saw] ¹⁸ disturbances; instead of [rests,] ¹⁹ troubles. Neither was it [possible] ²⁰ for him to make them stop [loving] ²¹ disturbance, nor was it possible [for him] ²² to put an end to it. He was [completely] powerless ²³ after his entirety and his [exaltation] ²⁴ deserted him.

Those who had come to be ²⁵ not knowing themselves ²⁶ did not know ²⁷ the fullnesses from which they had come forth, ²⁸ and they did not know ²⁹ the one who was a cause of ³⁰ their coming to be.

The Word, ³¹ since he was in ³² chaotic sorts, ³³ did not continue to bring ³⁴ forth (things) like emanations, ³⁵ those things that are in the fullness, ³⁶ the glories that have come about for the glorification ³⁷ of the Father. Rather, he brought ⁸¹·¹ forth little things, ² [held back] by the sicknesses ³ by which he too was held back. ⁴ It was [the] likeness of the disposition that was ⁵ unified, this one that ⁶ became a cause for the things ⁷ that do not themselves ⁸ exist from the beginning.

Until the one who brought ⁹ forth these things that were in this way ¹⁰ needed into the deficiency, until he ¹¹ judged those who had come to be on account of ¹² him not in accordance with reason—which is the judgment ¹³ that became condemnation—¹⁴ he worked against them to destruction, ¹⁵ that is, the ones who worked against the condemnation ¹⁶ and whom the wrath follows, whereas ¹⁷ it (the wrath) accepts and redeems (them) ¹⁸ from their opinion and ¹⁹ rebellion, since from it ²⁰ [is] the return, which is ²¹ also called "repentance." ²² The Word turned ²³ to [another] opinion and another thought. ²⁴ Once he turned away from evil things, ²⁵ he turned to good things. ²⁶ After the return came ²⁷ the thought of things that are ²⁸ and the petition for the one who returned ²⁹ himself to the good.

³⁰ He who was in the fullness ³¹ is whom he prayed to and remembered first. ³² Then (he remembered) his siblings ³³ individually and (yet) always ³⁴ with each other. Then (he remembered) all of them together. ³⁵ But before all these, (he remembered) the Father. ⁸²·¹ The prayer of the agreement was ² a help for ³ he himself being returned ⁴ and (for) the entirety, because a cause ⁵ for his remembering ⁶ of those

ⲁⲧⲣⲉϥⲣ̄ ⲡⲙⲉⲉⲩ[ⲉ] ⁶ ⲛ̄ⲛⲉⲧϣⲟⲟⲡ ⲛ̄ϣⲁⲣⲡ̄ ⲡⲉ- ⁷ ⲧⲣⲟⲩⲣ̄ ⲡⲉϥⲙⲉⲉⲩⲉ, ⲉⲧⲉ ⲡⲁ- ⁸ ⲉⲓ ⲡⲉ ⲡⲙⲉⲩⲉ
ⲉⲧⲱϣ ⲁⲃⲁⲗ ⁹ ⲙ̄ⲡⲟⲩⲁⲉⲓⲉ, ⲉϥⲧⲥⲟ ⲙ̄ⲙⲁϥ.

¹⁰ ϫⲉ ⲡⲓⲥⲁⲡⲥⲡⲥ̄ ⲧⲏⲣϥ̄ ⲛ̄ⲧⲉϥ ⲙ̄ⲛ̄ ¹¹ ⲡⲓⲣ̄ <ⲡ>ⲙⲉⲉⲩⲉ ⲛⲉⲩϣⲟⲟⲡ ⲛ̄ϩⲛ̄- ¹² ϭⲟⲙ ⲉⲛⲁϣϣⲟⲩ
ⲕⲁ<ⲧⲁ> ⲡⲓϩⲟⲣⲟⲥ ¹³ ⲟⲛ ⲉⲧⲙ̄ⲙⲉⲩ, ϫⲉ ⲙ̄ⲛ̄ ⲗⲁⲩⲉ ¹⁴ ϣⲟⲟⲡ ⲉϥⲟⲩⲁϭϥ̄ ⲛ̄ⲧⲉϥ ⲙ̄ⲡⲙⲉⲩ[ⲉ].

¹⁵ ϫⲉ ⲛⲓϭⲁⲙ ϭⲉ ⲛⲉⲛⲁⲛⲟⲩⲟⲩ ⲡ[ⲉ], ¹⁶ ⲁⲩⲱ ⲛⲁⲩⲟⲩⲁⲉⲓ ⲛ̄ϩⲟⲩⲟ ⲁⲛⲁ ⲡ[ⲓ]- ¹⁷ ⲧⲁⲛⲧⲛ̄.
ⲛⲉⲧⲙ̄ⲙⲉⲩ ⲅⲁⲣ ⲛⲁ ⲡ[ⲓ]- ¹⁸ ⲧⲁⲛⲧⲛ̄ ⲛ̄ⲧⲁⲩ ⲛⲁ ⲟⲩⲥⲓⲁ ⲛ̄ⲕⲣ[ⲟϥ] ¹⁹ ⲛⲉ. ⲁⲃⲁⲗ ϩⲛ̄ⲛ ⲟⲩⲫⲁⲛⲧ[ⲁⲥⲓⲁ]
²⁰ ⲛ̄ⲧⲉ ⲟⲩⲧⲁⲛⲧⲛ̄ ⲙ̄ⲛ̄ ⲟⲩⲙⲉ[ⲩⲉ] ²¹ ⲙ̄ⲙⲛ̄[ⲛ]ϫⲁⲥⲓϩⲏⲧ ⲉϥϣ[ⲟⲟⲡ ⲙ̄]- ²² ⲡⲉⲧⲉⲁⲩϣⲱⲡⲉ.
ⲛⲉⲉⲓ ⲛ̄ⲁ[ⲉ ⲛ]- ²³ ⲧⲁⲩ ϩⲛ̄ⲛⲁⲃⲁⲗ ⲛⲉ ϩⲙ̄ ⲡⲓ[ⲙ]ⲉⲩⲉ ²⁴ ⲉⲛⲧⲁϥⲣ̄ ϣⲁⲣⲡ̄ ⲛ̄ⲥⲟⲩϣ[ⲛ]ⲟⲩ.

²⁵ ϫⲉ ⲛⲉⲉⲓ ϭⲉ ⲉⲧⲙ̄ⲙⲉⲩ ⲛⲁ ⲟⲩ- ²⁶ ⲱ; ⲙ̄ⲡⲣⲏⲧⲉ ⲛ̄ⲛⲟⲩⲱ<ⲃ>ϣⲉ ⲛⲉ ²⁷ ⲁⲩⲱ ⲟⲩϩⲓ̈ⲛⲏⲃ
ⲉϥϩⲁⲣⲱ, ⲉⲩⲟ̈ ²⁸ ⲙ̄ⲡⲣⲏⲧⲉ ⲛ̄ⲛⲉⲧⲡ̄ⲣ̄ ⲣⲉⲥⲟⲩⲉ ²⁹ ⲉⲩϣⲧⲣ̄ⲧⲁⲣⲧ̄, ⲛⲉⲉⲓ ⲉⲧⲉϣⲁⲣⲉ- ³⁰ ⲟⲩϩⲓ̈ⲛⲏⲃ
ⲟⲩⲁϩϥ̄ ⲛ̄ⲥⲱⲟⲩ ⲉⲩ- ³¹ ⲭⲗ̄ⲭⲁⲗⲧ ⲛ̄ϭⲓ ⲛⲉⲧⲡⲉⲣ ⲣⲉⲥⲟⲩ- ³² ⲉ. ⲛⲓⲕⲉⲕⲟⲟⲩⲉ ⲇⲉ ⲉⲩⲟ ⲙ̄- ³³ ⲡⲣⲏⲧⲉ
ⲛ̄ϩⲛ̄ϩⲁⲉⲓⲛⲉ ⲛ̄ⲟⲩⲁⲉⲓⲛ ³⁴ ⲛⲉϥ, ⲉⲩϭⲁϣⲧ̄ ⲁⲃⲁⲗ ⲁϫⲱϥ ³⁵ ⲙ̄ⲡⲣ̄ⲣⲉ ⲙ̄ⲡⲣⲏ, ⲉⲁⲥϣⲱⲡⲉ ⲁ- ³⁶
ⲧⲣⲟⲩⲛⲉⲩ ⲁϩⲛ̄ⲣⲉⲥⲟⲩⲉ ⲛ̄ϩⲏⲧϥ̄ ³⁷ ⲉⲩⲟⲩ<ϩ>ⲁⲗϭ ⲙⲁⲙⲛⲉ ⲛ̄ⲧⲟⲩ. ⁸³·¹ ⲙⲉⲛ ⲏⲇⲏ ⲁⲥⲱϫⲛⲉ ²
[ⲁ]ⲛⲓⲡⲣⲟⲃⲟⲗⲟⲩ ⲛ̄ⲧⲉ ⲡⲓⲙⲉⲩⲉ. ³ [ⲛⲉ]ⲙ̄ⲛ̄ⲧⲟⲩ ϩⲟⲩⲟ ⲙ̄ⲙⲉⲩ ⲡⲉ ⁴ [ⲛ̄]ⲧⲟⲩⲟⲩⲥⲓⲁ, ⲁⲩⲱ ⲁⲛ
ⲛⲉ- ⁵ [ⲙ]ⲛ̄ⲧⲉⲩ ⲧⲁⲉⲓⲟ ⲙ̄ⲙⲉⲩ ⲡⲉ ⲛ̄ϩⲟⲩⲟ.

⁶ [ϫ]ⲉ ⲉϥϣⲏϣ ⲉⲛ ⲙ̄ⲛ̄ ⲛⲉⲧⲣ̄ ϣⲣⲡ̄ ⁷ ⲛ̄ϣⲱⲡⲉ, ⲉϣϫⲡⲉ ⲛⲉⲩⲥⲁⲧⲡ̄ ⲁⲛ ⁸ [ⲁ]ⲛ̄ⲧⲁⲛⲧⲛ̄ ⲛⲉ,
ⲡⲁⲉⲓ ⲟⲩⲁⲉⲉⲧϥ̄ ⁹ [ⲡ]ⲉⲧⲟⲩϫⲁⲥⲉ ⲁⲣⲁⲩ ⲙ̄ⲙⲟϥ, ϫⲉ ¹⁰ [ϩ]ⲛ̄ⲛⲁⲃⲁⲗ ϩⲛ̄ⲛ ⲟⲩⲅ̄ⲛ̄ϣⲙⲏ ⲉⲛ ¹¹
ⲛⲁⲛⲟⲩⲥ ⲛⲉ.

ϫⲉ ⲛ̄ⲧ[ⲁ]ⲩⲉⲓ ⲉ- ¹² ⲃⲟⲗ ⲉⲛ ϩⲛ̄ ⲡϣⲱⲛⲉ ⲛ̄ⲧⲁϩ- ¹³ ϣⲱⲡⲉ, ⲉⲧⲉ ϯⲅⲛⲱⲙⲏ ⲉⲧ- ¹⁴ ⲛⲁⲛⲟⲩ
ⲛ̄ⲧⲟⲟⲧϥ̄, ⲛ̄ⲥⲉ ⲡⲉ- ¹⁵ [ⲧ]ⲁϩϣⲓⲛⲉ ⲛ̄ⲥⲉ ⲡⲉⲧⲣ̄ ϣⲁⲣⲡ̄ ¹⁶ ⲛ̄ϣⲱⲡⲉ. ⲉⲁϥⲧⲱⲃⲥ̄, ⲁⲩⲱ ⲁϥϫⲓⲧϥ̄ ¹⁷
ⲙ̄ⲙⲓⲛ ⲙ̄ⲙⲟϥ ⲙ̄ⲡ[ⲉ]ⲧⲛⲁ- ¹⁸ [ⲛⲟ]ⲩϥ ⲁⲩⲱ ⲁϥⲥⲓⲧⲉ ⲛ̄ϩⲏⲧⲟⲩ ¹⁹ [ⲛ̄]ⲟⲩⲡⲣⲟⲉⲣⲉⲥⲓⲥ ⲛ̄ϣⲓⲛⲉ ²⁰
[ⲁ]ⲩⲱ ⲛ̄ⲧⲱⲃⲥ̄ ⲛ̄ⲧⲟⲟ[ⲧ]ϥ̄ ⲙ̄ⲡⲉⲧ- ²¹ [ⲧ]ⲁⲉⲓⲁⲉⲓⲧ ⲉⲧⲣ̄ ϣⲁⲣⲡ̄ ⲛ̄ϣⲟⲟⲡ, ²² [ⲁ]ⲩⲱ ⲁϥⲥⲓⲧⲉ
ⲛ̄ϩⲏⲧⲟⲩ ⲛ̄ⲛⲟⲩⲙⲉⲩⲉ ²³ [ⲁⲣ]ⲁϥ ⲁⲩⲱ ⲟⲩⲙⲁⲕⲙⲉⲕ, ⲁⲧⲣⲟⲩ- ²⁴ [ⲙ]ⲉⲩⲉ ϫⲉ ⲟⲩⲛ̄ ⲛⲟϭ ⲁⲣⲁⲩ
ϥϣⲟ- ²⁵ [ⲟⲡ] ϩⲁ ⲧⲟⲩⲉϩⲏ, ⲉⲙⲡⲟⲩⲙ̄ⲙⲉ ²⁶ [ϫⲉ] ⲉⲩ ⲡⲉⲧⲉⲛⲉϥϣⲟⲟⲡ. ⲉⲩϫⲡⲟ ²⁷ [ⲙ]ⲡⲓϯ ⲙⲉⲧⲉ
ⲙ̄ⲛ̄ ϯⲙⲛ̄ⲧⲙⲁ- ²⁸ ⲉ̄[ⲓ] ⲛ̄ⲟⲩⲉⲣⲏⲩ ⲁⲃⲁⲗ ϩⲙ̄ ⲡⲙⲉⲩⲉ ²⁹ ⲉⲧⲙ̄ⲙⲉⲩ {ⲉⲧⲙⲙⲉⲩ}, ⲁⲩⲉⲓⲣⲉ ϩⲣⲏⲓ̈ ³⁰
ϩⲛ̄ ϯⲙⲛ̄ⲧⲟⲩⲉⲓⲉ ⲙ̄ⲛ̄ ϯⲅⲛⲱ- ³¹ ⲙⲏ ⲛ̄ⲟⲩⲱⲧ, ϩⲱⲥ ⲁⲃⲁⲗ ϩⲛ̄ ϯ- ³² ⲙⲛ̄ⲧⲟⲩⲉⲓ ⲙ̄ⲛ̄ ϯⲅⲛⲱⲙⲏ
ⲛ̄- ³³ ⲟⲩⲱⲧ ⲉⲁⲩϫⲓ ⲙ̄[ⲡ]ⲧⲣⲟⲩϣⲱⲡⲉ.

³⁴ ϫⲉ ⲛ̄ⲧⲁⲩ ϭⲉ ⲁⲩϭⲣ[ⲱ] ⲁⲣⲁⲟⲩ ³⁵ ⲛ̄ⲧⲙⲛ̄ⲧ{ⲙⲛ}ⲙⲁⲉ[ⲓⲟ]ⲩⲉϩ ⲥⲁϩⲛⲉ ³⁶ ϫⲉ ⲛⲁⲩⲧⲁⲉⲓⲁⲉⲓ-
[ⲧ] ⲛ̄ϩⲟⲩⲟ ⁸⁴·¹ ⲁⲛⲓϣⲁ[ⲣ]ⲡ ⲉⲛⲧⲁϥ[ⲓⲧ]ⲟⲩ [ⲁ]- ² ϩⲣⲏⲓ̈ ⲁϫⲱⲟⲩ. ⲛⲉⲙⲡⲉ `ⲛⲉ´ⲧⲙⲏ[ⲉⲩ] ³
ⲑⲃⲃⲓⲁⲩ. ⲛⲉⲩⲙⲉⲩⲉ ⲁⲣⲁⲟ[ⲩ] ⁴ ϫⲉ ϩⲉⲛϣⲱⲡⲉ ⲁⲃⲁⲗ ⲙ̄ⲙⲁ[ⲩ] ⁵ ⲟⲩⲁⲉⲉⲧⲟⲩ ⲛⲉ
ⲁⲩⲱ ϩ[ⲉ]- ⁶ ⲛⲁⲧⲁⲣⲭⲏ ⲛⲉ. ⲉⲩⲉⲓⲛⲉ ⲁ[ⲃⲁⲗ] ⁷ ⲛ̄ϣⲁⲣⲡ̄ ⲕⲁⲧⲁ ⲡⲟⲩⲙⲓⲥⲉ, ⲛ̄[ⲉⲁⲩ]- ⁸ ϯ ⲡⲉ

82.9 ⲉϥⲧⲥⲟ: read ⲉϥⲧⲥⲟ<ⲧ>ⲟ.
82.16 ⲛⲁⲩⲟⲩⲁⲉⲓ: read ⲛⲉⲩⲟⲩⲁⲉⲓ.
83.36 ⲛⲁⲩⲧⲁⲉⲓⲁⲉⲓ[ⲧ]: read ⲛⲉⲩⲧⲁⲉⲓⲁⲉⲓ[ⲧ].

who have existed from the beginning ⁷ was his being remembered, that ⁸ is, the thought that summons from ⁹ afar, bringing him back.

¹⁰ All his prayers and ¹¹ remembering were numerous powers ¹² <after the fashion of> that boundary, ¹³ because there is nothing ¹⁴ barren in his thought.

¹⁵ The powers were good, ¹⁶ and they were greater than those belonging to the ¹⁷ likeness. For those belonging to the ¹⁸ likeness are those belonging to the substance of [falsehood.] ¹⁹ From an illusion ²⁰ of likeness and a [thought] ²¹ of conceit [arises] ²² that which they came to be. They ²³ are from the thought ²⁴ that first knew them.

²⁵ To what do these aforementioned (beings) belong? ²⁶ They are like the forgetfulness ²⁷ and deep sleep, ²⁸ like those who dream disturbing dreams, ²⁹ those whom ³⁰ sleep pursues while those who dream ³¹ are surrounded. ³² But the others are ³³ like some (beings) of light ³⁴ to him, awaiting ³⁵ the dawning of the sun, since it happened ³⁶ that they saw in him ³⁷ dreams that are genuinely sweet. ⁸³·¹ Immediately it ended ² the emanations of the thought. ³ They no longer had ⁴ their substance, and they also ⁵ did not have honor any more.

⁶ Though he is not equal to those who ⁷ came into being first, if they were superior ⁸ [to] the likenesses, he alone ⁹ is [the] one by whom they are more exalted than those, because ¹⁰ they are not from a ¹¹ good opinion.

They came ¹² forth not from the illness that had ¹³ come to be, from which is the good ¹⁴ opinion, but (from) the ¹⁵ one who sought after the preexistent one. ¹⁶ After he prayed, he both brought ¹⁷ himself to the good ¹⁸ and sowed within them ¹⁹ an inclination to seek ²⁰ and pray to the ²¹ glorified one who preexists, ²² and he sowed within them a thought ²³ [about] him and a consideration, so that they ²⁴ might think that something greater than themselves ²⁵ preexists them, though they did not know ²⁶ what it was. Begetting ²⁷ agreement and mutual affection ²⁸ from that thought, ²⁹ they acted in ³⁰ unity and unanimity, ³¹ since from ³² unity and unanimity ³³ they had received their being.

³⁴ They were [stronger] than them ³⁵ in the love of power ³⁶ because they were honored more ⁸⁴·¹ than the first ones, who had been elevated ² above them. Those ones had not ³ humbled themselves. They thought concerning themselves ⁴ that they are beings (coming forth) from [themselves] ⁵ alone and ⁶ are without a beginning.

ⲁⲅⲛ̄ ⲛⲟⲩⲉⲣⲏⲟⲩ ⲛ̄ϭⲓ ⲡ[ⲓⲗⲁ]- ⁹ ⲅⲙⲁ ⲥⲛⲉⲩ, ⲉⲩⲙⲓϣⲉ ⲁⲭⲛ̄ [ⲡⲟⲩ]- ¹⁰ ⲁⲅ ⲥⲁⲅⲛⲉ ⲁⲃⲁⲗ
ⲙ̄ⲡⲓⲥⲙⲁⲧ ⲛ̄- ¹¹ ϣⲱ[ⲡ]ⲉ, ⲁⲧⲣⲟⲩⲱⲙⲥ̄ ϩⲁ ϩⲛ̄- ¹² ϭⲟⲙ ⲁⲩⲱ ϩⲁ ϩⲛⲛⲟⲩⲟⲩⲥⲓ[ⲁ] ¹³ ⲕⲁⲧⲁ
ⲡⲧⲱϣⲉ ⲙ̄ⲡϯ ⲁ[ϩⲛ] ¹⁴ ⲛⲟⲩⲉⲣⲏⲩ, ⲉⲩⲛ̄ⲧⲉⲩ ⲛ̄ⲧⲙⲛ̄[ⲧ]- ¹⁵ ⲙⲁⲉⲓⲟⲩⲉϩ ⲥⲁϩⲛⲉ ϩⲱⲟⲩ [ⲁⲛ] ¹⁶
ⲁⲩⲱ ϩⲛ̄ⲕⲉⲕⲟⲟⲩⲉ ⲁⲛ ⲧⲏⲣⲟⲩ ⲙ̄- ¹⁷ ⲡⲓⲣⲏⲧⲉ. ⲁⲃⲁⲗ ϩⲛ̄ ⲛⲉⲉⲓ ⲉⲥⲥⲱⲕ ¹⁸ ⲙ̄ⲙⲁⲩ ⲧⲏⲣⲟⲩ ⲛ̄ϭⲓ
ϯⲙⲛ̄ⲧ[ⲙⲁ]- ¹⁹ ⲉⲓⲉⲁ[ⲩ] ⲉⲧϣⲟⲩⲉⲓⲧ ⲁϩⲟ[ⲩⲛ] ²⁰ ⲁⲧⲉⲡⲓⲑⲩⲙⲓⲁ ⲛ̄ⲧⲙⲛ̄ⲧ[ⲙⲁ]- ²¹ ⲉⲓⲟⲩⲉϩ
ⲥⲁϩⲛⲉ, ⲉⲙⲛ̄ ⲟⲩ[ⲉⲉⲓ] ²² ⲙ̄ⲙⲁⲩ ⲉⲓⲣⲉ ⲙ̄ⲡⲙⲉⲉⲩ[ⲉ] ²³ ⲉⲧⲭ[ⲁ]ⲥⲓ ⲁⲩⲱ ⲥⲉⲣ̄ ϩⲟⲙ[ⲟ]- ²⁴ ⲗⲟⲅ̣ⲓ
ⲙⲙⲁϥ ⲉⲛ.

ϫⲉ ⲛⲓϭ[ⲁⲙ] ²⁵ ⲛ̄ⲧⲉ ⲡⲓⲙⲉⲩⲉ ⲛⲉⲩⲥ[ⲃⲧ]- ²⁶ ⲁⲉⲓⲧ ϩⲛ̄ ⲛⲓⲣⲉ ⲛ̄ⲡⲉⲧⲣ̄ ϣ[ⲣ̄ⲡ] ²⁷ ⲛ̄ϣⲱⲡⲉ, ⲛⲉⲉⲓ
ⲉⲧⲟⲩϣⲟ̣[ⲟⲡ] ²⁸ ⲛ̄ⲛⲉⲓⲛⲉ ⲛ̄ⲧⲉⲩ. ϫⲉ ϯⲧⲁⲝ̣[ⲓⲥ] ²⁹ ⲛ̄ⲇⲉ ⲛⲉⲉⲓ ⲙ̄ⲡⲓⲣⲏⲧⲉ ⲛ̄[ⲉ]ⲟⲩ- ³⁰ ⲛ̄ⲧⲉⲥ
ⲙ̄ⲙⲉⲩ ⲙ̄ⲡϯ ⲙⲉ̣ⲧⲉ ³¹ ϣⲁⲣⲁⲥ ⲙⲛ̄ ⲛⲉⲥⲉⲣⲏⲟⲩ, ⲛⲉⲥ- ³² ϯ ⲇⲉ ⲛⲧⲁϥ ⲟⲩⲃⲉ ϯⲧⲁⲝⲓⲥ ⲛ̄- ³³ ⲧⲉ ⲛⲁ
ⲡⲓⲧⲁⲛⲧⲛ̄, ⲉϯⲧⲁⲝⲓⲥ ³⁴ ⲛ̄ⲇⲉ [ⲛ]ⲁ ⲡⲓⲧⲁⲛⲧⲛ̄ ⲣ̄ ⲡⲟⲗⲉⲙⲟⲥ ³⁵ ⲟⲩⲃⲉ ⲛ̣[ⲓ]ⲉⲓⲛⲉ, ⲁⲩⲱ ⲉⲥⲉⲓⲣⲉ ³⁶
ⲟⲩⲃⲏ[ⲥ] ⲟⲩⲁⲉⲉⲧⲥ ⲉⲧⲃⲉ ⲧⲉⲥ- ³⁷ ⲙⲛ̄ⲧⲃⲁⲗⲉⲕϥ̄. ⁸⁵·¹ ⲁ[ⲃ]ⲁⲗ ⲙ̄ⲡⲉⲉⲓ ⲁⲥ ̣ [12–14] ²
ⲧⲉ ⲙ̄ⲙⲉⲛ ⲙ̄ⲙⲁⲩ [9–11 ⲟⲩ-] ³ ⲃⲉ ⲛⲟⲩⲉⲣⲏⲩ ϩⲁϩ[12–14] ⁴ ⲧⲁⲛⲁⲅⲕⲏ ⲕⲁⲩⲟⲩ ⲁ̣[12–14] ⁵ ⲁⲛ
ⲁⲧⲣⲟⲩⲁⲙⲁϩⲧⲉ [12–14] ⁶ ⲛⲁϥ ⲟⲩⲁϣⲓⲉ ⲉⲛ ⲡⲉ ⲟ̣[11–13] ⁷ ⲙⲛ̄ ⲡⲟⲩⲕⲱϩ ⲙⲛ̄
ⲧ̣[ⲟⲩ]ⲙ̣ⲛ̄ⲧⲃⲁ....⁸ ⲙⲛ̄ ⲧⲃⲗ̄ⲕⲉ ⲙⲛ̄ ⲧⲙⲛ̄ⲧⲭⲓ ⲛ̄ϭⲁⲛⲥ ⲙⲛ̄ ⲧ[ⲉ]- ⁹ ⲡⲓⲑⲩⲙⲓⲁ ⲙⲛ̄ ⲧⲙⲛ̄ⲧⲁⲧⲥⲁⲩⲛⲉ
ⲉⲥⲁⲙ[ⲁ]- ¹⁰ ϩⲧⲉ ⲉⲩⲭⲡⲟ ⲛ̄ϩⲛ̄ϩⲩⲗⲏ ⲉⲩϣ̄ⲃⲃⲓⲁⲉⲓⲧ ⲙ̄[ⲛ] ¹¹ ϩⲛ̄ϭⲟⲙ ⲙ̄ⲙⲓⲛⲉ ⲙⲓⲛⲉ, ⲉⲩⲧⲉϩⲧⲁϩⲧ̄
ⲉ̣[ⲩ]- ¹² ⲁϣ ⲙⲛ̄ ⲛⲟⲩⲉⲣⲏⲩ. ⲉⲡⲗⲟⲅⲟⲥ ⲉⲛⲧⲁϩϣⲱⲡⲉ ¹³ ⲛⲉⲩ ⲛ̄ⲗⲁⲉⲓⲥⲉ ⲛ̄ϫⲡⲟ, ⲉⲡϥ̄ⲛⲟⲩⲥ
ϭⲁϣⲧ̄ ¹⁴ ⲉϩⲟⲩⲛ ⲉⲡⲟⲩⲱⲛϩ̄ ⲁⲃⲁⲗ ⲛ̄ⲧⲉ ⲑ[ⲉⲗ]ⲡ̣[ⲓⲥ] ¹⁵ ⲉⲧⲛⲁϣⲱⲡⲉ ⲛⲉϥ ⲙ̄ⲡⲥⲁ ⲛϩⲣⲉ.

ϫⲉ ⲡⲗⲟⲅⲟ̣[ⲥ] ¹⁶ ⲉⲛⲧⲁϩⲕⲓⲙ ⲛ̣ⲉⲟⲩⲛⲧⲉϥ ⲙ̄ⲙⲉⲩ ⲛ̄- ¹⁷ ⲑⲉⲗⲡⲓⲥ ⲙⲛ̄ ⲡϭⲱϣⲧ̄ ⲁⲃⲁⲗ ⲁⲭⲱϥ ⲙ̄- ¹⁸
ⲡⲉⲧϫⲁⲥⲓ. ⲛⲁ ϯϩⲁⲉⲓⲃⲉⲥ ⲙⲉⲛ ⲁϥⲛⲁϩ- ¹⁹ ⲟⲩϥ ⲛ̄ⲥⲁⲃⲁⲗ ⲙ̄ⲙⲁⲩ ⲕⲁⲧⲁ ⲥⲙⲁⲧ ⲛⲓⲙ, ²⁰ ϩⲱⲥ ⲉⲩϯ
ⲟⲩⲃⲏϥ ⲁⲩⲱ ϩⲛ̄ⲁⲧⲉⲑⲃⲓⲁⲩ ²¹ ⲛⲉϥ ⲛⲉ ⲙ̄ⲡϣⲁ. ⲁϥⲙ̄ⲧⲁⲛ ⲇⲉ ⲙ̄ⲙⲁϥ ²² ⲁⲭⲛ̄ ⲛⲁ ⲡⲓⲙⲉⲉⲩⲉ.
ⲁⲩⲱ ⲡⲉⲉⲓ ⲉⲧⲕⲏ ²³ ⲁϩⲣⲏⲓ̈ ⲙ̄ⲡⲓⲣⲏⲧⲉ ⲁⲩⲱ ⲉϥϣⲟⲟⲡ ϩⲛ̄ ⲡⲓ- ²⁴ ⲧⲱϣⲉ ⲉⲧϫⲁⲥⲉ, ⲉϥⲉⲓⲣⲉ
ⲙ̄ⲡⲙⲉⲩ- ²⁵ ⲟⲩⲉ ⲙ̄ⲡⲉⲧⲁϩϣⲧⲁ, ⲁⲡⲗⲟⲅⲟⲥ ⲙⲓⲥⲉ ²⁶ ⲙ̄ⲙⲁϥ ϩⲛ̄ⲛ ⲟⲩⲙⲛ̄ⲧⲁⲧⲛⲉⲩ ⲁⲣⲁⲥ ²⁷ ϩⲛ̄
ⲛⲉⲧⲁϩϣⲱⲡⲉ ⲕⲁⲧⲁ ⲡⲓⲙⲉⲩⲉ, ⲕⲁⲧⲁ ²⁸ ⲡⲉⲉⲓ ⲉⲧⲉⲛⲉϥϣⲟⲟⲡ ⲛⲙⲙⲉⲩ ⲡⲉ, ²⁹ ϣⲁⲧⲉⲡⲟⲩⲁⲉⲓⲛ
ⲡⲣ̄ⲣⲉ ⲛⲉϥ ⲁⲃⲁⲗ ⲙ̄- ³⁰ ⲡⲥⲁ ⲛϩⲣⲏⲓ̈ ⲛ̄ⲣⲉϥⲧⲛ̄ϩⲟ, ⲡⲉⲉⲓ ⲛ̄ⲧⲁⲩⲭⲡⲁϥ ³¹ ⲁⲃⲁⲗ ϩⲙ̄ ⲡⲓⲙⲉⲩⲉ
ⲛⲧⲙⲛ̄ⲧⲛⲁⲓ̈ⲥⲁⲛ ³² ⲇⲉ ⲛ̄ⲛⲓⲡⲗⲏⲣⲱⲙⲁ ⲉⲧⲣ̄ ϣⲣ̄ⲡ ⲛ̄ϣⲟⲟⲡ.

³³ ϫⲉ ⲡⲓⲥⲗⲁⲧⲉ ⲉⲛⲧⲁϩϣⲱⲡⲉ ⲁⲛⲁⲓ̈ⲱ[ⲛ] ³⁴ ⲛ̄ⲧⲉ ⲡⲓⲱⲧ ⲛ̄ⲛⲓⲡⲧⲏⲣϥ̄ ⲉⲧⲉⲙ̄ⲡⲟⲩϣⲡ̄ ³⁵ ⲙ̄ⲕⲁϩ,
ⲁⲩⲭⲓⲧϥ̄ ⲁⲣⲁⲩ ϩⲱⲥ ⲉⲡⲟⲟⲩ ⲡⲉ ³⁶ ϩⲛ̄ⲛ ⲟⲩⲙⲛ̄<ⲧ>ϩⲁⲉⲓⲣⲁⲟⲩϣ ⲙⲛ̄ ⲟⲩⲙⲛ̄ⲧⲁⲧⲣ ⲃⲱ[ⲛ] ³⁷
ⲁⲩⲱ ϩⲛ̄ⲛ ⲟⲩⲙⲛ̄ⲧϩⲗϭⲉ ⲉⲛⲁϣⲱⲥ. ⁸⁶·¹ [ⲁⲩϫⲓⲧϥ̄ ⲛⲛⲓⲡ]ⲧⲏⲣϥ̄ ⲁⲧⲣⲟⲩⲧⲥⲉⲃⲟ ⲁⲡ- ² [ϣⲧⲁ

84.26 ⲙ̄ⲡⲉⲧⲣ̄: read ⲙ̄ⲛⲉⲧⲣ̄.
84.29 ⲛ̄ⲇⲉ: read ⲛ̄ⲧⲉ.
84.34 ⲛ̄ⲇⲉ: read ⲛ̄ⲧⲉ.
85.29 ϣⲁⲧⲉ: read ϣⲁⲛⲧⲉ.
85.32 ⲇⲉ: read ⲛ̄ⲧⲉ.
85.36 ⲙⲛ̄<ⲧ>ϩⲁⲉⲓⲣⲁⲟⲩϣ: read ⲙⲛ̄<ⲧ>ϥϩⲁⲉⲓⲣⲁⲟⲩϣ.

Bringing [forth] [7] first according to their birth, [8] the two orders fought with one another, [9] struggling for command [10] on account of their way of [11] being, with the result that they sunk below [12] powers and below substances [13] in accordance with the matter of the infighting, [14] having also a [15] love of power [16] and all other things of [17] this sort. [18] From these the vain love of glory lures [19] them all [20] to the desire for the love [21] of power, while not one [22] of them produces the exalted thought [23] or confesses [24] it.

The [powers] [25] of this thought were prepared [26] in the deeds of the preexistent <ones>, [27] those of which they [are] [28] the semblances. Since the [order] [29] of those of this kind had [30] agreement within [31] it, but it [32] fought against the order of [33] those belonging to the likeness, while the order [34] of [those] belonging to the likeness waged war [35] against these semblances, and it works [36] against it alone on account of its [37] anger. [85.1] From this it [. . .] [2] them [. . .] [3] against each other [. . .] [4] the necessity placed them for [. . .] [5] in order that they might prevail [. . .] [6] for him it was not a multitude [. . .] [7] and their jealousy and [their . . .] [8] and anger and brutality and [9] desire and clutching ignorance [10] produce empty matter and [11] powers of every kind, mixed in a [12] multitude with each other. Whereas the Word, who came to be [13] for them a cause of begetting, his mind stared [14] into the revelation of the [hope] [15] that would come to him from above.

The Word [16] that had moved had [17] hope and the anticipation of [18] the one who is exalted. From those belonging to the shadow he [19] separated himself in every manner, [20] since they fight against him and are greatly disrespectful [21] to him. He found comfort [22] in those belonging to the thought. And as for the one established [23] in this way and who is within the [24] exalted limit, remembering [25] the deficient one, the Word produced [26] him invisibly [27] among those that had come about according to the thought, according to [28] the one who was with them, [29] until the light radiated upon him from [30] above as a bringer of life, the one who has been begotten [31] by the thought of the brotherly love [32] of the preexistent fullnesses.

[33] The stumbling, which came to the eternities [34] of the Father of the entireties who did not endure [35] hardship, was given to them as though it were theirs [36] in a providential, innocent, [37] and abundantly sweet manner. [86.1] [It was given to the] entire-

аваλ ϩι]τοοτϥ̄ ⲙ̄ⲡⲓⲟⲩⲉⲉⲓ ⲡⲁ- ³ [ⲉⲓ ⲉⲧⲟⲩⲧⲁϫ]ⲣⲟ ⲧⲏⲣⲟⲩ ⲁⲃⲁλ ϩⲓ̈ⲧⲟⲟⲧϥ̄ ⁴ [ⲟⲩⲁⲉⲉⲧϥ̄]
ⲁλⲁϭ ⲛ̄ϣⲧⲁ.

ϫⲉ ϯⲧⲁ- ⁵ [ϫⲓⲥ ⲉⲧⲁϩϣ]ⲱⲡⲉ ⲛⲉϥ ⲛ̄ⲧⲁⲥϣⲱⲡⲉ ϩⲛ̄ ⁶ ⲛⲉⲧⲁϩⲡϣ[ⲧ] ⲁ[ⲡ]ϫⲓⲥⲉ
ⲙⲛ̄ ⲡⲉⲧⲁϩⲛⲧϥ̄ ⲛⲉϥ ⁷ ⲁⲃⲁλ ⲙ̄ⲙⲟϥ ⲁⲩⲱ ⲁⲃⲁλ ϩⲙ̄ ⲡⲭⲱⲕ ⲧⲏⲣϥ̄. ⁸ ⲡⲉⲧⲁϩⲡⲱⲧ ⲙⲉⲛ
ⲁⲡϫⲓⲥⲉ ⲁϥϣⲱⲡⲉ ⲛ̄ⲣⲉϥ- ⁹ ⲥⲁⲡⲥⲡ ϩⲁ ⲡⲉⲧⲁϩⲣ̄ ϣⲧⲁ ⲟⲩⲃⲉ ⲧⲡⲣⲟ- ¹⁰ ⲃⲟλⲏ ⲛ̄ⲧⲉ ⲛⲁⲓⲱⲛ
ⲉⲛⲧⲁϩϣⲱⲡⲉ ⲕⲁⲧ[ⲁ] ¹¹ ⲛⲉⲧϣⲟⲟⲡ. ⲛ̄ⲧⲁⲩ ⲛ̄ⲇⲉ ⲛ̄ⲧⲁⲣⲉϥⲥⲉⲛ- ¹² ⲥⲱⲡⲟⲩ, ⲁⲩϯ ⲙⲉⲧⲉ ⲙⲛ̄
ⲟⲩⲣⲉϣⲉ ⲙⲛ̄- ¹³ ⲛ̄ ⲟⲩⲱϣⲉ ⲉϩⲛⲉⲩ, ⲙⲛ̄ ϩⲛ̄ⲥⲩⲙⲫⲱⲛⲓⲁ ¹⁴ ⲙ̄ⲡϯ ⲙⲉⲧⲉ, ⲁⲧⲣⲟⲩⲣ̄ ⲃⲟⲏⲑⲓⲁ
ⲁⲡⲉ[ⲧⲁϩ]- ¹⁵ ⲣ̄ ϣⲧⲁ. ⲁⲅⲉⲓ ⲁⲩⲙⲁ ⲙⲛ̄ ⲛⲟⲩⲉⲣⲏⲟⲩ, ¹⁶ ⲉⲩⲣ̄ ⲁⲓⲧⲓ ⲙ̄ⲡⲓⲱⲧ ϩⲛ̄ⲛ ⲟⲩⲙⲉⲉⲩⲉ ⲉⲩⲣ̄
ϣⲉⲩ ¹⁷ ⲁⲧⲣⲉⲥϣⲱⲡⲉ ⲛ̄ϭⲓ ϯⲃⲟⲏⲑⲓⲁ ⲁⲃⲁλ ⲙ̄- ¹⁸ ⲡⲥⲁ ⲛϩⲣⲏⲓ̈, ⲛ̄ⲧⲟⲟⲧϥ̄ ⲙ̄ⲡⲓⲱⲧ, ⲁⲩⲉⲁⲩ ⲛⲉϥ,
¹⁹ ϩⲱⲥ ⲉⲛⲉϥⲛⲁϣ ϫⲱⲕ ⲛ̄ⲕⲉⲣⲏⲧⲉ ⲉⲛ ⲛ̄ϭⲓ ²⁰ ⲡⲉⲛⲧⲁϩⲣ̄ ϣⲧⲁ, ⲉⲓⲙⲏⲧⲓ ϥⲣ̄ ϩⲛⲉϥ ⲛ̄ϭⲓ ⲡⲓ- ²¹
ⲡλⲏⲣⲱⲙⲁ ⲙ̄ⲡⲓⲱⲧ, ⲉⲛⲧⲁϥⲥⲁⲕϥ̄ ⲛⲉϥ ²² ⲛ̄ϥⲟⲩⲁⲛϩϥ̄ ⲁⲩⲱ ⲛ̄ϥϯ ⲙ̄ⲡⲉⲧⲁϩⲣ̄ ²³ ϣⲧⲁ. ⲁⲃⲁλ
ϭⲉ ϩⲛ̄ ⲡⲓϯ ⲙⲉⲧⲉ, ϩⲛ̄ⲛ ⲟⲩ- ²⁴ ⲱϣⲉ ⲙ̄ⲡⲣⲉϣⲉ ⲉⲛⲧⲁϩϣⲱⲡⲉ, ⲁⲩ- ²⁵ ⲉⲓⲛⲉ ⲁⲃⲁλ ⲙ̄ⲡⲓⲕⲁⲣⲡⲟⲥ
ⲉⲩⲭⲡⲟ ²⁶ ⲛ̄ⲧⲉ ϯⲙⲛ̄ϯ ⲙⲉⲧⲉ ⲡⲉ ⲉⲟⲩⲉⲉⲓ ²⁷ ⲛ̄ⲟⲩⲱⲧ ⲡⲉ ⲉⲡⲁ ⲛⲓⲡⲧⲏⲣϥ̄ ⲡⲉ, ⲉϥⲟⲩ- ²⁸ ⲱⲛϩ̄
ⲁⲃⲁλ ⲙ̄ⲡⲓⲙⲟⲩⲛⲕ̄ ϩⲣⲟ ⲛ̄ⲇⲉ ²⁹ ⲡⲓⲱⲧ ⲉⲧⲉⲁⲩⲙⲉⲩⲉ ⲁⲣⲁϥ ⲛ̄ϭⲓ ⲛⲁⲓⲱⲛ, ³⁰ ⲉⲩϯ ⲉⲁⲩ ⲉⲩⲧⲱⲃϩ̄
ⲛ̄ⲧⲃⲟⲏⲑⲓⲁ ⲙ̄ⲡⲟⲩ- ³¹ ⲥⲁⲛ ϩⲛ̄ ϯⲅⲛⲱⲙⲏ ⲉⲛⲧⲁⲡⲓⲱⲧ ⲁⲡϥ̄ ³² ⲙ̄ⲙⲉⲩ ⲁⲣⲁⲥ. ϩⲱⲥ ϩⲛ̄ ⲟⲩⲱϣⲉ
ⲙⲛ̄ ³³ ⲟⲩⲣⲉϣⲉ ⲉⲩϣⲁⲉⲓⲛⲉ ⲙ̄ⲡⲓⲕⲁⲣ- ³⁴ ⲡⲟⲥ ⲉⲃⲟλ. ⲁⲩⲱ ⲡⲓϯ ⲙⲉⲧⲉ ⲛ̄ⲧⲉ ³⁵ ⲡⲟⲩⲱⲛϩ̄ ⲛ̄ⲧⲉ
ⲡⲙⲟⲩϫϭ ⲛ̄ⲧⲉϥ ³⁶ ⲛ̄ⲙⲙⲉⲩ, ⲉⲧⲉ ⲡϣⲏⲣⲉ ⲡⲉ ³⁷ ⲛ̄ⲇⲉ ⲡⲟⲩⲱϣⲉ ⲛ̄ⲧⲉϥ, ⲁϥⲟⲩⲁⲛϩϥ̄. ⁸⁷·¹
ⲁⲡϣⲏⲣⲉ ⲛ̄ⲇⲉ ⲡⲱⲕ ⲛ̄ϩⲏⲧ ⲛ̄ⲇⲉ ² ⲛⲓⲡⲧⲏⲣϥ̄ ⲁϥⲧⲉⲉⲓϥ ⲛ̄ⲟⲩϩⲃⲥⲟⲩ ³ ϩⲓ̈ⲱⲟⲩ, ⲡⲉⲉⲓ ⲉⲧⲉ
ⲁⲃⲁλ ϩⲓ̈ⲧⲟⲟⲧϥ̄ ⁴ ⲁϥϯ ⲙ̄ⲡⲭⲱⲕ ⲙ̄ⲡⲉⲛⲧⲁϩⲣ̄ ϣⲧⲁ, ⁵ ⲁⲩⲱ ⲁϥϯ ⲙ̄ⲡⲧⲁⲭⲣⲟ ⲛ̄ⲛⲉⲧϫⲏⲕ, ⁶
ⲡⲉⲉⲓ ⲉⲧⲟⲩⲙⲟⲩⲧⲉ ⲁⲣⲁϥ ϩⲛ̄ⲛ ⲟⲩⲙⲛ̄ⲧ- ⁷ ϫⲁⲉⲓⲥ ϫⲉ « ⲥⲱⲧⲏⲣ » ⲁⲩⲱ « ⲡⲣⲉϥⲥⲱⲧⲉ » ⁸
ⲁⲩⲱ « ⲡⲉⲩⲇⲟⲕⲏⲧⲟⲥ » ⲁⲩⲱ « ⲡⲓⲙⲛ̄ⲣⲓⲧ, » ⁹ « ⲡⲁⲉⲓ ⲉⲧⲁⲩϯ ϩⲟ ⲁⲣⲁϥ » ⲁⲩⲱ
« ⲡⲭⲣⲓⲥⲧⲟⲥ » ⲁⲩⲱ ¹⁰ « ⲡⲟⲩⲁⲉⲓⲛ ⲛ̄ⲛⲉⲧⲧⲏϣ, » ⲕⲁⲧⲁ ⲛⲉⲧⲁⲩ- ¹¹ ⲛ̄ⲧϥ̄ ⲁⲃⲁλ ⲙ̄ⲙⲁⲩⲟⲩ,
ⲉⲁϥϣⲱⲡⲉ ⲛ̄- ¹² ⲛⲓⲣⲉⲛ ⲛ̄ⲛⲓⲙⲛ̄<ⲧ>ⲉϩⲟ ⲁⲣⲉⲧϥ̄ <ⲉⲧ>ⲧⲟⲉⲓ ¹³ ⲁⲣⲁϥ. ⲏ ⲟⲩ ⲅⲁⲣ ⲡⲉ ⲡⲕⲉⲣⲉⲛ
ⲁⲭⲟⲟϥ ¹⁴ ⲁⲣⲁϥ ⲛ̄ⲥⲁ ⲡϣⲏⲣⲉ, ⲛ̄ⲑⲉ ⲉⲧⲁⲛϣⲣ̄ⲡ ¹⁵ ⲛ̄ϫⲟⲟⲥ, ⲉⲡⲉⲓ ⲡⲉ ⲡⲥⲁⲩⲛⲉ ⲛ̄- ¹⁶ ⲧⲉ ⲡⲓⲱⲧ
ⲉⲛⲧⲁϥⲟⲩⲱϣⲉ ⲁⲧⲣⲟⲩⲥⲟⲩ- ¹⁷ ⲱⲛϥ̄;

ϫⲉ ⲟⲩ ⲙⲟⲛⲟⲛ ϫⲉ ϩⲁⲛⲛⲁⲓⲱⲛ ¹⁸ ⲭⲡⲟ ⲙ̄ⲡⲙⲟⲩ<ⲛ>ⲕ ⲛ̄ϩⲟ ⲛ̄ⲇⲉ ⲡⲓⲱⲧ ⲉⲛⲧⲁⲩ- ¹⁹ ϯ ⲉⲁⲩ
ⲛⲉϥ, ⲡⲉⲧⲥⲏϩ ϫⲛ̄ ⲛ̄ϣⲁⲣⲡ̄, ⲁλⲗⲁ ²⁰ ⲁⲩⲭⲡⲟ ⲙ̄ⲡⲟⲟⲩ ϩⲱⲟⲩ ⲁⲛ, ϫⲉ ⲛⲉ<ⲓ>ⲁⲓⲱⲛ ²¹ ⲛⲉⲉⲓ ⲉⲧϯ
ⲉⲁⲩ ⲁⲩⲭⲡⲟ ⲙ̄ⲡⲟⲩⲙ<ⲟⲩⲛ>ⲕ̄ ⲛ̄- ²² ϩⲟ ⲙⲛ̄ ⲡⲟⲩϩⲟ. ⲁⲩⲭⲡⲁⲩ ⲛ̄ⲛⲟⲩⲙⲛ̄ⲧ- ²³ ⲙⲁⲧⲁⲉⲓ ⲛⲉϥ,
ⲙ̄ⲡⲣⲏⲧⲉ ⲛ̄ⲛⲟⲩⲣ̄ⲣⲟ, ²⁴ ⲉⲛⲁ ⲡⲓⲙⲉⲩⲉ ⲉⲩⲛ̄ⲧⲉⲩ ⲛ̄ⲛⲟⲩⲙⲛ̄ⲧ- ²⁵ ϣⲃⲏⲣ ⲛ̄ⲛⲁⲙⲁⲥⲧⲉ ⲁⲩⲱ
ⲟⲩⲙⲛ̄ϯ ⲙⲉ- ²⁶ ⲧⲉ ϩⲛ̄ⲛ ⲟⲩⲙⲟⲩϫϭ. ⲁⲅⲉⲓ ⲁⲃⲁλ ²⁷ ⲛ̄ⲛⲟⲩϩⲟ ⲉϥⲟ ⲛ̄ϩⲁϩ {ⲛ̄ϩⲁϩ} ⲛ̄ϩⲟ, ϫⲉ- ²⁸
ⲕⲁⲥⲉ ⲡⲉⲧⲟⲩⲛⲁⲣ̄ ⲃⲟⲏⲓ ⲛⲉϥ ⲁϥ- ²⁹ ⲛⲁⲛⲉⲩ ⲁⲛⲉⲧⲁϥⲧⲱⲃϩ̄ ⲙ̄ⲙⲁⲩ ³⁰ ⲛ̄ⲧⲃⲟⲏⲑⲓⲁ. ϥⲛⲉⲩ ⲁⲛ
ⲁⲡⲉⲧⲁϩ- ³¹ ⲧⲉⲉⲥ ⲛⲉϥ.

86.6 ⲛⲉⲧⲁϩⲡϣ[ⲧ]: read ⲡⲉⲧⲁϩⲡϣ[ⲧ].
86.28 ⲛ̄ⲇⲉ: read ⲛ̄ⲧⲉ.
87.1 ⲛ̄ⲇⲉ: read ⲛ̄ⲧⲉ.
87.8 ⲙ̄ⲛ̄ⲣⲓⲧ: read ⲙⲉⲣⲓⲧ.
87.18 ⲛ̄ⲇⲉ: read ⲛ̄ⲧⲉ.

ties so that they might learn about the [2] [deficiency] caused by the one from whom [3] [alone] they all were [strengthened] [4] to put an end to deficiency.

The [5] [order that] was his came about from [6] <the one> who rushed to [the] height and the one that brought itself forth from him [7] and from the entire perfection. [8] The one who rushed to the height became an [9] intercessor for the one who introduced deficiency with the [10] emanation of the eternities that had come to be according to [11] the things that exist. After he prayed [12] to them, they approved with joy and [13] contentment, since they were pleased, and with one [14] accord, so that they would help the [15] deficient one. They came to a place together, [16] requesting from the Father with a virtuous thought [17] that assistance would come from [18] above, from the Father, for his glory, [19] since the deficient one would not be able to be made perfect any other way, [20] unless it was willed by the [21] fullness of the Father, which he had drawn to himself, [22] revealed, and given to the [23] deficient one. Then from the agreement, in a [24] joyful contentment that had come to be, they [25] brought forth the fruit, which was the product [26] of the agreement, being a unity, [27] the property of the entireties, [28] revealing the countenance of [29] the Father, about whom the eternities thought, [30] giving glory and praying for assistance for their [31] brother in an opinion concerning which the Father counted himself [32] with them. Thus with contentment and [33] joy they bring forth the [34] fruit. And the agreement of [35] the revelation of his mixing [36] with them, which is [37] his beloved Son, he revealed. [87.1] The Son of the goodwill of [2] the entireties draped himself upon them as a garment, [3] through which [4] he gave perfection to the one who was deficient, [5] and he gave strength to those who are perfect, [6] this one who is properly called [7] "Savior" and "Redeemer" [8] and "Well-Pleasing" and "Beloved," [9] "the one to whom prayers have been given" and "Christ" [10] and "the Light of those ordained," in accordance with those [11] from whom he was brought forth, because he has become the [12] names of the assignments given [13] to him. Still, what other name can be assigned [14] to him except "Son," which we said earlier, [15] since he is the knowledge of [16] the Father whom he wanted them to [17] know?

Not only did the eternities [18] produce the countenance of the Father whom they [19] glorified, as was written before, but [20] they produced their own as well, since the eternities [21] that glorified produced their countenance [22] and face. They were produced as an [23] army for him, as if for a king, [24] since those belonging to thought have a [25] powerful partnership and a blended [26] unity. They came forth [27] as a face with many expressions, so that [28] the one that was to receive assistance [29] might see those to whom he had prayed [30] for assistance. Moreover, he sees the one that [31] gave it to him.

ⲭⲉ ⲡⲓⲕⲁⲣⲡⲟⲥ ⲉⲧⲁⲛ- [32] ⲣ̄ ϣⲣⲡ̄ ⲛ̄ϫⲟⲟⲥ ⲛ̄ⲧⲉ ⲧ̄ⲙⲛ̄ⲧ̄ ⲙⲉ- [33] ⲧⲉ ⲛⲉϥ, ϩⲁ ⲧⲉϩⲟⲩⲥⲓⲁ ⲛ̄ⲧⲉ ⲛⲓⲡⲧⲏ- [34] ⲣϥ̄. ⲡⲓⲱⲧ ⲛ̄ⲅⲁⲣ ⲁϥⲕⲱ ⲛ̄ϩⲏⲧϥ̄ ⲛ̄- [35] ⲛⲓⲡⲧⲏⲣϥ̄ ⲉⲓⲧⲉ ⲛⲉⲧⲣ̄ ϣⲁⲣⲡ̄ ⲛ̄ϣⲱⲡⲉ [36] ⲉⲓⲇⲉ ⲛⲉⲧϣⲟⲟⲡ ⲉⲓⲧⲉ ⲛⲉⲧⲛⲁϣⲱⲡⲉ. [88.1] ⲛⲉⲩϣⲓⲕⲁⲛⲟⲥ ⲡⲉ. ⲁϥⲟⲩⲱⲛϩ̄ [2] ⲁⲃⲁⲗ ⲛ̄ⲛⲉⲛⲧⲁϥⲕⲁⲁⲩ ⲛ̄ϩⲏⲧϥ̄. [3] ⲙ̄ⲡⲉϥⲧⲉⲧⲟⲩ, ⲉⲁϥⲣ̄ ⲉⲡⲓⲧⲣⲉⲡⲉⲓ ⲛⲉϥ. [4] ⲁϥⲣ̄ ϩⲙ̄ⲙⲉ ⲁⲧⲟⲓⲕⲟⲛⲟⲙⲓⲁ ⲙ̄ⲡⲧⲏⲣϥ̄ [5] ⲕⲁⲧⲁ ⲧ̄ⲉϩⲟⲩⲥⲓⲁ ⲉⲧⲧⲟⲉⲓ ⲛⲉϥ [6] ϫⲛ̄ ⲛ̄ϣⲁⲣⲡ̄ ⲙⲛ̄ ⲧϭⲟⲙ ⲛ̄ⲇⲉ ⲡⲓϩⲱⲃ. ⲡⲉ- [7] ⲉⲓ <ⲡⲉ> ⲡⲣⲏⲧⲉ ⲉⲛⲧⲁϥⲣ̄ ϩⲏⲧⲥ̄ ⲉⲛⲧⲁϥⲉⲓⲣⲉ [8] ⲙ̄ⲡⲟⲩⲱⲛϩ̄ ⲛ̄ⲧⲉϥ.

ⲭⲉ ⲡⲉⲉⲓ ⲉⲧⲉ- [9] ⲣⲉⲡⲓⲱⲧ ϣⲟⲟⲡ ⲛ̄ϩⲏⲧϥ̄, ⲁⲩⲱ ⲡⲉⲉⲓ [10] ⲉⲧⲉⲣⲉⲛⲓⲡⲧⲏⲣϥ̄ ϣⲟⲟⲡ ⲛ̄ϩⲏⲧϥ̄, ⲁϥⲉ- [11] ⲉⲓϥ ⲛ̄ϣⲁⲣⲡ̄ ⲁⲡⲁⲉⲓ ⲉⲧⲉⲛⲁϥϣⲁⲁⲧ [12] ⲛ̄ⲧⲟⲛⲛⲉϥ. ⲁϥⲧⲥⲉⲃⲁϥ ⲁⲛⲉⲉⲓ ⲉⲧⲁⲛⲁϥ- [13] ϣⲓⲛⲉ ⲛ̄ⲥⲁ ⲡⲟⲩϭⲛ̄ⲛⲉϥ ⲛ̄ϩⲱ, ⲁⲃⲁⲗ ϩⲓ̈- [14] ⲧⲛ̄ ⲡ̄ⲣⲣⲉ ⲙ̄ⲡⲟⲩⲁⲉⲓⲛ ⲉⲧⲙ̄ⲙⲉⲩ ⲉⲧ- [15] ϫⲏⲕ ⲁⲃⲁⲗ. ⲁϥϫⲁⲕϥ̄ ⲁⲃⲁⲗ ⲛ̄ϣⲁⲣⲡ̄ [16] ⲙ̄ⲡⲓⲣⲉϣⲉ ⲛ̄ⲁⲧϣⲉϫⲉ ⲁⲣⲁϥ. ⲁϥ- [17] ϫⲁⲕϥ̄ ⲛⲉϥ ⲁⲃⲁⲗ ⲛ̄ⲛⲟⲩⲡⲉⲧϫⲏⲕ, [18] ⲁⲩⲱ ⲁϥ† ⲛⲉϥ ⲁⲛ ⲙ̄ⲡⲓⲕⲁⲧⲁ ⲟⲩⲉⲉⲓ [19] ⲟⲩⲉⲉⲓ. ⲡⲁⲉⲓ ⲅⲁⲣ ⲡⲉ ⲡⲧⲱϣⲉ ⲙ̄- [20] ⲡϣⲁⲣⲡ̄ ⲛ̄ⲣⲉϣⲉ. ⲁⲩⲱ ⲁⲛⲥⲓⲧⲉ [21] ⲁⲛ ⲛ̄ϩⲣⲏⲓ ⲛ̄ϩⲏⲧϥ̄ ϩⲛ̄ ⲟⲩⲙⲛ̄ⲧⲁⲧⲛⲉⲩⲥ [22] ⲁⲣⲁⲥ ⲛ̄ⲛⲟⲩⲗⲟⲅⲟⲥ ⲉϥⲧⲛϣ ⲛ̄ⲛⲟⲩ- [23] ⲉⲡⲓⲥⲧⲏⲙⲁ. ⲁⲩⲱ ⲁϥ† ⲛⲉϥ ⲛ̄ⲟⲩϭⲁⲙ [24] ⲁⲧⲣⲉϥⲡⲱⲣϫ̄ ϥⲛⲟⲩϩⲉ ⲁⲃⲁⲗ ⲙ̄ⲙⲁϥ [25] ⲛ̄ⲛⲉⲧ{ⲧ}ⲟⲉⲓ ⲛ̄ⲛⲁⲧⲣ̄ ⲡⲓⲑⲉ ⲛⲉϥ. [26] ⲡⲉⲉⲓ ⲙⲉⲛ ⲡⲉ ⲡⲣⲏⲧⲉ ⲉⲛⲧⲁϥϫⲁⲉⲓⲁϥ [27] ⲁⲃⲁⲗ ⲙ̄ⲙⲓⲛ ⲙ̄ⲙⲟϥ ⲛⲉϥ. ⲛⲁⲉⲓ ⲛ̄ⲇⲉ [28] ⲛ̄ⲧⲁⲩ ⲛ̄ⲧⲁϩϣⲱⲡⲉ ⲉⲧⲃⲛⲛⲧϥ̄ ⲁϥⲟⲩ- [29] ⲱⲛϩ̄ ⲛⲉⲩ ⲛ̄ⲛⲟⲩⲥⲙⲁⲧ ⲛ̄ϫⲱⲃⲉ [30] ⲙ̄ⲙⲁⲩ. ⲁⲩⲉⲓⲣⲉ ϩⲛ̄ⲛ ⲟⲩⲙⲛ̄ⲧ† [31] ϣϭⲁ ⲛⲉⲩ, ⲉϥⲟⲩⲱⲛϩ̄ ⲙ̄ⲙⲁϥ ⲛⲉⲩ [32] ⲛ̄<ⲥ>ϣⲛⲉ, ⲉϥⲥⲱⲕ ⲙ̄ⲙⲁϥ ⲛⲉϥ [33] ⲕⲁⲧⲁ ⲡⲥⲙⲁⲧ ⲛ̄ⲣ̄ⲛⲃⲃⲣⲏϭⲉ. ⲁⲩⲱ [34] ⲙ̄ⲡϩⲗⲏⲙ ⲁⲃⲁⲗ ⲉⲧⲉⲩⲛ̄ⲧⲉϥⲩ ϣⲁ [35] ⲛⲟⲩⲉⲣⲏⲩ ⲉⲁϥⲗⲱ, ⲁϥⲗⲁϭϥ̄ ⲛ̄- [89.1] ϩⲣⲏⲓ ϩⲛ̄ ⲡⲓⲟⲩⲱⲛϩ̄ ⟦ⲁ⟧ⲃ⟦ⲁⲗ⟧ ⲁⲡⲥϣⲛⲉ, [2] ⲡⲉⲉⲓ ⲉⲧⲉⲛ̄ⲥⲉⲧⲁⲙⲁⲉⲓⲧ ⲁⲣⲁϥ ⲉⲛ, [3] ⲉⲛⲥⲉϭⲁϣⲧ̄ ⲁⲃⲁⲗ ⲁϫⲱϥ ⲉⲛ, ⲉⲙ- [4] ⲡⲟⲩⲥⲟⲩⲱⲛϥ̄. ⲉⲧⲃⲉ ⲡⲉⲉⲓ ⲁⲩⲧⲣⲉⲩ- [5] ⲣ̄ ϩⲟⲧⲉ, ⲁⲩϩⲁⲉⲓⲉ ⲁϩⲣⲏⲓ, ⲉⲙⲡⲟⲩϣ [6] ϭⲓ ϩⲁ ⲡⲣⲟϭ ⲙ̄ⲡⲟⲩⲁⲉⲓⲛ ⲉⲧ† ⲉϩⲟⲩⲛ ⲁ- [7] ϩⲣⲉⲩ. ⲡⲓⲧⲁⲅⲙⲁ ⲇⲉ ⲥⲛⲉⲩ ⲛⲉⲩⲙⲛ̄<ⲧ>- [8] † ϣϭⲁ ⲛⲉⲩ ⲡⲉ ⲡⲉⲧⲁ<ϩ>ⲟⲩⲱⲛϩ̄. ⲙ̄ⲡⲓⲣⲏⲧⲉ [9] ⲇⲉ ⲛ̄ⲇⲉ ⲛⲁ ⲡⲓⲙⲉⲉⲩⲉ ⲛⲉⲁⲩ† ⲣⲉⲛ [10] « ⲛ̄ⲛⲟⲩϣⲏⲙ, » ϩⲱⲥ ⲉⲩⲛ̄ⲧⲉⲩ ⲙ̄ⲙⲉⲩ [11] ⲛ̄ⲛⲟⲩⲙⲉⲩⲉ ϣⲏⲙ ϫⲉ ⲟⲩⲛ̄ⲧⲉⲩ ⲡⲉⲧ- [12] ϫⲁⲥⲓ,— ϥϣⲟⲟⲡ ϩⲁ ⲧⲉⲩⲉϩⲏ,—ⲁⲩⲱ ⲉⲩⲛ̄- [13] ⲧⲉⲩ ⲙ̄ⲙⲉⲩ ⲉⲩⲥⲓⲧⲉ ⲛ̄ϩⲏⲧⲟⲩ ⲙ̄ⲡⲛ̄- [14] ⲉⲓⲱⲣⲙ̄ ⲁⲃⲁⲗ ⲁϫⲱϥ ⲙ̄ⲡⲉⲧϫⲁⲥⲉ ⲉⲧ- [15] ⲛⲁⲟⲩⲱⲛϩ̄ ⲁⲃⲁⲗ. ⲉⲧⲃⲉ ⲡⲉⲉⲓ ⲁⲩⲣ̄ ⲁⲥ- [16] ⲡⲁⲍⲉ ⲛ̄ⲧⲉϥϭⲓⲛⲟⲩⲱⲛϩ̄ ⲁⲃⲁⲗ, ⲁⲩⲱ [17] ⲁⲩⲟⲩⲱϣⲧ̄ ⲙ̄ⲙⲁϥ. ⲁⲩϣⲱⲡⲉ ⲙ̄ⲙⲛ̄- [18] ⲧⲣⲉ ⲛⲉⲩ ⲛ̄ⲅⲛⲱⲙⲏ. ⲁⲩⲣ̄ ϩⲟⲙⲟⲗⲟⲅⲓ [19] ⲙ̄ⲡⲟⲩⲁⲉⲓⲛ ⲉⲛⲧⲁϩϣⲱⲡⲉ ⲉⲩϫⲱ- [20] ⲣⲉ ⲁⲛⲉⲧ† ⲟⲩⲃⲏⲟⲩ ⲡⲉ. ⲛⲁ ⲡⲓ- [21] ⲧⲁⲛⲧⲛ̄ ⲇⲉ ⲛ̄ⲧⲁⲩ [22] ⲁⲩⲧⲣⲣⲉ ⲙ̄ⲡϣⲁ, ϩⲱⲥ ⲉⲙⲡⲟⲩϣ ⲥⲱⲧⲙ̄ ⲁⲃⲁⲗ ⲁϫⲱϥ [23] ⲛ̄ⲧⲁⲣⲭⲏ, ϫⲉ ⲟⲩⲛ ⲟⲩϩⲱ ⲙ̄ⲡⲓⲣⲏ- [24] ⲧⲏ ⲡⲉ. ⲉⲧⲃⲉ ⲡⲉⲉⲓ ⲁⲩϩⲁⲉⲓⲉ ⲁϩⲣⲏⲓ [25] ⲁⲡϣⲓⲕⲉ ⲡⲉ ⲛ̄ⲧⲙⲛ̄ⲧⲁⲧⲥⲁⲩⲛⲉ, [26] ⲉⲧⲉ ⲡⲉⲧⲟⲩⲙⲟⲩⲧⲉ ⲁⲣⲁϥ ϫⲉ « ⲡⲕⲉⲕⲉⲓ » [27] {ϩ}ⲉⲧϩⲉ ⲥⲁ ⲛⲃⲟⲗ ⲁⲩⲱ « ⲡⲭⲁⲟⲩⲥ » ⲁⲩⲱ [28] « ⲉⲙⲛ̄ⲧⲉ » ⲁⲩⲱ « ⲡⲛⲟⲩⲛ. » ⲁϥⲕⲱ ⲙ̄ⲡⲥⲁ ⲛ̄- [29] ϩⲣⲏⲓ ⲙ̄ⲡⲇⲁⲅⲙⲁ ⲛ̄ⲇⲉ ⲛⲁ ⲡⲓ- [30] ⲙⲉⲩⲉ ϩⲱⲥ ⲉⲁϥϣⲱⲡⲉ ⲉϥ- [31] ϫⲱⲣⲉ ⲁⲣⲁⲟⲩ. ⲁⲩⲣ̄ ⲁⲍⲓⲟⲩ ⲁⲧⲣⲟⲩ- [32] ϣⲱⲡⲉ ⲉⲩⲣ̄ ⲁⲣⲭⲉⲥⲑⲁⲓ ⲁϫⲛ̄ ⲡⲕⲉⲕⲉⲓ [33]

88.6 ⲛ̄ⲇⲉ: read ⲛ̄ⲧⲉ.
88.20 ⲁⲛⲥⲓⲧⲉ: read ⲁϥⲥⲓⲧⲉ.
88.32 ⲛⲉϥ: read ⲛⲉⲩ.
89.6 ⲡ̄ⲣⲟϭ: read ⲡϣϭⲁ?
89.9 ⲛ̄ⲇⲉ: read ⲛ̄ⲧⲉ.
89.18 ⲛⲉⲩ: read ⲛⲉϥ.
89.29 ⲛ̄ⲇⲉ: read ⲛ̄ⲧⲉ.

The fruit of the agreement with him, which we [32] previously discussed, [33] is under the authority of the entireties. [34] For the Father has placed [35] the entireties within him, whether those that preexist, [36] those that are, or those that will be. [88.1] He was able (to do it). He revealed [2] those he placed within him. [3] In his giving of them, he entrusted (them) to him. [4] He guided the arrangement of the entirety [5] according to the authority given to him [6] from the beginning and according to the power of the matter. This [7] <is> how he acted and brought about [8] his revelation.

As for the one [9] in whom the Father exists, and the one [10] within whom the entirety exists, he created [11] him before the one who lacked [12] vision. He taught him about those who were [13] looking for their ability to see, through [14] the radiance of that [15] perfect light. He perfected him first [16] with ineffable joy. He [17] perfected him for himself as one who is perfect, [18] and, moreover, he give him what is suitable for each [19] one. For this is the manner of [20] the first joy. And <he> sowed [21] within him invisibly [22] a word ordained for [23] knowledge. And he gave him an ability [24] to separate and cast away from himself [25] those who are disobedient to him. [26] In this way he displayed [27] himself to him. But to those [28] who came about on account of him he [29] revealed a form inaccessible [30] to them. They acted with hostility [31] among themselves, when suddenly he revealed himself to them, [32] drawing himself to <them> [33] in the form of lightning. And [34] after he stopped the altercation they had with [35] each other, he remedied it [89.1] with the sudden revelation, [2] which they were not told about, [3] did not see (coming), and [4] did not know about. For this reason they were [5] afraid, and they fell down, since they were not able to [6] endure the strike from the light that shone down [7] upon them. What appeared was a [8] strike to the two orders. Just as [9] those belonging to thought had received the name [10] "small," so too do they have [11] a small-minded thought that they have the [12] exalted one—he preexists them—and yet they [13] have sown within them an [14] astonishment at the exalted one who [15] will become revealed. For this reason they [16] welcomed his revelation, and [17] they worshipped him. They became [18] resolute witnesses to <him.> They acknowledged [19] the light that had come to be as something stronger [20] than those who opposed them. Those belonging to the [21] likeness were greatly frightened, [22] since they were not able to hear about him [23] in the beginning, that there is a countenance [24] like this. For this reason they fell down [25] into the depth of ignorance, [26] which is called "the Outer Darkness" [27] and "Chaos" and [28] "Hell" and "the Abyss." He established what was [29] beneath the order of those belonging to the [30] thought, since it was [31] stronger than they are. They were worthy of [32] becoming rulers over the ineffable darkness, [33] since it is theirs, [34] and it is the lot

ⲛ̄ⲛⲁⲧⲭⲟⲟⲩ, ϩⲱⲥ ⲉⲡⲉⲧⲉ ⲡⲟⲟⲩ ⲡⲉ, [34] ⲁⲩⲱ ⲡⲕⲗⲏⲣⲟⲥ ⲉⲛⲧⲁϩⲧⲉϩⲁⲩ ⲡⲉ. ⲁϥⲕⲁ- [35] ⲁϥ ⲛⲉⲩ ⲭⲉ ⲥⲉⲛⲁⲣ̄ ϣⲉⲩ ϩⲱⲟⲩ ⲁⲧⲟⲓ- [36] ⲕⲟⲛⲟⲙⲓⲁ ⲉⲧⲁϣⲱⲡⲉ, [90.1] ⲧⲁⲉⲓ ⲉⲛⲧⲁϥⲁⲃⲱⲟⲩ ⲁⲣⲁⲥ.

ⲭⲉ ⲟⲩⲛ̄ ⲟⲩⲛⲁ[ϭ] [2] ⲛ̄ϣⲓⲃⲏ ⲙ̄ⲡⲟⲩⲱⲛϩ̄ ⲁⲃⲁⲗ ⲙ̄ⲡⲉⲧϩⲱⲡⲉ [3] ⲙ̄{ⲛ̄}ⲡⲉⲛⲧⲁϩⲱⲧⲁ ⲙⲛ̄ ⲛⲉⲧⲛⲁϣⲱⲡⲉ ⲉⲧⲃⲏ- [4] ⲛⲧϥ̄. ⲛ̄ⲧⲁϥ ⲛ̄ⲅⲁⲣ ⲁϥⲟⲩⲁⲛϩϥ̄ ⲛⲉϥ ϩⲓ̈ ⲥⲁ ⲛ- [5] ϩⲟⲩⲛ ⲙ̄ⲙⲟϥ, ⲉϥϣⲟⲟⲡ ⲛ̄ⲙⲙⲉϥ ⲉϥⲟ ⲛ̄- [6] ϣⲃⲏⲣ ⲛ̄ϣⲱⲡ ⲛ̄ⲕⲁϩ ⲛ̄ⲙⲙⲉϥ, ⲉϥⲙⲟⲩ- [7] ⲧⲛⲉ ⲙ̄ⲙⲁϥ ⲕⲁⲧⲁ ϣⲏⲙ ϣⲏⲙ, ⲉϥⲧⲣⲉϥ- [8] ⲡⲁⲩⲣⲏ, ⲉϥϥⲓ ⲙ̄ⲙⲁϥ ⲁϩⲣⲏⲓ, ⲉϥⲧ̄ ⲙ̄ⲙⲁϥ [9] ⲛⲉϥ ϣⲁⲃⲟⲗ ⲁⲅⲁⲡⲟⲗⲁⲩⲥⲓⲥ ⲁⲃⲁⲗ ϩⲛ̄ ⲟ[ⲩ]- [10] ϭⲛ̄ⲛⲉⲩ. ⲛⲁⲉⲓ ⲛ̄ⲇⲉ ⲛ̄ⲧⲁⲩ ⲉⲧϩⲉ ⲛⲥⲁ ⲛ- [11] ⲃⲟⲗ, ⲁϥⲟⲩⲁⲛϩϥ̄ ⲛⲉⲩ ϩⲛ̄ⲛ ⲟⲩⲡⲱⲧ ⲙⲛ̄- [12] ⲛ ⲟⲩⲧ̄ ϣϭⲁ, ⲁⲩⲱ ⲁϥⲥⲁⲕϥ̄ ⲛⲉϥ ⲥⲉϩⲛ̄ⲧϥ̄, [13] ⲉⲙ̄ⲡⲉϥⲧⲉⲉϥ ⲛⲉⲩ ⲁⲧⲣⲟⲩⲉⲓⲁⲣϩϥ̄.

[14] ⲭⲉ ⲛ̄ⲧⲁⲣⲉϥⲣ̄ ⲟⲩⲟⲉⲓⲛ ⲛ̄ϭⲓ ⲡⲗⲟⲅⲟⲥ [15] ⲉⲧⲁϣⲧⲁ, ⲁϥⲣ̄ ϩⲏⲧϭ̄ ⲛ̄ϭⲓ ⲡⲉϥⲡⲗⲏⲣⲟⲩ- [16] ⲙⲁ. ⲁϥⲣ̄ ⲃⲁⲗ ⲁⲛⲉⲉⲓ ⲉⲧⲉⲛⲁⲩϣⲧⲁⲣ- [17] ⲧⲣ̄ ⲙ̄ⲙⲟϥ ⲛ̄ϣⲁⲣⲡ̄. ⲁϥϣⲱⲡⲉ ⲛ̄ⲁⲧ- [18] ⲧⲱϩ ⲛ̄ⲙⲙⲉϥ, ⲁϥⲕⲁⲕϥ̄ ⲁϩⲏⲟⲩ ⲙ̄- [19] ⲡⲓⲙⲉⲉⲩⲉ ⲉⲧⲙ̄ⲙⲉⲩ ⲙ̄ⲙⲛ̄ⲧⲭⲁⲥⲓϩⲏⲧ. [20] ⲁϥⲭⲓ ⲙ̄ⲡⲙⲟⲩⲭϭ ⲙ̄ⲡⲙ̄ⲧⲁⲛ ϩⲙ̄ [21] ⲡⲧⲣⲟⲩⲕⲃϩⲱⲟⲩ ⲁⲩⲱ ⲛ̄ⲥⲉⲑⲃⲃⲓⲁⲩ [22] ⲛⲉⲩ ⲛ̄ϭⲓ ⲛⲉⲉⲓ ⲉⲧⲟⲉⲓ ⲛ̄ⲁⲧⲡⲓⲑⲉ [23] ⲛ̄ⲙⲙⲉϥ ⲛ̄ϣⲁⲣⲡ̄. ⲁⲩⲱ ⲁⲩⲣⲉϣⲉ [24] ⲁϩⲣⲏⲓ ⲁⲭⲛ̄ ⲧⲉⲡⲓⲥⲕⲟⲡⲏ ⲛ̄ⲛⲉϥⲥⲛⲏⲩ [25] ⲉⲛⲧⲁⲩϭⲛ̄ ⲡⲉϥϣⲓⲛⲉ. ⲁϥⲧ̄ ⲇⲉ ⲛ̄ⲛⲟⲩ- [26] ⲉⲁⲩ ⲙⲛ̄ ⲟⲩⲥⲙⲟⲩ ⲁⲛⲉⲧⲁϩⲟⲩ{ϩ}ⲁⲛ- [27] ϩⲟⲩ ⲛⲉⲩ ⲁⲩⲃⲟⲏⲑⲓⲁ, ⲉϥϣⲡ̄ ϩⲙⲁⲧ [28] ⲭⲉ ⲁϥⲣ̄ ⲃⲁⲗ ⲁⲛⲉⲧⲣ̄ ⲥⲧⲁⲇⲓⲁⲍⲉ ⲙ̄ⲙⲟϥ [29] ⲉϥⲣ̄ ⲙⲁϩⲉⲓⲉ ⲙ̄ⲛ ⲟⲩⲧⲁⲉⲓⲟ ⲛ̄ⲧⲙⲛ̄ⲧ- [30] ⲛⲟϭ ⲙⲛ̄ ⲛⲉⲧⲁⲟⲩⲁⲛϩⲟⲩ ⲛⲉⲩ ⲁⲃⲁⲗ ϩⲛ̄- [31] ⲛ ⲟⲩⲧⲱϣⲉ. ⲁϥⲭⲡⲟ ⲛ̄ϩⲛ̄ϩⲓⲕⲱⲛ ⲉⲩⲟⲩ- [32] ⲁⲛϩ̄ ⲛ̄ⲇⲉ ⲛⲓϩⲟ ⲉⲧⲁⲛϩ̄, ⲉϩⲛ̄ⲡⲉⲧⲁ- [33] ⲛⲓⲧ ⲛⲉ ⲛ̄ⲇⲉ ⲡⲉⲧⲛⲁⲛⲟⲩⲟⲩ, ⲉⲩϣⲟ- [34] ⲟⲡ ⲛ̄ⲧⲉ ⲛⲉⲧϣⲟⲟⲡ, ⲉⲩⲉⲓⲛⲉ ⲙⲉⲛ [35] ⲁⲣⲁⲟⲩ ⲛ̄ⲥⲁⲉⲓⲉ, ⲉⲩϣⲏϣ ⲛ̄ⲇⲉ ⲁⲣⲁⲟⲩ [36] ⲉⲛ ⲙⲁⲙⲓⲉ, ⲁⲃⲁⲗ ⲭⲉ ϩⲛ̄ⲁⲃⲁⲗ ϩⲛ̄ ⲟⲩ- [37] ⲧⲱⲧ ⲛ̄ⲙⲙⲉϥ ⲉⲛ <ⲛⲉ>, ⲙ̄ⲡⲉⲧⲁϥϭⲛ̄ⲧⲟⲩ [91.1] [ⲁ]ⲃⲁⲗ ⲙ̄ⲡⲉⲛⲧⲁϥⲟⲩⲁⲛϩϥ̄ ⲛⲉϥ. ⲁⲗⲗⲁ [2] ϩⲛ̄ⲛ ⲟⲩⲥⲟⲫⲓⲁ ϩⲛ̄ ⲟⲩ{ⲛⲉⲩ}ⲉⲡⲓⲥⲧⲏ- [3] ⲙⲏ ⲉϥⲣ̄ ϩⲱⲃ, ⲉϥⲙⲟⲩⲭϭ ⲙ̄ⲡⲗⲟⲅⲟⲥ ⲛ̄ⲙ̄- [4] ⲙⲉϥ ⲧⲏⲣϥ̄. ⲉⲧⲃⲉ ⲡⲁⲉⲓ ϭⲉ ⲛⲉⲛⲧⲁϩⲉⲓ [5] ⲁⲃⲁⲗ ⲙ̄ⲙⲁϥ ϩⲛ̄ⲛⲁϭ ⲛⲉ, ⲛ̄ⲑⲉ ⲉⲧⲉ [6] ⲟⲩⲛⲁϭ ⲙ̄ⲁⲙⲛⲉ ⲡⲉ ⲡⲉⲧϣⲟⲟⲡ.

[7] ⲭⲉ ⲙⲛ̄ⲛⲥⲁ ⲡⲧⲣⲉϥⲣ̄ ⲙⲁϩⲉⲓⲉ ⲙ̄ⲡⲥⲁ- [8] ⲉ ⲛ̄ⲛⲉⲉⲓ ⲉⲛⲧⲁϥⲟⲩⲱⲛϩ̄ ⲁⲣⲁϥ, [9] ⲁϥⲣ̄ ϩⲟⲙⲟⲗⲟⲅⲓ ⲙ̄ⲡϩⲙⲁⲧ ⲁⲭⲛ̄ ⲡⲉⲓⲧ̄- [10] ⲉⲡⲓⲥⲕⲟⲡⲏ. ⲁϥⲉⲓⲣⲉ ⲙ̄ⲡϩⲱⲃ ⲛ̄ϭⲓ ⲡⲗⲟ- [11] ⲅⲟⲥ, ⲛ̄ⲧⲟⲟⲧⲟⲩ ⲛ̄ⲛⲉⲉⲓ ⲉⲛⲧⲁⲩⲧⲉϩⲟ [12] ⲛ̄ⲧⲃⲟⲏⲑⲓ ⲛ̄ⲧⲟⲟⲧⲟⲩ, ϩⲁ ⲡⲥⲙⲓⲛⲉ [13] ⲛ̄ⲛⲉ{ⲉⲓ} ⲉⲛⲧⲁϩϣⲱⲡⲉ ⲉⲧⲃⲛⲏⲧϥ̄, ⲁⲩⲱ [14] ⲁⲧⲣⲟⲩⲭⲓ ⲛ̄ⲛⲟⲩⲡⲉⲧⲛⲁⲛⲟⲩϥ ⲉϥ- [15] ⲙⲉⲩⲉ ⲁⲧⲣⲉϥⲧⲱⲃϩ̄ ⲛ̄ⲧⲟⲓⲕⲟⲛⲟ- [16] ⲙⲓⲁ ⲛ̄ⲛⲉⲧⲁϩⲉⲓ ⲁⲃⲁⲗ ⲙ̄ⲙⲁϥ ⲧⲏ- [17] ⲣⲟⲩ, ⲉⲧⲥⲙⲁⲛⲧ ⲁⲧⲣⲉⲥⲧⲉϩⲁⲩ. ⲉⲧⲃⲉ [18] ⲡⲉⲉⲓ ⲛⲉⲧⲉ ⲁϥⲛ̄ⲧⲟⲩ ⲁⲃⲁⲗ ⲕⲁⲧⲁ [19] ⲧ̄ⲡⲣⲟⲁⲓⲣⲉⲥⲓⲥ ϩⲛ̄ ϩⲛ̄ϩⲁⲣⲙⲁ ⲛⲉ, ⲛ̄- [20] ⲑⲉ ⲛ̄ⲛⲉⲉⲓ ⲉⲛⲧⲁⲩϣⲱⲡⲉ, ⲛⲉⲉⲓ ⲉⲛ- [21] ⲧⲁⲩⲟⲩⲱⲛϩ̄, ⲭⲉ ⲉⲩⲛⲁⲭⲱⲃⲉ ⲛ̄ϩⲉⲛ- [22] ⲙⲁ ⲧⲏⲣⲟⲩ ⲛ̄ϩⲛ̄ϩⲃⲏⲩⲉ ⲉⲧⲙ̄ⲡⲥⲁ ⲛ̄ⲡⲓ- [23]

90.1 ⲉⲛⲧⲁϥⲁⲃⲱⲟⲩ: read ⲉⲛⲧⲁϥⲧⲁϣⲟⲩ.
90.23 ⲁⲩⲣⲉϣⲉ: read ⲁⲩⲣⲉϣⲉ.
90.28 ⲥⲧⲁⲇⲓⲁⲍⲉ: read ⲥⲧⲁⲥⲓⲁⲍⲉ.
90.32 ⲛ̄ⲇⲉ: read ⲛ̄ⲧⲉ.
90.33 ⲛ̄ⲇⲉ: read ⲛ̄ⲧⲉ. ⲡⲉⲧⲛⲁⲛⲟⲩⲟⲩ: read ⲛⲉⲧⲛⲁⲛⲟⲩⲟⲩ.
91.8 ⲉⲛⲧⲁϥⲟⲩⲱⲛϩ̄: read ⲉⲛⲧⲁϩⲟⲩⲱⲛϩ̄ (or ⲉⲛⲧⲁⲩⲟⲩⲱⲛϩ̄).

assigned to them. He allowed [35] them too to be useful in the [36] arrangement that will come to be, [90.1] which he had [ordained] for them.

There is a great [2] difference between the revelation of the one who came about [3] <from> the one who was deficient and those who will come to be on account of [4] him. For he revealed himself to him [5] within him, since he was with him as [6] a companion, suffering with him, giving [7] him rest little by little, in order for him [8] to grow, lifting him up, giving himself [9] to him utterly for enjoyment in [a] [10] vision. But to those present outside, [11] he revealed himself to them fleetingly and [12] aggressively, and he withdrew himself to himself suddenly, [13] without allowing them to perceive him.

[14] After the Word that was deficient was illuminated, [15] his fullness acted. [16] He fled from those who disturbed [17] him initially. He became [18] unmixed with them, and he stripped off [19] that arrogant thought. [20] He received the mixture of the rest when [21] those who were disobedient [22] to him initially kneeled and humbled themselves [23] before him. And <he> rejoiced [24] at the vision of his siblings [25] who had visited him. He offered [26] glory and praise to those who had revealed [27] themselves to him as an aid, while (also) giving thanks [28] because he had evaded those who had been at odds with him [29] and marveled at and honored the [30] greatness and those who revealed themselves to him [31] through destiny. He produced revealed images [32] of the living faces, pleasing [33] among good things, existing [34] among existing things, like [35] them in beauty, but not equal to them [36] in truth, because <they are> not from a [37] mixing with him, between the one who brought them [91.1] forth and the one who revealed himself to him. But [2] wisely and thoughtfully [3] he acts, mixing the Word with [4] himself completely. For this reason, then, those who came [5] forth from him are great, just as [6] that which exists is truly great.

[7] After his amazement at the beauty [8] of those who had appeared to him, [9] he expressed thanks for the [10] visit. The Word did this, [11] through those who had received [12] aid, for the establishment [13] of those who had come to be on account of him, and (he did this) [14] so that they might receive a good thing, since he [15] thought to pray for the assembly [16] of all those who had come forth from him, [17] which is established so that it might set them up. For [18] this reason those he chose to bring forth [19] are chariots, [20] just as those who came to be, those [21] who have appeared, so that they might pass through [22] all places of things that are below, [23] so that to each

ⲧⲛ̅, ⲁⲧⲣⲟⲩϯ ⲛ̅ⲧⲭⲱⲣⲁ ⲙ̅ⲡⲟⲩⲉⲉⲓ ²⁴ ⲡⲟⲩⲉⲉⲓ ⲛⲉϥ ⲉⲧⲥⲙⲁⲛ̅ⲧ̅ ⲛ̅ⲑⲉ ⲉⲧϥ̅- ²⁵ ϣⲟⲟⲡ. ⲡⲉⲉⲓ
ⲙⲉⲛ ⲟⲩϣⲁⲣⲱ̅ⲣ̅ ⲇⲉ ⲛ̅- ²⁶ ⲛⲁ ⲡⲓⲧⲁⲛⲧⲛ̅ ⲡⲉ, ⲟⲩⲙⲛ̅ⲧ̅ⲣ̅ ⲡⲉⲧⲛⲁⲛⲟⲩϥ ²⁷ ⲛ̅ⲇⲉ ⲛ̅ⲧⲁϥ ⲛ̅ⲛⲁ
ⲡⲓⲙⲉⲉⲩⲉ, ⲟⲩⲱⲛ̅ϩ̅ ²⁸ ⟦ⲛ̅ⲇⲉ ⲛ̅ⲧⲁϥ ⲛ̅ⲛⲁ ⲡⲓⲙⲉⲉⲩⲉ⟧ ²⁹ ⲛ̅ⲇⲉ ⲁⲃⲁⲗ ⲛ̅ⲛⲉⲉⲓ ⲉⲧⲉ ⲁⲃⲁⲗ ⲛⲉ ϩⲛ̅ ³⁰
ⲡⲓⲧⲱϣⲉ, ⲉⲛⲧⲁϩⲣ̅ ⲟⲩⲉⲉⲓ ⲟⲩⲱⲧ ³¹ ⲉϥϣⲱⲡ ⲙ̅ⲕⲁϩ, ⲉϩⲛ̅ⲥⲡⲉⲣⲙⲁ ⲛⲉ ³² ⲉⲙⲡⲁⲧⲟⲩϣⲱⲡⲉ
ⲟⲩⲁⲉⲉⲧⲟⲩ.

ϫⲉ ³³ ⲡⲉⲧⲁⲟⲩⲱⲛ̅ϩ̅ ϭⲉ ⲛⲉⲩⲙⲟⲩⲛⲅ ⲛϩⲟ ⲡⲉ ³⁴ ⲛ̅ⲇⲉ ⲡⲓⲱⲧ ⲁⲩⲱ ⲡⲓϯ ⲙⲉⲧⲉ. ⲛⲉⲩⲟⲩ- ³⁵
ϩⲃ̅ⲥⲟⲩ ⲧⲉ ⲛ̅ⲇⲉ ⲭⲁⲣⲓⲥ ⲛⲓⲙ, ⲁⲩⲱ ⲟⲩϩⲣⲉ ⲡⲉ, ³⁶ ⲉϥϣⲟⲟⲡ ⲛ̅ⲛⲉⲉⲓ ⲉⲛⲧⲁⲡⲗⲟⲅⲟⲥ ⲛ̅ⲧⲟⲩ ³⁷
ⲁⲃⲁⲗ ⲉϥⲧⲱⲃϩ ⲉϥϫⲓ ⲙ̅ⲡⲓⲉⲁⲩ ⲙⲛ̅ ³⁸ ⲡⲓⲧⲁⲉⲓⲟ. ⁹²·¹ ⲡⲁⲉⲓ ⲉⲛⲧⲁϥϯ ⲉⲁⲩ ⲙ̅ⲙⲟϥ ⲉϥⲧⲁⲓⲟ, ²
ⲉϥⲉⲓⲁⲣ̅ⲙ̅ ⲛ̅ⲇⲉ ⲁⲛⲉⲧⲁϥⲧⲱⲃϩ̅ ⲙ̅ⲙⲁⲩ, ³ ⲁⲧⲣⲉϥϫⲁⲕⲟⲩ ⲁⲃⲟⲗ ϩⲓⲧⲟⲟⲧⲟⲩ ⲛ̅ⲛⲓϩⲓ̈- ⁴ ⲕⲱⲛ
ⲉⲛⲧⲁϥⲛ̅ⲧⲟⲩ ⲁⲃⲁⲗ.

ϫⲉ ⲁϥⲟⲩⲱϩ ⁵ ⲁⲧⲟⲟⲧϥ̅ ⲛ̅ϩⲟⲩⲟ ⲛ̅ϭⲓ ⲡⲗⲟⲅⲟⲥ ⲁⲭⲛ̅ ⁶ ⲡⲓϭⲛ̅ϯ ⲧⲟⲟⲧϥ̅ ⲛ̅ⲛⲟⲩⲉⲣⲏⲟⲩ ⲁⲩⲱ ⲁ- ⁷
ⲭⲛ̅ ϯϩⲉⲗⲡⲓⲥ ⲛ̅ⲇⲉ ⲡⲓϣⲡ ⲱⲡ, ⲉⲩⲛ̅- ⁸ [ⲧ]ⲉⲩ ⲙ̅ⲙⲉⲩ ⲙ̅ⲡⲟⲩⲣⲁⲧ ⲙⲛ̅ ⲡⲓⲙ̅ⲧⲁⲛ ⁹ ⲉⲧⲛⲁϣⲁϥ
ⲁⲩⲱ ϩⲛ̅ϩⲏⲇⲟⲛⲏ ⲛ̅ⲁⲧ- ¹⁰ ϫⲱϩⲙⲉ. ⲁϥϫⲡⲟ ⲛ̅ⲛⲉⲛⲧⲁϥⲉⲓⲣⲉ ¹¹ ⲙ̅ⲡⲟⲩⲙⲉⲉⲩⲉ ⲛ̅ϣⲁⲣⲡ̅, ⲉⲛⲥⲉϩⲁ-
¹² ⲧⲏϥ ⲉⲛ, ⲉⲩⲛ̅ⲧⲉϥ ⲙ̅ⲙⲉⲩ ⲙ̅ⲡϫⲱⲕ. ¹³ ⟦ⲁϥϫⲡⲟ ⲛ̅ⲛⲉⲧⲁϥⲉⲓⲣⲉ ⲙ̅ⲡⲟⲩⲙⲉⲉⲩⲉ ¹⁴ ⲛ̅ϣⲁⲣⲡ̅⟧
ϯⲛⲟⲩ ⲉⲡⲁ ⲡϭⲓⲛⲉⲩ ϩⲁⲧⲛϥ̅, ¹⁵ ⲉϥϣⲟⲟⲡ ϩⲛ̅ⲛ ⲟⲩϩⲉⲗⲡⲓⲥ ⲙⲛ̅ⲛ ⲟⲩ- ¹⁶ ⲛⲁϩⲧⲉ ⲛ̅ⲇⲉ ⲡⲓⲱⲧ
ⲉⲧϫⲏⲕ ϣⲁ ⲛⲓⲡⲧⲏ- ¹⁷ ⲣϥ̅. ⲉⲩⲟⲩⲁⲛ̅ϩ̅ ⲙⲉⲛ ⲛⲉϥ ⲉⲙⲡⲁⲧϥ̅- ¹⁸ ⲙⲟⲩϫϭ ⲇⲉ ⲛⲙ̅ⲙⲉϥ ϫⲉⲕⲁⲥⲉ
ⲛⲉⲧⲁϩ- ¹⁹ ϣⲱⲡⲉ ⲛⲟⲩⲧⲉⲕⲟ ϩⲣⲏⲓ̈ ϩⲙ̅ ⲡⲓϣⲱϣⲧ̅ ²⁰ ⲁⲭⲁϥ ⲛ̅ⲧⲉ ⲡⲟⲩⲁⲉⲓⲛⲉ, ϫⲉ ⲥⲉⲛⲁ- ²¹
ϣⲱⲡ ⲁⲣⲁⲩ ⲉⲛ ⲛ̅ϯⲛⲁϭ ⲙ̅ⲙⲁⲉⲓⲛ ²² ⲉⲧϫⲁⲥⲉ.

ϫⲉ ⲡⲓⲙⲉⲩⲉ ⲇⲉ ⲛ̅ⲇⲉ ⲡⲗⲟ- ²³ ⲅⲟⲥ, ⲉⲛⲧⲁϥⲥⲧⲁϥ ⲁϩⲟⲩⲛ ⲁⲡⲉϥⲥⲙⲛ̅- ²⁴ ⲛⲉ ⲁⲩⲱ ⲁϥⲣ̅ ⲭⲁⲉⲓⲥ
ⲁⲭⲛ̅ ⲛⲉⲧⲁϩ- ²⁵ ϣⲱⲡⲉ ⲉⲧⲃⲏⲧϥ̅, ⲛⲉϣⲁⲣⲟⲩⲙⲟⲩ- ²⁶ ⲧⲉ ⲁⲣⲁϥ ϫⲉ « ⲁⲓⲱⲛ » ⲁⲩⲱ
« ⲧⲟⲡⲟⲥ » ⲛ̅- ²⁷ ⲛⲉⲉⲓ ⲧⲏⲣⲟⲩ ⲉⲛⲧⲁϥⲛ̅ⲧⲟⲩ ⲁⲃⲁⲗ ²⁸ ⲕⲁⲧⲁ ⲡⲓⲧⲱϣⲉ, ⲁⲩⲱ ϣⲁⲩⲙⲟⲩⲧⲉ ²⁹
ⲁⲣⲁϥ ⲁⲛ ϫⲉ « ⲟⲩⲥⲩⲛⲁⲅⲱⲅⲏ ⲛ̅ⲛⲟⲩ- ³⁰ ϫⲁⲉⲓⲧⲉ, » ⲁⲃⲁⲗ ϫⲉ ⲁϥⲧⲁⲗϭⲟϥ ϩⲛ̅ ³¹ ⲡⲭⲱⲣⲉ,
ⲉⲧⲉ ⲡⲓⲙⲉⲉⲩⲉ ⲡⲉ ⲉⲧⲟ- ³² ⲉⲓ ⲛ̅ϩⲁϩ ⲛ̅ⲣⲏⲧⲉ, ⲁϥⲥⲧⲁϥ ⲁϩⲟⲩⲛ ³³ ⲁⲡⲓⲙⲉⲉⲩⲉ ⲛ̅ⲟⲩⲱⲧ. ⲙ̅ⲡⲣⲏⲧⲏ
³⁴ ⲁⲛ ⲉϣⲁⲩⲙⲟⲩⲧⲉ ⲁⲣⲁϥ ϫⲉ « ⲁⲡⲟ- ³⁵ ⲑⲏⲕⲏ, » ⲉⲧⲃⲉ ⲡⲓⲙ̅ⲧⲁⲛ ⲉⲛⲧⲁϥ- ³⁶ ⲭⲓⲧϥ̅, ⲉϥϯ
ⲛⲉϥ ⲟⲩⲁⲉⲉⲧⲩ. ⁹³·¹ ⲁⲩⲱ ϣⲁⲩⲙⲟⲩⲧⲉ ⲁⲣⲁϥ ⲁⲛ ϫⲉ « ϣⲉ- ² ⲗⲉⲉⲧ, » ⲉⲧⲃⲉ ⲡⲟⲩⲣⲁⲧ ⲙ̅ⲡⲉⲉⲓ
ⲉⲛ- ³ ⲧⲁϩⲧⲉⲉⲓϥ ⲁⲭⲛ̅ ⲑⲉⲗⲡⲓⲥ ⲛ̅ⲕⲁⲣⲡⲟⲥ ⁴ ⲙ̅ⲡⲧⲱⲧ, ⲉⲛⲧⲁⲟⲩⲱⲛ̅ϩ̅ ⲛⲉϥ. ϣⲁ- ⁵ ⲣⲟⲩⲙⲟⲩⲧⲉ
ⲁⲣⲁϥ ⲁⲛ ϫⲉ « ⲙⲛ̅ⲧⲣ̅ⲣⲟ, » ⁶ ⲉⲧⲃⲉ ⲡⲥⲙⲓⲛⲉ ⲉⲛⲧⲁϥϫⲓⲧϥ̅ ⲉϥⲧⲉ- ⁷ ⲗⲏⲗ ⲁⲭⲛ̅ ⲡⲉⲙⲁϩⲧⲉ
ⲛ̅ⲛⲉⲧϯ ⲁϩⲏⲧϥ̅. ⁸ ⲁⲩⲱ ϣⲁⲩⲙⲟⲩⲧⲉ ⲁⲣⲁϥ ϫⲉ « ⲡⲣⲉϣⲉ ⁹ ⲛ̅ⲧⲉ ⲡⲭⲁⲉⲓⲥ, » ⲉⲧⲃⲉ ⲡⲁⲗⲏⲗ

91.27 ⲛ̅ⲇⲉ: read ⲛ̅ⲧⲉ.
91.34 ⲛ̅ⲇⲉ: read ⲛ̅ⲧⲉ.
91.35 ⲛ̅ⲇⲉ: read ⲛ̅ⲧⲉ.
91.37 ⲭⲓ: read ϯ.
92.2 ⲛ̅ⲇⲉ: read ⲇⲉ.
92.7 ⲛ̅ⲇⲉ: read ⲛ̅ⲧⲉ.
92.16 ⲛ̅ⲇⲉ: read ⲛ̅ⲧⲉ.
92.21 ⲙⲁⲉⲓⲛ: read ⲙⲁⲉⲓⲉ?
92.22 ⲛ̅ⲇⲉ: read ⲛ̅ⲧⲉ.
92.28 ⲛ̅ⲇⲉ: read ⲛ̅ⲧⲉ.

one might be given the region ²⁴ established just as he ²⁵ is. Now this is a frustration for ²⁶ those belonging to the likeness, but a good thing ²⁷ for those of the thought, a revelation ²⁸ ⟦ . . . ⟧ ²⁹ of those who are from ³⁰ the ordinance, which was a unity ³¹ though painful, being seeds ³² that have not come to be alone.

³³ The one who had appeared was a countenance ³⁴ of the Father and the agreement. He was a garment ³⁵ of all grace, and he was nourishment, ³⁶ which exists for those whom the Word brought ³⁷ forth while praying and <giving> glory and ³⁸ honor. ⁹²·¹ This is the one to whom he gave glory and honor, ² while beholding those to whom he had prayed, ³ so that he might perfect them through the images ⁴ that he had brought forth.

The Word contributed ⁵ more to ⁶ their mutual assistance and ⁷ to the peace of the promise, since ⁸ they have gladness and much rest ⁹ and undefiled enjoyment. ¹⁰ He produced those he had ¹¹ remembered first, while they ¹² were not with him, (resulting in them) having perfection. ¹³ ⟦ . . . ⟧ ¹⁴ Now, when the one belonging to the vision is with him, ¹⁵ he dwells in hope and ¹⁶ trust in the perfect Father as much as the eternities. ¹⁷ He appears to him when he has not yet ¹⁸ mixed with him so that those that have ¹⁹ come to be might not die by gazing ²⁰ upon the light, because they will ²¹ not be able to accept for themselves the great, ²² exalted love.

The thought of the Word, ²³ who had returned to his position ²⁴ and ruled over those who had ²⁵ come to be on account of him, was called ²⁶ "Eternity" and "Place" by ²⁷ all those whom he brought forth ²⁸ according to the ordinance, and it is also called ²⁹ "Synagogue of ³⁰ Salvation," because he healed himself from ³¹ the dispersion, which is the thought that has ³² many ways, and returned ³³ to the unified thought. In a similar way, ³⁴ it is called "Storehouse," ³⁵ because of the rest that he received, ³⁶ giving (it) to himself only. ⁹³·¹ It is also called ² "Bride," because of the gladness of the one ³ who gave himself in the hope of fruit ⁴ from the agreement, which he revealed to him. ⁵ Moreover, it is called "Kingdom," ⁶ because of the confirmation that he received while rejoicing ⁷ at the victory over those who oppose him. ⁸ And it is called "the Joy ⁹ of the Lord," because of the joy

92.21–22 "great, exalted love": or "great, exalted stature."

ε[ΝΤΑϤ]- ¹⁰ Τεειϥ ϩΙϢϢϤ. ΕΠΟΥΟΕΙΝ ϢΟΟΠ ¹¹ ϩΑΤΗϤ, ΕϤϯ ΝΕϤ ⲚΤⲰΒΒΙⲰ ⲚⲚΙΠⲉ[Τ]- ¹²
ΝΑΝΟΥΟΥ ΕΤϢΟΟΠ ⲚϩΗΤϤ̄ ¹³ ΑΥⲰ ΠΙΜΕΥΕ ⲚΤΕ ϯⲘⲚΤΕΛΕΥΘⲈ- ¹⁴ ΡΟϹ.

ϪΕ ΠΙΑΙⲰΝ ϬΕ, ΕΝΤΑΝⲢ ϢⲢⲠ̄ ¹⁵ ⲚϪΟΟϤ, ϤⲚ̄ΠϹΑ ⲚϩΡΕ ⲘⲠ{ΔΙΑ}ΤΑΓΜΑ ¹⁶ ϹΝΕϤ ⲚⲚΕΕΙ
ΕΤϯ ΟΥΒΕ ΝΕΥΕΡΗΟΥ. ¹⁷ ϤΟϊ ⲚΑΤϢΒΗΡ ⲚΝΕΤΑΜΑϩΤΕ, ΑΥⲰ ¹⁸ ϤΟϊ `Ⲛ´ΝΑΤ<Τ>Ⲱϩ ⲘⲚ
ΝΙϢⲰΝΕ ⲘⲚ ΝΙϬⲰ- ¹⁹ ϪΒΕ, ΝΑ ΠΙΜΕΥΕ ⲘⲚ ΝΑ ΠΙΤΑΝ- ²⁰ ΤⲚ̄.

ϪΕ ΠΕΤΕΑΠΛΟΓΟϹ ϬΕ ΚΑΑϤ Ⲙ̄- ²¹ ΜΟϤ ΑϩΡΗϊ, ΕϤϪΗΚ ΑΒΑΛ ⲘΠΙΡΕϢΕ, ²² ΝΕΥΟΥΑΙⲰΝ ΠΕ
ΕΥⲚΤΕϤ ⲘΜΕΥ ²³ ⲘΠϹΜΑΤ ⲘϤϢΒ, ΕΥⲚΤΕϤ ΔΕ ²⁴ ΑΝ ⲘΠΤΕϩΟ ΑΡΕΤϤ ⲚΤΛΑΕΙϬΕ, ΕΤΕ ²⁵
ΠΕΤΑϩΟΥΑΝϩϤ ΠΕ. ΕΥϩΙΚⲰΝ ΠΕ ²⁶ ⲚΝΕΕΙ ΕΤϢΟΟΠ ϩⲚ ΠΠΛΗΡⲰΜΑ, ²⁷ ΝΕΕΙ ΕΝΤΑϨϢⲰΠΕ
ΑΒΑΛ ϩⲚ ΠϩΟΥ- ²⁸ Ο ⲚΤΑΠΟΛΑΥϹΙϹ ⲚΔΕ ΠΕΤϢΟ- ²⁹ ΟΠ ϩⲚ ΟΥΡΕϢΕ. ⲚΤΑϤ Ⲛ̄ΔΕ ΠΜΟΥ- ³⁰
ΝⲔ Ⲛ̄ϩΟ ⲘΠΕΤΑϩΟΥΑΝϩϤ ΑΒΑΛ, ³¹ ϩⲚ ΠΙϪⲰⲔ Ⲛ̄ϩΗΤ ΜΝ ΠϢⲢΜΕ ³² ΑϩΟΥΝ ⲘⲚ ΠϢⲰΠ ⲰΠ
ϩΑ ΠΡΑ Ⲛ̄Ε- ³³ ΤΑϤⲢ ΑΙΤΙ ⲘΜΑΥΟΥ. ΝΕΟΥⲚ̄ΤΕϤ ³⁴ ⲘΜΕΥ ΠΕ ⲘΠΛΟΓΟϹ ⲚΤΕ ΠϢΗΡΕ ³⁵ ⲘⲚ
ΤΕϤΟΥϹΙΑ ⲘⲚ ΤΕϤϬΟΜ ⲘⲚ ΤΕϤ- ³⁶ ΜΟΡΦΗ, ΕΤΕ ΠΑΕΙ ΕΝΤΑϤΟΥⲰϢΕ <ⲘΜΑϤ> ³⁷ ΑΥⲰ
ΑϤϢⲰⲔ Ⲛ̄ϩΗΤ ΑΡΑϤ, ⁹⁴.¹ ΕΤΕ ΠΕΤΑΥΤⲰΒϩ̄ ⲘΜΑϤ ΠΕ ϩⲚ ΟΥΑΓΑ[ΠΗ]. ² ΝΕΟΥΑΕΙΝΕ ΠΕ ΑΥⲰ
ΝΕΥΟΥⲰϢΕ ΠΕ Α- ³ ΤΡΕϤΤΕϩΟ ΑΡΕΤϤ ΑΥⲰ ΝΕΥΟΥⲰⲢϥ ΠΕ ⁴ ΑΥϹΒΟΥ ΠΕ ΑΥⲰ <Ⲛ>ΑΥΒΕΛ
ΠΕ <Ε>ΟΥϬⲚ̄ΝΕϤ Ⲛ̄- ⁵ ϩΟ, ΝΕΕΙ ΕΤΕΥΟΥⲚΤΕϤϹΕ ⲘΜΕΥ Ⲛ̄- ⁶ ΤΕ ΝΕΤϪΑϹΕ. ΑΥⲰ ΝΕΟΥϹΟΦΙΑ
ΠΕ ⁷ ΑΠΕϤΜΕΥΕ ΟΥΒΕ ΝΕΤϩΙ ΠϹΑ ΝΠΙΤⲚ̄ Α[Τ]- ⁸ ΟΙΚΟΝΟΜΙΑ. ΑΥⲰ ΟΥΛΟΓΟϹ ΠΕ ΑΥϬⲚ̄- ⁹
ϢΕϪΕ ΠΕ ΑΥⲰ ΠϪⲰⲔ ⲚΝΕϩΒΗΥΕ ΠΕ ¹⁰ [ΑΒΑ]Λ ϩⲚ ΠΙΡΗΤΕ. ΑΥⲰ ΝΕΕΙ ΝΕ ΕΝ- ¹¹ ΤΑϨϪΙ
ΜΟΡΦΗ ⲚΜΜΕϤ ΚΑΤΑ ΤϩΙ- ¹² ⲔⲰΝ ΔΕ ⲘΠΛΗΡΟΥΜΑ, ΕΥⲚΤΕΥ Ⲙ̄- ¹³ ΜΕΥ ΝΟΥΕΙΑΤΕ ΕΤΕ
ΝΕΤΑ<ΤΑ>ϩϩΟ<Ο>Υ ΑΝ [Α]- ¹⁴ ϩΟΥΝ, ΕΠΟΥΕΙ ΠΟΥΕΙ ΕΥΧΑΡΑΚΤΗ- ¹⁵ [Ρ]ΙΟΝ ΠΕ ⲚΤΕ
ΠΟΥΕΙ ΠΟΥΕΙ ⲚΝΙϩΟ, ¹⁶ ΝΕΕΙ ΕΤΕ ϩⲚ̄ΜΟΡΦΗ ΝΕ ⲘⲘⲚ̄ϩΑΟΥΤ, ¹⁷ ΕϩⲚ̄ΝΑΒΑΛ ϩⲘ ΠΙϢⲰΝΕ
ΕΝ ΝΕ, ΕΤΕ ¹⁸ ΤΑΕΙ ΤΕ ΤⲘⲚ̄ΤϹϩΙΜΕ, ΑΛΛΑ ϩⲚ̄ΝΑΒΑΛ ¹⁹ ϩⲚ ΠΕΕΙ ΝΕ ΗΔΗ ΕΝΤΑϨⲔⲰ ⲚϹⲰϤ
Ⲙ̄- ²⁰ ΠΙϢⲰΝΕ. ΕΥⲚΤΕϤ ⲘΜΕΥ ⲘΠΡΕΝ ²¹ « ⲚΤΕⲔⲔΛΗϹΙΑ, » ϩⲚ̄Ν ΟΥϯ ΜΕΤΕ ²² ΓΑΡ ΕΥΕΙΝΕ
ⲘΠϯ ΜΕΤΕ ϩⲚ ΤϹΑΟΥϩϹ̄ ²³ ⲚΝΕΝΤΑϩΟΥΑΝϩΟΥ.

ϪΕ ΠΕΕΙ ΜΕΝ ²⁴ ΕΤΑϨϢⲰΠΕ ΚΑΤΑ ΤϩΙⲔⲰΝ ⲘΠΟΥ- ²⁵ ΔΕΙΝΕ ⲚΤΑϤ ϩⲰⲰϤ ϤϪΗⲔ ΑΒΑΛ, ²⁶
ϩⲰϹ ΕΥϩΙⲔⲰΝ ΠΕ ⲚΤΕ ΠΟΥΟΕΙΝ ²⁷ ⲚΟΥⲰΤ ΕΤϢΟΟΠ, ΕΤΕ ⲚΤΑϤ ΠΕ ΝΙ- ²⁸ ΠΤΗΡϤ̄. ΕϢϪΕ
Ⲛ̄ΑϤϬΑϪⲂ ΑΠΑΕΙ ΕΤΕ ²⁹ ΝΕΥϩΙⲔⲰΝ ⲚΤΕϤ ΠΕ, ΑΛΛΑ ΟΥⲚΤΕϤ ³⁰ ⲘΜΕΥ ⲚΤΕϤⲘⲚ̄ΤΑΤΠⲰϢΕ,
ΑΒΑΛ ³¹ ⲚΔΕ ϪΕ ΜΟΥⲚϤ̄ ⲚϩΟ ΠΕ ⲚΤΕ ΠΟΥ- ³² ΔΕΙΝ ΠΕ ⲚΑΤΠⲰϢΕ. ⲚΝΕΕΙ Ⲛ̄ΔΕ Ⲛ̄- ³³
ΤΑϤ ΕΝΤΑϨϢⲰΠΕ ΚΑΤΑ ΤϩΙⲔⲰΝ ³⁴ ⲘΠΟΥΕΙ ΠΟΥΕΙ ⲚΝΑΙⲰΝ, ϩⲚ ³⁵ ΤΟΥϹΙΑ ΜΕΝ ⲚΤΑΥ
ΝΕ ϩⲚ ΠΕΤΕΝⲢ ³⁶ ϢⲢⲠ ⲚϪΟΟϤ, ϩⲚ ΤϬΟΜ Ⲛ̄ΔΕ ϹΕϹΝϢ ³⁷ ΕΝ, ΑΒΑΛ ϪΕ ϩⲚ ΠΟΥΕΙ ΠΟΥΕΙ
{Ⲛ̄- ³⁸ ΔΕ ΠΟΥΕΙ ΠΟΥΕΙ} Ⲛ̄ΔΕΥ ΤΕ. ϩΡΗϊ ³⁹ ΝΕΝ ϩⲚ ΠΜΟΥϪϬ ϢΑ ΝΟΥΕΡΗΥ, ⁴⁰ ΟΥⲚΤΕΥ

94.12 ΔΕ: read ⲚΤΕ.
94.31 Ⲛ̄ΔΕ: read ΔΕ.
94.32 Ⲛ̄ΔΕ: read ΔΕ.
94.36 ϹΝϢ: read ϢΝϢ.
94.38 Ⲛ̄ΔΕΥ: read ⲚΤΕΥ.

in [which he] [10] clothed himself. The light is [11] with him, giving him repayment for the [12] good things that dwell in him [13] and the thought of freedom [14] (which also dwells in him).

This eternity, which we discussed earlier, [15] is above the two orders [16] of those that oppose each other. [17] It is not a companion to those who hold sway, and [18] it is not mixed with the illnesses or the [19] weaknesses, those belonging to the thought or those belonging to the [20] likeness.

What the Word placed [21] himself within, being perfect in joy, [22] was an eternity, having [23] the form of a thing, but also having [24] the establishment of the cause, which [25] is the one who revealed himself. It (the eternity) is an image [26] of those existing in the fullness, [27] those who have come to be from the exceeding [28] enjoyment of the one who exists [29] joyfully. And it, the [30] countenance of the one who revealed himself, [31] (was) in the sincerity [32] and the onset and the promise concerning the [33] things he requested. It possessed [34] the name of the Son [35] and his being and his power and his [36] form, who is the one <whom> he loved [37] and with whom he was pleased, [94.1] who was prayed to lovingly. [2] It was a light and a desire [3] for his establishment and an openness [4] to learning and an eye for seeing a [5] face, things that it possessed from [6] the exalted ones. It was also wisdom [7] for his thought against the things below [the] [8] assembly. It is also a word for speaking [9] and the perfection of things [10] like this. And these are the ones that have [11] received form with him in accordance with the image [12] of the fullness, having [13] their fathers, who are those who <made> them <alive> again, [14] since each one is a copy [15] of each of the faces, [16] those that are forms of maleness, [17] because they are not the illness, which [18] is femaleness, but are from [19] this one who already renounced [20] the illness. It has the name [21] "Church," for approvingly [22] they resemble the approval in the gathering [23] of those who have revealed themselves.

What [24] came to be according to the image of the [25] light is also perfect, [26] since it is an image of the light [27] that dwells alone, which is the [28] totalities. Even if it were inferior to the one [29] of which it is an image, it still has [30] its indivisibility, since [31] it is the countenance of the indivisible light. [32] But those [33] who came to be in accordance with the image [34] of each one of the eternities, in [35] essence are those (described) in what we [36] said before, but in power are not equal, [37] because it (the power) is in each one [38] { . . . } of them. In [39] the mixing with each other, [40] they have

ⲙ̄ⲙⲉⲩ ⲙ̄ⲡⲱϣⲱ, {ⲙ̄}ⲡⲟⲩ- ⁹⁵·¹ ⲉⲉ[ⲓ] ⲇⲉ ⲡⲟⲩⲉⲉⲓ ⲙ̄ⲡⲟⲩⲛⲁϩ ⲡⲱϥ ² {ⲛ̄ⲇⲉ} ⲁⲃⲁⲗ. ⲉⲧⲃⲉ ⲡⲉⲉⲓ
ϩⲛ̄ⲡⲁⲑⲟⲥ ³ ⲛⲉ, ⲡⲁⲑⲟⲥ ⲛ̄ⲅⲁⲣ ⲡⲉ ⲡϣⲱⲛⲉ, ϩⲱⲥ ⁴ ⲉϩⲛ̄ⲭⲡⲟ ⲉⲛ ⲛⲉ ⲁⲃⲁⲗ ϩⲛ̄ ⲡⲧⲱⲧ ⲛ̄- ⁵ ⲇⲉ
ⲡⲗⲏⲣⲱⲙⲁ, ⲁⲗⲗⲁ ⲁⲃⲁⲗ ϩⲛ̄ ⲡⲁⲓ ⁶ ⲏ̄ⲇⲏ ⲉⲧⲉⲙⲡⲁⲧϥ̄ϫⲓ ⲙ̄ⲡⲓⲱⲧ. ⲉⲓ<ⲉ> ⁷ ⲡⲧⲱⲧ ⲙⲛ̄ ⲡⲉϥⲡⲧⲏⲣϥ̄
ⲁⲩⲱ ⲡⲟⲩⲱϣⲉ ⁸ ⲛⲉ ⲟⲩⲡⲉⲧⲣ̄ ϣⲉⲩ ⲡⲉ ⲁⲧⲟⲓⲕⲟⲛⲟⲙⲓⲁ ⁹ ⲉⲧⲛⲁϣⲱⲡⲉ. ⲉⲁⲩⲛⲉⲩⲉ ⲁⲣⲁⲩⲟⲩ ¹⁰
ⲁⲧⲣⲟⲩϫⲱⲃⲉ ⲛ̄ⲛⲧⲟⲡⲟⲥ ⲉⲧⲛ̄ⲡⲥ[ⲁ] ⲛ̄- ¹¹ [ⲡ]ⲓⲧⲛ̄, ⲉⲛⲥⲉⲛⲁϣ ϭⲙϭⲟⲙ ⲛ̄ⲇⲉ ⲉⲛ ¹² ⲛ̄ϫⲓ ⲛ̄ⲧⲟⲡⲟⲥ
ⲁϥϣⲱⲡ ⲙ̄ⲡⲟⲩϭⲛ̄ⲉⲓ ⲥⲉ- ¹³ ϩⲏⲧⲟⲩ ⲛ̄ϭⲗⲟⲙ ⲉⲓⲙⲏⲧⲓ ⲕⲁⲧⲁ ⲟⲩϭⲉ[ⲓ] ¹⁴ ⲟⲩⲉⲉⲓ ⲛ̄ⲇⲉ ⲡⲟⲩⲉⲉⲓ
ⲡⲟⲩⲉⲉⲓ. ⲉⲩⲁ[ⲛⲁⲅ]- ¹⁵ ⲕⲁⲓⲟⲛ ⲡⲉ {ⲡⲉ} ⲡⲟⲩϭⲛ̄ⲉⲓ, ⲉⲡⲓⲇⲏ ϩⲱ[ⲃ] ¹⁶ ⲛⲓⲙ ⲉⲩⲛⲁϫⲱⲕ ⲁⲃⲁⲗ
ϩⲓⲧⲟⲟⲧⲟⲩ.

¹⁷ ϫⲉ ⲛ̄ⲧⲁⲩ ϭⲉ ⲧⲏⲣⲟⲩ, ϩⲁⲡⲁ`ϩ´ϩⲁⲡⲗⲱⲥ, ¹⁸ ⲛⲉⲧⲣ̄ ϣⲣⲡ̄ ⲛ̄ϣⲟⲟⲡ ⲙⲛ̄ ⲛⲉⲧϣⲟⲟⲡ ⲧ[ⲉ]- ¹⁹
ⲛⲟⲩ ⲙⲛ̄ ⲛⲉⲧⲛⲁϣⲱⲡⲉ, ⲁϥϫⲓ ⲙ̄- ²⁰ ⲡⲛⲉⲩ ⲁⲣⲁⲩ ⲛ̄ϭⲓ ⲡⲗⲟⲅⲟⲥ, ⲉⲁⲩⲛ̄- ²¹ ϩⲟⲩⲧϥ̄
ⲁⲧⲟⲓⲕⲟⲛⲟⲙⲓⲁ ⲛ̄ⲛⲉⲧⲕⲏ ²² ⲁϩⲣⲏⲓ ⲧⲏⲣⲟⲩ. ϩⲛ̄ϩⲁⲉⲓ`ⲛⲉ´ ⲙⲉⲛ ⲏ̄ⲇⲏ ²³ ϩⲛ̄ ⲛⲉϩⲃⲏⲟⲩⲉ ⲉⲩⲣ̄ ϣⲉⲩ
ⲁⲧⲣⲟⲩ- ²⁴ ϣⲱⲡⲉ, ⲛ̄ⲥⲡⲉⲣⲙⲁ ⲇⲉ ⲉⲧⲛⲁϣⲁ- ²⁵ ⲡⲉ ⲉⲩⲛ̄ⲧⲉϥⲥⲉ ⲛ̄ϩⲏⲧϥ̄, ⲁⲃⲁⲗ ϩⲓⲧⲛ̄ ²⁶
ⲡϣⲡⲱⲡ ⲉⲛⲧⲁϩϣⲱⲡⲉ ⲙ̄ⲡⲁⲉⲓ ²⁷ ⲉⲛⲧⲁϥⲣ̄ ⲃⲁⲕⲏ ⲙ̄ⲙⲁϥ, ϩⲱⲥ ⲉⲡⲁ ²⁸ ϩⲛ̄ⲥⲡⲉⲣⲙⲁ ⲡⲉ
ⲉⲩⲛⲁϣⲱⲡⲉ. ⲁⲩⲱ ²⁹ ⲁϥϫⲡⲟ ⲙ̄ⲡⲉϥⲙⲓⲥⲉ, ⲉⲧⲉ ⲡⲉⲉⲓ ³⁰ ⲡⲉ ⲡⲟⲩⲱⲛϩ̄ ⲁⲃⲁⲗ ⲙ̄ⲡⲉⲉⲓ ⲉⲛⲧⲁϥ- ³¹
ⲣ̄ ⲃⲁⲕⲏ ⲙ̄ⲙⲟϥ. ⲡⲥⲡⲉⲣⲙⲁ ⲇⲉ ⲛ̄- ³² ϣⲡⲱⲡ ⲉⲩⲣⲁⲉⲓⲥ ⲁⲣⲁϥ ⲁϩⲉⲛⲟⲩⲁ- ³³ ⲉⲓϣ, ⲁⲧⲣⲟⲩϣⲱⲡⲉ
ⲉⲁⲩⲧⲁϣⲟⲩ ⲛ̄- ³⁴ ϭⲓ ⲛⲉⲛⲧⲁⲩⲧⲁϣⲟⲩ ⲉⲩⲭⲁⲩ ⲁⲃⲁⲗ ³⁵ ϩⲓⲧⲛ̄ ⲧϭⲛ̄ⲉⲓ ⲙ̄ⲡⲥⲱⲧⲏⲣ ⲁⲩⲱ ⲛⲉⲧ- ³⁶
ⲛⲙ̄ⲙⲉϥ, ⲛⲉⲉⲓ ⲉⲛⲧⲁⲩ ⲛⲉ ⲛ̄ϣⲁ- ³⁷ ⲣⲉⲡ ⲁⲩⲥⲁⲩⲛⲉ ⲙⲛ̄ ⲟⲩⲉⲁⲩ ⲛ̄ⲇⲉ ³⁸ ⲡⲓⲱⲧ.

ϫⲉ ⲡⲉⲧⲉϣϣⲉ ⲡⲉ, ⲛ̄ϩⲣⲏⲉⲓ ⁹⁶·¹ [ϩ]ⲛ̄ ⲡⲧⲱⲃϩ̄ ⲉⲛⲧⲁϥⲉⲓⲣⲉ ⲙ̄ⲙⲁϥ ⲙⲛ̄ ⲡⲛ̄[ⲟⲩ]- ² ϩⲟⲩ ⲁϩⲟⲩⲛ
ⲉⲛⲧⲁϩϣⲱⲡⲉ ⲉⲧⲃⲏⲧ[ϥ], ³ ϫⲉⲕⲁⲥ ϩⲛ̄ϩⲁⲉⲓⲛⲉ ⲛⲉⲛ ⲉⲩⲛⲁⲧⲉⲕⲟ ⁴ ϩⲛ̄ⲕⲉⲕⲁⲩⲉ ⲉⲩⲛⲁⲣ̄
ⲡⲉⲧⲛⲁⲛⲟⲩϥ ⁵ ⲛⲉⲩ, ϩⲛ̄ⲕⲉⲕⲁⲩⲉ ⲇⲉ ⲁⲛ ⲉⲩⲛⲁ- ⁶ ⲛⲁϩⲟⲩ ⲁⲃⲁⲗ. ⲁϥⲣ̄ ϣⲟⲣⲡ̄ ⲛ̄ⲥⲟⲃⲧⲉ ⁷
ⲛ̄ⲧⲕⲟⲗⲁⲥⲓⲥ ⲛ̄ⲛⲉⲉⲓ ⲉⲧⲟⲉⲓ ⲛ̄ⲁⲧ- ⁸ ⲣ̄ ⲡⲓⲑⲉ, ⲉϥⲣ̄ ⲭⲣⲁⲥⲑⲉ ϩⲛ̄ ⲟⲩⲧ ϭⲟⲙ ⁹ ⲙ̄ⲡⲉⲧⲁϩⲟⲩⲱⲛϩ̄,
ⲡⲉⲉⲓ ⲉⲛⲧⲁϥϫⲓ ¹⁰ ⲛ̄ⲧⲟⲟⲧϥ̄ ⲛ̄ⲧⲉϫⲟⲩⲥⲓⲁ ⲛ̄ⲇⲉ ⲛ̄ⲓⲡⲧⲏⲣ[ϥ], ¹¹ ⲁⲧⲣⲉϥⲡⲱⲣϫ̄ ⲁⲃⲁⲗ ⲙ̄ⲙⲁϥ.
ⲛ̄[ⲧ]ⲁϥ ¹² ⲉⲧϩⲉ ⲥⲁ ⲛⲡⲓⲧⲛ̄, ⲁⲩⲱ ϥⲕⲁⲁϥ ⲁⲛ ¹³ ⲉϥⲛⲏϩ ⲁⲃⲁⲗ ⲙ̄ⲡⲉⲧϫⲁⲥⲉ ϣⲁⲧⲉ[ϥ]- ¹⁴
ⲥⲁⲃⲧⲉ ⲛ̄ⲧⲟⲓⲕⲟⲛⲟⲙⲓⲁ ⲛ̄ⲛⲉⲧ- ¹⁵ ϩⲉ ⲥⲁ ⲛⲃⲟⲗ ⲧⲏⲣⲟⲩ <ⲛ̄>ϥⲧ̄ ⲛ̄ⲧⲭⲱⲣⲁ ¹⁶ ⲙ̄ⲡⲟⲩⲉⲉⲓ ⲡⲟⲩⲉⲉⲓ
ⲉⲧⲧⲉϩⲟ ⲙ̄ⲙⲁϥ.

¹⁷ ϫⲉ ⲡⲗⲟⲅⲟⲥ ⲁϥⲧⲉϩⲁϥ ⲁⲣⲉⲧϥ̄ ⲛ̄- ¹⁸ ϣⲟⲣⲡ̄, ⲉϥⲧⲥⲁⲉⲓⲟ ⲛ̄ⲛⲓⲡⲧⲏⲣϥ̄, ϩⲱⲥ ¹⁹ ⲉⲩⲁⲣⲭⲏ ⲡⲉ
ⲁⲩⲱ ⲟⲩⲗⲁⲉⲓϭⲉ ⲡⲉ ²⁰ ⲁⲩⲱ ⲟⲩϩⲏⲅⲉⲙⲱⲛ ⲡⲉ ⲛ̄ⲛⲉⲧⲁϩ- ²¹ ϣⲱⲡⲉ ⲙ̄ⲡⲥⲙⲁⲧ ⲙ̄ⲡⲓⲱⲧ, ⲡⲁⲉⲓ
ⲉⲛ- ²² ⲧⲁϩϣⲱⲡⲉ ⲛ̄ⲗⲁⲉⲓϭⲉ ⲙ̄ⲡⲧⲉϩⲟ ²³ ⲁⲣⲉⲧϥ̄, ⲉⲧⲣ̄ ϣⲣⲡ̄ ⲛ̄ϣⲟⲟⲡ ⲙⲛ̄ⲛⲥⲱϥ. ²⁴ ⲁϥⲧⲥⲉⲛⲟ

94.39 ⲛⲉⲛ: read ⲙⲉⲛ.
95.4–5 ⲛ̄ⲇⲉ: read ⲛ̄ⲧⲉ.
95.11 ⲛ̄ⲇⲉ: read ⲇⲉ.
95.12 ⲛ̄ϫⲓ: read ⲛ̄ϭⲓ.
95.13 ⲛ̄ϭⲗⲟⲙ: read ⲛ̄ⲕⲗⲟⲙ.
95.14 ⲛ̄ⲇⲉ: read ⲛ̄ⲧⲉ.
95.37 ⲛ̄ⲇⲉ: read ⲛ̄ⲧⲉ.
96.3 ⲛⲉⲛ: read ⲙⲉⲛ.
96.8 ⲧϭⲟⲙ: read ϭⲟⲙ.
96.10 ⲛ̄ⲇⲉ: read ⲛ̄ⲧⲉ.

equality, but each [95.1] one has not shaken off what is uniquely its own. [2] For this reason they are passions, [3] for passion is illness, since [4] they are offspring not of the agreement of [5] the fullness, but of this one [6] before he even received the Father. <Indeed> [7] the agreement with his totality and the will [8] were useful to the assembly [9] that was to come to be. They were inclined [10] to pass through the places [11] below, since the places will not be able [12] to endure their sudden and hasty coming [13] unless (they come) [14] one by one. Their coming is a [15] necessity, since everything [16] will be perfected through them.

[17] Therefore, in summary, [18] the Word received the vision of all things, those that preexist and those that exist now [19] and those that will [20] come to be, since [21] he was entrusted with the assembly of all things that exist. [22] Some are already [23] in the things suitable for [24] coming to be, but the seeds that will come to be [25] he has within himself, because of [26] the promise that came about for that [27] which he conceived, as a thing belonging to [28] seeds that will come to be. And [29] he bore his children, that is, [30] the manifestation of what he conceived. [31] Yet the promised seed [32] is watched over for a time, [33] so that those who have been commissioned to be sent [34] might be commissioned [35] by the coming of the Savior and those [36] with him, those who are first [37] in knowledge and glory of [38] the Father.

It is fitting, from [96.1] the prayer that he made and the [2] return that came about on account of it, [3] that some will be destroyed [4] while others will do well [5] for themselves, while still others [6] will be distinguished. He first prepared [7] the correction for those who were [8] disobedient by utilizing a power [9] of the one who appeared, the one from whom he had received [10] authority over all things, [11] resulting in his separation from him. He [12] is the one who is below, and, moreover, he keeps himself [13] separate from what is exalted until [he] [14] prepares the assembly of [15] all external things <and> gives [16] to each one the region determined for it.

[17] The Word established himself [18] first, while making beautiful the entireties, as [19] a beginning and cause [20] and commander of those who have [21] come to be in the form of the Father, the one [22] who became the cause of the [23] establishment, which

ⲚⲚⲒϨⲒⲔⲰⲚ ⲈⲦⲢ̄ ϢⲢⲠ Ⲛ̄- 25 ϢⲞⲞⲠ, ⲚⲈⲈⲒ Ⲛ̄ⲦⲀϥⲚ̄ⲦⲞⲨ ⲀⲂⲀⲖ ϨⲚ̄- 26 Ⲛ ⲞⲨ<ⲈⲨ>ⲬⲀⲢⲒⲤⲦⲒⲀ ⲘⲚ̄
ⲞⲨⲈⲀⲨ. ⲈⲒⲦⲀ 27 ⲀϥⲤⲀⲈⲒⲰ Ⲙ̄ⲠⲘⲀ Ⲛ̄ⲚⲈⲈⲒ ⲈⲚⲦⲀϥ- 28 Ⲛ̄ⲦⲞⲨ ⲔⲀⲦⲀ ⲞⲨⲈⲀⲨ, ⲠⲈⲦⲞⲨⲘⲞⲨⲦⲈ 29
ⲀⲢⲀϥ ϪⲈ « ⲠⲀⲢⲀⲆⲒⲆⲞⲤ » ⲘⲚ̄ « ⲦⲀ- 30 ⲠⲞⲖⲀⲨϪⲒⲤ » ⲘⲚ̄ « ⲠⲞⲨⲚⲀϥ Ⲉ{ϥ}ⲦⲘⲎϨ 31 Ⲛ̄ⲦⲢⲞⲪⲎ »
ⲘⲚ̄ « ⲠⲞⲨⲚⲀϥ », ⲚⲈⲈⲒ ⲈⲦⲢ̄ 32 ϢⲢⲠ̄ Ⲛ̄ϢⲞⲞⲠ. ⲀⲨⲰ ⲀⲂⲀⲖ 33 Ⲛ̄ⲘⲚ̄ⲦⲚⲀϥⲢⲈ ⲚⲒⲘ ⲈⲦϢⲞⲞⲠ ϨⲚ̄
34 ⲠⲖⲎⲢⲞⲨⲘⲀ, ⲈϥⲦⲞⲨϪⲞ Ⲛ̄ⲦϨⲒⲔⲰⲚ. 35 ⲈⲒⲆⲀ ⲀϥⲤⲀⲈⲒⲞ Ⲛ̄ⲦⲘⲚ̄ⲦⲢ̄ⲢⲞ, ⲈⲤ- 36 ⲞⲈⲒ Ⲙ̄ⲠⲢⲎⲦⲈ
Ⲛ̄ⲚⲞⲨⲠⲞⲖⲒⲤ ⲈⲤ- 37 ⲘⲎϨ ⲀⲂⲀⲖ Ⲙ̄ⲠⲈⲦⲀⲚⲒⲦ ⲚⲒⲘ, Ⲉ- 38 ⲦⲈ ⲦⲘⲚ̄ⲦⲘⲀⲈⲒⲤⲀⲚ ⲦⲈ ⲀⲨⲰ 39 ϮⲚⲞϬ
Ⲙ̄ⲘⲚ̄ⲦⲀⲪⲐⲞⲚⲞⲤ, ⲈⲦⲘⲎϨ 97.1 ⲀⲂⲀⲖ Ⲛ̄ⲚⲒⲠⲚⲈⲨⲘⲀ ⲈⲦⲞⲨⲀⲀⲂ ⲘⲚ̄ [ⲚⲒ]- 2 ϬⲞⲘ ⲈⲦⲬⲞⲞⲢ ⲈⲦⲞⲨⲢ̄
ⲠⲞⲖⲒⲦⲈⲨϬ 3 Ⲙ̄ⲘⲞⲞⲨ, ⲚⲈⲈⲒ ⲈⲦⲈⲀⲠⲖⲞⲄⲞⲤ 4 Ⲛ̄ⲦⲞⲨ ⲀⲂⲀⲖ ⲀⲨⲰ ⲀϥⲦⲰⲔ ⲀⲢⲈⲦϥ 5 ϨⲚ̄Ⲛ ⲞⲨϬⲞⲘ.
ⲈⲒⲆⲀ ⲠⲦⲞⲠⲞⲤ Ⲛ̄- 6 ⲦⲈⲔⲔⲖⲎⲤⲒⲀ ⲈⲦⲤⲞϨⲞⲨ ϨⲘ̄ ⲠⲈⲈⲒⲘ[Ⲁ], 7 ⲈⲨⲚ̄ⲦⲈϥ Ⲙ̄ⲘⲈⲨ Ⲙ̄ⲠⲤⲘⲀⲦ Ⲛ̄ⲦⲈⲔ- 8
ⲔⲖⲎⲤⲒⲀ ⲈⲦϢⲞⲞⲠ ϨⲚ̄ ⲚⲀⲒⲰⲚ ⲈⲦϮ [Ⲉ-] 9 ⲀⲨ Ⲙ̄ⲠⲒⲰⲦ. ⲘⲚ̄ⲚⲤⲀ ⲚⲀⲒ ⲠⲦⲞⲠⲞⲤ 10 Ⲙ̄ⲠⲚⲀⲢⲦⲈ ⲘⲚ̄
ⲠⲤⲰⲦⲘ̄ ⲀⲂⲀ[Ⲗ ϨⲚ̄] 11 ⲐⲈⲖⲠⲒⲤ, ⲚⲀⲈⲒ ⲈⲚⲦⲀϥϪⲒⲦⲞⲨ Ⲛ̄Ϭ[Ⲓ ⲠⲖⲞ- 12 Ⲅ]ⲞⲤ Ⲛ̄ⲦⲀⲢⲈⲠⲞⲨⲀⲈⲒⲚ
ⲞⲨⲰⲚϨ Ⲁ[ⲂⲀⲖ]. 13 ⲈⲒⲆⲈ ϮⲆⲒⲀⲐⲈⲤⲒⲤ ⲈⲦⲈ ⲠϢⲖⲎⲖ ⲠⲈ [ⲘⲚ̄] 14 ⲠⲤⲀⲠⲤⲠ̄, ⲚⲈⲈⲒ ⲈⲚⲦⲀⲠⲔⲰ`Ⲉ´
ⲀⲂⲀⲖ [ⲞⲨ]- 15 ⲀϨϥ ⲚⲤⲰⲞⲨ ⲀⲨⲰ ⲠϢⲈϪⲈ ϨⲀ ⲠⲢ[Ⲁ Ⲙ̄]- 16 ⲠⲈⲦⲚⲀⲞⲨⲰⲚϨ.

ϪⲈ ⲚⲒⲦⲞⲠⲞⲤ ⲦⲎⲢⲞ[Ⲩ] 17 Ⲙ̄ⲠⲚⲈⲨⲘⲀⲦⲒⲔⲞⲚ ϨⲚ̄Ⲛ ⲞⲨϬⲞⲘ Ⲙ̄- 18 ⲠⲚⲈⲨⲘⲀⲦⲒⲔⲎ. ⲤⲈⲚⲎϨ ⲀⲂⲀⲖ
Ⲛ̄ⲚⲀ 19 ⲠⲒⲘⲈⲨⲈ, ⲈⲤⲔⲎ ⲀϨⲢⲎⲒ Ⲛ̄ϬⲒ ⲦϬⲞⲘ ϨⲚ̄- 20 Ⲛ ⲞⲨϨⲒⲔⲰⲚ, ⲈⲦⲈ ⲠⲀⲈⲒ ⲈⲦⲠⲰⲢⲬ̄ Ⲙ̄- 21
ⲠⲖⲎⲢⲞⲨⲘⲀ ⲀⲠⲖⲞⲄⲞⲤ, ⲈⲦϬⲞⲘ ⲈⲦⲢ̄ 22 ⲈⲚⲈⲢⲄⲒ ⲀⲦⲢⲞⲨⲢ̄ ⲠⲢⲞⲪⲎⲦⲈⲨⲈ ϨⲀ Ⲡ̄[ⲢⲀ] 23
Ⲛ̄ⲚⲈⲦⲚⲀϢⲰⲠⲈ ⲈⲤⲔⲰ Ⲛ̄ⲚⲀ ⲠⲒⲘⲈⲨ[Ⲉ], 24 ⲈⲚⲦⲀϨϢⲰⲠⲈ ⲀⲠⲈⲦⲢ̄ ϢⲞⲢⲠ Ⲛ̄ϢⲞ- 25 ⲞⲠ,
ⲈⲤⲔⲰ Ⲙ̄ⲘⲀⲨ ⲈⲚ ⲀⲦⲰϢ ⲘⲚ̄ ⲚⲈⲦ- 26 ⲀϨϢⲰⲠⲈ ϨⲚ̄Ⲛ ⲞⲨⲚⲈⲨ Ⲛ̄ϨⲞ Ⲛ̄ⲚⲈⲦϨⲀ- 27 ⲦⲎϥ.

ϪⲈ ⲚⲀ ⲠⲒⲘⲈⲈⲨⲈ ϨⲰⲞⲨ ⲀⲚ ⲠⲀⲒ 28 ⲈⲦϨⲒⲂⲞⲖ Ⲙ̄ⲘⲞϥ ⲤⲈⲐⲂⲂⲒⲀⲈⲒⲦ. ⲤⲈ- 29 ⲦⲞⲨϪⲰ Ⲙ̄ⲠⲈⲒⲚⲈ
ϨⲰⲚⲞⲨ Ⲙ̄{Ⲡ}ⲠⲖⲎⲢⲰ- 30 ⲘⲀⲦⲒⲔⲞⲚ, Ⲛ̄ϨⲞⲨⲞ ⲆⲈ ⲈⲦⲂⲈ ⲦⲔⲞⲒ- 31 ⲚⲰⲚⲒⲀ Ⲛ̄ⲚⲒⲢⲈⲚ
ⲈⲚⲦⲀⲨⲤⲀⲈⲒⲀⲈⲒⲦ 32 Ⲛ̄ϨⲎⲦⲞⲨ.

ϪⲈ ⲠⲒⲚⲞⲨϨⲞⲨ ⲀϨⲞⲨⲚ ϥⲞⲂ- 33 ⲂⲒⲀⲈⲒⲦ Ⲛ̄ⲚⲀ ⲠⲒⲘⲈⲈⲨⲈ, ⲀⲨⲰ ⲠⲒⲚⲞ- 34 ⲘⲞⲤ ϨⲰⲰϥ ⲀⲚ
ϥⲞⲐⲂⲂⲒⲀⲈⲒⲦ ⲚⲈⲨ Ⲛ̄- 35 ⲦⲈ ⲦⲔⲢⲒⲤⲒⲤ ⲈⲦⲈ ⲠⲒⲦⲀϪⲞⲨ ⲠⲈ ⲀⲨⲰ 36 ϮⲂⲀ̄ⲔⲈ.

ⲆⲈ ⲚⲈⲈⲒ Ⲥ{Ⲉ}ⲐⲂⲂⲒⲀⲈⲒⲦ ⲚⲈⲨ 37 ϨⲰⲰⲤ Ⲛ̄ϬⲒ ϮϬⲞⲘ ⲈⲦⲠⲰⲢⲬ̄ Ⲛ̄ⲚⲈⲦ- 38 ϨⲈ ⲤⲀ ⲚⲠⲒⲦⲚ̄ Ⲙ̄ⲘⲀⲨ,
ⲈⲤⲚⲞⲨϪⲈ Ⲙ̄ⲘⲀⲨ 39 ⲀⲠⲞⲨⲀⲈⲒⲈ, ⲈⲤⲔⲰ Ⲙ̄ⲘⲀⲨ ⲈⲚ 98.1 [ⲀⲠ]ⲰⲖⲀ̄ϥ ⲀϨⲢⲎⲒ ⲀϪⲚ ⲚⲀ ⲠⲒⲘⲈⲈⲨⲈ
Ⲙ̄[Ⲛ̄] 2 ⲠⲒⲚⲞⲨϨ ⲈϨⲞⲨⲚ, ⲈⲦⲈ ⲦⲈⲈⲒ ⲦⲈ ⲐⲢ̄ⲦⲈ ⲘⲚ̄ 3 ⲦⲀⲠⲞⲢⲒⲀ ⲀⲨⲰ ⲦⲂϢⲈ ⲀⲨⲰ Ϯ<Ⲥ>ⲀⲢⲘⲈⲤ
ⲀⲨⲰ 4 Ⲧ{Ⲛ̄}ⲘⲚ̄ⲦⲀⲦⲤⲀⲨⲚⲈ ⲀⲨⲰ ⲚⲈⲦⲀϨϢⲰⲠⲈ 5 ⲔⲀⲦⲀ ⲞⲨⲦⲀⲚⲦⲚ̄ ⲀⲂⲀⲖ ϨⲚ̄ ⲞⲨⲪⲀⲚⲦⲀⲤⲒⲀ.
6 ⲀⲨⲰ Ⲛ̄ⲦⲀⲨ ϨⲰⲚⲞⲨ ⲤⲈⲘⲞⲨⲦⲈ ⲀⲢⲀⲨ Ⲛ̄- 7 ϨⲢⲎⲒ ϨⲚ̄ ⲚⲒⲢⲈⲚ ⲈⲦϪⲀⲤⲒ, ⲚⲈⲈⲒ ⲈⲚⲦⲀⲨ- 8 ⲐⲂⲂⲒⲰ.
ⲘⲚ̄Ⲛ ⲞⲨⲤⲀⲨⲚⲈ Ⲛ̄ⲚⲈⲚⲦⲀⲨⲈⲒ 9 ⲈⲂⲞⲖ Ⲙ̄ⲘⲞⲞⲨ ϨⲚ̄ ⲞⲨⲘⲈⲨⲈ Ⲙ̄ⲘⲚ̄ⲦⲬⲀⲤⲒ- 10 [ϨⲎ]Ⲧ ⲘⲚ̄
ⲞⲨⲘⲚ̄ⲦⲘⲀⲈⲒⲞⲨϨϨ ⲤⲀϨⲚⲈ 11 [Ⲙ]Ⲛ̄ ⲞⲨⲘⲚ̄ⲦⲀⲦⲢ̄ ⲠⲒⲐⲈ ⲘⲚ̄ ⲞⲨⲘⲚ̄[ⲦϪⲒ] 12 [Ϭ]ⲞⲖ.

97.36 ⲆⲈ ⲚⲈⲈⲒ: read ⲚⲈⲈⲒ ⲆⲈ.
98.1 [Ⲡ]ⲰⲖⲀ̄ϥ: read [Ⲡ]ⲰⲢⲀ̄ϥ.

was first to exist after him. [24] He adorned the preexisting images, [25] those that he had brought in [26] thanksgiving and glory. Next [27] he made beautiful the place of those whom he had [28] brought forth in glory, (the place) that is called [29] "Paradise" and "the [30] Enjoyment" and "the Joy that is full of [31] nourishment" and "the Joy," those that [32] preexist. And with [33] every goodness that exists in [34] the fullness, it protects the image. [35] Next he made beautiful the kingdom, [36] like a city [37] filled with every pleasant thing, which [38] is brotherly love and [39] great abundance, which is filled [97.1] with holy spirits and [2] strong powers that govern [3] them, those that the Word [4] brought forth and established [5] in power. Next (he made beautiful) the place of [6] the Church that is gathered in this place, [7] having the form of the [8] Church that dwells in the eternities that glorify [9] the Father. After these things (he made beautiful) the place [10] of faith and obedience (that comes) from [11] hope, these that the [Word] received [12] after the light was revealed. [13] Then (he made beautiful) the disposition that is prayer [and] [14] the petition, these that forgiveness and talk [of] [15] the one who would appear [16] followed.

All the spiritual places [17] are in a spiritual power. [18] They are distinct from those belonging to [19] the thought, because the power is established in [20] an image, which is what separates [21] the fullness from the Word, because the power that makes it [22] possible for them to prophesy about [23] the things that will occur appoints those belonging to the thought, [24] which came to be in what preexists, [25] not permitting them to interact with those who have [26] come to be in a vision of the face of the things that are with [27] him.

Those belonging to the thought that is [28] outside are humble. They [29] preserve the image of the fullness, [30] even more on account of the fellowship [31] of the names by which they are made [32] beautiful.

The return is [33] humble to those belonging to the thought, and the [34] law is also humble to those of [35] the judgment, which is the condemnation and [36] the anger.

Yet also humble to them {is} [37] the power that divides those who [38] fall beneath them, since it casts them [39] far away, not allowing them [98.1] [to] spread out upon those belonging to the thought and [2] the return, that is, the fear and [3] the perplexity and the oblivion and the error and [4] the ignorance and the things that have come to be [5] according to a likeness and a phantasm. [6] And these too, which are humble, are given [7] names that are [8] lofty. There is no knowledge for those who have come forth [9] from an arrogant thought [10] and love of power [11] and disobedience and [12] [lying].

ϫⲉ ⲡⲟⲩⲉⲉⲓ ϭⲉ ⲡⲟⲩⲉⲉⲓ {ϭⲉ} ⲁⲩϯ ¹³ [ⲣ]ⲉⲛ ⲁⲣⲁⲟⲩ, ϫⲉ ⲡⲓⲇⲁⲅⲙⲁ ⲥⲛⲉⲩ ⲛ̄- ¹⁴ [ϩ]ⲣⲏⲓ̈ ϩⲛ̄ⲛ
ⲟⲩⲣⲉⲛ. ⲉϣⲁⲣⲟⲩⲙⲟⲩⲧⲉ ⲙⲉⲛ ¹⁵ [ⲁ]ⲛⲁ ⲡⲓⲙⲉⲩⲉ ⲙⲛ̄ ⲛⲁ ⲡⲓⲉⲓⲛⲉ ϫⲉ ¹⁶ « ⲛⲓⲟⲩⲛⲉⲙ » ⲁⲩⲱ
« ⲯⲩⲭⲓⲕⲟⲛ » ⲁⲩⲱ ¹⁷ « ⲛⲓⲥⲉⲧⲉ » ⲁⲩⲱ « ⲛⲓⲙⲏⲧⲉ.» ⲛⲁ ⲡⲓⲙⲉⲉⲩⲉ ¹⁸ ⲇⲉ ϩⲱⲟⲩ ⲙ̄ⲙⲛ̄ⲧϫⲁⲥⲓϩⲏⲧ
ⲙⲛ̄ ⲛⲁ ⲡⲓ- ¹⁹ ⲧⲁⲛⲧⲛ̄ ⲥⲉⲙⲟⲩⲧⲉ ⲁⲣⲁⲩ ϫⲉ « ⲛⲓϭⲃⲟⲩⲣ, » ²⁰ « ϩⲩⲗⲓⲕⲟⲛ, » « ⲛ̄ⲕⲉⲕⲉ, » ⲁⲩⲱ
« ⲛ̄ϩⲁⲉⲟⲩⲉ. »

ϫⲉ ²¹ ⲙⲛ̄ⲛⲥⲁ ⲧⲣⲉϥⲧⲉϩⲟ ⲁⲣⲉⲧϥ̄ ⲛ̄ϭⲓ ⲡⲗⲟⲅⲟⲥ ²² ⲙ̄ⲡⲟⲩⲉⲉⲓ ⲡⲟⲩⲉⲉⲓ ϩⲛ̄ ⲧⲉϥⲧⲁϫⲓⲥ, ⲉⲓ- ²³ ⲧⲁ
ⲛⲓϩⲓ̈ⲕⲱⲛ ⲙⲛ̄ ⲛⲓⲉⲓⲛⲉ ⲁⲩⲱ ⲛⲓⲧⲁⲛⲧⲛ̄, ²⁴ ⲛ̄ⲡⲁⲓⲱⲛ ⲙⲉⲛ ⲛⲇⲉ ⲛⲓϩⲓⲕⲱⲛ ⲁϥⲉⲣⲏϩ ²⁵ ⲉⲣⲟϥ
ⲉϥⲧⲟⲩⲃⲁⲉⲓⲧ ⲁⲃⲁⲗ ϩⲛ̄ ⲛⲉⲧϯ ⲁ- ²⁶ ϩⲧⲏϥ ⲧⲏⲣⲟⲩ, ϩⲱⲥ ⲉⲩⲧⲟⲡⲟⲥ ⲡⲉ ⲛ̄ⲟⲩⲣⲁⲧ ²⁷ ⲡⲉ. ⲛⲁ
ⲡⲓⲙⲉⲩⲉ ⲇⲉ ⲛ̄ⲧⲁϥ ⲁϥⲟⲩⲱⲛϩ̄ ²⁸ ⲁⲣⲁⲟⲩ ⲙ̄ⲡⲓⲙⲉⲩⲉ ⲉⲛⲧⲁϥⲕⲁⲕϥ̄ ⲁ- ²⁹ ϩⲏⲟⲩ ⲙ̄ⲙⲟϥ,
ⲉϥⲟⲩⲱϣⲉ ⲁⲧⲣⲉϥⲥⲁⲕⲟⲩ ³⁰ ⲁⲩⲕⲟⲓⲛⲱⲛⲓⲁ ⲛ̄ϩⲩⲗⲓⲕⲟⲛ, ⲉⲧⲃⲉ ⲟⲩ- ³¹ ⲥⲩⲥⲧⲁⲥⲓⲥ ⲛⲉⲩ ⲙⲛ̄ⲛ
ⲟⲩⲙⲁ ⲛ̄ϣⲱⲡⲉ ³² ⲁⲩⲱ ϫⲉⲕⲁⲥⲉ ⲟⲛ ⲉⲩⲛⲁϫⲡⲟ ⲛ̄ⲛⲟⲩ- ³³ ⲁⲫⲟⲣⲙⲏ ⲛ̄ϭⲱϫⲃ̄ ⲁⲃⲁⲗ ϩⲓⲧⲛ̄
ⲡⲥⲁ- ³⁴ ⲕⲟⲩ ϣⲁ ⲛⲉⲧⲑⲁⲩ, ϫ<ⲉ> ⲛ̄ⲛⲟ`ⲩ´ⲣ̄ ϩⲟⲩⲉ ³⁵ ⲟⲩⲛⲁϭ ⲙ̄ⲙⲁⲩ ⲛ̄ϩⲣⲏⲓ̈ ϩⲛ̄ ⲡⲉⲁϥ ³⁶
ⲙ̄ⲡⲟⲩⲕⲱⲧⲉ ⲛ̄ⲥⲉⲡⲱⲛⲉ ⲁⲃⲁⲗ, ³⁷ ⲁⲗⲗⲁ ϫⲉⲕⲁⲥⲉ ⲛ̄ⲧⲟϥ ⲉⲩⲛⲁϭϣϣ̄ⲧ ³⁸ ⲁⲡⲟⲩϣⲱⲛⲉ
ⲉⲛⲧⲁⲩⲙ̄ⲕⲁϩ ⲙ̄ⲙⲟϥ, ⁹⁹·¹ ϫⲉⲕⲁⲥⲉ ⲉⲩⲛⲁϫⲡⲟ ⲛⲛⲟⲩⲙⲁ- ² ⲉⲓⲉ ⲙⲛ̄ ⲟⲩϣⲓⲛⲉ ⲉⲩⲙⲏⲛ ⲛ̄ⲥⲉ ⲡⲉ-
³ ⲧⲉⲟⲩⲛ̄ ϭⲟⲙ ⲙⲙⲟϥ ⲛ̄ⲗⲁϭⲉ ⲉⲣⲟ- ⁴ ⲟⲩ ϩⲛ̄ ⲡⲓϭⲱϫⲃ̄. ⲛⲉⲉⲓ ⲇⲉ ϩⲱⲟⲩ ⁵ ⲉⲧⲉ ⲛⲁ ⲡⲓⲧⲁⲛⲧⲛ̄
ⲛⲉ, ⲁϥⲕⲱ ⲉϩⲣⲁⲓ̈ ⁶ ⲉⲭⲱⲟⲩ ⲙ̄ⲡⲓⲗⲟⲅⲟⲥ ⲛ̄ⲧⲥⲁⲉⲓⲟ ⲁⲧⲣⲉϥ- ⁷ ⲛ̄ⲧⲟⲩ ⲁⲩⲙⲟⲣⲫⲏ. ⲁϥⲕⲱ`ⲉ´
ⲁϩⲣⲏⲓ̈ ⲁ- ⁸ ϫⲱⲟⲩ ⲁⲛ ⲙ̄ⲡⲓⲛⲟⲙⲟⲥ ⲛ̄ⲧⲉⲕⲣⲓⲥⲓⲥ. ⁹ ⲉⲧⲓ ⲁⲛ ⲁϥⲕⲱⲉ ⲁϩⲣⲏⲓ̈ ⲁⲭⲱⲟⲩ ⲛ̄[ⲛⲓ]- ¹⁰
ϭⲟⲙ ⲉⲧⲁⲛⲛⲟⲩⲛⲉ ⲛ̄ⲧⲟⲩ ⲁⲃ[ⲁⲗ ¹¹ ϩⲛ̄] ϯⲙⲛ̄ⲧⲙⲁⲉⲓⲟⲩϩ ⲥⲁϩⲛⲉ. ⲁϥ[ⲕⲁ- ¹² ⲁ]ⲩ ⲉⲩⲁⲣⲭⲉⲓ
ⲁⲭⲱⲟⲩ, ϫⲉⲕⲁⲥⲉ ⲁⲃⲁ[ⲗ ¹³ ϩⲓ̈]ⲧⲛ̄ ⲡⲥⲙⲓⲛⲉ ⲙ̄ⲡⲗⲟⲅⲟⲥ ⲉⲧ<ⲧ>ⲥⲁⲉ[ⲓⲏ]- ¹⁴ ⲟⲩ ⲏ ⲁⲃⲁⲗ ϩⲓⲧⲛ̄
ⲧⲁⲡⲓⲗⲏ ⲙ̄ⲡⲛ̄[ⲟⲙⲟⲥ] ¹⁵ ⲏ ⲁⲃⲟⲗ ϩⲓⲧⲛ̄ ϯϭⲟⲙ ⲙⲙⲛ̄ⲧⲙⲁⲉ[ⲓ]- ¹⁶ ⲟⲩⲉϩ ⲥⲁϩⲛⲉ ⲁⲅⲁ<ⲁ>ⲣⲏϩ
ⲁⲧⲧⲁϫⲓⲥ ¹⁷ ⲛ̄ⲛⲉⲧⲁϩⲟⲩⲱⲙ ⲙ̄ⲙⲟⲥ ⲛ̄ⲛⲉⲧⲑⲁⲩ, ¹⁸ ϣⲁⲛⲧⲉϥⲣ̄ ϩⲛⲉϥ ⲁⲣⲁⲟⲩ ⲛ̄ϭⲓ ⲡⲗⲟⲅⲟⲥ, ¹⁹
ⲉⲩⲣ̄ ϣⲉⲩ ⲁⲧⲟⲓ̈ⲕⲟⲓⲛⲟⲙⲓⲁ.

ϫⲉ ⲡⲧⲱⲧ ²⁰ ⲛ̄ⲧⲙⲛ̄ⲧⲙⲁⲉⲓⲟⲩϩ ⲥⲁϩⲛⲉ ⲙ̄ⲡⲧⲁⲅ- ²¹ ⲙⲁ ⲥⲛⲉⲩ ϥⲥⲁϩⲛⲉ ⲙ̄ⲙⲟϥ ⲛ̄ϭⲓ ⲡⲗⲟⲅⲟⲥ. ²²
ⲛⲉⲉⲓ ⲙⲛ̄ ⲛⲉⲉⲓⲕⲉⲕⲁⲩⲉ ⲧⲏⲣⲟⲩ ⲁϥⲣ̄ ²³ ϩⲙⲟⲧ ⲛⲉⲩ ⲛ̄ⲧⲟⲩⲉⲡⲓⲑⲩⲙⲓⲁ. ⲁϥϯ ⲛ̄- ²⁴ <ϯ>ⲧⲁϫⲓⲥ
ⲙ̄ⲡⲟⲩⲉⲉⲓ ⲡⲟⲩⲉⲉⲓ ⲛⲉϥ ⲉⲧ- ²⁵ ⲧⲉϩⲟ ⲙ̄ⲙⲁϥ, ⲁⲩⲱ ⲁⲩⲟⲩⲉⲓ ⲥⲁ- ²⁶ ϩⲛⲉ ⲙ̄ⲙⲟⲥ ϫⲉⲕⲁⲥⲉ ⲡⲟⲩⲉⲓ
ⲡⲟⲩⲉ- ²⁷ ⲉⲓ ⲉϥⲛⲁϣⲱⲡⲉ ⲛⲛⲁⲣⲭⲱⲛ ⲛ̄ⲛⲟⲩ- ²⁸ ⲧⲟⲡⲟⲥ ⲙⲛ̄ ⲟⲩϩⲱⲃ. ϥⲕⲱⲉ ⲙ̄ⲡⲙⲁ ²⁹
ⲙ̄ⲡⲉⲧϫⲁⲥⲉ ⲁⲣⲁϥ ⲁⲧⲣⲉϥⲟⲩⲁϩ ³⁰ ⲥⲁϩⲛⲉ ⲛⲓⲕⲉⲧⲟⲡⲟⲥ ϩⲛ̄ⲛ ⲟⲩϩⲱⲃ ³¹ ⲉϥϣⲟⲟⲡ ϩⲛ̄ ⲡⲕⲗⲏⲣⲟⲥ
ⲙ̄ⲫⲱⲃ ³² ⲉⲧⲁⲧⲉϩⲁϥ ⲁⲉⲙⲁⲣⲧⲉ ⲙ̄ⲙⲁϥ ³³ ⲁⲃⲁⲗ ⲙ̄ⲡⲥⲙⲁⲧ ⲛ̄ϣⲱⲡⲉ. ⲁⲧⲣⲉ- ³⁴ ϩ̄ⲣⲉϥⲟⲩⲉϩ
ⲥⲁϩⲛⲉ ϣⲱⲡⲉ ⲙⲛ̄ ³⁵ ⲛⲉⲧⲟⲃⲃⲓⲁⲉⲓⲧ ϩⲛ̄ ϩⲛ̄ⲙⲛ̄ⲧϫⲁⲓ̈ⲥ ³⁶ ⲙⲛ̄ ϩⲛ̄ⲙⲛ̄ⲧϭⲁⲩⲁⲛ ⲛⲇⲉ ⲛⲓⲁⲅ- ³⁷
ⲅⲉⲗⲟⲥ ¹⁰⁰·¹ [ⲙ]ⲛ̄ ⲛⲓⲁⲣⲭⲁⲅⲅⲉⲗⲟⲥ, ⲛⲉϩⲃⲏⲩⲉ ² [ⲉ]ⲩⲟⲉⲓ ⲙ̄ⲙⲓⲛⲉ ⲙⲓⲛⲉ ⲁⲩⲱ ⲉⲩϣⲃ̄ⲃⲓⲁ[ⲉⲓⲧ]. ³
ⲡⲟⲩⲉⲓ ⲡⲟⲩⲉⲓ ⲛ̄ⲛⲁⲣⲭⲱⲛ ⲙⲛ̄ ⲡⲉϥ- ⁴ ⲅⲉⲛⲟⲥ ⲙⲛ̄ ⲧⲉϥⲁϫⲓⲁ ⲉⲧⲉⲁⲡⲉϥⲕⲗⲏ- ⁵ ⲣⲟⲥ ⲧⲉϩⲁϥ
ⲁⲣⲁⲩ, ⲕⲁⲧⲁ ⲑⲉ ⲉⲛⲧⲁⲩ- ⁶ ⲟⲩⲱⲛϩ̄, ⲛⲉϥⲁⲣⲏϩ, ⲉⲁⲩⲛ̄ϩⲟⲩⲧϥ̄ ⁷ ⲙⲉⲛ ⲁⲧⲟⲓⲕⲟⲛⲟⲙⲓⲁ ⲁⲩⲱ ⲙⲛ̄
ⲗⲁⲩ- ⁸ ⲉ ⲉϥⲟⲉⲓ ⲛ̄ⲁⲧⲟⲩⲉϩ ⲥⲁϩⲛⲉ ⲁⲩⲱ ⁹ ⲙⲛ̄ ⲗⲁⲩⲉ ⲉϥⲟⲉⲓ ⲛ̄ⲁⲧⲧⲣ̄ⲣⲟ ϫⲓⲛ ¹⁰ [ⲁⲣⲏ]ϫϥ̄ ⲛ̄ⲙⲡⲏⲩⲉ
ϣⲁ ⲁⲣⲏϫϥ̄ ⲙ̄ⲡ- ¹¹ [ⲕⲁϩ] ϣⲁ ϩⲣⲏⲓ̈ ⲁⲛⲕⲣ̄ⲕⲛⲟⲩ ⲙ̄ⲡ[ⲕⲁϩ ¹² ⲙ]ⲛ̄ ⲛⲉⲧⲛ̄ⲡⲥⲁ ⲛⲡⲓⲧⲛ̄ ⲙ̄ⲡⲕⲁ[ϩ].

98.24 ⲛⲇⲉ: read ⲛⲧⲉ.
99.36 ⲛ̄ⲇⲉ: read ⲛ̄ⲧⲉ.
100.11 ⲕⲣ̄ⲕⲛⲟⲩ: ϭⲣϭⲛⲟⲩ.

Therefore, to each one he gave [13] a name, because the two orders are [14] in a name. Those belonging [15] to the thought and those belonging to the image are called [16] "the Right ones" and "Soulish" and [17] "the Flaming ones" and "the Middle ones." Yet those belonging to the arrogant thought [18] and those belonging to the [19] likeness are called "the Left ones," [20] "Material," "the Dark ones," and "the Last ones."

[21] After the Word established [22] each one in its order, whether [23] the images or the semblances or the likenesses, [24] he kept the eternity of the images [25] pure from all those who fight [26] against it, since it is a place of joy. [27] But to those belonging to the thought he revealed [28] the thought that he had stripped [29] from himself, because he wanted to lure them [30] into a material fellowship, on account of [31] their system [32] and place of existence and so that they might bear a [33] penchant for smallness by means of their attraction [34] to evil things, so that they might not [35] rejoice any more in the glory [36] of their surroundings and be poured out, [37] but so that they might see [38] the illness from which they suffer, [99.1] so that they will bear love [2] and perpetual seeking after the one [3] for whom it is possible to cure [4] them from smallness. But also over those [5] who belong to the likeness, he placed [6] the Word of beauty in order to [7] bring them into a form. He placed over [8] them the law of judgment as well. [9] Next he also placed over them [the] [10] powers that the roots brought forth [11] [from] the love of power. He [stationed] [12] them as rulers over them, so that by means of [13] the confirmation of the Word that is beautiful [14] or by means of the threat of the [law] [15] or by means of the power of the love of [16] power the order [17] might be guarded from those who submitted it to evil things, [18] until the Word is pleased by them, [19] because they are of value to the assembly.

The agreement [20] concerning the love of power by the [21] two orders the Word knows. [22] To these and all the others he [23] granted their desire. He gave [24] to each one a proper rank, [25] and it was determined [26] that each one [27] would become ruler over a [28] place and a matter. He concedes the place [29] of the one exalted over him so that he can [30] command the other places in a matter [31] that is in the allotted matter [32] incumbent upon him to oversee [33] because of (his) manner of being. Consequently, [34] commanders and [35] subordinates came to be in positions of authority [36] and subjugation among the [37] angels [100.1] and archangels. Accordingly the tasks [2] are of different kinds and variegated. [3] Each of the rulers and his [4] race and his benefit [5] to which his allotment lays claim, just as they were [6] revealed, was on guard, since it had [7] the assembly and none [8] is without a command and [9] none lacks kingship from [10] the end of the heavens to the end of the [11] [earth] to the foundations of the [earth] [12] and

ο[ΥΝ̄ ¹³ Ρ̄]ΡΟ, ΟΥΝ̄ ϪΑΕΙⲤ, ΑΥⲰ ΝΕΤ[Ο]Υ[ЄϨ] ¹⁴ ⳟⲀϨΝЄ ⲘⲘΑΥ, ϨΑЄΙΝЄ ⲘЄΝ Ⲁ- ¹⁵ ṬⲢΟΥϮ
ⲔΟⲖⲀⲤⲒⲤ, ϨⲚ̄ⲔЄⲔⲀⲨЄ ¹⁶ ⲀⲦⲢΟΥϮ ϨⲀⲠ, ϨⲚ̄ⲔЄϨⲀЄΙΝЄ ⲀⲦⲢΟΥ- ¹⁷ Ϯ Ṃ̄ⲦⲀΝ ΝⲤЄⲦⲀⲖϬΟ,
ϨⲚ̄ⲔЄⲔⲀⲨЄ ⲀⲦⲢΟΥ- ¹⁸ Ϯ ⲤⲂⲰ, ϨⲚ̄ⲔЄⲔⲀⲨЄ ⲀⲦⲢΟΥⲀⲢЄϨ.

ϪЄ ΝΙ[ⲀⲢ]- ¹⁹ Ϫ̄ⲰⲚ ⲦⲎⲢΟΥ ⲀⲨⲔⲰЄ Ⲛ̄ⲚΟΥⲀⲢⲬⲰⲚ [Ⲁ]- ²⁰ ϨⲢⲎⲒ̈ ⲀⲬⲰΟΥ ЄⲘⲚ̄ ⲖⲀⲨЄ ΟΥЄϨ
ⲤⲀϨΝЄ ²¹ ⲘⲘΟϤ, ЄΝⲦⲀϤ ⲠЄ ⲠΟΥϪⲀЄΙⲤ ⲦⲎⲢΟΥ, ²² ЄⲦЄ ⲠⲀЄΙ ⲠЄ ⲠⲒⲘΟΥΝⲔ̄ Ⲛ̄ϨΟ ЄΝⲦⲀⲠⲖΟ- ²³
ⲄΟⲤ ΝⲦϤ ⲀⲂⲀⲖ ϨⲚ̄ ⲠⲒⲘЄЄΥЄ Ⲛ̄ⲦЄϤ ²⁴ ⲔⲀⲦⲀ ⲠⲒΝЄ Ⲙ̄ⲠⲒⲰⲦ Ⲛ̄ⲆЄ ΝⲒⲠⲦⲎⲢϤ̄. ЄⲦⲂЄ ²⁵ ⲠЄЄⲒ
ϤⲦⲤⲀЄⲒⲀЄⲒⲦ Ⲛ̄ϨⲢⲎⲒ̈ ϨⲚ̄ {Ϩ}ⲢЄ<Ν> ΝⲒⲘ, ²⁶ ЄΥΟΥЄⲒΝЄ Ⲛ̄ⲦЄϤ <ⲠЄ>, ЄⲠⲀ ΝⲒⲀⲢЄⲦⲎ ⲦⲎⲢΟΥ
ⲠЄ ²⁷ ⲘⲚ̄ ⲠⲀ ΝⲒЄⲀΥ ⲦⲎⲢΟΥ. ⲤЄⲘΟΥⲦЄ ⲄⲀⲢ ⲀⲢⲀϤ ²⁸ ϨⲰⲰϤ Ϫ̄Є « Ⲓ̈ⲰⲦ » ⲀⲨⲰ « ΝΟΥⲦЄ »
ⲀⲨⲰ « ⲢЄϤ- ²⁹ Ⲣ̄ ϨⲰⲂ » ⲀⲨⲰ « Ⲣ̄ⲢΟ » ⲀⲨⲰ « ⲔⲢⲒⲦⲎⲤ » ⲀⲨⲰ « ⲦΟⲠΟⲤ » ³⁰ ⲀⲨⲰ
« ⲘΟΝⲎ » ⲀⲨⲰ « ΝΟⲘΟⲤ. »

Ϫ̄Є ⲠⲀЄⲒ ϬЄ ³¹ ⲀϤⲢ̄ ⲬⲢⲀⲤⲐⲀⲒ Ⲙ̄ⲘΟϤ Ⲛ̄ϬⲒ ⲠⲖΟⲄΟⲤ Ⲙ̄ⲠⲢⲎ- ³² ⲦЄ Ⲛ̄ΝΟΥϬⲒϪ, ⲀⲦⲢЄϤⲦⲤⲀЄⲒⲰ
ⲀⲨⲰ Ⲛ̄Ϥ- ³³ Ⲣ̄ ϨⲰⲂ ⲀΝЄⲦⲘ̄ⲠⲤⲀ ΝⲠⲒⲦⲚ̄. ⲀⲨⲰ ΝϤⲢ̄ ³⁴ ⲬⲢⲀⲤⲐⲀⲒ Ⲙ̄ⲘΟϤ Ⲙ̄ⲠⲢⲎⲦЄ Ⲛ̄ΝΟΥⲢΟ,
Ⲁ- ³⁵ ⲦⲢЄϤϢЄϪЄ ⲀΝЄⲦΟΥΝⲀⲢ̄ ⲠⲢΟϤⲎⲦЄΥЄ ³⁶ Ⲙ̄ⲘΟΥ.

Ϫ̄Є ΝЄⲦЄⲀϤϪΟΟϬ ЄϤⲢ̄ ϨⲰⲂ ³⁷ ⲀⲢⲀΥ. ЄⲀϤΝЄϤ ⲀⲢⲀΥ Ϫ̄Є ϨⲚ̄ΝΟϬ ΝЄ ⲀΥⲰ ³⁸ ΝⲀΝΟΥΟΥ ⲀΥⲰ
ϨⲚ̄ⲘⲀϨЄⲒЄ ΝЄ, ⲀϤΟΥ- ³⁹ ΝⲀϤ Ⲙ̄ⲘΟϤ ⲀΥⲰ ⲀϤ[ⲦЄ]ⲖⲎⲖ, ϨⲰⲤ ^{101.1} ЄϢϪЄ Ⲛ̄ⲦⲀϤ Ⲛ̄ϨⲢⲎⲒ̈ ϨΝ
ΝЄϤⲘЄΥЄ ² ⲠЄⲦϪΟΥ Ⲙ̄ⲘΑΥ ⲀΥⲰ ЄϤЄⲒⲢЄ Ⲙ̄- ³ ⲘⲀΥ, ЄϤΟЄⲒ Ⲛ̄ⲀⲦⲤⲀΥΝЄ Ϫ̄Є ⲠⲔⲒⲘ ⁴ ЄⲦΟΟⲦϤ̄
ⲀⲂⲀⲖ ⁵ ϨⲚ̄ ⲠЄⲠΝЄΥⲘⲀ, ⲠЄⲦⲔⲒⲘ Ⲁ- ⁵ ⲢΟϤ ϨⲚ̄ ΟΥⲦⲰϢЄ ⲀΝЄⲦϤ̄ΟΥⲀϢΟΥ.

⁶ Ϫ̄Є ΝЄⲦⲀϢⲰⲠЄ ⲀⲂⲀⲖ Ⲙ̄ⲘⲀϤ ⲀϤϪΟΟΥ, ⁷ ⲀΥⲰ ⲀΥϢⲰⲠЄ ⲔⲀⲦⲀ ⲠⲒΝЄ Ⲙ̄ⲠΝЄΥⲘⲀⲦⲒⲔΟ[Ⲥ]
⁸ Ⲛ̄ⲦΟⲠΟⲤ, ΝЄЄⲒ ЄⲦⲀΝⲢ̄ ϢⲢⲠ̄ Ⲛ̄ϪΟΟΥ ⁹ ϨⲘ̄ ⲠⲖΟⲄΟⲤ ϨⲀ ⲠⲢⲀ Ⲛ̄ΝⲒϨⲒ̈ⲔⲰΝ.

Ϫ̄[Є Ο]Υ ⲘΟΝΟ[Ν] ¹⁰ <Ν>ЄϤⲢ̄ ϨⲰⲂ ⲀⲖⲖⲀ ΝЄϤϪⲠΟ ⲀΝ, ϨⲰ[Ⲥ ⲠЄ]Ϯ- ¹¹ ЄⲀϤⲔⲀⲀⲦ Ⲛ̄ЄⲒⲰⲦ
Ⲛ̄ⲦΟⲒⲔΟΝΟⲘⲒ[Ⲁ ¹² Ⲛ̄ⲦЄ]Ϥ, ⲔⲀⲦⲀⲢⲀϤ ⲘⲚ̄ Ⲛ̄ⲤⲠЄⲢⲘⲀ Ϩ[Ⲛ̄ ¹³ ⲠⲒⲠ]ΝЄΥⲘⲀ ⲆЄ ЄⲦⲤⲀⲦⲠ̄ Є Ⲧ´ΝⲀЄⲒ
ⲀϨⲢⲎⲒ̈ [Ⲛ̄- ¹⁴ ⲦΟΟ]ⲦϤ̄ ⲀΝⲒⲦΟⲠΟⲤ ЄⲦⲚ̄ⲠⲤⲀ Ⲁ ΝⲠⲒ[Ⲧ]Ⲛ̄. ¹⁵ Ο[Υ ⲘΟ]ΝΟΝ ЄϤϪΟΥ ⲀΝ Ⲛ̄ϨⲚⲰϢЄ- ¹⁶
Ϫ̄Є Ⲙ̄ⲠΝЄΥⲘⲀⲦⲒⲔΟΝ ЄΝⲰϢ ΝЄ, <ⲀⲖⲖⲀ> ϨⲚ̄ ¹⁷ [Ο]ΥⲘⲚ̄ⲦⲀⲦΝЄΥ ⲀⲢⲀⲤ ¹⁸ ⲀⲂⲀⲖ ϨⲒⲦⲚ̄
ⲠΝЄΥⲘⲀ, ЄⲦϮ ϨⲢⲀΥΟΥ ¹⁹ ⲀΥⲰ ЄⲦϪⲠΟ ΝΝΟϬ ⲀⲦЄϤΟΥⲤⲒⲀ ²⁰ ⲔⲀⲦⲀⲢⲀϤ.

Ϫ̄Є Ⲛ̄ⲦⲀϤ ⲀⲂⲀⲖ ϨⲚ̄ ²¹ ⲦЄϤΟΥⲤⲒⲀ ϨⲰⲤ ЄΥΝΟΥⲦЄ ⲠЄ ²² ⲀΥⲰ ΝЄⲒⲰⲦ Ⲙ<Ν> ⲠⲔЄϢⲰϪⲠ̄ Ⲛ̄- ²³
ΝⲒⲢЄΝ ⲦⲎⲢΟΥ ЄⲦ´Ⲧ´ⲀЄⲒΗⲨ, ΝЄϤ- ²⁴ ⲘЄΥЄ ⲀⲢⲀϤ Ϫ̄Є ϨⲚ̄ΝⲀⲂⲀⲖ ²⁵ ϨⲚ̄ ⲦЄϤΟΥⲤⲒⲀ ΝЄ. ⲀϤⲦЄϨΟ
ⲀⲢЄ- ²⁶ ⲦϤ̄ Ⲛ̄ΝΟΥⲘ̄ⲦΟΝ ΝЄⲦΟΥⲢ̄ ⲠⲒΘЄ ²⁷ ΝⲘ̄ⲘЄϤ. ΝЄЄⲒ ⲆЄ ЄⲦⲢ̄ ⲠⲒΘЄ ²⁸ ΝⲘ̄ⲘЄϤ ЄΝ,
ⲀϨⲚ̄ⲔΟⲖⲀⲤⲒⲤ ²⁹ ϨⲰⲰϤ. ЄϤϢΟΟⲠ ϨⲀⲦⲎϤ ϨⲰⲰϤ ³⁰ ⲀΝ Ⲛ̄ϬⲒ ΟΥⲠⲀⲢⲀⲆⲒⲆΟⲤ ⲀΥⲰ ΟΥ- ³¹
ⲘⲚ̄ⲦⲢ̄ⲢΟ ⲀΥⲰ ⲠⲔЄϢⲰϪⲠ̄ ³² ⲦⲎⲢϤ̄ ЄⲦϢΟΟⲠ ϨⲘ̄ ⲠⲀⲒⲰΝ ³³ ЄⲦϢΟΟⲠ ϨⲀ ⲦЄϤϬⲢⲎ. ЄΥⲤⲀⲦⲠ
³⁴ Ⲛ̄ΝⲦΟΥⲂЄ ЄⲦⲂЄ ⲠⲘЄЄΥЄ ЄⲦΝⲀ- ³⁵ ϨⲂ ⲀⲢ[ⲀΟ]Υ, ЄⲦΟЄⲒ Ⲙ̄ⲠⲢⲎⲦЄ ^{102.1} [Ν]ΝΟΥϨⲀЄⲒⲂЄⲤ ⲘⲚ̄
ΟΥϨⲂⲤ, Ⲙ̄ⲠⲢⲎ- ² [Ⲧ]Ⲏ ⲀϪΟΟⲤ, Ϫ̄Є ϤΝЄΥ ЄΝ Ϫ̄<Є> ⲀⲢЄΝЄⲦ- ³ ϢΟΟⲠ Ⲱ ΝЄϢ Ⲛ̄ⲢⲎⲦⲚ.

102.3 Ⲱ ΝЄϢ: read ΟЄⲒ Ⲛ̄ЄϢ.

the places below the earth. There are [13] kings, there are lords, and those who command [14] them, some for [15] giving correction, others [16] for passing judgment, others for [17] giving rest and healing, others for [18] teaching, and others for protecting.

Over [19] all the rulers he placed a ruler [20] whom no one commanded, [21] since he is Lord over all, [22] that is, the countenance that the Word [23] brought forth in his thought [24] in accordance with the image of the Father of the entireties. Because [25] of this he is made beautiful by every <name>, [26] which <is> an image of him, since he is the one who belongs to all excellence [27] and all glory. For he is also called [28] "Father" and "God" and "Demiurge" [29] and "King" and "Judge" and "Place" and [30] "Continuance" and "Law."

Therefore [31] the Word made use of him as [32] a hand, in order to make beautiful and [33] work on the things below. He also [34] made use of him as a mouth, in [35] order to say the things that will be [36] prophesied.

The things he has spoken he does. [37] Upon seeing that they were great and [38] good and marvelous, he [39] rejoiced and was happy, as [101.1] if he in his own thought [2] is the one that said and did [3] them, since he was unaware that the movement [4] in him was from the spirit, the one who moves [5] him in a determined manner toward the things he desires.

[6] The things that came to be from him he spoke, [7] and they came to be according to the image of spiritual [8] places, those that we previously mentioned [9] in the discussion of the images.

[Not] only [10] <was> he working, but, as [the one] [11] appointed as the father of [his] assembly, [12] he also gave birth alone by seed and [by [13] the] spirit that is chosen and that will come down [14] [through] him to the places below. [15] [Not] only does he speak [16] spiritual words that are his own, <but> (he also speaks) [17] invisibly [18] through the spirit, which gives voice [19] and bears things greater than its [20] own essence.

Since he in [21] his essence is God [22] and Father <and> all the rest of the honorific [23] names, he [24] thought that they are (qualities) of [25] his own essence. He established [26] a rest for those who obey [27] him. But for those who do not obey [28] him, (he established) punishments [29] as well. Also with him is [30] a paradise and a [31] kingdom and all the rest of the things [32] that exist in the eternity [33] that exists before him. They are better [34] than the imprints because the thought that is yoked [35] to them, which is like [102.1] a shadow and a cloak, so [2] to speak, because he does not see [3] in what way the things that exist (truly exist).

ϫⲉ ⲁϥⲧⲉϩⲟ ⁴ ⲛⲉϥ ⲛ̄ϩⲉⲛⲣⲉϥⲣ̄ ϩⲱⲃ ⲁⲣⲉⲧⲟⲩ ⲙⲛ̄ ⁵ ϩⲉⲛⲣⲉϥϣⲙ̄ϣⲉ, ⲉⲩⲣ̄ ϩⲩⲡⲟⲩⲣⲅⲓⲁ ⁶
ⲛ̄ⲛⲉⲧⲛ̄ⲁⲉⲧⲟⲩ ⲙⲛ̄ ⲛⲉⲧⲩⲛⲁⲭⲟ- ⁷ ⲟⲩ, ϫⲉ ⲙⲁ ⲛⲓⲙ ⲉⲛⲧⲁⲩⲣ̄ ϩⲱⲃ ⲁ- ⁸ ⲣⲁⲩ, ⲁⲩⲕⲱϣ
ⲙ̄ⲡⲉϥⲙⲟⲩⲛⲅ̄ ⲛ̄ϩⲟ ⁹ ⲛ̄ϩ[ⲏ]ⲧⲟⲩ ⲛ̄ϩⲣⲏⲓ̈ ϩⲙ̄ ⲡⲉϥⲣⲉⲛ ⲉϥⲧⲥⲁ- ¹⁰ [ⲉ]ⲁⲉⲓⲧ, ⲉϥⲣ̄ ϩⲱⲃ ⲁⲩⲱ
ⲉϥϣⲉϫⲉ ¹¹ [ⲛ]ⲛⲉⲧⲩⲛⲁⲙⲉⲩⲉ ⲁⲣⲁⲟⲩ.

ϫⲉ ⲁ[ϥ]- ¹² ⲧⲉϩⲟ ⲁⲣⲉⲧⲟⲩ ⲛ̄ϩⲛ̄ϩⲓⲕⲱⲛ ⲛ̄[ϩⲣⲏⲓ̈] ¹³ ϩⲛ̄ ⲛⲉϥⲧⲟⲡⲟⲥ ⲛ̄ⲇⲉ ⲡⲟⲩⲁ[ⲉⲓⲛ] ¹⁴
ⲉⲛⲧⲁϩⲟⲩⲱⲛϩ̄ ⲁⲩⲱ ⲛ̄ⲧⲉ [ⲛⲉⲧⲟ] ¹⁵ ⲙ̄ⲡⲛⲉⲩⲙⲁⲧⲓⲕⲟⲥ, ⲉϩⲛ̄[ⲁⲃ]ⲁⲗ ¹⁶ ϩⲛ̄ ⲧⲉϥⲟⲩⲥⲓⲁ ⲛⲉ.
ⲙ̄ⲡⲣⲏⲧⲉ ϫⲉ ⲛⲁⲩ- ¹⁷ ⲧⲁⲉⲓⲁⲉⲓⲧ ϭⲉ ϩⲛ̄ ⲙⲁ ⲛⲓⲙ ⲛ̄ⲧⲟⲟⲧϥ̄ ¹⁸ ⲉⲩⲧⲃ̄ⲃⲟ, ⲁⲃⲁⲗ ⲙ̄ⲡⲙⲟⲩⲛⲅ̄ ⲛ̄ϩⲟ ¹⁹
ⲙ̄ⲡⲉⲧⲁϩⲕⲁⲩⲉ, ⲁⲩⲱ ⲁⲩⲧⲉϩⲟ- ²⁰ ⲛⲟⲩ ⲁⲣⲉⲧⲟⲩ <ⲛ̄>ϩⲛ̄ⲡⲁⲣⲁⲇⲓⲇⲟⲥ ²¹ ⲙⲛ̄ ϩⲛ̄ⲙⲛ̄ⲧⲣ̄ⲣⲟ ⲁⲩⲱ
ϩⲙ̄ⲙⲧⲟⲛ ²² ⲙⲛ̄ ϩⲉⲛϣⲱⲡ ⲙⲛ̄ ϩⲉⲛⲙⲛ̄ϣⲉ ²³ ⲛ̄ⲣⲉϥϣⲙ̄ϣⲉ ⲛ̄ⲧⲉϥ ⲙ̄ⲡⲟⲩ- ²⁴ ϣⲉ, ⲁⲩⲱ ⲛⲁⲉⲓ
ⲉϩⲛ̄ϫⲁⲉⲓⲥ ⲛⲉ ⲛ̄ⲛⲁⲣ- ²⁵ ⲭⲏ ⲛⲉ, ⲉⲩⲕⲁⲁⲧ ⲁϩⲣⲏⲓ̈ ⲉⲡⲉⲧⲟⲓ̈ ²⁶ ⲛ̄ϫⲁⲉⲓⲥ, ⲡⲉⲛⲧⲁϩⲕⲟⲟⲩⲉ.

ϫⲉ ²⁷ ⲙⲛ̄ⲛⲥⲁ ⲧⲣⲉϥⲥⲁⲧⲙ̄ ⲁⲣⲁϥ ²⁸ ⲙ̄ⲡⲓⲣⲏⲧⲏ ⲕⲁⲗⲱⲥ ⲁⲛⲓⲟⲩⲁⲉⲓ-²⁹ ⲛⲉ, ⲛⲁⲉⲓ ⲉⲧⲉ
ϯⲕⲁⲧⲁⲣⲭⲏ ³⁰ ⲙⲛ̄ ϯⲥⲩⲥⲧⲁⲥⲓⲥ, ⲁⲩⲕⲁⲁⲩ ⲁⲭⲛ̄ ³¹ ⲡⲓⲧⲥⲁⲉⲓⲱ ⲛ̄ⲛⲉⲧⲙ̄ⲡⲥⲁ ⲛ̄ⲡⲓⲧⲛ̄. ³² ⲁⲩⲕⲓⲙ
ⲁⲣⲁϥ ⲙ̄ⲡⲓⲣⲏⲧⲉ ⲛ̄ϭⲓ ⲡⲛⲉⲩ- ³³ ⲙⲁ ⲛ̄ⲛⲁⲧⲛ̄ⲛⲉⲩ ⲁ[ⲣⲁϥ] ⲁⲧⲣⲉϥ- ¹⁰³.¹ ⲟⲩⲱϣⲉ ⲁⲛ ⲁⲣ̄ ⲟⲓⲕⲟⲛⲟⲙⲓ
ⲁⲃⲁⲗ ϩ[ⲓ]- ² ⲧⲛ̄ ⲡⲓⲣⲉϥϣⲙ̄ϣ ⲛ̄ⲧⲉϥ ϩⲱⲱϥ, ⲡⲁ- ³ ⲉⲓ ⲉⲛⲧⲁⲩⲣ̄ ⲭⲣⲁⲥⲑⲁⲓ ⲙ̄ⲙⲟϥ ϩⲱ- ⁴ ⲱϥ ⲁⲛ
ⲙ̄ⲡⲓⲣⲏⲧⲏ ⲛ̄ⲛⲟⲩϭⲓϫ ⲁⲩⲱ ⁵ ⲙ̄ⲡⲓⲣⲏⲧⲉ ⲛ̄ⲛⲟⲩ{ⲣ̄}ⲣⲟ ⲁⲩⲱ ⲙ̄ⲡⲣⲏⲧ[ⲏ] ⁶ ⲉⲩⲛ̄ ϩⲱ ϩⲁⲧⲏϥ, ⲛⲉⲉⲓ
ⲉⲧϥⲉⲓⲛⲉ ⲙ- ⁷ ⲙⲁⲩ, ⲟⲩⲧⲁϫⲓⲥ ⲙⲛ̄ ⲟⲩⲁⲅⲁⲡⲏ ⲁ[ⲩⲱ] ⁸ ⲟⲩϩⲣ̄ⲧⲉ, ϫⲉⲕⲁⲥⲉ ⲛⲁⲉⲓ ⲉⲛⲧⲁⲩ[ⲉⲓ]- ⁹
ⲣⲉ ⲛ̄ⲛⲟⲩⲙⲛ̄ⲧⲁⲧⲥⲃⲱ ⲛ̄[ⲙⲙⲉⲩ ⲉⲩ]- ¹⁰ ⲛⲁϣⲱϭ <ⲧ>ⲧⲁϫⲓⲥ ⲉⲛⲧⲁ[ⲩⲧⲉⲉⲓⲥ ⲁⲧⲟⲩ]- ¹¹ ⲁⲣⲏϩ
ⲁⲣⲁⲥ, ⲉⲩⲥⲁⲛϩ̄ ⲛ̄ⲛⲥ̄[ⲛⲁϩ ⲛ̄- ¹² ⲛⲁ]ⲣⲭⲱⲛ ⲉⲧϩⲓϫⲱⲟⲩ ϩⲛ̄ⲛ ⲟⲩⲙⲛ̄[ⲧ- ¹³ ⲧⲱ]ⲥ.

ⲡⲧⲱⲕ ⲁⲣⲉⲧϥ̄ ⲧⲏⲣϥ̄ ⲛ̄ⲇⲉ ϯϩⲩ[ⲗⲏ ¹⁴ ϣ]ⲡ[ⲁϣ] ⲁϥϣⲟⲙⲛ̄ⲧ. ⲛⲓϭⲟⲙ ⲙⲉⲛ [ⲉⲧⲭⲟ- ¹⁵ ⲟⲣ] ⲛⲁⲉⲓ
ⲉⲛⲧⲁⲡⲗⲟⲅⲟⲥ ⲙ̄ⲡⲛⲉⲩⲙⲁ[ⲧⲓⲕⲟⲥ ¹⁶ ⲛ̄ⲧⲟ]ⲩ ⲁⲃⲁⲗ ⲕⲁⲧⲁ ⲟⲩⲫⲁⲛⲧⲁⲥ[ⲓⲁ ¹⁷ ⲙⲛ̄[ⲛ]
ⲟⲩⲙⲛ̄ⲧϫⲁⲥⲓϩⲛ̄ⲧ ⲁϥⲕⲁ[ⲁⲩ] ¹⁸ ϩⲛ̄ ⲧϣⲁⲣⲡ̄ ⲛ̄ⲧⲁϫⲓⲥ ⲙ̄ⲡⲛⲉⲩⲙⲁⲧⲓⲕⲟ[ⲛ]. ¹⁹ ⲛⲉⲧⲁϩⲁⲛⲉⲉⲓ
ϭⲉ ⲛ̄ⲧⲟⲩ ⲁⲃⲁⲗ ϩⲛ̄ ϯ- ²⁰ ⲙⲛ̄ⲧⲙⲁⲉⲓⲟⲩϩⲉ ⲥⲁϩⲛⲉ ⲁϥⲕⲁⲁⲩ ²¹ ϩⲛ̄ ⲧⲭⲱⲣⲁ ⲛ̄ⲧⲙⲏⲧⲉ,
ⲉϩⲛ̄ϭⲟⲙ ⲛ̄[ⲉ] ²² ⲛ̄ⲙⲛ̄ⲧⲙⲁⲉⲓⲟⲩϩⲉ ⲥⲁϩⲛⲉ ⲁⲧⲣⲟⲩ[ⲣ̄] ²³ ϫⲁⲉⲓⲥ ⲁⲩⲱ ⲛⲥⲉⲟⲩⲉϩ ⲥⲁϩⲛⲉ ⲙ̄[ⲡ]-
²⁴ ⲧⲉϩⲟ ⲁⲣⲉⲧϥ̄ ⲉⲧϩⲓ ⲥⲁ ⲛ̄ⲡⲓⲧⲛ̄ ⲙⲛ [ⲟⲩ]- ²⁵ ⲁⲛⲁⲅⲕⲏ ⲙⲛ̄ ⲟⲩϫⲛ̄ϫⲛⲁⲁϩ. ⲛⲉⲉⲓ ⲇⲉ ²⁶
ⲛ̄ⲧⲁϩϣⲱⲡⲉ ⲁⲃⲁⲗ ϩⲛ̄ ⲡⲓⲫⲑⲟⲛⲟⲥ ²⁷ ⲙⲛ̄ ⲡⲓⲕⲱϩ ⲙⲛ̄ ⲛⲓⲕⲉϫⲡⲟ ⲧⲏⲣⲟⲩ ²⁸ ⲁⲃⲁⲗ ϩⲛ̄
ⲛⲓⲧⲱϣⲉ ⲙ̄ⲡⲓⲣⲏⲧⲉ. ⲁϥⲕⲁⲩ- ²⁹ ⲉ ⲛ̄ⲛⲟⲩⲧⲁϫⲓⲥ ⲛ̄ⲣⲉϥϣⲙ̄ϣⲉ, ⲉⲩⲁ- ³⁰ ⲙⲁⲣⲧⲉ ⲛ̄ⲛⲉϩⲁⲉⲟⲩ,
ⲉⲩⲟⲩⲁϩ ⲥⲁϩⲛⲉ ³¹ ⲛ̄ⲛⲉⲧϣⲟⲟⲡ ⲧⲏⲣⲟⲩ ⲁⲩⲱ ⲡⲓⲙⲓⲥⲉ ⲧⲏⲣ[ϥ̄], ³² ⲛⲉⲉⲓ ⲉⲧⲉ ⲁⲃⲁⲗ
ϩⲓⲧⲟⲟⲧⲟⲩ ⲛⲉ ⲛⲓϣⲁ- ³³ ⲛⲉ ⲉϩⲛ̄ⲣⲉϥⲧⲉⲕⲟ ⲥⲉⲧⲟⲟⲧⲟⲩ ⲛⲉ, ⲉⲩ- ³⁴ ⲉⲗⲱⲗ ⲁⲭⲛ̄ⲛ ⲟⲩϫⲡⲟ,
ⲉⲩϣⲟⲟⲡ ⲁⲩ- ³⁵ ⲗⲁⲅⲉ ⲙ̄ⲡⲙⲁ ⲉⲧⲉ ϩⲛ̄ⲁⲃⲁⲗ ⲙ̄ⲙⲁϥ ³⁶ ⲛⲉ ⲁⲩⲱ ⲉⲩⲛⲁⲛⲁⲩϩⲟⲩ ⲁⲛ ⲁⲣⲁϥ. ³⁷
ⲁⲩⲱ ⲉⲧⲃⲉ ⲡⲁⲓ ⲁϥⲕⲱ ⲁϩⲣⲏⲓ̈ ⲁϫⲱ- ³⁸ ⲟⲩ ⲛ̄ϩⲛ̄ϭⲟⲙ ⲛ̄ⲣⲉϥⲟⲩⲁϩ ⲥⲁϩⲛⲉ, ⲉⲩⲣ̄ ³⁹ ϩⲱⲃ
ⲉⲩ[ⲙ̄]ⲏⲛ ⲁⲧϩⲩⲗⲏ, ϫⲉⲕⲁⲥⲉ ¹⁰⁴.¹ ⲛ̄ϫⲡⲟ ⲛ̄ⲛⲉⲧϣⲱⲡⲉ ⲉⲩⲛⲁϣⲱ- ² ⲡⲉ ⲁⲛ ⲉⲩⲙⲏⲛ. ⲡⲉⲉⲓ ⲅⲁⲣ
ⲡⲉ ⲡⲟⲩ- ³ ⲉⲁⲩ.

102.13 ⲛ̄ⲇⲉ: read ⲛ̄ⲧⲉ.
103.13 ⲛ̄ⲇⲉ: read ⲛ̄ⲧⲉ.

He established [4] workers and [5] servants, who provided assistance [6] with the things he will do and what he will say, [7] because every place in which he works, [8] he places his countenance [9] in his beautiful name, [10] working and speaking [11] the things about which he thinks.

[He] [12] established [13] in his places images of light [14] that appeared and (images) of [those who are] spiritual, [15] although they are from [16] his essence. Since in this way they were [17] honored as pure in every place by him, [18] from the countenance [19] of the one who placed them, and they were [20] established <as> paradises [21] and kingdoms and rests [22] and promises and throngs [23] of servants of his will, [24] and they are lords of ruling, [25] though they are placed below the one who is [26] Lord, the one who placed them.

[27] After he listened to them appropriately[28] about the lights, [29] those that are the beginning [30] and system, he placed them over [31] the beauty of the things below. [32] The invisible spirit moved him so [33] that he might [103.1] desire to manage by means of [2] his own servant, whom [3] he also made use of [4] as a hand and [5] mouth as though [6] it were his face, (and his servant is also) the things he brings, [7] order and threat [8] and fear, so that those [with whom] he has done [9] something ignorant might [10] look down upon <the> order that [had been given to them to] [11] guard, since they are bound by the [bonds of [12] the] rulers that constrict them [13] [tightly].

The entire establishment of matter is divided in three. The [strong] [15] powers that the spiritual Word [16] [brought] forth according to a phantasm [17] and arrogance he placed [18] in the first spiritual order. [19] Next those that these brought forth from the [20] love of power he placed [21] in the region of the middle, since they are powers [22] from the love of power, in order that they might [23] rule and command [24] compellingly and forcefully [the] [25] establishment below. But those [26] that came forth from envy [27] and jealousy and all the other offspring [28] of the fashion of this sort he placed them [29] in a subservient order, [30] ruling over the peripheral things, commanding [31] all the things that exist and every generation, [32] those from whom come illnesses [33] that destroy quickly, who are [34] impatient for begetting, who are [35] something from the place from which they come [36] and to which they will return. [37] And for this reason, he placed over [38] them commanding powers, [39] working [regularly] on matter, so that [104.1] the offspring of those that had come to be might also come to be [2] regularly. For this is their [3] glory.

[4] >>>>>——————————————————————>>>>>>>>>>>>>>>>>>>>>>>>>>>———-

[5] ⲭⲉ ϯϩⲩⲗⲏ ⲉⲧϩⲉⲧⲉ ⲟⲩⲧⲉ ϯⲙⲟⲣ- [6] ⲫⲏ ⲛ̄ⲧⲉⲥ ⲟⲩⲗⲁⲉⲓϭⲉ <ⲧⲉ> ⲉⲧⲉ ϯⲙⲛ̄ⲧ- [7] ⲁⲧⲛⲉⲩ ⲉⲧϣⲟⲟⲡ ⲁⲃⲁⲗ ϩⲓⲧⲛ̄ ⲛⲓϭⲟⲙ [8] [. . .] ⲉ ⲛⲉⲩ ⲛ̄ϩⲏⲧⲥ̄ ⲧⲏⲣⲟⲩ ⲉⲛⲟⲩ- [9] [. . . .] ⲉⲩⲭⲡⲟ ϩⲁⲧⲛⲟⲩ ⲁⲩⲱ ⲉⲩ- [10] [ⲧⲉⲕ]ⲟ.

ⲭⲉ ⲡⲙⲉⲩⲉ ⲉⲧⲕⲁⲁⲧ [ⲛ̄]- [11] ϩⲣⲏⲓ̈ ⲛ̄ⲧⲙⲏⲧⲉ ⲛ̄ⲛⲓⲟⲩ[ⲛⲉⲙ ⲙⲛ̄] [12] ⲛⲓϭⲃⲟⲩⲣ ⲟⲩϭⲟⲙ ⲙ̄ⲙⲛ̄[. . . .]ⲉ̣ [13] ⲡⲉ. ⲛⲁⲉⲓ ⲧⲏⲣⲟⲩ ⲉⲧⲁⲛⲓϣ[ⲁⲣⲉ]ⲡ [14] ⲛⲁⲟⲩⲁϣⲟⲩ ⲁⲉⲟⲩ, ⲙ̄ⲡⲣⲏ[ⲧⲉ ⲁ]ⲭⲟ- [15] ⲟⲥ, ⲭⲉ ⲟⲩⲉⲓⲛⲉ ⲙ̄ⲙⲁⲩⲟⲩ ⲁⲃⲁⲗ, [16] ⲙ̄ⲡⲣⲏⲧⲏ ⲛ̄ⲛⲟⲩϩⲁⲉⲓⲃⲉⲥ ϩⲓⲧⲛ̄ ⲟⲩ- [17] ⲥⲱⲙⲁ ⲉⲥⲟⲩⲏϩ ⲛ̄ⲥⲱϥ, ⲛⲉⲉⲓ ⲉⲧⲉ [18] ⲛ̄ⲛⲟⲩⲛⲉ <ⲛⲉ> ⲛ̄ⲛⲓⲧⲥⲉⲛⲱ ⲉⲧⲟⲩⲁⲛ[ϩ] [19] ⲁⲃⲁⲗ, ⲭⲉ ⲡⲓⲥⲁⲃⲧⲉ ⲧⲏⲣϥ̄ ⲙ̄ⲡ- [20] ⲧⲥⲁⲉⲓⲱ ⲛ̄ⲧⲉ ⲛⲓϩⲓ̈ⲕⲱⲛ ⲙⲛ̄ ⲛⲓⲉⲓ- [21] ⲛⲉ ⲙⲛ̄ ⲛⲓⲧⲁⲛⲧⲛ̄ ⲉⲣⲉⲛ̄ⲧⲁⲩ- [22] ϣⲱⲡⲉ ⲉⲧⲃⲉ ⲛⲉⲧⲣ̄ ⲭⲣⲓⲁ ⲛ̄ⲛⲟⲩ- [23] ⲥⲁⲛⲉϣ ⲙⲛ̄ⲛ ⲟⲩⲥⲃⲱ ⲙⲛ̄ ϯⲙⲟⲣ- [24] ⲫⲏ, ⲭⲉⲕⲁⲥⲉ ⲉⲣⲉⲧⲙⲛ̄ⲧⲁϩⲏⲙ [25] ⲛⲁϫⲓ ⲛ̄ⲛⲟⲩⲡⲁⲩⲣⲉⲓ ⲕⲁⲧⲁ ϣⲏⲙ [26] ϣⲏⲙ, ϩⲱⲥ ϩⲓⲧⲛ̄ ⲡⲉⲓⲛⲉ ⲛ̄ⲛⲟⲩⲉⲓⲉⲗ. [27] ⲉⲧⲃⲉ ⲡⲉⲉⲓ ⲛⲅⲁⲣ ⲛ̄ⲧⲁϥⲧⲥⲉⲛⲟ ⲙ̄- [28] ⲡⲣⲱⲙⲉ ⲛ̄ϩⲁⲏ, ⲉⲁϥⲣ̄ ϣⲁⲣⲡ ⲛ̄- [29] ⲥⲁⲃⲧⲉ ⲁⲩⲱ ⲁϥ{ϥ}ⲣ̄ ϣⲁⲣⲡ ⲛ̄- [30] ⲥⲁϩⲛⲉ ⲛⲉϥ ⲛ̄ⲛⲉⲧⲉϩⲁϥⲧⲥⲉⲛⲁⲩ- [31] ⲟⲩ ⲉⲧⲃⲏⲏⲧϥ̄.

ⲭⲉ ⲡⲧⲥⲉⲛⲟ ⲙ̄- [32] ⲡⲣⲱⲙⲉ ⲉϥⲟⲉⲓ ⲙ̄ⲡⲣⲏⲧⲉ ⲙ̄ⲡⲕⲉ- [33] ϣⲱϫⲡ ϩⲱⲱϥ ⲁⲛ. ⲛⲉϥⲕⲓⲙ ⲁⲣⲁϥ [34] ⲛ̄ϭⲓ ⲡⲗⲟⲅⲟⲥ ⲙ̄ⲡⲛⲉⲩⲙⲁⲧⲓⲕⲟⲥ ϩⲛ̄ [35] ⲟⲩⲙⲛ̄ⲧⲁⲧⲛⲉⲩ ⲁⲣⲁⲥ, ⲉϥⲭⲱⲕ [36] ⲛ̄ⲇⲉ ⲙ̄ⲙⲟϥ ⲉⲃⲟⲗ [ϩ]ⲛ̣̄ ⲡⲓⲧϩⲙⲓ- [105.1] ⲟⲣⲅⲟⲥ ⲙⲛ̄ ⲛⲉϥⲁⲅⲅⲉⲗⲟⲥ ⲛ̄ⲣⲉϥϣⲙ- [2] ϣⲉ, ⲉⲩⲣ̄ ϣⲃⲏⲣ ⲙ̄ⲡⲗⲁⲥⲥⲉ ⲛ̄ⲙⲙⲏϣ[ⲉ ⲉϥ]- [3] ϫⲓ ⲡⲓⲙⲉⲩⲉ ⲙⲛ̄ ⲛⲉϥⲁⲣⲭⲱⲛ. ⲉϥⲟⲉⲓ [4] ⲙ̄ⲡⲣⲏⲧⲉ ⲛ̄ⲛⲟⲩϩⲁⲉⲓⲃⲉⲥ ⲛ̄<ϭⲓ ⲡ>ⲣⲙⲛ̄ⲕⲁϩ [5] ⲭⲉⲕⲁⲥⲉ ⲉϥⲛⲁⲣ̄ ⲡⲣⲏⲧⲉ ⲙⲛ̄ [ⲛⲉⲧ]- [6] ϣⲟⲟⲧ ⲁⲃⲁⲗ ⲛ̄ⲛⲓⲡⲧⲏⲣϥ̄. ⲁⲩⲱ [ⲟⲩ]- [7] ⲥⲁⲃⲧⲉ ⲛ̄ⲧⲉⲩ ⲧⲏⲣⲟⲩ ⲡⲉ, ⲛⲓⲟⲩⲛⲉⲙ [8] ⲙⲛ̄ ⲛⲓϭⲃⲟⲩⲣ, ⲉⲡⲟⲩⲉⲉⲓ ⲡ[ⲓⲟ]ⲩⲉⲉⲓ ⲛ̄[ⲛⲓⲧⲁ]- [9] ⲅⲙⲁ ⲉϥϯ ⲙⲟⲣⲫⲏ ⲙ̄[. . . . . . .] [10] ⲉⲧϥϣⲟⲟⲡ ⲙ̄ⲙⲟⲥ.

ⲭⲉ ϯ[. . . . .ⲉⲛ]- [11] ⲧ[ⲁ]ϥⲛ̄ⲧⲥ̄ ⲁⲃⲁⲗ ⲛ̄ϭⲓ ⲡⲗⲟⲅⲟⲥ [ⲉⲛⲧⲁϥ]- [12] ⲣ̄ ϣⲧⲁ ⲙ̄ⲡⲥⲙⲁⲧ, ⲉⲛⲧⲁϥϣ[ⲱⲡⲉ] [13] ϩⲛ̄ ⲡⲁϣⲱⲛⲉ, ⲛⲁⲥⲉⲓⲛⲉ ⲁⲣⲁϥ ⲉⲛ [14] ⲁⲃⲁⲗ ⲭⲉ ⲁϥⲛ̄ⲧⲥ̄ ⲁⲃⲁⲗ ϩⲛ̄ⲛ ⲟⲩϣⲱ[ⲃϣ] [15] ⲛ̄[ⲛ]ⲟⲩⲙⲛ̄ⲧⲁⲧⲥⲁⲩⲛⲉ ⲙⲛ̄ⲛ ⲟⲩ[ϣⲧⲁ], [16] ⲙⲛ̄ ⲡ[ⲕ]ⲉϣⲱϫⲡ ⲧⲏⲣϥ̄ ⲛ̄ⲁϣⲱⲛ[ⲉ], [17] ⲉⲁϥϯ [18] ⲛ̄ⲧϣⲁⲣⲡ ⲙ̄ⲙⲟⲣⲫⲏ ⲭⲉ ⲛ̄ⲧⲁ[ϥ] ⲡⲗⲟⲅⲟⲥ ⲁⲃⲁⲗ ϩⲓⲧⲛ̄ ⲡⲇⲏⲙⲓⲟⲩⲣⲅⲟⲥ [19] ⲁⲃⲁⲗ ϩⲛ̄ⲛ ⲟⲩⲙⲛ̄ⲧⲁⲧⲥⲁⲩⲛⲉ ⲁⲧⲣⲉϥ- [20] ϫⲓ ⲥⲁⲩⲛⲉ ⲭⲉ ⲟⲩⲛ̄ ⲡⲉⲧϩⲁⲥⲉ ϣⲟ- [21] ⲟⲡ ⲁⲩⲱ ⲛ̄ϥⲙ̄ⲙⲉ ⲭⲉ ϥⲣ̄ [22] ⲭⲣⲓⲁ ⲙ̄ⲙ[ⲁϥ]. ⲉⲧⲉ ⲡⲉⲉⲓ ⲡⲉ ⲉⲧⲁ<ϩ>ⲁⲡⲣⲟⲫⲏⲧⲏⲥ ⲙ[ⲟⲩ]- [23] ⲧⲉ ⲁⲣⲁϥ ⲭⲉ « ⲛⲓϥⲉ ⲛ̄ⲱⲛϩ̄ [24] » ⲁⲩⲱ « ⲡⲛ[ⲟ]- ⲉⲓ ⲛ̄ⲇⲉ ⲡⲁⲓⲱⲛ ⲉⲧϩⲁⲥⲉ » ⲁⲩⲱ « [ⲡⲓ]- [25] ⲁⲧⲛⲉⲩ ⲁⲣⲁϥ, » ⲁⲩⲱ ⲧⲉⲉⲓ [26] ⲧⲉ ϯϯⲩ[ⲭⲏ] ⲉⲧⲁⲛϩ̄ ⲉⲧⲁϩⲧⲛ̄ϩⲟ ⲛ̄ⲧⲉϫⲟⲩⲥ[ⲓⲁ] [27] ⲉⲧⲉⲛⲁⲥⲙⲟⲟⲩⲧ ⲛ̄ϣⲟⲣⲡ̄. ⲡⲓⲡⲉⲧ- [28] ⲙⲟⲟⲩⲧ ⲅⲁⲣ ⲛ̄ⲧⲉ ϯⲙⲛ̄ⲧⲁⲧⲥⲁⲩ[ⲛⲉ].

[29] ⲭⲉ ⲡⲉⲧⲉϣϣⲉ ϭⲉ ⲙⲉⲛ ⲡⲉ ⲁⲧⲣ̄ⲕⲱ [30] ⲁϩⲣⲏⲓ̈ ⲛ̄ⲧⲯⲩⲭⲏ ⲙ̄ⲡϣⲁⲣⲡ ⲛ̄ⲣⲱⲙⲉ, [31] ⲭⲉ ⲟⲩⲁⲃⲁⲗ ϩⲛ̄ ⲡⲓⲗⲟⲅⲟⲥ ⲡⲉ ⲙ̄ⲡⲛⲉⲩ- [32] ⲙⲁⲧⲓⲕⲟⲥ, ⲉϥⲙⲉⲉⲩⲉ ⲛ̄ϭⲓ ⲡⲓⲣⲉϥ- [33] ⲥⲱⲛⲧ ⲭⲉ ⲡⲱϥ ⲡⲉ, ⲉⲡⲓⲇⲏ

105.17 ⲭⲉ: read ⲛ̄ϭⲓ.

105.23–24 ⲡⲛ[ⲟ]ⲉⲓ: this word could be from either νοῦς ("mind"; for the declined form, see 54.15) or an orthographic variant of πνοή ("breath").

105.28 ⲛ̄ⲧⲉ: read ⲧⲉ.

[5] The matter that flows through its form [6] <is> a cause through which the [7] invisibility that exists through the powers [8] [. . .] they all [9] [. . .] they beget before them and they [10] [defile].

The thought that resided [11] in the middle of those of the [right and] [12] left is a power of [. . .]. [13] All those that the [first] ones [14] will desire to make, in a manner of speaking, [15] an image of theirs, [16] like a shadow following a [17] body, these that [18] are the roots of the visible order, [19] that is, the entire preparation of the [20] ordering of the images and likenesses [21] and semblances have [22] come to be on account of those in need of [23] nourishment and teaching and formation, [24] so that the smallness [25] will receive growth little [26] by little, as through the image of a mirror. [27] For this reason he created [28] humanity last, having first [29] prepared and first [30] provided for him the things that he had made [31] on his account.

The creation of [32] humanity was like (the creation) of [33] everything else as well. [34] The spiritual Word moved him [35] invisibly, perfecting [36] him through the creator [105.1] and his ministering angels, [2] who partnered in the forming of multitudes, [once he] [3] consulted with his rulers. [4] <The> earth being is like a shadow, [5] so that he might resemble [those] [6] cut off from the entireties. He is also [a] [7] product of all of them, those on the right [8] and those on the left, because each [one] of [the] orders [9] he formed [. . .] [10] which he exists.

The [. . .] [11] that the Word [who was] [12] deficient in form brought forth, who [came to be] [13] in sickness, did not resemble him [14] because he brought it forth out of [15] [forgetfulness], ignorance, and [deficiency], [16] and [of] all other illnesses, [17] yet he, the [18] Word, gave the first form through the creator [19] out of ignorance in order to [20] receive knowledge that the exalted one exists [21] and know that he needs [him]. [22] This is what the prophet termed [23] "living spirit" and "the [24] mind of the exalted eternity" and "[the] [25] invisible one," and this is the living soul [26] that has enlivened the power [27] that was dead initially. For what [28] is dead is ignorance.

[29] Therefore, it is fitting that we expound [30] upon the soul of the first human, [31] that it is from the spiritual Word, [32] even though the [33] creator thinks that it is his, since

105.23–24 "the mind": or "breath."

ⲁⲃⲁⲗ ϩⲓⲧⲟ- ³⁴ ⲟⲧϥ ⲡⲉ ⲙ̄ⲡⲣⲏⲧⲏ ⲛ̄ⲛⲟⲩ{ⲣ̄}ⲣⲟ ⲡⲉⲧⲁⲩ- ³⁵ ⲛⲓϭⲉ ⲙ̄ⲙⲁϥ. ⲁϥⲧⲛ̄ⲛⲟⲟⲩ ϩⲱⲱϥ
ⲁⲛ ³⁶ ⲁⲡⲓⲧⲛ̄ ⲛ̄ϭⲓ ⲡⲓⲣⲉϥⲥⲱⲛⲧ̄ ⲛ̄ϩⲛ̄ⲯⲩⲭ[ⲏ]- ³⁷ ⲟⲩ ⲁⲃⲁⲗ ϩⲛ̄ ⲧⲉϥⲟⲩⲥⲓⲁ, ⲉⲩⲛ̄ⲧ[ⲉϥ] ³⁸ ϩⲱⲱϥ
ⲁⲛ ⲙ̄ⲙⲉⲩ ⲙ̄ⲡⲓϭⲛ̄ⲭⲡⲟ ¹⁰⁶·¹ ϫⲉ ⲟⲩϣⲱⲡⲉ ⲁⲃⲁⲗ ϩⲛ̄ ⲡⲓⲛⲉ ² ⲙ̄ⲡⲉⲓⲱⲧ. ⲁⲩⲉⲓⲛⲉ ⲁⲃⲁⲗ ϩⲱⲟⲩ ³
ⲛ̄ϭⲓ ⲛⲓϭⲃⲟⲩⲣ ⲙ̄ⲡⲣⲏⲧⲉ ⲛ̄ϩⲛ̄ⲣⲱ- ⁴ ⲙⲉ, {`ϥ´} ⲉⲛⲟⲩⲟⲩ ⲛⲉ, ⲉⲩⲛ̄ⲧⲉⲩ ⲙ̄- ⁵ ⲙⲉⲩ ⲙ̄ⲡⲧⲁⲛⲧⲛ̄
ⲙ̄ⲡϣⲱⲡ<ⲉ>.

⁶ ϫⲉ ⲧⲟⲩⲥⲓⲁ ⲙ̄ⲡⲛⲉⲩⲙⲁⲧⲓⲕⲟⲛ ⲟⲩ- ⁷ ⲉⲓ[ⲉ] ⲧⲉ, ⲁⲩⲱ ⲟⲩⲉⲓⲛⲉ ⲛ̄ⲟⲩⲱⲧ ⲧⲉ, ⁸ [ⲁⲩⲱ ⲁⲛ ⲡⲓ]-
ϣⲱⲛⲉ ⲛ̄ⲧⲉⲥ ⲡⲉ ⲡⲧⲱϣⲉ ⁹ [ϩⲛ̄ ϩⲁ]ϩ ⲛ̄ⲥⲙⲟⲧ. ⲧⲟⲩⲥⲓⲁ ⲇⲉ ¹⁰ [. .] . . ⲛⲛⲉⲉⲓⲯⲩⲭⲓⲕⲟⲛ
ⲡⲉⲥⲧⲱϣⲉ ¹¹ [ϩ]ⲁⲧⲣ̄, ⲉⲩⲛ̄ⲧⲉⲥ ⲙ̄ⲙⲉⲩ ⲙ<ⲡ>ϭⲓⲛⲙ̄ⲙⲉ ¹² ⲙⲛ̄ ⲑⲟⲙⲟⲗⲟⲅⲓⲁ ⲙ̄ⲡⲉⲧϫⲁⲥⲉ, ¹³
[ⲁ]ⲩⲱ ⲥⲣⲁⲕⲉ ⲉⲛ ⲁⲡⲉⲧⲑⲁⲩ ⲉⲧⲃⲉ ¹⁴ ⲡⲣⲓⲕⲉ ⲙ̄ⲡⲓⲙⲉⲩⲉ. ⲧⲟⲩⲥⲓⲁ ⲇ[ⲉ] ϩⲱⲱⲥ ¹⁵ ⲛ̄ϩⲩⲗⲓⲕⲟⲛ
ⲡⲉⲥⲟⲩⲁⲉⲓ ϣⲃⲃⲓⲁⲉⲓⲧ ¹⁶ ⲁⲩⲱ ϩⲛ̄ ϩⲁϩ ⲛ̄ⲥⲙⲁⲧ· ⲛⲉⲩϣⲱⲛⲉ ⲇⲉ ¹⁷ ⲡⲉ ⲉⲛⲧⲁϩϣⲱⲡⲉ ϩⲛ̄ ϩⲁϩ
ⲛ̄ⲥⲙⲟⲧ ¹⁸ ⲛ̄ⲣⲓⲕⲉ.

ϫⲉ ⲡⲓϣⲁⲣⲡ̄ ⲇⲉ ⲛ̄ⲣⲱⲙⲉ ⲟⲩ- ¹⁹ ⲡⲗⲁⲥⲙⲁ ⲡⲉ ⲉϥⲧⲏϩ ⲡⲉ, ⲁⲩⲱ ⲟⲩⲧⲥⲉ- ²⁰ ⲛⲟ ⲡⲉ ⲉϥⲧⲏϩ ⲡⲉ,
ⲁⲩⲱ ⲟⲩⲕⲟⲩ ⲁϩⲣⲏⲓ ²¹ ⲡⲉ ⲛ̄ⲇⲉ ⲛⲓϭⲃⲟⲩⲣ ⲡⲉ ⲙⲛ̄ ⲛⲓⲟⲩⲛⲉⲙ ²² ⲡⲉ, ⲁⲩⲱ ⲟⲩⲡⲛⲉⲩⲙⲁⲧⲓⲕⲟⲥ
ⲛ̄ⲗⲟⲅⲟⲥ ²³ ⲉⲧⲉϥⲅⲛⲱⲙⲏ ⲡ`ⲏ´ϣ ⲁⲡⲉⲥⲛⲉⲩ ⲧⲟⲩⲉⲓⲉ ²⁴ ⲧⲟⲩⲉⲓⲉ ⲛⲛⲓⲟⲩⲥⲓⲁ, ⲛⲉⲉⲓ ⲉⲛⲧⲁϩϫⲓ ²⁵
ⲡ{ⲣ}ⲉϥϣⲱⲡⲉ ⲁⲃⲁⲗ ⲙ̄ⲙⲁⲩ. ⲁⲃⲁⲗ ²⁶ ⲙ̄ⲡⲉⲉⲓ ⲥⲉϫⲟⲩ ⲙ̄ⲙⲁⲥ ⲁⲛ ϫⲉ ⲁⲩ- ²⁷ ϫⲱ ⲛⲉϥ
ⲛ̄ⲛⲟⲩⲡⲁⲣⲁⲇⲓⲥⲟⲥ ⲁⲧⲣⲉϥ- ²⁸ ⲟⲩⲱⲙ ⲁⲃⲁⲗ ϩⲛ̄ ⲧⲣⲉ ⲛ̄ϣⲟⲙⲧⲉ ²⁹ ⲙ̄ⲙⲓⲛⲉ ⲛ̄ϣⲏⲛ, ⲉⲩⲟⲩϭⲟⲙ
ⲡⲉ ⲛ̄ⲇⲉ ⲧ- ³⁰ ⲧⲁⲝⲓⲥ ⲉⲥϩⲁⲧⲣ̄ ⲛ̄ϣⲟⲙⲛ̄ⲧ ⲛ̄ⲣⲏⲧⲉ, ³¹ ⲉⲛⲧⲁϥ ⲡⲉⲧϯ ⲛ̄ⲛⲁⲡⲟⲗⲁⲩⲥⲓⲥ.

ϫⲉ ϯ- ³² ⲙⲛ̄ⲧⲉⲩⲅⲉⲛⲏⲥ ⲛ̄ϯⲟⲩⲥⲓⲁ ⲉⲧⲥⲁⲧⲡ̄, ³³ ⲉⲧϣⲟⲟⲡ ⲛ̄ϩⲏⲧϥ̄, ⲛⲉⲥϫⲁⲥⲓ ⲡⲉ ⲛ̄ϩ ⲟⲩ- ³⁴ ⲟ
ⲡⲉ. ⲁⲥⲧⲥⲉⲛⲟ, ⲁⲩⲱ ⲙⲁⲥϯ ϣϭⲁ ³⁵ ⲛⲉⲩ ⲡⲉ. ⲁⲃⲁⲗ ⲙ̄ⲡⲁⲉⲓ ⲁⲩⲛ̄ⲧϥ̄ ⲁ- ³⁶ ⲃⲁⲗ ⲛ̄ⲛⲟⲩⲉϩ ⲥⲁϩⲛⲉ,
ⲉⲩⲣ̄ ⲁⲡⲉⲓⲗⲏ ³⁷ ⲁⲩⲱ ⲉⲩⲉⲓⲛⲉ ⲁϫⲱϥ ⲛ̄[ⲟⲩ]ⲛⲟϭ ⲛ̄ϭⲓⲛ- ¹⁰⁷·¹ ⲇⲩⲛⲟⲥ, ⲉⲧⲉ ⲡⲙⲟⲩ ⲧⲉ. ⲁϯⲁⲡⲟ-
² ⲗⲁⲩⲥⲓⲥ ⲛ̄ⲇⲉ ⲛⲉⲧⲑⲁⲩ ⲟⲩⲁⲉⲧⲥ̄ ³ ⲛ̄ⲇⲉ ⲁϥⲕⲁⲁϥ ⲁⲧⲣⲉϥⲟⲩⲱⲙ ⁴ ⲁⲃⲁⲗ ⲙ̄ⲙⲁⲥ, ⲁⲩⲱ ⲡⲕⲉϣⲏⲛ
ⲉⲧⲉⲩ- ⁵ ⲛ̄ⲧⲉϥ ⲙ̄ⲡⲕⲉϩⲱⲧⲣⲉ ⲙ̄ⲡⲟⲩⲕⲁ[ⲁϥ] ⁶ ⲁⲟⲩⲱⲙ ⲁⲃⲁⲗ ⲙ̄ⲙⲁϥ, ⲛ̄ϩⲟⲩⲟ ⁷ ⲛ̄ϩⲟⲩⲟ ⲡⲁ
ⲡⲱⲛϩ, ϫⲉⲕⲁ[ⲥ]ⲉ ⲛ̄[ⲟⲩ]- ⁸ ϫⲡⲟ ⲛ̄ⲛⲟⲩⲧⲁⲉⲓⲟ ⲉ[. . . . .]- ⁹ ⲙⲛⲟⲩ
ⲁⲩⲱ ϫⲉⲕⲁⲥⲉ ⲛ̄[ⲟⲩ. . . .]- ¹⁰ ⲣⲁⲟⲩ ⲁⲃⲁⲗ ϩⲓ ϯϭⲟⲙ ⲉⲧⲁⲩ ⲉ[ⲧⲟⲩ]- ¹¹ ⲙⲟⲩⲧⲉ ⲁⲣⲁⲥ ϫⲉ
« ⲡϩⲁϥ. » ⲟⲩⲡⲁⲛⲟⲩⲣ[ⲅⲟⲥ] ¹² ⲛ̄ⲇⲉ ⲇⲉ ⲛ̄ϩⲟⲩⲟ ⲁⲛⲓϭⲁⲙ ⲧⲏⲣⲟⲩ ⲉ[ⲧ]- ¹³ ϩⲁⲩⲟⲩ. ⲁϥⲣ̄
ⲁⲡⲁⲧⲁ ⲙ̄ⲡⲣⲱⲙⲉ [ⲁⲃⲁⲗ] ¹⁴ ϩⲓⲧⲛ̄ ⲡⲧⲱϣⲉ ⲛ̄ⲇⲉ ⲛⲁ ⲡⲓⲙⲉⲩ[ⲉ] ¹⁵ ⲙⲛ̄ ⲛⲉⲡⲓⲑⲩⲙⲓⲁ. ⲁⲥⲧⲣⲉϥⲣ̄
ⲡⲁⲣⲁⲃⲁ ¹⁶ ⲛ̄ⲧⲉⲛⲧⲟⲗⲏ ϫⲉⲕⲁⲥ ⲉϥⲛⲁⲙⲟⲩ. ¹⁷ ⲁⲩⲱ ⲧⲁⲡⲟⲗⲁⲩⲥⲓⲥ ⲧⲏⲣⲥ̄ ⲉⲧⲙ̄ⲡⲙⲁ ⲉ- ¹⁸
ⲧ̄ⲙⲙⲉⲩ ⲁⲩⲛⲟϫϥ̄ ⲁⲃⲁⲗ ⲛ̄ϩⲏⲧⲥ̄.

ϫⲉ ¹⁹ ⲡⲉⲉⲓ ⲡⲉ ⲡⲛⲟⲩϫⲉ ⲁⲃⲁⲗ ⲉⲛⲧⲁⲩⲉ[ϥ] ²⁰ ⲛⲉϥ, ⲉⲁⲩⲛⲁϫϥ̄ ⲁⲃⲁⲗ ⲛ̄ⲛⲓⲁⲡⲟⲗⲁ[ⲩ]- ²¹
ⲥⲓⲥ ⲛ̄ⲇⲉ ⲛⲁ ⲡⲓⲧⲁⲛⲧⲛ̄ ⲙⲛ̄ ⲛⲁ ⲡⲉⲓⲛ̄[ⲉ]. ²² ⲉⲩϩⲱⲃ ⲛ̄ⲇⲉ ϯⲡⲣⲟⲛⲟⲓⲁ ⲡⲉ, ϫⲉⲕ[ⲁⲥⲉ] ²³

106.21 ⲛ̄ⲇⲉ: read ⲛ̄ⲧⲉ.
106.29 ⲛ̄ⲇⲉ: read ⲛ̄ⲧⲉ.
106.37–107.1 ϭⲓⲛⲇⲩⲛⲟⲥ: read ⲕⲓⲛⲇⲩⲛⲟⲥ.
107.12 ⲇⲉ: read ⲡⲉ?
107.14 ⲛ̄ⲇⲉ: read ⲛ̄ⲧⲉ.
107.15 ⲁⲥⲧⲣⲉϥ: read ⲁϥⲧⲣⲉϥ.
107.21 ⲛ̄ⲇⲉ: read ⲛ̄ⲧⲉ.

it is from [34] him in the manner of a mouth through which one [35] breathes. Moreover, the creator also sent [36] down souls [37] from his being, since [he] [38] also has (the ability of) begetting [106.1] because he is one that has come into being from the image [2] of the Father. Those on the left also brought forth, [3] in a way, humans [4] of their own, having [5] the likeness of being.

[6] The spiritual being [7] is a unity, and it is a solitary image, [8] [and] its sickness is the propensity [9] [in many] forms. But as for the being [10] . . . of the soulish ones, its propensity [11] is twofold, since it has <the> knowledge [12] and the confession of the one who is exalted, [13] and it is not inclined toward evil on account of [14] the inclination of the thought. But as for the material being itself, [15] its course is different [16] and in many forms; it was an illness [17] that came to be in many kinds [18] of inclination.

The first human is a [19] mixed molded form, and he is a [20] mixed creation, and he is a remnant [21] of those on the left and those on the right, [22] and a spiritual word [23] whose opinion is divided between each [24] one of the two substances, those from which he has received [25] his being. For [26] this (reason) it is said that paradise was [27] planted for him so that he might [28] eat from the food of the three [29] kinds of tree, since it is a garden of the [30] triple order, [31] being that which bears fruit.

The [32] noble generation that is elect, [33] which dwells in him, was more exalted. [34] It created, and it did not injure [35] them. For this reason they gave [36] a command, issuing a threat [37] and bringing upon him [a] great [107.1] trial, which is death. [2] Only the fruit [3] of those that are evil did he permit him to taste, [4] and the other tree that [5] had the twofold (fruit) [he] was permitted [6] to eat, not to mention [7] the (tree) belonging to life, so that [they [8] might] not bear the honor for [. . .] [9] and so that [they would] not [. . .] [10] through the evil power [that is] [11] called "the snake." [12] Yet he is more wicked than all the evil powers. [13] He deceived the human [14] through the propensity of those things belonging to the thought [15] and the desires in order to lead <him> to toss aside [16] the command with the result that he would die. [17] And from all fruitful benefit of that place, [18] he was cast out.

[19] This is the banishment that was done [20] to him, when he was deprived of the fruitful benefits [21] of the things belonging to the likeness and image. [22] It was a

ⲉⲩⲛⲁϭⲛⲧⲥ̄ ⲉⲩⲟⲩⲁⲉⲓϣ ϣⲏⲙ ⲡⲉ ²⁴ ⲉⲧⲉⲣⲉⲡⲣⲱⲙⲉ ⲛⲁϫⲓ ⲛ̄ⲧⲁⲡⲟⲗⲁⲩ- ²⁵ ⲥⲓⲥ ⲛ̄ⲇⲉ
ⲛⲓⲡⲉⲧⲛⲁⲛⲟⲩⲟⲩ ϣⲁ ⲁ- ²⁶ ⲛⲏϩⲉ, ⲉⲧⲉⲣⲉⲡⲓⲙⲁ ⲛ̄ⲙ̄ⲧⲟⲛ ϣⲟⲟⲡ ²⁷ ⲛ̄ϩⲏⲧⲟⲩ. ⲡⲉⲉⲓ ⲉⲧⲉⲁϥⲧⲁϣϥ̄
ⲉⲁϥⲣ̄ ²⁸ ϣⲁⲣⲡ̄ ⲡ{`ⲙⲟ´}ⲙⲟⲩⲕⲙⲟⲩⲕϥ ⲛ̄ϭⲓ ⲡⲛⲉⲩⲙⲁ ²⁹ ⲁⲧⲣⲉϥϫⲓ ⲙ̄ⲡ`ⲓ´ⲣⲉ{ⲛ} ⲛ̄ϭⲓ
ⲡⲣⲱⲙⲉ ³⁰ ⲡⲓⲛⲟϭ ⲙ̄ⲡⲉⲑⲁⲩ ⲉⲧⲉ ⲡⲉⲉⲓ ⲡⲉ ⲡⲙⲟⲩ, ³¹ ⲉⲧⲉ ϯⲙ̄ⲛ̄ⲧⲁⲧⲥⲁⲩⲛⲉ ⲧⲉ ⲛ̄ⲇⲉ ⲡⲧⲏⲣϥ̄ ³²
ⲧⲉⲗⲉⲩⲧⲏⲥ, ⲁⲩⲱ {ⲛ̄ⲧⲣ̄}ⲛ̄ⲧϥ̄ϫⲓ ⲙ̄ⲡⲓⲣⲁ ⲁⲛ ³³ ⲡⲉ ⲛ̄ⲛⲓⲡⲉⲧϩⲁⲩⲟⲩ ⲧⲏⲣⲟⲩ ⲉⲧϣⲁ- ³⁴
ⲣⲟⲩϣⲱⲡⲉ ⲁⲃⲁⲗ ϩⲙ̄ ⲡⲉⲉⲓ, ⲁⲩⲱ ³⁵ ⲙ̄ⲛ̄ⲛ̄ⲥⲁ ⲛⲓϣⲟϭⲉ ⲉⲧϣⲟⲟⲡ ϩⲛ̄ ⲛⲉⲉⲓ ³⁶ ⲙ̄ⲛ̄ ⲛⲓⲗ[ⲉ]ϩ, ⲛ̄ϥϫⲓ
ⲉⲃⲟⲗ ϩⲙ̄ ⲡⲓⲛⲟϭ ¹⁰⁸·¹ ⲙ̄ⲡⲉⲧⲛⲁⲛⲟⲩϥ, ⲉⲧⲉ [ⲡ]ⲉⲉⲓ ⲡⲉ ⲡⲓ- ² ⲱⲛϩ̄ ϣⲁ ⲛⲓⲉⲛⲏϩⲉ, ⲉⲇⲉ ⲡⲁⲉⲓ ⲡⲉ
³ ⲡⲥⲁⲩⲛⲉ ⲛ̄ⲇⲉ ⲛⲓⲡⲧⲏⲣϥ̄ ⲉⲧⲟⲩⲁϩ ⁴ ⲁⲩⲱ ⲡϫⲓ ⲁⲃⲁⲗ ϩⲛ̄ⲛⲁⲅⲁⲑⲟⲛ ⲧⲏⲣⲟⲩ. ⁵ ⲉⲧⲃⲉ
ⲧⲡⲁⲣⲁⲃⲁⲥⲓⲥ ⲙ̄ⲡⲓϣⲁⲣⲡ̄ ⲛ̄ⲣⲱ- ⁶ [ⲙ]ⲉ ⲁⲡⲙⲟⲩ ⲣ̄ ϫⲁⲉⲓⲥ. ⲁϥⲣ̄ ⲥⲩⲛⲏⲑⲓⲁ ⁷ [ⲛ̄]ⲣⲱⲙⲉ ⲛⲓⲙ
ⲁⲧⲣⲉϥ`ⲟ´ⲟⲩⲧ ⲙ̄ⲙⲟⲟⲩ ⁸ [ⲕ]ⲁⲧⲁ ⲡⲟⲩⲱⲛϩ̄ ⲁⲃⲁⲗ ⲛ̄ⲧⲉϥⲙⲛ̄ⲧ- ⁹ [. . . ⲉ]ⲧϣⲟⲟⲡ ⲛⲉϥ
ⲉⲥⲧⲟⲉⲓ ⲛⲉϥ ¹⁰ [. . .] ⲙ̄ⲛ̄ⲧⲣ̄ⲣⲟ ⲉⲧⲃⲉ ⲟⲓⲕⲟⲛⲟⲙⲓ- ¹¹ [ⲁ] ⲉⲧⲁⲛⲣ̄ ϣⲣⲡ̄ ϫⲟⲟⲥ ⲛ̄ⲇⲉ ⲡⲉⲓ- ¹²
ⲟⲩⲱϣⲉ ⲛ̄ⲧⲉ ⲡⲓⲱⲧ.

¹³ [ ] >>>>>>>>>>>>>>>>>>>——————————————————

¹⁴ [ϫ]ⲉ ⲡⲟⲩⲉⲉⲓ ⲡⲟⲩⲉ̈ⲓ ϭⲉ ⲛ̄ⲛⲓⲇⲁⲅⲙⲁ, ¹⁵ [ⲛ]ⲓⲟⲩⲛⲉⲙ ⲙ̄ⲛ̄ ⲛⲓϭⲃⲟⲩⲣ, ⲁⲩϣⲁ- ¹⁶ ⲥⲱϩⲟⲩ
ⲁⲛⲟⲩⲉⲣⲏⲟⲩ ⲁⲃⲁⲗ ϩⲓⲧⲛ̄ ¹⁷ ⲡ`ⲓ̈´ⲙⲉⲉⲩⲉ ⲉⲧⲕⲏ ⲁϩⲣⲏⲓ̈ ⲟⲩⲧⲟⲟⲩ, ¹⁸ ⲡⲁⲓ̈ ⲉⲧϯ ⲛⲉⲩ
ⲛ̄ⲛⲟⲩϩⲟⲓⲕⲟⲛⲟⲙⲓⲁ ¹⁹ ⲙ̄ⲛ̄ ⲛⲟⲩⲉⲣⲏⲩ, ϣⲁⲣⲉⲥϣⲱⲡⲉ ⲛ̄- ²⁰ ⲥⲉⲉⲓⲣⲉ ⲙ̄ⲡⲥⲛⲉⲩ ⲕⲁⲧⲁ ⲟⲩⲕⲱϩ ²¹
ⲛ̄ⲛⲓϩⲃⲏⲩⲉ ⲛ̄ⲟⲩⲱⲧ, ⲉⲩⲣ̄ ⲙⲓⲛⲉ ⲙ̄- ²² ⲙⲁⲩ ⲛ̄ϫⲓ ⲛⲓⲟⲩⲛⲉⲙ ⲙ̄ⲛ̄ ⲛⲓϭⲃⲟⲩⲣ, ²³ ⲁⲩⲱ ⲛⲓϭⲃⲟⲩⲣ
ϩⲱⲟⲩ ⲉⲩⲣ̄ ⲙⲓⲛⲉ ⲙ̄- ²⁴ ⲙⲁⲩ ⲙ̄ⲛ̄ ⲛⲓⲟⲩⲛⲉⲙ. ⲁⲩⲱ ⲥⲁⲡ ⲁⲥ- ²⁵ ϣⲁ<ⲁ>ⲣⲭⲉⲥⲑⲁⲓ ⲁⲉⲓⲣⲉ ⲛ̄ⲛⲟⲩⲡⲉ-
²⁶ ⲑⲁⲩ ⲛ̄ϭⲓ ϯⲧⲁⲝⲓⲥ ⲉⲑⲁⲩ ϩⲛ̄ⲛ ⲟⲩ- ²⁷ ⲥⲙⲁⲧ ⲙ̄ⲙⲛ̄ⲧⲁⲧⲑⲏⲧ, ϣⲁⲣⲉϥ- ²⁸ ⲕⲱϩ ⲛ̄ϭⲓ ϯⲧⲁⲝⲓⲥ
ⲙ̄ⲙⲛ̄ⲧϩⲏⲡ, ϩⲛ̄- ²⁹ ⲛ ⲟⲩϩⲟ ⲛ̄ⲣⲙⲉϥⲛ̄ϫⲛ̄ϭⲟⲛⲥ ⲁϩⲣⲏⲓ̈, ³⁰ ⲉϥⲣ̄ ϩⲱⲃ ϩⲱⲥ ⲁⲛ ⲁⲡⲡⲉⲑⲁⲩ,
³¹ ⲙ̄ⲡⲓⲣⲏⲧⲉ ⲉⲩϭⲟⲙ ⲧⲉ ⲛ̄ⲣⲙⲉϥ- ³² ⲛ̄ϫⲛ̄ϭⲟⲛⲥ ⲁϩⲣⲏⲓ̈ ⲧⲉ. ⲥⲁⲡ ⲇⲉ ϩⲱ- ³³ ϣϥ ⲁⲛ
ϣⲁⲣⲉϯⲧⲁⲝⲓⲥ ⲙ̄ⲙⲛ̄ⲧ<ⲁⲧ>ϩⲏⲧ ³⁴ ϩⲟⲩ ⲧⲟⲟⲧⲥ̄ ⲁⲣ̄ ϩⲱⲃ ⲉⲛⲁⲛⲟⲩϥ, ⲉⲥ- ³⁵ ⲧⲛ̄ⲧⲱⲛⲥ ⲁⲣⲁⲥ,
ϫⲉ ϯⲧⲁⲝⲓⲥ ⲉⲧ- ³⁶ ϩⲏⲡ ⲉⲥⲕⲱϩ ⲁⲉⲓⲣⲉ ⲙ̄ⲙⲁϥ. ϩⲱⲥ ³⁷ ⲁⲛ ⲡⲉⲉⲓ ⲡⲉ ⲡⲣⲏⲧⲉ ⲉⲧϣⲟⲟⲡ ⲛ̄- ³⁸
ⲛⲉⲧⲧⲏⲕ ⲁⲣⲉⲧⲟⲩ, ⲙ̄ⲡ[ⲓⲣⲏ]ⲧⲉ ϩⲛ̄ ⲛⲓ- ¹⁰⁹·¹ ϩⲃⲏⲩⲉ ⲉⲛⲧⲁⲩϣⲱⲡⲉ. ⲉⲩⲉⲓⲛⲉ[² ⲛ̄ⲛⲓϩⲃⲏⲩⲉ
ⲛ̄ⲛⲁⲧⲉⲓⲛⲉ ⲁⲛⲟⲩⲉⲣ[ⲏⲩ], ³ ⲉⲙⲡⲟⲩϭⲛ̄ϭⲟⲙ ⲙ̄ⲙⲉ ⲁⲧⲗⲁⲉⲓϩ[ⲉ] ⁴ ⲛ̄ⲛϩⲃⲏⲩⲉ ⲉⲧϣⲟⲟⲡ ⲛ̄ϫⲓ
ⲛⲉⲉⲓ ⲉⲧ[ⲉ]- ⁵ ⲙ̄ⲡⲟⲩⲧⲁⲙⲁⲩ. ⲁⲃⲁⲗ ⲙ̄ⲡⲁⲉⲓ ⁶ ⲁⲩⲉⲓⲛⲉ ⲁⲛ ⲁϩⲟⲩⲛ ⲛ̄ⲕⲉⲣⲏⲧⲉ, ⁷ ϩⲉⲛϩⲁⲉⲓⲛⲉ
ⲉⲩϫⲱ ⲙ̄ⲙⲁⲥ ϫ[ⲉ ⁸ ⲛⲉⲧϣⲟⲟⲡ ⲉⲩϣⲟⲟⲡ ⲛ̄ϩⲣⲏⲓ̈ ϩⲛ̄ [ⲟⲩ]- ⁹ ⲡⲣⲟⲛⲟⲓⲁ. ⲉⲧⲉ ⲛⲉⲧ[ϭⲁ]ϣⲧ̄ ⲛⲉ
¹⁰ ⲁⲡⲥⲙⲓⲛⲉ ⲙ̄ⲡⲕⲓⲙ ⲙ̄ⲡ[ⲥ]ϭⲛ̄ⲧ ¹¹ ⲙ̄ⲛ̄ ⲧⲙⲛ̄ⲧⲣ̄ ⲡⲓⲑⲉ. ϩⲛ̄ⲕⲉⲕⲁⲩⲉ ⲉⲩ- ¹² ϫⲱ ⲙ̄ⲙⲟⲥ ϫⲉ
ⲟⲩⲁⲗⲟⲧⲣⲓⲟⲛ ⲡⲉ. ¹³ ⲉⲧⲉ ⲛⲉⲉⲓ ⲛⲉ ⲉⲧⲥϭⲁϣⲧ̄ ⲁⲧⲛ̄ⲧⲁⲣ! ¹⁴ ⲙⲓⲛⲉ ⲙ̄ⲛ̄ ⲧⲙⲛ̄ⲧⲁⲧϣⲉⲡ ⲛ̄ⲛⲓϭⲟⲙ ¹⁵
ⲙ̄ⲛ̄ ⲡⲉⲑⲁⲩ. ϩⲛ̄ⲕⲉⲕⲁⲩⲉ ⲉ[ⲩ]- ¹⁶ ϫⲟⲩ ⲙ̄ⲙⲁⲥ ϫⲉ ⲡⲉⲧⲏⲡ ⲁϣϣⲱⲡⲉ ¹⁷ ⲛⲉ. ⲛⲉⲧϣⲟⲟⲡ ⲉⲧⲉ
ⲛⲉⲉⲓ ⲛⲉ ⲛ̄ⲧ[ⲁⲩ]- ¹⁸ ⲥⲣ̄ϥⲉ ⲁⲡⲓϩⲱⲃ. ϩⲛ̄ⲕⲉⲕⲁⲩⲉ ⲉⲩ- ¹⁹ ϫⲱ ⲙ̄ⲙⲁⲥ ϫⲉ ⲟⲩⲕⲁⲧⲁ ⲫⲩⲥⲓⲥ ⲡ[ⲉ].
²⁰ ϩⲛ̄ⲕⲉⲕⲁⲩⲉ ⲉⲩϫⲱ ⲙ̄ⲙⲁⲥ ϫⲉ ⲛⲟⲩ- ²¹ ⲡⲉⲧϣⲟⲟⲡ ⲟⲩⲁⲉⲉⲧϥ. ⲡϩⲟⲩⲟ ⲇⲉ ²² ⲧⲏⲣϥ̄ ⲛ̄ⲧⲁⲩⲡⲱϩ
ϣⲁ ⲛⲓⲥⲧⲟⲓⲭⲓ[ⲟⲛ], ²³ ⲉⲧⲟⲩⲁⲛϩ̄ ⲁⲃⲁⲗ ⲙ̄ⲡⲟⲩⲥⲟⲩⲱⲛ ϩⲟⲩⲟ ²⁴ ⲁⲣⲁⲟⲩ.

108.2 ⲉⲇⲉ: read ⲉⲧⲉ.
108.3 ⲛ̄ⲇⲉ: read ⲛ̄ⲧⲉ.
108.22 ⲛ̄ϫⲓ: read ⲛ̄ϭⲓ.
108.28 ϩⲏⲡ: read ϩⲏⲧ?

matter of providence, so that [23] it might be discovered that the brief amount of time [24] until the human will receive the fruit [25] of things that are eternally good, [26] in which is the place of rest. [27] This the spirit destined when he [28] first considered [29] that the human should experience the [30] great evil that is death, [31] which is the ignorance of the entire totality, [32] and, moreover, that he should experience [33] all of the evil things that [34] come to be from this, and [35] after the impetuosities [36] and anxieties that accompany these things, he should receive the greatest [108.1] good, which is [2] eternal life, namely, [3] the sound knowledge of the entireties [4] and the reception of all good things. [5] Because of the transgression of the first human [6] death ruled. It customarily [7] killed every human [8] in accordance with the appearance of its [9] [. . .] given to it [10] [. . .] kingdom because of the [11] assembly of the [12] will of the Father, which we previously discussed.

[14] If each order, [15] those on the right and those on the left, is [16] joined to another by [17] the thought that is placed between them, [18] that which gives them their ordering [19] with each other, it happens that [20] both act according to a zeal [21] for works alone, since those on the right resemble [22] those on the left, [23] and those on the left also resemble [24] those on the right. And if occasionally [25] the evil order begins to do [26] evil in an [27] ignorant manner, [28] the <wise> order emulates, with [29] a face of a man of violence, [30] doing what is evil as well, [31] just as if it were a power of a man [32] of violence. Other times [33] the ignorant order [34] attempts to do what is good, becoming [35] like it, since the hidden order [36] is also eager to do it. Just as [37] it is with the way that exists with [38] the things that are established, so too with the [109.1] things that have come about. Since they bring [2] things unlike one another, [3] those who were not informed were not able to know the cause [4] of the things that [5] exist. Therefore, [6] they have brought forth other approaches, [7] some saying that the things that [8] exist have their being in [9] providence. These are those who [observe] [10] the establishment and persistence [11] of the motion of creation. Others [12] say that it is something hostile. [13] They are those who observe the [ ] [14] and lawlessness of the powers [15] and wickedness. Others [16] say that which is destined to happen are the things that exist. [17] These are those who [18] were occupied with this matter. Others [19] say that it is in accordance with nature. [20] Others say that it is a thing [21] that exists alone. The majority, however, [22] all who have reached as far as the visible elements, [23] do not know anything more [24] than them.

ϫⲉ ⲛⲉⲧⲁϩϣⲱⲡⲉ ⲛ̄ⲥⲟⲫⲟⲥ ²⁵ ⲕⲁⲧⲁ ⲛ̄ϩⲉⲗⲗⲏⲛ ⲙ̄ⲛ ⲛⲓⲃⲁⲣⲃⲁⲣⲟⲥ ²⁶ ⲁⲩⲣ̄ ⲁⲡⲁⲛⲧⲁ ϫⲉ
ⲛⲉⲧⲁϩϣⲱⲡⲉ ⲛ̄ⲥⲟⲫⲟⲥ ²⁵ ⲕⲁⲧⲁ ⲛ̄ϩⲉⲗⲗⲏⲛ ⲙ̄ⲛ ⲛⲓⲃⲁⲣⲃⲁⲣⲟⲥ ²⁶ ⲁⲩⲣ̄ ⲁⲡⲁⲛⲧⲁ ⲁⲛⲓϭⲟⲙ
ⲉⲛⲧⲁⲩ- ²⁷ ϣⲱⲡⲉ ⲕⲁⲧⲁ ⲟⲩⲫⲁⲛⲧⲁⲥⲓⲁ ⲙ̄ⲛ̄- ²⁸ ⲛ ⲟⲩⲙⲉⲩⲉ ⲉϥϣⲟⲩⲉⲓⲧ. ⲛⲛⲉⲛⲧⲁⲩ- ²⁹ ⲉⲓ ⲁⲃⲁⲗ
ϩⲛ̄ ⲛⲁⲉⲓ, ⲕⲁⲧⲁ ⲡⲓⲕⲟⲗ̄ϩ̄ ⲁϩⲟⲩⲛ ³⁰ ⲁⲛⲟⲩⲉⲣⲏⲩ ⲙ̄ⲛ ⲡⲥⲙⲁⲧ ⲛ̄ϯⲙⲛ̄ⲧⲁ- ³¹ ⲡⲟⲥⲧⲁⲇⲏⲥ ⲉⲁⲩⲣ̄
ⲉⲛⲉⲣⲅⲓ ⲛ̄ϩⲏⲧⲟⲩ, ³² ⲁⲩⲱ ⲁⲩϣⲉϫⲉ ϩⲣⲏⲓ ϩⲛ̄ⲛ ⲟⲩⲧⲁⲛⲧⲛ̄ ³³ ⲙ̄ⲛ ⲟⲩⲙ̄ⲛ̄ⲧϫⲁⲥⲓϩⲏⲧ ⲙ̄ⲛⲛ
ⲟⲩⲙⲉⲉⲩⲉ ³⁴ ⲙ̄ⲫⲁⲛⲧⲁⲥⲓⲁ ϩⲁ ⲡⲣⲁ ⲛ̄ⲛⲉⲉⲓ ⲉⲛ- ³⁵ ⲧⲁⲩⲙⲉⲩⲉ ⲁⲣⲁⲩ ⲙ̄ⲙⲛ̄ⲧⲣⲙ̄ⲛϩⲏⲧ. ³⁶ ⲉⲁϥⲣ̄
ⲁⲡⲁⲧⲁ ⲙ̄ⲙⲁⲩ ⲛ̄ϭⲓ ⲡⲓⲧⲁϥⲧⲛ̄ ³⁷ ⲉⲩⲙⲉⲩ[ⲉ] ϫⲉ ⲛⲧⲁⲩⲧⲁϩⲉ ⲧⲙⲏⲉ ¹¹⁰·¹ [ⲉ]ⲛⲧⲁⲩⲧⲉϩⲉ ϯⲡⲗⲁⲛⲏ.
ϩⲛ̄ ⲛⲓⲣⲉⲛ ² ϣⲏⲙ ⲉⲛ ⲟⲩⲁⲉⲉⲧⲟⲩ ⲉⲛ, ⲁⲗⲗⲁ ³ ⲛ̄ⲧⲁⲩ ⲛⲓϭⲟⲙ ⲧⲁⲛⲧⲛ ⲉⲥⲱϣⲧ̄ ⲙ̄- ⁴ ⲙⲁⲩ, ϩⲱⲥ
ⲉⲛⲧⲁⲩ ⲡⲉ ⲡⲧⲏⲣϥ̄. ⁵ ⲁⲃⲟⲗ ⲙ̄ⲡⲁⲉⲓ ⲁⲥϣⲱⲡⲉ ⲉⲡⲓ- ⁶ [ⲇ]ⲁⲅⲙⲁ ⲉⲩϩⲗⲏⲙ ⲁⲃⲁⲗ ⲉϥϯ ⁷ ⲟⲩⲃⲏϥ
ⲟⲩⲁⲉⲉⲧϥ̄, ⲉⲧⲃⲉ ⲧⲙⲛ̄ⲧⲣⲉϥ- ⁸ ⲙⲓϣⲉ ⲙ̄ⲙⲛ̄ϩⲁⲥⲓϩⲏⲧ ⲛ̄ⲇⲉ ⁹ ⲟⲩϩ [ⲛⲛⲓⲭ]ⲡⲟ ⲙ̄ⲡⲁⲣⲭⲱⲛ ⲉⲧⲣ̄
ϩⲩ- ¹⁰ ⲡⲉ[ⲣ]ⲉ̣[ⲥ]ⲥⲉ, ⲉⲧϣⲟⲟⲡ ϩⲁ ⲧⲉϥ- ¹¹ ⲉϩⲛ. ⲉⲧⲃⲉ ⲡⲉⲉⲓ ⲙ̄ⲡⲉⲗⲁⲩⲉ ¹² ϣⲱⲡⲉ ⲉϥϯ ⲙⲉⲧⲉ ⲙ̄ⲛ
ⲛⲉϥⲉⲣⲏ- ¹³ ⲟⲩ, ⲙ̄ⲛ ⲗⲁⲩⲉ ⲛϩⲱⲃ ⲟⲩⲇⲉ ⲙ̄ⲛⲧ- ¹⁴ ⲫⲓⲗⲟⲥⲟⲫⲟⲥ ⲟⲩⲇⲉ ϩⲛ̄ⲙⲛ̄ⲧⲥⲉⲉⲓⲛ ¹⁵ ⲟⲩⲇⲉ
ϩⲛ̄ⲙⲛ̄ⲧ̄ϩ̄´ⲣⲏⲧⲱⲣ ⲟⲩⲇⲉ ϩⲛ̄- ¹⁶ ⲙ̄ⲛ̄ⲧⲙⲟⲩⲥⲓⲕⲟⲛ ⲟⲩⲇⲉ ϩⲛ̄ⲙⲛ̄ⲧ- ¹⁷ ⲟⲣⲅⲁⲛⲟⲛ, ⲁⲗⲗⲁ ϩⲛ̄ⲉⲁⲩ ⲛⲉ
ϩⲓ ¹⁸ ⲙ̄ⲛⲧⲣⲉϥⲙ̄ⲙⲉ. ⲁⲥϣⲱⲡⲉ ⲉⲥⲁ- ¹⁹ ⲙⲁϩⲧⲉ ⲁⲭⲛ̄ ⲧⲙⲛ̄ⲧⲁⲧϯ ϩⲣⲁⲩⲟⲩ, ²⁰ ⲉⲩⲙⲁϭϫ ⲉⲧⲃⲉ
ⲧⲙⲛ̄ⲧⲁⲧⲧⲉⲟⲩ- ²¹ [.]ⲉ̣ ⲉⲧⲉ ⲛⲉⲧⲁⲙⲁϩⲧⲉ, ⲉⲧϯ ⲛⲉⲩ ²² ⲛⲛⲙⲙⲉⲩⲉ.

ϫⲉ ⲛⲉⲉⲓ ⲉⲛⲧⲁϩϣⲱ- ²³ ⲡⲉ ⲁⲃⲁⲗ ϩⲛ̄ ⲡⲧⲉⲉⲛⲟ ⲛ̄ⲇⲉ ϩⲛ̄- ²⁴ ϩⲉⲃⲃⲣⲉⲟⲥ, ⲛⲁⲉⲓ ⲉⲧⲥⲏϩ ⲁⲃⲁⲗ
ⲛ̄ⲛⲓ- ²⁵ ϩⲩⲗⲏ ⲉⲧϫⲱ ⲙ̄ⲡⲧⲩⲡⲟⲥ ⲛ̄ⲛϩⲉⲗⲗⲏⲛ, ²⁶ ⲛ̄ϭⲟⲙ ⲛ̄ⲛⲉⲧⲁⲙⲉⲉⲩⲉ ⲁⲣⲁⲩ ²⁷ ⲧⲏⲣⲟⲩ ⲁⲭⲟⲟⲩ
ⲁⲛⲓⲟⲩⲛⲉⲙ, ⲛ̄ϭⲟⲙ ²⁸ ⲉⲧⲕⲓⲙ ⲁⲣⲁⲩ ⲧⲏⲣⲟⲩ ⲁⲧⲣⲟⲩⲙⲉⲩⲉ ²⁹ ⲛ̄ϣⲉϫⲉ ⲙ̄ⲛ ⲟⲩⲉⲓⲛⲉ,
<ⲁⲩ>ⲛ̄ⲧ{ⲁⲩ}ⲟⲩ ⲁⲩⲱ ³⁰ ⲁⲩⲁⲙⲁϩⲧⲉ ϩⲱⲥ ⲁⲧⲣⲟⲩⲧⲉϩⲟ ⲛ̄- ³¹ ⲧⲙⲏⲉ, ⲁⲩⲣ̄ ⲭⲣⲁⲥⲑⲁⲓ ⲁⲛⲓϭⲟⲙ
ⲉ- ³² ⲧⲉϩⲧⲁϩⲧ̄ ⲉⲧⲣ̄ ⲉⲛⲉⲣⲅⲓ ⲛ̄ϩⲏⲧⲟⲩ. ³³ ⲙⲛ̄ⲛⲥⲁ ⲛⲁⲉⲓ ⲁⲩⲧⲉϩⲟ ⲛ̄ⲧⲁⲝⲓⲥ ⲛ̄- ³⁴ ⲇⲉ
ⲛⲓⲁⲧ<ⲧ>ⲁϩⲧ̄ϩ̄, ⲙ̄ⲡⲉⲧⲟⲩⲧⲉϩⲟ, ⲡⲟⲩ- ³⁵ ⲉⲉⲓ ⲟⲩⲁⲉⲉⲧϥ̄ ⲉⲧⲕⲁⲁⲧ ⲕⲁⲧⲁ ⲡⲓ- ³⁶ ⲛⲉ ⲙ̄ⲡⲓⲛⲉ
ⲙ̄ⲡⲱⲧ. ⲉⲩⲁⲧⲛⲉⲩ ⲁⲣⲁϥ ¹¹¹·¹ [ⲉ]ⲛ ⲡⲉ ϩⲛ̄ ⲧⲉϥⲫⲩⲥⲓⲥ ⲡⲉ, ⲁⲗⲗⲁ ⲟ[ⲩ- ² ⲥ]ⲟⲫⲓⲁ ⲧⲉ ⲧϩⲁⲃⲉ̄
ⲁⲃⲁⲗ ⲁⲭⲱϥ, ϫⲉⲕⲁ[ⲥ] ³ ⲉϥⲛⲁⲧⲟⲩϫⲟ ⲡⲧⲩⲡⲟⲥ ⲙ̄ⲡⲓⲁⲧⲛⲉⲩ ⁴ ⲁⲣⲁϥ ⲛⲁⲙⲏⲉ. ⲉⲧⲃⲉ ⲡⲉⲉⲓ
ⲙ̄ⲡⲉ- ⁵ [ϩ]ⲁϩ ⲛ̄ⲁⲅⲅⲉⲗⲟⲥ ⲧⲉϩⲁϥ ⲁⲛⲉⲩ ⲁⲣⲁϥ. ⁶ ⲁⲩⲱ ⲛ̄ⲕⲉⲣⲱⲙⲉ ϩⲱⲟⲩ ⲁⲛ ⲛ̄ⲧⲉ ⁷ ⲡⲅⲉⲛⲟⲥ
ⲙ̄ⲙⲛ̄ⲧϩⲉⲃⲣⲁⲓⲟⲥ ⲉⲧⲁⲛ- ⁸ ϣⲣⲡ ⲛⲭⲟⲟⲩ, ⲉⲧⲉ ⲛⲓⲇⲓⲕⲁⲓⲟⲥ ⲛⲉ ⁹ ⲙ̄ⲛ ⲛ̄ⲡⲣⲟⲫⲏⲧⲏⲥ, ⲙⲡⲟⲩⲙⲉⲩⲉ
ⲁⲗⲁⲩⲉ ¹⁰ ⲙ̄ⲡⲟⲩϫⲟⲩ ⲗⲁⲩⲉ {ⲙ̄ⲡⲟⲩϫⲉ ⲗⲁⲩⲉ} ¹¹ ⲕⲁⲧⲁ ⲟⲩⲫⲁⲛⲧⲁⲥⲓⲁ ⲏ ⲁⲃⲁⲗ ϩⲛ̄ ¹² ⲟⲩⲧⲁⲛⲧⲛ̄
ⲏ ⲁⲃⲁⲗ ϩⲛ̄ⲛ ⲟⲩⲙⲉⲉⲩⲉ ¹³ ⲉϥϩⲁⲃⲉ̄, ⲁⲗⲗⲁ ⲡⲟⲩⲉⲉⲓ ⲡⲟⲩⲉⲉⲓ ¹⁴ ⲁⲃⲁⲗ ϩⲛ̄ ⲧϭⲁⲙ ⲉⲧⲉⲛⲉⲣⲅⲓ
ⲛ̄ϩⲏⲧϥ̄, ¹⁵ ⲁⲩⲱ ⲉϥⲥⲱⲧⲙ̄ ⲁⲛⲉⲛⲧⲁϥⲛⲉⲩ ¹⁶ ⲁⲣⲁⲩ ⲁⲩⲱ ⲁϥⲥⲟⲧⲙⲟⲩ `ⲁϥϫⲟⲟⲩ´ ϩⲛ̄ⲛ
ⲟⲩⲛⲁⲧ[. .] ¹⁷ ⲧⲉ. ⲉⲩⲛ̄ⲧⲉⲩ ⲙ̄ⲙⲉⲩ ⲙ̄ⲡⲓϯ ⲙⲉⲧⲉ ¹⁸ ⲙ̄ⲙⲛ̄ⲧϩⲗⲏⲙ ϣⲁ ⲛⲟⲩⲉⲣⲏⲩ ⲕⲁⲧⲁ [ⲡⲓ]- ¹⁹
ⲥⲙⲁⲧ ⲛ̄ⲛⲉⲧⲣ̄ ⲉⲛⲉⲣⲅⲓ ⲛ̄ϩⲏⲧⲟⲩ, ²⁰ ⲉⲟⲩⲧⲟⲩϫⲱ ⲙⲡⲓⲛⲟⲩϭⲉ ⲙ̄ⲛ ⲡⲓϯ ⲙⲉ- ²¹ ⲧⲉ ϣⲁ ⲛⲟⲩⲉⲣⲏⲩ
ⲙⲁⲗⲓⲥⲧⲁ ⲛ̄ϩⲣⲏⲓ ²² ϩⲛ̄ ϯϩⲟⲙⲟⲗⲟⲅⲓⲁ ⲛ̄ⲇⲉ ⲡⲉⲧϫⲁⲥⲉ ²³ ⲁⲣⲁⲩ. ⲁⲩⲱ ⲟⲩⲛ ⲡⲉⲧⲛⲉⲉϥ ⲁⲣⲁⲩ,
²⁴ ⲡⲉⲉⲓ ⲉⲧⲉⲁⲩⲕⲁⲁϥ ϩⲱⲥ ⲉⲩⲣ̄ ⲭⲣⲓⲁ ²⁵ ⲙ̄ⲙⲟϥ, ⲉⲁⲡⲗⲟⲅⲟⲥ ⲙ̄ⲡⲛⲉⲩⲙⲁⲧⲓⲕⲟⲛ ²⁶ ϫⲡⲁϥ ⲛⲙ̄ⲙⲉⲩ

110.8 ⲛ̄ⲇⲉ: read ⲛ̄ⲧⲉ.
110.19 ⲁⲭⲛ̄: emend to ⲛ̄ϭⲓ.
110.20 ⲉϥⲙⲁϭϫ: emend to ⲉⲥⲛⲁϫϭ.
110.23 ⲧⲉⲉⲛⲟ: read ⲅⲉⲛⲟⲥ?
110.23 ⲛ̄ⲇⲉ: read ⲛ̄ⲧⲉ.
110.26 ⲛ̄ⲛⲉⲧⲁⲙⲉⲉⲩⲉ: read ⲛ̄ⲛⲁⲉⲓ ⲉⲧⲁⲩⲙⲉⲉⲩⲉ?
110.33–34 ⲛ̄ⲇⲉ: read ⲛ̄ⲧⲉ.
111.20 ⲛⲟⲩⲭϭ: read ⲙⲟⲩⲭϭ.
111.22 ⲛ̄ⲇⲉ: read ⲛ̄ⲧⲉ.

Those who were wise [25] among the Greeks and Barbarians [26] approach the powers that [27] have come about on account of fantasy and [28] empty thought. Those who have [29] come from these, in accordance with the conflict [30] with each other and the [31] rebellious manner they have active among them, [32] also spoke in a likely, [33] arrogant, and [34] fantastical way about the things that [35] they thought of as wisdom. [36] However, the likeness deceived them [37] when they thought that they had arrived at the truth, [110.1] (but) they had arrived at error. (This is the case) not only with the small names, [2] moreover, but [3] the powers themselves appear to obstruct [4] them, as though they are the entirety. [5] From this it happened that the [6] order is caught up fighting [7] against itself alone, because the hostility [8] of arrogance of [9] the offspring of the ruler who [10] is superior, who exists before his [11] beginning. On account of this nothing [12] came about giving assent with its counterparts, [13] nothing, neither [14] philosophy, nor medicine, [15] nor rhetoric, nor [16] music, nor [17] logic, but they are opinions and [18] theories. Ineffability prevailed [19] because it was mixed, [20] because of the unutterable nature [21] of those who prevail, who give them [22] thoughts.

As for these things that came [23] about from the Hebrew <race>, [24] things written by the [25] material ones who speak in the manner of the Greeks, [26] the powers of those <that think> about [27] them all, so to speak, about those on the right, [28] the powers that move them all to meditate on [29] words and an image, <they brought> them, and [30] they seized them in order to reach [31] the truth, and they consulted the confused powers [32] at work within them. [33] After these things they reached the order of [34] the unmixed things, the one that is established, the [35] unity that is an [36] image of the image of the Father. It is not invisible [111.1] in its nature, but [2] wisdom is the cloak upon it, so that [3] it will preserve the type of the one who is truly invisible. [4] For this reason, [5] many angels are unable to see it. [6] And other people of [7] the Hebrew race that we [8] discussed previously, which are the righteous ones [9] and the prophets, did not think anything [10] or say anything [11] according to fantasy or from [12] a likeness or from a secret thought, [13] but each one [14] by the power at work within him, [15] and while listing to the things that he saw [16] and he heard, he spoke them in a [. . .] [17] They have the unified harmony [18] toward each other in accordance with [the] [19] pattern of those working within them, [20] since they preserve the mixture and the harmony [21] with each other mainly [22] by the confession of the one exalted [23] over them. And there is one who is better than they are, [24] one who was appointed, since they needed [25] him,

ноүееі, ечр̄ хрıа м̄- ²⁷ петхасе нноүгелпıс мн̄н оүб̄ш- ²⁸ ш̄т абал ката пıмееүе
ете пе- ²⁹ ееı пе псперма н̄ноүхаеıте. ³⁰ аүш оүлогос нречр̄ оүаеıн пе, ете ³¹
пıмееүе пе мн̄ нıхпо н̄теч мн̄ ³² нıпроболн̄ н̄теч не. нıдı`к´аıос мн̄ ³³
неıпрофнтнс, етан̄ш̄рп̄ н̄хооү, ³⁴ еүтоүхо н̄гомологıа мн̄ †- ³⁵ мн̄тмн̄тре нте
ноүеıате га пра ³⁶ м̄петнееч, нееı н̄таүш̄- ³⁷ пе ¹¹²·¹ [е]үб̄аш̄т абол н̄са †[ге]
лпıс мн̄ ² пıсш̄тм̄ абол, ечсате н̄гнто[ү] ³ н̄б̄ı <пı>сперма н̄сап̄с аүш н̄ш̄ıне, ⁴
пееı етсате н̄грнı `г´ н̄ гаг, нееı ⁵ ентагш̄ıне н̄са пıтш̄к аретч̄. ⁶ чоүанг̄ абал
чсш̄к м̄маү а- ⁷ м̄р̄ре петхасе, аташ̄е аеıш̄ ⁸ мен н̄нееı гш̄с га пра н̄оүееı н̄- ⁹
оүш̄т. аүш неоүееı н̄оүш̄т пе- ¹⁰ тр̄ енергı м̄маү еүш̄ехе. се- ¹¹ ш̄ббıаеıт {а}ен
н̄хе ноүneч мн̄ ¹² ноүш̄ехе етбе паш̄еıте ¹³ м̄нетагт̄ неү н̄теш̄рıа
мн̄ ¹⁴ пıш̄ехе. етбе пееı нетагсш̄- ¹⁵ тм̄ абал нса нентаүхооү ¹⁶ етбе пееı, серг̄
лаγе ен абал ¹⁷ н̄теγоү, алла гн̄н оүш̄ıбн ¹⁸ аүхı н̄нетснг. еүр̄ гермннеγ- ¹⁹ е
м̄маү аүтего аретоү ²⁰ н̄гн̄гересıс енаш̄ш̄оү нетаү- ²¹ ш̄ооп ш̄а гоүн етеноү
гате нı<ı>- ²² оүдаеı. гн̄гаеıне мен се- ²³ хоγ м̄мас хе оγееı пе ²⁴ пноүте,
ентагташ̄е оеıш̄ ²⁵ н̄неıграфноγ н̄ес. гн̄ке- ²⁶ каγе еγхоγ м̄мас хе гаг ²⁷ не.
гн̄гаеıне мен еγхш̄ м̄- ²⁸ мас хе оүгаплоγн пе пноγ- ²⁹ те аүш неγгнт н̄оүш̄т
пе ³⁰ гн̄ тфγсıс. гн̄кекаγе еγхоγ ³¹ м̄мас хе печеıре гатре мн̄ ³² пкш̄е агрнı
м̄петнаноүч ³³ мн̄ петоγаγ. гн̄кекаγе ан ³⁴ еγхш̄ м̄мас хе н̄тач пе преч- ³⁵ р̄ гш̄б
апентагш̄ш̄пе. гн̄кекаγ- ³⁶ е де ан еγхш̄ м̄мо[с] хе абал ¹¹³·¹ [гı]тн̄ нее[ıа]
ггелос петачр̄ гш̄б.

хе ² [п]гаг ог мн̄тречмееγе м̄- ³ пıрнте пгаг н̄рнте пе аүш пгаг ⁴ н̄смат
ннıграфноγ, пентагт̄ ⁵ неγсаг м̄пномос. ндаγ н̄де м̄- ⁶ профнтнс
м̄поγхе лаγе абал ⁷ м̄моγ м̄ıн м̄моγ оγаеет[о]γ, ⁸ алла поγееı поγееı
н̄гнтоγ аба[л] ⁹ м̄пентачнеγ арооγ аγш ачса- ¹⁰ тмеч н̄тоотч̄ м̄пташ̄е аеıш̄
м̄- ¹¹ псш̄тнр. пееı пентачташ̄е аеıш̄ ¹² м̄моч, еıкефалаıон пе м̄поγта- ¹³ ш̄е
оеıш̄ [[н̄]] петеачхооγ га пра м̄- ¹⁴ пб̄ıн̄еı. м̄псш̄тнр, ете пıб̄ıнеı ¹⁵ пе.
сап де еγш̄ехе гарач н̄б̄ı н̄- ¹⁶ профнтнс гш̄с ечнаш̄ш̄пе. ¹⁷ сап де ан гш̄с
епсш̄тнр ш̄ехе ¹⁸ абал гн̄ рш̄оγ, аγш хе чнаеı н̄б̄ı ¹⁹ псш̄тнр н̄чр̄
гмот н̄нетемпоγ- ²⁰ соγш̄нч̄. емпоγр̄ ш̄бнр н̄р̄ гомо- ²¹ логı н̄ноγернγ тнроγ
н̄лаγе, ²² поγееı де поγееı, абол гм̄ печ- ²³ гш̄б ентачхı енергı абал м̄- ²⁴ моч
атречш̄ехе гарач [[ечме]] ²⁵ аγш птопос етачш̄ш̄пе ечнеγ ²⁶ арач, ечмееγе
хе абол м̄моч ²⁷ пе петоγнахпач аγш хе ечна- ²⁸ еı абал гм̄ пма етм̄маγ.
енпе- ²⁹ оγан м̄маγ м̄ме хе ечн̄ннγ ³⁰ абал тш̄н н абол гн̄ нıм петоγ- ³¹ нахпач,
алла пееı оγаееτч̄ ³² пентагр̄ печм̄пш̄а н̄хоос, ете ³³ петоγнахпач м̄мач
пе аγш ³⁴ н̄чш̄ш̄п м̄каг м̄мач пе. га пра ³⁵ де м̄пентагр̄ ш̄рп̄ н̄ш̄ооп м̄мач ³⁶
аγш петачоеı м̄мач аннгε тмет, ³⁷ н̄атхпоч н̄натм̄каг н̄те ³⁸ плогос,
ен{ен}тагш̄ш̄пе гн̄ сарг̄, ¹¹⁴·¹ м̄печеı апоγмеγе. [аγ]ш пее[ı] ² пе пш̄ехе

112.11 н̄хе: read н̄б̄ı.
113.5 ндаγ н̄де: read нтаγ де.

whom the spiritual Word [26] also produced with them, as one needing [27] the exalted one in hope and [28] anticipation in accordance with the thought that [29] is the seed of salvation. [30] He is also an illuminating word, which [31] is the thought and his offspring and [32] his emanations. The righteous ones and [33] the prophets, whom we mentioned before, [34] since they preserve the confession and the [35] testimony concerning [36] the great one from their fathers, those who [37] were [112.1] searching for the hope and [2] the hearing, in them [3] the seed of prayer and seeking is sown, [4] that which is sown among many, those [5] have sought after the establishment. [6] It appears, and it draws them to [7] love the exalted one, to proclaim [8] these things as concerning a [9] unity. And it was a unity that [10] acted in them as they spoke. Their [11] visions and [12] words are not changed because of the multitudes [13] of those who have given them the vision and [14] the word. Therefore, those who have listened [15] to the things that they said [16] on account of this, they do not reject anything [17] from them, but [18] receive the Scriptures differently. By interpreting [19] them they establish [20] the numerous heresies that [21] exist to the present day among the [22] Jews. Some [23] say that God is one, [24] who made a proclamation [25] in these ancient Scriptures. [26] Others say that they are many. [27] Some say [28] that God is simple [29] and that he was a mind single [30] in nature. Others say [31] that his work is linked with [32] the establishment of good [33] and evil. Still others [34] say that it is he who is the [35] creator of that which has come to be. But others [36] say that by [113.1] means of angels he created.

[2] The many notions of [3] this sort are the many ways and many [4] images of the Scriptures, that which produced [5] their teachers of the law. Yet their [6] prophets did not say anything by [7] themselves alone, [8] but each one of them (spoke) [9] about what he had seen and [10] heard from the preaching of [11] the Savior. This is what he preached, [12] the main point of their [13] preaching being what he said concerning [14] the coming of the Savior, which is this coming. [15] At times the prophets speak about it [16] as if it will occur. [17] Other times (they speak) as if the Savior speaks [18] from their mouth, and (they say) that the Savior will come [19] and have mercy upon those who have not [20] known him. They have not all come together in professing [21] something, [22] but each one, on the basis of the [23] thing from which he has received the ability [24] to speak about him [25] and (on the basis of) the place that he has seen, [26] thinks that from it [27] is where he will be born and that he will [28] come from that place. None [29] of them knew from where he would come [30] or by whom [31] he would be born, but he alone [32] is the one worthy to be spoken about, [33] the one who will be born and [34] who will suffer. Now concerning [35] what he was previously [36] and what he is eternally, [37] an unbegotten and impassable one from [38] the Word, who came to be in the flesh, [114.1] he did not enter into their thought. [And] this [2] is the Word from whom

ⲉⲛⲧⲁⲩϫⲓ ⲉⲛⲉⲣⲅⲓ ⲁⲣⲁ[ϥ] [3] ⲁⲧⲣⲟⲩϫⲟⲟⲥ ϩⲁ ⲡⲣⲁ ⲛ̄ⲧⲉϥⲥⲁⲣⳅ [4] ⲉⲧⲛⲁⲟⲩⲱⲛϩ̄. ⲉⲩϫⲟⲩ ⲙ̄ⲙⲟⲥ
ϫⲉ ⲟⲩ- [5] ϫⲡⲟ ⲁⲃⲟⲗ ⲛ̄ϩⲏⲧⲟⲩ ⲧⲏⲣⲟⲩ ⲧⲉ, ϩⲁ- [6] ⲑⲏ ⲇⲉ ⲛ̄ϩⲱⲃ ⲛⲓⲙ ϫⲉ ⲟⲩⲁⲃⲁⲗ ⲧⲉ [7] ϩⲙ̄
ⲡⲓⲗⲟⲅⲟⲥ ⲙ̄ⲡⲛⲉⲩⲙⲁⲧⲓⲕⲟⲥ ⲧⲉ, [8] ⲉⲧⲉ ⲛ̄ⲧⲁϥ ⲡⲉ ⲧⲗⲁⲉⲓⲥⲉ ⲛ̄ⲛⲉⲛ- [9] ⲧⲁϩϣⲱⲡⲉ, ⲡⲉⲉⲓ
ⲉⲧⲉⲁⲡⲥⲱⲧⲏⲣ ϫⲓ [10] ⲛ̄ⲧⲉϥⲥⲁⲣⳅ ⲁⲃⲁⲗ ϩⲓⲧⲟⲟⲧϥ̄. ⲛⲉⲁⲩⲣ̄ [11] ⲃⲁⲕⲏ ⲙⲉⲛ ⲙ̄ⲙⲁϥ ⲡⲉ ϩⲙ̄
ⲡϭⲓⲛⲟⲩ- [12] ⲱⲛϩ̄ ⲁⲃⲁⲗ ⲙ̄ⲡⲟⲩⲟⲉⲓⲛ, ⲕⲁⲧⲁ ⲡϣⲉ- [13] ϫⲉ ⲙⲡϣ`ⲡ´ ⲱⲡ, ⲙ̄ⲡⲉϥϭⲛⲟⲩⲱⲛϩ̄
ⲁⲃⲁⲗ [14] ϩⲛ̄ ⲧⲙⲛ̄ⲧⲥⲡⲉⲣⲙⲁ. ⲟⲩⲇⲉ ⲥⲡⲉⲣⲙⲁ [15] ⲛ̄ⲅⲁⲣ ⲛ̄ⲇⲉ ⲛⲉⲧϣⲟⲟⲡ ⲡⲉⲧϣⲟⲟⲡ, [16]
ⲉⲁϥϫⲡⲁϥ ⲛ̄ⲇⲉ ϩⲛ̄ ⲡϫⲁⲉ. ⲡⲁⲉⲓ ⲇⲉ [17] ⲉⲛⲧⲁⲡⲱⲧ ⲧⲱϣⲉ ⲙ̄ⲡⲓϭⲱⲗⲡ̄ ⲁⲃⲁⲗ [18] ⲛ̄ⲇⲉ
ⲡⲟⲩϫⲁⲉⲓⲧⲉ ⲛ̄ϩⲏⲧϥ̄, ⲉⲧⲉ ⲡⲉ- [19] ⲉⲓ ⲡⲉ ⲡϫⲱⲕ ⲛ̄ⲇⲉ ⲡϣⲡ ⲱⲡ, ⲉⲁⲛⲉⲓ- [20] ⲟⲣⲅⲁⲛⲟⲛ ⲧⲏⲣⲟⲩ
ϣⲱⲡⲉ ⲛⲉϥ ⲛ̄ⲡϭⲓⲛ- [21] ⲉⲓ ⲁϩⲣⲏⲓ̈ ⲙ̄ⲡⲃⲓⲟⲥ, ⲛⲉⲉⲓ ⲉⲧⲉⲁϥⲉⲓ ⲁ- [22] ϩⲣⲏⲓ̈ ϩⲓⲧⲟⲟⲧⲩ. ⲉⲟⲩⲉⲉⲓ ⲡⲉ
ⲡⲉϥⲓⲱⲧ, [23] ⲁⲩⲱ ⲛ̄ⲧⲁϥ ⲟⲩⲁⲉⲉⲧϥ̄ ⲡⲉⲧϣⲟⲟⲡ [24] ⲛⲉϥ ⲛ̄ⲓ̈ⲱⲧ ⲕⲁⲧⲁ ⲟⲩⲙⲛⲉ, ⲡⲓⲁⲧ- [25] ⲛⲉⲩ
ⲁⲣⲁϥ ⲙⲉⲛ ⲛ̄ⲁⲧⲥⲟⲩⲱⲛϥ̄ ⲛ̄- [26] ⲁⲧⲧⲉϩⲁϥ ϩⲛ̄ ⲧⲉϥⲫⲩⲥⲓⲥ, ⲉⲧⲉ [27] ⲡⲛⲟⲩⲧⲉ ⲡⲉ ϩⲛ̄ ⲡⲉϥⲟⲩⲱϣⲉ
ⲟⲩ- [28] ⲁⲉⲉⲧϥ̄ ⲙⲛ̄ ⲡⲉϥϩⲙⲟⲧ, ⲙⲛ̄ ⲡⲉⲧⲉ- [29] ⲁϥⲧⲉⲉⲓϥ ⲙ̄ⲙⲓⲛ ⲙ̄ⲙⲟϥ ⲁⲧⲣⲟⲩⲛⲉⲩ [30] ⲁⲣⲁϥ
ⲛ̄ⲥⲉⲥⲟⲩⲱⲛϥ̄ ⲛ̄ⲥⲉⲧⲉϩⲁϥ.

ϫⲉ [31] ⲡⲉⲉⲓ ⲡⲉ ⲉⲧⲉⲁⲡⲛ̄ⲥⲱⲧⲏⲣ ϣⲱⲡⲉ [32] ⲙ̄ⲙⲁϥ ⲁⲃⲁⲗ ϩⲛ̄ⲛ ⲟⲩⲙⲛ̄ⲧϣⲃⲏⲣ ⲛ̄- [33] ϣⲱⲡ ⲛ̄ⲕⲁϩ
ⲉϥⲟⲩⲱϣⲉ, ⲉⲧⲉ ⲡⲉⲧⲁⲩ- [34] ϣⲱⲡⲉ ⲙ̄ⲙⲁϥ ⲡⲉ. ϫⲉ ⲉⲣⲉⲛ̄ⲧⲁϥⲟⲩ- [35] ⲱⲛϩ̄ ⲁⲃⲁⲗ ⲉⲧⲃⲏⲧⲟⲩ
ϩⲛ̄ⲛ ⲟⲩⲡⲁⲑⲟⲥ [36] ⲛ̄ⲁⲧⲟⲩⲱϣⲉ. ⲁⲩϣⲱⲡⲉ ⲛ̄ⲥⲁⲣⳅ ϩⲓ ⲧⲩ- [37] ⲭⲏ, ⲉⲧⲉ ⲡⲉⲉⲓ ⲡⲉ ⲁⲛⲏϩⲉ,
ⲉⲧⲉⲙⲁⲣⲧⲉ [38] ⲙ̄ⲙⲁⲩ ⲁⲩⲱ ⲙⲛ̄ ϩⲛ̄ⲧⲉⲕⲟ [39] ⲉϣⲁⲩⲙⲟⲩ. ⲛⲉⲧⲁϩ[ϣⲱⲡ]ⲉ ⲇⲉ ϩⲱϣ ꜣ [115.1]
[ⲡ]ⲣⲱⲙⲉ [ⲛⲛ]ⲁⲧⲛⲉⲩ ⲁⲣⲁϥ ϩⲛⲛ ⲟⲩ- [2] [ⲙ]ⲛ̄ⲧⲁⲧⲛⲉⲩ ⲁⲣⲁⲥ ⲁϥⲧⲥⲉⲃⲁⲩ ⲁⲣⲁ [3] {[ϩ]-
ⲛ̄ ⲟⲩⲙⲛ̄ⲧⲁⲧⲛⲉⲩ ⲁⲣⲁⲥ ⲁⲛ}.

ϫⲉ ⲟⲩ [4] ⲙⲟⲛⲟⲛ ⲁϥϫⲓ ⲁⲣⲁⲟⲩ ⲙ̄ⲡⲓⲙⲟⲩ ⲛ̄ⲧⲉ[ⲩ]- [5] ⲟⲩ ⲛⲉⲧⲉⲁϥⲙⲉⲩⲉ ⲁⲣⲁⲟⲩ ⲁⲧⲣⲉϥⲧⲟⲩ- [6]
ϫⲁⲩⲟⲩ, ⲁⲗⲗⲁ ⲧⲟⲩⲕⲉⲙⲛ̄ⲧϣⲏⲙ ⲁ̣[ⲛ] [7] ⲡⲉⲛⲧⲁⲩⲉⲓ ⲁϩⲣⲏⲓ̈ ⲁⲣⲁⲥ ⲉⲁⲩⲛⲉⲥⲧⲟ̣[ⲩ] [8] ⲕⲁⲧⲁ
ⲡⲥⲱⲙⲁ ⲙⲛ̄ ⲧⲩⲭⲏ ⲁϥϫ̣[ⲓⲧⲥ] [9] ⲁⲛ <ⲉ>ⲃⲟⲗ ⲙ̄ⲡⲉⲉⲓ ϫⲉ ⲁϥⲧⲣⲟⲩ ⲙ̄ⲙ[ⲁ]ⲥ̣ [10] ⲁⲩⲱ
ⲁϥⲧⲣⲟⲩⲙⲉⲥⲧϥ̄ ⲛ̄ⲛⲟⲩⲗⲓⲗⲟⲩ ⲛ̄- [11] ⲥⲱⲙⲁ ⲧⲩⲭⲏ

ϫⲉ ϩⲣⲏⲓ̈ ϩⲛ̄ ⲛ̄ⲕⲉⲕⲁⲩⲉ [12] ⲧⲏⲣⲟⲩ ⲉⲛⲧⲁⲩⲣ̄ ⲕⲟⲓⲛⲱⲛⲓ ⲁⲣⲁⲟⲩ ⲙⲛ̄ [13] ⲛⲉⲛⲧⲁϩⲁⲉⲓⲉ ⲁⲩⲱ ⲉⲩϫⲓ
ⲙ̄ⲡⲟⲩⲟⲓ̈ⲛ, [14] ⲛⲉⲁϥⲉⲓ ⲉϥϩⲁⲥⲓ ⲛ̄ϩⲏⲧⲟⲩ ⲡⲉ, ⲁⲃⲁⲗ [15] ϫⲉ ϩⲛ̄ ⲟⲩⲙⲛ̄ⲧⲁⲧⲣ̄ ⲛⲟⲃⲉ ⲁⲩⲱ ϩⲛ̄ ⲟⲩ-
[16] ⲙⲛ̄ⲧⲁⲧⲧⲱⲗⲙ ⲁⲩⲱ ϩⲛ̄ ⲟⲩⲙⲛ̄ⲧ- [17] ⲁⲧϫⲱϩⲙ̄ ⲡⲉⲛⲧⲁϥⲧⲣⲟⲩⲱ ⲙ̄ⲙⲁϥ [18] ⲁⲩϫⲡⲟϥ. ϩⲙ̄
ⲡⲃⲓⲟⲥ ⲉϥϣⲟⲟⲡ, ϩⲙ̄ ⲡⲃⲓⲟⲥ [19] ⲁⲃⲁⲗ ϫⲉ ⲛ̄ⲧⲁⲩ ⲙⲛ̄ ⲛⲉⲧⲙⲙⲉⲩ ϩⲛ̄- [20] ⲛ ⲟⲩⲡⲁⲑⲟⲥ ⲙⲛ̄ⲛ
ⲟⲩⲅⲛⲱⲙⲏ ⲉ{ⲛ}ⲥⲡⲁ- [21] ⲛⲉ ⲁⲃⲁⲗ ⲛ̄ⲧⲉ ⲡⲗⲟⲅⲟⲥ ⲉⲛⲧⲁϩⲕⲓⲙ, [22] ⲉⲛⲧⲁⲥⲧⲉϩⲁⲩ ⲁⲧⲣⲟⲩϣⲱⲡⲉ
ⲛ̄ⲥⲱ- [23] ⲙⲁ ϩⲓ ⲧⲩⲭⲏ. ⲡⲉⲉⲓ ⲇⲉ ⲛ̄ⲧⲁϥ <ⲡⲉⲧ>ⲉⲁϥϫⲓ [24] ⲁⲣⲁϥ ⲙ̄ⲡⲣⲉϥⲉⲓ ϩⲁ ⲛⲉⲧⲁⲛⲣ̄ ϣⲣⲡ̄ [25]
ⲛ̄ϫⲟⲟⲩ.

114.11 ⲙ̄ⲙⲁϥ: read ⲙ̄ⲙⲁⲥ.
114.15 ⲛ̄ⲇⲉ: read ⲛ̄ⲧⲉ.
114.16 ⲉⲁϥϫⲡⲁϥ: read ⲉⲁⲩϫⲡⲁϥ.
114.16 ⲛ̄ⲇⲉ: read ⲛ̄ⲧⲉ.
115.4 ⲁⲣⲁⲟⲩ: read ⲁⲣⲁϥ.
115.7 ⲛⲉⲥⲧⲟ̣[ⲩ]: read ⲛⲉⲥⲧⲟ̣[ⲩ].

they received the ability [3] to speak about his flesh [4] that would become apparent. They say that it is a [5] product of all of them, but that before [6] all things it is a product [7] of the spiritual Word, [8] who is the cause of the things that [9] have come to be, this one [10] from whom the Savior received his flesh. He became [11] pregnant with <it> at the revelation [12] of the light, in accordance with the [13] word of the promise, at his revelation [14] in the seminality. [15] For the one who exists is not a seed of the things that exist, [16] since he was produced later. This one [17] by whom the Father ordained the revelation [18] of salvation, who [19] is the completion of the promise, for him all of the [20] implements for the [21] coming into life came to be, those through which he descended. [22] His Father is one, [23] and he alone is truly a Father [24] to him, the [25] invisible, unknowable, [26] unfathomable in his nature, who [27] alone is God in his will [28] and his form, and the one who [29] has granted that he alone might be seen [30] and known and understood.

[31] This is the one whom our Savior became [32] in a companionship of [33] willful suffering, which is that which they were. [34] For he became manifest [35] in an undesirable suffering on account of them. [36] They became flesh and soul, [37] that is, eternally, which detain [38] them and with corruptible things [39] they die. But those who have [come to be], [115.1] the invisible human taught [2] invisibly [3] about himself.

Not [4] only did he take upon <himself> the death of those [5] whom he thought to [6] save, but their smallness [7] to which they had descended after they had been <born> [8] in body and soul he [received] [9] because he permitted himself to be conceived [10] and born as a child in [11] body (and) soul.

Among all the others [12] who fellowshipped with them and [13] those who descended and received the light, [14] he came as one exalted over them, because [15] without sin and [16] stain and defilement [17] he allowed himself [18] to be conceived. He dwells in life, in life [19] because they and those with them are in [20] passion and changing opinion [21] from the Word who moved, [22] who set them up to be body [23] and soul. But this is <the one who> received [24] to himself the one coming from those we mentioned [25] earlier.

ⲭⲉ ⲁϥϣⲱⲡⲉ ⲁⲃⲁⲗ ⲛ̄ⲡⲓϭⲛ̄- ²⁶ ⲛⲉⲩ ⲉⲧⲡ̄ⲣⲣⲓⲱⲟⲩ ⲁⲩⲱ ⲡⲓⲙⲉⲩⲉ ⲛ̄ⲛⲁⲧ- ²⁷ ⲡⲱⲛⲉ ⲁⲃⲁⲗ ⲛ̄ⲧⲉ
ⲡⲗⲟⲅⲟⲥ ⲉⲛⲧⲁϥⲥⲧⲁϥ ²⁸ ⲉϩⲟⲩⲛ ⲙ̄ⲙⲓⲛ ⲙ̄ⲙⲟϥ ⲙⲛ̄ⲛⲥⲁ ⲡⲉϥⲕⲓⲙ ²⁹ ⲁⲃⲁⲗ ϩⲛ̄ ϯⲟⲓⲕⲟⲛⲟⲙⲓⲁ,
ⲙ̄ⲡⲓⲣⲏⲧⲉ ⲡⲉⲛ- ³⁰ ⲧⲁⲩϫⲓ ⲥⲱⲙⲁ ϩⲓ ⲯⲩⲭⲏ ⲛ̄ϭⲓ ⲛⲉⲛⲧⲁ<ϩ>- ³¹ ⲉⲓ ⲛ̄ⲙⲙⲉϥ ⲙⲛ̄ ⲟⲩⲧⲉϩⲟ
ⲁⲣⲉⲧϥ ³² ⲙⲛ̄ ⲟⲩⲥⲙⲓⲛⲉ ⲙⲛ̄ ⲟⲩϩⲉⲡ ⲛ̄- ³³ ϩⲃⲏⲩⲉ. ⲁⲩⲙⲉⲩⲉ ⲙⲉⲛ ϩⲱⲟⲩ ⲁⲣⲁⲩ- ³⁴ ⲟⲩ
ⲁⲧⲣⲟⲩⲉⲓ.

ⲭⲉ ⲛ̄ⲧⲁⲣⲟⲩⲙⲉⲩⲉ ⲁ- ³⁵ ⲡⲥⲱⲧⲏⲣ, ⲁⲩⲉⲓ <ⲁⲩⲉⲓ> ⲇⲉ ⲛ̄ⲧⲁⲣⲉϥⲙ̄ⲙⲉ ³⁶ ⲁⲩⲉⲓ. ⲙⲉⲛ ϩⲱⲟⲩ ⲁⲛ
ⲉⲩⲭⲁⲥⲓ ϩⲛ̄ ϯ- ³⁷ ⲡⲣⲟⲃⲟⲗⲏ ⲕⲁⲧⲁ ⲥⲁⲣⲝ ⲛ̄ϩⲟⲩⲟ ⲁⲛⲉⲛ- ³⁸ ⲧⲁⲩⲛ̄ⲧⲟⲩ ⲁⲃⲁⲗ ϩⲛ̄ⲛ ⲟⲩϣⲧⲁ,
ⲁⲃⲁⲗ ¹¹⁶·¹ ⲭⲉ ⲛ̄ⲧⲁⲩ ϩⲱⲟⲩ ⲁⲛ ⲙ̄[ⲡⲓ]ⲣⲏ[ⲧ]ⲉ ² ⲛⲉⲩϫⲓ ⲡⲣⲟⲃⲟⲗⲏ ⲛ̄ⲥⲱⲙⲁ ⲙⲛ̄ ³ ⲛ̄ⲥⲱⲙⲁ
ⲙ̄ⲡⲥⲱⲧⲏⲣ ⲁⲃⲁⲗ ϩⲓⲧⲛ̄ ⁴ ϯϭⲛⲟⲩⲱⲛϩ̄ ⲁⲃⲁⲗ ⲙⲛ̄ ϯϭⲛ- ⁵ ⲙⲟⲩϫϭ ⲛ̄ⲙⲙⲉϥ. ⲛⲉⲉⲓⲕⲉ- ⁶ ⲕⲉⲩⲉ
ⲛⲉ ⲛⲁ ϯⲟⲩⲥⲓⲁ ⲛ̄ⲟⲩⲱⲧ ⁷ ⲛⲉ, ⲁⲩⲱ ⲛ̄ⲧⲁⲥ ⲣⲱ ⲧⲉ {`ⲧⲉ´} ϯⲡⲛⲉⲩ- ⁸ ⲙⲁⲧⲓⲕⲏ ⲇⲉ. ⲧⲟⲓⲕⲟⲛⲟⲙⲓⲁ
ⲛ̄ⲇⲉ ⁹ ⲛ̄ⲧⲁⲥ<ⲥ>ϣⲃⲃⲓⲁⲉⲓⲧ. ⲟⲩⲱⲧ ⲧⲁⲉⲓ ¹⁰ ⲟⲩⲱⲧ ⲧⲁⲉⲓ. ϩⲛ̄ϩⲁⲉⲓⲛⲉ ⲙⲉⲛ ¹¹ ⲉⲛⲧⲁⲩⲉⲓ ⲉⲃⲟⲗ
ϩⲛ̄ⲛ ⲟⲩⲡⲁⲑⲟⲥ ¹² ⲙⲛ̄ ⲟⲩⲡⲱϣⲉ ⲉⲩϣⲁⲁⲧ ⲛ̄ⲛⲟⲩ- ¹³ ⲧⲗ̄ϭⲟ. ϩⲛ̄ⲕⲉⲕⲉⲟⲩⲉ ϩⲣ̄ⲛⲛⲁⲃⲁⲗ ¹⁴ ϩⲛ̄
ⲟⲩⲧⲱⲃϩ̄ ⲛⲉ ⲁⲧⲣⲟⲩⲧⲗ̄ϭⲱ ⲛ̄- ¹⁵ ⲛⲉⲧϣⲱⲛⲉ, ⲉⲁⲩⲕⲁⲁⲩ ⲁⲧⲣⲟⲩ- ¹⁶ ⲣ̄ ⲑⲉⲣⲁⲡⲉⲩⲉ ⲛ̄ⲛⲉⲧⲁϩⲉⲓ.
ⲉⲧⲉ ¹⁷ ⲛⲓⲁⲡⲟⲥⲧⲟⲗⲟⲥ ⲛⲉ ⲙⲛ̄ ⲛⲓⲣⲙ̄ϯ ϣⲙ̄ ¹⁸ ⲛⲟⲩϥⲉ. ⲛ̄ⲙⲁⲑⲏⲧⲏⲥ ⲛ̄ⲇⲉ ⲛ̄ⲧⲁⲩ ¹⁹ ⲙ̄ⲡⲥⲱⲧⲏⲣ
ⲛⲉ, ϩⲛ̄ⲥⲁϩ ⲇⲉ ⲛ̄ⲧⲁⲩ ²⁰ {ⲛ̄}ⲛⲉ ⲛⲉⲉⲓ ⲉⲧⲣ̄ ⲭⲣⲉⲓⲁ ⲛ̄ⲥⲃⲟⲩ. ⲉⲓ ⲁⲣⲁ ²¹ ⲉⲧⲃⲉ ⲉⲩ ϭⲉ ⲁⲩⲣ̄ ⲕⲟⲓⲛⲱⲛⲓ
ⲁⲛⲓⲡⲁ- ²² ⲑⲟⲥ ϩⲱⲟⲩ ⲁⲛ, ⲛⲉⲉⲓ ⲉⲧⲁⲩⲣ̄ ⲕⲟⲓⲛⲱ- ²³ ⲛⲓ ⲁⲣⲁⲟⲩ ⲛ̄ϭⲓ ⲛⲉⲛⲧⲁⲩⲛ̄ⲧⲟⲩ ⲁⲃⲟⲗ ²⁴
ϩⲛ̄ⲛ ⲟⲩⲡⲁⲑⲟⲥ, ⲉϣⲡⲉ ϩⲛ̄ⲉⲓⲛⲉ ²⁵ ⲁⲃⲁⲗ ⲛⲉ ⲕⲁⲧⲁ ϯⲟⲓⲕⲟⲛⲟⲙⲓⲁ ⲙⲛ̄ ²⁶ <ⲡ>ⲥⲱⲧⲏⲣ ⲕⲁⲧⲁ
ⲡⲥⲱⲙⲁ, ⲡⲉⲉⲓ ⲉⲧⲉⲙ̄- ²⁷ ⲡϥ̄ⲣ̄ ⲕⲟⲓⲛⲱⲛⲓ ⲁⲛⲓⲡⲁⲑⲟⲥ;

ⲭⲉ ⲛ̄- ²⁸ ⲧⲁϥ ⲙⲉⲛ ⲡⲥⲱⲧⲏⲣ ⲛⲉⲟⲩϩⲓⲕⲱⲛ ²⁹ ⲡⲉ ⲛ̄ⲇⲉ ⲟⲩⲉⲉⲓ `ⲛ̄´ⲟⲩⲱⲧ, ⲉⲧⲉ ⲛ̄- ³⁰ ⲧⲁϥ ⲡⲉ
ⲡⲧⲏⲣϥ̄ ⲕⲁⲧⲁ ⲡⲥⲱⲙⲁ. ³¹ ⲉⲧⲃⲉ ⲡⲁⲉⲓ ⲁϥⲧⲟⲩⲭⲟ ⲡⲥⲙⲁⲧ ⲛ̄- ³² ⲧⲙ̄ⲛ̄ⲧⲁⲧⲡⲱϣⲉ, ⲧⲉⲉⲓ
ⲉⲧⲉⲣⲉ- ³³ ⲧⲙ̄ⲛ̄ⲧⲁⲧⲡⲁⲑⲟⲥ ϣⲟⲟⲡ ⲁⲃⲁⲗ ⲛ̄- ³⁴ ϩⲏⲧⲥ̄. ⲛⲁⲉⲓ ⲛ̄ⲇⲉ ⲛ̄ⲧⲁⲩ ⲉϩⲛ̄ϩⲓⲕⲱⲛ ³⁵ ⲛⲉ ⲛ̄ⲇⲉ
ⲡⲟⲩⲉⲉⲓ ⲡⲟⲩⲉⲉⲓ ⲉⲧⲁϩ- ³⁶ ⲟⲩⲱⲛϩ̄ ⲁⲃⲁⲗ. ⲉⲧⲃⲉ ⲡⲉⲉⲓ ⲥⲉ- ³⁷ ϫⲓ ⲁⲣⲁⲩ ⲙ̄ⲡⲓⲡⲱϣⲉ ⲁⲃⲁⲗ
ϩⲓⲧⲟⲟⲧϥ̄ ⲙ̄- ³⁸ ⲡⲥⲙⲁⲧ, ⲉⲁⲩϫⲓ ⲙⲟⲣⲫⲏ ⲁⲡⲓϫⲱ ⲉⲧ- ³⁹ ϣⲟⲟⲡ ϩⲛ̄ ⲡⲥⲁ ⲛⲡⲓⲧⲛ̄ [ⲛ̄ⲧⲡ]ⲉ. ⲡⲉⲉⲓ
ⲁⲛ ¹¹⁷·¹ [ⲡ]ⲉⲧⲣ̄ ⲕⲟⲓⲛ[ⲱⲛⲓ] ⲁⲧⲕⲁⲕⲓⲁ ⲉⲧϣⲟⲟⲡ ⲛ̄- ² [ϩ]ⲣⲏⲓ̈ ϩⲛ̄ ⲛ̄ⲧ[ⲟ]ⲡⲟⲥ ⲉⲛⲧⲁⲩⲡⲱϣ
ϣⲁⲣⲟ- ³ [ⲟ]ⲩ. ⲉⲁⲡⲟⲩⲱϣⲉ {ⲉⲁⲡⲟⲩⲱϣⲉ} ⲅⲁⲣ ⁴ ϣⲣⲱ ⲁⲣⲙ̄ ⲡⲧⲏⲣϥ̄ ϩⲁ ⲡⲛⲁⲃⲉⲓ ϫⲉⲕⲁⲥⲉ
⁵ ϩⲙ̄ ⲡⲟⲩⲱϣⲉ ⲉⲧⲙ̄ⲙⲉⲩ ⲉϥⲛⲁⲛⲁⲉ ⁶ ⲙ̄ⲡⲧⲏⲣϥ̄ ⲛ̄ⲥⲉⲛⲟⲩϩⲙⲉ, ⲉⲟⲩⲉⲉⲓ ⲟⲩ- ⁷ ⲁⲉⲉⲧϥ̄
ⲡⲉⲧ<ⲧ>ⲛⲁϣ ⲁϯ ⲱⲛϩ̄ ⲡⲕⲉϣⲱϫⲡ ⁸ ⲧⲏⲣϥ̄ ⲉϥⲣ̄ ⲭⲣⲓⲁ ⲙ̄ⲡⲛⲟⲩϩⲙⲉ. ⲉⲧⲃⲉ ⁹ ⲡⲉⲉⲓ ⲁⲃⲁⲗ ϩⲛ̄
ⲛⲉⲉⲓ ⲙ̄ⲡⲓⲣⲏⲧⲉ ⲡⲉⲛ- ¹⁰ ⲧⲁϥⲣ̄ ⲁⲣⲭⲉⲥⲑⲁⲓ ⲛ̄ϫⲉ ϩⲙⲟⲧ ⲁϯ ⲛⲓⲧⲁ- ¹¹ ⲉⲓⲟ ⲉⲛⲧⲁⲩⲧⲁϣⲉ
ⲟⲉⲓϣ ⲙ̄ⲙⲟϥ ⲁⲃⲁⲗ ¹² ϩⲓⲧⲟⲟⲧϥ̄ ⲛ̄ⲓⲏⲥⲟⲩⲥ, ⲛⲉⲉⲓ ⲉⲧⲥ{ⲙ̄ⲡ}ⲙ̄ⲡϣⲁ ⲁⲃⲁⲗ ¹³ ϩⲓⲧⲟⲟ<ⲧⲟ>ⲩ⟦⟦ϥ⟧⟧
ⲁⲧⲣⲟⲩⲧⲁϣⲉ ⲁⲉⲓϣ ⲙ̄ⲡⲕⲉϣⲱ- ¹⁴ ϫⲡ, ⲉϥⲕⲏ ⲁϩⲣⲏⲓ̈ ⲛ̄ϭⲓ ⲥⲡⲉⲣⲙⲁ ⲛ̄ⲇⲉ ¹⁵ ⲡⲥ`ϣ´ⲡ ⲱⲡ
ⲛ̄ⲇⲉ ⲓⲏⲥⲟⲩⲥ ⲡⲉⲭⲣⲓⲥⲧⲟⲥ, ⲡⲉⲉⲓ ⲛ̄ⲧⲁⲛⲣ̄ ¹⁶ ⲇⲓⲁⲕⲟⲛⲓ ⲙ̄ⲡⲟⲩⲱⲛϩ̄ ⲁⲃⲟⲗ ⲙⲛ̄ ⲡⲓⲙⲟ[ⲩ]- ¹⁷

116.8 ⲇⲉ: read ⲧⲉ. ⲛ̄ⲇⲉ: read ⲇⲉ.
116.18 ⲛ̄ⲇⲉ: read ⲇⲉ.
116.29 ⲛ̄ⲇⲉ: read ⲛ̄ⲧⲉ.
116.34 ⲛ̄ⲇⲉ: read ⲇⲉ.
116.35 ⲛ̄ⲇⲉ: read ⲛ̄ⲧⲉ.
117.14 ⲛ̄ⲇⲉ: read ⲛ̄ⲧⲉ.
117.15 ⲛ̄ⲇⲉ: read ⲛ̄ⲧⲉ.

He came into being from the dazzling vision [26] and the unchanged thought [27] of the Word who turned himself [28] to him alone after his movement [29] from the assembly, just as [30] those who [31] came forth with him received a body and soul and a foundation [32] and a confirmation and a judgment of [33] things. They also thought that [34] they should come.

After they contemplated [35] the Savior, they came, and <they came> when he knew. [36] They also were more exalted in the [37] emanation according to the flesh than those who [38] were brought forth from a deficiency, [116.1] because in this way [2] they also received their bodily emanation along with [3] the body of the Savior through [4] the revelation and the [5] mixing with him. These others are those belonging to one being, and it is indeed the spiritual (being). But the assembly [9] is different. This is one thing; [10] that is another. Some [11] have come forth from passion [12] and division, lacking a [13] cure. Others are from [14] prayer, so that they cure [15] those who are sick, since they have been appointed to [16] cure those who have descended. [17] These are the apostles and the [18] evangelists. They are the disciples [19] of the Savior, and they are teachers [20] in need of instruction. [21] Why then did they also associate with the passions [22] with which those who have been brought forth [23] from passion associate, [24] if they are brought forth [25] bodily according to the assembly and [26] <the> Savior, who did [27] not associate with the passions?

[28] The Savior was an image [29] of the solitary one, he who [30] is the entirety embodied. [31] For this reason he kept the form of [32] invisibility, from which [33] passionlessness derives. [34] But they are images [35] of each thing that has [36] appeared. For this reason they [37] receive for themselves the division from [38] the form, after they have received form for the sowing that [39] occurs beneath [heaven]. Additionally, this [117.1] is what it has in common with the evil that dwells [2] in the places that they have reached. [3] For the will [4] subjected the entirety to sin so that [5] by that will he might have mercy [6] upon the entirety and they might be saved, since a [7] single one is appointed to give life whereas all the others [8] need salvation. Therefore, [9] it was from these sorts (of considerations) that it [10] began to receive grace to give the [11] honors that were preached [12] by Jesus, these that are worthy [13] for him to preach to the others, [14] since a seed of [15] the promise of Jesus Christ, whom we have [16] served in the revelation

ⲭⲉ. ⲡⲓϣⲡ ⲱⲡ ϭⲉ ⲛⲉⲩⲛ̄ⲧⲉϥ ⲙ̄ⲙⲉⲩ ¹⁸ ⲡⲉ ⲙ̄ⲡϭⲛ̄ⲧⲥⲉⲃⲁⲩ ⲁⲩⲱ ⲡϭⲛ̄ⲥⲧⲁⲩ ¹⁹ ⲉϩⲟⲩⲛ
ⲁⲡⲉⲧⲁϣⲟⲟⲡ ⲙ̄ⲙⲁϥ ϫⲛ̄ ⲛ̄- ²⁰ ϣⲟⲣⲡ̄, ⲡⲁⲉⲓ ⲉⲧⲉⲩⲛ̄ⲧⲉⲩ ⲁⲃⲟⲗ ⲛ̄- ²¹ ϩⲏⲧϥ̄ ⲛ̄ⲧ̄ⲗ̄ⲗⲉ
ⲁⲧⲣⲟⲩⲥⲧⲟ ⲁϩⲟⲩⲛ ²² ⲁⲣⲁϥ, ⲉⲧⲉ ⲡⲉⲧⲟⲩⲙⲟⲩⲧⲉ ⲉⲣⲟϥ ϫⲉ ²³ « ⲡⲥⲱⲧⲉ » ⲡⲉ. ⲁⲩⲱ ⲛ̄ⲧⲁϥ ⲡⲉ
ⲡⲣ̄ ⲃⲟⲗ ⲉⲃⲟⲗ ²⁴ ⲛ̄ⲧⲟⲟⲧⲥ̄ ⲛ̄ⲧⲁⲓⲭⲙⲁⲗⲱⲥⲓⲁ ⲁⲩⲱ ⲡϫⲓⲛ ²⁵ ⲛ̄ⲧⲙⲛ̄ⲧⲣⲙ̄ϩⲉ. ⲧⲉⲕⲭⲙⲁⲗⲱⲥⲓⲁ
`ⲛ̄´ ⲇⲉ ²⁶ ⲛⲉⲉⲓ ⲉⲛⲧⲁⲩⲣ̄ ϭⲁⲩⲟⲩⲁⲛ ⲛ̄ⲧⲙⲛ̄ⲧⲁⲧ- ²⁷ ⲥⲁⲩⲛⲉ ⲉⲥⲟⲉⲓ ⲛ̄ⲛⲣ̄ⲣⲟ ϩⲛ̄ ⲛⲉⲥⲧⲟⲡⲟⲥ. ²⁸
ⲧⲙⲛ̄ⲧⲣⲙ̄ϩⲉ ⲇⲉ ⲡⲉ ⲡⲓⲥⲁⲩⲛⲉ ⲛ̄ⲧⲉ ²⁹ ⲧⲙⲏⲉ ⲉⲧϣⲟⲟⲡ ϩⲁⲑⲏ ⲇⲉ ⲙ̄ⲡⲁⲧⲉ- ³⁰ ⲧⲙⲛ̄ⲧⲁⲧⲥⲁⲩⲛⲉ
ϣⲱⲡⲉ ⲉϥⲟⲉⲓ ⲛ̄ⲣⲣⲟ, ³¹ ϣⲁ `ⲁ´ⲛⲏϩⲉ ϩⲛ̄ⲛ ⲟⲩⲙⲛ̄ⲧⲁⲧⲁⲣⲭⲏ ⲙⲛ̄- ³² ⲛ ⲟⲩⲙⲛ̄ⲧⲁⲧϩⲁⲛ,
ⲉⲟⲩⲡⲉⲧⲛⲁⲛⲟⲩϥ ³³ ⲡⲉ ⲁⲩⲱ ⲟⲩϫⲁⲉⲓⲧⲉ ⲛ̄ⲛϩⲃⲏⲩⲉ ³⁴ ⲧⲉ ⲁⲩⲱ ⲟⲩⲣ̄ ⲃⲟⲗ ⲉⲃⲟⲗ ⲧⲉ ⲛ̄ⲧⲟⲟⲧⲥ̄ ³⁵
ⲛ̄ⲧϥⲩⲥⲓⲥ ⲙ̄ⲙⲛ̄ⲧϭⲁⲩⲟⲩⲁⲛ ⲧⲁ- ³⁶ ⲉⲓ ⲛ̄ⲧⲁⲩϣⲱⲡ ⲙ̄ⲕⲁϩ ⲙ̄ⲙⲁⲥ.

ϫⲉ ⲛⲉ- ³⁷ ⲛ̄ⲧⲁⲩⲛ̄ⲧⲟⲩ ⲁⲃⲁⲗ ϩⲛ̄ⲛ ⲟⲩⲙⲉⲉⲩⲉ ³⁸ ⲉϥⲑⲃⲃⲓⲁⲉⲓⲧ ⲛ̄ⲧⲉ ⲧⲙⲛ̄ⲧⲁⲡⲟⲗ[ⲁ], ³⁹ ⲉⲧⲉ
ⲡⲉⲉⲓ ⲡⲉ, ⲉⲥⲛⲁ ϣⲁ ⲛⲉⲧϩⲁⲩ ¹¹⁸·¹ ⲁⲃⲁⲗ ϩⲓⲧⲛ̄ ⲡⲓⲙⲉⲩⲉ ⲉⲧⲥ[ⲱ]ⲕ̣ ⲙ̄ⲙⲁⲩ ² ⲁⲡⲓⲧⲛ̄
ⲁⲧⲙ̄ⲛ̄ⲧ`ⲙⲁⲓ´ⲟⲩⲁϩ ⲥⲁϩⲛⲉ, ⲁⲩⲭⲓ ⲇⲉ ³ ⲙ̄ⲡⲓⲕⲧⲏⲙⲁ ⲉⲧⲉ ⲧⲙⲛ̄ⲧⲣⲙ̄ϩⲉ ⲇⲉ, ⁴ ϩⲙ̄ ⲡϩⲟⲩⲟ
ⲙ̄ⲡϩⲙⲁⲧ ⲉⲛⲧⲁϩϭϣⲱⲧ̄ ⁵ ⲁϫⲛ̄ ⲛ̄ϣⲏⲣⲉ. ⲉⲩⲟⲩϣⲟⲣϣⲣ̄ ⲛ̄ⲇⲉ ⲡⲉ ⲙ̄- ⁶ ⲡⲁⲑⲟⲥ ⲡⲉ ⲁⲩⲱ
ⲟⲩⲧⲉⲕⲟ ⲛⲉⲩⲟⲩ ⲡⲉ ⲛ̄- ⁷ ⲛⲁⲉⲓ ⲉⲧⲉⲁϥⲛⲁϩⲟⲩ ⲉⲃⲟⲗ ⲙ̄ⲙⲟϥ ⁸ ⲟⲩⲁⲉⲉⲧϥ̄ ⲛ̄ϣⲟⲣⲉⲡ, ⲉⲁϥⲡⲁⲣⲭⲟⲩ
⁹ ⲁⲃⲟⲗ ⲙ̄ⲙⲟϥ ⲛ̄ϭⲓ ⲡⲗⲟⲅⲟⲥ ⲉⲛⲧⲁϩϣⲱⲡⲉ ¹⁰ ⲛⲉⲩ ⲛ̄ⲗⲁⲉⲓϭⲉ ⲙ̄ⲡⲧⲟⲩϣⲱⲡⲉ ⲉⲡⲟⲩ- ¹¹ ⲧⲉⲕⲟ,
ⲉⲁϥⲁⲣⲏϩ ⲁⲣⲁϥ ⲁ<ⲡ>ϩⲁⲉ ⲛ̄ⲧⲟⲓⲕⲟ- ¹² ⲛⲟⲙⲓⲁ ⲉⲁϥⲕⲁⲉ ⲁⲧⲣⲟⲩϣⲱⲡⲉ ¹³ ϫⲉ ⲛⲉⲩⲣ̄ ϣⲉⲩ
ϩⲱⲟⲩ ⲁⲛ ⲡⲉ ⲁⲛⲉⲧⲁⲩⲧⲁ- ¹⁴ ϣⲟⲩ.

ϫⲉ ⲧⲙⲛ̄ⲧⲣⲱⲙⲉ ⲁⲥϣⲱⲡⲉ ¹⁵ ⲉⲥⲟⲉⲓ ⲛ̄ϣⲟⲙⲛ̄ⲧ ⲛ̄ⲣⲏⲧⲉ ⲕⲁⲧⲁ ⲟⲩⲥⲓⲁ ¹⁶ ⲇⲉ· ⲧⲡⲛⲉⲩⲙⲁⲧⲓⲕⲏ
ⲙⲛ̄ ⲧⲯⲩⲭ<ⲓⲕ>ⲏ ¹⁷ ⲙⲛ̄ ⲧϩⲩⲗⲓⲕⲏ, ⲉⲥⲧⲟⲩⲭⲟ ⲙ̄ⲡⲧⲩⲡⲟⲥ ¹⁸ ⲛ̄ⲧⲇⲓⲁⲑⲉⲥⲓⲥ ⲙ̄ⲡⲓϣⲟⲙⲛ̄ⲧ ⲛ̄ⲣⲏⲧⲏ
ⲛ̄- ¹⁹ ⲇⲉ ⲡⲗⲟⲅⲟⲥ {ⲧⲉ}, ⲧⲉⲉⲓ `ⲉⲧⲉ´ ⲁⲃⲁⲗ ⲛ̄ϩⲏⲧⲥ ²⁰ ⲁⲩⲉⲓⲛⲉ ⲁⲃⲁⲗ ⲛ̄ⲛⲓϩⲩⲗⲓⲕⲟⲛ ⲙⲛ̄ ⲛⲓⲯⲩ- ²¹
ⲭⲓⲕⲟⲛ ⲙⲛ̄ ⲛⲓⲡⲛⲉⲩⲙⲁⲧⲓⲕⲟⲛ. ⲧⲟⲩⲉⲓⲉ ⲧⲟⲩⲉⲓⲉ ²² ⲛ̄ⲛⲟⲩⲥⲓⲁ ⲙ̄ⲡⲓϣⲟⲙⲛ̄ⲧ ⲛ̄ⲅⲉⲛⲟⲥ ⲁⲃⲁⲗ ²³
ϩⲓⲧⲛ̄ ⲡⲉⲥⲕⲁⲣⲡⲟⲥ ⲉⲩⲥⲟⲩⲱⲛ ⲙ̄ⲙⲟⲥ, ²⁴ ⲁⲩⲱ ⲛⲉⲙ̄ⲡⲟⲩⲥⲟⲩⲱⲛⲟⲩ ⲇⲉ ⲛ̄ϣⲟⲣⲡ̄, ²⁵ ⲁⲗⲗⲁ ϩⲙ̄
ⲡⲟⲛϭⲓ ⲙ̄ⲡⲥⲱⲧⲏⲣ, ⲡⲁⲓ̈ ²⁶ ⲉⲛⲧⲁϥⲣ̄ ⲟⲩⲁⲉⲓⲛ ⲁⲛⲉⲧⲟⲩⲁⲁⲃ ϣⲁ- ²⁷ ⲣⲟⲟⲩ ⲁⲩⲱ ⲡⲟⲩⲉⲓ ⲡⲟⲩⲉⲓ
ⲁϥⲟⲩⲁⲛϩϥ̄ ²⁸ ⲁⲃⲁⲗ ⲙ̄ⲡⲉⲧⲉ ⲛ̄ⲧⲁϥ ⲡⲉ.

ϫⲉ ⲡⲓⲅⲉ- ²⁹ ⲛⲟⲥ ⲙⲉⲛ ⲙ̄ⲡⲛⲉⲩⲙⲁⲧⲓⲕⲟⲥ, ⲉϥⲟ- ³⁰ ⲉⲓ ⲙ̄ⲡⲣⲏⲧⲏ ⲛ̄ⲛⲟⲩⲟⲉⲓⲛ ⲁⲃⲁⲗ ϩⲛ̄ⲛ ⲟⲩ- ³¹
ⲟⲉⲓⲛ ⲁⲩⲱ ⲙ̄ⲡⲣⲏⲧⲉ ⲛ̄ⲛⲟⲩⲡⲛⲉⲩⲙⲁ ⲁⲃⲁⲗ ³² ϩⲛ̄ⲛ ⲟⲩⲡⲛⲉⲩⲙⲁ, ⲛ̄ⲧⲁⲣⲉⲧⲉϥϣⲁⲡⲉ ³³ ⲟⲩⲱⲛϩ̄
ⲁⲃⲁⲗ, ⲁϥⲡⲱⲧ ⲁϩⲟⲩⲛ ⲁⲣⲁϥ ³⁴ ⲥⲉϩⲛ̄ⲧϥ̄. ⲁϥϣⲱⲡⲉ ⲛ̄ⲛⲟⲩⲥⲱⲙⲁ ³⁵ ⲥⲉϩⲛ̄ⲧϥ̄ ⲛ̄ⲧⲉϥⲁⲡⲉ.
ⲁϥⲭⲓ ⲙ̄ⲡⲥⲁⲩ- ³⁶ ⲛⲉ ϩⲛ̄ ⲟⲩϭⲉⲡⲏ ⲙ̄ⲡϭⲱⲗⲡ̄ ⲁⲃⲁⲗ. ³⁷ [ⲡ]ⲓⲯⲩⲭⲓⲕⲟⲛ ⲇⲉ ⲛ̄ⲅⲉⲛⲟⲥ ϩⲱⲥ
ⲟⲩⲟⲉⲓⲛ ⲡⲉ ³⁸ ⲁⲃⲁⲗ ϩⲛ̄ⲛ ⲟⲩⲕⲱϩⲧ̄, ⲉⲁϥⲱⲥⲕ̄ ⲁⲭⲓ ⲥⲁⲩⲛⲉ ¹¹⁹·¹ ⲙ̄ⲡⲉⲛⲧⲁϩⲟⲩⲱⲛϩ̄ ⲛⲉϥ
ⲁⲃⲁⲗ. ⲛ̄ϩⲟⲩⲟ ² {ⲛ̄ϩⲟⲩⲟ} ⲁⲡⲱⲧ ϣⲁⲣⲁϥ ϩⲛ̄ ⲟⲩⲛⲁϩⲧⲉ. ³ ϩⲓⲧⲛ̄ ⲟⲩⲥⲙⲏ ⲉⲩ ⲧ̄ ⲥⲃⲱ
ⲛⲉϥ ⲛ̄ϩⲟⲩⲟ ⁴ ⲁⲩⲱ ⲛⲉⲩϩⲱ ⲙ̄ⲡⲣⲏⲧⲉ ⲉϥⲟⲩⲏⲟⲩ ⁵ ⲁⲃⲁⲗ ⲉⲛ ⲛ̄ⲧϩⲉⲗⲡⲓⲥ ⲕⲁⲧⲁ ⲡⲓϣⲡ ⲱⲡ, ⁶
ⲉⲁϥⲭⲓ ⲙ̄ⲡⲣⲏⲧⲉ ⲁϩⲟⲟⲥ ϫⲉ ϩⲛ̄ ⲟⲩ- ⁷ ⲥⲙⲟⲧ ⲛ̄ⲛⲁⲣⲏⲃ ⲙ̄ⲡⲧⲁⲭⲣⲟ ⲛ̄ⲛⲉ- ⁸ ⲧⲛⲁϣⲱⲡⲉ.
ⲡⲓϩⲩⲗⲓⲕⲟⲛ ⲛ̄ⲇⲉ ⲛ̄- ⁹ ⲧⲁϥ ⲛ̄ⲅⲉⲛⲟⲥ ⲟⲩϣⲙⲙⲟ ⲡⲉ ⲛ̄ⲣⲏ- ¹⁰ ⲧⲉ ⲛⲓⲙ. ϩⲱⲥ ⲉⲩⲕⲉⲕⲉⲓ ⲡⲉ

117.25 `ⲛ̄´ ⲇⲉ: read ⲛ̄ⲧⲉ.
118.11 ⲁⲣⲁϥ: read ⲁⲣⲁⲩ.
118.16 ⲇⲉ: read ϫⲉ.
118.18–19 ⲛ̄ⲇⲉ: read ⲛ̄ⲧⲉ.

and mixing, [17] was established. The promise had [18] the teaching and the return [19] to what they were from the [20] beginning, from which they have [21] the drop in order to return [22] to him, which is what they call [23] "the redemption." And it is the freedom from [24] imprisonment and the power [25] of freedom. The imprisonment of [26] those who were captives of ignorance [27] reigns in its places. [28] But the freedom is the knowledge of [29] the truth that exited before [30] ignorance came to be in a position of power, [31] eternally without beginning and [32] end, since it is what is good [33] and salvation of things [34] and a release from [35] the enslaved nature [36] in which they have suffered.

Those [37] who have been brought forth in a [38] base thought of vanity, [39] that is, it gravitates toward evil things [118.1] through the thought that [draws] them [2] down to the love of power, they have received [3] the possession that is freedom, [4] from the greatness of the image that looked [5] upon the children. Yet it was a disturbance of [6] the passion and a corruption of [7] those things that he tossed aside from [8] himself initially, [9] when the Word, who is [10] for them a cause of their being and [11] corruption, separated them from himself, while keeping <them> at <the> end of the assembly [12] and permitting them to exist [13] because they too were useful for the things that were [14] destined.

Humanity came into being [15] in three manners according to essence: [16] the spiritual, the soulish, [17] and the material, preserved by the type [18] of the threefold disposition [19] of the Word, from which [20] were brought forth the material, [21] soulish, and spiritual. Each one [22] of the essences of the three races [23] is known by its fruit, [24] and yet they were not known at first, [25] but (only) at the coming of the Savior, the one [26] who illuminated the holy ones [27] and revealed [28] what each one is.

The spiritual race, [29] since it is [30] like light from [31] light and like spirit from [32] spirit, when its head [33] appeared, it rushed to him [34] immediately. Immediately it became a body [35] of its head. It received the knowledge [36] of the revelation quickly. [37] Now the soulish race (is) as light [38] from fire, since it hesitated to receive knowledge [119.1] of the one who appeared to it. (It hesitated) even more [2] to rush to him in faith. [3] From a voice it receives teaching, rather, [4] and this was sufficient, since it is not distant [5] from the hope in accordance with the promise, [6] since it received, in a manner of speaking, as a [7] pledge the guarantee of things [8] to come. But as for the material (race), [9] it is a foreign race in [10] every way. Since it is dark, it

ечна- ¹¹ наг̅ч̅ авал м̅пρρε м̅поγαειν ¹² χε печογωн̅г̅ авал ρ̅ каталγε м̅- ¹³ моч.
гωс емпечхι м̅печб̅ноγ- ¹⁴ ееι, <оγ>авал н̅гоγо пε αγω оγ- ¹⁵ масте пε ω̣α
пχαειс атреч- ¹⁶ оγαν̅г̅ч̅ пε.

χε πιгενос м̅пнεγματικον ¹⁷ ч̅нахι м̅поγгме тηρ̅ч̅ ката ¹⁸ ρητε νιμ. πιгγλικον
н̅δε ч̅нахι ¹⁹ птεко ката ρητε νιμ, ка<та> πρητε ²⁰ н̅оγεει εч̅ς̣ αρτηч̣. πιψγχικον
δ̣[ε] ²¹ н̅гενος, гωс εγ̅н̅ ζ̅н̅ тмητε πε ζ̅м̅ ²² печб̅н̅н̅τ̅ч̅ авал αγω печкω α- ²³ ζρηϊ
гωωч̣ αν, ч̣ζατρε ката печтωω ²⁴ απαгαθον μ̅ν̅ пкакон. ч̣хι αραч̣ ²⁵ м̅пιζετε
авал εчкη αζρηϊ ζ̅н̅- ²⁶ н оγωнε μ̅ν̅ πιпωт αζоγν ²⁷ παντως αν ανιπετνανоγоγ.
²⁸ неει μεν ετεαпλогос н̅τоγ авал ²⁹ ката πετ̅ρ̅ ω̣ρ̅π̅ н̅ω̣ооπ н̅δε π̅ч̅- ³⁰ μεεγε,
εч̣ειρε м̅πμεγε м̅пετ- ³¹ χасι αγω εчтωβ̅ζ̣ м̅поγχαειτε, ³² оγ̅н̅тεч м̅μεγ
м̅поγχεειτε н̣ạ[пс]- ³³ ω̣νε. παντως сεναнογгме ε[твε] ³⁴ πιμεγε н̅ноγχαειτε.
ката πε[н]- ³⁵ таγντ̅ч̣ авал м̅μαч̣, πρητε ζω̣[оч̣] ³⁶ αν πε [пε]ε̣[ι] ετεαναει
н̅τоγ αβ[αλ] ³⁷ м̅μ[αч̣], ¹²⁰·¹ ειδε м̅н̅таггελος ειδε м̅н̅τρω̣- ² με. ката тгомоλогια
χε оγ̅н̅ ³ πεταει εч̣ζασε н̅гоγо αραγ, ⁴ αγω ката πσαπ̅с̅ м̅н̅ πὸν̅ω̣ινε н̅- ⁵ σωч̣,
сεναтεζο гωоγ αν м̅поγ- ⁶ χαειτε н̅нεταζ̅н̅тоγ авал, гωс ⁷ εζ̅н̅навол νε ζ̅н̅
†διαθεсιс νε ⁸ ετναноγоγ νε. неει αγκαγε αγ- ⁹ ω̣μω̣ε απтαω̣ε αειω̣ м̅пб̅неї ¹⁰
м̅псωтηρ εταч̣наω̣ωπε, αγω ¹¹ печч̣оγ̅ноγ̅г̅ авал ετεαчεϊ. ει- ¹² δε аггελос
ειδε ρωμε, εαγ- ¹³ т̅н̅νooγч̣ απω̣μω̣ε н̅наει, αγχι н̅- ¹⁴ тоγсια м̅поγω̣ωπε
ζ̅м̅ πρωβ. νε- ¹⁵ ει н̅δε н̅таγ ετε ζ̅навоλ νε ζ̅н̅ ¹⁶ πιμεεγε м̅м̅н̅тμαειоγεζ ¹⁷ сагνε,
неει ενταζ̣ω̣ωπε авал ¹⁸ ζ̅м̅ пκωλζ̅ αζоγν н̅нετ̅† оγ- ¹⁹ βηч̣, ετε неει νε
ετεαπιμεγε ²⁰ н̅тоγ авал {авал}, н̅нεει б̣ε, ²¹ гωс εζ̅н̅тζ̅τ̅ζ̣ νε, ε<γ>нахι
н̅тоγζαн ²² гωс ζ̅н̅´ оγω̣νε. нετναн̅тоγ ²³ μεν авал ζ̅н̅ тμ̅н̅тμαειоγεζ ²⁴ сагνε
εттω̣ει νεγ м̅πρос оγα- ²⁵ ειω̣ м̅н̅ ζενсηγ, н̅сε† εαγ м̅- ²⁶ πχоϊс м̅πεαγ, н̅сεкω
н̅сωоγ ²⁷ н̅тоγβ̅λ̅κε, сεναхι н̅тω̣ββιω м̅- ²⁸ поγθββιо, н̅δε πιμογν αζоγν ²⁹
ω̣авоλ πε. неει δε н̅таγ ετνα- ³⁰ с̅λλαζ̅λ̅ ετвε τεπιθγμια ³¹ н̅тм̅н̅тμαει·ε´αγ,
н̅сεм̅ρρε πεαγ ³² πрос оγαειω̣, н̅сερ̣ πωω̣ χε τε- ³³ ζоγсια ερε н̣´ таγτν̅ζоγтоγ
арас ³⁴ πρос н̅сноγ м̅н̅ ζ̅ноγоειω̣ ετεγ- ³⁵ н̅теγсоγ, αγω ετвε †λαειб̣ε {м̅} ³⁶
м̅поγ̅ρ̅ гомоλογι м̅πω̣ηρε м̅πноγ- ³⁷ τε ¹²¹·¹ χε πχαειс м̅птηρ̅ч̅ πε αγω ² πсωτηρ
πε, αγω м̅{м̅}поγ̅н̅тоγ ³ авол н̅τм̅н̅тρεч̣оргη м̅н̅ †- ⁴ м̅н̅†н̅тωноγ ανεтθαγоγ,
νε- ⁵ ει сεναхι н̅ноγζαπ н̅тоγм̅н̅т- ⁶ ατсαγνε м̅н̅ тоγм̅н̅тагнωμων, ⁷ ετε
†м̅н̅тω̣οπ н̅каζ τε, м̅н̅ неει ⁸ εταζсωρμε, неει ετε ζαεινε ⁹ тηρоγ ρικε
авал н̅τεγоγ· αγω ¹⁰ <†>м̅н̅тπεθαγ н̅гоγо гωсте атроγ- ¹¹ ρ̅ гωβ гωоγ αν анεεϊ
αζоγн απχο- ¹² ειс ετε нετεω̣ω̣ε εν νε, εν- ¹³ таγ̅ρ̅ гωβ {араγ} арач̣ н̅б̣ι н̅б̣ом

119.29 н̅δε: read н̅тε.
119.32 оγ̅н̅τεч: read оγ̅н̅τεγ.
120.3 πεταει: read πετοει.
120.28 н̅δε: read ετε.
120.30 The meaning of с̅λλαζ̅λ̅ is unknown, but it may be related to λαζλζ "to be high" (C149b).
121.9 н̅τεγоγ: read н̅ζητоγ?

avoids [11] the illumination of the light [12] because its appearance destroys [13] it. Since it has not received its oneness, [14] it is in excess, and it is [15] hostile to the Lord at his [16] manifestation.

The spiritual race [17] will receive total salvation in [18] every way. The material (race) will receive [19] destruction in every way, just as [20] one who fights against him. But the soul-ish [21] race, since it is in the middle in [22] its coming forth and its creation [23] as well, is double in its disposition [24] to good and evil. It receives [25] (its) established departure [26] immediately and (its) complete flight [27] to those that are good. [28] As for those whom the Word brought forth [29] according to the first being of his [30] thought, when he remembered the [31] exalted one and prayed for salvation, [32] <they> have salvation [33] immediately. They will be saved entirely [because of] [34] the salvific thought. Just as [35] he was brought forth from him, so too [36] were these brought forth from [37] [him], [120.1] whether angel or [2] human. In accordance with the confession that there is [3] one who is more exalted than them, [4] and in accordance with the prayer and the search [5] for him, they will also reach the [6] salvation of those who have been brought forth, since [7] they are from the disposition [8] that is good. These were [9] appointed for service of the announcement of the coming [10] of the Savior, which was to occur, and [11] his manifestation that had come about. Whether [12] angels or humans, when [13] he was sent as the service for them, they received as a matter of fact [14] the substance of their being. But these [15] who are from [16] the thought of the love of power, [17] those who have come about from [18] the assault of those who oppose [19] him, these whom the thought had [20] brought forth, these, [21] since they are mixed, <they> will receive their end [22] quickly. Those who will be brought [23] forth from the love of [24] power that is given to them at [25] a time and for periods of time, and who will glorify [26] the Lord of glory, and who will leave behind [27] their anger, they will receive their reward for [28] their humility, which is the eternal perseverance. [29] But those who will [30] be arrogant because of the desire [31] for domination, and who love glory [32] for a time, and who forget that the [33] power that they were entrusted with [34] (was given) occasionally and at times [35] they have, and for this reason [36] they did not profess that the Son of [37] God [121.1] is Lord of all and [2] Savior, and they were not delivered [3] from the wrath and the [4] likeness to the evil ones, these [5] will receive judgment for their [6] ignorance and their senselessness, [7] which is suffering, along with those [8] in error, any of those [9] who turned away <from them>; and [10] a wickedness even greater so that they [11] also did to the Lord [12] things that were not

ⲛ- [14] ϭⲃⲟⲩⲣ ϣⲁϩⲣⲏⲓ̈ ⲁⲡⲉϥⲙⲟⲩ. ⲁⲩϭⲱ ⲙ̄- [15] ⲙⲉⲩ ϫⲉ « ⲧⲛ̄ⲛⲁϣⲱⲡⲉ ⲉⲛⲟⲉⲓ ⲛ̄ⲁⲣ- [16]
ⲭⲱⲛ ⲛ̄ⲧⲉ ⲡⲧⲏⲣϥ̄, ⲉϣϫⲉ ⲥⲉⲛⲁϣ [17] ϩⲱⲧⲃ̄ ⲁⲡⲉⲛⲧⲁⲩⲧⲁϣⲉ ⲁⲉⲓϣ ⲙ̄ⲙⲁϥ [18] ⲛ̄ⲛⲣ̄ⲣⲟ
ⲙ̄ⲡⲧⲏⲣϥ̄. » ⲉⲁⲩϩⲓ̈ⲥⲉ ⲉⲩⲉⲓⲣⲉ ⲛ̄- [19] ⲛⲉⲉⲓ ⲛ̄ϭⲓ ⲛ̄ⲣⲱⲙⲉ ⲙⲛ̄ ⲛ̄ⲁⲅⲅⲉⲗⲟⲥ, ⲛⲉⲉⲓ [20] ⲉⲧⲉ ϩⲛ̄ⲁⲃⲁⲗ
ⲉⲛ ⲛⲉ ϩⲛ̄ ⲧ̄ⲇⲓⲁⲑⲉⲥⲓⲥ ⲉⲧ- [21] ⲛⲁⲛⲟⲩⲥ ⲛ̄ⲇⲉ ⲛⲓⲟⲩⲛⲉⲙ, ⲁⲗⲗⲁ ⲟⲩ- [22] ⲁⲃⲁⲗ ⲧⲉ ϩⲛ̄
ⲧ̄ⲙⲛ̄<ⲧ>ϩⲉϩⲧϩ ⲧⲉ. ⲁⲩⲱ [23] {ⲁⲩⲱ} ⲁⲩⲣ̄ ϣⲁⲣⲡ̄ ⲛ̄ⲥⲱⲧⲡ̄ ⲛⲉⲩ ⲙ̄- [24] ⲡⲧⲁⲉⲓⲟ, ⲉⲩⲟⲩⲱϣⲉ ⲡⲉ
ⲡⲣⲟⲥ ⲟⲩⲁⲉⲓϣ [25] ⲁⲩⲱ ⲧⲉⲡⲓⲑⲩⲙⲓⲁ, ⲉϥϣⲟⲟⲡ ⲛ̄ϭⲓ ⲡ- [26] ⲙⲁⲉⲓⲧ ⲛ̄ⲙⲧⲁⲛ ⲛ̄ϣⲁ ⲉ{ⲓ̓}ⲛ̀ⲏ́ⲉϩⲉ
ⲁⲃⲁⲗ [27] ϩⲓ̈ⲧⲛ ⲡⲓⲑⲃⲃⲓⲟ ⲁⲩⲟⲩϫⲉⲉⲓⲧⲉ ⲛ̄- [28] ⲛⲉⲉⲓ ⲉⲧⲉⲛⲁ⟦ϩ⟧ⲙⲟⲩϩⲙⲉ ⲛ̄ⲇⲉ [29] ⲛⲓⲟⲩⲛⲉⲙ.
ⲙⲛ̄ⲛ̄ⲥⲁ ⲧⲣⲟⲩϩⲟⲙⲟⲗⲟⲅⲓ [30] ⲙ̄ⲡϫⲁⲉⲓⲥ ⲁⲩⲱ ⲡⲓⲙⲉⲉⲩⲉ ⲙ̄ⲡⲉ- [31] ⲧⲁⲛⲓⲧ ⲁⲧⲉⲕⲕⲗⲏⲥⲓⲁ ⲁⲩⲱ
ⲡⲓϩⲱⲥ ⲛ̄- [32] ⲛⲉⲧϩⲃⲃⲓⲏⲩ ⲛ̄ⲙⲙⲉⲥ ⲁⲡⲉⲧⲉ ⲟⲩⲛ̄ ϭⲟⲙ [33] ⲙ̄ⲙⲟⲟⲩ ⲧⲏⲣ⟦ⲟⲩ⟧ϥ, ⲙ̄ⲡⲉⲧⲁⲛⲓⲧ ⲁⲉⲉϥ
[34] ⲛⲉⲥ, ⲁⲧⲣⲟⲩⲕⲟⲓⲛⲱⲛⲓ ⲁⲛⲉϣⲱⲛⲉ [35] ⲙⲛ̄ ⲛⲉⲥⲙ̄ⲕⲟⲟϩ ⲁⲃⲁⲗ ϩⲓ̈ⲧⲛ̄ ⲡⲥⲙⲁⲧ ⲛ̄- [36]
ⲛⲉⲩⲅⲛⲱⲙⲱⲛ ⲁⲡⲓⲡⲉⲧⲛⲁⲛⲟⲩϥ [37] ⲁⲧ̄ⲉⲕⲕⲗⲏ[ⲥ]ⲓⲁ, ⲉⲩⲛⲁϫⲓ ⲛ̄ⲧ̄ⲕⲟⲓⲛⲱ- [38] ⲛⲓⲁ ϩⲛ̄ [ⲧⲉⲥϩ]
ⲉ̄ⲗⲡⲓⲥ. ⲡⲉⲉⲓ ⲛ̄ⲇⲉ ⲁϫⲟⲟⲥ [122.1] ϩⲁ ⲡⲣⲁ ⲛ̄ⲛⲣⲱⲙⲉ ⲙⲛ̄ ⲛ̄ⲁⲅⲅⲉⲗⲟⲥ [2] ⲙ̄ⲡⲣⲏⲧⲉ ⲉⲧⲉⲣⲉⲡⲓⲙⲁⲉⲓⲧ
ϣⲟⲟⲡ [3] ⲛ̄ⲛⲁⲉⲓ ⲉⲧⲉ ϩⲛ̄ⲛⲁⲃⲁⲗ ⲛⲉ ϩⲛ̄ ⲡⲓ- [4] ⲇⲁⲅⲙⲁ ⲛ̄ⲇⲉ ⲛⲓϭⲃⲟⲩⲣ ⲁⲡⲥⲱⲣⲙⲉ· [5] ⲟⲩ ⲙⲟⲛⲟⲛ
ϫⲉ ⲁⲩϭⲱⲗⲉ ⲙ̄ⲡⲭⲟⲓ̈ⲥ [6] ⲁⲃⲟⲗ ⲁⲩⲱ ⲁⲩⲣ̄ ϣⲁⲭⲛⲉ ⲉⲩϩⲁⲩ ⲁⲣⲁϥ, [7] ⲁⲗⲗⲁ ⲧⲕⲉⲉⲕⲕⲗⲏⲥⲓⲁ
ϩⲱⲱⲥ ⲁⲛ [8] ⲉϣϣⲟⲟⲡ ⲛ̄ϭⲓ ⲡⲟⲩⲙⲁⲥⲧⲉ ϣⲁⲣⲁⲥ [9] ⲙⲛ̄ ⲡⲟⲩⲕⲱϣ ⲙⲛ̄ ⲡⲟⲩⲫⲑⲟⲛⲟⲥ, [10]
ⲁⲩⲱ ⲧⲉⲉⲓ ⲧⲉ ⲧⲗⲁⲉⲓϭⲉ ⲛ̄ⲡⲧⲁϫⲱ [11] ⲛ̄ⲛⲉⲉⲓ ⲉⲧⲁϩⲕⲓⲙ ⲉⲁⲩϥⲓⲧⲟⲩ ⲁϩⲣⲏⲓ̈ [12] ⲁⲛⲉⲡⲓⲣⲁ
ⲛ̄ⲧⲉⲕⲕⲗⲏⲥⲓⲁ.

ϫⲉ ⲧ̄ⲙⲛ̄ⲧ- [13] ⲥⲱⲧⲡ̄ ⲛ̄ⲇⲉ ⲟⲩϣⲃⲏⲣ ⲛ̄ⲥⲱⲙⲁ ⲇⲉ [14] ⲁⲩⲱ ⲟⲩϣⲃⲏⲣ ⲛ̄ⲛⲟⲩⲥⲓⲁ ⲧⲉ ⲙⲛ̄ [15]
ⲡⲥⲱⲧⲏⲣ ⲉⲥⲟⲉⲓ ⲙ̄ⲡⲣⲏⲧⲉ ⲛ̄ⲛⲟⲩⲙⲁ [16] ⲛ̄ϣⲉⲗⲉⲉⲧ ⲉⲧⲃⲉ ⲧⲉⲥⲙⲛ̄ⲧⲟⲩⲉⲓ ⲛ̄- [17] ⲟⲩⲱⲧ ⲙⲛ̄
ⲡⲉⲥⲧⲱⲧ ϣⲁⲣⲁϥ. ϩⲁⲑⲏ ⲅⲁⲣ [18] ⲙ̄ⲙⲁⲉⲓⲧ ⲛⲓⲙ ⲉⲣⲉⲁϥⲉⲓ ⲉⲧⲃⲏⲏⲧⲥ̄ [19] ⲛ̄ϭⲓ ⲡⲉⲭⲣⲏⲥⲧⲟⲥ.
ⲧ̄ⲙⲛ̄<ⲧ>ϣⲃⲙⲉ ⲛ̄ⲇⲉ [20] ⲛ̄ⲧⲁϥ ⲉⲩⲛⲧⲉⲥ ⲙ̄ⲙⲉⲩ ⲛ̄ⲧⲭⲱⲣⲁ [21] ⲛ̄ⲛⲉⲧⲟⲩⲛⲁϫ ⲙ̄ⲡⲙⲁ ⲛ̄ϣⲉⲗⲉ- [22]
ⲉⲧ ⲁⲩ ⲉⲧⲣⲁⲟⲩⲧ ⲉⲧⲣⲁϣⲉ ⲁ- [23] ϩⲣⲏⲓ̈ ⲁϫⲛ̄ ⲡⲙⲟⲩϫϭ̄ ⲙ̄ⲡⲁ ⲧ̄ϣⲉⲗⲉⲉⲧ [24] ⲙⲛ̄ ⲧ̄ϣⲉⲗⲉⲉⲧ.
ⲧ̄ⲙⲛ̄<ⲧ>ϣⲃⲙⲉ ϭⲉ [25] ⲡⲉⲥⲧⲟⲡⲟⲥ ⲉⲧⲛⲁϣⲱⲡⲉ ⲛⲉⲥ, ⲡⲉ ⲡⲁⲓⲱⲛ [26] ⲛ̄ⲇⲉ ⲛⲓϩⲓ̈ⲕⲱⲛ, ⲙ̄ⲡⲙⲁ
ⲉⲧⲉⲙ̄ⲡⲁⲧⲉ [27] ⲡⲗⲟⲅⲟⲥ ⲧⲱⲧ ⲙ̄ⲡⲡⲗⲏⲣⲱⲙⲁ. ⲁⲩⲱ [28] ⲡⲁⲉⲓ ⲉϥⲣⲉϣⲉ ⲁⲩⲱ ⲉϥⲣⲁ- [29] ⲟⲩⲧ
ⲙ̄ⲙⲟϥ, ⲉϥⲣ̄ ϩⲉⲗⲡⲓⲍⲉ ⲙ̄ⲙⲁϥ [30] ⲁⲣⲁϥ, ⲛ̄ϭⲓ ⲡⲣⲱⲙⲉ ⲛ̄ⲧⲉⲕⲕⲗⲏⲥⲓⲁ, [31] ⲁϥⲡⲱϣⲉ ⲙ̄ⲡⲛⲉⲩⲙⲁ
ⲯⲩⲭⲏ ⲥⲱⲙⲁ ϩⲛ̄ [32] ⲧⲟⲓⲕⲟⲛⲟⲙⲓⲁ ⲙ̄ⲡⲁⲉⲓ ⲉⲧⲙⲉⲩⲉ ϫⲉ [33] ⲛⲉⲟⲩⲉⲉⲓ ⲛ̄ⲟⲩⲱⲧ ⲡⲉ, ⲉϥϣⲟⲟⲡ
ⲛ̄ϩⲏⲧϥ̄ [34] ⲡⲉ ⲛ̄ϭⲓ ⲡⲣⲱⲙⲉ ⲡⲉⲉⲓ ⲉⲧⲉ ⲛ̄ⲧⲁϥ ⲡⲉ [35] ⲡⲧⲏⲣϥ̄, ⲁⲩⲱ ⲛ̄ⲧⲁϥ ⲛ̄ⲧⲁⲩ ⲧⲏⲣⲟⲩ ⲡⲉ. [36]
ⲁⲩⲱ ⲡⲁⲉⲓ ⲉⲩⲛ̄ⲧⲉϥ ⲙ̄ⲙⲉⲩ ⲙ̄- [37] ⲡⲓⲣⲉⲧⲉ ⲁⲃⲁⲗ ϩⲓ̈ⲧⲛ̄ ⲡⲓ_[.]_ⲉ ⲉⲧⲁⲣⲉⲛ- [123.1] ⲧⲟⲡⲟⲥ ⲛⲁϣⲁⲡϥ̄,
ⲁⲩⲱ ⲟⲩⲛ̄ⲧⲉϥ [2] ⲙ̄ⲙⲉⲩ ⲛ̄ⲛⲓⲙⲉⲗⲟⲥ ⲉⲧⲁⲛⲣ̄ ϣⲣⲡ̄ [3] ⲛ̄ϫⲟⲟⲩ. ⲛ̄ⲧⲁⲣⲟⲩⲧⲁϣⲉ ⲁⲉⲓϣ [4] ⲙ̄ⲡⲥⲱⲧⲉ,
ⲁϥϫⲓ ⲥⲁⲩⲛⲉ ⲙⲉⲛ ⲥⲉ- [5] ⲛ̄ⲧϥ̄ ⲛ̄ϭⲓ ⲡⲣⲱⲙⲉ ⲉⲧϫⲏⲕ ⲁⲃⲁⲗ, [6] ⲁⲧⲣⲉϥⲧⲥⲟ ⲉϩⲟⲩⲛ ϩⲛ̄ ⲟⲩⲥⲉⲡⲏ
ⲁⲧⲉϥ- [7] ⲙ̄ⲛ̄ⲧⲟⲩⲉⲉⲓ ⲛ̄ⲟⲩⲱⲧ, ⲁⲡⲙⲁ ⲉⲧⲉ [8] ⲟⲩⲁⲃⲁⲗ ⲛ̄ϩⲏⲧϥ̄ ⲡⲉ, ⲁⲧⲣⲉϥⲧⲥⲟ [9] ⲁⲙⲉⲩ ⲁⲛ ϩⲛⲛ
ⲟⲩⲣⲉϣⲉ, ⲁⲡⲙⲁ ⲉ- [10] ⲧⲉ ⲟⲩⲁⲃⲁⲗ ⲛ̄ϩⲏⲧϥ̄ ⲡⲉ, ⲁⲡⲙⲁ ⲉⲧⲉ- [11] ⲁϥϩⲉⲧⲉ ⲁⲃⲁⲗ ⲙ̄ⲙⲟϥ. ⲛⲉϥⲙⲉ-
[12] ⲗⲟⲥ ⲇⲉ ⲁⲩⲣ̄ ⲭⲣⲓⲁ ⲛ̄ⲛⲟⲩⲙⲁ ⲛ̄ϫⲓ ⲥⲃⲱ, [13] ⲡⲉⲉⲓ ⲉⲧϣⲟⲟⲡ ϩⲣⲏⲓ̈ ϩⲛ̄ ⲛ̄ⲧⲟⲡⲟⲥ ⲉⲧⲧⲥ[ⲉ]- [14]

121.14–15 ⲁⲩϭⲱ ⲙ̄ⲙⲉⲩ: read ⲁⲩⲭⲱ ⲙ̄ⲙⲁⲥ?

121.21 ⲛ̄ⲇⲉ: read ⲛ̄ⲧⲉ.

121.28 ⲙⲟⲩϩⲙⲉ: read ⲛⲟⲩϩⲙⲉ.

121.28 ⲛ̄ⲇⲉ: read ⲛ̄ⲧⲉ.

122.12 ⲡⲓⲣⲓⲁ: read ⲡⲉⲓⲣⲁ.

122.13 ⲇⲉ: read ⲧⲉ.

122.26 ⲛ̄ⲇⲉ: read ⲛ̄ⲧⲉ.

appropriate, [13] which the powers of the [14] left did to him leading to his death. They <said>, [15] "We will become [16] rulers of the entirety, if [17] the one who has been proclaimed [18] the king of the entirety is able to be killed." (They said this) when they labored to do [19] these things, they being the humans and angels, [20] who are not from the good disposition [21] of those on the right, but [22] from the mixture. And [23] they first chose for themselves honor, though it was a wish [25] and desire (only) for a time, while the [26] path of eternal rest is [27] through humility for salvation of [28] those of [29] the right ones who will be saved. After they confess [30] the Lord and the thought of what is [31] pleasing to the church and the hymn of [32] those who are humble along with it (the church) to the [33] highest degree, in what is pleasing to do [34] for it, in participating in its struggles [35] and its afflictions in the manner of [36] their understanding of what is good [37] for the church, they will participate [38] in [the] hope. Now this is to be said [122.1] concerning how humans and angels [2] who are [3] from the [4] order of the left have a path to error: [5] not only did they reject the Lord [6] and conspire to do evil to him, [7] but toward the church also [8] (they directed) their hatred [9] and their envy and their jealousy, [10] and this is the cause for the condemnation [11] of those who have moved, having stirred themselves [12] for the trials of the church.

Now the [13] election is a partner in the body [14] and being with [15] the Savior, since it is like a bridal chamber [16] on account of its unity [17] and its agreement with him. For, before [18] each space, [19] the Christ came on account of it (the election). Now as for the calling, [20] it has the place [21] of those who rejoice at the bridal chamber [22] and who are glad and rejoice [23] at the joining of the bridegroom [24] and the bride. The calling's [25] place, which will come to be for it, is the eternity [26] of the images, where [27] the Word has not yet joined with the fullness. And [28] when the human of the church was joyful and [29] glad at this, since he was hoping [30] for it, [31] he divided spirit, soul, and body in [32] the ordering of the one who thinks that [33] he is a unity, even though the human dwelling within him [34] is the one who is the [35] entirety, and he is all of them. [36] And this one has [37] the departure from the . . . that the [123.1] places will receive, and he has [2] the parts that we [3] spoke about earlier. When [4] the redemption was proclaimed, the perfect human received knowledge [5] immediately, [6] in order to return quickly to his [7] unity, to the place [8] whence he came, in order to return [9] there joyously, to the place [10] whence he came, to the place [11] whence he departed. But his [12] members needed a place of instruction, [13] which is the places

ⲛⲁⲉⲓⲧ, ⲁⲧⲣⲉϥϫⲓ ⲉⲓⲛⲉ ⲁⲃⲁⲗ ϩⲓⲧⲟⲟ- ¹⁵ ⲧⲟⲩ ⲁⲛⲛⲓϩⲓⲕⲱⲛ ⲁⲛⲓⲧⲩⲡⲟⲥ ⲛ̄ϣⲁⲣⲡ̄, ¹⁶ ⲙ̄ⲡⲥⲙⲁⲧ ⲛⲛⲟⲩⲉⲉⲓⲉⲗ, ϣⲁⲛⲧⲉ ¹⁷ ⲙ̄ⲙⲉⲗⲟⲥ ⲙ̄ⲡⲥⲱⲙⲁ ⲧⲏⲣⲟⲩ ⲛ̄- ¹⁸ ⲧⲉⲕⲕⲗⲏⲥⲓⲁ ⲛ̄ⲛⲟⲩⲙⲁ ⲛ̄ⲟⲩⲱⲧ ¹⁹ ⲛ̄ⲥⲉϫⲓ ⲛ̄ⲧⲁⲡⲟⲕⲁⲧⲁⲥⲧⲁⲥⲓⲥ ϩⲓ ⲟⲩ- ²⁰ ⲥⲟⲡ, ⲉⲁⲩⲟⲩⲁⲛϩⲟⲩ ⲁⲃⲁⲗ ⲙ̄ⲡⲓⲥⲱ- ²¹ ⲙⲁ ⲉⲧⲟⲩⲁϫ, ⲛ̄{ϭⲓ}ϯⲁⲡⲟⲕⲁⲧⲁ- ²² ⲥⲧⲁⲥⲓⲥ ⲁϩⲟⲩⲛ ⲁⲡⲓⲡⲗⲏⲣⲱⲙⲁ. ²³ ⲟⲩⲛ̄ⲧⲉϥ ⲙ̄ⲙⲉ{ϥⲟ}ⲩ ⲛⲟⲩϯ ⲙⲉⲧⲉ ²⁴ ⲛ̄ϣⲁⲣⲡ̄, ⲛ̄ⲛⲟⲩⲱⲧ ϣⲁ ⲛⲟⲩⲉⲣⲏⲩ, ²⁵ ⲉⲧⲉ ⲡⲓⲙⲉⲧⲉ ⲡⲉ ⲉⲧϣⲟⲟⲡ ⲙ̄ⲡⲓⲱⲧ ²⁶ ϣⲁⲛⲧⲉⲛ̄ⲡⲓⲡⲧⲏⲣⲡ̄ϥ ϫⲓ ⲙⲟⲩⲛ̄ⲅ ⲛ̄ϩⲟ ²⁷ ⲁϩⲟⲩⲛ ⲁⲣⲁϥ. ϯⲁⲡⲟⲕⲁⲧⲁⲥⲧⲁⲥⲓⲥ ⲇⲉ ²⁸ ⲛ̄ϩⲁⲉ, ⲙⲛ̄ⲛⲥⲁ ⲧⲣⲉⲡⲧⲏⲣϥ̄ ⲟⲩ- ²⁹ ⲁⲛϩϥ̄ ⲁⲃⲁⲗ ⲙ̄ⲡⲉⲧⲉ ⲛ̄ⲧⲁϥ ⲡⲉ, ⲡⲱϩ- ³⁰ ⲣⲉ ⲉⲧⲉ ⲛ̄ⲧⲁϥ ⲡⲉ ⲡⲥⲱⲧⲉ, ⲉⲧⲉ ³¹ ⲡⲉⲉⲓ ⲡⲉ ⲡⲓⲙⲁⲉⲓⲧ ⲁϩⲟⲩⲛ ⲁⲡⲓⲁⲧ- ³² ϣⲁⲡϥ̄ ⲛ̄ⲉⲓⲱⲧ, ⲉⲧⲉ ⲡⲉⲉⲓ ⲡⲉ ⲡⲓⲥⲧⲟ ³³ ⲁϩⲟⲩⲛ ⲁⲡⲉⲧⲣ̄ ϣⲣⲡ̄ ⲛ̄ϣⲟⲟⲡ. ⲛ̄ⲥⲉ- ³⁴ ⲟⲩⲁⲛϩⲟⲩ ⲁⲃⲁⲗ ⲛ̄ϭⲓ ⲛⲓⲡⲧⲏⲣϥ̄ ⲛ̄- ³⁵ ⲡⲁⲉⲓ ϩⲛ̄ ⲟⲩⲙⲛ̄ⲧϫⲁⲉⲓⲥ ⲉⲧⲉ ³⁶ ⲡⲉⲉⲓ ⲡ[ⲉ ⲡ]ⲁⲧ]ⲣ̄ ⲛⲟⲉⲓ ⲙ̄ⲙⲁϥ ⲁⲩⲱ ⲡⲓ- ³⁷ ⲁⲧϫⲟⲟϥ ¹²⁴·¹ ⲁⲩⲱ ⲡⲓⲁⲧⲛⲉⲩ ⲁⲣⲁϥ ⲁⲩⲱ ⲡⲓ- ² ⲁⲧⲁⲙⲁϩⲧⲉ ⲙ̄ⲙⲁϥ, ϩⲱⲥⲇⲉ ⲛ̄ϥ- ³ ϫⲓ ⲙ̄ⲡⲓⲥⲱⲧⲉ. ⲉⲩⲣ̄ ⲃⲟⲗ ⲟⲩⲁⲉⲉ- ⁴ ⲧϥ̄ ⲉⲛ ⲡⲉ ⲁⲧⲙⲛ̄ⲧϫⲁⲉⲓⲥ ⲛ̄ϭⲓ ⲛⲓ- ⁵ ϭⲃⲟⲩⲣ, ⲟⲩⲇⲉ ⲁⲛ ⲟⲩϯ ϩⲱ ⲟⲩⲁ- ⁶ ⲉⲉⲧϥ̄ ⲉⲛ ⲡⲉ ⲛ̄ⲧⲟⲟⲧϥ̄ ⲛ̄ⲧⲉⲝⲟⲩⲥⲓⲁ ⁷ ⲛ̄ⲇⲉ ⲛⲓⲟⲩⲛⲉⲙ, ⲛⲉⲉⲓ ⲉⲧⲉⲁⲛ- ⁸ ⲙⲉⲩⲉ ⲁⲡⲟⲩⲉⲉⲓ ⲡⲟⲩⲉⲉⲓ ⲙ̄ⲙⲁⲩ ⁹ ϫⲉ ⲁⲛⲁⲛ ϩⲛ̄ϭⲁⲟⲩⲁⲛ ⲛ̄ⲧⲉϥ ⲁⲩⲱ ¹⁰ ϩⲛ̄ϣⲏⲣⲉ, ⲛ̄ⲉⲉⲓ ⲉⲧⲉⲙⲁⲣⲉϩⲗⲉ ϯ ¹¹ ⲟⲩⲱ ⲛ̄ⲧⲟⲟⲧⲟⲩ ⲛ̄ϭⲗⲟⲙ ⲉⲓⲙⲏ- ¹² ⲧⲓ ⲛ̄ϥϣⲱⲡⲉ ⲛⲉⲩ ⲛ̄ⲕⲉⲥⲟⲡ, ⲁⲗⲗⲁ ¹³ ⲟⲩⲙⲛ̄ⲧⲣ̄ ⲥⲁ ⲛϩⲣⲏⲓ ⲁⲛ ⲡⲉ ⲡⲓⲥⲱⲧⲉ ¹⁴ ⲁ{ⲩⲱ}ⲛⲓⲃⲁⲑⲙⲟⲥ ⲉⲧϣⲟⲟⲡ ϩⲛ̄ ⲡ- ¹⁵ ⲡⲗⲏⲣⲱⲙⲁ ⲁⲩⲱ {ⲙ}ⲛ̄ⲛⲉⲛⲧⲁⲩϯ ⲣⲉⲛ ¹⁶ ⲁⲣⲁⲩ ⲧⲏⲣⲟⲩ ⲁⲩⲱ ⲉⲩⲣ̄ ⲛⲟⲓ ⲙ̄ⲙⲁⲩ ¹⁷ ⲕⲁⲧⲁ ⲧϭⲟⲙ ⲙ̄ⲡⲟⲩⲉⲉⲓ ⲡⲟⲩⲉⲉⲓ ⲛ̄- ¹⁸ ⲛⲁⲓⲱⲛ, ⲁⲩⲱ ⲟⲩⲙⲛ̄ⲧⲁϣ ⲁϩⲟⲩⲛ ¹⁹ ϣⲁ ⲡⲉⲧⲕⲁⲣⲁⲉⲓⲧ ⲡⲙⲁ ⲉⲧⲉ ⲙⲛ̄ ²⁰ ⲭⲣⲓⲁ ⲛ̄ⲥⲙⲏ ⲙ̄ⲙⲉⲩ ⲟⲩⲇⲉ ⲁ- ²¹ ⲧⲣⲟⲩⲙ̄ⲙⲉ ⲟⲩⲇⲉ ⲁⲧⲣⲟⲩⲣ̄ ⲛⲟⲓ ²² ⲟⲩⲇⲉ ⲁⲧⲣⲟⲩⲣ̄ ⲟⲩⲟⲉⲓⲛ ⲁⲣⲁⲟⲩ, ²³ ⲁⲗⲗⲁ ϩⲛ̄ϩⲃⲏⲩⲉ ⲧⲏⲣⲟⲩ ⲛⲉ ⲉⲩⲟ ⲛ̄- ²⁴ ⲟⲩⲟⲉⲓⲛ ⲉⲛⲥⲉⲣ̄ ⲭⲣⲓⲁ ⲉⲛ ⲛ̄ⲧⲣⲟⲩⲣ̄ ²⁵ ⲟⲩⲟⲉⲓⲛ ⲁⲣⲁⲩ.

ϫⲉ ⲟⲩ ⲙⲟⲛⲟⲛ ⲛ̄- ²⁶ ⲣⲙ̄ⲛⲕⲁϩ ⲟⲩⲁⲉⲧⲟⲩ ⲥⲉⲣ̄ ⲭⲣⲓⲁ ⲙ̄- ²⁷ ⲡⲓⲥⲱⲧⲉ, ⲁⲗⲗⲁ ⲛ̄ⲕⲉⲁⲅⲅⲉⲗⲟⲥ ²⁸ ϩⲱⲟⲩ ⲁⲛ ⲥⲉⲣ̄ ⲭⲣⲓⲁ ⲙ̄ⲡⲓⲥⲱⲧⲉ ⲙⲛ̄ ²⁹ ϯϩⲓⲕⲱⲛ ⲁⲩⲱ ⲛⲓⲕⲉⲡⲗⲏⲣⲱⲙⲁ ⲛ̄- ³⁰ ⲇⲉ ⲛⲁⲓⲱⲛ ⲁⲩⲱ ⲛⲓϭⲟⲙ ⲙ̄ⲙⲁϩⲉⲓⲉ ⲛ̄<ⲡ>ϯ <ⲟⲩ>- ³¹ ⲁⲉⲓⲛ. ϫⲉⲕⲁⲥ ⲛ̄ⲧⲛ̄ⲧⲙ̄ⲣ ⲁⲡⲟⲣⲓ ϩⲁ ⲡⲣⲁ ³² ⲛ̄ⲕⲉⲟⲩⲉⲉⲓ, ⲁⲗⲗⲁ ⲛ̄ⲧⲁϥ ϩⲱⲱϥ ⲁⲛ ³³ ⲡϣⲏⲣⲉ, ⲡⲁⲉⲓ ⲉⲧⲕⲏ ⲛ̄ⲧ[ⲟ]ⲡⲟⲥ ⲛ̄- ³⁴ ⲥⲱⲧⲉ ⲙ̄ⲡⲧⲏⲣϥ̄, ⲁ[ϥⲣ ⲭⲣⲓ] ⲁ ⲙ̄ⲡⲥⲱⲧⲉ ¹²⁵·¹ ϩⲱⲱϥ ⲁⲛ, ⲉⲧⲉ ⲡⲣⲉϥϣⲱⲡⲉ ⲛ̄- ² ⲣⲱⲙⲉ ⲡⲉ, ⲉⲁϥⲧⲁⲁϥ ⲙ̄ⲙⲓⲛ ³ ⲙ̄ⲙⲟϥ ⲛ̄ⲟⲩⲁⲛ ⲛⲓⲙ ⲛⲉⲉⲓ ⲉⲧⲛ̄ⲣ̄ ⲭⲣⲓ- ⁴ ⲁ ⲙ̄ⲙⲟⲟⲩ, ⲁⲛⲁⲛ ϩⲛ̄ ⲥⲁⲣⲝ, ⲉⲧⲟⲉⲓ ⁵ ⲛ̄ⲛⲉⲕⲕⲗⲏⲥⲓⲁ ⲛ̄ⲧⲉϥ. ⲡⲁⲉⲓ ⁶ ϭⲉ ⲛ̄- ⁶ ⲧⲁⲣⲉϥϫⲓ ⲙ̄ⲡⲓⲥⲱⲧⲉ ⲛ̄ϣⲁⲣⲡ̄ ⲁⲃⲁ[ⲗ] ⁷ ϩⲓⲧⲛ̄ ⲡⲗⲟⲅⲟⲥ ⲉⲧⲁϩⲓ ⲁⲡⲓⲧⲛ̄ ⲁϫⲱϥ ⁸ ⲡⲕⲉϣⲱϫⲡ̄ ⲧⲏⲣϥ̄ ⲁⲩϫⲓ ⲥⲱⲧⲉ ⲁⲃⲁ[ⲗ] ⁹ ϩⲓⲧⲟⲟⲧϥ̄, ⲛⲉⲉⲓ ⲉⲛⲧⲁϩϫⲓⲧϥ̄ ⲁⲣⲁⲩ. ¹⁰ ⲛⲉⲛⲧⲁϩϫⲓ ⲛ̄ⲅⲁⲣ ⲙ̄ⲡⲉⲧⲁϩϫⲓ ⲁⲩ- ¹¹ ϫⲓ ⲁⲛ ⲙ̄ⲡⲉⲧϣⲟⲟⲡ ⲛ̄ϩⲏⲧϥ̄.

ϫⲉ ⲁⲃⲁⲗ ¹² ⲛ̄ⲛⲣⲱⲙⲉ ⲉⲧϣⲟⲟⲡ ϩⲛ̄ ⲥⲁⲣⲝ ⲛⲉⲩ- ¹³ ⲣ̄ ϩⲏⲧⲥ̄ ⲛ̄ϯ ⲙ̄ⲡⲓⲥⲱⲧⲉ, ⲡϣⲣⲡ̄ ⲙ̄ⲙⲓ[ⲥⲉ] ¹⁴ ⲛ̄ⲧⲉϥ ⲁⲩⲱ ϯⲁⲅⲁⲡⲏ ⲛ̄ⲧⲉϥ, ⲡⲓϣⲱϩ- ¹⁵ ⲣⲉ ⲉⲛⲧⲁϩϣⲱⲡⲉ ϩⲛ̄ ⲥⲁⲣⲝ, ⲉⲁⲩⲣ̄ ⲁ- ¹⁶ ϫⲓⲟⲩ ⲛ̄ϭⲓ ⲛ̄ⲁⲅⲅⲉⲗⲟⲥ ⲉⲧϣⲟⲟⲡ ϩⲛ̄ ⲧⲡ[ⲉ] ¹⁷ ⲁⲡⲓⲡⲟⲗⲓⲧⲉⲩⲉ ⲁⲧⲣⲟⲩⲣ̄ ⲡⲟⲗⲓⲧⲉⲩⲙⲁ ¹⁸ <ⲛ>ⲙ̄ⲙⲁϥ

124.2 ϩⲱⲥⲇⲉ: read ϩⲱⲥⲧⲉ.

124.4 ⲛ̄ϭⲓ: read ⲛ̄ⲧⲉ?

124.5 ϯ ϩⲱ: read ϯ ⲟⲩⲱ?

124.7 ⲛ̄ⲇⲉ: read ⲛ̄ⲧⲉ.

124.29–30 ⲛ̄ⲇⲁⲉ: read ⲛ̄ⲧⲉ.

125.12–13 ⲛⲉⲩⲣ̄: the ink trace might also suggest ⲛⲉϥⲣ̄, in which case the referent is the Father.

125.17 ⲡⲟⲗⲓⲧⲉⲩⲉ . . . ⲡⲟⲗⲓⲧⲉⲩⲙⲁ: read ⲡⲟⲗⲓⲧⲉⲩⲙⲁ . . . ⲡⲟⲗⲓⲧⲉⲩⲉ.

that are [14] adorned, so that he might receive from them a likeness [15] to the images, to the archetypes, [16] in the manner of a mirror, until [17] all the members of the body of [18] the church (are) in a single place [19] and receive the restoration at the same [20] time, having been revealed as the [21] saved body, the restoration [22] into the fullness. [23] It has an initial accord, [24] an agreement with one another, [25] which is an accord that dwells in the Father [26] until the entireties receive countenances [27] (from) within him. But the restoration is [28] at the end, after the entirety [29] reveals what it is, the Son [30] who is the redemption, that [31] is, the path toward the incomprehensible [32] Father, that is, the return [33] to what preexists. The eternities [34] reveal themselves properly in [35] that one, who [36] is the unknowable and [37] ineffable [124.1] and invisible and [2] ungraspable one, so that it [3] might receive the redemption. Not only [4] was it freedom from the rule <of> those [5] on the left, nor was it [6] only <release> from the power [7] of those on the right, those [8] to each of whom we thought [9] we were slaves and [10] children, those from whom no one [11] escapes quickly without [12] becoming theirs again, but [13] the redemption is an ascending to [14] the stages in the [15] fullness and to those who have named [16] themselves and who think of themselves [17] according to the power of each one of [18] the eternities, and (it is) an entry into [19] the silent place that has no [20] need for a voice nor for [21] knowing nor for conceiving [22] nor for illumination, [23] but (it is a place where) all things are [24] light, even though they do not need to be [25] illuminated.

Not only do [26] earthly humans need [27] redemption, but also the angels [28] need redemption along with [29] the image and the rest of the fullnesses [30] of the eternities and the marvelous powers of illumination. [31] So that we might not be perplexed concerning [32] the other ones, he too, [33] the Savior, the one who is the place of [34] redemption for the entirety, [needed] the redemption [125.1] as well, the one who became [2] human, since he gave himself [3] for everything that we needed, [4] we in the flesh, who are [5] his church. [6] After he first received redemption from [7] the Word that went down to him, [8] all the rest received redemption from him, [9] those who had received him to themselves. [10] For those who had received the one who had received [11] received what dwells in him.

Among [12] humans dwelling in the flesh [13] redemption started to be given, his first-born [14] and his love, the [15] Son who came to be in flesh, while [16] the angels above requested [17] administration so that they might administer [18] with him upon the

ⲛ̄ϩⲣⲏⲓ̈ ϩⲓϫⲙ̄ ⲡⲕⲁϩ. ⲉⲧⲃⲉ ⲡⲉ- [19] ⲉⲓ ϣⲁⲣⲟⲩⲙⲟⲩⲧⲉ ⲁⲣⲁϥ ϫⲉ « ⲡⲓⲥⲱⲧⲉ [20] ⲛ̄ⲁⲅⲅⲉⲗⲟⲥ ⲛ̄ⲧⲉ ⲡⲓⲱⲧ, » ⲡⲉⲛⲧⲁϩ- [21] ⲥⲁⲗⲥⲗ̄ ⲛ̄ⲛⲉⲉⲓ ⲉⲛⲧⲁϩϣⲱⲡ{ⲉ} ϩⲓⲥⲉ [22] ϩⲁ ⲡⲧⲏⲣϥ̄ ⲉⲧⲃⲉ ⲡⲓⲥⲁⲩⲛⲉ ⲛ̄ⲧⲉϥ, [23] ⲁⲃⲁⲗ ϫⲉ ⲁⲩϯ ⲛⲉϥ ⲙ̄ⲡⲉϩⲙⲟⲧ [24] ϩⲁⲑⲏ <ⲛ>ⲟⲩⲁⲛ ⲛⲓⲙ.

ϫⲉ ⲡⲓⲱⲧ ⲁϥⲣ̄ ϣⲁ- [25] ⲣ̄ⲡ ⲁⲡⲓⲥⲁⲩⲛⲉ ⲛ̄ⲧⲉϥ, ⲉϥϣⲟⲟⲡ [26] ϩⲙ̄ ⲡⲓⲙⲟⲕⲙⲉⲕ ⲛ̄ⲧⲉϥ ϩⲁⲑⲏ ⲉⲙ- [27] ⲡⲁⲧⲉⲗⲁⲩⲉ ϣⲱⲡⲉ ⲁⲩⲱ ⲉⲩⲛ̄ⲧⲉϥ [28] ⲙ̄ⲙⲉⲩ ⲁⲛ ⲛ̄ⲛⲉⲉⲓ ⲉⲧⲉⲁϥⲟⲩⲁⲛϩϥ̄ [29] ⲛⲉⲩ. ⲁϥⲕⲱ ⲙ̄ⲡⲱⲧⲁ ⲁϫⲛ̄ ⲡⲣⲉϥ- [30] ϭⲱ ⲛ̄ϩⲉⲛⲥⲛⲟⲩ ⲙⲛ̄ ϩⲉⲛⲟⲩⲁⲉⲓϣ [31] ⲁⲩⲉⲁⲩ ⲙ̄ⲡⲉϥⲡⲗⲏⲣⲱⲙⲁ, ⲉⲡⲓⲇⲏ [32] ⲡⲧⲣⲟⲩⲣ̄ ⲁⲧⲥⲁⲩⲛⲉ ⲙ̄ⲙⲁϥ ⲟⲩⲛ- [33] ⲧⲉϥ ⲙ̄ⲙⲉⲩ ⲛⲛⲟⲩⲗⲁⲉⲓϭⲉ ⲛ̄ϭⲓ [34] ⲡⲉϥϭⲛⲉⲓⲛⲉ ⲁⲃⲁⲗ [35] ⲙ̄ⲡⲉϥ[ϯ] ⲙⲉⲧⲉ. [13–15] [126.1] ⲛ̄ⲧⲉϥ. ⲙ̄ⲡⲣⲏⲧⲉ ⲛ̄ϯⲙⲛ̄ⲧϫⲓ ⲥⲁⲩ- [2] ⲛⲉ ⲁⲣⲁϥ ⲟⲩⲱⲛϩ ⲁⲃⲁⲗ ⲛ̄ϯⲙⲛ̄ⲧⲁ- [3] ⲫⲑⲟⲛⲟⲥ ⲛ̄ⲧⲉϥ ⲧⲉ ⲁⲩⲱ ⲡⲟⲩⲱⲛϩ [4] ⲁⲃⲁⲗ ⲙ̄ⲡⲣ̄ⲟⲩⲟ ⲛ̄ϯⲙⲛ̄ⲧϩⲗ̄ϭⲉ ⲛ̄ⲧⲉϥ [5] ⲡⲉ, ⲉⲧⲉ ⲡⲉⲉⲓ ⲡⲉ ⲡⲙⲉϩ ⲥⲛⲉⲩ ⲛ̄ⲉⲁⲩ, [6] ⲉⲧⲉ ⲡⲉⲉⲓ ⲡⲉ ⲡⲣⲏⲧⲉ ⲉⲧⲉⲁⲩϭⲓⲛⲉ [7] ⲙ̄ⲙⲁϥ ⲙ̄ⲙⲉⲛ ⲉϥⲟⲉⲓ [8] ⲛ̄ⲗⲁⲉⲓϭⲉ ⲛ̄ϯⲙⲛ̄ⲧⲁⲧⲥⲁⲩⲛⲉ, ⲉϥⲟⲉⲓ ⲇⲉ ⲁⲛ [9] ⲛ̄ⲣⲉϥϫⲡⲟ ⲙ̄ⲡⲓⲥⲁⲩⲛⲉ.

ϫⲉ ϩⲛ̄ⲛ ⲟⲩ- [10] ⲥⲟⲫⲓⲁ ⲉⲥϩⲏⲡ ⲁⲩⲱ ⲛ̄ⲁⲧⲧⲉϩⲁⲥ [11] ⲁϥϭⲁⲣⲉϩ ⲁⲡⲓⲥⲁⲩⲛⲉ ϣⲁ ϩⲁⲉ, ϣⲁⲛ- [12] ⲧⲉⲛⲓⲡⲧⲏⲣϥ̄ ϩⲓⲥⲉ ⲉⲩⲕⲱⲧⲉ ⲛ̄ⲥⲁ [13] ⲡⲛⲟⲩⲧⲉ ⲡⲓⲱⲧ, ⲉⲧⲉⲙ̄ⲡⲉⲗⲁⲩⲉ [14] ϭⲛ̄ⲧϥ̄ ⲁⲃⲁⲗ ϩⲓⲧⲛ̄ ⲧⲉϥⲥⲟⲫⲓⲁ ⲙ̄ⲙⲓⲛ [15] {ⲙ̄ⲙⲓⲛ} ⲙ̄ⲙⲟϥ ⲙⲛ̄ ⲧⲉϥϭⲟⲙ. ⲉϥϯ [16] ⲙ̄ⲙⲟϥ ⲁⲧⲣⲟⲩϫⲓ ⲥⲁⲩⲛⲉ ⲙ̄ⲡϩⲟⲩⲉ [17] ⲙⲉⲩⲉ ⲁⲡⲓⲛⲟϭ ⲛ̄ⲧⲁⲉⲓⲟ ⲛ̄ⲧⲉϥ, ⲉⲧⲉ- [18] ⲁϥϯ ⲙ̄ⲙⲟϥ, ⲁⲩⲱ ϯⲗⲁⲉⲓϭⲉ ⲉⲧⲉⲁϥ- [19] ⲧⲉⲉⲥ, ⲉⲧⲉ ϯⲉⲩⲭⲁⲣⲓⲥⲧⲉⲓⲁ ⲛ̄ⲧⲉϥ ⲧⲉ [20] ⲛ̄ⲁⲧⲱϫⲛⲉ, ⲡⲁⲉⲓ ⲉⲧⲉ ⲁⲃⲁⲗ ϩⲓⲧⲟⲟ- [21] ⲧ<ϥ̄> ⲛ̄ϯⲙⲛ̄ⲧⲁⲧⲕⲓⲙ ⲛ̄ⲇⲉ ⲡⲉϥϣⲁϫⲛⲉ, [22] ⲉϥⲟⲩⲱⲛϩ ⲙ̄ⲙⲟϥ ⲉⲃⲟⲗ ϣⲁ ⲉⲛⲏϩⲉ [23] ⲁⲛⲉⲉⲓ ⲉⲧⲁⲣ ʼⲡ´ⲙ̄ⲡϣⲁ ⲙ̄ⲡⲓⲱⲧ ⲛ̄- [24] ⲁⲧⲥⲟⲩⲱⲛϥ̄ ϩⲛ̄ ⲧⲉϥⲫⲩⲥⲓⲥ, ⲁⲧⲣⲟⲩ- [25] ϫⲓ ⲙ̄ⲡⲓⲥⲁⲩⲛⲉ ⲛ̄ⲧⲉϥ ϩⲙ̄ ⲡⲉϥⲟⲩⲱϣⲉ [26] ϫⲉ ⲡⲧⲣⲟⲩⲉⲓ ⲁⲡⲉⲓⲣⲁ ⲁⲛ ⲛ̄ϯ- [27] ⲙⲛ̄ⲧⲁⲧⲥⲁⲩⲛⲉ ⲙⲛ̄ ⲛⲉⲥⲙ̄ⲕⲟⲟϩ.

[28] ϫⲉ ⲛⲁⲉⲓ ⲉⲛⲧⲁϥⲣ̄ ϣⲁⲣⲡ̄ ⲙ̄ⲙⲉⲩⲉ [29] ⲁⲣⲁⲩ ⲁⲧⲣⲟⲩⲧⲉϩⲟ ⲙ̄ⲡⲓⲥⲁⲩⲛⲉ ⲙⲛ̄ [30] ⲛⲓⲡⲉⲧⲛⲁⲛⲟⲩⲟⲩ ⲉⲧϣⲟⲟⲡ ⲛ̄ϩⲏⲧϥ̄, [31] ⲛⲉⲩⲙⲁⲕⲙⲉⲕ—ⲉⲧⲉ ϯⲥⲟⲫⲓⲁ ⲛ̄- [32] ⲧⲉ ⲡⲓⲱⲧ—ϫⲉⲕⲁⲥⲉ ⲉⲩⲛⲁϫⲓ ϯ- [33] ⲡⲉ ⲛ̄ⲛⲓⲡⲉⲧⲉⲁⲩⲟⲩ ⲁⲩⲱ ⲛ̄ⲥⲉⲣ̄ ⲅⲩ- [34] ⲙⲛⲁⲍⲉ ⲙ̄ⲙⲁⲩ ⲛ̄ϩⲣⲏⲓ ⲛ̄ϩⲏⲧⲟⲩ, [35] ⲙ̄ⲡⲣⲏⲧⲏ ⲛⲛⲟⲩ..... ⲡⲣⲟⲥ ⲟⲩⲁⲓ̈ⲱ [36] [ϣ]ⲏⲙ ϫⲉⲕⲁⲥⲉ ⲉⲩⲛⲁ]ϫⲓ ⲛ̄ⲧⲁⲡⲟ- [37] [ⲗⲁⲩⲥⲓⲥ ⲛⲛⲓⲡⲉⲧⲛⲁⲛⲟ]ⲟⲩ ϣⲁ ⲁⲛⲏ- [38] ϩ[ⲉ ⲧⲙⲉⲧ]. [127.1] ⲉⲩⲛ̄ⲧⲉⲩ ⲙ̄ⲙⲉⲩ ⲙ̄ⲡⲓϣⲓⲃⲉ ⲙⲛ̄ [2] ⲡⲓϭⲛϭⲟⲩ ⲛ̄ⲕⲱ ⲛ̄ⲥⲱⲟⲩ ⲙⲛ̄ ⲧⲗⲁ- [3] ⲉⲓⲥⲉ ⲛ̄ⲛⲉⲧϯ ⲟⲩⲃⲏⲩ ⲁⲩⲧⲁⲓⲟ [4] ⲙⲛ̄ⲛ ⲟⲩⲑⲁⲩⲙⲁⲥⲧⲟⲛ ⲛ̄ⲛⲉⲧⲭⲁ- [5] ⲥⲉ, ⲁⲧⲣⲉϥϣⲱⲡⲉ ⲉϥⲟⲩⲁⲛϩ̄ [6] ⲁⲃⲁⲗ ϫⲉ ϯⲙⲛ̄ⲧⲁⲧⲥⲁⲩⲛⲉ ⲛ̄- [7] ⲛⲉⲧⲛⲁⲣ̄ ⲁⲧⲥⲟⲩⲱⲛ ⲡⲓⲱⲧ ⲛⲉⲩ- [8] ϣⲱⲡⲉ ⲛ̄ⲧⲉⲩ ⲡⲉ. ⲡⲁⲉⲓ [9] ⲉⲧⲁϥϯ ⲛⲉⲩ ⲙ̄ⲡⲓⲥⲁⲩⲛⲉ ⲛ̄ⲧⲉϥ ⲛⲉⲩⲟⲩϭⲟⲙ [10] ⲛ̄ⲧⲉϥ ⲡⲉ ⲁⲧⲣⲟⲩⲧⲉϩⲁⲥ ϫⲉ ⲡⲓⲥⲁⲩ- [11] ⲛⲉ ⲙⲉⲛ ϩⲛ̄ⲛ ⲟⲩⲙⲛ̄ⲧϫⲁⲉⲓⲥ ⲥⲉ- [12] ⲙⲟⲩⲧⲉ ⲁⲣⲁϥ ϫⲉ « ⲡⲓⲥⲁⲩⲛⲉ ⲛ̄ⲛⲉ- [13] ⲧⲟⲩⲛⲁⲙⲉⲉⲩⲉ ʼⲁⲣⲁⲩʼ ⲧⲏⲣⲟⲩ » ⲁⲩⲱ « ⲡⲓⲁ- [14] ϩⲟ » ⲁⲩⲱ « ⲡⲓⲟⲩ{ϩ}ⲱϩ ⲛ̄ⲧⲉ ⲁⲧⲟⲟⲧⲟⲩ [15] ⲁⲣ̄ ϩⲟⲩⲉ ⲥⲁⲩⲛⲉ ⲡⲉ » « ⲡⲟⲩⲱⲛϩ ⲁ- [16] ⲃⲁⲗ ⲛ̄ⲛⲉⲛⲧⲁⲩⲥⲟⲩⲱⲛⲟⲩ ⲛ̄ϣⲟ- [17] ⲣ̄ⲡ » ⲁⲩⲱ « ⲡⲓⲙⲁⲉⲓⲧ ⲁϩⲟⲩⲛ ⲁⲡⲓϯ [18] ⲙⲉⲧⲉ ⲁⲩⲱ ⲁϩⲟⲩⲛ ⲁⲡⲉⲧⲣ̄ ϣⲟ- [19] ⲣ̄ⲡ ⲛ̄ϣⲟⲟⲡ, » ⲉⲧⲉ ⲡⲉⲉⲓ ⲡⲉ ⲡϫⲓⲛ [20] ⲛ̄ϯⲙⲁⲉⲓⲛ ⲛ̄ⲇⲉ ⲛⲁⲉⲓ ⲉⲛⲧⲁϩⲕⲱ [21] ⲛ̄ⲥⲱⲟⲩ ⲛ̄ⲧⲟⲩⲙⲁⲉⲓⲛ ⲉⲧⲉ ⲧⲱⲟⲩ [22] ⲧⲉ ⲛ̄ϩⲣⲏⲓ ⲛ̄ⲧⲟⲓⲕⲟⲛⲟⲙⲓⲁ ⲛ̄ⲧⲉ [23] ⲡⲟⲩⲱϣⲉ ϫⲉⲕⲁⲥⲉ ⲉⲣⲉⲧϩⲁⲛ ⲛⲁ- [24] ϣⲱⲡⲉ ⲙ̄ⲡⲣⲏⲧⲉ ⲉⲧⲁⲣⲉⲧⲁⲣⲭⲏ ⲟⲓ̈ [25] ⲙ̄ⲙⲁϥ.

125.33 ⲛ̄ϭⲓ: read ⲛ̄ⲧⲉ?
126.21 ⲛ̄ⲇⲉ: read ⲛ̄ⲧⲉ.
127.14 ⲛ̄ⲧⲉ: read ⲇⲉ.
127.19–20 ϫⲓⲛ ⲛ̄ϯⲙⲁⲉⲓⲛ: read ϭⲓ ⲛ̄ϯⲙⲁⲉⲓⲛ.
127.20 ⲛ̄ⲇⲉ: read ⲛ̄ⲧⲉ.

earth. For this [19] reason he is called "the redemption [20] of the angels of the Father," the one who [21] consoled those who were suffering [22] under the entirety because of his knowledge, [23] because he was given the grace [24] before anyone else.

The Father foreknew [25] him, since he was [26] in his thought before [27] anything had come to be and since he had [28] those to whom he has revealed him. [29] He placed the deficiency upon the one who [30] remains for certain times and periods [31] as a glory for his fullness, since [32] their ignorance of him [33] is a cause <of> [34] his bringing forth of his [35] unity [. . .] his. [126.1] Just as the reception of knowledge [2] about him is a manifestation of [3] his lack of jealousy and the revelation [4] of his abounding sweetness, [5] that is, the second glory, [6] so also has [7] he been found to be the cause [8] of ignorance, even though he is [9] one who produces knowledge.

In a [10] wisdom hidden and incomprehensible [11] he kept the knowledge until the end, until [12] the entireties became weary searching for [13] God the Father, whom no one [14] found from his own [15] wisdom or power. He gives [16] himself in order that they might receive knowledge of the immense [17] thought about his great glory, which [18] he has given, and (about) the cause he has [19] given, which is his never-ending thanksgiving, [20] the one who, from [21] the immovability of his counsel, [22] reveals himself eternally [23] to those worthy of the Father [24] unknowable in his nature, so that they might [25] receive knowledge of him by his wish [26] that they come to experience [27] ignorance and its pain.

[28] Those about whom he first thought [29] that they should attain knowledge and [30] the good things that are in it [31] were contemplating—which is the wisdom of [32] the Father—so that they might [33] taste the evil things and might [34] train themselves in them, [35] just as a [. . .] for a [short] time [36] [so that they might] receive the [37] [enjoyment of the good things] [38] forever. [127.1] They have change and [2] constant renunciation and the [3] cause of those who oppose them as a distinction [4] and excellence of those who are exalted, [5] so that is comes to be apparent [6] that the ignorance of [7] those who will be ignorant of the Father [8] was their being. The one who gives them [9] knowledge of him was one of his powers [10] for (helping) them to attain the [11] knowledge properly is called [12] "knowledge of [13] all that will be thought of" and "the [14] treasury" and "the repetition [15] for increase of knowledge," "the revelation [16] of the things that were known initially," [17] and "the path toward [18] unity and the preexistent one," [19] that is, the increase [20] of those who have left [21] behind their importance that was theirs [22] in the ordering of [23] the will so that the end might [24] be like the [25] beginning.

Ϫⲉ ⲠⲒⲂⲀⲠⲦⲒⲤⲘⲀ ⲉⲦϢⲟⲟⲠ [26] ϨⲚⲚ ⲞⲨⲘⲚⲦϪⲀⲈⲒⲤ, ⲠⲈⲈⲒ ⲈⲦⲞⲨ- [27] ⲚⲀϢⲈ ⲀϨⲢⲎⲒ̈ ⲀⲢⲀϤ ⲚϬⲒ ⲚⲒⲠⲦⲎⲢϤ̄ [28] ⲚⲤⲈϢⲰⲠⲈ ⲚϨⲎⲦϤ̄, ⲘⲚ ϬⲈⲂⲀ- [29] ⲠⲦⲒⲤⲘⲀ ⲤⲀ ⲠⲈⲦⲘ̄ⲘⲈⲨ ⲞⲨⲀⲈⲈⲦϤ̄, [30] ⲈⲦⲈ ⲠⲈⲈⲒ ⲠⲈ ⲠⲤⲰⲦⲈ ⲀϨⲞⲨⲚ [31] ⲈⲠⲚⲞⲨⲦⲈ ⲠⲒⲰⲦ ⲘⲚ̄ ⲠϢⲎⲢⲈ ⲘⲚ̄ [32] ⲠⲚⲈⲨⲘⲀ ⲈⲦⲞⲨⲀⲀⲂ, ⲈⲀⲤϢⲰⲠⲈ [33] ⲚϬⲒ ϮϨⲞⲘⲞⲖⲞⲄⲒⲀ ⲀⲂⲀⲖ ϨⲒⲦⲚ̄Ⲛ ⲞⲨ- [34] ⲚⲀϨⲦⲈ ⲀϨⲞⲨⲚ ⲀⲚⲒⲢⲈⲚ ⲈⲦⲘ̄ⲘⲈⲨ, [35] ⲚⲈⲈⲒ [ⲈⲦⲈ Ⲟ] ⲨⲢⲉⲚ ⲚⲞⲨⲰⲦ ⲠⲈ Ⲛ̄- [36] ⲆⲈ ⲠⲒϢⲘ̄ ⲚⲞⲨϬⲈ, [128.1] ⲈⲀⲨⲚ̄ϨⲞⲨⲦ ⲚⲚⲈⲦⲈⲀⲨⲬⲞⲞⲨⲈ [2] ⲚⲈⲨⲞⲨ ϪⲈ ⲤⲈϢⲞⲞⲠ. ⲈⲀⲂⲀⲖ Ⲙ̄- [3] ⲠⲀⲈⲒ ⲈⲨⲚ̄ⲦⲈⲨ ⲘⲘⲈⲨ ⲘⲠⲞⲨ- [4] ϪⲀⲈⲒⲦⲈ ⲚϪⲒ ⲚⲀⲒ̈ ⲈⲦⲀ<Ϩ>ⲚⲀ- [5] ϬⲦⲈ ϪⲈ ⲤⲈϢⲞⲞⲠ. ⲈⲦⲈ ⲠⲈⲈⲒ [6] ⲠⲈ ⲦⲠⲈϨⲞ ⲘⲈⲚ ϨⲚ ⲞⲨⲘⲚⲦⲀⲦ- [7] ⲚⲈⲨ ⲀⲢⲀⲤ Ⲙ̄ⲠⲒⲰⲦ ⲘⲚ ⲠϢⲎⲢⲈ [8] ⲘⲚ̄ ⲠⲚⲈⲨⲘⲀ ⲈⲦⲞⲨⲀⲀⲂ ϨⲚⲚ ⲞⲨⲚⲀϨ- [9] ⲦⲈ {ⲆⲈ} Ⲛ̄ⲀⲦⲢ̄ ϨⲎⲦ ⲤⲚⲈⲨ. ⲀⲨⲰ ⲈⲀⲨ- [10] Ⲣ̄ ⲘⲚ̄ⲦⲢⲈ ⲘⲘⲞⲞⲨ, ⲀⲨⲰ ϨⲚ ⲞⲨ- [11] ϨⲈⲖⲠⲒⲤ ⲈⲤⲦⲀⲬⲢⲀⲈⲒⲦ ⲈⲨⲀⲘⲀ- [12] ϨⲦⲈ Ⲙ̄ⲘⲀⲨ, ϪⲈⲔⲀⲤⲈ ⲈϤⲚⲀϢⲰ- [13] ⲠⲈ ⲈⲠϪⲰⲔ ⲚⲚⲈⲚⲦⲀⲨⲚⲀϨⲦⲈ [14] ⲀⲢⲀⲨ ⲠⲈ <ⲚϬⲒ> ⲠⲒⲦⲤⲞ ⲀϨⲞⲨⲚ ⲀⲢⲀⲨ ⲀⲨⲰ [15] ⲠⲒⲰⲦ ⲚⲘ̄ⲘⲈⲨ ⲞⲨⲀⲈⲒ ⲠⲈ, ⲠⲒⲰⲦ [16] ⲠⲚⲞⲨⲦⲈ, ⲠⲈⲈⲒ Ⲛ̄ⲦⲀⲨⲢ̄ ϨⲞⲘⲞⲖⲞⲄⲒ Ⲙ̄ⲘⲀϤ [17] ϨⲚⲚ ⲞⲨⲚⲀϨⲦⲈ ⲀⲨⲰ ⲠⲈⲈⲒ ⲈⲚⲦⲀϨ- [18] ϯ Ⲛ̄ⲚⲞⲨⲘⲞⲨϬϬ ⲚⲘ̄ⲘⲈϤ ϨⲚⲚ ⲞⲨ- [19] ⲤⲀⲨⲚⲈ.

Ϫⲉ ⲠⲒⲂⲀⲠⲦⲒⲤⲘⲀ Ⲛ̄ⲦⲀⲚ- [20] ϢⲢ̄Ⲡ̄ Ⲛ̄ϪⲞⲞϤ ⲤⲈⲘⲞⲨⲦⲈ ⲀⲢⲀϤ [21] ϪⲈ « ϨⲂⲤⲞⲨ Ⲛ̄ⲚⲈⲈⲒ ⲈⲦⲈⲘⲀⲨⲔⲀ- [22] ⲔⲞⲨ ⲀϨⲎⲨ Ⲙ̄ⲘⲞϤ, » ϪⲈ ⲚⲈⲈⲒ ⲈⲦ- [23] ⲚⲀⲦⲈⲈⲒϤ ϨⲒⲰⲞⲨ ⲀⲨⲰ ⲚⲈⲈⲒ ⲈⲚⲦⲀϨ- [24] ϪⲒ ⲤⲰⲦⲈ ⲈⲨⲢ̄ ⲪⲞⲢⲒ Ⲙ̄ⲘⲞϤ. ⲀⲨⲰ ⲤⲈ- [25] ⲘⲞⲨⲦⲈ ⲀⲢⲀϤ ϪⲈ « ⲠⲦⲀⲬⲢⲞ Ⲛ̄ϯ- [26] ⲦⲘⲎⲈ ⲠⲈⲈⲒ ⲈⲦⲈⲘ̄ⲚⲦϤ̄ ϨⲈⲈⲒⲈ [27] Ⲙ̄ⲘⲈⲨ. » ϨⲚ ⲞⲨⲘⲚ̄ⲦⲀ<Ⲧ>ⲢⲒⲔⲈ ⲘⲚ ⲞⲨ- [28] ⲘⲚ̄ⲦⲀⲦⲔⲒⲘ ⲈϤⲈⲘⲀϨⲦⲈ [29] Ⲙ̄ⲘⲀⲨ ⲈⲨⲀⲘⲀϨⲦⲈ Ⲙ̄ⲘⲀϤ ⲚϬⲒ ⲚⲈⲈⲒ Ⲛ̄- [30] ⲦⲀⲢⲬⲒ Ⲛ̄ⲀⲠⲞⲤⲦⲀⲤⲒⲞⲤ. ⲤⲈⲘⲞⲨ- [31] ⲦⲈ ⲀⲢⲀϤ ϪⲈ « ⲘⲚ̄ⲦⲔⲀⲢⲰⲤ » ⲈⲦⲂⲈ [32] ⲠⲤϬⲢⲀϨⲦ ⲘⲚ ⲦⲘⲚ̄ⲦⲀⲦϢⲦⲞⲢⲦⲢ̄. [33] ⲤⲈⲘⲞⲨⲦⲈ ⲀⲢⲀϤ ⲀⲚ ϪⲈ « ⲘⲀ Ⲛ̄ϢⲈⲖⲈ- [34] ⲈⲦ » ⲈⲦⲂⲈ ⲠⲒⲘⲈⲦⲈ ⲘⲚ ϮⲘⲚ̄Ⲧ- [35] ⲀⲦⲠⲰϢⲈ ⲈⲦⲈ ⲚⲀⲈ[Ⲓ Ⲛ̄]Ⲉϯ[Ⲟ] ⲨⲤⲀⲨⲚⲈ [36] ϪⲈ ⲀⲨⲤⲞⲨⲰⲚϤ̄. ⲀⲨⲰ Ⲥ[ⲈⲘⲞⲨ]ⲦⲈ ⲀⲢⲀϤ [129.1] ⲀⲚ ϪⲈ « ⲠⲞⲨⲀⲈⲒⲚ Ⲛ̄ⲀⲦϨⲰⲦⲠ̄ [2] ⲀⲨⲰ Ⲛ̄ⲀⲦⲔⲰϨⲦ, » ⲈϤ‘ ⲞⲨⲀⲈⲒⲚ ⲈⲚ, [3] ⲀⲖⲖⲀ ⲚⲈⲦⲀϨⲢ̄ ⲪⲞⲢⲒ Ⲙ̄ⲘⲀϤ ⲈⲨ- [4] ⲈⲒⲢⲈ Ⲙ̄ⲘⲀⲨ Ⲛ̄ⲞⲨⲀⲈⲒⲚ. ⲈⲦⲈ [5] ⲚⲀⲈⲒ ⲀⲚ ⲚⲈ ⲈⲚⲦⲀϤⲢ̄ ⲪⲞⲢⲒ ⲘⲘ[Ⲁ]Ⲩ. [6] ⲀⲨⲰ ⲤⲈⲘⲞⲨⲦⲈ ⲀⲢⲀϤ ⲀⲚ ϪⲈ « ⲠⲒ- [7] ⲰⲚϨ ϢⲀ ⲈⲚⲎϨⲈ, » ⲈⲦⲈ ⲠⲈⲈⲒ ⲠⲈ ⲠⲒ- [8] ⲀⲦⲘⲞⲨ. ⲀⲨⲰ ⲤⲈⲘⲞⲨⲦⲈ ⲀⲢⲀϤ « Ⲙ̄- [9] ⲠⲈⲦϢⲞⲞⲠ Ⲙ̄ⲘⲀϤ ⲦⲎⲢϤ̄ ϨⲀⲠⲖⲰⲤ [10] ϨⲚⲚ ⲞⲨⲘⲚ̄ⲦϪⲀⲈⲒⲤ Ⲙ̄ⲠⲈⲦⲀⲚⲒⲦ [11] ϨⲚⲚ ⲞⲨⲘⲚ̄ⲦⲀⲦⲠⲰϢⲈ ⲘⲚ [12] ⲞⲨⲘⲚ̄[Ⲧ]- ⲀⲦϤⲒ ⲘⲚ ⲞⲨⲘⲚ̄ⲦⲀⲦϢⲦⲀ ⲘⲚ ⲞⲨ- [13] ⲘⲚ̄ⲦⲀⲦⲢⲒⲔⲈ, ϢⲀ ⲠⲀⲈⲒ ⲈⲦϢⲞⲞⲠ [14] Ⲛ̄ⲚⲈⲦⲀⲢⲬⲒ ϨⲚ. » ⲈⲨ Ⲛ̄ⲄⲀⲢ ⲠⲈ ⲠⲔⲈ- [15] ⲞⲨⲈⲒ ⲀⲘⲞⲨⲦⲈ ⲀⲢⲀϤ Ⲙ̄ⲘⲀϤ [16] Ⲛ̄ⲤⲀ « `Ⲡ`ⲘⲞⲨⲦⲈ » ⲈϤⲞⲈⲒ Ⲛ̄ⲚⲒⲠⲦⲎⲢϤ̄, [17] ⲈⲦⲈ ⲠⲈⲈⲒ ⲠⲈ, ⲔⲀⲚ ⲈⲨϢⲀⲚⲘⲞⲨⲦⲈ [18] ⲀⲢⲀϤ Ⲛ̄ⲚⲒⲢⲈⲚ {ⲚⲚⲒⲢⲈⲚ} Ⲛ̄ⲀⲦⲀⲠⲞⲨ, [19] ⲈⲢⲈⲀⲨⲬⲞⲞⲨ ⲀⲨϬⲚϢⲈϪⲈ Ⲙ̄ⲘⲀϤ. [20] Ⲙ̄ⲠⲒⲢⲎⲦⲈ ⲈϤⲚ̄ⲠⲤⲀ Ⲛ̄ϨⲢⲎⲒ Ⲛ̄ϢⲈϪⲈ [21] ⲚⲒⲘ ⲀⲨⲰ ϤⲚ̄ⲠⲤⲀ Ⲛ̄ϨⲢⲎⲒ Ⲛ̄ϨⲢⲀⲨ ⲚⲒⲘ [22] ⲀⲨⲰ ϤⲚ̄ϮⲀ Ⲛ̄ϨⲢⲎⲒ Ⲛ̄ⲚⲞⲨⲤ ⲚⲒⲘ [23] ⲀⲨⲰ ϤⲚ̄ⲠⲤⲀ Ⲛ̄ⲦⲠⲈ [24] Ⲛ̄ⲞⲨⲀⲚ ⲚⲒⲘ ⲀⲨⲰ ϤⲚ̄ⲠⲤⲀ Ⲛ̄ϨⲢⲎⲒ Ⲙ̄ⲘⲚ̄ⲦⲔⲀⲢⲰⲤ [25] ⲚⲒⲘ, ⲠⲀⲈⲒ ⲠⲈ ⲠⲢⲎⲦⲈ ⲈⲦϢⲞⲞⲠ [26] {ⲀⲨⲰ ⲠⲈⲈⲒ ⲠⲈ ⲠⲈ ⲠⲢⲎⲦⲈ ⲈⲦϢⲞⲞⲠ} [27] Ⲙ̄ⲘⲀⲤ ϨⲀⲦⲈ ⲚⲈⲦϢⲞⲞⲠ Ⲛ̄ⲠⲈ- [28] ⲦⲈ Ⲛ̄ⲦⲀϤ ⲠⲈ. ⲠⲀⲈⲒ ⲠⲈ

---

127. 35–36 Ⲛ̄Ⲇⲉ: read Ⲛ̄Ⲧⲉ.

128.4 Ⲛ̄ϪⲒ: read Ⲛ̄ϬⲒ.

128.6 ⲦⲠⲈϨⲞ: read ⲠⲦⲈϨⲞ.

128.14 ⲠⲒⲦⲤⲞ: read ⲠⲒⲤⲦⲞ.

128.30 ⲀⲠⲞⲤⲦⲀⲤⲒⲞⲤ: read ⲀⲠⲞⲔⲀⲦⲀⲤⲦⲀⲤⲒⲤ.

129.22 ϤⲚ̄ϮⲀ: read ϤⲚ̄ϮⲀ.

The baptism that exists [26] properly, to which the entireties [27] will descend [28] and within which they will be, there is no other [29] baptism outside of this one alone, [30] which is the redemption into [31] God the Father and the Son and [32] the Holy Spirit, [33] when the confession occurs out of [34] faith in those names, [35] [which] are a single name [36] of the gospel, [128.1] when they believe what has been said [2] to them, namely, that they exist. On account of [3] this those who believed [4] that they exist have their [5] salvation. This [6] is the attainment in an [7] invisible manner of the Father and the Son [8] and the Holy Spirit in a [9] faith without doubt. And when they [10] testified about them, also with a [11] secure hope they grasped [12] them, so that the return to them might become [13] the perfection of those who had faith [14] in them and (so that) [15] the Father might united with them, the Father [16] God, who was confessed [17] in faith and who [18] gave (them) their union with him in [19] knowledge.

The baptism that we [20] previously discussed is called [21] "garment of those who do not [22] strip themselves of it," because those who [23] will clothe themselves in it and those who have [24] received redemption wear it. It is also [25] called "the strength of the [26] truth that does not have destruction." [27] Without wavering and [28] movement it grasps [29] those who [30] have received the <restoration> even as they grasp him. It is called [31] "silence" on account of [32] the tranquility and imperturbability. [33] It is also called "bridal chamber" [34] on account of the agreement and the [35] lack of division of those who know that [36] they have known him. It is also [called] [129.1] "the light that never sets [2] and has no flame," since it does not illuminate, [3] but those who have worn it [4] are made into light. [5] They are those whom he wore. [6] Additionally it (baptism) is called "the [7] life eternal," that is, [8] immortality. It is also called [9] "that which exists completely, plainly, [10] properly, in what is beautiful, [11] indivisibly, [12] steadfastly, flawlessly, [13] unwaveringly, to the one who exists [14] for those who have received a beginning." For what else [15] is there to call it [16] except "the call," since it is for the entireties, [17] that is, even if it is called [18] countless names, [19] they are spoken with reference to it. [20] Just as it surpasses every word [21] and every sound [22] and every mind [23] and everything [24] and every silence, [25] so too [26] (*scribal error*) [27] is it with those who are what [28] it is. This is their discovery [29] of what

ⲡⲉⲧⲟⲩϭⲓⲛⲉ ²⁹ ⲙ̄ⲙⲁϥ ⲙ̄ⲡⲉⲧⲉ ⲛ̄ⲧⲁϥ ⲡⲉ, ϩⲛ̄ ⲟⲩ- ³⁰ ⲙⲛ̄ⲧⲁⲧϫⲟⲟϥ ⲙⲛ̄ ⲟⲩⲙⲛ̄ⲧ- ³¹ ⲁⲧⲣ̄ ⲛⲟⲓ̈
ⲛ̄ϩⲱ, ⲁⲡϣⲱⲡⲉ ϩⲛ̄ ⲛⲉⲧ- ³² ⲥⲁⲩⲛⲉ, ⲁⲃⲁⲗ ϩⲓⲧⲛ̄ ⲡⲉⲧⲁⲩⲧⲉϩ[ⲟ] ³³ ⲙ̄ⲙⲁϥ, ⲉⲧⲉ ⲡⲉⲉⲓ ⲡⲉ
ⲉⲛⲧⲁⲩ- ³⁴ ϯ ⲉⲁ̣[ⲩ ⲛ]ⲉϥ.

ϩⲁ ⲡⲣⲁ ⲛ̄ϯⲙⲛ̄ⲧⲥⲱⲧⲡ̄ ¹³⁰·¹ ⲕⲁⲛ ⲉⲩⲛ̄ ϩⲟⲩⲉ ϩⲁϩ ⲛ̄ⲕⲱⲃ ⲁ- ² ⲧⲣⲛ̄ϫⲟⲟⲥ, ⲛ̄ⲑⲉ ⲉⲧⲉϣϣⲉ ⲁ- ³
ϫⲟⲟⲥ, ⲛⲁⲉⲓ ⲛ̄ⲇⲉ ϩⲱⲟⲩ ϩⲁ ⁴ ⲡⲣⲁ ⲛ̄ⲛⲁ ⲡⲓⲧⲱϩⲙⲉ—ⲡⲉⲉⲓ ⲅⲁⲣ ⁵ ⲡⲉ ⲡⲣⲏⲧⲉ ⲉⲧⲟⲩⲙⲟⲩⲧⲉ
ⲁⲛⲓ- ⁶ ⲟⲩⲛⲉⲙ ⲙ̄ⲙⲁϥ—ⲟⲩⲁⲛⲁⲅⲕⲁⲓⲟⲛ ⁷ ϭⲉ ⲡⲉ ⲁⲧⲣⲛ̄ⲟⲩ{ϩ}ⲱϩ ⲁⲧⲟⲟⲧⲛⲉ ⁸ ⲁϣⲉ<ϫⲉ
ϩ>ⲁⲣⲁⲩⲟⲩ ⲁⲩⲱ ϥⲣ̄ ϣⲉⲩ ⲉⲛ ⁹ ⲁⲧⲙ̄ⲧⲛ̄ⲣ̄ ⲡⲟⲩⲙⲉⲩⲉ. ⲁⲛϣⲉϫⲉ ¹⁰ ϩⲁⲣⲁⲩ—ⲉϣⲡⲉ ⲟⲩⲛ̄ ϩⲱ
ⲛ̄ϩⲣⲏⲓ̈ ¹¹ ϩⲛ̄ ⲛⲉⲧϩⲏ ϩⲛ̄ⲛ ⲟⲩϣ̣ⲓ. ⲡⲱⲥ ⲁⲛ- ¹² ϫⲟⲟⲥ; ⲁⲃⲁⲗ ϩⲛ̄ⲛ ⲟⲩⲙⲉⲣⲟⲥ, ¹³ ⲉⲡⲓⲇⲏ
ⲁⲉⲓϫⲟⲟⲥ ϫⲉ ⲛⲉⲧⲁϩⲉⲓ ¹⁴ ⲧⲏⲣⲟⲩ ⲁⲃⲁⲗ ϩⲓⲧⲛ̄ ⲡⲗⲟⲅⲟⲥ, ⲉⲓ- ¹⁵ ⲇⲉ ⲁⲃⲁⲗ ϩⲛ̄ ⲡⲓⲧⲁϫⲱ ⲛ̄ⲇⲉ ¹⁶
ⲛⲉⲧϩⲁⲟⲩ ⲉⲓⲇⲉ ⲁⲃⲁⲗ ϩⲛ̄ ¹⁷ ϯⲃⲁ̄ⲕⲉ ⲉⲧϯ ⲟⲩⲃⲏⲟⲩ ⲙⲛ̄ ⲡⲓ- ¹⁸ ⲛⲟⲩϩⲟⲩ ⲁⲃⲁⲗ ⲙ̄ⲙⲁⲩ, ⲉⲧⲉ ⲡⲓ- ¹⁹
ⲛⲟⲩϩⲟⲩ ⲛ̄ⲇⲉ ⲛ̄ⲧⲁϥ ⲡⲉ ⲁϩⲟⲩⲛ ²⁰ ⲛ̄ⲛⲉⲧϫⲁⲥⲉ ⲁⲩⲱ ⲡⲓⲥⲁⲡⲥ̄ ⲙⲛ̄ ²¹ ⲡⲓⲣ̄ ⲡⲙⲉⲩⲉ ⲛ̄ⲛⲉⲧⲣ̄ ϣⲣⲡ
ⲛ̄- ²² ϣⲟⲟⲡ ⲙⲛ̄ⲛ ⲟⲩϩⲉⲗⲡⲓⲥ ⲙⲛ̄ⲛ ⲟⲩ- ²³ ⲛⲁϩⲧⲉ ⲁⲧⲣⲉϥ[ϫ]ⲓ ⲙ̄ⲡⲟⲩϩⲁⲉⲓ- ²⁴ ⲧⲉ ⲛ̄ⲇⲉ ⲡϩⲱⲃ
ⲉⲧⲛⲁⲛⲟⲩϥ, ²⁵ ⲉⲁⲩⲣ̄ ⲁϫⲓⲟⲩ ⲙ̄ⲙⲟⲟⲩ ⲁⲃⲁⲗ ϫⲉ ²⁶ ϩⲛ̄ϣ̄ϣⲱⲡⲉ ⲛⲉ ⲁⲃⲁⲗ ϩⲛ̄ ⲛⲓⲇⲓⲁ- ²⁷ ⲑⲉⲥⲓⲥ
ⲉⲧⲛⲁⲛⲟⲩⲟⲩ, ⲉⲩⲛ̄ⲧⲉⲩ ²⁸ ⲙ̄ⲙⲉⲩ ⲛ̄ⲧⲗⲁⲉⲓϭⲉ ⲙ̄ⲡⲟⲩϫⲡⲟ, ²⁹ ⲉⲩⲟⲩⲅⲛⲱⲙⲏ ⲇⲉ ⲁⲃⲁⲗ ϩⲙ̄ ⲡⲉⲧ-
³⁰ ϣⲟⲟⲡ. ⲉⲧⲓ ⲁⲛ ϫⲉ ⲛⲉⲙⲡⲁⲧⲉⲡⲗⲟ- ³¹ ⲅⲟⲥ ϫⲓ ⲙ̄ⲙⲁϥ ⲙ̄ⲙⲓⲛ ⲙ̄ⲙⲁϥ ⲛⲙ̄- ³² ⲙⲉⲩ ϩⲛⲛ
ⲟⲩⲙⲛ̄ⲧⲁⲧⲛⲉⲩ ⲁⲣⲁⲥ ³³ ⲉϥⲟⲩⲱϣ, ⲡⲉⲧϫⲁⲥⲉ ⲁϥⲟⲩⲱϩ ³⁴ ⲁⲧⲟⲟⲧϥ ⲁⲛ ⲙ̄ⲡ`ⲉ´ⲓ̈ⲙⲉⲩⲉ ⲁⲃⲁⲗ
ϫⲉ ³⁵ ⲛⲉⲁⲩϣⲱⲡⲉ ⲉⲩⲣ̄ [ϩⲁ]ⲉ ⲛⲉϥ, ¹³¹·¹ ⲡⲉⲉⲓ ⲛ̄ⲧⲁϩϣⲱⲡⲉ ⲛ̄ⲗⲁⲉⲓϭⲉ ⲙ̄- ² ⲡⲧⲣⲟⲩϣⲱⲡⲉ.
ⲉⲙⲡⲟⲩϥⲓⲧⲟⲩ ³ ⲁϩⲣⲏⲓ̈ ⲉϥⲟⲩⲁϫ, ϩⲱⲥ ⲉⲙⲛ̄ ⲗⲁⲩⲉ ⁴ ϣⲟⲟⲡ ϩⲁ ⲧⲟⲩϩⲏ. ⲁⲗⲗⲁ ⲥⲉϩⲟ- ⁵
ⲙⲟⲗⲟⲅⲓ ϫⲉ ⲟⲩⲛ̄ⲧⲉⲩ ⲁⲣⲭⲏ ⁶ ⲙ̄ⲙⲉⲩ ⲙ̄ⲡⲧⲟⲩϣⲱⲡⲉ, ⲁⲩⲱ ⲥⲉ- ⁷ ⲟⲩⲱϣ <ⲙ̄>ⲡⲉⲉⲓ·
ⲁⲧⲣⲟⲩⲥⲟⲩⲱⲛϥ̄ ⁸ ⲉⲧⲉ ⲡⲉⲧϣⲟⲟⲡ ϩⲁ ⲧⲟⲩϩⲏ ⲡⲉ. ⁹ ⲛ̄ϩⲟⲩⲟ ϭⲉ ⲛ̄ϩⲟⲩⲟ ϫⲉ ⲁⲩⲟⲩⲱϣ̄ⲧ ¹⁰
ⲙ̄ⲡⲟⲩⲱⲛϩ̄ ⲁⲃⲁⲗ ⲙ̄ⲡⲟⲁⲉⲓⲛ ¹¹ ⲙ̄ⲡⲣⲏⲧⲉ ⲛ̄ⲛⲟⲩⲃⲃⲣⲏϭⲉ, ⲁⲩⲱ ¹² ⲁⲩⲣ̄ ⲙⲛ̄ⲧⲣⲉ ϫⲉ ⲛ̄ⲧⲁϥⲟⲩⲱⲛϩ̄
¹³ [ⲁⲃ]ⲁⲗ ⲁⲩⲟⲩϫⲁⲉⲓ ⲛ̄ⲧⲉ{ⲛⲉⲟ}ⲩ.

¹⁴ [ϫ]ⲉ ⲟⲩ ⲙⲟⲛⲟⲛ ⲛⲉⲧⲁϩⲉⲓ̄ ⲁⲃⲁⲗ ¹⁵ ⲙ̄ⲡⲗⲟⲅⲟⲥ, ⲛⲉⲧⲁⲛϫⲟⲩ ⲙ̄- ¹⁶ ⲙⲟⲥ ⲁ[ⲣⲁ]ⲩⲟⲩ ⲟⲩⲁⲉⲧⲟⲩ
ⲛⲉ ϫⲉ ¹⁷ ⲥⲉⲛⲁⲧⲉϩⲉ ⲡϩⲱⲃ ⲉⲧⲛⲁⲛⲟⲩϥ, ¹⁸ ⲁⲗⲗⲁ ⲛⲉⲧⲁⲛⲁⲉⲓ ϩⲱⲟⲩ ⲁⲛ ϫⲡⲁⲩ ¹⁹ ⲕⲁⲧⲁ
ⲛⲓⲇⲓⲁⲑⲉⲥⲓⲥ ⲁⲛ ⲉⲧⲛⲁ- ²⁰ ⲛⲟⲩⲟⲩ ⲥⲉⲛⲁⲣ̄ ⲕⲟⲓⲛⲱⲛⲓ ϩⲱⲟⲩ ²¹ ⲁⲛ ⲁⲡⲓⲙ̄ⲧⲟⲛ ⲕⲁⲧⲁ ⲧⲙⲛ̄ⲧϩⲟⲩⲟ
²² ⲙ̄ⲡⲉϩⲙⲟⲧ. ⲁⲩⲱ ⲛⲉⲉⲓ ⲉⲛⲧⲁⲩ- ²³ ⲛ̄ⲧⲟⲩ ⲁⲃⲁⲗ ϩⲛ̄ ⲧⲉⲉⲓⲉⲡⲓⲑⲩ- ²⁴ ⲙⲓⲁ ⲛ̄ⲧⲉ ⲧⲙⲛ̄ⲧⲙⲁⲉⲓⲟⲩⲉϩ
²⁵ ⲥⲁϩⲛⲉ, ⲉⲩⲛ̄ⲧⲉⲩ ⲙ̄ⲙⲉⲩ ⲙ̄ⲡⲓ- ²⁶ ⲥⲓⲧⲉ ⲛ̄ϩⲏⲧⲟⲩ, ⲉⲧⲉ ⲧⲉⲉⲓ ⲧⲉ ⲧⲙ̄<ⲛ̄>ⲧ- ²⁷ ⲙⲁⲉⲓⲟⲩⲉϩ
ⲥⲁϩⲛⲉ, ⲥⲉⲛⲁϫⲓ ²⁸ ⲛ̄ⲧⲱⲃⲃⲓⲱ ⲛ̄ⲛⲓⲡⲉⲧⲛⲁⲛⲟⲩⲟⲩ, ²⁹ ⲛ̄ϭⲓ ⲛⲁⲉⲓ ⲉⲛⲧⲁⲣ̄ ϩⲱⲃ ⲙⲛ̄ ⲛⲁⲉⲓ ³⁰
ⲉⲧⲉⲩⲛ̄ⲧⲉⲩ ⲙ̄ⲙⲉⲩ ⲛ̄ϯⲡⲣⲟⲁⲓⲣⲉ- ³¹ ⲥⲓⲥ ⲛ̄ⲛⲓⲡⲉⲧⲛⲁⲛⲟⲩⲟⲩ, ⲉⲩϣⲁⲣ̄ ϩ- ³² ⲛⲉⲩ ϩⲛⲛ ⲟⲩⲅⲛⲱⲙⲏ
ⲛ̄ⲥⲉⲟⲩⲱ- ³³ ϣⲉ ⲁⲕⲱ ⲛ̄ⲥⲱⲟⲩ ⲛ̄ⲧⲙⲛ̄ⲧⲙⲁ- ³⁴ ⲉⲓⲉⲁⲩⲟ ⲉⲧϣⲟⲩⲉⲓⲧ ⲡⲣⲟⲥ ⲟⲩ- ³⁵ ⲥⲛⲟⲩ
ⲛ̄[ⲥⲉⲣ̄] ⲡⲟⲩⲁϩ ⲥⲁϩⲛⲉ ⲙ̄ⲡⲭⲟⲓⲥ ¹³²·¹ ⲙ̄ⲡⲉⲁⲩ, ⲁⲛⲧⲓ ⲡⲓⲧⲁⲉⲓⲟ ⲡⲣⲟⲥ ⲟⲩ- ² ⲁⲉⲓϣ ϣⲏⲙ, ⲛ̄ⲥⲉⲣ̄
ⲕⲗⲏⲣⲟⲛⲟⲙⲓ ³ ⲛ̄ⲧⲙⲛ̄ⲧⲣ̄ⲣⲟ ϣⲁ ⲉⲛⲉϩ.

130.1 ⲛ̄ⲕⲱⲃ: read ⲛ̄ϩⲱⲃ.
130.15 ⲛ̄ⲇⲉ: read ⲛ̄ⲧⲉ.
130.19 ⲛ̄ⲇⲉ: read ⲇⲉ.
130.23 ⲁⲧⲣⲉϥ: read ⲁⲧⲣⲉⲩ.
130.24 ⲛ̄ⲇⲉ: read ⲛ̄ⲧⲉ.
131.3 ⲉϥⲟⲩⲁϫ: read ⲉⲩⲟⲩⲁϫ.

it is, [30] ineffably and inconceivably [31] in (its) face, for the coming into being in those [32] who know, through what they have attained, [33] that is the one [34] to whom they give glory.

Concerning the election, [130.1] even if there are many more things [2] for us to say, as it is fitting to [3] say, concerning [4] those of the calling—for this [5] is the way those [6] on the right are called—it is necessary [7] for us to continue [8] to <speak> about them and it is helpful for us not [9] to forget about them. We have spoken [10] about them— if there is enough in [11] what (came) before in abundance. How have we [12] spoken? Partially, [13] since I said that all those who have come [14] forth from the Word, either [15] from the condemnation of [16] the evil ones or from [17] the anger that fights against them and the [18] turning from them, which is the [19] turning toward [20] the exalted ones and the petition and [21] the remembrance of those who preexist [22] and hope and [23] faith that <they> might [receive] their salvation [24] from good work, [25] since they have been made worthy because [26] they are beings from the [27] good disposition, having [28] the cause of their begetting, [29] an opinion from the one who [30] exists. Still more (I said) that before the Word had [31] concerned himself with [32] them invisibly [33] by willing, the exalted one added [34] to his thought because [35] they came to be in need of him, [131.1] the one who had become a cause of [2] their coming into being. They did not elevate themselves [3] when <they> were saved, as though nothing [4] preexisted them. Rather, they [5] confess that they have a beginning [6] to their being, and they [7] want this: to know him [8] who preexists them. [9] More than anything, (I said) that they worshipped [10] the revelation of the light [11] that was in the form of lightning, and [12] they testified that it had appeared [13] as <their> salvation.

[14] Not only those who have come forth from [15] the Word, those about whom we said [16] only that [17] they would accomplish the good work, [18] but also those whom these produced [19] in accordance with the good dispositions [20] will participate [21] in the rest in accordance with the abundance [22] of grace. And those who were brought forth [23] from the desire [24] of the love of [25] power, since they have the [26] seed within them, that is the [27] love of power, will receive [28] a reward for (their) good deeds, [29] namely, those who worked and those [30] who are predisposed [31] to good things, should they be willing [32] in opinion and desire [33] to renounce the [34] vain, temporary era [35] [and keep] the commandment of the Lord [132.1] of glory, rather than fleeting glory, [2] and inherit [3] the eternal kingdom.

ⲦⲈⲚⲞⲨ ⲆⲈ [4] ⲞⲨⲀⲚⲀⲄⲔⲀⲒⲞⲚ ⲠⲈ ⲀⲦⲢⲚ̅[ⲅ̅]ⲰⲦⲢⲈ [5] Ⲛ̅ⲚⲖⲀⲈⲒⳠⲈ ⲘⲚ̅ ⲚⲈⲚⲈⲢⲄⲒⲀ Ⲛ̅ⲆⲈ [6] ⲠⲒⳠⲘⲞⲦ ⲰⲀⲢⲀⲨ ⲘⲚ̅ ⲚⲒⲀⲪⲞⲢⲘⲎ, [7] ⲈⲠⲈⲦⲈⲰⲰⲈ ⲠⲈ ⲀⲦⲢⲚ̅ⲬⲞⲨ Ⲙ̅ⲠⲈⲚ- [8] ⲦⲀⲚⲢ̅ ⲰⲢⲠ̅ Ⲛ̅ⲬⲞⲞϤ Ⲛ̅ⲆⲈ ⲠⲒⲞⲨⲬⲀ- [9] ⲈⲒⲦⲈ Ⲛ̅ⲆⲈ ⲚⲒⲞⲨⲚⲈⲘ ⲦⲎⲢⲞⲨ [10] Ⲛ̅ⲆⲈ ⲚⲒⲀⲦ<Ⲧ>ⲀⳠⲦⲈ̅ ⲘⲚ̅ ⲚⲈⲦ<Ⲧ>ⲀⳠⲦⲀⳠⲦ [11] ⲦⲎⲢⲞⲨ, ⲀⳠⲰⲦⲢⲈ Ⲙ̅ⲘⲀⲨ [ⲘⲚ̅] [12] ⲚⲞⲨⲈⲢⲎⲨ. ⲀⲨⲰ ⲠⲒⲘ̅ⲦⲞⲚ [ⲈⲦⲈ] [13] ⲠⲈⲈⲒ ⲠⲈ ⲠⲞⲨⲰⲚ̅Ⳡ ⲀⲂⲀⲖ Ⲙ̅[ⲠⲒ]- [14] ⲤⲘⲀⲦ ⲈⲚⲦⲀⲨⲚ[Ⲁ]ⳠⲦⲈ <Ⲛ̅Ⳡ̅ⲎⲦϤ̅>, ⲠⲈⲈⲒ [15] ⲀⲦⲢⲚ̅ⲦⲈⳠⲀϤ ⲀⲢⲈⲦϤ̅ ⳠⲚ̅Ⲛ ⲞⲨ- [16] ⲰⲈϪⲈ ⲈⲠⲈⲦⲈⲰⲰⲈ ⲠⲈ. ⲈⲚⲰⲀ- [17] Ⲣ̅ ⳠⲞⲘⲞⲖⲞⲄⲒ ⲄⲀⲢ Ⲛ̅Ⲧ̅Ⲙ̅Ⲛ̅Ⲧ̅ⲢⲢⲞ [18] ⲈⲦⳠ̅Ⲛ̅ ⲠⲈⲬⲢⲒⲤⲦⲞⲤ, ⲀⲨⲢ̅ ⲂⲞⲖ ⲈⲂⲞⲖ Ⲛ̅ⲦⲞ- [19] ⲞⲦϤ̅ Ⲙ̅ⲠⲒⳠⲀⳠ Ⲛ̅ⲢⲎⲦⲈ ⲦⲎⲢϤ̅ ⲀⲨⲰ Ⲧ- [20] Ⲙ̅Ⲛ̅ⲦⲀⲦⲰⲰⲰ ⲘⲚ̅ ⲠⲰⲒⲂⲈ. Ⲧ̅ⳠⲀⲚ [21] ⲄⲀⲢ ⲚⲀϪⲒ ⲠⲰⲰⲠⲈ ⲀⲚ Ⲛ̅ⲞⲨⲈⲈⲒ Ⲛ̅- [22] ⲞⲨⲰⲦ Ⲛ̅ⲐⲈ ⲀⲚ ⲈⲦⲈ ⲞⲨⲈⲈⲒ Ⲛ̅- [23] ⲞⲨⲰⲦ ⲦⲈ ⲦⲀⲢⲬⲎ, ⲠⲘⲀ ⲈⲦⲈ ⲘⲚ̅ [24] ⳠⲞⲞⲨⲦ ⲘⲚ̅ ⲤⳠⲒ̈ⲘⲈ ⲞⲨⲆⲈ ⳠⲘⳠⲈⲖ [25] Ⳡ̅Ⲓ ⲈⲖⲈⲨⲐⲈⲢⲞⲤ ⲞⲨⲆⲈ ⲘⲚ̅ ⲤⲂ̅ⲂⲈ [26] Ⳡ̅Ⲓ Ⲙ̅Ⲛ̅ⲦⲀⲦⲤⲂ̅ⲂⲈ ⲞⲨⲆ[Ⲉ] ⲘⲚ̅ ⲀⲄⲄⲈ- [27] ⲖⲞⲤ ⲞⲨⲆⲈ ⲘⲚ̅ ⲢⲰⲘⲈ, ⲀⲖⲖⲀ ⲠⲦⲎⲢϤ̅ [28] Ⳡ̅Ⲛ̅ ⲠⲦⲎⲢϤ̅ ⲠⲈⲬⲢⲒⲤⲦⲞⲤ. ⲈⲰ ⲠⲈ ⲠⲢⲎⲦⲎ [29] Ⲙ̅ⲠⲈⲦⲈⲚⲈϤⲰⲞⲞⲠ ⲈⲚ Ⲛ̅ⲰⲀⲢⲠ̅; [30] ⲈⲨⲚⲀⳠⲚ̅ⲦϤ̅ ⲈϤⲚⲀⲰⲰⲠⲈ. Ⳡ̅Ⲓ [31] ⲈⲰ ⲠⲈ ⲦⲪⲨⲤⲒⲤ Ⲙ̅ⲠⲈⲦⲈ ⲞⲨⳠⲘ̅- [32] ⳠⲈⲖ {ⲈⲚ} ⲠⲈ; ⲈϤⲚⲀϪⲒ ⲘⲀ ⲘⲚ̅ ⲞⲨ- [133.1] ⲈⲖⲈⲨⲐⲈⲢⲞⲤ. ⲤⲈⲚⲀϪⲒ ⲠⲚⲈⲨ Ⲛ̅- [2] ⲄⲀⲢ Ⲛ̅ⳠⲞⲨⲞ Ⲛ̅ⳠⲞⲨⲞ ⳠⲚ̅Ⲛ ⲞⲨⲪⲨⲤⲒⲤ [3] ⳠⲚ̅Ⲛ ⲞⲨⲰⲈϪⲈ ⲰⲎⲘ ⲞⲨⲀⲈⲈⲦϤ̅ [4] ⲈⲚ, ⲀⲦⲢⲞⲨⲚⲀⳠⲦⲈ, ⲞⲨⲀⲈⲈⲦϤ̅ Ⳡ̅Ⲓ- [5] ⲦⲚ ⲞⲨⲤⲘⲎ, ϪⲈ ⲠⲈⲈⲒ ⲠⲈ ⲠⲢⲎⲦⲈ [6] ⲈⲦⲰⲞⲞⲠ, ϪⲈ ⲞⲨⲈⲒⲈ Ⲛ̅ⲞⲨⲰⲦ ⲆⲈ [7] Ⲧ̅ⲀⲠⲞⲔⲀⲦⲀⲤⲦⲀⲤⲒⲤ ⲀⳠⲞⲨⲚ ⲀⲠⲈ- [8] ⲦⲈⲚⲈϤⲰⲞⲞⲠ. ⲔⲀⲚ ⲈⲨⲚ̅ ⳠⲀⲈⲒⲚⲈ [9] ϪⲀⲤⲈ ⲈⲦⲂⲈ ⲦⲞⲒⲔⲞⲚⲞⲘⲒⲀ, ⲈⲀⲨⲔⲀⲨ- [10] Ⲉ Ⲛ̅ⲖⲀⲈⲒⳠⲈ Ⲛ̅ⲚⲈⲦⲀⳠⲰⲰⲠⲈ, [11] ⲈⲨⲢ̅ ⳠⲞⲨⲈ ⲈⲚⲈⲢⲄⲒⲀ ⲈⳠⲚ̅ⲪⲨⲤⲒⲔⲎ ⲚⲈ, [12] [Ⲁ]ⲨⲰ ⲈⲨⲢ̅ ⳠⲚⲈⲨ ⲈⲦⲂⲈ ⲚⲈⲦⲘ̅ⲘⲈⲨ, [13] [ⲤⲈⲚ]ⲀϪⲒ Ⲛ̅Ⲧ̅Ⲙ̅Ⲛ̅Ⲧ̅ⲢⲢⲞ ⲘⲚ̅ ⲠⲒⲦⲀⲬⲢⲞ [14] [ⲘⲚ̅] ⲠⲒⲞⲨⲬⲀⲈⲒⲦⲈ Ⲛ̅ϬⲒ ⲀⲄⲄⲈⲖⲞⲤ [15] [Ⳡ̅Ⲓ Ⲕ]ⲈⲢⲰⲘⲈ. ⲚⲀⲈⲒ ϬⲈ ⲚⲈ ⲚⲖⲀⲈⲒⳠⲈ.

[16] ϪⲈ ⲚⲈⲦⲀⳠⲞⲨⲰⲚ̅Ⳡ Ⳡ̅Ⲛ̅ ⲤⲀⲢⳠ ⲀⲨⲚⲀⳠ- [17] ⲦⲈ ⲀⲢⲀϤ Ⳡ̅Ⲛ̅ ⲞⲨⲘ̅Ⲛ̅ⲦⲀⲦⲢ̅ ⳠⲎⲦ [18] ⲤⲚⲈⲨ ϪⲈ ⲠⲰⲎⲢⲈ ⲠⲈ Ⲙ̅ⲠⲒⲀⲦⲤⲞⲨ- [19] ⲰⲚ[Ϥ] Ⲡ[Ⲉ] Ⲛ̅ⲚⲞⲨⲦⲈ ⲠⲈ, ⲠⲈⲈⲒ ⲈⲦⲈ- [20] Ⲙ̅ⲠⲞⲨϢⲈϪⲈ ⲀⲢⲀϤ Ⲛ̅ⲰⲞⲢⲠ̅ [21] ⲀⲨⲰ ⲘⲠⲞⲨϢ ⲚⲈⲨ ⲀⲢⲀϤ. ⲀⲨⲰ [22] ⲀⲨⲔⲰ Ⲛ̅ⲤⲰⲞⲨ Ⲛ̅ⲚⲞⲨⲚⲞⲨⲦⲈ [23] ⲈⲚⲦⲀⲨⲰ̅Ⲙ̅ⲰⲈ Ⲙ̅ⲘⲞⲞⲨ Ⲛ̅ⲰⲞⲢⲠ̅ [24] ⲀⲨⲰ Ⲛ̅ⲬⲞⲈⲒⲤ, ⲚⲈⲈⲒ ⲈⲦⲰⲞⲞⲠ [25] Ⳡ̅Ⲛ̅ ⲦⲠⲈ ⲀⲨⲰ ⲚⲈⲦⲰⲞⲞⲠ Ⳡ̅ⲒϪⲘ̅ [26] ⲠⲔⲀⳠ. ⲚⲈⲈⲒ ⲘⲈⲚ ⳠⲀⲐⲎ [27] Ⲙ̅ⲠⲀ- ⲦⲞⲨϤⲒⲦⲞⲨ ⲀⳠⲢⲎⲒ̈, Ⲁ[Ⲗ]ⲖⲀ ⲈⲦⲒ ⲈϤⲞ- [28] ⲈⲒ Ⲛ̅ⲖⲒⲖ[Ⲟ]Ⲩ, ⲀⲨⲢ̅ ⲘⲚⲦⲢⲈ ϪⲈ ⲎⲆⲎ [29] ⲀϤⲢ̅ ⲀⲢⲬⲈⲤⲐⲀⲒ Ⲛ̅ⲦⲀⲰⲈ ⲀⲈⲒⲀⲰ), [30] ⲀⲨⲰ ⲠⲤⲀⲠ ⲈϤⲔⲎ ⲀⳠⲢⲎⲒ̈ Ⳡ̅Ⲛ̅ ⲠⲦⲀⲪⲞⲤ [31] Ⲉ[ϤⲞⲒ Ⲛ̅]ⲢⲰⲘⲈ ⲈϤⲘⲞⲞⲨⲦ, Ⲛ̅Ⲁ- [32] [ⲄⲄⲈ]ⲖⲞⲤ ⲆⲈ ⲚⲈⲨⲘⲈⲨⲈ ϪⲈ ϤⲀⲚⳠ, [33] [Ⲛ̅ⲤⲈⲬⲒ Ⲛ̅]ⲦⲞⲞⲦϤ̅ Ⲙ̅ⲠⲰⲚ̅Ⳡ [134.1] Ⲛ̅ⲦⲞⲞⲦϤ̅ Ⲙ̅ⲠⲈⲦⲀⳠⲘⲞⲨ. ⲚⲞⲨⲰⲘ̅- [2] ⲰⲈ ⲆⲈ ⲚⲀⲞⲨⲀⲰⲞⲨ Ⲛ̅ⲰⲞⲢⲠ̅ [3] ⲈⲦⲚⲀⲰⲰⲞⲨ ⲘⲚ̅ ⲚⲞⲨⲘⲀⳠⲈⲒⲈ, ⲚⲀ- [4] ⲈⲒ ⲈⲦⲈⲚⲈϤⲰⲞⲞⲠ Ⳡ̅Ⲛ̅ ⲠⲈⲢⲠⲈ Ⳡ̅Ⲁ [5] ⲚⲀⲈⲒ, {Ⲧ}ⲈⲈⲦⲞⲨ Ⲛ̅ⲞⲨⲀⲈⲒ <Ⲁ>Ⲧ̅ⳠⲞⲘ[Ⲟ]ⲖⲞ- [6] ⲄⲒⲀ. ⲈⲦⲈ ⲦⲈⲈⲒ ⲦⲈ ⲞⲨⲚ ϬⲀⲘ Ⲙ̅ⲘⲀⳠ [7] Ⳡ̅Ⲁ ⲚⲈⲈⲒ ⲈⲈⲒⲢⲈ Ⲙ̅ⲘⲀⲤ ⲀⲂⲀⲖ Ⳡ̅Ⲓ- [8] ⲦⲚ̅ ⲠⲦⲢⲞⲨⲠⲰⲦ ⲀⳠⲞⲨⲚ ⲀⲢⲀϤ.

132.5 Ⲛ̅ⲆⲈ: read Ⲛ̅ⲦⲈ.
132.8 Ⲛ̅ⲆⲈ: read Ⲛ̅ⲦⲈ.
132.9 Ⲛ̅ⲆⲈ: read Ⲛ̅ⲦⲈ.
132.10 Ⲛ̅ⲆⲈ: read Ⲛ̅ⲦⲈ.
132.18 ⲀⲨⲢ̅: read ⲀⲚⲢ̅.
133.6 ⲆⲈ: read ⲦⲈ.
133.16 ⲚⲈⲦⲀⳠⲞⲨⲰⲚ̅Ⳡ: read ⲠⲈⲦⲀⳠⲞⲨⲰⲚ̅Ⳡ?

Now [4] it is necessary for us to join [5] the causes with the effects of [6] the grace and motivations upon them, [7] since it is fitting for us to say what [8] we discussed earlier about the salvation [9] of all those of the right (and) [10] of the unmixed ones and all the mixed ones, [11] to join them [with] [12] each other. And the rest, [which] [13] is the manifestation of [the] [14] form <in> which they believed, [15] (it is necessary) that we establish it in a [16] fitting discussion. For when we [17] confessed the kingdom [18] in Christ, <we> became free from [19] all the many forms and the [20] inequality and the difference. For the end [21] will receive the singular being [22] just as the beginning [23] is singular, the place where there is no [24] male and female, nor slave [25] and free, nor circumcision [26] and uncircumcision, neither angel [27] nor human, but [28] Christ is all in all. What is the nature [29] of the one who did not exist at first? [30] It will be discovered that he will exist. And [31] what is the nature of the one who is a slave? [32] He will receive a place with a [133.1] free person. For they will receive the vision [2] more and more by nature and not only [3] by lesser word, [4] so that they believe, only through [5] voice, that this is the way [6] it is, that the restoration into [7] what once was is a [8] unity. Even if there are some who are [9] exalted because of the assembly, since they have established [10] causes of the things that have come into being, [11] since they are natures with greater energy, [12] and since they are pleasing on account of these (characteristics), [13] angels [and] humans will receive the kingdom and the strength [14] [and] the salvation. [15] These, therefore, are the causes.

[16] The <one> who appeared in the flesh they believed [17] without hesitation [18] that he is the Son of the unknown [19] God, the one [20] not previously spoken about [21] and not able to be seen. And [22] they set aside their gods [23] whom they had worshipped initially [24] and lords, those who are in [25] heaven and those upon [26] the earth. Before [27] they took them up, and even while he was [28] a child, they testified that he had already [29] begun to preach, [30] and at the time that he was in the tomb [31] as a dead man the [32] [angels] thought that he was alive, [33] [and they received] life from [134.1] he who had died. [2] They desired initially [3] that their numerous services and wonders, [4] which were in the temple for [5] them, be made continually <for> the confession. [6] That is, it is possible to do it [7] for them through [8] their advance toward him.

ϫⲉ ⁹ ⲡⲓⲥⲁⲃⲧⲉ ⲉⲧⲙ̄ⲙⲉⲩ ⲉⲧˋⲉˊⲙⲁⲩϫⲓ ¹⁰ ⲙ̄ⲙⲟϥ ⲉϩⲟⲩⲛ ⲁⲩϭⲁⲗⲉϥ ⲁⲃⲟⲗ ¹¹ ⲉⲧⲃⲉ
ⲡⲉⲧⲉⲛⲛⲉⲩⲟⲩⲱⲧ ⲙ̄ⲙⲟϥ ¹² ⲉⲛ ⲙ̄ⲡⲙⲁ ⲉⲧⲙ̄ⲙⲉⲩ, ⲁⲗⲗⲁ ⲉ̣[ⲩ†ⲙ]- ¹³ ⲡⲉⲭⲣⲓⲥⲧⲟⲥ, ⲡⲉⲉⲓ
ⲉⲧⲉⲛⲉⲩⲙⲉⲩⲉ [ⲁⲣⲁϥ] ¹⁴ ⲁⲧⲣⲉϥϣⲱⲡⲉ ⲙ̄ⲡⲙⲁ ⲉⲧ[ⲙ̄ⲙⲉⲩ], ¹⁵ ⲡⲙⲁ ⲉⲛⲧⲁⲅⲉⲓ ⲁⲃⲁⲗ ⲙ̄ⲙ[ⲁϥ]
¹⁶ ⲛ̄ⲙ̄ⲙⲉϥ, ⲁⲃⲁⲗ ⲛ̄ⲟⲩⲙⲁ ⲛ̄ⲛⲟⲩ[ⲧ]ⲉ ¹⁷ ϩⲓ̈ ϫⲁⲉⲓⲥ ⲛⲉⲉⲓ ⲉⲧⲉⲛⲉⲩⲱ̄ⲙ̄ϣⲉ ¹⁸ ⲙ̄ⲙⲁⲩ ⲉⲩⲣ̄
ⲑⲉⲣⲁⲡⲉⲩⲉ ⲙ̄- ¹⁹ ⲙⲁⲩ ⲉⲩⲣ̄ ϩⲩⲡⲏⲣⲉ† [ⲙ]ⲙⲁⲩ ²⁰ ⲛ̄ⲛⲣⲉⲛ ⲉⲛⲧⲁⲩϫⲓⲧⲟⲩ [ⲁ]ⲡⲟⲩϣⲉⲡ. ²¹
ⲁⲩⲧⲉⲉⲓⲧⲟⲩ ⲙ̄ⲡⲉⲧⲟⲩⲙⲟⲩⲧⲉ ²² ⲁⲣⲁϥ ⲙ̄ⲙⲁⲩ [ϩ]ⲛ̄ⲛ ⲟⲩⲙⲛ̄ⲧϫⲁ- ²³ ⲉⲓⲥ. ⲛⲉⲉⲓ ⲛ̄ⲇⲉ ⲙⲛⲛ̄ⲥⲁ
ⲧⲉϥ- ²⁴ ⲁⲛⲁⲗⲏⲙⲯⲉⲱⲥ ⲁⲩϫⲓ ⲡⲓⲣⲁ ²⁵ ⲁⲙⲙⲉ ϫⲉ ⲛ̄ⲧⲁϥ ⲡⲉ ⲡⲟⲩϫⲁⲓ̈ⲥ, ²⁶ ⲡⲉⲉⲓ ⲉⲧⲉ ⲙⲛ̄ ⲗⲁⲩⲉ
ⲟ̄ ˋⲛ̄ˊϫⲁⲉⲓⲥ ²⁷ ⲁⲣⲁϥ. ⲁⲩ† ⲛⲁϥ ⲛ̄ⲟⲩⲙⲛ̄ⲧⲣ̄ⲣⲁⲉⲓ, ²⁸ ⲁⲩⲧⲱ[ϣ]ⲛ̄ ⲁⲃⲁⲗ [ϩ]ⲛ̄[ⲛ] ⲟⲩⲟⲣⲟ- ²⁹
ⲛⲟⲥ, ⲁⲩϣⲉϣⲧⲟⲩ ⲁⲃ[ⲁⲗ] ⲛ̄ⲛⲟⲩ- ³⁰ ϭⲣⲏⲡⲉ. ⲡⲉⲉⲓ ⲛ̄ⲇⲉ ⲁϥⲟⲩⲁⲛϩ̄ϥ ⲛⲉⲩ, ³¹ ⲁⲛⲓⲗⲁⲉⲓϭⲉ
ⲉⲧⲁⲛⲣ̄ ϣ[ⲣ]ⲡ̄ ⲛ̄ϫⲟⲟⲩ, ³² ⲛ̄ⲛⲟⲩϫⲁⲉⲓⲧⲉ ⲙⲛ̄ ⲡⲓⲛ[ⲟⲩϩ ⲁⲩ]- ³³ ⲙⲉⲩⲉ ⲉⲧⲛⲁⲛⲟⲩϥ ϣⲁ [. . .
^{135.1} . . . .] ϣⲃⲏⲣ ⲁⲩⲱ ⲛⲓⲁⲅⲅⲉⲗⲟⲥ ² [. . .].̣ ⲁⲩⲱ ⲡⲓϩⲁϩ ⲙ̄ⲡⲉⲧⲛⲁⲛⲟⲩ- ³ [ⲟⲩ ⲉⲛ]ⲧ̣ⲁⲅⲉⲅⲉ
ⲛⲙ̄ⲙⲉⲥ. ⲧⲁⲉⲓ ⲧⲉ ⁴ [ⲑⲉ ⲉ]ⲧ̄[ⲉ]ⲁⲩⲛ̄ϩⲟⲩⲧⲟⲩ ⲁⲛⲓϣⲙ̄ϣⲉ ⁵ ⲉ̣ⲧⲉⲓⲣⲉ ⲙ̄ⲡⲉⲧⲛⲁⲛⲟⲩϥ ⲛ̄ⲛⲓⲥⲱ- ⁶
ⲧⲡ̄ ⲉⲩⲉⲓⲛⲉ ⲙ̄ⲡⲟⲩϫⲓ ⲛ̄ϭⲟⲛⲥ̄ ⲁ- ⁷ ϩⲣⲏⲓ̈ ⲉ̣[ⲧ]ⲡ̣ⲉ. ⲁⲩϫⲛ̄ⲧⲁⲩ ⲁⲛⲏϩⲉ ⁸ ⲛ̄ⲧⲙⲛ̄ⲧ[ⲁ]ⲧⲑⲃⲃⲓⲁⲩ
ⲛ̄ⲧⲙⲛ̄ⲧⲁⲧⲡⲗⲁ- ⁹ ⲛⲁ ⲙ̄ⲡ[ⲥⲱ]ⲛ̣ⲧ, ⲉⲩⲙⲏⲛ ⲁϩⲟⲩⲛ ⲉⲧⲃⲏ- ¹⁰ ⲧⲟⲩ ϣ[ⲁⲧ]ⲟⲩⲉⲓ ⲧⲏⲣⲟⲩ ⲁⲡⲃⲓⲟⲥ
ⲁⲩⲱ ¹¹ ⲛ̄ⲥⲉⲉ[ⲓ ⲁⲃ]ⲁⲗ ϩⲙ̄ ⲡⲃⲓⲟⲥ, ⲉⲣⲉⲛⲟⲩ- ¹² [ⲥ]ⲱⲙ̣[ⲁ ⲙⲏⲛ ϩ]ⲓ̈ϫⲙ̄ ⲡⲕⲁϩ, ⲉⲩⲣ̄ ϩⲩⲡⲏⲣⲉⲧⲓ ¹³
[. . . . .].[ⲧ]ⲏⲣⲟⲩ ⲛ̄ⲧⲉⲩ, ⲉⲩⲉⲓⲣⲉ ⲙ̄- ¹⁴ [ⲙⲁ]ⲩ̣ⲟ̣ⲩ ⲛ̄ⲕⲟⲓⲛⲱⲛⲟⲥ ⲁⲛⲟⲩⲙⲕⲟ- ¹⁵ [ⲟϩ] ⲙⲛ̄ [ⲛ]
ⲟⲩⲇⲓⲱⲅⲙⲟⲥ ⲙⲛ̄ ⲛⲟⲩ- ¹⁶ [ⲗⲱ]ϫ̣ϩ, ⲛ̣[ⲉ]ⲉⲓ ⲉⲛⲧⲁⲅⲉⲓⲛⲉ ⲙ̄ⲙⲁⲩ ¹⁷ [ⲁϩ]ⲣⲏⲓ̈ ⲁϫⲛ̣ ⲛⲉⲧⲟⲩⲁⲁⲃ
ϩⲁⲑⲏ ⲙ̄ⲙⲁⲓ̈ⲧ ¹⁸ [ⲛⲓ]ⲙ.

ϫⲉ ⲛ̄ⲣⲙ̄ⲛϣⲙ̄ϣⲉ ⲛ̄ⲇⲉ ⲛⲉⲧ- ¹⁹ [ϩⲁ]ⲩⲟⲩ, ϩⲱⲥ ⲉⲥⲙ̄ⲡϣⲁ ⲛ̄ϣⲁⲣⲱⲣ̄ ²⁰ [ⲛϭⲓ ⲧⲙ]-
ⲛ̄ⲧⲡⲉⲑⲁⲩⲟⲩ ⲛ̄ϩⲣⲏⲓ̈ ²¹ [ϩⲛ] ⲟⲩ[. . .]ⲓⲛⲉ. ⲁⲃⲁⲗ ϩⲓⲧⲛ̄ †ⲡⲟ- ²² [. .] ⲁ̣[.]ⲣ̣ⲙ̄ ⲉⲧⲛⲡⲥⲁ ⲛϩⲣⲏⲓ
ⲛ̄- ²³ ⲕⲟⲥⲙⲟⲥ ⲛⲓ[ⲙ], ⲉⲧⲉ ⲡⲓⲙⲉⲩⲉ ²⁴ ⲛ̄ⲧⲉⲩⲟⲩ ⲡ[ⲉ] ⲉⲧⲛⲁⲛⲟⲩϥ ⲡⲉ ²⁵ ⲙⲛ̄ †ⲙⲛ̄ⲧϣⲃⲏⲣ,
ⲉⲥⲛⲁⲣ̄ ⲡⲙⲉⲩⲉ ²⁶ ⲙ̄ⲙⲁⲩⲟⲩ ⲛ̄ϭⲓ †ⲉⲕⲕⲗⲏⲥⲓⲁ ²⁷ ⲙ̄ⲡⲣⲏⲧⲉ ⲛ̄ϩⲛ̄ϣⲃⲏⲣ ⲉⲛⲁⲛⲟⲩⲟⲩ ²⁸ ⲁⲩⲱ
ϩⲛ̄ϩⲙ̄ϩⲉⲗ ⲉⲩⲛϩⲁⲧ, ⲉⲁⲥϫⲓ ²⁹ ⲥⲱⲧⲉ ⲁ[ⲃⲁⲗ ϩ]ⲛ̣ [ⲡⲉⲧ†] ϣ̄ⲃⲃⲓⲱ. ³⁰ ⲉⲓⲉ ⲡ[ⲓⲥⲙ]ⲁⲧ ⲡⲉ
ⲉⲧϣⲟⲟⲡ ϩⲙ̄ ³¹ [ⲡⲙⲁ ⲛϣ]ⲉⲗ[ⲉ]ⲉⲧ ⲁⲩⲱ †[. . ³² . . . . ϣ]ⲟⲟⲡ ϩⲙ̄ ⲡⲉⲥⲛⲉⲓ ⲉ[. . ³³ . . . .]ⲉⲧ
ⲛ̄ϩⲣⲏⲓ ϩⲛ̄ ⲡⲓⲙⲉⲩⲅ[ⲉ] ³⁴ ⲛ̄ⲧⲉ ⲧⲙⲛ̄<ⲧ>† ⲙⲛ ⲡⲉⲧⲁⲣⲁⲥ ⲉⲓ[. .] ^{136.1} ⲡⲉⲭⲣⲏⲥⲧⲟⲥ ⲡⲉⲧⲛ̄ⲙ̄ⲙⲉⲥ
[ⲁⲩⲱ ⲡⲓ]- ² ϭⲛϭⲱϣⲧ ⲁⲃⲁⲗ ⲛ̄ⲧⲉ [ⲡ]ⲓϣ[ⲧ ⲙ]- ³ ⲡⲧⲏⲣϥ, ⲉⲥⲛⲁϫⲡⲟ ⲛⲉⲩ [ⲛϩ]ⲉ̣ⲛ[ⲁⲅ]- ⁴
ⲅⲉⲗⲟⲥ ⲛ̄ⲣⲙ̄ⲙⲉϥⲣ̄ ϩⲙ̄ⲙⲉ ⲙⲛ ⁵ ⲛⲣⲱⲙⲉ ⲉϥϣⲙ̄ϣⲉ.

ϫⲉ ⲥⲉⲛⲁ- ⁶ ⲣ̄ ⲡⲙⲉⲩⲉ ⲙ̄ⲡⲟⲩⲙⲉⲩⲉ[ⲉ] ⲉⲧⲁⲛⲓⲧ. ⁷ ⲙ̄ⲙⲛ̄ⲧⲣⲉϥϣⲙ̄ϣⲉ ⲛ[ⲉⲥ] ⲛⲉ. ⲥ̣ⲛ̣[ⲁ]- ⁸ † ⲛⲉⲩ
ⲛ̄ⲧⲟⲩϣⲃ̄ⲃⲓⲱ [ⲙ]ⲡⲉⲧⲟⲩ- ⁹ ⲛⲁⲙⲉⲩⲉ ⲉⲣⲟϥ ⲧⲏⲣϥ̄ ⲛ̄ϭⲓ ⲛⲁⲓⲱ[ⲛ]. ¹⁰ ⲟⲩⲡⲣⲟⲃⲟⲗⲏ ⲛ̄ⲧⲉⲩ ⲡ[ⲉ],
ϫⲉⲕⲁⲥ[ⲉ] ¹¹ ⲙ̄ⲡⲣⲏⲧⲉ ⲉⲧⲉⲁⲡⲉⲭ[ⲣⲓⲥⲧⲟⲥ ⲣ̄ ⲡ]ⲉϥ- ¹² ⲟⲩⲱϣⲉ, ⲉⲛⲧⲁϥⲉⲓⲛⲉ[ⲉ] ⲁⲃ[ⲁⲗ ⲛϥ]- ¹³
ϫⲓⲥⲉ ⲛ̄ⲛⲁⲉⲓⲛ ⲛ̄ⲧⲉ[ⲕ]ⲕⲗ̣[ⲏ]ⲥ̣ⲓ̣ⲁ [ⲛϥ]- ¹⁴ † ⲙ̄ⲙⲁⲩ ⲛⲉⲥ, ⲙ̄ⲡⲣⲏⲧⲉ ϩ]ⲟⲱϥ [ⲛ]- ¹⁵ ⲧⲁⲉⲓ
ⲉⲧⲛⲁϣⲱⲡⲉ ⲙ̄[ⲙ]ⲉⲩⲉ ⲛ[ⲛⲉ]- ¹⁶ ⲉⲓ. ⲁⲩⲱ ⲛ̄ⲣⲱⲙⲉ ⲉϥ† ⲛⲉⲩ ⲛ̄ⲛ[ⲟⲩ]- ¹⁷ ⲙⲁ ⲛ̄ϣ̄ϣⲱⲡⲉ ϣⲁ
ⲁⲛⲏϩⲉ, ⲛⲉ[ⲉⲓ] ¹⁸ ⲉⲧⲟⲩⲛⲁϣⲱⲡⲉ ⲛ̄ϩⲏⲧⲟⲩ, [ⲉⲩⲕⲱ]- ¹⁹ ⲉ ⲛ̄ⲥⲱⲟⲩ ⲙ̄ⲡⲥⲱⲕ ⲁ[ⲡⲓ]ⲧⲛ̄ ²⁰
ⲙ̄ⲡϣⲧⲁ, ⲉⲛⲉⲥⲥⲱⲕ ⲙ̄ⲙⲁ[ⲩ] ²¹ ⲁϩⲣⲏⲓ̈ ⲛ̄ϭⲓ ⲧϭⲟ[ⲙ] ⲛ̄ⲧⲉ ⲡⲗⲏⲣⲱⲙⲁ ²² ϩⲛ̄ ⲧⲙⲛ̄ⲧⲛⲟϭ

134.23 ⲛ̄ⲇⲉ: read ⲇⲉ.
134.30 ⲛ̄ⲇⲉ: read ⲇⲉ.
135.18 ⲛ̄ⲇⲉ: read ⲇⲉ.
136.22 ⲛ̄ⲇⲉ: read ⲛ̄ⲧⲉ.

⁹ That preparation that they did not receive ¹⁰ they returned ¹¹ because of the one who was not sent ¹² from that place, but they [gave to] ¹³ Christ, [about] whom they thought ¹⁴ that he was in [that] place, ¹⁵ the place whence they had come ¹⁶ with him, from a place of gods ¹⁷ and lords, those whom they worshipped, ¹⁸ served, ¹⁹ (and) submitted to in ²⁰ the names they had received on loan. ²¹ They were given to the one who is called ²² by them properly. ²³ Yet after his ²⁴ ascension they received the opportunity ²⁵ to know that he is their lord, ²⁶ he over whom no one is lord. ²⁷ They gave him their kingdoms, ²⁸ and they rose up from their thrones, ²⁹ and they were stopped (from wearing) their ³⁰ crowns. But he revealed himself to them, ³¹ for the reasons we discussed earlier, ³² their salvation and the [return to a] ³³ good thought until [. . . ¹³⁵·¹ . . .] friend and the angels ² [. . .] and the multitude of good ³ [that] they did with it. In this ⁴ [way] they were entrusted with the services ⁵ that benefit the elect ones ⁶ by bringing their injustice up ⁷ to heaven. They tested them eternally ⁸ for arrogance from the lack of going astray ⁹ from the [creation], continuing on account ¹⁰ of them until they all come to live and ¹¹ [leave] life, while their ¹² bodies [remain] upon the earth, serving all their ¹³ [. . .], participating ¹⁴ [with] them in their ¹⁵ troubles and persecutions and ¹⁶ oppressions, which were brought ¹⁷ upon the holy ones in ¹⁸ [every] place.

As for the servants of the ¹⁹ wicked things, since wickedness is worthy of destruction, ²⁰ [. . .] ²¹ Because of the ²² [. . .] which is above ²³ all worlds, which is ²⁴ their good thought ²⁵ and the friendship, the church will ²⁶ remember them ²⁷ as good friends ²⁸ and genuine servants, after it receives ²⁹ redemption [from the one who gives] gifts. ³⁰ Then the [form] that is in ³¹ [the] bridal chamber and the [. . . ³² . . .] dwells in its house [. . . ³³ . . .] in the thought ³⁴ of the giving and the one who [. . .] ¹³⁶·¹ Christ, the one with it, [and the] ² expectation of [the Father of] ³ the entirety, since it will produce for them ⁴ guiding angels and ⁵ human servants.

They will ⁶ think pleasing thoughts. ⁷ They are worshippers for [it.] It will ⁸ give them their gift [for] ⁹ all that the eternities will think about. ¹⁰ He is their emanation, so that ¹¹ just as [Christ accomplished] his ¹² will, which he brought [forth and] ¹³ elevated the magnitude of the church [and] gave ¹⁴ them to it, so too ¹⁵ will it be a thought for ¹⁶ them. And to humans he gives [their] ¹⁷ eternal places of being, those ¹⁸ in which they will dwell once they [leave] ¹⁹ behind the downward pull ²⁰ of deficiency and the ²¹ power of the fullness draws [them] up ²² into the greatness of

135.30 "[form]": or "[grace]."

ⲛⲇⲉ ⲛ̄ⲧⲙⲛ̄ⲧⲁ- ²³ ⲫⲑⲟⲛⲟⲥ ⲙⲛ̄ [ⲧ̄]ⲙⲛ̄ⲧⲣⲗⲟϭⲉ ⲛ̄ⲇⲉ ²⁴ ⲡⲓⲁⲓⲱⲛ ⲉⲧⲣ̄ ϣⲣ̄<ⲡ> ⲛ̄ϣⲟⲟⲡ. [ⲧⲉ]ⲉⲓ
²⁵ ⲧⲉ ⲧⲫⲩⲥⲓⲥ ⲙ̄ⲡϫⲡⲟ ⲧⲏⲣϥ̄ ⲛ̄- ²⁶ ⲛⲉⲧⲉⲩⲟⲩⲛⲧⲉ⳽ⲥⲟⲩ ⲉϥⲡⲣ̄ⲣⲉ ²⁷ ⲛⲉⲩⲟⲩ [ⲣⲛ̄] ⲟⲩⲣⲁⲉ[ⲓⲛ]
ⲉⲛⲧⲁϥ- ²⁸ ⲟⲩⲱⲛ̄[ⲣ] ⲁⲃⲁⲗ ⲛ̄ϭⲓ[. . .].... ²⁹ ⲣ̄. ⲡⲣⲏⲧⲉ ⲙ̄ⲡⲉϥ[7–9 ³⁰ ⲧ]ⲉ ⲉⲧⲛⲁϣϣⲡⲉ [7–9
³¹ ⲁ]ⲛ, ⲙ̄ⲡⲣⲏⲧⲉ ⲙ̄ⲡⲉϥϫ̄[. . . . ³² ⲉⲣ]ⲉⲡϣⲓⲃⲉ ⲟⲩⲁⲉⲉⲧϥ̄ ⲁ[ⲛ] ϣⲟ- ³³ [ⲟⲡ] ⲣⲣⲏ̈ . . [ⲣ]ⲛ̄
ⲛⲉⲛⲧⲁⲩ[ϣ]ⲃ̄ⲧⲟⲩ ⲁ[.] ¹³⁷·¹ [11–13]ⲟⲟ[. .] ² [11–13]ⲉⲉ[. .] ³ [.]ⲁ⳽[9–11]ⲉ[. .] ⁴ ⲛⲉⲧⲧ[8–10]
ⲗ ⲣⲓⲧⲟ- ⁵ ⲟⲧϥ̄ ⲛ̄ⲧ[ⲉ 6–8] ⲁⲥⲟⲩ ⁶ ⲣⲙ̄ ⲡⲥⲙⲁ[ⲧ.] [. .] [. . .] ϫⲟⲟϥ, ⁷ ⲉⲣⲉⲛⲓⲣⲩⲗⲓⲕⲟⲛ
ⲛⲁϣⲱϫⲡ̄ ϣⲁ ⁸ ⲫⲁⲉ ⲁⲩⲧⲉⲕⲟ, ⲉⲛⲥⲉⲛⲁⲧ̄ ⲁ- ⁹ [ⲃⲁ]ⲗ ⲁⲩ[ⲣ]ⲉⲛ ⲛ̄ⲧⲉⲩ, ⲉϣⲡⲉ ¹⁰ [ⲛⲉⲩⲛ]
ⲁⲧⲥⲧⲟ ⲡⲁⲗⲓⲛ ⲁⲡⲉⲧⲉⲛ- ¹¹ [ϥⲛⲁ]ϣϣ[ⲡⲉ ⲉ]ⲛ. ⲉⲛⲑⲉ ⲉⲧⲉ ⲛⲉⲩ- ¹² [7–9]ⲉ ⲛ̄ⲥⲉϣⲟⲟⲡ ⲉⲛ ¹³
[6–8] ⲁⲗⲗⲁ ⲛⲉⲁⲩⲧ̄ ⲣⲛⲟⲩ ¹⁴ [ⲣⲙ̄ ⲡⲉⲟ]ⲩⲁⲉⲓϣ ⲉⲧⲉⲁⲩϣⲱ- ¹⁵ [ⲡⲉ ⲛⲣⲏⲧ]ϥ ⲟⲩⲧⲱⲟⲩ ⲉⲛⲥⲉ ¹⁶
[. . . . ⲉⲛ] ⲛ̄ϣⲁⲣⲡ̄. ⲉϣⲡⲉ ⲣ[. . .¹⁷ . . . .]ⲉ ⲁⲣ̄ ϭⲉⲣⲱⲃ ⲣⲁ ¹⁸ [ⲡⲣⲁ] ⲙ̄ⲡ[ⲓⲁⲙ]ⲁⲣⲧⲉ ⲉⲧⲉⲩⲛ̄-
¹⁹ ⲧⲉⲩ ⲙ̄ⲙⲉ[ⲩ] ⲙ̄ⲡⲓⲥⲁⲃⲧⲉ ²⁰ [. . .]ϣⲛ ⲁⲣⲣ[ⲉ]ⲩⲟⲩ. ⲉⲉⲓⲣ̄ ⲭⲣⲁ- ²¹ [ⲥⲑⲁ]ⲓ ⲅⲁⲣ ⲁ[ⲛ]ⲟⲕ ⲉⲉⲓⲙⲏⲛ
²² [ⲛ̄ⲣⲣⲏ]ⲓ̈ ⲣⲛ̄ ⲛⲓϣⲉϫⲉ, ⲙ̄ⲡⲓⲛⲟⲩ ²³ [ⲁ]ⲛⲉϥⲙⲉⲩⲉ. ⲣⲉⲛⲡⲣⲉ- ²⁴ [ⲥⲃⲩⲧⲉⲣⲟⲥ. . . .] ⲉⲛϥ- ²⁵
[11–13 ⲙⲛ̄]ⲧⲛⲟϭ ¹³⁸·¹ [. .] [13–15] ² [. . .]ⲡⲧ [13–15] ³ [. .]ⲟⲩ[9–11]ⲁⲃ ⲧⲏ- ⁴ [ⲣ]ⲟⲩ .
[9–11]ⲉ ⲁⲅⲅⲉ- ⁵ ⲗⲟⲥ ⲉ[9–11]ⲡⲛ̄ϣⲣ ⁶ ϫⲉ ⲁ[. . .] [ⲣⲣ]ⲁⲩ [ⲛ̄]ⲥⲁⲗⲡⲓⲅⲍ ⁷ ⲉϥⲛⲁⲧⲁϣⲉ [ⲁ]ⲉⲓϣ
ⲛ̄ⲧⲛⲟϭ ⲛ̄ⲁⲙ<ⲛ̄>ⲏ- ⁸ ⲥⲧⲉⲓⲁ ⲉⲧϫⲏⲕ ⲁⲃⲁⲗ ⲣⲛ̄ ⲡⲓⲙⲁ ⁹ ⲛ̄ϣⲁⲉⲓⲉ ⲉⲧⲥⲁⲉⲓⲁ[ⲉ]ⲓⲧ, ⲙ̄[ⲡⲓⲙⲁ] ¹⁰
ⲛ̄ϣⲉⲗⲉⲉⲧ ⲉⲧⲉ ⲡⲓⲙⲁⲉⲓⲉ [ⲡⲉ] ¹¹ ⲛ̄ⲇⲉ ⲡⲛⲟⲩⲧⲉ ⲡⲓ[ϣⲧ]. .[. .] ¹² ⲕⲁⲧⲁ ⲧϭⲟⲙ ⲉⲧⲥⲁⲩ[7–9] ¹³
ⲛ̄ⲇⲉ ⲧⲙⲛ̄ⲧⲛⲟϭ [7–9] ¹⁴ ⲧⲙⲛ̄ⲧⲣⲗⲟϭⲉ ⲛ̄ⲇ[ⲉ 6–8] ¹⁵ ⲛ̄ⲧⲉϥ, ⲉϥⲟⲩⲱ[ⲣⲉ ⲙ̄ⲙⲓⲛ] ¹⁶ ⲙ̄ⲙⲟϥ
ⲁⲛⲓⲙⲛ̄ⲧⲛⲟ[ϭ 6–8] ¹⁷ ⲁⲅⲁⲑⲟⲛ ⲛ̄ⲧⲉϥ ⲡ[7–9] ¹⁸ ⲡⲥⲙⲟⲩ ⲡⲉⲙⲁⲣⲧⲉ [. .] [. . .] ¹⁹ ⲁⲃⲁⲗ ⲣⲓ̈ⲧⲛ̄
ⲧⲙ̄[. .]ⲗⲉ ⲡϫⲁⲓⲥ ⲡ[ⲥⲱ]- ²⁰ ⲧⲏⲣ ⲡⲣⲉϥⲥ[ⲱⲧ]ⲉ ⲛ̄ⲁ ⲡⲓⲙⲉⲣ [.] ²¹ ⲛ̄ⲇⲉ ⲧⲁⲅⲁⲡ[ⲏ] ⲧⲏⲣⲟⲩ,
ⲁ[ⲃⲁⲗ] ²² ⲣⲓⲧⲛ̄ ⲡⲛⲉⲩⲙⲁ [ⲉ]ⲧⲟⲩⲁⲁⲃ ⲛ̄[ⲧⲉϥ] ²³ ϫⲓⲛ [ⲧ]ⲉⲛⲟⲩ ϣⲁⲃⲟⲗ ϣⲁ [ⲛⲓⲅⲉⲛⲉⲁ] ²⁴
ⲛ̄ⲇⲉ ⲛⲓⲅⲉⲛⲉⲁ ϣⲁ ʼⲁʼⲛⲏⲣ ⲛ̄[ⲇⲉ] ²⁵ ⲛ̄ⲇⲉ ⲛⲉⲛⲏⲣⲉ. [ⲣ]ⲁⲙⲏⲛ.

136.23 ⲛ̄ⲇⲉ: read ⲛ̄ⲧⲉ.
138.11 ⲛ̄ⲇⲉ: read ⲛ̄ⲧⲉ.
138.13 ⲛ̄ⲇⲉ: read ⲛ̄ⲧⲉ.
138.14 ⲛ̄ⲇ[ⲉ]: read ⲛ̄ⲧ[ⲉ].
138.21 ⲛ̄ⲇⲉ: read ⲛ̄ⲧⲉ.

the [23] benevolence and sweetness of [24] the preexisting eternity. [This] [25] is the nature of the entire begetting of [26] those whom he had when he radiated [27] upon them [in] a light that had [28] appeared, namely, [. . . .] [29] Just as his [. . . [30] is] which will come to be [. . .], [31] so too is his [. . .] [32] since the change alone is [33] among those who have changed. [. . .] [137.1-4] Those who [. . .] from [5] him of [. . .] [6] in the form [. . .] say, [7] yet the material ones will remain until [8] the end for destruction, because they will not give [9] over their [names], if [10] [they would] return again to what [11] [will not be]. Just as they were [12] [. . .] they were not [13] [. . .] but they were useful [14] [in the] time that they were [15] [in] it among them, yet they [16] [. . .] first. If [. . . [17] . . .] to do another thing [18] concerning the control that they [19] have over the preparation [20] [. . .] before them. For though I am [21] using these words continually, [22] I did not know [23] his thoughts. Some [24] [elders . . .] him [25] greatness [. . . [138.1-3] . . .] [4] entirely [. . .] angel [5] [. . .] [6] because [. . .] trumpet [7] he will announce the great reprieve [8] that is perfect in the eastern place [9] of beauty, in [the] [10] bridal chamber that [is] the love [11] of God the [Father . . .] [12] according to the power that [. . .] [13] of the greatness [. . .] [14] the sweetness [of . . .] [15] him, since he revealed himself [16] to the greatness [. . .] [17] his good, the [. . .] [18] the blessing, the might [. . .] [19] through the [. . .] the Lord, the [20] Savior, the Redeemer of those belonging to the one filled [. . .] [21] with love completely, through [22] his Holy Spirit [23] from now through [all] [24] generations for ever and [25] ever. Amen.

XI. *GOSPEL OF PHILIP*

The *Gospel of Philip* is the third tractate in Nag Hammadi codex II. While the title of the work is ancient, it is misleading, since the work is not a gospel nor does Philip feature prominently in it. Philip's name may have become part of the work's title simply because he is the only disciple mentioned in the text, though the three Marys also make appearances, Jesus's mother, his aunt, and Mary Magdalene, and the latter enjoys a much closer relationship with Jesus than Philip does.

The *Gospel of Philip* is a collection of short passages belonging to various genres, including aphorisms, dialogues, sermons, and epistles, that have been brought together in an anthology. Often connecting these passages, however, are key words that recur throughout the text. These serve to link seemingly disparate passages together. These connecting words lend the *Gospel of Philip* as a whole an air of coherence, and many scholars interpret the work as though it was composed as a coherent work, inviting eager students to study the text and uncover the mystical connections between seemingly related teachings.

Others, however, consider the text to be an eclectic miscellany, a composite text created by someone who was taking notes or copying extracts from a variety of Valentinian works. Those who hold this view find a parallel in the *Excerpts of Theodotus*, a series of extracts made by Clement of Alexandria from a variety of Valentinian sources. An important difference between the *Excerpts of Theodotus* and the *Gospel of Philip* is, however, that Clement includes among the Valentinian excerpts comments of his own. No similar comments appear in the *Gospel of Philip*.

Whatever the intent of the author or compiler of the *Gospel of Philip*, the text contains valuable information about Valentinian biblical interpretation and ritual practice. The focus on ritual is particularly striking in the *Gospel of Philip*, where as many as five rituals are discussed: baptism, chrism, the Lord's Supper, redemption, and the bridal chamber.

⁵¹·²⁹ ογϩεβραιος ⲣ̅ⲣⲱⲙⲉ [ϣ]ⲁϥⲧⲁⲙⲓⲉ ϩⲉⲃⲣⲁⲓ- ³⁰ ⲟⲥ, ⲁⲩⲱ ϣⲁⲩⲙⲟⲩⲧⲉ [ⲉⲡⲁ]ⲉⲓ ⲛ̅ⲧⲉⲉⲓⲙⲓⲛⲉ
³¹ ϫⲉ « ⲡⲣⲟⲥⲏⲗⲩⲧⲟⲥ. » ⲟⲩⲡ[ⲣⲟⲥⲏ]ⲗⲩⲧⲟⲥ ⲇⲉ ⲙⲁϥ- ³² ⲧⲁⲙⲓⲉ ⲡⲣⲟⲥⲏⲗⲩⲧⲟⲥ. [. . . . .]. ⲉ
ⲙⲉⲛ ³³ ⲥⲉϣⲟⲟⲡ ⲛ̅ⲑⲉ ⲉⲧⲟⲩϣ[. . . . .] ³⁴ ⲁⲩⲱ ⲥⲉⲧⲁⲙⲉⲓⲟ ⲛ̅ϩ̅ⲛ̅ⲕⲟⲟ[ⲩⲉ. . . . . . . ⁵²·¹
ⲇⲉ] ⲙⲟⲛⲟ[ⲛ ⲉⲥ]ⲣⲱϣⲉ ⲉⲣⲟⲟⲩ ϣⲓⲛⲁ ⲉⲩⲛⲁ- ² ϣⲱⲡⲉ.

ⲡ[ϩⲙ]ϩⲁⲗ ⲙⲟⲛⲟⲛ ⲉϥϣⲓⲛⲉ ⲁⲣⲉ- ³ ⲗⲉⲩⲑⲉⲣⲟ[ⲥ]· ⲙⲁϥϣⲓⲛⲉ ⲇⲉ ⲛ̅ⲥⲁ ⲧⲟⲩⲥⲓⲁ ⁴ ⲙ̅ⲡⲉϥϫⲟⲉ[ⲓ]
ⲥ. ⲡϣⲏⲣⲉ ⲇⲉ ⲟⲩ ⲙⲟⲛⲟⲛ ϫⲉ ⁵ ϥⲟ ⲛ̅ϣⲏⲣⲉ, ⲁⲗⲗⲁ ⲧⲕⲗⲏⲣⲟⲛⲟⲙⲉⲓⲁ ⲙ̅ⲡⲉⲓ- ⁶ ⲱⲧ. ϣⲁϥⲥⲁϩⲥ̅
ⲛ̅ⲥⲱϥ ⲛⲉⲧⲣ̅ⲕⲗⲏⲣⲟⲛⲟⲙⲉⲓ ⁷ ⲛ̅ⲛⲉⲧⲙⲟⲟⲩⲧ ⲛ̅ⲧⲟⲟⲩ ϩⲱⲟⲩ ⲥⲉⲙⲟⲟⲩⲧ, ⁸ ⲁⲩⲱ ⲉⲩⲕⲗⲏⲣⲟⲛⲟⲙⲉⲓ
ⲛ̅ⲛⲉⲧⲙⲟⲟⲩⲧ. ⲛⲉ- ⁹ ⲧⲣ̅ⲕⲗⲏⲣⲟⲛⲟⲙⲉⲓ ⲙ̅ⲡⲉⲧⲟⲛϩ̅ ⲛ̅ⲧⲟⲟⲩ ⲥⲉⲟⲛϩ̅, ¹⁰ ⲁⲩⲱ ⲥⲉⲣ̅ⲕⲗⲏⲣⲟⲛⲟⲙⲉⲓ
ⲙ̅ⲡⲉⲧⲟⲛϩ̅ ⲙ̅ⲛ̅ ⲛⲉⲧ- ¹¹ ⲙⲟⲟⲩⲧ. ⲛⲉⲧⲙⲟⲟⲩⲧ ⲙⲁⲩⲣ̅ⲕⲗⲏⲣⲟⲛⲟⲙⲉⲓ ¹² ⲗ̅ⲗⲁⲁⲩ. ⲡⲱⲥ ⲅⲁⲣ
ⲡⲉⲧⲙⲟⲟⲩⲧ ϥⲛⲁⲕⲗⲏⲣⲟⲛⲟ- ¹³ ⲙⲉⲓ; ⲡⲉⲧⲙⲟⲟⲩⲧ ⲉϥϣⲁⲕⲗⲏⲣⲟⲛⲟⲙⲉⲓ ⲙ̅- ¹⁴ ⲡⲉⲧⲟⲛϩ̅ ϥⲛⲁⲙⲟⲩ
ⲁⲛ, ⲁⲗⲗⲁ ⲡⲉⲧⲙⲟⲟⲩⲧ ¹⁵ ⲉϥⲛⲁⲱⲛϩ̅ ⲛ̅ϩⲟⲩⲟ.

ⲟⲩϩⲉⲑⲛⲓⲕⲟⲥ ⲣ̅ⲣⲱ- ¹⁶ ⲙⲉ ⲙⲁϥⲙⲟⲩ, ⲙ̅ⲡⲉϥⲱⲛϩ̅ ⲅⲁⲣ ⲉⲛⲉϩ ϩⲓⲛⲁ ¹⁷ ⲉϥⲛⲁⲙⲟⲩ. ⲡⲉⲛⲧⲁϩⲡⲓⲥⲧⲉⲩⲉ
ⲉⲧⲙⲉ ⲁϥ- ¹⁸ ⲱⲛϩ̅, ⲁⲩⲱ ⲡⲁⲓ̈ ϥⲟ ⲛ̅ⲇⲩⲛⲉⲩⲉ ⲉⲙⲟⲩ ϥⲟⲛϩ̅ ¹⁹ ⲅⲁⲣ. ϫⲓⲙ ⲡϩⲟⲟⲩ ⲛ̅ⲧⲁ ⲡⲭⲣⲓⲥⲧⲟⲥ
ⲉⲓ, ⲥⲉⲥⲱⲛⲧ ⲙ̅- ²⁰ ⲡⲕⲟⲥⲙⲟⲥ ⲥⲉⲣ̅ⲕⲟⲥⲙⲉⲓ, ⲛ̅ⲙ̅ⲡⲟⲗⲉⲓⲥ ⲥⲉ- ²¹ ϥⲓ, ⲙ̅ⲡⲉⲧⲙⲟⲟⲩⲧ ⲉⲃⲟⲗ. ⲛ̅ϩⲟⲟⲩ
ⲛⲉⲛϣⲟ- ²² ⲟⲡ ⲛ̅ϩⲉⲃⲣⲁⲓⲟⲥ ⲛⲉⲛⲟ ⲛ̅ⲟⲣⲫⲁⲛⲟⲥ ⲛⲉⲩ- ²³ ⲛ̅ⲧⲁⲛ ⲛ̅ⲧⲙ̅ⲙⲁⲁⲩ, ⲛ̅ⲧⲁⲣⲛ̅ϣⲱⲡⲉ ⲇⲉ
ⲛ̅- ²⁴ ⲭⲣⲏⲥⲧⲓⲁⲛⲟⲥ, ⲁⲉⲓⲱⲧ ϩⲓ ⲙⲁⲁⲩ ϣⲱⲡⲉ ⲛⲁⲛ.

²⁵ ⲛⲉⲧⲥⲓⲧⲉ ϩⲛ̅ ⲧⲡⲣⲱ ϣⲁⲩⲱⲥϩ̅ ϩⲙ̅ ⲡϣⲱⲙ. ²⁶ ⲧⲡⲣⲱ ⲡⲉ ⲡⲕⲟⲥⲙⲟⲥ· ⲡϣⲱⲙ ⲡⲉ ⲡⲕⲉⲁⲓ- ²⁷
ⲱⲛ. ⲙⲁⲣⲛ̅ⲥⲓⲧⲉ ϩⲙ̅ ⲡⲕⲟⲥⲙⲟⲥ ϫⲉⲕⲁⲁⲥ ²⁸ ⲉⲛⲛⲁⲱⲥϩ̅ ϩⲙ̅ ⲡϣⲱⲙ. ⲇⲓⲁ ⲧⲟⲩⲧⲟ ϣϣⲉ ²⁹ ⲉⲣⲟⲛ
ⲉⲧⲙ̅ⲧⲣⲛ̅ϣⲗⲏⲗ ϩⲛ̅ ⲧⲡⲣⲱ. ⲡⲓⲉⲃⲟⲗ ³⁰ ϩⲛ̅ ⲧⲡⲣⲱ ⲡⲉ ⲡϣⲱⲙ. ⲉⲣϣⲁ ⲟⲩⲁ ⲇⲉ ⲱⲥϩ̅ ³¹ ϩⲛ̅
ⲧⲉⲡⲣⲱ ⲉϥⲛⲁⲱⲥϩ̅ ⲁⲛ ⲁⲗⲗⲁ ⲉϥⲛⲁϩⲱ- ³² ⲗⲉ, ϩⲱⲥ ⲡⲁⲉ[ⲓ ⲛ̅]ⲧⲉⲉⲓⲙⲓⲛⲉ ⲉϥⲛⲁⲧⲉⲩ- ³³ ⲉ
ⲕⲁⲣⲡⲟⲥ [ⲛⲁϥ] ⲁⲛ. ⲟⲩ ⲙⲟⲛⲟⲛ ⲉϥⲛ̅ⲛⲏⲩ ³⁴ ⲉⲃⲟ[ⲗ . . . . .] ⲁⲗⲗⲁ ϩⲙ̅ ⲡⲕⲉⲥⲁⲃⲃⲁⲧⲟⲛ ³⁵
[. . . . . . ⲟ]ⲩⲁⲧⲕⲁⲣⲡⲟⲥ ⲧⲉ.

ⲁⲡⲉⲭⲣⲓⲥⲧⲟⲥ ⲉⲓ ⁵³·¹ ϩⲟⲉⲓⲛⲉ ⲙⲉⲛ ⲉⲧⲣⲉϥⲧⲟⲟⲩⲥ[ⲉ, ϩ]ⲛ̅ⲕⲟⲟⲩⲉ ² ⲇⲉ ⲉⲧⲣⲉϥⲛⲁϩⲙⲟⲩ, ϩⲛ̅ⲕⲟⲟ[ⲩ]
ⲉ ⲉⲧⲣⲉϥⲥⲟ- ³ ⲧⲟⲩ. ⲛⲉⲧⲟ ⲛ̅ϣ̅ⲙⲙⲟ ⲛ̅ⲧⲁϥⲧⲟⲟⲩⲥⲉ. ⲁϥⲁ- ⁴ ⲁⲩ ⲛ̅ⲛⲉⲧⲉ ⲛⲟⲩϥ ⲛⲉ,
ⲁⲩⲱ ⲁϥⲛⲟⲩϩ ⁵ ⲛ̅ⲛⲉⲧⲉ ⲛⲟⲩϥ, ⲛⲁⲉⲓ ⲛ̅ⲧⲁϥⲕⲁⲁⲩ ⲛ̅ⲛⲉⲟⲩ- ⁶ ⲱ ϩⲙ̅ ⲡⲉϥⲟⲩⲱϣ. ⲟⲩ ⲙⲟⲛⲟⲛ
ϫⲉ ⲛ̅ⲧⲁⲣⲉϥ- ⁷ ⲟⲩⲱⲛϩ̅ ⲉⲃⲟⲗ ⲁϥⲕⲱ ⲛ̅ⲧⲯⲩⲭⲏ ⲛ̅ⲧⲁⲣⲉϥ- ⁸ ⲟⲩⲱϣ, ⲁⲗⲗⲁ ϫⲓⲛ ⲫⲟⲟⲩ
ⲉⲡⲕⲟⲥⲙⲟⲥ ϣⲟ- ⁹ ⲟⲡ ⲁϥⲕⲱ ⲛ̅ⲧⲯⲩⲭⲏ ⲙ̅ⲡⲥⲟⲡ ⲉⲧⲉϥⲟⲩ- ¹⁰ ⲱϣ. ⲧⲟⲧⲉ ⲁϥⲉⲓ ⲛ̅ϣⲟⲣⲡ
ⲉϥⲛⲁϥⲓⲧ̅ⲥ̅, ⲉⲡⲉⲓ ¹¹ ⲛ̅ⲧⲁⲩⲕⲁⲁⲥ ⲛ̅ⲛⲉⲟⲩⲱ. ⲁⲥϣⲱⲡⲉ ϩⲁ ⲛⲗⲏ- ¹² ⲥⲧⲏⲥ, ⲁⲩⲱ ⲁⲩϥⲓⲧ̅ⲥ̅
ⲛ̅ⲁⲓⲭⲙⲁⲗⲱⲧⲟⲥ, ⲁϥⲛⲟϩ- ¹³ ⲙⲉⲥ ⲇⲉ. ⲁⲩⲱ ⲛⲉⲧⲛⲁⲛⲟⲩⲟⲩ ϩⲙ̅ ⲡⲕⲟⲥⲙⲟⲥ ¹⁴ ⲁϥⲥⲟⲧⲟⲩ ⲁⲩⲱ
ⲛⲉⲑⲟⲟⲩ.

ⲡⲟⲩⲟⲉⲓⲛ ⲙ̅ⲛ̅ ⲡⲕⲁ- ¹⁵ ⲕⲉ, ⲡⲱⲛϩ̅ ⲙ̅ⲛ̅ ⲡⲙⲟⲩ, ⲛ̅ⲟⲩⲛⲁⲙ ⲙ̅ⲛ̅ ⲛ̅ϩⲃⲟⲩⲣ, ¹⁶ ⲛ̅ⲥⲛⲏⲩ ⲛⲉ ⲛ̅ⲛⲟⲩⲉⲣⲏⲩ.
ⲙ̅ⲛ̅ ϭⲟⲙ ⲛ̅ⲥⲉⲡⲱⲣϫ ¹⁷ ⲁⲛⲟⲩⲉⲣⲏⲩ. ⲉⲧⲃⲉ ⲡⲁⲉⲓ ⲟⲩⲧⲉ ⲛⲉⲧⲛⲁⲛⲟⲩ- ¹⁸ ⲟⲩ ⲛⲁⲛⲟⲩⲟⲩ, ⲟⲩⲧⲉ
ⲛⲉⲑⲟⲟⲩ ⲥⲉϩⲟⲟⲩ, ¹⁹ ⲟⲩⲧⲉ ⲡⲱⲛϩ̅ ⲟⲩⲱⲛϩ̅ ⲡⲉ, ⲟⲩⲧⲉ ⲡⲙⲟⲩ ⲟⲩ- ²⁰ ⲙⲟⲩ ⲡⲉ. ⲇⲓⲁ ⲧⲟⲩⲧⲟ
ⲡⲟⲩⲁ ⲡⲟⲩⲁ ⲛⲁⲃⲱⲗ ²¹ ⲉⲃⲟⲗ ⲁⲧⲉϥⲁⲣⲭⲏ ϫⲓⲛ ϣⲟⲣⲡ. ⲛⲉⲧϫⲟⲥⲉ ²² ⲇⲉ ⲁⲡⲕⲟⲥⲙⲟⲥ
ϩⲛ̅ⲛⲁⲧⲃⲱⲗ ⲉⲃⲟⲗ ⲛⲉ· ²³ ϩⲛ̅ϣⲁ ⲉⲛⲉϩ ⲛⲉ.

51.29 A Hebrew makes a Hebrew, 30 and this kind of person is called 31 "proselyte." But a proselyte does not 32 make a proselyte. 33 They are like the . . . 34 and they make others [. . . 52.1 But it] suffices for them simply to 2 exist.

The slave seeks only to be 3 free; he does not seek after the property 4 of his master. But the son is not only 5 a son; he also claims the inheritance of the Father. 6 Those who inherit 7 the dead are themselves dead, 8 and they inherit the dead. 9 (But) those who inherit the living are alive, 10 and they inherit the living and the 11 dead. The dead do not inherit 12 anything. For how can the dead inherit? 13 If the one who is dead inherits 14 the living he will not die, but the one who is dead 15 will become alive still more.

A gentile 16 does not die, because he has never lived in order that 17 he might die. The one who has believed in the truth has 18 lived, and this one is in danger of dying because he is alive. 19 From the day Christ came, 20 the world has been created, the cities 21 have been adorned, and the dead have been taken. When we were 22 Hebrews we were orphans and we had (only) 23 our mother, but once we became 24 Christians, a father and mother came about for us.

25 Those who sow in the winter reap in the summer. 26 The winter is the world; the summer is the other eternity. 27 Let us sow in the world so that 28 we might reap in the summer. For this reason it is fitting 29 for us not to pray in the winter. What follows 30 the winter is the summer. But if one reaps 31 in the winter he will not reap but tear out, 32 since this kind (of farming) will not produce 33 fruit [for him]. Not only does it come 34 forth [. . .] but also on the Sabbath 35 [. . .] it is barren.

Christ came 53.1 to purchase some, 2 to preserve others, and to redeem others. 3 Those who were foreign he bought. He made 4 them his own, and he separated 5 his own, those whom he had given as pledges 6 by his will. It was not only that when he had 7 appeared he laid down the soul when he 8 desired, but from the day that the world existed 9 he laid down the soul at the time he desired. 10 Then he came first so that he would take it, since 11 it had been given as pledges. It came to be in the possession of thieves, 12 and it was taken captive, but he saved 13 it. The good (people) in the world 14 he redeemed along with the bad (people).

Light and darkness, 15 life and death, right and left, 16 they are brothers with each other. It is not possible for them to be divided 17 from one another. For this reason neither are the good 18 good, nor the evil evil, 19 nor is life a life, nor death a 20 death. On account of this each one will dissolve 21 into its beginning. But those who are exalted 22 over the world are indissoluble; 23 they are eternal.

ⲚⲢⲀⲚ ⲈⲦⲞⲨϯ Ⲙ̄ⲘⲞⲞⲨ ⲀⲚ- ²⁴ ⲕⲟⲥⲘⲓⲕⲟⲥ ⲞⲨⲚ̄ⲦⲈⲨ Ⲙ̄ⲘⲀⲨ Ⲛ̄ⲞⲨⲚⲞϭ Ⲙ̄- ²⁵ ⲡⲗⲀⲚⲎ. ⲤⲈⲠⲰϫⲤ
ⲄⲀⲢ Ⲙ̄ⲠⲞⲨϩⲎⲦ ⲈⲂⲞⲖ ²⁶ ϨⲚ̄ ⲚⲈⲦⲤⲘⲞⲚⲦ ⲈϨⲞⲨⲚ ⲈⲚⲈⲦⲤⲘⲞⲚⲦ ²⁷ ⲀⲚ. ⲀⲨⲰ ⲠⲈⲦⲤⲰⲦⲘ̄ «
ⲈⲠⲚⲞⲨⲦⲈ » ⲈϤⲚⲞ- ²⁸ ⲈⲒ ⲀⲚ Ⲙ̄ⲠⲈⲦⲤⲘⲞⲚⲦ ⲀⲖⲖⲀ ⲀϤⲢⲚⲞⲈⲒ Ⲙ̄- ²⁹ ⲠⲈⲦⲤⲘⲞⲚⲦ ⲀⲚ. ⲦⲈⲈⲒϨⲈ ⲞⲚ
Ⲙ̄ⲠⲈⲒⲰⲦ ³⁰ ⲘⲚ̄ ⲠϢⲎⲢⲈ ⲘⲚ̄ ⲠⲠⲚ̣ⲈⲨⲘⲀ ⲈⲦⲞⲨⲀⲀⲂ ⲘⲚ̄ ³¹ ⲠⲰⲚϨ ⲘⲚ̄ ⲠⲞⲨⲞⲈⲒⲚ̣ ⲀⲨⲰ ⲦⲀⲚⲀⲤⲦⲀ-
³² ⲤⲒⲤ ⲘⲚ̄ ⲦⲈⲔⲔⲖⲎⲤⲒⲀ̣ [ⲘⲚ̄] Ⲛ̄ⲔⲞⲞⲨⲈ ⲦⲎⲢⲞⲨ. ³³ ⲈⲨⲢ̄ⲚⲞⲈⲒ ⲀⲚ Ⲛ̄ⲚⲈ[ⲦⲤⲘⲞ]Ⲛ̣Ⲧ, ⲀⲖⲖⲀ ⲈⲨⲢ̄- ³⁴
ⲚⲞⲈⲒ Ⲛ̄ⲚⲈⲦⲤⲘⲞⲚ[Ⲧ ⲀⲚ ⲠⲖ]ⲎⲚ ⲀⲨⲤⲈ- ³⁵ ⲂⲞ ⲀⲚⲈⲦⲤⲘⲞⲚⲦ. Ⲣ̄ⲢⲀ̣[Ⲛ Ⲛ̄ⲦⲀⲨⲤ]Ⲁ̣ⲦⲘⲞⲨ ³⁶ ⲤⲈϢⲞⲞⲠ
ϨⲘ̄ ⲠⲔⲞⲤⲘⲞ[Ⲥ . . . . . .] ⁵⁴·¹ ⲀⲠⲀ]ⲦⲀ. [Ⲉ]Ⲛ̣[ⲈⲨ]Ϣ[Ⲟ]ⲞⲠ ϨⲘ̄ ⲠⲀⲒⲰⲚ, ⲚⲈⲨⲚⲀ- ² Ⲣ̄ⲞⲚⲞⲘⲀⲌ̣[Ⲉ]
ⲀⲚ ϨⲘ̄ ⲠⲔⲞⲤⲘⲞⲤ ⲖⲖⲀⲀⲨ Ⲛ̄- ³ ϨⲞⲞⲨ. ⲞⲨⲦⲈ Ⲙ̄ⲠⲞⲨⲔⲀⲀⲨ ϨⲚ̄ Ⲛ̄ϨⲂⲎⲨⲈ Ⲛ̄- ⁴ ⲔⲞⲤⲘⲒⲔⲞⲚ. ⲞⲨⲚ̄ⲦⲀⲨ
Ⲙ̄ⲘⲀⲨ Ⲛ̄ⲚⲞⲨϨⲀⲎ ϨⲘ̄ ⁵ ⲠⲀⲒⲰⲚ.

ⲞⲨⲢⲀⲚ ⲞⲨⲰⲦ ⲘⲀⲨⲦⲈⲨⲞⲨⲀϤ ⁶ ϨⲘ̄ ⲠⲔⲞⲤⲘⲞⲤ, ⲠⲢⲀⲚ Ⲛ̄ⲦⲀ ⲠⲈⲒⲰⲦ ⲦⲀⲀϤ ⁷ Ⲙ̄ⲠϢⲎⲢⲈ, ϤϪⲞⲤⲈ
ⲈⲞⲨⲞⲚ ⲚⲒⲘ, ⲈⲦⲈ ⲠⲀ- ⁸ ⲈⲒ ⲠⲈ ⲠⲢⲀⲚ Ⲙ̄ⲠⲈⲒⲰⲦ. ⲚⲈⲢⲈ ⲠϢⲎⲢⲈ ⲄⲀⲢ ⁹ ⲚⲀϢⲰⲠⲈ ⲀⲚ ⲈⲒⲰⲦ
ⲤⲀⲂⲎⲖ Ϫ Ⲉ ⲀϤϯ ϨⲒ- ¹⁰ ϢⲰϤ Ⲙ̄ⲠⲢⲀⲚ Ⲙ̄ⲠⲈⲒⲰⲦ. ⲠⲈⲈⲒⲢⲀⲚ ⲚⲈ- ¹¹ ⲦⲈⲨⲚ̄ⲦⲀ`ⲩ´ϥ ⲤⲈⲢ̄ⲚⲞⲈⲒ ⲘⲈⲚ
Ⲙ̄ⲘⲞϤ, ⲤⲈϢⲀ- ¹² Ϫ Ⲉ ⲆⲈ ⲈⲢⲞϤ ⲀⲚ. ⲚⲈⲦⲈⲘⲚ̄ⲦⲀⲨϤ ⲆⲈ ⲤⲈ- ¹³ Ⲣ̄ⲚⲞⲈⲒ Ⲙ̄ⲘⲞϤ ⲀⲚ.

ⲀⲖⲖⲀ ⲀⲦⲘⲈ Ϫ ⲠⲈ ϨⲈⲚⲢⲀⲚ ¹⁴ ϨⲘ̄ ⲠⲔⲞⲤⲘⲞⲤ ⲈⲦⲂⲎⲦⲚ̄. ⲚⲀⲈⲒ ⲈⲘⲚ̄ϭⲞⲘ ¹⁵ ⲀⲤⲈⲂⲞ ⲈⲢⲞⲤ ⲬⲰⲢⲒⲤ
Ⲣ̄ⲢⲀⲚ. ⲞⲨⲈⲒ ⲞⲨⲰⲦ ¹⁶ ⲦⲈ ⲦⲘⲈ· ⲤⲞ Ⲛ̄ϨⲀϨ ⲀⲨⲰ ⲈⲦⲂⲎⲦⲚ̄ ⲈⲦⲤⲈ- ¹⁷ ⲂⲞ ⲈⲠⲀⲈⲒ ⲞⲨⲀⲀϤ ϨⲚ̄
ⲞⲨⲀⲄⲀⲠⲎ ϨⲒⲦⲚ̄ ¹⁸ ϨⲀϨ. ⲀⲚⲀⲢⲬⲰⲚ ⲞⲨⲰϢ ⲀⲢ̄ⲀⲠⲀⲦⲀ Ⲙ̄- ¹⁹ ⲠⲢⲰⲘⲈ ⲈⲠⲈⲒⲆⲎ ⲀⲨⲚⲀⲨ ⲈⲢⲞϤ
ⲈⲨⲚ̄ⲦⲀϤ ²⁰ Ⲙ̄ⲘⲀⲨ Ⲛ̄ⲞⲨⲤⲨⲄⲄⲈⲚⲈⲒⲀ ϢⲀ ⲚⲈⲦⲚⲀ- ²¹ ⲚⲞⲨⲞⲨ ⲚⲀⲘⲈ. ⲀⲨϤⲒ ⲠⲢⲀⲚ Ⲛ̄ⲚⲈⲦⲚⲀ- ²²
ⲚⲞⲨⲞⲨ ⲀⲨⲦⲀⲀϤ ⲀⲚⲈⲦⲚⲀⲚⲞⲨⲞⲨ ⲀⲚ ²³ Ϫ ⲈⲔⲀⲀⲤ ϨⲒⲦⲚ̄ Ⲣ̄ⲢⲀⲚ ⲈⲨⲚⲀⲢ̄ⲀⲠⲀⲦⲀ Ⲙ̄- ²⁴ ⲘⲞϤ ⲀⲨⲰ
Ⲛ̄ⲤⲈⲘⲞⲢⲞⲨ ⲈϨⲞⲨⲚ ⲀⲚⲈⲦⲚⲀ- ²⁵ ⲚⲞⲨⲞⲨ ⲀⲚ. ⲀⲨⲰ Ⲙ̄ⲘⲚ̄ⲚⲤⲰⲤ ⲈϢϪ Ⲉ ⲈⲨ- ²⁶ ⲈⲒⲢⲈ ⲚⲀⲨ
Ⲛ̄ⲞⲨϨⲘⲞⲦ. Ⲛ̄ⲤⲈⲦⲢⲞⲨⲤⲈϨⲰⲞⲨ ²⁷ ⲈⲂⲞⲖ Ⲛ̄ⲚⲈⲦⲚⲀⲚⲞⲨⲞⲨ ⲀⲚ ⲀⲨⲰ Ⲛ̄ⲤⲈ- ²⁸ ⲔⲀⲀⲨ ϨⲚ̄
ⲚⲈⲦⲚⲀⲚⲞⲨⲞⲨ. ⲚⲀⲈⲒ ⲚⲈⲨⲤⲞ- ²⁹ ⲞⲨⲚ Ⲙ̄ⲘⲞⲞⲨ. ⲚⲈⲨⲞⲨⲰϢ ⲄⲀⲢ ⲈⲦⲢⲞⲨ- ³⁰ ϬⲒ ⲠⲈⲖⲈⲨⲐⲈⲢ[Ⲟ]
Ⲥ Ⲛ̄ⲤⲈⲔⲀⲀϤ ⲚⲀⲨ Ⲛ̄- ³¹ ϨⲘϨⲀⲖ ϢⲀ ⲈⲚⲈϨ.

ⲞⲨⲚ ϨⲚ̄ⲆⲨⲚⲀⲘⲒⲤ ³² ϢⲞⲞⲠ ⲈⲨϯϨ[. . .] ⲠⲢⲰⲘⲈ. ⲈⲤⲈⲞⲨⲰϢ ³³ ⲀⲚ ⲀⲦⲢⲈϤⲞⲨ[Ϫ ⲀⲈⲒ] Ϫ ⲈⲔⲀⲀⲤ
ⲈⲨⲚⲀϢⲰ- ³⁴ ⲠⲈ ⲈⲨⲘ[. . . . .]Ⲗ ⲈⲢϢⲀ ⲠⲢⲰⲘⲈ ⲄⲀⲢ ³⁵ ⲞⲨⲬ̣[ⲀⲈⲒ, Ⲛ̄ⲚⲞⲨ]ϢⲰⲠⲈ Ⲛ̄ϬⲒ ϨⲚ̄ⲞⲨⲤⲒⲀ
³⁶ [. . . . . . .] ⲀⲨⲰ ⲚⲈⲨⲦⲀⲖⲈ ⲐⲎⲢⲒⲞⲚ ⁵⁵·¹ ⲈϨⲢⲀ ̈Ⲓ Ⲛ̄Ⲛ̄ⲆⲨⲚⲀⲘⲒⲤ ⲚⲈ [Ϩ]Ⲛ̄[Ⲑ]ⲎⲢⲒⲞⲚ ⲄⲀⲢ ² ⲚⲈ
ⲚⲈⲦⲞⲨⲦⲈⲖⲞ ⲈϨⲢⲀ ̈Ⲓ ⲚⲀ[Ⲩ] ⲚⲈⲨⲦⲈⲖⲞ ³ ⲘⲈⲚ Ⲙ̄ⲘⲞⲞⲨ ⲈϨⲢⲀ ̈Ⲓ ⲈⲨⲞⲚϨ, Ⲛ̄ⲦⲀⲢⲞⲨⲦⲈ- ⁴ ⲖⲞⲞⲨ ⲆⲈ
ⲈϨⲢⲀ ̈Ⲓ, ⲀⲨⲘⲞⲨ. ⲠⲢⲰⲘⲈ ⲀⲨⲦⲈⲖⲞϤ ⁵ ⲈϨⲢⲀ ̈Ⲓ Ⲙ̄ⲠⲚⲞⲨⲦⲈ ⲈϤⲘⲞⲞⲨⲦ, ⲀⲨⲰ ⲀϤⲰⲚϨ.

⁶ ϨⲀ ⲦⲈϨⲎ ⲈⲘⲠⲀⲦⲈ ⲠⲈⲬⲢⲒⲤⲦⲞⲤ ⲈⲒ ⲚⲈ ⲘⲚ̄ ⲞⲈⲒⲔ ⁷ ϨⲘ̄ ⲠⲔⲞⲤⲘⲞⲤ Ⲛ̄ⲐⲈ Ⲙ̄ⲠⲠⲀⲢⲀⲆⲒⲤⲞⲤ, ⲠⲘⲀ ⁸
ⲚⲈⲢⲈ ⲀⲆⲀⲘ Ⲙ̄ⲘⲀⲨ, ⲚⲈⲨⲚ̄ⲦⲀϤ ϨⲀϨ Ⲛ̄ϢⲎⲚ ⁹ Ⲛ̄Ⲛ̄ⲦⲢⲞⲪⲎ Ⲛ̄ⲚⲈⲐⲎⲢⲒⲞⲚ ⲚⲈ ⲘⲚ̄ⲦⲀϤ ⲤⲞⲨⲞ ¹⁰
Ⲛ̄ⲦⲦⲢⲞⲪⲎ Ⲙ̄ⲠⲢⲰⲘⲈ. ⲚⲈⲢⲈ ⲠⲢⲰⲘⲈ ⲤⲞ- ¹¹ ⲈⲒϢ Ⲛ̄ⲐⲈ Ⲛ̄ⲚⲈⲐⲎⲢⲒⲞⲚ, ⲀⲖⲖⲀ Ⲛ̄ⲦⲀⲢⲈ ⲠⲈⲬⲢⲒⲤⲦⲞⲤ ¹²
ⲈⲒ, ⲠⲦⲈⲖⲒⲞⲤ Ⲣ̄ⲢⲰⲘⲈ, ⲀϤⲈⲒⲚⲈ Ⲛ̄ⲞⲨⲞⲈⲒⲔ ¹³ ⲈⲂⲞⲖ ϨⲚ̄ ⲦⲠⲈ ϢⲒⲚⲀ ⲈⲢⲈ ⲠⲢⲰⲘⲈ ⲚⲀⲢ̄ⲦⲢⲈ- ¹⁴
ⲪⲈⲤⲐⲀⲒ ϨⲚ̄ ⲦⲦⲢⲞⲪⲎ Ⲙ̄ⲠⲢⲰⲘⲈ. ⲚⲈⲢⲈ Ⲛ̄- ¹⁵ ⲀⲢⲬⲰⲚ ⲘⲈⲈⲨⲈ Ϫ Ⲉ ϨⲚ̄ ⲦⲞⲨϬⲞⲘ ⲘⲚ̄ ⲠⲞⲨ- ¹⁶ ϢⲰ
ⲈⲨⲈⲒⲢⲈ Ⲛ̄ⲚⲈⲦⲞⲨⲈⲒⲢⲈ Ⲙ̄ⲘⲞⲞⲨ, ⲚⲈ- ¹⁷ ⲢⲈ ⲠⲠⲚⲈⲨⲘⲀ ⲆⲈ ⲈⲦⲞⲨⲀⲀⲂ ϨⲚ̄ ⲞⲨⲠⲈⲐⲎⲠ ¹⁸ ⲚⲈϤⲈⲚⲈⲢⲄⲈⲒ

54.16–17 ⲈⲦⲤⲈⲂⲞ: possibly ⲈⲨⲤⲈⲂⲞ.

Names given to [24] worldly things have great [25] error. For they divert their mind from [26] what is correct to what is incorrect. [27] And the one who hears "God" [28] does not perceive that which is correct, but perceives [29] what is incorrect. It is this way also with the Father [30] and the Son and the Holy Spirit and [31] life and light and resurrection [32] and the Church and all the rest. [33] What is correct is not perceived, but what is incorrect [34] is perceived unless what is correct [35] is perceived. The names that are heard [36] are in the world [. . .] [54.1] deceive. If they were in the eternity, they would not be [2] names in the world at any time. [3] Nor were they placed among the worldly things. [4] They have a limit in [5] the eternity.

A single name is not uttered [6] in the world, the name that the Father gave [7] to the Son, it is above everything, this [8] is the name of the Father. For the Son [9] would not become Father unless he clothed [10] himself in the name of the Father. As for this name, [11] those who have it know it, but they [12] do not speak it. Those who do not have it, [13] do not know it.

But truth produced names [14] in the world on our account. As for these (names), it is not possible [15] to know it (i.e., truth) without them. Truth [16] is one thing; it is also many on our account in order to teach [17] about this one thing in love through [18] many things. The rulers wanted to deceive [19] the man, since they saw him having [20] a kinship with the things that are [21] truly good. They took the name of those things that are good [22] and gave it to those things that are not good [23] so that through the names they might deceive [24] him and bind them to those things that are [25] not good. And afterward what a gift they [26] make for them! They cause them to be removed [27] from those things that are not good, and [28] place them among the good. These things they knew. [29] For they wanted [30] to take the free man and make him for them [31] a slave forever.

Powers [32] exist [. . .] the man. They do not want [33] him to be [saved] so that they might become [34] [. . .] For if man [35] is [saved], sacrifices ought not occur [36] [. . .] In fact animals were offered [55.1] up to the powers. For the animals [2] were those to whom they sacrificed. They were offering [3] them up alive, but when they offered them [4] up, they died. Man was offered [5] up to God dead, and he became alive.

[6] Before Christ came there was no bread [7] in the world just as Paradise, the place [8] where Adam was, had many trees [9] for the nourishment for the animals, (but) no wheat [10] for the nourishment of man. Man would eat [11] like the animals, but after Christ [12] came, the Perfect Man, he brought bread [13] from heaven so that man might be [14] nourished by the nourishment of man. The [15] rulers thought that by their power and will [16] they were doing the things they did, [17] but the Holy Spirit in secret

ⲙ̄ⲡⲧⲏⲣϥ ⲉⲃⲟⲗ ϩⲓⲧⲟⲟⲧⲟⲩ ¹⁹ ⲛ̄ⲑⲉ ⲉⲧϥⲟⲩⲱϣ. ⲧⲁⲗⲏⲑⲉⲓⲁ ⲥⲉⲥⲓⲧⲉ ⲙ̄ⲙⲟⲥ ²⁰ ⲙ̄ⲙⲁ ⲛⲓⲙ,
ⲧⲉⲧϣⲟⲟⲡ ϫⲓⲛ ⲛ̄ϣⲟⲣⲡ. ⲁⲩ- ²¹ ⲱ ⲟⲩⲛ ϩⲁϩ ⲛⲁⲩ ⲉⲣⲟⲥ ⲉⲩⲥⲓⲧⲉ ⲙ̄ⲙⲟⲥ, ϩⲛ̄- ²² ⲕⲟⲩⲉⲓ ⲇⲉ
ⲉⲧⲟⲩⲛⲁⲩ ⲉⲣⲟⲥ ⲉⲩⲥⲓⲧⲉ ⲉⲩ[[ϩ]]ⲱⲥ`ϩ΄ ⲙ̄ⲙⲟⲥ.

²³ ⲡⲉϫⲉ ϩⲟⲉⲓⲛⲉ ϫⲉ ⲁⲙⲁⲣⲓⲁ ⲱ ⲉⲃⲟⲗ ϩⲙ̄ ²⁴ ⲡⲡⲛⲉⲩⲙⲁ ⲉⲧⲟⲩⲁⲁⲃ. ⲥⲉⲣⲡⲗⲁⲛⲁⲥⲑⲉ· ⲟⲩ ⲡⲉ- ²⁵
ⲧⲟⲩⲭⲱ ⲙ̄ⲙⲟϥ ⲥⲉⲥⲟⲟⲩⲛ ⲁⲛ. ⲁϣ ⲛ̄ϩⲟ- ²⁶ ⲟⲩ ⲉⲛⲉϩ ⲡⲉⲛⲧⲁ ⲥϩⲓⲙⲉ ⲱ ⲉⲃⲟⲗ ϩⲛ̄ ⲥϩⲓ- ²⁷ ⲙⲉ;
ⲙⲁⲣⲓⲁ ⲧⲉ ⲧⲡⲁⲣⲑⲉⲛⲟⲥ ⲉⲧⲉ ⲙ̄ⲡⲉ ²⁸ ⲇⲩⲛⲁⲙⲓⲥ ϫⲁϩⲙⲉⲥ. ⲉⲥϣⲟⲟⲡ ⲛ̄ⲛⲟⲩ- ²⁹ ⲛⲟϭ ⲛ̄ⲛⲁⲛⲟϣ
ⲛ̄ⲛϩⲉⲃⲣⲁⲓⲟⲥ ⲉⲧⲉ ⲛⲁ- ³⁰ ⲡⲟⲥⲧⲟⲗⲟⲥ ⲛⲉ ⲁⲩⲱ [ⲛ̄]ⲁⲡⲟⲥⲧⲟⲗⲓⲕⲟⲥ. ³¹ ⲧⲉⲉⲓⲡⲁⲣⲑⲉⲛⲟⲥ ⲉⲧ[ⲉ]
ⲙ̄ⲡⲉ ⲇⲩⲛⲁⲙⲓⲥ ³² ϫⲟϩⲙⲉⲥ ⲟⲩ[. . . . .ⲁ]ⲛⲇⲩⲛⲁⲙⲓⲥ ³³ ϫⲟϩⲙⲟⲩ, ⲁⲩⲱ ⲛ̄[ⲉϥⲛⲁϫ]ⲟⲟⲥ ⲁⲛ
ⲛ̄ϭⲓ ³⁴ ⲡϫⲟⲉⲓⲥ ϫⲉ « ⲡⲁⲉ[ⲓⲱⲧ ⲉⲧϩ]ⲛ̄ ⲙ̄ⲡⲏⲩⲉ » ³⁵ ⲉⲓⲙⲏⲧⲓ ϫⲉ ⲛⲉⲩⲛ̄ⲧⲁ[ϥ ⲙ̄ⲙⲁⲩ] ⲛ̄[ⲕ]
ⲉⲉⲓⲱⲧ, ³⁶ ⲁⲗⲗⲁ ϩⲁⲡⲗⲱⲥ ⲁϥϫⲟⲟ[ⲥ ϫⲉ « ⲡⲁⲉⲓⲱⲧ ».]

³⁷ ⲡⲉϫⲉ ⲡϫⲟⲉⲓⲥ ⲛ̄ⲙ̄ⲙⲁⲑ[ⲏⲧⲏⲥ ϫⲉ « . . . ⁵⁶·¹ ⲉⲃ]ⲟⲗ ϩⲛ̄ [ⲏ]ⲉⲓ ⲛⲓⲙ ⲉⲛⲓ ⲉϩⲟⲩⲛ ⲉⲡⲏⲉⲓ ²
ⲙ̄ⲡⲉⲓⲱⲧ. ⲙ̄ⲡⲣ̄ϫⲓⲟⲩ<ⲉ> ⲇⲉ ⲛ̄ⲧⲟϥ ϩⲛ̄ ⲡⲏ- ³ ⲉⲓ ⲙ̄ⲡⲉⲓⲱⲧ, ⲛ̄ⲧⲉⲧⲛ̄ϥⲓ ⲉⲃⲟⲗ. »

ⲓⲏⲥⲟⲩⲥ ⲟⲩⲣⲁⲛ ⁴ ⲡⲉ ⲉϥϩⲏⲡ· ⲡⲉⲭⲣⲓⲥⲧⲟⲥ ⲟⲩⲣⲁⲛ ⲡⲉ ⲉϥⲟⲩⲟⲛϩ ⁵ ⲉⲃⲟⲗ. ⲇⲓⲁ ⲧⲟⲩⲧⲟ ⲓⲏⲥⲟⲩⲥ
ⲙⲉⲛ ϥϣⲟⲟⲡ ⲁⲛ ⁶ ϩⲛ̄ ⲗⲁⲁⲩ ⲛ̄ⲁⲥⲡⲉ, ⲁⲗⲗⲁ ⲡⲉϥⲣⲁⲛ ⲡⲉ ⲓⲏⲥⲟⲩⲥ ⁷ ⲛ̄ⲑⲉ ⲉⲧⲟⲩⲙⲟⲩⲧⲉ
ⲉⲣⲟϥ ⲙ̄ⲙⲟⲥ. ⲡⲉⲭⲣⲓⲥⲧⲟⲥ ⁸ ⲇⲉ ⲡⲉϥⲣⲁⲛ, {ⲡⲉ} ⲙ̄ⲙⲛ̄ⲧⲥⲩⲣⲟⲥ ⲡⲉ ⲙⲉⲥ- ⁹ ⲥⲓⲁⲥ. ⲙ̄ⲙⲛ̄ⲧⲟⲩⲁⲉⲓⲁⲛⲓⲛ
ⲇⲉ ⲡⲉ ⲡⲭⲣⲓⲥⲧⲟⲥ. ⲡⲁⲛ- ¹⁰ ⲧⲱⲥ ⲛ̄ⲕⲟⲟⲩⲉ ⲧⲏⲣⲟⲩ ⲟⲩⲛ̄ⲧⲁϥ ⲙ̄ⲙⲁⲩ ¹¹ ⲕⲁⲧⲁ ⲧⲁⲥⲡⲉ
ⲙ̄ⲡⲟⲩⲁ ⲡⲟⲩⲁ ⲛ̄ϩⲏⲧⲟⲩ. ¹² ⲡⲛⲁⲍⲁⲣⲏⲛⲟⲥ ⲡⲉⲧⲟⲩⲟⲛϩ ⲉⲃⲟⲗ ⲡⲉ ¹³ ⲙ̄ⲡⲡⲉⲑⲏⲡ. ⲡⲉⲭⲣⲓⲥⲧⲟⲥ—
ⲟⲩⲛ̄ⲧⲁϥ ⲟⲩⲟⲛ ⲛⲓⲙ ¹⁴ ϩⲣⲁⲓ̈ ⲛ̄ϩⲏⲧϥ ⲉⲓⲧⲉ ⲣⲱⲙⲉ ⲉⲓⲧⲉ ⲁⲅⲅⲉⲗⲟⲥ ¹⁵ ⲉⲓⲧⲉ ⲙⲩⲥⲧⲏⲣⲓⲟⲛ—ⲁⲩⲱ
ⲡⲉⲓⲱⲧ.

ⲛⲉⲧϫⲱ ¹⁶ ⲙ̄ⲙⲟⲥ ϫⲉ ⲁⲡϫⲟⲉⲓⲥ ⲙⲟⲩ ⲛ̄ϣⲟⲣⲡ ⲁⲩⲱ ¹⁷ ⲁϥⲧⲱⲟⲩⲛ ⲥⲉⲣ̄ⲡⲗⲁⲛⲁ. ⲁϥⲧⲱⲟⲩⲛ
ⲅⲁⲣ ¹⁸ ⲛ̄ϣⲟⲣⲡ ⲁⲩⲱ ⲁϥⲙⲟⲩ. ⲉⲧⲙ̄ ⲟⲩⲁ ϫⲡⲉ ¹⁹ ⲧⲁⲛⲁⲥⲧⲁⲥⲓⲥ ⲛ̄ϣⲟⲣⲡ, ϥⲛⲁⲙⲟⲩ ⲁⲛ. ϥⲟⲛϩ
²⁰ ⲛ̄ϭⲓ ⲡⲛⲟⲩⲧⲉ· ⲛⲉⲣⲉ ⲡⲏ ⲛⲁⲙ<ⲟⲩ>.

ⲙ̄ⲛ̄ ⲗⲁ- ²¹ ⲁⲩ ⲛⲁϩⲱⲡ ⲛ̄ⲟⲩⲛⲟϭ ⲙ̄ⲡⲣⲁⲅⲙⲁ ⲉϥⲧⲁ- ²² ⲉⲓⲏⲩ ϩⲛ̄ ⲟⲩⲛⲟϭ ⲛ̄ϩⲱⲃ, ⲁⲗⲗⲁ ϩⲁϩ
ⲛ̄ⲥⲟⲡ ²³ ⲁⲟⲩⲁ ϩⲛ̄ⲧⲃⲁ ⲉⲧⲉ ⲙⲛ̄ⲧⲟⲩ ⲏⲡⲉ ⲁϥⲛⲟϫⲟⲩ ²⁴ ⲁⲩϩⲱⲃ ϩⲁ ⲟⲩⲁⲥⲥⲁⲣⲓⲟⲛ. ⲧⲁⲉⲓ ⲧⲉ ⲑⲉ
ⲛ̄- ²⁵ ⲧⲯⲩⲭⲏ. ⲟⲩϩⲱⲃ ⲉϥⲧⲁⲉⲓⲏⲩ ⲡⲉ, ⲁⲥϣⲱ- ²⁶ ⲡⲉ ϩⲛ̄ⲛⲟⲩⲥⲱⲙⲁ ⲉϥϣⲏⲥ.

ⲟⲩⲛ̄ ϩⲟⲉⲓⲛⲉ ²⁷ ⲣ̄ ϩⲟⲧⲉ ϫⲉ ⲙⲏⲡⲱⲥ ⲛ̄ⲥⲉⲧⲱⲟⲩⲛ ⲉⲩⲕⲁ- ²⁸ ⲕ ⲁϩⲏⲩ. ⲉⲧⲃⲉ ⲡ[ⲁ]ⲉⲓ ⲥⲉⲟⲩⲱϣ
ⲉⲧⲱⲟⲩⲛ ²⁹ ϩⲛ̄ ⲧⲥⲁⲣⲝ, ⲁⲩⲱ [ⲥ]ⲉⲥⲟⲟⲩⲛ ⲁⲛ ϫⲉ ⲛⲉⲧⲣ̄- ³⁰ ⲫⲟⲣⲉⲓ ⲛ̄ⲧⲥ[ⲁⲣⲝ ⲛ̄ⲧⲟ]ⲟⲩ ⲡⲉ
ⲉⲧⲕⲏⲕ ⲁϩⲏⲩ, ³¹ ⲛⲁⲉⲓ ⲉⲧⲉ[. . . . .] ⲙ̄ⲙⲟⲟⲩ ⲉⲕⲁⲕⲟⲩ ³² ⲉϩⲣⲏⲓ [. . . . ⲉⲧⲕ]ⲁⲕ ⲁϩⲏⲩ ⲁⲛ. « ⲙⲛ̄
ⲥⲁⲣⲝ ³³ [ϩⲓ ⲥⲛⲟϥ ⲛⲁ]ⲣ̄ ⲕⲗⲏⲣⲟⲛⲟⲙⲉⲓ ⲛ̄ⲧⲙⲛ̄ⲧⲉ- ³⁴ [ⲣⲟ ⲙ̄ⲡⲛⲟ]ⲩⲧⲉ. » ⲛⲓⲙ ⲧⲉ ⲧⲁⲉⲓ
ⲉⲧⲛⲁⲕⲗⲏ- ⁵⁷·¹ ⲣⲟⲛⲟⲙⲉⲓ ⲁⲛ; ⲧⲁⲉⲓ ⲉⲧϩⲓⲱⲱⲛ. ⲛⲓⲙ ⲇⲉ ⲧⲉ ² ⲧⲁⲉⲓ ϩⲱⲱⲥ ⲉⲧⲛⲁⲕⲗⲏⲣⲟⲛⲟⲙⲉⲓ;
ⲧⲁ ⲓⲏⲥⲟⲩⲥ ³ ⲧⲉ ⲙⲛ̄ ⲡⲉϥⲥⲛⲟϥ. ⲇⲓⲁ ⲧⲟⲩⲧⲟ ⲡⲉϫⲁϥ ϫⲉ, ⁴ « ⲡⲉⲧⲁⲟⲩⲱⲙ ⲁⲛ ⲛ̄ⲧⲁⲥⲁⲣⲝ
ⲁⲩⲱ ⲛ̄ϥⲥⲱ ⲙ̄- ⁵ ⲡⲁⲥⲛⲟϥ ⲙⲛ̄ⲧⲁϥ ⲱⲛϩ ϩⲣⲁⲓ̈ ⲛ̄ϩⲏⲧϥ. » ⲁϣ ⁶ ⲧⲉ; ⲧⲉϥⲥⲁⲣⲝ ⲡⲉ ⲡⲗⲟⲅⲟⲥ

[18] was executing all things through them [19] as it wished. Truth, [20] which existed from the beginning, is sown everywhere. Indeed [21] many see it being sown, [22] but few are those who see it being reaped.

[23] Some said Mary conceived [24] by the Holy Spirit. They are wrong; [25] they do not know what they are saying. When [26] did a woman ever conceive by a woman? [27] Mary is the virgin whom no [28] power defiled. It is a [29] great anathema of the Hebrews who are the [30] apostles and the apostolic people. [31] This virgin whom no power [32] defiled [. . .]. The powers [33] defiled themselves, and the Lord [would] not have said, [34] "My [Father who is] in heaven," [35] unless [he] had another Father, [36] but simply he (would have) said, "[My Father.]"

[37] The Lord said to the disciples, "[. . .] [56.1] from every house, when we come into the house [2] of the Father. But do not steal it from the house [3] of the Father, and do not make off (with it)."

Jesus is a [4] hidden name; Christ is a revealed name. [5] For this reason Jesus does not exist [6] in any language, but his name is Jesus [7] as he is called. But as for his name Christ, [8] in Syriac it is Messiah. [9] But in Greek it is Christ. Doubtless [10] all others have it [11] according to the language of each one of them. [12] The Nazarene is the one who reveals [13] what is hidden. Christ—and the Father—have everyone [14] within him, be they man or angel [15] or mystery.

Those who say [16] the Lord died first and (then) [17] rose are in error. For he rose [18] first and (then) died. If one does not acquire [19] the resurrection first, he will not die. God lives; [20] that one would die.

No one [21] will hide a great matter that is [22] valuable in a great thing, but many times [23] one has cast invaluable things [24] into something (worth) less than a penny. This is like [25] the soul. It is a valuable thing, and it came about [26] in a despised body.

Some [27] fear lest they rise naked. [28] For this reason they desire to rise [29] in the flesh, and they do not know that those who [30] carry flesh upon themselves are naked, [31] those who [. . .] them being naked [32] [. . . who] are not naked. "Flesh [33] [and blood will] not inherit the kingdom [34] [of] God." What is it that you will [57.1] not inherit? That which is upon us. What is [2] it also that will inherit? That which belongs to Jesus [3] and his blood. For this reason he said, [4] "The one who does not eat my flesh and drink [5] my blood does not have life within him." What [6] is it? His flesh is the Word, and his blood [7] is the Holy Spirit. The one who has received these things has

ⲁⲩⲱ ⲡⲉϥⲥⲛⲟϥ ⁷ ⲡⲉ ⲡⲡⲛⲉⲩⲙⲁ ⲉⲧⲟⲩⲁⲁⲃ. ⲡⲉⲛⲧⲁϩϫⲓ ⲛⲁⲉⲓ ⲟⲩⲛ- ⁸ ⲧⲉϥ ⲧⲣⲟⲫⲏ ⲁⲩⲱ
ⲟⲩⲛⲧⲁϥ ⲥⲱ ϩⲓ ⲃ̄ⲥⲱ. ⁹ ⲁⲛⲟⲕ ϯϭⲛ ⲁⲣⲓⲕⲉ ⲁⲛⲕⲟⲟⲩⲉ ⲉⲧϫⲱ ⲙ̄ⲙⲟⲥ ¹⁰ ϫⲉ ⲥⲛⲁⲧⲱⲟⲩⲛ ⲁⲛ.
ⲉⲓⲧⲉ ⲛ̄ⲧⲟⲟⲩ ⲙ̄ⲡⲉⲥ- ¹¹ ⲛⲁⲩ ⲥⲉϣⲟⲟⲡ ϩⲛ ⲟⲩϣⲧⲁ. ⲕ̄ϫⲱ ⲙ̄ⲙⲟⲥ ¹² ϫⲉ ⲧⲥⲁⲣⲝ ⲛⲁⲧⲱⲟⲩⲛ ⲁⲛ,
ⲁⲗⲗⲁ ϫⲟⲟⲥ ⲉⲣⲟ- ¹³ ⲉⲓ ϫⲉ ⲁϣ ⲡⲉⲧⲛⲁⲧⲱⲟⲩⲛ ϣⲓⲛⲁ ⲉⲛⲁⲧⲁ- ¹⁴ ⲉⲓⲟⲕ; ⲕ̄ϫⲱ ⲙ̄ⲙⲟⲥ ϫⲉ
ⲡⲡⲛⲉⲩⲙⲁ ϩⲛ ⲧⲥⲁⲣⲝ, ¹⁵ ⲁⲩⲱ ⲡⲉⲉⲓⲕⲉⲟⲩⲟⲉⲓⲛ ⲡⲉ ϩⲛ ⲧⲥⲁⲣⲝ. ⲟⲩⲗⲟ- ¹⁶ ⲅⲟⲥ ⲡⲉ ⲡⲉⲉⲓⲕⲉ ⲉϥϩⲛ
ⲧⲥⲁⲣⲝ ϫⲉ ⲡⲉⲧⲕⲛⲁ- ¹⁷ ϫⲟⲟⲥ, ⲉⲕϫⲉ ⲗⲁⲁⲩ ⲁⲛ ⲙ̄ⲡⲃⲟⲗ ⲛ̄ⲧⲥⲁⲣⲝ. ¹⁸ ϩⲁⲡⲥ̄ ⲡⲉ ⲉⲧϣⲟⲩⲛ ϩⲛ
ⲧⲉⲉⲓⲥⲁⲣⲝ ⲉϩⲱⲃ ¹⁹ ⲛⲓⲙ ϣⲟⲟⲡ ⲛ̄ϩⲏⲧⲥ̄ ϩⲙ ⲡⲉⲉⲓⲕⲟⲥⲙⲟⲥ. ²⁰ ⲛⲉⲧϯ ϩⲓⲱⲟⲩ ⲛ̄ⲛϩⲃⲥⲱ ⲥⲉⲥⲟⲧⲡ
ⲁⲛⲛ̄- ²¹ ϩⲃⲥⲱ. ϩⲛ ⲧⲙⲛ̄ⲧⲉⲣⲟ ⲛ̄ⲙⲡⲏⲩⲉ ⲛ̄ϩⲃⲥⲱ ²² ⲥⲉⲥⲟⲧⲡ ⲁⲛⲉⲛⲧⲁⲩⲧⲁⲁⲩ ϩⲓⲱⲟⲩ.

ϩⲓⲧⲛ̄ ²³ ⲟⲩⲙⲟⲟⲩ ⲙⲛ̄ ⲟⲩⲕⲱϩⲧ ⲉⲩⲧⲟⲩⲃⲟ ⲙ̄ⲡⲙⲁ ²⁴ ⲧⲏⲣϥ—ⲛⲉⲧⲟⲩⲟⲛϩ ϩⲓⲧⲛ̄ ⲛⲉⲧⲟⲩⲟⲛϩ
ⲉ- ²⁵ ⲃⲟⲗ, ⲛⲉⲑⲏⲡ ϩⲓⲧⲛ̄ ⲛⲉⲑⲏⲡ. ⲟⲩⲛ ϩⲟ- ²⁶ ⲉⲓⲛⲉ ⲉⲩϩⲏⲡ ϩⲓⲧⲛ̄ ⲛⲉⲧⲟⲩⲟⲛϩ ⲉⲃⲟⲗ. ²⁷ ⲟⲩⲙ̄ⲙⲟⲟⲩ
ϩⲛ ⲟⲩⲙⲟⲟⲩ, ⲟⲩⲛ̄ ⲕⲱϩⲧ ²⁸ ϩⲛ̄ⲛⲟⲩⲭⲣⲓⲥⲙⲁ.

ⲁⲓⲏⲥⲟⲩⲥ ϥⲓⲧⲟⲩ ⲛ̄ϫⲓⲟⲩⲉ ²⁹ ⲧⲏⲣⲟⲩ. ⲙ̄ⲡⲉϥⲟⲩⲱ[ⲛϩ] ⲅⲁⲣ ⲉⲃⲟⲗ ⲛ̄ⲑⲉ ³⁰ ⲉⲛⲉϥϣⲟⲟⲡ
[ⲛϩ]ⲏ[ⲧⲥ, ⲁ]ⲗⲗⲁ ⲛ̄ⲧⲁϥⲟⲩⲱⲛϩ ³¹ ⲉⲃⲟⲗ ⲛ̄ⲑⲉ ⲉⲧ[ⲟⲩⲛⲁϣ]ϭ̄ⲙ ϭⲟⲙ ⲛ̄ⲛⲁⲩ ³² ⲉⲣⲟϥ ⲛ̄ϩⲏⲧⲥ̄.
ⲛ[ⲁⲉⲓ ⲇⲉ ⲧⲏ]ⲣⲟⲩ ⲁϥⲟⲩ- ³³ ⲱⲛϩ ⲉⲃⲟⲗ ⲛⲁⲩ ⲁϥ[ⲟⲩⲱⲛϩ] ⲉⲃⲟⲗ ⲛ̄[ⲛ]- ³⁴ ⲛⲟϭ ϩⲱⲥ
ⲛⲟϭ· ⲁϥⲟⲩⲱ[ⲛϩ ⲉⲃⲟⲗ ⲛ̄]- ³⁵ ⲛ̄ⲕⲟⲩⲉⲓ ϩⲱⲥ ⲕⲟⲩⲉⲓ· ⲁϥ[ⲟⲩⲱⲛϩ ⲉⲃⲟⲗ] ⁵⁸·¹ [ⲛ̄ⲛ]ⲁⲅⲅⲉ[ⲗ]-
ⲟⲥ ϩⲱⲥ ⲁⲅⲅⲉⲗⲟⲥ ⲁⲩⲱ ² ⲛ̄ⲣⲣⲱⲙⲉ ϩⲱⲥ ⲣⲱⲙⲉ. ⲉⲧⲃⲉ ⲡⲁⲉⲓ ⲁⲡⲉϥ- ³ ⲗⲟⲅⲟⲥ ⲁϥϩⲟⲡϥ ⲉⲟⲩⲟⲛ
ⲛⲓⲙ. ϩⲟⲉⲓⲛⲉ ⁴ ⲙⲉⲛ ⲁⲩⲛⲁⲩ ⲉⲣⲟϥ, ⲉⲩⲙⲉⲉⲩⲉ ϫⲉ ⲛⲁⲩⲛⲁⲩ ⁵ ⲉⲣⲟⲟⲩ ⲙ̄ⲙⲓⲛ ⲙ̄ⲙⲟⲟⲩ. ⲁⲗⲗⲁ
ⲛ̄ⲧⲁⲣⲉϥⲟⲩ- ⁶ ⲱⲛϩ ⲉⲃⲟⲗ ⲛ̄ⲛⲉϥⲙⲁⲑⲏⲧⲏⲥ ϩⲛ̄ⲛⲟⲩⲉⲟ- ⁷ ⲟⲩ ϩⲓϫⲙ ⲡⲧⲟⲟⲩ, ⲛⲉϥⲟ ⲁⲛ ⲛ̄ⲕⲟⲩⲉⲓ.
ⲁϥ- ⁸ ϣⲱⲡⲉ ⲛ̄ⲛⲟϭ ⲁⲗⲗⲁ ⲛ̄ⲧⲁϥⲣ̄ ⲙ̄ⲙⲁⲑⲏⲧⲏⲥ ⁹ ⲛ̄ⲛⲟϭ ϫⲉⲕⲁⲁⲥ ⲉⲩⲛⲁϣϭⲙ ϭⲟⲙ ⲛ̄ⲛⲁⲩ ¹⁰
ⲉⲣⲟϥ ⲉϥⲟ ⲛ̄ⲛⲟϭ.

ⲡⲉϫⲁϥ ⲙ̄ⲫⲟⲟⲩ ⲉⲧⲙ̄- ¹¹ ⲙⲁⲩ ϩⲛ ⲧⲉⲩⲭⲁⲣⲓⲥⲧⲉⲓⲁ, ϫⲉ « ⲡⲉⲛⲧⲁϩϩⲱⲧⲣ̄ ¹² ⲙ̄ⲡⲧⲉⲗⲉⲓⲟⲥ
ⲡⲟⲩⲟⲉⲓⲛ ⲉⲡⲡⲛⲉⲩⲙⲁ ⲉⲧⲟⲩ- ¹³ ⲁⲁⲃ ϩⲟⲧⲣ̄ ⲛ̄ⲁⲅⲅⲉⲗⲟⲥ ⲉⲣⲟⲛ ϩⲱⲱⲛ ⲁⲛ- ¹⁴ ϩⲓⲕⲱⲛ. »
ⲙ̄ⲡⲣ̄ⲕⲁⲧⲁⲫⲣⲟⲛⲉⲓ ⲙ̄ⲡⲉⲓⲉⲓⲃ, ⲁϫⲛ̄- ¹⁵ ⲧϥ ⲅⲁⲣ ⲙⲛ̄ ϣϭⲟⲙ ⲉⲛⲁⲩ ⲉⲡⲣⲟ. ⲙⲛ̄ ⲗⲁⲁⲩ ¹⁶ ⲛⲁϣϯ
ⲡⲉϥⲟⲩⲟⲉⲓ ⲉϩⲟⲩⲛ ⲉⲡⲣⲣⲟ ⲉϥ- ¹⁷ ⲕⲏⲕⲁϩⲏⲩ.

ⲡⲣ̄ⲙⲡⲉ ⲛⲁϣⲉ ⲛⲉϥϣⲏⲣⲉ ¹⁸ ⲛ̄ϩⲟⲩⲟ ⲁⲡⲣ̄ⲙ̄ⲕⲁϩ. ⲉϣϫⲉ ⲛ̄ϣⲏⲣⲉ ⲛⲁ- ¹⁹ ⲇⲁⲙ ⲛⲁϣⲱⲟⲩ,
ⲕⲁⲓⲧⲟⲓⲅⲉ ϣⲁⲩⲙⲟⲩ, ⲡⲟ- ²⁰ ⲥⲱ ⲙⲁⲗⲗⲟⲛ ⲛ̄ϣⲏⲣⲉ ⲙ̄ⲡⲧⲉⲗⲉⲓⲟⲥ ⲣ̄ⲣⲱ- ²¹ ⲙⲉ, ⲛⲁⲉⲓ ⲉⲙⲁⲩⲙⲟⲩ
ⲁⲗⲗⲁ ⲥⲉϫⲡⲟ ⲙ̄ⲙⲟ- ²² ⲟⲩ ⲟⲩⲟⲉⲓϣ ⲛⲓⲙ; ⲡⲉⲓⲱⲧ ⲧⲁⲙⲉⲓⲟ ϣⲏ- ²³ ⲣⲉ, ⲁⲩⲱ ⲡϣⲏⲣⲉ ⲙⲛ̄
ϭⲟⲙ ⲙ̄ⲙⲟϥ ⲛ̄ϥⲧⲁ- ²⁴ ⲙⲓⲉ ϣⲏⲣⲉ. ⲡⲉⲛⲧⲁⲩϫⲡⲟϥ ⲅⲁⲣ ⲙⲛ̄ ϭⲟⲙ ²⁵ ⲙ̄ⲙⲟϥ ⲛ̄ϥϫⲡⲟ, ⲁⲗⲗⲁ
ⲉⲡϣⲏⲣⲉ ϫⲡⲟ ²⁶ ⲛⲁϥ ⲛ̄ϩⲛ̄ⲥⲛⲏⲩ ⲛ̄ϩⲛ̄ϣⲏⲣⲉ ⲁⲛ. ⲛⲉⲧⲟⲩ- ²⁷ ϫⲡⲟ ⲙ̄ⲙⲟⲟⲩ ⲧⲏⲣⲟⲩ
ϩⲙ ⲡⲕⲟⲥⲙⲟⲥ ²⁸ ⲉⲩϫⲡⲟ ⲙ̄ⲙⲟⲟ[ⲩ] ⲉⲃⲟⲗ ϩⲛ ⲧⲫⲩⲥⲓⲥ, ⲁⲩ- ²⁹ ⲱ ⲛ̄ⲕⲟⲟⲩⲉ ϩⲙ̄ [ⲡⲁⲉ]ⲓ
[ⲉⲧ]ⲟⲩϫⲡⲟ ⲙ̄ⲙⲟⲟⲩ ³⁰ ⲉⲃⲟⲗ ⲛ̄ϩⲏⲧϥ [......]ϣ ⲉⲃⲟⲗ ⲙ̄ⲙⲁⲩ. ³¹ ⲉⲡⲣⲱⲙⲉ ϫ̣[ⲓ

57.8 ⲃ̄ⲥⲱ: read ϩⲃⲥⲱ.

57.10 ⲉⲓⲧⲉ: read ⲉⲓⲧⲁ (following Till)?

57.34 [ⲛ̄]: superlinear stroke visible.

58.15 ⲡⲣⲟ: read ⲡ̄ⲣⲣⲟ?

⁸ nourishment, and he has drink and clothing. ⁹ I find fault with those who say ¹⁰ that it will not rise. Therefore, both ¹¹ of them are in error. You say ¹² that the flesh will not rise, but tell ¹³ me what will rise so that we might glorify ¹⁴ you? You say that the spirit is in the flesh, ¹⁵ and this light is also in the flesh. This also is a ¹⁶ word in the flesh, since (regardless of) what you shall ¹⁷ say, you say nothing outside of the flesh. ¹⁸ It is necessary to rise in this flesh, since ¹⁹ everything dwells in it in this world. ²⁰ Those who clothe themselves in garments are better than the ²¹ garments. In the kingdom of heaven the garments ²² are better than those who wear them.

Through ²³ water and fire every place is purified ²⁴—that which is revealed through that which is revealed, ²⁵ that which is hidden through that which is hidden. Some ²⁶ are hidden through that which is revealed. ²⁷ Water in water, there is fire ²⁸ in a chrism.

Jesus took them ²⁹ all stealthily. For he did not appear as ³⁰ he was, but he appeared ³¹ as one that could not be seen. ³² [But to each of these] he ³³ appeared. He [appeared] to [the] ³⁴ great as great; he appeared to ³⁵ the small as small; he [appeared ⁵⁸·¹ to the] angels as an angel and ² to humans as a human. For this reason his ³ Word hid itself from everyone. Some ⁴ actually saw him, though they thought that they were seeing ⁵ themselves. But after he appeared ⁶ to his disciples in glory ⁷ upon the mountain, he was not small. He had ⁸ become great, but he made the disciples ⁹ great so that they might be able to see ¹⁰ him as someone great.

He said on that day ¹¹ in the Eucharist, "The one who has joined ¹² the perfect light to the Holy Spirit ¹³ joins angels to us also, (we who are) the ¹⁴ images." Do not despise the lamb, since without ¹⁵ it it is not possible to see the <king.> No one ¹⁶ will be able to approach the king if he ¹⁷ is naked.

The heavenly man has more children ¹⁸ than the earthly man. If the children of Adam ¹⁹ are numerous, although they indeed die, how much more ²⁰ (numerous are) the children of the perfect man, ²¹ those who do not die but are ²² always born? The Father creates a son, ²³ and the son is not able to create ²⁴ a son. For the one who is created is not able ²⁵ to create, but the son creates ²⁶ brothers for himself, not children. All those who are ²⁷ created in the world ²⁸ are created in nature, and ²⁹ others in that which they are born ³⁰ are [. . .] there. ³¹ Man receives nourishment

ⲙ̄ⲡⲥⲟ]ⲉⲓϣ ⲉⲃⲟⲗ ϩⲙ̄ ⲡⲣ̄- ³² [ⲣ]ⲏⲧ ⲉϩⲟ[ⲩⲛ ⲉⲡⲧⲟ]ⲡⲟⲥ ⲙ̄ⲡⲥⲁ ⲛⲧⲡⲉ ³³ [. . . . .] ⲙ̄ⲙⲟϥ
ⲉⲃⲟⲗ ϩⲛ̄ ⲧⲧⲁⲡⲣⲟ. ³⁴ [ⲁⲩⲱ ⲉⲛⲉ]ⲁⲡⲗⲟⲅⲟⲥ ⲉⲓ ⲉⲃⲟⲗ ⲙ̄ⲙⲁⲩ, ⁵⁹·¹ ⲛⲉϥⲛⲁⲥⲟⲉⲓϣ ⲉⲃⲟⲗ ϩⲛ̄
ⲧⲧⲁⲡⲣⲟ, ⲁⲩ[ⲱ] ² ⲛⲉϥⲛⲁϣⲱⲡⲉ ⲛ̄ⲧⲉⲗⲉⲓⲟⲥ. ⲛ̄ⲧⲉⲗⲉⲓⲟⲥ ⲅⲁⲣ ³ ϩⲓⲧⲛ̄ ⲟⲩⲡⲉⲓ ⲉⲩⲱ ⲁⲩⲱ
ⲉⲩⲭⲡⲟ. ⲇⲓⲁ ⲧⲟⲩⲧⲟ ⁴ ⲁⲛⲟⲛ ϩⲱⲱⲛ ⲧⲛ̄ϯ ⲡⲓ ⲉⲣⲛ̄ ⲛ̄ⲛⲉⲣⲏⲩ, ⁵ ⲉⲛϫⲓ ⲙ̄ⲡⲱ ⲉⲃⲟⲗ ϩⲛ̄ ⲧⲭⲁⲣⲓⲥ
ⲉⲧϩⲛ̄ ⲛ̄- ⁶ ⲛ̄ⲛⲉⲣⲏⲩ.

ⲛⲉ ⲟⲩⲛ̄ ϣⲟⲙⲧⲉ ⲙⲟⲟϣⲉ ⲙⲛ̄ ⁷ ⲡϫⲟⲉⲓⲥ ⲟⲩⲟⲉⲓϣ ⲛⲓⲙ· ⲙⲁⲣⲓⲁ ⲧⲉϥⲙⲁⲁⲩ ⁸ ⲁⲩⲱ ⲧⲉⲥⲥⲱⲛⲉ
ⲁⲩⲱ ⲙⲁⲅⲇⲁⲗⲏⲛⲏ ⲧⲁ- ⁹ ⲉⲓ ⲉⲧⲟⲩⲙⲟⲩⲧⲉ ⲉⲣⲟⲥ ϫⲉ ⲧⲉϥⲕⲟⲓⲛⲱⲛⲟⲥ. ¹⁰ ⲙⲁⲣⲓⲁ ⲅⲁⲣ ⲧⲉ
ⲧⲉϥⲥⲱⲛⲉ, ⲁⲩⲱ ⲧⲉϥⲙⲁⲁⲩ ¹¹ ⲧⲉ, ⲁⲩⲱ ⲧⲉϥϩⲱⲧⲣⲉ ⲧⲉ.

« ⲡⲉⲓⲱⲧ » ⲙⲛ̄ « ⲡϣⲏ- ¹² ⲣⲉ » ⲛ̄ϩⲁⲡⲗⲟⲩⲛ ⲛⲉ ⲣ̄ⲣⲁⲛ. « ⲡⲡⲛⲉⲩⲙⲁ ⲉⲧⲟⲩⲁⲁⲃ » ¹³ ⲟⲩⲣⲁⲛ
ⲡⲉ ⲛ̄ⲇⲓⲡⲗⲟⲩⲛ. ⲥⲉϣⲟⲟⲡ ⲅⲁⲣ ⲙ̄- ¹⁴ ⲙⲁ ⲛⲓⲙ. ⲥⲉⲙ̄ⲡⲥⲁ ⲛⲧⲡⲉ· ⲥⲉⲙ̄ⲡⲥⲁ ⲙⲡⲓ- ¹⁵ ⲧⲛ̄· ⲥⲉϩⲛ̄
ⲡⲉⲑⲏⲡ· ⲥⲉϩⲛ̄ ⲛⲉⲧⲟⲩⲟⲛϩ ¹⁶ ⲉⲃⲟⲗ. ⲡⲡⲛⲉⲩⲙⲁ ⲉⲧⲟⲩⲁⲁⲃ ϥϩⲙ̄ ⲡⲟⲩⲱⲛϩ ¹⁷ ⲉⲃⲟⲗ· ϥϩⲙ̄ ⲡⲥⲁ
ⲙⲡⲓⲧⲛ̄· ϥϩⲙ̄ ⲡⲉⲑⲏⲡ· ¹⁸ ϥϩⲙ̄ ⲡⲥⲁ ⲛⲧⲡⲉ.

ⲥⲉϣⲙ̄ϣⲉ ⲛ̄ⲛⲉⲧⲟⲩ- ¹⁹ ⲁⲁⲃ ϩⲓⲧⲛ̄ ⲛ̄ⲇⲩⲛⲁⲙⲓⲥ ⲙ̄ⲡⲟⲛⲏⲣⲟⲛ. ²⁰ ⲥⲉⲟ ⲅⲁⲣ ⲛ̄ⲃⲁⲗⲉ ϩⲓⲧⲙ̄ ⲡⲡⲛⲉⲩⲙⲁ
ⲉⲧⲟⲩⲁⲁⲃ ²¹ ϫⲉⲕⲁⲁⲥ ⲉⲩⲛⲁⲙⲉⲉⲩⲉ ϫⲉ ⲉⲩⲣ̄ϩⲩⲡⲏⲣⲉ- ²² ⲧⲉⲓ ⲛ̄ⲛⲟⲩⲣⲱⲙⲉ ϩⲟⲡⲟⲧⲉ ⲉⲩⲉⲓⲣⲉ
ⲛ̄ⲛⲉ- ²³ ⲧⲟⲩⲁⲁⲃ. ⲉⲧⲃⲉ ⲡⲁⲉⲓ ⲁⲩ⟦ⲙ̄⟧ⲙⲁⲑⲏⲧⲏⲥ ⲣ̄- ²⁴ ⲁⲓⲧⲉⲓ ⲙ̄ⲡϫⲟⲉⲓⲥ ⲛ̄ⲛⲟⲩϩⲟⲟⲩ ⲉⲧⲃⲉ ⲟⲩ-
²⁵ ϩⲱⲃ ⲛ̄ⲧⲉ ⲡⲕⲟⲥⲙⲟⲥ. ⲡⲉϫⲁϥ ⲛⲁϥ ϫⲉ, ²⁶ « ⲉⲣⲓⲁⲓⲧⲉⲓ ⲛ̄ⲧⲉⲕⲙⲁⲁⲩ, ⲁⲩⲱ ⲥⲛⲁϯ ⲛⲁⲕ ²⁷ ⲉⲃⲟⲗ
ϩⲛ̄ ⲁⲗⲗⲟⲧⲣⲓⲟⲛ. »

ⲡⲉϫⲉ ⲛⲁⲡⲟⲥⲧⲟ- ²⁸ ⲗⲟⲥ ⲛ̄ⲛ̄ⲙⲁⲑⲏⲧⲏⲥ ϫⲉ, « ⲧⲙ̄ⲡⲣⲟⲥⲫⲟ- ²⁹ ⲣⲁ ⲧⲏⲣⲥ̄ ⲙⲁⲣⲉⲥϫⲡⲟ [ⲛ̄]ⲁⲥ
ⲛ̄ⲟⲩϩⲙⲟⲩ. » ³⁰ ⲛⲉⲩⲙⲟⲩⲧⲉ [ⲉⲧⲥⲟⲫⲓ]ⲁ ϫⲉ « ϩⲙⲟⲩ. » ⲁϫⲛ̄ⲧⲥ̄ ³¹ ⲙⲁⲣⲉ ⲡⲣⲟⲥⲫ[ⲟⲣⲁ ϣⲱ]
ⲡⲉ ⲉϥϣⲏⲡ. ⲧⲥⲟ- ³² ⲫⲓⲁ ⲇⲉ ⲟⲩⲥⲧⲉⲓⲣ[ⲁ ⲧⲉ ⲁϫⲛ̄] ϣⲏⲣⲉ. ⲇⲓⲁ ⲧⲟⲩ- ³³ ⲧⲟ ⲉⲩⲙⲟⲩⲧⲉ ⲉⲣⲟ[ⲥ
ϫⲉ « ⲡⲕⲉ]ⲥⲉⲡⲉⲓ ⲛ̄- ³⁴ ϩⲙⲟⲩ. » ⲡⲙⲁ ⲉⲧⲟⲩⲛⲁϣ[. . . . .]ⲛϣ ³⁵ ⲛ̄ⲧⲟⲩϩⲉ ⲡⲡⲛⲉⲩⲙⲁ ⲉⲧⲟⲩⲁⲁⲃ
[. . . . . . ⁶⁰·¹ ⲁⲩ]ⲱ ⲛⲁϣ[ⲉ] ⲛⲉⲥϣⲏⲣⲉ.

ⲡⲉⲧⲉⲩⲛ̄ⲧⲁϥϥ ² ⲛ̄ϭⲓ ⲡⲉⲓⲱⲧ ⲛⲁ ⲡϣⲏⲣⲉ ⲛⲉ, ⲁⲩⲱ ⲛ̄ⲧⲟϥ ϩⲱ- ³ ⲱϥ, ⲡϣⲏⲣⲉ ⲉⲛ ϩⲟⲥⲟⲛ ϥⲟ
ⲛ̄ⲕⲟⲩⲉⲓ, ⲙⲁⲩ- ⁴ ⲡⲓⲥⲧⲉⲩⲉ ⲛⲁϥ ⲁⲛⲉⲧⲉ ⲛⲟⲩϥ. ϩⲟⲧⲁⲛ ⲉϥ- ⁵ ϣⲁϣⲱⲡⲉ ⲣ̄ⲣⲱⲙⲉ, ϣⲁⲣⲉ
ⲡⲉϥⲉⲓⲱⲧ ϯ ⲛⲁϥ ⁶ ⲛⲉⲧⲉⲩⲛ̄ⲧⲁⲃⲥⲉ ⲧⲏⲣⲟⲩ.

ⲛⲉⲧⲥⲟⲣⲙ, ⲛⲉⲧⲉ ⲡ- ⁷ ⲡⲛⲉⲩⲙⲁ ϫⲡⲟ ⲙ̄ⲙⲟⲟⲩ, ϣⲁⲩⲥⲱⲣⲙ ⲟⲛ ⲉⲃⲟⲗ ⁸ ϩⲓⲧⲟⲟⲧϥ ⲇⲓⲁ ⲧⲟⲩⲧⲟ
ⲉⲃⲟⲗ ϩⲓⲧⲙ̄ ⲡⲓⲡⲛⲉⲩⲙⲁ ⁹ ⲟⲩⲱⲧ ϥϫⲉⲣⲟ ⲛ̄ϭⲓ ⲡⲕⲱϩⲧ ⲁⲩⲱ ϥⲱϣⲙ̄.

¹⁰ ⲕⲉⲟⲩⲁ ⲡⲉ ⲉⲭⲁⲙⲱⲑ ⲁⲩⲱ ⲕⲉⲟⲩⲁ ⲡⲉ ¹¹ ⲉⲭⲙⲱⲑ. ⲉⲭⲁⲙⲱⲑ ⲧⲉ ⲧⲥⲟⲫⲓⲁ ϩⲁⲡⲗⲱⲥ, ¹²
ⲉⲭⲙⲱⲑ ⲇⲉ ⲧⲉ ⲧⲥⲟⲫⲓⲁ ⲙ̄ⲡⲙⲟⲩ ⲉⲧⲉ ⲧⲁ- ¹³ ⲉⲓ ⲧⲉ {ⲧⲥⲟⲫⲓⲁ ⲙ̄ⲡⲙⲟⲩ ⲉⲧⲉ ⲧⲁⲉⲓ ⲧⲉ} ⲉⲧⲥⲟ- ¹⁴
ⲟⲩⲛ ⲙ̄ⲡⲙⲟⲩ ⲧⲁⲉⲓ ⲉⲧⲟⲩⲙⲟⲩⲧⲉ ⲉⲣⲟⲥ ϫⲉ ¹⁵ « ⲧⲕⲟⲩⲉⲓ ⲛ̄ⲥⲟⲫⲓⲁ. »

ⲟⲩⲛ̄ ϩⲛ̄ⲑⲏⲣⲓⲟⲛ ϣⲟⲟⲡ ¹⁶ ⲉⲩϩⲩⲡⲟⲧⲁⲥⲥⲉ ⲙ̄ⲡⲣⲱⲙⲉ, ⲛ̄ⲑⲉ ⲙ̄ⲡⲙⲁⲥⲉ ¹⁷ ⲙⲛ̄ ⲡⲉⲓⲱ ⲙⲛ̄ ϩⲛ̄ⲕⲟⲟⲩⲉ
ⲛ̄ⲧⲉⲉⲓⲙⲓⲛⲉ. ⲟⲩ- ¹⁸ ⲛ̄ ϩⲛ̄ⲕⲟⲟⲩⲉ ϣⲟⲟⲡ ⲉⲩϩⲩⲡⲟⲧⲁⲥⲥⲉ ⲁⲛ, ¹⁹ ⲉⲩⲟⲩⲁⲧ ϩⲛ̄ ⲛⲉⲣⲏⲙⲓⲁ. ⲡⲣⲱⲙⲉ

60.6 ⲛⲉⲧⲉⲩⲛ̄ⲧⲁⲃⲥⲉ: read ⲛⲉⲧⲉⲩⲛ̄ⲧⲁϥⲥⲉ

from the promise [32] in [the] heavenly [place . . .] [33] him from the mouth. [34] [And if] the word had gone forth from there, [59.1] it would be nourished from the mouth, and [2] it would be perfect. For the perfect [3] conceive and give birth by a kiss. Because of this [4] we too kiss one other, [5] since we conceive from the grace that is in [6] one another.

There were three who walked with [7] the Lord always: Mary, his mother, [8] and her sister, and Magdalene, the one [9] who is called his companion. [10] For Mary is his sister, and she is his mother, [11] and she is his union.

"The Father" and "the Son" [12] are unified names. "The Holy Spirit" [13] is a double name. For they dwell in every [14] place. They are above; they are below; [15] they are in what is hidden; they are in what is manifest. [16] The Holy Spirit is in what is manifest; [17] it is in what is below; it is in what is hidden; [18] it is in what is above.

The saints [19] are worshipped by evil powers. [20] They are blinded by the Holy Spirit [21] so that they might think that they serve [22] a man when they make the saints (objects of worship). [23] Because of this a disciple [24] asked the Lord one day about a [25] worldly thing. He said to him, [26] "Ask your mother, and she will give you [27] another person's (things)."

The apostles [28] said to the disciples, "Our whole offering, [29] may it produce salt." [30] [Wisdom] is called "salt." Without it [31] an offering [is] not acceptable. But Wisdom [32] [is] barren, [without] child. For this reason [33] [she] is called "[the abundance] of salt." [34] The place where they will [. . .] [35] in their (own) way, the Holy Spirit [. . . [60.1] and] her children are numerous.

What the father has [2] belongs to the son, and the son alone, [3] as long as he is small, is not [4] entrusted with the things that are his. When he [5] becomes a man, his father gives him [6] all the things he has.

Those who stray, those whom the [7] Spirit bears, they stray by [8] means of it. For this reason, by means of the same spirit, [9] fire burns and is quenched.

[10] Echamoth is one (being), and Echmoth is another. [11] Echamoth is simply Wisdom, [12] but Echmoth is Wisdom of death, that [13] is, one who knows [14] death, the one who is called [15] "the little Wisdom."

There are submissive animals, [16] like the calf [17] and the donkey and others like these. There are [18] others that are not submissive, [19] which are alone in deserts. Man

60.15 "submissive animals": literally, "animals placed under man."

ⲥⲕⲁⲉⲓ ⲛ̅- ²⁰ ⲧⲥⲱϣⲉ ϩⲓⲧⲛ̅ ⲛ̅ⲑⲏⲣⲓⲟⲛ ⲉⲧⲣ̅ⲩⲡⲟⲧⲁⲥⲥⲉ, ²¹ ⲁⲩⲱ ⲉⲃⲟⲗ ϩⲙ̅ ⲡⲁⲉⲓ ϥⲥⲟⲉⲓϣ ⲛ̅ⲧⲟϥ
ⲙⲛ̅ ⲛ̅- ²² ⲑⲏⲣⲓⲟⲛ, ⲉⲓⲧⲉ ⲛⲉⲧⲣ̅ⲩⲡⲟⲧⲁⲥⲥⲉ ⲉⲓⲧⲉ ⲛⲉⲧ- ²³ ⲣ̅ⲩⲡⲟⲧⲁⲥⲥⲉ ⲁⲛ. ⲧⲁⲉⲓ ⲧⲉ ⲑⲉ
ⲙ̅ⲡⲧⲉⲗⲓⲟⲥ ²⁴ ⲣ̅ⲣⲱⲙⲉ ϩⲓⲧⲛ̅ ϩⲛ̅ⲇⲩⲛⲁⲙⲓⲥ ⲉⲧⲣ̅ⲩⲡⲟⲧⲁⲥ- ²⁵ ⲥⲉ ⲉϥⲥⲕⲁⲉⲓ, ⲟⲩⲟⲛ ⲛⲓⲙ ⲉϥⲥⲟⲃⲧⲉ
ⲉⲧⲣⲟⲩ- ²⁶ ϣⲱⲡⲉ. ⲉⲧⲃⲉ ⲡⲁⲉⲓ ⲅⲁⲣ ⲉⲡⲙⲁ ⲧⲏⲣϥ ⲁϩⲉ- ²⁷ ⲣⲁⲧϥ, ⲉⲓⲧⲉ ⲛⲉⲧⲛⲁⲛⲟⲩⲟⲩ ⲉⲓⲧⲉ
ⲛⲉⲑⲟⲟⲩ, ²⁸ ⲁⲩⲱ ⲛⲟⲩⲛⲁⲙ ⲙⲛ̅ ⲛ̅ϭⲃⲟⲩⲣ. ⲡⲉⲡⲛⲉⲩⲙⲁ ⲉⲧⲟⲩ- ²⁹ ⲁⲁⲃ ϥⲙⲟⲟⲛⲉ ⲟ[ⲩⲟ]ⲛ ⲛⲓⲙ,
ⲁⲩⲱ ϥⲣⲁⲣⲭⲉⲓ ³⁰ ⲛ̅ⲛⲇⲩⲛⲁⲙⲓⲥ ⲧ[ⲏⲣⲟ]ⲩ̅, [ⲛ̅]ⲉⲧⲣ̅ⲩⲡⲟⲧⲁⲥⲥⲉ ³¹ ⲁⲩⲱ ⲛⲉⲧⲣ̅ⲩⲡ[ⲟⲧⲁⲥⲥⲉ ⲁ]ⲛ
ⲙⲛ̅ ⲛⲉⲧⲟⲩⲁⲧ. ³² ⲕⲁⲓ ⲅⲁⲣ ϥϭⲱϣ[. . . .]ϣ ⲱⲧⲡ ⲙ̅ⲙⲟⲟⲩ ⲉ- ³³ ϩⲟⲩⲛ ϫⲉ[ⲕⲁⲁⲥ . .]
ϣⲁⲛⲟⲩⲱϣ, ⲛⲟⲩϣ- ³⁴ [ⲃ]ⲱⲕ [ⲉⲃⲟⲗ.]

[ⲡⲉⲛⲧ]ⲁⲩⲡⲗⲁⲥⲥⲉ ⲙ̅ⲙⲟϥ ⲛⲉ ³⁵ [. . . ⲁⲩⲱ ⲛ]ⲉⲕⲛⲁϩⲉ ⲁⲛⲉϥϣⲏⲣⲉ ⲉⲩⲟ ⁶¹·¹ ⲙ̅ⲡⲗⲁⲥⲙⲁ
ⲛ̅ⲉⲩⲅⲉⲛⲏⲥ. ⲉϥϫⲉ ⲙ̅ⲡⲟⲩⲣ̅- ² ⲡⲗⲁⲥⲥⲉ ⲙ̅ⲙⲟϥ ⲁⲗⲗⲁ ⲁⲩϫⲡⲟϥ, ⲛⲉⲕⲛⲁ- ³ ϩⲉ ⲁⲡⲉϥⲥⲡⲉⲣⲙⲁ
ⲉϥⲟ ⲛ̅ⲉⲩⲅⲉⲛⲏⲥ. ⲧⲉ- ⁴ ⲛⲟⲩ ⲇⲉ ⲁⲩⲡⲗⲁⲥⲥⲉ ⲙ̅ⲙⲟϥ ⲁϥϫⲡⲟ. ⲁϣ ⁵ ⲛ̅ⲉⲩⲅⲉⲛⲉⲓⲁ ⲡⲉ ⲡⲁⲉⲓ;
ϣⲟⲣⲡ ⲁⲧⲙ̅ⲛⲧⲛⲟ- ⁶ ⲉⲓⲕ ϣⲱⲡⲉ, ⲙ̅ⲙⲛ̅ⲛⲥⲱⲥ ϥⲱⲧⲃⲉ, ⲁⲩⲱ ⲁⲩ- ⁷ ϫⲡⲟϥ ⲉⲃⲟⲗ ϩⲛ̅
ⲧⲙ̅ⲛⲧⲛⲟⲉⲓⲕ. ⲛⲉⲡϣⲏ- ⁸ ⲣⲉ ⲅⲁⲣ ⲙ̅ⲫⲟϥ ⲡⲉ. ⲇⲓⲁ ⲧⲟⲩⲧⲟ ⲁϥϣⲱⲡⲉ ⁹ ⲛ̅ϩⲁⲧⲃⲣⲱⲙⲉ ⲛ̅ⲑⲉ
ⲙ̅ⲡⲉϥⲕⲉⲉⲓⲱⲧ, ⲁⲩ- ¹⁰ ⲱ ⲁϥⲙⲟⲩⲟⲩⲧ ⲙ̅ⲡⲉϥⲥⲟⲛ. ⲕⲟⲓⲛⲱⲛⲓⲁ ⲇⲉ ¹¹ ⲛⲓⲙ ⲛ̅ⲧⲁϩϣⲱⲡⲉ ⲉⲃⲟⲗ ϩⲛ̅
ⲛⲉⲧⲛⲉ ⲁⲛ ⲛ̅- ¹² ⲛⲟⲩⲉⲣⲏⲩ ⲟⲩⲙ̅ⲛ̅ⲧⲛⲟⲉⲓⲕ ⲧⲉ.

ⲡⲛⲟⲩⲧⲉ ¹³ ⲟⲩϫⲟⲓⲧ ⲡⲉ. ⲛ̅ⲑⲉ ⲛ̅ⲛⲭⲱϭⲉ ⲉⲧⲛⲁⲛⲟⲩⲟⲩ ¹⁴—ϣⲁⲩⲙⲟⲩⲧⲉ ⲉⲣⲟⲟⲩ ϫⲉ
« ⲛⲁⲗⲏⲑⲓⲛⲟⲛ »—ϣⲁⲩ- ¹⁵ ⲙⲟⲩ ⲙⲛ̅ ⲛⲉⲛⲧⲁⲩϫⲱϭⲉ ϩⲣⲁⲓ ⲛ̅ϩⲏⲧⲟⲩ, ⲧⲁ- ¹⁶ ⲉⲓ ⲧⲉ ⲑⲉ
ⲛ̅ⲛⲉⲛⲧⲁⲡⲛⲟⲩⲧⲉ ϫⲟϭⲟⲩ. ⲉ- ¹⁷ ⲡⲉⲓⲇⲏ ϩⲛ̅ⲛⲁⲧⲙⲟⲩ ⲛⲉ ⲛⲉϥϫⲱϭⲉ, ϣⲁⲩ- ¹⁸ ⲣ̅ ⲁⲧⲙⲟⲩ ⲉⲃⲟⲗ
ϩⲓⲧⲟⲟⲧϥ ⲛ̅ⲛⲉϥⲡⲁϩⲣⲉ. ¹⁹ ⲡⲛⲟⲩⲧⲉ ⲇⲉ ⲣ̅ⲃⲁⲡⲧⲓⲍⲉ ⲛ̅ⲛⲉⲧϥ̅ⲣ̅ⲃⲁⲡⲧⲓ- ²⁰ ⲍⲉ ⲙ̅ⲙⲟⲟⲩ ϩⲛ̅ ⲟⲩⲙⲟⲟⲩ
ⲙⲛ̅ [[ⲟⲩ]]ϭⲟⲙ.

²¹ ⲛ̅ⲧⲉ ⲗⲁⲁⲩ ⲛⲁⲩ ⲁⲗⲁⲁⲩ ϩⲛ̅ ⲛⲉⲧⲥⲙⲟⲛⲧ ²² ⲉⲓⲙⲏⲧⲓ ⲛ̅ⲧⲉ ⲡⲉⲧⲙ̅ⲙⲁⲩ ϣⲱⲡⲉ ⲛ̅ⲑⲉ ²³
ⲛ̅ⲛⲉⲧⲙ̅ⲙⲁⲩ. ⲛ̅ⲑⲉ ⲙ̅ⲡⲣⲱⲙⲉ ⲁⲛ ⲉϥ- ²⁴ ϩⲙ̅ ⲡⲕⲟⲥⲙⲟⲥ. ϥⲛⲁⲩ ⲉⲡⲣⲏ ⲉϥⲟ ⲣ̅ⲣⲏ ²⁵ ⲁⲛ, ⲁⲩⲱ
ϥⲛⲁⲩ ⲉⲧⲡⲉ ⲙⲛ̅ ⲡⲕⲁϩ ⲙⲛ̅ ⲛ̅- ²⁶ ⲕⲉϩⲃⲏⲩⲉ ⲧⲏⲣⲟⲩ ⲉⲛⲧⲟϥ ⲁⲛ ⲡⲉ ⲛⲉⲧⲙ̅- ²⁷ ⲙⲁⲩ. ⲧⲁⲉⲓ ⲧⲉ ⲑⲉ
ϩⲣⲁⲓ ϩⲛ̅ ⲧⲙⲉ. ⲁⲗⲗⲁ ⲁⲕ- ²⁸ ⲛⲁⲩ ⲉⲗⲁⲁⲩ ⲛ̅ⲧⲉ ⲡⲙⲁ ⲉⲧⲙ̅ⲙⲁⲩ ⲁⲕϣⲱ- ²⁹ ⲡⲉ ⲛ̅ⲛⲉⲧⲙ̅ⲙⲁⲩ.
ⲁⲕⲛⲁⲩ ⲁⲡⲡⲛⲉⲩⲙⲁ· ⲁⲕ- ³⁰ ϣⲱⲡⲉ ⲙ̅ⲡⲛⲉⲩⲙⲁ. ⲁⲕⲛⲁ[ⲩ ⲁ]ⲡⲭⲣⲓⲥⲧⲟⲥ· ⲁⲕϣⲱⲡⲉ ³¹
ⲛ̅ⲭⲣⲓⲥⲧⲟⲥ. ⲁⲕⲛⲁⲩ ⲁⲡ[ⲉⲓⲱⲧ· ⲕ]ⲛⲁϣⲱⲡⲉ ⲛ̅ⲉⲓ- ³² ⲱⲧ. ⲇⲓⲁ ⲧⲟⲩⲧⲟ [ⲛ̅ⲛⲉⲉⲓⲙⲁ] ⲙⲉⲛ ⲕⲛⲁⲩ
³³ ⲁϩⲱⲃ ⲛⲓⲙ, ⲁⲩⲱ ⲕ̅[ⲛⲁⲩ ⲉⲣⲟ]ⲕ ⲁⲛ ⲟⲩⲁⲁⲕ, ³⁴ ⲕⲛⲁⲩ ⲇⲉ ⲉⲣⲟⲕ ⲙ̅ⲡ̅[ⲙⲁ ⲉⲧⲙ̅]ⲙⲁⲩ. ⲡⲉⲧ- ³⁵
ⲕⲛⲁⲩ ⲅⲁⲣ ⲉⲣⲟϥ ⲉⲕⲛⲁϣ[ⲱⲡⲉ ⲙ̅]ⲙ̅ⲟϥ.

³⁶ ⲧⲡⲓⲥⲧⲓⲥ ϫⲓ, ⲧⲁⲅⲁⲡⲏ ⲥϯ. ⲙ[ⲛ̅ ⲗⲁⲁⲩ ⲛⲁϣ- ⁶²·¹ ϫⲓ] ⲁϫⲛ̅ ⲧⲡⲓⲥⲧⲓⲥ. [ⲙ]ⲛ̅ ⲗⲁⲁⲩ ⲛⲁϥϯ
ⲁϫⲛ̅ ² ⲁⲅⲁⲡⲏ. ⲉⲧⲃⲉ ⲡⲁⲉⲓ, ϫⲉⲕⲁⲁⲥ ⲙⲉⲛ ⲉⲛⲁϫⲓ, ³ ⲧⲛ̅ⲣ̅ⲡⲓⲥⲧⲉⲩⲉ, ϣⲓⲛⲁ ⲇⲉ ⲛⲁⲙⲉ ⲛ̅ⲧⲛ̅ϯ,
ⲉⲡⲉⲓ ⁴ ⲉⲣϣⲁ ⲟⲩⲁ ϯ ϩⲛ̅ ⲟⲩⲁⲅⲁⲡⲏ ⲁⲛ ⲙ̅ⲛ̅ⲧⲉϥ ⲱ- ⁵ ⲫⲉⲗⲉⲓⲁ ϩⲙ̅ ⲡⲉⲛⲧⲁϥⲧⲁⲁϥ. ⲡⲉⲛⲧⲁϩϫⲓ
⁶ ⲡⲭⲟⲉⲓⲥ ⲁⲛ ⲟ ⲛ̅ⲛ̅ϩⲉⲃⲣⲁⲓⲟⲥ ⲉⲧⲓ.

ⲛ̅ⲁⲡⲟ- ⁷ ⲥⲧⲟⲗⲟⲥ ⲉⲧϩⲓ ⲧⲛ̅ⲛⲉϩ ⲧⲉⲉⲓϩⲉ ⲛⲉⲩⲙⲟⲩ- ⁸ ⲧⲉ ϫⲉ· « ⲓⲏⲥⲟⲩⲥ, ⲡⲛⲁⲍⲱⲣⲁⲓⲟⲥ,
ⲙⲉⲥⲥⲓⲁⲥ, » ⲉⲧⲉ ⁹ ⲡⲁⲉⲓ ⲡⲉ, « ⲓⲏⲥⲟⲩⲥ, ⲡⲛⲁⲍⲱⲣⲁⲓⲟⲥ, ⲡⲉⲭⲣⲓⲥⲧⲟⲥ. » ⲡϩⲁⲉ ¹⁰ ⲣ̅ⲣⲁⲛ ⲡⲉ

61.18 ϩⲓⲧⲟⲟⲧϥ: read ϩⲓⲧⲟⲟⲧⲟⲩ.

plows [20] the field by means of submissive animals, [21] and from this he nourishes himself and the [22] animals, both those submissive and those [23] not submissive. In this way the perfect [24] man by means of powers that are submissive [25] plows, preparing everyone to come [26] to be. For on account of this every place [27] stands, the good and the wicked, [28] the right and the left. The Holy Spirit [29] nourishes everyone, and it rules over [30] [all] the powers, those submissive [31] and those [not] submissive as well as those that are alone. [32] For indeed he [...] imprison them [33] within [so that...] if [...] desire, they will not be able [34] [to escape.]

The one who has been fashioned [35] [... and] you would find his children [61.1] nobly fashioned. If he was not [2] fashioned but born, you would [3] find his seed noble. [4] But now he has been fashioned and born. What [5] nobility is this? Adultery first [6] came to be, later murder, and [7] he was born in adultery. [8] For he was the child of the snake. For this reason he became [9] a murderer like his father, and [10] he murdered his brother. But all intercourse [11] that occurs between those unlike [12] each other is adultery.

God [13] is a dyer. Just as good dyes [14]—they are called "true"—[15] dissipate with the things dyed in them, so [16] too is it with those whom God has dyed. [17] Since his dyes are immortal, they [18] create immortality by means of his colors. [19] But God baptizes what he baptizes [20] in water and power.

[21] No one sees any of the established things [22] unless he becomes like [23] them. (This is) unlike the man [24] in the world. He sees the sun while not being the sun, [25] and he sees heaven and earth and [26] all other things while not being them. [27] This is the way it is with truth. But you [28] saw something of that place and became [29] those things. You saw spirit; you [30] became spirit. You saw Christ; you became [31] Christ. You saw the [Father; you] will become a [32] father. For this reason [in these places] you see [33] everything, and you do not [see] yourself alone, [34] but you see yourself in that [place.] [35] For what you see you shall [become.]

[36] Faith receives, love gives. [No one will be able [62.1] to receive] without faith. No one will be able to give without [2] love. Because of this, so that we might receive, [3] we believe, and so that truly we might give, since [4] if one does not give in love, he has no [5] benefit from what he has given. The one who has not received [6] the Lord is still a Hebrew.

The [7] apostles who preceded us referred (to him) in this way: [8] "Jesus, the Nazarean, Messiah," that [9] is, "Jesus, the Nazarean, the Christ." The last [10] name is "Christ,"

61.19 "baptizes": or "dips."

« ΠЄΧΡΙСΤΟС, » ΠϢΟΡΠ ΠЄ « ΙΗСΟΥС, » ΠЄΤϨ𝕹 [11] ΤΜΗΤЄ ΠЄ « ΠΝΑΖΑΡΗΝΟС. »
« ΜЄССΙΑС » [12] ΟΥ𝕹ΤΑϤ СΗΜΑСΙΑ С𝕹ΤЄ ΑΥϢ « ΠЄΧΡΙСΤΟС » [13] ΑΥϢ « ΠЄΤϢΗΥ. »
« ΙΗСΟΥС » Μ̄ΜΝ̄ΤϨЄΒΡΑΙΟС ΠЄ [14] « ΠСϢΤЄ. » « ΝΑΖΑΡΑ » ΤЄ « ΤΑΛΗΘЄΙΑ. » « ΠΝΑ- [15]
ΖΑΡΗΝΟС » ⟦ΝЄ⟧ ϬЄ ΤЄ ΤΑΛΗΘЄΙΑ. « ΠЄ{Π}ΧΡΙСΤΟС » [16] Ν̄ΤΑΥϢΙΤϤ· « ΠΝΑΖΑΡΗΝΟС
» Μ̄𝕹 « ΙΗСΟΥС » [17] ΝЄΝΤΑΥϢΙΤΟΥ.

ΠΜΑΡΓΑΡΙΤΗС ЄΥϢΑΝ- [18] ΝΟΧϤ ЄΠΙΤ𝕹 ЄΠΒΟΡΒΟΡΟΝ ϢΑϤϢϢ- [19] ΠЄ {ϢΑϤϢϢΠЄ ΑΝ}
ЄϤϢΗС Ν̄ϨΟΥΟ, [20] ΟΥΤЄ ЄΥϢΑΤΑϨСϤ Ν̄ΝΑΠΟΒΑΡСΙΜΟΝ [21] ЄϤΝΑϢϢΠЄ <ΑΝ> ЄϤΤΑЄΙΗΥ.
ΑΛΛΑ ΟΥ𝕹ΤΑϤ [22] Μ̄ΜΑΥ Μ̄ΠΤΑЄΙΟ ϨΑϨΤ𝕹 ΠЄϤΧΟЄΙС [23] ΟΥΟЄΙϢ ΝΙΜ. ΤΑЄΙ ΤЄ ΘЄ Ν̄ΝϢΗΡЄ
Μ̄- [24] ΠΝΟΥΤЄ ϨΝ̄ ΝЄΤΟΥΝΑϢϢΠЄ Ν̄ϨΗΤΟΥ. [25] ЄΤΙ ΟΥ𝕹ΤΑΥ Μ̄ΜΑΥ Μ̄ΠΤΑЄΙΟ ϨΑϨΤΜ̄ ΠΟΥ- [26]
ЄΙϢΤ.

ЄΚϢΑΧΟΟС, ΧЄ « ΑΝΟΚ ΟΥЇΟΥΔΑЇ, » [27] Μ̄𝕹 ΛΑΑΥ ΝΑΚΙΜ. ЄΚϢΑΧΟΟС ΧЄ, « ΑΝΟΚ ΟΥ- [28]
ϨΡϢΜΑΙΟС, » Μ̄𝕹 ΛΑΑΥ ΝΑΡ̄ΤΑΡΑССЄ. ЄΚϢΑ- [29] ΧΟΟС, ΧЄ « ΑΝΟ[Κ Ο]ΥϨЄΛΛΗΝ
ΟΥΒΑΡΒΑ- [30] ΡΟС ΟΥϨΜ̄ϨΑΛ̄ [ΟΥЄΛЄΥ]ΘЄΡΟС, » Μ̄𝕹 ΛΑΑΥ [31] ΝΑϢΤΟΡΤΡ̄. ЄΚ[ϢΑΧΟΟС],
ΧЄ « ΑΝΟΚ ΟΥΧΡΗ- [32] СΤΙΑΝΟС, » Π[. . . . . .] ΝΑΝΟЄΙΝ. Ν̄ΓЄΝΟΙ- [33] ΤΟ Ν̄ΤΑϢ[. . . . Ν̄Τ]-
ЄЄΙΜЄΙΝЄ ΠΑЄΙ Є- [34] [Τ]Є [. . . . .] ΝΑϢϨΥΠΟΜЄΙΝЄ ΑΝ Є- [35] [СϢΤΜ̄ ЄΠ]ЄϤΡΑΝ.

ΠΝΟΥΤЄ ΟΥΑΜΡϢ- [63.1] ΜЄ ΠЄ. ΔΙΑ ΤΟΥΤΟ С[ЄϢϢ]ϢΤ Μ̄ΠΡϢΜ[Є] [2] ΝΑϤ. ϨΑ ΤЄϨΗ
ЄΜΠΑΤΟΥϢϢϢΤ Μ̄ΠΡϢ- [3] ΜЄ, ΝЄΥϢϢϢΤ Ν̄ΘΝΘΗΡΙΟΝ ΝЄ. ϨΝ̄ΝΟΥ- [4] ΤЄ ΓΑΡ ΑΝ ΝЄ
ΝΑЄΙ ЄΤΟΥϢϢϢΤ ΝΑΥ.

[5] Ν̄СΚЄΥΟС Ν̄ΝΑΒΑϬΗЄΙΝ ΜΝ̄ Ν̄СΚЄΥΟС [6] ΒΒΛϬЄ ϢΑΥϢϢΠЄ ЄΒΟΛ ϨΙΤΜ̄ ΠΚϢϨΤ, [7] ΑΛΛΑ
Ν̄СΚЄΥΟС Ν̄ΝΑΒΑϬΗЄΙΝ ЄΥϢΑ- [8] ΟΥϢϬΠ ΠΑΛΙΝ ϢΑΥΤΑΜΙΟΟΥ Ν̄ΤΑΥ- [9] ϢϢΠЄ ΓΑΡ ЄΒΟΛ
ϨΝ̄ ΟΥΠΝЄΥΜΑ. Ν̄СΚЄΥΟС [10] ΔЄ ΒΒΛ̄ϬЄ ЄΥϢΑΟΥϢϬΠ ϢΑΥΤΑΚΟ [11] Ν̄ΤΑΥϢϢΠЄ ΓΑΡ
ΧϢΡΙС ΝΙϤЄ.

ΟΥЄΙϢ [12] ЄϤΚϢΤЄ ϨΑ ΟΥϢΝЄ ʼΝ̄ΝΟΥΤʼ ΑϤΝ̄ ϢЄ Μ̄ΜΙΛΟС [13] ЄΒΟΛ ЄϤΜΟΟϢЄ. Ν̄ΤΑΡΟΥΚΑΑϤ
ЄΒΟΛ, [14] ΑϤϨЄ ЄΡΟϤ ΟΝ ЄϤϨΜ̄ ΠΙΜΑ ΠΙΜΑ. [15] ΟΥΝ̄ ϨΡ̄ΡϢΜЄ ϢΟΟΠ ϢΑΥΝ̄ ϨΑϨ Μ̄ΜΟ- [16] ΟϢЄ
ЄΒΟΛ, ΑΥϢ ΜΑΥΠΡΟΚΟΠΤЄ Є- [17] ΛΑΑΥ Μ̄ΜΑ. Ν̄ΤΑΡЄ ΡΟΥϨЄ ϢϢΠЄ ЄΡΟ- [18] ΟΥ, ΟΥΤЄ
Μ̄ΠΟΥΝΑΥ ЄΠΟΛΙС ΟΥΤЄ [19] ΚϢΜΗ, ΟΥΤЄ ΚΤΙСΙС ΟΥΤЄ ΦΥСΙС ΜΝ̄ [20] ΔΥΝΑΜΙС ΜΝ̄ ΑΓΓЄΛΟС.
ЄΙΚΗ ΑΝΤΑΛΑΙ- [21] ΠϢΡΟС ϨΙСЄ.

ΤЄΥΧΑΡΙСΤЄΙΑ ΠЄ ΙΗСΟΥС ЄΥ- [22] ΜΟΥΤЄ ΓΑΡ ЄΡΟϤ Μ̄ΜΝ̄ΤСΥΡΟС ΧЄ « ΦΑ- [23] ΡΙСΑΘΑ, »
ЄΤЄ ΠΑЄΙ ΠЄ, « ΠЄΤΠΟΡϢ ЄΒΟΛ. » [24] ΑΙΗСΟΥС ΓΑΡ ЄΙ ЄϤСΤΑΥΡΟΥ Μ̄ΠΚΟСΜΟС.

[25] ΑΠΧΟЄΙС ΒϢΚ ЄϨΟΥ[Ν] ЄΠΜΑ Ν̄ΧϢϬЄ [26] Ν̄ΛЄΥЄΙ. ΑϤϤΙ ϢΒЄСΝΟΟΥС Ν̄ΧΡϢΜΑ, [27]
ΑϤΝΟΧΟΥ ΑΤΡΟϨΤЄ. ΑϤΝ̄ΤΟΥ ЄϨΡΑЇ [28] ЄΥΟΒϢ ΤΗΡΟΥ, ΑΥϢ ΠЄΧΑϤ, ΧЄ « ΤΑЄΙ [29] ΤЄ ΘЄ
Ν̄ΤΑϤЄΙ Μ̄ΜΟϬ Ν̄ϬΙ ΠϢΗΡ⟦Є Μ̄- [30] ΠϢΗΡ⟧Є Μ̄ΠΡϢΜ[Є Є]Ϥ[Ο] Ν̄ϬΘΙΤ. »

62.35 [ЄΠ]ЄϤΡΑΝ: reading from earliest images; see Stephen Emmel, "Unique Photographic Evidence for Nag Hammadi Texts, CG I, 1–5." *BASP* 15 (1978): 113.

the first is "Jesus," the one in [11] the middle is "Nazarean." "Messiah" [12] has two meanings, both "Christ" [13] and "the worthy one." "Jesus" in Hebrew is [14] "the redemption." "Nazara" is "the truth." "The [15] Nazarean," then, is "the truth." "The Christ" [16] has been measured; "the Nazarean" and "Jesus" [17] are those who have been measured.

As for the pearl, when it is [18] cast down into filth it becomes [19] greatly despised, [20] nor when it is anointed with balsam [21] will it become valued. But it [22] always has value to its master. [23] This is the way it is with the children of [24] God in the places they might be. [25] Nonetheless they have value to their father.

If you say, "I am a Jew," [27] no one will waver. If you say, "I am a [28] Roman," no one will be agitated. If you [29] say, "I am a Greek, a barbarian, [30] a slave, [a] free person," no one [31] will be disturbed. [If] you [say,] "I am a Christian," [32] the [. . .] will tremble. May it be [33] that [. . . of] this sort, this [34] [which . . .] will not be able to stand firm to [35] [hear] his name.

God is a human eater. [63.1] For this reason the human [is sacrificed] [2] to him. When the human was not yet sacrificed, [3] animals were sacrificed. [4] For those to whom they are sacrificed are not gods.

[5] Glass vessels and earthen vessels [6] are from the earth, [7] but glass vessels are made again when they [8] break, since they have [9] come to be through breath. But earthen vessels [10] when they break are destroyed, [11] since they came to be without breath.

A donkey [12] that turns a millstone travels one hundred miles [13] when walking. Once released, [14] it finds itself again in the same place. [15] There are people that make many journeys, [16] and they progress to [17] no place. After evening comes upon [18] them, they do not see city or [19] village, neither (things) man made nor natural, no [20] power or angel. Vainly have (these) miserable ones [21] labored.

The Eucharist is Jesus, since [22] it is called in Syriac "Pharisatha," [23] that is, "the one who is spread out." [24] For Jesus came to crucify the world.

[25] The Lord entered into Levi's dyehouse. [26] He took up seventy-two colors, [27] and he tossed them into the kettle. He brought them out [28] completely white, and he said, "In this [29] way the Son [30] of Man came [as] a dyer."

62.12–13 Behind the association between "Christ" and "the worthy one" is a Greek wordplay between χριστός and χρηστός.

63.9 "breath": or "spirit."

ⲧⲥⲟ- ³¹ ⲫⲓⲁ, ⲉⲧⲟⲩⲙⲟⲩⲧ[ⲉ ⲉⲣⲟ]ⲥ ϫⲉ « ⲧⲥⲧⲓⲣⲁ, » ⲛ̄- ³² ⲧⲟⲥ ⲧⲉ ⲧⲙⲁⲁ[ⲩ ⲛ̄ⲛⲁⲅ]ⲅⲉⲗⲟⲥ
ⲁⲩⲱ [ⲧ]ⲕⲟⲓ- ³³ ⲛⲱⲛⲟⲥ ⲙ̄ⲡⲥ[ⲱⲧⲏⲣ. ⲙⲁ]ⲣⲓⲁ ⲧⲙⲁⲅ[ⲇⲁ]- ³⁴ ⲗⲏⲛⲏ ⲛⲉⲣⲉ ⲡⲥ[ⲱⲧⲏⲣ ⲙⲉ]
ⲙ̄ⲙⲟ[ⲥ ⲛ̄]- ³⁵ ϩⲟⲩⲟ ⲁⲙ̄ⲙⲁⲑⲏⲧ[ⲏⲥ ⲧⲏⲣⲟⲩ. ⲛⲉϥ]- ³⁶ ⲁⲥⲡⲁⲍⲉ ⲙ̄ⲙⲟⲥ ⲁⲧⲉⲥ[. . . . . ⲛ̄ϩⲁϩ] ³⁷
ⲛ̄ⲥⲟⲡ. ⲁⲡⲕⲉⲥⲉⲉⲡⲉ ⲙ̄[ⲙⲁⲑⲏⲧⲏⲥ ⁶⁴·¹ . . .] ⲉⲣⲟ [.] [. .]ⲙⲁ. ⲡⲉϫⲁⲩ ⲛⲁϥ ϫⲉ· ² « ⲉⲧⲃⲉ ⲟⲩ
ⲕⲙⲉ ⲙ̄ⲙⲟⲥ ⲡⲁⲣⲁⲣⲟⲛ ⲧⲏⲣⲛ̄; » ⲁϥ- ³ ⲟⲩⲱϣⲃ̄ ⲛ̄ϭⲓ ⲡⲥⲱⲧⲏⲣ, ⲡⲉϫⲁϥ ⲛⲁⲩ {ⲡⲉ- ⁴ ϫⲁϥ
ⲛⲁⲩ} ϫⲉ· « ⲉⲧⲃⲉ ⲟⲩ ϯⲙⲉ ⲙ̄ⲙⲱⲧⲛ̄ ⲁⲛ ⁵ ⲛ̄ⲧⲉⲥϩⲉ; ⲟⲩⲃⲗ̄ⲗⲉ ⲙⲛ̄ ⲟⲩⲁ ⲉϥⲛⲁⲩ ⲉⲃⲟⲗ ⁶ ⲉⲩϩⲙ̄
ⲡⲕⲁⲕⲉ, ⲙ̄ⲡⲉⲥⲛⲁⲩ ⲥⲉϣⲟⲃⲉ ⲉⲛⲟⲩ- ⁷ ⲉⲣⲏⲩ ⲁⲛ. ϩⲟⲧⲁⲛ ⲉⲣϣⲁ ⲡⲟⲩⲟⲉⲓⲛ ⲉⲓ, ⲧⲟⲧⲉ ⁸
ⲡⲉⲧⲛⲁⲃⲟⲗ ϥⲛⲁⲛⲁⲩ ⲉⲡⲟⲩⲟⲉⲓⲛ, ⲁⲩⲱ ⁹ ⲡⲉⲧⲟ ⲃ̄ⲃⲗ̄ⲗⲉ ⲉϥⲛⲁϭⲱ ϩⲙ̄ ⲡⲕⲁⲕⲉ. »

ⲡⲉ- ¹⁰ ϫⲉ ⲡϫⲟⲉⲓⲥ ϫⲉ· « ⲟⲩⲙⲁⲕⲁⲣⲓⲟⲥ ⲡⲉ ⲡⲉⲧϣⲟ- ¹¹ ⲟⲡ ϩⲁ ⲧⲉϩⲏ ⲉⲙⲡⲁⲧⲉϥϣⲱⲡⲉ.
ⲡⲉⲧϣⲟ- ¹² ⲟⲡ ⲅⲁⲣ ⲁϥϣⲱⲡⲉ, ⲁⲩⲱ ϥⲛⲁϣⲱⲡⲉ. »

ⲡϫⲓ- ¹³ ⲥⲉ ⲙ̄ⲡⲣⲱⲙⲉ ϥⲟⲩⲟⲛϩ ⲁⲛ ⲉⲃⲟⲗ, ⲁⲗⲗⲁ ¹⁴ ϥϣⲟⲟⲡ ϩⲙ̄ ⲡⲉⲑⲏⲡ. ⲉⲧⲃⲉ ⲡⲁⲉⲓ ϥⲟ ⲛ̄- ¹⁵
ϫⲟⲉⲓⲥ ⲁⲛⲉⲑⲏⲣⲓⲟⲛ ⲉⲧϫⲟⲟⲣ ⲉⲣⲟϥ, ⲉⲧⲛⲉ- ¹⁶ ⲁⲩ ⲕⲁⲧⲁ ⲡⲉⲧⲟⲩⲟⲛϩ ⲉⲃⲟⲗ ⲙⲛ̄ ⲡⲉⲑⲏⲡ. ¹⁷ ⲁⲩⲱ
ⲡⲁⲉⲓ ϯ ⲛⲁⲩ ⲙ̄ⲡⲙⲟⲩⲛ ⲉⲃⲟⲗ. ⲉⲣϣⲁ ¹⁸ ⲡⲣⲱⲙⲉ ⲇⲉ ⲡⲱⲣϫ ⲉⲣⲟⲟⲩ ϣⲁⲩⲙⲟⲩⲟⲩⲧ ¹⁹ ⲛ̄ⲛⲟⲩⲉⲣⲏⲩ
ⲛ̄ⲥⲉⲡⲱϩⲥ ⲛ̄ⲛⲟⲩⲉⲣⲏⲩ. ²⁰ ⲁⲩⲱ ⲁⲩⲟⲩⲱⲙ ⲛ̄ⲛⲟⲩⲉⲣⲏⲩ ϫⲉ ⲙ̄ⲡⲟⲩϩⲉ ²¹ ⲉⲧⲣⲟⲫⲏ. ⲧⲉⲛⲟⲩ ⲇⲉ
ⲁⲩϩⲉ ⲉⲧⲣⲟⲫⲏ ⲉⲃⲟⲗ ²² ϫⲉ ⲁⲡⲣⲱⲙⲉ ⲣ̄ ϩⲱⲃ ⲉⲡⲕⲁϩ.

ⲉⲣϣⲁⲟⲩⲁ ²³ ⲃⲱⲕ ⲉⲡⲉⲥⲛⲧ ⲉⲡⲙⲟⲟⲩ ⲛ̄ϥⲉⲓ ⲉϩⲣⲁⲓ ⲉⲙ- ²⁴ ⲡⲉϥϫⲓ ⲗⲁⲁⲩ ⲛ̄ϥϫⲟⲟⲥ ϫⲉ· « ⲁⲛⲟⲕ
ⲟⲩⲭⲣⲏ- ²⁵ ⲥⲧⲓⲁⲛⲟⲥ, » ⲛ̄ⲧⲁϥϫⲓ ⲙ̄ⲡⲣⲁⲛ ⲉⲧⲙⲏⲥⲉ. ⲉϥ- ²⁶ ϣⲁϫⲓ ⲇⲉ ⲙ̄ⲡⲡⲛⲉⲩⲙⲁ ⲉⲧⲟⲩⲁⲁⲃ
ⲟⲩⲛ̄ⲧⲁϥ ⲙ̄- ²⁷ ⲙⲁⲩ ⲛ̄ⲧⲇⲱⲣⲉⲁ ⲙ̄ⲡⲣⲁⲛ. ⲡⲉⲛⲧⲁϩϫⲓ ⲛ̄ⲟⲩ- ²⁸ ⲇⲱⲣⲉⲁ ⲙⲁⲩϭⲓⲧⲥ̄ ⲛ̄ⲧⲟⲟⲧϥ,
ⲡⲉⲛⲧⲁϩϫⲓ ⲇⲉ ²⁹ ⲉϫⲱϥ ⲉⲧⲙⲏⲥⲉ ϣⲁⲩϣⲁⲧϥ. ⲧⲁⲉⲓ ⲧⲉ ⲑⲉ ³⁰ ⲉⲧϣⲟ[ⲟ]ⲡ ⲛⲁⲛ ⲉⲣϣⲁⲟⲩⲁ
ϣⲱⲡⲉ ϩⲛ̄ ³¹ ⲟⲩⲙⲩⲥⲧⲏⲣⲓⲟ[ⲛ].

[ⲡⲙ]ⲩⲥⲧⲏⲣⲓⲟⲛ ⲙⲡⲅⲁ- ³² ⲙ[ⲟⲥ] ⲟⲩⲛⲟϭ [ⲡⲉ. ⲁϫⲛ̄]ⲧϥ̄ ⲅⲁⲣ ⲛⲉⲡⲕⲟⲥ- ³³ [ⲙⲟ]ⲥ ⲛⲁϣⲱ[ⲡⲉ]
ⲁⲛ. ⲧⲥ]ⲩⲥⲧⲁⲥⲓⲥ ⲅⲁⲣ ⲙ̄- ³⁴ [ⲡⲕⲟ]ⲥⲙⲟ[ⲥ. . . . .]ⲙⲉ. ⲧⲥⲩⲥⲧⲁⲥⲓⲥ ⲇⲉ ³⁵ [. . . . . ⲡϫ]
ⲁⲙⲟⲥ. ⲉⲣⲓⲛⲟⲉⲓ ⲛ̄ⲧⲕⲟⲓ- ³⁶ [ⲛⲱⲛⲓⲁ . . . ϫ]ⲱϩⲙ̄ ϫⲉ ⲟⲩⲛ̄ⲧⲁⲥ ⲙ̄ⲙⲁⲩ ³⁷ [. . . . . . .] ⲇⲩⲛⲁⲙⲓⲥ.
ⲧⲉⲥϩⲓⲕⲱⲛ ⁶⁵·¹ ⲉⲥϣⲟⲟⲡ ϩⲛ̄ ⲟⲩϫⲱ[ϩⲙ̄].

[ⲛ̄]ⲟⲭ[ⲏⲙ]ⲁ ⲙⲡⲛⲉⲩⲙ[ⲁ] ² ⲛ̄ⲁⲕⲁⲑⲁⲣⲧⲟⲛ, ⲟⲩⲛ̄ ϩⲟⲟⲩⲧ ⲛ̄ϩⲏⲧⲟⲩ ⲟⲩ- ³ ⲛ̄ ϩⲛ̄ⲥϩⲓⲟⲙⲉ.
ⲛ̄ϩⲟⲟⲩⲧ ⲙⲉⲛ ⲛⲉ ⲉⲧⲣ̄ⲕⲟⲓ- ⁴ ⲛⲱⲛⲉⲓ ⲁⲙⲯⲩⲭⲁ ⲉⲧⲣⲡⲟⲗⲓⲧⲉⲩⲉⲥⲑⲉ ⁵ ϩⲛ̄ⲛⲟⲩⲥⲭⲏⲙⲁ
ⲛ̄ⲥϩⲓⲙⲉ. ⲛ̄ⲥϩⲓⲟⲙⲉ ⲇⲉ ⁶ ⲛⲉ ⲛⲉⲧⲧⲏϩ ⲙⲛ̄ ⲛⲉⲧϩⲛ̄ ⲟⲩⲥⲭⲏⲙⲁ ⲛ̄- ⁷ ϩⲟⲟⲩⲧ ⲉⲃⲟⲗ
ϩⲓⲧⲛ̄ ⲟⲩⲁⲧⲧⲱⲧ. ⲁⲩⲱ ⲙⲛ̄ ⁸ ⲗⲁⲁⲩ ⲛⲁϣⲣ̄ ⲃⲟⲗ ⲉⲛⲁⲉⲓ ⲉⲩⲉⲙⲁϩⲧⲉ ⲙ̄- ⁹ ⲙⲟϥ ⲉϥⲧⲙ̄ϫⲓ
ⲛ̄ⲟⲩϭⲟⲙ ⲛ̄ϩⲟⲟⲩⲧ ⲙⲛ̄- ¹⁰ ⲛⲟⲩⲥϩⲓⲙⲉ, ⲉⲧⲉ ⲡⲛⲩⲙⲫⲓⲟⲥ ⲡⲉ ⲙⲛ ¹¹ ⲧⲛⲩⲙⲫⲏ. ⲟⲩⲁ ⲇⲉ ϫⲓ
ⲉⲃⲟⲗ ϩⲙ̄ ⲡⲛⲩⲙ- ¹² ⲫⲱⲛ ⲛ̄ϩⲓⲕⲟⲛⲓⲕⲟⲥ. ϩⲟⲧⲁⲛ ⲉⲣϣⲁ ⲛ̄ⲥϩⲓ- ¹³ ⲙⲉ ⲛ̄ⲁⲧⲥⲃⲱ ⲛⲁⲩ
ⲁⲩϩⲟⲟⲩⲧ ⲉϥϩⲙⲟⲟⲥ ¹⁴ ⲟⲩⲁⲁϥ, ϣⲁⲩϩⲱϭⲉ ⲉϩⲣⲁⲓ ⲉϫⲱϥ ⲛ̄ⲥⲉ- ¹⁵ ⲥⲱⲃⲉ ⲛⲙ̄ⲙⲁϥ ⲛ̄ⲥⲉϫⲟϩⲙⲉϥ.

64.8 ⲡⲉⲧⲛⲁⲃⲟⲗ: read ⲡⲉⲧⲛⲁⲩ ⲉⲃⲟⲗ.
64.30 ⲉⲣϣⲁⲟⲩⲁ: reading of earliest images; see Emmel, 114.

Wisdom, [31] who is called "the barren one," [32] is the mother [of the] angels and [the] companion [33] of the [Savior. As for Mary] Magdalene, [34] the [Savior loved her] [35] more than [all] the disciples. [He would] [36] kiss her on her [. . .] [37] often. The remaining [disciples [64.1] . . .]. They said to him, [2] "Why do you love her more than all of us?" [3] The Savior answered, and he said to them, [4] "Why do I not love you [5] in the way (I love) her? When a blind person and a sighted person [6] are in the dark, the two are no different from each other. [7] (Yet) when the light comes, then [8] the sighted person will see the light, and [9] the blind person will remain in the dark."

[10] The Lord said, "Blessed is the one who exists [11] before he has come to be. For the one who exists [12] has come to be and he will come to be."

The [13] superiority of man is not apparent, but [14] it is in what is hidden. Because of this he is [15] master over the animals that are stronger than he is, which are great [16] in accordance with what is apparent and what is hidden. [17] And he gives them survival. But if [18] man is separated from them, they kill [19] each other and bite each other. [20] And they ate each other because they did not find [21] food. But now they have found food because [22] man has worked the land.

If someone [23] goes down into the water and comes up having [24] not received anything and says, "I am a [25] Christian," he has received the name on loan. But if he [26] receives the Holy Spirit, he has [27] the name as a gift. As for the one who has received a [28] gift, it is not taken from him, but as for the one who has received [29] it as a loan, it needs (to be taken from him). This is how [30] it is for us if someone comes to be in [31] a mystery.

[The] mystery of marriage [32] [is] great. For [without] it the world [33] would [not] have come to be. For [the] structure of [34] [the] world [. . .]. But the structure [35] [. . .] marriage. Consider the [fellowship [36] . . . defilement] because it has [37] [. . .] power. Its image [65.1] dwells in [defilement].

As for [the] forms of unclean spirit, [2] there are males among them (and) there are [3] females. The males are those that unite [4] with the souls that reside in a female [5] form. But the females [6] are those that mix with those in a male form [7] by means of an unmixed one. And [8] nothing will be able to escape from them, since they seize it [9] when it is not able to receive a male power or [10] a female (power), that is, the bridegroom and [11] the bride. But one receives from (them) within the [12] imaged bridal chamber. When ignorant women [13] see males sitting [14] alone, they pounce upon him

63.36 "on her [. . .]": There are many feminine singular nouns that can fit in this lacuna, including mouth (ⲡⲁⲓϭⲉ or ⲧⲁⲡⲣⲟ), cheek (ⲟⲩⲟϭⲉ), foot (ϭⲁⲗⲟⲝ), and forehead (ⲧⲉϩⲛⲉ).

ⲧⲉⲉⲓⲣⲉ ¹⁶ ⲟⲛ ⳍⲣⲣⲱⲙⲉ ⲛ̄ⲁⲧⲥⲃⲱ ⲉⲩϣⲁⲛⲛⲁⲩ ⲉⲩ- ¹⁷ ⲥⳍⲓⲙⲉ ⲉⲥⳍⲙⲟⲟⲥ ⲟⲩⲁⲁⲧⲥ̄ ⲉⲛⲉⲥⲱⲥ, ¹⁸ ϣⲁⲩⲡⲓⲑⲉ ⲙ̄ⲙⲟⲥ ⲛ̄ⲥⲉⲣⲃⲓⲁⲍⲉ ⲙ̄ⲙⲟⲥ, ¹⁹ ⲉⲩⲟⲩⲱϣ ⲉⲭⲟⳍⲙⲉⲥ. ⲉⲩϣⲁⲛⲛⲁⲩ ⲇⲉ ²⁰ ⲁⲡⳍⲟⲟⲩⲧ ⲙⲛ̄ ⲧⲉϥⳍⲓⲙⲉ ⲉⲩⳍⲙⲟⲟⲥ ⳍⲁ- ²¹ ⲧⲛ̄ ⲛⲟⲩⲉⲣⲏⲩ, ⲙⲁⲣⲉ ⲛ̄ⳍⲓⲟⲙⲉ ϣⲃⲱⲕ ⲉ- ²² ⳍⲟⲩⲛ ϣⲁ ⲡⳍⲟⲟⲩⲧ ⲟⲩⲧⲉ ⲙⲁⲣⲉ ⲛ̄ⳍⲟⲟⲩⲧ ²³ ϣⲃⲱⲕ ⲉⳍⲟⲩⲛ ϣⲁ ⲧⲥⳍⲓⲙⲉ. ⲧⲁⲉⲓ ⲧⲉ ⲑⲉ ²⁴ ⲉⲣϣⲁ ⲑⲓⲕⲱⲛ ⲙⲛ̄ ⲡ[ⲁ] ⲅⲅⲉⲗⲟⲥ ⳍⲱⲧⲣ̄ ⲉ- ²⁵ ⲛⲟⲩⲉⲣⲏⲩ, ⲟⲩⲧⲉ ⲙⲛ̄ [ⲗ]ⲁⲁⲩ ⲛⲁϣⲣ̄ⲧⲟⲗⲙⲁ ²⁶ ⲁⲃⲱⲕ ⲉⳍⲟⲩⲛ ϣⲁ ⲫ[ⳍⲟ] ⲟⲩⲧ ⲏ ⲧⲥⳍⲓⲙⲉ.

²⁷ ⲡⲉⲧⲛ̄ⲛⲏⲩ ⲉⲃⲟⲗ ⳍⲙ̄ ⲡⲕⲟⲥⲙⲟⲥ ⲛ̄ⲥⲉ- ²⁸ ⲧⲙ̄ϣⲉⲙⳍⲁⲥⲧⲉ ⲙ̄ⲙⲟϥ ⲉⲧⲓ ϫⲉ ⲛⲉϥⳍⲙ̄ ²⁹ ⲡⲕⲟⲥⲙⲟⲥ, ϥⲟⲩⲟ[ⲛⳍ] ⲉⲃⲟⲗ ϫⲉ ϥϫⲟⲥⲉ ³⁰ ⲁⲧⲉⲡⲓⲑⲩⲙⲓⲁ ⲙ̄ⲡ[. .]ϥ[. .]ⲉ̣[.]ⲛ̄ ⲑⲣ̄ⲧⲉ. ³¹ ϥⲟ ⲛ̄ϫⲟⲉⲓⲥ ⲁⲭⲛ̄ [. . .]ⲥ̣[.]ⲥ ϥⲥⲟⲧⲡ ⲉ- ³² ⲡⲕⲱⳍ. ⲉϣϫⲉ [. . . . .]ⲩ ⲉⲓ ⲥⲉⲁⲙ[ⲁ]ⳍⲧⲉ ³³ ⲙ̄ⲙⲟϥ, ⲥⲉϣⲟ̄ϭ[ⲧ ⲙ̄ⲙⲟϥ.] ⲁⲩⲱ ⲡϣ[ⲥ ⲉϥ]- ³⁴ ⲛⲁϣⲣ̄ ⲃⲟⲗ ⲁⲛⲛ̣[ⲟϭ ⲛ̄ⲇⲩⲛ]ⲁⲙⲓ[ⲥ . . .] ³⁵ ⲧⲉ; ⲡⲱⲥ ϥⲛⲁϣⳍ[. . . . . . .
. . . . .] ³⁶ ⲕⲓⲥ; ⲟⲩⲛ̄ ⳍⲟⲉⲓⲛⲉ ⲉ[ⲩϫⲱ ⲙ̄ⲙⲟⲥ ϫⲉ·] ³⁷ « ⲁⲛⲟⲛ ⳍⲙ̄ⲡⲓⲥⲧⲟⲥ, » ⳍⲟⲡϣ[ⲥ . . . . . ⁶⁶·¹ ⲛⲉⲡ]ⲛⲉⲩⲙⲁ [ⲛ̄ⲁⲕⲁⲑⲁⲣⲧⲟ]ⲛ ⳍⲓ ⲇⲁⲓⲙⲟⲛⲓⲟⲛ. ² ⲛⲉⲩⲛ̄ⲧⲁⲩ ⲅⲁⲣ ⲙ̄ⲙⲁ[ⲩ] ⲙ̄ⲡⲛⲉⲩⲙⲁ ⲉⲧⲟⲩⲁⲁⲃ ³ ⲛⲉ, ⲙⲛ̄ ⲡⲛⲉⲩⲙⲁ ⲛ̄ⲁⲕⲁⲑⲁⲣⲧⲟⲛ ⲛⲁⲣ̄ⲕⲟⲗⲗⲁ ⁴ ⲉⲣⲟⲟⲩ. ⲙ̄ⲡⲣ̄ ⳍⲟⲧⲉ ⳍⲏⲧⲥ̄ ⲛ̄ⲧⲥⲁⲣⳍ, ⲟⲩⲇⲉ ⁵ ⲙ̄ⲙ̄ⲙⲉⲣⲓⲧⲥ̄. ⲉⲕϣⲁⲣ̄ ⳍⲟⲧⲉ ⳍⲏⲧⲥ̄, ⲥⲛⲁⲣ̄ ϫⲟ- ⁶ ⲉⲓⲥ ⲉⲣⲟⲕ· ⲉⲕϣⲁⲛⲙⲉⲣⲓⲧⲥ̄, ⲥⲛⲁⲟⲙ<ⲕ>ⲕ, ⲛ̄ⲥⲟϭ<ⲧ>ⲕ.

⁷ ⲏ ⲛ̄ϥϣⲱⲡⲉ ⳍⲙ̄ ⲡⲉⲉⲓⲕⲟⲥⲙⲟⲥ ʼⲏʼ ⳍⲛ̄ ⲧⲁⲛⲁ- ⁸ ⲥⲧⲁⲥⲓⲥ ⲏ ⳍⲛ̄ ⲛ̄ⲧⲟⲡⲟⲥ ⲉⲧⳍⲛ̄ ⲧⲙⲏⲧⲉ, ⁹ ⲙⲏ ⲅⲉⲛⲟⲓⲧⲟ ⲛ̄ⲥⲉⳍⲉ ⲉⲣⲟⲉⲓ ⲛ̄ⳍⲏⲧⲟⲩ. ⲡⲉ- ¹⁰ ⲉⲓⲕⲟⲥⲙⲟⲥ ⲟⲩⲙ̄ ⲡⲉⲧⲛⲁⲛⲟⲩϥ ⲛ̄ⳍⲏⲧϥ ¹¹ ⲟⲩⲙ̄ ⲡⲉⲑⲟⲟⲩ. ⲛⲉϥⲡⲉⲧⲛⲁⲛⲟⲩⲟⲩ ⲙ̄ⲡⲉ- ¹² ⲧⲛⲁⲛⲟⲩⲟⲩ ⲁⲛ ⲛⲉ, ⲁⲩⲱ ⲛⲉϥⲡⲉⲑⲟⲟⲩ ⳍⲙ̄- ¹³ ⲡⲉⲑⲟⲟⲩ ⲁⲛ ⲛⲉ. ⲟⲩⲛ̄ ⲡⲉⲑⲟⲟⲩ ⲇⲉ ⲙⲛ̄- ¹⁴ ⲥⲁ ⲡⲉⲉⲓⲕⲟⲥⲙⲟⲥ ⲉⳍⲙ̄ⲡⲉⲑⲟⲟⲩ ⲛⲁⲙⲉ ⲛⲉ, ¹⁵ ⲧⲉⲧⲟⲩⲙⲟⲩⲧⲉ ⲉⲣⲟⲥ ϫⲉ· « ⲧⲙⲉⲥⲟⲧⲏⲥ. » ⲛ̄ⲧⲟϥ ¹⁶ ⲡⲉ ⲡⲙⲟⲩ. ⳍⲱⲥ ⲉⲛϣⲟⲟⲡ ⳍⲙ̄ ⲡⲉⲉⲓⲕⲟⲥ- ¹⁷ ⲙⲟⲥ, ϣϣⲉ ⲉⲣⲟⲛ ⲉϫⲡⲟ ⲛⲁⲛ ⲛ̄ⲧⲁⲛⲁⲥⲧⲁ- ¹⁸ ⲥⲓⲥ ϫⲉⲕⲁⲁⲥ ⲉⲛϣⲁⲕⲁⲁⲕⲛ ⲁⳍⲏⲩ ⲛ̄ⲧⲥⲁⲣⳍ, ¹⁹ ⲉⲩⲛⲁⳍⲉ ⲉⲣⲟⲛ ⳍⲛ̄ ⲧⲁⲛⲁⲡⲁⲩⲥⲓⲥ ⲛ̄ⲧⲛ̄ⲧⲙ̄- ²⁰ ⲙⲟⲟϣⲉ ⳍⲛ̄ ⲧⲙⲉⲥⲟⲧⲏⲥ. ⳍⲁⳍ ⲅⲁⲣ ⲥⲉⳍⲡⲗⲁ- ²¹ ⲛⲉⲥⲑⲉ ⳍⲛ̄ ⲧⳍⲓⲏ. ⲛⲁⲛⲟⲩⲥ ⲅⲁⲣ ⲉⲉⲓ ⲉⲃⲟⲗ ²² ⳍⲙ̄ ⲡⲕⲟⲥⲙⲟⲥ ⳍⲁ ⲧⲉϥⳍⲏ ⲉⲙⲡⲁⲧⲉ ⲡⲣⲱⲙⲉ ²³ ⲣ̄ ⲛⲟⲃⲉ.

ⲟⲩⲛ̄ ⳍⲟⲉⲓⲛⲉ ⲙⲉⲛ ⲟⲩⲧⲉ ⲥⲉⲟⲩⲱϣ ²⁴ ⲁⲛ ⲟⲩⲧⲉ ⲙⲛ̄ ϭⲟⲙ ⲙ̄ⲙⲟⲟⲩ· ⳍⲛ̄ⲕⲟⲟⲩⲉ ⲇⲉ ²⁵ ⲉⲩϣⲁⲛⲟⲩⲱϣ ⲙⲛ̄ ⳍⲏⲩ ϣⲟⲟⲡ ⲛⲁⲩ ϫⲉ ²⁶ ⲙ̄ⲡⲟⲩⲉⲓⲣⲉ. ⲉⲡ[ⲟⲩ]ⲱϣ ⲅⲁⲣ ϥⲉⲓⲣⲉ ⲙ̄ⲙⲟ- ²⁷ ⲟⲩ ⲛ̄ⲣⲉϥⲣ̄ⲛⲟⲃⲉ̣. [ⲉ]ⲩⲧⲙ̄ⲟⲩⲱϣ ⲇⲉ, ⲧⲇⲓ- ²⁸ ⲕⲁⲓⲟⲥⲩⲛⲏ ⲛⲁⳍⲱⲡ ⲉⲣⲟⲟⲩ ⲙ̄ⲡⲉⲥⲛⲁⲩ. ²⁹ ⲁⲩⲱ ⲡⲟⲩⲱϣ ⲁⲛ [ⲡⲉ], ⲛ̄ⲡⲉⲓⲣⲉ ⲁⲛ.

ⲟⲩⲁⲡⲟ- ³⁰ ⲥ̣ⲧⲟⲗⲓⲕⲟⲥ [ⳍⲛ̄ ⲟ[ⲩ]ⲟⲡⲧⲁⲥⲓⲁ ⲁϥⲛⲁⲩ ⲁⳍⲟ- ³¹ ⲉⲓⲛⲉ ⲉⲩⲟⲧⲡ [ⲉⳍⲟⲩ]ⲛ̄ ⲉⲩⲏⲉⲓ ⲛ̄ⲕⲱⳍⲧ, ⲁⲩ- ³² ⲱ ⲉ[ⲩ]ⲙⲏⲣ ⳍⲛ̄ [ⲡⲉⲓⲏⲉⲓ] ⲛ̄ⲕⲱⳍⲧ, ⲉⲩⲛⲏϫ ³³ [. . .]ⲛ̄ ⲛ̄ⲕⲱⳍⲧ [. . . . .]ⲧⲟⲩ ⲙ̄ⲙⲟⲟⲩ ⳍⲛ̄ ³⁴ [. .ⲡⲓ]ⲥ̣ⲧⲓ̣[ⲥ] ⲛ̄[. . . .], ⲁⲩⲱ ⲡⲉϫⲁⲩ ⲛⲁⲩ ³⁵ [ϫⲉ· « . . . . ϭ]ⲟⲙ ⲙ̄ⲙⲟⲟⲩ

65.30 ⲙ̄ⲡ[. .]ϥ[. .]ⲉ̣[.]ⲛ̄: transcription from earliest images; see Emmel, 114.

65.31 ⲁⲭⲛ̄ [. . .]ⲥ̣[.]ⲥ: transcription from earliest images; see Emmel, 114.

66.6 ⲛ̄ⲥⲟϭ<ⲧ>ⲕ: or ⲛ̄ⲥ<ⲥ>ⲟϭⲕ.

66.29–30 ⲁⲡⲟⲥⲧⲟⲗⲓⲕⲟⲥ [ⳍⲛ̄: transcription from earliest images; see Emmel, 114.

66.31 ⲉⲩⲟⲧⲡ [ⲉⳍⲟⲩ]ⲛ: transcription from earliest images; see Emmel, 114.

and [15] play with him and defile him. In this way, [16] moreover, when ignorant men see [17] beautiful women sitting alone, [18] they persuade her and overpower her, [19] wanting to defile her. But when they see [20] the male and his female sitting [21] with each other, the female is not able to enter [22] into the male, nor is the male [23] able to enter into the female. This is the way (it is) [24] when the image and the angel join with [25] each other, neither will anyone be able to dare [26] to enter into the [male] or the female.

[27] The one who comes out of the world and [28] is (no longer) able to be seized because he was in [29] the world, he is manifest because he is above [30] the desire of the [. . .] fear. [31] He is lord over [. . .]. He is better than [32] jealousy. If [. . .] comes, they grasp [33] him, they strangle [him]. And how will [he] [34] be able to escape the [great powers . . . ? [35]] How will he be able to [. . .]? [36] Some [say,] [37] "We are faithful," in such a manner that [. . . the unclean] spirits [66.1] and demons. [2] For if they had the Holy Spirit, [3] no unclean spirit would unite [4] with them. Do not fear the flesh, nor [5] love it. If you fear it, it will become a lord [6] over you; if you love it, it will swallow you, and it will strangle you.

[7] Unless he comes to be in this world or in the resurrection [8] or in the place that is in the middle, [9] may it never be that I am found among them. In this [10] world there is good (and) [11] there is evil. Its good things [12] are not good things, and its evil things are not [13] evil things. But there is evil following [14] this world that is truly evil, [15] what is called "the middle." It [16] is death. While we are in this world, [17] it is fitting for us to bear for ourselves the resurrection [18] so that when we strip off the flesh, [19] we might be found in rest and not [20] walk in the middle. For many [21] err on the way. For it is good to depart from [22] the world before one has [23] sinned.

Some neither desire [24] nor are able; but others, [25] when they desire, no benefit exists for them because [26] they did not act. For [their] will makes them [27] sinners. But when they do not desire, [28] justice will be hidden from them in both instances. [29] There is no desire, no action.

An [30] apostolic person in [a] vision saw some people [31] trapped [in] a house on fire, [32] imprisoned in [this house] of fire, casting [33] [. . .] of fire [. . .] them in [34] [. . . faith] of [. . .], and they said to them, [35] "[. . .] possible for them to be saved?" [36] [. . .]

66.6 "it will strangle you": or "it will paralyze you."

ⲁⲛⲟⲩⳏⲙ; » ³⁶ [..........]« ⲙ̄ⲡⲟⲩⲟⲩⲱϣ. ⲁⲩϫⲓ ³⁷ [.......]ⲕⲟⲗⲁⲥⲓⲥ ⲡⲁⲉⲓ
ⲉⲧⲟⲩⲙⲟⲩⲧⲉ ⁶⁷·¹ ⲉⲣⲟϥ ϫⲉ· « ⲡⲕⲁⲕⲉ ⲉⲧ[.....]ⲗ » ϫⲉ ϥ [..].

² ⲉⲃⲟⲗ ⳏⲛ̄ ⲟⲩⲙⲟⲟⲩ ⲙⲛ̄ ⲟⲩⲕⲱϩⲧ ⲛ̄ⲧⲁ ⲧⲯⲩⲭ[ⲏ] ³ ⲙⲛ̄ ⲡⲡⲛⲉⲩⲙⲁ ϣⲱⲡⲉ. ⲉⲃⲟⲗ ⳏⲛ̄ ⲟⲩⲙⲟⲟⲩ
ⲙⲛ̄ ⁴ ⲟⲩⲕⲱϩⲧ ⲙⲛ̄ⲛⲟⲩⲟⲉⲓⲛ ⲛ̄ⲧⲁ ⲡϣⲏⲣⲉ ⲙ̄- ⁵ ⲡⲛⲩⲙⲫⲱⲛ. ⲡⲕⲱϩⲧ ⲡⲉ ⲡⲭⲣⲓⲥⲙⲁ· ⲡⲟⲩⲟ- ⁶
ⲉⲓⲛ ⲡⲉ ⲡⲕⲱϩⲧ. ⲉⲉⲓϣⲁϫⲉ ⲁⲛ ⲁⲡⲉⲉⲓⲕⲱϩⲧ ⁷ ⲉⲧⲉ ⲙⲛ̄ⲧⲁϥ ⲙⲟⲣⲫⲏ, ⲁⲗⲗⲁ ⲡⲕⲉⲟⲩⲁ ⲉⲧⲉ
<ⲧⲉ>ϥ- ⁸ ⲙⲟⲣϥⲏ ⲟⲩⲁⲃϣ ⲉⲧⲟ ⲛ̄ⲟⲩⲟⲉⲓⲛ ⲉⲛⲉⲥⲱϥ ⁹ ⲁⲩⲱ ⲉⲧ† ⲛ̄ⲧⲙⲛ̄ⲧⲥⲁ.

ⲧⲁⲗⲏⲑⲉⲓⲁ ⲙ̄ⲡⲉⲥⲉⲓ ¹⁰ ⲉⲡⲕⲟⲥⲙⲟⲥ ⲉⲥⲕⲁⲕ ⲁϩⲏⲩ. ⲁⲗⲗⲁ ⲛ̄ⲧⲁⲥⲉⲓ ⳏⲛ̄ ¹¹ ⲛ̄ⲧⲩⲡⲟⲥ ⲙⲛ̄ ⲛ̄ϩⲓⲕⲱⲛ.
ϥⲛⲁϫⲓⲧⲥ̄ ⲁⲛ ⲛ̄ⲕⲉⲣⲏ- ¹² ⲧⲉ. ⲟⲩⲛ̄ ⲟⲩϫⲡⲟ ⲛ̄ⲕⲉⲥⲟⲡ ϣⲟⲟⲡ ⲙ̄ⲛ̄ⲛⲟⲩ- ¹³ ϩⲓⲕⲱⲛ ⲛ̄ϫⲡⲟ ⲛ̄ⲕⲉⲥⲟⲡ.
ϣϣⲉ ⲁⲗⲏⲑⲱⲥ ¹⁴ ⲁⲧⲣⲟⲩϫⲡⲟⲟⲩ ⲛ̄ⲕⲉⲥⲟⲡ ϩⲓⲧⲛ̄ ⲧϩⲓⲕⲱⲛ. ⲁϣ ¹⁵ ⲧⲉ ⲧⲁⲛⲁⲥⲧⲁⲥⲓⲥ; ⲁⲩⲱ
ⲑⲓⲕⲱⲛ ϩⲓⲧⲛ̄ ⲑⲓⲕⲱⲛ ¹⁶ ϣϣⲉ ⲉⲧⲣⲉⲥⲧⲱⲟⲩⲛ. ⲡⲛⲩⲙⲫⲱⲛ ⲙⲛ̄ ⲑⲓ- ¹⁷ ⲕⲱⲛ ϩⲓⲧⲛ̄ ⲑⲓⲕⲱⲛ ϣϣⲉ
ⲉⲧⲣⲟⲩⲉⲓ ⲉϩⲟⲩⲛ ¹⁸ ⲉⲧⲁⲗⲏⲑⲉⲓⲁ ⲉⲧⲉ ⲧⲁⲉⲓ ⲧⲉ ⲧⲁⲡⲟⲕⲁⲧⲁⲥⲧⲁⲥⲓⲥ. ¹⁹ ϣϣⲉ ⲁⲛⲉⲧϫⲡⲟ ⲁⲛ
ⲙ̄ⲙⲁⲧⲉ ⲙ̄ⲡⲣⲁⲛ ⲙ̄- ²⁰ ⲡⲉⲓⲱⲧ ⲙⲛ̄ ⲡϣⲏⲣⲉ ⲙⲛ̄ ⲡⲡⲛⲉⲩⲙⲁ ⲉⲧⲟⲩⲁⲁⲃ, ²¹ ⲁⲗⲗⲁ
ⲁ<ⲛⲉⲛⲧⲁ>ⲩϫⲡⲟⲟⲩ ⲛⲁⲕ ϩⲱⲟⲩ. ⲉⲧⲙ̄ ⲟⲩⲁ ϫⲡⲟ- ²² ⲟⲩ ⲛⲁϥ, ⲡⲕⲉⲣⲁⲛ ⲥⲉⲛⲁϥⲓⲧϥ ⲛ̄ⲧⲟⲟⲧϥ.
²³ ⲟⲩⲁ ⲇⲉ ϫⲓ ⲙ̄ⲙⲟⲟⲩ ϩⲙ̄ ⲡⲭⲣⲓⲥⲙⲁ ⲙ̄ⲡⲥⲟϭ[ⲛ] ²⁴ ⲛ̄ⲧⲇⲩⲛⲁⲙⲓⲥ ⲙ̄ⲡⲥⲧⲁⲩⲣ[ⲟ]ⲥ. ⲧⲁ[ⲉ]ⲓ ⲛⲉ
ⲛⲁⲡⲟⲥⲧⲟ- ²⁵ ⲗⲟⲥ ⲙⲟⲩⲧⲉ ⲉⲣⲟⲥ ϫⲉ, « [ⲧⲟ]ⲅⲩⲁⲙ ⲙⲛ̄ ⲧⲉϩⲃⲟⲩⲣ, » ²⁶ ⲡⲁⲉⲓ ⲅⲁⲣ ⲟⲩⲕⲉⲧⲓ
ⲟⲩ[ⲭⲣⲏ]ⲥⲧ[ⲓ]ⲁⲛⲟⲥ ⲡⲉ, ⲁⲗⲗⲁ ²⁷ ⲟⲩⲭⲣⲓⲥⲧⲟⲥ ⲡⲉ.

ⲁⲡϫⲟⲉⲓ[ⲥ ⲣ̄] ϩⲱⲃ ⲛⲓⲙ ϩⲛ̄ⲛⲟⲩ- ²⁸ ⲙⲩⲥⲧⲏⲣⲓⲟⲛ· ⲟⲩⲃⲁⲡⲧⲓⲥⲙⲁ ⲙⲛ̄ ⲟⲩⲭⲣⲓⲥ- ²⁹ ⲙⲁ
ⲙⲛ̄ⲛⲟⲩⲉⲩⲭⲁⲣ[ⲓⲥⲧ]ⲓⲁ ⲙⲛ̄ⲛⲟⲩⲥⲱⲧⲉ ³⁰ ⲙⲛ̄ⲛⲟⲩⲛⲩⲙⲫⲱⲛ.

[..]. [.]. ⲡ[ⲉⲭ]ⲁϥ ³¹ ϫⲉ· « ⲁⲉⲓ ⲉⲧⲣⲁⲉⲓⲣⲉ [ⲛ̄ⲛⲁ ⲡⲥⲁ ⲙⲡⲓⲧ]ⲛ̄ ⲛ̄- ³² ⲑⲉ ⲛ̄ⲛⲁ ⲡⲥⲁ ⲛ̄[ⲧⲡⲉ,
ⲁⲩⲱ ⲛⲁ ⲡⲥⲁ ⲛ̄]ⲃⲟⲗ ³³ ⲛ̄ⲑⲉ ⲛ̄ⲛⲁ ⲡⲥ[ⲁ ⲛϩⲟⲩⲛ, ⲁⲩⲱ ⲉⲧⲣⲁϩⲟⲧ]- ³⁴ ⲣⲟⲩ ⲙ̄ⲡⲙⲁ ⲉⲧⲙ̄[......
»..... ⲛⲉ]- ³⁵ ⲉⲓⲙⲁ ϩⲓⲧⲛ̄ ϩⲛ̄ⲧⲩ[ⲡⲟⲥ.........] ³⁶ ⲛⲉⲧϫⲱ ⲙ̄ⲙⲟⲥ ϫⲉ· [« ⲟⲩⲛ̄
ⲟⲩⲣⲙ̄ⲙⲡⲉ, ⲁⲩⲱ] ³⁷ ⲟⲩⲛ̄ ⲟⲩⲉⲓ ⲙ̄ⲡⲥⲁ ⲛⲧⲡⲉ [ⲙ̄ⲙⲟϥ. » ⲥⲉⲣⲡⲗⲁ]- ³⁸ ⲛⲁⲥⲑⲉ. ⲡⲉⲧⲟⲩⲟⲛϩ
ⲅ[ⲁⲣ ⲉⲃⲟⲗ ⲡⲣⲙ̄ⲙ]- ⁶⁸·¹ ⲡⲉ ⲉⲧⲙ̄ⲙⲁⲩ ⲡ[ⲉ]ⲧⲟ[ⲩ]ⲙⲟⲩⲧⲉ ⲉⲣⲟϥ ϫⲉ ² « ⲡⲉⲧⲙ̄ⲡⲥⲁ ⲛⲡⲓⲧⲛ̄, »
ⲁⲩⲱ ⲡⲉⲧⲉ ⲡⲉⲑⲏⲡ ³ ϣⲟⲟⲡ ⲛⲁϥ, ⲡⲉⲧⲙ̄ⲙⲁⲩ ⲡⲉ ⲉⲧⲛ̄ⲧⲡⲉ ⲙ̄- ⁴ ⲙⲟϥ. ⲛⲁⲛⲟⲩⲥ ⲅⲁⲣ ⲛ̄ⲥⲉϫⲟⲟⲥ
ϫⲉ· « ⲡⲥⲁ ⲛ- ⁵ ϩⲟⲩⲛ ⲁⲩⲱ ⲡⲉⲧⲙ̄ⲡⲥⲁ ⲛⲃⲟⲗ, ⲙⲛ̄ ⲡⲉⲧⲛ̄- ⁶ ⲡⲥⲁ ⲛⲃⲟⲗ ⲙ̄ⲡⲥⲁ ⲛⲃⲟⲗ. » ⲉⲧⲃⲉ
ⲡⲁⲓ̈ ⲁⲡϫⲟ- ⁷ ⲉⲓⲥ ⲙⲟⲩⲧⲉ ⲁⲡⲧⲁⲕⲟ ϫⲉ « ⲡⲕⲁⲕⲉ ⲉⲧϩⲓ ⲡⲥⲁ ⲛ- ⁸ ⲃⲟⲗ, » ⲙⲛ̄ ϭⲉ ϣⲟⲟⲡ
ⲙ̄ⲡⲉϥⲃⲁⲗ. ⲡⲉϫⲁϥ ⁹ ϫⲉ· « ⲡⲁⲉⲓⲱⲧ ⲉⲧϩⲙ̄ ⲡⲉⲑⲏⲡ. » ⲡⲉϫⲁϥ ϫⲉ· ¹⁰ « ⲃⲱⲕ ⲉϩⲟⲩⲛ
ⲉⲡⲉⲕⲧⲁⲙⲉⲓⲟⲛ, ⲛ̄ⲅϣ̄ⲧⲁⲙ ¹¹ ⲙ̄ⲡⲉⲕⲣⲟ ⲉⲣⲱⲕ, ⲛ̄ⲅϣⲗⲏⲗ ⲁⲡⲉⲕⲉⲓⲱⲧ ¹² ⲉⲧϩⲙ̄ ⲡⲉⲑⲏⲡ, ⲉⲧⲉ
ⲡⲁⲉⲓ ⲡⲉ, ⲡⲉⲧϩⲓ ⲥⲁ ⲛ- ¹³ ϩⲟⲩⲛ ⲙ̄ⲙⲟⲟⲩ ⲧⲏⲣⲟⲩ. » ⲡⲉⲧϩⲓ ⲥⲁ ⲛϩⲟⲩⲛ ¹⁴ ⲇⲉ ⲙ̄ⲙⲟⲟⲩ ⲧⲏⲣⲟⲩ
ⲡⲉ ⲡⲡⲗⲏⲣⲱⲙⲁ. ⲙ̄- ¹⁵ ⲙⲛ̄ⲛⲥⲱϥ ⲙⲛ̄ ϭⲉ ⲙ̄ⲡⲉϥⲥⲁ ⲛϩⲟⲩⲛ. ⲡⲁ- ¹⁶ ⲉⲓ ⲡⲉ ⲉⲧⲟⲩϣⲁϫⲉ ⲉⲣⲟϥ
ϫⲉ· « ⲡⲉⲧⲙ̄ⲡⲥⲁ ⲛ- ¹⁷ ⲧⲡⲉ ⲙ̄ⲙⲟⲟⲩ. »

"They did not desire. They received ³⁷ [. . .] chastisement, that which is called ⁶⁷.¹ "the darkness that [. . .]" that he [. . .].

² From water and fire have the soul ³ and spirit come to be. From water and ⁴ fire and light has the child of ⁵ the bridal chamber (come to be). Fire is the chrism; light ⁶ is the fire. I am not speaking about this fire ⁷ that does not have form, but the other one that has ⁸ a white form, which is luminous and beautiful ⁹ and which exudes beauty.

Truth did not come ¹⁰ into the world stripped naked. Rather it came in ¹¹ types and images. It (the world) will not receive it any other way. ¹² There is a rebirth and an ¹³ image of a rebirth. It is truly necessary ¹⁴ that they be reborn through the image. What ¹⁵ is the resurrection? ¹⁶ It is necessary for the image to rise through the image. It is necessary for the bridal chamber and the ¹⁷ image to come through the image into ¹⁸ truth, that is, the restoration. ¹⁹ It is necessary not only for us to produce the name of ²⁰ the Father and the Son and the Holy Spirit, ²¹ but also for <those who have> produced ²² them for you. If one does not produce them for himself, the other name will be taken from him. ²³ But one receives them in the chrism of the [ointment] ²⁴ of the power of the cross. This (power) the apostles ²⁵ called "[the] right and the left," ²⁶ since this one is no longer a Christian, but ²⁷ he is a Christ.

The Lord [did] everything in a ²⁸ mystery: a baptism and a chrism ²⁹ and a Eucharist and a redemption ³⁰ and a bridal chamber.

[. . .] he [said], ³¹ "I have come to make [the things below] like ³² the things [above, and the things outside] ³³ like the things [inside, and to join] ³⁴ them in the place that [. . ." these] ³⁵ places in the [type . . .] ³⁶ those who say, ["There is a heavenly man, and] ³⁷ there is one above [him." They are] ³⁸ wrong. [For] the one who is manifest, that [heavenly man], ⁶⁸.¹ the one they call ² "the one below," and the one to whom the hidden things ³ belong, this one is the one above ⁴ him. For it would be better for them to say, "The inside ⁵ and the outside, and the outside ⁶ of the outside." For this reason the Lord ⁷ called defilement "the darkness outside." ⁸ No other is outside of it. He said, ⁹ "My Father who is in what is hidden." He said, ¹⁰ "Go into your storehouse, and close ¹¹ your door behind you, and pray to your Father ¹² who is in what is hidden, that is, the one who is within ¹³ them all." But the one who is within ¹⁴ them all is the fullness. ¹⁵ After it, no other is within. This is the one ¹⁶ about whom they say, "The one above ¹⁷ them."

67.22 "the other name": presumably the name "Christian" (see 67.26).

ϩⲁ ⲧⲉϩⲏ ⲙ̄ⲡⲉⲭⲣⲓⲥⲧⲟⲥ ⲁϩⲟⲉⲓⲛⲉ ¹⁸ ⲉⲓ ⲉⲃⲟⲗ ⲉⲃⲟⲗ ⲧⲱⲛ ⲟⲩⲕⲉⲧⲓ ⲙ̄ⲡⲟⲩϣ- ¹⁹ ⲃⲱⲕ ⲉϩⲟⲩⲛ, ⲁⲩⲱ ⲁⲩⲃⲱⲕ ⲉⲧⲱⲛ ⲟⲩⲕⲉⲧⲓ ²⁰ ⲙ̄ⲡⲟⲩϣⲓ ⲉⲃⲟⲗ. ⲁϥⲉⲓ ⲇⲉ ⲛ̄ϭⲓ ⲡⲉⲭⲣⲓⲥⲧⲟⲥ. ⲛⲉⲛ- ²¹ ⲧⲁϩⲃⲱⲕ ⲉϩⲟⲩⲛ ⲁϥⲛ̄ⲧⲟⲩ ⲉⲃⲟⲗ, ⲁⲩⲱ ⲛⲉⲛ- ²² ⲧⲁϩⲃⲱⲕ ⲉⲃⲟⲗ ⲁϥⲛ̄ⲧⲟⲩ ⲉϩⲟⲩⲛ.

ⲛ̄ϩⲟⲟⲩ ²³ ⲛⲉⲣⲉ ⲉⲩϩⲁ [ϩ]ⲛ̄ ⲁ[ⲇ]ⲁⲙ ⲛⲉ ⲙⲛ̄ ⲙⲟⲩ ϣⲟⲟⲡ. ²⁴ ⲛ̄ⲧⲁⲣⲉⲥⲡⲱⲣϫ [ⲉⲣ]ⲟϥ ⲁⲡⲙⲟⲩ ϣⲱⲡⲉ. ⲡⲁ- ²⁵ ⲗⲓⲛ ⲉϥϣⲁⲃϣ[ⲕ ⲉϩ]ⲟⲩⲛ ⲛ̄ϥϫⲓⲧϥ ⲉⲣⲟϥ, ⲙⲛ̄ ²⁶ ⲙⲟⲩ ⲛⲁϣⲱⲡⲉ.

« [ⲡ]ⲁⲛⲟⲩⲧⲉ ⲡⲁⲛⲟⲩⲧⲉ ⲉ- ²⁷ ⲧⲃⲉ ⲟⲩ ⲡϫⲟⲉⲓⲥ [ⲁ]ⲕⲕⲁⲁⲧ ⲛ̄ⲥⲱⲕ; » ⲛ̄ⲧⲁϥϫⲉ ²⁸ ⲛⲁⲉⲓ ϩⲓ ⲡⲥⲧⲁⲩⲣⲟⲥ. [ⲛⲉ]ⲁϥⲡⲱⲣϫ ⲅⲁⲣ ⲙ̄ⲡⲙⲁ ²⁹ ⲉⲧ[ⲙ̄]ⲙⲁⲩ.

[.].. [. . .] ⲛ̄ⲧⲁⲩϫⲡⲟϥ ⲉⲃⲟⲗ ϩⲙ̄ ³⁰ ⲡⲉⲧ[. . . . . . ⲉ]ⲃⲟⲗ ϩⲓⲧⲙ̄ ⲡⲛⲟⲩⲧⲉ.

³¹ ⲁⲡ[. . . . . . . .ⲉⲃ]ⲟⲗ ϩⲛ̄ ⲛⲉⲧⲙⲟⲟⲩⲧ ³² .[. . . . . ϣ]ⲟⲟⲡ, ⲁⲗⲗⲁ ⲛⲉ- ³³ [. . . . .] ⲉϥⲟ ⲛ̄ⲧⲉⲗⲉⲓⲟⲛ ³⁴ [. . . . .] ⲛ̄ⲥⲁⲣⲝ, ⲁⲗⲗⲁ ⲧⲉⲉⲓ ³⁵ [. . . . . . ⲟⲩⲥ]-ⲁⲣⲝ ⲧⲉ ⲛ̄ⲁⲗⲏⲑⲉⲓⲛⲏ ³⁶ [. . . . . .] ⲟⲩⲁⲗⲏⲑⲉⲓⲛⲏ ⲁⲛ ⲧⲉ, ⲁⲗ- ³⁷ [ⲗⲁ. . . . .] ⲛ̄ϩⲓⲕⲱⲛ ⲛ̄ⲧⲁⲗⲏⲑⲉⲓⲛⲏ.

⁶⁹·¹ ⲙⲁⲣⲉ ⲡⲁⲥⲧⲟⲥ ϣⲱⲡⲉ ⲛ̄ⲛⲑⲏⲣⲓⲟⲛ, ⲟⲩ- ² ⲧⲉ ⲙⲁϥϣⲱⲡⲉ ⲛ̄ⲛϩⲙ̄ϩⲁⲗ ⲟⲩⲧⲉ ⲛ̄ⲥϩⲓⲙⲉ ³ ⲉϥϫⲟϩⲙ ⲁⲗⲗⲁ ϣⲁϥϣⲱⲡⲉ ⲛ̄ϩⲛ̄ⲣⲱⲙⲉ ⁴ ⲛ̄ⲉⲗⲉⲩⲑⲉⲣⲟⲥ ⲙⲛ̄ ϩⲛ̄ⲡⲁⲣⲑⲉⲛⲟⲥ.

ⲉⲃⲟⲗ ⁵ ϩⲓⲧⲙ̄ ⲡⲛⲉⲩⲙⲁ ⲉⲧⲟⲩⲁⲁⲃ ⲥⲉϫⲡⲟ ⲙⲉⲛ ⲙ̄ⲙⲟⲛ ⁶ ⲛ̄ⲕⲉⲥⲟⲡ. ⲥⲉϫⲡⲟ ⲇⲉ ⲙ̄ⲙⲟⲛ ϩⲓⲧⲛ̄ ⲡⲉ- ⁷ ⲭⲣⲓⲥⲧⲟⲥ ϩⲙ̄ ⲡⲥⲛⲁⲩ. ⲥⲉⲧⲱϩⲥ ⲙ̄ⲙⲟⲛ ϩⲓⲧⲙ̄ ⲡ- ⁸ ⲡⲛⲉⲩⲙⲁ. ⲛ̄ⲧⲁⲣⲟⲩϫⲡⲟⲛ ⲁⲩϩⲟⲧⲣⲛ̄. ⲙⲛ̄ ⲗⲁⲁⲩ ⁹ ⲛⲁϣⲛⲁⲩ ⲉⲣⲟϥ ⲟⲩⲧⲉ ϩⲙ̄ ⲙⲟⲟⲩ ⲟⲩⲧⲉ ϩⲛ̄ ¹⁰ ⲉⲓⲁⲗ ⲭⲱⲣⲓⲥ ⲟⲩⲟⲉⲓⲛ ⲟⲩⲧⲉ ⲡⲁⲗⲓⲛ ⲕⲛⲁϣ- ¹¹ ⲛⲁⲩ ⲁⲛ ϩⲛ̄ ⲟⲩⲟⲉⲓⲛ ⲭⲱⲣⲓⲥ ⲙⲟⲟⲩ ϩⲓⲁⲗ. ¹² ⲇⲓⲁ ⲧⲟⲩⲧⲟ ϣϣⲉ ⲁⲣⲃⲁⲡⲧⲓⲍⲉ ϩⲙ̄ ⲡⲥⲛⲁⲩ ¹³ ϩⲙ̄ ⲡⲟⲩⲟⲉⲓⲛ ⲙⲛ̄ ⲡⲙⲟⲟⲩ. ⲡⲟⲩⲟⲉⲓⲛ ⲇⲉ ¹⁴ ⲡⲉ ⲡⲭⲣⲓⲥⲙⲁ.

ⲛⲉⲩⲛ̄ ϣⲟⲙⲧ ⲛ̄ⲏⲉⲓ ⲙ̄ⲙⲁ ¹⁵ ⲛ̄ϯⲡⲣⲟⲥⲫⲟⲣⲁ ϩⲛ̄ ⲑⲓⲉⲣⲟⲥⲟⲗⲩⲙⲁ· ⲡⲟⲩ- ¹⁶ ⲁ ⲉϥⲟⲩⲉⲛ ⲉⲡⲁⲙⲛ̄ⲧⲉ ⲉⲩⲙⲟⲩⲧⲉ ⲉⲣⲟϥ ¹⁷ ϫⲉ « ⲡⲉⲧⲟⲩⲁⲁⲃ, » ⲡⲕⲉⲟⲩⲁ ⲉϥⲟⲩⲏⲛ ⲉⲡⲥⲁ- ¹⁸ ⲣⲏⲥ ⲉⲩⲙⲟⲩⲧⲉ ⲉⲣⲟϥ ϫⲉ « ⲡⲉⲧⲟⲩⲁⲁⲃ ⲙ̄- ¹⁹ ⲡⲉⲧⲟⲩⲁⲁⲃ, » ⲡⲙⲁϩϣⲟⲙⲧ ⲉϥⲟⲩⲏⲛ ⲁ- ²⁰ ⲡⲁⲉⲓⲃⲧⲉ ⲉⲩⲙⲟⲩⲧⲉ ⲉⲣⲟϥ ϫⲉ « ⲡⲉⲧⲟⲩⲁⲁⲃ ²¹ ⲛ̄ⲛⲉⲧⲟⲩⲁⲁⲃ. » ⲡⲙⲁ ⲉϣⲁⲣⲉ ⲡⲁⲣⲭⲓⲉⲣⲉⲩ[ⲥ] ²² ⲃⲱⲕ ⲉϩⲟⲩⲛ ⲉⲙⲁⲩ ⲟⲩⲁ[ⲁ]ϥ. ⲡⲃⲁⲡⲧⲓⲥⲙⲁ ²³ ⲡⲉ ⲡⲏⲉⲓ « ⲉⲧⲟⲩⲁⲁⲃ, » [ⲡ]ⲥⲱ[ⲧ]ⲉ « ⲡⲉⲧⲟⲩⲁⲁⲃ ²⁴ ⲙ̄ⲡⲉⲧⲟⲩⲁⲁⲃ, » « ⲡⲉⲧ[ⲟⲩⲁ]ⲁⲃ ⲛ̄ⲛⲉⲧⲟⲩⲁⲁⲃ » ²⁵ ⲡⲉ ⲡⲛⲩⲙⲫⲱⲛ. ⲡ[ⲃⲁⲡⲧⲓ]ⲥⲙⲁ ⲟⲩⲛ̄ⲧⲁϥ ²⁶ ⲙ̄ⲙⲁⲩ ⲛ̄ⲧⲁⲛⲁⲥⲧⲁⲥ[ⲓⲥ ⲙⲛ̄ ⲡ]ⲥⲱⲧⲉ, ⲉⲡⲥⲱ- ²⁷ ⲧⲉ ϩⲙ̄ ⲡⲛⲩⲙⲫⲱⲛ. [ⲉⲡⲛⲩ]ⲙⲫⲱⲛ ⲇⲉ ²⁸ ϩⲙ̄ ⲡⲉⲧϫⲟⲥⲉ ⲉⲣⲟ[. . . .]ⲛ̄[.]ⲟⲟ.[.] ²⁹ ⲕⲛⲁϩⲉ ⲁⲛ ⲉⲧⲉϥ[. . . . .]ⲧⲱⲡ [. . . .] ³⁰ ⲛⲉ ⲛⲉⲧϣⲗⲏⲗ [. . . . .] ³¹ ⲑⲓⲉⲣⲟⲥⲟⲗⲩⲙ[ⲁ. . . . . . . .ⲑⲓⲉⲣⲟ]- ³² ⲥⲟⲗⲩⲙⲁ ⲉⲩϣ[. . . . . ⲑⲓⲉⲣⲟⲥⲟ]- ³³ ⲗⲩⲙⲁ ⲉⲩϭⲱϣ[ⲧ. . . . .] ³⁴ ⲛⲁⲉⲓ ⲉⲧⲟⲩⲙⲟⲩ[ⲧⲉ ⲉⲣⲟⲟⲩ ϫⲉ « ⲡⲉⲧⲟⲩ]- ³⁵ ⲁⲁⲃ ⲛ̄ⲛⲉⲧⲟⲩⲁⲁⲃ » [. . . . . . . ⲁⲡⲉϥⲕⲁ]- ³⁶ ⲧⲁⲡⲉⲧⲁⲥⲙⲁ ⲡⲱϩ ⲕⲉ[. . . . .] ³⁷ ⲡⲁⲥⲧⲟⲥ ⲉⲓ ⲙⲏ ⲑⲓⲕⲱⲛ [. . . . . . . ⲉⲧ]- ⁷⁰·¹ [ⲙ̄]ⲡⲥⲁ ⲛⲧⲡ[ⲉ.] ⲉⲧ[ⲃ]ⲉ [ⲡ]ⲁⲉⲓ ⲁⲡⲉϥⲕⲁⲧⲁ- ² ⲡⲉⲧⲁⲥⲙⲁ ⲡⲱϩ[ϩ] ϫⲓⲛ ⲡⲥⲁ ⲛⲧⲡⲉ ϣⲁ ³ ⲡⲥⲁ ⲙⲡⲓⲧⲛ̄. ⲛⲉϣϣⲉ ⲅⲁⲣ ⲉϩⲟⲉⲓⲛⲉ ⁴ ϫⲓⲛ ⲡⲥⲁ ⲙⲡⲓⲧⲛ̄ ⲛ̄ⲥⲉⲃⲱⲕ ⲉⲡⲥⲁ ⲛⲧⲡⲉ.

69.11 ϩⲓⲁⲗ: i.e. ϩⲓ ⲉⲓⲁⲗ
69.24 ⲡⲉⲧ[ⲟⲩⲁ]ⲁⲃ: transcription from earliest images; see Emmel, 114.

Before Christ some [18] came from where they were no longer able to go into, and they went to where they were no longer [20] able to come from. But Christ came. Those who [21] went in he brought out, and those [22] who went out he brought in.

When [23] Eve was in Adam there was no death. [24] After she separated [from] him death came about. [25] If he goes in again and receives himself to himself, [26] death will cease to be.

"My God, my god, [27] why, Lord, have you forsaken me?" He said [28] these things upon the cross. For he had departed from [29] that place.

[. . .] He was begotten in [30] that which [. . .] from God.

[31] The [. . .] from those who are dead [32] . [. . .] exist, but [33] the [. . .] who is perfect [34] [. . .] of flesh, but this [35] [. . .] is [a] true flesh [36] [. . .]. It is not true, but [37] [. . .] image of what is true.

[69.1]The bridal chamber is not for the animals, nor [2] is it for slaves or defiled women. [3] Rather, it is for [4] free men and virgins.

Through [5] the Holy Spirit we are in fact begotten [6] again. But we are begotten through [7] Christ in the two. We are anointed through the [8] Spirit. When we were begotten, we were joined. No one [9] will be able to see himself either in water or in [10] a mirror without light, nor again will you be able [11] to see in light without water or a mirror. [12] For this reason it is necessary to baptize in the two, [13] in light and water. Now the light [14] is the chrism.

There were three buildings [15] for sacrifice in Jerusalem: one [16] facing west called [17] "the holy," another facing south [18] called "the holy of [19] the holy," (and) the third facing [20] east called "the holy [21] of the holies," the place in which only the high priest [22] enters. Baptism [23] is the building that is "the holy," redemption is "the holy [24] of the holy," "the [holy] of the holies" [25] is the bridal chamber. [Baptism] has [26] the resurrection [and the] redemption, (and) the redemption [27] (occurs) within the bridal chamber. But [the] bridal chamber is [28] in what is exalted above [. . .] [29] you will not [. . .] [30] are those who pray [. . .] [31] Jerusalem [. . .] [32] Jerusalem [. . .] [33] Jerusalem watching [. . .] [34] those that are called "[the] holy [35] of the holies" [. . . its] [36] veil [was] torn [. . .] [37] bridal chamber except the image [. . .] [70.1] above. For this reason its veil [2] was torn from top to [3] bottom. For it was necessary for some [4] from below to go above.

⁵ ⲛⲉⲛⲧⲁϩϯ ϩⲓⲱⲟⲩ ⲙ̄ⲡⲧⲉⲗⲉⲓⲟⲛ ⲛ̄ⲟⲩ- ⁶ ⲟⲉⲓⲛ ⲙⲁⲣⲟⲩⲛⲁⲩ ⲉⲣⲟⲟⲩ ⲛ̄ϭⲓ ⲛ̄ⲇⲩⲛⲁ- ⁷ ⲙⲓⲥ, ⲁⲩⲱ ⲙⲁⲩϣⲉⲙⲁϩⲧⲉ ⲙ̄ⲙⲟⲟⲩ. ⲟⲩ- ⁸ ⲁ ⲇⲉ ⲛⲁϯ ϩⲓⲱⲱϥ ⲙ̄ⲡⲓⲟⲩⲟⲉⲓⲛ ϩⲙ̄ ⁹ ⲡⲙⲩⲥⲧⲏⲣⲓⲟⲛ ϩⲙ̄ ⲡϩⲱⲧⲣ̄.

ⲛⲉⲙⲡⲉⲧ- ¹⁰ ⲥϩⲓⲙⲉ ⲡⲱⲣϫ ⲉϥⲟⲟⲩⲧ, ⲛⲉⲥⲛⲁⲙⲟⲩ ¹¹ ⲁⲛ ⲡⲉ ⲙⲛ̄ ⲫⲟⲟⲩⲧ. ⲡⲉϥⲡⲱⲣϫ ⲛ̄ⲧⲁϥ- ¹² ϣⲱⲡⲉ ⲛ̄ⲁⲣⲭⲏ ⲙ̄ⲡⲙⲟⲩ. ⲇⲓⲁ ⲧⲟⲩⲧⲟ ¹³ ⲁⲡⲉⲭⲣⲓⲥⲧⲟⲥ ⲉⲓ ϫⲉⲕⲁⲁⲥ ⲡⲡⲱⲣϫ ⲛ̄ⲧⲁϩ- ¹⁴ ϣⲱⲡⲉ ϫⲓⲛ ϣⲟⲣⲡ ⲉϥⲛⲁⲥⲉϩⲱϥ ⲉⲣⲁⲧϥ ¹⁵ ⲡⲁⲗⲓⲛ ⲛ̄ϥϩⲟⲧⲣⲟⲩ ⲙ̄ⲡⲥⲛⲁⲩ. ⲁⲩⲱ ⲛⲉⲛ- ¹⁶ ⲧⲁϩⲙⲟⲩ ϩⲙ̄ ⲡⲡⲱⲣϫ ⲉϥⲛⲁϯ ⲛⲁⲩ ⲛ̄ⲛⲟⲩ- ¹⁷ ⲱⲛϩ ⲛ̄ϥϩⲟⲧⲣⲟⲩ. ϣⲁⲣⲉⲧⲥϩⲓⲙⲉ ⲇⲉ ¹⁸ ϩⲱⲧⲣ̄ ⲁⲡⲉⲥϩⲁⲉⲓ ϩⲣⲁⲓ̈ ϩⲙ̄ ⲡⲡⲁⲥⲧⲟⲥ. ¹⁹ ⲛⲉⲛⲧⲁϩⲱⲧⲣ̄ ⲇⲉ ϩⲙ̄ ⲡⲡⲁⲥⲧⲟⲥ ⲟⲩⲕⲉ- ²⁰ ⲧⲓ ⲥⲉⲛⲁⲡⲱⲣϫ. ⲇⲓⲁ ⲧⲟⲩⲧⲟ ⲁⲉⲩϩⲁ ²¹ ⲡⲱⲣϫ ⲁⲁⲇⲁⲙ ϫⲉ ⲛ̄ⲧⲁⲥϩⲱⲧⲣ̄ ⲉⲣⲟϥ ²² ⲁⲛ ϩⲙ̄ ⲡⲡⲁⲥ[ⲧⲟ]ⲥ.

ⲧ̄ⲯⲩⲭⲏ ⲛ̄ⲁⲇⲁⲙ ⲛ̄- ²³ ⲧⲁⲥϣⲱⲡⲉ ⲉ̣[ⲃ]ⲟⲗ ϩⲛ̄ⲛⲟⲩⲛⲓϥⲉ. ⲡⲉⲥ- ²⁴ ϩⲱⲧⲣ̄ ⲡⲉ ⲡⲡ[ⲛⲉⲩⲙ]ⲁ̣. ⲡ[ⲉ] ⲛⲧⲁⲩⲧⲁⲁϥ ⲛⲁϥ ²⁵ ⲧⲉ ⲧⲉϥⲙⲁⲁⲩ. ⲁⲩ[ϥⲓ] ⲛ̄ⲧⲉϥⲯⲩⲭⲏ, ⲁⲩϯ ²⁶ ⲛⲁϥ ⲛ̄ⲛⲟⲩ[ⲡⲛⲉⲩⲙⲁ ⲉ]- ⲡⲉⲥⲙⲁ. ⲉⲡⲉⲓ ⲛ̄- ²⁷ ⲧⲁⲣⲉϥϩⲱⲧⲣ̄, [ⲁϥϫ]ⲱ ⲛ̄ϩⲛ̄ϣⲁϫⲉ ⲉⲩϫⲟ- ²⁸ ⲥⲉ ⲁⲛⲇⲩⲛⲁ[ⲙⲓⲥ]. ⲁⲩ̄ⲣ̄ⲃⲁⲥⲕⲁⲛⲉ ⲉⲣⲟϥ ²⁹ [. . . .]ⲣϫ [. . . ⲡϩ]ⲱⲧⲣ̄ ⲙ̄ⲡⲛⲉⲩⲙⲁ- ³⁰ [ⲧⲓⲕ.] . . ⲁ[. . . . .]ⲕⲏ ⲧⲉⲑⲏⲡ ⲁⲩ- ³¹ [. . . . .] ⲉ̣ⲓϭⲉ ⲛ̄ϭⲓ ⲡⲉ- ³² [. . . . .] ̣ ⲛⲁⲩ ⲟⲩⲁⲁⲩ ³³ [. . . . . ⲡ]ⲁⲥⲧⲟⲥ ϣⲓⲛⲁ ³⁴ [. . . . .] ⲟⲩ.

ⲁⲓⲏⲥⲟⲩⲥ ϭⲱⲗⲡ ³⁵ [ⲉⲃⲟⲗ. . . . .ⲡⲉⲓⲟ]ⲣⲇⲁⲛⲏⲥ ⲡⲡⲗⲏ- ³⁶ [ⲣⲱⲙⲁ ⲛ̄ⲧⲙⲛ̄ⲧⲉ]ⲣⲟ ⲛ̄ⲙ̄ⲡⲏⲩⲉ. ⲡⲉⲛ- ³⁷ [ⲧⲁⲩⲭⲡⲟϥ ϩ]ⲁ ⲧⲉϩⲏ ⲙ̄ⲡⲧⲏⲣϥ ⲡⲁ- ⁷¹·¹ ⲗⲓⲛ ⲁⲩⲭⲡⲟϥ. ⲡ[ⲉ]ⲛ[ⲧ]ⲁⲩ[ⲟ]ϩⲥϥ̄ ⲛ̄ϣⲟⲣ[ⲡ] ² ⲡⲁⲗⲓⲛ ⲁⲩⲧⲟϩⲥϥ̄. ⲡ[ⲉⲛ]ⲧⲁⲩⲥⲟⲧϥ̄ ⲡⲁ- ³ ⲗⲓⲛ ⲁϥⲥⲱⲧⲉ.

ⲉϣϫⲉ ϣϣⲉ ⲉϫⲱ ⲛ̄ⲟⲩ- ⁴ ⲙⲩⲥⲧⲏⲣⲓⲟⲛ ⲁⲡⲉⲓⲱⲧ ⲙ̄ⲡⲧⲏⲣϥ ϩⲱⲧⲣ̄ ⁵ ⲁⲧⲡⲁⲣⲑⲉⲛⲟⲥ ⲛ̄ⲧⲁⲉⲓ ⲁⲡⲓⲧⲛ̄, ⲁⲩⲱ ⁶ ⲁⲩⲕⲱⲧ ⲣ̄ ⲟⲩⲟⲉⲓⲛ ⲉⲣⲟϥ ⲙ̄ⲫⲟⲟⲩ ⲉⲧⲙ̄- ⁷ ⲙⲁⲩ. ⲁϥϭⲱⲗⲡ ⲉⲃⲟⲗ ⲙ̄ⲡⲛⲟϭ ⲙ̄ⲡⲁⲥⲧⲟⲥ. ⁸ ⲉⲧⲃⲉ ⲡⲁⲉⲓ ⲡⲉϥⲥⲱⲙⲁ ⲛ̄ⲧⲁϥϣⲱⲡⲉ ⁹ ⲙ̄ⲫⲟⲟⲩ ⲉⲧⲙ̄ⲙⲁⲩ. ⲁϥⲉⲓ ⲉⲃⲟⲗ ϩⲙ̄ ⲡⲡⲁ- ¹⁰ ⲥⲧⲟⲥ ⲛ̄ⲑⲉ ⲙ̄ⲡⲉⲛⲧⲁϥϣⲱⲡⲉ ⲉⲃⲟⲗ ¹¹ ϩⲙ̄ ⲡⲛⲩⲙⲫⲓⲟⲥ ⲙⲛ̄ ⲧⲛⲩⲙⲫⲏ. ⲧⲁ- ¹² ⲉⲓ ⲧⲉ ⲑⲉ ⲁⲓⲏⲥⲟⲩⲥ ⲧⲉϩⲟ ⲙ̄ⲡⲧⲏⲣϥ ⲉⲣⲁⲧϥ ¹³ ϩⲣⲁⲓ̈ ⲛ̄ϩⲏⲧϥ ⲉⲃⲟⲗ ϩⲓⲧⲛ̄ ⲛⲁⲉⲓ. ⲁⲩⲱ ¹⁴ ϣϣⲉ ⲉⲧⲣⲉ ⲡⲟⲩⲁ ⲡⲟⲩⲁ ⲛ̄ⲙ̄ⲙⲁⲑⲏⲧⲏⲥ ¹⁵ ⲙⲟⲟϣⲉ ⲉϩⲟⲩⲛ ⲉⲧⲉϥⲁⲛⲁⲡⲁⲩⲥⲓⲥ.

¹⁶ ⲁⲁⲇⲁⲙ ϣⲱⲡⲉ ⲉⲃⲟⲗ ϩⲛ̄ ⲡⲁⲣⲑⲉⲛⲟⲥ ¹⁷ ⲥⲛ̄ⲧⲉ, ⲉⲃⲟⲗ ϩⲙ̄ ⲡⲡⲛⲉⲩⲙⲁ ⲁⲩⲱ ⲉⲃⲟⲗ ¹⁸ ϩⲙ̄ ⲡⲕⲁϩ ⲙ̄ⲡⲁⲣⲑⲉⲛⲟⲥ. ⲉⲧⲃⲉ ⲡⲁⲉⲓ ¹⁹ ⲁⲩⲭⲡⲉ ⲡⲉⲭⲣⲓⲥⲧⲟⲥ ⲉⲃⲟⲗ ϩⲛ̄ ⲟⲩⲡⲁⲣⲑⲉⲛⲟⲥ ²⁰ ϫⲉⲕⲁⲁⲥ ⲡⲉⲥⲗⲟⲟⲧⲉ ⲛ̄ⲧⲁϩϣⲱⲡⲉ ²¹ ϩⲛ̄ ⲧⲉϩⲟⲩⲉⲓⲧⲉ ⲉϥⲛⲁ̣[ⲥ]ⲉϩⲱϥ ⲉⲣⲁⲧϥ.

²² ⲟⲩⲛ̄ ϣⲏⲛ ⲥⲛⲁⲩ ⲣⲏⲧ [ϩ]ⲙ̄ ⲡⲡⲁⲣⲁⲇⲓ- ²³ ⲥⲟⲥ. ⲡⲟⲩⲁ ϫⲡⲉ ⲑ[ⲏⲣⲓⲟⲛ]· ⲡⲟⲩⲁ ϫⲡⲉ ²⁴ ⲣⲱⲙⲉ. ⲁⲁⲇⲁⲙ ⲟ[ⲩⲱⲙ] ⲉⲃⲟⲗ ϩⲙ̄ ⲡϣⲏⲛ ²⁵ ⲛ̄ⲧⲁϩϫⲡⲉ ⲑⲏⲣⲓ[ⲟⲛ]. ⲁϥϣ[ⲱ]ⲡⲉ ⲛ̄ⲑⲏ- ²⁶ ⲣⲓⲟⲛ. ⲁϥϫⲡⲉ ⲑⲏ[ⲣⲓⲟⲛ]. ⲉⲧⲃⲉ ⲡⲁⲓ̈ ⲥⲉ- ²⁷ ⲣ̄ⲥⲉⲃⲉⲥⲑⲉ ⲁⲛⲉⲑ[ⲏⲣⲓⲟⲛ ⲛ̄ϭ]ⲓ ⲛ̄ϣⲏⲣⲉ ²⁸

⁵ Those who have been clothed in the perfect light ⁶ the powers do not see, ⁷ and they are not able to seize them. But one ⁸ will clothe himself in this light in ⁹ the mystery in the union.

If the ¹⁰ woman had not separated from the man, she ¹¹ would not have died along with the man. His separation ¹² became the beginning from death. For this reason ¹³ Christ came so he might rectify the division that ¹⁴ came about from the beginning ¹⁵ and again join the two, and so that to those ¹⁶ who have died in the division he might give ¹⁷ life and join them. But the woman ¹⁸ is joined to her husband in the bridal chamber. ¹⁹ But those who have joined in the bridal chamber will no longer ²⁰ be separated. For this reason Eve ²¹ separated from Adam because she had not joined to him ²² in the bridal chamber.

The soul of Adam ²³ came about from a breath. Its ²⁴ companion is the [spirit.] What has been given to him ²⁵ is his mother. His soul was taken, and he was given ²⁶ a [spirit] in its place. When ²⁷ he was joined, [he spoke] words more exalted ²⁸ than the powers. They envied ²⁹ him [. . .] spiritual companion ³⁰ [. . .] what is hidden ³¹ [. . .] namely, the ³² [. . .] to themselves alone ³³ [. . .] bridal chamber so that ³⁴ [. . .].

Jesus revealed ³⁵ [. . . the] Jordan. The fullness ³⁶ [of the kingdom] of heaven. The one ³⁷ who [was begotten] before the entirety ⁷¹·¹ was begotten again. The one who was anointed first ² was anointed again. The one who was redeemed has again ³ become redeemed.

Indeed it is necessary to speak a ⁴ mystery. The Father of the entirety joined ⁵ with the virgin who came down, and ⁶ a fire illuminated him on that day. ⁷ He appeared in the great bridal chamber. ⁸ For this reason his body came about on ⁹ that day. He came from the bridal chamber ¹⁰ as one who had come to be from ¹¹ the groom and the bride. This ¹² is how Jesus established the entirety ¹³ within it through these. Indeed ¹⁴ it is necessary to enable each of the disciples ¹⁵ to journey into his rest.

¹⁶ Adam came to be from two virgins, ¹⁷ from the spirit and from ¹⁸ the virgin earth. For this reason ¹⁹ Christ was begotten from a virgin ²⁰ so that the stumbling that came about ²¹ in the beginning might be set right.

²² Two trees grow in paradise. ²³ One produces [animals]; the other produces ²⁴ humans. Adam [eats] from the tree ²⁵ that bore animals. [He] became an animal. ²⁶ He bore [animals.] For this reason the children of Adam ²⁷ worship [animals.] ²⁸

ⲚⲀⲆⲀⲘ. ⲡϢⲎ[Ⲛ. . . . .] ̣[. . . . .] ²⁹ ⲔⲀⲢⲠⲞⲤ ⲠⲈ ̣[. . . . .] ³⁰ ⲠⲀⲈⲒ
ⲀⲨⲀϢ[. . . . .] ³¹ ⲞⲨⲰⲘ Ⲙ̄Ⲡ[. . . . .] ³² ⲔⲀⲢⲠⲞⲤ Ⲙ̄Ⲡ[. . . . .]
³³ ϪⲠⲞ Ⲛ̄ⲢⲢⲰⲘⲈ [. . . . .]- ³⁴ ϢⲦ Ⲙ̄ⲠⲢⲰⲘⲈ Ⲛ̄[. . . . .] ³⁵ ⲠⲚⲞⲨⲦⲈ ⲦⲀⲘⲈⲒⲈ
ⲠⲢϢ[ⲘⲈ . . . Ⲣ̄ⲢϢ]- ⁷²·¹ ⲘⲈ ⲦⲀⲘⲈⲒ̣Ⲉ Ⲡ[Ⲛ]ⲞⲨ[Ⲧ]Ⲉ. ⲦⲀⲈⲒ ⲦⲈ ⲐⲈ ⲐⲘ̄ ⲠⲔⲞⲤ- ² ⲘⲞⲤ· ⲈⲚⲢϢ[Ⲙ]Ⲉ̣
ⲦⲀⲘⲒⲈ ⲚⲞⲨⲦⲈ, ⲀⲨⲰ ⲤⲈⲞⲨ- ³ ϢϢⲦ Ⲛ̄ⲚⲞⲨⲦⲀⲘⲒⲞ. ⲚⲈϢϢⲈ ⲈⲦⲢⲈ Ⲛ̄ⲚⲞⲨ- ⁴ ⲦⲈ ⲞⲨⲰϢⲦ
Ⲛ̄ⲢⲢⲰⲘⲈ Ⲛ̄ⲐⲈ ⲈⲤϢⲞⲞⲠ Ⲙ̄- ⁵ ⲘⲞⲤ Ⲛ̄ϬⲒ ⲦⲀⲖⲎⲐⲈⲒⲀ.

Ⲛ̄Ⲛ̄ⲈϨⲂⲎⲨⲈ Ⲙ̄ⲠⲢϢ- ⁶ ⲘⲈ ϢⲀⲨϢϢⲠⲈ ⲈⲂⲞⲖ ϨⲚ ⲦⲈⳐⲆⲨⲚⲀⲘⲒⲤ. ⁷ ⲈⲦⲂⲈ ⲠⲀⲈⲒ ⲤⲈⲘⲞⲨⲦⲈ ⲈⲢⲞⲞⲨ
ϪⲈ « Ⲛ̄ⲆⲨ- ⁸ ⲚⲀⲘⲒⲤ. » ⲚⲈⳐϨⲂⲎⲨⲈ ⲚⲈ ⲚⲈⳐϢⲎⲢⲈ. Ⲛ̄ⲦⲀⳐ- ⁹ ϢϢⲠⲈ ⲈⲂⲞⲖ ϨⲚ ⲞⲨⲀⲚⲀⲠⲀⲨⲤⲒⲤ.
ⲈⲦⲂⲈ ¹⁰ ⲠⲀⲈⲒ ⲦⲈⳐⲆⲨⲚⲀⲘⲒⲤ Ⲣ̄ⲠⲞⲖⲒⲦⲈⲨⲈⲤⲐⲈ ¹¹ ϨⲢⲀⲒ̈ ϨⲚ ⲚⲈⳐϨⲂⲎⲨⲈ. ⲈⲦⲀⲚⲀⲠⲀⲨⲤⲒⲤ ⲆⲈ ¹²
ⲞⲨⲞⲚϨ ⲈⲂⲞⲖ ϨⲢⲀⲒ̈ ϨⲚ Ⲛ̄ϢⲎⲢⲈ. ⲀⲨⲰ ¹³ ⲔⲚⲀϨⲈ ⲈⲠⲀⲈⲒ ⲈⳐϪⲰⲦⲈ ϢⲀ ϨⲢⲀⲒ̈ ⲈⲐⲒⲔⲰⲚ, ¹⁴ ⲀⲨⲰ
ⲠⲀⲈⲒ ⲠⲈ ⲠⲢⲰⲘⲈ Ⲛ̄ϨⲒⲔⲞⲚⲒⲔⲞⲤ ¹⁵ ⲈⳐⲈⲒⲢⲈ Ⲛ̄ⲚⲈⳐϨⲂⲎⲨⲈ ⲈⲂⲞⲖ ϨⲚ ⲦⲈⳐϬⲞⲘ, ¹⁶ ⲈⲂⲞⲖ ⲆⲈ ϨⲚ
ⲀⲚⲀⲠⲀⲨⲤⲒⲤ ⲈⳐϪⲠⲞ Ⲛ̄ⲚⲈⳐ- ¹⁷ ϢⲎⲢⲈ.

ϨⲘ̄ ⲠⲈⲈⲒⲔⲞⲤⲘⲞⲤ Ⲛ̄ϨⲘ̄ϨⲀⲖ Ⲣ̄- ¹⁸ ϨⲨⲠⲎⲢⲈⲦⲈⲒ Ⲛ̄ⲈⲖⲈⲨⲐⲈⲢⲞⲤ. ϨⲚ ⲦⲘⲚ̄- ¹⁹ ⲦⲈⲢⲞ ⲚⲘ̄ⲠⲎⲨⲈ
ⲚⲈⲖⲈⲨⲐⲈⲢⲞⲤ ⲚⲀⲢ̄- ²⁰ ⲆⲒⲀⲔⲞⲚ[ⲈⲒ] Ⲛ̄Ⲛ̄ϨⲘ̄ϨⲀⲖ. Ⲛ̄Ⲛ̄ϢⲎⲢⲈ Ⲙ̄- ²¹ ⲠⲚⲨⲘⲪ[Ϣ]Ⲛ̄ [ⲚⲀ]-
Ⲣ̄ⲆⲒⲀⲔⲞⲚⲈⲒ Ⲛ̄Ⲛ̄ϢⲎ- ²² ⲢⲈ Ⲙ̄ⲠⲄⲀ[ⲘⲞⲤ. Ⲛ̄]ϢⲎⲢⲈ Ⲙ̄ⲠⲚⲨⲘⲪⲰⲚ ²³ ⲞⲨⲢⲀⲚ ⲞⲨ[Ⲱ]Ⲧ ⲠⲈ]ⲦⲈ
ⲞⲨⲚⲦⲀⳐⳐ « ⲦⲀⲚⲀ- ²⁴ ⲠⲀⲨⲤⲒⲤ. » Ⲉ[. . . Ⲛ]ⲞⲨⲈⲢⲎⲨ ⲤⲈⲢ̄ⲬⲢⲈⲒⲀ ⲀⲚ ²⁵ Ⲛ̄ϪⲒ ϨⲢⲂ [ⲈⲨⲚ̄ⲦⲀⲨ]
ⲦⲈⲐⲈⲰⲢⲈⲒⲀ Ⲙ̄ⲘⲀⲨ. ²⁶ [. . . .]Ⲫ[. . . . . .] ̣·ⲚⲤⲒⲤ ϨⲚ̄ϨⲞⲨⲞ ⲚⲈ ²⁷ [. . . . .]ⲤⲒⲀ ϨⲚ
ⲚⲈⲦϨⲚ̄ Ⲡ- ²⁸ [. . . . .]Ⲛ̄ ⲚⲈⲞⲞⲨ Ⲛ̄ⲚⲈ- ²⁹ [. . . . .]Ⲉ̣ Ⲙ̄ⲘⲞⲞⲨ ⲀⲚ.

ⲚⲈ- ³⁰ [. . . . . .Ⲃ]ⲰⲔ ⲈⲠⲒⲦⲚ̄ ⲈⲠⲘⲞ- ³¹ [ⲞⲨ. . . . . .] ⲈⲂⲞⲖ ⲈⳐⲚⲀⲤⲞⲦⳐ ³² [. . . . . . .] ̣
Ⲕ ⲈⲂⲞⲖ Ⲛ̄ϬⲒ ⲚⲈⲚⲦⲀϨ- ³³ [. . . . .] ̣ϨⲘ̄ ⲠⲈⳐⲢⲀⲚ. ⲠⲈϪⲀⳐ ⲄⲀⲢ ³⁴ [ϪⲈ· « ⲦⲀⲈⲒ ⲦⲈ Ⲑ]Ⲉ ⲈⲚⲀϪⲰⲔ
ⲈⲂⲞⲖ Ⲛ̄ⲆⲒⲔⲀⲒ- ⁷³·¹ ⲞⲤⲨⲚⲎ ⲚⲒⲘ. »

ⲚⲈⲦϪⲰ Ⲙ̄ⲘⲞⲤ ϪⲈ ⲤⲈⲚⲀ- ² ⲘⲞⲨ Ⲛ̄ϢⲞⲢⲠ ⲀⲨⲰ ⲤⲈⲚⲀ̣ⲦϢⲞⲨⲚ[[Ⲛ̄]] ⲤⲈ- ³ Ⲣ̄ⲠⲖⲀⲚⲀⲤⲐⲈ.
ⲈⲨⲦⲘ̄ϪⲒ Ⲛ̄ϢⲞⲢⲠ Ⲛ̄ⲦⲀⲚⲀ- ⁴ ⲤⲦⲀⲤⲒⲤ ⲈⲨⲞⲚϨ, ⲈⲨϢⲀⲘⲞⲨ ⲤⲈⲚⲀϪⲒ ⲖⲀ- ⁵ ⲀⲨ ⲀⲚ. ⲦⲀⲈⲒ ⲦⲈ ⲐⲈ
ⲞⲚ ⲈⲨϪⲰ Ⲙ̄ⲘⲞⲤ Ⲉ- ⁶ ⲠⲂⲀⲠⲦⲒⲤⲘⲀ ⲈⲨϪⲰ Ⲙ̄ⲘⲞⲤ ϪⲈ, « ⲞⲨⲚⲞϬ ⁷ ⲠⲈ ⲠⲂⲀⲠⲦⲒⲤⲘⲀ, » ϪⲈ
ⲈⲨϢⲀϪⲒⲦⳐ, ⲤⲈⲚⲀ- ⁸ ⲰⲚϨ.

ⲪⲒⲖⲒⲠⲠⲞⲤ ⲠⲀⲠⲞⲤⲦⲞⲖⲞⲤ ⲠⲈ- ⁹ ϪⲀⳐ ϪⲈ· « Ⲓ̈ⲰⲤⲎⲪ ⲠⲢⲀⲘϢⲈ ⲀⳐⲦⲰϬⲈ Ⲛ̄- ¹⁰ ⲚⲞⲨⲠⲀⲢⲀⲆⲈⲒⲤⲞⲤ
ϪⲈ ⲚⲈⳐⲢ̄ⲬⲢⲈⲒⲀ Ⲛ̄ϨⲚ̄- ¹¹ ϢⲈ ⲈϨⲞⲨⲚ ⲈⲦⲈⳐⲦⲈⲬⲚⲎ. Ⲛ̄ⲦⲞⳐ ⲠⲈⲚ- ¹² ⲦⲀϨⲦⲀⲘⲒⲞ Ⲙ̄ⲠⲤⲦⲀⲨⲢⲞⲤ
ⲈⲂⲞⲖ ϨⲚ Ⲛ̄- ¹³ ϢⲎⲚ Ⲛ̄ⲦⲀⳐⲦⲞϬⲞⲨ. ⲀⲨⲰ ⲠⲈⳐϬⲢⲞϬ ⲚⲈⳐ- ¹⁴ ⲞϢⲈ ⲀⲠⲈⲚⲦⲀⳐⲦⲞϬⳐ ⲚⲈ.
ⲠⲈⳐϬⲢⲞϬ ⲠⲈ ¹⁵ ⲒⲎⲤⲞⲨⲤ. ⲠⲦⲰϬⲈ ⲆⲈ ⲠⲈ ⲠⲈⲤⲦⲀⲨⲢⲞⲤ, ⲀⲖⲖⲀ ⲠϢⲎⲚ ¹⁶ Ⲙ̄ⲠⲰⲚϨ ϨⲚ ⲦⲘⲎⲦⲈ
Ⲙ̄ⲠⲀⲢⲀⲆⲈⲒⲤⲞⲤ. » ¹⁷ ⲀⲨⲰ ⲦⲂⲈⲚ̄ϪⲞⲈⲒⲦ Ⲛ̄ⲦⲀ ⲠⲈⲬⲢⲈⲒⲤⲘⲀ ϢⲀ- ¹⁸ ⲠⲈ ⲈⲂⲞⲖ Ⲛ̄ϨⲎⲦⲤ̄· ⲈⲂⲞⲖ
ϨⲒⲦⲞⲞⲦⳐ ⲀⲦⲀ- ¹⁹ ⲚⲀⲤⲦⲀⲤⲒⲤ.

71.28 ⲡϢⲎ[Ⲛ. . . . .] ̣[. . . . .]: transcription from earliest images; see Emmel, 114.

The tree [...] ²⁹ fruit is [...] ³⁰ this they [...] ³¹ eat the [...] ³² fruit of the [...] ³³ bears humans [...] ³⁴ of the man of [...] ³⁵ God creates man [... humans] ⁷²·¹ create God. This is how it is in the world: ² humans create gods, and they ³ worship their creations. It would be fitting for gods ⁴ to worship humans, just as truth exists ⁵ for itself.

The works of a person ⁶ come about from his ability. ⁷ For this reason, they are called "abilities." ⁸ His works are his children. They have ⁹ come about from rest. For ¹⁰ this reason his power dwells ¹¹ in his works. But the rest ¹² is apparent in children. ¹³ You will find this extends to the image, ¹⁴ and this is the imaged man, ¹⁵ doing his works with his might, ¹⁶ but from rest bearing his ¹⁷ children.

In this world slaves ¹⁸ serve the free. In the kingdom ¹⁹ of heaven the free will ²⁰ minister to the slaves. The children of ²¹ the bridal chamber [will] minister to the children ²² of [marriage. The] children of the bridal chamber ²³ have [only] one name: "rest." ²⁴ [...] one another, they do not need ²⁵ to receive form, [since they have] contemplation. ²⁶ [...] they are abundant ²⁷ [...] in those in the ²⁸ [...] glories of the ²⁹ [...] not them.

The ³⁰ [... go] down into the water ³¹ [...] he will be elected ³² [...] those who have ³³ [...] in his name. For he said, ³⁴ "[It is fitting] that we should perfect ⁷³·¹ all righteousness."

Those who say that they will ² die first and (then) rise ³ are in error. If they do not first receive the resurrection ⁴ while they are alive, when they die they will not receive anything. ⁵ So too when they speak about ⁶ baptism they say, "Great ⁷ is baptism," because if they receive it, they ⁸ will live.

Philip the apostle ⁹ said, "Joseph the carpenter planted in ¹⁰ paradise because he needed wood ¹¹ for his craft. It is he ¹² who made the cross from the ¹³ trees that he had planted. His seed ¹⁴ hung upon that which he planted. His seed is ¹⁵ Jesus. What he planted is the cross, but the tree ¹⁶ of life is in the middle of paradise." ¹⁷ The olive tree is where the chrism has come ¹⁸ from; from the chrism (is) the ¹⁹ resurrection.

ⲡⲉⲉⲓⲕⲟⲥⲙⲟⲥ ⲟⲩⲁⲙⲕⲱ- 20 ⲱⲥ ⲡⲉ. ⲛ̄ⲕⲉ ⲛⲓⲙ ⲉⲧⲟⲩⲱⲙ ⲙ̄ⲙⲟⲟⲩ 21 ϩⲣⲁⲓ̈ ⲛ̄ϩⲏⲧϥ ⲥⲉⲙⲟ[ⲩ]
ϩⲱⲟⲩ ⲟⲛ. ⲧⲁⲗⲏⲑⲉⲓ- 22 ⲁ ⲟⲩⲁⲙⲱⲛϩ ⲧⲉ. ⲉⲧⲃⲉ ⲡⲁⲉⲓ ⲙ̄ⲛ ⲗⲁⲁⲩ 23 ϩⲛ̄ ⲛⲉⲧⲥⲟⲛϩ ϩⲛ̄ ⲧ̣[ⲙⲉ]
ⲛⲁⲙⲟⲩ. ⲛ̄ⲧⲁⲓⲏⲥⲟⲩⲥ 24 ⲉⲓ ⲉⲃⲟⲗ ϩⲙ̄ ⲡⲙⲁ ⲉ[ⲧⲙ̄]ⲙⲁⲩ, ⲁⲩⲱ ⲁϥⲉⲓ- 25 ⲛⲉ ⲛ̄ϩⲛ̄ⲧⲣⲟⲫⲏ ⲉⲃⲟⲗ
ⲙ̄ⲙⲁⲩ. ⲁⲩⲱ ⲛⲉ- 26 ⲧⲟⲩⲱϣ ⲁϥϯ ⲛⲁⲩ [ⲛ̄ⲟ]ⲩⲱⲛ̣[ϩ] ϫⲉ[ⲕⲁⲁⲥ] 27 ⲛ̄ⲛⲟⲩⲙⲟⲩ.

ⲁⲡⲛ̄[ⲟⲩⲧⲉ] . . ⲉ ⲛ̄ⲟ̣[ⲩⲡⲁⲣⲁ]- 28 ⲇⲉⲓⲥⲟⲥ. ⲁⲡⲣⲱ[ⲙⲉ . . . . . ⲡⲁⲣⲁ]- 29 ⲇⲉⲓⲥⲟⲥ. ⲟⲩⲛ̄
ϩ[ⲉⲛ . . . . ϣⲟ]- 30 ⲟⲡ ⲙⲛ̄ ϩⲙ̄ⲡ[. . . . .] 31 ⲙ̄ⲡⲛⲟⲩⲧⲉ ϩⲙ̄ [. . . . .] 32
ⲙⲉ ⲛⲉⲧⲛ̄ϩⲏⲧ[ϥ . . . .] 33 ϯ ⲟⲩⲱϣ. ⲡⲓⲡⲁⲣⲁ[ⲇⲉⲓⲥⲟⲥ ⲡⲉ ⲡⲙⲁ ⲉ]- 34 ⲧⲟⲩⲛⲁϫⲟⲟⲥ
ⲛⲁⲉⲓ ϫⲉ· « [. . . . ⲟⲩⲱⲙ] 35 ⲙ̄ⲡⲁⲉⲓ ⲏ ⲙ̄ⲛⲟⲩⲱⲙ ⲙ̄[ⲡⲁⲉⲓ, ⲛ̄ⲑⲉ ⲉⲧⲕ]- 74.1 ⲟⲩⲱϣ. » ⲡⲁⲉⲓ
ⲡⲙⲁ [ⲉ]ϯⲛⲁⲟⲩⲱⲙ ⲛ̄ⲕⲉ ⲛⲓⲙ 2 ⲙ̄ⲙⲁⲩ ⲉϥϣⲟ[ⲟ]ⲡ ⲙ̄ⲙⲁⲩ ⲛ̄ϭⲓ ⲡϣⲏⲛ ⲛ̄ⲧ- 3 ⲅⲛⲱⲥⲓⲥ.
ⲡⲉⲧⲙ̄ⲙⲁⲩ ⲁϥⲙⲟⲩⲧ ⲁⲇⲁⲙ. ⲡⲉ- 4 ⲉⲓⲙⲁ ⲇⲉ ⲡϣⲏⲛ ⲛ̄ⲧⲅⲛⲱⲥⲓⲥ ⲁϥⲧⲛ̄ϩⲉ ⲡⲣⲱ- 5 ⲙⲉ.
ⲡⲛⲟⲙⲟⲥ ⲛⲉ ⲡϣⲏⲛ ⲡⲉ. ⲟⲩⲛ̄ ϭⲟⲙ 6 ⲙ̄ⲙⲟϥ ⲛ̄ϯ ⲧⲅⲛⲱⲥⲓⲥ ⲙ̄ⲡⲉⲧⲛⲁⲛⲟⲩϥ 7 ⲙⲛ̄ ⲡⲉⲑⲟⲟⲩ.
ⲟⲩⲧⲉ ⲙ̄ⲡⲉϥⲗⲁϭⲉ ⲉⲣⲟϥ ϩⲙ̄ 8 ⲡⲡⲉⲑⲟⲟⲩ ⲟⲩⲧⲉ ⲙ̄ⲡⲉϥⲕⲁⲁϥ ϩⲙ̄ ⲡⲡⲉⲧⲛⲁ- 9 ⲛⲟⲩϥ, ⲁⲗⲗⲁ
ⲁϥⲧⲁⲙⲓⲟ ⲛ̄ⲟⲩⲙⲟⲩ ⲛ̄ⲛⲉⲛⲧⲁϩ- 10 ⲟⲩⲱⲙ ⲉⲃⲟⲗ ⲛ̄ϩⲏⲧϥ. ϩⲙ̄ ⲡⲧⲣⲉϥϫⲟⲟⲥ ⲅⲁⲣ 11 ϫⲉ· « ⲟⲩⲱⲙ
ⲡⲁⲉⲓ ⲙ̄ⲛⲟⲩⲱⲙ ⲡⲁⲉⲓ, » ⲁϥϣⲱ- 12 ⲡⲉ ⲛ̄ⲁⲣⲭⲏ ⲙ̄ⲡⲙⲟⲩ.

ⲡⲭⲣⲉⲓⲥⲙⲁ ϭⲟ ⲛ̄ϫⲟ- 13 ⲉⲓⲥ ⲉⲡⲃⲁⲡⲧⲓⲥⲙⲁ, ⲉⲃⲟⲗ ⲅⲁⲣ ϩⲙ̄ « ⲡⲭⲣⲓⲥⲙⲁ » 14 ⲁⲩⲙⲟⲩⲧⲉ ⲉⲣⲟⲛ ϫⲉ
« ⲭⲣⲓⲥⲧⲓⲁⲛⲟⲥ, » ⲉⲧⲃⲉ 15 « ⲡⲃⲁⲡⲧⲓⲥⲙⲁ » ⲁⲛ. ⲁⲩⲱ ⲛ̄ⲧⲁⲩⲙⲟⲩⲧⲉ « ⲉⲡⲉ- 16 ⲭⲣⲓⲥⲧⲟⲥ »
ⲉⲧⲃⲉ « ⲡⲭⲣⲓⲥⲙⲁ. » ⲁⲡⲉⲓⲱⲧ ⲅⲁⲣ ⲧⲱϩⲥ 17 ⲙ̄ⲡϣⲏⲣⲉ, ⲁⲡϣⲏⲣⲉ ⲇⲉ ⲧⲱϩⲥ ⲛ̄ⲁⲡⲟⲥⲧⲟ- 18
ⲗⲟⲥ, ⲁⲛⲁⲡⲟⲥⲧⲟⲗⲟⲥ ⲇⲉ ⲧⲁϩⲥⲛ̄. ⲡⲉⲛ- 19 ⲧⲁⲩⲧⲟϩⲥϥ ⲟⲩⲛ̄ⲧⲉ`ϥ´ ⲡⲧⲏⲣϥ ⲙ̄ⲙⲁⲩ. ⲟⲩⲛ̄- 20
ⲧⲁϥ ⲧⲁⲛⲁⲥⲧⲁⲥⲓⲥ, ⲡⲟⲩⲟⲉⲓⲛ ⲡⲉⲥⲧⲁⲩⲣⲟⲥ, 21 ⲡⲡⲛⲉⲩⲙⲁ ⲉⲧⲟⲩⲁⲁⲃ. ⲁⲡⲉⲓⲱⲧ ϯ ⲛⲁϥ ⲙ̄ⲡⲁ- 22
ⲉⲓ ϩⲙ̄ ⲡⲛⲩ[ⲙ]ⲫⲱⲛ· ⲁϥϫⲓ. ⲁϥϣⲱⲡⲉ ⲛ̄ϭⲓ 23 ⲡⲉⲓⲱⲧ ϩⲙ̄ ⲡϣ[ⲏ]ⲣⲉ, ⲁⲩⲱ ⲡϣⲏⲣⲉ ϩⲙ̄ ⲡⲉⲓ- 24
ⲱⲧ. ⲧⲁⲉⲓ ⲧ[ⲉ ⲧⲙⲛ̄ⲧ]ⲉⲣⲟ ⲛ̄ⲙⲡⲏⲩⲉ.

ⲕⲁⲗⲱⲥ 25 ⲁⲡϫⲟⲉⲓⲥ ϫⲟⲟ[ⲥ ϫ]ⲉ· « ⲁϩⲟⲉⲓⲛⲉ ⲃⲱⲕ ⲉⲧⲙⲛ̄- 26 ⲧⲉⲣⲟ ⲛ̄ⲙⲡⲏⲩ[ⲉ] ⲉⲩⲥⲱⲃⲉ,
ⲁⲩⲱ ⲁⲩⲉⲓ ⲉⲃⲟⲗ 27 [. . . .] » [.]ⲉ̣ⲁⲩ[. . .]ⲟⲩⲁ ϫⲉ ⲟⲩⲭⲣⲏⲥⲧⲓⲁⲛⲟⲥ 28 [. . .] ⲉ̣ϫ̣ . . [. . . .] ⲟ̣ⲛ.
ⲁⲩⲱ ⲛ̄ⲧⲉⲩⲛⲟⲩ 29 [. . . . . ⲉⲡ]ⲓ̣ⲧⲛ̄ ⲉⲡⲙⲟⲟⲩ. ⲁϥⲉⲓ 30 [. . . . .] ⲁⲡⲧⲏⲣϥ
ⲉⲧⲃⲉ 31 [. . . . . ⲟⲩⲡ]ⲁⲓⲅⲛⲓⲟⲛ ⲡⲉ, ⲁⲗ- 32 [ⲗⲁ . . . . . ⲣ̄ⲕⲁⲧⲁⲫ]ⲣⲟⲛⲉⲓ ⲙ̄ⲡⲉⲉⲓⲡⲉ- 33
[. . . . .]ⲛ ⲉⲧⲙⲛ̄ⲧⲉⲣⲟ ⲛⲙ̄- 34 [ⲡⲏⲩⲉ . . . . . .]. ⲉϥϣⲁⲣ̄ⲕⲁⲧⲁⲫⲣⲟⲛⲉⲓ 35 [. . . . . . .ⲁ]-
ⲩⲱ ⲛ̄ϥϣⲟⲥϥ ϩⲱⲥ ⲡⲁⲓⲅⲛⲓ- 36 [ⲟⲛ . . . . ⲉⲃ]ⲟ̣ⲗ ⲉⲩⲥⲱⲃⲉ. ⲧⲉⲉⲓϩⲉ ⲟⲛ ⲧⲉ 75.1 ϩⲓ ⲡⲟⲉⲓⲕ ⲙⲛ̄
ⲡⲡⲟ[ⲧ]ⲏⲣⲓⲟⲛ ⲙⲛ̄ ⲡⲛⲏϩ, 2 ⲕⲁⲛ ⲟⲩⲛ̄ ⲕⲉⲟⲩⲁ ⲉϥϫⲟⲥⲉ ⲉⲛⲁⲉⲓ.

ⲁⲡ- 3 ⲕⲟⲥⲙⲟⲥ ϣⲱⲡⲉ ϩⲛ̄ ⲟⲩⲡⲁⲣⲁⲡⲧⲱⲙⲁ. 4 ⲡⲉⲛⲧⲁϩⲧⲁⲙⲓⲟϥ ⲅⲁⲣ ⲛⲉϥⲟⲩⲱϣ ⲁⲧⲁ- 5
ⲙⲓⲟϥ ⲉϥⲟ ⲛ̄ⲁⲧⲧⲁⲕⲟ ⲁⲩⲱ ⲛ̄ⲁⲑⲁⲛⲁⲧⲟⲥ. 6 ⲁϥϩⲉ ⲉⲃⲟⲗ, ⲁⲩⲱ ⲙ̄ⲡⲉϥⲙⲉⲧⲉ ⲁⲑⲉⲗⲡⲓⲥ. 7
ⲛⲉⲥϣⲟⲟⲡ ⲅⲁⲣ ⲁⲛ ⲛ̄ϭⲓ ⲧⲙⲛ̄ⲧⲁⲧⲧⲉⲕⲟ 8 ⲙ̄ⲡⲕⲟⲥⲙⲟⲥ, ⲁⲩⲱ ⲛⲉϥϣⲟⲟⲡ ⲁⲛ ⲛ̄ϭⲓ 9
ⲧⲙⲛ̄ⲧⲁⲧⲧⲁⲕⲟ ⲙ̄ⲡⲉⲛⲧⲁϩⲧⲁⲙⲓⲉ ⲡⲕⲟⲥ- 10 ⲙⲟⲥ. ⲥϣⲟⲟⲡ ⲅⲁⲣ ⲁⲛ ⲛ̄ϭⲓ ⲧⲙⲛ̄ⲧⲁⲧⲧⲁ- 11 ⲕⲟ
ⲛ̄ⲛⲉϩⲃⲏⲩⲉ, ⲁⲗⲗⲁ ⲛ̄ⲛ̄ϣⲏⲣⲉ. ⲁⲩⲱ ⲙⲛ̄ 12 ⲟⲩϩⲱⲃ ⲛⲁϣϫⲓ ⲛ̄ⲟⲩⲙⲛ̄ⲧⲁⲧⲧⲁⲕⲟ ⲉϥⲧⲙ̄- 13 ϣⲱⲡⲉ
ⲛ̄ϣⲏⲣⲉ. ⲡⲉⲧⲉ ⲙⲛ̄ ϭⲟⲙ ⲇⲉ ⲙ̄ⲙⲟϥ 14 ⲉϫⲓ, ⲡⲟⲥⲱ ⲙⲁⲗⲗⲟⲛ ϥⲛⲁϣϯ ⲁⲛ;

73.20 ⲉⲧⲟⲩⲱⲙ: read ⲉⲧⲟⲩⲟⲩⲱⲙ.
75.8 ⲛⲉϥϣⲟⲟⲡ: read ⲛⲉⲥϣⲟⲟⲡ.

This world is a corpse eater. [20] All things that are eaten [21] in it [die] as well. Truth [22] is a life eater. For this reason none [23] of those nourished by the [truth] will die. Jesus [24] came from that place, and he brought [25] nourishment from there. To those [26] who desired, he gave [life so that] [27] they might not die.

[God . . .] a paradise. [28] Man [. . .] paradise. [29] There are [. . .] [30] and [. . .] [31] of God in [. . .] [32] the things in [it . . .] [33] I desire. This paradise [is the place] [34] where they will say to me, "[. . . eat] [35] this or do not eat [that, as you] [74.1] desire." In this place where I will eat all things [2] is the tree of [3] knowledge. That one killed Adam. But in this [4] place the tree of knowledge made man alive. [5] The tree was the law. It is possible [6] for it to give knowledge of good [7] and evil. It neither recovered him from [8] evil nor placed him in [9] good, rather it created death for those who had [10] eaten from it. For when he said, [11] "Eat this, and do not eat that," it became [12] the beginning of death.

The chrism is better [13] than baptism, since on the basis of the (word) "chrism" [14] we have been called "Christians," not because (of the word) [15] "baptism." Also [16] "Christ" is named on account of the "chrism." For the Father anointed [17] the Son, and the Son anointed the apostles, [18] and the apostles anointed us. The one [19] who is anointed has the entirety. He has [20] the resurrection, the light, the cross, [21] the Holy Spirit. The Father gave this [22] to him in the bridal chamber; he received. The Father came to be [23] in the son, and the son (came to be) in the Father. [24] This [is the] kingdom of heaven.

Rightly [25] did the Lord say, "Some went into the kingdom [26] of heaven laughing, and they left [27] [. . . " . . .] a Christian [28] [. . .]. And immediately [29] [. . .] into the water. He came [30] [. . .] to the entirety because [31] [. . .] it is [a] foolish thing, but [32] [. . .] despise this [33] [. . .] the kingdom of [34] [heaven . . .]. If he despises [35] [. . .] and looks down on it as a foolish thing [36] [. . .] he is laughing. This is how it is [75.1] with the bread and the cup and the oil, [2] even if there is another one more exalted than these.

The [3] world came to be through a blunder. [4] For the one who created it wanted to [5] create it imperishable and immortal. [6] He failed, and he did not achieve the objective. [7] For the imperishability [8] of the world never came to be, and the imperishability [9] of the one who made the world [10] did not exist. For the imperishability [11] of things does not exist, but (the imperishability of) children (does). Nothing [12] will be able to receive imperishability if it does not [13] become a child. But the one that is not able [14] to receive, how much more will he be unable to give?

ⲡⲡⲟⲧⲏ- [15] ⲣⲓⲟⲛ ⲙ̄ⲡϣⲗⲏⲗ ⲟⲩⲛ̄ⲧⲁϥ ⲏⲣⲡ ⲙ̄ⲙⲁⲩ ⲟⲩ- [16] ⲛ̄ⲧⲁϥ ⲙⲟⲟⲩ, ⲉϥⲕⲏ ⲉϩⲣⲁⲓ̈ ⲉⲡⲧⲩⲡⲟⲥ ⲙ̄- [17] ⲡⲉⲥⲛⲟϥ ⲉⲧⲟⲩⲣ̄ⲉⲩⲭⲁⲣⲓⲥⲧⲉⲓ ⲉϫⲱϥ. ⲁⲩ- [18] ⲱ ϥⲙⲟⲩϩ ⲉⲃⲟⲗ ϩⲙ̄ ⲡⲡⲛⲉⲩⲙⲁ ⲉⲧⲟⲩⲁⲁⲃ, ⲁⲩ- [19] ⲱ ⲡⲁ ⲡⲧⲉⲗⲉⲓⲟⲥ ⲧⲏⲣϥ ⲣ̄ⲣⲱⲙⲉ ⲡⲉ. ϩⲟⲧⲁⲛ [20] ⲉⲛϣⲁⲛⲥⲱ ⲙ̄ⲡⲁⲉⲓ, ⲧⲛⲁϫⲓ ⲛⲁⲛ ⲙ̄ⲡⲧⲉ- [21] ⲗⲉⲓⲟⲥ ⲣ̄ⲣⲱⲙⲉ. ⲡⲙⲟⲟⲩ ⲉⲧⲟⲛϩ ⲟⲩⲥⲱⲙⲁ [22] ⲡⲉ. ϣϣⲉ ⲉⲧⲣⲛ̄ϯ ϩⲓⲱⲱⲛ ⲙ̄ⲡⲣⲱⲙⲉ ⲉⲧⲟⲛϩ. [23] ⲉⲧⲃⲉ ⲡⲁⲉⲓ ⲉϥⲉⲓ ⲉϥⲃⲏⲕ ⲉⲡⲓⲧⲛ̄ ⲉⲡⲙⲟ- [24] ⲟⲩ, ϣⲁϥⲕⲁⲕϥ ⲁϩⲏⲩ ϣⲓⲛⲁ ⲉϥⲛⲁϯ ⲡⲏ [25] ϩⲓⲱⲱϥ.

ϣⲁⲣⲉⲟⲩϩⲧⲟ ϫⲡⲉ ⲟⲩϩⲧⲟ. ⲟⲩ- [26] ⲣⲱⲙⲉ ϣⲁⲣⲉϥϫⲡⲉ ⲣⲱⲙⲉ. ⲟⲩⲛⲟⲩⲧⲉ [27] ϣⲁⲣⲉϥϫⲡⲉ ⲛⲟⲩⲧⲉ. ⲧⲁⲉⲓ ⲧⲉ ⲑⲉ ϩⲙ̄[ⲡⲁⲧ]- [28] ϣⲉⲗⲉⲉⲧ ⲙⲛ̄ ϩⲛ̄[ⲕⲉϣⲉ]ⲗⲉⲉⲧ. ⲁⲩ[ϣⲱ]- [29] ⲡⲉ ⲉⲃⲟⲗ ϩⲙ̄ ⲡⲛ[. . . . .]ⲛ̄[. . . . .] [30] ⲛⲉ ⲙⲛ̄ ⲓⲟⲩⲇⲁⲓ ⲟ[. . . . .] [31] ⲉⲃⲟⲗ ϩⲛ̄ ⲛ̄ⲓⲟ[. . . . .] [32] ϣⲟⲟⲡ, ⲁⲩⲱ ⲁⲛ[. . . . .] [33] ⲉⲃⲟⲗ ϩⲛ̄ ⲛ̄ ⲓⲟⲩⲇ[ⲁⲓ . . . .] [34] ⲛ̄ⲭⲣⲓⲥⲧⲓⲁⲛⲟⲥ. ⲁⲕ[. . . . .]- [35] ⲱ ⲁⲩⲙⲟⲩⲧⲉ ⲁⲛⲉⲉⲓⲙⲁ[. . . . . . .] [36] « ⲡⲅⲉⲛⲟⲥ ⲉⲧⲥⲟⲧⲡ ⲙ̄ⲡⲛ̄[ⲟⲩⲧⲉ » . . .] [76.1] ⲁⲩⲱ « ⲡⲁⲗⲏⲑⲉⲓⲛⲟⲥ ⲣ̄ⲣⲱⲙⲉ » ⲁⲩⲱ « ⲡϣⲏⲣⲉ [2] ⲙ̄ⲡⲣⲱⲙⲉ » ⲁⲩⲱ « ⲡⲥⲡⲉⲣⲙⲁ ⲙ̄ⲡϣⲏⲣⲉ ⲙ̄ⲡⲣⲱ- [3] ⲙⲉ. » ⲡⲉⲉⲓⲅⲉⲛⲟⲥ ⲛ̄ⲁⲗⲏⲑⲉⲓⲛⲟⲛ ⲥⲉⲣ̄ⲟⲛⲟ- [4] ⲙⲁⲍⲉ ⲙ̄ⲙⲟϥ ϩⲙ̄ ⲡⲕⲟⲥⲙⲟⲥ. ⲛⲁⲉⲓ ⲛⲉ ⲡⲙⲁ [5] ⲉⲧⲟⲩϣⲟⲟⲡ ⲙ̄ⲙⲁⲩ ⲛ̄ϭⲓ ⲛ̄ϣⲏⲣⲉ ⲙ̄ⲡⲛⲩⲙ- [6] ⲫⲱⲛ.

ⲉⲡϩⲱⲧⲣ̄ ϣⲟⲟⲡ ϩⲙ̄ ⲡⲉⲉⲓⲕⲟⲥⲙⲟⲥ [7] ϩⲟⲟⲩⲧ ϩⲓ ⲥϩⲓⲙⲉ—ⲡⲙⲁ ⲉⲧϭⲟⲙ ⲙⲛ̄ ⲧⲙⲛ̄ⲧ- [8] ϭⲱⲃ—ϩⲙ̄ ⲡⲁⲓⲱⲛ ⲕⲉⲟⲩⲁ ⲡⲉ ⲡⲉⲓⲛⲉ ⲙ̄ⲡϩⲱ- [9] ⲧⲣ̄, ⲉⲙⲙⲟⲩⲧⲉ ⲇⲉ ⲉⲣⲟⲟⲩ ⲛ̄ⲛⲉⲉⲓⲣⲁⲛ. ⲟⲩⲛ̄ ϩⲛ̄- [10] ⲕⲟⲟⲩⲉ ⲇⲉ ϣⲟⲟⲡ. ⲥⲉϫⲟⲥⲉ ⲡⲁⲣⲁ ⲣⲁⲛ [11] ⲛⲓⲙ ⲉⲧⲟⲩⲣ̄ⲟⲛⲟⲙⲁⲍⲉ ⲙ̄ⲙⲟⲟⲩ, ⲁⲩⲱ ⲥⲉ- [12] ϫⲟⲟⲥⲉ ⲉⲡϫⲱⲱⲣⲉ. ⲡⲙⲁ ⲅⲁⲣ ⲉⲧⲉ ⲟⲩⲛ̄ ⲃⲓⲁ [13] ⲙ̄ⲙⲁⲩ, ⲉϥϣⲟⲟⲡ ⲙ̄ⲙⲁⲩ ⲛ̄ϭⲓ ⲛⲉⲧⲥⲟⲧⲡ [14] ⲉⲧϭⲟⲙ. ⲛⲉⲧⲙ̄ⲙⲁⲩ ⲕⲉⲟⲩⲁ ⲁⲛ ⲡⲉ ⲁⲩⲱ ⲕⲉ- [15] ⲟⲩⲁ ⲡⲉ, ⲁⲗⲗⲁ ⲛ̄ⲧⲟⲟⲩ ⲙ̄ⲡⲉⲥⲛⲁⲩ ⲡⲓⲟⲩⲁ [16] ⲟⲩⲱⲧ ⲡⲉ. ⲡⲁⲉⲓ ⲡⲉ ⲉⲧϥⲛⲁϣⲓ ⲁⲛ ⲉϩⲣⲁⲓ̈ [17] ⲉϫⲛ̄ ⲫⲏⲧ ⲛ̄ⲥⲁⲣⲝ.

ⲟⲩⲟⲛ ⲛⲓⲙ ⲉⲧⲟⲩⲛ̄ⲧⲟⲩ [18] ⲡⲧⲏⲣϥ ⲙ̄ⲙⲁⲩ ϣϣⲉ ⲁⲛ ⲉⲧⲣⲟⲩⲉⲓⲙⲉ ⲙ̄- [19] ⲙⲟⲟⲩ ⲧⲏⲣⲟⲩ; ϩⲟⲉⲓⲛⲉ ⲙⲉⲛ ⲉⲩⲧⲙ̄ⲉⲓⲙⲉ [20] ⲙ̄ⲙⲟⲟⲩ ⲥⲉⲛⲁⲣ̄ⲁⲡⲟⲗⲁⲩⲉ ⲁⲛ ⲛ̄ⲛⲉⲧⲉ [21] ⲟⲩⲛ̄ⲧⲁⲩⲥⲉ. ⲛⲉⲧⲁϩⲥⲉⲃⲟ ⲇⲉ ⲉⲣⲟⲟⲩ, ⲥⲉⲛⲁ- [22] ⲣ̄ⲁⲡⲟⲗⲁⲩⲉ ⲙ̄ⲙⲟⲟⲩ.

ⲟⲩ ⲙⲟⲛⲟⲛ ⲡⲣⲱⲙⲉ [23] ⲛ̄ⲧⲉⲗⲉⲓⲟⲥ ⲥⲉⲛⲁϣⲉⲙⲁϩⲧⲉ ⲁⲛ ⲙ̄ⲙⲟϥ, [24] ⲁⲗⲗⲁ ⲥⲉⲛⲁϣⲛⲁⲩ ⲉⲣⲟϥ ⲁⲛ. ⲉⲩϣⲁⲛⲛⲁⲩ [25] ⲅⲁⲣ ⲉⲣⲟϥ, ⲥⲉⲛⲁⲉⲙⲁϩⲧⲉ ⲙ̄ⲙⲟϥ. ⲛ̄ⲕⲉⲣⲏⲧⲉ [26] ⲙⲛ̄ ⲟⲩⲁ ⲛⲁϣϫⲡⲟ ⲛⲁϥ [27] ⲛ̄ⲧⲉⲉⲓⲭⲁⲣⲓⲥ ⲉⲓ ⲙⲏ ⲛ̄ϥϯ ϩ[ⲓ]ⲱⲱϥ ⲙ̄ⲡⲧⲉⲗⲉⲓⲟⲛ ⲛ̄ⲟⲩⲟⲉⲓⲛ [28] [ⲁⲩⲱ] ⲛ̄ϥϣⲱ[ⲡⲉ ϩ]ϣⲱϥ ⲛ̄ⲧⲉⲗⲉⲓⲟⲛ ⲟⲩⲟ- [29] [ⲉⲓⲛ. ⲡⲉ]ⲛⲧⲁ[ϩⲧⲁⲁϥ] ϩⲓⲱⲱϥ ϥⲛⲁⲃⲱⲕ [30] [. . . . .] ⲡⲁⲉⲓ

75.28 ϩⲛ̄[ⲕⲉϣⲉ]ⲗⲉⲉⲧ: reading from earliest images; see Emmel, 114.

76.4 ⲡⲙⲁ: read ⲙ̄ⲙⲁ.

76.9 ⲉⲙⲙⲟⲩⲧⲉ: read ⲉⲛⲙⲟⲩⲧⲉ.

76.28 ⲛ̄ϥϣⲱ[ⲡⲉ ϩ]ϣⲱϥ: reading from earliest images; see Emmel, 114.

76.29 [ⲡⲉ]ⲛⲧⲁ[ϩⲧⲁⲁϥ]: reading from earliest images; see Emmel, 114.

The cup [15] of prayer contains wine and [16] water, because it is established as a type of [17] the blood for which thanks is given. [18] It is filled with the Holy Spirit, and [19] it is the possession of the wholly perfect human. When [20] we drink this, we will receive for ourselves the perfect [21] human. The living water is a body. [22] It is necessary for us to put on the living human. [23] For this reason when he comes and goes down into the water, [24] he undresses himself so that he might [25] put on that one (the living human).

A horse gives birth to a horse. A [26] human gives birth to a human. A god [27] gives birth to a god. This is how it is for the bridegroom [28] and the [bride]. They [come about] [29] from in the [...] [30] no Jew [...] [31] from [...] [32] exists, and [...] [33] from among the Jews [...] [34] Christians. You [...] [35] they are referred to here [...] [36] "the chosen race of [God ...]" [76.1] and "the true man" and "the son [2] of man" and "the seed of the son of man." [3] This true race is well known [4] in the world. These are the places [5] in which the children of the bridal chamber dwell.

While the union dwells in this world (as) [7] male and female—the place that is strong and [8] weakness—in the eternity the image of the union is different, [9] although we refer to them by these names. But [10] others exist. They are exalted above every name [11] that is named, and they [12] are exalted above the mighty. [13] For where there is strength, there those chosen [14] for power dwell. They are not different things, [15] but both of them are this one single [16] thing. This is the one that will not be able to rise up [17] to the heart of flesh.

As for all those who have [18] the entirety, is it not necessary for them to know [19] themselves entirely? Some who do not know [20] themselves will not benefit from those things [21] they have. But those who have learned about themselves, they will [22] benefit from them.

Not only will the [23] perfect human not be able to be detained, [24] but he will not be able to be seen. For if he is seen, [25] he will be detained. There is no other way [26] that someone will be able to produce for himself this grace unless [27] he should clothe himself in the perfect light [28] [and] also become the perfect [light. [29] The] one who [clothes]

76.14 "They are not different things": literally, "They are not one thing and another."

пе птєлєιον [31] [. . . . .] єтℝℕϣϣπε ℕ- [32] [. . . . .]ⲱⲥ єⲙⲡⲁⲧℕⲉⲓ
є- [33] [. . . . .] πⲉⲧⲁ⟦ϩ⟧ϫⲓ ⲡⲧⲏⲣϥ [34] [. . . . .] ⲁⲛⲉⲉⲓⲙⲁ. ϥⲛⲁϣ ℝ- [35]
[. . . . .]ⲡⲙⲁ єⲧℳⲙⲁⲩ, ⲁⲗⲗⲁ ϥⲛⲁ- [36] [. . .ⲧⲙⲉ]ⲥⲟⲧⲏⲥ ϩⲱⲥ ⲁⲧϫⲱⲕ ⲉⲃⲟⲗ. [77.1]
ⲙⲟⲛⲟⲛ ⲓⲏⲥⲟⲩⲥ ⲥⲟⲟⲩⲛ ℳⲡⲧⲉⲗⲟⲥ ℳⲡⲁⲉⲓ.

[2] ⲡⲣⲱⲙⲉ ⲉⲧⲟⲩⲁⲁⲃ ϥⲟⲩⲁⲁⲃ ⲧⲏⲣϥ, ϣⲁϩ- [3] ⲣⲁⲓ̈ ⲉⲡⲉϥⲥⲱⲙⲁ. ⲉϣϫⲉ ⲁϥϫⲓ ⲅⲁⲣ ℳⲡⲟ- [4] ⲉⲓⲕ
ϥⲛⲁⲁϥ ⲉϥⲟⲩⲁⲁⲃ. ⲏ ⲡⲡⲟⲧⲏⲣⲓⲟⲛ, [5] ⲏ ⲡⲕⲉⲥⲉⲉⲡⲉ ⲧⲏⲣϥ ⲉⲧϥϫⲓ ℳⲙⲟⲟⲩ, ⲉϥ- [6] ⲧⲟⲩⲃⲟ
ℳⲙⲟⲟⲩ. ⲁⲩⲱ ⲡⲱⲥ ϥⲛⲁⲧⲟⲩⲃⲟ [7] ⲁⲛ ℳⲡⲕⲉⲥⲱⲙⲁ;

ℕⲑⲉ ℕⲧⲁ ⲓⲏⲥⲟⲩⲥ ϫⲱⲕ ⲉⲃⲟⲗ [8] ℳⲡⲙⲟⲟⲩ ℳⲡⲃⲁⲡⲧⲓⲥⲙⲁ, ⲧⲁⲉⲓ ⲧⲉ ⲑⲉ ⲁϥ- [9] ⲡⲱϩⲧ
ⲉⲃⲟⲗ ℳⲡⲙⲟⲟⲩ. ⲉⲧⲃⲉ ⲡⲁⲉⲓ ⲧℕⲃⲏⲕ [10] ⲙⲉⲛ ⲉⲡⲓⲧℕ ⲉⲡⲙⲟⲟⲩ, ⲧℕⲃⲏⲕ ⲇⲉ ⲁⲛ [11] ⲉⲡⲓⲧℕ
ⲉⲡⲙⲟⲩ ϣⲓⲛⲁ ϫⲉ ⲛⲟⲩⲡⲁϩⲧℕ [12] ⲉⲃⲟⲗ ϩℳ ⲡⲡⲛⲉⲩⲙⲁ ℳⲡⲕⲟⲥⲙⲟⲥ. ϩⲟⲧⲁⲛ [13] ⲉϥϣⲁⲛⲛⲓϥⲉ,
ϣⲁⲣⲉϥⲧⲉ ⲧⲡⲣⲱ ϣⲱⲡⲉ. [14] ⲡⲡⲛⲉⲩⲙⲁ ⲉⲧⲟⲩⲁⲁⲃ ϩⲟⲧⲁⲛ ⲉϥϣⲁⲛⲛⲓϥⲉ, [15] ϣⲁⲣⲉ ⲧϣⲁⲙⲏ
ϣⲱⲡⲉ.

ⲡⲉⲧⲉⲩℕⲧⲁϥ ℳ- [16] ⲙⲁⲩ ℕⲧⲅⲛⲱⲥⲓⲥ ℕⲧⲙⲉ ⲟⲩⲉⲗⲉⲩⲑⲉⲣⲟⲥ [17] ⲡⲉ, ⲡⲉⲗⲉⲩⲑⲉⲣⲟⲥ ⲇⲉ ⲙⲁϥℝ
ⲛⲟⲃⲉ. « ⲡⲉ- [18] ⲧⲣⲉ ⲅⲁⲣ ℳⲡⲛⲟⲃⲉ ⲡϩℳϩⲁⲗ ℳⲡⲛⲟⲃⲉ [19] ⲡⲉ. » ⲧⲙⲁⲁⲩ ⲧⲉ ⲧⲁⲗⲏⲑⲉⲓⲁ,
ⲧⲧⲅⲛⲱⲥⲓⲥ ⲇⲉ [20] ⲡⲉ ⲡⲧⲱⲧ. ⲛⲉ<ⲧ>ⲧⲉⲥⲧⲟ ⲛⲁⲩ ⲁⲛ ⲁⲣ ⲛⲟⲃⲉ, [21] ⲉⲡⲕⲟⲥⲙⲟⲥ ⲙⲟⲩⲧⲉ ⲉⲣⲟⲟⲩ
ϫⲉ « ⲉⲗⲉⲩ- [22] ⲑⲉⲣⲟⲥ. » ⲛⲁⲉⲓ ⲉ<ⲧ>ⲧⲥⲧⲟ ⲛⲁⲩ ⲁⲛ ⲁⲣ ⲛⲟⲃⲉ, [23] ⲧⲧⲅⲛⲱⲥⲓⲥ ℕⲧⲁⲗⲏⲑⲉⲓⲁ «
ϫⲓⲥⲉ ℕϩⲏⲧ, » ⲉⲧⲉ [24] ⲡⲁⲉⲓ ⲡⲉ « ⲥⲉⲓⲣⲉ ℳⲙⲟⲟⲩ ℕⲉⲗⲉⲩⲑⲉⲣⲟⲥ. » [25] ⲁⲩⲱ ⲥⲧⲣⲟⲩϫⲓⲥⲉ ⲉⲡⲙⲁ
ⲧⲏⲣϥ. « ⲧⲁⲅⲁⲡⲏ [26] ⲇⲉ ⲕⲱⲧ. » ⲡⲉⲧⲁϩⲣ ⲉⲗⲉⲩⲑⲉⲣⲟⲥ ⲇⲉ ϩⲓ- [27] ⲧℕ ⲧⲅⲛⲱⲥⲓⲥ ϥⲟ ℕϩℳϩⲁⲗ
ⲉⲧⲃⲉ ⲧⲁⲅⲁ- [28] ⲡⲏ ℕⲛⲁⲉⲓ ⲉⲙⲡⲁⲧⲟⲩϣϥⲓ ⲉϩⲣⲁⲓ̈ [ℕⲧⲉ]- [29] ⲗⲉⲩⲑⲉⲣⲓⲁ ℕⲧⲅⲛⲱⲥⲓⲥ. ⲧⲅⲛⲱⲥ[ⲓⲥ
ⲇⲉ] [30] ⲥⲉⲓⲣⲉ ℳⲙⲟⲟⲩ ℕϣⲓⲕⲁⲛⲟⲥ ⲉⲥⲧ[ⲣⲟⲩ]- [31] ϣⲱⲡⲉ ℕⲉⲗⲉⲩ[ⲑ]ⲉⲣ[ⲟⲥ]. ⲧⲁⲅⲁⲡⲏ ⲙ[ⲁⲥϫⲉ]
[32] ⲗⲁⲁⲩ ϫⲉ ⲡⲱⲥ [ⲡⲉ . .]ⲟⲓ[.]. [. . .] [33] ⲡⲱⲥ ⲡⲉ. ⲙⲁⲥϫ[ⲟⲟⲥ ϫⲉ « ⲡⲁⲉⲓ ⲡⲱⲉⲓ ⲡⲉ,] » [34] ⲏ
« ⲡⲁⲉⲓ ⲡⲱⲉⲓ ⲡⲉ. » ⲁ[ⲗⲗⲁ « ℕ]ⲟⲩ[ⲉⲓ ⲧⲏⲣⲟⲩ] [35] ⲛⲟⲩⲕ ⲛⲉ. » ⲧⲁⲅⲁⲡⲏ ℳⲡⲛⲉⲩⲙ[ⲁⲧⲓⲕⲏ] [36]
ⲟⲩⲏⲣⲡ ⲧⲉ ϩⲓ ⲥⲧⲟⲉⲓ. ⲥⲉ̄ⲣⲁⲡⲟ[ⲗⲁⲩⲉ ℳ]- [78.1] ⲙⲟⲥ ⲧⲏⲣⲟⲩ ℕϭⲓ ⲛⲉⲧⲛⲁⲧⲟϩⲥⲟⲩ ℳⲙⲟⲥ. [2]
ⲥⲉ̄ⲣⲁⲡⲟⲗⲁⲩⲉ ϩⲱⲟⲩ ℕϭⲓ ⲛⲉⲧⲁϩⲉⲣⲁⲧⲟⲩ [3] ℳⲡⲟⲩⲃⲟⲗ, ϩⲱⲥ ⲉⲩⲁϩⲉⲣⲁⲧⲟⲩ ℕϭⲓ ⲛⲉⲧ- [4] ⲧⲟϩⲥ.
ⲛⲉⲧⲧⲁϩⲥ̄ ℕⲥⲟϭⲛ ⲉⲩϣⲁⲗⲟ ⲉⲧⲟⲩ- [5] ϣⲟⲩ ℕⲥⲉⲃⲱⲕ, ϣⲁⲣⲉⲛⲏ ⲉⲥⲉⲧⲟϩⲥ ⲁⲛ, [6] ⲙⲟⲛⲟⲛ
ⲉⲩⲁϩⲉ ⲉⲣⲁⲧⲟⲩ ℳⲡⲟⲩⲃⲟⲗ, ϣⲁⲩ- [7] ϭⲱ ⲟⲛ ϩℳ ⲡⲟⲩⲥⲧⲃⲱⲱⲛ. ⲡⲥⲁⲙⲁⲣⲓⲧⲏⲥ [8] ℕⲧⲁϥϯ
ⲗⲁⲁⲩ ⲁⲛ ⲁⲡⲉⲧϣⲟⲟϭⲉ ⲉⲓ ⲙⲏ [9] ⲏⲣⲡ ϩⲓ ⲛⲉϩ. ⲕⲉⲗⲁⲁⲩ ⲁⲛ ⲡⲉ ⲉⲓ ⲙⲏⲧⲓ ⲁ- [10] ⲡⲥⲟϭℕ. ⲁⲩⲱ
ⲁϥⲑⲉⲣⲁⲡⲉⲩⲉ ℕⲙⲡⲗⲏⲅⲏ, [11] « ⲧⲁⲅⲁⲡⲏ ⲅⲁⲣ ϩⲱⲃⲥ̄ ⲛⲟⲩⲙⲏⲏϣⲉ ℕⲛⲟ- [12] ⲃⲉ. »

ⲡⲉⲧⲉⲧⲥϩⲓⲙⲉ ⲙⲉ ℳⲙⲟϥ ⲛⲉⲧⲥⲛⲁ- [13] ϫⲡⲟⲟⲩ ⲉⲩⲉⲓⲛⲉ ℳⲙⲟϥ. ⲉϣⲱⲡⲉ ⲡⲉⲥ- [14]
ϩⲁⲉⲓ, ⲉⲩⲉⲓⲛⲉ ℳⲡⲉⲥϩⲁⲓ̈. ⲉϣⲱⲡⲉ ⲟⲩⲛⲟ- [15] ⲉⲓⲕ ⲡⲉ, ⲉⲩⲉⲓⲛⲉ ℳⲡⲛⲟⲉⲓⲕ ⲡⲟⲗⲗⲁⲕⲓⲥ. [16]
ⲉϣⲱⲡⲉ ⲟⲩⲛ `ⲥ´ϩⲓⲙⲉ ⲉⲥℕⲕⲟⲧⲕ ⲙⲛ ⲡⲉⲥ- [17] ϩⲁⲓ̈ ⲕⲁⲧⲁ ⲟⲩϩⲧⲟⲣ, ⲉⲡⲉⲥϩⲏⲧ ⲇⲉ ϩⲓ
ⲡⲛⲟ- [18] ⲉⲓⲕ ⲉϥⲁⲥℝⲕⲟⲓⲛⲱⲛⲉⲓ ℕⲙⲙⲁϥ, ⲡⲉⲧ- [19] ⲥⲁⲙⲁⲥⲧϥ ϣⲁⲥⲙⲁⲥⲧϥ ⲉϥⲓⲛⲉ
ℳⲡⲛⲟ- [20] ⲉⲓⲕ. ℕⲧⲱⲧℕ ⲇⲉ ⲛⲉⲧϣⲟⲟⲡ ⲙⲛ ⲡϣⲏ- [21] ⲣⲉ ℳⲡⲛⲟⲩⲧⲉ, ⲙⲛ̄ⲙⲣⲣⲉ ⲡⲕⲟⲥⲙⲟⲥ,

---

77.13 ϣⲁⲣⲉϥⲧⲉ: read ϣⲁϥⲧⲣⲉ.
77.20 ⲡⲧⲱⲧ: emend to ⲡⲉⲓⲱⲧ?

himself will go [30] [. . .] this is the perfect [31] [. . .] that we become [32] [. . .] we have not yet come to [33] [. . .] the one who has received the entirety [34] [. . .] to these places. He will be able to [35] [. . .] that place, but he will [36] [. . . the] middle as imperfect. [77.1] Only Jesus knows the end of this one.

[2] The priest is entirely holy, (even) in [3] his body. For if he has received bread, [4] he will make it holy. Or the cup, [5] or other things that he receives, he [6] purifies. So how will he not purify [7] the body also?

As Jesus perfects [8] the water of baptism, this is how he [9] emptied out death. For this reason we go [10] down into the water, but do not go [11] down into death so that we might be emptied [12] out into the spirit of the world. When [13] it (the spirit of the world) blows, it causes the winter to come about. [14] When the Holy Spirit blows, [15] the summer comes about.

The one who has [16] knowledge of the truth is free, [17] but the free person does not sin. For "the [18] one who sins is the slave to sin." [19] The mother is the truth, but knowledge [20] is the <Father>. Those who do not allow themselves to sin, [21] the world calls them "free." [22] Those who do not allow themselves to sin, [23] knowledge of the truth "puffs up," [24] which is what "it makes them free" (means). [25] And it makes them feel superior in every place. "But love [26] builds up." But the one who is free through [27] knowledge is a slave because of love [28] for those who have not yet been able to achieve [the] [29] freedom of knowledge. [But] knowledge [30] makes them able to [31] become free. Love [does not call] [32] something its own [. . .] [33] its own. It does not [say, "This is mine,"] [34] or "That is mine." [Rather,] (it says,) "All that is mine [35] is yours." Spiritual love is [36] wine and aroma. All those who anoint [78.1] themselves with it benefit from it. [2] Those who stand outside benefit also, [3] while those anointed stand (within). [4] If those anointed with the ointment withdraw from them [5] and depart, those not anointed, [6] who merely stand outside, they [7] still remain in their stench. The Samaritan [8] gave nothing to the wounded man except [9] wine and oil. It is nothing other than [10] the ointment. It healed the wounds, [11] for "love covers an abundance of [12] sins."

Those the woman is to bear [13] resemble the one whom she loves. If (she loves) her [14] husband, they resemble her husband. If he is an adulterer, [15] they often resemble the adulterer. [16] If a woman sleeps with her [17] husband out of necessity, yet her heart is with the adulterer [18] with whom she usually sleeps, the one [19] she will bear is born often resembling the adulterer. [20] But you who dwell with the child [21] of God, do

²² ⲁⲗⲗⲁ ⲙ̄ⲡⲣⲉ ⲡϫⲟⲉⲓⲥ ϣⲓⲛⲁ ⲛⲉⲧⲉⲧⲛⲁ- ²³ ϫⲡⲟⲟⲩ ⲛⲟⲩϣⲱⲡⲉ ⲉⲩⲉⲓⲛⲉ ⲙ̄ⲡⲕⲟⲥ- ²⁴ ⲙⲟⲥ, ⲁⲗⲗⲁ ⲉⲩⲛⲁϣⲱⲡⲉ ⲉⲩⲉⲓⲛⲉ ⲙ̄ⲡ- ²⁵ ϫⲟⲉⲓⲥ.

ϣⲁⲣⲉⲡⲣⲱⲙⲉ ⲧⲱϩ ⲙ̄ⲛ ⲡⲣⲱⲙⲉ. ²⁶ ϣⲁⲣⲉϩ̄ⲧⲟ ⲧⲱϩ ⲙ̄ⲛ ⲡϩ̄ⲧⲟ. ϣⲁⲣⲉ ⲡⲉⲓ- ²⁷ [ⲱ ⲧ]ⲱϩ ⲙ̄ⲛ ⲡⲉⲓⲱ. ⲛ̄ⲅⲉⲛⲟⲥ ⲛⲉϣⲁⲩⲧⲱϩ ²⁸ [ⲙ̄ⲛ] ⲛⲟⲩϣⲃ̄ⲣⲅⲉⲛⲟⲥ. ⲧⲁⲉⲓ ⲧⲉ ⲑⲉ ⲉϣⲁ- ²⁹ [ⲣⲉ]ⲡⲡⲛⲉⲩⲙⲁ ⲧⲱϩ ⲙ̄ⲛ ⲡⲡⲛⲉⲩⲙⲁ ⲁⲩⲱ ⲡⲗⲟ- ³⁰ [ⲅⲟⲥ] ϣⲁϥϥⲣ̄ⲕ[ⲟ]ⲓⲛⲱ[ⲛ]ⲉⲓ ⲙ̄ⲛ ⲡⲗⲟⲅⲟⲥ, ³¹ [ⲁⲩⲱ ⲡ] ⲟⲩⲟ[ⲉⲓⲛ ϣⲁ]ϥⲣ̄ⲕⲟⲓⲛⲱⲛⲉⲓ ³² [ⲙ̄ⲛ ⲡ]ⲟⲩⲟⲉⲓⲛ. ⲉⲕ]ϣⲁϣⲱⲡⲉ ⲛ̄ⲣⲱⲙⲉ, ³³ [ⲡⲣⲱⲙ]ⲉ ⲡⲉ[ⲧⲛⲁ]- ⲙⲉⲣⲓⲧⲕ. ⲉⲕϣⲁϣⲱⲡⲉ ³⁴ [ⲙ̄ⲡⲛⲉⲩⲙⲁ], ⲡⲡⲛⲉⲩⲙⲁ ⲡⲉⲧⲛⲁϩⲱⲧⲣ̄ ⲉⲣⲟⲕ. ⲉⲕ- ³⁵ [ϣⲁⲛϣ]ⲱⲡⲉ ⲛ̄ⲗⲟⲅⲟⲥ, ⲡⲗⲟⲅⲟⲥ ⲡⲉⲧ- ⁷⁹·¹ ⲛⲁⲧⲱϩ ⲛ̄ⲙ̄ⲙⲁⲕ. ⲉ[ⲕ]ϣⲁⲛϣⲱⲡⲉ ⲛ̄ⲟⲩ- ² ⲟⲉⲓⲛ, ⲟⲩⲟⲉⲓⲛ ⲡⲉⲧⲛⲁⲣ̄ⲕⲟⲓⲛⲱⲛⲉⲓ ³ ⲛ̄ⲙ̄ⲙⲁⲕ. ⲉⲕϣⲁⲛϣⲱⲡⲉ ⲛ̄ⲛⲁ ⲡⲥⲁ ⲛ- ⁴ ϩⲣⲉ, ⲛⲁ ⲡⲥⲁ ⲛϩⲣⲉ ⲛⲁⲙ̄ⲧⲟⲛ ⲙ̄ⲙⲟⲟⲩ ⁵ ⲉϩⲣⲁⲓ̈ ⲉϫⲱⲕ. ⲉⲕϣⲁⲛϣⲱⲡⲉ ⲛ̄ϩ̄ⲧⲟ ⁶ ⲏ ⲛ̄ⲉⲓⲱ ⲏ ⲙ̄ⲙⲁⲥⲉ ⲏ ⲛ̄ⲟⲩϩⲟⲟⲣ ⲏ ⲛⲉ- ⁷ ⲥⲟⲟⲩ ⲏ ϭⲉ ϩ̄ⲛ ⲛⲉⲑⲏⲣⲓⲟⲛ ⲉⲧⲛ̄ⲡⲥⲁ ⲛ- ⁸ ⲃⲟⲗ ⲙ̄ⲛ ⲛⲉⲧⲙ̄ⲡⲥⲁ ⲙⲡⲓⲧⲛ̄, ϥⲛⲁϣⲙⲉ- ⁹ ⲣⲓⲧⲕ ⲁⲛ ⲟⲩⲧⲉ ⲡⲣⲱⲙⲉ ⲟⲩⲧⲉ ⲡⲡⲛⲉⲩⲙⲁ ⲟⲩ- ¹⁰ ⲧⲉ ⲡⲗⲟⲅⲟⲥ ⲟⲩⲧⲉ ⲡⲟⲩⲟⲉⲓⲛ. ⲟⲩⲧⲉ ⲛⲁ- ¹¹ ⲡⲥⲁ ⲛⲧⲡⲉ ⲟⲩⲧⲉ ⲛⲁ ⲡⲥⲁ ⲛϩⲟⲩⲛ ⲥⲉ- ¹² ⲛⲁϣⲙ̄ⲧⲟⲛ ⲙ̄ⲙⲟⲟⲩ ⲁⲛ ϩⲣⲁⲓ̈ ⲛ̄ϩⲏⲧⲕ, ¹³ ⲁⲩⲱ ⲙ̄ⲛ̄ⲧⲁⲕ ⲙⲉⲣⲟⲥ ϩⲣⲁⲓ̈ ⲛ̄ϩⲏⲧⲟⲩ.

ⲡⲉ- ¹⁴ ⲧⲟ ⲛ̄ϩ̄ⲙ̄ϩⲁⲗ ⲉϩⲛⲁϥ ⲁⲛ ϥⲛⲁϣⲣⲉⲗⲉⲩ- ¹⁵ ⲑⲉⲣⲟⲥ. ⲡⲉⲛⲧⲁϩⲣⲉⲗⲉⲩⲑⲉⲣⲟⲥ ⲙ̄ⲡⲉϩ- ¹⁶ ⲙⲟⲧ ⲙ̄ⲡⲉϥϫⲟⲉⲓⲥ ⲁⲩⲱ ⲁϥⲧⲁⲁϥ ⲉⲃⲟⲗ ¹⁷ ⲟⲩⲁⲁϥ ⲁⲩⲙ̄ⲛ̄ⲧϩ̄ⲙ̄ϩⲁⲗ ⲟⲩⲕⲉⲧⲓ ϥⲛⲁϣ- ¹⁸ ⲣ̄ⲣⲉⲗⲉⲩⲑⲉⲣⲟⲥ

ⲧⲙ̄ⲛ̄ⲧⲟⲩⲟⲉⲓⲉ ⲙ̄ⲡⲕⲟⲥ- ¹⁹ ⲙⲟⲥ ϩⲓⲧⲛ̄ ϥⲧⲟⲟⲩ ⲛ̄ⲉⲓⲇⲟⲥ. ϣⲁⲩⲟⲗⲟⲩ ²⁰ ⲉϩⲟⲩⲛ ⲁⲧⲁⲡⲟⲑⲏⲕⲏ ϩⲓⲧⲛ̄ ⲟⲩⲙⲟⲟⲩ ²¹ ⲙ̄ⲛ̄ ⲛ̄ⲟⲩⲕⲁϩ ⲙ̄ⲛ̄ⲟⲩⲡⲛⲉⲩⲙⲁ ⲙ̄ⲛ̄ⲟⲩⲟⲉⲓⲛ. ²² ⲁⲩⲱ ⲧⲙ̄ⲛ̄ⲧⲟⲩⲟⲉⲓⲉ ⲙ̄ⲡⲛⲟⲩⲧⲉ ⲧⲉⲉⲓⲣⲉ ²³ ⲟⲛ ϩⲓⲧⲛ̄ ϥⲧⲟⲟⲩ, ϩⲓⲧⲛ̄ ⲟⲩⲡⲓⲥⲧⲓⲥ ⲙ̄ⲛ̄- ²⁴ ⲛⲟⲩϩⲉⲗⲡⲓⲥ ⲙ̄ⲛ̄ⲛⲟⲩⲁⲅⲁⲡⲏ ⲙ̄ⲛ ⲟⲩ- ²⁵ ⲅⲛⲱⲥⲓⲥ. ⲡⲛⲕⲁϩ ⲧⲉ ⲧⲡⲓⲥⲧⲓⲥ, ⲧⲁⲓ̈ ⲉⲛ- ²⁶ ϫⲉ ⲛⲟⲩⲛⲉ ϩⲣⲁⲓ̈ ⲛ̄ϩⲏⲧⲥ̄. ⲡⲙⲟ[ⲟ]ⲩ [ⲇⲉ] ²⁷ ⲧⲉ ⲑⲉⲗⲡⲓⲥ ⲉⲃⲟⲗ ϩⲓⲧⲟⲟⲧⲥ̄ ⲉ[ⲛⲥⲟ]- ²⁸ ⲉⲓϣ. ⲡⲡⲛⲉⲩⲙⲁ ⲧⲉ ⲧⲁⲅⲁⲡⲏ ⲉⲃⲟⲗ [ϩⲓⲧⲟ]- ²⁹ ⲟⲧϥ ⲉⲛⲁⲩⲝⲁⲛⲉ. ⲡⲟⲩⲟⲉⲓⲛ ⲇⲉ ⲧⲉ ³⁰ ⲧⲧⲛⲱⲥⲓⲥ ⲉⲃⲟⲗ [ϩ]ⲓⲧ[ⲟⲟ]ⲧⲥ̄ ⲧⲛ̄ⲡ[ⲱϩ]. ³¹ ⲧⲭⲁⲣⲓⲥ ⲥⲟ ⲛ̄ϥ[ⲧⲟⲟⲩ ⲙ̄]ⲙ̄[ⲉⲓⲛⲉ· ⲥⲟ ⲣ̄]- ³² ⲣ̄ⲙ̄ⲛ̄ⲕⲁϩ ⲥⲟ ⲣ̄ⲣ[. . . . .] ³³ ⲧⲡⲉ ⲛ̄ⲧⲉ ⲧⲡⲉ ⲁⲩ[. .] ϩ̄ⲛ [. .]

[ⲟⲩⲙⲁⲕⲁ]- ³⁴ ⲣⲓⲟⲥ ⲡⲉ ⲡⲁⲉⲓ ⲉⲙⲡⲉϥϣⲗ̄[. . . . ⲛ̄]- ⁸⁰·¹ ⲛⲟⲩⲯⲩⲭⲏ. ⲡⲁⲉⲓ ⲡⲉ ⲓⲏⲥⲟⲩⲥ ⲡⲭⲣⲓⲥⲧⲟⲥ. ⲁϥⲣ̄ⲁⲡⲁⲛ- ² ⲧⲁ ⲙ̄ⲡⲙⲁ ⲧⲏⲣϥ, ⲁⲩⲱ ⲙ̄ⲡⲉϥⲣ̄ⲃⲁⲣⲉⲓ ⲗ̄ⲗⲁⲁⲩ. ³ ⲉⲧⲃⲉ ⲡⲁⲉⲓ ⲟⲩⲙⲁⲕⲁⲣⲓⲟⲥ ⲡⲉ ⲡⲁⲉⲓ ⲛ̄ⲧⲉⲉⲓ- ⁴ ⲙⲓⲛⲉ ϫⲉ ⲟⲩⲧⲉⲗⲉⲓⲟⲥ ⲣ̄ⲣⲱⲙⲉ ⲡⲉ. ⲡⲁⲉⲓ ⲅⲁⲣ ⁵ ⲡⲗⲟⲅⲟⲥ ϫⲛⲟⲩⲛ ⲙ̄ⲙⲟⲛ ⲉⲣⲟϥ ϩⲱⲥ <ϥ>ⲙⲟⲕϩ ⁶ ⲁⲥⲉϩⲉ ⲡⲁⲉⲓ ⲉⲣⲁⲧϥ. ⲡⲱⲥ ⲧⲛ̄ⲛⲁϣⲣ̄ⲕⲁⲧⲟⲣ- ⁷ ⲑⲟⲩ ⲙ̄ⲡⲉⲉⲓⲛⲟϭ; ⲡⲱⲥ ⲉϥⲛⲁϯ ⲁⲛⲁⲡⲁⲩ- ⁸ ⲥⲓⲥ ⲛ̄ⲟⲩⲟⲛ ⲛⲓⲙ; ϩⲁ ⲧⲉϩⲏ ⲛ̄ϩⲱⲃ ⲛⲓⲙ ϣϣⲉ ⁹ ⲁⲛ ⲉⲗⲩⲡⲉⲓ ⲗ̄ⲗⲁⲁⲩ, ⲉⲓⲧⲉ ⲛⲟϭ ⲉⲓⲧⲉ ⲕⲟⲩⲉⲓ, ¹⁰ ⲏ ⲁⲡⲓⲥⲧⲟⲥ ⲏ ⲡⲓⲥⲧⲟⲥ, ⲉⲓⲧⲁ ⲁϯ ⲁⲛⲁⲡⲁⲩⲥⲓⲥ ¹¹ ⲛ̄ⲛⲉⲧⲙ̄ⲧⲟⲛ ⲙ̄ⲙⲟⲟⲩ ϩ̄ⲛ ⲛⲉⲧⲛⲁⲛⲟⲩⲟⲩ. ¹² ⲟⲩⲛ̄ ϩⲟⲉⲓⲛⲉ ⲉⲧⲟⲩⲛⲟϥⲣⲉ ⲧⲉ ⲉϯ ⲁⲛⲁ- ¹³ ⲡⲁⲩⲥⲓⲥ ⲙ̄ⲡⲉⲧϣⲟⲟⲡ ⲕⲁⲗⲱⲥ. ⲡⲉⲧⲣⲉ ¹⁴ ⲙ̄ⲡⲉⲧⲛⲁⲛⲟⲩϥ ⲙ̄ⲛ ϭⲟⲙ ⲙ̄ⲙⲟϥ ⲛ̄ϥϯ ¹⁵ ⲁⲛⲁⲡⲁⲩⲥⲓⲥ ⲛ̄ⲛⲁⲉⲓ. <ϥ>ϥⲓ ⲅⲁⲣ ⲁⲛ

78.23 ⲛⲟⲩϣⲱⲡⲉ: read ⲛ̄ⲛⲉⲩϣⲱⲡⲉ.
80.5 ϫⲛⲟⲩⲛ: read ϫⲛⲟⲩ.

not love the world, [22] but love the Lord so that those you will bear [23] might not come about resembling the world, [24] but come about resembling the [25] Lord.

The human has intercourse with the human. [26] The horse has intercourse with the horse. The donkey [27] has intercourse with the donkey. Nations have intercourse [28] [with] neighboring nations. In this way [29] the spirit has intercourse with the spirit, and the [30] [word] has intercourse with the word, [31] and light has intercourse [32] [with the light.] If [you] are born human, [33] [the human is the one that will] love you. If you come to be [34] [in the spirit], the spirit is the one that will join with you. [If] you [35] come to be in the word, the word is the one [79.1] that will have intercourse with you. If [you] come to be in light, [2] the light is the one that will have intercourse [3] with you. If you come to be one of those from above, [4] those from above will rest themselves [5] upon you. If you come to be a horse [6] or a donkey or calf or dog or [7] sheep or other animals that are outside [8] and below, then [9] neither human nor spirit nor [10] word nor light will be able to love you. Neither those above [11] nor those below nor those within [12] will be able to rest within you, [13] and you do not have a part in them.

The one [14] who is a slave unwillingly will not able to be free. [15] The one who has been free by the [16] grace of his master and has given [17] himself to slavery will no longer be able [18] to be free.

Farming the world [19] (occurs) in four kinds. They are gathered [20] into the storehouse through water [21] and earth and spirit and light. [22] And God's farming in the same way [23] (occurs) in four (kinds), in faith and [24] hope and love and [25] knowledge. Our earth is faith, in which [26] we are rooted. Water [27] is the hope through which [we] are nourished. [28] The spirit is the love through which [29] we grow. Light [is] [30] the knowledge through which we [ripen]. [31] Grace exists in [four manners: it is] [32] an earthly man, it is [. . .] [33] highest heaven [. . .].

[Blessed] [34] is the one who has not [. . .][80.1] a soul. This is Jesus Christ. He encountered [2] every place, and he did not burden anyone. [3] For this reason blessed is the one of this [4] sort because he is a perfect human. For [5] the word tells us about this one that it is difficult [6] to find. How will we be able to succeed [7] in this great thing? How will he give rest [8] to everyone? Above all it is not fitting [9] to grieve anyone, whether great or small, [10] or unbeliever or believer, and then give rest [11] to those resting upon good deeds. [12] There are some who profit from giving [13] rest to the one that lives happily. The one who does [14] a good deed is not able to give [15] rest to these

ⲙ̄ⲡⲉⲧⲉϩ- ¹⁶ ⲛⲁϥ. ⲙ̄ⲛ ϭⲟⲙ ⲇⲉ ⲙ̄ⲙⲟϥ ⲁⲗⲗⲩⲡⲉⲓ ⲉϥ- ¹⁷ ⲧⲙ̄ⲧⲣⲟⲩⲑⲗⲓⲃⲉ ⲙ̄ⲙⲟⲟⲩ. ⲁⲗⲗⲁ
ⲡⲉⲧⲁϣⲱ- ¹⁸ ⲡⲉ ⲕⲁⲗⲱⲥ ϩⲛ̄ⲥⲟⲡ ϣⲁϥⲁⲗⲗⲩⲡⲉⲓ ⲙ̄ⲙⲟ- ¹⁹ ⲟⲩ. ϥϣⲟⲟⲡ ⲁⲛ ⲛ̄ⲧⲉⲉⲓϩⲉ, ⲁⲗⲗⲁ
ⲧⲟⲩⲕⲁ- ²⁰ ⲕⲓⲁ ⲧⲉ ⲉⲧⲣ̄ⲗⲩⲡⲉⲓ ⲙ̄ⲙⲟⲟⲩ. ⲡⲉⲧⲉⲩⲛ̄ⲧⲁϥ ²¹ ⲙ̄ⲙⲁⲩ ⲛ̄ⲧϥⲩⲥⲓⲥ ϥϯ ⲟⲩⲛⲟϥ ⲙ̄ⲡⲉⲧⲛⲁ-
²² ⲛⲟⲩϥ. ϩⲟⲉⲓⲛⲉ ⲇⲉ ⲉⲃⲟⲗ ϩⲛ̄ ⲡⲁⲉⲓ ⲥⲉⲗ̄- ²³ ⲗⲩⲡⲉⲓ ⲕⲁⲕⲱⲥ.

ⲟⲩϫⲉϩ̣ⲛⲛⲏⲉⲓ ⲁϥϫⲡⲉ ²⁴ ⲛ̄ⲕⲁ ⲛⲓⲙ, ⲉⲓⲧⲉ ϣⲏⲣⲉ ⲉⲓⲧⲉ ϩⲙϩⲁⲗ̄ ⲉⲓⲧⲉ ²⁵ ⲧⲃⲛⲏ ⲉⲓⲧⲉ ⲟⲩϩⲟⲣ ⲉⲓⲧⲉ
ⲣⲓⲣ ⲉⲓⲧⲉ ⲥⲟⲩⲟ ²⁶ [ⲉⲓⲧⲉ] ⲉⲓⲱⲧ ⲉⲓⲧⲉ ⲧⲱϩ ⲉⲓⲧⲉ ⲭⲟⲣⲧⲟⲥ ⲉⲓⲧⲉ ²⁷ [. . .], ⲉⲓⲧⲉ ⲁϥ ⲁⲩⲱ
ⲃⲁⲗⲁⲛⲟⲥ. ⲟⲩⲥⲁⲃⲉ ²⁸ [ⲇⲉ ⲡ]ⲉ ⲁⲩⲱ ⲁϥⲉⲓⲙⲉ ⲛ̄ⲧⲧⲣⲟⲫⲏ ⲙ̄ⲡⲟⲩⲁ ²⁹ [ⲡⲟⲩⲁ]. ⲛ̣ϣⲏⲣⲉ̣ ⲙⲉⲛ
ⲁϥⲕⲉ ⲁⲣⲧⲟⲥ ϩⲁⲣⲱ- ³⁰ [ⲟⲩ. . . . .] ⲁ̣[. . . . ⲛ̄]ϩ̣ⲙ̣ϩ̣ⲁⲗ̄ ⲇⲉ ⲁϥⲕⲉ ⲕⲓ- ³¹ [. . . . .ϩⲁⲣⲱⲟⲩ ϩⲓ ⲉ]
ⲃⲣⲉ. ⲁⲩⲱ ⲛ̄ⲧⲃⲛⲟⲟⲩ ³² [ⲁϥⲛⲉϫ ⲉⲓ]ⲱ̣[ⲧ ϩ̣]ⲁ̣ⲣⲱⲟⲩ ϩⲓ ⲧⲱϩ ϩⲓ ⲭⲟⲣ- ³³ [ⲧⲟⲥ. ⲛ̄ⲟⲩ]-
ϩⲟⲟⲣ ⲁϥⲛⲉϫ ⲕⲉⲉⲥ ϩⲁⲣⲱⲟⲩ. ³⁴ [ⲁⲩⲱ ⲣ̄ⲣⲓⲣ ⲁ]ϥⲛⲉϫ ⲃⲁⲗⲁⲛⲟⲥ ϩⲁⲣⲱⲟⲩ ⁸¹·¹ ϩⲓ̈ ⲙⲁⲙⲟⲩ
ⲛ̄ⲟⲉⲓⲕ. ⲧⲁⲉⲓ ⲧⲉ ⲑⲉ ⲙ̄ⲡⲙⲁⲑⲏ- ² ⲧⲏⲥ ⲙ̄ⲡⲛⲟⲩⲧⲉ· ⲉϣⲱⲡⲉ ⲟⲩⲥⲁⲃⲉ ⲡⲉ ⲉϥ- ³ ⲁⲓⲥⲑⲁⲛⲉ
ⲛ̄ⲧⲙ̄ⲛⲧⲙⲁⲑⲏⲧⲏⲥ. ⲙ̄ⲙⲟⲣ- ⁴ ϥⲏ ⲛ̄ⲥⲱⲙⲁⲧⲓⲕⲏ ⲥⲉⲛⲁⲣ̄ⲁⲡⲁⲧⲁ ⲁⲛ ⲙ̄- ⁵ ⲙⲟϥ, ⲁⲗⲗⲁ
ⲉϥⲛⲁϭⲱϣⲧ ⲛ̄ⲥⲁ ⲧⲇⲓⲁⲑⲉ- ⁶ ⲥⲓⲥ ⲛ̄ⲧⲉϥⲯⲩⲭⲏ ⲙ̄ⲡⲟⲩⲁ ⲡⲟⲩⲁ, ⲛ̄ϥϣⲁ- ⁷ ϫⲉ ⲛⲙ̄ⲙⲁϥ. ⲟⲩⲛ̄
ϩⲁϩ ⲛ̄ⲑⲏⲣⲓⲟⲛ ϩⲙ̄ ⲡⲕⲟⲥ- ⁸ ⲙⲟⲥ ⲉⲩⲟ ⲙ̄ⲙⲟⲣⲫⲏ ⲣ̄ⲣⲱⲙⲉ. ⲛⲁⲉⲓ ⲉϥ- ⁹ ϣⲁⲥⲟⲩⲱⲛⲟⲩ, ⲣ̄ⲣⲓⲣ ⲙⲉⲛ
ϥⲛⲁⲛⲉϫ ⲃⲁ- ¹⁰ ⲗⲁⲛⲟⲥ ⲉⲣⲟⲟⲩ. ⲛ̄ⲧⲃⲛⲟⲟⲩ ⲇⲉ ϥⲛⲁⲛⲉϫ ¹¹ ⲉⲓⲱⲧ ⲉⲣⲟⲟⲩ ϩⲓ ⲧⲱϩ ϩⲓ ⲭⲟⲣⲧⲟⲥ.
ⲛ̄ⲟⲩ- ¹² ϩⲟⲟⲣ ϥⲛⲁⲛⲉϫ ⲕⲁⲁⲥ ⲉⲣⲟⲟⲩ. ⲛ̄ϩⲙ̄ϩⲁⲗ̄ ¹³ ϥⲛⲁϯ ⲛⲁⲩ ⲛ̄ϣⲟⲣⲡ. ⲛ̄ϣⲏⲣⲉ ϥⲛⲁϯ ⲛⲁⲩ ¹⁴
ⲛ̄ⲧⲉⲗⲉⲓⲟⲛ.

ϥϣⲟⲟⲡ ⲛ̄ϭⲓ ⲡϣⲏⲣⲉ ⲙ̄ⲡⲣⲱ- ¹⁵ ⲙⲉ, ⲁⲩⲱ ϥϣⲟⲟⲡ ⲛ̄ϭⲓ ⲡϣⲏⲣⲉ ⲙ̄ⲡϣⲏ- ¹⁶ ⲣⲉ ⲙ̄ⲡⲣⲱⲙⲉ.
ⲡϫⲟⲉⲓⲥ ⲡⲉ ⲡϣⲏⲣⲉ ⲙ̄- ¹⁷ ⲡⲣⲱⲙⲉ, ⲁⲩⲱ ⲡϣⲏⲣⲉ ⲙ̄ⲡϣⲏⲣⲉ ⲙ̄- ¹⁸ ⲡⲣⲱⲙⲉ ⲡⲉ ⲡⲉⲧⲥⲱⲛⲧ ϩⲓⲧⲙ̄
ⲡϣⲏ- ¹⁹ ⲣⲉ ⲙ̄ⲡⲣⲱⲙⲉ. ⲁⲡϣⲏⲣⲉ ⲙ̄ⲡⲣⲱⲙⲉ ϫⲓ ²⁰ ⲛ̄ⲧⲟⲟⲧϥ ⲙ̄ⲡⲛⲟⲩⲧⲉ ⲉⲧⲣⲉϥⲥⲱⲛⲧ. ⲟⲩⲛ- ²¹
ⲧⲁϥ ⲙ̄ⲙⲁⲩ ⲉⲧⲣⲉϥϫⲡⲟ. ⲡⲉⲛⲧⲁϩϫⲓ ⲉ- ²² ⲧⲣⲉϥⲥⲱⲛⲧ ⲟⲩⲥⲱⲛⲧ ⲡⲉ. ⲡⲉⲛⲧⲁϩϫⲓ ²³ ⲉϫⲡⲟ
ⲟⲩϫⲡⲟ ⲡⲉ. ⲡⲉⲧⲥⲱⲛⲧ ⲙ̄ⲛ ϭⲟⲙ ²⁴ ⲛ̄ϥϫⲡⲟ. ⲡⲉⲧϫⲡⲟ ⲟⲩⲛ̄ ϭⲟⲙ ⲛ̄ϥⲥⲱⲛⲧ. ²⁵ ⲥⲉϫⲱ ⲇⲉ
ⲙ̄ⲙⲟⲥ ϫⲉ· « ⲡⲉⲧⲥⲱⲛⲧ ϫⲡⲟ, » ²⁶ ⲁⲗⲗⲁ ⲡⲉϥϫⲡⲟ ⲟⲩⲥⲱⲛⲧ ⲡⲉ ⲉⲧ[ⲃⲉ . .] ²⁷
ⲛ̄ϫⲡⲟ, ⲛⲉϥϣⲏⲣⲉ ⲁⲛ ⲛⲉ, ⲁⲗⲗⲁ ⲛ̣[. . . .] ²⁸ ⲛⲉ. ⲡⲉⲧⲥⲱⲛⲧ ⲉϥⲣ̄ ϩⲱⲃ ϩⲛ̄ ⲟⲩ[ⲱⲛϩ] ²⁹ ⲉⲃⲟⲗ,
ⲁⲩⲱ ⲛ̄ⲧⲟϥ ϩⲱⲱϥ ϥⲟⲩⲟ[ⲛϩ ⲉ]- ³⁰ ⲃⲟⲗ. ⲡⲉⲧϫⲡⲟ ⲉϥϫⲡⲟ ϩⲛ̄ ⲟⲩⲡ[ⲉⲑⲏⲡ,] ³¹ ⲁⲩⲱ ⲛ̄ⲧⲟϥ
ϥϩⲏⲡ [.] [.]ⲩⲁ̣[. . . . . .] ³² ⲑⲓⲕⲱⲛ. ⲡⲉⲧⲥⲱ̣[ⲛⲧ ⲟ]ⲛ ⲉϥϩ[ⲱⲛⲧ ϩⲛ̄] ³³ ⲟⲩⲫⲁⲛⲉⲣⲟⲛ.
ⲡⲉⲧϫⲡⲟ ⲇ[ⲉ ⲉϥϫⲡⲉ] ³⁴ ϣⲏⲣⲉ ϩⲛ̄ ⲟⲩⲡⲉⲑⲏⲡ. ⲙ̄ⲛ [ⲗⲁⲁⲩ ⲛⲁϣ]- ³⁵ ⲥⲟⲟⲩⲛ ϫⲉ ⲁϣ
ⲡⲉ ⲫⲟ[ⲩ ⲉⲧⲉ ⲫⲟⲟⲩⲧ] ⁸²·¹ ⲙ̄ⲛ ⲧⲥϩⲓⲙⲉ ⲣ̄ⲕⲟⲓⲛⲱⲛⲉⲓ ⲙ̄ⲛ ⲛⲟⲩⲉⲣⲏⲩ ² ⲉⲓ ⲙⲏ ⲛ̄ⲧⲟⲟⲩ
ⲟⲩⲁⲁⲩ. ⲟⲩⲙⲩⲥⲧⲏⲣⲓⲟⲛ ⲅⲁⲣ ³ ⲡⲉ ⲡⲅⲁⲙⲟⲥ ⲙ̄ⲡⲕⲟⲥⲙⲟⲥ ⲛ̄ⲛⲉⲛⲧⲁϩϫⲓ ⁴ ϩⲓⲙⲉ. ⲉϣϫⲉ
ⲡⲅⲁⲙⲟⲥ ⲙ̄ⲡϫⲱϩⲙ ϥϩⲏⲡ, ⁵ ⲡⲟⲥⲱ ⲙⲁⲗⲗⲟⲛ ⲡⲅⲁⲙⲟⲥ ⲛ̄ⲁⲧϫⲱϩⲙ ⲟⲩ- ⁶ ⲙⲩⲥⲧⲏⲣⲓⲟⲛ
ⲡⲉ ⲛ̄ⲁⲗⲏⲑⲉⲓⲛⲟⲛ; ⲟⲩⲥⲁⲣⲕⲓ- ⁷ ⲕⲟⲛ ⲁⲛ ⲡⲉ, ⲁⲗⲗⲁ ⲉϥⲧⲃⲃⲏⲩ. ⲉϥⲏⲡ ⲁⲛ ⲁⲧⲉ- ⁸
ⲡⲓⲑⲩⲙⲓⲁ, ⲁⲗⲗⲁ ⲉⲡⲟⲩⲱϣ. ⲉϥⲏⲡ ⲁⲛ ⲉⲡⲕⲁ- ⁹ ⲕⲉ ⲏ ⲧⲟⲩϣⲏ, ⲁⲗⲗⲁ ⲉϥⲏⲡ ⲉⲡⲉϩⲟⲟⲩ ⲙ̄ⲛ ¹⁰
ⲡⲟⲩⲟⲉⲓⲛ. ⲟⲩⲅⲁⲙⲟⲥ ⲉϥϣⲁⲕⲱⲕ ⲁϩⲏⲩ, ¹¹ ⲁϥϣⲱⲡⲉ ⲙ̄ⲡⲟⲣⲛⲉⲓⲁ, ⲁⲩⲱ ⲧϣⲉⲗⲉⲉⲧ, ¹²
ⲟⲩ ⲙⲟⲛⲟⲛ ⲉⲥϣⲁϫⲓ ⲡⲥⲡⲉⲣⲙⲁ ⲛ̄ⲕⲉϩⲟ- ¹³ ⲟⲩⲧ, ⲁⲗⲗⲁ ⲕⲁⲛ ⲉⲥϣⲁⲛⲣ̄ ⲡⲃⲟⲗ ⲙ̄ⲡⲉⲥⲕⲟⲓ- ¹⁴
ⲧⲱⲛ ⲛ̄ⲥⲉⲛⲁⲩ ⲉⲣⲟⲥ, ⲁⲥⲡⲟⲣⲛⲉⲩⲉ. ⲙⲟⲛⲟⲛ ¹⁵ ⲙⲁⲣⲉⲥⲟⲩⲱⲛϩ ⲉⲃⲟⲗ ⲙ̄ⲡⲉⲥⲉⲓⲱⲧ ⲙ̄ⲛ ⲧⲉⲥ- ¹⁶
ⲙⲁⲁⲩ ⲙ̄ⲛ ⲡϣⲃⲏⲣ ⲙ̄ⲡⲛⲩⲙⲫⲓⲟⲥ ⲙ̄ⲛ ⲛ̄- ¹⁷ ⲛ̄ϣⲏⲣⲉ ⲙ̄ⲡⲛⲩⲙⲫⲓⲟⲥ. ⲛⲁⲉⲓ ⲉⲥⲧⲟⲉⲓ ⲛⲁⲩ ¹⁸
ⲉⲧⲣⲟⲩⲃⲱⲕ ⲉϩⲟⲩⲛ ⲙ̄ⲙⲏⲛⲉ ⲉⲡⲛⲩⲙⲫⲱⲛ. ¹⁹ ⲛ̄ⲕⲟⲟⲩⲉ ⲇⲉ ⲙⲁⲣⲟⲩⲣ̄ⲉⲡⲓⲑⲩⲙⲉⲓ ⲕⲁⲛ ²⁰

(people). For he does not take what [16] pleases him. He is not able to cause grief, since he [17] is not able to afflict them. Rather, the one who lives [18] happily occasionally grieves [19] them. He does not (act) in this way, but their [20] wickedness is what grieves them. The one who has [21] the nature (of the perfect human) gives joy to the good. [22] But some by all this are [23] terribly grieved.

A homeowner acquired [24] everything, whether a son or slave or [25] cow or dog or pig or wheat [26] [or] barley or chaff or grass or [27] [. . .] or meat and acorns. [He is] a wise man, [28] and he knew the food (to be eaten) by each [29] [one]. To the children he served bread. [30] [. . .] To the slaves he served [31] [. . . and] meal. And to the cows [32] [he tossed barley] and chaff and grass. [33] To the dogs he tossed bones. [34] [And to the pigs] he tossed acorns [81.1] and slop. This is how it is with the disciple [2] of God: if he is wise he [3] understands discipleship. The bodily forms [4] will not trick [5] him, but he will see the disposition [6] of the soul of each one, and he will speak [7] with him. Many animals in the world [8] are in human form. If he [9] recognizes them, to the pigs he will toss acorns. [10] To the cows he will toss [11] barley and chaff and grass. To the [12] dogs he will toss bones. To the slaves [13] he will give the basics. To the children he will give [14] advanced teaching.

The son of man exists, [15] and the son of the son [16] of man exists. The Lord is the son of [17] man, and the son of the son of [18] man is the one who creates through the son [19] of man. The son of man received [20] from God the ability to create. He has [21] the ability to beget. The one who has received [22] the ability to create is a creature. The one who has received [23] the ability to beget is begotten. The one who creates cannot [24] beget. The one who begets can create. [25] But it is said that "the one who creates begets," [26] but his (alleged) offspring is (merely) a creature because [27] [. . .] of begetting, they are not his children, rather [. . .] [28] they are. The one who creates works in [the open], [29] and he also is apparent. [30] The one who begets begets in [secret] [31] and he himself is hidden. [. . .] [32] the image. [Moreover,] the one who [creates creates] [33] manifestly. But the one who begets [begets] [34] children in private. [No one will be able] [35] to know when [the husband] [82.1] and wife have intercourse with each other [2] except the two of them. For [3] marriage in the world is a mystery for those who have taken [4] a wife. If the marriage of defilement is hidden, [5] how much more is the marriage of undefilement a [6] true mystery? It is not fleshly, [7] but pure. It belongs not to passion, but to the [8] will. It belongs not to the darkness [9] or night, but it belongs to the day and [10] light. If a marriage is open, [11] it becomes prostitution, and the bride, [12] not only when she receives the seed of the other man, [13] but even if she leaves her bed [14] and is seen, prostitutes (herself). [15] Let her reveal (herself) only to her father and her [16] mother and the friend of the groom and [17] the children of the groom. These are allowed [18] to go into the bridal chamber every day. [19] But others let them desire just [20]

ⲉⲥⲱⲧⲙ̄ ⲉⲧⲉⲥⲥⲙⲏ ⲛ̄ⲥⲉⲣ̄ⲁⲡⲟⲗⲁⲩⲉ ⲙ̄- ²¹ ⲡˋⲉⲥˊⲥⲟ̄ⲡ̄, ⲁⲩⲱ ⲙⲁⲣⲟⲩⲥⲟⲛϣ ⲉⲃⲟⲗ ⲡ̄ⲛ̄ ⲛ̄- ²²
ⲗⲉϥⲗⲓϥⲉ ⲉⲧⲣⲉ ⲉⲃⲟⲗ ϩⲓ ⲧⲣⲁⲡⲉⲍⲁ ⲛ̄ⲑⲉ ⲛ̄- ²³ ⲛⲟⲩϩⲟⲟⲣ. ⲟⲩⲛ ϩⲛ̄ⲛⲩⲙⲫⲓⲟⲥ ⲙⲛ̄ ϩⲛ̄- ²⁴ ⲛⲩⲙⲫⲏ
ⲏⲡ ⲉⲡⲛⲩⲙⲫⲱⲛ, ⲙⲛ̄ ⲟⲩⲁ ⲛⲁϣ- ²⁵ ⲛⲁⲩ ⲁⲡⲛⲩⲙⲫⲓⲟⲥ ⲙⲛ̄ ⲧⲛⲩⲙⲫⲏ ⲉⲓ ⲙⲏ ²⁶ [ⲛ̄ϥϣ]ⲱⲡⲉ
ⲙ̄ⲡⲁⲉⲓ.

ⲛ̄ⲧⲉⲣⲉⲁⲃⲣⲁϩⲁⲙ ²⁷ [. . . .] ⲉⲧⲣⲉϥⲛⲁⲩ ⲁⲡⲉⲧϥⲛⲁⲛⲁⲩ ⲉⲣⲟϥ. ²⁸ [ⲁϥⲥ]ⲃ̄ⲃⲉ ⲛ̄ⲧⲥⲁⲣⲝ̄
ⲛ̄ⲧⲁⲕⲣⲟⲃⲩⲥⲧⲓⲁ, ⲉϥⲧⲁ- ²⁹ [ⲙⲟ] ⲙ̄ⲙⲟⲛ ϫⲉ ϣϣⲉ ⲉⲧⲁⲕⲟ ⲛ̄ⲧⲥⲁⲣⲝ̄.

³⁰ [. . . .]ⲩ ⲛ̄ⲧⲉ [ⲡ]ⲕⲟⲥⲙⲟⲥ, ⲉⲛ ϩⲟⲥⲟⲛ ⲛⲟⲩ- ³¹ [ⲥⲁ ⲛϩⲟⲩ]ⲛ ϩⲏ[ⲡ, ⲥⲉ]ⲁϩⲉⲣⲁⲧⲟⲩ ⲁⲩⲱ
ⲥⲉⲟⲛϩ. ³² [ⲉⲩϣⲁⲛ]ⲟⲩⲱⲛ[ϩ ⲉⲃⲟ]ⲗ, ⲁⲩⲙⲟⲩ, ⲕⲁⲧⲁ ⲡⲡⲁ- ³³ [ⲣⲁⲇⲓⲅⲙ]ⲁ ⲙ̄ⲡⲣⲱⲙⲉ
ⲉⲧⲟⲩⲟⲛϩ ⲉⲃⲟⲗ· ³⁴ [ⲉⲛ ϩⲟⲥⲟ]ⲛ ⲙ̄ⲙⲁϩⲧ ⲙ̄ⲡⲣⲱⲙⲉ ϩⲏⲡ ϭⲟⲛϩ ⁸³·¹ ⲛ̄ϭⲓ ⲡⲣⲱⲙⲉ· ⲉⲩϣⲁϭⲱⲗⲡ
ⲛ̄ϭⲓ ⲛⲉϥⲙⲁϩⲧ, ² ⲥⲉⲣ̄ ⲡⲃⲟⲗ ⲛ̄ϩⲏⲧϥ ϥⲛⲁⲙⲟⲩ ⲛ̄ϭⲓ ⲡⲣⲱⲙⲉ. ³ ⲧⲉⲉⲓϩⲉ ⲟⲛ ⲙ̄ⲡϣⲏⲛ· ϩⲱⲥ
ⲉⲧⲉϥⲛⲟⲩⲛⲉ ⁴ ϩⲏⲡ, ϣⲁϥϯ ⲟⲩⲱ ⲛ̄ϥⲗⲉϩⲛⲧ. ⲉⲣϣⲁ ⲧⲉϥ- ⁵ ⲛⲟⲩⲛⲉ ϭⲱⲗⲡ ⲉⲃⲟⲗ, ϣⲁⲣⲉⲡϣⲏⲛ
ϣⲟ- ⁶ ⲟⲩⲉ. ⲧⲁⲉⲓ ⲧⲉ ⲑⲉ ϩⲓ ϫⲡⲟ ⲛⲓⲙ ⲉⲧϩ̄ⲙ ⲡⲕⲟⲥ- ⁷ ⲙⲟⲥ, ⲟⲩ ⲙⲟⲛⲟⲛ ϩⲓ ⲛⲉⲧⲟⲩⲟⲛϩ ⲉⲃⲟⲗ, ⁸
ⲁⲗⲗⲁ ϩⲓ ⲛⲉⲑⲏⲡ. ⲉϥ ϩⲟⲥⲟⲛ ⲅⲁⲣ ⲧⲛⲟⲩⲛⲉ ⁹ ⲛ̄ⲧⲕⲁⲕⲓⲁ ϩⲏⲡ ⲥϩⲟⲟⲣ. ⲉⲩϣⲁⲛⲥⲟⲩⲱⲛⲥ̄ ¹⁰ ⲇⲉ,
ⲁⲥⲃⲱⲗ ⲉⲃⲟⲗ. ⲉⲥϣⲁⲛⲟⲩⲱⲛϩ ⲇⲉ ⲉ- ¹¹ ⲃⲟⲗ, ⲁⲥⲱϫⲛ̄. ⲉⲧⲃⲉ ⲡⲁⲉⲓ ⲡⲗⲟⲅⲟⲥ ϫⲱ ⲙ̄- ¹² ⲙⲟⲥ
ϫⲉ· « ⲏⲇⲏ ⲧⲁϩⲉⲓⲛⲏ ⲥⲙ̄ⲙⲟⲛⲧ ⲁⲧⲛⲟⲩ- ¹³ ⲛⲉ ⲛ̄ⲛϣⲏⲛ. » ⲉⲥⲛⲁϣⲱϣⲧ ⲁⲛ—ⲡⲉⲧⲟⲩ- ¹⁴
ⲛⲁϣⲁⲁⲧϥ ⲡⲁⲗⲓⲛ ϣⲁϥϯ ⲟⲩⲱ—ⲁⲗⲗⲁ ⲉϣⲁ- ¹⁵ ⲣⲉ ⲧⲁϩⲉⲓⲛⲏ ⲃⲁⲗⲃ̄ⲗ ⲉⲡⲓⲧⲛ̄ ⲉⲡⲉⲥⲛⲧ ϣⲁⲛ-
¹⁶ ⲧⲉⲥⲛ̄ ⲧⲛⲟⲩⲛⲉ ⲉϩⲣⲁⲉⲓ. ⲁⲓⲏⲥⲟⲩⲥ ⲇⲉ ⲡⲱⲣⲕ ⲛ̄- ¹⁷ ⲧⲛⲟⲩⲛⲉ ⲙ̄ⲡⲙⲁ ⲧⲏⲣϥ, ϩⲛ̄ⲕⲟⲟⲩⲉ ⲇⲉ ⲕⲁ-
¹⁸ ⲧⲁ ⲙⲉⲣⲟⲥ. ⲁⲛⲟⲛ ϩⲱⲱⲛ ⲙⲁⲣⲉ ⲡⲟⲩⲁ ¹⁹ ⲡⲟⲩⲁ ⲛ̄ϩⲏⲧⲛ̄ ⲙⲁⲣⲉϥⲃⲁⲗⲃⲗⲉ ⲛ̄ⲥⲁ ⲧⲛⲟⲩ- ²⁰
ⲛⲉ ⲛ̄ⲧⲕⲁⲕⲓⲁ ⲉⲧⲛ̄ϩⲣⲁⲉⲓ ⲛ̄ϩⲏⲧϥ, ⲛ̄ϥⲡⲟⲣⲕ̄ⲥ̄ ²¹ ϩⲁ ⲧⲉⲥⲛⲟⲩⲛⲉ ϩ̄ⲙ ⲡⲉϥϩⲏⲧ. ⲉⲥⲛⲁⲡⲱⲣⲕ ²² ⲇⲉ
ⲉⲛ̄ϣⲁⲥⲟⲩⲱⲛⲥ̄. ⲉϣⲱⲡⲉ ⲇⲉ ⲧⲛ̄- ²³ ⲛⲟ ⲛ̄ⲁⲧⲥⲟⲟⲩⲛ ⲉⲣⲟⲥ, ⲥϫⲉ ⲛⲟⲩⲛⲉ ϩⲣ[ⲁ]ⲓ̈ ²⁴ ⲛ̄ϩⲏⲧⲛ̄,
ⲁⲩⲱ ⲥⲧⲉⲩⲟ ⲉⲃⲟⲗ ⲛ̄ⲛⲉⲥⲕⲁⲣ- ²⁵ ⲡⲟⲥ ϩⲣⲁⲓ̈ ϩ̄ⲙ ⲡⲛ̄ϩⲏⲧ. ⲥⲟ ⲛ̄ϫⲟⲉⲓⲥ ⲉⲣⲟⲛ. ²⁶ ⲧⲛ̄ⲛⲟ ⲛ̄ϩⲙ̄ϩⲁⲗ
ⲛⲁⲥ. ⲥⲣ̄ⲁⲓⲭⲙⲁⲗⲱ[ⲧ]ⲓ̈ⲍⲉ ²⁷ ⲙ̄ⲙⲟⲛ ⲉⲧⲣⲛ̄ⲉⲓⲣⲉ ⲛ̄ⲛⲉⲧⲛ̄ⲟⲩⲟϣ[ⲟⲩ ⲁⲛ,] ²⁸ ⲛⲉⲧⲛ̄ⲟⲩⲟϣⲟⲩ
ⲧⲛ̄ⲉⲓⲣⲉ ⲙ̄ⲙⲟⲟⲩ [ⲁⲛ. ⲥ]- ²⁹ ϭⲙ̄ ϭⲟⲙ ϫⲉ ⲙ̄ⲡⲛ̄ⲥⲟⲩⲱⲛⲥ̄. ϩⲱⲥ [ⲉⲥϣⲟ]- ³⁰ ⲟⲡ ⲙⲉⲛ ⲥⲣ̄ⲉⲛⲉⲣⲅⲉⲓ.
ⲧⲙ̄ⲛ̄ⲧⲁⲧⲥ[ⲟⲟⲩⲛ] ³¹ ⲉⲥϣⲟⲟⲡ ⲙ̄ⲙⲁⲁⲩ ⲛ̄ⲛⲡⲉ[ⲑⲟⲟⲩ ⲧⲏⲣⲟⲩ.] ³² ⲧⲙ̄ⲛ̄ⲧⲁⲧⲥⲟⲟⲩⲛ [ⲉⲥ]ⲛⲁϣⲉ
ⲁⲡ[ⲙⲟⲩ ϫⲉ] ³³ ⲛⲉⲧϣⲟⲟⲡ ⲉⲃⲟⲗ ϩ̄ⲛ ⲧⲙ̄ⲛ̄ⲧ[ⲁⲧⲥⲟⲟⲩⲛ] ³⁴ ⲟⲩⲧⲉ ⲛⲉⲩϣⲟⲟⲡ ⲁⲛ ⲟⲩⲧⲉ
[ⲥⲉϣⲟⲟⲡ ⲁⲛ] ³⁵ ⲟⲩⲧⲉ ⲥⲉⲛⲁϣⲱⲡⲉ ⲁⲛ. [. . . . . .] ⁸⁴·¹ ⲥⲉⲛⲁϫⲱⲕ ⲉⲃⲟⲗ ϩⲟⲧⲁⲛ ⲉⲣϣⲁ
ⲧⲁⲗⲏⲑⲉⲓⲁ ² ⲧⲏⲣⲥ ⲟⲩⲱⲛϩ ⲉⲃⲟⲗ. ⲧⲁⲗⲏⲑⲉⲓⲁ ⲅⲁⲣ ⲕⲁⲧⲁ ⲑⲉ ³ ⲛ̄ⲧⲙ̄ⲛ̄ⲧⲁⲧⲥⲟⲟⲩⲛ· ⲉⲥϩⲏⲡ ⲙⲉⲛ
ⲥⲣ̄ⲁⲛⲁ- ⁴ ⲡⲁⲩⲉ ϩⲣⲁⲓ̈ ⲛ̄ϩⲏⲧⲥ̄, ⲉⲥϣⲁⲟⲩⲱⲛϩ ⲇⲉ ⲉⲃⲟⲗ ⁵ ⲛ̄ⲥⲉⲥⲟⲩⲱⲛⲥ̄, ϣⲁⲩⲧⲛⲁⲥ ⲉⲟⲟⲩ
ϩⲟⲥⲟⲛ ⁶ ⲥⲟ̄ⲛ ϭⲟⲙ ⲉⲧⲙ̄ⲛ̄ⲧⲁⲧⲥⲟⲟⲩⲛ ⲁⲩⲱ ⲁⲧⲡⲗⲁ- ⁷ ⲛⲏ. ⲥϯ ⲛ̄ⲧⲙ̄ⲛ̄ⲧⲉⲗⲉⲩⲑⲉⲣⲟⲥ. ⲡⲉϫⲁϥ
ⲛ̄ϭⲓ ⁸ ⲡⲗⲟⲅⲟⲥ ϫⲉ· « ⲉⲧⲉⲧⲛ̄ϣⲁⲛⲥⲟⲩⲱⲛ ⲧⲁⲗⲏ- ⁹ ⲑⲉⲓⲁ, ⲧⲁⲗⲏⲑⲉⲓⲁ ⲛⲁⲣ̄ ⲧⲏⲛⲉ ⲛ̄ⲉⲗⲉⲩⲑⲉⲣⲟⲥ.
» ¹⁰ ⲧⲙ̄ⲛ̄ⲧⲁⲧⲥⲟⲟⲩⲛ ⲥⲟ ⲛ̄ϩⲙ̄ϩⲁⲗ. ⲧⲅⲛⲱⲥⲓⲥ ⲟⲩ- ¹¹ ⲉⲗⲉⲩⲑⲉⲣⲓⲁ ⲧⲉ. ⲉⲛϣⲁⲥⲟⲩⲱⲛ ⲧⲁⲗⲏⲑⲉⲓⲁ,
¹² ⲧⲛ̄ⲛⲁϩⲉ ⲁⲛⲕⲁⲣⲡⲟⲥ ⲛ̄ⲧⲁⲗⲏⲑⲉⲓⲁ ϩⲣⲁⲓ̈ ⲛ̄- ¹³ ϩⲏⲧⲛ̄. ⲉⲛϣⲁϩⲱⲧⲣ̄ ⲉⲣⲟⲥ, ⲥⲛⲁϫⲓ ⲙ̄ⲡⲛ̄ⲡⲗⲏ-
¹⁴ ⲣⲱⲙⲁ.

ⲧⲉⲛⲟⲩ ⲟⲩⲛ̄ⲧⲁⲛ ⲙ̄ⲙⲁⲩ ⲛ̄ⲛⲉⲧⲟⲩ- ¹⁵ ⲟⲛϩ ⲉⲃⲟⲗ ⲛ̄ⲧⲉ ⲡⲥⲱⲛⲧ. ϣⲁⲛϫⲟⲟⲥ ϫⲉ· ¹⁶ « ⲛ̄ⲧⲟⲟⲩ
ⲛⲉ ⲛ̄ϫⲱⲱⲣⲉ ⲉⲧⲧⲁⲉⲓⲏⲩ. ⲛⲉⲑⲏⲡ ¹⁷ ⲇⲉ ⲛⲉ ⲛ̄ϭⲱⲃ ⲉⲧϣⲏⲥ. » ⲧⲁⲉⲓ <ⲁⲛ> ⲧⲉ ⲑⲉ

to hear her voice and take pleasure in ²¹ her ointment, and let them feast on the ²²
scraps that fall from the table, like ²³ the dogs. Grooms and ²⁴ brides belong in the
bridal chamber, and no one will be able ²⁵ to see the groom and bride unless ²⁶ [he]
becomes this one.

When Abraham ²⁷ [. . .] for him to see what he was going to see. ²⁸ [He] circumcised the flesh of the foreskin, telling ²⁹ us that it is necessary to destroy the flesh.

³⁰ [. . .] of [the] world, as long as their ³¹ [insides] are hidden, stand and live. ³² [If
they] become apparent, they die, in accordance with the ³³ [model] of the visible
man: ³⁴ [as long as] the bowels of the man remain hidden, the man is alive; ⁸³·¹ if his
bowels are revealed, ² they come to be outside of him, and the man will die. ³ This
(is) also (how it is) with the tree: while its roots ⁴ remain hidden, it sprouts and
grows. If its ⁵ root becomes uncovered, ⁶ the tree shrivels up. This is how it is with
every birth in the world, ⁷ not only with those visible, ⁸ but (also) with those hidden. For as long as the root ⁹ of evil is hidden, it is strong. But if it is known, ¹⁰ it has
been destroyed. If it becomes uncovered, ¹¹ it has been destroyed. For this reason
the word says: ¹² "Already the ax is laid at the root ¹³ of the trees." It will not (merely)
cut—what ¹⁴ is cut sprouts again—but ¹⁵ the ax digs down until ¹⁶ it pulls the root
out. But Jesus unearths ¹⁷ the root of the entire place, but others (do it) ¹⁸ partially.
Let each ¹⁹ one among us also dig up the root ²⁰ of evil that is within him, and let
him unearth ²¹ its root in his heart. It will be unearthed ²² when we are aware of it.
But if we ²³ are ignorant of it, it takes root ²⁴ within you, and it produces its fruit ²⁵
in our heart. It becomes lord over us. ²⁶ We are slaves to it. It takes us captive, ²⁷
causing us to do things we [do not] want (to do), ²⁸ (and) the things we want (to
do), we [do not] do. [It] ²⁹ becomes powerful because we are not aware of it. While
[it exists,] ³⁰ it is indeed active. [Ignorance] ³¹ is the mother [of all evil.] ³² Ignorance
will lead to [death ³³ because] those from [ignorance] ³⁴ neither did they exist nor
do they exist nor ³⁵ will they exist. [. . .] ⁸⁴·¹ They will be perfected when all truth ²
appears. For truth is like ³ ignorance: when hidden it rests ⁴ within itself, but when
revealed ⁵ and recognized, it is glorified to the extent that ⁶ it is stronger than ignorance and error. ⁷ It gives freedom. The word said, ⁸ "If you know the truth, ⁹ the
truth will make you free." ¹⁰ Ignorance is a slave. Knowledge ¹¹ is a free person. If we
know the truth, ¹² we will find the fruit of truth within ¹³ us. If we unite with it, it
will receive our ¹⁴ fullness.

Now we have the ¹⁵ revealed things of creation. We say, ¹⁶ "They are strong who are
revered. But the hidden things ¹⁷ are the weak that are despised." This is not how it

84.13 "receive": or "bring."

ⲛ̅ⲛⲉⲧⲟⲩ- [18] ⲟⲛϩ ⲉⲃⲟⲗ ⲛ̅ⲧⲁⲗⲏⲑⲉⲓⲁ· ϩⲛ̅ⲅ̅ⲱⲃ ⲛⲉ, ⲁⲩⲱ [19] ⲥⲉϣⲏⲥ. ⲛⲉⲑⲏⲡ ⲇⲉ ⲛ̅ϫⲱⲣⲉ ⲛⲉ
ⲁⲩⲱ ⲥⲉⲧⲁ- [20] ⲉⲓⲏⲩ. ⲥⲉⲟⲩⲟⲛϩ ⲇⲉ ⲉⲃⲟⲗ ⲛ̅ϭⲓ ⲙ̅ⲙⲩⲥⲧⲏⲣⲓⲟⲛ [21] ⲛ̅ⲧⲁⲗⲏⲑⲉⲓⲁ ⲉⲩⲟ ⲛ̅ⲧⲩⲡⲟⲥ
ϩⲓ ϩⲓⲕⲱⲛ. ⲡⲕⲟⲓ- [22] ⲧⲱⲛ ⲇⲉ ϥϩⲏⲡ. ⲛ̅ⲧⲟϥ ⲡⲉ ⲡⲉⲧⲟⲩⲁⲁⲃ ϩⲙ̅ [23] ⲡⲉⲧⲟⲩⲁⲁⲃ.
ⲛⲉⲣⲉⲡⲕⲁⲧⲁⲡⲉⲧⲁⲥⲙⲁ ⲙⲉⲛ [24] ϩⲟⲃⲥ̅ ⲛ̅ϣⲟⲣⲡ ⲡⲱⲥ ⲉⲣⲉ ⲡⲛⲟⲩⲧⲉ ⲣ̅ⲇⲓⲟⲓⲕⲉⲓ [25] ⲛ̅ⲧⲕⲧⲓⲥⲓⲥ,
ⲉϥϣⲁⲡⲱϩ ⲇⲉ ⲛ̅ϭⲓ ⲡⲕⲁⲧⲁⲡⲉ- [26] ⲧⲁⲥ̣[ⲙ]ⲁ̣, ⲁⲩⲱ ⲛ̅ⲧⲉ ⲛⲁ ⲡⲥⲁ ⲛϩⲟⲩⲛ ⲟⲩⲱⲛϩ [27] [ⲉⲃⲟⲗ],
ⲥⲉⲛⲁⲕⲱ ⲇⲉ ⲙ̅ⲡⲉⲉⲓⲏⲉⲓ ⲛ̅ⲥⲱⲟⲩ [28] [ⲉϥⲟ] ⲛ̅ⲉⲣⲏⲙⲟⲥ, ⲙⲁⲗⲗⲟⲛ ⲇⲉ, ⲥⲉⲛⲁⲣ̅ⲕⲁⲧⲁ- [29] [ⲗⲩⲉ]
ⲙ̅ⲙⲟϥ. ⲧⲙ̅ⲛ̅ⲧⲛⲟⲩⲧⲉ ⲇⲉ ⲧⲏⲣⲥ̅ ⲥⲁⲡⲱⲧ [30] [ⲉⲃⲟⲗ] ⲛ̅ⲛⲉⲉⲓⲙⲁ, ⲉϩⲟⲩⲛ ⲁⲛ ⲉⲛⲉⲧⲟⲩⲁⲁⲃ [31]
[ⲛ̅ⲧⲉ ⲛ]ⲉ̣ⲧ̣[ⲟ]ⲩⲁⲁⲃ. ⲥⲛⲁϣⲧⲱⲥ ⲅⲁⲣ ⲁⲛ ⲙⲛ̅ ⲡⲟⲩ- [32] [ⲟⲉⲓⲛ ⲛ̅]ⲁ̣ⲧⲧⲱϩ ⲙⲛ̅ ⲡⲡⲗⲏⲣⲱⲙⲁ
ⲛ̅ⲁⲧ- [33] [ϣⲧⲁ, ⲁⲗ]ⲗ̣ⲁ ⲥⲛⲁϣⲱⲡⲉ ϩⲁ ⲛ̅ⲧⲛϩ ⲙ̅ⲡⲥⲧⲁⲩⲣⲟⲥ [34] [ⲁⲩⲱ ϩⲁ ⲛ]ⲉ̣ϥⲥⲃⲟⲉⲓ.
ⲧⲉⲉⲓϭⲓⲃⲱⲧⲟⲥ ⲛⲁϣⲱ- [35] [ⲡⲉ ⲙ̅ⲡⲟ]ⲩⲟⲩϫⲁⲉⲓ ⲛ̅ⲧⲁⲣⲉⲡⲕⲁⲧⲁⲕⲗⲩⲥ- [85.1] ⲙⲟⲥ ⲙ̅ⲙⲟⲟⲩ ⲉⲙⲁϩⲧⲉ
ⲉϩⲣⲁⲓ̈ ⲉϫⲱⲟⲩ. ⲉⲣϣⲁ [2] ϩⲛ̅ϩⲟⲉⲓⲛⲉ ϣⲱⲡⲉ ϩⲛ̅ ⲧⲫⲩⲗⲏ ⲛ̅ⲧⲙⲛ̅ⲧⲟⲩ- [3] ⲏⲏⲃ, ⲛⲁⲉⲓ ⲛⲁϣϭⲛ̅
ϭⲟⲙ ⲛ̅ⲃⲱⲕ ⲉϩⲟⲩⲛ ⲉ- [4] ⲡⲥⲁ ⲛϩⲟⲩⲛ ⲙ̅ⲡⲕⲁⲧⲁⲡⲉⲧⲁⲥⲙⲁ ⲙⲛ̅ ⲡⲁⲣ- [5] ⲭⲓⲉⲣⲉⲩⲥ. ⲉⲧⲃⲉ ⲡⲁⲉⲓ
ⲙ̅ⲡⲉ ⲡⲕⲁⲧⲁⲡⲉⲧⲁⲥ- [6] ⲙⲁ ⲡⲱϩ ⲙ̅ⲡⲥⲁ ⲛⲧⲡⲉ ⲟⲩⲁⲁⲧϥ, ⲉⲡⲉⲓ ⲛⲉⲩ- [7] ⲛⲁⲟⲩⲉⲛ ⲛ̅ⲛⲁ ⲡⲥⲁ ⲛⲧⲡⲉ
ⲟⲩⲁⲁⲧⲟⲩ, ⲟⲩⲧⲉ [8] ⲙ̅ⲡⲥⲁ ⲙ̅ⲡⲓⲧⲛ̅ ⲟⲩⲁⲁⲧϥ ⲁⲛ ⲛ̅ⲧⲁϥⲡⲱϩ, ⲉⲡⲉⲓ [9] ⲛⲁϥⲛⲁⲟⲩⲱⲛϩ ⲉⲃⲟⲗ ⲛ̅ⲛⲁ
ⲡⲥⲁ ⲙ̅ⲡⲓⲧⲛ ⲟⲩ- [10] ⲁⲁⲩ. ⲁⲗⲗⲁ ⲛ̅ⲧⲁϥⲡⲱϩ ⲛ̅ⲧⲡⲉ ⲉⲡⲓⲧⲛ̅. ⲁⲛⲁ [11] ⲡⲥⲁ ⲛⲧⲡⲉ ⲟⲩⲱⲛ ⲛⲁⲛ
ⲛ̅ⲛⲉⲧⲙ̅ⲡⲥⲁ ⲙⲡⲓ- [12] ⲧⲛ̅, ϫⲉⲕⲁⲁⲥ ⲉⲛⲛⲁⲃⲱⲕ ⲉϩⲟⲩⲛ ⲁⲡⲡⲉⲑⲏⲡ [13] ⲛ̅ⲧⲁⲗⲏⲑⲉⲓⲁ. ⲡⲁⲉⲓ
ⲁⲗⲏⲑⲱⲥ ⲡⲉ ⲡⲉⲧⲧⲁⲉⲓ- [14] ⲏⲩ, ⲉⲧⲟ ⲛ̅ϫⲱ`ⲱ´ⲣⲉ. ⲉⲛⲁⲃⲱⲕ ⲇⲉ ⲉϩⲟⲩⲛ ⲉⲙⲁⲩ [15] ϩⲓⲧⲛ̅ ϩⲛ̅ⲧⲩⲡⲟⲥ
ⲉⲩϣⲏⲥ ⲙⲛ̅ ϩⲛ̅ⲙⲛ̅ⲧϭⲱⲃ. [16] ⲥⲉϣⲏⲥ ⲙⲉⲛ ⲛ̅ⲛⲁϩⲣⲛ̅ ⲡⲉⲟⲟⲩ ⲉⲧϫⲏⲕ ⲉⲃⲟ[ⲗ]. [17] ⲟⲩⲛ̅ ⲉⲟⲟⲩ
ⲉϥϫⲟⲥⲉ <ⲉ>ⲉⲟⲟⲩ· ⲟⲩⲛ̅ ϭⲟⲙ ⲉϥϫⲟ- [18] ⲥⲉ ⲉϭⲟⲙ. ⲉⲧⲃⲉ ⲡⲁⲉⲓ ⲁⲛⲧⲉⲗⲉⲓⲟⲛ ⲟⲩⲉⲛ [19] ⲛⲁⲛ, ⲙⲛ̅
ⲛⲉⲑⲏⲡ ⲛ̅ⲧⲁⲗⲏⲑⲉⲓⲁ ⲁⲩⲱ ⲛⲉⲧⲟⲩ- [20] ⲁⲁⲃ ⲛ̅ⲛⲉⲧⲟⲩⲁⲁⲃ ⲁⲩϭⲱⲗⲡ ⲉⲃⲟⲗ, ⲁⲩⲱ ⲁ- [21] ⲡⲕⲟⲓⲧⲱⲛ
ⲧⲱϣ`ⲙ´ ⲙ̅ⲙⲟⲛ ⲉϩⲟⲩⲛ.

ⲉⲛ ϩⲟⲥⲟⲛ [22] ⲙⲉⲛ ϥϩⲏⲡ, ⲧⲕⲁⲕⲓⲁ ⲟⲩⲟⲥϥ̅, ⲙⲉⲛ ⲙ̅ⲡⲟⲩ- [23] ϫⲓⲧⲥ̅ ⲇⲉ ⲛ̅ⲧⲙⲏⲧⲉ ⲙ̅ⲡⲥⲡⲉⲣⲙⲁ
ⲙ̅ⲡⲡⲛⲉⲩⲙⲁ [24] ⲉⲧⲟⲩⲁⲁⲃ. ⲥⲉⲟ ⲛ̅ϩⲙ̅ϩⲁⲗ ⲛ̅ⲧⲡⲟⲛⲏⲣⲓⲁ. ϩⲟ- [25] ⲧⲁⲛ ⲇⲉ ⲉϥϣⲁϭⲱⲗⲡ ⲉⲃⲟⲗ,
ⲧⲟⲧⲉ ⲡⲟⲩⲟ- [26] ⲉⲓⲛ ⲛ̅ⲧⲉⲗⲉⲓⲟⲛ ⲛⲁϩⲁⲧⲉ ⲉⲃⲟⲗ ⲉϫⲛ̅ [ⲟ]ⲩⲟⲛ [27] ⲛⲓⲙ, ⲁⲩⲱ ⲛⲉⲧⲛ̅ϩⲏⲧϥ ⲧⲏⲣⲟⲩ
ⲥⲉⲛ[ⲁϫⲓ ⲭⲣⲓ]- [28] ⲥⲙⲁ. ⲧⲟⲧⲉ ⲛ̅ϩⲙ̅ϩⲁⲗ ⲛⲁⲣⲉⲗⲉⲩⲑⲉ[ⲣⲟⲥ, ⲁⲩⲱ] [29] ⲛ̅ⲥⲉⲥⲱⲧⲉ ⲛ̅ⲁⲓⲭⲙⲁⲗⲱⲧⲟⲥ.
« ⲧⲱϭⲉ [ⲛⲓⲙ ⲉⲙ]- [30] ⲡⲉⲡⲁⲉⲓⲱⲧ ⲉⲧϩⲛ̅ ⲙ̅ⲡⲏⲩⲉ ⲧⲟϭϥ [ⲥⲉⲛⲁ]- [31] ⲡⲟⲣⲕϥ. » ⲛⲉⲧⲡⲟⲣϫ
ⲥⲉⲛⲁϩⲱ[ⲧ]ⲣ̅ ⲛ̣[....] [32] ⲥⲉⲛⲁⲙⲟⲩϩ. ⲟⲩⲟⲛ ⲛⲓⲙ ⲉⲧⲛⲁⲃ̣[ⲱⲕ ⲉϩⲟⲩⲛ] [33] ⲉⲡⲕⲟⲓⲧⲱⲛ
ⲥⲉⲛⲁϫⲉⲣⲟ ⲙ̅ⲡⲟ[ⲩⲟⲉⲓⲛ ...] [34] ⲟ ⲅⲁⲣ ⲛ̅ⲑⲉ ⲛ̅ⲛⲅⲁⲙⲟⲥ ⲉⲧⲛⲛⲉ[........] [35] ϣⲱⲡⲉ
ⲛ̅ⲧⲟⲩϣⲏ. ⲡⲕⲱϩⲧ ϣⲁ̣[ϥ......] [86.1] ⲛ̅ⲧⲟⲩϣⲏ ϣⲁⲩϫⲉⲛⲉ. ⲙ̅ⲙⲩⲥⲧⲏⲣⲓⲟⲛ ⲇⲉ [2] ⲙ̅ⲡⲓⲅⲁⲙⲟⲥ
ⲛ̅ⲧⲟϥ ϣⲁⲩϫⲱⲕ ⲉⲃⲟⲗ ϩⲙ̅ ⲡⲉ- [3] ϩⲟⲟⲩ ⲙⲛ̅ ⲡⲟⲩⲟⲉⲓⲛ. ⲙⲁⲣⲉϥⲟⲟⲩ ⲉⲧⲙ̅ⲙⲁⲩ [4] ⲏ ⲡⲉϥⲟⲩⲟⲉⲓⲛ
ϩⲱⲧⲡ. ⲉⲣϣⲁ ⲟⲩⲁ ϣⲱⲡⲉ ⲛ̅- [5] ϣⲏⲣⲉ ⲙ̅ⲡⲛⲩⲙⲫⲱⲛ ϥⲛⲁϫⲓ ⲙ̅ⲡⲟⲩⲟⲉⲓⲛ. [6] ⲉⲧⲙ̅ ⲟⲩⲁ ϫⲓⲧϥ
ⲉϥⲛ̅ⲛⲉⲉⲓⲙⲁ, ϥⲛⲁϣⲓⲧϥ [7] ⲁⲛ ⲙ̅ⲡⲕⲉⲙⲁ. ⲡⲉⲧⲁϫⲓ ⲡⲟⲩⲟⲉⲓⲛ ⲉⲧⲙ̅ⲙⲁⲩ [8] ⲥⲉⲛⲁⲛⲁⲩ ⲁⲛ ⲉⲣⲟϥ
ⲟⲩⲧⲉ ⲥⲉⲛⲁϣⲉⲙⲁϩⲧⲉ [9] ⲁⲛ ⲙ̅ⲙⲟϥ. ⲁⲩⲱ ⲙⲛ̅ ⲗⲁⲁⲩ ⲛⲁϣ̅ⲣⲥⲕⲩⲗⲗⲉ ⲙ̅- [10] ⲡⲁⲉⲓ ⲛ̅ⲧⲉⲉⲓⲙⲉⲓⲛⲉ
ⲕⲁⲛ ⲉϥⲣ̅ⲡⲟⲗⲓⲧⲉⲩⲉⲥ- [11] ⲑⲁⲓ ϩⲙ̅ ⲡⲕⲟⲥⲙⲟⲥ ⲁⲩⲱ ⲟⲛ ⲉϥϣⲁⲉⲓ ⲉⲃⲟⲗ [12] ϩⲙ̅ ⲡⲕⲟⲥⲙⲟⲥ, ⲏⲇⲏ
ⲁϥϫⲓ ⲛ̅ⲧⲁⲗⲏⲑⲉⲓⲁ ϩⲛ̅ [13] ⲛ̅ϩⲓⲕⲱⲛ. ⲡⲕⲟⲥⲙⲟⲥ ⲁϥϣⲱⲡⲉ ⲛ̅ⲁⲓⲱⲛ. [14] ⲡⲁⲓⲱⲛ ⲅⲁⲣ ⲉϥϣⲟⲟⲡ
ⲛⲁϥ ⲙ̅ⲡⲗⲏⲣⲱ- [15] ⲙⲁ, ⲁⲩⲱ ⲉϥϣⲟⲟⲡ ⲛ̅ⲧⲉⲉⲓϩⲉ· ϥⲟⲩⲟⲛϩ ⲉⲃⲟⲗ [16] ⲛⲁϥ ⲟⲩⲁⲁϥ ⲉϥϩⲏⲡ ⲁⲛ ϩⲙ̅
ⲡⲕⲁⲕⲉ ⲙⲛ̅ ⲧⲟⲩ- [17] ϣⲏ, ⲁⲗⲗⲁ ⲉϥϩⲏⲡ ϩⲛ̅ⲛⲟⲩϩⲟⲟⲩ ⲛ̅ⲧⲉⲗⲉⲓⲟⲛ [18] ⲙⲛ̅ ⲟⲩⲟⲉⲓⲛ ⲉϥⲟⲩⲁⲁⲃ.

[19] ⲡⲉⲩⲁⲅⲅⲉⲗⲓⲟⲛ

[20] ⲡⲕⲁⲧⲁ ⲫⲓⲗⲓⲡⲡⲟⲥ

is with the revealed things [18] of truth: they are weak, and [19] they are despised. But the hidden things are strong and [20] revered. But the mysteries [21] of truth are revealed, since they are types and images. [22] Now the bridal chamber is hidden. It is the holy in [23] the holy. The curtain [24] first hid how God managed [25] the creation, but when the curtain is torn, [26] and the things inside are revealed, [27] this house will be deserted, [28] or rather, it will be [destroyed]. [29] The entire deity will depart [30] [from] these places, (but) not within the holies [31] [of] holies. For it will not be able to mix with the unmixed [32] [light] and the [limitless] fullness, [33] [but] it will be under the wings of the cross [34] [and under] its arms. This ark will become [35] [their] salvation when the flood [85.1] inundates them. If [2] some come to be part of the class of the priesthood, [3] they will be able to go into [4] the place behind the curtain with the high [5] priest. Because of this the curtain [6] did not tear at the top alone, since they (the two sides of the curtain) [7] would open only for those at the top, nor [8] did it tear at the bottom alone, since [9] it would have been shown only to those at the bottom. [10] Rather, it was torn from top to bottom. Those [11] at the top opened to us the things below, [12] so that we might go into the secret [13] of the truth. This truth is what is esteemed, [14] what is strong. But we should go in there [15] through despised types and weakness. [16] They are indeed despised when compared to glory that is perfect. [17] There is glory that is exalted above glory; there is power that is exalted [18] above power. For this reason perfect things have opened [19] to us, and the hidden things of truth, and the holies [20] of the holies have been revealed, and [21] the bridal chamber has beckoned us.

As long as [22] it is hidden, evil is idle, but it has not [23] been taken from the midst of the seed of the [24] holy spirit. They are the slaves of wickedness. But when [25] it is revealed, then the [26] perfect light will rush forth upon every one, [27] and all those in it will [receive] the chrism. [28] Then the slaves will be free, [and] [29] the prisoners will be released. ["Every] plant [30] that my father in heaven [did not] plant [will] [31] be uprooted." Those separated will be joined [. . .] [32] will be filled. Everyone who will [go into] [33] the bridal chamber will ignite the [light . . .]. [34] For [. . .] like marriages that are [. . .] [35] happen at night. The fire [. . .] [86.1] at night is extinguished. But the mysteries [2] of this marriage are perfected in the [3] day and the light. Neither that day [4] nor its light sets. If one becomes [5] a child of the bridal chamber, he will receive the light. [6] If one does not receive it while in this place, he will not be able to receive it [7] in the other place. The one who has received that light [8] will not be seen, nor will he be detained. [9] And no one will be able to vex [10] a person of this sort even while he dwells [11] in the world. And, moreover, when he leaves [12] the world, already he has received the truth in [13] the images. The world becomes the eternities. [14] For the eternity is for him a fullness, [15] and he exists in this way: it is revealed [16] to him alone, not hidden in the dark or the night, [17] but hidden in a perfect day [18] and holy light.

[19] The Gospel [20] according to Philip

XII. *VALENTINIAN EXPOSITION*

The *Valentinian Exposition* is the editorial title given to the highly fragmentary second tractate in Nag Hammadi codex XI. This text is often grouped with five ritual fragments that follow in sequence in the codex: On the Anointing, On Baptism A and B, and On the Eucharist A and B. The association of the *Valentinian Exposition* with the ritual fragments has influenced the interpretation of the text; it is often regarded as a catechism that prepares neophytes for ritual initiation. However, there is no reason to believe that the ritual fragments were intended to be read as a coda to the *Valentinian Exposition*. They are separated from the *Valentinian Exposition* with the same scribal markings that separate other tractates in the codex. Additionally, there is nothing in the content of the ritual fragments to suggest an affiliation with the *Valentinian Exposition* in particular, or Valentinian ritual practice more generally.

On its own terms, then, the *Valentinian Exposition* presents one Christian teacher's recounting of one version of Valentinian first principles, including the myth of Wisdom's error. An interesting feature of the text is the author's frequent interjections. These appear throughout the text and include his personal thoughts on the topic under discussion as well as acknowledgments of the views of others. The author also emphasizes the importance of faithfully interpreting Scripture and paying close attention to the teachings of other interpreters as well. These features suggest that the *Valentinian Exposition* is both a retelling of and a commentary on one version of the Valentinian Wisdom myth.

Despite the frequent use of first-person singular pronouns, the author is anonymous. The original language of composition was likely Greek, and given similarities with Valentinian first principles found in Irenaeus, *AH* book 1, the original composition likely dates to the last quarter of the second century C.E.

²²·¹ [o]ⲩⲧⲉ ⳩ⲛ [ ] ² [   ]ⲉⲓ ⲁⳕⲟ[ⲩⲛ   ] ³ [   ]ⲧⲭⲟⲣⲏⲅ[ⲓⲁ] ⁴ [   ]   ⲣ
ⲙ̄ⲙⲁⲉⲓ[ⲛ] ⁵ [   ] ⲛⲉⲧⲉ [ ] ⁶ [   ] ⲛ̄ⲡ̣ [   ] ⁷ (Lines 7–15 lacking) ¹⁶ [11–13
†ⲛⲁ]ⲭⲉ ⲡⲁⲙⲩⲥ- ¹⁷ [ⲧⲏⲣⲓⲟⲛ ⲁⲛⲉⲉⲓ ⲉⲧ]ⳙⲟⲟⲡ ⲛ̄ⲏⲉⲓ ⲙⲛ̄ ¹⁸ [ⲛⲉⲧⲛⲁⳙⲱⲡⲉ ⲛ̄]ⲏⲉⲓ. ⲛⲉⲉⲓ ⳝⲉ
ⲛⲉⲛ- ¹⁹ [ⲧⲁⳕⲙ̄ⲙⲉ ⲁⲡⲏ ⲉⲧ]ⳙⲟⲟⲡ ⲡⲓⲱⲧ ⲉⲧⲉ ²⁰ [ⲡⲉⲉⲓ ⲡⲉ . . . .]ⲉ ⲙ̄ⲡⲧⲏⲣϥ̄ ⲡⲓⲁⲧ- ²¹ [ⳙⲉⲭⲉ
ⲁⲣⲁϥ ⲉⲧ]ⳙⲟⲟⲡ ⳩ⲛ̄ ⲧⲙⲟⲛⲁⲥ. ²² [11–13] ⳩ⲛ ⲡⲕⲁⲣⲱϥ̄, ⲡⲕⲁ- ²³ [ⲣⲱϥ̄ ⲛ̄ⲇⲉ ⲡ]ⲉ ⲡⲥⳝⲣⲁⳕⲧ,
ⲉⲡⲉⲓ ⲟⲩⲛ ²⁴ [ⲛⲉϥⳙⲟⲟ]ⲡ ⲙ̄ⲙⲟⲛⲁⲥ ⲁⲩⲱ ⲛⲉⲙⲛ̄ ²⁵ [ⲗⲁⲩⲉ ⳙⲟ]ⲟⲡ ⳩ⲁⲧⲉϥ⳩ⲉⲏ. ⲉϥⳙⲟⲟⲡ ²⁶ [⳩ⲛ
ⲧⲁ̣]ⲩⲁⲥ ⲁⲩⲱ ⳩ⲛ̄ ⲡⲥⲁⲉⲓⲱ. ⲡⲉϥ- ²⁷ [ⲥ]ⲁⲉⲓⲱ ⲛ̄ⲇⲉ ⲡⲉ ⲧⲥⲓ̈ⲅⲏ. ⲛⲉⲩⲛ̄ⲧⲉϥ ⲛ̄- ²⁸ [ⲁ̣]ⲉ̣ ⲙ̄ⲙⲉⲩ
ⲙ̄ⲡⲧⲏⲣϥ̄ ⲉⲩⳙⲟⲟⲡ ⲛ̄⳩- ²⁹ [ⲣⲏⲓ̈] ⲛ̄⳩ⲏⲧϥ̄. ⲁⲩⲱ ⲡⲟⲩⲱⳙⲉ ⲙⲛ̄ ³⁰ ⲡⳙⲱⲡⲉ, ⲡⲙⲁⲉⲓⲉ ⲙⲛ̄ ⲡⳝⲱ,
³¹ ⲛ̣ⲉⲉⲓ ⳝⲉ ⳩ⲛ̄ⲁⲧⲭⲡⲁⲩ ⲛⲉ.

ⲡⲛⲟⲩⲧⲉ ³² [ⲁϥⲉ]ⲓ̣ ⲁⲃⲁⲗ ⲡ̄ⳙⲏⲣⲉ ⲡⲛⲟⲩⲥ ⲙ̄ⲡⲧⲏ- ³³ [ⲣ]ϥ̄ ⲉⲧⲉ ⲡⲉⲉⲓ ⲡⲉ ⳝⲉ ⲁⲃⲁⲗ ⳩ⲛ̄ ⲧⲛⲟⲩⲛⲉ
³⁴ ⲙ̄ⲡⲧⲏⲣϥ̄ ⲉⲣⲉⲡⲉϥⲕⲉⲙⲉⲩⲉ ⳙⲟⲟⲡ. ³⁵ ⲡⲉⲉⲓ ⲅⲁⲣ ⲛⲉⲟⲩⲛ̄ⲧⲉϥ⳩ ⲙ̄ⲙⲉⲩ ⳩ⲙ̄ ³⁶ ⲡⲛⲟⲩⲥ. ⲉⲧⲃⲉ
ⲡⲧⲏⲣϥ̄ ⲛ̄ⲅⲁⲣ ⲁϥϫⲓ ³⁷ ⲛ̄ⲟⲩⲙⲉⲩⲉ ⲛ̄ⳙⲙⲟ, ⲛⲉⲙⲛ̄ⲗⲁⲩⲉ ³⁸ ⲛ̄ⲅⲁⲣ ⳙⲟⲟⲡ ⳩ⲁⲧⲉϥ⳩ⲉⲏ ⲁⲃⲁⲗ. ⳩ⲙ̄
³⁹ ⲡⲙⲁ ⲉⲧⲙ̄ⲙⲉⲩ ⲛ̄ⲧⲁϥ ⲡⲉ ⲉⲛⲧⲁ⳩̄ⲕⲓⲙ ²³·¹⁶ (Lines 1–16 lacking) ¹⁷ ..[3–5].. [ ] ¹⁸ ⲁ̣ⲉⲓ ..
[. . .].̣ [4–6].̣ ⲟ̣[4–6] ¹⁹ ⲉⲥⲃⲉⲃⲉ ⲧ̣ⲉⲉⲓ ⳝⲉ [ⲧⲉ ⲧⲛ̄]ⲟⲩⲛⳕ [ⲙ̄ⲡⲧⲏ]- ²⁰ ⲣϥ̄ ⲁⲩⲱ ⲙⲟⲛⲁⲥ [ⲡⲉ
ⲉ]ⲙⲛ̄ⲗ[ⲁⲩⲉ ⳩ⲁ]- ²¹ ⲧⲉϥ⳩ⲉⲏ. ⲧⲙⲁ⳩̄ⲥⲛ̄[ⲧ]ⲉ ⲛ̄ⲇⲉ [4–6] ²² ⲉϥⳙⲟⲟⲡ ⳩ⲛ̄ ⲧⲥⲓ̈ⳅⲏ ⲁⲩⲱ
[ⲉϥⳙⲉ]- ²³ ⳝⲉ ⲛ̄ⲙ̄ⲙⲉϥ ⲟⲩⲁⲉⲉⲧϥ̄. ⲧⲙ̣[ⲁ⳩̄ϣⲟⲙⲧⲉ] ²⁴ ⲛ̄ⲇⲉ ⲕⲁⲧⲁ ⳝⲉ ⲛ̄ⲧⲁϥ ⲡⲉ[ⲛⲧⲁ⳩̄]- ²⁵
ⳙⲣϥ̄ ⲁⲃⲁⲗ ⲙ̄ⲙⲁϥ̄ ⲟⲩⲁⲉ[ⲉⲧϥ̄ ⳩ⲛ̄ ⲧ]- ²⁶ ⲙⲁ⳩̄ⲧⲟⲉ. ⲉϥⳙⲟⲟⲡ ⳩ⲛ̄ ⲧ̣[ⲙⲁ⳩̄]- ²⁷ ϣ̄ⲛ̄ⲧⳙⲉⲥⲉ
ⲁϥⳙⲣ̄ⲡ ⲉⲓⲛ[ⲉ ⲙ̄ⲙⲁϥ] ²⁸ ⲟⲩⲁⲉⲉⲧϥ̄, ⲁⲩⲱ ⳩ⲛ̄ ⲧⲙⲁ⳩̄ⲥⲛ̄[ⲧⲉ ⲁϥⲟⲩ]- ²⁹ ⲱⲛ⳩ ⲁⲃⲁⲗ
ⲙ̄ⲡⲉϥⲟⲩⲱⳙⲉ, [ⲁⲩⲱ] ³⁰ ⳩ⲛ̄ ⲧⲙⲁ⳩̄ⲧⲟⲉ ⲁϥ̄ⲡⲱⲣⳙ [ⲁⲃⲁ]ⲗ̣ ³¹ ⲙ̄ⲙⲁϥ ⲟⲩⲁⲉⲉⲧϥ̄.

ⲛⲉⲉⲓ ⲙ̄ⲙⲉⲛ ⲉ- ³² ⲧϥⲉ ⲧⲛⲟⲩⲛⲉ ⲙ̄ⲡⲧⲏⲣϥ̄, ⲙⲁⲣⲛ̄[ⲉⲓ] ³³ ⲛ̄ⲇⲉ ⲁ⳩ⲟⲩⲛ ⲁⲡⲉϥⲟⲩⲱⲛ⳥ ⲁⲃ[ⲁⲗ] ³⁴
ⲁⲩⲱ ⲧⲉϥⲙ̄ⲛ̄ⲧⲭⲣⲏⲥⲧⲟⲥ ⲙⲛ̄ ⲧⲉϥϥⲓ- ³⁵ ⲛ̄ⲉⲓ ⲁⲡⲓⲧⲛ̄ ⲙⲛ̄ ⲡⲧⲏⲣϥ̄ ⲉⲧⲉ ⲡⲉⲉⲓ ³⁶ ⲡⲉ ⲡⳙⲏⲣⲉ ⲡⲓⲱⲧ
ⲙ̄ⲡⲧⲏⲣϥ̄ ⲁⲩ- ³⁷ ⲱ ⲡⲛⲟⲩⲥ ⲙ̄ⲡⲡⲛⲉⲩⲙⲁ, ⲛⲉⲩⲛ̄- ³⁸ ⲧⲉϥ ⲛ̄ⲅⲁⲣ ⲙ̄ⲙⲉⲩ ⲙ̄ⲡⲉⲉⲓ ⲁⲧⲉϥ⳩ⲉ ⲙ̄ ²⁴·¹⁵
(Lines 1–15 lacking) ¹⁶ [17–19].̣ [ ] ¹⁷ [16–18]ⲛⳕ̣ ¹⁸ [. . . .]ⲡ̣ⲓ̣ [. . . .]ⳕ̣ ⲉⲧⲙ̄ⲙⲉⲩ. ⲟⲩⲡⲏ-
¹⁹ [ⲅⲏ ⲡⲉ] ⲡⲉⲉⲓ, [ⲟⲩⲡⲉ]ⲧⲟⲩⲱⲛ⳥ ⲁⲃⲁⲗ ⲡⲉ ²⁰ [⳩ⲛ̄ ⲧⲥ]ⲓ̈ⳅⲏ ⲁⲩ[ⲱ ⲟ]ⲩ̣ⲛⲟⲩⲥ ⲙ̄ⲡⲧⲏⲣϥ̄ ²¹ [ⲡⲉ
ⲉϥ]ⳙⲟⲟⲡ ⳩ⲛ̄ ⲟⲩⲙⲁ⳩̄ⲥⲛ̄ⲧⲉ ⲙⲛ̄ ²² [ⲡⲱ]ⲛ̣⳥̣. ⲛ̄ⲧⲁϥ ⲛ̄ⲅⲁⲣ ⲡⲉ ⲡⲣⲉϥⲧⲉⲩ- ²³ [ⲟ ⲁⲃⲁⲗ] ⲙ̄ⲡⲧⲏⲣϥ̄
ⲁⲩⲱ ⲑ[ⲩ]ⲡⲟⲥⲧⲁⲥⲓ[ⲥ] ²⁴ [6–8] ⲙ̄ⲡⲉⲓⲱⲧ ⲉⲧⲉ [ⲧ]ⲉ̣ⲉⲓ ⲧⲉ ⲧⲉⲛ- ²⁵ [ⲛⲟⲓⲁ ⲧ]ⲉ̣ ⲁⲩⲱ <ⲧ>ⳝⲓⲛ̄ⲛ̄ⲧϥ̄
ⲁⲡⲓⲧⲛ̄ ⲙ̄ⲡ- ²⁶ [ⲥⲁ ⲙ̄]ⲡⲥⲁⲛ̄ⲡⲓⲧⲛ̄.

ⲛ̄ⲧⲁⲣⲉϥⲟⲩⲱⳙⲉ ²⁷ [ⲛ̄ⳝⲓ] ⲡ̄ⳙⲣ̄ⲡ ⲛ̄ⲉⲓⲱⲧ ⲁϥⲟⲩⲁⲛ⳥ϥ̄ ⲁ- ²⁸ [ⲃⲁⲗ ⲛ̄]⳩ⲣⲏⲓ ⲛ̄⳩ⲏⲧϥ̄. ⲉⲡⲉⲓ ⲟⲩⲛ
ⲉⲧⲃ[ⲏ]- ²⁹ [ⲧϥ̄ ⲉⲣⲉ]ⲡⲟⲩⲱⲛ⳥ ⲁⲃⲁⲗ ⳙⲟⲟⲡ ⲙ̄ⲡ- ³⁰ ⲧⲏⲣϥ̄, ⲉⲉⲓⳙⲟⲩ ⲇⲉ ⲙ̄ⲙⲁϥ ⲁⲡⲧⲏⲣϥ̄ ³¹ ⳝⲉ
«ⲡⲟⲩⲱⳙⲉ ⲙ̄ⲡⲧⲏⲣϥ̄.» ⲁϥϫⲓ ⲇⲉ ⲙ̄- ³² ⲡⲙⲉⲩⲉ ⲛ̄ⲧⲙⲓⲛⲉ ⲉⲧⲃⲉ ⲡⲧⲏⲣϥ̄. ⲉⲉⲓ- ³³ [ⲭ]ⲟⲩ ⲇⲉ
ⲙ̄ⲙⲁⲥ ⲁⲡⲙⲉⲩⲉ ⳝⲉ «ⲡⲙⲟⲛⲟ- ³⁴ ⲅⲉⲛⲏⲥ.» ⲡⲛⲉⲩ ⲛ̄ⲅⲁⲣ ⲁⲡⲛⲟⲩⲧⲉ ⲛ̄- ³⁵ ⲧⲙⲏⲉ, ⲡⲉⲧ ⲉⲁⲩ
ⲛ̄ⲧⲛⲟⲩⲛⲉ ⲙ̄ⲡ- ³⁶ ⲧⲏⲣϥ̄. ⲉⲧⲃⲉ ⲡⲉⲉⲓ ⲛ̄ⲧⲁϥ ⲡⲉⲛⲧⲁϥ- ³⁷ ⲟⲩⲁⲛ⳩ϥ̄ ⲁⲃⲁⲗ ⲟⲩⲁⲉⲉⲧϥ̄ ⳩ⲙ̄ ⲡⲙⲟ-
³⁸ ⲛⲟⲅⲉⲛⲏⲥ, ⲁⲩⲱ ⲛ̄⳩ⲣⲏⲓ̈ ⲛ̄⳩ⲏⲧϥ̄ ³⁹ ⲁϥⲟⲩⲱⲛ⳩ ⲁⲃⲁⲗ ⲙ̄ⲡⲁⲧ̄ⳙⲉⲭⲉ ⲁ- ²⁵·¹⁶ (Lines 1–16
lacking) ¹⁷ [.].̣ [12–14]ⲡ̣.. [2–3] ¹⁸ [.]ⲛ⳥[. . . . .].̣ [5–7] ⲧⲙⲏⲉ [ⲁⲩ]- ¹⁹ ⲛⲉⲩ ⲁⲣ[ⲁ]ϥ
ⲉϥ⳩[ⲙⲁⲥⲧ] ⳩ ⲛ̄ ⲧⲙⲟⲛ̣[ⲁⲥ ⲁⲩ]- ²⁰ ⲱ ⳩ⲛ̄ ⲧⲁⲩⲁⲥ ⲁ[ⲩⲱ ⳩]ⲛ̄ ⲧⲧⲉⲧⲣⲁ̣[ⲥ ⲁϥ]- ²¹ ⳙⲣ̄ⲡ ⲛ̄ⲉⲓⲛⲉ
ⲁⲃⲁ[ⲗ] ⲙ̄ⲡⲙⲟⲛ[ⲟⲅⲉⲛⲏⲥ] ²² [.].̣ [.].̣ ⲁⲩⲱ ⲡ⳩ⲟⲣⲟⲥ ⲡⲉ[. . . .] ²³ [. . . . . ⲁ]ⲃⲁⲗ ⲙ̄ⲡⲧⲏⲣϥ̄
[6–8]- ²⁴ [. . . . . .]ϥ̄ ⲉϥⳙⲟⲟⲡ ²⁹⁵⁻⁶ ²⁵ [8–10].̣ ⲡ̣ⳙⲉ ⲛ̄[5–6] ²⁶ [. . . . .ⲡⲛⲟ]ⲩ̣ⲥ ⲡⲉ
ⲁⲩⲱ [5–6] ²⁷ (Two lines lacking) ²⁹ [5–7].̣ [ ] ³⁰ ⲙ̄ⲡⳙ̣[ⲏⲣⲉ ⲟ]ⲩⲁⲧ̣[ⳙ̣ⲉⲭ]ⲉ ⲁⲣⲁ[ϥ ⲡ]

22.1 [. . .] neither in [. . .] ² enter in [. . .] ³ the fortune [. . .] ⁴ remarkable [. . .] ⁵ those who [. . .] ⁶ of the ⁷ (Lines 7–15 lacking) ¹⁶ [I will] declare my mystery ¹⁷ [to those who] are mine and ¹⁸ [those who will be] mine. These are the ¹⁹ [ones who have known him who] exists, the Father, that ²⁰ is, [. . .] of the entirety, the ²¹ [. . .] one [who] exists in solitude. ²² [. . .] in silence, ²³ [and] silence [is] rest, since ²⁴ [he was] solitary, and no ²⁵ [one existed] before him. He exists ²⁶ [in the] pair and in the double. His ²⁷ double is silence. He had ²⁸ the entirety dwelling ²⁹ within him. And will and ³⁰ becoming, love and persistence, ³¹ these are unbegotten.

God ³² came forth, the Son, the Mind of the ³³ entirety, that is, his other thought also exists from the root ³⁴ of the entirety. ³⁵ For he had this one in ³⁶ the Mind. On account of the entirety he received ³⁷ a foreign thought, since nothing ³⁸ existed before him. From ³⁹ that place, he is the one that moved ²³·¹⁶ (Lines 1–16 lacking) ¹⁷ [. . .] ¹⁸ [. . .] ¹⁹ bubbling. This then [is the] root [of the] ²⁰ entirety and solitude lacking [anything] ²¹ before him. But the second [. . .] ²² dwells in silence and speaks ²³ with him alone. And the [fourth] ²⁴ in this way is the one [who has] ²⁵ enclosed himself [within the] ²⁶ fourth. Dwelling in the ²⁷ three hundred and sixtieth, he initially brought himself forth, ²⁸ and in the second [he] ²⁹ revealed his will, [and] ³⁰ in the fourth he set ³¹ himself apart.

These things are ³² concerning the root of the entirety, but let us [enter] ³³ into his revelation ³⁴ and his blessing and his ³⁵ descent and the entirety, that ³⁶ is, the Son, the Father of the entirety, and ³⁷ the mind of the spirit, ³⁸ for he had this before ²⁴·¹⁵ (Lines 1–15 lacking) ¹⁶ [. . .] ¹⁷ [. . .] ¹⁸ there. This one [is] a ¹⁹ spring, he is one who is manifest ²⁰ [in] silence and [he is the] mind of the entirety ²¹ that exists also with ²² [life]. For he is the one who sends ²³ [forth] the entirety and the reality ²⁴ [. . .] of the Father, that is, the ²⁵ [thought] and <the> ²⁶ descent.

Once the First Father willed, ²⁷ he revealed himself ²⁸ within him. Since then on account of ²⁹ [him] the revelation exists for the ³⁰ entirety, I call the entirety ³¹ "the will of the entirety." He received ³² the thought of this sort on account of the entirety. But I ³³ call the thought the "Only-³⁴ Begotten." For now God has brought truth, ³⁵ the one who glorifies the root of the ³⁶ entirety. For this reason he is the one who ³⁷ revealed himself in the ³⁸ Only-Begotten, and in him ³⁹ he revealed the ineffable one to [. . .] ²⁵·¹⁶ (Lines 1–16 lacking) ¹⁷ [. . .] ¹⁸ the truth. [They] ¹⁹ saw him [residing] in the monad [and] ²⁰ the Dyad [and] in the Tetrad. [He] ²¹ brought forth the Only-Begotten first ²² [. . .]. And the limit [is . . .] ²³ [. . .] from the entirety [. . .] ²⁴ [. . .] him, since they were [. . .] ²⁵ [. . .] hundred [. . .] ²⁶ [. . .] He is [the] mind and [. . .] ²⁷ [. . .] (Two lines lacking) ²⁹ [. . .] ³⁰ the Son. He is entirely indescribable

є [а]- ³¹ п̄тн̄[р̄ϥ] м̄птнр̄ϥ аүш птахро ³² м̄н [тєү]постасіс м̄птнр̄ϥ пк[а]- ³³
тап[єтас]ма н̄ ... пархіє- ³⁴ рєү[с 4–6]є п[єєі єтєүн]т[єϥ м̄]- ³⁵ мєү н̄тєхоусіа
м̄вшк агоүн а- ³⁶ нєтоүааϥ н̄нєтоүаа϶ єϥоү- ³⁷ [ш]н϶ м̄мєн агоүн м̄пєаү н̄- ³⁸
[н]аішн єϥєінє н̄дє авал н̄т- ³⁹ хорнгіа а{ү}т̄{с}ноүвє . танатолн ²⁶·¹⁷ (Lines
1–17 lacking) ¹⁸ [. .] н̄϶р[н̄ї 12–14] н̄- ¹⁹ [т]аϥоүан̄[р̄ϥ авал] єн[таϥ]пє п- ²⁰ [ар]-
хаіон н̄[.....] аүш [п]є϶о м̄- ²¹ [птн]ϥ. аүш [нє]ϥємаг̄тє м̄птн- ²² [р̄ϥ пн]
єтхасі [ап]тнр̄ϥ [а]нє[є]і м̄мєн ²³ [тєүо] пєхрнстос а[вал атр̄ϥ-] ²⁴ [тєгас] н̄϶є
н̄таүтє϶[аү гатєгн] ²⁵ [н̄тєс϶]ін̄нєі ап[іт̄н̄ 6–8] ²⁶ [....] араϥ хє [7–9] ²⁷
[7–9] . . [8–10] ²⁸ (One line lacking) ²⁹ . [8–10 ав]а̣л [... єн оүа]- ³⁰ ϶[оρат]ос
ар[аү п]є єү[϶ш ϶м̄] п϶о- ³¹ рос аүш оүн̄тєϥ м̄н̣[єү н̄]ϥ̣тоє ³² н̄϶ам оүрєспшр̄х̄
м̄[н̄ о]үрєс- ³³ [т]ах̄р̄о оүрє`с´[[ϥ]]т̄ морфн [а]үш оү- ³⁴ р[єсхпє оусіа анан
оүаєєт]н̄ ³⁵ мн єнє єішпє <є>н̄а̣р̣ноєі н̄ ³⁶ нєүпросшпон м̄н пхронос ³⁷ аүш
н̄топос нєєі н̄таган- ³⁸ єінє архоү авал хє а϶оүс [.] ²⁷·¹⁵ (Lines 1–15 lacking) ¹⁶
[15–17]єх̣[. .] ¹⁷ [15–17]н̄сєс[.] ¹⁸ [13–15 ав]а̣л ϶н̄ нім[а] ¹⁹ [12–14]п̣ тагапн̣
[.] ²⁰ [9–11]па̣р̣т авал [. .] ²¹ [.... п]пл̄ншма тн[р̄]ϥ̣ [. .] ²² [.....] пєϭш
р̄϶үп[ℹомє]- ²³ [нє н̄оүа]єіш нім аүш [....] ²⁴ [......]. каі гар ав[ал ϶н̄] ²⁵
[......] поүаєіш [4–6] ²⁶ [5–7] єі ϶оүо[.] [5–7] ²⁷ (One line lacking) ²⁸ [8–10
]ш[6–8]н̣[.] ²⁹ [6–8] тапо̣дєіхіс н̄тϥ[.]

³⁰ [...... єт]вє єү н̄дє хє оүрєс- ³¹ [пшр̄х̄ авал м̄н оүрєстахро ³² [аү]ш
оүрєсхпє оусіа м̄н оүрєс- ³³ [т̄ м]орфн н̄϶є н̄тагаг̄нкаує ³⁴ [хоо]с̣ с[є]хоү н̄гар
м̄маϥ ап϶о- ³⁵ [ро]с̣ хє [оү]н̄тєϥ м̄мєү н̄϶ам ³⁶ [с]н̄тє о[үр]єспшр[[х̄]]<х̄> авал
аүш ³⁷ [о]үрєс[та]хро єпєі спшр̄х̄ м̄- ³⁸ [п]вү[θо]с̣ авал ϶н̄ <н̄>аішн хєка- ²⁸·¹
[сє ...] ¹⁵ (Lines 1–15 lacking) ¹⁶ [..]є̣[¹⁷ нн т[¹⁸ нєєі ϭє ¹⁹ єі н̄оү[²⁰ [.] н̣.
м̄пв[үθос ²¹ [г]а̣р [т]є̣ тморфн̣ [²² [...]. є м̄пшт н̄т[мнє ²³ [аүхо]ос хє
пєхрн[стос ²⁴ [....]. є пєпнєүм[а ²⁵ [....] м̄мон[огєннс ²⁶ [....]. [о]үн̄тє[²⁷
[....].[.]. ... [²⁸ (One blank line)

²⁹ [.]т о[үтєтна]шшс [тє м̄н оүа]- ³⁰ нанкаіон атрн̄[шінє ϶н̄] ³¹ оүшр̄х̄ н̄϶оүо
м̄н̄ [оүϭш] ³² н̄са нграфаүєіє аүш [нєт]- ³³ тєүо н̄ннонма єтвє п[єєі] ³⁴ н̄гар
сєхоү м̄маϥ н̄ϭє[ї] ³⁵ нархаіос хє н̄та[ү]тєүа[ү] ³⁶ авал ϶іт̄м пноүт[є] мар[н̄] ³⁷
м̄мє н̄дє атєϥм̄[н̄т]рмм[а]- ³⁸ о н̄атон̄рєтс̄ аϥ[о]үшш[є] ²⁹·¹⁶ (Lines 1–16 lacking) ¹⁷ [16–17].ү[....] ¹⁸ [14–16]доүлєі[а] ¹⁹ [14–16]нп а̣т̣ ²⁰ [11–13 м̄]п[є]-
ϥшшпє ²¹ [11–13]рє м̄п[є]үвіос ²² [6–8 сєбш]ш̣т̣ ϶н̄ [оү]шр̄х̄ ²³ [апвівлі]а̣ион
н̄тгншсіс ²⁴ [5–7] н̄дє агоүн апп̣ро[сш]- ²⁵ [пон н̄нєү]єрнү

ттєт[рас .]- ²⁶ [..... астє]үо ава[л] н̣[....]р[. .] ²⁷ [9–11]... [... м̄]н̄ пш- ²⁸ [н]
є [9–11 т]єк̄к̄лн[²⁹ [с]і̣а [патсш]шнт [н̄дє а]ϥтєүо ³⁰ ава[л̄ м̄пл]огос м̄[н̄ п]-
шн϶ пло- ³¹ гос м̄[мє]н̄ [а]пєаү м̄[п]атшє- ³² хє а[ра]ϥ пшн̄϶ н̄д[є] апєаү н̄- ³³
тсі[гн] пршмє н̄дє апєϥє- ³⁴ аү [м̄м]ін м̄маϥ тє[к]клнсіа ³⁵ н̄дє [а]пєаү н̄тмнє
тєєі ϭє ³⁶ тє ттє[тр]а̣с єтоүхпо м̄мас ³⁷ ката [пта]нт̄н н̄[[п]]т̄атхпа[[ϥ]]с ³⁸

[to] ³¹ the entirety, and he is the strength ³² and [the] reality of the entirety, the ³³ veil of [. . .] the High ³⁴ Priest, [. . . the one who] has ³⁵ the ability to enter into ³⁶ the Holy of Holies, ³⁷ manifesting the glory of ³⁸ [the] eternities and brining forth the ³⁹ abundance to <the fragrance>. The east [. . .] ^{26.17} (Lines 1–17 lacking) ¹⁸ [. . .] in [. . .] who ¹⁹ revealed [himself . . .] as the ²⁰ first [. . .] and the storehouse of ²¹ [the] entirety. And he seized the entirety, ²² [the one who] is superior [to the] entirety. These ²³ [sent forth] Christ ²⁴ [to establish her] just as [they] were established [before] ²⁵ [she] came [down . . .] ²⁶ [. . .] it that [. . .] ²⁷ [. . .] ²⁸ (One line lacking) ²⁹ [. . .] ³⁰ [he is invisible] to those [remaining in] the boundary, ³¹ and he has four ³² powers: a divider and a ³³ strengthener, a form giver and a ³⁴ [substance maker. We alone] ³⁵ indeed would know ³⁶ their appearances and the time ³⁷ and the places that the ³⁸ semblances have strengthened because [. . .] ^{27.15} (Lines 1–15 lacking) ¹⁶ [. . .] ¹⁷ [. . .] ¹⁸ [. . .] from these places ¹⁹ [. . .] the love ²⁰ [. . .] emanated [. . .] ²¹ [. . . the] entire fullness [. . .] ²² [. . .] the endurance continues ²³ always and [. . .] ²⁴ [. . .] for and from [in] ²⁵ [. . .] the time [. . .] ²⁶ [. . .] greater [. . .] ²⁷ (One line lacking) ²⁸ [. . .] ²⁹ [. . .] the demonstration of his [. . .]

³⁰ [. . .] But why a ³¹ [divider] and a strengthener ³² [and] a substance maker and a ³³ form [giver] as others have ³⁴ [said]? For they say that the ³⁵ boundary has two powers, ³⁶ a divider and ³⁷ a strengthener, since it divides ³⁸ [the] depth from the eternities, so that ^{28.1} [. . .] ¹⁵ (Lines 1–15 lacking) ¹⁶ [. . .] ¹⁷ [. . .] These then [. . .] ¹⁹ [. . .] ²⁰ [. . .] of the depth [. . .] ²¹ [. . .] For [. . .] is the form [. . .] ²² [. . .] of the Father of [truth . . .] ²³ [. . . They] say that Christ [. . .] ²⁴ [. . .] the Spirit [. . .] ²⁵ [. . .] of the Only-Begotten ²⁶ [. . .] has [. . .] ²⁷ [. . .] ²⁸ (One blank line)

[It is] great [and] necessary for us to [seek with] greater precision and [persistence] the Scriptures and [those] who set forth the interpretations. For concerning [this] the ancients say, "[They] were announced by God." Now let [us] know this incomprehensible wealth. He desired ^{29.16} (Lines 1–16 lacking) ¹⁷ [. . .] ¹⁸ [. . .] bondage ¹⁹ [. . .] ²⁰ [. . .] he was [not] ²¹ [. . .] of their life ²² [. . . They look] unwaveringly at ²³ the book of knowledge, and ²⁴ [. . .] into the ²⁵ face of each other.

The tetrad ²⁶ [. . . emanated] ²⁷ [. . .] and ²⁸ Life [. . .] ²⁹ Church. [The uncreated one] emanated ³⁰ Word and Life. Word ³¹ is the glory of the ineffable one; ³² Life is the glory of ³³ Silence, but the human is for his own glory. ³⁴ The Church ³⁵ is for the glory of Truth. Therefore, this ³⁶ is the tetrad that was begotten according to ³⁷ [the] likeness of the unbegotten one. ³⁸ And the tetrad is begotten ^{30.15} (Lines 1–15 lack-

ⲁⲩⲱ [ⲧ]ⲧⲉⲧⲣⲁⲥ ⲉϣⲁⲣⲟⲩⲭⲡⲁⲥ 30.15 (Lines 1–15 lacking) 16 ⲛ̄[15–17 ⲁ]- 17 ⲃⲁⲗ ϩⲙ̄
[12–14] 18 ⲁⲩⲱ ⲧⲁ[15–17]- 19 ⲙⲉ ⲙⲛ̄ ⲧ ̣[14–16] 20 ⲧⲣⲓⲁⲕ[ⲟ]ⲛⲧⲁⲥ [ⲡⲁⲧⲉⲧⲣⲓⲁⲕⲟⲛ]- 21
ⲧⲁⲥ ϭⲉ ⲡⲉ ⲛ̄ⲛⲁ[ⲓⲱⲛ 5–7] 22 [. .]ⲥ ⲉ[ϥⲁ]ⲃⲁⲗ ϩⲛ̄ ̣[8–10] 23 [ⲥⲉ]ⲡⲏⲧ ⲁϩⲟⲩⲛ ⲛ̄ⲕⲟ[ⲓⲛⲱⲛⲟⲥ]
24 [ⲁⲗⲗⲁ ⲥ]ⲉⲉⲓ ⲁⲃⲁⲗ ⲛ̄[ⲟⲩⲱⲧ . .] 25 ⲡ[. . ϩ̄ⲛ ⲛ[. .]ⲱ[.] ⲙ̄[6–8] 26 ⲡⲟⲩ [. . .] ⲛⲓⲁⲧϣ
[9–11]- 27 ϩⲱ[ϣ̄ⲧ 12–14]ⲟ̣[. .] 28 ⲉⲡⲉⲓ [. . . . .] ̣[. [5–7]ⲟⲟ[.] 29 ϩⲙ̄ ⲡⲡ[ⲗⲏⲣ]ⲱⲙⲁ

ⲁⲗ[ⲗⲁ ⲁⲥ]ⲉⲓⲛⲉ 30 ⲙ̄ⲙⲉⲛ ⲁ[ⲃ]ⲁⲗ ⲛ̄ϭⲓ [ⲧ]ⲁ ̣[ⲉⲕⲁ] ⲧⲁⲃⲁ[ⲗ] 31 ϩⲙ̄ ⲡⲗⲟ[ⲅ]ⲟⲥ ⲙⲛ̄ ⲡⲁϣϥ[ⲛ]ϩ
ⲛ̄ϩⲛ̄- 32 ⲇⲉⲕⲁ ϩⲱⲥ ⲁⲧⲣⲉⲡⲡⲗ[ⲏⲣ]ⲱⲙⲁ 33 ϣⲱⲡ[ⲉ] ⲛ̄ⲟⲩϩⲉⲕⲁⲧⲟⲛ[ⲧⲁⲥ] ⲁⲩⲱ 34 ⲧⲁⲱⲁ[ⲉ]-
ⲕⲁⲥ ⲧⲁⲃⲁⲗ ϩⲙ̄ ⲡⲣⲱⲙ[ⲉ] 35 ⲙⲛ̄ ⲧⲉⲕⲕⲗⲏⲥⲓⲁ ⲁⲥⲉ[ⲓⲛⲉ] ⲁⲃⲁⲗ ⲁⲥ[ⲣ̄]- 36 ⲡⲙⲁⲁⲃ ϩⲱⲥ
ⲁⲧⲣⲉ[ⲧⲱ̄]ⲛ̄ⲧ ϣⲉ 37 ⲥⲉ ϣⲱⲡⲉ ⲛ̄ⲡⲡⲗⲏ[ⲣⲱ]ⲙⲁ ⲛ̄ⲧ- 38 ⲣⲁⲙⲡⲉ ⲁⲩⲱ ⲧⲣⲁⲙⲡ[ⲉ] ⲙ̄ⲡⲭⲁⲉⲓ[ⲥ]
31.14 (Lines 1–14 lacking) 15 [19–21].[16 [19–21]ⲃⲁ[ⲗ] 17 [19–21]ⲙ̄ 18 [15–17 ⲧⲉⲗⲉ]ⲓⲟⲥ
19 [15–17 ⲧ]ⲉⲗⲉⲓⲟⲛ 20 [14–16] ⲕⲁⲧⲁ ⲫⲟ 21 [14–16]ⲁⲛ ⲡⲉ ⲁⲣ̄ 22 [14–16 ϩⲟ]ⲣⲟⲥ ⲁⲩⲱ 23
[15–17]ϩⲟⲣⲟ[ⲥ] 24 [15–17]ⲛⲉ [. .] 25 [16–18] ̣[. . .] 26 (One line lacking) 27 [17–19 ⲡ]-
ⲙⲉⲅⲉ[ⲑⲟⲥ] 28 ⲉⲧϥ[13–15]ⲛ̄ⲧ̄ⲙ̄[ⲛ̄]- 29 ⲧⲭⲣ[ⲏⲥⲧⲟⲥ 7–9]ⲁϥ ⲡϣ- 30 ⲱⲛ̄ϩ̄ 6–8]ⲛ[. . . .]
ϣⲱⲡ ϩⲓ- 31 ⲥⲉ ⲡ[6–8]ⲉ ̣[. . . .]ⲧⲏ ϩⲓⲧⲙ̄ 32 ⲫⲟ ⲧ[6–8] ⲉⲓ[. . .ⲛ̄]ⲛ̄ⲁϩⲣⲉ 33 ⲡⲡ[ⲗⲏⲣⲱⲙⲁ. .]
. ⲁⲣ[. .]ⲉ ⲛ̄ⲧⲁϥⲟⲩ- 34 ⲁϣ[ϥ 6–8 ⲁⲩ]ϣ ⲁϥⲟⲩⲱϣⲉ 35 ⲁⲃϣ[ⲕ ⲁⲃⲁⲗ ϩⲛ̄] ⲧⲙⲁϩⲙⲁⲁⲃⲉ ⲉϥ- 36
ϣⲟⲟⲡ [ⲛ̄ⲥⲩⲍⲩⲅ]ⲟⲥ ⲙ̄ⲡⲣⲱⲙⲉ ⲙⲛ̄ 37 ⲧⲉⲕⲕⲗⲏ[ⲥⲓⲁ ⲉⲧⲉ] ⲧⲉⲉⲓ ⲧⲉ ⲧⲥⲟⲫⲓⲁ ⲁⲣ̄- 38 ⲧⲡⲉ ⲙ̄[6–8]
ⲛ̄ ⲡⲡⲗⲏⲣⲱⲙⲁ 32.13 (Lines 1–13 lacking) 14 [.].[15 ⲟⲩ[16 ⲡϥ[17 ⲛ̄ⲁ[ⲉ . . . ⲁⲩ]- 18 ⲱ ⲁⲥϣ[
19 ⲅⲟⲥ ⲉⲧⲉ[20 ⲛⲓⲁ ⲙ̄ⲛ[21 ⲛ̄ⲅⲁⲣ ⲁ[22 ⲙ̄ⲡⲧⲏ[ⲣϥ 23 [.]ⲧ̄ⲙ[24 [.].ⲟ.[25 [26 ⲫⲟ[27 ⲁⲩⲣ̄[28
ⲛ̄ⲁⲉ[14–16]. ⲩ . ⲉ 29 ⲧⲟⲩⲡ[14–16]ⲡ̄ⲧⲏ- 30 ⲣϥ ⲛ̄ϩ̄[13–15]ϥ ⲁⲩ- 31 ⲱ ⲛ̄ⲧⲁϥ[. . . .]. .[
7–9]ⲉ ⲁϥ- 32 ⲉⲓⲣⲉ ⲛ̄ [. . . .]ⲡ [5–7]ⲡⲙⲉⲩ- 33 ⲉ ⲙⲛ̄ ⲛ̄[. . .]ⲁⲩ[. . . ⲡⲡⲗ]ⲏⲣⲱ- 34 ⲙⲁ ϩⲓⲧⲙ̄
ⲡ[ⲗ]ⲟⲅⲟ[ⲥ 4–6] ⲛ̄ⲧⲉϥ- 35 ⲥⲁⲣⲝ ⲛⲉⲉⲓ ϭⲉ [4–6]ϯⲛⲉ 36 ⲙ̄ⲙⲁⲩ ⲛ̄ⲧⲁⲣⲉⲡ[ⲗⲟⲅⲟⲥ] ⲉⲓ ⲁϩⲟⲩⲛ
37 ⲁⲣⲁⲥ ⲕⲁ[[ⲑ]]ⲧⲁ ⲑⲉ [ⲛ̄ⲧⲁϩⲓ[ϣ̄ⲣⲡ ⲛ̄- 38 ϫⲟⲟⲥ ⲁⲩⲱ ⲡ[ⲏ ⲉⲧⲁϣ]ⲡⲉ ϣⲁ 39 ⲡⲁⲧϣⲁⲡϥ
ⲁ[ϥⲉⲓⲛⲉ] ⲁⲃⲁⲗ ⲛ̄ 33.10 (Lines 1–10 lacking) 11 [12–14 ⲙ̄]ⲡⲁⲧⲟⲩ 12 [13–15] ⲁⲃⲁⲗ ⲛ̄- 13 [
13–15]ϩⲁⲡϥ ⲁ- 14 [11–13]ⲡⲥⲩⲍⲩⲅⲟⲥ ⲁⲩ- 15 [ⲱ 9–11] ⲧϭⲓⲛⲏⲥⲓⲥ ⲙⲛ̄ 16 [.] ⲉⲩ [4–6]ⲧⲉⲩⲟ
ⲁⲃⲁⲗ ⲙ̄ⲡⲉ- 17 [ⲭ]ⲣⲏⲥⲧⲟ[ⲥ . . .]ⲣⲧⲉ ⲁⲩⲱ ⲛⲉⲥⲡⲉⲣ- 18 ⲙⲁ ⲛ̄[5–7] [. . .]. ⲃ ⲛ̄ⲛϣⲉ 19 ϫⲉ
ⲉ̣[. . . ⲛⲉⲛⲧⲩⲡ]ϣⲥⲓⲥ ⲙ̄ⲡⲱ̄- 20 ϣⲧ̄ ⲁ̣[5–7]. [ⲟ]ⲩⲙ̄ⲛ̄ⲧ-ⲉ- 21 ⲗⲉⲓ[ⲟ]ⲥ [ⲉⲡⲉⲓⲇⲏ] ⲟⲩⲙⲟⲣⲫⲏ
ⲛ̄ⲧⲉ- 22 ⲗⲉ[ⲓⲁ. . . . .]ⲉ [ⲁ]ⲃⲱⲕ ⲁⲧⲡⲉ ⲁϩⲟⲩⲛ 23 [ⲁⲡⲡⲗⲏⲣ]ⲱⲙ[ⲁ] ⲙ̄ⲡⲉϥⲟⲩⲱϣ[ⲉ] 24 [. .
ⲁ̄ⲣⲥⲩ]ⲛⲉⲩⲇⲟⲕⲉⲓ ⲙⲛ̄ ⲡϩⲓⲥⲉ [. .] 25 [. . . . ⲁⲩ]ⲣ̄ⲕⲱⲗⲩⲉ ⲙ̄ⲙⲁϥ ⲁⲅⲉ 26 [. . . .] ̣. ⲉ ⲙ̄ⲙⲁϥ ϩⲓⲧⲛ̄
[ⲡ]ϩⲟ- 27 ⲣⲟⲥ ⲉⲧⲉ ⲡⲉⲉⲓ ⲡⲉ ϩⲓⲧⲛ̄ ⲡ[ⲥ]ⲩⲍⲩ- 28 ⲅⲟⲥ ⲉⲡⲉⲓ[ⲇ]ⲏ ⲧⲉⲥⲇⲓⲟⲣⲑⲱⲥⲓⲥ ⲛⲁ- 29 ϣⲱⲡⲉ
ⲉⲛ ϩⲓⲧⲛ̄ ⲗⲁⲩⲉ ⲉⲓⲙⲏⲧⲓ 30 ϩⲓⲧⲛ̄ ⲡϣ̄ⲏⲣⲉ ⲙ̄ⲙⲓⲛ ⲙ̄ⲙⲁ<ⲥ> 31 ⲡⲉⲉⲓ ⲉⲧⲉ ⲡⲁϥ ⲧⲏⲣϥ ⲡⲉ ⲡⲡⲗⲏ-
32 ⲣⲱⲙⲁ ⲛ̄ⲧⲙ̄ⲛ̄ⲧⲛⲟⲩⲧⲉ ⲁϥⲣϩⲉⲛϥ 33 ⲛ̄ϩⲣⲏⲓ ⲛ̄ϩⲏⲧϥ ⲥⲱⲙⲁⲧⲓⲕⲱⲥ 34 ⲁⲕⲱϣ ⲛ̄ⲛϭⲁⲙ ⲁⲩⲱ
ⲁϥⲉⲓ ⲁⲡⲓⲧⲛ̄ 35 ⲛ̄<ⲉ>ⲉⲓ ⲛ̄ⲇⲉ ⲁϩⲁⲧⲥⲟⲫⲓⲁ ϣⲁⲡⲟⲩ 36 ⲛ̄ⲧⲁⲣⲉϥⲡⲱⲧ ⲁⲧⲡⲉ ⲁⲃⲁⲗ ⲛ̄- 37 ϩⲏⲧⲥ
ⲛ̄ϭ[ⲓ] ⲡⲉⲥϣ̄ⲏⲣⲉ ⲁⲥⲥⲟⲩ- 38 ϣⲱⲛⲥ [ⲛ̄ⲅ]ⲁⲣ ⲉⲥϣⲟⲟⲡ ϩⲛ̄ ⲟⲩ 34.9 (Lines 1–9 lacking) 10 ⲛⲉ[
13–15]- 11 ⲧⲣ̄ ⲁⲩⲱ [11–13 ⲁⲩ]- 12 ⲗⲟ ⲧⲟⲩ̣[12–14] 13 [.]ⲉ ⲛ̄ⲛⲥⲛ̄[ⲏⲩ 9–11] 14 ⲛⲉⲉⲓ ⲙ̄ⲡⲉⲩ ̣[
9–11] 15 ⲁϩⲓϣⲱⲡⲉ [4–6]. ⲕ̣ .[.] 16 ⲉⲩϣⲟⲩ ⲛⲉⲉ[ⲓ ⲛⲉ . .]ⲓⲥⲙⲟⲥ [ⲙ̄]- 17 ⲙⲉⲛ ⲁϥⲗⲟ ⲧⲉ[4–6
] ⲛ̄ⲁⲉ ⲁϩⲟ[ⲩⲛ] 18 ⲙⲛ̄ ⲛ̄ⲥϥ[9–11] ⲙ̄- 19 ⲙⲁⲥ ⲛⲉⲉ[ⲓ 6–8]ⲉⲩ ⲁⲣⲁⲓ 20 ⲡⲉ ⲛⲉⲉⲓ ⲉⲧⲛ̄[3–5 ⲛ]
ⲉⲉⲓ ⲛ̄- 21 ⲧⲁϩⲓⲙⲕⲙⲟⲩⲕ[5–6][.]ⲉⲓ ⲡⲓ- 22 [ⲙ]ⲟⲩ ⲁⲩⲗⲟⲧⲉⲩ̣[5–7]ⲁⲥ 23 [ⲁⲩ]ⲱ ⲁⲥⲣ̄ⲙⲉⲧ[ⲁ]
ⲛⲟ[ⲉⲓ ⲁⲩⲱ ⲁⲥ]- 24 [ⲣ̄]ⲁⲓⲧⲉⲓ ⲙ̄ⲡⲓⲱⲧ ⲛ̄ⲧⲙ̄[ⲛⲉ ⲉⲥⲭⲟⲩ] 25 ⲙ̄ⲙ[ⲁ]ⲥ ⲉⲥⲧⲱ ⲁϩⲓⲕ[ϣⲉ ⲛ̄ⲥⲱⲉⲓ]
26 ⲙ̄ⲡⲁⲥⲩⲍⲩⲅⲟⲥ ⲉⲧⲃⲉ [ⲡⲉⲉⲓ ϯⲙ̄ 27 ⲡⲃⲁⲗ ⲛ̄ⲡⲕⲉⲧⲁⲭⲣⲟ ϯⲙ̄ⲡϣⲁ 28 ⲛ̄ⲛⲉⲉⲓ ⲉⲧϣⲱⲡ ⲙ̄ⲙⲁⲩ
ⲛⲉ- 29 ⲉⲓϣⲟⲟⲡ ⲡⲉ ϩⲙ̄ ⲡⲡⲗⲏⲣⲱⲙⲁ 30 ⲉⲉⲓⲧⲉⲩⲟ ⲁⲃⲁⲗ ⲛ̄ⲛⲁⲓⲱⲛ ⲁⲩⲱ 31 ⲉⲉⲓϯ ⲕⲁⲣⲡⲟⲥ ⲙⲛ̄
ⲡⲁⲥⲩⲍⲩⲅⲟⲥ 32 ⲁⲥⲥⲟⲩⲱⲛ̄ⲥ ⲛ̄ⲇⲉ ϫⲉ ⲛⲉⲟⲩⲉⲩ ⲧⲉ 33 ⲁⲩⲱ ⲉⲩ ⲡⲉⲛⲧⲁϥϣⲱⲡⲉ ⲙ̄- 34 ⲙⲁⲥ

ing) [16] [. . .] [17] from [. . .] [18] and the [. . .] [19] and the [. . .] [20] triacontad. Therefore, [the one belonging to the] triacontad [21] is of the [eternities . . .] [22] [. . .] from [. . .] [23] [they] go in [together] [24] [but they] come out [alone . . .] [25] [. . .] in the [. . .] of [. . .] [26] [. . .] [27] look [. . .] [28] since [. . .] [29] in the fullness.

But [30] the [decad] from [31] Word and Life brought forth [32] decads so that the fullness [33] could come to be a hundred, and [34] the duodecad from Human [35] and Church [brought] forth and [made] [36] the triacontad in order to make the three hundred sixty [37] become the fullness of the [38] year, and the year of the Lord [31.14] (Lines 1–14 lacking) [15] [. . .] [16] [. . .] [17] [. . .] [18] [. . .] perfect [19] [. . .] perfect [20] [. . .] according to the face [21] [. . .] [22] [. . .] boundary and [23] [. . .] boundary [24] [. . .] [25] [. . .] [26] (One line lacking) [27] [. . . the] greatness [28] that he [. . .] of the [29] goodness [. . .] him. [30] Life [. . .] [31] difficult [. . .] by the face [32] [. . .] before [33] the [fullness . . .] that he wanted [34] [. . . and] he wanted to depart [35] [from] the thirteenth–since it [36] is a [pairing] of Human and [37] Church, [that] is, Wisdom–to [38] supersede [. . .] of the fullness. [32.13] (Lines 1–13 lacking) [14] [. . .] [15] [. . .] [16] [. . .] [17] but [. . . and] [18] it was [. . .] [19] [. . .] who [. . .] [20] [. . .] and [. . .] [21] For [. . .] [22] of the entirety [. . .] [23] [. . .] [24] [. . .] [25] [. . .] [26] [. . .] [27] they made [. . .] [28] but [. . .] [29] [. . .] the [30] entirety [. . .] and [31] he [. . .] he [32] made [. . .] the mind [33] and [. . . the] fullness [34] through the Word [. . .] his [35] flesh. These then [. . .] like [36] them. After the [Word] went into [37] it, as [I have] [38] said before, also the [one who exists] with [39] the Illimitable one [brought] forth [33.10] (Lines 1–10 lacking) [11] [. . .] before they [12] [. . .] from [13] [. . .] hide him from [14] [. . .] the pair and [15] [. . .] the movement and [16] [. . .] send forth [17] Christ [. . .] and the seeds [18] of [. . .] of the cross [19] because [. . . the] scars from the [20] nails [. . .] perfection. [21] [Since] a perfect form [22] [. . .] up into [23] [the fullness], he did not want [24] [. . . to] approve of the trouble [. . .] [25] [. . .] he was prevented [. . .] [26] [. . .] him by boundary, [27] that is, by the pairing, [28] since her correction will [29] not come about through anyone except [30] her own child, [31] the one who alone possesses the [32] fullness of divinity. He desired [33] within himself bodily [34] to leave the powers, and he went down. [35] These things that Wisdom experienced [36] after her child went up [37] from her, for she knew [38] that she was in a [34.9] (Lines 1–9 lacking) [10] [. . .] [11] [. . .] and [. . . they] ceased [. . .] [13] [. . .] siblings [. . .] [14] these of their [. . .] [15] I came to be [. . .] [16] who [are] these? [. . .] [17] On the one hand he stopped, on the other [. . .] into [18] and the [. . .] [19] her. These [. . .] to me, [20] these who [. . .] these [21] who thought [. . .] the [22] death. They were stopped [. . .] [23] [and] she repented [and she] [24] petitioned the Father of truth, [saying,] [25] "Given that I have [abandoned] [26] my partner, therefore I am [27] outside of strength as well. I have earned [28] the things I endure. [29] I was dwelling in the fullness, [30] sending forth eternities and [31] bearing fruit with my partner." [32] Yet she knew what she was [33] and what had happened to [34] her.

ⲁⲩϣⲡ ϩⲓⲥⲉ ϭⲉ ⲙ̄ⲡⲉⲥⲛⲉⲩ ³⁵ ⲡⲁϫⲉⲩ ⲥ̄ⲥ̄ϣⲃⲉ ⲉⲡⲉⲓ ⲁⲥϭⲱ ⲟⲩ- ³⁶ ⲁⲉⲉⲧⲥ̄ ⲁⲩⲱ ⲁⲥⲧⲁⲛⲧ̄ⲛ̄
ⲙ̄ⲡⲁⲧ- ³⁷ ϣⲁⲡϥ̄ ⲡⲁϫⲉϥ ⲥ̣[ⲱⲃ]ⲉ̣ ⲛ̄ⲇⲉ ⲉⲡⲉⲓ ³⁸ ⲁⲥϣⲁⲁⲧⲥ̄ ⲁⲃⲁⲗ [ϩ̄ⲙ ⲡ]ⲉⲥⲥⲩⲍⲩ- ³⁵·¹ [ⲅⲟⲥ ⁸
(Lines 1–8 lacking) ⁹ [15–17] [. .] ¹⁰ ⲁⲃ[ⲁ]ⲗ [7–9]ⲧⲥⲟⲫⲓⲁ̣ ¹¹ ⲙ̄ⲙⲉⲛ ⲁⲩϭⲱⲗ[ⲡ ⲙ̄ⲡⲥ]
ⲱⲛⲧ ⲉⲡ[ⲉⲓ ¹² ⲟⲩⲛ ⲛ̄ⲥⲡⲉⲣⲙⲁ̣ [ⲛ̄ⲧ]ⲥ̣ⲟⲫⲓⲁ ⲥⲉⲟⲉ[ⲓ] ¹³ ⲛ̄ⲁⲧϫⲱⲕ ⲁⲃⲁ[ⲗ ⲁⲩ]ⲱ ⲛ̄ⲁⲙⲟⲣⲫ[ⲟⲥ]-
¹⁴ ⲁⲓⲏ̣[ⲥ̄] ⲣⲉⲡⲓⲛ[ⲟⲉⲓ ⲛ̄]ⲟⲩⲕⲧⲓⲥⲓⲥ ⲛ̄[ϯ]- ¹⁵ ⲙⲓ[ⲛⲉ] ⲁϥⲥⲱ[ⲱⲛⲧ] ⲙ̄ⲙⲁϥ ⲛ̄ⲛ̄- ¹⁶ ⲥⲡⲉⲣⲙⲁ
ⲉⲣ[ⲉⲧⲥ]ⲟⲫⲓⲁ ⲣ̄ϩⲱϥ̄ ⲛ̄ⲛ̄- ¹⁷ ⲙⲉϥ ⲉⲡⲉⲓ ⲅⲁ̣[ⲣ ϩ̄]ⲛ̄ⲥⲡⲉⲣⲙⲁ ⲛⲉ ¹⁸ ⲁⲩⲱ ⲙ̄ⲛ̄[ⲙⲟⲣⲫⲏ] ⲙ̄ⲙⲁⲩ ⲁϥⲉⲓ
ⲁ- ¹⁹ ϩⲣⲏ̣ⲓ̈ ⲁⲩⲱ ⲁϥⲉⲓⲛⲉ ⲁⲃⲁⲗ ⲙ̄ⲡⲓ- ²⁰ ⲡⲗⲏ[ⲣⲱⲙⲁ ⲛ̄ⲧⲉ ϩ̄ⲛ̄[ⲁⲓ]ⲱⲛ ⲉⲩⲙ̄ⲡⲓ- ²¹ ⲧⲟⲡ[ⲟⲥ
ⲉⲛⲓⲁⲧ̄]ⲥ̣ⲱⲱⲛⲧ ϩⲱⲟ[ⲩ ⲛ̄]- ²² ⲛⲓⲁ̣[ⲓⲱⲛ ⲛⲉ] ⲛ̣ⲁⲛⲧⲩⲡⲟⲥ ⲙ̄ⲡ`ⲓ̀[ⲡ]- ²³ [ⲗ]ⲏ̣[ⲣⲱⲙ]ⲁ̣ ⲙ̄ⲛ̄
ⲡⲓⲱⲧ ⲡⲓⲁⲧϣ̣[ⲁ]- ²⁴ [ⲡϥ̄ ϩⲁ]ⲡⲁⲧⲥⲱⲱⲛⲧ ⲙ̄ⲙⲉⲛ ⲁ̣[ϥ]- ²⁵ [ⲛ̄ ⲡⲧⲩ]ⲡⲟⲥ ⲙ̄ⲡⲁⲧⲥⲁⲁⲛⲧϥ̄ ²⁶
[ⲁⲃⲁⲗ ⲁ]ⲃ̣ⲁⲗ ⲛ̄ⲅⲁⲣ ϩ̄ⲙ ⲡⲁⲧⲥⲁ ²⁷ ⲁ̣ⲛ̄ⲧϥ̄ ⲉⲣⲉⲡⲓⲱⲧ ⲉⲓⲛⲉ ⲁⲃⲁⲗ ⲁ- ²⁸ ϩⲟⲩⲛ ⲁⲧⲙⲟⲣⲫⲏ
ⲡⲥⲱⲱⲛⲧ ⲛ̄- ²⁹ ⲇⲉ ⲑⲁⲉⲓⲃⲉⲥ ⲧⲉ ⲙ̄ⲛⲉⲧϣ̄ⲣ̄ⲡ ⲛ̄- ³⁰ ϣⲟⲟⲡ ⲡⲉⲉⲓ ϭⲉ ⲓ̄ⲥ̄ ⲁϥⲥⲟ- ³¹ ⲱⲛⲧ
ⲛ̄ⲧⲕⲧⲓⲥⲓⲥ ⲁⲩⲱ ⲁϥⲇⲏⲙⲓ- ³² ⲟⲩⲣⲅⲉⲓ ⲁⲃⲁⲗ ϩ̄ⲛ ⲛ̄ⲡⲁⲑⲟⲥ ⲉⲧⲙ̄ ³³ ⲡⲕⲱⲧⲉ ⲛ̄ⲛ̄ⲥⲡⲉⲣⲙⲁ ⲁⲩⲱ
ⲁϥ- ³⁴ ⲡⲱⲣϫ̄ ⲙ̄ⲙⲁⲩ ⲁⲃⲁⲗ ⲛ̄ⲛⲟⲩⲉⲣⲏⲩ ³⁵ ⲁⲩⲱ ⲛ̄ⲡⲁⲑⲟⲥ ⲉⲧⲥⲁⲧⲡ̄ ⲁϥⲛ̄ⲧⲟⲩ ³⁶ ⲁϩⲟⲩⲛ
ⲁⲡⲡⲛⲉⲩⲙⲁ ⲛⲉⲑⲁⲩ ³⁷ ⲛ̄ⲇⲉ ⲁϩⲟⲩⲛ ⲁⲛⲥⲁⲣⲕⲓⲕⲟⲛ

ϣⲁ- ³⁸ ⲁⲣⲡ ϭⲉ [ⲁⲃ]ⲁ̣ⲗ ϩ̄ⲛ ⲛⲓⲡⲁⲑⲟⲥ ⲧⲏ- ³⁶·¹ [ⲣⲟⲩ ⁷ (Lines 1–7 lacking) ⁸ ⲡⲉⲛ̣[⁹ ⲟⲩⲧⲉ ⲛ̣[
4–6]...... ϣ ¹⁰ ⲙ̄ⲙⲁϥ [ⲉⲡⲉⲓ ⲟ]ⲩⲛ ⲧⲡⲣⲟⲛⲟⲓⲁ ¹¹ ⲁⲥⲧ [[ⲁⲙⲓⲟ]] ⲛ̄[ⲧⲇⲓⲟ]ⲣⲱⲥⲓⲥ ⲁⲧⲉⲩ- ¹² ⲟ̣
ⲁⲃⲁⲗ ⲛ̄ⲥ̣[ⲛ̄ϩ̣]ⲁⲉⲓⲃⲉⲥ ⲙ̄ⲛ ϩ̄ⲛ ¹³ ϩⲓⲕⲱⲛ ⲛ̄[ⲛⲉⲧ]ϣⲟⲟⲡ ϫ̣[ⲓⲛ] ⲛ̄- ¹⁴ ϣⲁⲣⲡ ⲙ̄ⲛ̄ [ⲛⲉⲧ]ϣⲟⲟⲡ
[ⲁⲩ]ⲱ ¹⁵ ⲛⲉⲧⲛⲁϣ̣ⲱ[ⲡⲉ ⲧ]ⲉⲉⲓ ϭ[ⲉ ⲧ]ⲉ̣ ⲧⲟⲓ- ¹⁶ ⲕⲟⲛ[ⲟ]ⲙ<ⲓ>ⲁ ⲙ̄ⲡ[ⲓⲣ̄]ⲡⲓⲥⲧⲉⲩⲉ ⲙ̄ⲙ̣[ⲁ]ⲥ ¹⁷
ⲛ̄ⲓ̄ⲏ̄ⲥ̄ ⲉⲧⲃⲉ [ⲡⲉⲛⲧ]ⲁ̣ϥϩⲉⲉⲓ ⲙ̄- ¹⁸ ⲡⲧⲏⲣϥ̄ ⲛ̄[6–8 ⲙ]ⲛ̄ ϩ̄ⲛ ¹⁹ ϩⲓⲕⲱⲛ ⲙ̄[ⲛ 8–10]

ⲛ̄- ²⁰ ⲧⲁⲣⲉϥⲉⲓⲛⲉ ⲁ̣[ⲃⲁⲗ ⲁⲛ ⲛ̄]ϭ̣ⲓ ²¹ ⲓ̄ⲏ̄ⲥ̄ ⲁϥⲉⲓⲛⲉ ⲁ[ⲃⲁⲗ ⲙ̄ⲙⲁⲩ] ⲙ̄- ²² ⲡⲧⲏⲣϥ̄ ⲛⲁⲡⲉⲡⲗⲏ[ⲣⲱⲙⲁ]
²³ ⲙ̄ⲛ ⲡⲥⲩⲍⲩⲅⲟⲥ ⲉⲧⲉ ⲛ̣[ⲉⲉⲓ ⲛ̣]ⲉ̣ ⲛ̄- ²⁴ ⲁⲅⲅⲉⲗⲟⲥ ϩⲁⲙⲁ ⲅⲁⲣ ϩ̄[ⲛ̄ ⲧⲥⲩⲧ]- ²⁵ ⲭⲱⲣⲏⲥⲓⲥ
ⲙ̄ⲡⲡⲗⲏ[ⲣⲱⲙⲁ] ²⁶ ϩⲁⲡⲉⲥⲥⲩⲍⲩⲅⲟⲥ ⲧ̣[ⲉ]ⲩ̣ⲟ [ⲁⲃⲁⲗ] ²⁷ ⲛ̄ⲛⲁⲅⲅⲉⲗⲟⲥ ⲉϥϣⲟⲟⲡ ϩ̄ⲙ ²⁸ ⲡⲟⲩⲱϣⲉ
ⲙ̄ⲡⲓⲱⲧ ⲡⲉⲉⲓ ⲛ̄- ²⁹ ⲅⲁⲣ ⲡⲉ ⲡⲟⲩⲱϣⲉ ⲙ̄ⲡⲓⲱⲧ ⲁ- ³⁰ ⲧⲙ̄ⲧⲣⲉⲗⲁⲩⲉ ϣⲱⲡⲉ ϩ̄ⲛ ⲡ- ³¹ ⲡⲗⲏⲣⲱⲙⲁ
ⲟⲩⲁ̣ϣ̣ⲛ̄ ⲥⲩⲍⲩⲅⲟⲥ ³² ⲡⲟⲩⲱϣⲉ ϭⲉ ⲙ̄ⲡⲓⲱⲧ ⲡⲉ ³³ ⲧⲉⲩⲟ ⲁⲃⲁⲗ ⲛ̄ⲟⲩⲁⲉⲓ{ⲛ̄}ϣ ⲛⲓⲙ ³⁴ ⲁⲩⲱ ϯ
ⲕⲁⲣⲡⲟⲥ ⲁⲧⲣⲉⲥϣ̣ⲡ̄ ³⁵ ϩⲓⲥⲉ ϭⲉ ⲛⲉⲡⲟⲩⲱϣⲉ ⲉⲛ ³⁶ ⲙ̄ⲡⲓⲱⲧ ⲡⲉ ⲉⲥϣⲟⲟⲡ ⲛ̄ⲅⲁⲣ ³⁷ ⲛ̄ϩⲣⲏⲓ̈
ⲛ̄ϩⲏⲧⲥ̄ ⲟⲩⲁⲉⲉⲧ<ⲥ> ⲟⲩ- ³⁸ ϣ̣ⲛ̄ ⲡⲉⲥⲥⲩⲍⲩ[ⲅⲟⲥ] ⲙⲁⲣⲛ̄ ³⁷·⁷ (Lines 1–7 lacking) ⁸ .[⁹ ... ⲟⲩⲉ̣
[¹⁰ ⲡⲙⲁϩⲥⲛⲉⲩ ⲁ̣[¹¹ ⲡϣⲏⲣⲉ ⲛ̄ⲕⲉⲟⲩ[ⲉⲉⲓ 3–5] ¹² ⲧⲉ ⲧ̄[ⲧ]ⲉⲧⲣⲁⲥ ⲙ̄ⲡⲕⲟ[ⲥ]ⲙⲟⲥ [ⲁⲩⲱ] ¹³
ϯ[ⲧ]ⲉ̣[ⲧ]ⲣⲁⲥ ⲁⲥⲧⲉⲩⲟ ⲁⲃⲁⲗ ⲛ̄ⲕ[ⲁⲣ]- ¹⁴ ⲡ[ⲟ]ⲥ ϩⲱⲥ ⲟⲩϩⲉⲃⲇⲟⲙⲁⲥ ⲡⲉ[¹⁵ ⲡⲡⲗⲏⲣⲱⲙ[ⲁ ⲙ̄]
ⲡⲕⲟ[ⲥ]ⲙ̣[ⲟⲥ ⲁϥ]- ¹⁶ ⲉⲓ ⲛ̄ⲇⲉ ⲁϩ̣[ⲟⲩⲛ ⲁϩ̄]ⲛ̣ϩ̣[ⲓⲕⲱⲛ] ¹⁷ ⲙ̄ⲛ ϩⲛ̄ϩ̣[ⲉⲓⲛⲉ ⲙ̄ⲛ ϩ̣]ⲛ̄ⲁⲅ[ⲅⲉⲗⲟⲥ] ¹⁸ ⲙ̄ⲛ
ϩ̄ⲛ̄ⲁⲣ[ⲭⲁⲅⲅⲉⲗ]ⲟⲥ ϩ̣[ⲛ̄ⲛⲟⲩ]- ¹⁹ ⲧⲉ ⲁⲩⲱ ϩ̄ⲛ[ⲗⲉⲓ]ⲧⲟⲩ[ⲣⲅⲟⲥ]

²⁰ ⲛ̄[ⲉ]ⲉ̣[ⲓ ⲧ]ⲏⲣⲟⲩ ⲛ̄ⲧⲁⲣⲟⲩ[ϣⲱ]- ²¹ ⲡ[ⲉ ϩⲓ]ⲧ̄ⲛ̄ ⲧⲡⲣⲟⲛⲟⲓⲁ [. . .] ²² ⲙ̣[. . . .]ⲉⲣ ⲛ̄ⲓ̄ⲏ̄ⲥ̄ ⲉϥ[. .]
²³ [. . .] ⲛ̄ⲛⲥⲡⲉⲣⲙⲁ̣ [. .] ²⁴ [. . .] ⲙ̄ⲡⲙⲟⲛⲟⲅⲉⲛⲏⲥ [. .] ²⁵ [. . .] ⲛ̄ⲧⲁⲩ ⲙ̄ⲙⲉⲛ ϩ̄ⲙ[ⲡⲛⲉⲩ]- ²⁶
[ⲙⲁ]ⲧⲓⲕⲟⲛ ⲛⲉ ⲁⲩⲱ ⲛ̄ⲥ[ⲁⲣ]ⲕⲓ- ²⁷ ⲕⲟⲛ ⲛ̄ⲛⲉ ⲟ̄ⲛ̄ⲧⲡⲉ ⲙ̄ⲛ ⲛⲉⲧ- ²⁸ ϩⲓⲝ̄ⲙ ⲡⲕⲁϩ ⲁϥⲧⲁⲙⲓⲟ ⲛⲉⲩ
²⁹ ⲛ̄ⲟⲩⲧⲟⲡⲟⲥ ⲛ̄ϯⲙⲓⲛⲉ [ⲁ]ⲩ̣ⲱ ³⁰ ⲟⲩⲥⲭⲟⲗⲏ ⲛ̄ϯⲙⲓⲛⲉ ⲁϩⲟⲩⲛ ⲁⲩ- ³¹ ⲥⲃⲱ ⲁⲩⲱ ⲁ<ϩ>ⲟⲩⲛ
ⲁⲩⲙⲟⲣⲫⲏ

Thus both of them suffered. [35] They said she laughs because she remained [36] alone and was like the [37] Uncontainable One. But he said she [laughs] because [38] she separated herself from her partner. [35.1] (Lines 1–8 lacking) [9] [. . .] [10] from [. . .] Wisdom [11] revealed [the] creation. Since [12] indeed the seeds [of] Wisdom are [13] imperfect [and] without form, [14] Jesus invented a creature of [this] [15] kind and created it with the [16] seeds while Wisdom worked with [17] him. For since they are seeds [18] and forms, he came [19] down [and brought] forth the [20] fullness [of] eternities in that [21] place, [since] even [the] uncreated ones [among] [22] the eternities belong to the type of the [23] [fullness] and the [illimitable] Father. [24] The uncreated one [25] [brought the] type of the uncreated one, [26] for from the uncreated [27] one the Father brings [28] form. But the creation [29] is a shadow of the things that preexist. [30] This Jesus, then, created [31] the creation, and he created [32] from the passions [33] surrounding the seeds. And he [34] divided them, [35] and the good passions he brought [36] into the spirit, but the bad passions [37] he put into the fleshly element.

So [38] first among all those passions [36.1] (Lines 1–7 lacking) [8] [. . .] [9] [. . .] [10] him, since providence [11] gave [the] correction to produce [12] shadows and [13] images of [those who] exist from [14] the beginning [and] [15] [those who] are and those who will be. This then is the [16] organization of faith [17] in Jesus on account of [the one who] inscribed [18] the entirety with [. . .] and [19] images and [. . .].

[20] After Jesus brought forth [again], [21] he brought [forth] for [22] the entirety those belonging to the fullness [23] and the pairing, that is, the [24] angels. For at once with [the] [25] consent of the fullness, [26] her partner produced [27] the angels, since he dwells in [28] the will of the Father. For this [29] is the will of the Father that [30] nothing happens in the [31] fullness outside of a pairing. [32] Moreover, the will of the Father is [33] to produce [34] and bear fruit always. Therefore, her suffering [35] was not [36] the will of the Father, for she dwells [37] within herself alone, apart [38] from her partner. Let us [37.7] (Lines 1–7 lacking) [8] [. . .] [9] [. . .] [10] the second [. . .][11] the child of another one [. . .] [12] is the tetrad of the world, [and] [13] this tetrad produced fruit [14] as though the fullness [of] the world were a hebdomad. [15] [It] entered [16] into [images] [17] and [likenesses] [18] and [angels] and archangels, [deities] [19] and [servants].

[20] After all these things [came about] [21] through providence [. . .] [22] [. . .] of Jesus, who [. . .] [23] [. . .] of the seeds [. . .] [24] [. . .] of the Only-Begotten [. . .] [25] [. . .]. They are spiritual [26] and fleshly, [27] those in the heavens and [28] upon the earth. He made them [29] a place of this kind and [30] a school of this kind for [31] teaching and form.

³² аϥрархесөаі σε ⲛ̄σι пееі ³³ ⲁⲛⲙⲓⲟⲩⲣⲅⲟⲥ атаміо ⲛ̄оу- ³⁴ рⲱме ката ⲧ̄ϥ₂ікⲱⲛ меⲛ
³⁵ ката піⲛе ⲛ̄ⲇе ⲛ̄ⲛетϣо- ³⁶ оп хіⲛ ⲛ̄ϣарⲡ̄ оуⲙа ⲛⲁϣ- ³⁷ пе ⲛ̄ϯⲙіⲛе пеⲛтаⲥ̄ⲣхрⲱ
³⁸ ⲙⲙаϥ̄ ⲛ̄ⲛсперⲙа ⲛ̄σι ³⁹ (Lines 1–9 lacking)

³⁸·¹⁰ [10–12]ͺͺ[ͺпⲱ]р̄ⲭ ¹¹ [7–9 п]ⲛ̣оуте ⲛ̄тароу ¹² [5–7]е̣і етве прⲱⲙе ¹³ [епⲇ]-
іⲁв̣[ол]ос ⲙ̄меⲛ оуееі пе ¹⁴ [ⲛ̄т]е̣ ⲛапⲛоуте аϥсе₂ⲱ̣ϥ а- ¹⁵ [в]ал аⲱ аϥтⲱрп
ⲛ̄тп̣[л]атеі- ¹⁶ [а т]н̄р̄с̄ ⲛ̄ⲛп̣[о]улⲱⲛ а̣[уⲱ] аϥ- ¹⁷ [р̄апⲱ]ѳеі ⲛ̣[еϥ ⲛ̄т]еϥⲛоуⲛе ⲙ̄-
¹⁸ [ⲙіⲛ] ⲙ̄ⲙ[аϥ авал ₂ⲙ̄ пⲙа е̣- ¹⁹ [ⲧⲙⲙ]е̣у ₂[ⲙ̣ͺͺͺͺ]а̣ ⲙ̄ⲛ ₂ⲛ̄- ²⁰ [ͺͺͺ ⲛ̄]сар[ⲍ ϥσ]а̣ле
ⲛ̄гар ⲙ̄- ²¹ [прⲱ]ⲙе ⲛ̄пⲛоуте а[у]ϣ апа- ²² [ͺͺͺͺ]аϥ̄ етве пееі а̣[ϥ]х̣[ⲡ]о ²³ [ⲛеϥ
ⲛ̄₂ⲛϣнре еу[ͺͺͺͺ]т ⲛ̄- ²⁴ [ͺͺͺͺͺ]ну ₂акаïⲛ ⲛ̄[ⲇе ͺͺ]н̣[ͺͺ] ²⁵ [ͺͺͺ] авел пеϥсаⲛ
а̣[ͺͺͺͺͺ] ²⁶ [ͺͺͺͺͺ]с гар ⲛіϥе а₂оу[ⲛ арау] ²⁷ ⲙ̄п[е]ϥпⲛеуⲙа аϥϣⲱ̣[пе] ²⁸ ⲛ̄σ[і]
пⲙіϣе ⲙ̄ⲛ тапос̣таⲥ̣і- ²⁹ а ⲛ̄ⲛаггелос ауⲱ тⲙⲛ̄трⲱ- ³⁰ ⲙе ⲛауⲛем ⲙ̄ⲛ наσвоур
ⲙ̣[ⲛ̄] ³¹ неѳⲛ тпе ⲙ̄ⲛ нет₂іхⲙ пка₂ ³² ⲛ̄пⲛеуⲙа ⲙ̄ⲛ ⲛ̄саркікоⲛ ³³ ауⲱ пⲇіаволос
на₂р̄ⲛ пⲛоу- ³⁴ те етве пееі ₂анаггелос р̄е- ³⁵ п̄іѳуⲙеі анϣеере ⲛ̄ⲛрⲱⲙе ³⁶ ауⲱ
ауеі апіⲧ̄ⲛ асар₂ ₂ⲱс- ³⁷ те ⲛ̄тепⲛоуте еіре ⲛ̄оукǎта- ³⁸ клусⲙос ауⲱ схеⲇоⲛ
аϥр̄ ³⁹ ₂тнϥ хе аϥсⲱⲱⲛт ⲙ̄пкос- ³⁹·¹ [ⲙос

² (Lines 1–7 lacking) ⁷ [ͺͺͺͺ]ͺ[⁸ [ͺͺͺ]таⲛ[⁹ [ͺ]ос ⲙ̄меⲛ[7–9 псу- ¹⁰ ⲍ]угос ⲙ̄ⲛ
тсо[фіа ⲙ̄ⲛ пⲥ̄ϣⲛ]- ¹¹ ре ⲙ̄ⲛ ⲛ̄аггелос ⲙ̣[ⲛ̄ ⲛ̄спер]- ¹² ⲙа псухугос ⲛ̄ⲇе пте[ͺͺͺͺͺ]
¹³ ауⲱ тсофіа ⲙ̄ⲛ інсоус ауⲱ [ⲛ̄агге]- ¹⁴ ло[с] ⲙ̄ⲛ ⲛ̄сперⲙа ₂ⲛ̄₂і[кⲱⲛ] ¹⁵ ⲛе [ⲙ̄]-
ппⲗнр[ⲱ]ⲙа пⲇн̄[ⲙі]- ¹⁶ оургос σе [а]ϥ̄р̄аеⲓвес [а]- ¹⁷ псухугос ⲙ̄ⲛ [п]-
ппⲗнрⲱⲙ[а ¹⁸ ау[ⲱ] інсоус ⲙ̄ⲛ [тсоф]іа ⲙ̄ⲛ ⲛ̄аг]- ¹⁹ ге[ло]с ⲙ̄ⲛ ⲛ̄сп[ер]ⲙа п[ͺ]
ͺ[ͺͺ] ²⁰ [ϯ еау] ⲛ̄тсофіа тⲍⲓк[ⲱⲛ] ²¹ [ϯ еау] ⲛ̄тⲙне пеау ⲛ̄ⲇе ⲛ̄- ²² [ⲛ̄спе]рⲙа ⲙ̄ⲛ
інс ⲛатⲥ[ігн] ²³ [ⲛе ⲙ̄ⲛ] п̄ⲙоⲛогеⲛн[с ауⲱ] ²⁴ [ⲛ̄агге]лос ⲛ̄ⲛ₂ауⲧ ⲙ̄ⲛ [ⲛ̄]- ²⁵
[сперⲙа]ⲧікоⲛ ⲛ̄ⲛс₂і[ⲙе] ²⁶ [₂ⲛ̄п]лнр[ⲱ]ⲙа тнроу [ⲛе ₂о]- ²⁷ таⲛ σе
ереϣаⲛтсофі[а] хі ²⁸ ⲙ̄псухугос ауⲱ інсоус ⲛ̄ϥ̄- ²⁹ хі ⲙ̄пехрнстос ⲙ̄ⲛ ⲛ̄[с]пер-
³⁰ ⲙа ⲙ̄ⲛ ⲛ̄аггелос тотⲟ[е п]і- ³¹ плнрⲱⲙа ϥ̄нахі ⲛ̄тсофіа ³² ₂ⲛ̄ оуреϣе ауⲱ
птнр̄[ϥ] на- ³³ ϣⲱпе ₂ⲛ̄ оу₂ⲱт̄р ау[ⲱ] ₂ⲛ̄ ³⁴ оуапоката̄стасіс ₂ⲙ̄ пееі ³⁵ ⲛ̄гар
₂анаіⲱⲛ аухі ⲙ̄п- ³⁶ ₂оуо аусоуⲱⲛоу ⲛ̄гар хе ³⁷ еуϣаⲛϣ̄еіе сеϣооп ³⁸
ⲛатϣ̄ϥеіе

³² This creator began ³³ to create a ³⁴ man according to his image and ³⁵ according to the likeness of those who exist ³⁶ from the beginning. It was a dwelling place ³⁷ of this kind that she made use of ³⁸ for the seeds, namely, ³⁹ (Lines 1–9 lacking)

³⁸·¹⁰ [. . . divide] ¹¹ [. . .] God. After they ¹² [. . .] on account of the man, ¹³ [since the] devil is one ¹⁴ [of] those who belong to God. He withdrew ¹⁵ and seized the ¹⁶ entire courtyard of the gates, [and] he ¹⁷ [drove out] his ¹⁸ [own] root from [that] place ¹⁹ in [. . .] and ²⁰ [. . . of] flesh, for [he] is surrounded by ²¹ the person of God. And [. . .] ²² [. . .] him. For this reason he [produced] ²³ [for himself] sons, who [. . .] ²⁴ [. . .] Now Cain [. . .] ²⁵ [. . .] Abel, his brother, [. . .] ²⁶ [. . .] for [. . .] breathed into [them] ²⁷ his spirit. And a battle ²⁸ with the apostasy ²⁹ of the angels and humanity began, ³⁰ those on the right against those on the left, and ³¹ those in heaven against those on earth, ³² the spirits against the fleshly, ³³ and the devil against ³⁴ God. For this reason the angels ³⁵ lusted after the daughters of humans, ³⁶ and they went down into flesh so ³⁷ that God would bring about a ³⁸ flood, and he nearly ³⁹ regretted that he made the world. ³⁹·¹

² (Lines 1–7 lacking) ⁷ [. . .] ⁸ [. . .] ⁹ [. . . the] ¹⁰ partner of Wisdom [and her] son ¹¹ and the angels and [the seeds]. ¹² But the pairing is the [. . .]¹³ and Wisdom and Jesus and [the angels] ¹⁴ and the seeds are [images] ¹⁵ [of] the fullness. Therefore, the ¹⁶ creator [casts] a shadow [over] ¹⁷ the pairing and [the] fullness ¹⁸ and Jesus and [Wisdom] and the ¹⁹ angels and the seeds. The [. . .] ²⁰ [gives glory] to Wisdom; the image ²¹ [gives glory] to the truth. [But] the glory [of] ²² [the] seeds and Jesus [are] those of [Silence] ²³ [and] the Only-Begotten. [And] ²⁴ [the angels] of the males and [the] ²⁵ seminal (angels) of the females ²⁶ [are] all fullnesses. ²⁷ Then when Wisdom receives ²⁸ her partner, and Jesus ²⁹ receives the Christ and the seeds ³⁰ and the angels, then [this] ³¹ fullness will receive Wisdom ³² with joy, and the entirety will ³³ become unified and ³⁴ reconciled. For in this ³⁵ the eternities have received ³⁶ increase. For they knew that ³⁷ if they change, they are ³⁸ unchanging.

Inscription

XIII. FLAVIA SOPHE

The Flavia Sophe inscription includes two funerary epigraphs written in hexameter. The first epigraph is also an acrostic, spelling out FLAB[IA SOPHE], the name of the deceased woman. L. Fortunati discovered the inscription at the third mile marker along the Via Latina east of Rome in the nineteenth century. It is the only inscription with a certain Valentinian character, and if it does in fact date from the late second or early third century C.E., it is one the earliest known Christian inscriptions.

The Valentinian character of the Flavia Sophe inscription rests on its use of characteristically Valentinian language, including the reference to the "bridal chamber," her aim to "behold the divine countenances of the eternities," and Christ's designation as the "Angel of the great counsel," a title known also from the *Excerpts of Theodotus.*[1]

Peter Lampe has included the Flavia Sophe inscription in a body of evidence to suggest that there was a community of wealthy and highly educated Valentinians active in the villas to the east of Rome.[2] Lampe's argument rests not simply upon the Flavia Sophe inscription, but also upon three additional pieces of material evidence discovered along the Via Latina: two additional inscriptions and one pictorial

---

1. Peter Lampe, *From Paul to Valentinus: Christians at Rome in the First Two Centuries* (Minneapolis, MN: Fortress Press, 2003), 292–318.

2. Lampe (*From Paul to Valentinus*) builds on the earlier work of Margherita Guarducci, "Valentiniani a Roma: Ricerche epigrafiche ed archeologiche," *Mitteilungen des Deutschen Archäologischen Instituts, Römische Abteilung* 80 (1973): 169–89; and Guarducci, "Ancora sui Valentiniani a Roma," *Mitteilungen des Deutschen Archäologischen Instituts, Römische Abteilung* 81 (1974): 341–43.

representation of the Eucharist. Upon closer inspection, however, the evidence for such a community comes up short. Among the four items Lampe discusses, only one, the Flavia Sophe inscription, contains characteristically Valentinian language or imagery. The remaining inscriptions and iconography are Christian, but not likely Valentinian. Rather than indicate the presence of a Valentinian community active in the suburban villas, the material evidence suggests that wealthy Christians of various theological leanings were active along the Via Latina as early as the second century, including at least one Valentinian woman named Flavia Sophe.[3]

3. For a detailed discussion of the material evidence, see Geoffrey Smith, "Identifying Justin's Valentinians," in *"Opponents": Conflicts with Rivals in Early Jewish and Christian Literature*, ed. Ulrich Mell and Michael Tilly (Tübingen: Mohr Siebeck, 2020), 353–80.

Front

Φῶς πατρικὸν ποθέουσα, σύναιμε, σύνευνε Σόφη μου,
Λουτροῖς χρεισαμένη Χριστοῦ μύρον ἄφθιτον, ἁγνόν,
Αἰώνων ἔσπευσας ἀθρῖσαι θεῖα πρόσωπα,
Βουλῆς τῆς μεγάλης μέγαν ἄγγελον, υἷὸν ἀληθῆ.
Ἰς ν]υμφῶνα μολοῦσα καὶ εἰς [παστ]οὺς ἀνοροῦσα
Ἄφθαρτο]ς πατρικοὺς κα[ὶ . . . . ον ἐστ[εφα]γώ[θης]
[Σ . . . . . .]

Back

Οὐκ ἔσχεν κοινὸν βιότου τέλος ἥδε θανοῦσα·
κάτθανε καὶ ζώει καὶ ὁρᾷ φάος ἄφθιτον ὄντως·
ζώει μὲν ζωοῖσι, θάνεν δὲ θανοῦσιν ἀληθῶς.
γαῖα, τί θαυμάζεις νέκυος γένος; ἢ πεφόβησαι;

Front

Yearning for the fatherly light, my sister and wife, Sophe,
Anointed in the baths of Christ with perfume unfading, pure,
You were eager to behold the divine countenances of the eternities,
The great angel of the mighty council, the true Son,
Processing [into] the bridal chamber and ascending into the fatherly chambers
Undefiled and [. . . you were crowned].

Back

She experienced no common end of life, this woman who died;
She died, yet she lives, and sees the truly unfading light;
She lives among those who live, but she died to those who are in reality dead.
Earth, why are you amazed by a corpse of this sort? Are you afraid?

BIBLIOGRAPHIES

VALENTINIANISM

Abramowski, Luise. "Marius Victorinus, Porphyrius und die römischen Gnostiker." *ZNW* 74 (1983): 108–28.

Aland, Barbara. "Erwahlungstheologie und Menschenklassenlehre: Die Theologie des Herakleon als Schliissel zum Verstandnis der christlichen Gnosis." In *Gnosis and Gnosticism: Papers Read at the Eighth International Conference on Patristic Studies (Oxford, September 3rd–8th 1979)*, edited by Martin Krause, 148–69. NHS 8. Leiden: Brill, 1977.

Armstrong, A. H. "Plotinus." In *The Cambridge History of Later Greek and Early Medieval Philosophy*, edited by A. H. Armstrong, 193–268. Cambridge: Cambridge University Press, 1967.

———, trans. *Plotinus.* 7 vols. Loeb Classical Library. Cambridge, MA: Harvard University Press, 1966–88.

Attridge, Harold W., ed. *Nag Hammadi Codex I.* 2 vols. Nag Hammadi Studies 22 and 23. Leiden: Brill, 1985.

———. "Valentinian and Sethian Apocalyptic Traditions." *JECS* 8 (2000): 173–211.

Barc, Bernard, ed. *Colloque international sur les textes de Nag Hammadi.* BCNH: Études 1. Quebec City: Presses de l'Université Laval, 1981.

Barnes, T. D. "Methodius, Maximus, and Valentinus." *JTS* 30 (1979): 47–55. [Reprinted in T. D. Barnes, *Early Christianity and the Roman Empire* (London: Variorum Reprints, 1984).]

Barr, James. *The Garden of Eden and the Hope of Immortality.* Minneapolis: Fortress Press, 1993.

Barry, Catherine, Wolf-Peter Funk, Paul-Hubert Poirier, and John D. Turner. *Zostrien* (NHC VIII, 1). BCNH: Textes 24. Quebec City: Presses de l'Université Laval, 2000.

Bartelink, G. J. M. "Quelques observations sur parrhesia dans la littérature paléochretiénne." In *Graecitas et Latinitas Christianorum primaeva*, Suppl. 3. Nijmegen, Netherlands: Dekker & van de Vegt, 1970.

Barth, Carola. *Die Interpretation des Neuen Testaments in der valentinianischen Gnosis.* TU 37.3. Leipzig: Hinrichs, 1911.

Bauer, Walter. *Griechisch-deutsches Wörterbuch zu den Schriften des Neuen Testaments und der frühchristlichen Literatur.* Edited by Kurt Aland and Barbara Aland. 6th ed. Berlin: Walter de Gruyter, 1988.

Baumstark, Anton. "Die Lehre des römischen Presbyters Florinus." *ZNW* 13 (1912): 306–19.

Baur, Ferdinand Christian. *Die christliche Gnosis oder die christliche Religions-Philosophie in ihrer geschichtlichen Entwicklung.* Tübingen: C. F. Osiander, 1835.

Bechtle, Gerald. *The Anonymous Commentary on Plato's "Parmenides."* Berner Reihe philosophischer Studien 22. Bern: Paul Haupt, 1999.

Bermejo Rubiero, Fernando. *Le escisión imposible: Lectura del gnosticismo valentiniano.* Plenitudo temporis 5. Salamanca: Publicaciones Universidad Pontificia, 1998.

Beyschlag, Karlmann. "Kallist und Hippolyt." *ThZ* 20 (1964): 103–24.

Bianchi, Ugo, ed. *The Origins of Gnosticism: Colloquium of Messina, 13–18 April 1966.* SHR 12. Leiden: Brill, 1967.

Blanc, Cecile. *Origene: Commentaire sur Saint Jean.* 5 vols. SC 120, 157, 222, 290, 385. Paris: Cerf, 1970–92.

Blass, F., and A. Debrunner. *A Greek Grammar of the New Testament and Other Early Christian Literature.* A translation and revision of the ninth–tenth German edition, incorporating supplementary notes of A. Debrunner, by Robert W. Funk. Chicago: University of Chicago Press, 1961.

Blomkvist, Vemund. "An Early Christian Inscription?" *ZNW* 88 (1997): 143–44.

Bohlig, Alexander. "Zur Vorstellung vom Lichtkreutz in Gnostizismus und Manichaismus." In *Gnosis: Festschrift fur Hans Jonas,* edited by Barbara Aland et al., 473–91. Göttingen: Vandenhoeck & Ruprecht, 1978. [Reprinted in Alexander Bohlig, *Gnosis und Synkretismus,* WUNT 47, 48 (Tübingen: Mohr-Siebeck, 1989), 135–63.]

Bradshaw, Paul F., Maxwell E. Johnson, and L. Edward Phillips. *The Apostolic Tradition: A Commentary.* Hermeneia. Minneapolis: Fortress Press, 2002.

Broek, R. van den. "The Creation of Adam's Psychic Body in the *Apocryphon of John*." In *Studies in Gnosticism and Hellenistic Religions Presented to Gilles Quispel on the Occasion of His 65th Birthday,* edited by R. van den Broek and M. J. Vermaseren, 38–57. EPRO 91. Leiden: Brill, 1981.

Brooke, A. E. *The Fragments of Heracleon, Newly Edited from the MSS with an Introduction and Notes.* Texts and Studies 1.4. Cambridge: The University Press, 1891. [Reprinted, Piscataway, NJ: Gorgias Press, 2004.]

Bultmann, Rudolf. *Theology of the New Testament.* 2 vols. London: SCM Press, 1952–55.

Burkert, Walter. *Lore and Science in Ancient Pythagoreanism.* Translated by Edwin L. Minar Jr. Cambridge, MA: Harvard University Press, 1972.

Casel, Odo. "Die Taufe als Brautbad der Kirche." *Jahrbuch fur Liturgiewissenschaft* 5 (1925): 144–47.

Casey, Robert P. "Note on Epiphanius *Panarion* XXXI 5–6." *JTS* 29 (1928): 34–40.

———. "Two Notes on Valentinian Theology." *HTR* 23 (1930): 275–98.

Castagno, A. Monaci. "Origene e Ambrogio: L'indipendenza dell'intellettuale e le pretese dell'patronato." In *Origeniana Octava: Origene e la tradizione alessandrina; Papers of the*

8th International Origen Congress, Pisa, 27–31 August 2001, edited by Lorenzo Perrone, 165–93. Leuven: Leuven University Press, 2003.

Cattenoz, Jean-Pierre. *Le baptême, mystère nuptial: Théologie de Saint Jean Chrysostome*. Collection Centre Notre-Dame de Vie: Série théologie 5. Venasque: Éditions du Carmel, 1993.

Charles, R. H., ed. *The Apocrypha and Pseudepigrapha of the Old Testament in English*. 2 vols. Oxford: Clarendon Press, 1913.

Charlesworth, James H., ed. *The Old Testament Pseudepigrapha*. 2 vols. Garden City, NY: Doubleday, 1983–85.

Chazon, Esther G. "Liturgical Communion with the Angels at Qumran." In *Sapiential, Liturgical, and Poetical Texts from Qumran: Proceedings of the Third Meeting of the International Organization for Qumran Studies, Oslo 1998, Published in Memory of Maurice Baillet*, edited by Daniel K. Falk, Florentino Garcia Martinez, and Eileen M. Schuller, 95–105. Studies on the Texts of the Judean Desert 35. Leiden: Brill, 2000.

Colpe, Carsten. "Heidnische, jüdische und christliche Überlieferung in den Schriften aus Nag Hammadi, VII." *JAC* 21 (1978): 125–46.

Connolly, R. Hugh. *The Liturgical Homilies of Narsai*. Texts and Studies 8.1. Cambridge: Cambridge University Press, 1909.

Conzelmann, Hans. *I Corinthians*. Hermeneia. Philadelphia: Fortress Press, 1975.

Corrigan, Kevin. "Platonism and Gnosticism: The Anonymous Commentary on the *Parmenides*; Middle or Neoplatonic?" In *Gnosticism and Later Platonism: Themes, Figures, and Texts*, edited by John Turner and Ruth Majercik, 141–77. Society of Biblical Literature Symposium Series 12. Atlanta: Society of Biblical Literature, 2000.

Cross, F. L., ed. *The Jung Codex: A Newly Recovered Gnostic Papyrus; Three Studies by H.-Ch. Puech, G. Quispel, and W. C. van Unnik*. London: Mowbray, 1955.

Dahl, Nils A. "Form-Critical Observations on Early Christian Preaching." In *Jesus in the Memory of the Early Church*, edited by Nils Dahl, 30–36. Minneapolis: Augsburg, 1976.

DeConick, April. "The Great Mystery of Marriage: Sex and Conception in Ancient Valentinian Traditions." *VC* 57 (2003): 307–42.

Denzey, Nicola. "Apolytrosis as Ritual and Sacrament: Determining a Ritual Context for Death in Second-Century Valentinianism." *JECS* 17.4 (2009): 525–61.

Desjardins, Michel. *Sin in Valentinianism*. Society of Biblical Literature Dissertation Series 108. Atlanta: Scholars Press, 1990.

———. "The Sources for Valentinian Gnosticism: A Question of Methodology." *VC* 40 (1986): 342–47.

Des Places, Édouard. *Oracles chaldaïques*. Paris: Les Belles Lettres, 1971.

Dibelius, Otto. "Studien zur Geschichte der Valentinianer." *ZNW* 9 (1908): 230–47, 329–40.

Dillon, John. *The Middle Platonists: A Study of Platonism, 80 B.C. to A.D. 220*. London: Duckworth, 1977.

Dodds, E. R. "The *Parmenides* of Plato and the Origin of the Neoplatonic One." *Classical Quarterly* 22 (1928): 129–42.

Dunderberg, Ismo. "From Thomas to Valentinus: Genesis Exegesis in the Fragment 4 of Valentinus and Its Relationship to Thomas." In *Thomasine Traditions in Antiquity: The Social and Cultural Worlds of the Gospel of Thomas*, edited by Risto Uro, Jon Ma Asgeirsson, and April D. De Corrick, 221–37. NHMS 59. Leiden: Brill, 2006.

————. *Gnostic Morality Revisited*. WUNT 347. Tübingen: Mohr Siebeck, 2015.

————. "The School of Valentinus." In *A Companion to Second-Century Christian "Heretics,"* edited by Antti Marjanen and Petri Luomanen, 64–99. VC Supplement. Leiden: Brill, 2005.

————. "Valentinian Teachers in Rome." In *Christians as a Religious Minority in a Multicultural City: Modes of Interaction and Identity Formation in Early Imperial Rome*, edited by Michael Labahn and Jurgen Zangenberg, 157–74. JSNTSup 243. London: T&T Clark International, 2004.

Dupont-Sommer, A. *La doctrine gnostique de la lettre <<wâw>> d'après une lamelle araméenne inédite*. Bibliothèque archéologique et historique 41. Paris: Paul Geuthner, 1946.

Edsman, Carl-Martin. *Le baptême de feu*. Acta seminarii i neotestamentici upsaliensis 9. Leipzig: A.-B. Lundequistska, 1940.

Edwards, M. J. "Gnostics and Valentinians in the Church Fathers." *JTS* 40 (1989): 26–47.

Emmel, Stephen. "Exploring the Pathway That Leads from Paul to Gnosticism: What Is the Genre of the *Interpretation of Knowledge* (NHC XI, I)?" In *Die Weisheit-Ursprünge und Rezeption: Festschrift für Karl Löning zum 65 Geburtstag*, edited by Martin Fassnacht et al., 257–76. Munster: Aschendorff, 2003.

————. "The Recently Published *Gospel of the Savior* ('Unbekanntes Berliner Evangelium'): Righting the Order of Pages and Events." *HTR* 95 (2002): 45–72.

Engberding, Hieronymus. "Die Kirche als Braut in der ostsyrischen Liturgie." *Orientalia christiana periodica* 3 (1937): 5–48.

Festugière, A.-J. *La révélation d'Hermès Trismégiste*. 4 vols. Paris: Gabalda, 1949–54.

————. "Notes sur les *Extraits de Théodote* de Clément d'Alexandrie et sur les fragments de Valentin." *VC* 3 (1949): 193–207.

Filoramo, Giovanni. *A History of Gnosticism*. Translated by Anthony Alcock. Oxford: Blackwell, 1990.

Finn, Thomas M. *The Liturgy of Baptism in the Baptismal Instructions of St. John Chrysostom*. SCA 15. Washington, DC: The Catholic University of America Press, 1967.

Fitzgerald, John T., ed. *Friendship, Flattery, and Frankness of Speech: Studies on Friendship in the New Testament World*. Supplementum Novum Testamentum 82. Leiden: Brill, 1996.

————. *Greco-Roman Perspectives on Friendship*. SBL Resources for Biblical Study 34. Atlanta: Scholars Press, 1997.

Fliedner, Friedrich. "Die ketzergeschichtlichen Angaben des Agapius und das System des Presbyters Florinus." Diss., Münster, 1942.

Foerster, Werner. *Gnosis: A Selection of Gnostic Texts*. Translated by R. M. Wilson. 2 vols. Oxford: Clarendon Press, 1972.

————. *Von Valentin zu Herakleon: Untersuchungen über die Quellen und die Entwicklung der valentinianischen Gnosis*. Beihefte zur *ZNW* 7. Giessen: Töpelmann, 1928.

Förster, Niclas. *Marcus Magus: Kult, Lehre und Gemeindeleben einer valentinianischen Gnostikergruppe*. Sammlung der Quellen und Kommentar. WUNT 114. Tübingen: Mohr-Siebeck, 1999.

Franzmann, Majella. *Jesus in the Nag Hammadi Writings*. Edinburgh: T&T Clark, 1996.

Fraser, P. M. *Ptolemaic Alexandria*. 3 vols. Oxford: Clarendon Press, 1972.

Fredouille, Jean-Claude. *Tertullien: Contre les Valentiniens*. SC 280, 281. Paris: Cerf, 1980–81.

Frend, W. H. C. "The Gnostic Sects and the Roman Empire." *JEH* 5 (1954): 25–37. [Reprinted in W. H. C. Frend, *Religion Popular and Unpopular in the Early Christian Centuries* (London: Variorum Reprints, 1976).]

Frennesson, Björn. *"In a Common Rejoicing": Liturgical Communion with Angels in Qumran*. Studia semitica upsaliensia 14. Diss., Uppsala University, 1999.

Funk, Wolf-Peter. *Concordance des textes de Nag Hammadi: Les codices XI et XIA*. BCNH: Concordances 6. Sainte-Foy: Presses de l'Université Laval, 2000.

Giversen, Søren, and B. Pearson. *Nag Hammadi Codices IX and X*. Nag Hammadi Studies 15. Leiden: Brill, 1997.

Greer, Rowan A. "The Dog and the Mushrooms: Irenaeus's View of the Valentinians Assessed." In *The Rediscovery of Gnosticism: Proceedings of the International Conference on Gnosticism at Yale, New Haven, Connecticut, March 28–31, 1978*, edited by Bentley Layton, 1:146–71. Studies in the History of Religions: Supp. to *Numen* 41. Leiden: Brill, 1980.

Gressmann, Hugo. "Jüdisch-Aramaisches bei Epiphanius." *ZNW* 16 (1915): 191–97.

Guarducci, M. "Ancora sui Valentiniani a Roma." *MDAI(R)* 81 (1974): 341–43.

———. "Valentiniani a Roma: Ricerche epigrafiche ed archeologiche." *MDAI(R)* 80 (1973): 169–89.

Guy, Laurie. "'Naked' Baptism in the Early Church: The Rhetoric and the Reality." *Journal of Religious History* 27 (2003): 133–42.

Hadot, Pierre. *Porphyre et Victorinus*. 2 vols. Études Augustiniennes 32, 33. Paris: Institut d'Études Augustiniennes, 1968.

———. "'Porphyre et Victorinus': Questions et hypotheses." *Res orientales* 9 (1996): 117–25.

Harnack, Adolf von. *Geschichte der altchristlichen Literatur bis Eusebius*. 2 pts. in 4 vols. Leipzig, 1896–1904. [Reprinted, Leipzig: Hinrich, 1958.]

———. *Marcion: Das Evangelium vom fremden Gott*. 2nd ed. Leipzig: Hinrich, 1924.

———. *Zur Quellenkritik der Geschichte des Gnosticismus*. Leipzig: O. Leiner, 1873.

———. "Zur Quellenkritik der Geschichte des Gnosticismus." *Zeitschrift für historische Theologie* 44 (1874): 143–226.

Heath, Thomas L. *A History of Greek Mathematics*. 2 vols. Oxford: Clarendon Press, 1921.

Hedrick, Charles W., ed. *Nag Hammadi Codices XI, XII, XIII*. NHS 28. Leiden: Brill, 1990.

Hedrick, Charles, and Paul Mirecki. *Gospel of the Savior: A New Ancient Gospel*. California Classical Library. Santa Rosa, CA: Polebridge, 1999.

Heinrici, Georg. *Die valentinianische Gnosis und die heilige Schriften*. Berlin: Wiegandt und Grieben, 1871.

Hellholm, David. "The 'Revelation-Schema' and Its Adaptation in the Coptic Gnostic Apocalypse of Peter." *SEA* 63 (1998): 233–48.

Henry, Paul, and Pierre Hadot. *Marius Victorinus: Traités théologiques sur la trinité*. 2 vols. SC 68, 69. Paris: Cerf, 1960.

Henry, Paul, and Hans-Rudolf Schwyzer. *Plotini Opera*. 3 vols. Oxford: Clarendon Press, 1964, 1977, 1982.

Herzhoff, Bernhard. "Zwei gnostische Psalmen." Diss., Bonn, 1973.

Hilgenfeld, Adolf. "Der Gnostiker Valentinus und seine Schriften." *ZWTh* 23 (1880): 280–300.

———. *Die Ketzergeschichte des Urchristentums urkundlich dargestellt*. Leipzig, 1884. [Reprinted, Hildesheim: Georg Olms, 1966.]

Hoffmann, R. Joseph. *Celsus: On the True Doctrine; A Discourse against the Christians.* Oxford: Oxford University Press, 1987.

Holzhausen, Jens. *Der "Mythos vom Menschen" im hellenistischen Ägypten: Eine Studie zum "Poimandres" (= CH I), zu Valentin und dem gnostischen Mythos.* Theophaneia 33. Bodenheim: Athenaum Hain Hanstein, 1994.

———. "Ein gnostischer Psalm?" *JAC* 36 (1993): 68–80.

———. "Gnosis und Martyrium." *ZNW* 85 (1994): 116–31.

———. "Irenäus und die valentinianische Schule: Zur Praefatio von *Adv. Haer.* 1." *VC* 55 (2001): 341–55.

———. "Valentinus and Valentinians." In *Dictionary of Gnosis and Western Esotericism,* edited by Wouter J. Hanegraaff et al., 2:1144–57. Leiden: Brill, 2005.

Hubner, Reinhard. *Die Einheit des Leibes Christi bei Gregor von Nyssa.* Philosophia patrum 2. Leiden: Brill, 1974.

———. "Thesen zur Echtheit und Datierung der sieben Briefe des Ignatius von Antiochien." *ZAC* 1 (1997): 44–72.

Johnson, Maxwell. "The Baptismal Rite and Anaphora in the Prayers of Sarapion of Thmuis: An Assessment of a Recent Judicious Reassessment." *Worship* 73 (1999): 140–68.

———, ed. *Living Water, Sealing Spirit: Readings on Christian Initiation.* Collegeville, MN: Liturgical Press, 1995.

Jonas, Hans. *Gnosis und spätantiker Geist.* Vol. 1, *Die mythologische Gnosis.* 3rd ed. FRLANT 51. Göttingen: Vandenhoeck & Ruprecht, 1964.

———. *Gnosis und spätantiker Geist.* Vol. 2, *Von der Mythologie zur mystischen Philosophie.* FRLANT 159. Göttingen: Vandenhoeck & Ruprecht, 1993.

———. *The Gnostic Religion: The Message of the Alien God and the Beginnings of Christianity.* 2nd ed. Boston: Beacon Press, 1963.

Kaestli, Jean-Daniel. "Valentinisme italien et valentinisme oriental: Leurs divergences à propos de la nature du corps du Christ." In *The Rediscovery of Gnosticism: Proceedings of the International Conference on Gnosticism at Yale, New Haven, Connecticut, March 28–31, 1978,* edited by Bentley Layton, 1:391–403. Studies in the History of Religions: Supp. to *Numen* 41. Leiden: Brill, 1980.

Kalbfleisch, Karl. *Die neuplatonische, fälschlich dem Galen zugeschriebene Schrift Πρὸς Γαῦρον περὶ τοῦ πῶς ἐμψυχοῦται τὰ ἔμβρυα aus der Pariser Handschrift zum ersten Male herausgeben.* Berlin: Königl. Akademie der Wissenschaften, 1895.

Kanzler, Rodolfo. "Di un nuovo cirnitero anonimo sulla via Latina." *Nuovo bullettino di archeologia cristiana* 9 (1903): 173–86.

Kehl, Alois. "Gewand." *RAC* 10:945–1025.

Koep, Leo. *Das himmlische Buch in Antike und Christentum.* Theophaneia 8. Bonn: Peter Hanstein, 1952.

Koschorke, Klaus. *Hippolyt's Ketzerbekämpfung und Polemik gegen die Gnostiker.* Göttinger Orientforschungen 6, Hellenistica 4. Wiesbaden: Harrassowitz, 1975.

———. "Patristische Materialien zur Spätgeschichte der valentinianischen Gnosis." In *Gnosis and Gnosticism: Papers Read at the Eighth International Conference on Patristic Studies (Oxford, September 3rd–8th 1979),* edited by Martin Krause, 120–39. NHS 17. Leiden: Brill, 1981.

Kramer, Hans Joachim. *Der Ursprung der Geistmetaphysik: Untersuchungen zur Geschichte des Platonismus zwischen Platon und Plotin.* 2nd ed. Amsterdam: B. R. Gruner, 1964.

Kretschmar, Georg. "Beiträge zur Geschichte der Liturgie, insbesondere der Taufliturgie, in Ägypten." *Jahrbuch for Liturgik und Hymnologie* 8 (1963): 1–54.

Kroll, Wilhelm. *De oraculis Chaldaicis.* Breslau, 1894. [Reprinted, Hildesheim: Georg Olms, 1986.]

Kübert, R. "Achamoth." *Biblica* 45 (1964): 254–55.

Labriolle, Pierre Champagne de. *La crise montaniste.* Paris: Ernest Leroux, 1913.

Lacombrade, Christian. *Synésios de Cyrène.* Vol. 1, *Hymnes.* Paris: Les Belles Lettres, 1978.

Lalleman, Pieter J. *The Acts of John: A Two-Stage Initiation into Johannine Gnosticism.* Studies on the Apocryphal Acts of the Apostles 4. Leuven: Peeters, 1998.

Lampe, G. W.ths}H. *A Patristic Greek Lexicon.* Oxford: Oxford University Press, 1961.

———. *The Seal of the Spirit: A Study in the Doctrine of Baptism and Confirmation in the New Testament and the Fathers.* 2nd ed. London: SPCK, 1967. [1st ed., 1951.]

Lampe, Peter. "An Early Christian Inscription in the Musei Capitolini." In *Mighty Minorities: Minorities in Early Christianity—Positions and Strategies: Essays in Honour of Jacob Jervell on His 70th Birthday, 21 May 1995,* edited by D. Hellholm, H. Moxnes, and T. K. Seim, 79–92. Oslo: Scandinavian University Press, 1995.

———. *From Paul to Valentinus: Christians at Rome in the First Two Centuries.* Minneapolis: Fortress Press, 2003.

Layton, Bentley. *The Gnostic Scriptures: A New Translation with Annotations and Introduction.* Garden City, NY: Doubleday, 1995.

———, ed. *Nag Hammadi Codex II,2–7 Together with XIII,2*, Brit. Lib. Or. 4926(1), and P. Oxy. 1, 654, 655.* 2 vols. NHS 20, 21. Leiden: Brill, 1989.

———. "Prolegomena to the Study of Ancient Gnosticism." In *The Social World of the First Christians: Essays in Honor of Wayne A. Meeks,* edited by L. Michael White and O. Larry Yarbrough, 334–50. Minneapolis: Fortress Press, 1995.

———, ed. *The Rediscovery of Gnosticism: Proceedings of the International Conference on Gnosticism at Yale, New Haven, Connecticut, March 28–31, 1978.* 2 vols. Studies in the History of Religions: Supp. to *Numen* 41. Leiden: Brill, 1980.

Le Boulluec, Alan. *La notion d'hérésie dans la littérature grecque, IIe-IIIe siècles.* 2 vols. Paris: Études Augustiniennes, 1985.

Lechner, Thomas. *Ignatius adversus Valentinianos? Chronologische und theologiegeschichtliche Studien zu den Briefen des Ignatius von Antiochien.* Supplementum *VC* 47. Leiden: Brill, 1999.

Leeper, Elizabeth A. "From Alexandria to Rome: The Valentinian Connection to the Incorporation of Exorcism as a Prebaptismal Rite." *VC* 44 (1990): 6–24.

Lesky, E. "Embryologie: A. Nichtchristlich. I. Griech.-röm." *RAC* 4:1228–41.

Lewis, I. M. *Ecstatic Religion: An Anthropological Study of Spirit Possession and Shamanism.* Harmondsworth, UK: Penguin, 1971.

Lewy, Hans. *Chaldaean Oracles and Theurgy: Mysticism, Magic, and Platonism in the Later Roman Empire.* New ed. by Michel Tardieu. Paris: Études Augustiniennes, 1978. [1st ed., Cairo, 1956.]

Lilla, Salvatore. *Clement of Alexandria: A Study in Christian Platonism and Gnosticism.* Oxford: Oxford University Press, 1971.

Lipsius, Richard. *Die Quellen der ältesten Ketzergeschichte, neu untersucht.* Leipzig: J. A. Barth, 1875.

———. "Ptolemaeus (1)." In *A Dictionary of Christian Biography, Literature, Sects, and Doctrines during the First Eight Centuries,* edited by W. Smith and H. Wace, 4:515–17. London, 1887.

———. "Valentinus (1)." In *A Dictionary of Christian Biography, Literature, Sects, and Doctrines during the First Eight Centuries,* edited by W. Smith and H. Wace, 4:1076–99. London, 1887.

———. *Zur Quellenkritik des Epiphanios.* Vienna: Wilhelm Braumuller, 1865.

Litwa, David. "The Wondrous Exchange: Irenaeus and the Eastern Valentinians on the Soteriology of Exchange." *JECS* 22.3 (2014): 311–41.

Logan, Alastair. *Gnostic Truth and Christian Heresy: A Study in the History of Gnosticism.* Edinburgh: T&T Clark, 1996.

———. "Post-baptismal Chrismation in Syria: The Evidence of Ignatius, the Didache, and the Apostolic Constitutions." *JTS* 49.1 (1998): 92–108.

Long, A.ths}A., and D.ths}N. Sedley. *The Hellenistic Philosophers.* 2 vols. Cambridge: Cambridge University Press 1987.

Lüdemann, Gerd. "Zur Geschichte des ältesten Christentums im Rom." *ZNW* 70 (1979): 86–114.

Lundhaug, Hugo. "Fragments of Early Christianity: An Analysis of a *Valentinian Exposition* (NHC XI,2) with the Liturgical Fragments On the Anointing, On Baptism A, On Baptism B, On the Eucharist A, On the Eucharist B (NHC XI,2a–e)." Diss. IKS, University of Oslo, 2000.

———. *Images of Rebirth: Cognitive Poetics and the Transformational Soteriology in the "Gospel of Philip" and the "Exegesis of the Soul."* NHMS 73. Leiden: Brill, 2010.

Mach, Michael. *Entwicklungsstadien des jüdischen Engelglaubens in vorrabbinischer Zeit.* Texte und Studien zum antiken Judentum 34. Tübingen: Mohr-Siebeck, 1992.

Mahé, Annie, and Jean-Pierre Mahé. *Le témoignage véritable (NH IX, 3): Gnose et martyre.* BCNH: Textes 23. Quebec City: Presses de l'Université Laval, 1996.

Mahé, Jean-Pierre. *Tertullien: La chair du Christ.* SC 216, 217. Paris: Cerf, 1975.

Majercik, Ruth. *The Chaldean Oracles: Text, Translation, and Commentary.* Studies in Greek and Roman Religion 5. Leiden: Brill, 1989.

———. "The Existence-Life-Intellect Triad in Gnosticism and Neoplatonism." *Classical Quarterly* 42 (1992): 475–88.

Marcovich, Miroslav. *Hippolytus Refutatio omnium haeresium.* Patristische Texte und Studien 25. Berlin: Walter de Gruyter, 1986.

Markschies, Christoph. "Die Krise einer Bibeltheologie in der Alten Kirche oder: Valentin und die valentinianische Gnosis zwischen philosophischer Bibelinterpretation und mythologischer Häresie." In *Gnosis und Manichaismus: Forschungen und Studien zu Texten von Valentin und Mani sowie zu den Bibliotheken von Nag Hammadi und Medinet Madi,* edited by Alexander Böhlig and Christoph Markschies, 1–37. BZNW 72. Berlin: De Gruyter, 1994.

———. "Die valentinianische Gnosis und Marcion-einige neue Perspektiven." In *Marcion und kirchengeschichtliche Wirkung,* edited by Gerhard May, Katharina Greschat, and Martin Meiser, 159–72. TU 150. Berlin: Walter de Gruyter, 2002.

———. "New Research on Ptolemaeus Gnosticus." *ZAC* 4 (2000): 225–54.

———. "Valentinian Gnosticism: Toward the Anatomy of a School." In *The Nag Hammadi Library after Fifty Years: Proceedings of the 1995 Society of Biblical Literature Commemoration*, edited by John Turner and Anne McGuire, 401–38. NHMS 44. Leiden: Brill, 1997.

———. "Valentinianische Gnosis in Alexandrien und Agypten." In *Origeniana Octava: Origene e la tradizione alessandrina; Papers of the 8th International Origen Congress, Pisa, 27–31 August 2001*, edited by Lorenzo Perrone, 331–46. Leuven: Leuven University Press, 2003.

———. *Valentinus Gnosticus? Untersuchungen zur valentinianischen Gnosis mit einem Kommentar zu den Fragmenten Valentins*. WUNT 65. Tübingen: J. C. B. Mohr, 1992.

Marucchi, Orazio. "Osservazioni sopra il cimitero anonimo recentamente scoperto sulla via Latina." *Nuovo bullettino di archeologia cristiana* 9 (1903): 301–14.

McDonnell, Kilian. *The Baptism of Jesus in the Jordan: The Trinitarian and the Cosmic Order of Salvation*. Collegeville, MN: Liturgical Press, 1996.

McGowan, Andrew. "Valentinus Poeta: Notes on θέρος." *VC* 51 (1997): 158–78.

McGuire, Anne. "Valentinus and the 'Gnostike Hairesis': An Investigation of Valentinus' Position in the History of Gnosticism." PhD diss., Yale University, 1983.

Meeks, Wayne. *The First Urban Christians: The Social World of the Apostle Paul*. New Haven: Yale University Press, 1983.

———. "The Image of Androgyne: Some Uses of the Symbol in Earliest Christianity." *HR* 13 (1974): 165–208.

Ménard, Jacques-É. *L'exposé valentinien: Les fragments sur le baptême et sur l'eucharistie (NH XI,2)*. BCNH: Textes 14. Quebec City: Presses de l'Université Laval, 1985.

Merlan, P. "Greek Philosophy from Plato to Plotinus." In *The Cambridge History of Later Greek and Early Medieval Philosophy*, edited by A. H. Armstrong, 11–32. Cambridge: Cambridge University Press, 1967.

Michl, J. "Engel I–IX." *RAC* 5:53–258.

Muller, Karl. "Beiträge zum Verständnis der valentinianischen Gnosis." *NGG*, 1920, 179–242.

Munier, Charles. "Initiation chrétienne et rites d'onction (IIe–IIIe siècles)." *RSR* 64 (1990): 115–25.

Musurillo, Herbert. *The Acts of the Christian Martyrs*. Oxford: Oxford University Press, 1972.

Neander, August. *Genetische Entwickelung der vornehmsten gnostischen Systeme*. Berlin: F. Dummler, 1818.

Nickel, Diethard. *Untersuchungen zur Embryologie Galens*. Schriften zur Geschichte und Kultur der Antike 27. Berlin: Akademie-Verlag, 1989.

Nickelsburg, George W.ths}E. *1 Enoch 1: A Commentary on the Book of Enoch, Chapters 1–36; 81–108*. Hermeneia. Minneapolis: Fortress Press, 2001.

Norden, Eduard. *Die antike Kunstprosa vom VI. Jahrhundert v. Chr. bis in die Zeit der Renaissance*. 3rd ed. 2 vols. Stuttgart: Teubner, 1915.

Orbe, Antonio. *Cristologia gnóstica: Introducción a la soteriologia de los siglos II y III*. 2 vols. Biblioteca de autores cristianos 384, 385. Madrid: Edica, 1976.

———. *En los albores de la exegesis Iohannea (Ioh. I, 3)*. Vol. 2 of *Estudios valentinianos*. Analecta Gregoriana 65. Rome: Apud aedes Universitatis Gregorianae, 1955.

————. *Hacia la primera teologia de la procesión del verbo.* Vol. 1 of *Estudios valentinianos.* Analecta Gregoriana 99–100. Rome: Apud aedes Universitatis Gregorianae, 1958.

————. *La teologia del Espiritu Santo.* Vol. 4 of *Estudios valentinianos.* Analecta Gregoriana 158. Rome: Libreria editrice dell'Universita Gregoriana, 1966.

Pagels, Elaine. "Gnostic and Orthodox Views of Christ's Passion: Paradigms for the Christian's Response to Persecution?" In *The Rediscovery of Gnosticism: Proceedings of the International Conference on Gnosticism at Yale, New Haven, Connecticut, March 28–31, 1978,* edited by Bentley Layton, 1:262–83. Studies in the History of Religions: Supp. to *Numen* 41. Leiden: Brill, 1980.

————. *The Johannine Gospel in Gnostic Exegesis: Heracleon's Commentary on John.* SBL Monograph Series 17. Atlanta: Scholars Press, 1989.

————. "The Valentinian Claim to Esoteric Exegesis of Romans as Basis for Anthropological Theory." *VC* 26 (1972): 241–58.

Painchaud, Louis. *L'Écrit sans titre: Traité sur l'origine du monde (NH II, 5 et XIII, 2 et Brit. Lib. Or. 4926[1]).* BCNH: Textes 21. Quebec City: Presses de l'Université Laval, 1995.

Perler, Othmar. *Ein Hymnus zur Ostemigil von Meliton? (Papyrus Bodmer XII).* Paradosis 15. Freiburg: Universitatsverlag, 1960.

Perrone, Lorenzo, ed. *Origeniana Octava: Origene e la tradizione alessandrina; Papers of the 8th International Origen Congress, Pisa, 27–31 August 2001.* Leuven: Leuven University Press, 2003.

Petrement, Simone. *A Separate God: The Origins and Teachings of Gnosticism.* Translated by Carol Harrison. San Francisco: HarperCollins, 1990. [First published as *Le Dieu separé: Les origines du gnosticisme* (Paris: Cerf, 1984).]

Phillips, L. Edward. *The Ritual Kiss in Early Christian Worship.* Alcuin/GROW Joint Liturgical Studies 36. Cambridge: Grove Books, 1996.

Plisch, Uwe-Karsten. *Die Auslegung der Erkenntnis (Nag Hammadi-Codex XI,1).* TU 142. Berlin: Akademie Verlag, 1996.

————. "Textverständnis und Übersetzung: Bemerkungen zur Gesamtübersetzung der Texte des Nag-Hammadi-Fundes durch den Berliner Arbeitskreis für Koptisch-Gnostische Schriften." *Hallesche Beiträge zur Orientwissenschaft* 26 (1998): 81–82.

Puech, Henri-Charles, and Gilles Quispel. "Les écrits gnostiques du Codex Jung." *VC* 8 (1954): 1–54.

Quispel, Gilles. "From Mythos to Logos." In Quispel, *Gnostic Studies,* 1:158–69.

————. *Gnostic Studies.* 2 vols. Uitgaven van het Nederlands Historisch-Archaeologisch Instituut te Istanbul 34.1–2. Istanbul: Nederlands Historisch-Archaeologisch Instituut in het Nabije Oosten, 1974–75.

————. "The Jung Codex and Its Significance." In *The Jung Codex: A Newly Recovered Gnostic Papyrus; Three Studies by H.-Ch. Puech, G. Quispel, and W. C. van Unnik,* edited by F. L. Cross, 35–78. London: Mowbray, 1955.

————. "La conception de l'homme dans la gnose valentinienne." In Quispel, *Gnostic Studies,* 1:37-57. [First published in *Eranos Jahrbuch* 15 (1947): 249–86.]

————. "The Original Doctrine of Valentine." *VC* 1 (1947): 43–73.

————. "The Original Doctrine of Valentinus the Gnostic." *VC* 50 (1996): 327–52.

————. "Valentinian Gnosis and the *Apocryphon of John.*" In *The Rediscovery of Gnosticism: Proceedings of the International Conference on Gnosticism at Yale, New Haven, Connecti-*

cut, March 28–31, 1978, edited by Bentley Layton, 1:118–27. Studies in the History of Religions: Supp. to *Numen* 41. Leiden: Brill, 1980.

———. "Valentinus and the Gnostikoi." *VC* 50 (1996): 1–4.

Richard, Marie-Dominique. *L'enseignement oral de Platon: Une nouvelle interprétation du platonisme*. Paris: Cerf, 1986.

Riley, Hugh M. *Christian Initiation: A Comparative Study of the Interpretation of the Baptismal Liturgy in the Mystagogical Writings of Cyril of Jerusalem, John Chrysostom, Theodore of Mopsuestia, and Ambrose of Milan*. SCA 17. Washington, DC: The Catholic University of America Press, 1974.

Riley, Marie. "Q. S. Fl. Tertulliani *Adversus Valentinianos*: Text, Translation, and Commentary." PhD diss., Stanford University, 1971.

Rudolph, Kurt. *Die Gnosis: Wesen und Geschichte einer spätantiken Religion*. 3rd ed. Göttingen: Vandenhoeck and Ruprecht, 1990.

Sagnard, François. *Clément d'Alexandrie: Extraits de Théodote*. SC 23. Paris 1970. [1st ed., 1948.]

———. *La gnose valentinienne et le témoignage de saint Irénée*. Études de philosophie médiévale 36. Paris: J. Vrin, 1947.

Salmon, G. "Heracleon." *DCB* 2:897–901.

Scarpat, Giuseppe. *Parrhesia greca, parrhesia cristiana*. 2nd ed. Studi biblici 130. Brescia: Paideia, 2001.

Schenke, Hans-Martin, Hans-Gebhard Bethge, and Ursula Ulrike Kaiser, eds. *Nag Hammadi Deutsch*. 2 vols. GCS N.F. 8 and 12; Koptisch-Gnostische Schriften II and III. Berlin: Walter de Gruyter, 2001 and 2003.

Schmid, J. "Brautschaft, heilige." *RAC* 2:528–64.

Scholten, Clemens. "Gibt es Quellen zur Sozialgeschichte der Valentinianer Roms?" *ZNW* 79 (1988): 244–61.

Schüngel, Paul. "Gnostische kontra neutestamentliche Soteriologie: Zu Valentins viertem Fragment." *VC* 50 (1996): 257–65.

Segelberg, Erik. *Gnostica, Mandaica, Liturgica*. Acta Universitatis Upsaliensis: Historia Religionum 11. Uppsala: Almquist & Wiksell, 1990.

———. *Maṣbūtā: Studies in the Ritual of the Mandaean Baptism*. Uppsala: Almqvist och Wiksells, 1958.

Simonetti, Manlio. *Testi gnostici in lingua greca e latina*. Scrittori greci e latini. Rome: Fondazione Lorenzo Valla/Mondadori, 1993.

Smith, Geoffrey. "Irenaeus, the Will of God, and Anti-Valentinian Polemics: A Closer Look at *Against the Heresies* I.12.1." In *Beyond the Gnostic Gospels: Studies Building on the Work of Elaine Pagels*, edited by Eduard Iricinschi et al., 93–47. STAC 82. Tübingen: Mohr Siebeck, 2013.

Smith, Morton. *Clement of Alexandria and a Secret Gospel of Mark*. Cambridge, MA: Harvard University Press, 1973.

Spinks, Bryan D. "Sarapion of Thmuis and Baptismal Practice in Early Christian Egypt: The Need for a Judicious Reassessment." *Worship* 72 (1998): 255–70.

Stead, Christopher. "In Search of Valentinus." In *The Rediscovery of Gnosticism: Proceedings of the International Conference on Gnosticism at Yale, New Haven, Connecticut, March 28–31, 1978*, edited by Bentley Layton, 1:75–95. Studies in the History of Religions: Supp. to *Numen* 41. Leiden: Brill, 1980.

———. "The Valentinian Myth of Sophia." *JTS* 20 (1969): 75–104.

Stenzel, Alois. *Die Taufe: Eine genetische Erklärung der Taufliturgie.* Innsbruck: Felizian Rauch, 1958.

Strack, H.ths}L., and P. Billerbeck. *Kommentar zum Neuen Testament aus Talmud und Midrasch.* 4 vols. Munich: Beck, 1922–28.

Strutwolf, Bolger. *Gnosis als System: Zur Rezeption der valentinianischen Gnosis bei Origenes.* Forschungen zur Kirchen- und Dogmengeschichte 56. Göttingen: Vandenhoeck & Ruprecht, 1993.

Tardieu, Michel. "'Comme a travers une tuyau': Quelques remarques sur le mythe valentinien de la chair céleste du Christ." In *Colloque international sur les textes de Nag Hammadi,* edited by Bernard Barc, 151–77. BCNH: Études 1. Quebec City: Presses de l'Université Laval, 1981.

———. "La gnose valentinienne et les oracles chaldaïques." In *The Rediscovery of Gnosticism: Proceedings of the International Conference on Gnosticism at Yale, New Haven, Connecticut, March 28–31, 1978,* edited by Bentley Layton, 1:194–231. Studies in the History of Religions: Supp. to *Numen* 41. Leiden: Brill, 1980.

———. "Recherches sur la formation de l'Apocalypse de Zostrien et les sources de Marius Victorinus." *Res orientales* 9 (1996): 7–114.

———. *Trois mythes gnostiques: Adam, Eros et les animaux d'Égypte dans un écrit de Nag Hammadi (II, 5).* Paris: Études Augustiniennes, 1974.

Theiler, Willy. *Die Vorbereitung des Neuplatonismus.* Problemata: Forschungen zur klassischen Philologie 1. Berlin, 1930.

Thomassen, Einar. "The Derivation of Matter in Monistic Gnosticism." In *Gnosticism and Later Platonism: Themes, Figures, and Texts,* edited by John Turner and Ruth Majercik, 1–17. Society of Biblical Literature Symposium Series 12. Atlanta: Society of Biblical Literature, 2000.

———. "Gnostic Semiotics: The Valentinian Notion of the Name." *Temenos* 29 (1993): 141–56.

———. "Λόγος ἀπὸ σιγῆς προελθών (Ignatius, Mag. 8:2)." In *Texts and Contexts: Biblical Texts in Their Textual and Situational Contexts; Essays in Honor of Lars Hartman,* edited by T. Fornberg and D. Hellholm, 847–67. Oslo: Scandinavian University Press, 1995.

———. "Notes pour la délimitation d'un corpus valentinien à Nag Hammadi." In *Les textes de Nag Hammadi et le problème de leur classification: Actes du colloque tenu à Quebec du 15 au 19 septembre 1993,* edited by L. Painchaud and A. Pasquier, 243–59. BCNH: Études 3. Quebec City: Presses de l'Université Laval, 1995.

———. "Orthodoxy and Heresy in Second-Century Rome." *HTR* 97 (2004): 241–56.

———. "The Platonic and the Gnostic 'Demiurge.'" In *Apocryphon Severini Presented to Søren Giversen,* edited by P. Bilde, H. Kjaer Nielsen, and J. Podemann Sørensen, 226–44. Aarhus: Aarhus University Press, 1993.

———. *The Spiritual Seed: The Church of the "Valentinians."* Leiden: Brill, 2008.

———. "The Valentinianism of the *Valentinian Exposition* (NHC XI,2)." *Muséon* 102 (1989): 225–36.

Thorn, Johan C. "'Harmonious Equality': The Topos of Friendship in Neopythagorean Writings." In *Greco-Roman Perspectives on Friendship,* edited by John T. Fitzgerald, 77–103. SBL Resources for Biblical Study 34. Atlanta: Scholars Press, 1997.

Thornton, Claus-Jurgen. *Der Zeuge des Zeugen: Lukas als Historiker der Paulusreisen.* WUNT 56. Tübingen: Mohr Siebeck, 1991.

Thraede, Klaus. "Ursprung und Formen des 'heiligen Kusses' im frühen Christentum." *JAC* 11/12 (1968/69): 124–80.

Tite, Philip. *Valentinian Ethics and Paraenetic Discourse: Determining the Social Function of Moral Exhortation in Valentinian Christianity.* NHMS 67. Leiden: Brill, 2009.

Tripp, David. "The Original Sequence of Irenaeus 'Adversus Haereses' I: A Suggestion." *Second Century* 8 (1991): 157–62.

Trompf, G. W. "The Conception of God in Hebrews 4:12–13." *Studia theologica* 25 (1971): 123–32.

Turner, John D. *Sethian Gnosticism and the Platonic Tradition.* BCNH: Études 6. Quebec City: Presses de l'Universite Laval, 2001.

Turner, John D., and Ruth Majercik, eds. *Gnosticism and Later Platonism: Themes, Figures, and Texts.* Society of Biblical Literature Symposium Series 12. Atlanta: Society of Biblical Literature 2000.

Turner, John, and Anne McGuire, eds. *The Nag Hammadi Library after Fifty Years: Proceedings of the 1995 Society of Biblical Literature Commemoration.* NHMS 44. Leiden: Brill, 1997.

Varghese, Baby. *Les onctions baptismales dans la tradition syrienne.* CSCO 512; Subsidia 82. Louvain: Peeters, 1989.

Veilleux, Armand. *La première Apocalypse de Jacques (NH V,3); La seconde Apocalypse de Jacques (NH V,4).* BCNH: Textes 17. Quebec City: Presses de l'Université Laval, 1986.

Volker, Walther. *Quellen zur Geschichte der christlichen Gnosis.* Sammlung ausgewählter kirchen- und dogmengeschichtlicher Quellenschriften, N.F. 5. Tübingen: Mohr Siebeck, 1932.

Volz, Paul. *Die Eschatologie der jüdischen Gemeinde im neutestamentlichen Zeitalter nach den Quellen der rabbinischen, apokalyptischen und apokryphen Literatur.* Tübingen: Mohr Siebeck, 1934. [Reprinted, Hildesheim: Georg Olms, 1966.]

Waldstein, Michael, and Frederik Wisse. *The Apocryphon of John: Synopsis of Nag Hammadi Codices II,1; III,1; and IV,1 with BG 8502,2.* NHMS 33. Leiden: Brill, 1995.

Wanke, Daniel. "Irenäus und die Häretiker in Rom: Thesen zur geschichtlichen Situation von *Adversus haereses.*" *ZAC* 3 (1999): 202–40.

Whittaker, John. "Valentinus Fr. 2." In *Kerygma und Logos: Beiträge zu den geistesgeschichtlichen Beziehungen zwischen Antike und Christentum; Festschrift fur Carl Andresen zum 70. Geburtstag,* edited by A. M. Ritter, 455–60. Göttingen: Vandenhoeck & Ruprecht, 1979. [Reprinted in John Whittaker, *Studies in Platonism and Patristic Thought* (London: Variorum Reprints, 1984), chap. 26.]

Wilamowitz–Moellendorf, Ulrich von. "Lesefruchte." *Hermes* 34 (1899): 203–30.

Williams, Michael A. "The Demonizing of the Demiurge: The Innovation of Gnostic Myth." In *Innovation in Religious Traditions,* edited by Michael A. Williams, Collett Cox, and Martin S. Jaffee, 73–107. Berlin: De Gruyter, 1992.

———. *The Immovable Race: A Gnostic Designation and the Theme of Stability in Late Antiquity.* NHS 29. Leiden: Brill, 1985.

———. "Negative Theologies and Demiurgical Myths in Late Antiquity." In *Gnosticism and Later Platonism: Themes, Figures, and Texts,* edited by John D. Turner and Ruth

Majercik, 277–302. Society of Biblical Literature Symposium Series 12. Atlanta: Society of Biblical Literature, 2000.

———. *Rethinking "Gnosticism": An Argument for Dismantling a Dubious Category*. Princeton: Princeton University Press, 1996.

———. "Stability as a Soteriological Theme in Gnosticism." In *The Rediscovery of Gnosticism: Proceedings of the International Conference on Gnosticism at Yale, New Haven, Connecticut, March 28–31, 1978*, edited by Bentley Layton, 2:819–929. Studies in the History of Religions: Supp. to *Numen* 41. Leiden: Brill, 1980.

Wilmet, Michel. *Concordance du Nouveau Testament sahidique*. Vol. 2, *Les mots autochtones*. 3 vols. CSCO 173, 183, 185; Subsidia 11 , 13, 15. Louvain: Secrétariat du CorpusSCO, 1957, 1958, 1959.

Winkler, Gabriele. "The Original Meaning of the Prebaptismal Anointing and Its Implications." In *Living Water, Sealing Spirit: Readings on Christian Initiation,* edited by Maxwell Johnson, 58–81. Collegeville, MN: Liturgical Press, 1995. [First published in *Worship* 52 (1978): 24–45.]

Wolbergs, Thielko. *Griechische religiöse Gedichte der ersten nachchristlichen Jahrhunderte I: Psalmen und Hymnen der Gnosis und des frühen Christentums*. Beiträge zur klassischen Philologie 40.1. Meisenheim am Glan: A. Hain, 1971.

Wucherpfennig, Ansgar. *Heracleon Philologus: Gnostische Johannesexegese im zweiten Jahrhundert*. WUNT 142. Tübingen: Mohr Siebeck, 2002.

Wunsche, Matthias. *Der Ausgang der urchristlichen Prophetie in der frühkatholischen Kirche: Untersuchungen zu den Apostolischen Vätem, den Apologeten, Irenäus von Lyon und dem antimontanistischen Anonymus*. Calwer theologische Monographien, B:14. Stuttgart: Calwer Verlag, 1997.

Wyrwa, D. "Julius Cassian." *LACL*, 409.

FRAGMENTS OF VALENTINUS

Dunderberg, Ismo. *Beyond Gnosticism: Myth, Lifestyle, and Society in the School of Valentinus*. New York: Columbia University Press, 2008. [Esp. 35–74.]

Heitsch, E. *Die griechischen Dichterfragmente der römischen Kaiserzeit*. 2nd ed. Vol. 1 Göttingen: Vandenhoeck & Ruprecht, 1963.

Markschies, Christoph. *Valentinus Gnosticus? Untersuchungen zur valentinianischen Gnosis mit einem Kommentar zu den Fragmenten Valentins*. WUNT 65. Tübingen: J. C. B. Mohr, 1992.

Thomassen, Einar. *The Spiritual Seed: The Church of the "Valentinians."* Leiden: Brill, 2008. [Esp. 430–90.]

Whittaker, John. "Valentinus Fr. 2." In *Kerygma und Logos: Beiträge zu den geistesgeschichtlichen Beziehungen zwischen Antike und Christentum; Festschrift für Carl Andresen zum 70 Geburtstag,* edited by A. M. Ritter, 455–60. Göttingen: Vandenhoeck and Ruprecht, 1979.

PTOLEMY'S *LETTER TO FLORA*

Fallon, Francis. "The Law in Philo and Ptolemaeus: A Note on the *Letter to Flora*." *VC* 30 (1976): 45–51.

Holl, K. *Epiphanius, Ancoratus und Panarion.* Vols. 1–3. GCS 25, 31, 37. Leipzig: Hinrichs, 1915, 1922, 1933.

Jorgensen, David. *Treasure Hidden in a Field: Early Christian Reception of the Gospel of Matthew.* Studies in the Bible and Its Reception. Berlin: De Gruyter, 2016.

Löhr, Winrich A. "La doctrine de Dieu dans la *Lettre à Flora* de Ptolémée." *RHPHR* 75 (1995): 177–91.

Quispel, Gilles. "La Lettre de Ptolémée à Flora." *VC* 2 (1948): 17–56.

———. *Ptolémée: Lettre à Flora.* 2nd ed. SC 24. Paris: Cerf, 1966.

FRAGMENTS OF HERACLEON

Blanc, C. "Le commentaire d'Héracléon sur Jean 4 et 8." *Augustinianum* 15 (1975): 81–121.

———. *Origène: Commentaire sur saint Jean.* 5 vols. SC 120, 157, 222, 290, 385. Paris: Éditions du Cerf, 1966, 1970, 1975, 1982, 1992.

Früchtel, L., O. Stählin, and U. Treu. *Clemens Alexandrinus.* 4th ed. Vol. 2. GCS 52.15. Berlin: Akademie, 1985.

Holzhausen, Jens. "Die Seelenlehre des Gnostikers Herakleon." In *Seele-anima,* edited by Jens Holzhausen, 278–300. BAK 109. Stuttgart: Teubner, 1998.

Janssens, Yvonne. "Héracléon: Commentaire sur l'Évangile selon Saint Jean." *Muséon* 72 (1959): 101–51, 277–99.

Kaler, Michael, and Marie-Pierre Bussières. "Was Heracleon a Valentinian? A New Look at Old Sources." *HTR* 99 (2006): 275–89.

Muhlenberg, Ekkehardt. "Wieviel Erlösungen kennt der Gnostiker Herakleon?" *ZNW* 66 (1975): 170–93.

EXCERPTS OF THEODOTUS

Casey, Robert. *The Excerpta ex Theodoto of Clement of Alexandria.* Studies and Documents 1. London: Christophers, 1934.

———. "Introduction." In *The Excerpta ex Theodoto of Clement of Alexandria,* edited and translated by Robert Casey, 3–38. London: Christophers, 1934.

McCue, James. "Conflicting Versions of Valentinianism? Irenaeus and the *Excerpta ex Theodoto.*" In *The Rediscovery of Gnosticism: Proceedings of the International Conference on Gnosticism at Yale, New Haven, Connecticut, March 28–31, 1978,* edited by Bentley Layton, 1:404–16. Studies in the History of Religions: Supp. to *Numen* 41. Leiden: Brill, 1980.

Orbe, Antonio. "La trinidad maléfica (A propósito de 'Excerpta ex Theodoto' 80,3)." *Gregorianum* 49 (1968): 726–61.

Sagnard, François, ed. and trans. *Clément d'Alexandrie, Extraits de Théodote.* SC 23. Paris: Éditions du Cerf, 1970.

ANONYMOUS *COMMENTARY ON THE PROLOGUE OF JOHN* IN IRENAEUS (*ADVERSUS HAERESES* 1.8.5)

Barth, Carola. *Die Interpretation des Neuen Testaments in der valentinianischen Gnosis.* TU 37.3. Leipzig: Hinrichs, 1911.

Foerster, Werner. *Von Valentin zu Herakleon: Untersuchungen über die Quellen und die Entwicklung der valentinianischen Gnosis.* Beihefte zur ZNW 7. Geissen: Töpelmann, 1928.

Harris, Brendan. "Irenaeus's Engagement with Rhetorical Theory in His Exegesis of the Johannine Prologue in *Adversus Haereses* 1.8.5–1.9.3." *VC* 72.4 (2018): 405–20.

Sagnard, François. *La gnose valentinienne et le témoignage de saint Irénée.* Études de philosophie médiévale 36. Paris: J. Vrin, 1947. [Esp. 306–15.]

Simonetti, Manlio. *Testi gnostici in lingua greca e latina.* Scrittori greci e latini. Rome: Fondazione Lorenzo Valla/Mondadori 1993. [Esp. 281–85, 479–81.]

Thomassen, Einar. *The Spiritual Seed: The Church of the "Valentinians."* Leiden: Brill, 2008. [Esp. 213–18.]

Williams, Frank. *The Panarion of Epiphanius of Salamis: Book I (Sects. 1–46).* 2nd ed. NHMS 63. Leiden: Brill, 2008. [Esp. 165–207.]

ANONYMOUS *LETTER* IN EPIPHANIUS (*PANARION* 31.5–6)

Casey, Robert P. "Note on Epiphanius *Panarion* XXXI 5–6." *JTS* 29 (1928): 34–40.

Chiapparini, Giuliano. *Il divino senza veli: La dottrina gnostica della "Lettera valentiniana" di Epifanio, Panarion 31 5–6; Testo, traduzione e commento storico-religioso.* Studia patristica mediolanensia 29. Milan: Vita e Pensiero, 2015.

Dibelius, Otto. "Studien zur Geschichte der Valentinianer." *ZNW* 9 (1908): 230–47, 329–40.

Simonetti, Manlio. *Testi gnostici in lingua greca e latina.* Scrittori greci e latini. Rome: Fondazione Lorenzo Valla/Mondadori, 1993. [Esp. 217–23, 455–58.]

Thomassen, Einar. *The Spiritual Seed: The Church of the "Valentinians."* Leiden: Brill, 2008. [Esp. 218–30.]

ANONYMOUS COMMENTARY ON THEROS

Markschies, Christoph. *Valentinus Gnosticus? Untersuchungen zur valentinianischen Gnosis mit einem Kommentar zu den Fragmenten Valentins.* WUNT 65. Tübingen: J. C. B. Mohr, 1992. [Esp. 218–59.]

McGowan, Andrew. "Valentinus Poeta: Notes on Theros." *VC* 51 (1997): 158–78.

Thomassen, Einar. *The Spiritual Seed: The Church of the "Valentinians."* Leiden: Brill. 2008. [Esp. 479–88.]

GOSPEL OF TRUTH

Aland, Barbara. "Gnosis und Christentum." In *The Rediscovery of Gnosticism: Proceedings of the International Conference on Gnosticism at Yale, New Haven, Connecticut, March 28–31, 1978,* edited by Bentley Layton, 1:319–50. Studies in the History of Religions: Supp. to *Numen* 41. Leiden: Brill, 1980.

Arai, Sasagu. *Die Christologie des "Evangelium Veritatis": Eine religionsgeschichtliche Untersuchung.* Leiden: Brill, 1964.

———. "Zur Lesung und Übersetzung des "Evangelium Veritatis": Ein Beitrag zum Verständnis seiner Christologie." *NT* 5 (1962): 214–18.

Attridge, Harold. "The *Gospel of Truth* as an Exoteric Text." In *Nag Hammadi, Gnosticism, and Early Christianity*, edited by C. W. Hedrick and R. Hodgson, 239–55. Peabody, MA: Hendrickson, 1986.

Barrett, C. K. "The Theological Vocabulary of the Fourth Gospel and the *Gospel of Truth*." In *Current Issues in New Testament Interpretation: Essays in Honor of Otto A. Piper*, edited by W. Klassen and O. F. Snyder, 210–23, 297–98. New York: Harper & Row, 1962.

Bellet, Paulinus, OP. "Analecta Coptica: 4. An Etymological Speculation in the *Gospel of Truth*." *CBQ* 40 (1978): 49–52.

Böhlig, Alexander. "Zur Ursprache des *Evangelium Veritatis*." *Muséon* 79 (1966): 317–33.

Cerfaux, Lucien. "De Saint Paul à 'L'Évangile de la Vérité.'" *NTS* 5 (1958–59): 103–12.

Christense, C. R. "John's Christology and the 'Gospel of Truth.'" *Gordon Review* 10 (1966): 23–31.

Colpe, Carsten. "Heidnische, jüdische und christliche Überlieferung in den Schriften aus Nag Hammadi, VII." *JAC* 21 (1978): 125–46.

Cramer, Maria. "Zur Deutung des Ausdrucks 'Gnosis' in *Evangelium Veritatis*." In *Studia Biblica et Orientalia 3, Oriens Antiquus*, 48–56. Analecta Biblica 12. Rome: Pontificio Istituto Biblico, 1959.

Dubois, Jean-Daniel. "Le context judaïque du 'nom' dans l'*Évangile de Vérité*." *Revue de théologie et de philosophie* 24 (1974): 198–216.

———. "Remarques sur le texte de l'*Évangile de Verité* (CG I,2)." *VC* 29 (1975): 138–40.

Emmel, Stephen. "Proclitic Forms of the Verb *ti* in Coptic." In *Studies Presented to Hans Jacob Polotsky*, edited by Dwight W. Young, 131–46. East Gloucester, MA: Pirtle and Poulson, 1981.

———. "Unique Photographic Evidence for Nag Hammadi Texts, CG I, 1–5." *BASP* 15 (1978): 251–61.

Freht, Gerhard. "Der erst 'Teil' des sogennanten *Evangelium Veritatis* (S. 16, 31–22,20): I. Kapitel⁴ I, Str. I–III; II. Kapitel⁴ I, STR. IV = Kapitel⁴ 2, Str. VII; III. Kapitel⁴ 2, STR VIII— Kapitel⁴ 3, Str. IX." *Orientalia* 30 (1961): 371–90; 31 (1962): 85–119; 32 (1963): 298–335.

Giversen, Søren. *Sandhedens Evangelium, De gnostiske handskrifter fra Nidalden*. Theologiske Studien. Copenhagen: Gads, 1957.

Grobel, Kendrick. *The Gospel of Truth: A Valentinian Meditation on the Gospel*. New York: Abingdon Press, 1960. [Esp. 92–95.]

Helderman, Jan. "Das *Evangelium Veritatis* in der neueren Forschung." *ANRW* II 25:5 (1988): 4054–106.

Jansen, Herman Ludin. "Spuren sakramentaler Handlungen im *Evangelium Veritatis*." *Acta orientalia* 28 (1964/65): 215–19.

Kasser, Rodolphe, Rodolphe Kasser, Michel Malinine, Henri-Charles Puech, Gilles Quispel, Jan Zandee, Werner Vycichl, and R. M. Wilson. *Evangelium Veritatis: Supplementum Photographicum*. Bern: Francke, 1975.

Koschorke, Klaus. *Die Polemik der Gnostiker gegen das kirchliche Christentum unter besonderer Berücksichtigung der Nag-Hammadi Traktate "Apokalypse des Petrus" (NHC VII,5) und "Testimonium Veritatis" (NHC IX,3)*. NHS 12. Leiden: Brill, 1978.

Kragerud, A. "*Evangelium Veritatis*: En oversettelse." *NTT* 66 (1965): 177–93.

Malinine, Michel, Henri-Charles Puech, and Gilles Quispel. *Evangelium Veritatis: Codex Jung f VIIIv–XVIv (pp. 16–32) f XIXr–XXIIr (pp. 37–43)*. Zurich: Rascher, 1956.

Ménard, Jacques-É. *L'Évangile de Vérité: Rétroversion grecque et commentaire*. Paris: Letouzey et Ané, 1962.

———. *L'Évangile de Vérité: Traduction française, introduction, et commentaire*. NHS 2. Leiden: Brill, 1972.

Munck, Johannes. "*Evangelium Veritatis* and Greek Usage as to Book Titles." *Studia theologica* 17 (1963): 133–38.

Orlandi, Tito. *Evangelium Veritatis*. Testi del vicino oriente antico 8.2. Brescia: Paideia, 1992.

Save-Söderbergh, Torgny. "Det koptiska 'Evangelium Veritatis.'" *Religion och Bibel* 17 (1958): 28–40.

———. *Evangelium Veritatis och Thomas-evangeliet*. Symbolae Biblicae Upsalienses; Supplementhäften til *Svensk Exegetisk Arsbok* 16. Uppsala: Wretmans, 1959.

Schenke, Hans-Martin. *Die Herkunft des sogennanten "Evangelium veritatis."* Berlin: Evangilescher Verlag, 1958.

Segelberg, Erik. "*Evangelium Veritatis*: A Confirmation Homily and Its Relation to the Odes of Solomon." *Orientalia Suecana* 8 (1959): 1–40.

Smith, Geoffrey. "Constructing a Christian Universe: Mythological Exegesis of Ben Sira 24 and John's Prologue in the *Gospel of Truth*." In *Jewish and Christian Cosmogony in Late Antiquity*, edited by Lance Jenott and Sarit Kattan Gribetz, 64–81. Textual Studies in Ancient Judaism 155. Tübingen: Mohr Siebeck, 2013.

Steenberg, M. C. "The *Gospel of Truth* and the Truth of the Gospel." *SP* 50 (2011): 89–104.

Thomassen, Einar. "Revelation as Book and Book as Revelation: Reflections on the *Gospel of Truth*." In *The Nag Hammadi Texts in the History of Religions: Proceedings of the International Conference at the Royal Academy and Sciences and Letters in Copenhagen, September 19–24, 1995, on the Occasion of the 50th Anniversary of the Nag Hammadi Discovery*, edited by Soren Giversen, Tage Petersen, and Jorgen Podemann Sorensen, 35–45. Det Kongelige Danske Videnskabernes Selskab: Historisk-filosofiske Skrifter 26. Copenhagen: C. A. Reitzel, 2002.

Till, Walter. "Das *Evangelium der Wahrheit*: Neue Übersetzung des vollständigen Textes." *ZNW* 50 (1959): 165–85.

———. "Die kairener Seiten des 'Evangeliums der Wahrheit.'" *Orientalia* 28 (1959): 170–85.

van Unnik, W. C. "The Recently Discovered *Gospel of Truth* and the New Testament." In *The Jung Codex: A Newly Recovered Gnostic Papyrus; Three Studies by H.-Ch. Puech, G. Quispel, and W. C. van Unnik*, edited by F. L. Cross, 81–129. London: Mowbray, 1955.

Williams, Jacqueline A. *Biblical Interpretation in the Gnostic "Gospel of Truth" from Nag Hammadi*. Society of Biblical Literature Dissertation Series 79. Atlanta: Scholars Press, 1988. [Esp. 179–83.]

TREATISE ON THE RESURRECTION

Bazan, Francisco Garcia. "La *Doctrina de resurrección* en S. Pablo y entre los gnósticos." *RevistB* 37 (1975): 341–52.

———. "*Sobre la Resurrección (Epistola a Reginos)*: Traducción, introducción y commentario." *RevistB* 38 (1976): 147–78.

Colpe, Carsten. "Heidnische, jüdische und christliche Überlieferung in den Schriften aus Nag Hammadi, VIII." *JAC* 22 (1979): 98–122.

Dehandschutter, Boudewijn. "L'Épître à Rhéginos (CG I,3): Quelques problèmes critiques." *OLP* 4 (1973): 101–11.

Frid, B. *De Resurrectione, Epistula ad Rheginum: Inledning och oversattning fran koptiskan.* Symbolae Biblicae Upsalienses: Supp. to *SEA* 19. Lund: Gleerup, 1967.

Gaffron, Hans-Georg. "Eine gnostische Apologie des Auferstehungsglaubens: Bemerkungen zur 'Epistula ad Rheginum.'" In *Die Zeit Jesu: Festschrift fur Heinrich Schlier,* edited by Gunther Bornkamm and Karl Rahner, 218–27. Freiburg: Herder, 1970.

Haardt, Robert. "'Die Abhandlung über die Auferstehung' des Codex Jung aus der Bibliothek gnosticher koptischer Schriften von Nag Hammadi: Bemerkungen zu ausgewählten Motiven, Teil I; Der Text." *Kairos* n.s. 11 (1969): 1–5.

———. "'Die Abhandlung über die Auferstehung' des Codex Jung aus der Bibliothek gnostischer koptischer Schriften von Nag Hammadi: Bemerkungen zu ausgewählten Motiven, Teil II; Die Interpretation." *Kairos* n.s. 12 (1970): 241–69.

Kraus, Martin. "Die Abhandlung über die Auferstehung." In *Die Gnosis,* edited by Werner Foerster, 2:85–163. Zurich: Artemis, 1971.

Layton, Bentley. *The Gnostic Treatise on Resurrection from Nag Hammadi.* HDR 12. Missoula, MT: Scholars Press, 1979.

———. "Vision and Revision: A Gnostic View of the Resurrection." In *Colloque international sur les textes de Nag Hammadi,* edited by Bernard Barc, 190–217. BCNH: Études 1. Quebec City: Presses de l'Université Laval, 1981.

Malinine, Michel, et al. *De Resurrectione (Epistula ad Rheginum): Codex Jung F.xxiir–F.xxvv (p. 43–50).* Zurich: Rascher, 1963.

Martin, Luther H. "The Anti-philosophical Polemic and Gnostic Soteriology in 'The Treatise on the Resurrection' (CG I, 3)." *Numen* 20 (1973): 20–37.

———. "The Epistle to Rheginos: Translation, Commentary, and Analysis." PhD diss., Claremont College, 1971.

———. "Note on 'The Treatise on the Resurrection' (CG I, 3) 48, 3–6." *VC* 27 (1973): 28r.

———. "'The Treatise on the Resurrection' (CG I, 3) and Diatribe Style." *VC* 27 (1973): 277–80.

Ménard, Jacques-É. "La notion de 'Résurrection' dans 'l'Épître à Rhéginos.'" In *Essays on the Nag Hammadi Texts in Honour of Pahor Labib,* edited by Martin Krause, 110–24. NHS 6. Leiden: Brill, 1975.

———. "L'Épître à Rhéginos et la Résurrection." In *Proceedings of the XII International Congress of the International Association for the History of Religions, Stockholm, Sweden, August 16–22, 1970,* edited by C. Jouco Bleeker et al., 189–99. Studies in the History of Religions: Supp. to *Numen* 31. Leiden: Brill, 1975.

Peel, Malcolm. *The Epistle to Rheginos: A Valentinian Letter on the Resurrection; Introduction, Translation, Analysis, and Exposition.* Philadelphia: Westminster, 1969.

———. *Gnosis und Auferstehung: Der Brief an Rheginus von Nag Hammadi.* Translated by W.-P. Funk. Rev. ed. Neukirchen-Vluyn: Neukirchener, 1974.

———. "Gnostic Eschatology and the New Testament." *NT* 12 (1970): 141–65.

Peretto, Elio. "L'Epistola a Rheginos: Il posta del corpo nella risurrezione." *Augustinianum* 18 (1978): 63–74.

Quispel, Gilles. "Note sur 'De Resurrectione.'" *VC* 22 (1968): 14–15.

Schenke, Hans-Martin. "Auferstehungsglaube und Gnosis." *ZNW* 59 (1968): 123–26.

Troger, Karl-Wolfgang. "Die Bedeutung der Texte von Nag Hammadi fur die moderne Gnosisforschung." In *Gnosis und Neues Testament: Studien aus Religionswissenschaft und Theologie*, 29–30. Berlin: Evangelische Verlagsanstalt, 1973.

van Unnik, Willem C. "The Newly Discovered 'Epistle to Rheginos' on the Resurrection." *JEH* 15 (1964): 141–52, 153–67.

Zandee, Jan. "De opstanding in de *Brief aan Rheginos* en in het *Evangelie van Philippus.*" *NTT* 16 (1962): 361–77.

TRIPARTITE TRACTATE

Attridge, Harold, and Elaine Pagels. "*The Tripartite Tractate:* I,5: 51.1–138.27." In *Nag Hammadi Codex I (The Jung Codex)*, edited by Harold Attridge, 1:159–337, 2:217–497. NHS 22–23. Leiden: Brill, 1985.

Bohlig, Alexander. "Zum Gottesbegriff des *Tractatus Tripartitus,* Nag Hammadi C. I,5." In *Kerygma und Logos: Beiträge zu den geistesgeschichtlichen Beziehungen zwischen Antike und Christentum; Festschrift fur Carl Andresen zum 70 Geburtstag*, edited by A. M. Ritter, 49–67. Göttingen: Vandenhoeck und Ruprecht, 1979.

Camplani, Alberto. "Per la cronologia di testi valentiniani: Il *Trattato tripartito* e la crisi ariana." *Cassiodorus* 1 (1995): 171–95.

Colpe, Carsten. "Heidnische, jüdische und christliche Überlieferung in den Schriften aus Nag Hammadi, VIII." *JAC* 22 (1979): 98–122.

Devoti, D. "Una summa di teologia gnostica; II *Tractatus Tripartitus.*" *Revista di storia e letteratura religiosa* 13 (1977): 326–53.

Dubois, Jean-Daniel. "Le sotériologie valentinienne du *Traité tripartite* (NHL 5)." In *Les textes de Nag Hammadi et le problème de leur classification*, edited by Louis Painchaud and Anne Pasquier, 221–32. BCNH: Études 3. Quebec City: Presses de l'Universite Laval, 1995.

———. "Le *Traité tripartite* (Nag Hammadi I, 5) est-il anterieure a Origene?" In *Origeniana Octava: Origene e la tradizione alessandrina; Papers of the 8th International Origen Congress, Pisa, 27–31 August 2001*, edited by Lorenzo Perrone, 303–16. Leuven: Leuven University Press, 2003.

Dunderberg, Ismo. "Lust for Power in the *Tripartite Tractate* (NHC I, 5)." In *Coptica, Manichaeica, Gnostica: Melanges Wolf-Peter Funk*, edited by Paul-Hubert Poirier and Louis Painchaud, 169–89. BCNH: Études 7. Quebec City: Laval University Press, 2006.

Emmel, Stephen. "Unique Photographic Evidence for Nag Hammadi Texts, CG I, 1–5." *BASP* 15 (1978): 251–61.

Kasser, Rodolphe, et al. *Tractatus Tripartitus.* 2 vols. Bern: Francke, 1973–75.

Luz, Ulrich. "Der dreiteilige Traktat von Nag Hammadi." *TZ* 33 (1977): 384–92.

Orbe, Antonio. "En torno a un tratado gnostico." *Gregorianum* 56 (1975): 558–66.

Perkins, Pheme. "Logos Christologies in the Nag Hammadi Codices." *VC* 35 (1981): 379–96.

Puech, Henri-Charles, and Gilles Quispel. "Le quatrième écrit du Codex Jung." *VC* 9 (1955): 65–102.

———. "Les écrits gnostiques du Codex Jung." *VC* 8 (1954): 1–51.

Schenke, Hans-Martin. "Zum sogennanten *Tractatus Tripartitus* des Codex Jung." *ZAS* 105 (1978): 133–41.

Thomassen, Einar. "The Structure of the Transcendent World in the *Tripartite Tractate* (NHC I, 5)." *VC* 34 (1980): 358–75.

Thomassen, Einar, and Louis Painchaud. *Le Traité tripartite (NH I, 5)*. BCNH: Textes 19. Quebec City: Presses de l'Université Laval, 1989.

Zandee, Jan. "Die Person der Sophia in der Vierten Schrift des Codex Jung." In *The Origins of Gnosticism: Colloquium of Messina, 13–18 April 1966*, edited by Ugo Bianchi, 203–14. Studies in the History of Religions: Supp. to *Numen* 12. Leiden: Brill, 1967.

———. *The Terminology of Plotinus and of Some Gnostic Writings, Mainly the Fourth Treatise of the Jung Codex*. Istanbul: Nederlands historisch-archaeologisch Instituut in het Nabije Oosten, 1961.

GOSPEL OF PHILIP

DeConick, April. "The True Mysteries: Sacramentalism in the *Gospel of Philip*." *VC* 55 (2001): 225–61.

Dunderberg, Ismo. "Valentinian Views about Adam's Creation: Valentinus and the *Gospel of Philip*." In *Lux Humana, Lux Aeterna: Essays on Biblical and Related Themes in Honour of Lars Aejmelaeus*, edited by Antti Mustakallio, 509–27. Publications of the Finnish Exegetical Society 89. Helsinki/Göttingen: The Finnish Exegetical Society/Vandenhoeck and Ruprecht, 2005.

Gaffron, Hans-Georg. "Studien zum koptischen Philippusevangelium unter besonderer Berucksichtignng der Sakramente." Diss., Friedrich-Wilhelms-Universität, 1969.

Isenberg, Wesley. "The Coptic Gospel According to Philip." PhD diss., University of Chicago, 1968.

Kasser, Rodolphe. "Bibliothèque Gnostique VIII: *L'Evangile selon Philippe*." *RTP* 20 (1970): 12–35.

Koschorke, Klaus. "Die 'Namen' im Philippusevangelium: Beobachtungen zur Auseinandersetzung zwischen gnostischem und kirchlichem Christentum." *ZNW* 64 (1973): 307–22.

Lundhaug, Hugo. "Begotten, Not Made, to Arise in This Flesh: The Post-Nicene Soteriology of the *Gospel of Philip*." In *Beyond the Gnostic Gospels: Studies Building on the Work of Elaine Pagels*, edited by Eduard Iricinschi et al., 235–71. STAC 82. Tübingen: Mohr Siebeck, 2013.

———. *Images of Rebirth: Cognitive Poetics and the Transformational Soteriology in the "Gospel of Philip" and the "Exegesis on the Soul."* NHMS 73. Leiden: Brill, 2010.

Ménard, Jacques-É. *L'Évangile selon Philippe: Introduction, texte, traduction, commentaire.* Strasbourg: Letouzey & Ane, 1967.

Schenke, Hans-Martin. "Das *Evangelium nach Philippus*: Ein Evangelium der Valentinianer aus dem Funde von Nag-Hamadi." In *Koptisch-gnostische Schriften aus dem Papyrus-Codices von Nag-Hamadi*, edited by J. Leipoldt and H.-M. Schenke, 31–65, 81–82. Theologische Forschung 20. Bamburg-Bergstedt: Herbert Reich-Evangelischer Verlag, 1960. [First published in *TLZ* 84 (1959): 1–26.]

———. *Das Philippus-Evangelium (Nag Hammadi-Codex 11,3)*. TU 143. Berlin: Akademie Verlag, 1997.

Segelberg, Erik. "The Antiochene Background of the *Gospel of Philip*." *BSAC* 18 (1966): 205–23. [Reprinted in Erik Segelberg, *Gnostica, Mandaica, Liturgica*, Acta Universitatis Upsaliensis: Historia Religionum 11 (Uppsala: Almquist & Wiksell, 1990) 31–49.]

———. "The Antiochene Origin of the 'Gospel of Philip.'" *BSAC* 19 (1967–68): 207–10. [Reprinted in Segelberg, *Gnostica, Mandaica, Liturgica*, 51–54.]

———. "The Coptic-Gnostic Gospel According to Philip and Its Sacramental System." *Numen* 7 (1960): 189–200.

Sevrin, Jean-Marie. "Les noces spirituelles dans l'*Évangile selon Philippe*." *Muséon* 87 (1974): 143–93.

———. "Pratique et doctrine des sacrements dans l'*Évangile selon Philippe*." Diss., Louvain, 1972.

Thomassen, Einar. "How Valentinian Is the *Gospel of Philip*?" In *The Nag Hammadi Library after Fifty Years: Proceedings of the 1995 Society of Biblical Literature Commemoration*, edited by John Turner and Anne McGuire, 251–79. NHMS 44. Leiden: Brill, 1997.

Trautmann, Catherine. "La parente dans l'*Évangile selon Philippe*." In *Colloque international sur les textes de Nag Hammadi*, edited by Bernard Barc, 267–78. BCNH: Études 1. Quebec City: Presses de l'Université Laval, 1981.

Tripp, David. "The 'Sacramental System' of the *Gospel of Philip*." *Studia patristica* 17 (1982): 251–60.

Turner, Martha. *The Gospel According to Philip: The Sources and Coherence of an Early Christian Collection*. NHMS 38. Leiden: Brill, 1996.

Wilson, R. M. *The Gospel of Philip*. New York: Harper & Row, 1962.

VALENTINIAN EXPOSITION

Foerster, Werner. *Von Valentin zu Herakleon: Untersuchungen über die Quellen und die Entwicklung der valentinianischen Gnosis*. Beihefte zur ZNW 7. Giessen: Töpelmann, 1928.

Gaffron, Hans-Georg. "Studien zum koptischen Philippusevangelium unter besonderer Berucksichtigung der Sakramente." Diss., Friedrich-Wilhelm Universität, 1969.

Lundhaug, Hugo. "Fragments of Early Christianity: An Analysis of a *Valentinian Exposition* (NHC XI,2) with the Liturgical Fragments On the Anointing, On Baptism A, On Baptism B, On the Eucharist A, On the Eucharist B (NHC XI,2a–e)." Diss. IKS, University of Oslo, 2000.

Sagnard, François. *La gnose valentinienne et le témoignage de saint Irénée*. Études de philosophie médiévale 36. Paris: J. Vrin, 1947.

Segelberg, Eric. "The Baptismal Rite According to Some of the Coptic-Gnostic Texts of the Nag Hammadi." *Studia patristica* 5 (1962): 117–28.

Thomassen, Einar. "The Valentinianism of the *Valentinian Exposition* (NHC XI,2)." *Muséon* 102 (1989): 225–36.

FLAVIA SOPHE INSCRIPTION

Carletti, Carlo. "'Preistoria' dell'epigrafia dei cristiani: Un mito storiografico ex maiorum auctoritate?" In *Origine delle catacombe romane: Atti della giornata tematica dei*

Seminari di archeologia cristiana (Roma, 21 marzo 2005), edited by Vincenzo Fiocchi Nicolai and Jean Guyon, 91–119. Vatican City: Pontificio Istituto di Archeologia Cristiana, 2006.

Coppo, Angelo. "Contributo all'interpretazione di un'epigrafe greca cristiana dei Musei Capitolini." *Rivista di archeologia cristiana* 46 (1970): 97–138.

Guarducci, Margherita. "Ancora sui valentiniani a Roma." *Mitteilungen des Deutschen Archäologischen Instituts, Römische Abteilung* 81 (1974): 341–43.

———. *From Paul to Valentinus: Christians at Rome in the First Two Centuries.* Minneapolis: Fortress Press, 2003. [Esp. 298–313.]

———. "Iscrizione cristiana del II secolo nei Musei Capitolini." *BCom* 79 (1963–64): 117–34.

———. "Valentiniani a Roma: Ricerche epigrafiche ed archeologiche." *Mitteilungen des Deutschen Archäologischen Instituts, Römische Abteilung* 80 (1973): 169–89.Lampe, Peter. "An Early Christian Inscription in the Musei Capitolini." *Studia theologica* 49 (1995): 79–92.

Moretti, Luigi. "Iscrizione greche inedite di Roma." *BCom* 75 (1953–55): 83.

Quispel, Gilles. "L'inscription de Flavia Sophe." In *Gnostic Studies,* 1:58–59. Uitgaven van het Nederlands Historisch-Archaeologisch Instituut te Istanbul 34.1–2. Istanbul: Nederlands Historisch-Archaeologisch Instituut in het Nabije Oosten, 1974–75. [First published in *Mélanges Joseph de Ghellinck, S.J.,* 201–14, Museum Lessianum: Section historique 13, 14 (Gembloux: J. Duculot 1951).]

Raoss, Mariano. "Iscrizione cristiana-greca di Roma anteriore al terzo secolo?" *Aevum* 37 (1963): 11–30.

Snyder, Gregory H. "The Discovery and Interpretation of the Flavia Sophe Inscription: New Results." *VC* 68 (2014): 1–59.

———. "Flavia's Neighborhood: The Physical Context for the Valentinian Inscriptions." An essay for a volume based on a conference held at the Norwegian Institute in Rome, Oct. 16–18, edited by Einar Thomassen and Christoph Markschies. NHMS. Leiden: Brill, forthcoming.

INDICES

The following indices include only key terms and themes that appear throughout the Valentinian corpus. For comprehensive Greek and Coptic indices, see the critical editions included in the bibliography. Roman numerals refer to the order of the writings in this collection (e.g., VIII = the *Gospel of Truth*). Numbers refer to specific sections and/or subsections or manuscript pages and lines. References to writings lacking such divisions are to page number in this volume.

SELECT GREEK INDEX

νοῦς (mind), IV 6. 52; VIII 16.36, 19.38, 37.10; IX
    46.24; X 54.15, 55.6, 55.22, 59.17, 63.23, 63.33,
    64.6, 64.9, 65.3, 66.16, 70.8, 70.90, 71.30,
    85.13, 105.23, 129.22; XII 22.32, 22.36, 23.37,
    24.20
νυμφών (bridal chamber), IV 64, 65, 68; XI 65.11,
    67.5, 67.16, 67.30, 69.25, 69.27, 72.21, 72.22,
    74.22, 76.5, 82.18, 82.24, 86.5; XIII 312

ὀγδοάδα (ogdoad), IV 63, 80; V 110, 112; VI 6.2,
    3, 4, 7, 8, 9
οἰκονομία (ordering), III 8, 11, 36; X 77.3, 77.10,
    88.4, 89.35, 91.15, 94.8, 95.8, 95.21, 96.14,
    99.19, 100.7, 101.11, 108.10, 108.17, 115.29, 116.8,
    116.25, 118.11, 122.32, 127.22, 133.9
ὁμολογία (agreement), II 5.7, 6.1, 7.8; III 4, 8, 19,
    26, 50; IV 50, 61; X 84.23, 89.18, 91.9, 106.12,
    111.22, 111.34, 113.20, 120.2, 120.36, 121.29,
    127.33, 128.16, 131.4, 132.17, 134.5
ὅρος (boundary, limit), III 20; IV 22, 26, 35, 42,
    64; VII 124; X 75.13, 76.33, 82.12; XII 25.22,
    26.30, 31.23, 33.26
οὐσία (being, substance), I 1; II 7.4, 7.6, 7.7; III
    43, 44, 45, 46; IV 45, 46, 47, 50, 59, 61, 67, 71;
    V 110; VIII 20.16; X 53.34, 58.37, 61.6, 82.18,
    83.4, 84.12, 93.35, 94.35, 101.19, 101.21, 101.25,
    102.16, 105.37, 106.6, 106.9, 106.14, 106.24,
    106.32, 116.6, 118.15, 118.22; 120.14, 122.14; XI
    52.3; XII 27.32

πάθος (passion), III 12, 38; IV 1, 23, 30, 33, 41, 45,
    46, 61, 67, 76; V 112; X 95.2, 95.5, 114.35, 115.20,
    116.11, 116.21, 116.23, 116.24, 116.27, 118.6; XII
    35.32, 35.35, 35.38
παράδεισος (Paradise), IV 51; VIII 36.37, 36.38;
    X 96.29, 101.30, 102.20, 106.27; XI 55.7, 71.22,
    73.10, 73.16, 73.27, 73.28, 73.33
πάτηρ (father), I 2; II 3.2, 3.4, 3.7, 5.5, 7.5, 7.6, 7.7;
    IV 1, 6, 7, 16, 30, 31, 33, 43, 45, 47, 61, 64, 76,
    80; V 110, 112; VI 5.5, 7, 6.1, 3, 4; VII 124
πείθω (to persuade), VI 6.7; IX 46.5, 46.7; X
    79.17, 80.8, 88.25, 90.22, 96.7, 98.11, 101.26,
    101.27, 109.11; XI 65.18
πιστεύω (to believe), II 7.8; IV 61, 67, 74, 76; IX
    46.4, 46.12, 46.8, 46.15, 46.20, 46.21; XI 52.17,
    60.4, 62.3; XII 36.16
πίστις (faith), I 5; IV 56; VI 5.8, 6.1; IX 46.5, 46.13;
    61.36, 62.1, 66.34, 79.23, 79.25
πλανάω (to wander, err), III 22; IV 70; IX
    49.34; X 135.8; XI 55.24, 56.17, 66.20, 67.37,
    73.3

πλάνη (error), III 22, 23, 24, 47; VIII 17.15, 17.29,
    17.36, 18.22, 22.21, 22.24, 26.19, 26.26, 31.25,
    32.37, 35.18; X 110.1; XI 78.18
πλάσμα (something formed), I 1; III 16; VIII 17.8,
    17.24, 21.35, 34.18; X 106.19
πλήρωμα (fullness), III 13, 18, 22; IV 21, 22, 23,
    26, 31, 32, 33, 34, 35, 36, 38, 41, 42, 43, 45, 65;
    V 112; VII 124; VIII 16.35, 34.30, 34.36, 35.8,
    35.29, 35.35, 36.10, 41.1, 41.14, 41.15, 43.15; IX
    44.33, 46.36, 49.4; X 59.36, 68.30, 70.1, 74.27,
    75.14, 77.5, 78.4, 78.20, 78.26, 78.31, 80.27,
    80.35, 81.30, 85.32, 86.21, 90.15, 93.26, 94.12,
    95.5, 96.34, 97.21, 122.27, 123.22, 124.25, 124.29,
    125.31, 136.21; XI 68.14, 70.35, 84.13, 84.32,
    86.14; XII 27.21, 30.32, 30.37, 31.38, 33.31,
    34.29, 35.20, 36.31, 37.15, 39.16, 39.18, 39.12,
    40.30
πνεῦμα (spirit), I 2, 3, 8; III 13, 17, 24, 27; IV 1, 3, 7,
    16, 23, 24, 38, 48, 55, 60, 61, 76, 77, 80, 81, 83;
    VI 6.7, 8; VII 124; VIII 24.11, 26.36, 27.4, 30.17,
    31.18, 34.11, 42.33, 43.17; IX 45.13; X 58.35, 64.9,
    66.27, 72.2, 72.18, 73.2, 73.5, 97.1, 101.4, 101.13,
    101.18, 102.32, 107.28, 118.31, 118.32, 122.31,
    127.32, 128.8, 138.24; XI 53.30, 55.17, 55.24, 57.7,
    57.14, 58.12, 59.12, 59.16, 59.20, 59.35, 60.7,
    60.8, 60.28, 61.29, 61.30, 63.9, 64.26, 65.1,
    66.1, 66.2, 66.3, 67.3, 67.20, 69.5, 69.8, 70.24,
    70.26, 71.17, 74.21, 75.18, 77.12, 77.14, 78.29
    , 78.34 , 79.9, 79.21, 79.28, 85.23; XII 23.37,
    28.24, 35.36, 38.27, 38.32, 42.34, 42.37
πνευματικός (spiritual), II 5.2, 5.8, 5.9, 5.10, 5.11,
    5.13, 6.4; III 2, 15, 20, 23, 24, 37; IV 1, 2, 7,
    48, 53, 54, 56, 57, 58, 61, 62, 63, 64, 82; VI 5.7,
    6.4; IX 45.40; X 63.36, 64.7, 97.17, 97.18, 101.7,
    101.16, 102.15, 103.18, 103.15, 104.33, 105.31,
    106.6, 106.22, 111.25, 114.7, 116.7, 118.16, 118.21,
    118.29, 119.16; XI 77.35
πολιτεύω (to inhabit), III 40; IV 59, 69; IX 49.11;
    X 97.2, 125.17, XI 65.4, 72.10, 86.10
πονηρός (evil), I 2; II 5.12, 7.5; III 40; IV 72; XI
    59.19
προβολή (emanation), IV 21, 67; V 110; VII 124;
    IX 45.12, X 63.35, 68.1, 70.25, 73.18, 80.34, 83.2,
    86.9, 111.32, 115.37, 116.2, 136.10
πρόνοια (foreknowledge), I 2; II 3.6; IV 74; X
    66.21, 66.22, 107.22, 109.9; XII 36.10, 37.21
προφήτης (prophet), III 4, 5, 10, 19; IV 24, 59; X
    97.22, 100.35, 105.22, 111.9, 111.33, 113.6, 113.16

σάββατον (Sabbath), II 5.8, 5.12; IV 49; VIII
    32.18, 32.23; XI 52.34

SELECT COPTIC INDEX

Founded in 1893,
UNIVERSITY OF CALIFORNIA PRESS
publishes bold, progressive books and journals
on topics in the arts, humanities, social sciences,
and natural sciences—with a focus on social
justice issues—that inspire thought and action
among readers worldwide.

The UC PRESS FOUNDATION
raises funds to uphold the press's vital role
as an independent, nonprofit publisher, and
receives philanthropic support from a wide
range of individuals and institutions—and from
committed readers like you. To learn more, visit
ucpress.edu/supportus.